HENRY MCBRIDE SERIES IN MODERNISM AND MODERNITY

The artistic movement known as modernism, which includes the historical avant-garde, produced the most radical and comprehensive change in Western culture since Romanticism. Its effects reverberated through all the arts, permanently altering their formal repertories and their relations with society at large, and its products still surround us in our workplaces and homes. Although modernism produced a pervasive cultural upheaval, it can never be assessed as an artistic movement alone: its contours took shape against the background of social, political, and intellectual change, and it was always bound up with large questions of modernity and modernization and with the intellectual challenge of sifting their meanings. Henry McBride (1867–1962) became perhaps the leading American critic of his time to write perceptively and engagingly on modern art. The Henry McBride Series in Modernism and Modernity, which focuses on modernism and the arts in their many contexts, is respectfully dedicated to his memory.

Marcel Proust A LIFE

William C. Carter

Yale University Press ∾ New Haven and London

This book has been published with assistance from the fund for the Henry McBride Series in Modernism and Modernity established by Maximilian Miltzlaff.

Designed by Rebecca Gibb. Set in Minion type by Keystone Typesetting, Inc., Orwigsburg, Pennsylvania. Printed in the United States of America by Vail-Ballou Press, Binghamton, New York.

Library of Congress Cataloging-in-Publication Data
Carter, William C., 1941–
Marcel Proust: a life / William C. Carter.
    p   cm. (Henry McBride series in modernism and modernity)
Includes bibliographical references and index.
ISBN 0–300–08145–6 (cloth : alk. paper).
1. Proust, Marcel, 1871–1922.   2. Novelists, French—20th century—Biography   I. Title.
[PQ2631.R63 Z545485 2000]
843'.912—dc21
[B]   99–053701

A catalogue record for this book is available from the British Library.

The paper in this book meets the guidelines for permanence and durability of the Committee on Production Guidelines for Book Longevity of the Council on Library Resources.

10   9   8   7   6   5   4   3   2   1

For Lynn, my love

Contents ∾

Preface ∾

MARCEL PROUST'S LIFE LEADS, after many false starts, to the production of a masterpiece: *À la recherche du temps perdu.* Since its publication in France in the first quarter of the twentieth century, this vast novel has never been out of print. Known for many years in English as *Remembrance of Things Past,* the title chosen by its distinguished translator C. K. Scott-Moncrieff, this work continues to delight readers in more than thirty languages throughout the world. Lecturing at Cornell University in the 1950s, Vladimir Nabokov, who declined to use Scott-Moncrieff's title, called *In Search of Lost Time* "the greatest novel of the first half of our century." Many eminent writers and critics consider the *Search* to be the major novel of the twentieth century and perhaps in the history of the genre.

Given the abiding interest in Proust and the wealth of fresh material available, a new life of Proust in English seems overdue. These sources of information—to name the most important since the first major English biography, by George D. Painter (two volumes, 1959 and 1965)—include more than five thousand letters in Philip Kolb's twenty-one-volume edition of Proust's correspondence; the seventy-five notebooks containing Proust's manuscripts at the Bibliothèque nationale; several new French editions of the *Search,* all with generous notes; a number of sketches and poems by an adolescent Proust (many cited here for the first time in

English); and a number of memoirs by people who knew the writer and his milieu intimately. Of the memoirs, the single most important is *Monsieur Proust,* by his legendary housekeeper Céleste Albaret, who witnessed Proust's daily life for the final eight years. *Marcel Proust: A Life* takes advantage of the new material, giving for the first time in English a detailed portrait of Proust's life and his odyssey as a writer in search of his vocation.

Proust's era, 1871–1922, which he depicted in the *Search,* was one of the most exciting and momentous in history. His life encompassed the fin-de-siècle, Belle Époque, and World War I years. Charles Péguy, a poet and contemporary of Proust's, observed in 1913, on the eve of the war in which he would perish, that the world had changed more in the previous thirty years than in all the centuries since Christ. Proust came of age in a world with no electricity or central heating, without rapid transit and mass communication. By 1910 he had witnessed the arrival of electric lighting, the telephone, the automobile, motion pictures, the Paris subway, and the airplane. He characterized his era as the "age of speed" and showed in the *Search* how these remarkable inventions changed daily life and the way people perceived time and space. By 1918 he had observed the catastrophic effects of World War I. His novel bears witness to the rich, complex workings of the mind and heart—memory, love, passion, both sacred and profane—and to the oceanic trans-formations that changed the horse-and-buggy world to one of aviation, Cubism, modern fashion, comfort, and hygiene.

In *Marcel Proust: A Life* I have attempted to reveal, in addition to the writer's intimate life, his aesthetic convictions and passionate devotion to his craft. My purpose has been to study this life and to understand, as well as one reasonably can, how Marcel Proust, generally considered by his peers a talented but frivolous dilettante, came to produce what is arguably the most brilliant sustained prose narration in the history of literature.

Although this biography takes into account all areas of Proust scholarship, I have given priority to his writings and letters and to the memoirs of those who knew him best. I have benefited immeasurably from the work of all who have made important contributions to Proustian studies.

I would like to thank those who helped me along the way. I am greatly indebted to the late Philip Kolb, author of many studies and editions of Proust's texts, especially his monumental edition of Proust's correspondence, without which this book and many others on Proust would not have been possible. Philip and his wife, Dorothy, whom I also wish to thank, became good friends who encouraged and assisted me in this and other projects. Another much regretted friend is Odile Gévaudan, the daughter of Odilon and Céleste Albaret, who offered hospitality, shared memories of her parents, and showed me her extensive collection of Proust memorabilia. I also miss my good friend and gifted photographer François-Xavier Bouchart, who served as a pleasant and knowledgeable tour guide to many out-of-the way Proustian locales that he had scouted and photographed for his book *Marcel Proust: La Figure des pays.* François died too young, but his wife, Nadine Beauthéac, also a good friend, has published many of the beautiful color photographs that he left behind in her book *Les Promenades de Marcel Proust.* I wish to thank Anne Borrel for making my many visits to the Proust Museum (La Maison Tante Léonie) at Illiers such a pleasant and rewarding experience. I am indebted to Florence Callu, head of the manuscript department at the Bibliothèque nationale and cataloguer of the Proust manuscripts, for graciously providing information and access to the Proust manuscripts on many occasions; to Mme Anne-Marie Bernard for her expert assistance in collecting the photographs for this book; and to Patrice Mante-Proust for lending photographs from the family collection. This biography has benefited immensely from the suggestions of delightful, accomplished friends who read it in manuscript and whom I thank for their generous assistance: Dr. L. M. Bargeron, Jr., Elyane Dezon-Jones, Shelby Foote, Blandine McLaughlin, and J. P. Smith. Their suggestions alerted me to many errors and omissions.

I want to thank Lawrence Rainey for bringing this book, in its early stages, to the attention of Yale University Press, and all those at the press for their interest and enthusiasm, especially Lara Heimert, who has guided me so well and with such kindness, and Dan Heaton, whose impressive editorial skills are combined with great stamina and a salutary sense of humor.

On the home front, I wish to thank the University of Alabama at Birmingham for supporting this project through sabbatical leaves; my colleagues in the Department of Foreign Languages and Literatures, for their interest and support, and for their understanding when I sometimes seemed rather distracted; the considerate and efficient staff at UAB's Mervyn H. Sterne Library, which houses one of the world's most extensive Proust collections; and Dr. James C. Martin, a colleague in the Department of Physics, who kindly rescued me more than once when I was baffled by computer difficulties. I am grateful to many students and friends in the Birmingham community whose interest in my Proust courses and projects have provided encouragement over many years.

My heartfelt gratitude goes to our good friend Marie-Colette Lefort, whose

gracious hospitality during many Paris sojourns made hard work a pleasant experience, and to Robert and Dixie Bowden, true friends of many years, with whom we
visited several Proustian sites, including my first trips to Beg-Meil and Belle-Île-en-
Mer. I wish to express my love and gratitude to my beautiful, accomplished daughters, who enchant and enliven my days, Josephine Carter Monmaney, Sarah Carter
Davis, and Susanna Carter, and, above all, to my wife, Lynn, for her love, patience,
encouragement, and invaluable assistance at every phase of this long and challenging enterprise.

PART I

Petit Marcel (1870–1889)

1   *Secret Places of the Heart*   ∾

THE FIRST DAYS OF SEPTEMBER 1870 were among the most calamitous in French history. In the town of Sedan, on the Meuse River near the Belgian border, Emperor Napoléon III and his troops found themselves surrounded by an invading Prussian army that overwhelmed the French with heavy shelling. Cut off from reinforcements, the emperor, whom Victor Hugo had dubbed Napoléon le Petit, gave the order to raise the white flag. The victorious Prussians demanded unconditional surrender. The capitulation agreement was signed by the French on Friday, September 2.

In Paris the next day, as news of the swift, humiliating defeat at Sedan spread throughout the capital, Dr. Adrien Proust, a middle-aged Catholic bachelor, a grocer's son originally from the small provincial town of Illiers, married Jeanne Weil, the daughter of a wealthy Parisian Jewish family. At twenty-one, the beautiful, dark-haired woman was fifteen years younger than the bridegroom. No one knows how Adrien and Jeanne met, but it is likely that they were introduced at a government-sponsored event or social gathering. Adrien had recently risen to the top ranks in public health administration, and Jeanne's family had many connections in official circles.

The wedding ceremony took place in the town hall of the city's tenth arrondissement, where the Weils lived and where Jeanne's father, Nathé, oversaw his successful business ventures. Nathé's father had made his fortune as a porcelain manufacturer, wealth that Nathé increased as a stockbroker. Jeanne's dowry was an impressive trousseau and two hundred thousand gold francs, a considerable fortune in any era. The bride's witnesses were her twenty-two-year-old brother Georges Weil, an attorney, and her great-uncle Adolphe Crémieux, an important political leader soon to join the frantic efforts to form a new government and defend Paris against the advancing Prussians. The following day, Crémieux accepted the appointment of Minister of Justice in the Government of National Defense. The groom's witness was Dr. Gustave Cabanellas, a distinguished physician and member of the Légion d'honneur. The union was a brilliant one for the provincial shopkeeper's son, proof of the new social status Adrien enjoyed as a scientist with excellent prospects for a stellar career. As a public health official, Dr. Proust's income was in the high range of ten thousand to twenty thousand francs a year.[1]

Everyone agreed that the bride and groom made a handsome couple. Each had strong, regular features and a clear, steady gaze. Jeanne seemed serene, her beauty contemplative, her natural mirth and quick wit subdued by the solemnity of the occasion and the looming national crisis. Perhaps her most striking feature was her large, almond-shaped eyes, eyes with heavy lids that gave her a slightly Oriental look. She usually wore her beautiful dark hair pulled up or braided. Being fairly tall for a woman, she carried her tendency toward plumpness well; her heaviness later became more marked and aggravated her health problems. Adrien was a fine-looking man with an air of quiet authority and confidence. Not yet needing glasses, his eyes had the clear look of a pioneering intellectual, but one who had maintained his provincial common sense, a seeker of knowledge and practical solutions. He, too, had fine black hair, though the line had begun to recede slightly above the temples; his beard and mustache were already flecked with strands of gray.

Jeanne and Adrien

Jeanne Weil was a sensitive, exceptionally intelligent, and well-educated young woman who had a profound appreciation of music and literature. Her schooling had been primarily classical. Because girls could not attend the lycées that functioned as preparatory schools for higher education, Jeanne studied at home, and probably also with private tutors. In addition to Latin and Greek, she learned to read and speak English and some German. She was a passionate admirer of the great French masters of the seventeenth century whose works formed the central element of her education: the plays of Molière, Racine, and Corneille, as well as the letters of Mme de Sévigné. From these and other beloved books that Jeanne read and reread, she used to copy out in a notebook, writing in a fine, slanted hand, her favorite passages, committing many of them to memory.[2] As befitted her modesty, she did so in secret. Her letters contain many literary allusions, and she quotes at ease not only from French classical writers and William Shakespeare but also from such modern novelists as Honoré de Balzac and Pierre Loti.[3] An accomplished pianist like her mother, she often played the works of Mozart and Beethoven for her family and friends. Those who knew her well delighted in her company, enjoying her subtle sense of humor fed by a strong sense of the ridiculous. With all her accomplishments and her fine mind, Jeanne was reserved, preferring simplicity to ostentation, natural dignity to any display of vanity.

Both her parents were descended from wealthy families who had made their fortunes in manufacturing and trade. The Berncastels and the Weils were powerful and rich members of the Jewish *haute bourgeoisie* of Paris, with many links to legal, financial, and political figures. Home for the Weils was a large six-room apartment at 40 bis rue du Faubourg-Poissonnière, in a neighborhood of stockbrokers and businessmen. This area also comprised the theater and opera district, an ideal location for a financier whose family loved plays and music.[4] Nathé Weil was a conservative who under the reign of Louis-Philippe had joined the National Guard. Nathé often scandalized his family by his avarice. At meals, he served mediocre wines to others while keeping a bottle of a better vintage well chilled at his feet for his own delectation.[5]

Jeanne resembled her mother, born Adèle Berncastel in 1824, an attractive, highly educated woman. Like many prominent Jewish families in France, the Berncastels had adopted the comte de Saint-Simon's recommendations for the education of women. The girls received a strong background in languages, literature, art, and music so that they could carry on the tradition of the brilliant salons of the Age of Enlightenment. With this in mind, Adèle's mother had sent her regularly to the salon of her aunt Amélie, whose husband, Adolphe Crémieux, had agreed to find the time in his busy political and social agenda to be her tutor. She could not have chosen a better mentor, for Adolphe was one of the outstanding statesmen of his era. An ardent republican, leader of the radical left and the Jewish community, Crémieux had been elected since 1842 to the Chamber of Deputies in various governments and had served as minister of justice in the provisional government of 1848. On October 24, 1870, less than two months after Jeanne's wedding, he signed the decree that bears his name, granting French citizenship to Algerian Jews. Crémieux was an enlightened political leader whose efforts led to the abolition of slavery in the French colonies and of the death penalty for political crimes.[6]

In the Crémieux salon, Adèle met some of the era's most distinguished writers and composers: Alphonse de Lamartine, Alfred de Musset, Gioacchino Rossini, Victor Hugo, George Sand—whose novels she loved—and Fromenthal Halévy, whose daughter Geneviève Bizet and grandson Jacques Bizet were to be closely associated with Proust. But above all other literary works, Adèle loved those of the seventeenth century, especially the *Mémoires* of the duc de Saint-Simon and the letters of Mme de Sévigné. To Marcel, his grandmother Adèle always seemed "more Sévigné than Sévigné herself." Witty, intelligent Mme de Sévigné (1629–96), whose letters are among the most famous in French literature, chronicled the entertainments and scandals at the world's most brilliant court, that of Louis XIV, the Sun King. Her letters also reveal her passionate devotion to her daughter, from whom she was separated for long periods of time. Adèle passed her admiration of Sévigné on to Jeanne and Marcel. For Proust, the marquise became a major literary inspiration for her way of narrating, as a chronicler of her epoch, and as a model of motherly devotion. In his novel, Proust endowed the Narrator's grandmother with the same love for Sévigné's letters.[7]

In addition to the artists Adèle encountered in her aunt's salon, she met prominent politicians and social reformers. Adèle and her aunt were invited to other salons, whose leaders they in turn entertained. The young woman quickly lost any sense of insecurity, feeling just as much at home in Comtesse d'Hausson-ville's liberal salon as among the more conservative guests who gathered around Princesse Mathilde, niece of Napoléon I and longtime salon hostess, whom Proust knew in the final decade of her life. By the time of her marriage, Adèle was a well-educated, gentle, and self-sacrificing woman, in many ways the opposite of her eccentric husband, Nathé. Her daughter Jeanne took after her in both temperament and taste.

What had Jeanne, the product of this milieu, thought of Adrien Proust when they first met? Intelligent, well brought up, and polite he certainly was, but he knew next to nothing about literature and music. What kind of life would she have with him? She must have sensed that he was a good man, solid, reliable, someone who might well become endearing. Being in love was not the most important consideration in the decision to marry. The most one could hope for was that love would follow marriage and last for a lifetime. This seems to have been true for Jeanne and Adrien. Proust later wrote about middle-class marriages in *Jean Santeuil:* "A love-match, that is to say a marriage based on love, would have been considered as a proof of vice. Love was something that came after marriage and lasted until death. No woman ever stopped loving her husband any more than she would have stopped loving her mother." Proust looked approvingly on "this couple whose union was not a matter of free choice, but the result of middle-class conventions and respectable notions, but who, for all that, will remain together until death breaks the bond."[8]

Mixed marriages, although rare under the Second Empire, occurred more frequently in wealthy Jewish families. The Weils accepted such a union for their daughter more readily because they did not observe the Sabbath or keep a kosher house. They went to temple only on major religious days, such as Yom Kippur.[9] As was customary in such marriages, Jeanne agreed to raise the children as Catholics. Out of respect for her parents, she refused to convert to Catholicism.

All evidence suggests that Adrien and Jeanne were devoted to each other. During their marriage, he had brief, discreet affairs with courtesans, actresses, and singers, without causing any apparent harm to his relationship with Jeanne. According to the mores of the time, virile men of the middle class were expected to indulge in such escapades. No one knows what Jeanne thought about her future husband when they met, but she and her parents must have believed in the prospects of this gentile doctor, just in his prime, who had arrived from nowhere and ascended in record time to the first rank of young scientists.

The Proust family, one of the oldest in the small town of Illiers, near Chartres, can be traced back as far as the sixteenth century. Adrien's ancestors, for the most part, belonged to the middle class and held administrative posts that, under the ancien régime, were normally reserved for notables. The records list Prousts who were bailiffs, elected representatives, and lawyers. In 1589 Jehan Proust was listed as a member of the Assembly of Notables, a civic institution dating from the Middle Ages. In 1621, when Louis XIII was king, Gilles Proust purchased the office of bailiff that passed down to his descendants, some of whom are buried in the church of Saint-Jacques in Illiers. With his new office Gilles became exempted from the poll tax paid by serfs and commoners and rose to the ranks of the upper bourgeoisie. In August 1633 Gilles's brother Robert was appointed tax collector, thereby assuming the annual obligations of supplying the marquis d'Illiers with the sum of 10,500 francs minted at Tours and of providing a candle at Candlemas for the cathedral of Notre-Dame de Chartres. Adrien's other ancestors remained in the lower middle class as merchants or farmers.

Adrien's father, François-Valentin Proust, was born in 1801, the youngest of seven children.[10] The family lived in the rue du Cheval-Blanc in an ancient house whose entrance had a low Romanesque arch and sandstone steps. When François-Valentin was in his mid-twenties, he married Catherine-Virginie Torcheux from the nearby village of Cernay. The couple established a general store at number 11, place du Marché, opposite the church of Saint-Jacques. There they earned their living by selling a variety of items, including honey, a chocolate touted as being good for your health, spices, cotton, pottery, hardware, spirits and liqueurs, and candles made from their own supply of wax.[11]

Their first child, Louise Virginie, born in 1826, died when she was only six. In 1828 Virginie gave birth to another girl, Françoise-Élisabeth-Joséphine Proust. Six years passed before their last child was born; on March 18, 1834, François-Valentin and Virginie became the parents of a son, Achille Adrien Proust.

As a child, Adrien was healthy and intelligent, a good boy endowed with an insatiable curiosity about his surroundings and a passion for learning. When he finished elementary school, the family decided that the serious, hardworking pupil should prepare for the priesthood by attending the seminary at the Collège impérial de Chartres, where he had won a scholarship. At the seminary he continued to be an excellent student. In 1853 he received his bachelor's degrees in literature and science and passed brilliantly the examination for his certificate of aptitude in the physical sciences. Despite the many greater awards and honorific titles that were later his, he always remained proud that the name Adrien Proust was engraved on the honor roll in the parlor of the old college in Chartres.[12]

After graduation Adrien declared himself free to follow his new calling, science; against his father's wishes, he abandoned the priesthood for medicine. To pursue his career he went to Paris and enrolled at the Academie de médecin, becoming the first of his family to leave Illiers and seek his fortune in the big city. Unknown and entirely on his own, he succeeded through hard work and concentration, advancing rapidly through the medical ranks until he occupied a position in the vanguard.

Adrien sensed that a new era was dawning. He ceased practicing his religion as he was drawn, like so many of his generation, to the great movement of scientific exploration. He determined to be part of the revolution in science that was taking place in the laboratories and amphitheaters across Europe in the second half of the nineteenth century. In France the founders of this new age were men who taught natural and physical sciences and stressed the importance of empirical experimentation. Such pioneers as Philippe Pinel had created new fields of study based on observation and experimentation rather than ignorance and superstition. Pinel's work with the insane, carried on for the most part during the turbulent times of the French Revolution and early Empire, had shown that mental illness was the result not of demons but of physiological and psychological problems. His observations and studies laid the foundation for the establishment of psychiatry as a field of medicine, demonstrating that the methods of observation used in other sciences were also applicable to the healing arts. Marie-François-Xavier Bichat's anatomical research led to the creation of histology, the microscopic study of the structure of human tissues. Bichat was the first to simplify anatomy and physiology by reducing the complex structures of organs to their elementary tissues. These and other revolutionary discoveries influenced Adrien's research and methods.

When his father died in Illiers on October 2, 1855, Adrien, though only twenty-one, had been studying medicine for two years. Death had robbed Adrien of the chance to prove to his father that he could become a distinguished physician. After attending his father's funeral, Adrien returned to Paris, where he excelled, winning prizes at the Academie de médecin for his hospital work and claiming top honors as a resident. His career advanced rapidly. In 1862 Adrien defended his thesis on "Idiopathic Pneumothorax" and received his medical degree. The following year he was named chief of clinic after another competitive state examination. From 1863 to 1866, he practiced medicine and continued his advanced studies. In 1866 he defended his doctoral thesis, "Différentes formes de ramollissement du cerveau" (Different types of softening of the brain), passing with honorable mention the *concours d'agrégation,* a competitive state examination for teaching posts that qualified him to teach in the Academie de médecin.

It was during the cholera epidemic of 1866, while chief of clinic at the Hôpital de la Charité, that Adrien began the work that eventually brought him international fame. At the beginning of the nineteenth century, Asiatic cholera had not spread far beyond India, but with the rapid expansion of trade between Asia and Europe, epidemics of the disease began to reach France and soon grew more frequent. In 1832, two years before Adrien was born, cholera killed 154 of Illiers's citizens and more than 100,000 people in France.[13] Another epidemic swept the country in 1849, carrying away more than 300,000 French souls. Although earlier plagues of cholera had ravaged France, the great epidemic of 1866, with a fatality rate of 50 percent, plunged the entire nation into mourning.[14]

Cholera, a severe infectious disease prevalent in warm regions where filth and poor sanitary conditions are found, is spread by contact with fecally contaminated food and water. After a short incubation period of only two or three days the victim begins to suffer terrible diarrhea and nausea leading to extreme dehydration. In the severe 1866 epidemic, Dr. Proust spent long hours at a stretch without rest, caring for his patients at great personal risk. Yet despite having taken all possible measures to save them, he could only stand by and watch helplessly as their conditions worsened. As dehydration reached a critical stage, the victims suffered horrible muscle cramps, the eyes became sunken, the cheeks hollow, the voice hoarse, and blood pressure dropped. Death quickly followed. Adrien understood that given the magnitude of the disease, individual treatment could never defeat cholera. The solution lay in prevention.

In spite of the vigilance of scientists, the plague of 1866 had spread by following a new, more rapid route from India to Suez and into Europe. Adrien, in addition to his responsibilities as a public health official, belonged to a group of young scientists who were studying hygiene and epidemiology under Doctors Tardieu and Fauvel. Like Fauvel, who conceived the idea of a *cordon sanitaire*, Adrien was convinced that the only way to prevent plagues was to define and implement principles of international hygiene. A cordon sanitaire would establish a boundary line of nations cooperating to enforce a strict system of quarantine for ships entering their waters. In his clinic, Dr. Proust began to test this idea, with excellent results, by isolating patients sick with cholera. Other doctors and scientists noticed his tireless efforts to combat the disease and his disregard of danger. Although it was nearly twenty years before the German bacteriologist Robert Koch isolated the bacillus that causes cholera, Adrien knew that such an agent must exist. If his theory about how cholera moved westward from India was correct, the deadly epidemics could be halted by creating a cordon sanitaire on Europe's eastern flank. In order to implement such a plan, he must first determine the routes by which the disease spread. Foreseeing the importance of an organized effort among nations to improve world health, he undertook a campaign to persuade political figures of the Second Empire to support his plan.

After the International Health Conference in Vienna in 1869, the minister of agriculture and commerce sent Dr. Proust to Russia and Persia on a mission to learn the routes by which cholera had arrived from Russia in the most recent epidemics. He would travel first to Astrakhan in Russia, then on to Persia, tracing the route followed by the epidemic of 1832. Then, for the return to Paris, he would take a southerly route: Mecca, Turkey, and Egypt, following the path taken by the 1849 and 1866 epidemics.

Adrien's voyage began under excellent conditions in the summer of 1869, when he boarded a car of the new Northern Railway bound for Moscow. The train, a model of nineteenth-century mass-transit technology, combined speed and comfort, and the service on board was superb, provided by an astonishingly large number of valets and waiters. But when Dr. Proust continued the journey from Moscow, conditions immediately became more primitive. He left the Russian capital in a wooden carriage known as a *kibitka,* a contraption that, as Balzac had remarked decades earlier when visiting Russia, "makes one feel in every bone the tiniest bump in the road."[15] Adrien had to endure jarring potholes in the road as he traveled in withering heat all the way to Saint Petersburg and on to Astrakhan. These hardships tested his physical stamina and courage but did not deter the determined doctor, more thankful than ever for his robust constitution.

To continue across the Caucasus Mountains and the high plateaus of Persia, Adrien mounted horses and eventually camels when he joined a caravan following the ancient routes across the desert. During this adventuresome trip, Dr. Proust lived and ate like the natives, whom he never tired of observing. Along the way he took notes, often while rocking in the saddle, learning as much as he could about customs and hygiene among the Persians. Reaching Teheran, he found himself, for the first time in weeks, in opulent surroundings when he was received by the shah of Persia and his minister of foreign affairs, who presented the brave physician with sumptuous carpets. The Persian officials were curious about the scientific nature of the doctor's voyage and hoped that their country would also benefit from his efforts to find relief from cholera. In Mecca, Adrien was appalled by the crush of pilgrims in the holy city to which each Muslim must make at least one pilgrimage before he dies. He watched as multitudes arrived and departed, living throughout their stay in the most primitive sanitary conditions, a sight that reinforced his convictions about how diseases spread. He journeyed on to Constantinople, where the Grand Vizier Ali Pasha gave him another magnificent reception.

After his arrival in Egypt, where he inspected the ports and ships bound for Europe, Adrien reviewed his observations and continued drafting his report, certain that he had uncovered the routes followed by the disease that sprang from the waters of faraway Indian lagoons to wind its long and deadly journey westward. The observations he made during this scientific expedition also confirmed his theory that cholera was spread by rats—always the first infected in new epidemics—which boarded ships mooring in Indian ports before sailing to Egypt, and then on to Europe.

After this long, arduous, often dangerous voyage, Dr. Proust had become an early authority on epidemiology. Henceforth he was a key member of France's delegation to international conferences on the prevention of epidemics and a tireless, outspoken advocate for the establishment of an international sanitation system against the spread of disease.

Adrien later proposed that all ships bound for Europe be quarantined at Suez, the only place where vessels from India and the Far East converged. In *La Défense de l'Europe contre la peste* (The defense of Europe against cholera), he wrote, "Egypt must be considered Europe's barrier against cholera." His theory and proposals were not immediately accepted. Some international political figures, keen on maintaining their countries' authority and autonomy, had been troubled by his statement that "questions of international hygiene reach beyond the borders established by politics."[16] Adrien's battle against cholera proved to him that being an accomplished, innovative scientist did not suffice. To his scientific skills he added those of diplomacy in order to overcome the resistance to his proposals made by some nations, especially Great Britain, which saw this French doctor's restrictive plans as a threat to the interests of its trading empire.[17] It took a series of international conferences and the Bombay plague of 1877 before governments began to take steps that eventually implemented all Dr. Proust's recommendations.

By November 26, 1869, Adrien had returned to Paris from his long mission and filed a report that was published the following summer in the government's *Journal officiel.* Sometime during this period, fresh from his successful and daring expedition, acclaimed by scientists and officials of the Second Empire, Adrien met Jeanne Weil. In early August 1870, he set out again to inspect entry points between France and other countries. By August 27 he had returned to Paris on an important personal mission: to sign the marriage contract between himself and Mlle Jeanne Clémence Weil. At the signing, the couple agreed to the creation of a joint estate as established by the Napoleonic Code.

On September 1, the day the battle at Sedan raged and sealed the fate of the Second Empire, Adrien moved into the new apartment that he and Jeanne would inhabit at 8, rue Roy, in the eighth arrondissement. The yearly rental of 2,500 francs indicated his new financial status. At age thirty-six, the busy, ambitious doctor was ready to take a wife and start a family.

Siege and War

After the Proust-Weil wedding and the banquet, over which hung the gloom of uncertainty about the country's future, the couple settled into their Right Bank apartment near the newly completed Church of Saint-Augustin. As Adrien and Jeanne put away their wedding finery, they could hear the noises of civil strife erupting in the streets as the Second Empire began its death throes. The following day, Jules Favre and Léon Gambetta led a revolutionary mob from the meeting of the legislature to the Hôtel de Ville, the city hall of Paris, and proclaimed the birth of the Third Republic.

When more details of the fate of the emperor and his army reached Paris, Adrien and Jeanne, who had many friends in high positions, grew even more alarmed and saddened. The Second Empire's sudden and disgraceful defeat shocked them. They, like many of their compatriots, had believed the rosy forecasts of vain, boastful leaders and generals. After the debacle at Sedan, nothing stood between the outer defenses surrounding Paris and the invading Prussian army. Only one short month before, in a world now vanished, Adrien had been invited to the Tuileries Palace, where Her Majesty Empress-Regent Eugénie had bestowed upon him the red ribbon of the Légion d'honneur for his heroic efforts against cholera. Now, with the humiliated and generally despised emperor a prisoner of the Prussians, the empress was preparing to flee incognito, escorted by her American-born dentist and friend Dr. John Evans, to exile in England. France was left to face the twin scourges of a military invasion that could only result in the siege of Paris and civil war, as the French divided into a number of seething factions, chiefly monarchists, republicans, and communists. Adrien, angry at the fiasco brought upon the nation by the ineptitude of both political and military leaders, determined to resume his normal activities in a world gone awry.

The siege of Paris began on September 19 when the Prussians surrounded the city and cut all lines of communication.[18] Henceforth balloon post and carrier pigeons were the only means—and very uncertain ones at that—of communicating with the outside world. It was clear that the Prussians intended to starve the city into submission. The government estimated that the food supply would last only until January 20. Food rationing began, with the immediate result of soaring prices. Many suppliers and speculators hoarded food out of greed. Once beef grew scarce and expensive, the slaughter of horses for meat became commonplace. In a short time, Parisians, creators of one of the world's most delectable cuisines, found themselves reduced to nibbling on dogs, cats, and even rats.

The capital now lived in fear of starvation, civil war, and bombardment by the Prussians. The French were poorly organized to handle an emergency on a vast scale, and the situation was made worse by the various factions within the capital who distrusted one another. In the poor districts, there was talk of rebellion, as a number of red divisions pushed for the creation of a revolutionary council that was to become known as the Commune. Some radicals suggested reinstating the Terror.

Both Adrien and Jeanne worried about the safety of their families. Even the region near Chartres and Illiers that had always seemed remote in times of national crisis was not safe. In October, Prussians sacked Châteaudun and occupied Chartres, only twenty or so kilometers northeast of Illiers. For several months Adrien had no word from his widowed mother. In December, desperate for news, he attempted to contact her by carrier pigeon. He sent an urgent message to a friend in Tours, the only destination accessible, where his family knew a draper named Esnault with whom his mother might have taken refuge: "Has she left Illiers? Is she with you? Is she all right? I beg you to send me answers to all these questions by carrier pigeon."[19] After some delay, Adrien received word that his mother had remained in Illiers safe from harm.

Adrien watched with alarm as Paris became filthy and rank. He saw conditions grow ripe for cholera, smallpox, and typhoid as garbage and human waste piled up in the streets, creating a terrible stench. With each passing day, the city resembled more and more the primitive countries he had visited on his scientific mission. Events soon justified his fears as the mortality rate doubled, then tripled.

Nathé Weil's extraordinary decision to leave Paris was perhaps the best gauge of the siege's severity. Among his eccentricities was a horror of spending the night anywhere except in his own bed. Once, before taking a brief excursion to the seaside resort of Dieppe, Nathé made certain he could return home by train the same evening. It was no different when he went on his daily visit to his half-brother Louis's estate at Auteuil, on the outskirts of Paris. There, the two men would dine, discussing business and arguing about politics as they ate. No matter how heated the discussion or how delicious the food and wine he consumed at his brother's expense, Nathé would never agree to stay the night, but always returned home to the rue du Faubourg Poissonnière. Now, with Paris becoming a cold, bleak, desperate city, slowly starving to death, Nathé made the single exception in his eighty-five years of life and took his wife to safety at Étampes. There, miserable but secure, they would wait for the madness to end.

Jeanne, eager to forget the chaotic world outside her new apartment, kept busy organizing the household and overseeing the servants. After trying various arrangements of the furniture, she found the one that worked best, making certain that her husband's favorite chair was close to the fire. She had quickly learned his needs and habits as well as the abilities and shortcomings of the servants. The young wife read and played the piano, occupying herself as best she could, but

Jeanne, like most Parisians, longed for one thing: the return to a normal life. One day, scarcely three months after her wedding, Jeanne realized that she was pregnant. Adrien, who had postponed marriage to pursue his medical career, received the news that he was to be a father with satisfaction. He regretted only that Jeanne must carry the baby during such violent and uncertain times.

The siege showed no signs of ending, and luck did not favor the beleaguered Parisians. By early December a severe winter began when the temperature sank to near freezing. Gas lines had been cut, firewood became scarce, and the food supply continued to dwindle at an alarming rate. Officials estimated that at best, no more than a month's supply of wood remained. Snow came early; on December 21 the temperature hit a bone-chilling minus fourteen degrees Celsius. When white bread was no longer available, the government launched a propaganda campaign to convince skeptical Parisians of the virtues of brown bread. By the end of December a number of animals in the zoo had been sold at high prices and butchered, including two beloved young elephants named Castor and Pollux.

Early in the new year of 1871, the Prussians grew impatient and began bombarding the city. On January 14 the writer and diarist Edmond de Goncourt, a neighbor of Uncle Louis Weil's at Auteuil, shot a blackbird, whose roosting habits he had observed, and ate him for supper. On January 19 the first bread rationing began, followed three days later by an alarming but not unexpected event. A group of furious, drunken communists and prisoners newly released from a Paris jail approached the Hôtel de Ville, where they exchanged fire with its defenders. This was the first incident in which French fired upon French. At last, on January 26, after a siege of 131 days and a bombardment that lasted 24, the government announced a truce agreement with the Prussians. An assembly would be elected to convene at Bordeaux, recently named the official seat of the French government, and debate a formal peace or a resumption of the war. The Prussians, who had every reason to be confident of their strength and the eventual outcome of peace or war, allowed Parisians to obtain fresh supplies of food and fuel.

No sooner had the truce been signed and elections held than the French conservative and liberal factions began fighting among themselves. Adolphe Thiers was chosen to preside at Versailles over a provisional government whose majority was conservative and favored the restoration of the monarchy. Meanwhile, the Communards and other leftists controlled Paris. From the beginning they distrusted the Versailles government because they believed that Thiers was too conservative and too eager to accept a humiliating peace with Prussia.

The treaty with Prussia imposed harsh terms on France: cession to Prussia of

Alsace and a large part of Lorraine, plus the payment within three years of a war indemnity equivalent to a billion dollars in gold francs. Until the indemnity was paid, Prussian troops would remain in northern France. Thiers, insensitive to the hardships Paris had endured during the siege and indifferent to the fury its citizens felt over the peace treaty, announced measures the workers of Paris found equally severe for them: all landlords were entitled to demand full back payment on rent suspended during the siege; the National Guard's daily salary of thirty sous would no longer be paid.

On March 18 the violent insurrection known as the Commune began when Thiers, in an attempt to disarm the Paris National Guard, decided to reclaim the cannons that had been moved to safety in the poorer districts of the city during the brief Prussian occupation. To recoup the weapons Thiers's generals had planned an early-morning raid. The action began well, but once the government troops had taken possession of the cannons, they realized that no one had thought to requisition enough horses to transport the large guns. When the Communards awoke to discover what had happened, intense fighting began, during the course of which the rebels summarily executed two of Thiers's generals. Paris found itself besieged by its own government.

Adrien refused to stay at home even on the days of heavy street fighting. As casualties mounted, Jeanne became frantic for his safety. Reminding him that she and the expected baby would need a husband and father, she urged him to be cautious while making his way through the dangerous, barricaded streets. Adrien explained that he had no choice; he was a doctor and must look after his patients and fulfill his teaching and administrative duties. If he had had the courage to travel on horseback through the most primitive regions of Russia, Persia, and Egypt, surely he could cross Paris to reach his office at the Hôpital de la Charité on the other side of the Seine.

One day in early spring, just after Dr. Proust left the apartment for the hospital, an insurgent aimed his rifle at the well-dressed bourgeois gentleman and fired. The bullet brushed Adrien's clothes, barely missing its mark. Adrien was shaken by the incident, but Jeanne, almost six months pregnant, became sick with fear over the dangers he refused to avoid. He had vital duties to occupy his time while she had to stay at home, made miserable by worry about his safety, that of her parents, and the prospects for the future of the unborn child. She accepted her husband's obligation to duty and admired his courage, but this did not make the situation easier for her, uncomfortably pregnant and living apart from her beloved mother. Jeanne's parents grew alarmed at her condition and decided they would all go to

Auteuil to await the birth of her baby. The traditional story has been that Jeanne fled with Adrien to the shelter of Uncle Louis's estate after the narrow miss of the sniper's bullet. But it is just as likely that the couple went there because it had become a family tradition to go to Auteuil during the warmer months, as did many other fashionable Parisians.[20] An 1855 guidebook describes Auteuil as the spring and summer playground of retired bankers and lawyers who arrived accompanied by their cooks, grooms, coachmen, and valets.[21]

Uncle Louis, recently widowed, had made his fortune early as a businessman; he owned a button and silverware factory and fine property in Paris on boulevard Haussmann, an address that his future great nephew was to make famous. Known for his sense of humor and kindheartedness, Louis gladly took in his niece and her husband. Louis lived in a spacious, comfortable house in the middle of a large garden that had the appearance of a bucolic haven. Although Auteuil was not as removed from danger as Jeanne would have liked, it was safer than the streets of central Paris and close enough for Adrien to ride the trolley from Auteuil to Saint-Sulpice, the stop nearest his hospital. This was presumably a safer way to reach his office than striking out on his own from rue Roy through the bitterly contested streets.

Thiers, whose generals commanded well-trained and disciplined troops, had decided that there would be no negotiating with the Communards, whom he considered no better than common criminals. In April, Thiers began bombarding the city, an unthinkable act to most Parisians. Auteuil, which lay between Versailles and Paris, suffered heavy damage from the shelling. Edmond de Goncourt, the noted writer and future founder of the Académie Goncourt, lived in a house that took many hits. One shell pierced the roof, but Goncourt's art treasures and memorabilia escaped harm. Auteuil's fourteenth-century church was so heavily damaged that it was later torn down and replaced by a modern church. When the bombardment ended, many homes had been reduced to piles of smoldering rubble, but Uncle Louis's property had not been hit. Jeanne and her family, although severely shaken, had remained safe from harm.

On May 16 the realist painter Gustave Courbet, who had become a zealous revolutionary, took part in the destruction of one of Paris's most famous monuments, the Vendôme Column. Erected to commemorate the military victories of Napoléon I, the column was a shrine sacred to veterans but viewed by the Communards as an affront to the Republic and the brotherhood of man. This act was among many that caused support for the Commune to erode. During the uprising's "bloody week," May 21–28, Paris burned. Many of the fires were set by *pétroleuses,* women who threw kerosene bombs into public buildings and private homes.

On May 28, Generals MacMahon and Galliffet entered the city. The Commune, ill prepared to fight, quickly collapsed. In the following days, the victors inflicted a brutal repression on the Paris rebels as Thiers's men rounded up more than seventeen thousand Communards, including many women and children, and executed them, dumping their bodies in mass graves. Peace had returned to the City of Light, but at a terrible price. Many areas lay in ruins, including the Palais-Royal, the Ministries of Justice and Finance, and most of the rue de Rivoli and the boulevard de Sébastopol. Fire had destroyed the Tuileries Palace, the vast section of the Louvre where Napoléon III and Empress Eugénie had hosted magnificent balls to the tunes of Jacques Offenbach's lively operettas. The war and civil strife had left many severe wounds that needed to heal; there was rebuilding to undertake, the creation of a new government and constitution, and the payment of a huge war indemnity. In June, Adolphe Thiers was elected president of the Third Republic. Despite its bloody beginning, France was to prosper under the Third Republic, the longest in its history.

Marcel

Adrien and the family decided that Jeanne, now in her last month of pregnancy, would remain at Auteuil until she gave birth and it was safe to return to the rue Roy apartment. On Monday, July 10, Saint Felicity's Day, a baby boy was born at eleven in the evening. Jeanne's labor was difficult and the baby seemed so weak that the family feared it would die. On July 13, at two in the afternoon, Adrien, the baby's grandfather Nathé Weil, and great-uncle Louis Weil went to the town hall in the sixteenth arrondissement, where they signed a birth certificate bearing the child's given names: Marcel-Valentin-Louis-Eugène-Georges Proust. During the next two weeks, Jeanne and Adrien slept little as they constantly took care of their baby, who remained in poor condition. Then, to their great relief, they realized that the little boy's life was no longer in danger, although he remained frail.

The family blamed the infant's precarious health on the privations, anxiety, and lack of proper nourishment Jeanne had endured during her pregnancy. They were also convinced that her distress when the sniper's bullet nearly struck down Adrien had aggravated her state of nervous exhaustion as she approached term. Jeanne adored her son as much as she feared for his future. Devoting herself entirely to looking after the baby, she did everything possible to increase his chances of survival and make him strong. The constant attention and worry made necessary by events and the infant's frail condition marked the beginning of an anxious, loving dependency. Bending over him, talking to him, encouraging him to be strong, she called him "my little Marcel" and "my little wolf."[22]

On Saturday, August 5, Marcel was baptized at the parish church of Saint-Louis d'Antin. Although neither parent continued to practice a religion, the Proust children were raised as Catholics. Later, the boy would be proud of his certificates of baptism and confirmation signed by the archbishop of Paris.[23] In spite of his great love for his mother, Marcel did not consider himself Jewish, although he never forgot or denied his heritage.

When Marcel was twenty-two months old, Jeanne gave birth to a second son. Jeanne and Adrien named Marcel's little brother Robert-Émile-Sigismond-Léon. In August 1873 the family, needing larger quarters because of the new baby and Adrien's rapidly advancing career, moved a short distance east to an apartment at 9, boulevard Malesherbes, not far from the church of the Madeleine.

The entrance to the building where the Proust family lived for the next twenty-seven years was a large, sculpted double wooden door. Inside was a spacious inner courtyard, at the back of which stood a stairwell leading to the second-story main entrance to the Proust apartment. The apartment contained four bedrooms: Marcel and Robert occupied the two at one end of the apartment between the kitchen and the bathroom. The parents' bedroom was at the other end, near the living room, dining room, and water closet. Dr. Proust converted the fourth bedroom into an office, where he received private patients and wrote his speeches and books. The apartment, typical of the oppressive bourgeois style of the era, was "a rather dark interior, crammed with heavy furniture, all windows air-tight with curtains, smothered with carpets, everything in black and red . . . not . . . far removed . . . from the dark bric-a-brac of Balzac's time."[24]

The birth of a sibling and the move to a new apartment at first shocked the toddler Marcel, whose love for his mother became more exclusive and tyrannical now that he had serious competition for her attention and caresses. In time, Marcel understood that his relation with her was unique and not in jeopardy, for Robert required little attention, preferring to roughhouse with children his own age, play outdoors, and impress his father with feats of athletic prowess. In the first photographs of the two little boys, Marcel adopts a protective attitude toward Robert, placing an arm around him or holding his hand.

Robert's earliest memories of Marcel were of a benevolent, tender older brother who "watched over me with an enveloping, infinite sweetness that was, so to speak, maternal."[25] Robert, like many second children, experienced none of the difficulties and traumas of the first. The family always believed that the younger brother had the advantage of being conceived and born in a stable time. Unlike Marcel, he was not subject to fits of hysteria and tantrums; most often, he seemed the epitome of a bright, happy, normal baby. Robust like his father, athletic, and diligent as a student, he seemed the ideal son. Robert did, of course, demonstrate typical childish behavior. He was possessive about toys, refusing to lend them to playmates his age, sharing only with Marcel, or with his father on those rare occasions when the doctor could spare a few minutes to play with his young sons, who delighted in the attention. Robert would say to Marcel: "You're nice; you'd never hurt me. Here, I'll lend you my tipcart!"[26] These memories from childhood were always infused with the sunshine of the countryside, whether in the more distant garden at Illiers or in nearby Auteuil.

In December 1873 Adrien published his acclaimed *Essai sur l'hygiène internationale*. The doctor had begun to concentrate on the specialization that was to occupy him for the rest of his life.[27] He added an appointment to his medical responsibilities when he became chief of the Sainte-Perrine hospital in Auteuil, creating a professional attachment to the little town just outside Paris. For the next twenty-five years, Uncle Louis's home at Auteuil was the Proust family's second home, a peaceful oasis where they spent most of the spring and early summer days. Louis had purchased his property in 1857 from actress Eugénie Doche, who had created one of the century's most celebrated roles, that of Marguerite Gautier in Dumas fils's play *La Dame aux camélias*. The atmosphere in the Auteuil house, redolent with the perfumes of courtesans and actresses, perfectly suited Uncle Louis, who adored beautiful actresses of easy virtue.[28] Eugénie had decorated her residence in the Napoléon III style, and Louis did not bother to alter the decor or furnishings. Valentine Thomson, a cousin who visited Marcel at Auteuil, described the furnishings as "grim, frumpy, solid furniture, smothered with frills of silk, dark and uninviting like a roomful of ancient, overdressed maiden aunts."[29]

Louis's house, built of quarrystones, was large, with spacious rooms, including a drawing room with a grand piano and a billiard room, decorated with flower stands, where the family sometimes slept when seeking a cooler room during heat waves.[30] Surrounding the dwelling was a sizable lot of 1,500 square meters. Two small buildings standing next to the street served as a stable for the horses and as servants' quarters. The garden contained a pond surrounded by hawthorn trees, whose blossoms Marcel also admired in Uncle Jules's garden in Illiers. Among the abundant flowers and trees that were to embellish the pages of his future novel, hawthorns occupy a privileged position. In the back of the garden stood a building used as an orangery.[31]

Jeanne and her mother must have liked the property immediately, not only for its beauty but because of Auteuil's place in literary history. Fashionable during the final third of Louis XIV's reign, Auteuil had been home to many of Jeanne and her mother's literary idols: Molière, Racine, and Boileau had all lived there at one time. So had the eighteenth-century painter Hubert Robert, celebrated for his romantic depictions of Roman ruins. In the nineteenth century, the village had been the temporary home of François-René de Chateaubriand and the beautiful hostess Mme de Récamier, as well as Victor Hugo.[32] The Goncourt brothers, Edmond and Jules, had purchased a house on the boulevard Montmorency, where they took up permanent residence in 1868. The two brothers were extraordinarily close and shared a passion for literature and collecting objets d'art. They had collaborated on pioneering plays, novels, and above all their diary, known as the *Journal des Goncourt*, which became their most famous work and a major chronicle of their era. In 1870 Jules died at Auteuil, leaving the older Edmond alone to continue their work.

For the almost daily trips to Paris, Jeanne and Adrien had a number of choices: they might take the family carriage or the Zone railway that took passengers to the Saint-Lazare station; to go directly to his home office, Dr. Proust could take the double-decker Auteuil-Madeleine omnibus, which his faithful servant Jean Blanc would keep waiting when it stopped at Louis's gate, while Adrien kissed his young family good-bye.[33] By taking the trolley that ran from Auteuil to Saint-Sulpice, he could easily reach the Left Bank and the Academie de médecin. On extremely hot days, the family would board one of the steamboats that ran from Auteuil to the center of Paris.

Louis, who seemed to relish the proverbial role of childless, rich uncle, eagerly adopted Jeanne's family. He invited many relatives and friends to copious Sunday dinners. For these reunions, servants would fill the dining room vases to overflowing with white roses cut from the garden. In the haven of Auteuil, this close-knit family delighted in one another's company and in the pleasures they shared: gossip, books, letters, and informal family concerts.

In 1876 Louis, in his most ostentatious display of avuncular affection, added a wing to the main house for Jeanne and her family. The addition contained two bedrooms on the second story, two on the third, and a large attic room on the top floor that was most likely used by Marcel and Robert as a study.[34] The boys adored Uncle Louis Weil, whom they would tease, calling him the "squire of Auteuil" or "the thin squire of Auteuil," a not so subtle allusion to Louis's expanding girth and reputation as a bon vivant and gourmet.[35]

When Robert was a toddler, Marcel enjoyed relatively good health. In warm weather the boys spent hours together outdoors. At Auteuil they played in the garden and wandered the paths between the arbors. On one occasion, after hiding their clothes in the bushes, they pretended to be savages and burst out stark naked in front of their flabbergasted family. But Marcel's favorite activity by far was reading. He would curl up in one of the large wicker chairs on the lawn and lose himself entirely in an adventure story such as Théophile Gautier's *Le Capitaine Fracasse* or another novel on his mother's approved list.

The house and garden at Auteuil remained vivid in Proust's memory. A few years before his death, he reminisced about the vanished dwelling in a preface he wrote for a friend's book.[36] His impressions, typically, play on all the senses: "This house where we lived with my uncle, in Auteuil in the middle of a big garden . . . was completely lacking in style. Yet I can hardly describe the happiness I felt when, after having come up rue La Fontaine in bright sunlight and in the fragrance of the linden-trees, I went up to my room for a moment." There he always recalled the smooth, lush, heavy blue satin Empire curtains, the simple odors of soap, and the reflections in the mirrored armoire. All the sights and smells inside the house were intensified by the cool, close air kept in by doors and windows shut against the heat. In the dining room, he chose a thick crystal glass from which he drank apple cider so chilled that when he swallowed it, the refreshing liquid "would press against the sides of my throat in an adherence that was total, delicious, and profound." The atmosphere of the room was transparent, congealed "like a block of marble veined by the odor of cherries already piled high in the fruit-dishes, and where the knives—in the most vulgar bourgeois style, but one that enchanted me—were posed on little prisms of crystal. The iridescences emanating from them did more than add a mystic quality to the smell of gruyère cheese and apricots. In the half light the crystal knife-rests projected onto the walls rainbow rays resembling ocelli, like those on a peacock's tail, that I found as marvelous as the stained-glass windows at Reims."[37]

The house and grounds at Auteuil, like the relatively few trips to Illiers, seem to have made a more lasting impression on Marcel than did the family apartment in Paris. With Marcel's constitution becoming stronger, the happy, carefree days returned for the Prousts. There were signs as well that France had begun to recover from the destruction left by the war and civil strife. The staggering indemnity to Prussia had been paid much sooner than required, a feat that amazed all observers.

France was about to enter a period of remarkable change and prosperity that became known as the Belle Époque.

Childhood

Jeanne Proust possessed a lively mind, an unfailing sense of humor, and a profound appreciation of literature and music, combined with common sense and a firm belief in traditional bourgeois values. Although somewhat shy and self-effacing, she was strict with her sons regarding proper dress and grooming, neatness, manners, handwriting, and language, including the use of dignified expressions. She later destroyed her adolescent sons' letters if the handwriting and contents did not meet her high standards of taste and refinement. She also tried, with no success, to teach Marcel the value of money.

His mother's influence was the most important in Marcel's life. Not only did he strive to be like her; nature had made him like her, at least in outward appearance. One had only to see them standing next to each other to realize that his face bore many of her traits: the same oval shape, the same large, dark eyes. As Jeanne gazed lovingly at the child whose visage reflected hers, her Marcel, her little wolf, she must have been aware that he appeared remarkably unwolflike. The boy was frail and anxious, and burst easily into tears. How to make him able to stand on his own should something happen to her? She wanted him to be strong and independent and devoted herself to that goal. Although he displayed all the symptoms of a mama's boy, Marcel does not seem to have been a sissy. He eagerly joined in childhood games, enjoyed fishing, and took horseback riding lessons.

With his father often away or working when at home, Marcel's mother and grandmother Adèle Weil supervised his cultural education, exposing him to what they considered the best works in literature and music, spending many hours nurturing and feeding his insatiable curiosity. They taught him languages, primarily German and Latin, and arranged for additional study with private tutors. In 1881, when he was nine, Marcel wrote a short letter in German to his grandmother on her birthday, wishing her much happiness and that she be spared a tooth extraction.[38] In the letter, he mentioned that he had considered writing her in Latin as well.

Marcel and Robert both took piano lessons because music was an important part of family life, both for study and pleasure. Jeanne often played classical music, especially Mozart and Beethoven. Toward the end of his life, Marcel recalled one of the many recitals held in the Weil household when a cousin, Louise Crémieux, an accomplished singer and actress, sang Mozart arias.[39]

Jeanne and her mother took turns introducing their favorite books to Marcel. When he was eight years old, the book he liked most was Alfred de Musset's *Histoire d'un merle blanc,* a tale that shares some features with *The Ugly Duckling.*[40] The rare white crow is rejected by his own kind because he is so different. Not only is he white but he is unusually sensitive and kind. To an amazing degree this story foreshadows young Marcel's rejection and misunderstanding by his high school classmates, many of whom did not know what to make of the gifted but eccentric boy.

Marcel's grandmother, who admired George Sand's pastoral novels, likely read to him from *La Mare au diable* (The devil's pond), *La Petite Fadette* (The little fairy), *Les Maîtres sonneurs* (The master bell ringers), and *François le Champi,* skipping the passages in which there was a hint of sexuality. *François le Champi,* a romance of country life, tells the story of a foundling (in the Berry dialect *champi* means a child abandoned in the fields) who is taken in by a very young miller's wife named Madeleine Blanchet. Unconsciously, François and his adoptive mother fall in love when he is old enough to leave home. Later he returns, finds the widowed Madeleine struggling to pay the debts amassed by her worthless husband, and becomes her protector. Slowly, they recognize their love. After they have confessed their devotion to each other on the spot where Madeleine discovered François as a foundling, they marry. *François le Champi,* with its strong incestuous theme, appears in *À la recherche du temps perdu,* where it underscores the child Narrator's excessive love for his mother.[41]

Proust, who as an adult considered Sand's novels inferior, remembered that her prose had breathed goodness and moral distinction, qualities that his mother's beautiful voice easily made apparent.[42] Moral distinction, best represented in the *Search* by the grandmother, was a virtue that Marcel learned to prize in his childhood. In *Jean Santeuil,* the mother initiates Jean into the love of poetry by reading to him from Alphonse de Lamartine's *Les Méditations,* Pierre Corneille's *Horace,* and Victor Hugo's *Les Contemplations.* She believes that "good books," even if poorly understood at first, can nourish the child's mind and benefit him later.[43]

When Marcel was older, his mother and grandmother read with him the great seventeenth-century works of which he acquired a special understanding and appreciation. He came to love the tragedies of Jean Racine, whose masterpiece *Phèdre,* in its depiction of obsessive, destructive jealousy, haunts the pages of the *Search.* Adèle remembered from her aunt's salon the actress Rachel, France's most acclaimed tragedienne of the first half of the century, whose greatest success had been as Phèdre. As the grandmother read scenes from Corneille's and Racine's plays to the captivated Marcel, she described the actress's astounding interpretations of the tragic heroines.

Adèle's enthusiasm and knowledge created in Marcel an intense curiosity about the theater. Later, he was particularly intrigued by Sarah Bernhardt, who had assumed the mantle of Rachel. It was said that Bernhardt had invented a more natural style of acting, surpassing even that of her illustrious predecessor. Marcel would cross boulevard Malesherbes and stand on the sidewalk in front of the Morris Column to read the theatrical posters advertising Bernhardt's reprisal of her role as Phèdre, a performance that had all of Paris buzzing with excitement. He studied the poster with extraordinary concentration, trying to divine from the intricacies of the lettering and the names before him the secret rituals of the theater. Marcel longed to be old enough to go to the theater and see the Divine Sarah in her most famous role.

Illiers

In 1847 Adrien's older sister, Élisabeth, had married Jules Amiot, descendent of an old and wealthy Illiers family and one of the most respected merchants in the town. Jules had spent many years in Algeria, where he and his brothers prospered as wine merchants and developed a taste for exotic curios. After his return to Illiers and his marriage, Jules operated a successful notions shop at 14, place du Marché, opposite the church of Saint-Jacques. It was to Jules and Élisabeth's house in the rue du Saint-Esprit that Adrien would return with his wife and two young sons during Easter and part of the summer holidays. At Easter the town was at its best, offering wildflowers and trees in bloom that Marcel adored and could not find in Paris.

In *Jean Santeuil*, Proust describes, in a humorous, affectionate way, the relationship between his parents (thinly disguised as M. and Mme Santeuil) by contrasting their personalities and aptitudes.[44] The passage, concerning plans for the annual Easter trip to Éteuilles (Illiers), begins with M. Santeuil's announcement that because Easter is early this year the weather at Éteuilles will not be warm. Mme Santeuil, who has "plenty of taste in matters of literature . . . and considerable skill in the running of a household," is "ignorant in matters of meteorology . . . and other of the sciences." She is "always amazed that Monsieur Santeuil should know that Easter would be early in any given year and found in this evident proof of his superiority yet one more reason for silently renewing her admiring praise and for reaffirming that vow of docile obedience which she had once registered in the secret places of her heart."[45]

On the Thursday before Easter, the Prousts usually went by rail from Paris to Chartres, where they changed trains for the short ride to Illiers. Seen from afar as the train approached, Illiers was contained in its steeple, just as is Combray in the *Search:* "Combray at a distance . . . was no more than a church epitomising the town, representing it, speaking of it and for it to the horizon, . . . as one drew near, gathering close about its long, dark cloak, sheltering from the wind, on the open plain, as a shepherdess gathers her sheep, the woolly grey backs of its huddled houses."[46]

Marcel and Robert were impatient to leave the train when it stopped briefly at the small station. The four Parisians usually walked to the Amiots' house from the station, carrying the blankets that had kept them warm on the train, along with their parcels and suitcases, down the rue du Chemin de fer, lined on both sides with linden trees. Turning left at the rue de l'Oiseau flesché, they passed in front of the ancient hostelry of the same name. Marcel always noticed the optician's sign consisting of a large pair of spectacles, one lens blue, the other orange, unaware that one day he would transport these glasses hanging high above the optician's shop into the fictional Combray, where they became a symbol of his book and his conception of the novel.[47] Crossing the intersection of the rue Saint-Hilaire, the family arrived in the rue du Saint-Esprit, where the Amiots lived in a gray, relatively modest row house with half-timbered walls. Jules Amiot had acquired the house, dating from the First Empire, when he returned to Illiers. After 1885 Jules enlarged the property and created another entrance at the back of the garden, behind the house, where he installed an iron gate opening onto the tiny Place Lemoine.

The Amiot household was ruled over by Ernestine Gallou, a remarkable servant who remained with the family for more than thirty years.[48] A solid, strong woman embodying the timeless virtues of rural France, she saw that the guests from Paris were comfortable and well fed. She needed all her strength and resources when the Prousts came to visit. Not only were there extra beds to make and mouths to feed, but one of the guests was Marcel, who, whether at home or on vacation, always gave servants additional work because of special requests deemed beneficial to his frailties. Prone to colds, allergies, insomnia, and indigestion, Marcel exploited his ailments to wield strict control over his environment whenever possible. He and his mother insisted that he be indulged, like a budding tyrant. In *Jean Santeuil,* the admonishments Mme Santeuil gives Ernestine on arriving are no doubt typical of those the real Ernestine received from Mme Proust: "I needn't remind you, Ernestine, that Master Jean must have a bottle in his bed, not just hot water, but boiling, so that he can't bear his hands on it: or that the top end of the bed must be made very high, almost uncomfortable—I'm sure you remember that—so that he can't possibly lie flat even if he wants to, four pillows, if you can spare four; it can't be too high."[49] But Marcel was ordinarily so benevolent, charming, and grateful that most of the members of the household were happy to oblige him. The dilemma for the family, at Illiers just as at Auteuil, was the degree to which he should be indulged. Weren't they spoiling him? Would it not be better to teach him fortitude and make him stronger? His parents, frightened like all good parents of being too strict or too indulgent, struggled to find the delicate balance that would be just right for their elder, complicated son.

Ernestine Gallou served her copious, delicious meals, made of the best fresh produce available in the market that day, in the dining room whose heavy furniture and dark wooden panels dated from the First Empire. At the end of the meal, Uncle Jules, who liked to cook, would mix together the strawberries and cream, always in identical proportions, stopping only when he obtained the exact shade of pink he sought, thus combining "the experience of a colorist and the divination of a gourmand."[50] He made the coffee in a glass apparatus that Ernestine, right on cue, brought to the table. The guests would delight at the spectacle of the hot, fragrant, brown liquid shooting to the top of the bell-shaped glass container. Sometimes, the family took coffee in the small salon, whose door, in the form of a Gothic arch filled with stained glass in hues of red, blue, green, and yellow, looked out onto the garden. Here, in this small sitting room, Jules displayed some of the African trinkets collected during his years in Algeria.

Before bedtime, as a last treat for the boys, the family watched a magic lantern show made possible by a brightly colored projector set on the top of one of the oil-burning lamps. Marcel and Robert watched in wonderment as images of Geneviève de Brabant and the wicked Bluebeard or the equally villainous Golo moved across the wall in "an impalpable iridescence, supernatural phenomena of many colours," sometimes leaping, if the projector moved, onto the curtains and doorknob.[51] After the slides and a bedtime story, the boys went to sleep in rooms whose bland style— broken only by uninteresting knickknacks lying on furniture tops—resulted no doubt from the childless household. As Marcel lay waiting for sleep to come or plotting a way to lure his mother back into the room for one more good-night kiss, he took no comfort from the pious religious images of the Virgin Mary and Christ on the wall. Sometimes he felt so lonely and desperate when his mother left him at night that he identified himself with the wretched man abandoned by his own father and nailed to the cross.

While in Illiers, Marcel also visited his elderly grandmother Proust in her tiny apartment above the store. Relatively little is known about her except that she was an invalid cared for by an old servant. She apparently did not make a lasting impression on either of her grandsons, for she is not mentioned in any meaningful way in any of the preserved letters or documents. Yet what we do know makes her a more likely model for the hypochondriacal Aunt Léonie in the *Search* than Proust's Aunt Élisabeth Amiot, generally considered the original model.[52]

Although on vacation, Marcel and his parents never let pass an opportunity for him to learn. He studied the rudiments of Latin with the canon Joseph Marquis, whose great interest in local history later inspired him to write a book.[53] When not declining Latin nouns and botanizing with the priest in his garden, the boy took long walks in the countryside and along the Loir River, following its towpath lined with poplar trees.[54] He and Robert also continued their piano lessons. Because the Amiots had never acquired a piano—an unthinkable situation for Jeanne—a worthy of the village who owned one allowed the boys to come for daily lessons and practice.[55] The normally bookish Marcel enjoyed fishing with cousins of varying degrees, or hiding with Robert in one of the ruined medieval towers, the only vestiges of an ancient fortified castle that stood between the town and the river.

Jules, whom Marcel called his "early rising, gardening uncle," indulged his passion for horticulture by spending a portion of his wealth on the creation of a large pleasure garden just beyond the banks of the gently flowing Loir. He called it the Pré Catelan, after a section of the Bois de Boulogne in Paris. It must have seemed natural to Marcel, a Parisian who often played in the Bois, for his Illiers uncle to name his own garden after the one in Paris. Although Jules's Pré Catelan was no more than a postage stamp compared to the one in the capital, for the little town of Illiers its proportions were impressive. The name held in common by the two principal gardens of his childhood may have provided the first linking in Marcel's mind of the two spaces, Auteuil and Illiers, that inspired his fictional Combray.

In his garden, Uncle Jules had dug an artificial pond, in which he planted water lilies and other aquatic flowers; he then stocked the water with fish for his nephews to catch. In *Jean Santeuil,* Jean's grandfather creates alongside the Loir an identical garden that rose gradually until it reached "the same height as the wide plain where La Beauce began, to which a gate provided a way of entrance. This high point of the garden was of considerable width and was occupied by a magnificent asparagus bed and by a small contrived pond." A "mechanical contraption" turned "by one of Monsieur Santeuil's father's horses . . . forced water up from the canal below where Jean . . . played his line for great carp which he soon had lying beside him on the grass among the buttercups."[56] From the pond flowed a narrow, meandering stream over which Marcel and Robert could jump with ease if they decided not to use one of the little footbridges that crossed the water here and there throughout the garden. The Pré Catelan seemed an earthly paradise for the boys, who liked to pretend they were knights or to play hide-and-seek or simply to throw stones into the water.

Uncle Jules had constructed in the middle of the garden, halfway up the gently sloping ground, a small, brick, gabled belvedere, known by the family as the "house of the archers," and furnished it so that his relatives and friends could read, rest, and meditate while enjoying the view. On the south end of the garden a magnificent row of hawthorn trees slowly rose up the side of the garden, leading to a large white gate that opened onto fields of blue cornflowers and brilliant red poppies fanning out to the west and south on the plain toward Méréglise and the château of Tansonville.

Amiot died unaware that his nephew's fame would one day draw visitors from over the world to admire his creation, the only surviving garden of Proust's childhood and the model in *Swann's Way* for Charles Swann's park at Tansonville near Combray.[57]

Adrien often took Marcel and Robert on walks to show them where he had played as a child. He pointed out to his boys how two different topographies come together at Illiers: the Beauce, a flat, windy plain that, as it moves westward, meets the Perche, whose hilly terrain is ravined by streams rolling down to feed the Loir River. The Beauce plain, naturally covered with herbaceous plants, is ideal for the cultivation of wheat, whereas the Perche's rocky forests are more suited for apple trees and livestock, primarily horses and cattle. Illiers prospered as the central marketplace for these two distinctive but complementary regions.

In the *Search*, the defining features of Combray's fictional topography approximate those of Illiers where the two walks—one the landscape of an ideal plain, the other a captivating river view—embody, for the child Narrator, two separate worlds: "My father used always to speak of the 'Méséglise way' as comprising the finest view of a plain that he knew anywhere, and of the 'Guermantes way' as typical of river scenery."[58] On the walk that became the "Méséglise" or "Swann's way," Adrien led his sons south of Illiers, out toward Vieuvicq and Tansonville, passing "fields of wheat undulating under the sharp wind that seemed to arrive in a straight line from Chartres."[59]

As Adrien and his sons made their way back from Tansonville, it was the steeple of Saint-Jacques, appearing now and then in the sky as they mounted a hillock or rounded a bend, that beckoned them home. This rather modest parish church contains vestiges of earlier constructions dating from the eleventh and fifteenth centuries; the choir stalls and enclosed pews date from the era of Louis XIII. The visitor enters through the old Romanesque doorway with double arches, all that remains of the original edifice. Perhaps the church's most striking feature is the beautiful wooden Gothic vault, whose brightly decorated beams were hewn from trees that had grown in nearby forests.

Proust later used a motif found in the church's sculpted wood as one of the most powerful symbols of his art. On either side of the wall behind the altar stands a wooden statue of a saint above whose head is placed a scallop shell, a motif repeated elsewhere on the paneling inside Saint-Jacques. Such shells are the emblem of Saint James and were worn in the Middle Ages by the pilgrims on their way to Santiago di Compostella in Spain. The church of Saint Jacques, as its name indicates, was a stopping point on the major pilgrim route. The scallop shells also provide the form of the little cakes known as madeleines, symbol of a key revelation in the Narrator's quest to find his vocation as a writer.[60]

On fine days in Illiers when Marcel walked south toward Tansonville and Vieuvicq, he might pass Montjouvin, with its old mill on the Thironne River, and stop to admire the water lilies. Next to the mill he explored the ancient park in whose thick foliage had been discovered a dolmen and a mysterious circle of monoliths. Not far from the river a sacred wood surrounded an ancient tomb called the Tombelle-de-Montjouvin. Here had stood an old castle, presumably built atop a dwelling dating from Paleolithic times.[61]

On his walks through the river country north of Illiers, Marcel spied on the large manor house at Mirougrain, built on a gentle slope overlooking a large lily pond in the middle of which floats a tiny island supporting a weeping willow tree. This house offers an extraordinary architectural feature and an intriguing history. In the decade before Marcel's birth, the property was acquired by a young woman whose grave in the Illiers cemetery bears the simple inscription Juliette Joinville, poet. After taking up residence at Mirougrain, Juliette, then only twenty, and her servants combed the woods looking for dolmens or any druidical stones, which she used to cover completely the façade of the house. Her determination to withdraw from the world and live in quiet seclusion produced the opposite effect. Everyone, including Marcel, who heard about the boulder-encrusted house wanted to see it and catch a glimpse of Juliette. Rumors spread that she had come to Mirougrain to hide because she had been spurned by her lover; others believed that she had re-treated here to receive secret, nocturnal visits from Emperor Napoléon III, a noto-rious womanizer.[62] Proust remembered the impressions evoked by this strange dwelling later when creating the composer Vinteuil's house in the *Search*. He adapted the name of the old mill Montjouvin but used the setting and atmosphere of Mirougrain, minus the dolmens, for the lesbian love scene between Vinteuil's daughter and her friend.

The names of the streets, old inns, manor houses, and ruined churches of Illiers and its surroundings—Tansonville, Méréglise, Montjouvin, Saint-Hilaire, rue de l'Oiseau flesché—continued to live in Proust's memory and imagination, until he used them, with slight alterations or none at all, as part of the material out of which he constructed Combray, a place that exists only in the pages of his book.

Of all Marcel's indelible impressions of childhood, the two most important were the beauty of flowers and the pleasures of reading. Although he enjoyed fishing and games with Robert and other playmates, he spent most of his time absorbed in books, which he read when the weather was fine in Uncle Louis's Auteuil garden or in the nearby Bois de Boulogne. In Illiers, Marcel's two favorite spots for reading were in the small garden behind the house or in the spacious belvedere in the Pré Catelan. In either spot, he spent "silent, sonorous, fragrant, limpid hours" at a stretch, reading the novels of Gautier, Sand, Balzac, or Hugo.[63] Sometimes he did not even hear the church bell strike the hour: "The fascination of my book, a magic as potent as the deepest slumber, had deceived my enchanted ears and had obliterated the sound of that golden bell from the azure surface of the enveloping silence."[64]

Young Marcel had the strong, playful imagination of any normal child, but he also possessed an amazing ability to see and the patience to remain still and concentrate, to the point of appearing lost in a trance, when he came upon an object of beauty that seized his attention: a woman, a church, or a flower. In Illiers he became intoxicated with the spectacle of nature, especially of flowers and trees that bloomed in the surrounding countryside. He marveled at the splendor of hawthorn trees and apple trees when covered with white or pink blossoms. Proust later depicted an astonishing variety of flowers as manifestations of beauty and as symbols of desire and sexuality.

On one trip to Illiers, Marcel fell in love with the hawthorn trees whose blooms of white and pink line the south side of the Pré Catelan. Sensitive also to the splendors of churches and the poetry of religious ceremonies, on one occasion, he, with Robert's assistance, placed hawthorn branches dripping with blossoms on the altar of the Virgin Mary.[65] Marcel was so captivated by these flowers that he insisted on going to the Pré Catelan and bidding them good-bye before returning to Paris.

The early draft of what became the "farewell to the hawthorns" in the *Search* recounted an incident involving Robert, forced by his parents to leave behind a pet goat. This incident most likely occurred in September 1878, when Marcel was seven, during a late summer vacation in Illiers or Auteuil.[66] On the day in question, Marcel and Robert were both angry with their parents for not having told them that their mother was leaving to visit a friend and was taking Robert with her. Marcel hated any separation from his mother and was hurt at being left behind. Robert, upset that he could no longer keep the little goat and his prized cart, took his revenge by hiding, in hopes that his mother would miss the train. Earlier in the day, a relative had taken him to be photographed, and Robert was still dressed as was deemed appropriate for a studio photograph of a very young boy. His mother had clad him in a dress with lace skirt, curled his hair, and tied it up with ribbons. Furious that he must leave his goat and toys, Robert had a tantrum, ripped off his clothes, pulled the ribbons from his hair, and yanked his curls in an attempt to straighten them. For good measure, he smashed his toys and then, to the consternation of his mother, defiantly sat down on the railway tracks. Robert even made a little speech for her to overhear: "My poor little goat, you're not the one who tried to make me sad, to separate me from those I love." He then began to weep.

Dr. Proust arrived and pried the child loose from the tracks, whereupon Robert told his father that he would never again lend him the goat cart, the worst punishment the little boy could imagine. Marcel, intensely upset with his parents' duplicity and betrayal, had to resist the urge to set the house ablaze. In the *Search,* this scene, after revisions, is given to the Narrator, when, as a child, his parents force him to leave his beloved hawthorns: " 'Oh, my poor little hawthorns,' I was assuring them through my sobs, 'it isn't you who want to make me unhappy, to force me to leave you. You, you've never done me any harm. So I shall always love you.' And, drying my eyes, I promised them that, when I grew up, I would never copy the foolish example of other men, but that even in Paris, on fine spring days, instead of paying calls and listening to silly talk, I would set off for the country to see the first hawthorn-trees in bloom."[67]

But as the Narrator remarks in a draft of the hawthorn passage, this promise, like most of those made in childhood, was not to be kept.[68] His oath of fidelity sprang from his desire to maintain the innocent and absolute affection of a child whose heart is filled with wonder and love.

Breathing

While engaged in the healthy activities of a normal boy, Marcel experienced the accidents and mishaps of childhood. At age eight, while playing on the Champs-Élysées, he tripped and broke his nose. The fall left him with a barely visible bump in his nose that, during his adolescence, he would fret about in a way that struck his friend Fernand Gregh as "coquettish."[69] But the incident that had lasting consequences occurred in the spring of 1881, when Marcel was nine. The Proust family, accompanied by friends, Dr. Simon Duplay and his wife, had enjoyed a long walk in the Bois de Boulogne. As they returned, Marcel suddenly developed severe difficulty in breathing and collapsed. He nearly died in the arms of his terrified father. Marcel had been brought down by his first attack of asthma, a condition that would plague him, altering his health, his morale, and his habits. After the first severe attack, he lived in fear of suffocation. Robert, who witnessed the seizure, recalled that from then on his older brother, now officially certified as nervous and sick, had to give up "outings in the open air, the beauty of the countryside, and the charm of flowers because of the threat to his lungs."[70] Although there were periods of respite, he suffered from asthma and respiratory problems for the rest of his life.

More than a decade after the first attack, Marcel described in a novella about love and jealousy, *L'Indifférent,* the sensation of suffocating and the fear of imminent death. He compared a child's first experience of breathlessness to the feeling of panic and doom that overcomes the lover upon learning that the beloved is soon to depart on a long voyage: "A child who has been breathing since birth, without being aware of it, does not realize how essential to life is the air that swells his chest so gently that he doesn't even notice it. But what happens if, during a high fever or a convulsion, he starts to suffocate? His entire being will struggle desperately to stay alive, to recapture his lost tranquillity that will return only with the air from which, unbeknownst to him, it was inseparable."[71]

Asthma reminded Proust of the sensation of sheer terror, of gasping for air, for life, that overtook him when he found out that his mother was leaving on a trip and, eventually—when he had become so dependent on her presence and comfortings—even when she came to his bed to tuck him in and kiss him good night before retiring. He did everything possible to make her stay. This separation, the most hateful experience he knew, was as unsettling to him as the moment in childhood when we learn the inevitability of solitude and death.

Years later, after his mother's death, Proust recalled the childhood episode in a letter to Maurice Barrès: "Our entire life together was only a period of training for her to teach me to live without her for the day when she would leave me, and this has been going on since my childhood when she would refuse to come back ten times and tell me good-night before going out for the evening."[72] Proust wrote a description of this scene, which he later referred to as the drama of the good-night kiss, in *Jean Santeuil.* Jean is seven years old when he experiences such dependency on his mother and is diagnosed by the doctor as suffering from a nervous condition.[73]

In the *Search,* Proust dramatized a similar scene, generally thought to be auto-biographical and to have taken place at Auteuil, depicting the Narrator's dependency as a child on the presence of his mother. It is the mother's habit to tuck him in and to give him one last kiss before going to bed. On nights when company is present and she is not free to come up to the room for the kiss, he is particularly upset. On one such night, he waits up for her and then implores her to remain with him. She does not want to yield to his nervous anxiety, but the usually stern father intervenes and capriciously tells her to stay with the boy. She reads to him *François le Champi,* and though she skips the love scenes, the incestuous nature of the story perfectly suits the occasion. The child, incredulous at the easy violation of a strict rule, feels fortunate but guilty for having caused his mother to abandon her convictions. He will spend the rest of his life trying to recover the will and energy he lost that night at Combray and to expiate the wrong done to his mother. This scene, representing Marcel's primary childhood nightmare of separation from his mother, illustrates how Proust eventually learned to make his private demons serve the plot and structure of his novel. His material and psychological dependency on his mother remained, until her death, one of the defining traits of his personality.

To cure himself of asthma and hay fever, young Proust underwent many nasal cauterizations, whose purpose was to destroy the erectile tissue and render his nasal passage insensitive to pollen: "I had such faith that I underwent 110 cauterizations, hardly pleasant. Doctor Martin told me, 'Now, go to the country, you will no longer suffer from hay fever.'" Marcel left with his parents for the country, but as soon as he encountered lilacs in bloom, he was "seized with such violent asthma attacks that, until they were able to bring me back to Paris, my hands and feet remained purple like those of drowning victims."[74] Marcel's asthma was severe and, at times, extremely dangerous.[75] The many painful treatments he endured are proof of his eagerness to be cured.

Adrien and Jeanne were both vigorous individuals who enjoyed long walks for their health. As a pioneer in hygiene and preventive medicine who believed in the scientific treatment of maladies, Adrien advocated discipline and a strict regimen. Jeanne even preferred to walk in strong gusts when vacationing on the beach. In one letter to her, Marcel hopes she is having such weather, because "you like a bracing wind."[76] In the *Search,* similar traits are given to the grandmother, whose love of walks in the rain and the freedom to breathe are marks of her simplicity and fundamental wellness in body and soul: "My grandmother, in all weather, even when the rain was coming down in torrents . . . was to be seen pacing the deserted rain-lashed garden, pushing back her disordered gray locks so that her forehead might be freer to absorb the health-giving draughts of wind and rain. She would say, 'At last one can breathe!' "[77]

As a child Marcel often vacationed with his mother and grandmother on the Normandy coast at resorts made popular by the expansion of the railroads. In September 1880 he went to the fashionable seaside resort of Dieppe, the beach closest to Paris and France's oldest seaside resort. After Marcel developed asthma, the Proust family began to spend longer periods of the summer vacation on the coast because Adrien believed the sea air would benefit his son's lungs. In a letter to his grandfather in September 1881, Marcel speaks of the pleasures of Puys, a small village near Dieppe. Only ten years old, the child explained why the Normandy coast would always hold such an attraction for him: Puys was "a very small village, very pleasant, very picturesque, that combines the pleasures of the countryside with those of the shore."[78] The joining of farmland and beach created a perspective that he never failed to admire.

Marcel, in an 1888 letter to his mother, evoked the memory of happy vacation days spent at Le Tréport, just north of Dieppe, where he simply enjoyed breathing the sea air and stretching his limbs as he walked the long shingle beach, backed by tall cliffs. In a notebook that Jeanne kept, she recorded another letter from Marcel in which he recalled being on the beach with his grandmother, huddled together as they conversed, while walking into the wind.[79]

On occasion, he accompanied his mother in Paris to the Deligny Baths, a large wooden structure anchored in the Seine near the Concorde Bridge. Jeanne, seeking relief for health problems, regularly bathed in the cold water.[80] After waiting in a cubicle for her to change into her swimming costume, Marcel would emerge to find Jeanne already bathing. The wooden platform on which he stood to watch her and the other swimmers rose and fell with the current of the river. Amazed and frightened, Marcel imagined that this strange, watery cavern was the entrance to the underworld. In *Jean Santeuil,* Proust depicted Jean's mother "splashing and laughing there, blowing him kisses and climbing again ashore, looking so lovely in her dripping rubber helmet, he would not have felt surprised had he been told that he was the son of a goddess."[81] Beautiful, yes, and powerful, too, but would she emerge safely from the dark, deep water? Would she remain with him or leave through an underground passage with one of the male bathers, abandoning her child forever as she pursued unknown, forbidden pleasures?

The child Marcel, in his constant fear of being abandoned by his mother and suffocating to death, sensed that we are always walking on thin ice. Just below the surface of what appears to be a solid, lovely world—Paris, and later Venice—churn the dark, icy waters of solitude and death. By the time Proust wrote the *Search,* his mother's loveliness and mythological attributes at the Deligny Baths had vanished. The memory had darkened even more, and the Narrator speaks of what he dreaded most, being abandoned by his mother. The scene, now set in the watery city of Venice, describes the Narrator's refusal, at the appointed time, to depart with his mother, who leaves for the train station without him. As he sits contemplating what to do next, the view of the dock basin of the Arsenal filled him with that "blend of distaste and alarm which I had felt as a child when I first accompanied my mother to the Deligny Baths, where, in that weird setting of a pool of water reflecting neither sky nor sun . . . I had asked myself whether those depths . . . were not the entry to Arctic seas." A gondolier begins singing in the distance, and "in this lonely, unreal, icy, unfriendly setting in which I was going to be left alone, the strains of *O sole mio,* rising like a dirge . . . seemed to bear witness to my misery."[82]

The miseries of childhood, along with its incomparable joys, were being stored to serve a larger purpose for the man Marcel was to become. On those spring and summer days when his father was too busy to go to Illiers, or when foul weather or Marcel's health made the trip seem ill advised, the boy had to remain in his room, unhappy, exiled from nature and the pleasures of the season. He evokes such a moment in *Jean Santeuil* when a fly buzzing awakens in Jean a vision of days gone by: "Then, all of a sudden, he would see a picture of that lovely Illiers time, with the apple-trees all in blossom in the paddock, the tiler hammering in the street, when he had gone fishing in the lake."[83] Marcel, in whose future lay endless days of isolation in his room, ultimately learned that there was only one way to return, only one way to know what it had really been like, by re-creating his lost world in a book.

Auteuil and Illiers, as later transformed by Proust into the mythical place he called Combray, contain the lost treasures of Proust's childhood:

> The Méséglise way with its lilacs, its hawthorns, its cornflowers, its pop-
> pies, its apple-trees, the Guermantes way with its river full of tadpoles, its
> water-lilies and its buttercups, constituted for me for all time the image
> of the landscape in which I should like to live, in which my principal re-
> quirements are that I may go fishing, drift idly in a boat, see the ruins of
> Gothic fortifications, and find among the cornfields . . . an old church,
> monumental, rustic, and golden as a haystack; and the cornflowers, the
> hawthorns, the apple-trees which I may still happen, when I travel, to
> encounter in the fields, because they are situated at the same depth, on
> the level of my past life, at once establish contact with my heart.[84]

2 A Sentimental Education   ᴗ

IN THE FALL OF 1882 Marcel, eleven years old, entered class 5 at the Lycée Condorcet.[1] The lycée's courtyard on the rue Caumartin had once been the cloister of a Capuchin monastery designed in 1779 by Alexandre-Théodore Brongniart, a noted architect who had also created the Palais de la Bourse, which houses the Paris stock exchange, and the Père-Lachaise cemetery, the city's largest and most famous burial ground. The more modern wings of the lycée, constructed around the time of Proust's birth, were equally severe and monastic but lacked the architectural nobility of the original structure. Yet the ambiance at Condorcet, compared to that of the austere, rigorous lycées on the Left Bank, seemed hospitable. Robert Dreyfus, who entered Condorcet in 1888 and become a close friend of Marcel's, recalled his visit to a Left Bank lycée, which had impressed him as a "huge fortress of Latin and Greek. . . . When I left the building of Louis-le-Grand, I breathed more easily the fresh air of liberty and I thanked fate for having made me a frivolous day student of the light and charming Condorcet." Dreyfus noted gratefully in his memoirs that Condorcet's administration even took into account students' preferences for teachers and courses.[2]

Jeanne must have felt that this atmosphere would be good for her high-strung, nervous son. Another advantage was Condorcet's proximity; the school was a pleasant ten-minute walk from home, and Marcel, like the other boys, could easily be escorted by a parent or a servant. A contemporary painting, *La Sortie du Lycée Condorcet* by Jean Béraud, shows fashionably dressed, well-to-do parents standing on the sidewalk outside the columned entrance of the lycée, the men wearing greatcoats and top hats, the women in long fur-lined coats and stylish hats, come to collect their equally smartly dressed sons, who hold their leather satchels stuffed with schoolbooks for homework assignments.

In spite of its reputation as a less rigorous lycée, Condorcet had a solid curriculum and a strong humanist tradition, with an emphasis on literature and philosophy. Among Condorcet's most distinguished graduates, before Proust's time, were the writers Edmond and Jules de Goncourt; the novelist and critic Charles-Augustin Sainte-Beuve; the poets Théodore de Banville and Paul Verlaine; the philosophers Hippolyte Taine and Henri Bergson; the scientist André-Marie Ampère; and three presidents of the Republic: Sadi Carnot, Jean Casimir-Perier, and Paul Deschanel. If Marcel, as his parents intended, decided to become a lawyer, a diplomat, or a politician, the school seemed an excellent choice.

The great lycées of the Left Bank, such as Louis-le-Grand, Saint-Louis, and Henri IV, were steeped in tradition and known for their iron discipline and fierce competition among the students. Unlike Condorcet, their mission was to prepare the intellectual crème de la crème of France's young (as well as a large number of provincials bent on conquering Paris) for admission to one of the prestigious Grandes Écoles. These schools are France's most renowned institutions of higher learning and include the École polytechnique, or school of engineering, and the École normale supérieure, which trains teachers for secondary and higher education. Although some of Marcel's classmates were preparing to compete for slots at the École normale supérieure, the boys at Condorcet were spared the exhausting intellectual training for the entrance exams. The students in the Left Bank lycées did not hide their disdain for the more relaxed atmosphere enjoyed by the Condorcet pupils, whom they refused to take seriously as academic competitors, calling them "melodious flute players."[3]

Among Condorcet's students were many sons of the smart society set of Paris, including many Jews or half-Jews like Marcel who considered education not a means to social advancement or the key to a brilliant career in a distinguished profession but the confirmation of their cultural heritage. The school had the reputation of being solidly intellectual, yet with a worldly bent. Some of the students, sons of wealthy industrialists and rich bourgeoisie, liked to show off their "impeccably elegant wardrobes."[4] Many of Marcel's classmates, as befitted the upper class of Third Republic France, were to pursue careers as philosophers, scientists, industrialists, doctors, engineers, statesmen, and diplomats.[5] A number of his closest friends from school distinguished themselves as journalists and writers.

If parents had any misgivings about Condorcet, it was that the administration was too lax. The mothers also worried about the proximity of the notorious *passage du Havre,* where prostitutes were known to practice their trade and where schoolboys considered it a rite of passage to lose their virginity as quickly as possible. Dreyfus thought these fears unfounded and recalled that what drew him and his friends to the passage was the presence of a well-stocked stationer's shop, where the boys purchased their school supplies, and a confectioner's boutique that sold "incomparable caramel creams."

The boys loved their school. Dreyfus wrote that the atmosphere at Condorcet resembled that of a "Lilliputian cénacle," whose subtle appeal made Marcel and his friends so impatient to arrive at school that they often came early to meet and talk under the meager shade of the trees in the courtyard before the first drumroll called them to class. Even the drumroll was music to their ears, reverberating across the quadrangle more like a pleasant tympanic invitation than a harsh military command.[6]

When school ended at three o'clock, Marcel and his friends often headed for the gardens along the Champs-Élysées or the Parc Monceau to have fun. Among his playmates were Lucie and Antoinette Faure, daughters of François-Félix Faure, a family friend and future president of France. On winter days the other children were amazed when Marcel arrived to play, frail and sensitive to the cold, his pockets stuffed with hot potatoes his mother had put there to keep his hands warm. He especially liked Antoinette, who was his age and had taught him to make caramels.[7] He was fascinated by her beautiful long eyelashes and once asked his mother's friend Comtesse Mirabeau, who had watched him and Antoinette playing, "Tell me, Madame, have you ever seen Antoinette's eyelashes?"[8]

Other friends included children from upper-middle-class Jewish families, some of whom he had known in elementary school at the Cours Pape-Carpentier, like Jacques Bizet, Robert Dreyfus, Henri de Rothschild, and Daniel Halévy. Jacques, a year younger than Marcel, was the son of the composer Georges Bizet and Geneviève Halévy, who was the daughter of one of France's most distinguished composers, Jacques Fromenthal Halévy. Jacques was not yet three when his father died, less than three months after the disastrous première of his opera *Carmen.* Jacques's cousin Daniel Halévy was the son of Ludovic Halévy, a distinguished librettist and playwright. Ludovic, along with Henri Meilhac, had written the libretto for *Carmen,* as well as for many of Jacques Offenbach's most popular operettas. Writing, for the Halévys, resembled a family profession, passed from generation to generation, a tradition Marcel would envy. At Pape-Carpentier, Marcel eagerly awaited the arrival of Jacques's mother, who called him "my dear little Marcel." Even as a child Marcel was struck by Mme Bizet's elegance and beauty.

At Condorcet Marcel completed his secondary education, met many of his lifelong friends, and discovered his sexual nature. Because of ill health and constant respiratory difficulties, school life for Marcel was difficult and required special arrangements: tutors, private lessons, and work sessions with his parents to supplement missed classes, especially during the early years. In his first year at the lycée, he supplemented his homework by reading as quickly as he could books that his mother and grandmother Weil purchased for him or selected at the lending libraries to which they subscribed in Paris and Auteuil. For the next two years Marcel studied natural sciences with Georges Colomb, a distinguished alumnus of the École normale supérieure. Colomb's pupils admired him for his dedication to his discipline, his sense of humor, and the clownish side of his personality, later shared with the general public in three books of humorous stories.[9]

Colomb's buffoonery was a trait much appreciated by Marcel, who enjoyed being a clown himself. Young Proust liked to show off in class and constantly passed notes and letters to his friends, often reading and writing them right under the noses of his professors. But Colomb was not merely a light entertainer; he proved to be a well-prepared and enthusiastic lecturer with an appreciation for details. His classes strongly influenced Marcel, who had already developed a liking for natural sciences, especially botany. The only surviving honors list for class 5, division D, shows that on August 3, 1883, not long after his twelfth birthday, Marcel received the fifth and lowest certificate of merit in French, the fourth certificate of merit in Latin composition, and the second-place prize for natural sciences.

In the fall of 1883 Marcel made his first communion. Although the Catholic religion remained an important part of his cultural heritage, especially when he undertook his studies of history and medieval art, there are no indications that he remained a practicing Catholic beyond this time.

Marcel enrolled in class 4, division A, in early October 1883. His teacher for French, Latin, and Greek was Professor Legouëz, a kind man nearing retirement, who failed to recognize Marcel's potential. The subject that Proust hated and in which he performed poorly, despite his parents' urgings and threats, was math. According to Robert Proust, Adrien was a born mathematician who, in order to please his father, had abandoned math to study medicine. As a child, Adrien had amazed his professors by deriving mathematical laws with his own calculations. When his sons were young, Adrien's idea of a relaxing, entertaining evening was to invite math professors from the École normale supérieure to come over and play at inventing imaginary numbers. He was disappointed that neither of his sons showed any particular aptitude for math. When Marcel had math assignments, Adrien worked them for him, while trying diligently to make certain the boy understood. Marcel would plead with him: "Stop, stop, I'm completely at sea."[10]

Marcel managed to complete the school year despite frequent absences because of ill health. He performed fairly well in languages and literature and kept up in his other classes. In the first two terms he obtained the highest marks out of the class of twenty-five. Then his poor health and many absences began to take their toll, and at year's end he won only a single prize in Colomb's class: a third certificate of merit in natural sciences. But he had worked especially hard at what he liked: writing. The results of his compositions, often written at the dining room table, can be seen in the surviving rough drafts with their scant revisions.

The first such homework paper begins with a floral sensation, "The air is scented." Hastily written over seven pages, this dramatic piece tells the story of a young mason who sacrifices his life to save a coworker with a wife and children. Presenting a variety of narrative elements, it opens with a Proustian springtime: the air is fragrant with lilacs and hawthorns in bloom. Marcel's classical literary heroes—La Fontaine, Racine, Boileau, and Bossuet—are evoked in quotations and allusions. Young Proust enjoyed displaying his considerable erudition, although at times the placement of a quotation or brief commentary detracts from the story. Although the handwriting remains that of a child who has barely reached adolescence, the narration shows a precocious ability to dramatize a story in an engaging voice.[11] The action is quick. There is even a street scene in which two wealthy aristocrats briefly exchange gossip, in language typical of their class. Proust seems to have been born with a keen ear for spoken dialogue. Except for one or two lapses in tone and taste, "The air is scented," was an impressive composition for a thirteen-year-old schoolboy.

Marcel also wrote an essay on a proposed theme from Tacitus relating a dramatic event that took place in the Roman senate: Agrippina had accused Gaius Calpurnius Piso of murdering her husband. Such training was the goal of classical education, in which students learned to "reproduce before producing, re-create before creating."[12] The text that Marcel wrote based on Tacitus showed, yet again, a confidence in expression and an ability to create drama and suspense, as well as an increased sureness of taste and tone. The young scholar must have been proud of his efforts, because he wrote at the top of the first page *Lege, quaeso*—Latin for "please read"—and placed his essay on the table where he knew his mother would find it.

Impressive as his essays were, Marcel had struggled through a difficult school year because of his health. Jeanne hoped the summer months of rest and recreation, combined with the proper amount of tutoring, would strengthen him for the future. On August 8, 1884, Marcel received his certificate of grammar, having passed all the subjects taught in class 4. In addition to French, Latin, Greek, and German, Marcel had studied Roman history, French geography, arithmetic (basic theory), plane geometry (elementary), geology, and botany. The curriculum was demanding, even for students with excellent health.

Meanwhile, Dr. Proust continued to distinguish himself in the field of medicine. On December 1, 1883, Adrien published another study on *Le Choléra: Étiologie et prophylaxie.* On March 30, 1884, the French government appointed him inspector general of health. When a cholera epidemic broke out in Toulon that June, Dr. Proust left immediately to direct efforts to prevent the disease from spreading beyond the city. He carried out this assignment, as the citizens of Toulon later acknowledged, with his customary energy and dedication.

In August, when the Proust family vacationed in the Normandy seaside town of Houlgate, Marcel's parents arranged for him to take Greek lessons. But he continued to be more interested in literature expressed in his own idiom. Though still too young to attend plays, he now dreamed of becoming a famous playwright.

At Proust's funeral nearly four decades later, an elderly man approached the art dealer René Gimpel and introduced himself, eager to have a witness for what he remembered. Gimpel failed to catch the man's name, but not what he said: "I was his Greek professor . . . in the summer at Houlgate where he had come to vacation with his family." The old man went on to say that although "little Marcel liked Greek a lot," he preferred to talk with him and his wife about writing, especially for the theater. Unlike the other children, Marcel did not like to play, but "always tried to lead my wife far from the bustle of the beach to more tranquil spots, in order to talk, he said, about literature." Marcel would ask the couple, " 'Do you think one day my plays will be performed at the Comédie-Française?' "[13]

When Marcel returned to school in class 3, he began studying physical sciences, continued to struggle in math and German, and read history with Régis Jalliffier. Proust admired Jalliffier, who, at thirty-eight, was the youngest teacher at Condorcet. Dreyfus believed that Marcel's passion for history had been kindled in his long conversations with Jalliffier.[14] In the *Search,* the Narrator listens to the "Muse who has gathered up everything that the more exalted Muses of philosophy and art have rejected, everything that is not founded upon truth, everything that is merely contingent, but that reveals other laws as well: the Muse of History."[15] In the course of his vast novel, which roughly spans French history from 1870 to 1920, Proust shows the dramatic social changes caused by the invention of machines of mass transit and communication, and by two pivotal events in his lifetime, the Dreyfus Affair and World War I.

Some of Marcel's schoolwork survives in rough draft, with many sentences crossed out, including a composition written for a private tutor and titled "Le Gladiator mourant" (The dying gladiator). Upon completion, Jeanne wrote the date, October 1, 1884, at the top of the essay and Marcel signed it, noting "Class 3A." This work tended to Christianize ancient Rome, as had the composition on Piso. In the gladiator story, Marcel alludes to the French classical playwright Pierre Corneille, whose plays celebrated duty and heroism in the face of overwhelming forces.[16] The nobility of the brave warrior in an alien land who "must die for the pleasure of the wicked" represents Proust's first experiment with one of his future major themes: the prisoner. The first soundings of other major Proustian themes are also found in this sketch: perversion and guilt.[17]

Another assignment that Proust wrote for a private tutor recounts an episode from the Roman sacking of Corinth. The hero is a proud Greek youth who defies the Roman general intent upon killing all the free citizens of Corinth once he succeeds in separating them from the slave boys, whom he intends to confiscate and exploit. The only way the cruel tyrant can distinguish between the two groups is to trick the free boys into revealing their education. He asks all the youths to write on a tablet for him, knowing that the illiterate slaves will be unable to perform this task. The youthful hero, though aware of the general's stratagem, writes a heroic passage from Homer, "Three times and four times happy those Danaans were who died then in wide Troy land," illustrating his own courage and scorn for the barbaric Romans.[18] Marcel ended this remarkably mature story with a paean to the moral value of literature and the "harmonious and divine music" of Homer's epic poem: "Literary studies allow us to disdain death, they lift us above earthly things by speaking to us about spiritual matters; they purify our feelings; and this reasoned courage, that is nearly philosophical, is far more beautiful than physical courage, than the intrepidity of the senses, because, in reality, it is spiritual courage."[19] Marcel's literary credo was already fixed by age thirteen and did not vary: literature is superior to life and its petty miseries.

Saturated with the glories of French prose and poetry from his constant reading and memorization, Proust became intimately attuned to the precision and musicality of language. Robert Dreyfus recounts how one day when Marcel was thirteen or fourteen, he observed the texture of the Arc de Triomphe seen in the light of the setting sun and scribbled on a sheet of paper two words that rang true and whose sonorous beauty made him dream: *granit rose* (pink granite). Marcel's sensitivity to the sounds of French was also evident in his homework assignments that some of his professors, like those fictionalized in *Jean Santeuil,* criticized for being "too poetical."[20]

In spite of many absences during the second term, Marcel's name appears on the February 14 honor roll. But on March 31 he withdrew from Condorcet for reasons of health. His schooling now depended entirely on his mother and private tutors. Over the summer he would have to make up the work he had missed after dropping out if he wanted to stay with his class.

The year proved to be a good one for Marcel's father. On Bastille Day, July 14, 1885, the city of Toulon gave Dr. Proust its Medal of Honor for the extraordinary services rendered during the cholera epidemic of 1884. In October he was awarded the Chair of Hygiene at the Faculté de médecine. At fifty-one, Adrien had reached the peak of his career. He had worked hard, and he happily accepted his rewards. Adrien must have thought that he had everything a man could want: fame, fortune, a beautiful, accomplished wife who adored him, two fine, intelligent sons. Marcel's poor health remained his only worry.

The Spa at Salies-de-Béarn

In August 1886 Mme Proust decided to bring Marcel and Robert with her to a health spa "to take the waters." Jeanne had read in her Baedeker that Salies-de-Béarn, not far inland from Biarritz, was a small town with saline waters, superior even to its German counterparts. The guidebook further stated that it was a spa of the first order, specializing in the treatment of "illnesses of women, children, lymphatism, and scrofula."[21] Perhaps this cure would benefit them all and improve Marcel's health by giving his resistance a boost before the fall term.

The decision to go to Salies-de-Béarn must have been made suddenly, for when Jeanne and her sons boarded the train in Paris around midnight, she had no hotel reservations for their stay. After a train ride that lasted until noon the next day, Jeanne and her boys finally arrived in Salies. They stopped first at the Hôtel de Paris, where they lunched on veal, potatoes, steak, eggs, and grapes. Then Jeanne instructed the boys to wait in the lobby and write letters or read while she went to look for rooms. Robert dutifully wrote to his grandmother, giving her all the details of the journey and remarking on the decidedly bovine atmosphere of their new surroundings: "Since our feet first touched ground in Salies, we have seen only oxen, oxen here, oxen there, oxen everywhere." By the time Robert reached the postscript, his mother had returned: "P.S. We haven't found out yet if Marcel will be able to fish here. Mother just informed me that we will be staying at the Hôtel de la Paix."

Over the next few days, despite the intense late-summer heat that Marcel found "sufficiently southern," the family settled in and began to enjoy the routine of taking the waters, reading, and, for the boys, playing croquet on the hotel lawn. Jeanne was especially pleased that her elder son's appetite had grown hearty. Marcel, in a holiday mood, wrote to his grandmother and expressed some embarrassment about the quantities he found himself consuming. Each meal consisted of five courses, and the morning and evening desserts were preceded by entremets. He described the cooking as divine and the portions gargantuan. At breakfast, he had "gulped down more than usual: a hard-boiled egg, two slices of steak, five whole potatoes, a drumstick and a thigh, and three servings of baked apples." And at 8:30 he enjoyed café au lait and bread! He entreated her not to show the letter to anyone lest his family and friends think the "delicate bibliophile is becoming an insatiable eater, the peaceful reader of Horace and Virgil . . . is transforming himself into an enormous Pantagruel."

In the course of this letter to his grandmother, Marcel, who had acquired his mother's and grandmother's ability to quote at ease from classical works, cited Corneille and Racine, parodied Molière, and played with words, transcribing them phonetically: *Fé tro cho pour sla (Fait trop chaud pour cela)*, which means " 'S too hot for that."[22] It was too hot and he was too ebullient to worry about his mother's strictures: decorum, grammar, coherent ideas, style, and handwriting, all items she checked when he handed his letters to her for approval before mailing.

His mother may have let this letter pass, but not without repercussions. The vivacious, familiar style could not have pleased her refined taste. One day when Marcel was eager to join his new friends already playing croquet on the hotel lawn, Jeanne made him sit down and write another letter in a loftier style to his grandmother. Marcel had struck a bargain with his mother's close friend, Mme Anatole Catusse, who had recently joined them at Salies. Known for her beautiful voice, Mme Catusse promised to sing a "little" aria if he started a pen portrait of her and a "big" aria if he finished it. Marcel, who loved to hear her sing the "divine melodies of Jules Massenet and Charles Gounod," agreed. He described Mme Catusse's "charming" face of "perfect beauty" in a letter that contained enough classical epithets, literary quotations and allusions, and other sophisticated rhetorical devices to satisfy the high cultural standards of the matriarchs. At the end Marcel could not resist saying how stupid he found the exercise, slipping in, after the final literary fanfare, a dangerously informal note: " 'Hello, Grandma, how are you?' Marcel." He informed his grandmother that he found Salies boring and that only Mme Catusse's conversation consoled him for his many sorrows and for the unpoetic atmosphere on the "terrace filled with chit-chat and tobacco smoke, where we spend our days."[23]

In September, Marcel wrote from Salies to his grandfather Weil, admitting somewhat ruefully that because no one in the family appreciated the "sublime" style of his earlier letters, he would try the bourgeois style. Marcel proceeded with a comic description of encounters with one of the hotel guests, a pretentious dentist "who had become a local celebrity by walking around holding, tucked under his arm, copies of the *Proceedings of the Anthropology Society,* of which he was a co-founder, causing the staff and clientele to believe he is a famous scientist."[24] Concluding his letter, Marcel summarized the beneficial results of the spa: "Mama is flourishing and Robert is prospering. I am rosy and dying of hunger at every meal."

Robert is prospering. In French—*Robert prospère*—the words rhyme syllable for syllable. It is an appropriate motto for the younger boy, healthy, robust, never known to give his parents any problems, and seemingly successful at everything, as he would continue to be by following in his father's footsteps. The phrase may have become a tag for him, one that Marcel and his parents were often heard to murmur with a knowing smile, when informed of his latest achievement: *Robert prospère.* As for Marcel, it remained unclear whether he could regain his health and overcome his emotional dependency on his mother. At Salies, Jeanne must have been encouraged by his outdoor activities, his serious dedication to his studies, his healthy glow, and, above all, his amazing appetite for good food.

Marcel ended his letter to his grandfather by asking for something that "interests me infinitely," the fulfillment of a long-standing promise. Nathé had promised Marcel his own subscription to *La Revue bleue,* whose theater reviews by Jules Lemaître the boy was eager to read on a regular basis. Redemption of the pledge had awaited Jeanne's approval, which she had given at last, as a reward for Marcel's hard work and hearty appetite. Before closing the letter to Nathé, Marcel asked about the servants. He had apparently undertaken to educate the chambermaid Augustine about literature and inquired about her progress in reading the list he had left with her.[25]

Sometime during 1885 Adrien Proust, freshly endowed with laurels for his most recent accomplishments, had his portrait painted in oil by Jules Lecomte de Nouÿ. Adrien's portrait, greatly admired by his family, shows the doctor in full academic robes, plume and parchment in hand, the image of a wise, learned, and benevolent man, face glowing with knowledge, wisdom, and compassion. In the lower right-hand corner, one's eyes are drawn to an arresting detail: an hourglass with the sand nearly two-thirds run out. One has only to look at Adrien's portrait to see time in the process of being lost. Even if the hourglass is only a stock image to remind the mighty of the earth of the vanity of all human enterprises, it is a remarkable coincidence for the father of a man whose primary theme will be the loss and recapturing of time.

In spite of his many accomplishments in the field of medicine, Adrien remained as helpless as any parent when faced with a child's chronic physical and psychological disorders. The stay at Salies-de-Béarn brought only temporary improvements. Marcel successfully completed his summer assignments, enabling him to enroll with his schoolmates in class 2, but health problems plagued him constantly during the fall. On December 31, 1885, because of Marcel's constant absences from school, his parents officially withdrew him from Condorcet. While absent from school he worked closely with his mother, especially on composition, and the family arranged once more for private lessons. They would do everything possible to strengthen and prepare him to repeat class 2 the next fall.

A few pieces of Marcel's work survive in the exercises he prepared with his mother and private tutors. In March 1886 he wrote "L'Éclipse" (The eclipse), an account of an episode from Christopher Columbus's fourth and final voyage to the Americas.[26] This text contains the earliest known example of a technique that would become an important feature in Proust's narrative style in the *Search*. Proust's ability to attribute, in a convincing way, multiple motives for a single action increases the richness of character and situation. In "L'Éclipse," shortly after a storm drives Columbus's fleet into Jamaica, the explorer sends some of his crew to Santo Domingo to find fresh ships. While they are absent, the natives revolt "either because they had wanted to seize the opportunity to free themselves from a control of which they had grown weary, or because they had been mistreated by the sailors of the great voyager, or, finally, because they had been persuaded to rebel by

Columbus's enemies." Here Marcel repeats historical conjecture, but later in his fiction, he often attributes multiple motives to his characters. Such enrichment reminds us of our own complexity and how little we really know about others and, sometimes, ourselves.

While working at home, Marcel also completed a school assignment known as an exercise in style, in which the student expresses himself freely on a simple theme. Normally such assignments filled about twenty lines, but Marcel, never short on ideas and inspiration, produced four pages on "Les Nuages" (Clouds).[27] These pages reveal the pleasure the apprentice novelist took in learning his craft, seeking the right word and an appropriate image. Of all the adolescent writings that survive, this text is the most distinctly Proustian in the subject matter and expression. The subject of clouds suited his contemplative nature and announced the future child Narrator's lyrical dialogues with hawthorn trees in bloom in the *Search:* "Man, moved spiritually by the mysterious and solemn calm of this poetical hour, likes to contemplate the sky; he may then discover in the clouds giants and towers and all the brilliant fantasies of his exalted imagination." The dreamer becomes lost in the clouds, then the "brilliant fantasies" disappear and he abruptly returns to earth with "the same disagreeable sensation one has in the morning on awakening from a beautiful dream." After stating that clouds make us dream because "their rapid passage plunges our soul into the most profound philosophical meditations," he expresses a major tenet of his philosophy that will guide his aesthetics and vision: "Man has in his heart a secret and slender thread that binds him so closely to all parts of nature."[28]

"Clouds" contains a number of allusions and quotations from works he had studied at Condorcet: *The Odyssey,* Victor Hugo's poem "L'Enfant," and works by the French classical poet Joachim Du Bellay. In addition to literary allusions, Marcel expressed a number of ideas then current: The external world is a product of the mind of which it is a mere projection; sorrow is the great inspirer of art that is then transfigured and magnified by art.[29] The meditation also shares a common theme with "The Dying Gladiator," one that is a major motif of the *Search,* the plight of the captive or the exiled. God is invoked in this piece, as he often is in *Jean Santeuil,* though not in the *Search.* The dreamer confides his sorrows to the clouds in the belief that they will rush to God and seek consolation for him. He pities the captives and exiles to whose misfortunes the clouds are the only witness and expresses his thanks to clouds who make of a person, who was only a wretch, a poet and a philosopher.

The Year of Augustin Thierry

It was probably during the fall visit of 1886 to Illiers that Marcel knew for certain that he wanted to be a writer. Mme Jules Amiot had died in June following an operation for a cancerous intestinal tumor, and that autumn the Proust family came to Illiers, perhaps in connection with her estate. It had been four years since his last trip, and Marcel, now in his mid-teens, feared that Illiers might bore him, especially because the season was rainy and the hawthorns were not in bloom. He had brought along for his reading Augustin Thierry's *La Conquête de l'Angleterre par les Normands* (Norman conquest of England), considered a masterpiece of historical narration. Robert Proust remembered that their grandmother Weil "was enamored of Augustin Thierry and never stopped talking to us about him."[30] Marcel intended to discover the reasons for his grandmother's adulation.

Thierry (1795–1856) had abandoned a promising career as a scientist to devote himself to history. His aim had been to revolutionize historical narrative, which he felt had paid too much attention to abstractions and political institutions. To meet his goal, he decided to adapt the novelistic techniques of Sir Walter Scott's popular historical novels to his own needs in telling the story of the French people, especially the rich and largely neglected chronicles of medieval times. True to the romantic spirit of his age, Thierry made ample and effective use of anecdote and local color.

In *La Conquête de l'Angleterre* published in 1825, Thierry recounted the story of the Saxons' resistance to the Norman invaders and celebrated the heroism of those who rebelled against foreign oppressors.[31] As Marcel sat at the dining room table in Illiers and read page after page of vivid, picturesque narration, he was captivated. After each reading session, Marcel felt himself bursting with energy, with a desire to comprehend and convey his own sensations and impressions. He would become so pent up that he had to leave the warmth and comfort of the house and rush out for long walks, often in drenching rain. Rather than deterring him, the showers seemed to augment his feeling of exhilaration: "And I walked back soaked, tired and joyful in the harmony of all things."[32]

In one of the first drafts for *Swann's Way*, written sometime in 1908–9, Proust evoked the reading of Thierry at Illiers that rainy autumn in the context of the Narrator and his family's visit to Combray to settle the estate of the fictitious Aunt Léonie: "Autumn had come; it was cold; while my parents conferred with the notary, M. Goupil, I read, in the 'living room' by the fireside, Augustin Thierry's *The Norman Conquest of England;* then, when I tired of reading, I went out, no matter what the weather: my body, which in the long spell of immobility while reading for hours, during which the movement of my ideas kept it moving in place, so to speak, was like a wound up top which, when suddenly released, felt the need to let go, to expend the accumulated energy in every direction."[33]

The ebullience Marcel felt during these readings in 1886 created in him a great urge to uncover and express the hidden secrets, the laws, the profound meaning behind impressions that he stored up from his walks: "the play of sunlight on a stone, a roof, the sound of a bell, the smell of fallen leaves." Yes, he wanted to be a writer. But how? And what would he write about?

In the final fictionalized version of these reading sessions at Illiers, the situation is the same, but the book or books read are not specified. The Narrator realizes, as he walks through the forest, that in spite of his great desire to express himself as forcefully as the authors he loves, he is incapable of doing so. He expels his pent-up energy and frustrations by shouting and beating the trees with his umbrella. The passage illustrates one of Proust's most successful narrative tricks, used with variations throughout the *Search:* he tells us in dazzling prose about his inability to write!

> The wind tugged at the wild grass growing from cracks in the wall and at the hen's downy feathers, which floated out horizontally to their full extent with the unresisting submissiveness of light and lifeless things. The tiled roof cast upon the pond, translucent again in the sunlight, a dappled pink reflection which I had never observed before. And, seeing upon the water, and on the surface of the wall, a pallid smile responding to the smiling sky, I cried aloud in my enthusiasm, brandishing my furled umbrella: "Gosh, gosh, gosh, gosh!" But at the same time I felt that I was in duty bound not to content myself with these unilluminating words, but to endeavour to see more clearly into the sources of my rapture.[34]

Marcel had found reading Thierry's history and the walks afterward so happily stimulating that once his parents were ready to return home he had no desire to leave Illiers; he could not have guessed that he would never return. But during the Illiers trip he had made an invaluable discovery: the conviction that he must devote his life to literature.

Sometime during this year, perhaps on the occasion of her birthday, Antoinette Faure, whose long eyelashes continued to captivate Marcel, asked him to answer questions about himself in an English keepsake book, then a fixture of the social scene. Although Marcel left five answers blank, he took his task seriously as he wrote in the book whose red cover bore in large letters the title *Confessions: An Album to Record Thoughts, Feelings, Etc.*[35] His answers, thoughtful and sincere, bear witness to the idealism of a young dreamer:

> *Your favourite virtue.* All those that are not specific to any one sect, the universal ones.
>
> *Your favourite qualities in a man.* Intelligence, moral sense.
>
> *Your favourite qualities in a woman.* Tenderness, naturalness, intelligence.
>
> *Your favourite occupation.* Reading, daydreaming, poetry, history, theater.
>
> *Your idea of happiness.* To live near those I love, surrounded by the beauties of nature, lots of books and musical scores, and not far from a French theater.
>
> *Your idea of misery.* To be separated from maman.
>
> *Your favourite color and flower.* I like all colors, and as for flowers, I don't know.
>
> *If not yourself, who would you be?* Not having to ask this question, I prefer not to answer it. However, I would have quite liked to be Pliny the Younger.
>
> *Where would you like to live?* In the realm of the ideal, or rather of my ideal.
>
> *Your favourite prose authors.* George Sand, Aug[ustin] Thierry.
>
> *Your favourite poets.* Musset.
>
> *Your favourite painters and composers.* Meissonier, Mozart, Gounod.
>
> *Your favourite heroes in real life.* A mixture of Socrates, Pericles, Mohammed, Musset, Pliny the Younger, Aug[ustin] Thierry.
>
> *Your favourite heroines in real life.* A woman of genius leading the life of an ordinary woman.
>
> *Your favourite heroes in fiction.* The romantic, poetic heroes, those who represent an ideal rather than a model.
>
> *Your favourite heroines in fiction.* Those who are more than women without betraying their sex, everything tender, poetic, pure, beautiful in every genre.
>
> *Your pet aversion.* People who do not sense what is good, who are ignorant of the tenderness of affection.

For what fault have you most toleration? For the private lives of geniuses.

Your favourite motto. One that cannot be summed up because its simplest expression is in all that is beautiful, good, and grand in nature.[36]

Certainly Marcel's answers about what makes him happy or miserable are straight from the heart: happiness for him always meant being near his mother. Proust's intense love for her was, with his passion for writing, the primary constant in his life. His answer that his heroine in real life is "a woman of genius leading the life of an ordinary woman" may have been inspired by the thought of his mother, who had taught him so much, and with such modesty, about music and literature.

The questionnaire reveals his deep interest in history and literature, and especially poetry and the theater. His heroes are authors of many cultures and include those of ancient Greek and Roman history and literature. Three writers he particularly admired during his adolescence are each mentioned twice: Alfred de Musset, Pliny the Younger, Augustin Thierry. Although the reasons for his admiration of George Sand and Augustin Thierry are clear and reflect his grandmother's influence, we do not know what interested him especially about Pliny the Younger (A.D. 62–113), a wealthy patrician and state official, who counted among his friends Quintilian, Martial, Suetonius, Tacitus, and the emperor Trajan. Perhaps Marcel had read in Latin class or with a private tutor selections from the famous letters that Pliny wrote during his hours of cultivated leisure, while out on hunts, or relaxing at one of his country villas. Pliny's letters contain vivid accounts of the social, literary, and political life of his times, one of the happiest of the empire. Proust, who would chronicle the lives of wealthy aristocrats and bourgeois under the Third Republic, may have recognized in Pliny a kindred spirit.

Alfred de Musset (1810–57) was a poet of the early romantic movement who, after George Sand broke his heart, sang the ecstasies and despairs of love in verses tinged with bitter irony. Marcel's great admiration for Musset's poetry diminished as he matured, to be replaced by an enduring love for the poems of Charles Baudelaire (1821–67), whose masterpiece, *Les Fleurs du mal,* inspired the symbolist movement and is considered by many to contain the greatest French poems of the modern era. Proust was to share many of Baudelaire's predilections, especially in his poems about nostalgia and the resuscitation of memory through the sensations of scent and taste.

The questionnaire shows that Marcel had an uncommon degree of self-awareness for an adolescent. During this period he acquired the habit—at first agreeable but soon to become obsessive—of intensive self-analysis. And he was just as curious about the experiences of others. Eager to know everything about anyone who interested him, he would stop and talk for hours with the young or old, asking many questions. Proust particularly enjoyed conversing with members of the servant class, including concierges and waiters. He often received scoldings from his mother when he arrived home late from school because he had dawdled in the street, treating himself to cakes and chatting at length with the concierge. Servants, he learned, possess special knowledge about food, clothing, and social customs, not to mention delicious gossip about the secret lives and foibles of many families and men about town.

Marcel had likely discovered a secret about himself: he found boys as beautiful and as attractive as girls. Maybe even more so. His answer in the questionnaire that the fault for which he had the most tolerance was the private life of a genius may indicate that he had become fully aware of his sexual nature and of society's abhorrence of its expression. Homosexual experimentation among schoolboys might, to some degree, be tolerated, but its open expression by mature men was not accepted by society at large. Men whose masculinity was impugned fought duels to restore their honor. Prominent homosexuals, such as Proust's future acquaintances Oscar Wilde and Prince Constantin Radziwill, paid blackmailers to keep their activities secret. People might be willing to look the other way, but the façade of respectability had to be maintained.

Marcel's proclaimed tolerance for the private lives of geniuses is an early indication of another distinction that would inform his aesthetic theories and influence his innovative method of characterization: the crucial difference between what Proust called one's social self and the creative self. One cannot, he would demonstrate, contrary to what most French critics believed, determine the value of a writer's work by appearances or breeding or social distinction.

The Champs-Élysées

For children like Marcel, who lived in or near the prosperous eighth arrondisse-ment, the Champs-Élysées gardens offered a splendid playground. There were puppet shows, donkey and goat carts to ride, vendors selling candies, lemonade, and other refreshments, and green swards of grass lined with chairs and benches from which parents and nannies could enjoy beautiful vistas of statues and archi-tecture as they read or knitted or chatted while watching the children play. In the late spring and early summer months the rows of tall chestnut trees that lined the streets would display their blooms of pink or white.

Marcel was sent to the gardens for his health, to allow his body to absorb the healing, invigorating rays of the sun, and here he encountered other adolescent friends: Robert Dreyfus, two years younger than he; a sweet girl named Blanche; Jeanne Pouquet, with whom Marcel later engaged in an innocent flirtation; and sisters Lucie and Antoinette Faure, whom he liked intensely. Proust's health concerned his friends; he seemed fragile and was subject to bouts of hay fever. When particularly unwell, Marcel would arrive and depart in a carriage, his body wrapped in woolens "like a fragile, precious trinket."[37]

Dreyfus left a vivid account of Marcel playing in the Champs-Élysées gardens.[38] Young Proust usually met his companions on the wide green lawn near two adjacent popular music halls, the Alcazar d'Été and the Théâtre des Ambassadeurs. On the grass stood a fountain in whose spray rose a bronze nymph, bathing and plaiting her hair. Beyond the fountain two carousels offered rides on hand-carved, brightly painted steeds of different dispositions, ranging from docile mares to fiery stallions. Most often, the children entertained themselves by playing hoops, shuttlecock, or prisoner's base, a tag game in which the players on one team seek to catch and imprison members of the other.[39] As the children played, they would often hear, wafting toward them over the grass, bits of song and the blare of bands from rehearsals at one of the music halls.

Although Marcel joined the others in playing tag, he preferred conversing with the boys and reciting lines from his favorite poems. Dreyfus, privileged to have known the "outdoor Proust," never forgot their talks as they walked along the path that ran beside the Alcazar while Marcel chatted about his beloved authors: Racine, Hugo, Musset, Lamartine, and Baudelaire. From his friend, Dreyfus heard for the first time the name Leconte de Lisle, the leading figure in the Parnassian movement. During this time Marcel also read with obvious delight Tolstoy's *Anna Karenina* and the novels of George Eliot. Marcel had read his way through many of the Greek and Roman classics, as well as those of French literature, and was now discovering modern Russian and English authors.

Dreyfus later realized that this little group of playmates had formed Marcel's first salon, where he brilliantly displayed "the luminous gifts of his magnificent artistic intelligence and his delicious sensitivity."[40] His amazed and often perplexed playmates at times grew impatient to return to their invigorating games of pursuit and capture, yet on the whole they provided a sympathetic audience. Although the little nucleus contained future industrialists, engineers, statesmen, diplomats, and generals, their predominant interests and talents were literary. They were joined occasionally by other playmates, such as future writers Louis de La Salle and Jean de Tinan.[41]

If Marcel's intellect and manners surprised his friends, his remarkably refined, sensitive behavior, his sweetness, and his extraordinary knowledge of literature astounded their mothers even more. From an early age, encouraged by his mother, Marcel delighted in pleasing others. Handsome, smothered in woolens even in warm weather, Marcel would rush to greet the women, young and old, bowing to them as they approached, and always able to find just the right words to touch them, whether he introduced topics that ordinarily concerned only adults or simply inquired about their health. Geneviève Bizet, who was intrigued by Marcel's graciousness and intelligence, was always pleased to see him and listen to his remarks and observations. His incessant chatter irritated others. Marcel enjoyed recounting the occasion when Mme Catusse surprised him by asking, "Are you never going to stop talking?"[42]

One day while playing in the garden, Marcel saw Marie de Benardaky, an "elegant, tall, and beautiful" blonde with whom he fell in love.[43] Of Greek and Russian descent, Marie was born in Russia to a wealthy family. Her father, a Polish nobleman, had made a fortune in the tea trade before becoming master of ceremonies at the court of the Russian czar. Once Marcel met Marie, nothing was more important than the afternoon trek to the Champs-Élysées to find his new girlfriend and her sister Nelly. Marcel's daily rendezvous with Marie became the source of conflicts with his parents, who sometimes had other activities planned, such as private lessons. Jeanne and Adrien were ambitious for their son, who needed to remain in top form and extremely competitive if he was to succeed in a distinguished profession. But once Marcel met the vivacious Marie, nothing was more important to him than the afternoon trek to the Champs-Élysées to find his new girlfriend.

His insistence on going to meet Marie on every occasion and in all kinds of weather alarmed his mother, bent as usual on keeping him wrapped safely in the cocoon of her love and concern. During this period of his life, Marcel was attracted to girls. Had his parents known that his sexual orientation would change, they might have been more careful about discouraging his relationship with Marie and other young women. To obtain permission to leave for the Champs-Élysées on days when the weather was less than perfect, he had to convince his mother that he would not become ill; but he would do anything to be with the "pretty, exuberant" Marie, the girl with the open, winsome smile whom he was to remember as "the intoxication and despair of his childhood" and one of "the great loves of his life."[44] Here is an early account of this infatuation from *Jean Santeuil:*

> But a day arrived when a sudden change came over him. He made the acquaintance of a little Russian girl, with a mass of black hair, bright, mocking eyes and rosy cheeks, who was possessed of all the glowing vitality and joy of living which were so sadly lacking in Jean. As soon, now, as he awoke in the morning he began to think of nothing but the moment when he would see her laughing at her play. All the time she was present, he stayed close beside her, taking part in games of prisoner's base, hide-and-seek and sliding. When she arrived about three o'clock in the Champs-Élysées with her governess and her sister, his heart beat so fast that he almost fell down, and [he] remained for a few moments with his face as white as a sheet before he could pull himself together.[45]

Marcel's affection for Marie was obvious to everyone. His friends, including her sister Nelly, were amused by his ardor and indulged him to a large degree, always letting him be on Marie's side in games.

Marcel's preoccupation with Marie did not prevent him from being well prepared for the 1886–87 school year. He earned good grades in all subjects except math. He studied history and geography with Alexandre Gazeau, a brilliant, lively teacher who would later serve as headmaster. Although Gazeau had little enthusiasm for geography, his history lessons held the class spellbound. Marcel's love of history and his hard work earned him top marks all three terms.

Another piece of work, written for M. Claude Courbaud's literature class, showed that Marcel was making up for lost time. He produced a fluent translation of a Latin text known to all French schoolboys of the period: Cicero's account of his discovery of Archimedes' tomb. The enlightened, cultivated Cicero was appalled at the neglect suffered by the tomb of the greatest mathematician of antiquity. Cicero's conclusion contained a statement to which Proust heartily subscribed, one that became a dominant motivation for his own writing: "It is by discovering the laws that govern human nature that one finds consolation for life's bitterness and its frailties."[46] Did Marcel keep this particular assignment because he realized that he would set out to discover such laws himself?

In March Mme Proust took Marcel, a few months shy of sixteen, to Paul Nadar's famous studio to have his picture taken. At least two poses were printed, one in which he looks directly at the camera and the other from a three-quarter angle. The photographs, typical of Nadar's superb work of the era, look like official portraits. The pose is formal, almost too stiff, as if the young man had been warned not to move. He is fashionably dressed in a jacket and a wide white collar, with a floppy cravat tied in a bow and a gold fob looped through a buttonhole. His crew-cut hair crowns an oval face of nearly perfect symmetry. Just beneath the left nostril there is a mole. His small, delicately shaped lips are dry, cracked, perhaps from too much exposure to the March wind. Above his lips one can detect the faint outline of a mustache about to appear. The thin, short eyebrows, like the dim mustache, are those of early puberty. Looking directly into his face one is transfixed by the striking large brown almond-shaped eyes that look sad. More than one observer would qualify them as "gazelle-like eyes" because of their soft, lustrous appearance. Perhaps they are only contemplative, observing far more than one would expect from even the most perceptive adolescent. The strong impression his stare made on his friends was the reason they all mention those eyes, those eyes that might have belonged to a melancholy Persian prince, those deep, sad, penetrating globes.

In 1887, at the end of the school year, Alexandre Gazeau chose Marcel to compete in the state examinations, an honor for which he had qualified by taking second-place prizes in history and geography. His performance was no doubt due to his keen interest in history, greatly intensified by the previous summer's reading of Thierry. Although he had always earned good grades in the subject, this was the only time he won a prize.

Marcel and approximately one hundred other top-ranked students from each lycée division reported to the Sorbonne on July 13, 1887, the eve of Bastille Day, and right in the middle of the Boulangist crisis.[47] Gen. Georges Boulanger was a popular military leader who had played a major role in suppressing the Commune and had become a hero of the right wing. He had been elected war minister the year before and seemed poised for even greater political heights. Many of his ultraconservative admirers hoped that he would engineer a coup and create a government with strong executive power. Demonstrations for the general were being organized throughout Paris. As Marcel entered the Sorbonne to take the history exam, he was conscious of the portentous events swirling around him.

The general history exam consisted of two questions, one on Philip II and the decline of Spain, the other on Asian Russia, for which a map was provided; Marcel wrote for five straight hours on the questions. He also participated in the inter-school Greek contest, but he failed to place in either history or Greek. He and his parents were disappointed, but on his lycée's awards day in August he took home, in addition to the history prize, the top merit award in Latin and the fourth merit award in French.

After the history exam, Marcel went to Auteuil to spend the night. On Bastille Day he witnessed, in addition to the traditional national holiday celebrations, a pro-Boulanger demonstration that made the streets even livelier than usual. Crowds of the general's partisans filled the streets on their way to Longchamp in the Bois to attend the colorful military review, the final and most popular event of the Bastille Day celebration.[48] As groups of celebrators rushed by, Marcel heard them singing the general's campaign songs, "Happy, triumphantly, we marched" and " 'It's Boulange, lange, lange' shouted out by everyone, women, workmen, even children from five to eight years old, who sing it perfectly in tune and with passion."[49]

The next day he wrote to Antoinette Faure, reporting on his recent activities and the street scenes he had witnessed: "My dear Antoinette, Would you believe that Mama has torn up a letter I wrote to you. The handwriting was too bad. Actually, I am inclined to think that my great praise of our good general, that 'simple and sublime' soldier, as the *Petit Boulanger* calls him, aroused Madame Jeanne Proust's old Orleanist-republican sentiments." Marcel had been only temporarily swayed by the highly visible and vocal endorsements of the general's campaign. He told Antoinette that he saw in the general a "very common and vulgar self-promoter," although he admitted that the mighty, spontaneous enthusiasm that greeted Boulanger had stirred in his heart feelings that were "primitive, indomitable, bellicose." Fortune did not smile on the general, who, shortly after being elected a deputy in 1889, was accused of conspiring with the monarchists against the Republic and was forced to flee France.

In spite of health problems and Jeanne's constant fretting over his outings, his handwriting, his hygiene, and his progress, Marcel enjoyed active games and even roughhousing, some of which took place between boys and girls. Such tussles were the occasions of his first awareness of sexual desire. Marie was the primary model for Gilberte in the *Search*, the first girl with whom the Narrator falls in love. Here is how Proust describes a wrestling match between the two over the possession of a letter in the Champs-Élysées garden:

She thrust it behind her back; I put my arms round her neck, raising the plaits of hair which she wore over her shoulders . . . and we wrestled, locked together. I tried to pull her towards me, and she resisted; her cheeks, inflamed by the effort, were as red and round as two cherries; she laughed as though I were tickling her; I held her gripped between my legs like a young tree which I was trying to climb; and, in the middle of my gymnastics, when I was already out of breath with the muscular exercise and the heat of the game, I felt, like a few drops of sweat wrung from me by the effort, my pleasure express itself in a form which I could not even pause for a moment to analyse; immediately I snatched the letter from her. Whereupon Gilberte said good-naturedly: "You know, if you like, we might go on wrestling a bit longer."[50]

This is the first episode in the novel in which the Narrator obviously experiences orgasm with another person—an orgasm that is, to say the least, adolescent, protected, and remote. In real life such an incident might just as easily have occurred with a boy. Wrestling, fighting, playing rough-and-tumble games—such sport often furnishes the first occasion when many youths feel desire, fleeting, denied, or embraced, for members of their sex. Would this feeling disappear as a bit of youthful ephemera or would such yearnings become permanently fixed? How could Marcel know? He did know that he was irresistibly drawn to the masculine beauty of his classmates, and he yearned to taste the pleasures of intimate sexual contact. If masturbation brought such bliss, if wrestling held such promise, he could only imagine what it must be like to spend his passion willfully on a beautiful, naked body. Perhaps he had been wrong to decline an older classmate's invitation to visit a brothel.

If he was to have no compunction about offering himself to his male friends, Marcel felt a healthy repugnance toward having sex with whores, then a common rite of passage for French schoolboys. Daniel Halévy recounts an incident that occurred when Marcel wandered into a beer hall frequented by prostitutes who worked in the Latin Quarter. Later, when he and Daniel were sitting on a bench alongside an unknown, respectable-looking woman, Marcel related his adventure among the prostitutes, concluding: "I went into a beer hall. I will never go there again. I felt as if I had left there a part of my moral being!" The woman, stupefied, stared at him while Marcel assumed a cocky air.[51] This remark, which Daniel immediately spread among their classmates, appeared to them the height of ridiculousness, another instance of Marcel's making a colossal fool of himself.

Although he disdained prostitutes, Marcel was eager for sexual experience and largely indifferent as to whether it was with a man or a woman. Daniel had told Marcel about a woman whom he had discovered in a shop on the slopes of Montmartre and whose beauty intrigued him.[52] One day after school, Daniel led him to the dairy shop, where the two boys stopped on the sidewalk and stared, watching Mme Chirade as she came and went, busy serving her customers delicious cheeses and creams. Marcel, struck by the splendor of her black hair, fair skin, and fine features, whispered in Daniel's ear: "How beautiful she is!" Then he compared her to Flaubert's exotic heroine: "Beautiful like Salammbô." After a short silence in which he remained absorbed in admiration, trying to imagine what it might be like to possess such a creature, he startled Daniel by asking, "Do you think we can sleep with her?"

Daniel had to admit that the thought had never occurred to him. Marcel's audacity inspired in Daniel a sudden respect for the friend he had considered a sissy. Fearing that their immobility and curiosity would attract attention, the schoolboys moved on down the sidewalk, distracted and lost in thought. Marcel, obviously inflamed by desire and eager for action, suggested, "Let's bring her some flowers."

A few days later, at an agreed-upon hour, the boys returned to Montmartre. Marcel carried an armload of roses purchased in a floral shop along the way. They felt like untried soldiers about to execute a difficult and dangerous maneuver. Arriving in front of the shop, they saw Mme Chirade in her usual place, tending to customers. Daniel, unaccountably shy, remained glued to the sidewalk, his eyes wide and darting, wondering whether his friend would dare. Marcel, holding the roses before him, advanced into the shop straight toward Mme Chirade. Daniel watched Marcel's back as he spoke to the captivating dark-haired woman, saw her smile, gently but firmly saying *Non* while shaking her head. Marcel apparently insisted, at which point, the beautiful lady, still smiling and determined, advanced in slow, invincible steps, forcing Marcel to retreat until, before he knew it, he found himself back out on the sidewalk standing next to his amazed and flustered friend. Mme Chirade had never for a second lost her composure or her graciousness. The boys, suddenly panicked at the audacity of their attempted seduction, raced home, Marcel still clutching the now useless roses.

"*Transparent nights*"

Marcel's illnesses, his extreme sensitivity, the insomnia that would plague him all his life, and the dreaded onset of asthma attacks all increased his nervous condition and his dependency on his mother. His frailty forced him to listen intently and constantly to his body as he sought clues to the causes of his misery. His body had become for his parents the center of constant, fretful attention as they monitored diet, sleep, exercise, and other activities, looking for any modifications that might make him healthier. Whenever Jeanne and her son were apart, he reported his condition to her in detail, pleased no doubt, with a child's natural narcissism, to preoccupy so fully her mother love. At age sixteen, he wrote to her from Auteuil one day in early fall:

> My enchanting little Mama,
> Let me first tell you that my stomach is *divine*. . . . I was *sure* I was going to digest well at night. But then came *transparent nights* with the feeling one has when asleep, about to wake up soon, etc., dreams, *foul* taste in my mouth on waking. One night (the night of the Louvre) I go to bed, I'm really worried about my digestion, but I've taken tea very late and eaten a heavy dinner (3 desserts). On waking I let out a spontaneous cry of surprise, exquisite taste in my mouth, calm, perfect sleep. Consequently I feel much better that day. The next afternoon I go to the Bois as usual on foot, then Uncle's carriage, etc. Troubled sleep, disgusting taste in my mouth.
> So this is what I said to myself.
> The *only* day followed by a good night was like this:
> No Bois except in a coupé, because I called for Uncle outside the Louvre, not at the Acacia Gardens.
> The next day I try not going to the Bois.
> I take tea, I dine (by pure chance) very substantially, even provoking some comments on Grandmother's part.
> No bad taste in my mouth.[53]

This practice of monitoring himself—eventually leading to self-diagnosis and self-medication—became a lifelong preoccupation.

In October, Marcel enrolled in class 1 and began his next to last year at Condorcet. He studied in Maxime Gaucher's and Victor Cucheval's sections in rhetoric B, where the two men shared the teaching. Gaucher taught French and Greek literature, Cucheval the literature of ancient Rome, together conducting "this year's circular journey from Homer to Chénier by way of Petronius."[54] The students all agreed that M. Gaucher, known as "an infinitely charming and liberal spirit," was one of Condorcet's outstanding professors. Robert Dreyfus remembered him as being "the liveliest and most indulgent professor at Condorcet, a man much admired for his wit, his mischievous and jovial nature, and the literary column he wrote as a critic for *La Revue bleue*."[55] Thus for nearly a year, cut short at the end by Gaucher's illness and death, Marcel had the good fortune of studying with an excellent teacher who was also a respected critic at a favorite review. Gaucher, who had a profound influence on Marcel, seems to have been the first teacher to appreciate his pupil's extraordinary literary gifts.

A nonconformist, an admired and respected writer endowed with literary taste, Gaucher did not refrain from using colloquialisms in class, a practice noted and frowned upon by inspectors. A wise teacher, Gaucher provoked questions more often than he provided conclusions. He wanted his students to be curious, open-minded, and industrious, to know that one does not begin a journey or a quest with the answers in hand. Marcel had already become indifferent to literary theories, worth nothing to a young writer who understood that each artist must find his own path to success. Gaucher's refreshing approach held his attention.

To develop his students' writing skills, Gaucher concentrated on training them to write original essays on literary topics that he proposed. One topic required the discussion of a statement by Denis Diderot: "Sensitivity is scarcely the quality of a great genius; it is not a genius's heart but his head that matters." In his notes for the essay, apparently left unfinished, Marcel disagreed with Diderot, giving the heart the major role. But intelligence also had a vital part to play in creating a work of art: "Sensitivity alone, unless it has been implemented by intelligence, will perhaps excite our emotions, never our admiration, nor the elevated pleasures of intelligence that a true work of art gives us because art provides us with the order, meaning, and harmonious logic that is usually hidden in life."[56] In his mature work, Proust would define the artist as someone who "makes things visible," who shows us how to see things that are usually concealed.

Another composition challenged the opinion of Charles-Augustin Sainte-Beuve (1804–69), France's most distinguished literary critic of the nineteenth century. Gaucher had given his pupils Sainte-Beuve's statement that those who passionately admire Corneille must have a certain liking for boastfulness, whereas those who are passionate admirers of Racine run the risk of having too much of what the French call taste. Marcel addressed the question in a remarkably authoritative voice formed by his years of serious, dedicated reading. His comments showed an apprentice writer's complicity with the masters he admires, a realization that each must possess a unique quality, a vision that made his work original. It would be absurd, he argued, to seize upon a writer's defining characteristic, whether Corneille's pride or Racine's refinement, and use that as the basis for accusing him of being excessive.

Poetry and literature are not the result of pure thought, he wrote, but bear the stamp of an individual temperament. A true writer will produce masterpieces, like Corneille's *Le Cid* or Racine's *Andromaque,* that are the highest expression of an artist's humanity, seeming to derive from the aggregate soul belonging to the tribe of man. We should love great artists not by taking their defects as the essence of their originality but rather by seeing their strengths as the foundation of their genius and the reasons for its development. Thus, to admire passionately Racine is simply to esteem the most profound and sincerest intuitions of so many charming, martyred lives. To admire fervently Corneille would be to love in its integral beauty, in its unalterable pride, the highest achievement of a heroic ideal.[57] Marcel's argument is lucid, his reasons informed yet commonsensical. One can detect here Proust's earliest predilection for Racine's plays, which, as he noted, "affirm the power of love."[58]

Gaucher appreciated Marcel's superior essays and asked him to read them aloud in order to encourage his classmates to improve their writing. One student Pierre Lavallée, recalled Marcel's essays as being "so rich in impressions and images, already quite 'Proustian' with their sentences larded with asides and parentheses. . . . I can still see and hear Marcel reading his papers aloud, and the excellent, the charming M. Gaucher commenting, praising, criticizing, then suddenly overcome with laughter at the stylistic boldness, which actually delighted him. It was the joy of his last days to have discovered among his students a born writer."[59]

The Latin teacher Victor Cucheval, soon to be awarded the Légion d'honneur for his scholarly achievements, was a strict Cartesian who had no patience with students he considered sluggards—a category to which he at first assigned Marcel. The boy's nonconformity and the idiosyncratic style he had already begun to develop did not appeal to the rigorous Cucheval, who judged Marcel's progress as mediocre and uneven, labeling him a daydreamer and mischief maker.[60] Marcel, often at odds with his teachers concerning their opinions about writers and art, had begun to experiment with a writing style unlike that expected of a schoolboy. Writing to Robert Dreyfus, a year behind him at Condorcet, Marcel, aware that he had already become the school eccentric, advised his friend not to emulate his experiments with style, his disputes with teachers, and his attempts to convince them that some contemporary writers merited reading:

I wrote papers that weren't at all like school exercises. The result was that two months later a dozen imbeciles were writing in decadent style, that Cucheval thought me a troublemaker, that I had disrupted the class, and that some of my classmates came to regard me as a poseur. Luckily it only lasted for two months, but a month ago Cucheval said: "He'll pass, because he was only clowning, but fifteen will fail because of him." They will want to cure you. Your comrades will think you're crazy or feeble-minded. For several months I read all my French papers aloud in class, I was hooted and applauded. If it hadn't been for Gaucher, I'd have been torn to pieces.[61]

Years later Proust took his revenge on Cucheval, whose unfortunate name, a schoolboy's delight, made him the butt of many jokes. Pronounced the same as *cul-cheval*, the professor's name sounded just like the words for *horse's ass*. In 1903 Proust, using the pseudonym Horatio, made fun of the poor man in a society column describing an elegant party for *Le Figaro*. Upon the arrival of each guest in the ballroom, the usher announces the name:

> "Your name, sir?"
> "M. Cucheval."
> "Oh, no, sir, I asked your name?"
> "Don't be insolent! M. Cucheval."
> And the usher felt obliged to consult the host:
> "Monsieur le baron, this gentleman says his name is M. Horse's Ass, must I announce him like that?"

The issue is left unresolved and the disconcerted baron runs off to consult the baroness.[62]

Marcel's name did not appear on the honors list at the end of the year, but at the awards ceremony on July 31, owing to Gaucher's enthusiastic endorsement, he won the most prestigious honor, first prize in French composition. He also received certificates of merit for Latin and Greek. In coming years, Marcel did not always find editors and reviewers who immediately recognized, as had Gaucher, the exceptional beauty of his prose.

Boys in Bloom

At Condorcet, the boys whom Marcel considered the most intelligent were Robert Dreyfus, Daniel Halévy, and Jacques Bizet.[63] Halévy and Bizet were also, according to classmate Fernand Gregh, by far the most undisciplined: "The two cousins competed in making an uproar. The naïve study-hall teacher, M. Martin, who wore blue spectacles, said to them one day, 'You know perfectly well that with your names, you'd never be expelled. . . .' They took advantage of the situation, the dastards!"[64]

Daniel Halévy had come to Condorcet in the autumn of 1887, when he was fifteen years old. Like Marcel, he was from a liberal, bourgeois Parisian family and had a Jewish ancestor in Germany.[65] An intelligent, gifted boy, tall, handsome, with hazel eyes, he had a difficult but solid friendship with Proust.[66] They shared many qualities and tastes, a love of literature, and a drive to succeed, but they were separated by other traits. Daniel, who liked to be seen as domineering and tough, tormented Marcel with his angry gestures and his ability to keep silent for days on end.

Among Proust's classmates, there was an extraordinary amount of budding literary talent, accompanied by frequent outbursts of schoolboy high jinks. Daniel Halévy, Robert de Flers, Robert Dreyfus, Fernand Gregh, and Louis de La Salle were among those who formed what Dreyfus described as "our intimate circle of schoolboys," all of whom became successful writers.[67] Halévy was to write biographies of Friedrich Nietzsche, Jules Michelet, and Sébastien Vauban. La Salle published a volume of poetry and a novel before his career was cut short. Dreyfus was a journalist on the staff of Le Figaro for years and an important historian of the Third Republic. He wrote the first major study of Comte Joseph Arthur Gobineau, author of Essai sur l'inégalité des races humaines (The inequality of human races), who has been called the "intellectual parent of Nietzsche" and the creator of the idea of the super-man.[68] Robert de Flers, novelist, playwright, and librettist, and Fernand Gregh, future author of ten volumes of poetry, were both later elected to the Académie française, a distinction not bestowed upon Proust.

On May 13, 1888, Marcel succumbed to the call of the muse and wrote a poem "To Daniel Halévy, while watching him during the first quarter hour of detention." This untitled and unfinished verse, written primarily in rhymed alexandrine couplets, is the first known poem by Proust. Unlike other writings that he soon sent to friends or submitted to the little literary magazines his circle created at Condorcet, this one contained no homoerotic longings. The young poet expressed his horror at the tyranny of the sun over those who have been disappointed in the pursuit of their heroic dream and who now "curse you, o cruel King, fierce and white / And dream of the fresh blueness of nights / Near mystical cats."[69] This poem shows the influence of Marcel's favorite poets; if Leconte de Lisle made him want to write Parnassian verses, his first poems also echo the rhythms and images of Paul Verlaine, Charles Baudelaire, and Charles Cros.[70]

Although Marcel's friends were amazed by his talent, they were often repulsed by his personality, his clinging possessiveness, his tireless preoccupation with *gentillesse* (kindness), and his direct homosexual overtures. The boys recognized that while Marcel was "close" to them, he was different, and that sufficed to awaken their distrust and provoke their harsh treatment of him. They found it hard to believe anyone could be so refined and so tactful, and they thought his behavior was an affectation. Only later did they realize that the "words that he wasted on us, 'niceness, tenderness,' conveyed quite sincerely and, in a timid, attenuated language, as we later understood, his deep need to be liked."[71]

Precocious in composition, Marcel was gifted at observing and analyzing others. He was also lucid regarding his own amorous inclinations and eager to engage in sexual experimentation. Like other adolescents overflowing with sexual energy in late-nineteenth-century France, he had three obvious choices: masturbation, visits to prostitutes, and sex with his classmates. Marcel may have been puzzled and even disturbed on becoming aware that his longings for sexual gratification were not of the kind considered normal, but he had no hesitation in avowing his feelings to his classmates. Perhaps he hoped that these desires were just an adolescent phase. Weren't there others who felt as he did or who, at least, were curious about intimate contact?

Jacques Bizet, one year behind Marcel, had entered Condorcet in 1887. Robert Dreyfus described young Bizet as being "well liked, a faithful friend, and full of joyful life."[72] Handsome and popular, Jacques appeared gifted, sensitive, a normal adolescent boy who loved the outdoors and hiking. But Jacques had a troubled, darker side he kept hidden from his friends. Geneviève Bizet was the child of two parents whose families had histories of depression and other psychological disorders. Jacques's troubles would not become evident until he reached adulthood.

Sometime during the winter of 1887–88, Marcel wrote Jacques saying that he greatly needed his friendship because he had so many problems and hinted that his family treated him badly. Exaggerating his difficulties to win sympathy, he said that his parents had threatened to send him away to boarding school in the provinces. He then asked Jacques to be his "reservoir," the recipient of his overflowing sorrows and love: "My only consolation when I am really sad is to love and be loved." He ended his short, desperate appeal with a declaration, "I embrace you and love you with all my heart."[73]

Like all adolescents, Marcel felt isolated and misunderstood. In drafts of *Jean Santeuil* and later the *Search,* he remembered the feeling of being alone, plotted against, a prisoner of his family, a feeling that roused in him "that old desire to rebel against an imaginary plot woven against me by my parents, who imagined that I would be forced to obey them, that defiant spirit which drove me in the past to impose my will brutally upon the people I loved best in the world, though finally conforming to theirs after I had succeeded in making them yield." Marcel, whom his classmates considered spoiled, would write in *Jean Santeuil* that his protagonist's childhood resembled a prison, that his "parental home had seemed to him a place of slavery."[74] No doubt he felt shackled by his parents' relentless bourgeois aspirations for him and society's hypocrisy regarding homosexual love.

Undeterred by the knowledge that the couplings he desired were generally considered perverse, Marcel expressed in his letters to his classmates, often humorously, his strong homosexual urges. These letters reveal an astonishingly mature and analytic voice, highly sensual and yet capable of self-parody without abandoning candor. Marcel put his own sensuality under a microscope, refused to be hypocritical by pretending to denounce sensual pleasures, and proposed a hedonistic moral code that embraced the needs of his mind and his body.

In the spring of 1888, Marcel, still enamored of Jacques, handed him a letter at school, inviting him to have sex. Jacques, indifferent to the proposal, passed his unwanted suitor a note declining the offer while Marcel was on his way to M. Choublier's history class. Once in his seat Marcel skimmed the letter and then, on the sheet of notebook paper intended for history notes, he wrote his reply. Pretending to accept the refusal, Marcel praised Jacques's intellectual gifts and gently pressed his case. He again offered an erotic, troubling flower—his own eager body—tinged with all the dangers of forbidden love. By asking Jacques if he might pluck his flower-penis and savor the tender yet dangerous bloom, was Marcel naïve or indifferent to exposure and ridicule? The letter pleads along these lines: It is all right to engage in such behavior now, because we are young, innocent, and inexperienced.

> My dear Jacques,
>   Under the stern eye of M. Choublier, I have just raced through your letter, propelled by my fear. I admire your wisdom, while at the same time deploring it. Your reasons are excellent, and I am glad to see how strong and alert, how keen and penetrating your thinking has become. Still, the heart—or the body—has it reasons that are unknown to reason, and so it is with admiration for you (that is, for your thinking, not for your refusal, for I am not fatuous enough to believe that my body is so precious a treasure that to renounce it required great strength of character) but with sadness that I accept the disdainful and cruel yoke you im-

pose on me. Maybe you are right. Still, I always find it sad not to pluck the delicious flower that we shall soon be unable to pluck. For then it would be fruit . . . and forbidden.[75]

Marcel, by juxtaposing reasons of the heart and body, made a wordplay on Blaise Pascal's famous maxim from his *Pensées:* "Le cœur a ses raisons, que la raison ne connaît point" (The heart has its reasons that reason does not know).[76] In French the words for heart, *cœur,* and body, *corps,* have a similar sound. But in spite of the image of flowers and the wittily altered maxim, Jacques was simply not interested and shrugged off the sly invitation. Dreyfus remembered that Jacques often laughed robustly at Marcel's attempts at seduction because the younger boy "only liked women, who also found him very attractive, and so did not see himself at all compromised by Marcel's bizarre behavior; on the contrary, it flattered him."[77] Bizet remained a close friend, as he indicated a year later when he gave Marcel a photograph of himself as a child, on the back of which he wrote: "To my dearest friend (with Halévy), 18 February 1889."[78] Marcel cannot have been happy at sharing first place in Jacques's heart with Halévy, for he, like his later fictional heroes, exhibited extreme jealousy in his affections. Jacques-Émile Blanche recalls a childhood friend of Marcel's who told Blanche that in playing with the future writer, he was "gripped with fear when I felt Marcel seize my hand and declare to me his need for total and tyrannical possession."[79]

That spring Marcel wrote Jacques another letter, revealing that Marcel's parents had discovered the nature of his sexual desires and his obsessive masturbation.[80] Jacques gave the letter to Halévy, who recorded it in his diary.[81] Before copying the letter, Daniel noted, "Poor Proust is absolutely crazy." Marcel had written in a rage when his mother forbade him to see Jacques or invite him over, "perhaps because she is worried about my affection that is somewhat excessive and that may degenerate (so she believes perhaps) into a . . . sensual affection."[82] Mme Proust apparently had good reason to be alarmed. Marcel goes on to say that she believes Jacques has some of the same faults as he: rebellious spirit, nervousness, unfocused mind; perhaps even onanism. Marcel described for Jacques the scene that erupted when his father caught him masturbating: "This morning, dearest, when my father saw me . . . he begged me to stop masturbating for at least four days." He continues melodramatically by saying that if his parents refuse him permission to invite Jacques, then he will love him "outside the walls" of the family prison, and the two friends will make their common abode in a nearby café.

This letter amazed Daniel, not only because of the intimate glimpse into the

Proust family's private struggle with Marcel's emotions and raging sexuality but also as a literary production. He expressed to his diary his astonishment that Proust had written the letter without crossing out a word: "This deranged creature is extremely talented, and I know NOTHING that is sadder and more marvelously written than these two pages." Halévy noted that we must tolerate excesses when one has genius, but he feared that Marcel's obsessions would destroy his gifts. "More talented than anyone else. He overexerts himself. Weak, young, he fornicates, he masturbates, he engages, perhaps, in pederasty! He will perhaps show in his life flashes of genius that will be wasted." Years later, when asked whether any of Proust's schoolmates had a premonition of his genius, Halévy answered that although they knew Marcel was obviously talented, no one believed he had "the will power ever to achieve a masterpiece."[83]

Marcel's parents, alarmed at his proclivities, searched for solutions. His father concluded that his son needed to visit a brothel and gave him ten francs. Marcel went to a brothel, but in his consternation broke a chamber pot and lost his erection and his money. Jeanne, fearing Adrien's wrath if he found out Marcel had been so careless with the money while failing to obtain the desired results, advised him to appeal to his grandfather. Marcel sent Nathé an urgent plea for thirteen francs: "Here's why. I so desperately needed to see a woman in order to put an end to my bad habit of masturbating that Papa gave me 10 francs to go to a brothel. But 1st in my agitation I broke a chamber pot 3 francs and 2d in this same agitated state I was unable to screw. So here I am still awaiting each hour 10 francs to satisfy myself and in addition 3 francs for the chamber pot." He ended his petition on a humorous, bravura note: "But I dare not ask papa for money again so soon and I hoped you will be able to come to my aid in this instance, which, as you know, is not only exceptional but unique: it can't happen twice in one lifetime that a person's too upset to screw."[84] Unfortunately, the outcome of Marcel's misadventure remains unknown.

Nathé was the model for M. Sandré in *Jean Santeuil,* where he is described as a "violent and sweet" man who worries only about his daughter's happiness, his son-in-law's career, and his grandson's health. Marcel made this observation about elderly couples: "Old people don't love each other, they love their children."[85] Nathé did have tender affection for his grandson, but he tried to remain stern as part of the family's efforts to teach the boy discipline. If the boy looked to his grandmother to guide him in reading and cultural interests, he turned to his grandfather for practical matters, usually involving money, whether a subscription for a literary journal or a visit to a prostitute.[86]

Toward the end of May, Marcel wrote Halévy a long note from M. Choublier's class: "Everyone is 'geographizing' zealously around me."[87] After denying that he is decadent, he lists for Daniel the writers of the century he admired above all others: "Musset, Hugo, Michelet, Renan, Sully-Prudhomme, Leconte de Lisle, Halévy, Taine, Becque, France." He also mentions Théodore de Banville and Heredia, certain works by Mallarmé, and the *Chansons* of Verlaine, which he found exquisite but with reservations.[88] After more literary chitchat, he expresses his desire to meet Halévy after school on those days when Halévy does not go home immediately. "Bizet will believe that I am starting with you the series of 'lists' that are, as you know, with me the sign of a burgeoning friendship." The list apparently refers to a ranking of friends in order of affection.[89]

After thanking Daniel for giving him the opportunity not to listen to the boring Choublier, Marcel added a postscript in which he invites Daniel to cofound a major art magazine. Then, changing subjects rapidly, he discusses someone Daniel suspected of being a pederast, which led Marcel to share some information about homosexuality among youths: "(. . . If this interests you and you promise me *absolute secrecy*, not to tell even Bizet, I will give you documents of very great interest, belonging to me, addressed to me) from young men and especially ones in age from eight to seventeen who love other guys, eager always to see them (as I do Bizet), who cry and suffer far from them, and who desire only one thing to embrace them and sit in their lap, who love them for their *flesh*, who devour them with their eyes, who call them darling, my angel, very seriously, who write them passionate letters, and who would not for anything in the world practice pederasty."

No doubt the conclusion of this single, long sentence was not what Daniel expected. One can be skeptical about Proust's naïveté or sincerity here. He ends the postscript with another paragraph stating what was to remain his view on ethics concerning sexual love between members of the same sex: "However, generally love wins out and they [the boys] masturbate together. But don't mock them and the friend of whom you speak, if he is like this. They are simply in love. And I do not understand why their love is any more unclean than normal love."[90] In his early twenties, Marcel elaborated this viewpoint, using an aesthetic argument to justify same-sex love in the short story "Avant la nuit" (Before nightfall).[91]

By seeking sexual partners among his classmates, was the adolescent Marcel playing with fire, and did he finally get burned? Letters from the family of Raoul Versini, a classmate at Condorcet, indicate that Marcel's flirtations may have placed him in a difficult situation.[92] Versini became a close friend with whom Marcel exchanged letters. Sometimes when Adrien and Jeanne were away, they allowed

Marcel to spend the night at Raoul's. Versini undertook to cure Marcel of his homosexual tendencies by lecturing him about its dangers. In a letter to Versini, Marcel confessed that he had gone too far with an older boy and agreed to perform "a very filthy act."[93] What allegedly took place is that the older boy, while begging Marcel to consent, presumably, to anal intercourse, took him by surprise "in a moment of madness" and being stronger, overpowered him. Marcel claimed that he had agreed only to certain fondlings and caresses: "I agreed at first, that was all." Immediately after the incident he related what had happened to a friend, Abel Desjardins, and then to his father, who, aware of his tendencies, did not condemn him too severely but considered his "error a surprise." This information, which cannot be substantiated because the letter was later destroyed, shows that his parents knew about his homosexuality.[94]

In the autumn of 1888, Marcel sent Daniel a sonnet with its title in capital letters, PEDERASTY, in which he celebrates the serene joys of boy love. He begins by saying that if he had a large sack of gold he would run away to an ideal country where he would like "forever to sleep, love or live with a warm boy, Jacques, Pierre or Firmin" and "breathe his scent until he dies . . . far from the mournful knell of importunate Virtue."[95]

Proust's great need to be liked, combined with his extraordinary sensitivity, often made him behave in an obsequious, unctuous manner that his friends found insincere and phony. So bizarre were his mannerisms, at once both endearing and infuriating, that his friends, realizing the French language contained no word to describe such behavior, invented one: Proustify.[96] On occasions when the boys had their fill of Proustifications, they responded by displaying coldness or indifference, or by pretending not to like him any more. To show their displeasure and to indicate to Marcel that he was unwanted, they would speak to him sharply or feign a shove, dismissing him rudely with a wave of the arm, causing his large, dark eyes to fill with sadness. Often miserable, feeling misunderstood and unloved by his family, he found no solace among his friends, who considered him peculiar at best. None was willing to offer him the consolation he sought. On the contrary, filled with adolescent insensitivity, when not overtly hostile, they enjoyed teasing and tormenting him.

As summer drew to a close, he had another source of misery: his mother's impending departure. She had decided to return to the spa at Salies-de-Béarn and to take Robert along with her, leaving Marcel behind. It is unclear why Marcel did not accompany her to the spa, since his first trip had been so successful, excepting bouts of boredom, a common and rather benign adolescent ailment. Perhaps this was part of the family strategy to wean him from his dependency upon her. One thing is certain; being separated from his mother remained his idea of misery.

From Auteuil on September 5, Marcel wrote to his "dearest Mama" on his last sheet of fancy paper that what issued from his pen would be the "purest truth," a pledge no doubt made necessary by her fear over how he might fare and behave without her. After a funny story about taking his Uncle George to the train station, an anecdote no doubt intended to prove that he was putting on a brave face and trying his best to amuse himself despite his wretchedness over her departure, Marcel related the "accidents" he experienced at dinner. These were weeping fits caused by her absence that, coming from a seventeen-year-old boy, scandalized the family members, guests, and servants present.[97]

Jeanne wrote back immediately to her "poor wolf," quickly assuring him that she was all the less inclined to criticize his weeping fits because "I had at least as much chagrin as you and I haven't stopped thinking about you. I cannot say that I wish you were here because you would have had no pleasure till now." She was not exaggerating, for a calamity had occurred during the night: a fire broke out and destroyed part of the building housing the baths, upsetting everyone's regimen and schedule. The fire, the smoke, the confusion, added to the oppressive heat of late summer, would have been, she wrote, particularly difficult for him. She expressed her pleasure on learning about the success of his morning walks and urged him to take a stroll every day for as long as he enjoyed going out.

Marcel's parents continued to worry about his weeping fits, sexual orientation, proclivities, obvious nervous disorders, and asthma. In moments of painful objectivity, Adrien forced himself to wonder whether his son would ever become strong and independent. Were not many of his tastes, habits, and mannerisms more feminine than masculine? Was Marcel not the epitome of a clinging mama's boy? Did the boy have the stamina, the will to make his way in life and excel in a profession? The busy doctor, whose own son provided a case history of many of the ills that he sought to prevent or cure, had little time or energy to spare on Marcel's problems. Could he count on his wife, naturally tenderhearted and kind, to follow the strict regimen necessary to educate the boy?

While Jeanne and Robert were at Salies, Marcel, who had managed to regain his composure, visited a classmate, Édouard Joyant, at Île-Adam. From there Marcel wrote Dreyfus again, trying to comprehend Halévy's heartless treatment of him. Marcel spoke about "the different persons of whom I am composed." Proust had ready begun developing his concept of multiple selves. He identified his "romantic" self, who thought Halévy really did want to know him, and his "distrustful" self, whose voice insisted that Halévy found him an unbearable nuisance.[98]

What is remarkable about many of Marcel's adolescent letters is that he used them not simply to express his emotions but to analyze them and try to comprehend his motivations and those of his classmates. He played roles himself and assigned different attitudes to his friends. He had already created for himself, years before he began trying to develop plots for stories, a laboratory in which to study the human personality and psychology. This practice, begun at such a young age, combined with his remarkable sensitivity, which allowed him to put himself in another's place, was to serve him well when, as a mature writer, he began populating the *Search* with fascinating, multifaceted characters.

Lying and fiction are, after all, synonymous. A child's imagination and penchant for making up stories are but efforts to reshape the world to make it more interesting or more to our liking—an impulse that often lasts into adulthood. Marcel's letters reveal his intense self-scrutiny and remarkable ability with words, his passion for literature, his at times nearly ravenous desire to be loved and find happiness, all combining to create a made-up world in which he finds or seeks, at times through duplicity and manipulation but with an unyielding determination, a world in which to be happy. He wanted to love and be loved, especially by his mother but also by his friends—and physically by boys he found attractive.

We must all create a world of fiction in which we alone can live. Our world never matches the one inhabited by those with whom we are most intimate. A writer, especially one of genius, creates a world we can all visit, like paupers touring a palace, wondering, as we explore its splendors, at the remarkable differences with our own more ramshackle abode, while struck by the persistence of human nature and emotion that makes us feel that we, too, could live in such a mansion. Proust always invites us in. After making a particularly revealing remark about an aspect of a character's personality or behavior that the reader could have thought unique, he deftly switches to a pronoun, *one* or *we*, and embraces us all, as in this maxim about how the young are necessarily uncertain of their talents and inclinations: "No one can tell at first that he is an invert, or a poet, or a snob, or a scoundrel."[99] Young Marcel could not tell either, and he continued to experiment with various personae, peering like Narcissus into the water, but seeing many reflections of himself. Ultimately, disguising himself as the egotist at the story's center, he wrote a book that places the reader at its heart, a book that perhaps more than any other, is about each of us and our many reflections in the mirror.

This practice of relentlessly investigating and grilling—and lying to—his acquaintances would become a hallmark of jealous lovers in Proust's fiction. His characters subscribe to the belief that in love and war all is fair, including mendacity. In their world, it is accepted, even expected, that lovers, especially, lie to each other. If one may be said to wear a mask in society, Proustian characters wear many masks for many reasons, at times voluntarily, at others because of social pressures or lust, to disguise ruthless social ambition, or to hide from their own scruples. The world at Condorcet was society in miniature, minus women. Soon Marcel was to make his entrance onto the grand stage of dissimulation, the world of high society, of vanity fair.

The adolescent Marcel, who incarnated the wretched, insecure mama's boy, was also a precocious psychologist, and a gifted comic and mimic of his friends and professors. He understood how ridiculous he must often appear, a spectacle he depicted in outbursts of self-parody. One beautiful September day, in an elated mood before heading off to a riding lesson, Marcel sent Dreyfus a caricature of himself. If he were a great lord, he would like to "order up a play" and behave any way he liked and declare his love to Jacques. As a compensation, he would drive in a carriage to the "Acacia Gardens, the place for elegant, wealthy Parisians to see and be seen. That, to my taste, is the height of Parisian beauty in 1888."[100]

Marcel next imagined two beautiful courtesans gossiping as they drive through the park. One asks the other if she knows "M. P." and then begins to tattle about Marcel's personality and his crushes on his schoolmates. She accuses Marcel of hypocrisy because, having given her to understand he had "quite a feeling" for her and after "pretending to love a comrade like a father he loves him like a woman." Even among the boys, Marcel remains fickle: "The nasty part of it, *ma chère*, is that after making a fuss over B he drops him and cajoles D, whom he soon leaves to fling himself at the feet of E and a moment later into the lap of F. Is he a whore, is he mad, is he a charlatan, is he an imbecile? . . . Perhaps . . . he's all these at once."[101]

Whether engaged in mischievous play, as in this letter, or suffering from the pangs of terrible rejection and jealousy, Marcel could not help himself: he constantly reinvented himself and his friends, always aware of the rich complexity of personality and behavior. Because of the mature Proust's absolute commitment to his vocation and his creation of "high" art, his joyful, playful side, along with his great gift for comedy, is sometimes overlooked.

The letter to Dreyfus seems to mark a turning point, as though by ridiculing himself Marcel could then turn to serious matters and a new set of fascinations with courtesans and society hostesses. Marcel had mentioned to his friend the idea of creating a newspaper in which he and his schoolmates could publish their writings. He had been reading the theater columns and books in which he caught glimpses of life in high society. In Marcel's depiction of courtesans gossiping maliciously as their carriage descended the Avenue des Acacias, Dreyfus thought he detected the influence of two writers currently enjoying success: Jules Lemaître and Paul Bourget. It was his eagerness to read Lemaître's articles on literature that had made Marcel beg his grandfather for the subscription to *La Revue bleue.*

Jules Lemaître, who also wrote drama reviews for the *Journal des débats* and *La Revue des Deux Mondes,* captivated his readers, including Marcel, with the wit and charm of his impressionistic, irony-tinged essays. Lemaître's own works for the stage were less well received than his reviews. Paul Bourget had earned his reputation as an important writer with two novels, *Cruelle énigme* (1885) and *André Cornélis* (1887). The next year he would publish *Le Disciple,* the work that established him as a master of the psychological novel. A regular guest in the salons of Princesse Mathilde, Comtesse Potocka, and the former Geneviève Bizet, now Mme Straus, Bourget had ample opportunity to observe the lives of the rich and famous and of the hangers-on admitted to their intimate circles. His novels detailed the life of the privileged classes, providing analyses of the moods and inner conflicts of the idle rich. This was the world young Marcel yearned to enter.

Although Bourget's most recent publication, *Gladys Harvey,* was not one of his most ambitious works, it soon attracted Marcel's attention. The novel portrayed the life of a *demimondaine,* as kept women were called, and was based on Bourget's current lover, Laure Hayman, who had been Uncle Louis Weil's mistress. Adrien Proust was Laure's doctor and, almost certainly, her lover.[102] In late fall Marcel met Laure at Auteuil, where she had come to call on his Uncle Louis. Louis, who maintained close ties with his former mistress, had been a great ladies' man in his day and kept a collection of photographs, which Marcel would inherit, of the celebrated actresses and cocottes he had known.[103] One of the most interesting was a photograph Adrien had received from Marie Van Zandt, an American singer at the Opéra-Comique who in 1883 created the role of Lakmé in Léo Delibes's opera. Two years earlier, Marie had inscribed to Adrien a photograph of herself dressed as a man. On the day Laure met Marcel, the thirty-seven-year-old courtesan and the schoolboy were quite taken with each other. Without knowing it, Marcel had just met the first model for one of the *Search*'s major characters: Odette de Crécy, the courtesan who becomes Mme Swann.

Marcel, on his outings to the Bois de Boulogne, often spotted such women, who represented his current idea of the epitome of Parisian elegance, like the two courtesans he had sketched in the self-parody. At the Pigeon Shooting Range, a private club in the Bois, he had seen Léonie Clomesnil pass by, a vision he would never forget. Each day many of the epoch's famous courtesans, such as Clomesnil, Liane de Pougy, la belle Otero, paraded past in their carriages. The most elegant and cultivated of these lovely, expensive women was Laure Hayman.

Odette was to share many of Laure's traits, and to have a mother who, out of hardship, decides to make her a courtesan. Odette, like Laure, has a collection of fine porcelain and a small town house in the rue de la Pérouse near the Arc de Triomphe. She is also infected with anglophilia, then fashionable, and sprinkles her sentences with English words. Through Laure, Marcel had his first glimpse at the world of the demimonde, of the milieu, mores, and customs of beautiful, clever, elegant, and expensive prostitutes. What distinguished Laure from Odette, and most other courtesans, was her education, her intelligence, and her talent, proven later, as a sculptor. Among Laure's conquests were some of the most distinguished noble names of Europe, the duke of Orléans, the king of Greece, and Karageorgevitch, pretender to the throne of Serbia, whom, it was thought, she really loved. If she earned more respect than most of her kind, it was in large part because she never ruined any of her lovers financially and had earned the title " 'the educator of dukes' for her attention to the arts of literature, manners, and love."[104]

On September 25, 1888, just before the beginning of the school year, Marcel wrote Dreyfus about his new friend without naming her: "A platonic passion for a famous courtesan, ending in an exchange of letters and photographs." He also alluded to the pretty Viennese girl he had met in dance class, hinting that he was involved in an "absorbing liaison" with her and that his attachment "threatens to go on at least a year for the greater good of the *café-concerts* and other places of the same kind, where one takes this sort of person." Nothing more is known about this Austrian beauty and her effect on Marcel. She may have caught his fancy briefly in dance class, but the relationship must have been much less absorbing than he led his friend to believe, for, unlike Marie de Benardaky, the Viennese girl was quickly forgotten.

Marcel ended the letter by wishing Dreyfus, for the new school year, "brilliant success in your studies, sincere friends, and beautiful mistresses."[105] The idea of acquiring beautiful mistresses must have amused the fifteen-year-old Dreyfus as a bit of sheer fantasy on Marcel's part, but such talk was certainly in keeping with Marcel's new man-about-town air. Marcel had spent a good summer; his health had improved, he had met and become friends with one of Paris's legendary beauties, and he was looking forward to his senior year at Condorcet, especially the philosophy class.

A Student of Philosophy

By the summer of 1888, Marcel had met Paul Desjardins, a teacher and moralist who wrote poetry, reviews, and essays, many of which were published in *La Revue bleue*. Rather stern and uncompromising as a moralist, Desjardins attacked what he viewed as the current scourges of intellectual life: religious skepticism and literary dilettantism. From a distinguished upper-bourgeois family, Desjardins had become friends with Adrien and Jeanne and occasionally accompanied Marcel and Robert on their outings. Sometimes he came to boulevard Malesherbes to read philosophy, usually the philosopher-poets Heracleitus and Lucretius, with Marcel.[106] For a period Desjardins would influence Marcel's ideas on morality and self-reliance, but teacher and pupil would soon drift apart because Desjardins hated society and considered Marcel a lost cause once he began frequenting the salons. The teacher remembered that Marcel, at the beginning of his senior year, looked like a "young Persian prince with large gazelle-like eyes under languishing eyelids; respectful, graceful, affectionate, anxious; a seeker of delights, for whom nothing was insipid; exasperated with the obstacles nature places before man's endeavors, especially before a man such as he, so frail;—striving to transform into action the passive existence that seemed to be his lot, drawn to the effusive, the excessive even in his own charming goodness."[107]

In addition to studying classical authors with Desjardins, Marcel had spent the summer reading a variety of books—those required by his professors and others for pleasure. By now, he knew by heart many of Musset's and Hugo's poems. In the fragmentary *Jean Santeuil,* Proust described his frame of mind during this period when he rebelled against reading only the classical works required by school: "Jean held the view that Verlaine and Leconte de Lisle were the greatest among all the poets . . . and felt deadly bored when he read the classical authors. . . . On rainy days [as he] sat pondering in his room, the great spreading poems of Leconte de Lisle which juggled with Time, and put into words of shattering power the conception of Life as a dream and the nothingness of things, were more alive for him, more profound, more stimulating than those classical works from which such mental unease is absent."[108] Having absorbed the lessons and style of the great French classical writers, Marcel was eager to hear new voices. Marcel's favorite novelists from early adolescence, Théophile Gautier, Pierre Loti, Alphonse Daudet, and George Sand, were being replaced by Maurice Barrès and Anatole France.

Maurice Barrès, whose distinctive voice was to influence the prewar generation, had recently published his first novel, *Sous l'œil des barbares,* volume one of a trilogy whose general title was *Le Culte du moi.* Barrès, who had the tastes and sensitivity of a fin-de-siècle aesthete, was drawn to the political arena as an active rightist politician who preached individualism and nationalism. In 1889 he was elected to the Chambre des Députés (France's lower legislative house) as a Boulangist candidate.

Anatole France had caught Marcel's attention with his Saturday literary chronicles in the leading daily newspaper *Le Temps.* Marcel enjoyed France's graceful, impressionistic, and urbane reviews so much that he began reading his other works. France, the son of a Parisian bookseller, had intended to be a poet, but soon abandoned verse for fiction. This was proved a wise decision when his first novel, *Le Crime de Sylvestre Bonnard,* published in 1881, brought him fame. In 1885 he had published *Le Livre de mon ami,* a thinly disguised and widely acclaimed autobiographical novel about his childhood, a topic of great interest to Proust.[109]

During his formative years, Marcel also read in translation such English novelists of the nineteenth century as Robert Louis Stevenson and George Eliot. Eliot's novels *Middlemarch* and *The Mill on the Floss* remained lifelong favorites. Soon he added novels by Tolstoy and Dostoyevsky, as well as *The Arabian Nights.* He later remembered these enchanting Oriental tales, which filled his "adolescence with wonder," when he began his own nocturnal narrative.[110]

Lately Marcel's readings had been troubled by a habit, begun when he was fourteen or fifteen, that was becoming obsessive: intense self-analysis. He attributed this self-scrutiny in part to his isolation because of poor health and the family preoccupation, in which he fully participated, of monitoring all his habits, symptoms, and bodily functions. In *Jean Santeuil,* Proust described himself as the anxious, hopeful schoolboy he was in 1888. All his "dreams of tenderness and melancholy," and the discoveries made therein, "had developed in him a habit of self-examination for which the study of philosophy had not provided the necessary food." So far he had found his "bearings and a natural nourishment in the exaltation produced in him by the reading of books which, no matter how superficially, gave him the sense of a philosophic background."[111]

The intelligent older boys whose opinion he respected considered Alphonse Darlu to be a "great philosopher" who possessed "the profoundest mind" of any teacher at Condorcet.[112] Marcel, weary from endless self-probings, hoped that philosophy held the key. On Monday, October 1, Marcel began his last year at Condorcet when he walked into the philosophy class at 8:15. He saw that he had as classmates Élie Halévy and Xavier Léon, both brilliant candidates for the École normale supérieure and future philosophers. Their presence alone guaranteed that he would face serious competition for top ranking in this class. By 8:30, the teacher had still not arrived and the boys grew restless. Marcel was nervous but confident. Some days earlier he had turned in the assigned summer essays, convinced they contained the best writing he had produced. His prospects for the school year seemed brighter because his health had improved.

Suddenly, Alphonse Darlu burst into the classroom.[113] Clutching a briefcase, he was out of breath and had obviously experienced some difficulty in getting to school. A redheaded man, the professor wore glasses and a scarf around his neck. Marcel noticed the red hair, a markedly oval-shaped face, accentuated by a dark beard neatly trimmed to a sharp point, a receding hairline, and a slightly bulbous nose on which rested a pair of glasses. The professor's stare was piercing, his demeanor serious—perhaps the result of all the years spent examining philosophi-cal problems and their social ramifications. Marcel soon learned that although Darlu never compromised his principles, his severity was only skin deep. At thirty-nine, Darlu was in his fourth year at Condorcet, where he had acquired the reputation of being an outstanding teacher who awakened many adolescent minds to the intellectual joys of philosophy. Marcel became one of Darlu's preferred disciples, always referring to him as "our dear master."

Proust, like his later fictional hero Jean Santeuil, may have been disconcerted by his first philosophy class. The transition from literature to philosophy, from the more subjective commentaries that characterize the study of literature to the rigorous system of logic required of philosophy students, could be daunting. As he struggled to follow the introductory lecture, he heard Darlu refer to difficult philosophical concepts delivered in a concatenation by a voice strangely accented. Darlu spoke with the heavy accent of his native city of Libourne, on the Dordogne River in southwestern France. He was articulate, eloquent even, but his odd pro-nunciation at first distracted the students. Marcel, fresh from his readings of Ernest Renan, Barrès, and France, might have expected to find the same graceful-ness, the same worldly charm and skepticism in the masters of philosophy. He felt himself growing desperate and weary as he attempted to follow all the ideas and connections that poured from Darlu's lips with a fluency which made Jean, who had never heard anything like it, feel so exhausted at the end of five minutes that he ceased to follow what was being said. Not once did the words "vanity of life" or "nirvana" come like a familiar and delightful refrain to recall his wandering attention. Never through the whole course of the lessons did there occur any of those sublime and sweet-scented images before which, throughout this headlong intellectual race, he might have paused for rest as at a flower-strewn wayside shrine. Nor was that all. He, who knew that there was no such thing as the "good" or the "true," was staggered to hear this man, about whose genius he had heard so much, speaking of goodness, truth and certainty.[114]

After the first day, as Marcel reviewed his notes and impressions, he realized that despite the complexity of the opening lecture for the novice in philosophy, the teacher's words had seemed addressed directly to him. The evening after his second day in class, he wrote to Darlu seeking a remedy to his intensive self-analysis that caused him to imagine his consciousness as containing multiple selves. He feared becoming too intellectual and losing his ability to "take complete pleasure in what used to be my highest joy, the works of literature." Now when he read a poem by Leconte de Lisle, even while he was "savouring the infinite delights of former days," his other self amused itself by looking for the causes of his pleasure; finding them "in a certain relationship between me and the work, specifically, it imagines conditions diametrically opposed to beauty, and ends by killing all my pleasure. For more than a year I have been unable to judge anything in a literary light, I am devoured by the need for set rules by which to judge works of art with certainty." He feared that the cure would require him to cease the constant contemplation of his inner life, a thought that struck him "as frightful." Marcel told his professor that he assumed his predicament was common in "persons of my age, whom ill health obliged in the past to live a good deal to themselves."[115] He urged Darlu to keep this letter confidential for fear of being ridiculed by his classmates, who already found him sufficiently odd.

Darlu's precise remedy to Marcel's problem is not known. Proust was to remember the danger of excessive intellectualization when creating his fictional writer Bergotte in the *Search*, whose last works are overly intellectual, indicating a dryness of the soul, a fatal condition for an artist. The question that tormented Marcel in his senior year, unanswered completely until the concluding volume of the *Search,* was whether art has intrinsic value. Does art point to any universal, eternal value? Can it transcend mere materialism and human vanity? Proust lived his entire life, however, as if the answer were a resounding "Yes!"

Darlu may not have had an easy solution to Marcel's problem of intensive self-analysis, but almost immediately Marcel began to enjoy the lectures. Darlu was a gifted orator and took great pleasure in the verbal exchanges and debates with his students. His method normally consisted of oral presentations by students, followed by questions, and finally a lecture. Darlu was so well prepared and adept at leading discussions that his lessons resembled brilliant conversations between a group of enlightened young men and their mentor. His classes were ideal for the bright, ambitious, literarily inclined young men at Condorcet. Marcel and Xavier Léon found the discussions with Darlu so engaging that they often would leave the classroom with their teacher, follow him home, and mount the stairs with him to his sixth-floor apartment on rue de la Terrasse without having exhausted the subject begun in the classroom.

The students, however, were often discouraged when Darlu returned assignments, because he was unrelenting in the high standards he set for them. He informed them in blunt, picturesque language when they had failed to meet his expectations, even when their compositions received the highest marks. Fernand Gregh remembered some of the comments Darlu wrote on compositions, sarcastic remarks that came after the praise for being in the top tier: "product of a sick mind" (to which for good measure he added Horace's original phrase, *ægri somnia vana*), or "Sganarelle philosophy," after Molière's comic, cowardly lackey. Darlu returned one essay to Marcel after having written three times diagonally across the page *Verbiage.* In *Jean Santeuil,* Professor Beulier, like Darlu, seeks to purge the influence of decadent writers from his students' essays.

Once Marcel handed in a composition in which he attempted to demonstrate how a scientist draws conclusions enabling him to derive a law from factual knowledge. Darlu, disappointed in the essay, wrote across the top of the first page that the composition was "extremely vague and superficial." He did allow that the topic was "very complex" but nonetheless awarded Marcel only four points out of a possible twenty.[116] The demanding professor added a remark in which the devastated pupil found a grain of encouragement: there was "some progress in composition."[117] This harsh appraisal was quite different from the praise Proust had received in Gaucher's classes.

The teachers we admire most are those who help us to know ourselves, who awaken within us a desire to learn and to succeed. Xavier Léon, speaking for his generation of Condorcet students in the introduction to his *Philosophie de Fichte,* credited Darlu with teaching him to know and love philosophy: "I owe him my destiny and my conscience: I owe him the best of myself."[118] Robert Proust, in the class after Marcel's, recalled the professor's vivid, imagistic way of speaking even when explaining the most complex philosophical ideas. Darlu's "teaching manner was personal and intuitive and he had a nearly poetic way of explaining things that Marcel loved."[119] As his main prop, Darlu used a splendid top hat that he "would place on the lectern . . . and produce philosophy from it as though he were a magician."[120] His methods were innovative and his purpose clear: he wanted to create unfettered minds, capable of thinking for themselves.

From Darlu, Marcel learned, as an antidote to Hippolyte Taine's positivism, the lessons of Platonic and Kantian idealism and rationalism. These philosophers, with the later addition of Ruskin's aesthetics, served Proust well until he advanced beyond their systems to formulate his own aesthetics and ethics.[121] Marcel admired in Darlu's discourses the strength of his convictions, which were free from any trace of religious mysticism, his Olympian self-assuredness, the enthusiastic love of philosophy that he conveyed to his students, and his belief in progress in civilization due to the succession of great minds in all domains of creativity. Darlu believed in science and philosophy, and in the role of religion in its proper domain; his idea of God was that of a spirit embodying truth.[122]

Sometime that autumn Marcel wrote to Daniel Halévy a letter showing that his thoughts in Darlu's class were, at times, on subjects less idealistic and transcendental than Plato and Kant. Daniel had apparently given Marcel a verbal lashing and called him a pederast. Proust replied, stating in the opening paragraph that his "ethical beliefs allow me to regard the pleasures of the senses as a splendid thing." He attempted to explain why affectionate caresses between boys need not be corrupt:

You think me jaded and effete. You are mistaken. If you are delicious, if you have lovely eyes which reflect the grace and refinement of your mind with such purity that I feel I cannot fully love your mind without kissing your eyes, if your body and mind, like your thoughts, are so lithe and slender that I feel I could mingle more intimately with your thoughts by sitting on your lap, if, finally, I feel that the charm of your person, in which I cannot separate your keen mind from your agile body, would refine and enhance "the sweet joy of love" for me, there is nothing in all that to deserve your contemptuous words, which would have been more fittingly addressed to someone surfeited with women and seeking new pleasures in pederasty. I am glad to say that I have some highly intelligent friends, distinguished by great moral delicacy, who have amused themselves at one time with a boy. . . . That was the beginning of their youth. Later on they went back to women.

Presenting homosexual love between innocent youths as a rite of passage, Proust gave the examples of Socrates and Montaigne—Proust later realized he was mistaken about Montaigne—who "permit men in their earliest youth to 'amuse themselves' so as to know something of all pleasures, and so as to release their excess tenderness." Such "sensual and intellectual friendships are better for a young man with a keen sense of beauty . . . than affairs with stupid, corrupt women." Although Marcel felt the "old Masters" were wrong, he did accept the "general tenor of their advice. Don't call me a pederast, it hurts my feelings."

Darlu then announced that he was going to question Marcel, who had to interrupt his letter and concentrate on philosophy. He ended with a quick request to Daniel: "But tell me what you mean by saying that your hands are not pure."[123] The indirect question, placed as though it were a casual afterthought, shows Marcel typically eager to learn all he could about his friends' secrets. The reference to "impure hands" was, Marcel surmised, a confession on Daniel's part that he engaged in masturbation. Marcel remained trapped in the struggle between a young man's desires to remain pure and to taste the forbidden fruit. Overflowing with tenderness, he sought an ethics that would sanction the possession of his masculine ideal: intelligent beauty.

Darlu may not have known that Marcel spent part of his class time writing letters justifying homosexual love between youths, but the professor was aware of his frequent infatuations with classmates. One day, after seeing Marcel at Condorcet with yet another new friend, Darlu asked him: "What number did you give him when he passed through the door of your heart?"[124] In his final year at Condorcet, Marcel was blithely hedonistic, appreciative of Anatole France's brand of epicureanism, which perfectly suited his tastes and humor.

At the beginning of the fall term, Robert and other friends had noticed a change in Marcel, who no longer cared for the games in the parks along the Champs-Élysées. Now that "his beautiful languorous eyes had attracted the attention" of celebrated courtesans, his desires had gone farther afield.[125] Marcel wanted to distance himself from the younger, bothersome boys who teased him about preferring the company of the older women who opened their salons to him. Laure

Hayman had recently given Marcel a copy of *Gladys Harvey,* autographed by Paul Bourget and bound in the flowered silk from one of her petticoats. She, too, had signed her name, dated October 1888, and penned some advice: "To Marcel Proust, Do not love a Gladys Harvey."

Laure, with her years of experience observing, teaching, and flattering men—a professional necessity—recognized Marcel's precocious, genuine gifts. He constantly amazed her by the acuity of his psychological observations, especially from one so young, expressed in words that were often as eloquent as the classical French of La Rochefoucauld or Blaise Pascal. Considering Marcel's pale skin and fine features, reminded of the figurines in her porcelain collection, she chose a new name for her young admirer: "my little psychologist in porcelain."[126]

Word of Marcel's nickname spread quickly among his classmates, delighted to have a new reason to tease him. Dreyfus remembered: "We laughed at school on learning that she was mad about Marcel Proust, taking him along wherever she went, that he attended her parties, where he was thrilled to meet dukes, writers, and future members of the Académie française."[127] Marcel's classmates, many of whom had literary ambitions, had reason to be jealous, but no one took him too seriously as a competitor. He was tremendously gifted, of course, but too delicate, too exquisite, and too frivolous.

Some of the boys who had received love letters from Marcel must have been confused. Could he possibly be having an affair with a woman who, from their point of view, was an ancient but celebrated courtesan, currently the subject of a novella by one of their favorite writers? Jacques-Émile Blanche, Proust's future portraitist, who knew both Marcel and Laure, believed there was more than mutual fascination between them. His friends had noticed him every morning walking with Laure, who obviously doted on her young protégé.[128]

Daniel Halévy wrote in his diary on December 5, 1888:

> Proust, Jacques, and I went for a walk. We pass in front of Laure
> Hayman's town house, and, naturally, Proust cannot resist the desire to
> drop in. He remains a quarter of an hour and comes back out with this
> witty rejoinder from Barbey d'Aurevilly, related by her—Bourget had in-
> vited him [Barbey] for a meal—
> Bourget: Is it true that you are a pederast?
> Barbey: My tastes, my age, my whole life inclines me in that direc-
> tion, but the ugliness of the sex in question has always prevented me
> from entirely becoming one.[129]

In Laure's salon, Marcel met bohemians and the well-to-do. Artists, bourgeois, and aristocrats rubbed elbows as they enjoyed fine food, entertainment, and choice Parisian gossip. Men like Adrien Proust and Louis Weil pursued the courtesans and actresses whom Laure invited. The actress Louise Théo, yet another close attachment of the energetic Uncle Louis, signed, perhaps at Marcel's request, one of her photographs: "To Marcel Proust, the nephew of my dear friend M. Louis Weil, with my sincere friendship."[130] While Mme Straus and others of Marcel's more distinguished female acquaintances would provide inspiration for the duchesse de Guermantes, Laure and Louise belonged to the group of actresses and courtesans who would pose for Odette de Crécy.

Little Magazines

Seventeen years old. Eleven o'clock in the evening. October. I am living in a sanctuary, in the midst of a spectacle.

In their final years at Condorcet, Daniel, Jacques, Marcel, and a few other classmates began producing short-lived little magazines of which they would circulate a few copies from hand to hand. In November 1887 the boys created *Le Lundi,* subtitled "Artistic and Literary Review," whose white cover bore an ink drawing of two cupids lifting a great, open book across whose pages was spread a quote from Paul Verlaine: "The triumphant eclecticism of the Beautiful."[131] The editors made multiple copies of each issue in purple ink and then sewed the pages together by hand. In the first issue, the contributors addressed their readers and pledged to publish the best that each literary school had to offer or any work they considered beautiful. Among the schools then in vogue, the notice listed naturalist, idealist, decadent, incoherent, and progressive. Proclaiming its independence, the review assured each reader that he would find something to his liking.

Although Marcel was the oldest and most gifted of these young writers, he did not take the initiative in the creation of these reviews; he left the editor-in-chief role to Daniel, who proved to be a good choice. *Le Lundi* had a long run: thirteen issues. Marcel published in its pages several pastiches of Jules Lemaître, who was a disciple of Sainte-Beuve.[132] Lemaître's widely read column of theater reviews, *Chronique d'art dramatique,* appeared each Monday in *Le Journal des débats* and was considered the last word on the theater by the young generation. In December 1887 Lemaître published *Contes de Noël* (Christmas Stories), his own pastiches of the writings of popular authors, printed under their names. This literary exercise of imitating the manner of a well-known author intrigued Marcel, who became an accomplished pasticheur.[133]

For *Le Lundi,* Marcel produced several causeries that show his ability to identify a writer's particular tics. Marcel's essay in the manner of Sainte-Beuve and Jules Lemaître, *Causerie d'art dramatique,* which appeared in the review's second issue on December 5, discussed the use of local color, said to be absent from classical tragedy, in Corneille's play *Horace.* This essay, like many the young men wrote for their reviews, is basically academic, reflecting literary debates taking place in the classroom.

Marcel's next article, *Causerie littéraire,* was more personal, for it discussed his admiration for Gautier's adventure novel *Le Capitaine Fracasse.* Defending a favorite writer against the distinguished but stuffy critic Ferdinand Brunetière, who deplored Gautier's lack of ideas, Marcel saw in Gautier a precursor of modern decadence in the good sense, similar to Anatole France, in whom he found not ideas and romantic angst but gracefulness. He confessed that the apparent charms of decadence as practiced by Gautier and France tempted him: "If I were ever to found a Republic in the manner of Plato, . . . all ideas would be banished from it, its citizens would look at the sky and dream."[134]

Marcel, who still dreamed of becoming a playwright, announced a play, *La Première Matinée de mai* (The first May morn), inspired, he told the review's readers, by *A Midsummer Night's Dream.* The play involved pagan May Day ceremonies, which appealed to him because of their non-Christian, Celtic origins. This is all we know about the play, which he apparently never wrote. Plays were not to be Proust's genre. Although he had a superb ear for dialogue and produced page after page of captivating and often humorous conversations for his characters, their words were only part of the rich Proustian music, solo voices that emerge on cue from the orchestral sounds of the symphony.

After a number of issues of *Le Lundi* had appeared, Daniel stepped forward during an editorial meeting and proclaimed himself the inventor and promoter of a new school: *subtle-ism.* Marcel, perhaps due to the new emphasis on subtleties and his own search for the exquisite, began to write mainly poems, only one of which survives because he used it later for his first book, *Les Plaisirs et les jours* (Pleasures and days). He wrote the poem about the seventeenth-century Dutch painter Aelbert Cuyp "before a class at Condorcet, after visiting the Louvre, where I had just seen the horsemen who have a pink feather in their hats."[135] Over the years Proust wrote many poems, often doggerel bits written in jest or in letters to amuse friends. The same penchants that kept him from writing successful plays also discouraged poems.

The demise of *Le Lundi* came in March 1888, when the contributors, putting aside subtleties, contested Halévy's policies and tastes, prompting Daniel to resign. But the boys' victory was hollow; without Daniel's supervision they were unable to produce the review. Although Halévy was clearly the leader when it came to directing the reviews, the boys looked to Marcel as their mentor in writing. In his memoir, Daniel describes Marcel as "our master, our guide in matters of taste in a school full of civil servants." These apprentice writers, Daniel noted, were preoccupied with style: "The French language, at that time, was in poor condition. Edmond de Goncourt, with his 'rare epithets' and his 'artistic writing,' had done a lot of damage."[136] Halévy said that only Proust understood the importance of Anatole France's influence on style through his use of "exquisite language."[137]

That fall Daniel wrote "Amour," a poem of fourteen quatrains in alexandrines.[138] Reeking of decadence and the grotesque, complete with a vampire, rotting bodies, and a nun, the fifteen-year old poet's work tells the story of a youth on his deathbed whose principal regret is that he must die a virgin. The nun, who is nursing him, comprehends his plight and enters his bed, where both die in ecstasy. Daniel spent hours on the poem before submitting it to Proust, who took "great care and kindness" in reading his rhymed adolescent sex fantasy: "And what a correction! . . . How many useful, harsh remarks penciled in the margins of my poor poem! Odious. Formless. Idiotic. Naturalist, ergo stupid."[139] Marcel did single out as *très bien* the fifth verse, describing the "pale, dying blond boy" with "vaporous ringed eyes." And certainly Marcel sympathized with the nun's willingness to grant the dying boy's wish.

If Marcel's comments seemed brutal even to thick-skinned Daniel, the critic softened the blows by claiming to know nothing about such matters. Proust did offer Halévy some heartfelt advice. He must free himself from the grip of the decadents, who had spoiled his ability to express his "thoughts sincerely, completely." As a cure, Daniel should "practice Latin discourses" and, above all, read the classics. Marcel listed Homer, Plato, Virgil, Tacitus, Shakespeare, Shelley, Emerson, Goethe, La Fontaine, Racine, Rousseau, Flaubert, Baudelaire—and, among contemporaries, Renan, France, and "*super omnes* Ludovic Halévy." If Marcel highly recommended Daniel's own father, this was no doubt because of the sure, light touch of Ludovic's libretti for Offenbach's operettas and the superb, moving realism of his lyrics for Bizet's *Carmen*. For excellent examples of fine writing, Daniel need look no further than home. Marcel then made a statement proving that though still a schoolboy, he understood the basis of creativity: "You will learn (by reading the classics) that if your mind is original and strong, your works will be so only if you are absolutely sincere. . . . Simplicity is infinitely elegant, naturalness has ineffable charm."[140] Like all advisers, Marcel at times had trouble consistently following his own advice, but at least he had identified the qualities to which he should aspire.

That fall, shortly after entering Alphonse Darlu's philosophy class, Marcel, Daniel, and Jacques created another review, this time with Marcel as secretary. Because some of their collaborators had to write their homework assignments on green paper for the eccentric Professor Eugène Linthilhac, who believed that such paper protected his eyes, the boys decided this hue would give their little magazine an original look and its name, *La Revue verte*.[141] A disagreement soon erupted among the members of the editorial staff because Marcel wanted the single copy of each issue to be destroyed once it had been read by the small select group for which it was intended, while Daniel, who had the instincts of an archivist, wanted to preserve a copy for himself. Marcel notified Halévy that his proposal was unacceptable.[142] Marcel's ultimatum, duly submitted on green paper, may have aborted the efforts of the little publishing group. Proust feared that if copies remained in circulation, professors and parents would read and censor them. He wanted to express himself frankly regarding his own feelings, including sexual longings. Marcel's ultimatum and a story by Jacques Bizet are the only surviving copy from this review.[143]

In November 1888 Marcel wrote a few sketches for a little magazine that he and his friends, switching colors, named *La Revue lilas* because its issues were produced in thin, pale mauve-colored notebooks purchased for a few cents at the stationer's shop in the passage du Havre.[144] No issue has survived, but Robert Dreyfus kept the battered manuscripts of two of Marcel's brief articles.[145] These are the first writings in which Marcel consciously fictionalizes his own voice in the first person.[146] Previously, as in "Clouds," there was a persona representing man in his contemplative, philosophical mode, or characters cast within stories or sketches provided by teachers or tutors.

The first text, consisting of two short paragraphs and dedicated to "my dear friend Jacques Bizet," begins "The sky is dark purple marked with shiny patches. Oh! my little friend why am I not in your lap, my face against your neck, why don't you love me?"[147] The narrator broods under a Baudelairian dark sky, heavy with ennui and suffocation, stifling all hope. These impressions evoke feelings of loneliness, boredom, claustrophobia, and, ultimately, insomnia. He hears noises drifting through the walls from an apartment where someone is playing a waltz and from a nearby room where dishes are being put away.

The second text, a schoolboy prose poem for Bizet about night and falling asleep, starts, "The lamp feebly lights the dark corners of my room." Although Proust is many years away from conceiving the *Search*, he will begin his great work with the Narrator slumbering in a dark room. Although he had yet to become the nocturnal storyteller, this early piece shows him meditating at late hours when "Everyone is asleep in the great silent apartment." He opens the window "to see one last time the sweet, wild face, completely round, of the friendly moon. I hear, it seems, the breath, very fresh, cold, of all the sleeping things—the tree from which seeps blue light—beautiful blue light transfiguring in the distance, at an intersection of streets, the pale, blue paving stones, like a polar landscape electrically illuminated. Overhead stretch out infinite blue fields where frail stars flourish."

In another remarkable anticipation of the sedentary life he will one day lead, Marcel described his bedside table cluttered with glasses, flacons, cool drinks, small expensively bound books, and letters of love and friendship. The adolescent writer has already placed himself at the center of his web to observe and record the universe around him: "Divine hour. Ordinary things, like nature, I have consecrated, being unable to vanquish them. I have clothed them with my soul and with intimate, splendid images. I am living in a sanctuary, in the midst of a spectacle. I am the center of things and each brings me magnificent or melancholy sensations that I enjoy. I have before my eyes splendid visions." Sensations and images from this luminously blue night—nocturnal solitude, moonlight streaming through open windows, the busy world in slumber, the tree seeping moonlight—all reappeared years later, cast in the mature prose of *Swann's Way*.[148]

Dreyfus also saved, from the fall of 1888, a prose poem about homosexuality, censored by the editors of *La Revue lilas*. The poet yearns to escape into an idealized, decadent world where such love is not merely tolerated but celebrated. A beautiful Greek boy named Glaukos, in love with philosophy, poetry, and other young men, surrounds himself with piles of letters expressing friendship as he sits nearly naked either in the sun or in a swank, decadent decor filled with rare blooms. (Marcel hesitated between an austere classical Greek setting and a contemporary lush scene.) Glaukos has many male friends, all of them beautiful, who delight in subtle thoughts. Some of them love him infinitely: "Often seated on the sturdy knees of one of them, cheek to cheek, bodies entwined, [Glaukos] discusses with him Aristotle's philosophy and Euripides' poems, while they embrace and caress each other, making elegant and wise remarks in the sumptuous room, near magnificent flowers."[149]

When not indulging in erotic literary and floral fantasies, Proust found inspiration in the theater and Jules Lemaître's reviews. In fall 1888 Marcel attended a number of operettas, operas, musical reviews, and vaudeville shows.[150] But what captured his attention were the classical plays of Racine and Corneille. On October 13, 1888, at the Odéon, Marcel saw a production of *Athalie* by Racine, whose tragedies were to be a major inspiration for the themes of jealousy and atavism in the *Search*. In his notes on *Athalie,* he indicated his admiration for the acclaimed classical actor Jean Sully Mounet, known as Mounet-Sully, who, like Sarah Bernhardt, had been accorded the epithet "divine."[151] Proust would spend years observing and noting the skills of such performers, both on the stage and in private salon readings, probing the secrets of their craft.

Le Beau Monde

In the fall of his last year at Condorcet, Marcel began frequenting the salons whose hostesses he had met through classmates. While remaining friends with the sons, Marcel now preferred the witty, worldly conversations of their mothers. Bewitched by the glamour of society, whose refined milieu suited his delicate nature, he wanted to know the details of its history, ceremonies, family connections, and secrets. Eager to please and genuinely thrilled at having been invited by a society *grande dame,* he lavished flattery and huge, expensive bouquets of flowers on the women who invited him to the most elegant drawing rooms of Paris. The hostesses who received him were happy to add a promising young recruit to the regular guest lists at their weekly gatherings. All the ladies admired his exquisite manners, his eagerness to please, his genius at turning a compliment, and, above all, his dazzling conversation.

Although Jacques Bizet spurned Marcel's amorous advances, he offered something that eventually would be more important than the withheld "delicious flower": entrance to his mother's drawing room. Geneviève Straus's salon had rapidly become one of the most brilliant in Paris. Early in her marriage to Georges Bizet, Geneviève, in need of distraction from her frequent bouts of melancholy, began inviting artists and musicians she knew from her father's and Bizet's circles. This group formed the nucleus of a small bohemian salon that met on Saturdays in her fourth-floor apartment at number 22, rue de Douai.[152]

Years after Bizet's death Émile Straus, a wealthy young lawyer for the Rothschild banking family, began to court Geneviève. Although something of a snob, Émile was an intelligent, highly capable, industrious man, who indulged himself only in his passion for collecting paintings and his fascination with Geneviève. He pressed her to marry him, but she refused. Her friends, convinced that Straus had nothing in common with Geneviève or with them, expressed relief.

Edmond de Goncourt, who met Straus at Princesse Mathilde's in 1883, several years before Émile married Geneviève, wrote a brief portrait of the lawyer in his diary that shows the anti-Semitism then prevalent in French society. Goncourt noted that Princesse Mathilde's salon was becoming "a real salon for Jewry, today increased by the entry of Straus who, it is whispered, is the illegitimate son of old Rothschild. In a novel, he would be the perfect type for a satanic eyeglasses merchant with his bestial eyelids that appear paralyzed and with a wrinkle as big as a horseshoe on his forehead."[153] Despite Goncourt's prejudices against Jews, he had an overall favorable opinion of the man, but not without reservations: "I find him intelligent, a keen observer, amiable with Jewish humility and a lawyer's somewhat excessive, glib chatter, but he has a damned Mephistophelean air about him that makes me distrust my inclination to like him."[154] The diabolical air may have been suggested by Straus's strange eyes, which disconcerted many who first met him. His eyes always remained half closed because of a slight paralysis, said to have resulted from an injury suffered during the siege of Paris.[155]

As Émile continued to court Geneviève, he invited her to Baronne Alphonse de Rothschild's salon, where she met the *gratin*, the utmost upper crust of Parisian society. Geneviève's beauty, taste, and extraordinary wit, combined with the name Bizet now in full posthumous glory, made her a star among the select. She found herself exalted, invited to all the best parties, but the popularity was nearly too much for a woman who, often ill and depressed, preferred to be alone. Then, suddenly, almost on a whim, the gratin made attendance at Geneviève's Saturday salon an obligation for the smart set. Her neighbors stared in bewilderment at the scene in front of the apartment building, where the street echoed with the beat of hooves as elegant broughams lined up to deposit the glamorous guests, the baronne de Rothschild, Comtesse Potocka, the duchesse de Richelieu, and Comtesse Chevigné among them. These elegant ladies, most of whom lived in sumptuous town houses, eagerly climbed the stairs at the back of the courtyard to join Geneviève's once intimate circle.

Straus had in large part orchestrated the evolution of her salon, making it an unqualified success. One day in 1886 Émile announced that Geneviève Bizet would become Mme Straus. The news alarmed her longtime friends because they still distrusted the lawyer, whom they considered indiscreet, abrupt, and insensitive. They tolerated him only because of his intelligence and obvious devotion to Geneviève.

One after the other her friends tried to dissuade her from accepting his proposal: "You're going to marry Straus! That will be tiresome." In a reply typical of the wit that delighted Proust, she asked, "What else can I do? It's the only way to get rid of him."

The Strauses moved into a grand town house at 134, boulevard Haussmann, not far from Proust's future address at number 102. Mme Straus was nearly forty when Marcel began attending her salon. Goncourt, that inveterate connoisseur and collector, could not resist describing Geneviève in her new and sumptuous interior: "She wears a dressing-gown of light, soft, puffed silk trimmed from head to toe in large flossy bows, as she sits lazily sunken into a deep armchair." The diarist noted "the feverish mobility of her soft, velvety eyes" and the "coquettishness" of her posturing as an invalid, while holding in her lap Vivette, the latest in a line of black poodles. "A charming decor surrounds the woman. On a panel, opposite her, is a splendid Nattier painting representing a great lady of the Regency in her flowing Naiad costume. . . . In the middle of the mantel, on whose cold marble the mistress of the house occasionally leans her forehead, stands an elegant statuette of white marble attributed to Coysevox."

Émile, during his long campaign to marry Geneviève, must have heard her express skepticism about love and marriage, as she did to Goncourt: "She speaks of love with a touch of bitterness, saying that after physical possession, it is indeed rare for two lovers to love each other equally and that inequality in love creates halting couples who don't walk in step. . . . Her words seem to allude to the state of her soul, giving a glimpse of her regret at having allowed herself to yield to tender entreaties."

It was rumored that one of the men to whom Geneviève had yielded was that notorious womanizer and distinguished surgeon Samuel Pozzi, a handsome, seductive man—admirably captured in one of Sargent's remarkable portraits—whose exploits had earned him the nickname *l'Amour médecin* (Dr. Love). But Geneviève quickly tired of talking about the disappointments of love and turned to lighter topics. She told Goncourt fascinating stories about her poodles, one of which had so hated baths that when his was being prepared, he "simulated the most convincing head cold one could imagine."[156]

In Mme Straus's round salon in the boulevard Haussmann, Marcel met the cream of the faubourg Saint-Germain aristocratic society and that of arts and letters, like Gabriel Fauré, Guy de Maupassant, Edgar Degas, Princesse Mathilde, Sarah Bernhardt, and Charles Haas.[157] Haas was, to Marcel's envious eyes, the quintessence of chic in manners, gestures, and wardrobe, the incarnation of the society man who belonged not only to the highly selective Cercle de la rue Royale but also to the ultrasnobbish Jockey Club, of which he was the only Jewish member. Haas, fifty-six, apparently paid Marcel little attention, but the young man studied him intently.

Émile's fortune made possible the acquisition of an impressive collection of paintings, which Marcel admired and studied, especially the works of the contemporary painters Claude Monet and Gustave Moreau. Straus's passion for collecting was so strong that he rarely resisted the opportunity to add a new work to his trove, leading Geneviève to complain to friends that she was encumbered with Boudins and Corots.

The constant object of Marcel's attention was Geneviève, so beautiful and so clever. An excellent conversationalist, she kept her remarks concise, never made speeches, remained calm but always ready with a witty remark. She lacked the cattiness and pettiness that typified so many leading hostesses. Her nephew Daniel Halévy said that she was too indifferent to what went on around her to be mean. Émile did take their entertaining seriously, organizing their receptions and repeating Geneviève's witticisms to everyone he encountered.[158] Eventually, her husband's presence became more tolerable to Geneviève's friends, who had to admit that though they still did not care much for Émile, the Straus salon was anything but boring.

Geneviève noticed that her guests were amused by Marcel, who seemed to possess encyclopedic knowledge, expressed with amazing eloquence on a number of subjects, literature especially, but also French history and botany. He played so naturally the role of a delicate, sensitive, and fawning page, eagerly attentive, producing magnificent flowers and exquisite compliments in great abundance. If most of the women were captivated by his kindness and manners, some of the men were disconcerted by this brilliant but strange adolescent. A number of Geneviève's regulars considered him nothing more than an interesting oddity. Years later Gustave Schlumberger recollected, "On a stool at the feet of Madame Geneviève Straus one constantly saw the bizarre Marcel Proust, still a young man, who since then has written books admired by some and quite incomprehensible to others, including myself."[159]

Just as Marcel had imagined he was in love with Jacques, he now became enamored of Geneviève Straus in her role as society hostess. Geneviève's photograph by Nadar, taken in 1887, shows a woman with strong features, whose beauty has not diminished. The many artists and society men who pursued Geneviève were struck by her svelte figure, her flawless olive-complexioned skin, and magnificent black eyes grown even more melancholy than when captured by painter Jules-

Élie Delaunay in his portrait of the young widow Bizet. Marcel found such beauty and prestige irresistible. Mme Straus, more amused than annoyed, discouraged his advances, thereby removing the only obstacle to the formation of a lifelong friendship. Over the years they would exchange letters, gossip, and information about their various ailments, which with time would make each more reclusive.

Through their sons, Marcel met Mmes Arthur and Henri Baignères, sisters-in-law who both had salons. Mme Arthur Baignères and her husband were close friends of the celebrated writer Alphonse Daudet, whose burlesque adventures of *Tartarin de Tarascon* Marcel had admired since the summer at Salies-de-Béarn. Marcel would soon be introduced to the Daudet family, with whom he would have a close lifelong relationship. Mme Arthur Baignères's son Paul, two years older than Marcel, had already developed a passion for art and owned a reproduction of a Vermeer painting. This reproduction may have provided Proust's first exposure to an artist whose work *The View of Delft* was to figure in a key scene in the *Search*.[160] Marcel soon became a weekly guest in both Baignèreses' drawing rooms, where the regulars were astonished to learn that the knowledgeable, articulate young man was still in high school.

Marcel's classmates denounced his seduction by high society. Believing that he was motivated by nothing more than egotism, they deplored his lack of seriousness. Society, labeled the "pink peril" by Robert Dreyfus, posed one of the chief dangers for writers in France. Rare was the artist who could resist the allure of a Parisian society hostess and all she could offer to one of the chosen few. Julien Benda, an acerbic essayist and critic, confessed to Dreyfus one day, "I've discovered why I don't go out in society; it's because no one invites me."[161] Marcel's friends could not fail to notice that he rarely declined an invitation, especially when he knew that members of the aristocracy would be present. Alarmed and irritated that he would risk wasting his exceptional talent, his classmates began to tease him about his servility toward people with noble titles. His behavior reinforced their conviction that he lacked discipline and would never be anything but a frivolous snob.

On March 19 Adrien's invalid mother died in Illiers, in her small second-floor apartment overlooking the town square. She was eighty years old. Nothing else is recorded about her passing or her funeral. Although we know that her grandsons visited her in Illiers and posed for at least one photograph with her, she does not seem to have been close to any members of the family. Perhaps this was because the family seldom went to Illiers and her inclinations and poor health forced her to stay at home. She must have always seemed distant and old-fashioned to her grandsons, especially when compared with the affectionate and cultivated grandmother Weil.

That spring Marcel met one of the leading writers and thinkers of his parents' generation when Ernest Renan came to have dinner with the family. Although Marcel had read and admired Renan's works earlier in the year, he rushed out to purchase copies for himself and asked the distinguished author to autograph his copy of *La Vie de Jésus* (The life of Jesus) and *Souvenirs d'enfance et de jeunesse* (Memories of childhood and youth).[162] Renan's studies of Christianity questioned the supernatural aspects of Christ's life. In his later years, Proust, while recognizing Renan's genius, saw *La Vie de Jésus* as "a kind of *Belle Hélène* of Christianity," a reference to Offenbach's operetta, indicating that he considered Renan delightful to read, but essentially lightweight as a philosopher.[163]

Proust's unqualified admiration went to novelist Anatole France. Darlu was a friend of France's and often discussed the writer's works with Marcel. Darlu and France each said the other possessed "a good brain."[164] When a critic attacked *Balthasar*, France's new collection of remarkably fine stories, for being "laborious, superficial, artificial, tedious, long-winded," and so on, Marcel sent France an anonymous letter by pneumatic mail, proclaiming his admiration for France's books.[165] Marcel told France that he always read the author's weekly Saturday chronicle in *Le Temps* and thought about him several times a day, although he found it difficult to imagine France's "physical presence."[166] But this was of no consequence, because what mattered was the spirit that emanated from his books: "With the memory of the hours of exquisite delight you have given me I have built, deep in my heart, a chapel filled with you." Marcel signed the letter, "A student of philosophy."[167] Proust soon met France in Mme Arman de Caillavet's salon, where the author was the star attraction.

Marcel was drawn to France's hedonism, in which he could find solace and some justification for many of his cherished dreams. France's delightful prose and fine humor tempered somewhat Darlu's rather austere conviction that there is a truth and that only truth matters. Marcel was to hesitate for some years between the arduous quest for truth and "the Epicurean gardens in bloom of Anatole France."[168] He later found that these two ways—at first, thought to be absolute and separate entities—were actually joined.

In the early summer months before graduation there was great excitement in Paris, as the city prepared to celebrate the centennial of the French Revolution with a world's fair. On April 1, as part of the fair, the City of Light inaugurated the world's tallest structure, which soared 984 feet (300 meters) into space. This controversial tower of indefinable symbolic value was something the likes of which no Frenchman had ever seen and for which most Parisians already felt prodigious

Gallic contempt. This incredibly expensive curiosity had been erected on the Left Bank of the Seine by a friend of the Prousts', an engineer named Gustave Eiffel.

At graduation, Marcel claimed his only top prize—but the most prestigious one of all—first place in French composition and third place in his class. For his award he received an edition of Jean de La Bruyère's *Caractères,* a classical work that contains shrewd, trenchant portraits and maxims describing the mores of court life under Louis XIV.[169] Marcel had made the most of his year studying philosophy with Darlu. In taking the composition prize, Proust beat all comers, even such accomplished veterans as Élie Halévy and Xavier Léon, both of whom were admitted to the École normale supérieure.[170]

The completion of his secondary education had been a long struggle for Marcel and his family, but now his health seemed genuinely improved. Perhaps he would leave behind the afflictions that had plagued his adolescence. His parents were relieved and proud that he had completed his lycée years near the top of a class with so many brilliant students.

Marcel cared for only two things, society and literature.[171] The new graduate, eager to compete with mature writers, dreamed of being published by a serious review. If only his parents would let him pursue a career as a writer! It was clear that he would never want for money, but respectability and duty as defined by his parents demanded that he pursue university studies and select a profession in law or government. He had officially reached manhood, but in his heart he would always be his mother's little Marcel. And yet he was ready, eager to make new friends—preferably well-born, handsome ones—and to face new challenges.

The first challenge Marcel and his classmates would face was being crafted on the other side of Paris on July 15, the very day the young men received their graduation certificates.[172] The French congress passed a law regarding military service that ended one year of voluntary enlistment and established obligatory service of three years. The new law provided a short grace period during which young men could still sign up for one year. Marcel was among the many who rushed to enroll.

PART II

Vanity Fair (1889–1895)

3   *Private Proust* ❧

AFTER GRADUATION, MARCEL PLANNED a series of visits and vacations with friends. In September, a few days before his mother and Robert went to Salies for her to take another cure, Marcel left on vacation with Horace Finaly and his family to the Belgian seaside resort of Ostend.[1] Horace, a Condorcet classmate who shared Proust's interest in metaphysics, was the son of Hugo Finaly, a wealthy Jewish banker.

By the time of Proust's visit, the ancient fishing port of Ostend had become one of Europe's most fashionable summer playgrounds. But Marcel, who missed his mother, saw only the somber hues of the immense gray sea. Although Marcel was genuinely fond of Horace and his family, he had never been so far away from his mother. He wrote to her at Salies, confessing his low morale and loneliness. She answered immediately, expressing her surprise that he was so upset and promising her "dear poor little wolf" that she would write every day.[2] Lest he regret not being with them in Salies, she painted a bleak picture. It was so hot that no one dared go out until after five. And Robert, for once in his life, had experienced some setbacks. He had been suffering from terrible nosebleeds, one of which had kept him up all night.[3] Robert, who was only sixteen, had elected to take the baccalaureate exam after his year in rhetoric and had failed. Fretting about Marcel's regimen in Ostend,

Jeanne wondered whether he was eating properly and asked him to send the details of his schedule and meals.

During this vacation spent apart, she replied to Marcel's plaintive letters, seeking to lift his spirits and offering advice. In one letter she even devised a form for him to use, showing how eager she was to monitor his routine: "Could you not also, dearest, date each of your letters, so that I can more easily follow things. Then tell me: arose at ——, went to bed at ——, hours outside ——, hours of rest ——, etc." Hoping that new books might distract Marcel, Jeanne had arranged for a bookseller to mail him a copy of Victor Hugo's play *Ruy Blas* and a book on nineteenth-century art. Because she knew that he was practicing his German with the Finalys, who spoke it fluently, she closed by sending him a thousand kisses: "Tausend Küsser."[4]

In mid-September Jeanne was alarmed to receive a letter from Marcel stating his intention to return home for a performance of *Tosca,* starring Sarah Bernhardt. She wrote immediately, urging him to remain with the Finalys until she and Adrien and he all converged, from their separate travels, on Paris at the end of the month. As for the stomach ailments of which he constantly complained, she warned him against taking a powdered medication he had procured, a remedy she considered detestable. At the end of her letter she joined Marcel in hoping the Republicans would carry the day in the upcoming elections and declared herself like him a member of the "intelligent liberal conservative party," her way of indicating the somewhat liberal yet independent political stance of their family.[5]

Having survived his separation from his mother, Marcel returned to Paris in late September. Less than two months remained before he must report for military duty at Orléans. Sometime in October he received an invitation to Mme Arman de Caillavet's salon, where he met the contemporary writer he admired the most: Anatole France.

Mme de Caillavet, née Léontine Lippmann, lived in a sumptuous town house at 12, avenue Hoche, near the Arc de Triomphe. Mme Arman, as she was called, had met France in 1883 and not long afterward became his mistress, despite being a married woman. Caillavet was said to be furious with jealousy at his wife's betrayal, but he remained discreet. All three parties went to extraordinary lengths to hide a liaison known to all. France practically lived in the house, where he took his meals with the couple, yet every day the three played the same comedy for the sake of appearances. France and Léontine began the day by making love in the writer's flat, then they returned to avenue Hoche for lunch. When guests came at tea time, France, hat in hand as though just arriving, would enter through the drawing-room door and announce, "I happened to be in the neighborhood and felt I had to pay my respects."[6] France divorced his wife, who was left to raise their two-year-old daughter Suzanne. Léontine, like Proust's future society hostess Mme Verdurin in the *Search*, had a nearly fanatical devotion to literature and the arts. Her liaison with France gave her the opportunity to create a literary salon in which he was the sun around whom lesser planets revolved.

Among the frequent guests at Mme Arman's Sunday receptions or Wednesday dinners were the playwrights Alexandre Dumas fils and Georges de Porto-Riche; the writers Jules Lemaître, Ernest Renan, and Pierre Loti; and such political figures as Georges Clemenceau and Raymond Poincaré, both future presidents of France. Proust also met Charles Maurras, who later became a leading conservative journalist and a zealous monarchist. By the time Marcel left Paris to begin basic training, he had become acquainted, through the Baignèreses, the Strauses, and the Caillavets, with many members of the capital's artistic, literary, and political elite.

On November 11, 1889, at the age of eighteen, Proust enlisted in Paris for a year of military service in the 76th Infantry Regiment, 1st Battalion, 2d Company, stationed at the Coligny barracks in the city of Orléans. The new law on military service provided that for the last time a volunteer would be able to choose his regiment. By selecting Orléans, Marcel could remain close to Paris and his family. By November 15, he had traveled south to his new city on the Loire River. In 1889 Orléans was a town of more than sixty thousand inhabitants and a rich history. In 1429 a peasant girl had earned glory and ultimately sainthood by liberating the city from the English, a triumph that earned Jeanne d'Arc the epithet of "maid of Orléans." Because Marcel loved history and had read works of ancient history as well as Augustin Thierry's books about the Norman invasion of England, he had long been interested in military strategy. In the questionnaire he completed at age thirteen, he had listed as his favorite painter Jean-Louis-Ernest Meissonier, who often depicted military scenes.[7] Proust was about to see for himself what a soldier's life was really like.

He reported to the Coligny barracks at 131, rue du Faubourg Bannier, where he underwent the standard induction procedure, received his kit, had his hair cut short, and was vaccinated. His military record describes Marcel as having dark brown eyebrows, brown hair, low forehead; his nose and mouth are listed as medium, his chin round, and his face oval. The slender volunteer's weight was not recorded, but he stood five feet, six inches. One week later, cadet Proust began the foot soldier's basic training, which included fencing, swimming, and calisthenics.

The minister of war had decreed that the last crop of volunteers be dispersed through all the companies and have the same obligations as the recruits from the lower classes. This meant that although Marcel was allowed to live among cadets who were more or less of his own social background, he trained with young men from extremely modest families.[8] Proust was later to choose friends and lovers from the working class; his initial encounters with such youths made a favorable impression.

The first description Proust wrote about his military experience is a short piece he entitled "Tableaux de genre du souvenir" (Memory's genre paintings), in which young men, usually of modest station, are caught at some ordinary moment in their lives. Marcel had been struck by the soldiers' physical beauty, combined with a simplicity to which he was unaccustomed: "The rural character of the places, the simplicity of some of my peasant comrades whose bodies were more beautiful and more agile, their minds more original, their hearts more spontaneous, their characters more natural than in the case of the young men I had known before, or those I knew afterwards."[9] This is the first time Proust expressed what will become a constant theme in the *Search*, his admiration for the naturalness and comeliness of the common people. Proust included "Memory's Genre Paintings," like most of the short stories he wrote over the next several years, in *Les Plaisirs et les jours* (later translated as *Pleasures and Regrets*), published in 1896.

Marcel adapted quickly to life in the barracks, with its spartan conditions. The hard, narrow bed, reveille, the dash to gulp down a cup of café au lait before leaving on a long march through the countryside, all had an unanticipated appeal for Marcel. In the barracks Marcel grew accustomed to the stench of tobacco and tried to be one of the boys. A scene from *Jean Santeuil* describes a similar impulse: "Jean, just a little intoxicated by the dinner and the gaiety (he had thought it incumbent upon himself to drink brandy and indulge in a cigar, holding the smoke for a long time in his mouth before expelling it, so as to persuade himself that he was just like his new acquaintances . . .), sat trembling with happiness at Henri's side under the great blanket."[10] He enjoyed being on familiar terms with the other trainees, using their language, calling a new friend "old man" or "chum," actions that made him feel like one of them.[11]

Eager as he was to adapt to military life, Marcel was beset by his usual health problems. Not long after his arrival the captain asked him to take a room in town because the violent coughing fits that often plagued him during the night disturbed the other cadets in their sleep. Lodging cadets in town violated the rules, but the officers looked the other way. Marcel found a suitable room for twenty-five francs a month near the barracks in a small house belonging to a Mme Renvoyzé, who offered room and board at 92, rue du Faubourg Bannier. Here Marcel took his meals with friends, served them wine sent by his parents from Paris, and enlisted Mme Renvoyzé to make him and his friends a rum and orange juice punch. He got along well with his landlady, whom he rewarded with large tips for her additional services, and he later recalled fondly their many "pleasant little chats."[12] In *Jean Santeuil,* Proust described the little house and Mme Renvoyzé, using her real name, and the evenings spent by the fire with his fellow cadets, who wrote letters, drank champagne (against the rules), and even read the *Manual of Military Theory.* The boys enjoyed playing pranks on one another, smoking cigars, and hiding the champagne from the officers.

Marcel's friends from Condorcet relished hearing tales of his adventures. A rumor circulated that Marcel was proving to be a soldier unlike any other, spoiled by his superiors to the point that his breakfast was brought to him in bed. This does not seem impossible, for Marcel, a mere private, had his own orderly. Although volunteers served in the ranks, they were treated more or less like officer-cadets and were permitted, regulations notwithstanding, to employ a comrade-in-arms to look after their uniforms and equipment.[13]

Many of the privileges Marcel enjoyed were no doubt due to his indulgent commanding officer Colonel Arvers, "who was sensitive to the prestige of his civilian rank and open to letters of recommendation" supplied by Proust's family. It was thanks in large part to Arvers's indulgence that Marcel, despite his precarious health, was able to survive his military training. The colonel excused "early morning parades, and jumping ditches during training in equitation."[14] But Marcel does not seem to have abused his privileges. There is evidence that, perhaps to his own surprise, he found life in the military a stimulating change from the cozy family nest.

Proust's immediate superior officer was an aristocratic lieutenant named Comte Armand-Pierre de Cholet, a handsome, elegant bachelor of twenty-five who belonged to the best clubs in Paris: the Cercle de la rue Royale, the Société Hippique, an equestrian club, and the exclusive Jockey Club. Cholet apparently liked this strange but zealous private. His demonstration of friendship seemed an inexplicable kindness that Proust remembered when creating the young aristocrat Comte Saintré in *Jean Santeuil* and, in the *Search,* Robert de Saint-Loup, an officer fascinated with military strategy.

Another of Marcel's superiors was company commander Captain Walewski, otherwise known as Comte Charles Colonna-Walewski, the grandson of France's most famous military genius: Napoléon Bonaparte. Walewski's father, Alexandre-Florian-Joseph Colonna, Comte Walewski, came into the world as the illegitimate son of Napoléon and his Polish lover Marie Laczynska. Marcel and his fellow cadets believed they saw in Captain Walewski a strong resemblance to his illustrious grandfather. Like Cholet, the count was a member of the Jockey Club, of which his father had been one of the founders. The club had been created to restore French horse breeding, after the decimation suffered during the Napoleonic Wars, to its former superior level.[15] Proust and his fellow cadets admired Walewski's "gentleness [and] his politeness as a commanding officer," traits his grandfather Bonaparte might not have considered the most important for a military officer.[16]

Marcel closely observed these two officers, each representing one of France's opposing political and historical forces: the ancient nobility, epitomized by Cholet, and the more recent nobility of the Empire represented by Walewski. Saintré, Cholet's counterpart in *Jean Santeuil,* "thought it good policy to show that he and his friends were ready to be on good terms with republicans and commoners, provided they were neither dirty, stupid nor blasphemous." The more conservative among Jean's friends and those who, like Cholet, descended from the old nobility, usually expressed, not surprisingly, "royalist or religious opinions."[17]

Comte Saintré and Prince Borodino, Walewski's equivalent in *Jean Santeuil,* regard each other with contempt. Borodino knows that Saintré's ancestors would never have employed Borodino's grandfather as a gamekeeper "because of his Jewish extraction and revolutionary opinions." Borodino returns Saintré's scorn, however, because he "had inherited a glorious name" of a great Napoleonic victory and "was the son of a War Minister who had been the Emperor's friend," whereas Saintré's grandfather had been an obscure, inglorious administrator during the great days of the Empire. Borodino lacks bloodlines and the prestige that comes from a long tradition; but men of the old nobility, like Saintré, had grown ineffectual, affected, and increasingly irrelevant.[18] Both were unaware that they belonged to a vanishing world whose extinction was to be accelerated by the industrial revolution and World War I. This future sea change became part of the *Search*'s historical tapestry.

At Orléans, Proust began accumulating mental notes about the social behavior of men in the ranks and of the officers who trained them. As a young man intensely curious about all the rituals and dramas of the human comedy, who loved his comrades in arms but was generally unfit for military life, Marcel saw that the army was, in many regards, a reflection of society at large.

Sundays

As a rule Marcel had leave only on Sundays. Since he had to report back to the barracks in the evening, he would board the train in Orléans early in the morning to hurry home to his mother, who usually met him at the Gare d'Austerlitz when the train arrived at 10:39 A.M. After a warm embrace, they rode home in a carriage, exchanging news and gossip all the way. In the summer they often boarded a steamboat at a dock near the train station and enjoyed the leisurely cruise down the Seine to the Pont Mirabeau, where they took a carriage for the short ride to Auteuil. After spending the day with his family, Marcel, eager to see his friends, paid a late afternoon visit to Mme de Caillavet's salon, where he always enjoyed conversing with Anatole France.

Some who met Marcel at Mme Arman's found him "handsome, even a bit too handsome, with over-brilliant, over-big eyes, and the disquieting beauty of a weak youth."[19] Others found the nineteen-year-old cadet slightly comical in a blue capote that was too big for him, wearing red epaulettes and trousers, "all bundled up in his uniform, his head thrown back and tilted to one side, nearly lying down in one of the large easy chairs that overflowed with cushions, making his warlike attire look ridiculous."[20]

Marcel quickly became friends with his hostess's son Gaston, the future author of highly successful comedies. Although Gaston had graduated from Condorcet only two years ahead of Marcel, they had never met at school. By the time Marcel enlisted, Gaston had nearly finished his military service as a gunner stationed at Versailles.[21] A bright, unpretentious man with a ready wit, Gaston treated Marcel with great respect, having noticed his remarkable intelligence and sensitivity. In their Sunday conversations the two soldiers exchanged ideas about literature, the theater, and music.

Gaston and Mme Arman were the first of his new friends who encouraged him to write.[22] Flattered because these two people lived in the presence of Anatole France, Marcel began to share with them—and even with France—his ideas for poems and stories in which he intended to depict life in the leisured class. One day France remarked how fond Marcel was of "intellectual life," to which the young man replied, "I am not at all fond of things of the intelligence, but only of life and of movement." France had missed the mark. Marcel attached little importance to intelligence; what he "really envied and admired was the grace of those who live instinctively."[23] Proust eventually grew weary of society people because he found too many who used intellectual pretentiousness to mask ignorance, prejudices, and snobbery.

Mme Arman's salon held another strong attraction for Marcel. Jeanne Pouquet was a beautiful, clever, vivacious girl of fifteen, who was practically engaged to Gaston. Marcel soon fell in love with Jeanne, but dared not court her: "My affection for Gaston . . . had an unsought-for vaccination effect. It made me immune to the acute suffering caused by my love for Mlle Pouquet."[24] This relationship set a pattern that Marcel would follow with future couples: he would "fall in love" with the fiancée or mistress of a man who appealed to him. Such an arrangement had a number of advantages: he could love the woman from a safe distance, exchange confidences with the man and woman about each other, observe the dynamics of sexual love, and have the illusion that he was an active participant experiencing all the joys, enthusiasms, and jealous sufferings of both partners. It was also an ideal vantage point for a novelist.

Marcel's lack of hope in wooing Jeanne did not prohibit him from seeking her out or attempting to become more closely attached. He arrived one day with a triumphant air at Mme Pouquet's home. Having found a little château to rent near Orléans, he had come to invite Jeanne and her mother, along with Gaston, Mme de Caillavet, and some of their friends for a sojourn in the country. Jeanne pointed out that if the château were small, it would not accommodate many friends. "We laughed at Marcel's silly ideas; but perhaps he was only enjoying his fantasies without really believing in them."[25]

Marcel had become fascinated with photographs. It was a fairly simple matter to obtain pictures of his male friends, but those of girls and women presented great obstacles. Exchanging photos was considered a gesture of intimacy, not to be taken lightly. The picture Marcel most coveted was Jeanne's. She always believed that the four poses he had taken of himself in uniform near the barracks were part of a scheme to obtain her photograph in return. He intended to give the photos to Jeanne and the girls he met while attending dancing lessons that Mme Pouquet had arranged for Jeanne and her friends. The idea of exchanging photographs scandalized the girls' mothers, who vetoed Marcel's proposal. When Gaston heard about Marcel's attempt to obtain a picture of Jeanne, he became furious and demanded an explanation. Marcel assured his friend that he meant no harm, and, to show his good will, he dedicated one of his photographs to Gaston.

When it came time for Marcel to leave Mme de Caillavet's drawing room, his friends loaded him down with sandwiches and cakes for the train ride back to Orléans. "Nothing was more comical than to see Marcel making his way around the drawing-room to say his good-byes, encumbered with his kepi and his little packages and hurried along by Gaston, who feared he'd miss his train."[26] Gaston would leave his other friends to accompany Marcel on the carriage ride to catch the 7:40 express train to Orléans. Once they had cleared the drawing room, Gaston and Marcel would rush down the stairs and jump into the carriage that had been waiting for half an hour. They promised the driver a huge tip if he got them to the station on time. Marcel, fearful of missing the express and having to take the slow train, knew that if he arrived late he stood an excellent chance of being confined to the barracks for four days. When the carriage finally reached the station, Marcel leapt from it before the driver could bring it to a complete stop. Gaston, wanting to make certain that his friend caught the train, followed close on Marcel's heels, all of which made the driver think he had been hoodwinked, so he ran after them shouting insults. This extraordinary scene was repeated nearly every Sunday. On one occasion, Gaston, under the spell of Marcel's conversation and charm, rode with him all the way to Orléans. Marcel thrived on the attention. On New Year's Day, 1890, Marcel praised Gaston so highly to his fellow cadets, who had never even met the paragon of thoughtfulness, that they sent him a "message conveying their respect!"[27]

Grief

On the weekend of December 13, for some reason Marcel's leave was canceled. The only consolation was that Horace Finaly had paid him a visit that Friday. His mother wrote that it was impossible for her to come visit him, as she did on occasion when he stayed in Orléans, because his grandmother had fallen ill. Despite the alarming news, Jeanne did not seem too concerned. Adèle was so good at hiding the seriousness of her sickness from those who loved her that at first the family failed to appreciate how rapidly her uremia was progressing. She also proved to be a somewhat difficult patient; her doctor had prescribed a milk diet, but she would take the liquid only in small doses and on condition that it not taste like milk.

Jeanne, who feared Marcel's morale might sink at the canceled leave and the long months ahead, told him that she had thought of a way to make the time of his enlistment seem shorter: "Take eleven bars of the chocolate you're so fond of, make up your mind to eat one and no more at the end of each month—you'll be amazed at how quickly they go—and your exile with them. I believe I'm talking nonsense, giving you stupid advice that will only aggravate your dyspepsia." She ended her letter by paraphrasing a line from Corneille, that old celebrator of duty and manly valor: "Keep well and win the battle, the reward will be your happiness and ours."[28]

By the time he came home on Christmas leave, Marcel had passed, if only barely, enough of the basic training requirements to be admitted to the instruction squadron. This made him eligible for promotion to the rank of noncommissioned officer. He was relieved at having advanced to the next level of soldiering, but he found the holidays to be dreary for the family, as concern mounted over his grandmother's condition. Shortly after he had returned to his post, Adèle's condition worsened, and she died on January 3, 1890, one month before her sixty-sixth birthday. Marcel had not arrived home in time to say good-bye to his grandmother, whose funeral he attended on January 5. In the days that followed, Marcel, who had adored his grandmother, did not seem strongly affected by her death.

His mother, whose grief was extreme, went into full mourning. In the coming year, she revisited the coast at Cabourg, where she sat on the beach and reread Mme de Sévigné's letters from the copy that her mother had always carried with her. She walked in the wind and the rain, just as her mother had loved to do, remembering days that would never return. In the *Search,* when depicting the Narrator's mother grieving over her mother's death, Proust remembered this vision of Jeanne Proust on the beach: "Dressed in black and carrying her mother's sunshade, advancing with timid, pious steps over the sands which beloved feet had trodden before her, . . . she looked as though she were going in search of a corpse which the waves would cast up at her feet."[29] For years afterward Jeanne mourned the dreadful dates of January 3 and 5. On those sad anniversaries of her mother's death and funeral she canceled all entertainment and social engagements. She did not insist that her family follow her example, but simply requested that "they should be true to what they genuinely felt."[30]

By January a flu epidemic reached Orléans. Before it ran its course, twenty-five thousand people—nearly half the population of the city—were laid low.[31] As bitter cold weather set in, warm fires and champagne parties were more appealing than ever after a day spent in military drills outdoors. In the evenings, the soldiers, despite their winter uniforms of long greatcoats and heavy shakos, returned from training exhausted and chilled to the bone. By February 7 the officers believed the cadets were ready for their first strenuous march. A local newspaper reported the occasion: "Today the 76th infantry regiment, drums and bugles leading the way, left their Coligny quarters around 11:30 for a route march that took them beyond the Loire River. Although they left in a light fog and heavy snow, the gallant regiment returned in the afternoon when the sun was beaming in all its splendor. The soldiers appeared to have bravely borne the hardships of their first march!"[32]

During this time when winter seemed eternal, Marcel and a fellow infantryman, André Mayrargues, were invited to dine at the official residence of the prefect, Paul Boegner.[33] A young gunner from the 30th artillery regiment, Robert de Billy, had also been invited. Billy, having spent the first three months of his training determined to achieve the military ideal of endurance and discipline, was proud of his progress and honored by the dinner invitation. Convinced, as he strode smartly toward the prefect's official residence, that his regiment was the best in France, and terrified at the thought of committing a gaffe in public before any noncommissioned officers, Billy intended to be a sterling representative of his regiment. He arrived bristling with swagger and fairly gleaming with polished leather and metal, wearing "boots as shiny as mirrors, brass buttons that had been patiently polished, white gloves freshly washed."[34] Such were the proud cadet's self-congratulatory thoughts when he entered the drawing room and promptly encountered the two infantrymen from the 76th Regiment: Proust and Mayrargues.

Billy did not find Marcel's spit and polish up to standard: the greatcoat was too loose for his slight body; his gait and his manner of speaking were certainly not those one expected from a soldier. But Billy was struck by the large, inquisitive eyes and his extraordinary, charming, supple sentences that drew one irresistibly toward him. "Marcel at nineteen was intensely curious and the variety of his questions astonished and perplexed me. Nourished on Platonic dialogues, he hoped by interrogating his friends on subjects about which they often knew nothing to discover a new point of view. But for him the world was not a succession of shadows in a cave. He was interested in substance and investigated how a personality is formed by diverse influences, apparently contradictory, but harmonized by life."[35]

Billy was at a loss to understand what appealed to him about this bizarre young man, not at all the kind of person with whom he would normally stand and chat. Yet something made him overlook Marcel's baggy uniform and unsoldierly mannerisms and wish to see him again. The encounter marked the beginning of a lifelong friendship that Billy later compared to Flaubert's unlikely pair of companions, Bouvard and Pécuchet, opposite in so many ways and yet strangely complementary. Billy had received a Protestant education and had traveled, unlike Marcel, who only dreamed of doing so, to a few major European cities and visited their art museums. Both men loved classical music. Billy, in order to further his appreciation, had regularly attended the concerts at the Conservatory. During their frequent conversations at Orléans, Marcel spoke to him about his years at Condorcet, especially about Darlu and the noble thoughts exchanged among his classmates in philosophy. To Billy, a graduate of the sterner, traditional Lycée Louis-le-Grand, such sentiments seemed exaggerated, perhaps even scornful, but at times he was willing to believe his new friend and to picture the Condorcet symposia as sublime.[36] Marcel, still under the spell of Darlu, considered himself a philosopher.

On March 3 Proust was admitted to the company college and became a second-class administrative officer in the territorial army. When spring finally arrived, the citizens of Orléans marveled at the exceptionally fine weather and the beauty of the first flowers, all of which seemed to enhance the spectacle of the freshly trained and synchronized troops drilling on the parade ground. The local newspaper described their marching in step as "simply admirable" and the sight of them trooping by as "marvelous."[37] Did Marcel sense that he too had changed? There were moments when he thought it possible that he might live apart from his family, that he might even pursue a career in the military.

In April, Jeanne wrote that she was finding some consolation for the loss of her mother in literature, particularly in Mme de Sévigné's letters. Quoting the marquise's declaration of devotion to her children, Jeanne wrote, " 'I know another mother who counts herself for nothing, who has wholly given herself over to her children.' Doesn't that apply perfectly to your grandmother? Except that she wouldn't have *said* it." Jeanne described for Marcel her activities of the day. Because Adrien was not coming home, she and Robert had lunched early. After cleaning the keyboard of Marcel's piano, as she described it, she sat down and practiced exercises for an hour, while Robert read his physics book. Sitting at the piano so long had made her "stiff and rheumatic," a more and more frequently heard complaint. After settling into a comfortable chair, she had dictated algebra problems to Robert. With his baccalaureate examination rapidly approaching, Robert was taking no chances this time. Some complaint by Marcel had apparently inspired her to consult Adrien, whose hygienic restrictions she relayed: "no swimming or riding for the present."[38]

In late June, Marcel stopped writing to his mother. The postponed grief for his grandmother at last overwhelmed him. Had the arrival of summer awakened memories of happy days with her at Auteuil and on the Normandy beaches? Only now did he realize the true dimensions of his loss.[39] Marcel withdrew into himself and confided in no one, not even his mother. When he resumed his letters to Jeanne, he apologized for not having written, telling her that he had spent his time weeping, lost in sadness, and had not wanted to add his sorrow to hers, which he knew to be nearly unbearable. She answered that he had been wrong not to write, that she could only be touched by knowing he was thinking of his grandmother, and she urged him not to make a practice of keeping silent for fear of making her sad, because such action would only defeat his purpose. She then tried to calm his grief: "Think of her, cherish her memory with me, but don't let yourself spend whole days in fits of tears that fray your nerves and that she would not have wanted. On the contrary, the more you think of her, the more you should try to be as she liked you to be, and to behave as she wanted you to behave."[40]

Marcel's superiors may have denied him some leaves in July or August, perhaps because his leggings were insufficiently polished or for other demerits, as happened at least six times during the year. Jeanne's August letters contain no mention of health problems or sadness. By the end of the summer Marcel had adjusted so well to life in the military and, with the end in sight, had begun to enjoy what he would later recall as one of the happiest periods of his life. He even skipped at least one Sunday trip to Paris. His mother wrote to him on Sunday morning August 10, with a touch of humor, "Since you said nothing about not coming, I stopped my presses yesterday."[41] Had she known he would not come home, she told him, paraphrasing *Macbeth*, he would have seen "Auteuil wood come to Orléans." If he would like to have lunch on Tuesday, she would come to Orléans as she had on a previous occasion.

Why did Jeanne not encourage Marcel to be more independent as she had a year before, when he was so miserable in Ostend? Why did she not rejoice that he was content to stay in Orléans with his fellow soldiers? Had she become sad and lonely since losing her mother? No one made her feel loved and cheered her more than Marcel; no one more savored, as they did together, the pleasures of reading and exchanging gossip. Marcel realized after her death that she had underestimated his ability to manage on his own, but as long as she lived they maintained a pattern of mutual emotional dependency.

On August 18 Jeanne informed Marcel that she had dispatched Robert to visit her father, whose health had not been good. That morning she had prohibited Nathé from taking his bath, because she was afraid that he was too unsteady and might fall. Since her mother's death, Jeanne had assumed the responsibility of looking after her father and his household. Although her brother Georges, now a judge, still lived at home, within less than a year, the forty-three-year-old bachelor surprised his family by deciding to marry a widow by the name of Amélie Oulman. The new couple moved to 22, place Malesherbes, and Nathé Weil found himself alone, with only his servants for company.

In the summer Marcel became a secretary at divisional headquarters, a post he soon lost because the chief of staff found his handwriting illegible.[42] This setback concerned his parents, who worried that their obviously gifted son lacked the discipline to succeed. In a letter Jeanne mentioned disapprovingly the situation of a friend's son, Marcel's age, who wanted to be a painter. He has his "master's degree in literature, but when it comes to choosing a career, he is childishly indecisive."[43] She made this observation with no further comment, yet Marcel could not have missed the point. His mother was anticipating a decision that was rapidly approaching: he would soon be out of the service and had no serious career plans.

In the final ranking of his class, Marcel finished near the bottom, sixty-third out of sixty-four. He still had the option of taking a second exam and becoming an officer. Years later Marcel maintained that his health had prevented his being a better soldier. His low ranking can be explained in part, no doubt, by his never having learned to swim. Nor did he receive any scores for the army gymnastics exercise known as the bridge-ladder, a rigorous drill in which the men had to move rapidly across a ladder laid flat over a trench.[44] Yet on the exam at the end of the year, he scored a fairly decent "assez bien."

By the end of the month the rarity of Marcel's letters angered his mother. After a scolding from her, he promised to make amends. Had he failed to write because he had been annoyed by the pointed reference to his lack of career plans, or had he simply been busy enjoying himself with his fellow soldiers? She accepted his apology, but not without conditions: he must "purchase ten notebooks with large sheets and two packages of white envelopes" and use these to write her sixty letters, approximately one for each remaining day of his military service.[45] Just when Marcel appeared to be showing signs of independence, his mother discouraged his pulling away.

In September the family celebrated Robert's graduation from the lycée with a baccalaureate in sciences and letters. Only seventeen, the younger son intended to enter the university and begin studies leading to a medical degree. As summer came to an end, Marcel accepted an invitation to spend his September vacation leave as the guest of his parents' friends M. and Mme Derbanne at Cabourg, a popular seaside resort in Normandy, just west of Trouville and Deauville. The stay was brief and not particularly pleasant, because he arrived fatigued and complaining of his usual ailments.

Marcel returned to the regiment on Monday, September 22. The next day he wrote to his father in the south of France to apologize for not having written daily as promised, explaining that because of his weariness he had spent most of his Cabourg leave in bed. Adrien was taking the waters at Aix-les-Bains as a guest of Dr. Henry Cazalis, a colleague who also wrote poetry, mainly Buddhist verses, under the pseudonym Jean Lahor. Cazalis was a friend of several writers, including Guy de Maupassant, also visiting him in Aix. At the height of his career as the author of numerous short stories, such as "Boule de suif" (Tallow ball) and "La Maison Tellier," and novels like *Une Vie* and *Bel-Ami*, Maupassant, at forty, had begun to suffer from the effects of tertiary syphilis and desperately sought remedies for his ills.[46] He feared most what might happen to his mind and his ability to write. Marcel, in his letter, wondered whether Maupassant would remember him from Mme Straus's salon. Although Marcel did not particularly admire Maupassant's works, he was pleased that his father had met the writer. Perhaps Adrien had seen that writing could bring fame and fortune. "I hope you liked Maupassant. I don't believe he knows me; I've only met him twice." Marcel then reported on his own condition: "I don't feel at all bad (except my stomach) and I'm not even suffering from the general melancholia, brought on by this year of absence that, if not its cause, can at least serve as a pretext and excuse for it. But I am finding it very hard to concentrate, to read, learn by heart, remember."

In closing, he told Adrien that before he had left Cabourg, some housemaids, no doubt attracted by his uniform, had scandalized his hosts by blowing kisses to him. Marcel said that the maids of Orléans, whom he had abandoned to go to Cabourg, were now taking their revenge. Always clever at weaving quotations into his letters, he cited a line of verse by Dr. Cazalis to explain one maid's fury at him for having "disdained the flowers of her naked breasts."[47] Could Adrien have taken any encouragement at his son's mention of naked breasts—even if shunned—or did he continue to fear that Marcel's sexual tastes were inclined in the wrong direction? Had Marcel's remark about an inability to concentrate been a hint that he was in no condition to begin his university studies on leaving the military?

At the end of Proust's year in the military, Lieutenant Cholet presented him with a signed photograph: "To Marcel Proust, volunteer cadet, from one of his torturers."[48] In the end the torture had been delicious. Contrary to tradition and expectations for most young men—above all, for one with his constitution, tastes, and personality—Proust had enjoyed his military year. His letters and writings never veer from depicting life in the service in the most positive, enthusiastic, and at times nearly lyrical terms. "It's curious," Proust wrote to a friend some fifteen years later, that we "should have seen the army, you as a prison, I as a paradise."[49] Once his year was up, Proust believed that he had ingratiated himself to the point where all the officers liked him and he had learned to make himself "so useful!" He attempted to reenlist, but the army turned him down.[50]

Discharged on November 14, Proust remained on the military roster as an active *sous-officier* or noncommissioned officer in the army reserve, for his training, though marginal, had been satisfactory.[51] When he came home to resume civilian life, his mother, who could now end her daily bulletins of love, support, and advice, carefully packed away his tailor-made uniform in a box that Proust was to keep for the rest of his life. Although his single ambition was to write, he could no longer postpone facing his parents' demands that he decide what university degree and professional goal he wished to pursue.

4   *A Modest Literary Debut*   ∾

ON HIS RETURN HOME FROM THE SERVICE, Marcel did not appear eager to attend parties, but on November 22, only a week after his discharge, he accepted an invitation to Mme Straus's Sunday reception. First he sent her a huge bouquet of giant chrysanthemums, which French horticulturists had learned to grow by imitating the Japanese. Then he wrote to say that he would come just this once, but first he had to see his tailor. Because he had gone straight from high school into the service, he had just realized how impoverished his civilian wardrobe had become. He ordered a new frock coat to wear because his jacket was "too frightful."[1]

Marcel, exhausted by his parents' relentless urgings, had finally agreed to attend law school and to consider the diplomatic service as a career. In late November he began an ambitious program of studies by enrolling in the Faculté de droit (School of law) and at the École libre des sciences politiques (Free school of political science), a course of studies for future French diplomats who must pass the foreign service examination. Marcel's only consolation on enrolling at the École libre des sciences politiques had been the delight of encountering Robert de Billy, who did want to be a diplomat.

Among Marcel's professors were Anatole Leroy-Beaulieu, Albert Sorel, Paul Desjardins, and Albert Vandal. Marcel did not particularly like his political science courses, except those taught by Sorel and Leroy-Beaulieu. Sorel, known for his strictness, was a distinguished historian who had already begun publishing his vast eight-volume history *L'Europe et la Révolution française*. Leroy-Beaulieu was one of the most eminent representatives of the French liberal tradition. Billy recalled that Marcel listened attentively to the lectures of Sorel and Leroy-Beaulieu but did not bother to take notes.[2]

In Vandal's class Marcel found it difficult not to be distracted by the professor's nervous tic, which caused one eye to flutter. While lecturing to his students about the maddeningly complex affairs of the Orient, Vandal relished telling stories intended to fix in their minds a particular treaty or major event. A favorite anecdote involved a Serb who, one day in Belgrade, went to draw water from a well. A Turkish soldier attempted to stop him, and when the Serb persisted, the Turk killed him. Vandal ended the often told tale with his standard dramatic summation: "Gentlemen, from that well sprang a conflagration that engulfed the entire Orient." Marcel, on hearing the emotional quiver in the voice and registering the batting eye that failed to hide the look of satisfaction on Vandal's face, seized his blank notebook and dashed off a poem, indicating his complete indifference to the subject matter and his contempt for the professor's pedagogic methods:

> Vandal, the fop, parades his wit
> Gabriel and Jean don't give a shit
> Nor does Robert, nor even Marcel
> Who's much less solemn than usual.[3]

At least Marcel had outgrown the practice of passing notes of seduction to the handsome boys in the class. No doubt he still felt the urge to do so, but the naïve, barely tolerated excesses of adolescence would be certain to provoke a scandal among adults. He had learned to be discreet.

After class, Marcel and Robert would walk toward the Right Bank and home. They were often accompanied by Gabriel Trarieux, a future symbolist poet, and Jean Boissonnas, who, like Billy, was to become a diplomat. The young men discussed poetry, aesthetics, paintings, and society—anything but political science.[4] Occasionally, Proust and Billy stopped by the Louvre Museum on the way home. As they roamed the vast galleries, Billy served as guide. His passionate interest in art and antiquities had been nurtured in secondary schooling, where art and art history were part of the curriculum. One visit to the museum had been inspired by Marcel's intense admiration of Charles Baudelaire's poem "Les Phares" (Guiding

Lights), in which the poet paid homage to great painters.[5] As Marcel and Robert viewed painting after painting, Marcel recited the lines that Baudelaire had written to evoke works of Michelangelo, Leonardo, Rembrandt, and others.

As Billy steered Marcel through the wing devoted to French painting, he realized that the works of the great seventeenth-century artist Nicolas Poussin held no interest for his friend. Marcel was drawn instead to the seaport paintings of Claude Lorrain, a precursor of impressionism who liked to paint harbors seen in the light of sunset, and to the more intimate sunsets of Dutch painter Aelbert Cuyp. The play of light, especially on water, enchanted Marcel. But the portrait that held Marcel's attention the longest was Van Dyck's painting of *The Duke of Richmond*. Billy had remarked that the splendid young men of the era whose portraits could be admired in museums throughout Europe were destined to be slaughtered during the civil war by Oliver Cromwell's unconquerable Ironsides regiment. Marcel remembered this theme of unforeseen tragedy awaiting the English youths in full flower when he wrote the poem addressed to Van Dyck that begins

Tu triomphes, Van Dyck, prince des gestes calmes,
Dans tous les êtres beaux qui vont bientôt mourir.[6]

You triumph, Van Dyck, prince of calm gestures,
In all the beautiful creatures who will soon die.

Proust's first independent publications were several pieces that appeared in the short-lived journal *Le Mensuel,* which, as its name indicated, appeared monthly in Paris.[7] During its one-year run beginning in October 1890, *Le Mensuel* published at least three pieces by Proust.[8] With its gray-blue cover and price of fifty centimes, *Le Mensuel* may not have had a much larger circulation than the little magazines the boys had created at Condorcet, but at least it was a real journal. Its first issue, proposing to readers a simple digest of the month's main events in politics, society, and the theater, was on sale in four bookstores in the eighth arrondissement, where Marcel no doubt discovered it and decided to become a contributor.[9] The February 1891 issue contained two of his pieces: a poem dedicated to a friend and entitled simply "Poésie" (Poetry) celebrated love; "Pendant la carême" (During Lent) reviewed a lecture series on the new singing sensation Yvette Guilbert.

Proust's generation had now reached adulthood and had begun to enjoy all the pleasures of the Belle Époque. The bohemian crowd of writers, painters, and musicians flocked to the café-concerts, cabarets, and music halls to ogle the cancan dancers and hear the most popular singers. Yvette Guilbert, whose trademark pair of long, black gloves can be admired in Henri de Toulouse-Lautrec's famous portrait, was considered the most intelligent and literary of the performers and one who delivered her songs in a nearly flawless diction. Her appearance in February at the Théâtre de l'Application caused a mighty traffic jam as the cabs and carriages of her eager fans crushed into the rue de Saint-Lazare.

Hugues Le Roux, a prolific novelist and journalist, had delivered five lectures on the chanteuse under the general title "Fin-de-siècle Ingenuity and Mlle Yvette Guilbert." In his review for Le Mensuel, Marcel gently scolded Le Roux for having delivered so many lectures on a popular entertainer, one more than another jour-nalist, Louis Ganderax, had devoted to Molière.[10] By attempting to formulate "scientific" theories on popular singing, Proust wrote, Le Roux had taken too seriously what was intended as pure entertainment, frequently of the most vulgar and salacious sort. Guilbert, one of the Belle Époque's legendary performers, was no different from the others insofar as content was concerned. Marcel, like all her fans, had too often relished the spicy delights of her songs to endorse Le Roux's amusing but unconvincing depiction of Yvette as an ingenue.

The same issue of Le Mensuel carried Marcel's poem dedicated to Gustave Laurens de Waru, a nobleman Marcel's age who was among the young men in his circle during his university years.[11] Gustave was the son of Comte Pierre Laurens de Waru, and his mother's sister was Comtesse Adhéaume de Chevigné, née Laure de Sade, a direct descendant of the infamous marquis. The poem that begins L'amour monte des cœurs comme une odeur de roses (Love rises from hearts like an odor of roses) lacks originality or any other distinction. A paean to love, it ends with the Baudelairian image of the poet drowning in the unnamed lover's indifferent, languorous, and mystical eyes.

Adrien read Marcel's pieces in Le Mensuel with a father's pride, proclaiming confidently, "Marcel will be elected to the Académie française." Dr. Proust may have exaggerated the merit of Marcel's essays, but he took the occasion to encour-age his son and bolster his morale. There was no harm in writing so long as it did not interfere with his studies. Writing, after all, was something one could do easily in one's spare time.

As Marcel explored the rarefied air of elegant salons and the private boxes in theaters and at the opera, he met beautiful women and handsome men whose chic, wit, and haughtiness quickly seduced him. He pandered to them, flattering them, seeing them much as they saw themselves, as divine creatures. Later, he would satirize their superficiality and pretentiousness, but now he reveled in their company as he studied the visible incarnations of lineage and rank, money and power, taste and glamour.

Marcel went to the theater as often as possible. On a Saturday in March he accompanied the Strauses, along with Jacques Bizet and Jacques Baignères, to the Odéon Theater to see the revival of *Germinie Lacerteux,* a famous play by the Goncourt brothers. The play, based on their naturalist novel, told the "true" story of their servant Rose Malingre, who, as a girl, had suffered rape and pregnancy, and had ended her days miserably in a workhouse. In the revival, the title role was played by the newly celebrated actress Réjane, whose performance devastated Marcel. He left the theater with his eyes red from weeping and claimed to have contracted a permanent sadness.[12]

The day following the play, he went to Mme Straus's Sunday reception. He had left home intending to study, but along the way he had seen some lilac branches and had been unable to resist the urge to bring some of the purple flowers to Mme Straus. He informed her that he had a ticket for the following Friday's performance of a play by Stanislas Rzewuski, *L'Impératrice Faustine.* Would she attend? He had, since reserving his ticket, found a more amusing alternative for the evening and would attend the play only if he could contemplate Mme Straus. As an additional sign of his devotion, he told her that Holy Friday was approaching, "the first anniversary of the first letter I received from you, and your handwriting, while remaining just as moving, is becoming more strangely new and as though I had never seen it."[13] Mme Straus, who adored Marcel, dismissed such nonsense.

Marcel, frustrated that Mme Straus did not take him seriously as a suitor, wrote to her in the guise of a spurned courtier, heading his letter "The truth about Madame Straus." It is a short letter meant to be frank about who she is, a woman with many appealing traits but of little substance. Yet he was overwhelmed by her beauty, wit, and charm. Above all, the letter is a literary exercise, a quick, lightweight sketch, in the tradition of seventeenth-century French moralists, which shows that Proust already saw his friends not just as themselves but as the products of his imagination. This is one of the first instances in which Proust observed salon behavior and hinted at its superficiality, albeit in a teasing, flattering manner:

> At first, you see, I thought you loved only beautiful things and that you understood them very well—but then I saw that you care nothing for them—later I thought you loved people, but I see that you care nothing for them. I believe that you love only a certain mode of life which brings out not so much your intelligence as your wit, not so much your wit as

your tact, not so much your tact as your dress. . . . Because you charm,
do not rejoice and suppose that I love you less. To prove the contrary . . .
I shall send you more beautiful flowers and you will be angry, Madame,
since you do not deign to favour the sentiments with which I have the
painful ecstasy to be

> The most respectful servant of your Sovereign Indifference
> Marcel Proust[14]

These flowers and their accompanying sycophantic prose proved to be no more
seductive, of course, than the roses he had, as a schoolboy, thrust upon Mme
Chirade in the dairy shop. Marcel was playacting, and no one, including himself,
took him seriously.

On May 1, at Gabriel Trarieux's, Marcel met a young man only two years older
than himself who shared his ambition to become a writer: André Gide.[15] Like many
of his generation, Gide was currently under the influence of the symbolists, but he,
unlike Marcel, was beginning to make a name for himself in literary circles as
opposed to social ones. At twenty-two Gide was a humorless young man, filled with
doubt and self-loathing, who shared Proust's sexual orientation but, having been
raised in a strict Calvinist environment, suffered from crushing guilt.

Gide, who was a meticulous diarist, must not have been impressed by his first
encounter with Marcel Proust, for there is no mention of him in Gide's diary
entries for 1891. Young Gide, despite serious misgivings about the influence of
society people on aspiring writers, had read Barbey d'Aurevilly's *Du dandysme et de
Georges Brummel* until he practically knew it by heart. Unlike Proust, Gide felt ill at
ease and made a poor impression with his "sad visage, his seriousness, and his
timidity."[16] Proust's and Gide's paths did not cross again for another two decades,
until Gide stood in Proust's way and denied him an opportunity to publish *Swann's
Way,* the first part of the *Search.*

The Court of Love

When summer arrived, Marcel pursued his law studies, enrolling for new courses
in June. But law was far from being his only preoccupation and certainly not his
greatest interest. He was often seen at the new tennis club on boulevard Bineau in
Neuilly with Jeanne Pouquet and her beau Gaston de Caillavet.[17] Gaston went
nearly every day to play tennis with his friends on a new hard court in the middle of

a vacant lot surrounded by a picket fence. The English enthusiasm for lawn tennis had spread to France, and new facilities were springing up here and there. Soon Marcel came along with his friends to the tennis court, not for the game but to be with Jeanne, whom he continued to adore. While the other young men strained to keep their eyes on the ball, Marcel could barely take his eyes off the vivacious, attractive girl. Not since the days when he had rushed breathless to the Champs-Élysées to find Marie de Benardaky at play had Marcel been so eager to spend time with a pretty girl. She was, he later recalled, the second great love of his youth.

In her memoirs Jeanne remembered that Marcel, unable to take part in so "violent" a game as tennis, came to the boulevard Bineau court to chat in the circle of girls and their mothers, who listened to him intently under the sparse shade provided by the young trees. The women quickly pressed Marcel into service by putting him in charge of the refreshments. Now the courtier arrived bearing a large box full of snacks. When the weather was especially hot, the ladies obliged him to go to a nearby café in search of beer and lemonade, which he brought back, moaning under the weight, in a hideous basket borrowed from the bartender.

Days at the court became an alfresco symposium, with Marcel holding forth while he and the women balanced drinks and napkins as they sat, nibbling and chatting. When a stray ball landed near Marcel, distracting him and the girls from their conversation, the athletes were pleased to have disrupted what Marcel referred to as the "court of love." Marcel would accuse the players of having fired the ball in their direction "with malice aforethought." Jeanne felt that Gaston and the other men were, perhaps without realizing it, jealous of Marcel because of the charm and tenderness that radiated from him and that he inspired in return. But Gaston knew that Jeanne's heart belonged to him and that Marcel, in spite of his great intelligence and ability to amuse, could never be taken seriously as a suitor.

Marcel spent his September vacation in Cabourg. While there he was frequently invited to visit the Arthur Baignèreses in their lovely villa, Les Frémonts, perched on a hill overlooking Trouville. From the villa Marcel admired the grand vistas of sea and farmland, remarking the contrasts between the vast sameness of the water to the north and west and the varied spectacle of the sloping countryside to the east and south, where lush, green fields were populated by sheep grazing in the apple orchards.[18]

During this stay he wrote a short piece entitled "Choses normandes" (Aspects of Normandy), describing that juxtaposition of rich, hilly farmland and the infinite perspective of the sea, for *Le Mensuel*'s September issue, which was to be its last. The essay also expressed his puzzlement at the vacation habits of his countrymen, who chose to leave the seashore just at the moment he found ideal, forsaking clear skies and gentle breezes because members of the leisured classes considered it elegant to leave the beaches at the end of August to go to the country.[19]

When Proust's hotel closed at the end of September, the Baignèreses invited him to be their guest at Les Frémonts, granting his wish to be unfashionable and remain on the coast well beyond the season. On October 1, before dinner, another guest at the villa, the painter Jacques-Émile Blanche, drew Marcel's portrait in pencil, a likeness that served as the basis for the full-length oil portrait he soon undertook. The pencil sketch reveals a more serious and introspective Marcel than the foppish man-about-town Blanche was to depict in the painting. Ten years Proust's senior, Blanche had long been a fixture of the social scene. Although Blanche lived near Uncle Louis in Auteuil, Marcel and the painter had met in a Paris salon. Their encounter at Les Frémonts was the beginning of a long and sometimes stormy friendship.

When Marcel returned to Paris for the beginning of a new academic year, he and his parents engaged again in heated debates about his future plans. During a visit, Nathé, to Marcel's horror, brought up the subject of a career, thus sparking another dispute. Writing to his grandfather, Marcel requested that Nathé not bring up the subject again until it had been resolved.[20] His parents, in whose house he lived and who controlled the purse strings, prevailed again, and on November 5 Marcel enrolled for his second year in law school and at the École libre des sciences politiques. A week later he was swooning with ecstasy because Mme Straus had written that she was still his friend: "These divine words of yesterday, when you proved that you are unsurpassed—as in everything—in the art of making hearts vibrate until they break."[21]

The visit of the Irish poet and novelist Oscar Wilde was the great event of Paris literary salons that late fall. Wilde, who had published his first and only novel, *The Picture of Dorian Gray,* a year earlier, had yet to write *Salomé* or the light comedies on which much of his fame rests today. His reputation in France, where his novel was not yet known, derived from his poems and fairy tales, as well as from his wit and eccentricities. Although Wilde's hosts may have been at pains to explain the precise nature of his accomplishments, they had no doubt that his gifts were authentic and would lead him to greatness. Everyone said that he was a gifted conversationalist, perhaps the most extraordinary *causeur* of his epoch. And even though he spoke the language of Racine and Molière with a deplorable English accent, his vocabulary was prodigious, his style eloquent, and fluent French poured from his large, voluptuous lips. Wilde relished being the new French sensation.

Like Proust, whom he soon met, Wilde enjoyed society because he "found in it both the satisfaction of his vanity and an inexhaustible source of fatuity."[22]

It was during this stay in Paris that Wilde remarked to Enrique Gomez Carrillo, a young Guatemalan diplomat he met at the Café d'Harcourt, "I have put all my talent into my works. I have put all my genius into my life."[23] Wilde, inspired by French art, especially Gustave Moreau's paintings and Stéphane Mallarmé's verses, began to write *Salomé*. Contemplating his attraction to the story of the veiled dancer and the Christian martyr, he remarked to Gomez, "I flee from what is moral as from what is impoverished. I have the same sickness as Des Esseintes."[24] Des Esseintes, one of late-nineteenth-century France's most famous literary characters, had been created by Joris-Karl Huysmans in a novel entitled *À rebours* (Against the grain, 1884). This figure with a strange sounding name is a hyperaesthete, a decadent hero said to have been inspired in large part by one of the most intriguing and vain men in Parisian society, Comte Robert de Montesquiou—a person with whom Proust was eager to become acquainted.

Whereas Montesquiou was svelte and supremely elegant, the arbiter of taste and fashion, Wilde was a large man with exaggerated features. In his journal Marcel Schwob, another of Wilde's French hosts, observed that his guest was addicted to opium-tainted cigarettes and absinthe and portrayed him as "a big man, with a large pasty face, red cheeks, an ironic eye, bad and protrusive teeth, a vicious childlike mouth with lips soft with milk ready to suck some more."[25] But when André Gide met Wilde he saw an altogether different person; the love-starved Gide gazed at a creature whose overpowering "beauty" captivated him. Gide's first diary entry for 1892, dated January 1, speaks of Oscar's disconcerting effect: "Wilde, I believe, did me nothing but harm. In his company I lost the habit of thinking."[26] For his part, Wilde was appalled at many aspects of Gide's character. Young André needed molding; most of all he had to liberate himself from his strict, conservative, religious upbringing. Wilde told Gide that his lips were "too straight, the lips 'of someone who has never lied. I must teach you to lie, so your lips will be beautiful and curved like those on an antique mask.' "[27] The previous summer Wilde had found for himself just such a pair of lips, beautiful and curved, on the face of a young English nobleman, Lord Alfred Douglas. Wilde, who was to become the most notorious homosexual celebrity of the era, was in many regards the polar opposite of the austere, virginal, deeply religious Gide. It was only after the transforming encounter with Wilde that Gide began to confront and display his own homosexuality.

Sometime that fall Wilde met Proust. According to Mme Arthur Baignères's two grandsons, it was in her drawing room that Jacques-Émile Blanche introduced the two writers. In their account of the meeting and the subsequent visit Wilde paid Marcel, Wilde was touched by the "enthusiasm for English literature evinced by Proust, by the intelligence revealed by his questions about Ruskin and George Eliot . . . and willingly accepted Marcel's invitation to dinner at boulevard Hauss-mann." Wilde arrived at the Proust apartment ahead of Marcel, who was running late. After having been shown into the drawing room, where he met Proust's parents, Wilde's "courage failed" him and he hid in the bathroom, which is where Marcel found him when he rushed in, breathless. Wilde then said, "Goodbye, dear M. Proust, goodbye." Marcel's parents told him that before Wilde had retreated to the bathroom, he had looked around the drawing room and commented, "How ugly your house is."

Is this account true? Two inaccuracies may indicate that the story is apoc-ryphal. In 1891 Proust had not read John Ruskin, none of whose works had been translated into French, a task to which Proust later applied himself; nor did he reside at 102, boulevard Haussmann, an address that was not to be his until fifteen years later, after the deaths of his parents. The same remark about "your ugly house" is given to Charlus in *The Search*, when he calls upon the Narrator. It is the same disparaging comment that another aesthete, Robert de Montesquiou, made a few years later on viewing the Proust apartment and the often decried furnishings. Wilde was certainly capable of such impertinence. At any rate, Marcel had ob-served, if only briefly, the man to whom he later alluded in his novel as a martyr to society's prejudices, a man who dared to yield to sexual temptation and whose petulance and pride led to his downfall and humiliation.[28]

Le Banquet

Early in 1892 Proust began collaborating on a monthly literary review created by a young poet, Fernand Gregh, and a small group of Condorcet graduates. Jacques Bizet had invited his friends with literary aspirations to meet in his mother's salon, where the founding took place. It was here that Gregh met Proust, who had graduated from Condorcet two classes ahead of him. In addition to Fernand, Jacques, and Marcel, the founders were Robert Dreyfus, Louis de La Salle, Daniel Halévy, and Horace Finaly. After a long debate over a variety of titles—those discussed included *Literary Anarchy, Paths in the Fog,* and *The Guitars*—Daniel Halévy, inspired by their Platonic ideals, proposed the one that was chosen: *Le Banquet,* the French title of Plato's *Symposium.*[29]

The founders agreed to pay monthly dues of ten francs, a sum they found considerable, but one that would guarantee their autonomy. With a budget of approximately one hundred francs a month Gregh believed they could print four hundred copies of a magazine with a professional look, especially with a good connection in the publishing world. Jacques had just the right contact through a close childhood friend, Eugène Reiter, now director of the newspaper *Le Temps*. It was like old times: Condorcet classmates writing, editing, and publishing their own works. Only now they could afford a real printer for their copy and letterhead for their correspondence.

Gregh, who met Proust just as he was nearing the peak of his society period, observed the "elegant young man in tails," with thick, dark hair, in his buttonhole a white camellia, the flower in vogue among the smart set. Marcel's spiffy appearance was somewhat attenuated by his shirtfront, which looked rather "fatigued" because it had been folded and unfolded so many times.[30] Gregh later remembered that friends, even those who were not homosexual, found Proust handsome. When Gregh told his new friend that he looked like a Neapolitan prince out of a Paul Bourget novel, Marcel laughed with delight. Marcel was aware of the impression he made and took some pride in the admiring glances that followed him as he moved through drawing rooms crowded with the era's beautiful people.[31] Gregh characterized as juvenile Marcel's preoccupation with the slight hump in his nose, caused by his childhood fall on the Champs-Élysées. But what astonished Gregh most was Proust's extraordinary intelligence: "His mind possessed resources that seemed truly infinite."[32] His brilliance was evident in conversation, and even in his flattering remarks, but especially in his "magnificent eyes . . . like those of a fly, with a thousand facets," allowing him to examine twenty sides of a subject, making him prodigiously inventive and ingenious.[33]

A letter from Marcel early in the year indicated that he had begun to adopt a schedule at variance with the rest of the world, one that was to provoke many family disputes and ultimately result in his reversing day and night. In a note inviting Gregh to an informal family dinner, Marcel asked him to stop by and inform a member of the household whether he could accept, but urged him not to ring the doorbell, for "I go to bed extremely late and sleep until nearly noon."[34]

Marcel's new hours were not well adapted to the needs of a university student, but they were perfectly suited to someone who wanted to make a career of a glamorous night life, including the society of Princesse Mathilde, the daughter of King Jerome of Westphalia and a niece of Napoléon I. Over seventy when Marcel met her at Mme Straus's, Princesse Mathilde represented the vestiges of Napoleonic glory.

Tremendously proud of her heritage, she boasted of her Corsican origin and took great pleasure in remarking to ancien régime nobles whenever they deplored the French Revolution: "The French Revolution! If it weren't for the French Revolution I would be selling oranges in the streets of Ajaccio."[35] In 1887 Mathilde abruptly ended her long friendship with the historian Hippolyte Taine after he published an article depicting Napoléon I as an upstart Italian condottiere. The next day the princess sent Mme Taine her calling card with the letters P.P.C. marked on it: *pour prendre congé* (to take leave), indicating that she was ending her relationship with the Taines. A wag suggested that the initials really stood for *princesse pas contente* (princess not happy).

Upon entering Mathilde's home in the rue de Berri, which fairly swarmed with eagles and bees—Napoleonic decorative motifs—Marcel felt that he had stepped back in time. Not only did the princess's residence, furnished in Empire Style, recall the glory days of the First Empire, her salon had hosted literary giants as well, such as Gustave Flaubert and Alexandre Dumas. Her soirée began early, with dinner served at 7:30. Like many hostesses she invited one group for dinner, after which others would arrive for the rest of the evening. When guests entered, Mathilde rose to greet the new arrivals, addressing each with a personal remark, giving the guest the impression that he or she was the evening's main attraction.

Proust noticed that the princess, who was short and plump, wore an enormous black pearl necklace, her favorite piece of jewelry. She had a passion for pearls and liked to add new and rare ones to the already magnificent string. Except for her pearls, Marcel found her simplicity remarkable, especially regarding birth and rank. Her "somewhat male gruffness" was somehow rendered endearing by an "extreme sweetness." Marcel's own charm, wit, and intelligence made an excellent impression. The veterans, who remembered how she used to dote on her recent, treacherous lover, the enameler and poet Claudius Popelin, began to refer to Marcel as Popelin the younger.[36]

When Proust began to attend the princess's salon, it was still dominated by an older generation of writers, intellectuals, and socialites. Among the contemporary writers whom Marcel encountered in her salon were Edmond de Goncourt, a veteran from the earliest days, now grown quite elderly; the poet José-Maria de Heredia, and the historian Gustave Schlumberger. Marcel also saw Émile and Geneviève Straus and noted that upon arriving, Émile looked around the room with a malicious air, no doubt rating the success of a rival salon.

The mixture of Mathilde's salon may have been too liberal for some. Here ancien régime aristocrats met and conversed with those upstarts from the Empire nobility. The princess also received members of chic Jewish society, many of whom had held important posts during the Second Empire. The Jewish element, increasingly numerous, provoked the outrage of the anti-Semites Edmond de Goncourt and Léon Daudet, who detested everything connected with Jews and the Empires, First and Second.[37] After one party, Daudet noted in his diary: "The imperial dwelling was infested with Jews and Jewesses."[38]

The princess had a favorite set of anecdotes about those in her entourage, especially her rather simple-minded reader, the baronne de Galbois. Proust, who savored good stories, remembered these examples of innocent imbecility when he created Mme de Varambon. In the *Search,* Mme de Varambon, who is the princesse de Parme's lady-in-waiting, repeats a number of naïve remarks that Proust collected from Mathilde's stories. One evening when snow had been forecast, Mme de Varambon tells a departing guest that he has nothing to fear. "It can't snow anymore because they have taken the necessary steps to prevent it: they've sprinkled salt in the streets!"[39]

For Proust, perhaps the most important acquaintance he made at Mathilde's salon was Charles Ephrussi, a respected art critic, the founder and director of the *Gazette des Beaux-Arts,* and author of a fine essay on Albrecht Dürer. Ephrussi, an important inspiration for Swann, had devoted his life to studying and appreciating art. He greatly admired Vermeer, whose paintings were to become increasingly important to Proust. Marcel questioned Ephrussi about paintings with such eagerness to learn more about them that the art critic invited the young man to view his fine collection, which included works by Gustave Moreau and Claude Monet.

One evening in March, returning home late from a party at which he had admired Comtesse Mailly-Nesle dressed in red, Marcel began to write "Cydalise," a sketch of a society woman.[40] By the time he had finished, the red dress had turned white and the portrait resembled more than anyone else Laure de Chevigné, with whom he had become infatuated that spring. He rose early every day to rush to the avenue Marigny, his "highway of hope," where he waited to see the lady glide by on her morning stroll.[41] Mme de Chevigné, whom he probably met in Mme Straus's salon in 1891, kept her own exclusive salon—one Proust could only dream of entering. Proud to be a descendant of the most notorious figure in French literary history, the marquis de Sade, Mme de Chevigné resented Marcel's spying on her and determined to remain aloof, a tactic that only heightened his curiosity.

Marcel saw in Mme de Chevigné's features traces of Gustave de Waru, an androgynous conflation of aunt and nephew of the sort that always fired Marcel's imagination and libido. Both these beautiful, desirable, yet distant creatures possessed a hooked nose he found "moving," and grace and glamour that surely indicated divine birth. In "Cydalise" the author sees the lady described as Hyppolyta at the theater, where Marcel often admired the fabulous beauties of Paris society. After describing her leaning "on the railing of her box," from which "her white-gloved arms rise straight to her chin," Proust wrote that Hyppolyta "makes one think of a bird dreaming on one elegant and slender leg. It is also charming to watch her feather fan fluttering and beating its white wing." Whenever he encounters "her sons or nephews, who have, all of them, the same beak-like nose, the thin lips, the piercing eyes and too delicate skins," he is moved by the recognition of "her race, the issue, I am sure, of a goddess and a bird." Such creatures, he wrote, add the "idea of the fabulous to the thrill of beauty."[42]

The texts that Proust began to write during this period and on through the *Jean Santeuil* era, which lasted until approximately 1900, constitute the writer's sketchbook, to which he would return and select items for further development. Proust used "Cydalise" many years later as the basis for a similar description of his most famous female aristocrat, the sublimely haughty Oriane de Guermantes, splendidly on display in her box at the opera. The young Narrator also rises mornings and rushes out to glimpse the worldly goddess, who resembles her nephew Saint-Loup, passing down the street.[43]

In the winter of 1891–92, Marcel had befriended a new acquaintance of Robert de Billy's, Edgar Aubert, two years older than himself. Billy, whose noble rank and Protestant religion allowed him to move freely among the Swiss aristocracy, had met Aubert during the summer and learned of his plans to come to Paris in the fall as an attaché to the Swiss embassy.[44] Edgar, the son of a distinguished Geneva magistrate, was a solid fellow with the straight thick neck of an athlete. Like Billy, he loved sports, especially tennis and mountain climbing.

To Marcel, Edgar seemed a sensitive person of strong character and resolve, but one who had not yet found his purpose in life. A good-looking young man with a fine mind and distinguished manners, he had all the qualities necessary to appeal to Proust. Billy described him as "full of personal charm and literary taste."[45] During the winter season Marcel and Robert took Edgar with them to a few of the salons, notably those of Mme Straus and Mme Henri Baignères, where their new friend won admirers with his "serene curiosity, his taste for elegance," and his cosmopolitan outlook, the result of having already lived in London and Berlin. At the Finalys', Edgar impressed everyone with his command of English. Marcel, clearly fascinated by the young polyglot, peppered Aubert with questions about literature and society in the English and German capitals and about his own family. Marcel occasionally met Edgar for lunch or a walk in the Tuileries Gardens.

When Marcel requested Edgar's photograph, the Genevan not only obliged but copied on the back a few lines of verse from an English poet. Marcel, who envied his fluency in English, had to read his favorite anglophone authors, like George Eliot and Ralph Waldo Emerson, in translation. As he scrutinized Edgar's face in the photograph, Marcel thought the verse rather mournful and worried about his friend's melancholy temperament, "his charming sadness."[46] Marcel's unrequited longings, so blatantly expressed in his high school texts, now were submerged in the mysterious, melancholy moods—not unlike those of Watteau's *Fêtes galantes*—of the sketches he penned for *Le Banquet*.

The April issue of *Le Banquet* contained several short pieces by Marcel, including "Cydalise." Forthcoming issues of the cooperative review were to contain similar pieces. "Les maîtresses de Fabrice" (Fabrice's mistresses) and "Snobs 1," from the May issue, allude perhaps to Mme Straus, who enjoyed "balls, horse-racing or even gambling."[47] At year's end Marcel wrote to her, again proclaiming: "I love mysterious women, since you are one, and I have often said so in *Le Banquet*, in which I would often have liked you to recognize yourself."[48] "Snobs," like a number of pieces from this year and the next, warns against the dangers of dissipating one's talents in society or one's virtues in snobbery.

The May 25 issue of *Littérature et critique* carried Marcel's laudatory review of Comte Armand-Pierre de Cholet's travel memoir, *Voyage en Turquie d'Asie: Arménie, Kurdistan et Mésopotamie*. Marcel praised his former lieutenant's display of superior intelligence and admirable energy, proven by his undertaking the difficult and dangerous expedition, and his compelling narration of its successful completion. Cholet's account, filled with "amusing legends" and picturesque observations, contained descriptions that have the "limpidity of watercolors," all told with the authentic accent that derives from scenes "directly observed, or better still, accomplished or endured personally, an accent always inimitable and that goes straight to the heart."[49]

In early June, Marcel wrote Gregh an angry letter about the contents of the latest issue of *Le Banquet*. Proust was incensed that Gregh and the others had accepted an article by Léon Blum containing his thoughts on the suicide of one of his friends. After calling Blum's article so nationalistic in tone that it might have been written by one of Maurice Barrès's lackeys, Proust attacked the piece as being dishonorable and stupid.[50] The reasons for his unusually harsh remarks are unclear. Blum, who was to distinguish himself as a critic, writer, and political leader, did not deserve such condemnation. Marcel's colleagues rejected his opinion. In spite of his virulent opposition and status as a member of *Le Banquet*'s review committee, Proust failed to stop publication of two additional articles by Blum in the July issue.

In the latter half of June, Proust took a series of exams in history and political science, which he passed without distinguishing himself.[51] On the Friday afternoon preceding the last exam on Saturday, he sent Mme Straus a bouquet of flowers with a letter, telling her he would have to miss her afternoon reception on Saturday because his history professor had ruined "my divine Saturday, my day of true happiness, by scheduling my examination in the afternoon rather than in the morning." Because she had teased him about being "lazy" and "interested only in society," he assured her that he had worked "very hard."

Posing

In July, Marcel began visits every Saturday morning to Jacques-Émile Blanche's home in Auteuil to sit for a full-length portrait in oil. The studio and family home were located in a beautiful garden with thick-branched trees; Proust wrote later that Jacques had found fame as a painter in Auteuil, whereas he had found only hay fever.[52] Blanche was a society painter, who frequently produced portraits of prominent figures from the intellectual and artistic milieus of Paris and London. His recent portraits of his compatriots included Edgar Degas, Maurice Barrès, Stéphane Mallarmé, and—just before Proust—André Gide.[53]

During the portrait sessions Blanche and Proust exchanged many stories about the salons they frequented. At idle moments Marcel noted the furnishings that reflected Blanche's taste for the latest British fashion: an English straw-bottomed chair, a mirror-wardrobe, Liberty curtains, and a reproduction of Whistler's portrait of *Pablo Sarasate*. The mingling of light from the lush garden outside with that reflected from the pistachio-colored door and the green water closet often gave the studio an aquarium-like atmosphere.[54]

Tall, well dressed, and somewhat effeminate, Blanche was, according to Proust, a great conversationalist but a difficult friend.[55] The relationship between Marcel and his portraitist was often strained, sometimes to the breaking point. Blanche delighted in gossip, often slandering his friends or setting them at odds with each other. Léon Daudet, a future friend of Marcel's and a chronicler of the era, wrote that he always avoided Blanche "like the plague."[56] But Marcel and Blanche, at the beginning of their relationship, enjoyed each other's company.

In his memoirs, Blanche recalled Marcel's normal attire when out in society: he wore butterfly collars and once a fading orchid as a boutonniere, "a gift no doubt from Lord Lytton the English Ambassador."[57] Later Proust "went in for pale green ties, loosely knotted, baggy trousers, and a frock coat with voluminous skirts." Blanche also remembered Proust's absentmindedness and extravagant, generous nature, all traits that made life endlessly complicated, not only for Marcel himself but for his friends, who were forced to run a permanent lost and found agency for him—though they were royally compensated:

> He carried a Malacca cane which he had a way of twirling whenever he
> stooped to pick up a dropped glove (his gloves were pearl gray with
> black stitching, and were always crumpled and dirty), or was engaged in
> putting on or taking off its fellow. He was forever leaving odd gloves
> about, or would implore their return by post, in exchange for a new pair,
> or for half a dozen new pairs, which he liked to present as a thank-you to
> anyone who would be kind enough to find his strays for him. The same
> thing was constantly happening to his umbrellas, which he left in cabs or
> in the halls of his friends' houses. No matter how dilapidated they might
> be, he continued to use them when his appeal for their return was an-
> swered, though he invariably bought the friend in question a new one at
> Verdier's. His top hats very soon took on the appearance of hedgehogs or
> Skye terriers, as a result of being brushed the wrong way, or rubbed
> against the skirts or furs of his driving companions.[58]

After each sitting, the painter and his model would have lunch with Jacques's father, Dr. Antoine Blanche, home from his nearby private asylum, where his patients included prominent writers, as well as Mme Straus and her relatives. As Proust later recorded, lunch included spontaneous psychological counseling from the good doctor, who "out of professional habit would from time to time urge me to remain calm and moderate. If I expressed an opinion that Jacques contradicted too vehemently, the doctor, admirable for his knowledge and goodness but accustomed to dealing with insane people, would sharply reprimand his son: 'Come, come, Jacques, don't torment him, don't perturb him.'" Then, turning to Marcel, " 'Pull yourself together, my child, try to remain calm; he doesn't believe one word of what he said; drink some cool water, in little sips, while you count to a hundred.' "[59]

Blanche did not record what his thoughts were while he painted Marcel, though he was struck by "the pure oval face of a young Assyrian."[60] But in retrospect he realized that even then he had noticed Marcel's seemingly indefinable age, a quality with which the novelist later endowed the Narrator. Was this striking, engaging person a child, an adolescent, a man? Blanche recorded that at twenty years of age, Proust had acquired this timeless "ambiguity." The best way to characterize him, his portraitist thought, was by the epithet "dear to Freud, . . . polymorphous."[61] Years later Blanche speculated about how Marcel, with "his needs for tyrannical possession," must have appeared to his Condorcet classmates, how he must already have borne "the troubling signs of the pure artist." Blanche wondered whether such a one elected by the gods can love, can be loved? He concluded that the answer was no; a person like Proust can only exist alone.[62] Blanche had identified an essential aspect of his subject's nature, attributable, no doubt, to the pure artist: polymorphous or Protean, Proust would become all the things and people he captured in his seamless, magical net of words and placed in the pages of his book.

Marcel's dominant traits, "unshakable energy and persistence," were evident at the time, but apparently serving no good purpose. His determination seemed aimed at tracking beautiful, elusive women or their male counterparts, young dukes with whom he began to dine more and more often. This was the Proust—the dandy and social climber—whom Blanche depicted in the portrait, an altogether different creature from the one he had quickly drawn in pencil that fall day in Trouville. In the oil portrait, not exhibited publicly until the following year, Marcel stares out at the world with the demeanor of a foppish snob, with the slightly bewildered air of a rising young man about town whose most serious thoughts are his physical appearance and the rank of the hostesses whom he assiduously courts.

The July issue of *Le Banquet* contained three untitled "études" or studies by Marcel. In the first he experiments with a universal theme that was to become a dominant one in the *Search,* dramatized with a Proustian twist: the absolute subjectivity or blindness of erotic desire and the inevitable disappointment that comes with possession.[63] The theme is stated in an opening maximlike sentence, then dramatized by the story: "Desire makes all things flourish, possession withers them." The second study speaks of the fear that society women have of expressing themselves, of being too serious, and of thus seeming to be vacuous.[64] The final study, of another embryonic theme, depicts a person's eyes as the windows through which her past may be read and hints at the false promises seen therein that the lover will believe. Remarks later made by Proust to Mme Straus suggest that this conceit was inspired by her dark, melancholy eyes. Those eyes, now blackened further by a decline into neurasthenia and an increasing dependency on drugs for solace, never ceased to fascinate Marcel.[65]

In late July or early August, Marcel wrote to Fernand, addressing him now as "my dear little Gregh," to complain about the impending series of law exams that forced him to study all day, and about his horrible asthma attacks that kept him up all night so that by evening he was drained of energy and will. To make matters worse, he was lonely; his family had gone to Auteuil, leaving him alone to cope with law books and suffocation. Could Gregh stop by for a moment?[66] One friend who did spend some time with Marcel was Aubert, whom he always found "so charming, witty, and kind."[67] The remaining summer days to be spent in Paris were rapidly drawing to an end, and soon he and his friends would be leaving to begin their long vacations. Aubert intended to vacation with Billy in Switzerland. Marcel would be going to Normandy, but first he must pass these infuriating exams on topics that held no interest for him.

Marcel took the first exam on August 4, with mixed results, receiving three white balls and three red ones, white indicating "satisfactory," the ominous red "barely satisfactory."[68] He was not alarmed at this point. Perhaps he was overly confident; perhaps he simply did not care.

On Sunday, August 7, despite another law exam scheduled for the coming week, Marcel made the short trip from Paris to Saint-Gratien to call upon Princesse Mathilde in her château de Catinat. There he met a distinguished, elderly gentleman right out of the history books he had been studying: Comte Vincent Benedetti, who had been France's ambassador to Berlin in 1870. It was Benedetti's famous, fruitless interview with Emperor Wilhelm I at Ems in July 1870, the purpose of which was to secure a renunciation to the Spanish throne from Prince Leopold of Hohenzollern-Sigmaringen, that provided Bismarck with the casus belli that precipitated the Franco-Prussian War. The count, whom Mathilde invited each year to be her houseguest for several months, impressed Marcel with his intelligence and grace.[69]

As the final days of summer 1892 approached, Marcel studied for his exams and made preparations for vacationing in Trouville as a guest of the Finalys, who had rented, on his recommendation, Les Frémonts from the Arthur Baignèreses. Inspired perhaps by Blanche's furnishings, Marcel had purchased a number of Liberty ties for his vacation. Billy and Aubert called to say good-bye before leaving for Saint-Moritz. Although Edgar remained uncertain about his future plans, he told Marcel, with the calm assurance of a strong, healthy youth: "No matter what happens I shall return." Marcel, who hated farewells and could not bear the thought of being deprived of such pleasant company, felt great relief on hearing Aubert's pledge. He still dreamed of a utopian life in which he would be surrounded by admiring, handsome youths.

From Auteuil during the second week of August, Marcel wrote to Billy at Saint-Moritz to tell him that he had failed the second half of his law exam, a disappointment that plunged his family into a "state of depression." Marcel provided no further details because he was too upset; he would leave, as planned, for Trouville the following Sunday. He closed by saying that he embraced Billy and Aubert, whom he loved with all his heart. "Do you see how useful sealed letters are? I could never have done that with a non-sealable letter."[70]

Trouville

Many of Marcel's friends were vacationing near Trouville. The Strauses had rented Mme Aubernon de Nerville's "adorable property," the Manoir de la Cour Brûlée located at the base of the hill that rose from the shore to Les Frémonts. Mme Straus had invited Fernand Gregh to vacation with them, naïvely believing that the aspiring poet and brilliant student would have a good influence on Jacques, who had begun to show early signs of instability that made his mother fear he might inherit the family disorders of depression and neurasthenia.[71] She hoped that Jacques's problems were merely those he shared with many his age, who, like Marcel, did not appear committed to studies and a serious career.

Although Marcel clearly enjoyed the summer and seemed relatively free from health problems, there was at least one alarming episode. One day he dropped by to see Fernand and Jacques, who were busy developing photographs in an improvised darkroom. Marcel waited in an adjoining room for them to finish. Suddenly, the two photographers heard Marcel make a strange noise. They rushed out to see what was happening and found him nearly unconscious in a corner of the room. Fortunately, Marcel recovered quickly from his mysterious malaise.[72] Had he feigned the spell to attract attention or was his distress genuine?

Fernand, who often came with Jacques to call at Les Frémonts, took a keen interest in the wealthy Jewish family that had rented the villa, and especially in Mary Finaly, Horace's nineteen-year-old sister. Horace, who eventually became director of the Bank of Paris and the Netherlands and, for a time, minister of finance, "was a somewhat short and stout young man, given to metaphysics and melancholy." But the most imposing figure was the family patriarch, the "great man," Baron Horace de Landau, who had made his fortune in Italy representing the Rothschilds during the railway boom of the 1860s.[73] M. de Landau relished being surrounded by his niece, whom he adored, and her family. After dinner a servant would bring the baron, still at table, an enormous German pipe that extended from his mouth nearly to the floor. As Landau talked and drew on the pipe, great clouds of smoke, as thick and steady as those from a locomotive, spewed from his mouth.

The Finalys were enchanted with Les Frémonts, finding the villa to be as beautiful as Marcel had promised. The house had been perfectly sited on the high hill to take full advantage of the property's extraordinary vistas. Fernand noticed that Marcel was attracted to Mary, with her pretty, rather pale face, and sea-green eyes, "a delightful girl, by turns laughing and serious, with whom we were all a little in love."[74] She and Marcel shared a love of music, and gazing into her eyes, he would quote Baudelaire's hypnotic line from "Chant d'automne" ("Autumnal"): "J'aime de vos longs yeux la lumière verdâtre" ("How sweet the greenish light of your long eyes!"), or hum the music Gabriel Fauré had composed for the poem.[75]

Marcel's mother sent brief letters about family activities at Auteuil: the suffocating heat wave that had blasted the Paris region, forcing them to sleep downstairs in the cooler confines of the billiard room, was at last abating. She also reported that they were reading Émile Zola's new novel *La Débâcle,* an account of Napoléon III's humiliating defeat at Sedan and its aftermath, a time she could never forget.

Marcel devoted most of his letter-writing time to his friends Billy and Aubert in Switzerland. A letter in late August to Billy expressed Proust's delight at the effect created by his Liberty ties of "every hue." He also mentioned a new friend, Comte Pierre de Segonzac, who had recently survived being struck by lightning, from whom Marcel regularly received letters ten pages long: "Finally, I have found the friend of my dreams, tender and epistolary. It is true that he only uses a single stamp and each time I have to pay thirty centimes for postage due. But what would one not do for love? Now I am going to crawl under the covers, but first I shake your hands quite affectionately. And even, if you like, I embrace you as well as my little Edgar Aubert."[76]

His mother sent a note in the morning mail complaining about the lack of letters from him. Jeanne seemed unwilling to believe that "no news was good news." Marcel was engaged with parties and other social activities. He had recently been to the racetrack at Deauville with Mme Straus and had lost money on a horse.[77] Had his flirtations with green-eyed Mary distracted him from answering his mother's last letter and two he had received from Aubert? Usually "tender and epistolary" himself, Proust had become rather lackadaisical regarding his duties. Perhaps he was concentrating on writing fiction. He used the back of the note from his mother to begin a story for *Le Banquet* on vanity.

"Violante ou la mondanité" (Violante, or worldly vanities), divided into four short chapters, was Proust's most effective sustained narration to date and contains a number of themes that were to be developed in the *Search:* the struggle of will against the forces of habit; one adolescent's loss of innocence to another already expert at enjoying the pleasures of the flesh; and an episode involving an attempted lesbian seduction.[78] He also wrote a prose poem entitled "La Mer" (The sea).[79]

While Marcel enjoyed the company at the villa and the nocturnal sessions with his muse, Billy and Aubert were making the most of their vacation in the Alps. The weather remained so splendid that the two friends spent many hours outdoors; they played tennis with a young Raja and climbed several summits. At the end of the vacation both men looked vigorous, their faces freshly tanned from the days spent on the courts and the slopes. Before saying good-bye and going their separate ways, they made plans to meet in Paris later in the autumn. Within a week of leaving Saint-Moritz, Billy received the heart-breaking news that on September 18 Aubert had died suddenly of acute appendicitis. Billy wrote immediately to Marcel at Trouville to convey the tragic news without stating the cause of death, perhaps because he had not yet been informed.

On Friday morning, September 23, Marcel received the "crushing letter" and wrote to Billy: "I'm very sad, my dear Robert, and I wish you were here with me so we could talk about Aubert together." Aubert's "return to Paris was one of the joys I was most looking forward to. He was so sure of returning, always saying '*In any case I shall be back next year.*' Now those words break my heart." Marcel regretted bitterly that he, usually so prompt in replying, had not taken time to answer Edgar's last two letters. "I beg you to write and tell me what his illness was, whether he knew how serious it was, what relations he has left behind, whether they resemble him, a thousand things that would not have interested me before, but are so precious to me now because they are the last things I shall know of him."[80] The death stunned Marcel, who mourned not only the company of the attractive young man so full of promise but the loss of all the information he had hoped to glean, the intimate exchange of memories, aspirations, enthusiasms, and projects. This death also reminded him of how little time one might have to accomplish one's goals. Other reminders, just as cruel and unexpected, were to follow.

At the end of September there was great excitement at the villa when Baron

Horace de Landau purchased Les Frémonts from the Baignèreses, for the sum of 152,000 francs, as a gift for his niece Mme Hugo Finaly.[81] For Marcel's part in bringing the two parties together, M. de Landau presented him with a sumptuous cane, which Gregh said looked like a cross between a sugar stick and a royal scepter.[82]

Confessions

After his return to Paris, Marcel and his parents decided that because he had failed the second part of his law exam in August, it would be wise for him to take private lessons with a M. Monnot to supplement his course work. Although he had a law exam scheduled for November 5, Marcel busied himself during October by reviewing Henri de Régnier's volume of poems *Tel qu'en songe* (As in a dream) for *Le Banquet*.[83] Only a few days before the exam he wrote to Laure Hayman a letter full of playful flattery.[84] With the exuberant missive to his "Dear friend, dear delight," came a bouquet of fifteen chrysanthemums. "I should so much have liked to attend that eighteenth-century party, to see those young people who . . . gathered around you. How well I understand them! That a woman who is merely desirable, a mere object of lust, should divide her worshippers and incite them against one another is only natural. But when a woman, like a work of art, reveals to us the most refined charm, the subtlest grace, the most divine beauty, the most voluptuous intelligence, a common admiration for her forges a bond and makes for brotherhood. The worship of Laure Hayman makes men co-religionists." He ended by proposing that the nineteenth century be called the "century of Laure Hayman, the reigning dynasty being that of the Saxes," and asking her to forgive him for "all this foolishness." He then asked permission to call on her after the exam. In the postscript he mentioned what may have been all along the purpose of his fanciful flattery: he angled for the opportunity to meet "the man whom I desire above all to see," her lover Paul Bourget, whom he had never had the luck to encounter.

While waiting for an introduction to Bourget, Marcel was kind enough to arrange for Gregh to meet an emerging philosopher whose reputation would endure. On November 7 Gregh received word that Marcel had succeeded in arranging a dinner with Henri Bergson. He instructed Gregh to arrive "at 7 sharp, no tails," because Bergson was in mourning.[85] Earlier in the year Marcel had been best man in the wedding when Bergson married Mme Proust's cousin Louise Neuburger. Although Gregh intended to become a poet, he was working toward an advanced degree in philosophy. There was no other luminary in the field whom Gregh would rather meet than Bergson. Bergson had already been singled out as the rising philosopher by the social snobs, as well as the intellectual ones who flocked to his public lectures.

Gregh recorded his impressions of this first dinner at the Prousts'. He knew that he was meeting another accomplished person in Dr. Proust, who struck him as a "superb man," though "a little too corpulent, but with a noble visage." Gregh observed that Robert resembled his father just as Marcel did his mother, who was a "delicious woman, an incomparable mother." Next to the hefty couple, Bergson's marked thinness was all the more evident, but he had an enormous head, and his slightest remarks sparkled with intelligence.[86] What amazed Fernand most, per-haps, was how intently Bergson, whose great introspection was evident, listened to others, as though every fiber of his being was tuned to the words being spoken.[87]

As 1892 drew to a close, Marcel continued to press Mme Straus to accord him more of her time by granting private interviews. He pleaded for a great Platonic love, complaining that he must always share her company with so many others. On the rare occasion when he succeeded in seeing her alone, he wrote, she never had more than five minutes, and even then "you are thinking of something else. But that's nothing so far. If one speaks to you of books, you find it pedantic, if one speaks to you of people, you find it indiscreet (if one informs) and curious (if one inquires), and if one speaks to you of yourself, you find it ridiculous." And just when he was on the point, for the hundredth time, of finding her "a lot less delicious . . . suddenly you grant some little favour that seems to indicate a slight preference, and one is caught again."[88] To which Mme Straus replied, ignoring his entreaties and assuring him of her friendship, that he was dotty.[89]

Sometime late in 1892 or early 1893 Marcel answered questions in a second keepsake book. A number of the queries were the same as in the first questionnaire, but in most cases his opinions had evolved or become more refined. His affection and admiration for his mother had not, would not ever change. "*My greatest misfortune would be:* Not having known my mother and grandmother." His favor-ite prose writers were no longer George Sand and Augustin Thierry but Anatole France and Pierre Loti, two contemporary writers, one of whom he could claim as a friend and mentor. Musset, the favorite poet of his adolescence, had been replaced by Charles Baudelaire, by far the one he most admired, and Alfred de Vigny. Marcel's heroes in real life remained his philosophy teachers, Darlu from the lycée and Émile Boutroux, a distinguished philosopher of science with whom he studied at the Sorbonne. His preferred musicians were a trio of Germans: Schumann, Beethoven, and Wagner, the last whose music had become the rage among many in

French society, creating a division between those who, like Proust, considered themselves Wagnerites and those who vehemently denounced this new foreign music. Marcel and his friends had discovered Wagner at the Sunday concerts they attended. Gregh described their astonishment as they listened, experiencing with each fragment "the ecstasy of a revelation."[90]

Proust's answers to what qualities he most preferred in a man or a woman reveal an increasingly complex view of human sexuality, acknowledging androgyny and its appeal for him. *My favorite qualities in a man:* "Feminine charm." *My favorite qualities in a woman:* "Manly virtue and openness in friendship." Another answer shows a new concern about his lack of will: *My greatest fault:* "Not to know how to, not to be able to 'will.' " He may have been made acutely aware of this personal flaw by his parents, who frequently lectured him about changing his behavior, going out less frequently, studying harder, and keeping normal hours; they urged him to stop spending so much money on flowers and other gifts for friends and hostesses, and to stop giving exorbitant tips.

Some of Marcel's answers contained touches of humor. Asked to name the military action he most admired, he replied enthusiastically, "My year of service!" But the majority of his replies show a need for affection. His favorite occupation was no longer, as it had been at sixteen, "reading, daydreaming, poetry, history, theater," but, in a single word, "loving." He wanted to be petted and spoiled and to live in a country "where certain things I desire would come true as though by enchantment and where feelings of tenderness would always *be shared.*"

Perhaps he feared that he would never find a true companion. Who could possibly satisfy his great need for affection and devotion? Although he genuinely liked women and was sensitive to their seductive charms, he seems already to have understood that he could not find fulfillment in their love. In spite of the obvious—perhaps too obvious—flirtations with attractive young women like Jeanne Pouquet, and occasional rumors about girlfriends or cousins he might marry, nothing indicates that Marcel or his parents ever considered marriage a serious prospect for him. In 1892, when Marcel was twenty-one and Gregh only nineteen, they wrote portraits of each other. Fernand took his title from the character Marcel had created for his sketches of Italian comedy, Fabrice, and in the first line stated Marcel's greatest wish: "Fabrice needs to be loved."[91]

On December 31, when the government announced the year's honors for distinguished service to France, Dr. Adrien Proust was named commander in the Légion d'honneur. Marcel, proud of his father's most recent distinction, celebrated the arrival of 1893 at the Finalys' sumptuous Paris mansion.

At the beginning of the new year Robert de Billy, much to Marcel's sorrow, left for Berlin, where he assumed his first diplomatic post as a trainee. Soon afterward Marcel wrote to Billy, confessing that he was not doing anything worthwhile. Paul Baignères had asked him to pose for a portrait, "providing a pretext for my recent inactivity."[92] Although he lamented the lack of any great change in his "sentimental life," he did boast of a new, attentive friend who came to see him nearly every day, "the young and charming and intelligent and good and affectionate Robert de Flers. Ah! you other Robert, hurry back to Paris to learn how one must love one's friends."[93] Flers, another of Le Banquet's authors, became, after Dreyfus and Billy, the third Robert in Proust's intimate circle. A student of law and literature, Flers was to have a distinguished career as a journalist and coauthor of light comedies with Gaston de Caillavet and, later, Francis de Croisset.

On January 25 Marcel enrolled in law school for the new term. The next day he wrote to Billy about a parcel that had arrived unexpectedly, containing a memento that Aubert had chosen for him. The unnamed souvenir and the prospect of a premature spring gave him the illusion of Edgar's presence. Then Marcel, turning to practical matters, informed Billy that only one day after registration he had already lost his assignment sheets: "Do be kind enough to give me another list of the four examinations I should take and the books I should read. . . . Don't forget." Did it occur to Proust that Billy might find it odd for him to request information, readily available at his law school in Paris, from a faraway friend in Berlin? Adrien, alarmed at Marcel's lack of progress and commitment, insisted that he continue the private law lessons at home with M. Monnot. Pierre Lavallée, a friend from Condorcet, who also wanted to increase his own chances of passing the exams, sometimes joined Marcel for the help sessions that would last until the end of July.

Marcel's last contribution to Le Banquet was an article in the February issue about a new club, which Proust apparently joined, where students from the École libre des sciences politiques staged mock parliamentary debates. In his piece Marcel heaped praise on his fellow students, many of whom were socially prominent and certain to be future deputies, at one point declaring that each of them was endowed with "true political genius."[94] Gregh, who feared that the debaters were being flattered and treated to Proustifications, placed a disclaimer at the bottom of Marcel's article, saying the opinions expressed were solely those of the author. Whether or not Marcel's feelings were wounded, the March issue, the eighth and the last, contained nothing by him. Without giving a reason or saying farewell to its readers, Le Banquet ceased to exist. Robert Dreyfus later wrote that the little magazine had run its course; the coffer was empty and the young writers had "played enough" at their declared vocation.[95]

Marcel, who had published fifteen sketches, stories, essays, and reviews, filling approximately forty pages in *Le Banquet,* began to entertain the idea of collecting these pieces and others unpublished, or to be written, into a volume. He had in mind several stories, some more ambitious than any he had written so far, to flesh out a small volume of "exquisite" prose. Surely, such a book would impress his father, please his mother, signal his accomplishment—however slight for the moment—and prove to all his determination to devote himself exclusively to writing.

He and his friends had reached the age where it was time not only to begin a career but to think of matrimony. On April 11 Gaston Arman de Caillavet married Jeanne Pouquet. In May the newlyweds left for an extended honeymoon trip to Italy, accompanied by Gaston's mother and Anatole France. Marcel envied Gaston's happiness and wondered whether he would ever depart on such a journey with his beloved, to a land filled with art treasures like those found in Rome, Florence, and Venice.

He feared not. He invented stories in which he was the male lover or the female lover; he cursed the exclusiveness of one sex and dreamed of being an androgyne or a hermaphrodite, some fabulous creature who would experience the delights of both sexes, who would not be condemned to wander in the desert of homosexual desire. Perhaps he envied Oscar Wilde, a writer who had achieved a name for himself, who had married and fathered two children and yet, so rumor said, kept young men for a different kind of love in a London hotel. Would he ever marry? Would he ever have a family? The thought of the entanglements, complications, and obligations of conjugal love horrified him. He intended to have only one master/mistress of his soul—literature.

Meanwhile, he continued to pay court to society ladies, pretending more and more as he spun tales in his mind that he was one himself and that, if he were, he would find the perfect lover—or if not, a cad who would make him sublimely unhappy. His friends had already divined who he was: polymorphous, ambiguous, and a pure artist. But what would he write? And how could he convince his parents to yield in the struggle to force him to choose a despised career?

5   *A Man About Town*   ❧

IN LATE 1892 OR EARLY 1893 Marcel began frequenting the salon of Madeleine Lemaire.[1] On Tuesdays in April and May, aristocrats, artists, writers, musicians, singers, actors, political figures, foreign ambassadors, and army generals, for whom the hostess had a soft spot, rushed to Lemaire's tiny home with its adjacent studio at 35, rue de Monceau, not far from the Arc de Triomphe. Although the glass-enclosed studio was quite large, inevitably a number of the guests, unable to find a vacant chair, remained standing in the garden under the lilac trees.

The aristocrats included Comte Boniface de Castellane, known to his friends as Boni, soon to become immensely rich by marrying the American railway heiress Anna Gould; Comtesse Adhéaume de Chevigné, the grand lady whom Marcel had shadowed in the streets; the duc and duchesse de Luynes; the duc and duchesse d'Uzès; the duc and duchesse de Brissac; as well as members of the Jewish aristocracy, such as the Rothschilds. The celebrated actors Sarah Bernhardt, Réjane, and Mounet-Sully often attended, as did the society painters Édouard Detaille, Jean Béraud, and Georges Clairin. Clairin, known familiarly as Jojotte, was Sarah Bernhardt's intimate friend and portraitist. Among the writers often present were Pierre Loti, Jules Lemaître, and Anatole France.

Madeleine's choice of friends and her genuine appreciation for the arts made her salon one of the most stimulating and amusing in Paris. A music lover, she offered her guests the occasion to listen to some of Paris's most distinguished composers. One might hear Camille Saint-Saëns, Jules Massenet, or Gabriel Fauré at the piano playing their own works or accompanying a singer. Madeleine, tall, lively, witty, and heavily made up, insisted upon silence during performances of music or poetry readings. If a guest dared to speak above a whisper, she did not hesitate to silence the offender.

Her daughter Suzette, unmarried at twenty-seven, also painted and helped her mother entertain. An accomplished watercolorist, Madeleine had won notoriety for her depictions of flowers, especially the roses she often painted on fans and sold dearly. One of her lovers, Alexandre Dumas fils, said that she had created more roses than anyone except God.[2] On his first visit to her studio, Marcel had admired the roses, both real and in watercolors, that seemed to be everywhere. Every Tuesday when the guests entered the studio, they saw the watercolor in progress that the hostess had just abandoned for their arrival. This ruse permitted them to admire her latest work while she maintained the pretense of being a serious artist, forced to lay down her brush because a large crowd of society people happened to drop in. Her friends were careful to maintain the fiction that the artist did not operate a salon. This pretense was somewhat belied at the soirée's conclusion when she would tell departing guests about the next week's attractions—on one occasion Francisco Tamagno and Jean de Reszké, two tenors much in demand—and urge them to make certain that they arrived early.

Marcel studied Mme Lemaire and the way she ruled her salon with an authoritarian air, her love of music, her way of doubling over in laughter, her hatred of "bores," and her hostility toward "deserters"—those who strayed away from the fold of the "faithful," as she called her adored regulars. He was often a guest in her château at Réveillon in Seine-et-Marne, where she spent the early part of summer, before moving on to her seaside villa in Dieppe in late August or early September.

On an April evening in 1893, when Mme Lemaire had resumed her Thursday dinner-receptions for a more select list of guests, Marcel met one of the most talented, extravagant, eccentric figures in French society, Comte Robert de Montesquiou-Fezensac. An account of the gala evening appeared in *Le Gaulois*'s April 14 edition, where "the great artist's" salon was described as "one of the intellectual centers of Parisian society." The newspaper reported that the actress Julia Bartet read to the elite audience, in an exquisite manner, poems by José-Maria de Heredia and Montesquiou. At thirty-eight, Montesquiou, eager to enter the poetry lists, had just published his first volume of verses, and the reading was intended to celebrate and publicize what the count saw as a literary milestone. After the reading, Madeleine brought Marcel to congratulate the count.

The hostess supposedly introduced Proust to Montesquiou as her delightful page, begging the conceited and often irascible count to be kind to the intimidated youth. Montesquiou, a connoisseur of masculine beauty, noted the attractive student's large eyes, exquisite manners, and eagerness to please. Recognizing Marcel's potential as an admiring disciple, Montesquiou gave him permission to call at his Paris home at 8, rue Franklin.

Montesquiou, arbiter of taste and epitome of aristocratic hauteur, poet, artist, critic, and patron of the arts, had already furnished novelist Joris-Karl Huysmans with the model for French literature's most renowned decadent aesthete, Des Esseintes. He was to supply Proust, over the years, with the major ingredients for one of his most famous characters, the disdainful, vituperative—at times hysterical—homosexual baron de Charlus. Montesquiou was descended from several marshals and statesmen, including the dashing D'Artagnan, hero of Alexandre Dumas's *The Three Musketeers*. Elegantly dressed, often in tones of gray and black as though he just stepped out of his portrait by Whistler, Montesquiou might remove a glove to show off "a single ring, simple and strange." Whether in conversation or reciting poems, the count displayed a remarkable set of mannerisms. As he spoke, his gesticulations became more and more impassioned until he lifted a finger high in the air and, his voice rising like a trumpet, he would stamp his foot, throw back his head, and release his hysterical laughter. Léon Daudet, who detested Montesquiou, noticed that after the outburst of "shrill laughter . . . as though seized by remorse, the count would place his hand over his mouth and rear back, until his inexplicable mirth ended, as though he had been inhaling 'laughing gas.'" Proust was amused by such a spectacle, while admiring the count's extraordinarily rich vocabulary and knowledge of the arts.[3]

Marcel also became acquainted with Montesquiou's lover and companion— some said slave—Gabriel d'Yturri. Gabriel was born in Argentina in 1864. In his teens, Gabriel had fled the country because of civil unrest.[4] After a stay in Lisbon he somehow made it to Paris, where he met Montesquiou in 1885 at the École des Beaux-Arts while viewing the Delacroix exhibition. In his memorial to Yturri, Montesquiou recalled that "this young Argentinian, only recently arrived in the capital, had heard talk of me here, in a manner that seduced him." Montesquiou was seduced as well by Yturri's dark brown eyes and his "features of a young hero of antiquity, proud, able-bodied, and graceful." The young man was also intelligent and enthusiastic, with a genuine passion for the arts. For Yturri, "Montesquiou represented . . . the whole historic past of France, all the painters, all the books, all the charms, and all the seductions of the intellect."[5] In a note to Montesquiou, written shortly after they met, Yturri indicated his eagerness to serve the count: "You know that I am devoted to you, body and soul, and for all my life. So use me as you wish. I would give everything to spare you any moment of sadness." Soon the count had Yturri located in an apartment near his and employed as his secretary. Immediately Yturri adopted as his own the tastes and habits of his master; he proved as adept in scouring for antiques as in planning entertainments for high society.[6]

Before the chance encounter with Montesquiou at the exhibition, Yturri had been selling ties at the Carnaval de Venise, a shirtmaker on the boulevard de la Madeleine.[7] Baron Doäzan, a flamboyant homosexual who wore makeup and perfumes, had already sought to engage Yturri as his secretary, but Montesquiou easily lured the young Argentinian away from the scandalous, ridiculous baron.[8] Doäzan was an intimate friend of another notorious homosexual, critic, poet, and scurrilous journalist, Jean Lorrain, soon to become Montesquiou's nemesis. Montesquiou's snatching of Yturri from Doäzan's clutches may have fueled Lorrain's jealous hatred of the count. Lorrain also worshiped Sarah Bernhardt, who paid far more attention to Montesquiou than to Lorrain, whose talents, tastes, and expertise were greatly inferior to those of his rival.

Montesquiou introduced Yturri to his own circle of family and friends as Don Gabriel de Yturri, bestowing on him a noble lineage. Although some remained skeptical, especially Montesquiou's father, most quickly understood that if they wanted the count's company they must accept his friend. Many who despised Montesquiou found Yturri likable, even charming. Léon Daudet, for example, thought Yturri "far superior in intelligence and sensitivity to his super-pretentious master." Only Yturri knew how to calm the count's fury.[9] Gabriel often said to Robert, as he was allowed to call him when the two were alone: "I came to humanize you."

Few Frenchmen dared, if they cared for their reputation and social standing, to display amorous affection for another man. Yet Montesquiou seemed not to fear the reaction of the most conservative members of his family and entourage. In his relationship with Yturri, his conduct appeared not only courageous but honorable, as he noted in the poem to his late companion from the 1906 edition of *Les Hortensias bleus* (Blue hydrangeas):

Un honneur me viendra d'avoir aimé sans feinte,
Ce qui n'inspire encore à d'autres, que la crainte.

Honor will come to me for having loved without feigning,
That which inspires so far in others only fear.

With Montesquiou, Marcel immediately assumed the role of fawning disciple. Not only did he find this extravagant person fascinating, but he knew that Montesquiou held the key to some of Paris's most exclusive salons. Marcel lost no time in writing to Montesquiou, asking if he could indeed call on the poet, signing the letter "Your most respectful, fervent and charmed Marcel Proust."[10] The count replied that he would receive Marcel on Thursday, April 20, at 4 P.M.

The appointment apparently went well, and Montesquiou showed his visitor the garden in which grew a number of rare and beautiful specimens, cared for by his Japanese gardener. Marcel sent Montesquiou an enormous bouquet of lilies and pale Florentine irises to thank him for the visit. In his thank-you note, Marcel informed Montesquiou that he had just purchased the count's book of poems *Les Chauves-souris* (The bats), on whose wings he was taking flight "to rise in your esteem."[11] In a reciprocal flourish, the count sent Marcel the deluxe edition of *Les Chauves-souris*, occasioning another letter of thanks in which Marcel used imagery indicating his eagerness to worship at the poet's shrine: this book would remain for him "an imperishable bouquet, a definite censer . . . of my memories, a glorious trophy for which I thank you with all my heart." Other letters and a telegram followed in which Marcel assured the count that his soul was "a rare and select garden like the one in which you allowed me to walk the other day."[12] Montesquiou, for the moment, appeared to be the perfect target for Proustifications.

On May 8 the 1893 Salon of the Champ de Mars opened its annual painting exhibition. Jacques-Émile Blanche showed eleven portraits, including Proust's in its original full-length version. Some viewers saw the painting as anything but flattering; Blanche himself referred to it as the "execrable" study, although "very lifelike."[13] Maurois later saw in the portrait "a mixture of the dandified and the limp which reminded one, for a brief moment, of Oscar Wilde."[14] Visitors to the exhibition must have wondered who this rather perplexed and foppish young man was. Proust later wrote a self-parodying description of the portrait in *Jean Santeuil*, where a similar likeness of Jean is attributed to one of Blanche's rivals, a society painter named La Gandara: "The radiant young man self-consciously posing before all Paris, with neither shyness nor bravado in his looks, gazing out from light-coloured elongated eyes with an air about them of fresh almonds, eyes less expressive of actual thought than seemingly capable of thought . . . beauty not perhaps thoughtful so much as pensive, the very visual sign of a delicate and happy life."[15]

In the same passage, Marcel evoked lightheartedly the family concerns about his social life and lack of seriousness. Jean's parents, who had "at first encouraged Jean to go out and about in society where he reveled in the position he had made for himself, were irritated now when they saw that he was no longer either working, reading, or even thinking, and for the last few months at least had shown no signs of anything approaching regret or shame." M. Sandré, based on Nathé Weil, expresses his opinion to his daughter: "That boy could have done anything he liked, but as things are now he will never do anything."[16] Such a prospect was rapidly becoming Jeanne and Adrien's greatest fear.

In early June, Paris's least enthusiastic law student asked his parents to preside at a dinner honoring his best friends. Marcel sent Billy the seating plan, over which he had agonized for hours. The status of six of these "best" friends—four counts and two viscounts—indicate Marcel's fascination with handsome young men with titles.[17] Among those invited were Fernand Gregh, Robert de Flers, and Léon Yeatman, a fellow law student. Robert Proust, soon to enter medical school, sat between Jacques Baignères and Count Gustave de Waru. On his mother's left Marcel placed a new English friend, Willie Heath, a cousin of Edgar Aubert's, whose place Heath had taken as an attractive and idealized young foreigner.[18] The place of honor on Mme Proust's right was occupied by the comte de Grancey.

In the letter to Billy, Marcel stated his intention to spend August in Saint-Moritz, if he passed his law exams—no doubt a paternal condition. Louis de La Salle had promised to accompany him to the resort and share the same pension. Marcel may have wished to visit, for sentimental reasons, the place where Aubert had spent the last happy days of his short life, a pilgrimage Marcel had likely discussed with Willie Heath.

Relatively little is known about Heath except that at age twelve he converted from Protestantism to Catholicism. In the spring of 1893 he and Marcel often met for leisurely strolls in the Bois de Boulogne. As they talked, Marcel observed Willie's "impenetrable, smiling eyes," which seemed "fastened upon an unspoken enigma." The two young men, their artistic nervous systems fully attuned to each other, ambled through the vast park in its springtime splendor, hatching utopian plans to "spend more and more of our lives with one another in a circle of men and women chosen for their great-heartedness, and sufficiently far removed from foolishness and vice and malice to give us a feeling that we were proof against the arrows of men's spite."[19]

It has been said that Aubert and Heath resembled each other.[20] Yet if the available photographs are accurate, the cousins looked nothing alike. Edgar Aubert was a solid-looking young man with strong features, albeit with somewhat dreamy eyes, as Marcel noted, whereas Willie Heath had the appearance of a young dandy with features as delicate as those of Laure Hayman's figurines. Heath, like many with whom Marcel became infatuated, seemed the very picture of the well-dressed aesthete, posing for his formal photograph in elegant tails with top hat, cane, and gloves, a flower in his boutonniere and a slim, leather-bound volume as an added prop. Apparently, Heath was not reticent and sarcastic as Aubert could be on occasion, and he eagerly joined Marcel in his dream of escaping to an idyllic colony of handsome youths, sensitive and loving.

During the early summer months, Marcel began what appeared to be a genuine flirtation with Mlle Germaine Giraudeau, whom he met at Pierre Lavallée's. Marcel had obtained Germaine's photograph and described it in such heated terms in her autograph book that the girl's confessor ordered her to tear out the page and destroy the passage, thereby denying herself—and anyone else—the opportunity to read it again.

Marcel had already begun using events from his life as grist for his literary mill and his flirtation with Germaine provided the occasion for a heterosexual fantasy. At times he may have considered marriage as a convenient screen for his true erotic longings, as do some homosexuals depicted in the *Search*. Although he asked Pierre Lavallée, in a July letter, whether he knew where Germaine was, Marcel quickly lost interest in her, as he always did in young, unattached women.[21]

In late June, Marcel received a prepublication copy of *Le Chef des odeurs suaves* (The commander of heavenly odors), Montesquiou's second collection of poems, devoted almost exclusively to flowers. Marcel, who adored flowers, wrote to thank the count: "Sir, I have been lying since this morning in this starry meadow, worshipping this heaven of flowers. I am dazzled by all these perfumes, intoxicated by so much light."[22] He continued his praise by quoting verses that he thought were the most marvelous Montesquiou had ever written and ended by comparing the poems to the creations of Richard Wagner and Leonardo da Vinci. In a postscript, he reminded Montesquiou to send the promised photograph.

When the count replied that it would be improper to send a photograph through the mail, Marcel suggested that, because they were both to attend parties at Madeleine Lemaire's and the princesse de Wagram's, perhaps Montesquiou would be so kind as to bring the photograph with him—a proposition that Montesquiou must have considered even more improper than using the postal service. Marcel then fished for an introduction to two ladies who were at the summit of Parisian society: "I shall also ask you . . . to point out to me some of those lady friends in whose circles you are most often spoken of (the Comtesse Greffulhe, the Princesse de Léon)."[23] Comtesse Greffulhe, Montesquiou's cousin, was the lady whom Proust was most eager to meet, because of her reputation as Paris's most beautiful and exalted hostess. A few days later Marcel wrote again to Montesquiou, with more praise for his poems: "In the midst of the torture that studying for my law exam is inflicting upon me and will continue to inflict until July 31, these verses are for me, as Baudelaire said, 'a divine opium.' " He also hinted that he would like to be invited to the count's property at Versailles.[24]

La Revue blanche

Marcel had recently submitted sketches, similar to those that had appeared in *Le Banquet,* to *La Revue blanche,* the first serious, independent review to publish his works. Founded in 1889 in Liège by Paul Leclercq, the review moved in 1890 to Paris, where it was taken over and financed by Alexandre and Thadée Natanson. The review, which often featured covers by such artists as Henri de Toulouse-Lautrec and Édouard Vuillard, rapidly became one of the most important and lively periodicals in France, closely associated with the symbolist and other modern literary movements. Among the writers it discovered or fostered were Paul Verlaine, Stéphane Mallarmé, Henri de Régnier, and André Gide.[25] Claude Debussy was its musical critic.

The editors obviously had a high opinion of Proust's work: the July–August issue included nine of his sketches. One of these, an amusing parody of Flaubert's comic novel *Bouvard and Pécuchet,* was dedicated to "my three dear Roberts" (his brother and friends Robert de Flers and Robert de Billy). "Bouvard and Pécuchet: Social Ambitions" showed Marcel's ability to mimic the manner, tone, and style of authors he admired. The topic also allowed him to amuse his friends by poking fun at his own intoxication with high society. Flaubert had taken grim delight in collecting clichés, pearls of human imbecility, that he used in his novels to reveal the shallowness and wrongheadedness of contemporary society. Bouvard and Pécuchet are two bachelor copyists who, due to an unexpected inheritance that makes them wealthy, take early retirement and become encyclopedic autodidacts.

In Proust's parody Bouvard and Pécuchet face the problem of how to succeed in high society.[26] "Now that we have a situation," said Bouvard, "why shouldn't we go into society?" Having decided that "contemporary literature is of prime importance" in achieving social status, they began to read numerous reviews and converse "on what they had read, endeavoring to imitate people in society. Bouvard would lean his elbow on the mantelpiece, toying cautiously, so as not to soil them, with a pair of light-colored gloves brought out for the occasion, calling Pécuchet 'Madame' or 'Général,' to complete the illusion."

In his satire, Proust pokes fun at the conventional wisdom that critics, dilettantes, and society people spouted about contemporary authors, including some of his acquaintances, such as Anatole France: Bouvard and Pécuchet "disparaged everything. Leconte de Lisle was too unemotional, Verlaine had too much sensibility. Mallarmé has more talent than the others, but is a brilliant talker. What a pity that such a gifted man should go mad as soon as he picks up his pen. As for France, he is a good writer but a bad thinker, the contrary of Bourget, who is profound but with no sense of form. They felt sad at the scarcity of genuine talent. . . . In short, everybody writes badly. According to Bouvard the excessive desire for originality is to blame; according to Pécuchet it is due to the decadence of our morals."

Bouvard and Pécuchet ultimately conclude that it is "better to avoid talking literature in society."[27] The story ends with a discussion of the Jews in French society, in which Proust enumerates disparaging remarks similar to ones found in the writings of many contemporaries, such as Edmond de Goncourt and Léon Daudet. While saying it was wrong to condemn the Jews, "(one must be liberal), Bouvard and Pécuchet admitted they detested being with them. All Jews once sold opera-glasses in Germany when they were young, have retained—and with a piety to which as impartial critics we must do justice—their religious observances. . . . They all have hooked noses, exceptional minds, and servile souls that think of nothing but making money."

Perhaps it was still possible when Proust wrote this to believe anti-Semitism a trivial matter, but within a few years one of the most traumatic affairs in French history was to prove that the roots of bigotry were deeply embedded in the soul of France.

Marcel was unquestionably extravagant; he earned nothing, spent prodigiously, and never seemed to know the value of money. What his parents saw as their duty to teach him fiscal responsibility he viewed as an unfair and parsimonious attitude. His contempt for their efforts is expressed in *Jean Santeuil,* where the hero's parents represent conservative bourgeois values: "One never went to evening parties, nor came home in a cab, any more than one changed one's clothes several times a day. One spent as little money as possible. Needless expenditures, generous gifts, fanciful indulgences, were looked upon as crimes, to be greeted with anger."[28] Marcel was aware of the advantages he enjoyed, but thrift or even moderation were not ideas he understood. He did not wish to offend those who were less well off, but for those he wanted to please or reward he saw excessive generosity as the appropriate way to express the love and gratitude with which he overflowed.

Toward the end of his life, Proust recalled his embarrassment as a wealthy adolescent when he became aware of distinctions among classes based primarily on money.[29] When he met fellow students at the Saint-Lazare station who were returning to Auteuil, he hid his first-class ticket and rode with them in a third-class wagon, trying to look as though he never traveled any other way. He also kept secret from the other young men in the neighborhood his invitations to social events, with unintended comic results. His neighbors assumed that he had no friends willing to invite him out. Although they pitied him, they decided—the rules of snobbery operating at all levels of society—that it would be best to keep Marcel away from people they considered smart. A young man from the neighborhood, accompanied by a couple named Dutilleul whom he wanted to impress, encountered Marcel and pretended not to know him in order to avoid an introduction.

This snub occurred on the very day Marcel was to attend the princesse de Wagram's ball. His parents, anticipating the showdown over Marcel's choice of a career and his extravagant ways, refused to let him use the family coach, whose horses had already been unharnessed for the evening, or even to hire a modest hackney cab. Adrien declared that the solution was obvious: Marcel had only to take the double-decker Auteuil-Madeleine bus that stopped right at their door and continued on toward the Seine, stopping at the avenue de l'Alma, where the princess had her town house. For a boutonniere Marcel had to settle for a rose cut from Uncle Louis's garden, without a silver-paper sheath.

Once on the bus whom should Marcel encounter but the young man who had wanted to avoid introducing him to the "smart" Dutilleuls. "Well," his neighbor exclaimed, "since you never go out, why are you in evening dress?" Marcel admitted that he was going to a ball. "Ah, so you do at least attend balls. Congratulations. And may I ask which one?" Not wanting to show off by uttering the word *princesse,*

Proust murmured he was going to "the Wagram Ball," unaware that a public ball for waiters and servants, held in the Salle Wagram, was known as the Wagram Ball. The young man seemed relieved, even pleased, "How delightful." But then he looked at Marcel sternly and admonished him, "My good fellow, one should not pretend to be invited out when one has no social connections to the point of being reduced to attending servants' balls, where you even have to pay admission!"

The day after Princesse Wagram's ball, Marcel, still under the spell of the fabulous evening, wrote to tell Montesquiou that he had finally seen Comtesse Greffulhe: "Her hair was dressed with Polynesian grace, and mauve orchids hung down to the nape of her neck." He had been particularly taken with her eyes: "The whole mystery of her beauty lies in the brilliance and especially the enigma of her eyes. I have never seen a woman so beautiful. I didn't ask to be introduced to her and I shall not even ask that of you, for apart from the indiscretion that might imply, it seems to me that speaking to her would agitate me rather painfully." He did ask the count however, to tell the lady what an "enormous impression" she had made.[30]

There is no reason to suspect Marcel of exaggerating. The countess, bejeweled, corseted, dressed in true elegance, with perfectly proportioned features, had a figure that could easily rival that of Venus on her pedestal at the Louvre. Née Princesse Élisabeth de Caraman-Chimay, Montesquiou's thirty-three-year-old cousin was at the height of her reign over Parisian society. Energetic, breathtakingly beautiful, she was an active patron of musical and artistic events. She had married the fabulously wealthy Belgian banking tycoon Henri Greffulhe, whose face, with its flattened, inexpressive features, Jacques-Émile Blanche likened to a king in a deck of cards. Proust recalled the countess nearly two decades later when he began to create her fictional counterpart, the duchesse de Guermantes, to whom he would impart Geneviève Straus's wit. Élisabeth Greffulhe was not shy about her position in Paris or even in the cosmos; her sense of self-importance rivaled that of Louis XIV. On one occasion she wrote to Montesquiou: "I have only been understood by you . . . and the sun!"[31]

A few days after the ball, Marcel had Montesquiou's photograph in his possession, a likeness that showed the count in profile with his hand on his forehead, deep in poetical meditation. The picture bore as its inscription the first line of his poem "Maestro," from Les Chauves-souris: "I am the Sovereign of Transitory Things."[32] In his letter of thanks, Marcel found the title too modest, telling the count that he also ruled over things eternal; then he observed: "I have long been aware that you far transcend the type of the exquisite decadent, whose features . . . have been imputed to you. But in these times without thought or will, in a word without genius, you alone excel by the twofold force of your meditation and your energy."[33] To which the satisfied count replied briefly, sparing a moment from ruling over the universe to congratulate himself on having formed such a disciple, one capable of reading poetry with the attitude he had recommended: "ingenious and sensitive, judicious and lucid."[34]

While studying for his law exams set for late July, both of which he would pass, Proust dashed off an unsigned review of Comte Henri de Saussine's novel *Le Nez de Cléopâtre* (Cleopatra's nose) for the *Gratis-Journal,* a free publicity sheet for Ollendorff publishers. Proust provided a text that would be any publicist's dream for blurbs, comparing the count to Zola, Stendhal, and Tolstoy, while claiming his novel displayed originality.

In the salon of the comte and comtesse de Saussine, Marcel met an unusually talented young pianist who also composed. Now nineteen, Léon Delafosse had been a child prodigy at thirteen, winning first prize at the Conservatory of Music. He had soon become the protégé of the Saussines, who were devoted music lovers and friends of Gabriel Fauré's and Claude Debussy's. Marcel, duly impressed by Léon's elegance, talent, and looks, began calling him the "Angel."

Many who heard Delafosse at the piano and saw his fine features might have thought that an angel was at play on the ivory keys. Fernand Gregh described him, in what was probably not intended as a compliment, as one of the "prettiest men" of his generation. Like Proust's future character Morel, a noted violinist who was the son of a valet, Léon was the child of a concierge and a mother who gave piano lessons. The mother's gift to her son had allowed him to rise above his class. Thanks to his grace and remarkable talent, Delafosse was welcomed into the best drawing rooms of Paris, where women swooned over his looks and his skillful, sensitive playing. He lived in an elegant apartment near the Bois and, on several occasions, invited Fernand, Marcel, and Louis de La Salle to lunch. Delafosse's guests were surprised that a young musician from an extremely modest background, who seldom gave concerts, could afford the sumptuous apartment and lifestyle. Had Delafosse a wealthy admirer who supported him? The young men, all of whom had artistic ambitions, talked about poetry and music and how to live while devoting all one's time and efforts to art. Shortly after Marcel and Léon became acquainted, the pianist set one of his poems, "Mensonges" (Lies), to music. The lies the poet spoke of were those he had found in love, love that was never true, that never fulfilled its promises.

Three Stories

In the summer of 1893, not long after seeing Mme Greffulhe at the ball, Proust wrote *L'Indifférent*, a novella whose beautiful, much sought-after heroine was most likely inspired by the countess.[35] Although marred by a lack of narrative sophistication and well-defined characters, *L'Indifférent* is an important work because it contains in embryonic form a number of themes and images that were to become permanent elements of Proust's fictional universe. The story is about Madeleine, who falls helplessly in love with Lepré, a man who cannot return her affection.[36] At the end of the story, she learns that Lepré leads a secret, scandalous life that explains his indifference to decent women. Lepré can make love only to prostitutes, whom he pursues relentlessly.[37] This trait is similar to that given to Swann, a highly eligible bachelor who, rather than making a good marriage and settling down, prefers to seduce servant girls and cooks.

Before leaving for his Swiss holiday, Proust wrote "Mélancolique Villégiature de Mme de Breyves" (The melancholy summer of Mme de Breyves), another story about unrequited love that was to be published in the September issue of *La Revue blanche*.[38] Here the narration is more skillful, perhaps because he had just treated the same theme and similar characters in *L'Indifférent*.

In the December 1893, issue of *La Revue blanche*, Proust published a story called "Avant la nuit," his first story about same-sex love.[39] In this story, Marcel attempts to justify homosexuality through a female narrator, Françoise. To relieve her conscience before dying, she confesses her reason for attempting suicide to her best friend, a man named Leslie. First, Françoise repeats Leslie's own words about not scorning Dorothy, a mutual friend who had been caught in a compromising situation with a chanteuse: Socrates, a wise and just man, tolerated homosexual behavior among his friends.

After acknowledging the superiority of natural, procreative love, Françoise argues that in instances of lovemaking whose purpose is not procreative there can be no "hierarchy among sterile loves," and therefore it is no less moral—or at any rate not more immoral—for a woman to find pleasure with another woman than with a person of the opposite sex. She then attributes such love to a "nervous alteration," observing that there are some people who see the color red as purple. This second justification for tolerating homosexual love appears based on physiological and psychological differences. One person's nervous system, through no fault of his own, may be constituted in an exceptional way. Françoise's final reason is aesthetic. Because both female and male bodies can be beautiful, there is no reason a "woman who is truly an artist" should "not fall in love with another woman. Among those with truly artistic natures, physical attraction or repulsion is modified by the contemplation of beauty." To illustrate her point, Françoise quotes the distinguished historian Jules Michelet, who used the example of the jellyfish, a creature some find beautiful, others repugnant. Jellyfish, when seen through Michelet's eyes, appear as "purple orchids of the sea."[40] Leslie, having listened to Françoise, attempts to disguise his horror at her confession and weeps with her, knowing that her self-inflicted bullet wound is mortal.

This story is Proust's first known attempt to depict and justify homosexual love. His wide range of explanations for homosexual desire, while remaining basically the same in import, are refined and greatly expanded in the *Search*, where he became the first writer to depict the continuum of human sexual expression. These three stories, written when Marcel was just twenty-two, may seem slight, but they contain important elements that were to be fully developed and orchestrated in his mature novel.

On Monday, August 7, Proust left for Saint-Moritz, where Louis de La Salle joined him at the lakeside Pension Veraguth a few days later. Marcel and Louis had brought along for summer reading the new French translation of Gabriele D'Annunzio's novel *L'innocente*. This work delighted Proust and may have influenced his method of characterization, especially the idea of a person embodying multiple selves.[41] Marcel's and Louis's athletic activities included fishing for trout, mountain climbing, a ride in a cable car into the Rigi—the mountain mass between the Lake of Lucerne and the Lake of Zug, and a hike up the Alp Grüm, from whose summit they could see all the way to Italy. Marcel later evoked the spectacular sight in a story: "Around us were sparkling glaciers. At our feet torrents ploughed through a wild country of the Engadine, darkly green." Far away in the distance Marcel saw "mauve slopes" that "intermittently revealed and hid a truly blue country—a shining avenue leading into Italy."[42]

While in Saint-Moritz, Marcel corresponded with three friends about an epistolary novel on which they had agreed to collaborate. This common effort may have been a last attempt to hold together the youthful band of aspiring writers after the demise of *Le Banquet*. The idea for the story in four voices seems to have been Proust's, inspired by *La Croix de Berny* (The Cross of Berny), a novel in letters written by the poet Théophile Gautier and three of his friends. In this collaboration, Proust played Pauline, Daniel Halévy an abbot, Louis de La Salle a general, and Fernand Gregh an artist. This experiment, like several that Proust undertook that year and next, required him to speak as a female narrator. In a letter from

Pauline de Dives to the abbot, Proust evoked the childhood days when he desperately hoped that bad weather would not prohibit him from playing in the Champs-Élysées garden with Marie de Benardaky. Reversing the roles, Marcel imagined himself to be a nostalgic Pauline longing for her childhood boyfriend.

This draft and other stories written this year showed Proust's growing fascination with names, especially unusual-sounding ones with historical links to French geography. Proust had been studying genealogy, history, and social connections by consulting various genealogical and social registers, such as *Tout-Paris,* the *Gotha,* and *High-Life.*[43] He had a character in a sketch—"À une snob" (To a snob), for the December issue of *La Revue blanche*—recognize the benefits of such knowledge, as a tool both for entertaining and for remembering history, activities that could be combined with gastronomy, if one knew the right people: "Reading about the battles won by the illustrious ancestors, you have recognized the names of their descendants whom you entertain at dinner, and by means of this mnemotechnics carry in your head the entire history of France."[44]

As Marcel sought the ideal family name for Pauline, he had her sign one letter as Pauline Dreux-Dives. Dives, a small town next to Cabourg, claims its place in history as the tiny port from which William the Conqueror set out to invade England. Dreux is one of three *sous-préfectures* of Illiers.[45] Although Proust expressed his fear that Pauline Dreux-Dives sounded too much like a railway line, he was inching toward an illumination vital to his future work. When Paris is added to those two locales to complete the triangle Paris-Illiers-Cabourg—or, as in his novel, Paris-Combray-Balbec—one of the world's most notable fictional maps will be nearly complete. Pauline soon perished; the characters' stations in life were defined, but the plot remained unfocused. The quartet grew tired of the game and abandoned Pauline. Proust likely lost interest because his own stories demanded his full attention.

In late August, Marcel left Saint-Moritz with sentiments that were bittersweet. Haunted by phantoms, both fictional and real, Proust wrote Billy that the memory of Edgar Aubert "pursued me throughout my beautiful trip, the thought of him who loved us so dearly and who is no longer with us, in whose clear eyes an unparalleled charm was mingled with irony and tenderness, faith and disillusionment. Poor Edgar, I reproached myself for the pleasure of looking at Lake Geneva, which he would never see again."[46]

Marcel extended his vacation by stopping at the Grand-Hôtel in Évian-les-Bains, a fashionable health resort on the southern shore of Lake Geneva. He remained in Évian until September, drafting more stories, often on hotel let-terhead, and a laudatory article on Montesquiou that he urged—unsuccessfully—Thadée Natanson to publish in *La Revue blanche*. If such a piece were published, its appearance would have the advantage of making public Montesquiou's friendship and trust in Marcel.

Career Choices

Marcel decided to add another leg to his nomadic vacation, the most extended in his life. But before continuing to Trouville, where he would join his mother at the Hôtel des Roches-Noires, he stopped in Paris to collect his proofs of "Mélancholi-que Villégiature de Mme de Breyves." Adrien had made it clear to Marcel that after Trouville, he would not be allowed to leave home again until he made a decision about a career.

Sometime during his long holiday, Marcel revealed to Pierre Lavallée his decision to publish his stories and sketches in a single volume. The determining factor may have been Madeleine Lemaire's agreement to illustrate the book. In a fall letter to Billy, Marcel modestly maintained that "the mediocrity of my book, the great licence of certain parts," had discouraged him from pursuing publication, but when Mme Lemaire agreed to illustrate his "little book," he realized that his writings would find their "way into the libraries of writers, artists, and persons of standing in all walks of life, who would otherwise have remained unaware of it and who will keep it only for the illustrations."[47]

Annoyed that his parents' ultimatum about a career choice prevented him from devoting all his energies to this book, Marcel consulted friends in an effort to placate his father and find a position that would not impinge upon his writing and social obligations. He wrote to Billy from Trouville, wondering whether he should try for a post at the Government Accounting Office or the Ministry of Foreign Affairs in Paris, both of which he viewed as "boring" and both of which required additional studies.[48] Another possibility under consideration was the École des chartes, which offered a three-year course of training for paleontologists and archivists.[49]

Marcel returned home from Trouville to find his father waiting to discuss his career plans. One morning in early fall, Marcel sat down at home and wrote a letter to his father, expressing his intentions and trepidations about such a decision:

My dearest papa,

I have kept hoping that I would finally be able to go on with the literary and philosophical studies for which I believe myself fit. But seeing that every year only subjects me to more and more practical discipline, I prefer to choose at once one of the practical careers you have suggested. I shall start studying in earnest with a view to the examination either for the Ministry of Foreign Affairs or for the École des Chartes, whichever one you prefer.—As for a law office, I should vastly prefer going to work for a stockbroker. And I assure you, I wouldn't stick it out for three days! I still believe that anything I do outside of literature and philosophy will be just so much time wasted.[50]

No doubt Proust would later find a sweet irony in the words "time wasted," for although he was apparently "wasting time" in his explorations of society and in his half-hearted attempts to choose a profession, the words *temps perdu* contain half the title of his future great work, the French phrase meaning both "wasted time" and "lost time." What seemed like Marcel's wastefulness and insouciance constituted a highly particularized apprenticeship. But who could have known that at the time? Not Marcel, who, in spite of his literary ambitions, was to experience years of disappointments and setbacks before finding his voice and the story he had to tell. And certainly not Adrien and Jeanne, who believed that a man must have a profession or "practical career" in order to succeed.

On October 10 Marcel received his law degree and reported for a two-week internship with a lawyer named Gustave Brunet. Although we have no details about Marcel's stint in the law office, the experience was his last in the legal field. Later in the month Marcel and his parents reached a truce through compromise. Although Marcel stood no closer to pursuing a serious career, he had at least agreed to become a librarian or curator. Such positions, although poorly paid, carried some prestige. Qualifying for one would entail acquiring yet another degree, but an easy one for Marcel to obtain: an advanced degree in literature. Marcel resigned himself to his fate as librarian; at least he would be surrounded by books, and he intended to maintain his writing schedule. Adrien did not feel particularly pleased with the choice, but what could one do with such an exasperating son? Before finally accepting an honorary, nonpaying, low-level post as librarian at the Bibliothèque Mazarine, Marcel consulted various friends, especially Charles Grandjean, inspector general of historic monuments, about a number of government posts, including editor at the senate, museum director, and inspector general of fine arts.

Grandjean had also served as an archivist at the senate, where he had been a colleague of Leconte de Lisle and Anatole France, both of whom had held posts as librarians.[51] The knowledge that two of the writers he admired most had been librarians likely influenced Marcel's decision to consider such a post.

Tragedy claimed another close friend. Willie Heath fell ill and died of dysentery on October 3. Within a year, Marcel had lost two young men whom he had idealized. The only known details of Heath's death are the scant ones found in Proust's letter to Billy: "After a most distinguished life he died with a heroic resignation . . . in the Catholic faith."[52] Marcel was devastated by these two deaths and sought a way to commemorate these lost young men.

Marcel revealed to Billy his plan of dedicating his "little book to two men whom I knew only a short time but whom I loved and still love with all my heart: Edgar Aubert—and Willie Heath." Heath's family seemed pleased with the idea, but he had been unable to contact Edgar's family. He asked Billy to write them on his behalf, saying that he would withdraw the dedication if they preferred, "understanding in advance the feelings that will dictate their response."[53] Aubert's family did decline the commemoration, perhaps because they were upset by the tone of certain letters Marcel had written to their son, letters the family had destroyed.[54] *Pleasures and Days,* still three long frustrating years from publication, was dedicated to Willie Heath alone.

Marcel, still determined to publish a piece on Montesquiou, asked permission to write the article about him that would undo the damage he had suffered by being lumped with "run-of-the-mill decadents." He proposed a title, "De la simplicité de M. de Montesquiou" (Concerning the simplicity of M. de Montesquiou), and offered to ride out to Versailles and consult the count in person.[55] This time the strategy worked; Montesquiou invited Marcel to come to lunch at his new residence, the Pavillon Montesquiou, at noon on Monday, October 30.

By the end of November, Proust, in order to obtain the library position, had agreed to pursue the advanced degree in literature and made arrangements to take private lessons with M. Mossot, a professor of rhetoric from Condorcet. Mme Lemaire had returned to Paris and was ready to begin work on the illustrations for his book, but he remained doubtful about the prospects of finding a publisher, given the time he must now devote to his studies. Discouraged, he soon enlisted Anatole France's aid in negotiating a contract with his publisher Calmann-Lévy, at the time France's most distinguished literary publishing house.[56] Marcel had even begun to think about publishing his book without Mme Lemaire's drawings— admitting to Grandjean, whom he consulted about the matter, that he was "quite

embarrassed" to have such thoughts—for if he must pay to have the book published, it would be much cheaper without the drawings. Sometime in the following
year, Calmann-Lévy agreed to publish *Pleasures and Days,* although the publisher
never issued a formal contract, despite Proust's efforts to obtain one.

Showing no signs of the illnesses that were soon to beset him and curtail his
activities, Marcel maintained a busy writing and social calendar. In mid-December,
he and Léon Yeatman went to see Sarah Bernhardt and Lucien Guitry in either
Phèdre or *La Dame aux camélias.* The two actors were giving alternate performances of Racine's masterpiece, much admired by Proust, and Dumas fils's popular melodrama at Bernhardt's Théâtre de la Renaissance. Bernhardt, now nearly
fifty, and world famous as the greatest French actress of all time, triumphed yet
again in two of her most memorable roles.

On Sunday, December 31, Marcel attended a dinner party at Chartres as the
guest of Pierre Lavallée. As Marcel celebrated the beginning of 1894 in the city near
Illiers, he must have calculated how far he had come since his last visit, at fifteen, when he had read Augustin Thierry and decided to become a writer. In the
past two years he had published more than thirty sketches and short stories and
written *L'Indifférent.* In the coming years, he was to draw from many of these pieces
to demonstrate the superficiality of society people. And he had begun to select,
perhaps without knowing it, themes that he would develop until they became
uniquely his. In one recent sketch called "L'Éventail" (The fan), time is not lost, but
the young writer anticipates that it will be. The lady in the story had painted on a
fan memories of her salon, a "little universe . . . that we shall never see again."[57] This
notion of moments rescued from oblivion, illustrated by the minor art of fan
painting, states Proust's main theme: time lost—and regained. But for now, like the
fan painter, Proust remained an artist in a minor genre, rendering exquisite little
pieces that might easily go unnoticed.

In the coming months, Marcel learned how difficult a friend and mentor
Montesquiou could be. The mercurial count's all-consuming ego demanded more
time, attention, and finesse than even Proust could provide, even though he continued to shower Montesquiou with compliments and gifts, sending him, among
many expressions of friendship and devotion, cherry trees and an unidentified
"pink" tree that Montesquiou's Japanese gardener "would recognize and know how
to nurture."[58]

In spite of some miscalculations as to what would please the count, Marcel did
score one major success when he introduced Léon Delafosse. In order to persuade
Montesquiou to meet Delafosse, Marcel had told him about the young man's keen

interest in the poems of *Les Chauves-souris,* which he found so beautiful that he had set some of them to music. Marcel told the poet that in his "humble opinion," the compositions were "exquisite."[59] The count, his curiosity aroused, took the bait and met the musician, who, the poet seemed to agree, was angelic. Soon Montesquiou, quite taken with Delafosse, assumed the role of protector and began grooming him for admission to his august circle.[60]

Shortly after New Year's Marcel became ill with what he described as pleuro-dynia; he suffered sharp pains in his side that forced him to reduce his schedule. His complaints about health problems became more frequent. By mid-January he was well enough to attend the Sunday Colonne concert that offered scenes from *Parsifal,* including one from act 2, in which the Flower Maidens appear. The enchanting, sensual music and the flower girls delighted Marcel, whose future Narrator, like Parsifal, would wander among a band of flower girls and seek to mingle with them.[61]

In February, Marcel wrote to Montesquiou, complaining that the past month had brought nothing but trouble. In addition to his health problems, Proust felt betrayed by Louis Ganderax, founder of *La Revue de Paris,* who had refused the article on Montesquiou and then reneged on his offer to pass it along to other publications. Montesquiou became enraged by the humiliation he was suffering at the hands of this inept disciple, who had promised him a larger public understanding but was making him look ridiculous instead—a condition any Frenchman, let alone Comte Robert de Montesquiou, found intolerable. In late winter Marcel confessed to Montesquiou that he was "persuaded that we cannot, at a certain level, comprehend each other." In the postscript he mentioned a peace offering, a little blue bird purchased from Traversa et Nivet, Montesquiou's bird supplier on the Quai du Louvre. The count should not make him wait too long to bring the bird or it would die.[62] Montesquiou was aware that Marcel had Greek and Latin lessons on the day when Delafosse would be working with him but sent him an invitation to lunch anyway, urging him to trick the ill-bred pedants, the "merchants of Greek and Latin," by taking the 11 o'clock train out to Versailles.[63] He also requested that Proust collect the bird and bring it with him.

Marcel did not attend the luncheon but stuck with his lessons and entrusted the blue bird to "the Angel." Aware that Montesquiou would be displeased at any apparent neglect, Marcel sent him a letter full of apologies and excuses. Having already used the excuse of his lessons so rapidly dismissed by the count, Marcel maintained that visiting a sick friend had made it impossible for him to come to Versailles. Then he spoke frankly to Montesquiou, telling him that he wished their friendship to be secure, that he longed to "arrive at last in port." In a plea for mutual trust, Marcel dared to lecture Montesquiou, briefly, on friendship: "I am not one of those who think that friendships, however rare they may be, should be easily gathered or discarded along the way. If undergoing a thousand difficulties *for* a friend brings great satisfaction, experiencing those difficulties *at* the hands of that friend mingles too much bitterness with friendship. I hope, dear Sir, that you will be eager to clear away so many clouds that perhaps my imagination alone has gathered."[64]

By the beginning of April, relations were smooth enough for Marcel, who had always enjoyed music hall performers, to invite Montesquiou and Yturri to the Folies-Bergère, where the star attractions were American-born dancing sensation Loïe Fuller and the Belle Otero, a lascivious Spanish dancer of remarkable beauty. Fuller, by using lighting of her own ingenious design and huge billowing veils that she extended with long wands, created spectacular effects as she danced across the stage, her swirling motions evoking many impressions, such as a butterfly hovering or an orchid unfolding its blossom. Mallarmé, who had seen her dance the year before, called her performance "at once an artistic intoxication and an industrial achievement."[65]

On April 20, Delafosse, under Montesquiou's sponsorship, gave the first of two concerts at the Salle Érard. A short time later, Marcel made one last frantic attempt to place the article on Montesquiou. Having already engaged a number of acquaintances in these futile efforts, he turned to Billy, who knew Henri Mazel, the director of *L'Ermitage*. "There's no point in telling him that it's a reject (!) from *la Revue blanche!*"[66] Proust stressed that the piece needed to appear immediately, in part because it was rapidly losing its timeliness as a piece to advertise *Le Chef des odeurs suaves*, but also because he needed to mollify the increasingly irascible count.

On Tuesday morning, May 1, Proust, alleging illness, wrote Montesquiou to apologize for not having replied sooner to an invitation to Versailles on Friday. He would arrive after lunch when Montesquiou and Delafosse had ended their work session. After indicating his eagerness to walk with the count and discuss their dreams for art and literature, he expressed his concern that Montesquiou continued to misjudge him because he did not really know him. He urged the count to abandon the "so complex and many-faceted character, so different from myself, which you persist in evoking." Montesquiou, by thinking him "simple of mind and complicated of character," had missed the mark. Marcel suggested that if the terms were reversed, "simple of character and complicated of mind," he could "at last obtain an identity."[67] Montesquiou, who seldom got along with anyone for very long, ignored his young friend's entreaties.

6   A Musical Prodigy   ∾

PROUST ATTENDED MADELEINE LEMAIRE'S salon on May 22, 1894, where a tenor from the Opéra-Comique sang while Delafosse played his six songs from Montesquiou's *Les Chauves-souris*. A few months earlier the composer had dedicated one of the songs, entitled "Baisers" (Kisses), to Marcel. For this performance Madeleine had arranged, as a surprise for the faithful, a kind of sound and light show: while the pianist-composer played a prelude, the astonished guests saw images of bats projected onto the wall. But this evening was to remain forever fixed in Marcel's memory because of the presence of another young prodigy whose talent far exceeded that of Delafosse: the darkly handsome Venezuelan Reynaldo Hahn.[1] Three years younger than Marcel, Reynaldo was only nineteen and already successful as a composer and a seasoned performer in the most exclusive drawing rooms. Recently, he had completed his first opera, *L'Île du rêve* (The isle of dreams), based on Pierre Loti's *Mariage de Loti*.

Reynaldo's heritage was the same Jewish-Catholic mixture as Proust's; his father, originally from Hamburg, was Jewish, and his mother, of Spanish origin, was Catholic. Reynaldo's mother was a beautiful, highly cultured woman, who adored poetry and music, whereas his father had the reputation of an astute businessman with a winsome personality. Unafraid of taking risks, the young couple left Europe for Caracas, Venezuela, where Carlos intended to make his fortune.

When Reynaldo was three, political turmoil undermined the stability of Venezuela. Fearing for his family's safety, Carlos liquidated all their assets and moved to Paris, where he had excellent business contacts. The Hahns chose as their new home a large, luxurious apartment at number 6, rue du Cirque, just off the Champs-Élysées not far from where Marcel had played as a child. At age six, Reynaldo made his artistic debut in the salon of Princesse Mathilde, singing in a thin voice arias from *opéras-bouffes* by Offenbach.

At ten, Reynaldo began his studies at the Paris Conservatory, where his friends and professors dubbed him the "little Venezuelan." Reynaldo loved being at the Conservatory and was happy in his family life. Unusually talented, he was also blessed with good looks and an engaging personality. In love with literature and the idea of setting words to music, he dreamed of writing an opera based on the adventures of Ulysses. While studying with three of the era's most accomplished composers—Jules Massenet, Charles Gounod, and Camille Saint-Saëns—he earned prizes in solfeggio and harmony. When Reynaldo was only sixteen, *Le Figaro* published his song based on a Victor Hugo poem, "Si mes vers avaient des ailes" (If only my poems had wings), which quickly became popular in the salons.[2] His professors considered him excellent in composition and piano playing—talents Massenet remembered when he recommended his pupil for an important commission from the noted author Alphonse Daudet. By the time he met Proust, Reynaldo had been a regular guest in the Daudet home for several years.

During adolescence, many of the young musician's happiest moments were spent with Cléo de Mérode, a dancer in the corps de ballet at the Opéra. Only seventeen when she met Reynaldo, Cléo was a ravishing beauty who, by thirteen, had already posed for Jean-Louis Forain and Edgar Degas. Reynaldo's precociousness, sparkling conversation, and wit impressed Cléo, as did the number of songs he had already published, inspired by poets such as Théodore de Banville, Victor Hugo, Henrich Heine, Leconte de Lisle, and Théophile Gautier. Reynaldo felt an intense friendship for the vivacious dancer, but one that lacked, apparently, the emotion Cléo aroused in her other male friends. Was he too timid? Was his interest only platonic? Or was he afraid of intimate contact because his true sexual longings lay in another direction—a direction he dared not explore in his conscious mind? Reynaldo brimmed with youthful purity, candor, and optimism, although his friends noticed a tendency to be ironic. None of them understood the reason for the melancholy streak in his personality, apparent in the profound look of sadness on his face.

Paris loved gossip. There was plenty of talk about Cléo and the men who pursued her. Among those who spoke of taboo subjects like homosexuality, it was rumored that Reynaldo had been the lover of his teacher and mentor, Camille Saint-Saëns, who had always lived as a closeted homosexual. When the composer of *Samson et Dalila* and *Le Carnaval des animaux* needed to escape the confines of respectability, he ran away to North Africa or the Canary Islands, where he could indulge in a "vice" to which he never alluded at home.[3]

At the time Reynaldo met Marcel, his attitude toward homosexuals was intolerant, as is revealed in letters to Édouard Risler, an accomplished pianist and fellow student at the Conservatory. Reynaldo wrote Risler that although he now attended the outdoor concerts in the Tuileries Gardens, there was one "drawback": "there are always a lot of *homosexuals*." In another letter he mentioned Paul Verlaine, who had served time in prison for shooting a fellow poet, his young protégé and lover Arthur Rimbaud: "I've heard that the great Verlaine's disciples attribute his talent to his horrible vice. Daudet told me so it must be true. Soon people will believe that to be a genius you have to shit on your music paper."[4]

Although Reynaldo still had to prove his genius, his talent had been firmly established the year before he met Marcel, when he set to music Verlaine's poems from *Chansons grises*. The light, graceful, haunting verses suited his style perfectly. Verlaine wept when he heard the beautiful melodies and even Edmond de Goncourt, who took little interest in music, was moved. A dashing performer, invariably referred to as handsome, Hahn had rapidly become the darling of the salons.

Reynaldo, like Marcel, had brown eyes, a dark complexion, and a small mustache. Accompanying himself at the piano, he frequently sang in his pleasant baritone voice selections from the delicate, vaporous *Chansons grises* to great acclaim at social gatherings. Marcel, who had always liked Verlaine's poetry, listened in amazement to the remarkable melodies created by this handsome youth. To Reynaldo singing seemed as effortless as breathing, even with a cigarette dangling from his mouth. Proust described his crooning, "his head thrown slightly back, . . . in the most beautiful, saddest and warmest voice ever heard."[5] Hahn's performance cast such a spell on Mme Lemaire's guests that she never had to call anyone to order when he sang. Everyone stopped talking and listened, a rare show of respect, even for great artists.

By the end of the year, Marcel's and Reynaldo's friendship would be firmly established. Although both relished the pleasures of the idle class, each pursued objectives important to his vocation. While Marcel assembled the stories he had published in little magazines and wrote new ones for his forthcoming book, Hahn, still studying composition at the Conservatory with Massenet, conducted, composed, and sought a producer for his opera.

A Literary Feast at Versailles

Early that spring Montesquiou had begun preparations for a spectacular party in late May to inaugurate the Pavillon Montesquiou, his new residence at Versailles. As usual, the poet entrusted the complicated arrangements to Yturri. As plans for the reception at Versailles advanced, Proust played the role of publicist and historiographer to Montesquiou's Sun King. He sent the poet, for his approval, a note announcing the event for La Patrie. The newspaper printed this on May 13, informing its readers that Comte Robert de Montesquiou would host an afternoon reception featuring "three artistic stars: Mesdames Sarah Bernhardt, Bartet, and Reichenberg."[6]

Montesquiou was accustomed to giving large, lavish parties as well as public lectures, to which wealthy and influential Parisians flocked, as part of his campaign to support those poets both living and dead whom he deemed worthy of his magnanimity. But nothing Montesquiou had ever planned could compare to this reception, intended to show off his new home and his new protégé, Delafosse, while allowing the beau monde to admire his latest poems. In spite of Montesquiou's misgivings about Marcel's effectiveness and the sincerity of his devotion, he invited him out to Versailles to discuss preparations for the reception. On May 9, Proust attended a small party that included Comtesse Greffulhe. The guests enjoyed a promenade, dinner, a theatrical performance, and, of course, the count reading some of his poems.

The weather was splendid for Montesquiou's "literary feast" on May 30. As the party began, Marcel scribbled notes on the back of his program for the article he would rush to the newspaper office when the party ended late in the afternoon. He described the events as they unfolded for the guests, beginning with their arrival down the wide avenue de Paris to Montesquiou's gate with its gilded ironwork. A smart tent had been set up near the entrance and a wide red carpet unfurled down the sandy path leading through the garden to the house, where, after treading on flower petals, the guests found the proud, smiling host waiting to greet them. Hidden away in a grove, an orchestra played. Under shade trees in a flat, cool part of the garden, a theater had been erected in the form of a temple, whose banner bore the word *Éphémère*. Robert de Montesquiou-Fezensac, who, like many of his contemporaries enjoyed word games, sometimes signed his initials in reverse order, FMR, creating the sounds of the French word for ephemeral. This word was especially apt for the dreamlike quality of the poet's feast.

It seemed that all the elite of Paris had come to see the count's new home. Many of the ladies carried parasols to shield their delicate, ivory skin from the sun, while the gentlemen wore their best top hats. There were titled ladies and gentleman galore, including the countesses Greffulhe, Fitz-James, Pourtalès, and Potocka, the princesses de Brancovan and de Chimay, and Comte Boni de Castellane. The poet José-Maria de Heredia and his three ravishing daughters were there, along with Henri de Régnier, Madeleine Lemaire and her daughter Suzette, Charles Ephrussi, M. and Mme Maurice Barrès, Mme Alphonse Daudet, M. and Mme Léon Daudet, Jean Béraud, Giovanni Boldini, and James Tissot. The prince de Sagan and the comte de Dion, rising to the uniqueness of the occasion, arrived in a strange new contraption, a vehicle powered by steam.

A discreet bell called for silence, and Delafosse came to the piano to play selections by Bach, Chopin, and Rubinstein. Then actors recited poems by Verlaine and Mme Desbordes-Valmore, and a madrigal penned by the host. Next Sarah Bernhardt, Julia Bartet, and Suzanne-Charlotte Reichenberg appeared to thunderous applause. The three exceptionally talented actresses read, by alternating stanzas, André Chénier's "Ode à Versailles."

During a short intermission, Montesquiou's guests enjoyed the "little wonders" of the garden, especially the Japanese hothouse, with its rare flowers and birds, or they partook of the refreshments awaiting them under the tent. Marcel rushed about greeting friends and noting the amazing bouquets of fine dresses in pink, mauve, yellow, lilac, purple, all creating an effect that was like a "sweet caress for the eyes." As he took notes, he consulted the ladies about the finer details of their dresses; he wanted his account to be flawless and worthy of its subjects. Delafosse returned to the piano and played his settings of Montesquiou's poems, sung with great feeling by the tenor Bagès. Then the actresses returned for more readings of poems by Leconte de Lisle, Heredia, and the host. For the newspaper article Proust made certain to quote stanzas of the count's verses. To conclude the celebration, Delafosse played a rhapsody by Liszt. Then it was over, the dream ended, and the crowd reluctantly left Versailles, "where, for a few hours, we believed we were living in the days of Louis XIV!"

Marcel dashed off his account, signed it "The Man-about-Town," and rushed to the editorial offices of *Le Gaulois*. When he awoke the next day, he pictured Montesquiou and the other exalted guests reading his story over their morning coffee with the greatest pleasures afforded by vanity, mingled with gratitude to their talented, diligent chronicler. When Marcel opened his newspaper, he saw to his horror that *Le Gaulois* had botched the article. He dispatched a letter to Montesquiou, giving a damage report and exculpating himself. Marcel had even taken the trouble, as he reminded the count, to let the ladies read what he had written and to correct any errors about their magnificent apparel. But the newspaper had dropped items, mixed others up, and simply rewritten much of his copy. The article had omitted Proust's name, which he had placed at the end of the guest list, but that was of no consequence "since I am not well known." But worst of all, they had dropped the names of Yturri, the "sublime organizer" of the feast, and other notables, including Prince Borghèse and Mme Howland. Through a strange metempsychosis, the flowers on Julia Bartet's dress had changed from periwinkles to cornflowers, but a more alarming alteration described Delafosse as having received a "kiss from Montesquiou's Muse."[7] Such bloopers must have made Jean Lorrain, soon to begin attacking Montesquiou in *Le Journal*, snicker with delight.

Fortunately for Marcel, a much shorter piece on the reception he had sent to *La Presse* appeared intact in the June 2 edition. The relieved author promptly sent Montesquiou a copy. Still fuming from Marcel's failure to publish his profile, Montesquiou told his young admirer that everything he undertook ended in an abortion. In mid-June, Proust wrote to Montesquiou, addressing him as "Dear Maestro," and expressed his own disappointment, after extraordinary efforts, at not having succeeded in placing the article. He blamed this failure on those envious of the count and said that the fault was certainly not that of "the great poet" but of "his clumsy singer," a view that matched Montesquiou's own. Marcel then wondered whether Montesquiou or Yturri could have the piece published in a newspaper friendly to them. He should have stopped there, but Marcel vowed, if all else failed, to found a review himself, even if for a single issue devoted to Montesquiou.[8] What Marcel had intended as a compliment was taken as an insult by the touchy count.

In July, Marcel, believing publication of his still untitled book would not be long in coming, completed and signed his long dedicatory note that began: "To my friend Willie Heath who died in Paris on October 3, 1893." Marcel evoked the youth, charm, and elegance of Heath by comparing him to portraits of English lords by Van Dyck, whose paintings Proust had celebrated in a poem. Proust suggested that Heath's pleasing but enigmatic look indicated a rich inner life that may have resulted from his delicate health. To illustrate his point, Proust recalled his childhood belief that no one in the Bible was more miserable than Noah when confined to the ark for many days and nights. Then, when Marcel became ill and had to remain for long days in his sickroom, he understood that never had Noah been able to see the world so clearly as from his place of confinement.

While Marcel was busy with tributes to Montesquiou and the unfortunate Heath, it was Reynaldo Hahn who most occupied his thoughts. In mid-July, he wrote to Hahn and expressed his eagerness for a meeting, using Léon Delafosse's trip to London as "the only pretext I have for asking you to see me." Proust proposed that they meet "any afternoon any time soon at my place or yours or on the terrace by the pond in the Tuileries or anywhere you like, I would be charmed to hear you relate to me Delafosse's success in London."[9] Hahn's reply is not known, but soon Marcel and Reynaldo were inseparable.

By the end of July, Montesquiou, busy making preparations to leave for the Engadine, contracted a sore throat. Marcel wrote immediately, lamenting Yturri's failure to inform him sooner and saying he would call soon to inquire about his health. He then enumerated all the services he would have provided, had he known: "I would have kept you company, brought your tisanes, answered people who inquired about your health, read to you, puffed your pillow, pulled up your covers, helped you to note the impressions your illness made on you, brought you flowers."[10] A courtier attending the Sun King's levee could not have offered more service. Montesquiou refused to acknowledge the disgraced courtier directly; he had Yturri reply to Marcel's letter about founding a review, which they considered a tasteless joke. Hurt that Montesquiou had not written himself, Marcel politely feigned delight with Yturri as intermediary, a role he filled "with such grace, power and charm."[11] Marcel closed by saying he fervently hoped to see them on Sunday.

That visit did not go well. The hapless Marcel had admired and then mislaid one of the count's favorite cravats, one he intended to wear in Saint-Moritz. Upon being informed of the missing tie, Marcel wrote that, although he did not remember handling the tie, he was sending three "modest Liberty ties that placed end to end would not equal the magnificent, somber fullness of the deceased." He had also been stung by Montesquiou's remark that he had no taste. To refute the count's unkind assertion, remarking that without taste he would be "incapable of loving as I do," Marcel engaged a defender whom he knew Montesquiou admired. With his own letter of remonstrance, Marcel enclosed a one-sentence note addressed to Montesquiou from Anatole France: "Dear Poet, How can you say that Marcel Proust has no taste since he speaks so eloquently about your verses?"[12] France had given what he thought to be irrefutable proof of Marcel's taste, but because Montesquiou thought his talent and genius obvious to all, he believed that detecting his greatness required no special gifts. Besides, Marcel's effectiveness in speaking about his poems was, to say the least, debatable. For now, Marcel remained the contemptible although faithful, adoring courtier, who protested against ill-treatment but kept running back for more.

Bengal Roses

After a bout of rheumatic fever that kept him in bed for a week, Marcel left Paris in mid-August for a month's vacation at Réveillon, Madeleine Lemaire's château in the Marne, where she and her daughter Suzette went for long stays and often entertained guests. This summer the Widows, as the two single women were affectionately known, had invited a number of guests, including Proust, Hahn, Delafosse, and a fellow painter, Raymond de Madrazo. Rounding out the company was a notable canine presence, Madeleine's beloved dog Loute, whose "extreme importance and high station" Marcel came to understand during this stay.[13] Madeleine adored her pet, to whom she talked constantly, convinced that the dog had acquired from her an appreciation of art and architecture. So certain was Madeleine of the canine's interest in architecture that she had visited the 1889 World's Fair once briefly so that Loute could admire the Eiffel Tower.

While awaiting Hahn's arrival, Marcel worked on another parody of *Bouvard and Pécuchet* for his book. This sketch, intended to thank Hahn for his many recent kindnesses, presents the two retired friends as music lovers. In his letters to Hahn, Proust continued the debate, begun in Paris, about music. Marcel had a better appreciation of contemporary music, whereas Hahn, whose best compositions are characterized by a natural simplicity, preferred the classical repertory, and above all worshiped Mozart. Marcel and Reynaldo especially disagreed about Wagner. Proust enumerated for his new friend what he admired most in *Lohengrin:* "You are hard on *Lohengrin,* I think. The herald and the king throughout, Elsa's dream, the arrival of the swan, the chorus of judgment, the scene between the two women, the refalado, the Grail, the leave-taking, the gift of the horn, the sword and the lamb, the prelude—isn't all that beautiful?"[14] He inquired about Reynaldo's progress in finding a producer for his opera *L'Île du rêve,* wondering whether he had been able to see Léon Carvalho, director of the Opéra-Comique.[15] Carvalho, despite Massenet's encouragement, declined the opportunity to stage *L'Île du rêve,* but Hahn was to have better luck with Carvalho's successor.

Shortly after Reynaldo's arrival at Réveillon on August 20, he wrote a letter to his English cousin Marie Nordlinger, who later became Proust's friend and collaborator on his translations of Ruskin. Hahn described Réveillon as "an old, interesting, artistic mansion" with "exquisite company." Mme Lemaire was "[all] smiles; her daughter Suzette accommodating; Delafosse svelte; Proust ecstatic and contemplative, an excellent lad of the first order," and Hahn himself, "brilliant." Always the epicurean, Reynaldo added a gastronomic note: "Fine, succulent cuisine. I work little and dream a lot—dreaming is the only true pleasure in life."[16]

Little is known about Suzette Lemaire, who seems to have been rather shy. Like her mother—though much less successfully—Suzette painted flowers, domesticated animals, and birds. While at Réveillon, Proust engaged in a flirtation with Suzette, unable to stop himself from speaking to her effusively about her charms and expressing, as he did with anyone he liked, feelings of great tenderness. In April, when Delafosse had published his setting of Marcel's poem "Mensonges," the poet had dedicated the piece to her. Marcel's attentiveness would soon land him in trouble; Suzette apparently believed that he was courting her.[17]

Many years later, Hahn recalled that he did not immediately recognize Marcel's superior qualities: "In our rare conversations, I had admired Marcel's ingenious amiability, the miraculous speed with which he understood everything, his sense of the comic, but I did not suspect his genius, which was only revealed to me little by little, and I didn't even suspect that he was someone extraordinary. I knew that he wrote, but he didn't talk about it; I had read nothing he had written and he in no way resembled the writers I knew."[18]

At Réveillon, one August day, when Marcel and Reynaldo went for a walk in the garden, an incident occurred that held a clue to Proust's ability to concentrate and observe. Hahn later recorded the event: "We were passing by a border of Bengal roses, when suddenly he fell silent and stopped. I stopped also, but then he started walking again and so did I. Soon he stopped again and asked me with that childlike sweetness that was somewhat sad that he always kept in his tone and voice: 'Would you be angry if I hung back a little? I'd like to look again at those little roses.'"

Reynaldo left Marcel and walked all the way around the castle until he came back to where he had left Marcel, who was still there staring "intently" at the roses. Reynaldo recalled that Marcel was bent forward, "his demeanor serious . . . his eyebrows slightly knitted as by an effort of impassioned attention, and with his left hand he obstinately pushed the end of his thin, little black mustache that he nibbled. I had the impression that he had heard me coming, that he saw me, but that he did not wish to speak or budge." Hahn began to circle the castle again and, after a minute, he heard Marcel calling him: "I turned around; he was running toward me. He caught up with me and asked me if 'I wasn't angry.' I assured him that I was not and, laughing, we picked up our conversation where we had left off. I did not ask him any questions about the episode of the roses; I made no remark, no joke: I somehow understood that I must not."

According to Hahn, this was the first of many such episodes, "mysterious moments when Marcel communicated totally with nature, with art, with life, in those 'profound minutes' when his entire being . . . entered into a trance where his superhuman intelligence and sensitivity . . . reached the root of things and discovered what no one else could see."[19] Proust later had his Narrator describe hawthorns in bloom: "I see them before my eyes, but at the same time I see them in me."[20] It was this stereoscopic vision, allowing him to see outward and inward, in the present and in the past, through a microscope and through a telescope, that eventually enabled him to create that particular, complex way of seeing that would become known as Proustian.

While Marcel was at Réveillon, the Proust family had a scare when Robert, who had gone for an extended ride on a tandem bike with his girlfriend, barely missed being crushed by a wagon transporting several tons of coal near Rueil, a pretty village on the outskirts of Paris. Jeanne, who had rushed to Robert's side on the day of the accident, wrote a few days later from Rueil to her "dear boy" at Réveillon, giving him an account and assuring him that although Robert had a nasty bruise where the wagon had rolled over his thigh, he had not been seriously hurt. Once the initial scare was over, Dick, as the family had affectionately nicknamed Robert, enjoyed himself thoroughly, comfortable in a room with a "view of the Seine, with a lovely backdrop of trees and greenery," and surrounded by his fellow interns from Ivry.[21]

During his medical school years Robert led a somewhat dissipated social life, often involved in escapades about which Marcel and his mother teased him. The girl with whom he had been biking near Rueil was Valentine Mestre, perhaps already his lover and eventually to become Horace Finaly's mistress. Like many pretty girls, she began as a cocotte and managed to rise far above her station. Early in the new century she married well and became Princesse Jean Soltykoff. Years later, Proust recalled in amazement the scene of his proper mother fraternizing at Robert's bedside "with the little cocotte who was taking care of him."[22]

By mid-September Marcel had joined his mother in Trouville for the annual seaside holiday. Shortly after his arrival Marcel wrote to Reynaldo, addressing him in English as "My little Master" and urging him to come to the Hôtel des Roches

Noires. Because Jeanne would be departing soon, Reynaldo could comfort Marcel after she left. Marcel was puzzled by something Reynaldo had called him in the last letter and asked: "Why 'Marcel the pony'? I don't care for this novelty. It makes me think of Jack the Ripper or Louis the Headstrong. Don't forget that it's not a nickname and that I am really and truly, Reynaldo, Your pony, Marcel."[23] In French, *pony* is a common term of endearment. Marcel, who seemed to fear that Hahn was using it lightheartedly, wanted to make certain that his friend, who liked to tease, meant what he said and that a special, affectionate bond was building between them.

This season at the beach was a quiet one. Since arriving, he and his mother had gone out with the Strauses and spent an evening with playwright Georges de Porto-Riche and his wife. The Strauses were enjoying their lovely villa, Le Clos des Mûriers, completed the year before "with a great deal of taste," according to *Le Gaulois*.[24] Marcel, free from health problems and with no one to distract him, wrote two short prose poems inspired by the moonlight at Trouville. Most of his efforts were spent on three stories, among the most important to be included in the forthcoming volume: "La Mort de Baldassare Silvande, vicomte de Sylvanie" (The death of Baldassare Silvande, viscount of Sylvania), "La Confession d'une jeune fille" (A girl's confession), and "La Fin de la jalousie" (The end of jealousy). He was glad to have a calm period in which to write; the only person whose company he desired was Reynaldo, who seemed reluctant to come.

Suzette occupied his thoughts too, but in a more distracting way. After Marcel arrived at Trouville, he feared that she might have misunderstood his intentions in flirting with her and wrote a long letter to clarify the nature of their relationship. Addressing her as Mademoiselle, he told her that in his thoughts he was still at Réveillon, "walking on the sand and in the park, trying to write to you in French but speaking Loute language."[25] In succeeding letters, he urged her to work and insisted upon the idea of friendship between them. He hoped that her mother was working "on something besides illustrating my little things which, in having even a bit of her time, are being given much more than they deserve." One can doubt Marcel's sincerity here, for he knew that publication of his book depended as much on Mme Lemaire's timely completion of the illustrations as on finding the right publisher. By way of encouraging Mme Lemaire, he praised to Suzette the illustrations her mother had finished during his stay at Réveillon: a dove that would be placed at the end of his dedication to Willie Heath and chrysanthemums, pansies, and a sketch of Violante's castle. All these, he said, "merge in my memory with the living occupants of Réveillon to add to my gratitude and my regrets."[26]

During his visit, Marcel decided to name his volume of stories and poems after his hostess's home in the country: *Le Château de Réveillon*. While preparing the final copy, Proust wrote to Montesquiou, asking permission to quote in his preface one or two of the "brilliant and beautiful lines you wrote on the flyleaf of Lemaire's copy of *Le Chef des odeurs suaves*. He also requested permission to dedicate one of the principal stories or poems to Montesquiou, as he intended to do for other "masters whom I admire or friends whom I love." After thanking Montesquiou for the nice letter from the Engadine, he confessed that its contents left him with a bittersweet impression: "The fact is that for some time your letters, whose intellectual and aesthetic quality I continue to value, have neither begun nor ended with a friendly word, and I suffer from their coldness of feeling."[27]

Montesquiou granted permission to use the quotes but seemed to fear a Proustian trick in the dedication. He wondered, regally, whether "we" would be allowed to see an advanced copy of the story dedicated to him, saying that "we" certainly hoped it was "the most beautiful one!"—or was Marcel "keeping back some new surprise resulting from so-called naïveté?"[28] Marcel attempted to dedicate many of the stories and poems in his book to friends, but Mme Lemaire opposed the idea, and all dedications, except the general one to Heath, were removed.

On Saturday evening, September 22, Marcel wrote another letter to Hahn to persuade him to come to Trouville for a brief visit, admitting that he was "a little sad this evening because of Mama's going away tomorrow." He was pleased with his progress: "I am working on a long piece and think it's rather good."[29] He liked the new story well enough to "use it as an excuse for omitting from my volume the story about Lepré, the opera, etc., which you are having copied." The story that he would substitute for *L'Indifférent,* whose shortcomings he recognized but did not know how to address, was "La Mort de Baldassare Silvande, vicomte de Sylvania." Marcel, who spoke to Hahn with a new simplicity, signed the letter, "I love you, my very dear friend."[30]

Amazed at Reynaldo's youth and accomplishments, Marcel alternated between addressing him as "my dear child" and as "my master." "La Mort de Baldassare Silvande," to appear in the *Revue hebdomadaire* the following year, was dedicated to Reynaldo. The story opens with an epigraph taken from Emerson: "The poets say that Apollo tended the flocks of Admetus; so too, each man is a God in disguise who plays the fool." Proust was convinced that he had found such a disguised god, and his name was Reynaldo.[31]

The story of Baldassare, whose theme owes much to Tolstoy's "Death of Ivan Ilyich," relates the final months in the life of Comte Baldassare, a handsome bachelor of thirty-five, strongly attracted to women.[32] The hero, who possesses many virtues and some common vices, chiefly vanity and jealousy, is slowly dying of a mysterious, incurable disease. Although Proust set the story in the mythological country of Silvania, the locale is really that of his favorite coastal spot, Les Frémonts in Normandy.[33] The viscount spends his last weeks in "an immense circular room entirely enclosed in glass. . . . Opposite the door, on entering one looked out over the sea and, turning the head a little, over lawns, pastures, and woods."

As a result of time spent alone suffering and staring at the sea, the nobleman comes to know himself, "the only guest he had neglected to invite to supper during his lifetime."[34] Baldassare, in spite of his moribund condition and the wisdom acquired through self-knowledge, occasionally experiences relapses of vanity and jealous passion. In one such scene, he asks Pia, with whom he had been in love, to promise not to attend the duchess of Bohemia's ball, where she and his new rival, Castruccio, are to lead the cotillion. She refuses to grant Baldassare's dying request. This victory of vanity over duty to a dying friend is a primitive version of the famous scene in the *Search* in which the duchesse de Guermantes, late for a party, cannot take the time to listen to Swann, who attempts to tell her that he is dying of cancer.

On September 24 Marcel received a letter from Hahn that disturbed him, because his friend seemed unwilling to come to Trouville. But perhaps Hahn was only teasing him. Marcel began a letter encouraging him to come and then, abruptly, changed his mind and canceled the invitation. Reynaldo had procrastinated too long; Marcel was nearly certain that the hotel would close for the season before his friend could arrive. Proust always hated to leave the coast at the end of the season. Once the extraordinary complications in getting him settled in new quarters had been accomplished and he had the entire staff of the hotel at his command, he became something of a squatter, never wanting to depart. He was usually the last guest to leave and often schemed to think of ways to stay even beyond the hotel's official closing.

The personnel of such establishments always adored Proust because, no matter how unreasonable his demands, he paid close attention to those who served him and the details of their lives, rewarding them with tips whose excessive amounts he tried to keep hidden from his parents. The information he gleaned from concierges, drivers, waiters, and other servants provided fascinating details about customs, language, and history—not to mention scandalous behavior. His novel owed as much, if not more, to this class as to that represented by Montesquiou and

Comtesse Greffulhe. The Proust of *Pleasures and Days,* who had always enjoyed the company and conversation of domestics, did not yet see how this material could be of any use except when it shed light on the behavior of the gratin, on whose glittering, rarefied world his attention remained sharply focused.

By the last week of September, Marcel was back in Paris, where he enrolled at the Sorbonne in Professor Egger's philosophy class. The family had also engaged Professor Darlu to give him private lessons. The ambitious stories he had been writing for his book made him less eager than ever to resume his university studies; he resented not being able to concentrate on the book that he hoped would establish him as a rising young author.

Marcel answered a letter from Suzette in which she had seemed to understand the limits of his interest in her. It is quite possible that she had never been romantically interested in him, but his tactics had placed her in an awkward position. He had given her reason to presume that he was wooing her, but now she was obliged to declare that she had thought nothing of it. In his reply, now that he felt safe, he skirted their mutually agreed upon pact of romantic noninterest when he addressed her as "My dear Mlle Suzette" and thanked her for having done him "a world of good." He invited her to tell him about her readings, "But . . . don't, I implore you, speak to me of what I write. Not that I don't feel a deep and heartfelt joy when I think you have liked it. Since I have never written *a line* for the pleasure of writing, but only to express something that struck my heart or my imagination, to tell me you like what I write is to tell me you like me, and that cannot leave me indifferent . . . "[35]

He ended the letter by telling her that he had neither the temperament nor the desire to be an ordinary man of letters and that she need not feel obliged to comment one way or the other on what he wrote: "But I haven't an ounce of vanity (unfortunately), not even of author's vanity, and when it seems to me that you feel obliged, as with a man of letters, to say a word either of criticism or praise, it makes me sad and gives me the impression that I am becoming a man of letters, instead of remaining purely and simply a man who bears you feelings of the most respectful friendship." The last word in the letter underscored his true feelings, in case his earlier remarks might mislead.

Proust wrote another story, "La Confession d'une jeune fille," about illicit heterosexual love. Like "Avant la nuit," this tale revealed the confession of a woman dying of a self-inflicted gunshot wound.[36] Having given up her lewd behavior to become engaged to a fine young man, the girl succumbs one evening to the temptations offered by an attractive dinner guest. Her mother, who happens to catch the daughter and young man in a moment of erotic passion, falls dead from the shock. As the girl lies dying, she recalls her childhood and the tender, loving relationship with her mother. Until she reached fifteen, her mother left her every summer at a country home called Les Oublis. The child, like Marcel, dreaded more than anything separation from her mother. Before departing, the mother would spend the first two days with her and "come to kiss me good night after I was in bed," a custom the mother had to abandon "because it caused me too much pleasure and too much pain, because due to my calling her back to say good night again and again I could never go to sleep." What grieved his own mother most was his lack of will, the shortcoming Proust had listed in the second questionnaire, at age twenty, as his chief weakness.[37] In "Confession," the girl's love for her mother was so intense that being ill brought the child joy because her mother had to return to her bedside at Les Oublis.[38] This episode is the prototype of the crucial good-night kiss scene in the *Search* that sets in motion the Narrator's long quest to regain his lost will and become an independent creative person.

Unlike the highly melodramatic tones of these early stories, the theme of matricide in the *Search* (or patricide in the later incident of Vinteuil, also from the *Search*) was to be understated. The Narrator's mother is spared death, but in the scene of the good-night kiss, when she is forced to yield to the child's weakness and spend the night in his room, the boy realizes, too late, that his action has harmed her. These dilemmas that Proust began to portray in his first mature stories— nerves, dependency on a mother's good-night kiss, sexual behavior considered dangerous or improper—originated in the aspects of his character of which his parents disapproved. In this regard, the *Search* can be seen as a long, magnificent apology to his parents, especially his mother.

Can "Confession" be read as Marcel's travestied admission of youthful homo-sexual debauchery? Illicit sex, in a variety of manifestations, intrigued Proust, as did the study of a number of vices, such as snobbery and obsessive jealousy. Years after the death of his parents, Proust admitted to Céleste Albaret that he occasion-ally visited a male brothel to observe through a peephole customers who paid to be whipped. Such voyeuristic moments were necessary to his investigations, he told Céleste, because he lacked imagination.[39]

The third story, completed in late 1894, focused on the major Proustian theme of jealousy. "La Fin de la jalousie" opens with two lovers pecking and cooing.[40] Honoré, a ladies' man who has always found it difficult to remain faithful for long, is mad about Mme Seaune, a widow with whom he has enjoyed a passionate, secret liaison for more than a year. A religious man, Honoré has prayed at mass to love

Françoise always. Leaving a party after midnight, Honoré walks home with M. de Buivres, who tells him that Mme Seaune is quite easy to possess, although perhaps too arduous in her affairs. This remark transforms Honoré. He becomes extremely jealous and interrogates Françoise, who swears she has always been faithful. Unable to sleep, he thinks of ways to trick her into revealing her betrayals. Above all, the thought of another man giving her pleasure torments him: "I am jealous of the other man's pleasure, I am jealous of her pleasure." In more rational moments he is ashamed of such thoughts. He returns to church and prays to no longer love her. Then, in order to feel secure and tranquil, he accompanies her everywhere. One day, in the Bois, a runaway horse collides with Honoré and crushes both his legs. Although the doctors are initially optimistic about his recovery, Honoré knows that he is lost.[41] Shortly after the accident, he feels as though a huge weight has been lifted from his body and he thinks he is dead. He understands that it is his jealous passion that has been lifted from him and only his pure love for Françoise remains. "And this was the end of his jealousy."

This story, Proust's favorite from his early years, contains in embryonic form the dynamics of nearly all the erotic relationships in the *Search*. The two most fully developed of these, Swann's obsession with Odette and the Narrator's with Albertine, follow the pattern of emotions that bind Honoré and Françoise. The man, self-confident if not downright cocky, decides, at some point, to abandon the woman. At the very moment when he is ready to carry out this resolution, he learns that she is absent without explanation, seeing someone else, or more than willing to end the relationship herself. He then is transformed into an obsessively jealous, dependent person. The lies and truths that Honoré tells Françoise are, in minia-ture, the models for Swann's future jealous interrogations and maneuvers with Odette, and for the Narrator's with Albertine, although, as always with Proust, he provides variations that are appropriate to the individual characters and circum-stances. The controlling emotions remain the same: jealous possession, insistence on exclusivity, and a love that is pathological and ultimately destructive to the person who harbors such feelings. Honoré is killed by a freak accident; Swann, because of his mania that made him waste, as he put it, years of his life on a woman who was not his type, eventually dies of cancer, fulfilling the prophesy of many metaphors depicting his "sickness" over Odette as an incurable disease or an inoperable tumor.[42]

These last stories, written when Proust was twenty-three, contain elements, including an occasional metaphor, in which one can see the promise of the future work, like the images depicting Honoré's eagerness to see his lover: "While dressing for dinner his thoughts were unconsciously hanging on the moment when he would see her again, just as an acrobat already touches the distant trapeze as he flies toward it, or as a musical phrase seems to reach the chord that will resolve it, drawing it across the distance separating them by the very force of the desire that presages and summons it."[43] These are fine touches, even though they lack the brilliance of mature Proustian analogies. The two metaphors showing Honoré's drifting thoughts may seem unrelated at first, but Proust effortlessly ties them together: the trapeze flies through the air to grasp and bring home the falling lover just as the musical phrase seizes the chord that saves it from dangling loose. Such moments of metaphorical magic are as rare in *Pleasures and Days* as they are bountiful in the *Search*.

One also notices, in the early work, Proust's search for the physiological and psychological laws that explain behavior. Depicting Honoré after a copious meal when metabolism detracts from the ability to concentrate, Proust gives a list of examples, each sufficient, each convincing, that enriches the observation: "Now in one of those purely physical moments when the soul within us hides behind the digesting stomach, behind the skin that still enjoys the recent shower and the sensation of fine linen, the mouth that smokes, the eye that takes delight in bare shoulders and bright lights, he repeated his prayer [to love Françoise always] with less conviction, no longer really believing in the miracle that would reverse the psychological law of his inconstancy, just as difficult to circumvent as the physical laws of gravitation or of death."[44]

Proust knew that these stories, along with the three he had written a year earlier, *L'Indifférent*, "Mélancolique Villégiature de Mme de Breyves," and "Avant la nuit," were his best work to date. He was still a young man in search of himself and often behaved like a poseur succumbing to the appeals of vanity. Self-conscious about the impression his penmanship and stationery would make on fashionable people, he had developed a somewhat affected but still legible handwriting. To impress rich aesthetes like Montesquiou, he purchased exotic writing paper and expensive, complicated pens, whose ink flow sometimes spoiled the effect of the beautiful paper. For a late October letter to Montesquiou's cousin Mme de Brantes, he chose gold ink and violet paper. He informed her that after a month of intensive work, he had produced three short stories and lots of poetry. So intense had been his concentration on writing that he had forgotten to register for the October exam for his advanced degree in philosophy. That would have to wait until April. The publication of his book mattered more to him than his university degree. He told Mme de Brantes that he still did not know when his book would appear, but informed her of its status, which included exciting news about two contributors. Without naming Hahn, he wrote that a "musician of genius—aged twenty—is composing music for the poetic part of the volume, and M. France is writing a preface." At this point in the letter, Marcel's fancy pen malfunctioned, and he stopped, saying that he would write again later with "more convenient ink."[45]

After being ill for several days, Marcel decided to consult the noted palmist Mme de Thèbes, who read so many alarming signs in the lines of his palm that she urged him to go "far away for a rest."[46] In a letter to Suzette, asking her to continue treating him like a brother and a child, he made an observation about what he had learned regarding friendship, love, and happiness. He admitted he was "touchy" and easily offended, but only with people he liked. "You'll say that's an odd way of showing my appreciation, I should save my touchiness for people I don't like. But where did you ever hear that one loves people to give them pleasure? One loves people because one can't help it." And as for happiness: "I am still too young to know what makes for happiness in life. But I know for sure that it's neither love nor friendship."[47] Marcel had reached this conclusion at a much earlier age than would his future Narrator.

In November, Robert, fully recovered from his biking accident, left for the 132d Infantry Regiment in Reims, where he would fulfill his military service. In December, when Robert came home on leave, he and Marcel went to a Sunday afternoon concert at the Conservatory to hear Beethoven's Fifth Symphony. Marcel wrote a review for *Le Gaulois,* in which he said little about the music but showed, using images of an army on the move and a ship at sea, the effect the symphony had on its listeners, creating "unity in each of us."[48] Marcel was struck by the realization that once the symphony was over, the feeling of elevation experienced in common by those who had heard it evaporated as everyone rushed off to take care of more practical business. This phenomenon caused Proust to observe with regret how quickly we "deny our souls," with which the music had brought us into contact, because of frivolous desires or habit. The essay ends with thoughts about "soul denial," the common condition in which we refuse to stop and peer into our inner being to find and apprehend that part of ourselves that responds to such beauty as that found in Beethoven's symphony. At this stage, Proust was engaged not so much in seeking lost time as he was in looking for his true self. Until he found it and the words to convey it, he would have nothing of value to give to others.

Marcel rushed to hand in an overdue paper on Socrates that Professor Egger was good enough to accept on December 17. The professor noted that Proust's essay was "difficult to read," especially because it lacked clear divisions, but that it was "extremely intelligent" and that the student "had understood everything."[49] The next day Marcel attended a party at the Arthur Baignèreses, where he met the distinguished novelist Alphonse Daudet and his wife. The Daudets, and especially their two sons Léon and Lucien, were to become Marcel's close friends. The following week Reynaldo, who had known the Daudets for some time, took Marcel to visit them in their home on the Left Bank.

Another year was rapidly drawing to a close, and Marcel still had no profession and no prospects for employment. He was finding it difficult to maintain his routine and reconcile his various activities: student, son, friend (the number of his relationships continued to grow), correspondent, society columnist, publicist, author, and fawning page to a number of "smart" people, chief among them Madeleine Lemaire and Robert de Montesquiou. His health seemed compromised by the life he was leading and his refusal to concentrate on what his parents viewed as his primary responsibilities: his studies and his career. Dr. Proust, who remembered his own hard climb to success after coming to Paris with nothing but the clothes on his back, must have thrown up his hands in frustration. How had he and Jeanne failed to instill in their elder son the character and discipline to forge a respectable, independent life? Marcel's extravagant spending and idleness violated a number of the family's most cherished principles. Robert, robust and practical, had already begun his internship and would soon be a practicing physician, while Marcel apparently intended to do nothing other than lead the life of a rich, spoiled dilettante.

Judas on Parade

In early January 1895 a heavy snowfall blanketed Paris, creating the sort of winter landscape that Marcel had dreaded as a child because it might prevent Marie from coming to the Champs-Élysées. On Saturday, January 5, on the other side of the Seine, a ceremony took place of which Proust, like most of his countrymen, took no notice, though what happened in the main courtyard of the École militaire was to affect their lives and change the course of French history. Diplomats, journalists, and some notables had been invited to witness the spectacle of an officer's humiliation. Even though the ceremony was not open to the public, a crowd of the curious and more conservative Parisians had assembled, in the bitter cold, outside the courtyard gates and jammed the adjacent streets.

Captain Alfred Dreyfus, who had been court-martialed in December for selling military secrets to the hated Germans, was about to be degraded. Among the notables present whom Proust knew were Léon Daudet and Maurice Barrès. Barrès, an anti-Semite who had been elected deputy from Nancy in 1889, later published his recollections of Dreyfus's degradation under the title "Judas on Parade."[50] Some in the impatient, angry crowd, outside the gates, began to shout "Death to the Jew," "Death to Judas," and Barrès, whose adrenaline had begun to surge, wrote that the event was "more exciting than the guillotine." The French Army, still smarting from the humiliating defeat by the Germans a quarter of a century before, had mustered all its might and rancor to destroy one obscure, innocent captain, whose only crime was to be a Jew. But no details of the evidence leading to his conviction of high treason were known, and because he had been court-martialed by unanimous vote after proceedings involving some of the military's most respected leaders, there was no reason for anyone to doubt the verdict. French Jews, if anything, felt that they, too, had been betrayed by Dreyfus.

Gen. Paul Darras, a domineering figure on horseback at the center of the courtyard, drew his sword, drums rolled, and from a far corner Captain Dreyfus emerged, escorted by a brigadier and four gunners. He walked resolutely, head high, and although he stumbled midway, he quickly recovered. The general rose in his stirrups, raised high his sword, and pronounced the official words of degradation: "Alfred Dreyfus, you are no longer worthy of bearing arms. In the name of the people of France, we dishonor you." Dreyfus, in a cracking but clear voice, shouted: "Soldiers, an innocent man is being degraded; soldiers, an innocent man is being dishonored. Long live France! Long live the Army!"[51] The crowd answered with shouts of "Death! Death to the Jew!" Then Sergeant-Major Bouxin proceeded to strip Dreyfus of his badges of rank, shred his clothing, and break his saber. An officer no more, the traitor Dreyfus would be sent to Devil's Island to begin serving his life sentence.

Léon Daudet, whose article "Le Châtiment" (The punishment) appeared in the next day's *Le Figaro*, had noted Dreyfus's demeanor as he passed close by on the way back to his cell: "His eyes dry, his gaze lost in the past, no doubt, since the future had died with his honor. He no longer had an age, a name, a complexion. His was the color of treason. His face was ashen, without relief, base, without appearance of remorse, foreign, to be sure, debris of the ghetto." Before departing, Daudet remarked to Barrès: "The wretch is not French." And Barrès elaborated: "Dreyfus does not belong to our Nation, and consequently, how could he betray it? The homeland of the Jews is where their money draws the greatest interest."[52]

Months would pass before a colonel discovered that Dreyfus had been framed and the real spy allowed to go unapprehended.

Marcel, unaware that anything extraordinary had taken place on the other side of the Seine, wrote his New Year's greetings. He sent a copy of "La Confession d'une jeune fille" to Montesquiou, wintering at Mme de Brantes's château du Fresne, where he was finishing a new volume of poetry. Marcel told the count that for the first time in three years he was beginning the new year "with a keener sense of divine grace and human freedom, with confidence in at least an inner Providence."[53] Perhaps his new faith in grace and freedom was due in part to his readings of Emerson, from whose essays he had gleaned epigraphs for some of the pieces in *Pleasures and Days.* On the morning of January 18 he wrote to Reynaldo, saying that he was "still in bed, drunk with reading Emerson." He was also pleased that Madeleine Lemaire had liked his poems about composers, a compliment he passed along to Reynaldo, giving him the credit for having quickened his pen: "One is always inspired when speaking of what one loves. The truth is that one should never speak of anything else."[54]

Among new friends whom Marcel began to see on a regular basis were Prince and Princesse Edmond de Polignac. Now sixty, the prince had married Winnaretta Singer, who was thirty years younger and the American heiress to the sewing machine fortune. When the couple married in 1893, it was rumored that Montesquiou and Comtesse Greffulhe had played matchmakers. Not only was the young lady extremely wealthy, she had a genuine knowledge and appreciation of the arts, especially music, which she played beautifully, as did the prince, who also composed. Winnaretta, who would become one of Paris's most prominent art patrons, was extraordinarily talented. In addition to her musical abilities, she painted and exhibited her works. The prince, who, at age thirty, had won first prize in composition at the Conservatory in 1865, maintained a studio in the rue Cortambert, where he hired large orchestras and choruses to perform his compositions. Winnaretta, whose mother was French, had long been a friend of Gabriel Fauré's, whom both the Polignacs, like Proust, greatly admired. Staunch Wagnerites, the prince and princess were among a number of smart Parisians who made the annual pilgrimage to Bayreuth.

Marcel continued to combine university studies, supplemented by the private lessons with M. Darlu, with a busy social life. The urgency to find a career had been put on hold until the final exams, set for March. His health occasionally led him to adopt a more reasonable schedule. On February 13 a high fever forced him to leave

Mme Aubernon de Nerville's salon in the middle of a comedy in which Robert de Flers was performing.

Nine days later Marcel wrote to Alphonse Daudet to thank him for inviting him to dinner that Sunday: "I cannot tell you, sir, how touched I am by your kindness. My fondest dreams when I was a child could not have held out a prospect as unlikely or as delightful as that of being so graciously received one day by the Master who even then inspired me with passionate admiration and respect."[55] Among those present would be Edmond de Goncourt and Daudet's two sons, Léon and Lucien, who were to give accounts of their recent trip to Stockholm. Marcel noticed Lucien's adolescent beauty and charm but remained immune to such temptations because of his devotion to Reynaldo. Goncourt, still handsome at seventy-four, with eyes that had lost none of their sparkle, made a gentle but imposing presence; his head of white hair, with matching mustache and goatee, framed the deceptively cherublike face of this literary and artistic grandee. Although he was the picture of a favorite teasing uncle, his pen could be vitriolic and bigoted. He continued to pour his loves and his hatreds into his famous diary, the seventh volume of which had been published the preceding year.

If Marcel delighted in his newfound friendship with the Daudet family, his relationship with Montesquiou remained uncertain. On the day after the Daudet dinner, Marcel wrote to the count to voice his frustration at not knowing where he stood. Repeating the analogy of a ship at sea, he stated that he longed more than ever to arrive safely in the harbor of Montesquiou's friendship and affection. But this time he demanded a resolution: a definite arrival in port or an "irreparable sinking."[56]

Montesquiou must have scoffed at the threat. What had he to fear from the likes of Marcel Proust? Still, Marcel could prove useful, despite the earlier fiascoes, in publicizing the next volume of poems, now nearly complete. On Sunday, February 24, *Le Figaro* announced the count's next party for the "ultraselect." Mlle Bartet would recite Montesquiou's poems written in honor of a trio of countesses: Greffulhe, Guerne, and Potocka. But the part of the program Marcel found most intriguing was the actress's recitation of "Offrande funéraire," one of the poems recently published in the *Revue de Deux Mondes* by an eighteen-year-old society girl who wished to remain anonymous.[57] Among those who would attend, in addition to the guests of honor, were Anatole France, Charles Haas, and the American painter James McNeill Whistler.

The following day Marcel had to decline an invitation from Montesquiou because he had agreed to be Mme Lemaire's escort to a performance of Hugo's *Hernani*. Perhaps his stern words to the count had not gone unheeded and he was entering, at last, calmer waters. In early March the count announced his intention to dedicate to Marcel the poem "Sérée" from his forthcoming collection, *Le Parcours du rêve au souvenir* (The path from dream to memory). Marcel thanked him for the proposed honor but said that he would prefer to decline it if the count intended to take away "with one hand what you give me regally with the other by mingling with your indulgence for the mind disdain for the heart."[58] Even with someone of the count's social stature, what Marcel prized most was affection.

Marcel wrote to Reynaldo, his "child," and informed him that he had recently spent some time at a party talking with fifty-year-old Gabriel Fauré, who is "really very nice." Fauré, who had a few years earlier composed a remarkable song cycle, *La Bonne Chanson,* set to Verlaine poems, told Marcel that Hahn must find it irritating to listen to Fauré's compositions, for Hahn's own versions of the same poems would seem definitive. Marcel had informed Fauré that, quite the contrary, Hahn performed Fauré's songs more often than his own and especially loved to sing Fauré's version of "Chant d'automne." Proust's admiration for Fauré continued to grow. Two years later he wrote the composer a letter to express his admiration for *Parfum impérissable,* which he found "intoxicating" as he played it day after day on the piano.[59]

Fauré, who lived in the same neighborhood as the Prousts, had become one of France's most distinguished musicians, considered by many to be the most advanced composer of his time. He respected the knowledge and appreciation of music that he found in Marcel and Mme Proust, whose skills at the piano he admired, particularly the "purity" with which Jeanne played.[60]

On March 1 Proust was among the guests, numbering more than three hundred, who attended a banquet in honor of Edmond de Goncourt's receiving the Légion d'honneur. On that gala occasion, there were tributes by many of France's most distinguished citizens: Alphonse Daudet, perhaps Goncourt's closest friend, Émile Zola, Georges Clemenceau, Raymond Poincaré, José-Maria de Heredia, and Auguste Rodin. Sarah Bernhardt read poems by Robert de Montesquiou. The evening ended with Yvette Guilbert's rendering of *La Soularde,* "in which . . . [she] proved herself," as Goncourt noted in his diary, "to be a great, a very great tragic actress, gripping your anguished heart."[61]

In late March, Marcel wrote to Reynaldo with the good news that he had passed his exam and would receive his license in philosophy. Of the 118 candidates who took the exam, Proust finished twenty-third. He had ended his days as a student, a status he had maintained for so long only because of his parents' insistence that he follow an acceptable career path.

After an asthma attack thwarted his plans for a spring vacation at Segrez, the country home of Pierre Lavallée, Marcel "dragged" around Paris, unable to decide whether to join his mother in Dieppe or to stay home. Perhaps his delicate bronchial tubes would benefit from the sea air. But he did not join his mother, despite feeling quite lonely; his father was traveling in the south of France, and Robert had gone to Illiers to visit Uncle Jules.[62]

An incident occurred one evening in late April that showed Marcel how much he had come to depend on Reynaldo's presence and affection. Marcel missed a rendezvous with Reynaldo because Mme Lemaire had insisted that he escort her to a silly affair called the "pink cotillion," given by Mme Edgar Stern. Confused about the time, Marcel arrived late for his appointment with Reynaldo, who had already left and was not to be found in any of their late-evening haunts. The anxiety he felt on not being able to find Reynaldo was nearly as awful as the sorrow and dread experienced as a child when he feared his mother would leave him.

The following morning, Marcel wrote to apologize for the confusion and indicated that his emotion over missing Reynaldo had been so intense that he might write about it: "Wait for my boy, lose him, find him, love him twice as much on hearing that he had come back . . . to get me, wait two minutes for him or make him wait for five, that for me is the true, throbbing, profound tragedy, which I shall perhaps write some day and which in the meantime I am living."[63] Marcel confessed to Reynaldo that he found it increasingly difficult to rise before noon. Often, after waking, he remained in bed to read *Le Figaro* and to write poems, sketches, and letters. After suggesting to Hahn a meeting time, he wondered whether they should not practice going for a week or two without seeing each other so as to harden themselves against future "tempests." But as practical and brave as this idea sounded, Marcel was not ready to make such a sacrifice: "Let's not begin yet, please." The missed appointment had made him realize the importance of his affection for Hahn.

While the French were persecuting an innocent Jew, the English were absorbed in a scandal of their own. In the spring, while Oscar Wilde's latest play, *The Importance of Being Earnest*, enjoyed a highly successful run at the Saint James's Theatre, the Irish writer found himself inextricably enmeshed in the gears of the British legal system. Pronounced guilty of sodomy and indecency on May 25, Wilde was sentenced to two years' hard labor. Wilde's troubles had begun when he brought a libel suit against the marquess of Queensberry, who had accused him of being a sodomite and of having had a bad influence on Queensberry's son Lord Alfred Douglas. The French poet Henri de Régnier had visited Wilde in London two years earlier, and he reported to Goncourt that the writer had flaunted his homosexuality: "Yes, he admits his pederasty. He once said: 'I've been married three times in my life, once with a woman and twice with men!'"[64]

In the months before the trial, Wilde had been hiring young males, usually unemployed, or gentleman's servants down on their luck who were willing to prostitute themselves. Wilde later claimed special privilege as an artist to explore evil while risking danger: "People thought it dreadful of me to have entertained at dinner the evil things of life, and to have found pleasure in their company. But then, from the point of view through which I, as an artist in life, approach them, they were delightful, suggestive and stimulating. It was like feasting with panthers; the danger was half the excitement."[65] Wilde had been devoured, not by panthers but by the British justice system.

Proust, shocked like many by Wilde's punishment, knew that prominent Parisian men also hired male prostitutes. Surely the British had sunk to a new low in cruelty and hypocrisy. In France, as in Britain, wealthy people employed a large retinue of servants. Homosexual men often recruited valets and drivers for their looks and willingness to render services quite different from the established duties of the job. Most homosexuals understood the need for discretion, and officials were willing to look the other way. A trial like the one that had destroyed Wilde was unthinkable in Paris. If anyone cast doubt publicly on a gentleman's virility, the demands of honor could be quickly satisfied by a duel. Proust, who had begun to write about homosexual love in stories like "Avant la nuit," was to make society's misunderstanding and unfair treatment of homosexuals a major theme in the *Search*, where he likened their persecution to that endured by the Jews during the Dreyfus Affair.

In May, Marcel attended a performance of *Tannhaüser*, whose newfound success among the French may illustrate what Proust said about works of art creating their own posterity. The Paris première of *Tannhaüser* in 1861 had been greeted with boos and catcalls. With the production that opened at the Opéra on May 13, 1895, Parisians now received Wagner's work with wild enthusiasm. Mme Straus was not among those applauding. She, like Reynaldo, disapproved of Wagner's excessive mysticism and mythologizing, which led the composer, according to them, to create fantastical figures who seemed inhuman. Deploring the public's and Marcel's infatuation with Wagner, Mme Straus preferred those works, like her father's and Bizet's, in which passions were voiced on a more earthly scale.

Marcel explained to Reynaldo why Mme Straus's remark that Wagner was "legendary rather than human" missed the point: "The more legendary Wagner is, the more human I find him, and in him the most magnificent artifice of the imagination strikes me only as the compelling symbolic expression of moral truths."[66] Hahn, who regarded with scorn most writers' opinions about music, found Proust just as unconvincing when it came to Wagner.

In a letter to Suzette, written during his Wagner debates with Reynaldo, Proust defined the point of basic disagreement: "I believe that the essence of music is to arouse the mysterious depths (which literature and generally speaking all finite modes of expression that make use either of words and consequently of ideas, which are determinate things, or of objects—painting, sculpture—cannot express) of our souls, which begin where all the arts aimed at the finite stop and where science as well stops, and which for that reason can be termed religious. This doesn't make much sense when said so quickly, it deserves a longer conversation."[67]

This longer conversation was postponed for nearly two decades and took place not with Suzette Lemaire but with his readers. Wagner's mysticism appealed to Proust's own, later evident in the *Search*, where his "religious" sentiments are expressed, albeit discreetly, in such epiphanies as the madeleine scene. Proust became enamored of music precisely because it expresses the ineffable by going beyond words. Music seemed the ideal and unique form of direct communication— what one would hear, he later wrote, if language and ideas had not been invented, "the means of communication between souls."[68]

In late May, preparing for what he hoped would be the imminent publication of *Pleasures and Days* (still entitled *Le Château de Réveillon*), Proust organized readings of his poems about painters and composers. He had also written to Henri Gauthier-Villars, known as Willy, a journalist who wrote for the *Revue blanche*, to inquire about the publication of other sketches or poems before their appearance in book form. Proust's letter was answered by Willy's wife, a young woman of twenty-four destined for literary fame as Colette. She had recently heard Marcel recite his poems and felt she must give him some advice: "I want to tell you how beautiful and perceptive we thought your glosses on painters the other evening. You mustn't spoil them as you do by reciting them badly, that's a terrible thing to do."[69] Marcel, whose brilliant conversation could hold his listeners enthralled for long periods and who performed hilarious imitations of his friends, proved shy and inept at reciting his own poetry. He took Colette's advice.

Marcel had planned a gala evening at Mme Lemaire's, where his poems "Portraits de peintres" and "Portraits de musiciens" were to be read.[70] Proust feared the reception his pieces might receive, a dread that intensified when he wrote out Montesquiou's invitation. Although Marcel usually debased himself when communicating with the count, this time he especially wanted to disarm the haughty arbiter of taste. After praising Hahn's music that would accompany his verses, Marcel confessed to Montesquiou how bad they were: "Some of my worst poems will be heard tomorrow in that same studio where such beautiful ones have been heard," referring, of course, to the count's own.[71] He asked Montesquiou to arrive early because Reynaldo's friend Édouard Risler had agreed to come from Chartres, where he was in the military, just to play the musical accompaniment to Marcel's poems. It was essential that the performance begin on time, for Risler must return to his regiment that evening.

Both *Le Gaulois* and *Le Figaro* gave accounts of the evening's dinner-reception at Madeleine Lemaire's for "très sélect" guests from the domains of art and aristocracy. Among those present were the princesse de Polignac, Montesquiou, the poet Heredia and his daughters, Comte Primoli, Anatole France, Carolus-Duran, and Charles Ephrussi. *Le Gaulois* praised Reynaldo as the "distinguished composer" of this "brilliant musical soirée"; Marcel's verses on celebrated painters were said to be "finely chiseled," each a "little gem."[72] But *Le Figaro*'s reporter cannot have been impressed with the little jewel-like poems; he failed to mention them or Proust's name. The article did praise Hahn's compositions, especially his setting of Gabriel Vicaire's poem "Le Cimetière de campagne," "a masterpiece of emotion."[73] It is easy to understand that the reporter overlooked Marcel's poems, not a line of which carried the conviction of the essay he was to write later in the year praising the quiet beauty of Jean-Baptiste Chardin's still lifes of ordinary objects.

Marcel did not have time to savor the recognition, however meager, from his society debut as a poet. He had two major distractions: a competitive exam for one of three vacant unpaid posts at the Bibliothèque Mazarine, one of France's national libraries; the other, more worrisome, the fear that Reynaldo was angry with him. The circumstances of the tiff are not known. Had Marcel seen someone he had promised Reynaldo never to see? Proust left the library during the exam period, risking a reprimand, to send Reynaldo a wire saying that he had not expected the visitor and urging him not to be angry. In the brief message he mentioned three times the hour of their date that evening, as though terrified that Reynaldo might not come. Whatever the problem, the two men patched things up. But Reynaldo, who according to Proust could be ill-humored and impatient, may have found life with Marcel too complicated at times.

The results of the exam were disappointing. Marcel's parents had hoped that because he had at last completed the university degrees necessary to compete for a post of some distinction, he would at least fulfill that rather modest goal. But he finished third in the competitive exam and was sent to the book depository in the rue de Grenelle on the Left Bank, the least desirable of the three available slots at the Bibliothèque Mazarine. Adrien and Marcel attempted to pull strings by asking their powerful friend Gabriel Hanotaux, minister of foreign affairs, to recommend that someone else who enjoyed better health be placed in the humiliating third slot. M. Franklin, the administrator at the Mazarine, observed, on declining the request, that "M. Proust seemed to me to be enjoying excellent health."[74] When this initiative to switch positions failed, Proust requested sick leave. While this request was pending, Marcel took a temporary assignment at the Mazarine, to which he reported only a few times before his sick leave was authorized. At the end of July he was granted a leave of two months, which he later succeeded in having extended until October 15.

In July, Marcel accompanied his mother to the Oranienhof, a German health resort located on the Nahe River in Kreuznach, an old picturesque town in Rhineland-Palatinate, known for its mineral springs. He took the waters with his mother in the morning and enjoyed late-evening boating excursions on the river, even though mosquitoes swarmed around him. It is possible, although there is no conclusive proof, that Marcel began writing some scenes there for his first attempted novel, known as *Jean Santeuil*.[75]

In June, Robert de Billy had married Jeanne Mirabaud, daughter of the wealthy financier Paul Mirabaud, director of the Banque de France. Fortunately for Marcel, bored so far from his friends, Billy and his wife were traveling near Kreuznach on an extended honeymoon and stopped by for a brief visit. Mme Proust greeted the new Mme de Billy with her "customary kindness." Billy, well on his way to achieving his professional and personal goals, seemed radiantly happy, his future assured.

Marcel, at twenty-five, handsome, wealthy, and single, watched his friends begin to marry and settle into their careers. It would have been normal for Proust's family to encourage him to take a wife, yet no serious attempt to find him a partner seems to have been made. Dr. Robert Soupault, who became acquainted with Marcel and his family as a medical student under Robert Proust, believed that although Marcel was homosexual, he was not exclusively so. Yet Soupault found it hard to imagine Marcel getting married and setting up a household, not because the writer found intimacy with women repugnant but simply because marriage "requires a modicum of practicality and self-denial of which he was quite incapable."[76]

By midsummer Proust's relations with Montesquiou had improved. The count wrote on July 24 to "My dear Marcel," inviting him to come the next day with his "brother Hahn" to see a few old friends. Montesquiou closed, "Until Thursday, I hope, and affectionately, FMR." Marcel answered his "dear Master," saying that he and Reynaldo were to leave on Friday for Dieppe, as guests of Mme Lemaire in her seaside villa, so he was reluctant to accept an invitation for the eve of their departure. After many flattering flourishes, Marcel signed the letter: "Your devoted disciple and friend."[77]

Marcel and Reynaldo did leave Paris, but not directly for Dieppe. Instead, they went to visit Reynaldo's sisters Maria and Clarita at Saint-Germain-en-Laye. After two exceptionally happy weeks with Hahn's sisters, the two men arrived in Dieppe on August 8. Marcel remembered his childhood, when he had first seen the old ramparts encircling the medieval village by the sea. From Madeleine's villa Marcel and Reynaldo watched the sea and the strollers on the fashionable boardwalk that ran along the shore.

Two days after their arrival, Reynaldo wrote Maria that he felt "great" and was enjoying himself in Dieppe, where he and Marcel took long walks. Then he described for Maria the deep nocturnal setting and the slumbering household: "It is four in the morning and I am writing while facing the sea, blue as a flower, or gray as the wing of a migratory bird. Everyone is sound asleep: the ladies downstairs, Marcel next door, but with one eye open, so that even the sound of my pen gives me terrible anxieties. He had a mild asthma attack. May his parents allow him this trip to Brittany that I so much desire!"[78]

Hahn, who had recently become acquainted with Sarah Bernhardt, whom he worshiped, had planned a trip to the actress's new summer home on Belle-Île-en-Mer, an island off the coast of Brittany. He was eager to visit that province and developed an itinerary that included other spots distinguished by the celebrated actress's frequent visits. She loved the region's hilly and rugged coastline, believing that its grand and wild nature matched her own.

During Marcel's stay in Dieppe, his better moments were spent listening to the sounds of the sea with Reynaldo and exploring the surrounding dunes and glens. As Marcel grew more relaxed, he enjoyed lying in the dunes and losing himself in nature. On one excursion to nearby Petit-Abbeville, his admiration of the beech woods inspired a prose poem, "Sous-bois" (Forest scene), for his forthcoming book.

From Auteuil, Jeanne continued to monitor her son's condition. Although he still sent daily bulletins on his bowel movements, breathing, sleep, and other bodily functions, she was not content with information she considered vague and reminded him of the precise categories they had used in letters when he was younger ("went to bed at ——; rose at ——," etc.) After admonishing him to handle his affairs in as orderly a manner as possible until he and his father were both back in Paris—an indication that a family council was needed to discuss his spending habits and career plans—she informed him that she had just received from the florist Mme Lemaître a huge bill that she would pay for him, as he had requested.[79]

During his last week as Mme Lemaire's guest, Marcel met one of France's most celebrated composers, Camille Saint-Saëns, also on holiday in Dieppe.[80] Saint-Saëns, who had been a student of Mme Straus's father, Fromenthal Halévy, and had in turn taught Gabriel Fauré, was in his sixtieth year; he was renowned for his many compositions, including symphonies, concertos, and operas, especially *Samson et Dalila*. Proust particularly admired his Sonata for Violin and Piano No. 1 in D Minor, a piece that he remembered when creating compositions for Vinteuil in the *Search*.

Although Madeleine, playing surrogate mother to both young men, remained concerned about their health, especially Marcel's, she had absolute faith in the salubrious atmosphere of Dieppe and the curative powers of her own ministrations. She wrote Maria that Reynaldo and Marcel would imperil their well-being if they left the refuge of her villa and affection: "Ah! if only they would give up their Brittany trip. I dare not mention it to them for fear of making them think about leaving—it seems to me that they will get more rest here than in bad hotels. I make them eat at regular hours. But once they are on their own who knows when they will take their meals?"[81]

When Madeleine saw that she could not dissuade her two young protégés from going to Brittany, she felt genuinely hurt. Not only did she dread losing such amiable and witty company, but her maternal instincts, which often bordered on the tyrannical, told her that they might be in danger if allowed to roam. Madeleine's determination to keep these two of her "faithful" close at hand, where she might manage their lives, was a trait Proust was to give to Mme Verdurin, the bourgeois society hostess in the *Search* who makes virtual prisoners of her group. One can hear comic echoes of Lemaire's possessiveness in this passage, in which Mme Verdurin, who always predicts disaster when any of her little clan travel without her, expresses her horror on learning that Dr. and Mme Cottard have planned a trip at Easter: "In Auvergne? To be eaten alive by fleas and all sorts of creatures! A fine lot of good that will do you!"[82] Marcel, not feeling as strong as he would have liked, but unwilling to disappoint Reynaldo, ignored Mme Lemaire's warnings and left on an extended vacation with the man he loved.

"A primitive and delightful spot"

On September 5 Marcel and Reynaldo sailed across the Bay of Biscay to Belle-Île-en-Mer, the largest of the islands that lie in the Atlantic Ocean off the Brittany Coast. As they sailed into the port of Le Palais, they observed the high walls of the seventeenth-century citadel, built by the famed military engineer Sébastien Le Prestre de Vauban. The spectacular scenery offers sheer seaside cliffs rising two hundred feet above the water. After centuries of battering the cliffs, the sea has, in many spots, carved out fantastic grottoes and rock formations, and when waves pound these jagged rocks, their force hurls thick spouts of spray high into the air.

In 1893, the year of Sarah Bernhardt's triumphant reprise of one of her most famous roles, Phèdre, she had purchased an old Napoleonic fort built on a high promontory with grand, sweeping vistas of the sea. With her usual zeal, Bernhardt converted the ancient fort into her summer home, complete with gardens, tennis courts, and other amenities that she, her entourage, and a large retinue of adoring servants began to enjoy in the summer of 1895.

Marcel and Reynaldo had barely arrived at Fort Sarah Bernhardt, where the flagpole flew a blue and white banner with the initials SB, when Mme Lemaire's predictions began to come true: Proust fell ill with a stomachache and fever. Soon he had but one thought: to return to the mainland as quickly as possible. Reynaldo, apparently indifferent to the island's savage beauty, readily agreed. The two friends left the following day, depriving Marcel of the opportunity to observe "la grande Sarah" in her island retreat.

Back on the mainland, they spent two days visiting various Brittany attractions, although sightseeing was difficult for Marcel, who slept poorly and suffered from diarrhea. On September 8 they reached the seaside village of Beg-Meil, where, on a gentle hill overlooking the sea, they found a small hotel, the Fermont. Run by a couple who had converted a farmhouse into a hotel, the establishment had become popular with painters, who stayed as late as possible in the season and often left their pictures behind as payment for the modest bills. Because the main building had only four or five rooms and all were taken, Hahn and Proust had to lodge in the annex, located approximately ninety meters away, in rooms that rented for two francs a night. They took their meals with the other guests in the hotel. Marcel, exhausted from his recent illnesses, desperately needed to settle down for a while.

Reynaldo registered first, listing his profession as musician; then Marcel took the pen and indicated his occupation not as librarian but as a man of letters—perhaps self-mockingly, for he had earlier cringed at the label assumed by so many inferior writers and poseurs. At least three of the other hotel guests were painters, and Beg-Meil, with the addition of a composer and a writer, suddenly resembled a miniature artists' colony. That evening after a pleasant dinner, Reynaldo wrote Maria to inform her of their whereabouts. He described for her Beg-Meil's natural beauty and lush vegetation. There were apple trees everywhere, as in Normandy, and "real Breton flowers, genista, heather, golden furze." Hahn decided to use this time in such a peaceful, secluded spot to finish the first section and the andante of his trio.[83]

Exploring the area around Beg-Meil, Proust found the air intoxicating and the views superb: "On one side there is the sea, very Breton and sad. On the other the Bay of Concarneau, which is blue with, in the background, a vista exactly like Lake Geneva."[84] Marcel began to feel much better; his recent stomach troubles disappeared, and he began to eat heartily.

Before embarking on the trip to Brittany, Proust had no idea that they would end up in such an isolated place. He had brought along books to read, Balzac's *Splendeurs et misères des courtisanes* and Thomas Carlyle's *Heroes and Hero-Worship* in a French translation, but no stationery or writing supplies. He scribbled a letter to Robert de Billy on the backs of two calling cards: "My dear Robert, . . . I am in a village where there is no paper. It's called Beg-Meil, the apple trees come down to the sea, and the smell of cider mingles with that of seaweed. The mixture of poetry and sensuality is just about right for me." He told Billy to watch for his story about Baldassare Silvande in *La Revue hebdomadaire*.[85]

Proust secured one sheet of decent writing paper and used it to inform Yturri that they had landed in "a primitive and delightful spot . . . where, however, there are not even any water closets. And indeed, this would be just the place to air Vigny's line:

Never leave me alone with nature.

For it is to nature that we consign everything, and I assure you that nothing is so *irritating* as the excessive zeal of the nettles, which try to make themselves *indispensable,* if you will forgive the pun, and their way of doing it is piquant but harsh."[86] Proust's pun alluded to the latest French euphemism for toilet paper, *indispensables.* He ended his letter by entreating Yturri to convey his "admiration and devotion to the great Poet."

Accustomed to the finest hotels, Marcel adapted well to his two-franc room and to all the other hardships, even to squatting in the bushes when he needed to evacuate his bowels. How had he found such an isolated spot? Sarah Bernhardt, who knew the region well, may have recommended Beg-Meil, but more likely the idea came from André Bénac, a railroad executive and close friend of Adrien's. The Bénacs had a house on the beach and a farm nearby, Kerengrimen, where, as Proust noted with delight, "apple trees slope down to the rocky beach."[87]

One of the painters with whom they immediately formed a bond was the American expatriate Thomas Alexander Harrison, a longtime visitor to Beg-Meil.[88] Harrison was a talented painter, one of whose works, *Blue Lake,* Reynaldo remembered seeing at Luxembourg Palace in Paris. Harrison rented a ramshackle studio constructed of unpainted planks on the Bénac farm. Fanatical about the beauty of the sunsets at Beg-Meil, every evening Harrison raced to the dunes to watch the sinking sun. Soon Marcel and Reynaldo joined him for the late afternoon dash to catch the sunsets, whose colors Hahn described to Maria: "We have seen the sea successively turn blood red, purple, nacreous with silver, gold, white, emerald green, and yesterday we were dazzled by an entirely pink sea specked with blue sails."[89]

The only problem with Beg-Meil, they discovered, was that the peaceful, natural beauty of the place made toil seem unnecessary and even foolish. The musician and the man of letters were working so little that by the end of September, Reynaldo confessed to Maria that he had not written a single note for his trio, though he had finished a few pieces begun earlier. But the location had inspired him to begin sketching a "Breton choral" work, eventually called *Là-bas* (Over there).[90]

Marcel had been thinking about new episodes for a story he began drafting sometime during the summer, most likely at Beg-Meil. These fragments became the basis for *Jean Santeuil,* the sprawling novel on which he worked intermittently for the next five years until the manuscript reached nearly a thousand pages. Proust named his hero Jean, probably as a tribute to his mother, whose name was the feminine form of the same name. While in Brittany he wrote descriptions based on his explorations of the coast, but he also wrote about the past, especially his childhood experiences in Paris, Auteuil, and Illiers, often transposing them to suit his fancy and the characters he sought to invent. Proust's encounter with Harrison inspired the character in *Jean Santeuil* known simply as the writer C, aspects of whom Proust would use for Elstir in the *Search,* who, like his original model, is a painter.[91]

Marcel and Reynaldo were so content in Beg-Meil that they decided to have their special thirty-three-day "Seaside Resorts" train passes, purchased for this trip, extended for another ten days into October.[92] Although this routine request would have been granted anyone, Proust thought it appropriate to ask M. Bénac, secretary general of the state railways, to handle the matter for him. Harrison, with his painter's eye and precise knowledge of the area, advised Marcel and Reynaldo how to use their extended railway passes to see the most beautiful vistas and sunsets. Proust later said that of all the places they visited along the coast, he "infinitely" preferred "Penmarch . . . a sort of mixture of Holland and the Indies and Florida (according to Harrison). Nothing could be more sublime than a tempest seen from there."[93] His preference went to Penmarch, no doubt, because of what he perceived to be its metaphorical nature, embodying not a single place but many. Proust usually preferred the complex to the simple, seeing many things in one; finding the harmony that unites them was a special faculty of his that he sought to develop.

A draft of *Jean Santeuil* inspired by Beg-Meil and Lake Geneva contains a sketch of a key theme of the future work: the phenomenon of memory ignited by a physical sensation; the examination of this sensation leads him to conclude that our true nature is outside time.[94] One day near Geneva, Jean, while driving in a carriage through farmland, suddenly sees Lake Geneva come into view: "Looking at the sea (at this hour it had almost the appearance of the sea) at the end of the road . . . Jean suddenly remembered. He saw it before him as the very sea he once had known, and felt its charm. In a flash, that life in Brittany which he had thought useless and unusable, appeared before his eyes in all its charm and beauty, and his heart swelled within him as he thought of his walks at Beg-Meil when the sun was setting and the sea stretched out before him." Then he wonders about the nature of the extraordinary memory phenomenon he is experiencing. He understands that what the poet needs to feed his imagination is memory experienced in the present, containing both the past and now. Jean then recalls a similar experience, provoked by the smell of "a deplorable wooden villa" where he and his family had vacationed by the sea: "The whole of that period of my life, with its hopes, its worries, its hungers, its hours of sleep or sleeplessness, its efforts to find joy in art—which ended in failure—its experiments in sensual gratification . . . its attempts to win the love of someone who had taken my fancy . . . all were caught up and made present in that smell." Jean finds that such recollections are total and "preserve the essence of both sense and memory."

This rough draft contains the elements of Proust's theory of involuntary memory that receives its definitive expression in the famous madeleine scene of the *Search*. Such early attempts to describe and comprehend this phenomenon indicate that there was not one precise moment in the writer's life when he bit into a madeleine and, in a frenzy of inspiration, began writing the *Search*. Proust recognized as early as *Jean Santeuil* the rich potential of such experiences, saying that they were "alive on a higher level than memory or than the present, so that they have not the flatness of pictures but the rounded fullness of reality, the ambiguity of feeling."[95] But he was years away from discovering how to make them serve a novel's plot.

The manuscript of *Jean Santeuil* contains the draft of an early-October letter to Raymond Poincaré, minister of education and future French president, requesting a month's extension of his sick leave from the library, from October 15 to November 15. Proust needed more time to complete the cure for "nervous asthma," from which he had "almost entirely recovered due to the two-month leave you so kindly granted me."[96] As usual, Marcel believed in going right to the top. If Marcel succeeded in extending his leave, he could visit Pierre Lavallée at Segrez or perhaps tour other areas of France with him during the late fall months. He saved the draft of this letter and used the back to write memories of Jean's days as a lycée student.[97]

On October 19 Marcel and Reynaldo left Beg-Meil on an excursion to see one of France's most spectacular and dangerous spots of natural beauty: the Pointe du Raz, whose high cliffs and jagged rocks are surrounded by a surging sea.[98] Proust noted with satisfaction that this gigantic granite rock was "literally Finisterre" (the end of the earth) and had been, according to Breton folklore, the object of a famous Breton curse.[99] The two Parisian tourists returned safely to the Fermont, surviving the dangers of the jagged and cursed sea-pounded cliff.

The following week Proust received catastrophic news: his request for additional sick leave had been denied.[100] This development dashed his plans for trips to Segrez, Réveillon, Dieppe, or other destinations he had contemplated. Marcel, who had no intention of working at the book depository, was to file another request for extended sick leave. As he prepared to leave Beg-Meil for Paris, he wondered whether his procrastinating illustrator had made any progress on her drawings for his long-awaited book.

PART III

A Man of Letters (1895–1899)

7 *Pleasures and Days* ∾

WHILE MARCEL AND REYNALDO WERE IN BRITTANY, Mme Lemaire contacted M. Jean Hubert, editor at Calmann-Lévy, regarding the production schedule of *Le Château de Réveillon.* During the remaining fall months Proust and Lemaire would each urge Hubert to intervene with the other in order to expedite matters. In one letter Mme Lemaire, citing Anatole France to back up her claims, beseeched Hubert to persuade Proust to make a few changes, such as eliminating certain pieces that were "somewhat muddled and of no interest" and shortening the rather long dedication.[1] Clearly, the young author required a great deal of assistance, and Mme Lemaire was eager to provide it.

Both the writer and his illustrator were to blame for the delays. If she had missed deadlines time and again by taking countless vacations and accepting too many other commissions, he had complicated matters by adding new stories, removing some of the older ones, and changing the order of the contents. By early November, Marcel began to lose patience and pleaded with Hubert to persuade Mme Lemaire to produce the illustrations with no further delay because he wanted a publishing date of February 1896. He also sought Hubert's advice on the delicate matter of his contract and royalties. Marcel admitted that because of his timidity he had never dared bring up the subject with the publisher Calmann-Levy, having had only one meeting with him. Did Hubert think they should agree on the amount Proust would receive for each volume? Would the costs of the reproduction method used considerably modify the amount? Nothing came of Proust's query, just as nothing had come of the single meeting with Calmann-Levy. Proust did not press the matter, and the book was published without a contract. His expectation that the book would sell enough copies to earn him royalties was naïve.

Proust's frustration with Calmann-Lévy and Lemaire was temporarily forgotten on October 29, when his story about the death of Baldassare appeared in the *Revue hebdomadaire,* dedicated to "Reynaldo Hahn, poet, singer and musician."[2] Proust was paid 150 francs for the story, apparently the first money he earned with his pen. Replying to Reynaldo, who had thanked him for the dedication, Marcel told his friend: "I would like to be master of all that you desire on earth in order to bring it to you—author of all you admire in art in order to dedicate it to you. I'm beginning in a very small way! but, who knows, if you encourage me . . . "[3]

Once introduced to Alphonse Daudet's circle by Reynaldo, Proust became acquainted with such distinguished writers among Daudet's friends as Edmond de Goncourt and Maurice Barrès. On November 14 Marcel and Reynaldo dined at the Daudets with the Parnassian poet and playwright François Coppée, a member of the Académie française, and the realist novelist Charles-Louis Philippe. Coppée had enjoyed enormous success with his poems and plays, including his 1869 play *Le Passant,* in which Sarah Bernhardt had won fame as Zanetto. Coppée, like the Daudets and Goncourt, was a staunch anti-Semite. In 1899, motivated primarily by the storm over the Dreyfus Affair, he was a founder of the notorious nationalist and racist Ligue de la patrie française.

At dinner that evening Marcel heard enough expressions of bigotry and inane remarks about literature to make him vent his disgust and sadness to Reynaldo in a letter the next day. If artists and intellectuals, France's most distinguished and celebrated citizens, held such stupid opinions, what, he wondered, could one expect from ordinary people? Because no one outside official circles had any reason to believe Dreyfus innocent, his plight had not yet captured public attention. The prejudices expressed by the Daudets and their circle, sentiments also prevalent throughout society, had made it easy, once it became evident that a spy was operating at the Ministry of War, for the army to identity a Jew as the traitor. In his letter to Hahn, Proust "noted with sadness . . . the frightful materialism, so surprising in 'intellectuals.' They account for character and genius by physical habits or race." Proust doubted whether any of the writers at dinner that evening understood "anything about poetry. A person who has no feeling for poetry and who is not moved by Truth, has never really read Baudelaire."[4]

On this occasion, Marcel held his tongue, apparently, when those around him uttered racist remarks. Derogatory comments about Jews, though he knew they were unfair, were commonplace and easily overlooked. Goncourt's account of the dinner mentions none of the details that appalled Marcel; the diarist had been intrigued by Mme Barrès's new hairdo and by Gustave Larroumet's accounts of the ferocious tortures practiced by Moroccan Islamics.[5]

Sometime in November, Proust wrote to Pierre Mainguet, publisher of the *Revue hebdomadaire,* wondering whether his readers might be interested in a "little study of the philosophy of art, if the term is not too pretentious, in which I try to show how great painters initiate us into a knowledge and love of the external world" by opening our eyes. The artist whom Proust had chosen as his example was Jean-Baptiste Chardin, whose still lifes reveal the beauty of the most common objects. Proust informed Mainguet that he had written an essay denouncing the "obscurity" of verses being written by young poets of the symbolist school, but he hesitated to offer it because he feared its vehemence would provoke the poets' desire for revenge when his own book appeared. Mainguet declined both pieces.[6]

In his study of Chardin, Proust expressed for the first time one of his "laws" or truths: art always results from the vision unique to each creative person and not from the beauty of the object depicted. A common kitchen utensil depicted by Chardin can be far more beautiful than, say, a string of pearls painted by a lesser artist. Or, as Proust later observed, applying the same principle to authors: "A mediocre writer who lives in a heroic age does not cease to be a mediocre writer."[7] Proust apparently put aside the Chardin essay, although he later attributed its basic ideas to his character Elstir.

Mad Laughter

Marcel was making plans for a dinner party to include his parents, Montesquiou, the Heredias, Antoinette and Lucie Faure—the "very intelligent daughters" of the president—as well as historian Gabriel Hanotaux, who had recently resigned as minister of foreign affairs.[8] At a secret October meeting of a "petty council" to decide what steps to take in thwarting the spy ring that was operating through the German embassy, Hanotaux had been the only official courageous enough to question the nature of the evidence used to court-martial Dreyfus. Hanotaux did not dwell on the matter because his chief concern, as befitted his office, had been the effect on diplomatic relations with Germany, if its embassy's involvement in espionage became publicly known.[9]

Just before the dinner party Montesquiou received a strange letter from Marcel and Lucien Daudet, who claimed that for the past week whenever they were together it was impossible for them to avoid "being seized and held by the most irrational, painful and irresistible laughter." Because they would be with Montesquiou and other friends that evening, the purpose of their letter was to beg his indulgence and ask that he warn the others: "Since Delafosse or Gregh might take offense, would you be so kind as to tell them not to be more sensitive than M. and Mme Daudet, who have been patiently tolerating this disorder for a week." Marcel and Lucien were particularly concerned about their behavior that evening because the reception would be attended by a distinguished friend of Montesquiou's whom he was eager for them to meet. Before affixing their signatures, the two hysterical young men assured Montesquiou of their affection and respect.[10] No doubt that remark made them giggle.

Lucien and Marcel had been playing a game that increased the likelihood of their breaking into mad laughter. They compiled lists of what they called *louchonneries,* trite or pretentious expressions, such as "the Big Blue" for the Mediterranean Sea or "our little soldiers" for the French army. Whenever Marcel and Lucien heard someone utter an expression from their list, the two would give each other a knowing look and Marcel would "modestly lower his eyes," in which Lucien would see "gleaming the diabolical light of uncontrollable laughter" that he found contagious.[11] In the beginning their fits of hilarity had been merely a game, but it soon became a problem, and they could not go anywhere together without making efforts to maintain a serious, respectful demeanor. Proust seemed to take pleasure in the juvenile game; before arriving at the Daudets, he would alert Lucien with telegrams asking him to warn his parents and appeal to their indulgence.

Although Lucien's parents tolerated this rude behavior, Montesquiou had no patience with such nonsense. He thought that Marcel and Lucien were attempting to spoil the exquisite aesthetic harmony of his parties. That evening, as soon as the two young men entered the room, Montesquiou's stern, suspicious demeanor sent them into peals of laughter, and they had to rush out of the room, suffocating and bent over double. Lucien said that Montesquiou never forgave them; years later the count still spoke of this "impropriety."

Montesquiou had other reasons to be displeased with Marcel. The count had heard that his disciple frequently did imitations of him at parties, mimicking his manner, gestures, voice, and even laughter. Marcel's admission of being unable to control his laughter gave Montesquiou the opportunity to raise the issue of these imitations. Although the count broached the subject with diffidence in his letter accepting the dinner invitation, Proust became alarmed and defensive. He denied that he persisted in imitating Montesquiou and, trying to put the best face on things, claimed to have done so only as an act of homage, because his body—he ingenuously claimed—had been unable to resist following his soul in taking the poet as his model: "If anyone has said more than this, and if they have spoken of caricature, I invoke your axiom: 'A remark repeated at second hand is rarely true.'" Then, prudently following the adage that the best defense is to attack, Marcel broached a grievance of his own. Someone had told him that Montesquiou had been less than generous in commenting about Proust's latest poems: "I was . . . somewhat humiliated to see that my 'latest creations,' as you call them, were held to be not very creative, and that you addressed me with . . . contemptuous tolerance."[12]

On December 8 Proust attended a program at the Conservatory, where Saint-Saëns played the piano part in a Mozart concerto. Afterward, he drafted an essay in which he examined the performer's effect on his audience. Around the same time, he submitted another article on Saint-Saëns to *Le Gaulois* and sent the composer a copy for his inspection, with the "homage of a respectful, passionate admirer," reminding the composer that they had met in Dieppe at Mme Lemaire's.[13] Proust's piece appeared on the newspaper's front page on the day of the dress rehearsal of *Frédégonde,* an opera, left unfinished by Ernest Guiraud, that Saint-Saëns had just completed. Guiraud provided one of Mme Straus's favorite anecdotes, which Proust would use in the *Search.* When she asked Guiraud, legendary for his absent-mindedness, whether his love child resembled her mother, the composer replied: "I don't know, I've never seen her without her hat."[14]

Despite "passionate" admiration for Saint-Saëns's work, Proust thought less highly of the composer's accomplishments than did his former pupil Reynaldo. But the haunting melody of one section of the first movement of Saint-Saëns's Sonata I for piano and violin, opus 75, captivated him. Marcel never tired of hearing it and asked Reynaldo to play it for him again and again, referring to it as the "little phrase." In *Jean Santeuil,* where Proust uses music by Saint-Saëns for Jean and Françoise's love song, he names the composer and the work. In the *Search* the same music, which Swann asks his mistress Odette to play for him again and again, is attributed to Proust's fictional composer Vinteuil.[15]

On December 24 Marcel received notification that he had been granted a year's leave from the Mazarine.[16] He now had the ideal situation: a title, though modest, with no duties. In the closing days of December, Proust, increasingly frustrated by Mme Lemaire's endless delays, wrote Hubert a series of letters aimed at compelling her to complete the illustrations. In one letter he urged Hubert to write to Mme Lemaire in a firm tone, because Marcel could do no more than pin his "hopes on the friendship of Mme Lemaire, who, since she has been holding me over the baptismal font of letters for the last four years . . . will not wish to hold me up for another year."[17] Marcel had doubled the number of years he had been suspended over the baptismal font, but for the eager young author the time spent waiting seemed far too long. By New Year's Eve, Proust knew that he had been betrayed when he learned about a meeting earlier in the week between Hubert and Lemaire at which the editor gave the illustrator permission to continue work on new pieces. Proust worried that the additional drawings for "Fragments de comédie italienne" (Scenes from Italian comedy) would draw the reader's eyes to the section that he considered the weakest in the book. But what riled him most was the missed opportunity to publish in February.

By year's end Marcel and Reynaldo's relationship had grown strained. Proust's affection for Reynaldo remained just as strong, but he had fallen in love with Lucien. Whether during their bouts of mad laughter across the dinner table at the Daudets' or during their meetings at the Louvre, which Lucien often visited as an art student, Proust had succumbed to the spell of Daudet's beauty. He marveled at the boy's features, delicate and sensual, his dreamy eyes, and his fine, olive complexion. Lucien's family, conservative and devoutly Catholic, chose to ignore his effeminate nature.

Why and how Marcel's passionate friendship with Reynaldo ended is not clear, but Proust's attraction to Lucien must have played a role. Aware since childhood of the career he wanted, Hahn was pursuing his goals as a composer and performer, and he had often found his romantic relationship with Marcel too complicated and above all too demanding. He fluctuated between jealousy and exasperation about Marcel's fussing over Lucien, who was practically a child. Marcel had just purchased an exceptionally fine article for Lucien's New Year's present: a beautiful eighteenth-century carved ivory box. When Lucien opened the box to admire its beauty, he felt certain that Marcel had enclosed his love.

After the holidays, Hubert remained caught between the impatient author and his meddlesome illustrator eager to correct what she considered the literary deficiencies of the work. Yielding to Mme Lemaire, Hubert wrote Anatole France a confidential letter, appealing to his "great authority," for Marcel was unwilling to "perfect" the text. Hubert and Lemaire deplored the rambling dedication and certain pieces that were somehow too involved and without interest. Even if, as they acknowledged might be the case, these elements endowed a beginner's work with charm, it was a charm with which they would gladly dispense.[17] France, unconvinced by their arguments or unwilling to intervene, ignored the request.

Early in the new year Paul Verlaine died, depriving the nation of the man many had considered France's greatest contemporary poet. Montesquiou was among those who spoke at the funeral on January 10. Proust, reflecting on Verlaine's achievement while struggling with alcoholism and living in the abject poverty to which his addictions had reduced him, commended Montesquiou for having "distinguished this moving contrast . . . between heavenly poetry and a hellish life."[18] Such distinctions became paramount to Proust's own aesthetics.

Sometime in the first quarter of the year Proust wrote the beginning pages of *Jean Santeuil,* in which Jean, vacationing in Beg-Meil, meets the novelist C. Marcel sent his draft to Reynaldo and asked whether it contained anything that recalled too obviously their being together, anything that was "too pony." If so, Hahn must help him to correct those parts. Then he spoke tenderly to Reynaldo, saying that he wanted him to be present in everything he wrote, "but like a god in disguise, invisible to mortals. Otherwise you'd have to write 'tear up' on every page."[19] Ultimately Hahn, like Lucien, was too close a friend to serve as a model for a character in Marcel's book, though part of the disguise Proust had in mind may be in the name of Jean's closest friend Henri de Réveillon, whose initials are Hahn's reversed. On March 1 a short-lived review, *La Vie contemporaine,* published Proust's novella *L'Indifférent.* Before publication Marcel inserted, as a compliment to Hahn, an oblique allusion to his opera *L'Île du rêve,* for which the composer still hoped to find a producer.

Toward the end of March Proust received, at last, the first proofs of his book, bearing the title *Le Château de Réveillon.* In April, while correcting the final proofs, he changed the title to *Les Plaisirs et les jours* (Pleasures and days). He realized that using the name of Lemaire's castle as the title of a book filled with her drawings might confuse his readers about its contents. For the new title he drew inspiration from Hesiod, whose works he had read in Leconte de Lisle's translation. But whereas the ancient writer had called his book *Works and Days,* Proust replaced chores by pleasures to indicate the vain, frivolous world inhabited by his characters. Finally, the long delayed project neared completion. On April 21 Anatole France signed and dated his preface. One week later the press campaign began when *Le Gaulois* announced the book's imminent publication.

Early in May, Proust dashed off a note to Lucien at Rodolphe Julian's academy. He apologized for disturbing him during his art class again—he swore this would be the last time—and asked to meet him outside the academy. Proust inquired about Lucien's brother, Léon, who had fallen gravely ill with typhoid fever from having eaten tainted oysters while in Venice.[20] Because the disease often proved fatal, the Daudet family passed many anxious hours before it became apparent that Léon would survive. Proust informed Lucien that he had set out that morning for the Daudet home to inquire about his brother's condition but that, on arriving in the full sunlight at the place de la Concorde, he had begun to sneeze violently and had to turn back.[21]

On May 10 Uncle Louis fell ill and died, at age eighty, in his home at 102, boulevard Haussmann. Marcel and his mother went to sit with the body. He sent a kind note to Laure Hayman, who had been the old man's mistress and friend: "Madame, My poor old uncle Louis Weil died yesterday at five in the afternoon, without suffering, without consciousness, without having been ill (a case of pneumonia that had made its appearance that same morning)."[22] Proust, who knew how fond Laure was of his uncle, had not wanted her to learn about his death from the newspapers. On the day of the funeral, Marcel received a note from Laure, conveying her condolences and expressing her frustration at being unable to attend the funeral without raising eyebrows. The funeral procession began in front of Louis's home and proceeded, with the mourners walking behind the horse-drawn hearse, to Père-Lachaise cemetery. The family no doubt wished to discourage Laure's presence at the funeral, but Marcel informed her of the time and place and protested, perhaps too much, that she would be most welcome: "But what *madness* to suppose you would shock anyone at all. They can only be *touched* by your presence."[23]

To the family's relief Laure did not attend, but just as the procession neared the cemetery, a boy, pedaling fast on a bicycle bearing a floral wreath, caught up with the mourners. Laure's attempt to be discreet while paying her respects had not succeeded; the family had requested no flowers. Marcel wrote to Laure a few days later, explaining that only asthma and choking fits had prevented his writing sooner to tell her "how amazed, how moved and overwhelmed I was at your so touching, so beautiful, so 'chic' thought of the other day." When he had found out the wreath was from her, he had "burst into tears, less out of grief than admiration.

Proust's father, Dr. Adrien Proust (1834–1903), around the time he married Jeanne Weil.

Mme Adrien Proust (1849–1905). *Photo: Bibliothèque nationale de France*

An early childhood portrait of Marcel, right, and his younger brother, Robert, in Scottish costume. *Mante-Proust Collection*

Marcel, left, and Robert around 1882.
Photo: Bibliothèque nationale de France

Marie de Benardaky, described by Proust as "the love of my life" during his school days. They often met to play on the Champs-Élysées.

Marcel, in boater, with Antoinette Faure and another young friend in the Parc Monceau. *Mante-Proust Collection*

Marcel at age fifteen, March 24, 1887.
*Paul Nadar/©Arch. Phot. Paris/*CNMHS

Alphonse Darlu's philosophy class at the
Lycée Condorcet. Proust, second row, far
left, is in his senior year, 1888–89. *Mante-
Proust Collection*

Proust in the infantry at Orléans, 1889–90. *Mante-Proust Collection*

Robert de Billy, future diplomat and close friend of Proust's. They met at Orléans during their year of military service. *Mante-Proust Collection*

Proust, seated at left, with Mme Geneviève Straus and other friends, shortly after his discharge from the army. *Photo: Bibliothèque nationale de France*

During his university years Proust sports a Liberty tie and a camellia boutonniere.
Mante-Proust Collection

Proust at the feet of Jeanne Pouquet at the tennis court on boulevard Bineau.
Photo: Bibliothèque nationale de France

Singer, pianist, and composer Reynaldo Hahn, 1898. Proust and Hahn met in the salon of Madeleine Lemaire and became lifelong friends. *Paul Nadar/©Arch. Phot. Paris/*CNMHS

The Parisian aristocrat Comte Robert de Montesquiou, 1895. A poet, art critic, and aesthete, Montesquiou was the primary model for Proust's baron de Charlus. *Paul Nadar/©Arch. Phot. Paris/*CNMHS

Comtesse Élisabeth Greffulhe, 1896. A cousin of Montesquiou's, the countess was considered the most beautiful salon hostess in Parisian society, and one of the most accomplished. *Paul Nadar/©Arch. Phot. Paris/CNMHS*

Dr. Adrien Proust, 1886, at the height of his distinguished medical career. *Photo: Bibliothèque nationale de France*

Mme Proust with her sons, Marcel and Robert, 1893. *Photo: Bibliothèque nationale de France*

Portrait of Proust as a young socialite by Jacques-Émile Blanche, oil on canvas, 1893. *Réunion des Musées Nationaux-ADAGP*

Proust with friends Robert de Flers, left, and Lucien Daudet, 1893. *Photo: Bibliothèque nationale de France*

Mme Geneviève Straus, 1887. A society hostess renowned for her salon and her wit, she remained a close friend to Proust throughout his life. *Paul Nadar/©Arch. Phot. Paris/CNMHS*

Laure Hayman, 1879. A celebrated courtesan of the Belle Époque, Laure was the mistress of Proust's great-uncle Louis Weil. She inspired Proust's creation of Odette de Crécy. *Paul Nadar/©Arch. Phot. Paris/CNMHS*

I was so hoping you would be at the cemetery so I could take you in my arms." Marcel conveyed to Laure as tactfully as possible what happened to her offering: at the cemetery, when Jeanne heard about the flowers, she said she wanted Louis to be buried with Laure's wreath.[24] Louis had managed to leave the world enveloped in sweet fragrances from a beloved courtesan.

Jeanne and her brother Georges inherited the apartment building on boulevard Haussmann. The following year they sold the Auteuil property to a developer, who promptly razed the house and adjacent structures in order to construct several apartment buildings that occupied all the land.[25] The home where Marcel and Robert had been born, the garden of their childhood, and the family summer retreat of many years had disappeared overnight.

During the year Marcel lamented the disappearance of the Auteuil property as well as his growing awareness of the effects of old age on his parents in a draft for *Jean Santeuil:* "Monsieur and Madame Santeuil had greatly changed since the day when we first made their acquaintance in the little garden at Auteuil, on the site of which three or four six-storeyed houses had now been built."[26] As though to underscore the passage of time, Adrien drew up his will later in the month. With his mother in mourning for her uncle, Marcel curtailed his social life for a brief period. In mid-May, he declined an invitation to a sumptuous ball given by Mme Emilio Terry at her home in the Bois de Boulogne.

Although none of Marcel's friends considered him a Jew, he noticed that race was becoming a frequent topic of conversation and controversy in social circles and in the newspapers. Émile Zola, alarmed at the vehemence of the anti-Semite press, published an article in *Le Figaro* on May 16, "Pour les juifs" (For the Jews), to defend the Jews against the rabid attacks to which they were frequently subjected. Many Jews were willing to overlook outbursts of intolerance rather than defend themselves and risk setbacks in their goal of assimilation into French society.

Marcel considered himself Catholic, but he never denied his lineage. Montesquiou, who had made denigrating remarks about Jews in a group that included Proust, received a letter explaining why Marcel had said nothing: "Dear Sir, Yesterday I did not answer the question you put to me about the Jews. For this very simple reason: though I am a Catholic like my father and brother, my mother is Jewish. I am sure you understand that this is reason enough for me to refrain from such discussions." Proust went on to say that he did not share Montesquiou's ideas about Jews, or rather, that he was "not free to have the ideas I might otherwise have on the subject."[27] Proust stated his position and his independence, but he might have been less ambiguous about the ethical implications of racist remarks. Like many others, he failed to see the real dangers of intolerance, dangers that became more evident over the next several years as the Dreyfus Affair became a national obsession.

Marcel and Reynaldo had not settled into a new modus vivendi since the turbulence caused by Marcel's infatuation with Lucien. Their efforts to find a balance appeared in their negotiations and in Hahn's intermittent attempts to be generous and understanding. On May 21 Hahn wrote a letter reproaching Marcel for the excessive attention he paid Lucien. He informed Marcel that he would be free later in the day, but urged him not to pass up an evening with Lucien solely for his sake. Reynaldo even apologized for having scolded Marcel, observing that "life is so short and so boring" that Marcel was right not to forgo "those things (even the most trivial) that amuse or give pleasure, when they are blameless or harmless— thus, forgive me, dear little Marcel. I am sometimes quite unbearable; I'm aware of it. But we're all so imperfect. A thousand tendernesses, Reynaldo."[28] Marcel, perhaps less in love with Lucien than he thought, could not bring himself to break with Reynaldo. He soon attempted to assert in an absurd way more control over Hahn.

Marcel spent the last Tuesday in May with Lucien reading *Les Hortensias bleus,* Montesquiou's latest volume of poetry, with a preface by José-Maria de Heredia.[29] While impatiently awaiting the publication of his own book, Marcel congratulated several friends who had cause to celebrate. He wired congratulations to Robert de Flers, whose recent book *Vers l'orient* had received an award from the Académie française. That evening Marcel went to Mme Lemaire's soirée for the première of Reynaldo's Breton choral work *Là-bas,* begun when they were so happy at Beg-Meil. Hahn's composition was sung with great success, according to the next day's *Le Gaulois.* Among the many guests who had come to hear Hahn's music were Anatole France, Montesquiou, the Strauses, and Minister of Finance Raymond Poincaré.

Our Young Man

On June 9 *Le Gaulois* and *Le Figaro* carried on their front pages France's preface to *Pleasures and Days* and announced the book's publication for Saturday, June 12.[30] In the preface France recognized Proust's "marvelous sense of observation, a flexible, penetrating and truly subtle intelligence," and he spoke of the book's "hothouse atmosphere," where the reader is kept "among the sophisticated orchids." Although Proust was young, France insisted that the author was "not in the least innocent. But he is so sincere, so real that he becomes ingenuous, and is charming. . . . There is something of a depraved Bernardin de Saint-Pierre in him, of a guileless Petronius."

To oppose Petronius's urbane debauchery, France had chosen the eighteenth-century writer Bernardin de Saint-Pierre, author of *Paul et Virginie,* a tale of two children brought up in poverty and innocence far from society's corrupting influence. By calling Bernardin depraved and Petronius innocent to indicate the bipolar nature of Proust's characters in *Pleasures and Days,* France must have had in mind stories like "Violante ou la mondanité" and "La Confession d'une jeune fille," in which innocence becomes depraved, and "La Fin de la jalousie," in which depravity is redeemed and made innocent. France ended by saying how lucky for the book that it could "go through the city all decked and scented with the flowers Madeleine Lemaire has strewn through its pages with that divine hand which dispenses roses still wet with dew."

Friends and reviewers who noted France's preface, Hahn's music, and Lemaire's drawings wondered whether *Pleasures and Days* was a book or a social event. Gossipers, including Fernand Gregh, soon spread the word that Mme Arman had written the preface and that France had merely signed it. According to Gregh, Mme Arman had confided to him that France, "the God of our youth," had only added a few words here and there—such as the concluding tribute to Lemaire's flowers—to make it more "Francienne."[31]

Is this story true? Perhaps, but there are good reasons to believe that France did write the preface. In her memoirs, Jeanne Pouquet recalled that Mme Arman obtained the preface from France, as she did prefaces for Charles Maurras and other protégés, because she thought that France's fame obliged him to help his young friends make their literary debuts.[32] The text seems to bear Anatole France's ironic tone.[33] France's secretary Jean-Jacques Brousson claimed in his memoirs that Mme Arman wrote it because "Anatole France protested against having to provide a preface for a book by an author who wrote 'endless sentences that leave you breathless' and that 'roam about aimlessly.' "[34] But "endless sentences," and a discursive style, charges later leveled against Proust by some critics of the *Search,* do not characterize *Pleasures and Days,* whose sentences have a classical simplicity unlike Proust's mature manner. The testimonies of Gregh and Brousson notwithstanding, the evidence does not support their claims.[35]

Marcel had finally been baptized at the font of authorship, but the experience fell short of his expectations. While nervously awaiting the first reviews, he busied himself dispatching signed copies of the hefty, deluxe volume to friends. Some, like

Pierre Loti, who sent Proust a polite thank-you note, did not even bother to cut the pages. Of the fifty *grand luxe* copies, twenty contained an original watercolor by Madeleine Lemaire. Montesquiou received the deluxe copy no. 1, printed on Japanese vellum. In autographing Pierre Lavallée's copy—one of the thirty copies printed on rice paper—Proust referred to his work in progress: "I say my book as though I were never to write another. You know well enough that is not true."[36]

In addition to the deluxe copies, nearly 1,500 unbound copies were waiting for booksellers' orders to arrive. With a selling price of 13 francs, 50 centimes, nearly four times the normal price for a book, there were precious few customers. Proust gave away many copies, but after a while, even he hesitated to purchase copies at author's price. Proust soon understood that the cost of the book was killing sales. Despite his entreaties, Calmann-Lévy refused to publish an affordable edition until the expensive one sold out.

The first review appeared on June 26, 1896, in *La Liberté*, raising Proust's hopes for the book's success. In a lengthy, laudatory article, Paul Perret noted the melancholy nature and dangerous desires harbored by certain characters in the "short, fine, and often cruel stories."[37] He said that the author was a "true modern because he conveys the present soul state, the profound ennui in daily life, with a touch of decadence." *Pleasures and Days* offered a variety of pieces on a small scale: "short stories, very psychological in nature, fairly bold, always interesting, descriptions and landscapes, poems, even music." He remarked in passing that the illustrator was much better at rendering the faces of flowers than those of humans. Perret admired the poetical expression of the psychological insights, citing, for example, the sentence "Desire makes all things flourish, possession withers them; it is better to dream one's life than to live it, although in living life one dreams it still."[38] Perret even thought that the book might act as a social "force" because "Marcel Proust is also a fine satirist." This critic, who did not know the author, had seen what Marcel's friends could not. There was more to Proust than a social sycophant, and his book marked a promising debut: "This young man, richly endowed, has put in his first work all he has seen, felt, thought, and observed. *Pleasures and Days* thus becomes the literary mirror of a soul and mind."

Édouard Rod's review, in the June 27 issue of *Le Gaulois*, basically seconded France's "marvelous" preface and saw in Proust a budding moralist in the tradition of La Bruyère.[39] Sensing the critic's reservations, Proust thanked Rod for the review and urged him, if ever he had a free moment, "to read the first story in my book ('The death of Baldassare Silvande'), which you may not find too displeasing."[40]

On July 1 Léon Blum, whom Proust had treated so unkindly when he wrote for

Le Banquet, published a short, judicious review in the *Revue blanche,* in which he praised Proust for having "combined all the genres and all their charms."[41] After hailing Proust's talents, Blum addressed him "affectionately" and with some "severity," saying that the author possessed such facility of style and intellectual powers that he must be careful not to squander these gifts. Blum suggested that perhaps this debut had been too fortunate and too easy: "And I await with great impatience and confidence his next book." Proust awaited his next production with equal impatience, but with less assuredness than Blum. He did not lack the determination to write—it was what he lived for—but he felt at sea on the makeshift raft of *Jean Santeuil*'s assorted planks.

On the same day that Blum's encouraging review appeared, another, ridiculing Montesquiou, Proust, and their distinguished prefacers, came out in *Le Journal.* Jean Lorrain, a scurrilous figure who wrote poetry and novels in the decadent vein, bedeviled many of Paris's elite with his weekly newspaper column "Pall-Mall Semaine." That day's short piece excoriated the two members of the Académie française, France and Heredia, for having set a dangerous precedent. Lorrain blamed them for encouraging such dilettantes as Proust and Montesquiou by penning "obliging prefaces for pretty society boys who desperately want to become writers and shine in the salons."[42] Although Montesquiou was hardly a boy, Lorrain lumped him together with all his minions. Lorrain decried the folly of France and Heredia for certifying such works as *Les Hortensias bleus* by Montesquiou and *Pleasures and Days,* because such recognition "turned the head of all the little Montesquitoes—the lesser or greater poets who frequent Mme Lemaire's." Mocking the count and his friends, Lorrain referred to Heredia as "Herediou" and Mme Arman as "Mme Arman de Caillavou," blaming her salon for having offered Parisians this "substitute" for Montesquiou, "until now alone of his kind—the young and charming Marcel Proust. Pooh and Boo!"[43] Lorrain did not address the literary qualities of *Les Hortensias bleus* or *Pleasures and Days* but contented himself, for now, with attacking what he saw as their pretentiousness.

Jean Lorrain, at forty-two, in many ways resembled a grotesque caricature of Montesquiou. Completely lacking in refinement, he was a homosexual, but one who preferred rough trade. His vulgar attacks on prominent figures had earned him thrashings and banishment from more than one salon, but such retribution did not stop Lorrain from taking cheap shots at society figures whom he envied— and Montesquiou topped his list. Proust apparently thought it best to disregard Lorrain's attack, which, while regrettable, contained nothing that assailed his honor. He would leave it to Montesquiou, his elder, to respond. Montesquiou, who had for some time been the butt of Lorrain's jibes, also let the matter pass, indicating that Lorrain was so far beneath his contempt as to be invisible.

In mid-July, Fernand Gregh wrote a brief, mean-spirited, equivocal review of *Pleasures and Days* for the *Revue de Paris*, in which he did not even mention Proust's writings. Instead, he blamed the unnamed author for having assembled around him too many fairy godmothers and fathers: "Each fairy had brought his own particular grace: melancholy, irony, and a particular melody. And all have guaranteed success."[44] Here Gregh was far off the mark; *Pleasures and Days* was to know no measure of success. He later revised his opinion, after Proust had achieved fame, and said that the total failure of *Pleasures and Days* was due to its oversized format, exorbitant price, and luxurious presentation. Although Gregh later praised certain aspects of the book, such as its fine psychological analyses, he deplored the overly precious, exquisite feelings that too often showed "Proust's first manner, when he acts like a child, sucking his finger, because he could be like that. But what did he not embody? His complexity exhausts analysis."[45] But Gregh admitted that those passages in which Proust mocks high society should have made his friends prick up their ears. Proust's first book, Gregh maintained, had given few clues about where he was headed, and his friends missed them.[46] Marcel's friends recognized his intelligence, his talent, and his remarkable ability with words, but they were convinced that he was squandering his gifts in the glitter and chic of salon life.

Although one could argue that *Pleasures and Days* was a critical success, especially for a first book, it was a publishing and public relations fiasco. This volume, although unpurchased and unread, along with Jacques-Émile Blanche's portrait of Marcel as the young aesthete dandy, cemented in the minds of many the image of Proust as a social dilettante, not to be taken seriously. *Le Gaulois*'s introductory paragraph to France's preface had used two adjectives to describe Marcel's talent that haunted him in the future: *délicat et fin*. Delicate and fine: two words that suggested the feelings of a precious aesthete, someone whose favorite adjective might be *exquisite*, someone who might be a decadent Narcissus rather than an original creative force.

Jealousy

Marcel, Reynaldo, and Pierre Lavallée spent a June afternoon in the Jardin des Plantes, where they were enthralled by the spectacle of transpierced doves, which bear on their breasts a red spot resembling blood. Reynaldo noted in his journal that the doves resembled nymphs who, having killed themselves over love, had been changed by a god into birds.[47] The image of mythological birds martyred for love appealed to Proust, and years later, when seeking a chapter title for his novel, he considered "Les Colombes poignardées."

Later that month, Hahn accompanied Sarah Bernhardt and her troupe to London. Hahn had already begun taking notes in his journal for the biography he would write many years later of the actress whom he and legions adored. On June 20, just after his return, Reynaldo and Marcel faced a crisis. Feeling that Hahn was slipping away from him, Marcel proposed a pact according to which each promised to tell the other everything about himself, especially about any sexual encounters, past, present, and future. Reynaldo, out of weariness or a desire to placate Marcel, agreed to the absurd proposal and swore to uphold it. Marcel had become, in many ways, the obsessed lover he had depicted in "La Fin de la jalousie." An unpublished text from this period reveals his anguish. One is not, he observed, jealous of the happiness of the person one loves but of the pleasure she gives or the pleasure she takes. There are no remedies: "Intelligence is disarmed when faced with jealousy as with sickness and with death."[48] The preposterous pact and Marcel's fragile physical and emotional condition were to aggravate the misunderstandings between the two men.

The Proust family had not fully recovered from Uncle Louis's death when Nathé Weil fell ill on June 28. Two days later he died at the age of eighty-two; like his brother, Louis, he had not lingered in illness. Jeanne was so sick with grief that Marcel wondered whether she could go on living. Reynaldo, who was in Hamburg, became concerned about Marcel's morale after the double bereavement and offered to return to Paris and comfort his friend. Marcel declined the offer because he thought the sacrifice would be too great and not really necessary: "I assure you that if the rare moments when I am tempted to jump on the train so as to see you straight away became intolerably frequent, I would ask you to let me join you, or beg you to come back. But this is quite unlikely." He did ask Reynaldo for reassurance that he remained faithful, using the word *mosch*, apparently a code word in their private language for homosexual: "Just tell me from time to time in your letters no mosch, have seen no mosch, because, even though you imply as much, I'd be happier if you'd say it now and then." He looked forward to Reynaldo's return when his journey was done and declared that he would be "very very happy when I'm able to embrace you, you whom along with Mama I love best in all the world."[49]

Proust used the remainder of the letter to tell Reynaldo what he had heard about Comte Boni de Castellane's fête in the Bois, one of the most spectacular of the Belle Époque. Boni's lavish party had been made possible by his marriage to the American railway heiress Anna Gould. For the occasion, eighty thousand Venetian lanterns had been hung in the Bois, whose many fountains were illuminated, and twenty-five swans had been released into the lakes. Proust was amused at the imprecise nature of the sumptuous event: it seemed to have been all things to all people. A delighted Mme Lemaire had compared it to the golden age of Versailles, "pure Louis XIV, you know," whereas Mme de Framboise had told him, "You'd have thought you were living in Athens." Arthur Meyer, on the other hand, wrote in *Le Gaulois,* "One felt one was living in the days of Lohengrin." Marcel gleefully pointed out to Reynaldo the hypocrisy of high society in attending the unprecedented event when one of its most prominent members, Louis-Charles-Philippe-Raphaël, duc de Nemours, had died on June 26 at the age of eighty-two. "You know there were 3,000 people at that fête. *Le Figaro* adds solemnly: 'All of Parisian society was there. We shall give no names. For though the whole of society was there, it was there incognito, because of the death of Monseigneur the Duc de Nemours.' Seeing that no masks were worn, I can't help wondering what their incognito consisted of. It's a good dodge for going out when in mourning."[50]

Marcel also discussed his vacation plans with Reynaldo, in hopes that they could spend some time together. He might soon go to Versailles with his mother, and in August to the seashore with her for a month or more. Or if Reynaldo preferred they could all go to Bex or another Swiss resort. Then he admitted that his mother wanted only to "spend a month with me, she wants me to 'have a good time' for the rest of the season."[51] Proust's parents were developing a strategy to make him more independent; one of its main elements called for him to spend more time on his own away from his mother.

In early July, Jeanne and Adrien retreated to the countryside near Passy to spend a quiet few days together. Marcel wrote to her in a black mood; the recent loss of his grandfather had finally struck him, making the mortality of his parents seem more real. Adrien, while not thinking seriously of retiring, had, at age sixty-two, reduced his activities somewhat. He would leave some of the more arduous inspection tours to younger colleagues and spend more time at home with his wife and his elder son, whom he loved dearly, though he did not understand him.[52]

Marcel began to show the strain of recent events as summer progressed, always the most difficult season for his respiratory system. His health suddenly worsened and he became depressed. He seldom felt good or rested, and his asthma and hay fever lingered. He began smoking medicated Espic cigarettes and, assisted by his mother and servants, burning Legras antiasthma powders to relieve his respiratory conditions. He also urged his mother, in the highly unlikely event that she encountered Montesquiou or Yturri, to tell them that because the family was in mourning, she "absolutely" did not want him to attend the ceremony at Douai dedicating the monument to poet Marceline Desbordes-Valmore. He then spoke of his sadness at not seeing her: "And yet, to what purpose? When one sees, as we saw the other day, how everything ends, why grieve over sorrows or dedicate oneself to causes of which nothing will remain. Only the fatalism of the Moslems seems to make sense."[53] Marcel's melancholy, pessimistic attitude lingered.

On July 16 a prominent figure of Marcel's grandparents' generation passed away. Edmond de Goncourt died of pneumonia in the Daudets' country home at Champrosay. Proust wrote immediately to express his sorrow to Lucien, knowing how attached he had been to the elderly writer whom the Daudets considered a member of the family. Marcel, who had been thinking a lot about death, found it "beautiful" that Goncourt had died "surrounded by all of you. And so gently! For when it comes to death, sudden is gentle." When his time came, he intended to face the end squarely: "I . . . want to know it when I die, if I am not too ill."[54]

Edmond bequeathed his estate to found a literary society of ten writers that in 1902 became the Académie Goncourt. According to the terms of the will, the members were to meet monthly over dinner at a restaurant. Alphonse Daudet was among the founding members and its first president, though the society did not function officially until 1903, when it awarded its first prize. The Prix Goncourt quickly became France's most prestigious literary prize, given annually to the best imaginative prose work.

Contrary to the title of Marcel's book, the days of 1896 brought few pleasures. The summer was a season of grieving and remembering, particularly for Marcel's mother, who sent him a photograph of his grandfather that he found a very good likeness. But more than the family's losses, Marcel's health and phobias tormented him; he was losing confidence and hope. Nothing seemed right. At two in the morning on July 16, Marcel wrote a rambling note to his mother telling her that he had left his iodine at Mme Arman's and asking whether she could think of anything to do about it. He expressed his displeasure that the *Revue blanche* had published the day before the article he had sent six months ago decrying obscurity in poetry, without informing him or sending him proofs. He had supposed that they had thrown his piece in the waste bin.[55] He feared his mother's disapproval that an article by him had appeared, even without his knowledge, during a period of mourning. He mentioned an appointment at Calmann-Lévy, where he hoped to interest the publisher in the novel he was writing, and another with Dr. Brissaud, an authority on asthma, that would prevent his visiting Reynaldo at Saint-Cloud.[56]

Neurasthenia

In the course of his career Dr. Proust, who held the Chair of Hygiene (public health) in the School of Medicine, edited seventeen volumes of medical manuals that offered practical advice on various conditions. The message in all of these manuals, such as *How to Live with Your Diabetes, How to Live with Your High Blood Pressure,* and so on, was "practice good hygiene and you will live a long and healthy life."[57]

In 1896 Dr. Proust asked Professor Édouard Brissaud, a distinguished director at the Hôpital Saint-Antoine, to write the book on asthma for this medical series. In his text, *How to Live with Your Asthma,* the learned professor concluded that the condition resulted from a "pure neurosis." Marcel frequently consulted Brissaud's book and may have initially blamed himself for his malady. Brissaud noted that although one does not necessarily die from a disease caused by a neurosis, there is no cure and no treatment. Proust may have ultimately rejected the doctor's thesis about asthma; he later described Brissaud as handsome, charming, vastly intelligent, and "a bad doctor."[58] But the overall effect of Brissaud's book, now considered to be a compendium of errors, was negative, for Proust later used its conclusions as an excuse to experiment with self-medication and to refuse treatments in clinics that might have provided lasting benefits.

Adrien and a colleague, Dr. Gilbert Ballet, were writing another book, to be published in October 1897, for their series. *L'Hygiène du neurasthénique* (How to live with your neurasthenia) prescribed treatment for this newly named disorder, which primarily afflicted members of the upper classes, those who supposedly used their brains more than their muscles. This manual read like a case study of Marcel. Among the debilitating symptoms of neurasthenia were dyspepsia, insomnia, hypochondria, asthma, hay fever, and abusive masturbation. Of particular interest, considering Adrien's experience in raising his elder son, are the pages on the dangers that high society posed for such patients. Parisian high life, with its endless series of visits, dinners, balls, soirées, and other obligations, easily led to dangerous excesses: for example, fatigue resulting from meals that were too long and too heavy; staying up late and losing sleep, or sleeping at irregular hours. Who could be surprised, the authors asked, if such a regimen often produced psychosomatic asthma?[59]

Dr. Proust apparently remained convinced that there was nothing physically wrong with Marcel.[60] In the manual Proust and Ballet pointed out that neurasthenia often developed in those who pursue vain pleasures rather than selecting a career suitable to their milieu and abilities.[61] Furthermore, neurasthenic patients are highly suggestible and prone to phobias, such as the fear of drafts, germs, or noise.[62] Marcel had already developed the first and last of these phobias and did not neglect to acquire the one related to germs. The example of patients who suffer from auditory hypersensitivity can be seen as prophetic of Proust's later retreats to his famous cork-lined room: In order to "escape noise, such patients shut themselves up in their rooms and live in veritable reclusion."[63] Jeanne and Adrien had already seen the endless housekeeping complications that arose when a grown, unemployed son needed to sleep all day, when noises indoors and out increased a thousandfold.

There was more. Abulia, or the loss of willpower, was described as another debilitating trait of the neurasthenic. Marcel exhibited this symptom in his endless hesitations about career choices and vacation plans. Nothing, observed the hygienists, is more painful to such patients than making a decision.[64] Had Marcel not already lived the experience, he could have taken the chief motivation for his protagonist right out of his father's book. The Narrator's quest is largely a lifelong attempt to regain his will, lost as a child in the scene of the good-night kiss. From that moment on, until he regains his will on the verge of old age, he considers himself certified as suffering from abulia, which constitutes the greatest obstacle the Narrator must surmount in his quest to become a creative person: Lack of will, he observes, is "that greatest of all vices," for it makes resisting the others impossible.[65]

A recommended treatment for patients such as Marcel was to isolate them from family and familiar surroundings. If the overwrought patient left his family and the milieu in which his neurasthenia originated to vacation in a calm, pleasant spot in the countryside or at a sanatorium, he would quickly regain his mental equilibrium; new images would occupy his mind and his hypochondriacal preoccupations would begin to disappear.[66] Proust's parents were planning such a treatment, without telling Marcel why, for his next vacation.

Soon after Reynaldo's return from Hamburg, a quarrel erupted with Proust that made Hahn threaten to break their pact of fidelity and confession. The rift had apparently started when Marcel tried to guess the name of the person to whom Reynaldo was attracted and whom he refused to discuss. Marcel protested furiously Hahn's refusal to divulge the name and tell all, saying that his silence, if maintained, would be a breach of his oath: "That you should tell me everything has been my hope, my consolation, my mainstay, my life since the 20th of June." Marcel admitted that the oath he had forced on Reynaldo was cruel but accused him of even greater cruelty and implored him to keep his promise: "If my fantasies are absurd, they are the fantasies of a sick man, and for that reason should not be crossed. Threatening to finish off a sick man because his mania is exasperating is the height of cruelty." Marcel closed by saying that he often deserved reproaches himself and by asking Reynaldo to be indulgent to his pony.[67] His lucidity in recognizing the nature of his mania and his frankness in admitting it were, as it turned out, positive signs. But first, there would be more difficult moments to endure.

Not long afterward, Marcel wrote Hahn another letter filled with recriminations, acknowledging that their friendship had considerably diminished; he cited among his grievances Hahn's refusal to accompany him home after a soirée at Madeleine's, preferring instead to remain for supper.[68] He repeated Hahn's warning, made earlier in the evening, that one day Marcel would regret having made him promise to tell all. Marcel declared that he had attempted to remain faithful to Reynaldo in order to avoid painful confessions: "Wretch, you don't understand, then, my daily and nightly struggles where the only thing that holds me back is the thought of hurting you." Then he observed, "Just as I love you much less now, you no longer love me at all, and that my dear little Reynaldo I cannot hold against you." He signed the letter, "Your little pony, who after all this bucking, returns alone to the stable where you once loved to say you were the master." Marcel recognized that the love affair was over, but fortunately not their mutual affection and the joy they took in each other's company.

Proust seized an opportunity to publicize his book when Charles Maurras asked him for a photograph to run with the review he was writing of *Pleasures and Days* for the *Revue encyclopédique*. Eager to look his best for his first published photograph, Proust decided to have new pictures made by the distinguished photographer Otto, who immortalized prominent Parisians and whose studio was conveniently located in the place de la Madeleine, only a few steps from Proust's apartment. By late July, Proust had sent the photograph for the brief but highly prescient review that was to appear on August 22. Maurras saw in Proust a new moralist who "shows such a wide variety of talents that one is bewildered at having to register them all in so young a writer."[69] He praised Proust's style for its "pure, transparent" language and hailed him as a writer around whom the new generation could gather.[70] A new author could hardly have wished for a better review, but as gratifying as it was, Maurras's words of praise did not increase sales.

On August 8, in hopes of improving his health, Marcel and his mother boarded a train at the Gare de Lyon for Mont-Dore, a spa in the mountains of central France that was noted for its treatment of asthma. From Mont-Dore a more composed Marcel wrote Reynaldo and, repentant, proposed that their pact be annulled: "Forgive me if I've hurt you, and in the future don't tell me anything since it upsets you. You will never find a more affectionate, more understanding (alas!) and less humiliating confessor. . . . Forgive me for having added, out of egoism as you say, to the sorrows of your life." Marcel proclaimed again his love for Reynaldo: "I have no sorrows, only an enormous tenderness for my boy, whom I think of, as I said of my nurse when I was little, not only with all my heart, but with all me." At the end of the letter Marcel declared himself cured of jealousy.[71] His obsessive preoccupation with Reynaldo established a pattern of behavior that he was to dissect and analyze with brutal lucidity in the principal pairs of lovers in the *Search:* Swann and Odette, the Narrator and Albertine, and Charlus and Morel.

If the calm atmosphere of Mont-Dore enabled Marcel to resolve the emotional conflict with Reynaldo, it brought no relief to his asthma. He and his mother had at first blamed the spa for his failure to improve, then realized that the real source of his trouble came from the farmers of the Auvergne, who were busy making hay, thus saturating the air with allergens. During his stay he read Dumas's *La Dame de Monsoreau* and, at a somewhat slower pace, Rousseau's *Confessions;* he also worked intermittently on the drafts of *Jean Santeuil.*

Marcel wrote an apologetic letter to Lucien, worrying that his exemption from this year's reserve training would not be approved and that he would have to report for duty at Versailles on August 31. Trying to resolve this problem before leaving Paris had prevented him from saying good-bye to his "dear little one. I think of you so often that it's unbelievable." He told Lucien that he was so unhappy with his lack of progress at Mont-Dore that if his condition did not improve soon, he would take the train to Paris. Did Lucien, he wondered, still harbor some feelings of friendship for him? Or had he completely forgotten him? He invited Lucien to come over and select one of the photographs from Otto, promising many "ridiculous poses from which to choose." Although he signed the letter "Your little Marcel," his relationship with Lucien had cooled from love to friendship.[72]

In late August, Marcel and his mother returned to Paris. Soon his parents left, as usual, on their separate ways for vacation, Jeanne to the Hôtel Royal in Dieppe, Adrien to his favorite watering spot in Vichy. Marcel would remain in Paris until he decided where to spend the fall vacation, a choice that would be largely determined by his health. Before leaving for the coast, Jeanne, having decided their apartment needed a face-lift, made arrangements for painters to come and for new carpet to be laid while she and Adrien were away. On September 2 Marcel, waiting in bed at 9:30 for Félicie to bring his breakfast tray and the morning paper, wrote his daily letter to his mother. He was obviously pleased with himself for having returned home the evening before at eleven, but he had not gone to bed immediately because his chest "felt rather oppressed," despite his having smoked several Espic cigarettes during the day. He decided that he should burn some of his antiasthma powders, whose smoke he inhaled seeking to relieve his bronchial tubes. Because this was the first time he carried out what he called a "fumigation," the procedure "took ages." Once in bed, his chest continued to feel tight, and he arose to take two capsules of amyl. He fell asleep quickly, although he woke at 5:30 A.M., panting severely. He got out of bed and burned a mound of Escouflaire and Legras powders. This habit of fumigating was to become an enduring ritual.

Marcel wrote his mother again on Sunday, September 6, with a request. He needed to know where he should send the copies of *Pleasures and Days* he intended to give Robert de Flers, on vacation, and Robert de Billy, now posted to the French embassy in London.[73] Would she write and find out their addresses and do the same for Laure Hayman, also vacationing? He was making an effort, he told her, though he admitted he was "a bit of a grumbler," to show her that she need not worry. Having pressed his mother into service as his remote secretary, he then urged her, "Go for walks, bathe, don't *think* too much, don't tire yourself by making your letters to me too long, and let me thank you once more for the tranquillity of these last few weeks, which you made me spend so happily."[74] He hoped she would report that the wind was blowing hard on the coast, for she believed high winds were good for her health. To reassure her of his equilibrium and good intentions, he told her that he was going "to work a bit on a little episode" for his novel. He congratulated himself for having written at least one "breezy" letter in which he had complained about nothing and expressed concern for her happiness and well-being. He considered it a tour de force.

The remaining September letters to his mother chronicle his constant difficulty breathing and sleeping and his mostly successful attempts to avoid resorting to soporifics. He asked the lending library for the *Correspondence* of Schiller and Goethe and *Par les champs et par les grèves* (Across fields and shores), Flaubert's book on Brittany, another indication that he was working on *Jean Santeuil*. He admitted his discouragement at not having found the story line, at not being able to conceive it as a whole. But he had filled one notebook of *"110 large pages,"* a quantity he underscored in the letter to his mother. As he continued to fill pages and accumulate copy, he wondered where he was headed. Before he began working on *Jean Santeuil*, he had written short stories, sketches, essays, and poems. Proust was finding that the novel was not for him an instinctive genre.

Robert, interning at Necker Hospital, visited Marcel on September 16. The two brothers discussed the pros and cons of Robert's spending the night at home, but he decided to return and sleep at the hospital. Robert accompanied Marcel as far as Mme de Brantes's town house, where a soirée was in progress. There the brothers parted, Robert to tend to his patients, Marcel to amuse the party goers. Proust always said the night air was easier to breathe.

His health problems, however, whether real or psychosomatic, made him profoundly unhappy. His letters flowed from Paris to his mother in Dieppe, detailing his ailments and his increasing reliance on drugs to alleviate his symptoms, news that alarmed Mme Proust, who feared the habit-forming dangers of drugs containing narcotics. Marcel blamed the need for a sleeping potion on the disturbance caused by the painters she had hired: "I must confess to you, I was woken up so early by the painters that I had to take a cachet of trional (.8 of a grain), as I couldn't go on sleeping so little. And I was going to ask your permission to flee to Dieppe to escape the painters. But what you say of the noise there has put a spoke in that wheel."[75] Two days later Marcel confessed again with regret, knowing his mother would be upset, that he had taken amyl in the evening and trional in the morning. But now he would have to contend with the carpet layers, who planned to begin work at 9:15, when he would still be in bed. Greatly annoyed by this arrangement, he urged his mother to write to the workmen and insist on a different schedule.

After more admonitions from Jeanne, he wrote, "I am continuing to abstain rigorously from trional, amyl and valerian." Sensing the need to reassure her about his condition, he wrote that he had been to dinner with a friend in the Bois de Boulogne and had "felt well ever since, which hasn't happened for ages." He had resumed work on his novel and vowed not to miss another day in order to have his manuscript ready for submission by February, but he lacked confidence in his ability to produce a worthy novel. He felt certain that the result would be detestable. In a postscript he urged Jeanne to remain in Dieppe, where she could continue to recuperate *"for me,* when it would do me so much good, until October 15? Papa would be much freer here without you during the celebrations for the Czar's visit."[76]

Paris was preparing for a state visit by Czar Nicholas II of Russia, October 6–8. President Faure and Nicolas II would lay the cornerstone for what would become the city's most elegant bridge, the Pont Alexandre III, to commemorate the alliance between France and Russia dating from 1892. As a leading international health authority who had visited Russia, as well as a close friend of the president's, Dr. Proust would be invited to many of the events surrounding the czar's visit.

Jeanne, despite her son's entreaties, did not wish to remain in Dieppe and by September 24 had moved nineteen miles up the coast to Le Tréport, where she resumed her bathing treatments in the sea. Jeanne told Marcel about a new luxury she was enjoying. The spa had the same sort of writing tables as at home, except that at Le Tréport they were illuminated by electric lighting. She was finding the treatment beneficial and had already begun to sleep much better. Another modern innovation at which she marveled was the excellent mail service, which made her correspondence with Marcel resemble a "conversation." A letter he had mailed at a quarter past noon was handed to her four hours and fifteen minutes later. She had heeded his pleas about the carpet layers and asked their manservant Jean to arrange for the workers to come after lunch, if possible, and if not, after 10 A.M. If necessary, the men could make two trips to finish the job. The family had begun making concessions to Marcel's schedule, which continued to shift toward a more nocturnal existence.[77]

Jeanne informed Marcel that she planned to stay in Le Tréport until October or until the baths began to wear on her. She wanted him to spend his vacation away from her and urged him to try Saint-Cloud, where she knew he would find Reynaldo. If Jeanne believed that her grieving depressed him, she was mistaken. He would have been only too happy to console her and distract her and be comforted in turn by her presence and love. His parents' insistence on his having "a good time" later in the fall was to have unfortunate results. Jeanne and Adrien were desperate for measures that would pull Marcel back from the life of an invalid, a state into which he seemed to be declining for reasons they believed were primarily neurotic.

A Thousand Tender Kisses

Marcel finally narrowed his autumn vacation choices to Segrez and Fontainebleau, whose forest was said to be splendid in the fall. Around mid-October he wrote to Jean Lazard, a friend who lived in Fontainebleau, to inquire about conditions and requested an answer by return mail. Such a prompt reply might have appeared reasonable to Marcel, but his correspondent must have been taken aback by all the questions asked in the letter. Marcel required a room or two located in a salubrious spot—but not by the river—in a quiet lodging with no noisy neighbors in the adjoining room; he also wanted to know the cost if he should decide to take a small apartment.

Marcel found it more and more impossible to make decisions about travel destinations and departure times and so hesitated until the last possible minute to choose between Fontainebleau and Segrez. When he finally left for Fontainebleau on October 19, his departure was so hasty that he forgot to pack a number of items. Upon arriving at his destination, the Hôtel de France et d'Angleterre, he immediately felt homesick and miserable. Nonetheless, he wrote asking his mother to end the forgotten items. Marcel's choice of Fontainebleau may also have been influenced by Léon Daudet's decision to retreat to that town in order to finish his fifth novel *Suzanne,* to be published in November. Marcel must have envied his friend's productivity.

When Marcel's mother received his letter the following morning, she became alarmed and went across the street to Cerisier's bakery, where she tried unsuccessfully to use a new means of communication: the telephone. The bakery's telephone apparently could be used only for local calls. Electric lighting and the telephone, two wonders of late nineteenth-century technology, had begun to change the lives of millions of people. Marcel, usually so curious about technological advances, had for some reason been reluctant to use the telephone. Although the Prousts had neither a telephone nor electric lighting at home, Jeanne had urged her increasingly dependent son, who hated being away from her, to experiment with the telephone as a direct way of remaining in contact when they were separated.

Frustrated at not being able to reach Marcel, Mme Proust went home for lunch. At one o'clock, she wrote him a letter promising to send his tie pin, watch, coat, hat, and his new umbrella, which she and the servants had as yet been unable to find. After posting the letter, she tried to call him again from another station. Finally, after much waiting, the call went through. During the conversation, which seemed miraculous to Marcel, bringing his mother and her incredible sweetness so near, he told her Fontainebleau was cold, damp, and dreary and argued his case for returning home immediately. That evening Jeanne wrote for the second time that day, urging him to be patient and attempt to "acclimatize" himself. She suggested Illiers as an alternative vacation choice because he had been "wonderfully well" there in cold weather. After sending him a "thousand kisses," she added a postscript to her "dear boy" that expressed her greatest concern: "I am waiting impatiently to hear what sort of night you have had and whether you have managed to break all ties with that insidious Trional."[78]

After the phone call Marcel felt miserable from having heard his mother's fragile, disembodied voice, confirming his suspicions about the intensity of her suffering over the loss of her parents and giving him the "first terrible inkling of what had broken forever within her."[79] He nearly panicked and rushed back to her. In spite of his distress, he summoned the discipline to write down his impressions of the exceptional communication and emotions it had provoked. He sent his mother what he wrote, more for sentimental than literary reasons, to show her how much he loved her and how wretched he was. He was no longer the independent, carefree Marcel of a year ago, who had prolonged his stay at Beg-Meil for as long as possible to remain on vacation with Reynaldo, while eagerly exploring the coast and taking notes for his novel. How much had changed in one year; he and Reynaldo had quarreled and separated; Marcel's "dear little Lucien" had displaced but not replaced the more stable and reliable Reynaldo; his grandfather and uncle had died; *Pleasures and Days* had been published and gone largely unnoticed. And now his body and emotions were betraying him through sickness and neuroses, and he seemed mired down in his writing. He had never been so unhappy.

In the fictionalized account that he later included in *Jean Santeuil*, Proust reversed the order of events: Jean panics and then speaks to his mother on the phone.[80] Proust captured for his character the struggle between the forces of habit and comforts of home and the strange, hostile environment in which he had landed. The passage abounds in images suggesting incarceration, claustrophobia, and suffocation, future themes of the *Search*, where so many characters become prisoners of their manias.

The day after the phone call, Marcel wrote to his mother and listed all the things that were wrong. From the moment he arrived at Fontainebleau, nothing inside or outside the hotel had pleased Proust, from the way the bed was set up in his room ("All the things I need, my coffee, my tisane, my candle, my pen, my matches etc. etc. are to the right of me, so that I keep having to lie on my bad side, etc.") to the colors of the forest ("still all green"), the town itself ("no character"), and the terrible weather that persisted ("It's pouring"). Still, "I had no asthma last night. And it's only just now, after a bad sneezing fit, that I had to smoke a little." He then told her about the terrible hours he had spent after their phone conversation, which he described as the most distressing time in his life. Later in the evening, needing someone to talk to, he had gone to the station at eleven o'clock to meet Léon Daudet, who was returning from a brief trip to Paris. Daudet had insisted on their taking their meals together, which must have sounded like good news to Jeanne.

Because his many complaints about feeling sick and miserable had failed to persuade his mother to allow him to return, he tried another way to hit a sensitive nerve: the great expense. He detailed the costs of keeping a fire burning in his room and the extra lamps required because in the off-season there was no lighted parlor, only the lights in one's room. Surely, she could see he would do better to come home? If his parents wanted him to breathe non-Parisian air to see whether his asthma improved, he suggested sleeping at home but going out to Versailles every day to write. Finally, Marcel made one request that sounded positive: "Do ask Papa for something to stop my nervous laugh. I'm afraid of irritating Léon Daudet." And he added a bit of good news: "No Trional."[81]

Marcel's mention of cost did not faze his mother. Although Jeanne always regarded thrift as a cardinal virtue, she felt that no expense would be too great if she could persuade her elder son to manage on his own. She was encouraged by his readiness to control his nervous laughter, a disorder he had treated so lightly but that now embarrassed him. Jeanne much preferred that he spend time with the older, mature Daudet brother, who was married and pursuing a career as a journalist, critic, and novelist. In his memoirs Léon recalled that he and Marcel spent "a charming week" together, "walking by day in the forest, chatting in the evening by the fireplace, in the deserted . . . drawing-room."[82] With his extraordinary politeness, Marcel succeeded in hiding from Daudet how tiresome he found their conversations, especially at mealtime. But Daudet did observe how extraordinarily sensitive Marcel seemed to be and likened him to someone who had been "flayed alive."[83]

In Marcel's next letter he told his mother that relocating was out of the question. Apparently, he did not intend to leave her side ever again. He told her that he had "lost his faith in country places." And a new worry had seized hold of him: he was afraid that he would be unable to pay his hotel bill because of the charges he had run up, and to make matters worse, he had lost a lot of money through a hole in his pocket. He confirmed his determination to work, but he must first find a place where he would feel well enough to write. If writing was difficult under the present circumstances, he could at least read the books from which he expected to draw inspiration. He asked his mother to send *"immediately"* several of Balzac's novels, including *Le Curé de village,* the Shakespeare volume with *Julius Caesar* and *Antony and Cleopatra,* the first volume of Goethe's *Wilhelm Meister,* and *Middlemarch* by George Eliot.[84]

Later that morning, after they had posted their letters, he and his mother spoke briefly on the telephone. Mme Proust now seemed resigned to letting him come home because of the disastrous report, but she would send the books and wait and see. The phone connection had been so bad that she couldn't make out certain titles, but she would receive his letter with the list at seven that evening.[85] Things only grew worse. In his next letter Marcel said: "I write to you in a state of deep dejection." The missing money, he wrote, "after annoying me at first now takes on fantastic proportions." He went so far as to say that he now understood "people who kill themselves for nothing at all." He made an urgent request for money— "Please send me a lot too much"—because his greatest fear was being unable to purchase a train ticket if he decided to return home.

Even a visit from Lucien had, surprisingly, made matters worse. They quarreled and parted on icy terms. Marcel composed a letter to his mother telling her that he was "worn out with remorse, racked with conscience, crushed with dejection." He would give Fontainebleau one more day. Reluctant to send such a bleak letter, he left it on the table and went to bed. The next morning at 9:30 he added a postscript: "I've had a good night, I'm very refreshed but also very congested." But he told her that his reservations about Fontainebleau remained just as strong.[86] Then he mailed the letter.

That morning Jeanne sent Marcel a wire and then one hundred francs, along with most of the books requested. That evening, after receiving his doleful letter, she wrote again, advising him to combat his anxieties and stop tormenting himself. He was not to be concerned about the bill. "If I knew you were flourishing over there, I would find the costs very sweet!"[87]

Marcel, far from flourishing, returned to Paris, having written many fewer pages in Fontainebleau than he had intended. Other than the telephone episode, which he would use with few changes in the *Search*, the only other text that was clearly written at Fontainebleau was an episode concerning Jean's attempts at seducing a married woman after he became bored with his mistress.[88]

Once home, Marcel's condition improved, and he resumed many of his normal activities. He and his friends were soon intrigued by the publication of the single most important piece of evidence used in the secret trial to convict Dreyfus. On November 10 *Le Matin* published a photograph of a secretly obtained facsimile of the *bordereau*, the memorandum sent by the spy in the French army to the German embassy. It listed the top secret documents detailing French weaponry and the plans for troop deployment in the event of an attack that the spy would sell to the Germans. Publication of the bordereau had an electrifying effect. Col. Georges Picquart, who had become chief of counterintelligence the year following Dreyfus's conviction and whom the army suspected of leaking the document, was forced into exile.[89] Commandant Marie-Charles-Ferdinand-Walsin Esterhazy, the real spy, became terrified that his handwriting might be identified. Although it would take years to break down the wall of secrecy and sort out the mountain of evidence that the French high command had forged against Dreyfus, the publication of the bordereau was the first major step toward an appeal and new trial.

One December evening at a party given by Reynaldo's mother, Marcel met his friend's twenty-year-old English cousin, Marie Nordlinger, a young artist who had come to France to continue her studies. She and Proust liked each other immediately and became friends. Marie later encouraged his interest in the English art critic John Ruskin and assisted in his translations of two of Ruskin's works.

Marcel maintained his close ties with Laure Hayman, who by the end of the year had asked him to drop "Madame" and use her given name. He sent her a vase for her collection and, along with it, a keepsake from Uncle Louis, a tie pin she might use for one of her hats; he hoped it would appeal to her "sentiment of friendship" without offending her taste.[90]

In early November he wrote to Fernand Gregh, thanking him for the inscribed copy of his book of verse *La Maison de l'enfance*. Proust, who had not forgiven Gregh's unkind notice for *Pleasures and Days,* couched his expression of gratitude for his friend's book in such guarded and ambiguous terms that afterward he dared not send the letter. The week before Christmas, while leafing through the *Revue de Paris,* Proust had seen a new note Gregh had written about *Pleasures and Days.* In his brief second notice, Gregh again praised the preface, Hahn's music, and Lemaire's drawings, but this time he mentioned Proust's text and said that it stood well on its own. In short, Gregh recommended *Pleasures and Days* as a "very beautiful gift book." The Christmas shoppers paid no attention to Gregh's advice— or if they did, they recoiled at the price.[91]

8   *The Duelists*   ❧

SOMETIME DURING LATE 1896 OR EARLY 1897, Marcel, grown increasingly high-strung and nervous, exploded in anger at his mother. The precise cause of the confrontation is not clear, but it apparently erupted over his lavish spending habits, requests for new and expensive wardrobe items, or such activities as taking Laure Hayman out every morning for a springtime drive, often followed by lunch—pleasures that, as he confessed to Mme Straus, cost him so much that he "hadn't a penny left for flowers."[1] Such extravagant behavior, given his inability to work and earn any money, posed a serious problem for his parents, who were concerned about both the family budget and Marcel's utter disregard for money. The altercation with his parents occurred when Marcel, angered at their attempt to rein him in and humiliated because he thought their manservant Jean had overheard the scolding, flew into a rage and smashed a valuable vase. Afterward from his room, Marcel wrote his parents a letter of apology. Later in the evening, he received this note from his mother:

My dear boy,

Your letter has done me good—your father and I were feeling very badly. I assure you that I didn't mean for one moment to say anything whatsoever in front of Jean and if I did it was quite unintentional. Let's never speak of it again. From now on let the broken glass be what it is at temple—a symbol of indissoluble union.

Your father wishes you good night and I kiss you tenderly.

J. P.

PS. I have to come back to the subject after all: be sure not to go into the dining room with bare feet, because of the glass.[2]

Proust left two versions of the incident, one in *Jean Santeuil*, the other related almost two decades afterward to his housekeeper Céleste Albaret.[3] Neither account provides complete details about the altercation; each ends with the symbolic union of mother and son. The crisis had erupted over a pair of gloves.[4] Marcel had become infatuated with a demimondaine who lived in the Bois; after many attempts, he finally received her permission to call. Wanting to appear as elegantly attired as possible, he had entreated his mother to buy him a new tie and "the most beautiful pair of yellow gloves she could find." Jeanne returned with a very pretty sailor-knot tie but without the coveted yellow gloves. Instead, she had purchased a gray pair she thought he would like. He was infuriated. In his anger and haste to punish his mother, he seized a beautiful antique vase she prized and smashed it on the floor. His mother had not flinched, but said simply: " 'Well, my little Marcel, this will be what it is in Jewish weddings. You broke the cup; our love will only be the greater.' " Marcel ran to his room, shut the door, and wept for hours over the great pain he had caused his mother. The story, as related by Proust to Céleste, had an amusing ending. When he arrived for his rendezvous with the cocotte, wearing his new tie, gloves, and carrying a huge bouquet of flowers, what he saw, instead of the elegant, romantic interlude he had pictured, was a scene from a Flaubert novel: a bailiff and his men were busy repossessing the fancy harlot's furnishings.

An unpublished source claims that Marcel's tantrum was caused by his mother's condemnation of a photograph showing Marcel with Robert de Flers and Lucien Daudet. Marcel, beaming with bemused contentment, is seated with Robert standing behind him and Lucien next to him, his forearm on Proust's shoulder. Lucien gazes down at Marcel in a way that could be described as amorous. Did this picture spark a violent argument between Proust and his parents because it reminded them of his homosexual inclinations?[5]

In his New Year's greetings to Montesquiou, Marcel pledged anew his gratitude and admiration, although "somewhat wounded" by the "unmerited disaffection"

the count had made him feel.[6] Montesquiou, still indignant because Marcel had
snubbed the ceremony at Douai and continued to amuse their friends with his
imitations, replied: "My dear Marcel, It is the transparent subterfuge of those who
feel themselves at fault to pretend to think they have been injured and try to hide
their real guilt behind a false susceptibility." Marcel should appreciate, as had their
mutual friends, "my indulgence towards your congenial and somewhat evasive
person," and the poet reminded his disciple, that although he might at times judge
him severely, he had also had "only too many occasions to acknowledge your many
virtues, among others honesty and delicacy. And I am pleased to do so when you
are not present. Indulgence, however, has never meant sycophancy." His New Year's
gift to Marcel was "my voice, crying out in the social wilderness, where your good
qualities are rather going to seed." Shrewdly observing that Marcel made of his
faults the virtues of his books, Montesquiou quoted from *Pleasures and Days* and
declared that the length of his letter showed a "pledge of my interest," of which,
he hinted, Marcel would "have better proof." Montesquiou planned to include
a chapter from Proust's book in his forthcoming anthology *Roseaux pensants*
(Thinking reeds).

Proust, who had been unaware of Montesquiou's intentions about *Pleasures
and Days,* expressed gratitude in his reply for the unusually long letter and attempted to justify his behavior. He assured the count of his eagerness to "re-enlist"
in the rolls of Montesquiou's friends, a position he admitted having abandoned:
"My admiration for you has remained unchanged and always shall. I had merely
ceased to harbour the slightest feeling of friendship." Montesquiou, while genuinely well disposed toward him, enjoyed taunting Marcel and returned his letter as
though he were a professor marking a composition, complete with a grade and
marginal comments: "The highest mark being 20, this little epistolary exercise
deserves no more than *minus fifteen.* The teacher." Montesquiou attributed another
comment by Proust to bitterness over not having received from the count a written
appreciation of *Pleasures and Days.*[7] Marcel's book was soon to receive attention
from the most undesirable source.

An Affair of Honor

On February 3 Jean Lorrain wrote a second virulent article in *Le Journal,* in which
he mocked Marcel and his friends by attacking *Pleasures and Days.* Lorrain maintained that France had written the preface because he could not deny his beautiful

prose to Mme Arman, in whose home he had dined so often. He characterized Proust's book as filled with "inane flirtations in a dated, pretentious, and precious style." What really distinguished Proust's "delicate volume" as the epitome of its genre were Madeleine Lemaire's illustrations. Lorrain described the drawing for "La Mort de Baldassare Silvande," whose title he misspelled, as "two jugs," for "Violante ou la mondanité," "two rose leaves," remarking parenthetically, "I'm not making this up." Then, aiming at Proust and his illustrator, Lorrain intoned sarcastically, "Madame Lemaire's ingenuity has never been so perfectly adapted to an author's talent." Commenting on the rarefied, silly-sounding names of some of Proust's aristocratic specimens, such as Heldemonde, Aldegise, and Hercole, Lorrain noted that such appellations represented the pure aristocracy of the old regime, and he called for the whip to punish the offender. Lorrain saved the worst blow for last: "Rest assured," he alerted his readers, "that for his next book, M. Marcel Proust will obtain a preface from M. Alphonse Daudet . . . who will not be able to refuse this preface either to Mme Lemaire or to his son Lucien."[8]

Like everyone else, Lorrain had noticed Lucien's pretty face and effeminate nature, traits the journalist despised. In his newspaper column, the acid-penned chronicler consistently attacked men in the social limelight who shared his homosexual inclinations. Effete homosexuals especially aroused his ire, although Lorrain himself often appeared bejeweled and perfumed, his mustache dyed red with henna. Lorrain fancied boys also, but—like Proust's baron de Charlus—he favored tough ones, sailors or butcher boys, from the lower classes. His letters and memoirs tell of narrow escapes from severe beatings; once sailors, offended by his blatant sexual advances, attempted to drown him.

Marcel knew that he could not let pass Lorrain's insinuation that he and Lucien were lovers, and he challenged the columnist to a duel. In spite of his nervous, sickly condition, Marcel did not fear exposing himself to danger, perhaps even death. Léon Daudet said that although Marcel was normally the most amiable of men, when offended, he responded like dynamite, or a lion that had been given a flick of the finger.[9] This powder-keg temper is a trait Proust gave first to Jean Santeuil and then to the Narrator, neither of whom hesitates to fight a duel when provoked.[10]

Marcel chose as his seconds Jean Béraud, a distinguished painter, and Gustave de Borda, a socialite with a delightful wit, whose dexterity and finesse in so many duels had earned him the nickname "Sword-Thrust Borda." Securing Borda's services provided Marcel with a warranty of distinction and integrity. Béraud, whom Proust knew well from Madeleine Lemaire's salon, was an excellent choice, given his expertise in handling such matters. He was particularly eager to serve in this instance because he had been piqued by Lorrain's attacks on his friends. As his seconds Lorrain chose the painter Octave Uzanne and the novelist Paul Adam. The four seconds met at Béraud's residence but were unable to resolve their differences, and a duel was judged necessary. It would be fought with pistols on Saturday, February 6, in the forest of Meudon just outside Paris. Proust's primary worry, he later told Montesquiou, was not the bullets but having to rise, dress, and go out in the morning. Fortunately, his seconds were able to arrange an afternoon confrontation.

Saturday dawned cold and rainy. Reynaldo was among those who accompanied Marcel on the carriage ride, through woods filled with oak and birch trees, to the meeting place at the Tour de Villebon. Once both parties had arrived, the men went quickly about their business. After stepping off twenty-five paces, each duelist fired one shot at the other, neither scoring a hit. Proust had apparently taken aim at Lorrain, because his bullet hit the ground almost on the journalist's right foot.[11] After the exchange of fire, the seconds for both parties declared the matter resolved. Was it Marcel's decision not to shake hands with the despised scandalmonger, or did his seconds prevent him from making the gesture of reconciliation?[12] Later that day Hahn noted briefly in his diary: "Today Marcel fought with Jean Lorrain, who had written an odious article about him in Le Journal. For the last three days he has shown a sangfroid and firmness that appear incompatible with his nerves, but that does not surprise me at all."[13] Marcel's pluck had also impressed Béraud, a veteran of many such confrontations.[14] Perhaps the real Marcel was not, after all, the one depicted by Blanche in the portrait but the one who had enjoyed military life and had sought to prolong his enlistment. Paul Morand, a diplomat and writer who knew Proust later in life, said that although Proust was often depicted as being weak and effeminate, nothing was further from the truth: "Proust had a lot of authority, what the English called 'poise,' . . . and, at the same time, lots of courage. He looked you right in the eye, with a somewhat defiant air, like D'Artagnan, head back. He was very courageous."[15]

On the day following the duel, as was customary, Le Figaro, Le Gaulois, and Le Journal printed an account of the proceedings, signed by all the seconds.[16] On Sunday morning Mme Arman wrote to Marcel to thank him "for your sweet thought and take you to my heart for being so brave and coming back to us safe and sound from your adventure." As for the "monster" Lorrain, she regretted that Proust's aim had not been better.[17]

The duel came at the time when Proust had promised to deliver the manuscript of Jean Santeuil to Calmann-Lévy. The formless mass of its pages was nowhere near ready for submission. Marcel had been far too optimistic about finishing the manuscript, whose pages he had multiplied without imposing any order or structure. For the remainder of 1897, Proust's productivity would reach its lowest level for the years during which he labored on Santeuil's story. Lorrain's attacks on *Pleasures and Days* may have intensified Proust's misgivings about his ability to complete the work. Would his new hero Jean be seen as pandering to the beau monde of the faubourg Saint-Germain? And what about the names he had chosen? Would Sentleur, M. d'Utraine, Rustinlor, M. de Traves, Mme d'Alériouvres, and so forth be received with the same derision?[18] Although somewhat discouraged and still at sea about where the story was heading, Proust did not abandon *Jean Santeuil,* which remained his only literary project, and drafts would continue to pile up over the next few years, like leaves without a central trunk and branches, pages without a plot or unifying point of view.

The Marcel most people thought they knew was the one Jacques-Émile Blanche had depicted: the spoiled, idle socialite. Now Lorrain's articles had tarred him as an effeminate snob who only dabbled in literature, an unflattering image that persisted in the minds of many, including friends, whose warnings about the dangers of high society seemed fulfilled. A group of these friends, indifferent to the disappointment and humiliation he had already suffered, soon mounted another attack, meant to be funny, on his hapless first book.

At the end of February, Marcel became confused about Lucien's schooling and thought that he had just passed his baccalaureate exams. He sent the supposed graduate a congratulatory telegram, saying that he had heard the news by chance and gently reproached Lucien for not having informed him. This oversight, Marcel remarked, suited Lucien's apparent determination to avoid him. The demise of Marcel's intimate relationship with Lucien had been a slow drifting apart, noticeably different from the flashes of jealousy, spite, hurt feelings, reproaches, and sorrow that marked the end of his passionate friendship with Reynaldo.

With spring approaching, the duel behind him, and his love life at a lull, Marcel began to think of adding a historical backdrop to *Jean Santeuil.* Writing to congratulate Édouard Rod on his recent novel *Là-Haut,* Proust flattered the author by linking Rod's book to what he especially admired in one of George Eliot's novels: "It is this panoramic painting, not only of places but also of events that I so loved in a novel like *Middlemarch.*" Proust thought that if he could construct the right historical panorama for *Jean Santeuil,* he could then devote his attention to the depiction of individual passions, show the import and consequences of apparently trivial events, and decode them to reveal the general laws of the human condition. Easy in theory, perhaps, such a program was nonetheless extremely ambitious.

Marcel had known for some time that he wanted to be a writer, but he had never specifically declared that he wanted to be a novelist. He had proved that he could write sketches and fully developed short stories of some merit, but he feared that the formless pages of *Jean Santeuil* would never constitute a novel. Now, perhaps inspired in part by Rod's novel and *Middlemarch*, he began to take a closer look at national events, attempting—like Balzac, Stendhal, and Flaubert, his great predecessors in the French novel—to set his story against the social and political background of his day.

On March 14 Marcel invited Prince Constantin de Brancovan to attend a session at the Chamber of Deputies, for which he had obtained two tickets through President Félix Faure's office. The debate concerned Greece's takeover of Crete, then under Turkish rule, and the ensuing international crisis. France, along with other European powers, had already committed troops to prevent Greece from annexing Crete. In the coming months Marcel attended other sessions in the legislature and trials related to the Dreyfus Affair. Although Proust followed the Dreyfus case closely, the cause célèbre interested him less as material for a novel than did Jean's friendship with Henri de Réveillon, the intrigues of salon life, or the beauty of flowers, mountains, and the sea. While listening to the trials, Marcel took notes and wrote portraits of the key figures, but as with everything he wrote for *Jean Santeuil,* the purpose of his journalistic notes remained unclear.

In his final year as a medical student, Jacques Bizet had rented a small studio apartment on the top floor of a fine old house on the Île Saint-Louis.[19] In spite of its modest size, Jacques converted the space into a study and seductive bachelor pad, one of whose finest features was a narrow terrace from which Bizet and his friends enjoyed a superb view of the rooftops of Paris. Among the regulars were Fernand Gregh and Daniel Halévy, determined, like Proust, to make their marks as writers, and the future lawyers Robert Dreyfus and Léon Yeatman.

Bizet and his group enjoyed staging amateur theatricals, musical reviews, and shadow plays inspired by those presented at the famous cabaret Le Chat noir. Casting about for an appropriate subject for a satirical review, the group quickly hit upon the idea of roasting Marcel and his recent publishing fiasco. The silhouettes and decors for the show, entitled "Les Lauriers sont coupés" (The laurel wreaths have been cut), were created by artist friends who were exceptionally talented: Jean-Louis Forain, Jacques-Émile Blanche, and Paul Baignères. The title may have come from Maurras's review of *Pleasures and Days,* which he ended by saying that in Ancient Greece, a new, distinguished young poet was presented with "myrtle, rose, and laurel."[20] Robert Dreyfus was recruited to help with Bizet's production, as well as two "nice little chanteuses," whose contributions to the enterprise may not have been solely lyrical. The producers selected the cast according to the special talents of each. Yeatman, who imitated Proust's voice and intonation to perfection, took the lead role, but only after some persuasion, because he feared offending the hypersensitive author. Dreyfus recorded in his diary what the audience heard while silhouettes of Proust and Ernest La Jeunesse, who wrote for *La Revue blanche,* were projected on a screen:

> Proust, to Ernest La Jeunesse: Did you read my book?
>
> La Jeunesse: No, sir, it is too expensive.
>
> Proust: Alas, that's what everyone says. . . . And you, Gregh, did you read it?
>
> Gregh: Yes, I cut the pages in order to review it.
>
> Proust: And did you, like the others, find it too expensive?
>
> Gregh: Oh, no, no, you certainly get your money's worth.
>
> Proust: You're quite right! M. France's preface, four francs, Mme Lemaire's illustrations, four francs, Reynaldo Hahn's music, four francs, my prose, one franc. A few poems by me, half a franc.
>
> The total comes to 13 francs 50 centimes, that's not outrageous for the money.
>
> La Jeunesse: But, Sir, there's a lot more than that in the *Almanach Hachette* and it only costs twenty-five centimes!

The little show was something of a hit; *La Vie parisienne* even published a flattering notice. As word of the review spread, Bizet was astonished to see many members of the social set mounting the steps to his small apartment. "Lauriers" had a long run for a private, nonprofessional production: three consecutive evenings, March 18–20. Marcel, although deeply wounded when he heard about the review, tried to be a good sport. His friends thought that they had been gentle in their satire, but although Marcel said nothing to any of them, they got wind of his unhappiness.[21] Marcel had escaped unharmed from his duel with Lorrain only to be wounded in his pride by the barbs of his friends' mockery. *Pleasures and Days* had attracted a fair amount of attention, but not the kind of which he had dreamed.

A Conflagration and Another Duel

Marcel enjoyed a busy winter season of dinner parties and evenings at the theater and opera. He occasionally saw Hahn's captivating cousin Marie Nordlinger. In January he accompanied her to the Louvre to see the tiara of Saïtapharnès, a scandalous fake that had rocked the Paris art world. In the following summer Reynaldo took Marcel and Marie to visit the studio of Alexander Harrison, the painter who had befriended them at Beg-Meil.

Marcel saw Montesquiou more often during this period, sometimes accompanying him on visits and excursions.[22] In mid-April *Le Figaro* published poems by the count that Delafosse had set to music. That merited a congratulatory letter from Marcel, who said that he found the poems ravishing. He also informed Montesquiou that he intended to go to the Palais des Beaux-Arts and view the count's portrait by Giovanni Boldini.[23] Boldini's canvas, the most talked about painting in the 1897 salon, showed the vain count holding and admiring a cane that had belonged to Louis XV. The resourceful Yturri had acquired this treasure for Montesquiou's remarkable cane collection at the sale of Edmond de Goncourt's estate.[24] The count, who had already been portrayed by Whistler, Blanche, and La Gandara, may have regretted posing with the cane, given the ridicule and danger to which this decision was about to expose him.

Various Paris wits had their fun at Montesquiou's expense as they described his picture. Geneviève Straus said he looked like "a toad headed for the strawberries."[25] Jean Lorrain, who particularly enjoyed goading the count, informed his readers: "We see him again this spring, executed by Boldini, the habitual deformer of little, agitated, and grimacing ladies, otherwise known as the Paganini of the peignoirs."[26] Lorrain did not scruple to make an obscene suggestion: the caption of the picture of Montesquiou gazing at the cane, should be, "Where shall I put it? or Indecision."[27]

On May 4 tragedy struck Paris at a charity bazaar organized by some of the city's most fashionable women. The Bazaar de la Charité had set up its counters, where luxury items and novelties were to be sold by volunteers under a huge, striped canvas tent on a vacant lot, surrounded on three sides by buildings. As an added attraction, a huge movie projector had been hoisted high above the stands to project a new film, "L'Escamotage d'une dame chez Robert Houdin" (The disappearance of a woman at Robert Houdin's) by Georges Méliès.[28] Across the top of the tent a vast awning had been stretched as a shield against the light and heat. Streams of elegant ladies and gentlemen arrived, clad in all their finery—the women wearing large, flowery *chapeaux* and the men sporting their top hats, scenting the air, as they moved about, with the finest French perfumes and colognes.

Suddenly, a fire broke out near the film projector and spread to the awning. Amid shouts of "Fire!" the flames spread rapidly, engulfing the awning and the tent, whose panels of burning canvas rained down on the crowd below. Thick clouds of smoke filled the tent, which began to reverberate with horrible screams and moans. Most of the crowd ran away from the fire toward the back of the tent, where the exit was blocked. Men and women, their clothes aflame, rushed toward the others, in a vain attempt to escape the inferno. Bodies began to pile up; many died from asphyxiation. Geneviève Straus, who had been in the tent when the fire started, somehow knew that the only way to safety lay in walking straight into the fire. That moment of aplomb saved her life.[29]

After the catastrophe, which claimed 140 lives, rumors circulated that a few society men from Paris's best clubs had used their canes to clear women out of their way as they beat a path to safety. Montesquiou, who had remained at home that day, was named as one of the offenders. To compound the offense, the rumor added that Montesquiou had been seen later at the morgue, using his cane to brush aside articles of clothing as he studied the charred remains of victims, among whom he expected to find relatives and friends. Lorrain wasted no time in giving credence to this slander in his column. Evoking the Boldini portrait of the count "hypnotized in the adoration of his cane," Lorrain accused Montesquiou of being a coward and a brute, a man who used his cane as a "cudgel for living women and as tongs for dead women, henceforth sadly renowned in the annals of masculine elegance!"[30] Montesquiou again ignored Lorrain's vile insults; a man of noble birth, a direct descendent of D'Artagnan, could not engage in combat with a gutter journalist. Trouble soon came from an altogether different quarter.

On May 21 the Académie française awarded Fernand Gregh's *La Maison de l'enfance* the Prix Archon-Despérouse, with its purse of two thousand francs. Proust, who had seen his own book become an object of derision, sent Gregh a congratulatory note that the recipient found rather perfunctory.[31] Was Marcel slightly jealous, as well as disappointed, because he believed *Pleasures and Days,* for all its flaws, superior to Gregh's book? Or was he simply too preoccupied with a large dinner party he had planned, whose date had to be suddenly advanced to accommodate Anatole France, set to depart on his usual springtime cruise?

The list of distinguished gentlemen invited to dine chez Proust on May 24 included Robert de Montesquiou, Boni de Castellane, Anatole France, Reynaldo Hahn, Jean Béraud, Gustave de Borda, Édouard Rod, Gaston de Caillavet, and one of Montesquiou's portraitists, La Gandara. Ladies were not included because Mme Proust was still in mourning and could not make an appearance. The guest list had been more troublesome to draw up than usual, and not only because of the exclusion of lady friends. The Dreyfus Affair had begun to complicate social events by making it difficult if not impossible to invite all one's friends, some of whom inevitably were no longer on speaking terms, having taken opposite sides in the increasingly emotional debate about whether or not Dreyfus was guilty. According to the brief account in the next day's *Le Gaulois,* Proust's dinner was a success: "The celebrated Dr. Proust, father of M. Marcel Proust," having put in an appearance welcomed by all, "withdrew, leaving his son to do the honors at this beautiful dinner, during the course of which wit at its most Parisian never ceased to sparkle."[32]

Montesquiou may have believed that the terrible rumors circulating about him after the Bazar de la Charité disaster had died down. Unfortunately for him, the rumors persisted. The count soon received the same insulting accusation to his face from a quarter much superior to Jean Lorrain's mire. On June 5 Montesquiou had asked Baronne Adolphe de Rothschild to show him and some of his artist friends her impressive collection of artworks and curios. After the viewing of the collection, Delafosse was to give a concert. Among those who accompanied the count were La Gandara, the designer and glassmaker Émile Gallé, and the carica-turist Sem. The baroness had also invited the poet Henri de Régnier, his wife, and her two sisters. Montesquiou, who had long been at odds with Régnier, recalled the incident that occurred when the group took their hats and canes to leave. One of the sisters, commenting on Robert's beautiful cane, had remarked, "with a frankly hostile tone, that it was of a size to clear a way for oneself in a catastrophe."[33] Régnier suggested that a fan or a muff would suit Montesquiou better.[34] Montes-quiou, greatly offended, decided to demand satisfaction. He chose as his seconds Maurice Barrès and the portly marquis de Dion; Régnier asked the historian Henry Houssaye and the much in demand Jean Béraud to represent him.[35] Although Régnier seemed willing to find some accommodation, Montesquiou declined somewhat discourteously all attempts to avoid a fight.

Proust, who read about the impending duel in *Le Figaro* of June 8, wrote immediately to the feuding poets, expressing his fears for their safety and remind-ing each that he was a friend of the other. The duelists met the following afternoon at the pont de Neuilly. Montesquiou, his illustrious swashbuckling ancestor not-withstanding, did not make an impressive swordsman as he flailed his blade around in the air. The duel ended when Régnier wounded Montesquiou's thumb. The two adversaries refused to shake hands, making reconciliation impossible.

Montesquiou retired to his family's château de Charnisay at Preuilly in Touraine to nurse his wounded hand. Marcel wrote to him there, expressing his relief that no greater harm had come to the count, who had been, "everyone said, so brave."[36]

Montesquiou began to look with displeasure upon Léon Delafosse, with whom he had become bored. The count had launched the musician in high society by arranging for him to play for such hostesses as Mme Lemaire and Mme de Pourtalès and by sponsoring concerts in the Salle Érard—not to mention featuring him at his own magnificent parties. But Montesquiou had recently detected signs not only of ingratitude but of disloyalty on the part of his protégé. Léon enjoyed—too much, Montesquiou may have thought—the company of the Brancovans, distant relatives of the count's. Princesse Rachel Brancovan, a longtime friend of Paderewski's, was an excellent pianist. When Delafosse performed for her circle, he was among true connoisseurs, who appreciated his talents, and he found it impossible to hide his pleasure. Montesquiou decided that the time had come to break with Delafosse and banish him from his entourage. Yturri begged him to reconsider, asking him where would he ever find "so gifted an interpreter to explain his moods and calm his tempers."[37]

On June 17 Delafosse, unaware of the count's malicious intentions, performed at a party his settings of Montesquiou's poems, as he had faithfully done for so long. Delafosse received the first indication of having fallen from favor when he was refused permission to dedicate a composition to Comtesse Greffulhe. In an outburst as mad as those Proust later attributed to the baron de Charlus, Montesquiou put the "arriviste" in his place: "Little people never see the efforts one makes to descend to their level and never climb up to one's own!" He then threatened to make certain that the doors that had opened to the musician through the count's "sovereign protection" were slammed shut, reducing Delafosse to "strumming some Moldavian or Bessarabian clavichord for a pittance. You have only been an instrument of my thought, you will never be more than a musical mechanic." A short time later when Montesquiou and Delafosse chanced to cross paths and his former protégé attempted to greet him, the count observed in a superb display of hauteur: "It is natural that one bows when passing the cross, but one must not expect the cross to return the bow."[38]

All the count's friends had fun with the pianist's name (*de la fosse,* meaning "from the pit"): Mme Howland called him "this little pit"; for Mme de Brossia he became "the dead-end pit." Montesquiou replied to those who asked what had become of Delafosse, "He fell into his name." Marcel joined the chorus of those who mocked Delafosse, adopting another of Montesquiou's play on words: *brouillé,* which is used when one is on bad terms with another, also means "scrambled" in cooking. Marcel, who had anointed Delafosse the Angel, now echoed Montesquiou's derisive epithet and referred to the disgraced musician as the *œuf brouillé* or scrambled egg.[39]

Proust remembered Montesquiou's antics, including his infatuation with Delafosse, when he depicted Charlus's passion for the violinist Morel. Although Charlus was a creation of Proust's imagination, some aspects of his character were directly inspired by Montesquiou, including his colossal pride and the tendency to violent outbursts. In *The Guermantes Way,* Charlus becomes annoyed at the Narrator for not having understood his overtures of friendship. When the perplexed youth attempts to apologize for whatever offense he might have committed, Charlus explodes: "Do you suppose that it is within your power to offend me? You are evidently not aware to whom you are speaking? Do you imagine that the envenomed spittle of five hundred little gentlemen of your type, heaped one upon another, would succeed in slobbering so much as the tips of my august toes?"[40] Such conceited acrimony sounded like vintage Montesquiou.

In June, Montesquiou abandoned the Pavillon Montesquiou at Versailles for another home, which he named the Pavillon des Muses, opposite the Bois de Boulogne in the fashionable Paris suburb of Neuilly. On entering the dining room guests saw the count's portrait by Whistler next to the majestic fireplace. Boldini's portrait of the count with the notorious cane greeted visitors from an easel in the White Salon, just to the right of the door opening into the Salon des Roses.[41]

On June 23 Proust wrote to thank Montesquiou for the laudatory remarks he had written about *Pleasures and Days* in his latest book, *Roseaux pensants.*[42] Montesquiou had returned Marcel's many favors by reprinting a story and characterizing his prose as "silken" and his verses as "harmonious."[43] Marcel explained that if he were not so unwell he would have come in person to thank the count. Due to terrible sleepless nights, he often went to bed at eight in the morning and slept until three in the afternoon. This bizarre sleep pattern had not yet become fixed, but it was becoming more frequent, a development that alarmed his long-suffering parents, who, try as they might, could do little to alter their son's regimen. Letters like the one to Montesquiou contained what was to become a familiar refrain to Marcel's friends: "Don't call too early."[44] Too early for Marcel now meant before two or three in the afternoon.

After nearly thirty years of happy summer retreats at Auteuil, Adrien and Jeanne found it difficult to admit that those days had gone forever. In July they rented a chalet in the Parc-des-Princes at the entrance to the Bois, only a few minutes from where Uncle Louis's house had stood in rue La Fontaine. The Proust family, determined to act as though little had changed, kept to its old routine as much as possible. Dr. Proust went daily to the Hôtel-Dieu, either in the omnibus or by the trolley that ran from Auteuil to Saint-Sulpice. Marcel helped his parents maintain the illusion that little had changed by taking the train from the Saint-Lazare station to Auteuil nearly every evening to dine with them. As he observed his parents that summer, he registered the unmistakable signs of approaching old age: their skin was wrinkled, their hair gray, and both were too corpulent and incapable of moving about with ease. He soon had a fresh reminder of how quickly time speeds away with those we love.

On July 15 Reynaldo's father Carlos died in his country home at Saint-Cloud, near Paris. Marcel went immediately to console his grieving friend. Upon returning to Paris, he wrote Reynaldo, inquiring whether he could help in any way: "Unless you tell me to, I won't come. I am thinking of you though, my poor boy. I love you with all my heart."[45] Barely able to tolerate travel and the countryside during pollen season, Marcel did not wish to return to Saint-Cloud unless Reynaldo insisted.

Marcel and Reynaldo had long watched the stoic suffering of another father, Alphonse Daudet, wracked with pain caused by the final stages of syphilis contracted in his youth. In August, just before Marcel's departure for Germany, *La Presse* published his essay on Daudet, in which he praised the writer's noble quest for "truth, beauty, courage," and his heroic endurance while struggling against a painful, debilitating disease.[46]

Marcel and his mother returned to the Oranienhof at Kreuznach because she believed that the treatments there were beneficial to her health. Because Marcel disliked this spa and they were to remain for several weeks, he intended to devote much of his time to reading works he hoped would inspire his writing. He sent a quick note to Lucien, asking which authors or books he should add to his list. He especially sought advice about British and Russian writers whose works he had heard praised. He peppered Lucien with questions; he wanted to know who wrote *The Brothers Karamazov*. "And has Boswelle's [*sic*] *Life of Johnston* [*sic*] been translated?" And finally, "What's the best of Dickens (I haven't read anything)?"[47] Over the course of his life he showed a preference, among foreign authors, for British and Russian novelists.

Proust did not limit his research to bookish sources. On September 1 he solicited advice of Mme de Brantes, whose social knowledge and taste he had come to appreciate. She was taking the waters at Marienbad, too far away, he lamented, or he would gladly have paid her a visit, for there was no one at Kreuznach whom he knew or even wished to meet. Desiring information about old regime aristocrats, he had read, on Mme de Brantes's recommendation, Balzac's *La Duchesse de Langeais;* he "didn't think much of it," but he found in Balzac's novel *Gobseck* some portraits of old nobles of the kind he needed for his novel. He sought character traits not to imitate, he said, but for inspiration. Mildly chastising Mme de Brantes for never having been willing to tell him anything, he asserted that she might be his best source for the information: "In five minutes a clever woman or a man of taste can sum up the experiences of several years." He promised to show her his sketch of the duc de Réveillon so that she could tell him how accurately he had portrayed the "tics, the prejudices, the habits" of such a personage. Etiquette among the nobility interested him particularly; for example, he inquired of Mme de Brantes whether offering the left hand was meant to show contempt and, if so, was that because of "not being *well born* or of not being in society?"[48] Proust continued to amass information about etiquette in high society, much of which he later used, often for comic effect, in scenes showing how members of the upper crust greeted, or refused to greet, people whom they considered their inferiors. Robert Dreyfus recalled that during the years Proust was writing *Jean Santeuil,* he studied the fabulous denizens of high society with the same diligence that an entomologist applied to the observation of ant colonies.[49]

In Paris on October 24, Marcel attended a concert featuring Hahn's composition "Nuit d'amour bergamasque." Marcel pronounced the work charming and noted with satisfaction that it had received two rounds of applause.[50] When a favorable review appeared in *Le Journal,* Marcel wrote immediately to thank a new acquaintance at the newspaper, the journalist and novelist Louis de Robert, whose novel *Papa* had been published the same day as *Pleasures and Days.*[51] What had particularly caught Proust's attention was the novel's hero, a young man who wanted to become a writer. Alluding to *Jean Santeuil,* Proust told Robert that his example would "perhaps encourage" him to create such a youth. Until now he had seriously doubted whether a book with such a protagonist could succeed. Many years later, Louis de Robert was to advise Proust about preparing *Swann's Way* for publication.

In July, President Faure, on the occasion of the publication of Adrien Proust's book *La Défense de l'Europe contre la peste,* thanked him personally for his tireless, effective efforts against disease. Dr. Proust had persevered in his determination to protect Europe from cholera epidemics. In February he had traveled to Venice, where he and a colleague represented France at the International Health Conference. The conference had been convened because a fresh outbreak of cholera in Bombay had alarmed European officials, who feared the plague might spread westward. In October, President Faure and his wife invited Dr. and Mme Proust to accompany them to Rambouillet, whose medieval château had recently been designated the presidential summer residence. Marcel may have urged his parents to find out, should the opportunity arise, where the president stood on the Dreyfus case.

The Dreyfus Scandal

In October an incident occurred in Mme Straus's salon that showed the increasing tension in French society over the Dreyfus Affair. A longtime friend of the Strauses, Joseph Reinach, a politician and lawyer, revealed to those present that Commandant Esterhazy was almost certainly the spy and the author of the bordereau. On hearing Reinach's remarks, which they considered outrageous and treasonous, Edgar Degas, Jules Lemaître, Jean-Louis Forain, and Gustave Schlumberger, four men who had enjoyed the Strauses' hospitality and friendship for many years, rose in disgust and left the salon, never to return.[52] Reinach, who became the first major historian of the Dreyfus Affair, made the Straus salon a center of Dreyfusard activity.

The following month the Dreyfus Affair finally erupted throughout French society. On November 13 Auguste Scheurer-Kestner, vice president of the senate and an elder statesman of unimpeachable integrity, published in *Le Figaro* a letter declaring that Dreyfus was innocent and that the real spy was known to authorities. Scheurer-Kestner offered the public no proofs, but his reputation was such that anyone who had been neutral or had entertained doubts should have been impressed by his stance.

On November 15 Mathieu Dreyfus, who, alongside Dreyfus's wife, had been fighting for three years to prove his brother's innocence, sent to Minister of War Jean-Baptiste Billot an open letter denouncing Esterhazy as the traitor and author of the bordereau. Ten days later Zola published his first article in *Le Figaro* supporting Dreyfus's cause by defending Auguste Scheurer-Kestner, now under attack for having spoken in Dreyfus's favor. Zola concluded his defense with the sentence that soon became famous as a slogan for the Dreyfusards: "La Vérité est en marche, et rien ne l'arrêtera" (Truth is on the march, and nothing can stop it).[53]

Zola's second article defending the Jews appeared in *Le Figaro* on December 1. On that day Daniel Halévy, in a bitter mood because of the maddening scandal, went to the opera, where he met Fernand Gregh, Louis de La Salle, and Jacques Baignères. Once in the great hall and under the spell of the music, Daniel tried to forget briefly the controversy swirling around Dreyfus. After the opera, the four friends went to Weber's café in the rue Royale, a favorite meeting place just around the corner from the Proust apartment. Here they talked until 1:30. Their conversation centered around art and reality, "the forgetting of everything in the presence of a beautiful work of art." Gregh got carried away and proclaimed that "art is the only reality since it is absolutely unreal." Daniel, unwilling to take flight on aesthetic paradoxes, reflected that in these sorry days reality gripped them only too tightly; he stubbornly maintained that "the most exalted work of art is the virtue of the strong."[54] He and his friends must find and enlist distinguished public figures strong enough and brave enough to confront Dreyfus's enemies, vanquish villainy, and exonerate Dreyfus and the Jews. Their idealistic hopes were soon dashed.

On the way home Fernand related to Daniel what he had seen a day earlier when he had stopped by the offices of *Le Figaro*. Léon Daudet and Maurice Barrès, two staunch anti-Semites, had come to pressure the newspaper's director, Ferdinand de Rodays, to adopt a "neutral" editorial stance by closing the paper's columns to Zola and all who questioned Dreyfus's guilt and the integrity of the army. Meanwhile, the government continued to pretend that there was no developing crisis. On December 4 Prime Minister Jules Méline, who opposed revision and hoped the clamor for a retrial would die down and vanish, reassured his countrymen: "I will say right away what will be the last word in this debate: There is no Dreyfus Affair. There is none at present and there will be no Dreyfus Affair."[55] Méline's comments were far from being the last word; his countrymen were on the verge of a painful, divisive debate that would take years to resolve.

Zola's third and last article in *Le Figaro* appeared on December 5. The newspaper that had long stood for openness and justice reacted to a deluge of canceled subscriptions and refused to publish any more articles critical of the army. Daudet, Barrès, and their allies had succeeded in blocking Zola's access to one of the capital's most influential dailies.

As Marcel and others in his circle worked to collect signatures from prominent men willing to support Zola's efforts, Halévy grew disgusted with the cravenness of many writers to whom they appealed. He noted in his diary: "Life is proving to be ignoble."[56] On December 12 Jacques Bizet showed Daniel a letter from Porto-Riche in which the playwright abandoned the cause. On the same day Marcel wrote Daniel to inform him that Anatole France had signed their petition supporting Zola's crusade. Marcel's early success had made him optimistic: "I will try to obtain for you all possible signatures." On reflection, he wondered whether he should ask Jules Massenet, as intended, because he had just remembered that the composer's brother was a general. He decided to try Massenet anyway, but he recommended against Daniel's proposal that Alphonse Daudet be asked to sign the petition, saying that such an appeal would be unkind, given the author's chronic pain. Even so, Marcel said that he would speak to Daudet privately about signing: "If it disturbs him, he won't do it." Proust's success did not cheer Daniel and Jacques for long, because they had but a single signature—albeit a distinguished one—on the sheet that should have been covered with names of courageous leaders who stood for justice. Anatole France, Daniel reflected, noticing the irony, was "the immoralist and the skeptic, who had so often attacked Zola."[57] France, who had been a member of the Académie française for only a year, was rapidly becoming disillusioned with the politics of his fellow "Immortals." The Academy, like most of France's traditional institutions, was made up almost exclusively of anti-Dreyfusards. Once he became committed to Dreyfus's case, France refused to attend meetings.[58]

Nothing could deter Émile Zola, who had committed his honor, his fame, and his fortune to the cause. The energy and spirit he had marshaled to create the hundreds of characters in the twenty novels of the Rougon-Macquart series now were channeled into the effort to save Dreyfus and the soul of France. His pamphlet to youth would attempt to reinvigorate his young countrymen's sense of justice. When Daniel and Fernand reported their lack of success to Zola, he suggested that they use their petition as a reply to his appeal to youth. Jacques and Daniel decided to abandon the solicitation of Paris's most prominent citizens because they were too cowardly. Instead, they heeded Zola's advice and concentrated on their peers.[59]

On December 13 Zola's "Letter to Youth" went on sale as a brochure urging the students of the Latin Quarter and all young intellectuals to rally to Dreyfus's cause. Marcel followed the events through the newspapers and by exchanging information with friends and acquaintances, many of whom occupied—or were intimately connected with those who did occupy—high places in the government. Proust later claimed to have been the first Dreyfusard because he obtained France's signature, but in fact he participated only briefly in the first part of the campaign.[60]

Shortly after Zola's letter was published, death took a distinguished writer who had often rivaled and opposed the author of *Germinal*. On December 16 Alphonse Daudet suffered a stroke; he died the following day. Marcel and Reynaldo had hurried to comfort the family on receiving news that Alphonse's condition was desperate. Proust's short tribute, "Adieux," appeared in *La Presse* on December 19, the day before the funeral.[61]

In early January 1898, Esterhazy had gone before a court-martial, whose true purpose was to erase doubts about his guilt. Zola became outraged when he realized that the real spy would be proclaimed innocent by the army and the press. Using his fury to invigorate his accustomed eloquence, Zola composed an open letter to President Faure. Fully aware of the personal, financial, and legal dangers to which he was exposing himself, the writer used his prestige and wide readership to fix attention on the list of indictments he was preparing to hurl at those he knew to be guilty. Like his most recent pieces, this letter would go on sale in brochure form, but ideally it should also appear in a widely circulated Paris daily. At the last moment Zola had the idea of bringing his letter to Ernest Vaughan, the director of *L'Aurore.* Both Vaughan and Georges Clemenceau, a politician who also served as the newspaper's political editor, "were immediately enthusiastic." Clemenceau came up with the sensational title "J'accuse."[62]

"J'accuse" appeared in a special edition on the morning of January 13. At the end of the letter to the president and the nation, Zola enumerated the accusations that provided the title. He began with the officer he believed to be at the origin of the whole sorry business: "I accuse Lieutenant-Colonel du Paty de Clam of having been the diabolical artisan of the judicial error, without knowing it, I am willing to believe, and then of having defended his nefarious work for three years through the most grotesque and culpable machinations." Then followed a number of paragraphs, each beginning with the resounding and damning *J'accuse* until Zola had named Generals Billot, Mercier, de Boisdeffre, Gonse, and de Pellieux, Commandant Ravary, the three handwriting experts, and the offices of war. Finally, he wrote, "I accuse the first Court Martial of having violated the law in convicting a defendant on the basis of a document kept secret, and I accuse the second Court Martial of having covered up that illegality on command by committing in turn the juridical crime of knowingly acquitting a guilty man."

Zola's letter hit the streets like a bombshell, no doubt one of the most deafening explosions ever produced in France by a single pen. At the end of his letter, Zola had listed the press laws that he was violating and called for his own prosecution to begin at once. The following day *L'Aurore* published a petition, known as the "Manifesto of the Intellectuals," condemning "the violation of juridical norms in the 1894 trial and the iniquities surrounding the Esterhazy affair."[63] The several hundred names on the petition had been collected by a group of aspiring writers that included Marcel Proust, Fernand Gregh, the Halévy brothers Élie and Daniel, and Jacques Bizet. Robert Proust had also signed the petition. In addition to their own signatures and those of other friends, such as Léon Yeatman, Robert de Flers, and Louis de La Salle, the petition bore the names of both Émile Zola and Anatole France.[64]

Adrien was furious with his sons for publicly acknowledging their support of Alfred Dreyfus and for placing their father in an embarrassing situation with his colleagues and his close friend Félix Faure. Dr. Proust belonged to the government establishment and shared, like most of his colleagues in medicine, many of their conservative, rightist views.[65] For a week he refused to speak to Marcel and Robert.

On January 13 Col. Georges Picquart was arrested and confined to the fortress of Mont-Valérien. Because he would be the principal witness for Zola's defense, the military decided to discredit him further before the trial. On February 1 he appeared before an investigatory board composed of directors from the general staff, who by a vote of four to one recommended that Picquart be retired from the army "for reason of grave misdeeds while in office."[66] The army immediately made the recommendation public in order to cast doubt on the testimony Picquart would soon give in criminal court.

Marcel, fascinated by the scandal's latest turns and the courageous role assumed by one of France's most acclaimed writers, sought passes to attend Zola's trial, which was to last from February 7 to February 23. Zola was represented by Fernand Labori, a distinguished and fearless lawyer, who defended Picquart later in the year and, in 1899, Dreyfus himself at the retrial of the court-martial at Rennes. Although Labori lost all three cases—cases that were unwinnable in the current climate—no one questioned his zeal and skill in defending his famous clients. Marcel easily obtained the passes; the real challenge for him was to rise early and arrive at the courtroom on time. In *Jean Santeuil,* Proust used his own experience at the trial to describe his hero's attendance: "For a month past his whole way of life had changed. Every morning he started early from home so as to arrive in good time for the Zola trial at the Cour d'Assises, taking with him no more than a few sandwiches and a small flask of coffee, and there he stayed, fasting, excited, emotionally on edge, till five o'clock."[67]

An event Marcel had long anticipated coincided with the Zola trial and competed for his attention. After years of waiting, Hahn's opera *L'Île du rêve* was finally to be produced. Albert Carré, who had succeeded Carvalho as director of the Opéra-Comique, selected Hahn's opera for his first production. Rehearsals began just as the Zola trial was getting under way. Marcel, eager to aid in the preparations for the March 23 première, divided his time between the trial at the Palais de Justice and rehearsals at the Opéra-Comique.

What Proust wrote about Zola's trial for *Jean Santeuil* was sketchy at best. The figure at the trial who captivated Proust was Picquart, a genuine hero, a man of unflinchable moral rectitude, who, though anti-Semitic himself, had risked his career, reputation, liberty, and even his life in the name of justice. Marcel saw in Picquart a philosopher, a courageous idealist.[68] His depiction of Picquart's gait, rapid, confident, and free, anticipates that of Saint-Loup, the character who in the *Search* was to represent a certain military ideal. On February 26, not long after Zola had been found guilty of defaming the army, the army dismissed the uncompromising Picquart from its ranks.

In *Jean Santeuil* there is very little about the actual events of the affair.[69] In the section about the Zola trial, there is nothing about Zola, nearly nothing about his lawyer, and little else connected with the actual trial. This raises the questions of how many sessions Marcel actually attended and why he did not glean more from the experience. If Marcel had hoped his close-hand observation of a major political and social crisis would enable him to coalesce the plotless, structureless pages of his manuscript into a coherent, compelling narrative, he must have been disappointed. Historical writing and social commentary were major concerns of his future novel, but told in relation to the private odyssey of an individual whose purpose in the world would remain hidden for a long time. He ultimately concluded that the "realist" novel, with its accumulation of details and facts, was far inferior to the product of the creative imagination. Although Proust never entirely shunned the muse of history, his forte was to be the exploration of perception and human psychology. Historical events, like salon intrigues, held his attention primarily when useful in discovering the psychological laws that govern human behavior.

By the time Proust wrote his mature novel, he understood exactly the best use to make of the cause célèbre. In the *Search*, the Dreyfus Affair shows how social entities thought to be enduring evolve under the influence of cultural and social upheavals: "It was true that the social kaleidoscope was in the act of turning and . . . the Dreyfus case was shortly to relegate the Jews to the lowest rung of the social ladder."[70] Proust had already witnessed examples of betrayal in the Straus and Caillavet salons when emotion overcame reason and people suddenly ended lifelong friendships. The affair, which in many cases made new enemies of old friends and new friends of people previously shunned because of status, rearranges the social constellations of the *Search*. For Mme Swann, who, because of her scandalous past as a cocotte, must start at the bottom of the heap, the Dreyfus case is a godsend, allowing her to associate with women from the best circles, now recruiting newcomers not according to distinctions of birth and breeding and social rank but based on whose side they had taken in the affair.[71] If choosing sides against Dreyfus gives a boost to Odette's ambitions to scale the social ladder, Mme Verdurin, whose sole raison d'être is her salon, suffers a major setback in society by supporting Dreyfus: "Mme Verdurin . . . though a sincere Dreyfusard . . . would nevertheless have been glad to discover a social counterpoise to the preponderant Dreyfusism of her salon. For Dreyfusism was triumphant politically but not socially. Labori, Reinach, Picquart, Zola were still, to people in society, more or less traitors, who could only keep them estranged from the little nucleus. And so, after this incursion into politics, Mme Verdurin was anxious to return to the world of art."[72]

His public support of Dreyfus lost Marcel few friends. Billy said that Marcel managed his relations so well because he had a keen sense of justice but detested cliques.[73] Marcel did suffer at least one social casualty, though. For Jacques-Émile Blanche, who loved gossip and delighted in setting his friends against each other, the Dreyfus Affair presented the opportunity for endless feuding. Marcel's relationship with Blanche became strained because of Dreyfus, and they stopped speaking to each other for thirteen years. Blanche speculated that Dreyfus's plight had awakened in Marcel an awareness of his Jewish heritage that had been submerged by his Catholic upbringing and the solid professional and social status of his bourgeois family.

According to Léon Blum, who was Jewish, one's racial status did not determine a Jewish intellectual's decision to become a Dreyfusard.[74] Proust, who in any case had never considered himself Jewish, wanted truth and justice to prevail. He and his brother had been raised in accordance with the marriage contract signed by his parents, as Catholics who enjoyed all the benefits of a well-established bourgeois family. Although Proust's religious beliefs as an adult wavered between atheism, agnosticism, and deism, he was to receive a Christian burial. Marcel never attempted to deny his Jewish heritage—he had reminded Montesquiou of it when the count made a disparaging remark about Jews—but defending his mother's race was not his motive for supporting Dreyfus.

Proust later recalled that during the Dreyfus years an anti-Semitic newspaper, *La Libre Parole,* had mentioned him as one of the "young Jews" who had attacked Barrès for his anti-Semitic views. Marcel's first impulse had been to rectify the statement that he was a Jew, but given the political climate he decided not to do so.[75] He took Dreyfus's side because of his own ideals. Proust made no objections if a friend harbored doubts about Dreyfus's innocence, as he explained to Constantin de Brancovan, when he sided with the Dreyfusards.[76] What could not be disputed, by any objective observer, was that little if any of the evidence used to convict Dreyfus had been valid.

One consequence of the affair was to make Jews who had been thoroughly assimilated into French society remember their origins. Unfortunately, the controversy also created many anti-Semites, as friends who harbored latent bigotry saw in Jews whom they had loved new incarnations they now loathed. Before Dreyfus, Blanche noted, there had been no noticeable distinctions made between one's Jewish and Christian friends; the word *anti-Semite* had no meaning.[77]

In Proust's circle there was a dramatic example of how the Dreyfus Affair changed people. Edgar Degas and Ludovic Halévy, now in their sixties, had been close friends since childhood. Although Halévy had converted to Catholicism, like many assimilated Jews, he had never sought to hide his heritage.[78] Ludovic's sons Élie and Daniel worshiped Degas, who had been a part of the Halévy circle before they were born. Daniel noted in his journal in 1890, long before the Dreyfus Affair, that the Halévys considered Degas "not just an intimate friend but a member of our family." For years the painter had come to their house for Thursday dinner and lunches several times a week. Degas had made so many drawings of the Halévys in their home that the works filled two large "Halévy Sketchbooks." The breakup came in the autumn of 1897, when Degas sat silently through dinner, at the end of which he rose and left without ever again saying a word to the Halévys.

How did Marcel the idealist maintain his close friendship with a rabid anti-Semite and anti-Dreyfusard like Léon Daudet? Even before the Dreyfus scandal created new bigots like Degas, Daudet had not hidden his anti-Semitism. But with Marcel and Léon the difference of opinion over Dreyfus never became a personal matter, while Marcel and Blanche quarreled over the issue and stopped speaking for years.

As for Montesquiou, he lost no friends over the affair. To the count, who had never lacked inspiration for ending friendships and banishing people from his circle, the Dreyfus business must have seemed like an unneeded luxury. Montesquiou chose not to take it too seriously and to remain blithely above the fray, although he tended to believe that Dreyfus was an innocent man. He was heavily influenced in this by his adored cousin Élisabeth de Greffulhe, who was well connected with Kaiser Wilhelm II and his court and had likely been informed through private channels that Dreyfus had never spied for Germany. According to Léon Daudet's book on the Dreyfus Affair, Mme de Greffulhe went to Berlin to hear from the emperor's own lips that Dreyfus was not a traitor. Daudet, of course, believed that this report, too, was part of the Jewish conspiracy.[79]

By summer the family's attention centered not on Marcel's health but on his mother's. A fibroid uterine tumor of considerable size had been discovered and had to be removed. Adrien, who knew the risks involved, had been nearly mad with anxiety. To lessen the chances of Jeanne's being upset, Adrien, Marcel, and Robert decided to tell no one beyond the immediate family about the operation until it was over. Dr. Terrier, a colleague of Adrien's, would perform the surgery. On July 6 Mme Proust underwent a major and difficult pelvic operation, lasting three hours, during which an unusually large, but apparently benign, tumor was removed. There had been moments during the ordeal when the surgeons feared that she would die.

Dr. Proust and his sons, greatly relieved that she had survived the operation, now grew concerned about her recovery. It was evident that it would be a long time before she regained her strength. They decided that it would be better not to tell her that she had nearly died. When Marcel visited her on the day after the operation, she, unaware of his extreme anguish over nearly having lost her forever, managed to be witty and, as always, to brighten his existence. In an unanticipated reversal of roles, Marcel began to serve as his mother's attendant and protector. Jeanne's doctors refused to let her rise from the bed; they also forbade many normal activities, including her favorite: reading. Looking after his mother, concentrating his energy on her illness and recovery, seemed to make him stronger and more independent. As her recovery progressed, he made plans to visit friends and perhaps even travel abroad, once she was well again. Jeanne suffered two minor complications in August, which prevented Marcel from seeing Léon Yeatman and visiting Montesquiou at Versailles. He wrote to Léon, telling him that he hoped to see him later at the seaside in September, perhaps in Dieppe, where he would accompany his mother if she was able to go.

Adrien and Marcel continued to observe Jeanne's recovery in the hospital and waited for her to decide where to spend the late summer vacation. Until then their own plans must remain uncertain. By the end of August, Robert, unable to obtain postponement of his army reserve training, reported to Châlons for the annual twenty-eight days of exercises. Jeanne was now well enough for Adrien to leave for Vichy, where he believed the thermal springs, used from Roman times, rejuvenated his gall bladder and kidneys. Marcel would remain with Jeanne and accompany her on vacation; unlike her husband, she remained devoted to the shores of Normandy.[80]

In July there had been startling developments in the Dreyfus Affair. The unscrupulous Esterhazy had swindled his nephew Christian out of his savings.

When Christian understood how his uncle had taken advantage of his innocence and trust, he denounced the culprit to the authorities and informed them that Esterhazy had forged telegrams sent to Picquart with the intention of implicating him in the spy case. On July 12, one week before a jury found Zola guilty again of defaming the French army, Esterhazy was arrested and charged with robbing his nephew and sending fraudulent telegrams.[81] The next day Picquart was arrested again and imprisoned in Mont-Valérien on the charge of having divulged secret military documents. He was held there, often in solitary confinement, for nearly a year. Later in the summer the army finally discharged Esterhazy on the true but vague grounds of "habitual misconduct."

The arrest of the real traitor set in motion a series of events that precipitated the beginning of the end for those who had framed and prosecuted Dreyfus. On August 13 Col. Hubert-Joseph Henry was identified as the forger of the bordereau, the principal document used to convict Dreyfus at his secret trial. Charles Maurras, a royalist and rabid anti-Semite, characterized Henry's crime as a "patriotic forgery."[82] After confessing to a number of such "patriotic" forgeries used as evidence to convict Dreyfus, Henry was placed in the same prison that held Picquart. On August 31 he committed suicide. Generals de Boisdeffre and de Pellieux resigned. In September, Du Paty de Clam, heavily implicated in the many criminal and treasonous acts of Major Esterhazy, was forced to retire from active service.

On September 31 Marcel attended Jaurès's public lecture on the Dreyfus Affair. Gregh was there, too, and read a poem that he had written to Picquart. Marcel decided to send Colonel Picquart an inscribed copy of *Pleasures and Days* to help the prisoner pass the hours more quickly. Getting a parcel to Picquart, kept under tight security, proved extremely difficult, but "after no end of trouble," Proust succeeded in having the book smuggled into the colonel's cell.[83] There is no record of Picquart's response to the thoughtful writer.

By October, Mme Proust was home from the clinic, fully recovered and feeling quite well. She soon left for Trouville, accompanied by Marcel and her maid. After their arrival Marcel reported to his father that Jeanne had made the trip without difficulty and seemed to be doing well. Using the elevator for comfort and to conserve her energy, Jeanne had at four o'clock gone down to the garden, where she remained until six-thirty without feeling tired in the least. The Proust men were relieved to see so many signs of her recuperation.

Not long after his arrival Marcel made a day trip up the coast to Dieppe to see Reynaldo, a guest at Madeleine Lemaire's villa, where he was composing a work he called "Destiny."[84] Marcel enjoyed walking with Reynaldo and Mme Lemaire along the cliff overlooking the sea. It was like old times—or nearly so. Back in Trouville, Marcel, in a nostalgic mood, wrote to Reynaldo, saying how he missed their happy days together and suggesting ways in which those moments could be revived. He proposed they meet halfway between Trouville and Dieppe, or if that wasn't possible, he would try to visit Reynaldo in the fall, wherever he might be. Having evoked the bittersweet memories of the days when they were intimate, he congratulated Reynaldo on the public letter he had written in support of Picquart. But then Marcel returned to his affection for Reynaldo, calling him "My dear little one" and telling him that his recent silence, far from being the silence that precedes oblivion, was "like undying embers that brood an ardent, intact love."[85] He had no other love. "Is it the same with you? See you soon, Marcel" In the first postscript he sounded the nostalgic note again by wondering if Beg-Meil would tempt Reynaldo at all; then he asked for news of Dieppe: "Send gossip."[86] Reynaldo always remained devoted to Marcel, but he did not share Marcel's inclination to resume their passionate friendship.

9 *Am I a Novelist?* ❧

MARCEL LEFT HIS MOTHER IN HIS father's care at Trouville and returned to Paris to prepare for a trip to Amsterdam. There he planned to see an unprecedented Rembrandt exhibition that brought together 125 of the great master's paintings.[1] *Le Figaro*'s art critic, Arsène Alexandre, had heralded the show with great enthusiasm, saying that never again would one have the opportunity to see so many Rembrandts.[2] Little is known about Proust's brief trip to Holland, except that he stayed at the Amstel Hotel and saw the Rembrandt paintings.

Although the trip to Holland was short and left Marcel's heart untouched, the paintings he viewed had inspired some thoughts about creativity. Back in Paris he continued working on the Moreau essay and began one on Rembrandt. In the Rembrandt essay Proust evoked some of the paintings that he had presumably seen in the Amsterdam exhibition, *The Woman Taken in Adultery, Esther,* and *Homer,* as well as others that he knew from the Louvre: *The Slaughtered Ox, Christ at Emmaüs,* and *The Good Samaritan.*[3] He observed that "these are not just the things that Rembrandt painted, they are things that appealed to him." It is the discovery of his true subjects that leads an artist to create his unique world. Once Rembrandt had found what was "real to him," he strove to "convey it in its entirety," rendering all such subjects "in a sort of golden medium, as if they had all been painted in similar light."[4] Rembrandt's discovery of his own light in the domain of the true self was accompanied by a feeling of ecstasy that he then conveyed to the viewer, enabling him or her to see the world through Rembrandt's eyes: "The light that bathes his portraits and his pictures is in some way the very light of his thought, the kind of personal light in which we view things when we are thinking for ourselves. One cannot doubt that he had realised that this was his own proper light, and that when he saw by it, what he saw became full of riches for him . . . and that then he felt the joy which portends that we are nearing some high event, that we are about to create."[5]

In preparation for the Moreau essay, Proust visited that artist's house on a day when he was "feeling out of my element, and disposed to hearken to inner voices."[6] On his death at seventy-two, Gustave Moreau had left his home and its contents of some eleven thousand paintings, drawings, and watercolors to his country.[7] Noted for his fanciful treatment of mythological and biblical subjects, he filled his canvases with exotic flowers and jewels and depictions of violence. Proust, who could have seen Moreau's paintings in either the Straus collection or that of Charles Ephrussi, was drawn to Moreau's depiction of young men of androgynous beauty.

In the Moreau essay, which contains a variation on the theme of the unique world that each artist makes visible, Marcel shows the artist at labor, like a spider, driven by an irresistible force of nature. Proust observed that when artists "inhabit their inner souls—they act by virtue of a sort of instinct which, like an insect's, is reinforced by a privy knowledge of the magnitude of their task and the shortness of their days, and so they put by every other obligation in order to create the dwelling where their posterity will live . . . and that being done, are ready to die."[8] Already deeply discouraged during the period when he wrote these lines, Proust could hardly know that by the time he began spinning in earnest his own enormous, intricate web, another decade would have passed. Once he finally undertook to write the *Search*, the presumed "shortness" of his days and the "magnitude" of his own chosen task forced him to race against time.

The Muse of History required Marcel's attention again when on November 24 Picquart, "accused of forgery and violation of the espionage law," appeared before the war council for his court-martial.[9] Proust and a number of his friends had signed a petition supporting Picquart that ran in *L'Aurore:* "In the name of flouted justice, the undersigned protest the measures taken against Colonel Picquart, the heroic artisan of revision, just as revision is going into effect."[10] When the petition appeared in the newspaper without his name, Proust wrote to the publisher to complain: "I know my name will add nothing to the list. But the fact of figuring on the list will add to my name; one doesn't miss an occasion to inscribe one's name on a pedestal."[11] Proust apparently did not mail his letter in time to make the second list, which appeared on Sunday, November 27, but one who did was "Reynaldo Hahn, musician."[12] In *Le Siècle*'s Sunday supplement, another petition on Picquart's behalf had been signed by Comte Mathieu de Noailles and some of Marcel's closest friends: Robert de Flers, Fernand Gregh, and Léon Yeatman.[13] Proust's name finally appeared the following day in *L'Aurore*'s third list of petitioners. The petitions had no effect on the government; Picquart remained incarcerated until the following June, when Esterhazy could no longer deny that he was the real spy.

Tea and Mimosa

Shortly after December 25 Proust wrote to Marie Nordlinger in England to thank her for her Christmas card.[14] In his meditative letter Marcel touched on topics that preoccupied him and were to form the philosophical underpinnings of his future work: the soul and its material encasement in the body, the passage of time and through time, the slow, unconscious accumulation of memories, largely ignored by the superficial, egotistical, social self. As Marcel sounded the depths of his being, he perceived only a faint echo indicating the unknown treasures that might lie buried beneath the sands of time. The scent of tea and mimosa furnished the *sesame* that opened, at least briefly in 1898, the door to the treasure trove. He spoke first about Christmas cards and other symbols and why we need them:

> If we were creatures only of reason, we would not believe in anniversaries, holidays, relics or tombs. But since we are also made up in some part of matter we like to believe that it too has a certain reality and we want what holds a place in our hearts to have some small place in the world around us and to have its material symbol, as our soul has in our body. And while little by little Christmas has lost its truth for us as an anniversary, it has at the same time, through the gentle emanation of accumulated memories, taken on a more and more living reality, in which candlelight, . . . the smell of its tangerines imbibing the warmth of heated rooms, the gaiety of its cold and its fires, the scent of tea and mimosa, return to us overlaid with the delectable honey of our personality, which we have unconsciously been depositing over the years during which—engrossed in selfish pursuits—we paid no attention to it, and now suddenly it sets our hearts to beating.

The text, along with the one in *Jean Santeuil* in which Lake Geneva recalls Beg-Meil, a passage that cannot be dated with any certainty, is the first known attempt by Proust to elucidate what became a key moment in the *Search:* the experience he later called involuntary memory.[15] Is it mere coincidence that another major Proustian talisman appears at the end of this letter to Marie? "I shall be very happy to renew acquaintance with your rare and precious wit and your grace as fresh as a branch of hawthorn."

The texts written in 1898 and 1899 for *Jean Santeuil,* just before he abandoned the novel, indicate that he now thought the key to his work lay submerged in the past. Proust recognized the importance of the insights expressed in the letter to Marie and transposed them for a scene in *Jean Santeuil.*[16] There they are inspired by another of his muses, the young and beautiful poet Anna de Noailles, to whom he gave the fictional name Vicomtesse Gaspard de Réveillon. Proust attempted to sketch and state the inspirational importance of such intoxicating, fleeting episodes, like the one evoked by tea and mimosa:

> Poems being precisely the commemoration of our inspired moments
> which in themselves are often a sort of communication of all that our
> being has left of itself in moments past, . . . the concentrated essence of
> ourselves which we exude without realizing that we are doing so, which a
> perfume smelled in that past time, a remembered light shining into our
> room, will suddenly bring back so vividly, that it fills us with . . . intox-
> ication, so that we become completely indifferent to what is usually
> called "real life," in which it never visits us unless that life be at the same
> time a past life, so that freed for a moment from the tyranny of the pres-
> ent, we feel something that spreads out beyond the actual minute.[17]

In the *Search,* Proust was to turn this around, as hinted here, and say that such moments of vivid, spontaneous memory and their conscious application in the creative process are the real life and that our usual daily life in its habitual and vain actions is a sham existence, a life lived on the surface, and hence, a life lost. In the continuation of the same passage from *Jean Santeuil,* he transposed the experience described to Marie, maintaining the holiday season and its atmosphere, but replacing the scent of mimosa with that of tangerines.

Proust's words do not convey the fervor of such ecstasy because he does not fully comprehend its importance and relation to the story he is trying to tell. The transfer of his own intense emotions and deeply felt insights to a third person and minor character like the poetess would not succeed; the current work had no structure or plot solid enough to support such revelations. Proust's creative vision would not come into sharp focus until he realized that his hero and spokesman must be himself, disguised somewhat but endowed with a remarkably seductive and intimate voice through which he would speak directly to the reader, pouring into the listener's ear the rich music of his enchanting, nocturnal musings.[18]

If the past lay concealed in material objects—whose tastes, textures, smells, or sounds provoked in him the ephemeral but intense reliving of past moments where they had been encountered before—what was the nature of this phenomenon and how could it be used in telling a story? The answer did not become apparent for many years.

A Publicist

Proust started the new year, the last of the century, in his usual fashion by writing to his friends. He congratulated Montesquiou on yet another book, *Les Autels privilégiés* (Privileged altars), for which Proust had written a brief publicity notice under the pseudonym Fantasia. He began thinking of the role he might play when the increasingly prolific count's new collection of poems, *Les Perles rouges* (The red pearls), appeared in the spring.[19]

Marcel thanked France for sending an inscribed copy of *L'Anneau d'améthyste* (The amethyst ring), the third part of his Bergeret chronicle, recently published in book form.[20] Proust, fulsome in his praise, compared this work favorably to Balzac's *Comédie humaine* and Saint-Simon's memoirs, two monuments of French literature, which were to be important models for his own future saga of life during the Third Republic. Then he compared France's humor to that of Molière and Cervantes, "relished by simple folk" and by "the sophisticated as well."[21]

Long an avid reader of British and American literature, Proust now became interested in the process of translation itself. On February 2 he wrote to Robert d'Humières, Kipling's translator, to thank him for the French version of Kipling's story "The Kidnapping of Mowgli," which had just appeared in the *Revue de Paris*. Marcel told d'Humières that the translation had given him one of the greatest literary joys he had ever experienced.[22] He then peppered d'Humières with questions about Kipling's life, the origin of his rather special preoccupation with wild beasts, kidnappings, and treks on the backs of elephants and monkeys and panthers. Marcel peered, intoxicated, into the exotic wilds of English literature—a refreshing, if brief, escape from concerns about the cannibalistic political crisis at home. The Dreyfus case was about to receive another twist of fate, one that encouraged to some degree those who sought to exonerate the prisoner on Devil's Island.

On the afternoon of February 16 Félix Faure retired to a back bedroom in the presidential suite with his mistress, Mme de Steinheil.[23] Around 5 o'clock the guards on duty heard hysterical shouts coming from the presidential suite. They rushed in and found Faure lying unconscious on the bed. His nude mistress was quickly wrapped in a blanket and hurried out a side door.[24] Faure's doctors arrived quickly, but there was nothing they could do for the stricken president, who had suffered a cerebral hemorrhage. He died that evening.

Faure's successor was Émile Loubet, a man proud of his humble origins and said to be a Dreyfusard. Because the late president had taken an essentially anti-Dreyfusard stance, the anti-Semitic press quickly charged that the Jews had killed Faure.[25] The reaction of Proust and his parents to Faure's death went unrecorded, but they must have grieved the loss of their old friend and pitied his wife and daughters, Antoinette and Lucie, while deploring the humiliation the family had suffered.

In February, Léon Daudet sent Marcel an inscribed copy of his novel *Sébastien Gouvès*. As Marcel read Daudet's novel, his second since their 1896 stay at Fontainebleau, where they had compared ideas about the books each would write, he wondered whether he would ever finish his own ambitious novel on which he had concentrated nearly all his literary efforts since the summer and fall of 1895. In his letter thanking Léon for sending the novel, Marcel, generous as always in his praise, compared Léon to Tolstoy, Goethe, and Balzac. He found in Daudet's character Mercier a portrait of evil that he would not have found believable until recently, because earlier he "absolutely" did not believe in evil. "Now I've had experience of it." His conversion to belief in evil had resulted from all the despicable acts committed by trusted public servants blinded by bigotry in their condemnation of an honest man. Not only had the Dreyfus Affair made Marcel see the veracity of a character like Mercier, but it had made accessible to him books that he had not understood before. Now he grasped for the first time, he told Léon, many of Balzac's, Shakespeare's, and Goethe's characters who incarnate evil. Marcel was strikingly candid in using the principal culprits in the Dreyfus case to epitomize evil in a letter to Daudet, who shared all the prejudices and hatreds of those men and who saw them first as heroes and, at worst, as victims of an international Jewish conspiracy. The bond of friendship that bound Marcel and Léon was impervious to the tensions of their radically opposed political and racial views.

Proust may indeed have understood evil after the Dreyfus Affair, but he would never portray evil that dark. His true vein was to be that of a comic, satirical moralist. Contrary to what he wrote to Daudet, his faith in goodness, notwithstanding his relentless satirizing of petty vices, remained unshakable. Proust saw too clearly the beauties of the world and the dignity of the human spirit, expressed through creativity, to dwell on the hideous face of evil.

Amid the rash of duels being fought over the Dreyfus case, in late February, Gaston de Caillavet challenged a critic to a sword fight after reading a theatrical review he judged offensive to his mother. Gaston had adapted France's novel *Le Lys rouge* (The red lily) for the stage, and it had premièred at the Théâtre du Vaudeville with Réjane and Lucien Guitry, two of Paris's best actors. Pierre Veber had written an acid review in *La Vie parisienne* about the play. Gaston and Pierre crossed sabers on the Île de la Grande Jatte and wounded each other slightly—Gaston on the hand, Verber on the arm—before their seconds stopped the fight.[26]

Marcel went immediately to Mme de Caillavet's home on avenue Hoche, hoping to find Gaston there. Because Marcel had once had a crush on Jeanne, he usually thought it best, out of discretion, not to call on Gaston at home. Having just missed his friend, Proust wrote to "My dear, my good Gaston," expressing his concern and complimenting Gaston on his conduct: "so fine, so perfect, so 'superb' (in the Latin sense)." He asked Gaston to convey to his wife the humble respects of her old admirer.[27] Marcel still enjoyed the illusion that he had been a serious suitor to Jeanne.

After the première of Gaston's play, Marcel attended a light supper given by Mme de Caillavet in honor of the novelist France. The hostess invited the cast of the play, Madeleine Lemaire, the rising newspaper publisher and political star Georges Clemenceau, and the writers Paul Hervieu, Marcel Prévost, Robert de Flers, and Tristan Bernard. Marcel, who seemed to enjoy better health in the late winter and early spring, devoted a fair amount of his time and energy to such artistic gatherings during the first half of the year. In April he became producer, stage manager, impresario, and host for a dinner party celebrating Montesquiou's latest outpourings from the muse, *Les Perles rouges,* a collection of ninety-three sonnets inspired by Versailles.

On April 15, in a rare burst of organizational zeal, Marcel wrote to Montesquiou to plan the rehearsal schedule with actress Cora Laparcerie and to compile the guest list for the dinner Marcel would host on Monday, April 24. On that occasion Laparcerie would recite poems by the writers Marcel knew best and whose works he tirelessly championed: Montesquiou, France, and the new, promising poet whose verses he admired, Anna de Noailles. The prickliest problem, as always, was the guest list. On that point no one in all of Paris, perhaps in the world, proved more difficult than Montesquiou. He had a long list of prominent Parisians who he believed had offended him, or who simply had been insufficiently adroit in show-ing their appreciation. Once the host had winnowed out the undesirables, there remained the problem of establishing whom to invite to the reading but not the dinner afterward, where space would be limited.

Among the most distinguished dinner guests was Gabriel Fauré, but his pres-ence complicated matters because he would have to slip out for fifteen minutes and run over to the Salle Pleyel to be present at a performance of one of his composi-tions. Proust asked the count to be so kind as to send the names of those proscribed, because he was making out his invitations as he thought of people he would like to include and did not want to inflict on the poet "the fastidious torture" of consulting him about each name. Marcel promised not to take his eyes off the "fatal circle" that enclosed those in disgrace.[28] Nervous about Montesquiou's own intentions, espe-cially if he were displeased about the guest list, Proust reminded the count that he was expecting him and Yturri on Monday for dinner at eight.

To Marcel's relief the party turned out to be a great success. Those present included one of Montesquiou's favorites, Comtesse Emmanuela Potocka, and, among others, Mme de Brantes, Madeleine and Suzette Lemaire, the Strauses, the newspaper editor Léon Bailby, Baron Edmond de Rothschild, Marquis Boni de Castellane, Prince Giovanni Borghese, Jean Béraud, and Charles Ephrussi. After Mlle Laparcerie read a few of Montesquiou's sonnets, the poet himself favored the guests with several more *Perles rouges*.[29]

When Marcel read the papers the next day, disaster, so often at hand when he attempted to ingratiate himself with Montesquiou, had struck again. *Le Figaro*'s account of the brilliant soirée did not mention the count or the publication of his *Perles rouges*, thwarting, from Montesquiou's perspective, the main purpose of the dinner. The newspaper had also created a major social crisis for the Proust family by printing that the "elite of the scientific world" had been invited. Adrien's colleagues must have wondered about their sudden demotion. Proust dashed off a letter to Montesquiou, deploring the omission, saying that the newspaper "de-prived me of the pleasure and pride I would have drawn from this honour. . . . I was obliged to spend my day with Charles Ephrussi on the one hand and Bailby on the other, looking for ways of remedying this state of affairs."[30] Ephrussi, a man of humble origins as a Polish Jew, had become a scholar, art critic, founder and director of *La Gazette des Beaux-Arts*, and an extremely well-connected Parisian.

He was just the sort of person Marcel needed to help straighten out the social mess created by *Le Figaro*. On April 26 the newspaper ran the desired rectification, twice mentioning Montesquiou's triumph as author and "exquisite reciter" and trumpeting his forthcoming book.[31]

If Proust had published no new books, he could still give away copies of an old one, especially because the publisher of *Pleasures and Days* had a large stockpile of unsold copies. The latest recipient was Vicomte Clément de Maugny, whom Marcel now considered one of his best friends.[32] When he sent the inscribed book to Clément in July, he included a letter in which he said that their "lives have been so affectionately mingled in these last two years that you have a kind of retrospective title to the thoughts and imaginings of my previous life." Marcel called his volume a likeness of himself when younger: "One often shows a photograph of oneself as a child to a friend who has made one's acquaintance later. So it is with this book, which introduces you to a Marcel you did not know."[33] He spoke of the era during which he wrote the pages collected in the volume as belonging to the past; new sorrows had replaced old ones: "What makes us weep changes, but the tears are the same. It seems to me that close as you have been to the wellsprings of my joys and sorrows during the years when you were my confidant and friend, you must, in reading these pages, feel more keenly than would anyone else, what remains in them of storms that will never return."[34]

Proust's attention soon turned to the political winds now rising again over the Dreyfus Affair. On August 7 Dreyfus's new trial began in Rennes. Having heard, after the first several days, that things were not going well for the revisionists at Rennes, Proust wrote to Joseph Reinach, inquiring whether this was true and requesting information about the retrial. In the early morning of August 14 a would-be assassin fired a shot at Dreyfus's lawyer Labori, injuring him slightly. Proust sent a telegram to Labori, expressing his relief that the "good invincible giant" had escaped serious injury.[35]

For the fall vacation Marcel decided to accompany his parents to Évian-les-Bains on the French shore of Lake Geneva. Jeanne and Adrien had booked rooms for themselves at the Splendide Hôtel, a new, fashionable resort. Knowing that the best hotels would be filled during the high season, Marcel began to worry about whether or not he could find accommodations suited to his particular needs. A number of his wealthy and titled friends owned or rented villas and châteaux around the lake near Évian. These included Vicomte Clément de Maugny, whose ancestral château was near Thonon-les-Bains, and Constantin de Brancovan, whose family owned a large lakeside estate, the Villa Bassaraba, at Amphion-les-

Bains. In mid-August, Marcel wrote to Constantin and involved the gracious prince in a complicated search for the perfect lodgings.

Marcel was considering a hotel at Amphion; it needn't be sumptuous, only clean. The advantages he sought in hotels were "solitude and silence," not easy to come by in popular resorts at the height of the season. The most important consideration was that the hotel not be completely booked, so that he could have an isolated room where he could sleep as late as he wished without hearing anyone walking in the room overhead or those adjoining. As Proust struggled over the years with insomnia, his noise phobia worsened. He asked Constantin, as someone familiar with the area, for information about hotels, rooms for rent, or even apartments, if they were not too expensive. Marcel's parents would arrive in Évian before him and his mother would scout the area with the same mission. He also engaged Clément to investigate hotels in the vicinity of Thonon. To no one's surprise, Marcel seemed hesitant about the trip, but he told Constantin, at the end of his letter, that if he did come to the lake he would be very pleased to see him from time to time when the prince had nothing to do. In the postscript he returned to the problem of the hotel, saying that he would be very interested to know whether it had shutters and thick curtains on the windows, so that when they were shut in the daytime the room could be made as dark as night. And whether the hotel staff was amiable.

Constantin, in an admirable example of noblesse oblige, replied quickly in such detail that Marcel thanked the "dear prince" for having provided the information with the "minutiae of a mother and the intelligence of a doctor."[36] Constantin had even gone so far as to invite Marcel to stay at the Villa Bassaraba, where, in addition to the château, there were several other guest houses on the large estate. Marcel said that his asthma would be the deciding factor. If he had difficulty breathing at the lakeside, he would leave after two days. But if not, he might remain indefinitely. Amused at the thought that Constantin, on reading these words, would be saying to himself in great terror: "He's coming to stay at the Villa!" Marcel reassured his friend that he sought only repose, not delightful company. But he would be greatly pleased if he were allowed to visit often.

The following week Marcel's mother inspected the hotels near Évian and thought that Marcel would be lodged more "silently" in the annex of the Hôtel Beaurivage in Évian. Marcel still hesitated, finding it nearly impossible to commit to the journey. Should he come to Évian, he asked Constantin to see him, if possible, soon after his arrival, because the first evenings in a strange place always made him profoundly sad.

A Season by the Lake

By late August or early September, Marcel arrived in Évian-les-Bains where he joined his parents at the sumptuous Splendide Hôtel, an establishment whose name seemed fully justified. After Napoléon III and Empress Eugénie inaugurated the thermal spa in 1856, Évian-les-Bains rapidly became the place for the wealthy to take the waters. Jeanne, who always went to spas in the late summer and early fall, had decided this year to try the new hotel, whose amenities included a library, first-class cuisine, and a celebrated wine cellar. The city, eager to attract those tourists who liked to gamble, had recently opened a casino.[37]

From the hilltop hotel Marcel admired the magnificent vistas of pristine blue water and snow-capped mountains, whose lower slopes were dotted with châteaux and villas. He was delighted with the charming, spacious suite his mother had chosen for him in the hotel, where, after close inspection, he found no traces of humidity on the wallpaper or anywhere else. Dampness, he had concluded, pre-cipitated asthma attacks and other ills. He enjoyed taking his meals in the spacious dining room, whose long façade of conservatory windows, especially when lit and seen from the exterior at night, reminded him of a huge aquarium in which rare creatures swam and fed.

During the season a number of Marcel's friends and acquaintances populated the lakeshore. The Brancovans were staying at their Villa Bassaraba just west of Évian at Amphion-les-Bains. Princesse Rachel Bassaraba de Brancovan had invited her son Constantin, daughters Anna and Hélène, and their husbands. Constantin's two beautiful sisters had married well; Anna's husband was Comte Mathieu de Noailles; Hélène had wed Prince Alexandre de Chimay. The Brancovan family occupied the château, chalet, and pavilion, while their guests were lodged in quarters known as the Farmhouse. On rainy days a carriage called at each lodging to bring family members and guests to the main house for meals and festivities.[38]

Princesse Bassaraba invited the prince and princesse de Polignac, fellow music lovers who were, in Marcel's opinion, "delicious" company for all, but especially for the hostess, who devoted her time to playing the piano works of Chopin and Haydn.[39] Marcel later wrote his mother that Princesse Bassaraba, in addition to her musical talent, was noted for excessive nervousness, kindness, and loftiness of spirit. She was so excitable that her new son-in-law M. de Noailles, on witnessing her frequent extravagant behavior, could only "smile disdainfully and say: what do you expect, she's nervous."[40]

The princess's other guests included Prince Antoine Bibesco, a Romanian diplomat, and Abel Hermant. Shortly after arriving, Marcel wrote to Bibesco, requesting that he and Constantin call him by his first name. Antoine, a Brancovan cousin six years younger than Marcel and destined to become one of his closest friends, apparently did not remain long at Villa Bassaraba. It is likely that he returned to Romania to complete his military service. Abel Hermant, a satirist and drama critic for *Gil Blas* and *Le Figaro,* was on excellent terms with the younger Brancovans, who enjoyed his endless stories about what went on behind the scenes in the theaters and drawing rooms of Paris. Geneviève Straus considered Hermant one of the best additions to her salon, but her nephew Daniel Halévy, who could be rather severe, wrote in his diary that Abel's conversation was an endless stream of insolent gossip.

A group photograph taken at the villa shows Marcel, perhaps thinner than he had been in recent years, standing in the back row next to Constantin. Just in front of them are the prince de Polignac, Mme Bartholoni, and her daughter Jeanne, standing next to Léon Delafosse, the Bartholonis' guest at Coudrée. Marcel's favorite Bartholoni daughter, the mischievous, vivacious Kiki, had apparently not accompanied her mother that day. Seen in the foreground of the picture are the princesse de Polignac, then Anna de Noailles and Hélène de Caraman-Chimay. Perched next to the sisters is Abel Hermant, looking elegant in spats and bow tie, and sporting a perfectly groomed handlebar mustache. The picture captured the aristocratic, cultivated, and artistic society that Marcel loved.

The Villa Bassaraba, with its music and poetry lovers, became the central gathering place for Marcel and his friends. On fine days the guests wandered through the gardens that sloped gently down to the lake. Over the years the princess had planted many Asian trees and plants, including rose bushes from Japan and other exotic or tropical specimens, like orange trees in tubs, magnolias, palm trees, and cedars. The Oriental garden theme included a pond where carps swam beneath a grotto. Guests could also play tennis, though the court seemed more often a meeting place for troubadours than for athletes. Anna, who loved being the center of attention, frequently recited her poems to the youngish crowd gathered there on fine days to hit an occasional ball or catch the poet's latest rhymes amid the festivities.[41]

In past years the Brancovan yacht, the *Romania,* had waited at its pier to ferry guests on their social rounds up and down the vast lake. Unfortunately for Marcel and his friends, this year the yacht needed repairs and could not be sailed. Marcel especially regretted the boat's disrepair when he calculated the expense of visiting his friends while striving to remain within the spending limits set by his mother.[42]

Each visit to the villa set him back ten to twenty francs, depending on the required combination of carriage, train, and ferry. When possible, he went on foot to meet friends or took transportation to a point nearby and walked the rest of the way.

There were many friends to call upon or who might join him at the Splendide for dinner. Pierre de Chevilly's family owned the château of Montjoux, one kilometer from Thonon-les-Bains. One year younger than Marcel, Pierre was another of his friends who later entered the diplomatic service. On a hill near the Chevillys' stood the austere château de Maugny, which belonged to Clément de Maugny's family. The ancient, fortresslike castle, built in the fifteenth century, reminded Proust of the one described by Théophile Gautier in a favorite novel of his childhood, *Le Capitaine Fracasse*. The Maugnys had constructed a more modern château, lighter, in the Renaissance style, at Lausenette. During his stay at Évian, Marcel had occasion to call on Clément in both his castles. Not too many kilometers westward from the Chevillys and Maugnys, Marcel's friends the Bartholonis were staying in their château de Coudrée. Léon Delafosse, whom Montesquiou had hoped to banish from high society, had eagerly accepted an invitation to spend September with his friends. While staying with the Bartholonis, the pianist entertained his hosts by performing works by Beethoven and Chopin that he was preparing for a concert in Geneva.[43]

The first part of Marcel's stay at Évian passed quickly, the time consumed with visits to his friends, especially to those closest by at the Villa Bassaraba. Then on September 9 the dreaded day arrived: it was time for his mother to leave him and return to Paris with Adrien. While biding her farewell on the hotel terrace, Marcel engaged in a series of wrenching embraces that embarrassed his parents and infuriated his father, who could not refrain from making a few critical remarks. After she left his side and climbed into the carriage, onlookers noticed how distraught Marcel appeared. Soon after his parents left, Marcel walked past the casino, where he saw a poster announcing the verdict in the Rennes trail. Dreyfus had been found guilty by a vote of 5 to 2, with "major extenuating" circumstances, and sentenced to ten years in prison. In the letter Marcel wrote his mother the next day, he told her about seeing the "shameful verdict posted at the Casino to the great joy of the entire Casino staff."[44]

That evening Marcel went to the Villa Bassaraba for dinner. He had decided that fumigating with his antiasthma powder before sitting down for dinner would alleviate or perhaps prevent the onset of his asthma. Constantin, with customary hospitality, offered Marcel the use of his pavilion. Just as Marcel was going in to fumigate, he heard sighs and turned to see the "little Noailles girl (the poetess) passing by, sobbing as though her heart would break, and crying out between sobs: 'How could they do such a thing? How did they dare go and tell him? What will the foreigners think and the whole world? How could they?' " Marcel, who had not always been kindly disposed toward Anna, was so moved by her distress over Dreyfus that he began to have a better opinion of her.

The precise nature of Proust's initial reservations about Anna, who was to become a trusted and admired friend, is not clear. He had not known what to make of this strange, beautiful young woman who held such promise as a poet. Perhaps he thought her flighty, too much her mother's daughter with her high-strung, nervous nature. At times her speech could be shocking, as when in a parlor game at the Brancovans' she answered a query about Alphonse Bertillon, the handwriting "expert" in the Dreyfus case, by saying "I don't know. I never slept with him." Constantin found his sister's answer quite amusing and repeated it to Marcel, who had been surprised that a young woman of her class would make such a remark in company.[45] He soon became one of Anna de Noailles's most ardent admirers.

Relationships among the Brancovans at the villa, as with the French everywhere, continued to be strained by the Dreyfus Affair and the retrial.[46] Some members of the Brancovan family considered Anna's husband, Mathieu, guilty of class betrayal for having signed the pro-Dreyfus petition. On hearing the Rennes verdict, the prince de Chimay fled the villa to go hunting, leaving behind his gorgeous young wife, Hélène, and, much to the satisfaction of Constantin and Abel, his new motorcar. Marcel explained to Jeanne that the reason for the prince's departure was the Affair: "though quite moderate he doesn't see eye to eye with the rest of the family and they would make life impossible for him." Marcel, who thought Hélène one of the most beautiful women he had ever seen, told his mother that the prince would not likely "bag any game that comes up to his wife."[47]

Marcel worried about the demoralizing effect the Rennes verdict would have on his mother and whether or not she could control his volatile brother, who sometimes, especially during the worst moments of the affair, threatened to commit rash actions. She should tell Robert not to behave like a hothead, and he urged her not to be "too sad about the verdict. It's sad for the army, for France, and for the judges who have had the cruelty to ask an exhausted Dreyfus to make another effort to be brave. As to the verdict itself, it will be quashed juridically. Morally it already has been."[48]

Proust found it difficult to follow his own advice. A week later, with Dreyfus still incarcerated, Marcel asked his mother to find out through Adrien's colleague and friend Dr. Samuel Pozzi whether it was true, as rumored, that Dreyfus was dying. Events soon proved Marcel's initial optimism well founded. The government offered Dreyfus a pardon, which he accepted—though with some bitterness, for to do so implied guilt. But the once-robust captain was in frail condition and needed to end the long season in hell for himself and his family, who now must find the strength to fight for the restoration of his good name and reinstatement in the army.

After his mother's departure from Évian, Marcel took stock of his clothes and accessories and consulted her about his needs. Since unpacking he had not been able to find any tiepins. Had Eugénie, he wondered, put any in when she packed his things? If not, should he buy some? And white ties? He decided not to bother Eugénie about this; he could probably find some in the unlikely event that he needed any. "I forgot to tell you that I still don't have any sponges. Should I buy some?"[49] But the wardrobe question that worried Mme Proust most was the matter of hats. Marcel had not arrived at the lake with a suitable chapeau for calling on smart people. To his mother's chagrin, he had brought only a warped boater— unsuitable for the cold, windy, rainy days of fall by the lake—and a dirty gray trilby that should have been discarded. Marcel told his mother that Mlle Kiki Bartholoni shared her opinion about his appearance: "She would like me to be better dressed and says she's amazed that I can't manage it with Eppler in the house." M. Eppler, a gentlemen's tailor, had his shop in the courtyard at 9 boulevard Malesherbes, where the Prousts lived.[50] Marcel enjoyed flirting with Kiki and even claimed to be "a little in love with her."[51] As for the boater he continued to wear at Évian, Marcel would be happy to follow his mother's instructions, but he tried to convince her that the drenching rain, in which he had been caught while returning from visiting Clément at the château de Lausenette, had worked a miracle on his hat, straightened the straw and made it as good as new.

In the daily letters to his mother, Marcel reported on the weather (generally unfavorable), his health, sleep, appetite, bodily functions, thoughts, anxieties, encounters, gossip, outings with friends, work (of which he did little), readings, and, as his cash dwindled, his expenses. She had hardly left Évian when he began worrying about how much he should tip the servants (chambermaid, valet, and waiter) and whether he should move to less expensive quarters. Even though far away, Jeanne influenced his every move.

On September 12 he confessed to her, knowing that she would be displeased and alarmed, that he had taken some Trional. He offered a number of excuses for his action: successive and fatiguing conversations with guests at the villa; a walk with Mme de Polignac, who had gotten them lost on the road, causing a longer walk than planned, during which they encountered Princesse Brancovan, a "combination of nervous twitches and Oriental extravagance." At that point Marcel, to his great dismay, was seized by an uncontrollable fit of laughter in front of the princess. Then he had spent another nearly sleepless night and, to top it off, "this morning the noise of the omnibus at half past six was exceptional." He had seen no other solution except to take a little Trional, which produced a restorative sleep. He reassured his mother that this latest incident was an exception and that, quoting her admonition, "we are not backsliding into medicines." He reminded her that he had not taken any Trional for twelve days.[52] A week later, he reassured her again in a postscript, "Still no Trional (that's understood)."[53]

Sometime before his stay at Évian, Marcel had befriended a man several years his senior, a roofer's son by the name of Pierre Poupetière, who had fallen on hard times and appealed to Marcel for financial assistance.[54] Marcel, who in turn depended on his mother's generosity, informed her from Évian that he had not given Poupetière any money for months and wanted to discourage his solicitations. He expressed his sympathy for the roofer and wondered how well they, who enjoyed the advantages of wealth, would have fared had they been in the unfortunate Poupetière's place, without money and a position in society.[55] In spite of his sympathetic philosophizing, Proust intended to end the relationship and instructed his mother to send Poupetière "25 francs *in your name*." Marcel would write him a stinging letter, encouraging him to pull himself together and look after himself.[56] His mother followed the instructions, an act that caused Marcel, he wrote her, "great joy," primarily because he knew the unfortunate man had at least received some money.[57]

Pierre Poupetière may have been the first in the long line of servants and members of the working class whom Proust would attempt to aid with cash gifts or by helping them to find better situations. With some of these future waiters, valets, chauffeurs, and male secretaries, his relationships may have gone beyond philanthropy. But what inspired him to assist them in the first place appears to have been genuine concern for their well-being and his ability—which was to serve him well as a writer—to identify with the misfortunes of others.

Sometime during this vacation Proust met Pierre de Chevilly's twenty-three-year-old sister Marie, whom he found "ravishing."[58] Marie had been eager to meet Marcel, about whom she had heard much. She knew that he had already acquired a certain reputation as a much sought-after social butterfly, a strange, hypochondriacal man with exquisite manners. Marcel and Marie met when Pierre planned an excursion for the three of them to visit the Bartholonis at Coudrée. Pierre hired a rickety old carriage, something of a local institution, to call for Marcel at the Splendide and then circle back to Montjoux, where he and Marie would be waiting. When the carriage arrived in Montjoux, Marcel alighted to meet his friend's sister and to see what features nature might have borrowed from her brother to create Marie. Although it was a hot day, Marcel arrived with a wool scarf wrapped twice around his neck; he apologized for the strange garment, saying that he feared chills that might trigger his asthma or hay fever. For the ride to Coudrée, Pierre insisted on taking the jump seat so that Marcel and Marie could sit in the back of the carriage. Pierre, normally reticent about matters he considered intellectual, listened to his sister and Marcel talk about poems they liked. Marie recited recent verses by Anna de Noailles and lines from Victor Hugo's "Booz endormi," one of Marcel's favorite poems. Then Marcel, struck by the sensations of crossing the countryside in an ancient carriage next to an attractive young lady, quoted lines from Vigny's *La Maison du berger,* in which the poet, accompanied by a beautiful woman named Eva, crosses meadows in a shepherd's wagon.

At the Bartholonis' the lady of the manor welcomed them. Léon Delafosse was present, but not Marcel's favorite, Kiki. As Marie listened in astonishment to the conversation between Marcel and Léon, she realized that if a stranger heard the two men talking he might suppose that Marcel was the musician and Léon the writer, so well informed was each about the other's art. But Delafosse's comments, she noted, were more technical and learned than the spontaneous, impulsive remarks that seemed to spring from Marcel's heart.

The afternoon passed quickly for the little group as they listened to Mme Bartholoni's recollections of life at the court of Napoléon III and Empress Eugénie, where, as a lady-in-waiting to the empress, she had won distinction for her beauty and wit. As their hostess evoked this vanished era, Marie noticed that Marcel appeared more eager to listen to the others than to exhibit his own knowledge. Mme Bartholoni's reminiscences about the imperial court had fired Marcel's imagination. On the return ride to Montjoux he kept the conversation focused on the Second Empire. He had been particularly impressed by the harmony that reigned between Mme Bartholoni, her Empire style furniture, and the memorabilia of the period with which she had surrounded herself.

Marcel found Pierre's sister charming, and Marie felt the stirrings of an "intense friendship."[59] Marcel was much less enchanted with the father. On one visit to the Chevillys', as Marcel reported to Jeanne, he had to listen to M. de Chevilly complain about the invasion of Jews at the Splendide, a circumstance that the old man assumed made his guest miserable. Marcel chose to ignore the remark, especially because he knew that Pierre was sick about the Dreyfus verdict. Realizing that Chevilly senior was an "old fool befuddled by *La Libre Parole,*" Marcel thought that he would be doing his family a favor by avoiding an argument, and so he replied: "I have no idea who is at the hotel, everyone keeps to himself." M. de Chevilly urged Marcel to stay at Thonon next year, where the clientele was "more French, not so cosmopolitan."[60]

Marcel had a literary assignment he needed to complete, one he already regretted having accepted, but for which he had received a five hundred–franc advance. He had agreed to collaborate with Robert de Flers on an epistolary romance to appear in installments in the newspaper *La Presse*. In mid-September, just as his first letter was about to go to press, Marcel received a wire from his editor, Léon Bailby, who was in a panic because he had lost the titles and other information for the series. Marcel, annoyed at the expense of sending a long, complicated wire to Bailby, told his mother that if the newspaper lost his copy again, his five hundred francs would be gone.[61]

On September 19 *La Presse* published Proust's first letter, in which Bernard d'Algouvres must struggle to hide his suspicions when Françoise, the woman he loves, is away with a group that includes a man Bernard knows she finds attractive. Not only did the precious, rarefied names Proust used in *Lettres de Perse et ailleurs* (Letters from Persia and elsewhere) recall those he had used earlier for the frivolous snobs in *Pleasures and Days,* but so did the setting of drawing-room romance. Marcel, uninspired as Bernard, took bits from *Pleasures and Days* and even some of the scenes he had drafted for *Jean Santeuil* and pieced together the first letter. Robert de Flers's reply appeared the following day. A week after publication of the first letter, Marcel was still complaining about the "stupid collaboration." *La Presse* published Proust's (Bernard's) second letter to Françoise on October 12, after which, all parties, apparently, were happy to let the series end.

While at Évian, Marcel tried to write two articles on Montesquiou's recent volumes, but his heart was not in lavishing praise on the insatiable count. There was little he did care to write about now, as another piece written about this time shows. In the draft of an essay on the decline of inspiration, Marcel deplored his current stagnation. He would gladly abandon all the uninspired pages he had written for "one minute of the mysterious power" that came during moments of genuine creativity. The words no longer rushed out of him in waves, "a single idea no longer gave birth to thousands."[62] His inkwell and his pocketbook had both nearly run dry.

Alarmed at what he had spent during the first half of his stay, he began to refuse dinner invitations to the more distant villas. The weather had shifted to a more turbulent pattern, changing from bright, sunny days to sudden downpours and cold winds. He attributed his sore wrists to these meteorological shifts that had perhaps brought on a touch of rheumatism. Dr. Jules Cottet put Marcel's arm in a sling, which prevented him from making movements that would have hurt him during sleep, but it made dressing and undressing awkward. Then, the solicitous doctor, after trying a cold spray, had massaged his wrists with morphinated iodine ointment.[63]

Marcel admitted to his mother that Jules Cottet was paying him a great deal of attention: "I will make no secret to you of the fact that Dr. Cottet seems to have gone quite overboard about me. *Does he spend the winter in Paris?* You realize (and I only add this stupid remark because of my mother's imagination) and I say overboard in a good sense, so don't go imagining that it's an evil connection, great gods!!!!!!" Apparently, his mother had reason to fear men who were overly solicitous of her son, always susceptible to exhibitions of tenderness.

During the days that followed, Marcel bought quantities of thermogene wadding, which he put on fresh every morning and evening, wrapping himself in the material, in a vain attempt to keep warm. Other guests began to depart as the season ended and colder weather set in, but not Marcel. Once he became accustomed to a place and its people, it was as difficult to convince him to leave as it had been to persuade him to come in the first place. He asked his mother how large a tip he should give to the waiter, the "pale Raphael," who served him at lunch and dinner. Because many guests had already left, Raphael now served lunch to no one but Marcel.

Marcel soon made another request. He had received a letter from Reynaldo, informing him that Dr. Pozzi had operated on Anatole France and removed a worrisome cyst. For some reason Proust believed France was not doing well and asked Jeanne to check daily on the writer's condition.

If any of Marcel's friends had happened to pass by the Splendide Hôtel in the early afternoon on Friday, September 22, they would have beheld a rare sight: Marcel sitting outdoors in the bright sunlight, writing his daily letter to his mother.[64] He gave her an account of the literary pilgrimage he had made with Constantin and Abel the day before to the château of Coppet, whose current proprietors were the comte and comtesse d'Haussonville. The comte d'Haussonville was the great-grandson of one of France's most distinguished women of letters, the baronne de Staël-Holstein (1766–1817), better known as Mme de Staël, to whom Coppet owed its literary fame. Essayist, novelist, and one of the great precursors of French romanticism and comparative literature, Mme de Staël had lived in her family's château at Coppet during the Revolution. Later when Napoléon exiled her from Paris because he considered her meddlesome and outspoken, she returned to the family château on Lake Geneva. Her love affair with Benjamin Constant inspired him to write *Adolphe,* one of the most acclaimed of French novels. Proust was naturally curious about the daily life of such a talented writer.

The weather had been perfect for the excursion. Constantin and Abel decided to make the trip in the prince de Chimay's motorcar. To spare Marcel the constant exposure to the cold wind he would have suffered had he accompanied them all the way from Évian in the automobile, they suggested that he take the train as far as Geneva. His two friends met him there at the station for the drive out to Coppet.[65] This is the first known instance of Proust's riding in an automobile, an experience he found fascinating and exhilarating. As the blur of trees against the blue backdrop of the lake flew past his astonished eyes, he thought of his brother's passion for vehicles of speed. He told his mother: "In the motor car everything struck me as amazing, and I'd like to describe every one of the chauffeur's movements to Dick, who would no doubt say: 'Why, of course.'" Proust became—health and schedule permitting—an avid motorist and wrote some of the first texts describing how the car altered notions of time and space, influenced fashion, and even changed the way we view art and architecture. As the prince's car raced toward Coppet, Marcel strained his eyes to take in the impressions that seemed to be speeding away from him in all directions.[66]

On their arrival at Coppet, the three motorists learned that the comtesse d'Haussonville had gone to Geneva for lunch. Marcel took advantage of her absence to search for Mme de Staël's ghostly presence, viewing each room in great detail. Leaving Coppet, Marcel and his friends drove to Prégny, where Mme Adolphe (Julie) de Rothschild was also out. Marcel told Jeanne that, having forgotten his calling cards, he had signed his name on the cards Constantin left for both ladies. From Prégny the motorists returned to Geneva, and Marcel boarded the train for Évian, arriving late. Before turning in, he went to say good-bye to Jules Cottet, due to leave the next morning. The doctor, who lived nearby at Féternes, occasionally returned to visit his fascinating patient.

During the excursion, Constantin and Abel had made remarks that greatly annoyed Marcel. Thoughtful in their attempts to make the trip to Coppet as comfortable for him as possible, they had not hidden their opinion regarding his condition, a diagnosis, he was furious to learn, that his own father had influenced. Fuming about the matter in the letter to his mother, he told her that when his friends attempted to persuade him to ride in the motorcar with them, "Constantin said I just imagined that cold air was bad for me, because Papa told everyone there was nothing wrong with me and my asthma was purely imaginary. I know only too well when I'm awake in the morning here that it's quite real and I wish in your next letter you'd say something like: 'Your father was furious about your riding in a motor car. You know very few things are bad for you, but that nothing is worse for your asthma than cold air.' "[67] Marcel wanted to show her letter to his skeptical friends, who on this point found Dr. Proust more persuasive than Marcel. Even Reynaldo had recently attributed Marcel's condition to "nervous asthma" that made it impossible for him to fall asleep until 8 or 9 A.M.[68]

Had Dr. Proust misdiagnosed his most famous patient: his son? His refusal to see Marcel's condition as a physiological disease may have been the origin of the writer's profound distrust of doctors, source of the satire to which members of the medical profession are subjected in the *Search*. Adrien's error may have encouraged his son's practice of self-diagnosis and treatment.

Toward the end of his stay Marcel, who had already bemoaned his lack of enthusiasm and motivation for working on his novel and essays, grew weary of society. He told his mother that he wished to avoid contact with his friends through letters as well; he asked her not to reveal that the pain in his wrist had vanished so that he would have an excuse to "shirk troublesome letters."[69] At times Marcel felt that the beautiful expanse of lake and valley and mountains from Évian to Geneva constituted not one of nature's great landscapes but an endless series of drawing rooms and social obligations. In a letter written twenty years later to Clément de Maugny's wife, Rita, he spoke of the first summer visits to Évian with genuine nostalgia, but at the time he knew that he was allowing his social duties to postpone the day when he would begin to work in earnest. In the *Search*, he remembered the little train, transferred from the shores of Lake Geneva to those of the Normandy coast. As the Narrator waits on the platform, he has the impression that many of those who meet the little train at its various stops to chat with its passengers have walked from the manor to the nearest platform "simply because they had nothing better to do than to converse for a moment with people of their acquaintance." These platforms had become "a setting for social intercourse like any other," and "these halts of the little train, which itself appeared conscious of the role that had been allotted to it, had contracted a sort of human kindliness: patient, of a docile nature, it waited as long as one wished for the stragglers, and even after it had started, would stop to pick up those who signalled to it."[70]

By the third week in September, Marcel realized that his funds were nearly depleted. He had charmed the personnel, ingratiating himself with exquisite manners, treating them as his equals, if not superiors, and plying them with generous tips. But Marcel admitted to his mother that he felt uncomfortable handing out such tips because the funds were not his: "I feel as though I'm trying to look generous with your money."[71] The habit of tipping extravagantly each person who had served him as he left the Splendide was not only expensive but complicated. Marcel had already resolved that if he returned next year, he would "give a lump sum for all the tips so as not to have to begin again with each departure."[72] The hotel servants were not indifferent to Marcel's largesse. The omnibus driver, to whom Marcel had given ten francs, came to thank him, telling Marcel that since he'd been working in hotels he'd never known anyone so kind to employees, a choice of words that Marcel characterized as "a charming euphemism." Finally, the driver asked permission to shake his hand.[73]

While Marcel lingered at the Splendide, plotting ways to stay until the last possible minute, some of the staff departing for other posts on the Riviera were on the verge of tears when they appeared at his room to say good-bye. Even the hotel manager, M. de Ferrière, had been won over and had taken extreme measures to insulate Marcel from noise, ordering carriages for the departing guests so that the large omnibus, kept in a shed near Marcel's room, would not have to be moved. Given the incredible demands he made on servants, Marcel worried whether he would have enough for the final round of tips, because he continued to spend large sums on thermogene wadding. He asked his mother to send a big packet of thermogene wadding and Espic cigarettes, along with the book on Ruskin by Robert de La Sizeranne entitled *Ruskin et la religion de la Beauté*.[74] Marcel's interest in Ruskin had become intense; he was eager to have La Sizeranne's book because it quoted a number of passages in which Ruskin described the Alps and Italy.

Toward the end of his season on the lake, Marcel began to think of traveling to Italy instead of returning directly to Paris. By the end of September, still undecided about where to go after Évian, he wrote to ask his mother's opinion. Writing in great haste because Cottet had come from Féternes to accompany him on a visit to Pierre, Marcel outlined what he considered the choices for staying on the lake or traveling. Reaching a decision had taken on a new urgency, for he had just learned that the hotel would close any day now. If he found a traveling companion, he could return home by way of the Italian lakes and Venice. He thought of Fréderic (Coco) de Madrazo, who had been interested in going to Italy, and asked his mother to see whether Reynaldo knew where to locate him.[75]

Although Jeanne had just sent him three hundred francs, as usual the "much more than needed" proved to be only half what he really required, though he did have a credit on his hotel bill. Then there was the matter of the two hundred francs he had borrowed earlier from Reynaldo and promised to repay by October 1. He proposed that she send a generous check for him to endorse and forward to Reynaldo.[76] Marcel had found the ideal solution to his financial dilemma: his mother would provide all the money to pay his debts, then he would engage Hahn to reimburse himself with the funds from his mother's check and use the balance to pay off his remaining debtors.

At the end of the letter he alerted his mother to be cautious should Anatole France approach her about Marcel's being a suitable husband for his daughter Suzanne Thibault, now eighteen years old. "Apparently he has thought of me for his daughter and since I would never do it you must be prudent."[77] The idea of marriage horrified him. If nothing else, he could not imagine adding the complications of having a spouse to a daily routine that already overwhelmed him.

On Sunday, October 1, Marcel took a boat tour around Lake Geneva. The weather was magnificent, and Marcel came back to the hotel thrilled by the "beautiful excursion."[78] Jules Cottet had come to dine with him at the Splendide, where they chatted until after midnight. By this time, despite generous outpourings of cash and Proustian charm, he had exasperated the skeletal crew of servants, already overdue at their next jobs in Nice, who had remained at the Splendide solely to wait on him. By midweek, with time and money running low, Marcel informed his mother that he had taken the drastic measures of buying thermogene wadding himself and of posting his letters and wires.[79] He thought he had enough money to tip the valet de chambre, Otto, and the Brancovans' coachman. He had not abandoned hope of seeing a mountain, such as Zermatt or Chamonix: "It's pointless to advise me to avoid risks since I don't feel like climbing!" And naturally, were he to go to Italy, he certainly did not expect to stay in a palace like the Splendide, nor would he have the endless comings and goings in carriages across the countryside. She must know how eager he was to return home and see her, but if he postponed their reunion it was only because he knew his returns were always "definitive." It is doubtful whether such assurances convinced Jeanne that Marcel could do anything thriftily.

Having spent hours planning a trip to Italy, dreaming of the mountains and Lake Como and Venice, Italian art and architecture, all to be seen through Ruskin's lenses, Marcel finally decided to postpone the trip until the following spring and warmer weather. Realizing that he had stretched his stay and the patience of the depleted staff to the limit, he left the Splendide Hôtel in haste on October 8. During his stay he had made no progress on the novel that occupied his thoughts less and less. On the way home to Paris he caught a cold that lingered over the coming weeks.

Jean Santeuil

Only a few days after his return from Évian, Proust went to the Bibliothèque nationale and starting reading works by John Ruskin. It is likely that Proust first became aware of Ruskin sometime in 1897 when he read Robert de La Sizerranne's *Ruskin et la religion de la Beauté.*[80] A *Jean Santeuil* draft alludes to a quotation by Ruskin from the book: "Ruskin tells us to describe everything, that we must not brush aside a certain object, because everything is poetical."[81]

The first translations of Ruskin in French had appeared in Paul Desjardins's *Bulletin de l'Union pour l'action morale,* to which Proust subscribed. Between 1893 and 1903 this review published short excerpts from Ruskin's books on Venice (*Saint Mark's Rest* and *The Stones of Venice*), and from *Sesame and Lilies, The Seven Lamps of Architecture,* and *Unto This Last.*[82] Earlier in 1899 Proust had begun exchanging books by Ruskin with an acquaintance, François d'Oncieu, whom he contacted again on his return from Évian.[83] Oncieu began to call daily and often accompanied Proust on his research trips to the Bibliothèque nationale. The Ruskin work that initially fascinated Proust most was *The Seven Lamps of Architecture,* a chapter of which he first read in an 1895 edition of *La Revue générale.* Within a few months Proust claimed to know the book by heart. In 1899 George Elwall published the first French translations of complete works by Ruskin: *The Seven Lamps of Architecture* and *The Crown of Wild Olive.*[84]

Following a practice that became standard for Proust, he soon engaged a number of friends in his quest for information and books, in English or French, about Ruskin. His mother remained his closest collaborator and factotum. Due to his strange hours, it was not always easy for the two translators to work together, even though they lived under the same roof. One October midnight, Marcel stood outside his parents' room for fifteen minutes, wanting to give his mother instructions but afraid to enter because he heard his father blowing his nose, but not rustling the newspaper, a sign that Adrien was awake but might still be trying to fall asleep. Marcel left a note to his "dear little Mama," asking if she would "be an angel tomorrow morning and translate for him on large sheets, preferably without writing on the back or leaving any blanks and squeezing it all in," the passage he had shown her from Ruskin's *Seven Lamps of Architecture.* He also requested that she translate another passage he had partly circled in blue pencil and that she keep the original with her copy. He reported the good news that he felt better, was fumigating less, and intended to go straight to bed without medication. He confessed to having uncorked the bottle of Vichy water. In a postscript he proposed an alternate chore if she did not have time to copy both passages. Would she send a sealed telegraph-card to François d'Oncieu, requesting that he come because Marcel had a little task for him to perform?[85] Satisfied that he had instructed his troops for the next day's engagements, Marcel went to bed.

At some point during this period when his interest in Ruskin began to absorb him, Proust realized that he had to decide whether to continue working on *Jean Santeuil* or put it aside. He had been audacious, after the publication of *Pleasures and Days*, to abandon the short story form, in which he had shown promise, to attempt a long novel. In the draft of a preface for *Jean Santeuil*, Marcel wondered about the nature of the book he struggled to create: "Should I call this book a novel? It is something less, perhaps, and yet much more, the very essence of my life."[86] He saw, though not clearly, what he wanted to achieve, but did not yet know how to transpose the "very essence" of his life into a work of fiction. He had experimented with various genres and with first- and third-person narratives, but he had not been able to bring his story into sharp focus, nor had he found the narrative voice in which to tell it.

In such earlier stories as "Avant la nuit," "La Confession d'une jeune fille," "La Fin de la jalousie," and *L'Indifférent,* Proust had confronted the problems of jealous passion and homosexual love, but in *Jean Santeuil,* these major themes, while present, occupy few of the surviving pages. Jean, as the jealous suitor who interrogates and spies on Mme S., forcing her to confess to a lesbian encounter, anticipates Swann's mental torture of Odette and the Narrator's similar treatment of Albertine. Proust also sketched the portrait of M. de Lamperolles, who abhors any sign of effeminacy in men. He is, like the future characters Charlus and his nephew Saint-Loup, obsessed by virility because he desires members of his own sex. Lamperolles ultimately commits suicide when a Polish violinist who had blackmailed him for the remaining two hundred thousand francs of his fortune elopes with a rich young woman. Lamperolles's physical appearance and circumstances were closely modeled on those of Baron Doäzan.[87] This first sketch of a male homosexual bears no traces of Montesquiou, as will the *Search*'s baron de Charlus. One of the most important undeveloped Proustian themes in *Jean Santeuil* is time. There are, however, hints of the importance that time will assume in the evolution of Proust's thoughts and writings. Time, for Marcel, had not been lost.

In his preface notes, Proust wrote that *Jean Santeuil* consisted of parts that he had reaped from experience, without adding anything extraneous, a book that "had not been made but harvested" from life.[88] He had identified a key problem: *Jean Santeuil* was the raw material for a book, but not the book itself; a book had to be made, not gathered up like so many scraps. The absent elements were the vital organs of fiction: plot, point of view, and structure.

"Am I a novelist?" The answer, he had decided, was no. But was he a writer? Yes. He refused to be one of those bogus writers who claim to be men of letters because they had found nothing else to do. Although Marcel had failed to prove to his father that he was a budding literary genius, he knew that he had to write. Nothing ever made him recant the notice that he had given his father after one of their many discussions about career choices: "I still believe that anything I do outside of literature and philosophy will be just so much time wasted."[89]

Although deeply discouraged when he abandoned *Jean Santeuil,* Proust had learned more than he realized. He stood closer to his goal than he knew, but was unable to see, in the ruins of his discarded manuscript, the makings of the world the Narrator would inhabit.

By the time of *Jean Santeuil* and some of Marcel's essays, the Proustian palette is largely composed—he has the color, the nuances, the signature brushstrokes, and a myriad of details from which to draw. Even his drafts show the hallmarks of the mature style and manner. He excels in observations about how people behave, in producing multiple motivations for characters' actions; he summarizes in maxim-like statements his laws, produces a wealth of examples to prove his points, examples drawn from his extensive readings and erudition, from conversations at home or in other learned environments or culled from the superficialities of salon chatter. Often his examples are from botany, biology, or zoology, as he studies intently the flora and fauna of his era. Included here is the servant class, absent from *Pleasures and Days.* Marcel seemed to know everything and to have it all at his fingertips. He had even amazed Alphonse Daudet with his extraordinary powers, causing the older writer to remark, "Marcel Proust is the devil."[90]

How could one know as much at such a young age without having made a Faustian pact with old Mephistopheles? The one thing Proust did not know—and its absence tormented him, then and for years to come—was the story. What plot could he find sturdy enough to support the characters, scenes, images, moods, sensations that he wanted to describe? Could all he wanted to say be put into a book? How to find the harmony, the unification, the masterstroke to make all the disparate pieces work together and delight the reader?

Even in its fragmented, unpolished state, the manuscript of *Jean Santeuil* is, next to the *Search,* Proust's most important text, because it represents his first determined effort to write a novel, and, when read in light of the *Search,* it contains many elements—themes, characters, situations—that he was to refashion in the mature work. This is not to say, of course, that when he began writing his great novel, it was simply a matter of returning to *Jean Santeuil* and picking up the pieces. But much of the raw material for the new work can be found in its drafts. Once a vision, anecdote, character trait, dream had caught Proust's attention, he seldom let go of it. He would note next to choice bits in the manuscript: "Place this somewhere." Like a master mosaicist, he abhorred tossing aside a beautiful, translucent piece of glass.

Jean Santeuil's chief interest lies in the autobiographical details Proust selected to transpose, and in the drafts containing characters, themes, and episodes that point toward the mature work.[91] In attempting to tell the story of Jean, Proust had begun to analyze the process of creativity and the discovery of self in those moments of illumination and joy that he called the search for the "true life"—not the daily humdrum of surface impressions and sensations, but life at its most plentiful, when the profound, inner self consciously connects with the mystery and wonder of being alive. The transcription of such experiences, he believed, was more important than the transcriber, and when he had written them all down, he would have no serious objection to dying.[92]

When writing the *Search,* Proust remembered his own dilemma as an apprentice novelist stuck in the tangled web of *Jean Santeuil* and depicted a discouraged Narrator vainly seeking a topic: "Since I wished some day to become a writer, it was high time to decide what sort of books I was going to write. But as soon as I asked myself the question, and tried to discover some subject to which I could impart a philosophical significance of infinite value, my mind would stop like a clock, my consciousness would be faced with a blank, I would feel either that I was wholly devoid of talent or that perhaps some malady of the brain was hindering its development."[93]

Proust must have been amused when he discovered a decade later that his own failure at novel writing could be used as the story line: the search for a vocation or how to become a (great) writer.[94] But for the present, he had to find a substitute for *Jean Santeuil,* something into which he could channel his ambitions and creative impulses, and something his parents would view as a worthy undertaking. He made what friends must have considered an odd choice—for he knew little or no

English—a study and translation of the works of John Ruskin, a project he apparently chose with his mother's encouragement.[95]

Through reading Ruskin, Marcel had become passionately interested in an art form from another era: cathedrals in the French style, but seen through the culture and language of a man who was not French. Since his youth Proust had felt a profound affinity with writers in English, whether British or American. "It's odd," he wrote, that "from George Eliot to Hardy, from Stevenson to Emerson, there's no other literature that has a power over me comparable to English and American. Germany, Italy, quite often France, leave me indifferent. But two pages of *The Mill on the Floss* are enough to make me cry."[96]

From the time he began *Jean Santeuil* until he wrote the *Search*, Proust's intentions and method of composition never changed. He knew, as he had stated in the pages of the Santeuil story, that he must still attempt to write the book of his life, the essence and quintessence of the experience gleaned while searching for the truth.[97] But he did not know how to shape all he knew and felt into a novel. Could he find in Ruskin and architecture a consolation for the failure of *Jean Santeuil* or the secret of how to succeed as a writer? Did Ruskin's writings on certain cathedrals hold the key to construction, to architecture in the novel, while providing a treatise on aesthetics, perhaps the vast philosophical subject that so far had eluded him? Surveying the extensive ruins of his novel, it was as if Proust saw lying before him many key elements of a Gothic cathedral, but lacking the notion of such an edifice, he could not join the various pieces and make them rise from the ground as a marvelous structure.

By December 1899 Proust had determined to pursue his interest in Ruskin and Gothic architecture. Thinking of Marie Nordlinger and her great compatriot, he wrote to her about his miserable health and his lack of progress as a writer, then announced his new project: "I have not been very happy since I had the honour of seeing you. My health, which was none too good before, has got still worse. And unfortunately my imagination . . . seems to have been affected by my weariness. I have been working for years on a very long-term project, but without getting anywhere. And there are times when I wonder if I do not resemble Dorothea Brooke's husband in *Middlemarch* and if I am not a collector of ruins. For the past fortnight I have been working on a little piece quite different from what I usually write, about Ruskin and certain cathedrals."[98]

Out of this "little piece" on Ruskin and cathedrals grew the essays that make up the preface to Proust's translation of *The Bible of Amiens.*

PART IV

A Voluntary Servitude (1900–1906)

10 *Ruskin and Certain Cathedrals* ∾

THE THIRD REPUBLIC, whose beginning had been so bloody and precarious, had enjoyed nearly three decades of unprecedented prosperity and technological progress. The Paris Chemin de fer métropolitain, known as the Métro, still considered one of the best mass transit systems in the world, began operations in 1900. Two grand exhibition halls, the Petit and Grand Palais, opened to the public. The 1900 Paris World's Fair, with its extravagant exhibitions lining the Left Bank of the Seine, drew huge crowds eager to see demonstrations of the latest technological wonders as well as exotic entertainments. The fair represented the triumph and swan song of Art Nouveau. The timeless and divine Sarah Bernhardt, at a very young sixty-six, triumphed as a boy Napoléon in *L'Aiglon.* Lalique's showcase, adorned with black velvet bats and a bronze grill of butterfly women, caused a sensation.

Paris streets bustled with an astonishing variety of pedestrians, ambulatory vendors, drivers and their horses, and a number of the new automobiles. A stroller like Marcel Proust or the young photographer Jacques-Henri Lartigue could see the past and the future on parade, as horse-drawn carriages made way for the new vehicles. Automobile production in France was increasing at an astounding rate, from two hundred in 1894 to fourteen thousand by 1905.[1] In 1900, anticipating the hordes of new tourists who would be exploring all of France, gliding along the roads on Michelin tires, the company created the green Michelin Guides that remain, a century later, standard companions for travelers.

Proust left no thoughts on the dawning of the new century, but there are many examples of his fascination with the new technology of mass transportation and communication, fields that supplied him with many analogies about how our perception of time and space is changed by the increased speed in daily life. Passages in *Jean Santeuil*, written during the fin-de-siècle years, note the first electric streetlights, still quite rare, and the earliest automobiles.[2] A character in *Jean Santeuil* faces the new dilemma of whether to acquire a horse or an automobile as the better means of transportation. In his parody of *Bouvard et Pécuchet*, Proust characterized his era as that of steam, universal suffrage, and the bicycle, and later as a "locomotive" and "an epoch of speed."[3] As the century turned, what held Proust's attention were the equally extraordinary but ancient technological wonders of medieval engineering that built the great French cathedrals.

Ruskin Pilgrimages

In early January, Anatole France had recovered from surgery to remove a cyst, but he was at pains to convince Marcel that he was better. Such insistence was necessary because his young friend kept showering him with attention and expensive gifts. Marcel had called on France and brought him a quantity of "excellent syrups," and the next day, feeling that the Master needed something for his soul as well, he sent France a beautiful and very costly Rubens drawing. France protested: "Marcel, Really, I can't countenance such folly." He assured Marcel that the accompanying letter was "so good!" that it alone would have cured him.[4]

Proust himself needed healing but found no relief. His respiratory problems grew more severe. In the second half of January, he experienced an especially bad asthma attack, during which he wrote a note to his mother and asked her not to enter his room before 9:30 or 10:00 because he was in a terrible state. Then he quickly wrote diagonally across the page: "You can come in and stand *in front of* me for an instant. It seems to me that makes me choke less."[5]

On January 20 John Ruskin died of influenza at Brantwood, his home on Coniston Lake, at the age of eighty-one. Proust read the news in the next day's edition of *Le Figaro* and wrote immediately to Marie Nordlinger to express his sadness, "a wholesome sadness, . . . replete with consolations, for I am shown how paltry a thing death is when I see how vigorously this dead man still lives, how I admire him."[6] He made an even greater effort to understand Ruskin. A month earlier Proust had wanted to ask Marie's advice about the essays he was writing on Ruskin, but fear of boring her had made him ask another English friend instead.[7] He apologized for not thanking her sooner for sending him her own copy of the 1869 edition of *The Queen of the Air,* with her "charming" notes in the margins.[8] On the day the book arrived he had just finished writing a sentence for an essay stating that the most generous gift a person can bestow is one the giver has long used himself. "To sensitive souls," he had written "these are the most precious of presents." And only a moment later he had received "this book bearing the marks of your personal use, so delicate a gift—and what is it but a book by Ruskin! O preestablished harmonies!"[9] Reynaldo added his harmonies to Proust's effort by undertaking a commemorative composition, *Les Muses pleurant la mort de Ruskin* (The muses mourning the death of Ruskin).

Proust lost no time. That January he began to visit towns whose medieval architecture Ruskin had described. One of his first trips was to Rouen, where he talked with the verger Julien Édouard, who had known Ruskin during the six months the Englishman had spent there studying the cathedral. A natural and charming interviewer, Marcel chatted away with Édouard, taking in all the information the verger's memories could provide. He learned that the verger showed tourists only the church of Saint-Ouen and not the cathedral. When Proust asked what Ruskin had said about Saint-Ouen, Édouard answered that Ruskin deemed it the most beautiful Gothic monument in the world. The reply amused Marcel, who knew that in *The Seven Lamps of Architecture* Ruskin had called the church "frightful!"[10]

Proust's obituary article "John Ruskin" was published on January 27 in *La Chronique des arts et de la curiosité.* Writing at the turn of the century, Proust thought it appropriate to begin with a census. There had been a recent rumor that Tolstoy, at seventy-two, was near death. Now with Ruskin gone, Nietzsche insane, and Tolstoy and Ibsen apparently at the ends of their careers, "Europe is losing one after the other of her great directors of conscience." After sketching the facts of Ruskin's life, Proust mentioned some of his works and marveled at the Englishman's productivity: 160 different titles that constituted "veritable breviaries of wisdom and aesthetics." One of those works had particularly held Proust's attention. In his last books Ruskin had returned to his early years, which had harbored "an indelible charm" now forever fixed in his unfinished autobiography *Praeterita.* Proust's long detour by way of Ruskin eventually led him back to the indelible charms of his own childhood, and to the unfinished sketches of *Jean Santeuil,* large portions of which evoked those same lost years.

For the next five years Proust devoted himself to studying a number of Ruskin's works, most of which had not been translated into French. At times he felt overwhelmed by the enormity of the task, especially for someone who knew almost no English, whose health plagued him, and who seemed incapable of keeping his notes and manuscripts in order. Although his admiration of Ruskin never waned during what he referred to as "a voluntary servitude," he began to question and ultimately challenge the wisdom of some of the Englishman's beliefs.[11] This intense involvement with the works of Ruskin, entailing the study of French history, geography, architecture, and the Bible, was to prove crucial to the development of Proust's own style and aesthetics.

In February, deeply immersed in Ruskin's works, he wrote Marie again, thanking her for the "many exquisite thoughts and the precious articles you sent." If she were to send more fragments of letters or passages from Ruskin, he particularly sought comments on French cathedrals other than Amiens, "apart from *The Seven Lamps of Architecture, The Bible of Amiens, Val d'Arno, The Lectures on Architecture and Painting,* and *Praeterita,* because I know those books by heart." But if she ever came across something in his other works about Chartres, Abbeville, Reims, or Rouen, those would interest him very much. She must not conclude from this that he wanted her to search, he said, because all his essays were finished.[12] Proust had exaggerated in announcing the completion of the essays, but his claim was only slightly premature. In an extraordinary burst of energy and enthusiasm, he wrote and published, between January and August, five essays on Ruskin. From these he would draw most of the text for the preface to his translation of *The Bible of Amiens.*

On February 13 *Le Figaro* published Proust's article "Pèlerinages ruskiniens en France" (Ruskin pilgrimages in France), in which he wrote about the cathedral cities that had been important to Ruskin: Rouen, Abbeville, Beauvais, Chartres, and, especially, Amiens. In the article Proust announced a series of studies and translations that was to begin with *La Bible d'Amiens.* Paul Ollendorff, in response to the new interest in Ruskin and his work, offered to publish Proust's translation of *The Bible of Amiens.* Nearly two years passed before Proust completed and submitted the manuscript to Éditions Ollendorff.

In mid-February, Marcel's much abused leave from the Mazarine Library ran out. He wrote Pol Neveux, chief assistant in the Ministry of Education and Fine Arts, the government department responsible for the library, and acknowledged that his last year of leave (the fifth) had expired and, therefore, he should return to the Mazarine, but his health, of course, prohibited the resumption of his duties. As incredible and pointless as it seems, Marcel asked Neveux if he could renew his leave, postpone his return, request indefinite leave, or "something else?" Should he take steps with "close friends of the Minister?" But this time there was no remedy, and as of March 1 the invisible assistant librarian could no longer claim to hold an official position.[13] It seems reasonable to assume that his parents were not surprised by this outcome. They must have long since abandoned any illusions about Marcel's ability to perform tasks requiring regular attendance, minimal organizational skills, and professional exchanges with colleagues. They were disappointed but resigned.

In early March, Marcel wrote to Marie again, saying how touched he was by her kindness and all the trouble she had taken to assist him. He forbade her to send him so much as one newspaper article. From now on, he insisted, she must send only references. He also thanked her for her "charming" verses that evoked in his memory the "delicious bouquet of spring flowers" that she had brought him once from an excursion, the sort of outing he would have loved, had his hay fever not prohibited it.

Marie complained in her letter sent with the poems of not being a learned person, which provoked Proust to reply with a deeply held belief about language and art: "Strictly speaking, no knowledge is involved, for there is none outside the mysterious associations effected by our memory and the tact which our invention acquires in its approach to words." The poet must find his own way in the sea of words by using a navigational system that remained mysterious. The charts, when discovered and retrieved, always lay within. "Knowledge, in the sense of something which exists ready-made outside us and which we can learn as in the Sciences—is meaningless in art." He quoted Victor Hugo's verse: "Know that the word is a living being." Marcel assured Marie that her letters and poems proved that she did know this: "And consequently you love words, you don't harm them, you play with them, you entrust your secrets to them, you teach them to paint, you teach them to sing."[14]

In April, Proust published two articles on Ruskin in different periodicals. The *Mercure de France* published "Ruskin à Notre-Dame d'Amiens," which was to become part two of the preface to *La Bible d'Amiens*. Proust wrote that his purpose was "to give the reader the desire and the means to spend a day in Amiens on a sort of Ruskin pilgrimage." He observed that we often "visit the place where a great man was born and the place where he died; but does he not inhabit even more the places he admired above all others, whose beauty is the very thing we love in his books?"[15] Proust explained Ruskin's title for his book on Amiens Cathedral: "The porch of Amiens is not merely a stone book, a stone Bible, in the vague sense in which Victor

Hugo would have understood it: it is 'the Bible' in stone." Referring his readers to Claude Monet's "sublime" series of the façade of Rouen Cathedral, Proust sketched in words the façade of Amiens at different hours and in different lights, "blue in the mist, brilliant in the morning, sunsoaked and sumptuously gilded in the afternoon, rose and already softly nocturnal at sunset."[16]

He had gone to Amiens, Proust told his readers, to find "Ruskin's soul . . . which he imparted to the stones of Amiens as deeply as their sculptors had imparted theirs, for the words of genius can give, as well as does the chisel, an immortal form to things. Literature, too, is a 'lamp of sacrifice,' consuming itself to light the coming generations."[17] In the essay "John Ruskin," which appeared in the *Gazette des Beaux-Arts,* Proust insisted on the universality of Ruskin and his search for truth: "For the man of genius cannot give birth to immortal works except by creating them in the image, not of his mortal being, but of the humanity he bears within himself. . . . The work of Ruskin is universal. He sought the truth, and found beauty even in chronological tables and social laws."[18] Proust found in such statements a confirmation of his own idealistic goals, held since youth and first ratified by Darlu in his philosophy class at Condorcet. These words resound again in Proust's own *Search:* universality, humanity, the search for truth. Ruskin, in many ways, led him back to where he began; during the journey, by seeing where he agreed and disagreed with Ruskin, Proust discovered his own destination.

In the spring, Proust's parents initiated a more practical search: they wanted to find a new apartment. It had been nearly three decades since the Prousts had moved into their apartment on boulevard Malesherbes. During that time traffic, and the accompanying noise and dust, had increased substantially on the wide, major artery the boulevard had become. Because Jeanne, who had been so ill two years earlier, often showed signs of fatigue and Marcel's recent asthma attacks had been so severe, the family needed a quieter neighborhood with purer air.[19] The search for a new residence went on until fall.

In the last week of April, Marcel began a letter to Marie to enclose with his essay. He asked her to read carefully the notes at the bottom of the pages where he referred to her as "the so-distinguished English artist."[20] Had he remembered to thank her for *The Queen of Air?* He would send her a copy he had and keep the one that she had so kindly offered him. Just as Marcel was finishing the letter to Marie, her note arrived, telling him that she was in Florence. Delighted at the thought of a reunion in Italy, he quickly added a postscript to his letter: "If you go to Venice let me know because it is possible . . . that I will come!"[21]

Sojourn in Venice

Reynaldo, who had spent the winter in Rome with his mother, had invited Marie to visit them in Italy. He would take her to Florence with Coco de Madrazo and perhaps—but here, Reynaldo told Marie, "an enormous question mark arises"—he would also travel to Venice, where Marcel intended to go.[22] The giant question mark, of course, was Marcel's health and ability to make the necessary arrangements for such a trip and then actually depart. But the miracle did occur and, as Marie remembered, on a "radiant May morning," she, her aunt Mme Caroline Hindrichsen, and Reynaldo were waiting when Marcel and his mother arrived in Venice.[23] Mrs. Hindrichsen was another passionate art lover whom Proust had met when he was introduced to Marie at the Hahns' in 1896.

Jeanne and Marcel had booked rooms for several weeks at the Hotel Europa, formerly the Palazzo Guistiniani. Like other Venetian palaces, the fifteenth-century Gothic-style edifice had been converted into a hotel with luxurious accommodations, including an elevator and central heating. Marcel could scarcely believe his happiness. As he later told Mme Straus: his dream was now his address. Among the works by Ruskin that Marcel and his mother had brought along were *The Bible of Amiens,* on which they, along with Marie, continued to work, and, as guidebooks, *The Stones of Venice* and *Saint Mark's Rest: The History of Venice, Written for the Help of the Few Travellers Who Still Care for Her Monuments.*[24] In his preface to *La Bible d'Amiens,* Proust explained how Ruskin's works had provided the impetus for the trip to Venice. His response to reading Ruskin had been so intense that "all at once the universe regained an infinite value in my eyes." Believing his "days to be numbered," Marcel had left for Venice "in order to be able before dying to approach, touch, and see incarnated in decaying but still-erect and rosy palaces, Ruskin's ideas on domestic architecture of the Middle Ages."[25]

According to Marie Nordlinger, only a few hours after Marcel's arrival, she and he, sitting in the shadow of Saint Mark's Basilica, began correcting the "proofs of our translation of the *Bible.*"[26] The pages they worked on were apparently those to be published in the August issue of the *Gazette des Beaux-Arts.* Much later she recalled how Marcel and his mother would collaborate. His mother, writing in her fine hand, began by translating Ruskin's original text literally, word by word. In this way she filled several yellow, green, and red school notebooks. Marcel then took his mother's rough translations and began to polish them, making a note of items whose precise meaning he would have to check and others, such as architectural terms or particular sculptures or paintings, that required research for the notes he would include in the French edition. Marie, as a native speaker of English and an artist, became an invaluable collaborator on Marcel's Ruskin translations.

Marcel and his mother frequently visited Saint Mark's, where they read Ruskin's description of the baptistery. On days when his mother preferred to rest, Marcel explored the fabled city with Marie. As they walked, she often read to Marcel from *Saint Mark's Rest,* while he jotted down notes on the splendors of the Venetian palaces and churches. Marcel seemed determined to track every painting and shrine described by Ruskin. As they visited one church or museum after another, Proust enjoyed the Venetian experience of being ferried about in a gondola. In the *Search* the Narrator remarks that any Venetian outing, "even when it was only to pay calls or to leave visiting cards, was threefold and unique in this Venice where the simplest social coming and going assumed at the same time the form and charm of a visit to a museum and a trip on the sea."[27]

In his Ruskin preface, Proust told his readers how he and his friends explored Venice with Ruskin's books as guides and offered some tips of his own: "The best place to read" the chapter in *Saint Mark's Rest* on Saint Jerome and the lion "is in the church of San Giorgio dei Schiavoni. . . . One takes a gondola and, in a quiet canal, a little before reaching the shimmering, sparkling infinity of the lagoon, one comes upon this 'Shrine of Slaves' where one can see (when the sun illuminates them) the paintings Carpaccio devoted to Saint Jerome."[28] On cloudless days when the sun beat down, Marcel, though he adapted well to the hot weather, enjoyed retreating to the "dark and dazzling baptistery," whose "freshness" became a sanctuary from the excessive heat.[29] Days of extreme heat often featured afternoon thunderstorms. Marie remembered once when "during a stormy, dark hour" she and Marcel took shelter inside the baptistery and read passages from *The Stones of Venice.*[30]

The sights of Venice captivated Marcel, but his asthma was relentless. He spent most nights awake, struggling to breathe. Although he did get up early enough to see the city during daylight, he never saw the sunrise. A photograph taken on a sunny day shows Marcel, wearing a coat and hat, seated on a terrace. With his chin resting on his hand, he contemplates the Venetian vistas of town, sea, and sky.

While in Venice, Proust encountered one of his favorite Parisian society women, Hélène de Caraman-Chimay, with whom he examined the Acrean pillars in front of Saint Mark's. Afterward he invited the young princess, whose beauty he never ceased to admire, to the hotel, where he introduced her to his mother.[31]

In the *Search*, the Narrator, while working on Ruskin translations, visits Venice with his mother, one of many points at which Proust's life and that of his future protagonist intersect: "After lunch when I was not going to roam about Venice by myself, I went up to my room to get ready to go out with my mother and to collect the exercise books in which I would take notes for some work I was doing on Ruskin."[32] His depiction of the mother was woven in part from recollections of Jeanne in Venice. Especially vivid were the memories of her sitting and reading a book at the hotel window while waiting for him. The Narrator arrives in a gondola and sees her in the window: "As soon as I called to her from the gondola, she sent out to me, from the bottom of her heart, a love which stopped only where there was no longer any corporeal matter to sustain it, on the surface of her impassioned gaze which she brought as close to me as possible . . . in a smile which seemed to be kissing me."[33]

Even more poignant perhaps is the Narrator's recollection of his mother sitting in Saint Mark's while he read Ruskin's descriptions of the interior. Whenever Proust thought of Saint Mark's, he saw this vision of his mother (still in mourning for his grandmother), "with her red cheeks and sad eyes and in her black veils, whom nothing can ever remove from that softly lit sanctuary of St. Mark's where I am always sure to find her because she has her place reserved there as immutably as a mosaic."[34] Jeanne Proust is as "immutably present" as the Narrator's mother in the pages of the *Search* as she was in her son's memory. The primary difference in her fictional incarnation is the removal of her Jewish heritage. The mother in the novel, like her son, has no given or family name, but she, as in traditional French families, is Catholic.

From Venice, Marcel, his mother, and Reynaldo made a final pilgrimage to Padua, an excursion that Proust evoked in the "Sojourn in Venice" section of the *Search*.[35] Still following in Ruskin's footsteps, they made the trip to see Giotto's famous frescoes of the Vices and Virtues in the Arena Chapel. Proust described these frescoes in *Swann's Way*, where they are given an important narrative role. Before leaving Padua, the visitors rushed to the Eremitani church to view Andrea Mantegna's famous frescoes. Proust's favorite, later evoked in *Swann's Way*, was the one depicting the life of Saint James.[36] Marcel told Montesquiou that this was "one of the paintings he liked best in the whole world."[37]

Upon her return to Paris, Mme Proust's rheumatism became so severe that she took to bed. When Lucien invited Marcel to have dinner at the World's Fair, he declined. With his mother temporarily bedridden, he did not want to abandon his father, who had been alone while they were in Venice. He was concerned about his father's health because Adrien had not been feeling well and expected to have his gall bladder removed. As it turned out, the surgery proved unnecessary.

Later in June, Marcel received an invitation from Montesquiou to have dinner and then view some of the fair's attractions. Montesquiou particularly wanted to see the exhibition "Paris in 1400," which replicated a medieval Paris neighborhood, with boutiques, a wax museum, and other curiosities of the time. Proust replied immediately, accepting the invitation to dinner at Weber's but not to the fair, saying that he did not feel well and needed to return home by ten so that his mother would not be alone on the fourth anniversary of her father's death. Marcel's concern about his family was genuine, but his intense work on Ruskin may have influenced his decision to curtail his social activity.

On August 8 Dr. and Mme Proust returned to Évian, where she hoped to improve her rheumatism, he to find relief from kidney stones. They were accompanied by their good friends Dr. and Mme Simon Duplay. A week after their arrival, Jeanne wrote Marcel that his father felt extremely fit. On evenings when they did not go to the theater, they played dominoes with the Duplays, who were amused by Adrien's delight when he won. Jeanne's letters gave Marcel details of her daily baths and the quantities of spring water she consumed. She did not recommend that Marcel join them, as he wished, because there was such a noisy crowd at the hotel that she feared he would be unable to sleep for two hours straight. In another letter she again discouraged his plans to come, emphasizing that the hotel society was not brilliant, just numerous and loud. Furthermore, she had decided to cut short her stay to return home and oversee the move into their new apartment.

Marcel, eager to travel during the season when his allergies bothered him least, considered going to Évian even if his parents were no longer there. Marcel and his parents dreaded moving to their new apartment while he was staying at home. Not only would it be impossible to maintain his bizarre hours and rituals during the move, but they feared the effect of all the dust on his asthma. In late August he wrote Constantin, saying that he would soon come to Évian if he rid himself of a mild sore throat. But Italy still lured him. Now that the flowers were no longer in bloom, perhaps he could fulfill his old dream of visiting Florence and return home via Venice. In mid-October, Proust, unable to find a traveling companion, departed alone for Italy. The only proof of his presence in Venice is the guest book he signed on October 19 at the monastery of the Mekhitarist Fathers on San Lazzaro Island. Nothing more is known about this trip. Is it possible that Marcel, like his future Narrator, wandered through the working-class quarters of Venice, casting covetous glances at attractive young women or men?[38]

Proust had left Venice with many impressions etched in his memory, though he had no idea to what purpose. He returned to Paris and a new residence at 45, rue de Courcelles, not far from his old neighborhood but in a much quieter street. The apartment was even closer to the lovely, elegant Parc Monceau, where, Jeanne remembered, Marcel and Robert had played as children. Old friends, such as Madeleine Lemaire, lived just down the street, as did Marcel's new friend Prince Antoine Bibesco. The third-floor apartment, bigger and more comfortable than the one the Prousts had left, seemed ideally suited to them. Jeanne's good friend Mme Catusse had advised her on the furnishings and decor.

The death of an Englishman had largely determined the course of Proust's writing for the next several years. But Proust apparently took little notice that autumn when another writer died, closer to home, on the other side of the Seine. On November 30 an Irishman, once the toast of London and Paris, died in a cheap room at the Hôtel d'Alsace. Oscar Wilde, ex-convict, expatriate, poet, playwright, and one of the era's great wits, had made an inglorious exit. *Le Figaro* ran an obituary on December 1; two days later Wilde was buried in the cemetery of Bagneux.[39] Proust must have reflected at the time that Wilde's prosecution and downfall had been precipitated solely by his sexual behavior. He was to remember Wilde's example when he was finally ready to write extensively about sexuality and society's attitudes toward it. But for the present, Gothic architecture, not sexual orientation, was the subject that preoccupied him.

"I have very little joy"

Proust often worked all night on the translation of *The Bible of Amiens.* Until nearly dawn he sat at the dining room table, bent over Ruskin's pages in the same pose he had assumed when writing his stories and *Jean Santeuil.* Now he labored under the glare of a bare lightbulb, a habit that was to damage his eyes. Early in the morning before retiring, he left his mother instructions for the day's work. His working all night and sleeping most of the day can hardly have pleased Jeanne, who may have agreed to assist him with the Ruskin translation as part of her strategy to help him establish a regular schedule with normal meals and working hours. That year and the next she made a determined effort to change his habits and his impossible schedule, which varied daily without ever matching the hours of the others in the household. His parents were certain that his bizarre hours aggravated whatever health problems he had and would create new ones. Now that he slept until late afternoon, no one knew when to serve him or what meal he was to have. If he woke at five and had lunch, that meant that he had not taken breakfast and would not be hungry for dinner when everyone else was at table. Marcel had reduced his meals to one a day, resulting in a weight loss that alarmed his parents. But if he seldom went out in the sun and took almost no exercise, how could he expect to have a normal appetite?

On January 24 Marcel attended a musicale soiree at Mme Lemaire's in honor of the cellist André Hekking and the violinist Lucien Capet. At home after the party Marcel, suffering from respiratory problems, selected the pages for Jeanne to translate and laid out her book and dictionary. He requested in his nightly note that she not disturb the litter of papers, books, and writing instruments he had left strewn across the living room and into Robert's room. Marcel confessed that he had done little good work that night. He wondered what mixture of the air inhaled that evening had caused his breathing difficulties, making him fall farther behind on the translation. This exasperated him.

Marcel did not, however, let his commitment to translate Ruskin interfere with his social calendar and his promotion of works by literary aristocrats. He began the year with a modest review—his only publication for 1901—of Montesquiou's *Pays des aromates,* a sumptuous booklet for the 1900 World's Fair exhibition on the history of the perfume industry. Mme Klotz, who owned the Pinaud perfumery, had commissioned Montesquiou to write the little book as a companion piece to the exhibition, featuring Victor Klotz's extraordinary collection of perfume bottles, and other paraphernalia related to the history of the perfume industry. Marcel ended his short notice by evoking a favorite Baudelairian theme, "le Parfum impérissable du Passé" (the imperishable Perfume of the Past).[40]

In May, Marcel attended Montesquiou's parties at Neuilly that centered around the reopening of the Pavillon des Muses, where the count received his friends on Thursdays between four and seven during the last months of spring. Early in the month Marcel planned a party at which Mlle Laparcerie would recite two new poems by Anna de Noailles. After returning from Neuilly early one morning, Marcel wrote the young poet, having looked at the poems she had sent for the actress to read. Two years before, on reading lines of hers for the first time—"But what matters it to the summer, drunk with flowering, / If the dust of the roses irks the winter"—he had felt the awakening of "a new literary passion."[41] From now on Marcel would devote to Anna and her poems the same enthusiastic admiration he had heaped on Montesquiou. In spite of such attention, she did not feel well enough to attend the evening at the Prousts' in honor of her first volume of poetry, *Le Cœur innombrable* (Unbounded heart), but Mathieu came to represent his ailing wife. After the birth of her son, Anna had suffered from nervous depression and had, on the advice of Dr. Brissaud, spent three months that winter in Dr. Sollier's sanatorium near Paris.[42] Some years later Proust sought treatment in the same clinic.

Marcel wrote Anna to say how sad her illness had made him, while depriving him "of the mysterious pleasure . . . of seeing you listen to your poetry." Who better than Marcel to sympathize with missed opportunities because of poor health and shattered nerves? "But one must not rail too much at illness," he wrote. "Often it is under the burden of too great a soul that the body gives way. Nervous states and enchanting poems may very well be inseparable manifestations of one and the same tempestuous power."[43] Talent and ambition could exact a heavy price.

Proust experimented with the telephone, one of the modern conveniences the family had installed in the new apartment. In late May, Marcel, bursting with exciting news, attempted to telephone Anna. Receiving no answer on the second try, he wrote instead that he had heard from Reynaldo, who was traveling in Brussels with Sarah Bernhardt. Hahn had taken *Le Cœur innombrable* on the trip and was so wild about it that he had read the poems to Sarah. She became "enthusiastic" and "thinks you are the greatest of poets, a great genius, etc." Sarah had immediately memorized the "Offering to Pan" and would recite it the next Thursday at the Pavillon des Muses. Marcel, insisting on secrecy, asked Anna not to repeat this news to anyone other than "*the Princesse de Chimay / fairer than the month of May,* if that would give you an opportunity to tell her I love her madly and would move her to indulgence."[44] Marcel, who understood Anna's ego, added, regarding Bernhardt's reading of her poem: "I beg you not to suppose that I tell you of this event in the belief that it should fill you with pride! You understand of course that I shall always regard such things merely as flowers in your path to set your feet upon." Then, with a touch of humor that also served to flatter, he talked about his own health, deplorable as usual, but perhaps he had contracted his current bout of hay fever not from the Bois but from reading her wonderful poems that evoked so many flowers. He promised to "take every medicine that has ever been invented in the hope of being present on Thursday, but I'm useless before nine in the evening and not much better after that."[45]

Not only did Marcel attend Montesquiou's party on May 30, but his mother accompanied him.[46] *Le Gaulois* reported that "Mme Sarah Bernhardt had returned from Brussels expressly to read these beautiful poems with musical adaptations by M. Francis Thomé." Montesquiou's guests also heard pieces written and performed by Reynaldo Hahn, the "exquisite composer." Anna de Noailles, replying to accept an invitation for June 19 to another large dinner party in her honor at the Prousts', expressed her "sorrow and disgust with life and all these unfortunate displays of vanity."[47]

At his large dinner party—there were about sixty guests—Marcel tried a dangerous stratagem: that of seating people next to each other who normally should have been at each other's throats. Léon Daudet was surprised to learn that the "ravishing young lady" next to him was the daughter of a well-known Jewish banker. Daudet's wonder increased as he realized other tables resembled his own, where "rabid enemies" calmly "chewed their cold-jellied chicken within two meters of each other." He attributed this tour de force, which no one else in Paris could have achieved, to the "torrents of understanding and good will that emanated from Marcel, spreading in whirlwinds and spirals through the dining room."[48] The host was delighted that his risky little experiment in social chemistry had succeeded. He modestly explained to Daudet that everything depended on how smoothly and adroitly the introductions, the first contacts, were carried out. Marcel had done this brilliantly, insulating those seated at each table in generous buffers of his charm.

In spite of his passion for Ruskin's writings and Gothic architecture and his abiding fascination for the glamorous world of high society in which he now moved with complete ease, Marcel was unhappy and took a dark view of his present circumstances and prospects. In January he had written to Constantin, in Bucharest, and unburdened himself about his sad state and bleak outlook: "Constantly ill, bereft of pleasures, aim, activity, and ambition, fully aware that my life is behind me, knowing the sorrow I bring on my parents, I have very little joy." Given all these woes, Constantin understood the great importance feelings of friendship had for him.[49] Marcel's need for affection from his friends remained insatiable.

His friends continued to marry and pursue their careers, undertakings that drew them farther away from Marcel. He would no longer be able to engage in innocent flirtations with Kiki Bartholoni, whose wedding to Octave Deschamps was planned for early June. Proust wrote to Léon Yeatman, who had been the matchmaker, and asked, "When will you marry me off?"[50] Léon must have smiled at the challenge. On June 24 Robert de Flers married Geneviève Sardou. Earlier in the year Robert had joined forces with Gaston de Caillavet to produce a "delicious" opéra-bouffe called *The Labors of Hercules*.[51]

Marcel was tormented by the insignificance of his accomplishments. On July 10, his thirtieth birthday, Marcel called on Yeatman in his law office and announced: "Today I'm thirty years old, and I've achieved nothing!" Léon must have protested, but Proust remained discouraged. Nearly all his friends had launched successful careers or begun establishing themselves as writers. He had not only failed at novel writing, but he still lived at home and depended on his parents for everything, even spending money.

In mid-August Proust's parents vacationed at Zermatt. His mother had asked him to surprise her on her return from Switzerland by gaining weight during her absence. Marcel's letters to Zermatt now included, along with the usual information about his health, enthusiastic itemizations of all he had eaten. His efforts sounded genuine; he often ate huge amounts. The trouble was that often he took a single gargantuan meal. Lucien, who occasionally joined him at dinner, had even told Marcel frankly that his "voracity" at mealtime was repellent.[52] On one occasion he reported to his mother that he had consumed two steaks, a huge plate of fried potatoes, Swiss cheese, a serving of cream cheese, two croissants, and a bottle of Pousset beer.[53] In spite of his constant complaints about asthma and other disorders during his parents' vacation, he did make efforts, always short-lived, to rise earlier and take regular meals.

Marcel went to see the princesse de Polignac, who had invited him to call and talk about the late prince. He had died on August 8, and Marcel had attended his funeral, where he had seen many members of the aristocracy, including one of his favorites, the princesse de Caraman-Chimay.[54] In a letter to his mother, Marcel related the visit, during which the American heiress talked about her last days with her husband. The nights she had spent sitting by the dying prince's side, talking about Mark Twain until three in the morning, reminded Marcel of his "poor little Mama, at Auteuil, wearing yourself out" sitting up at night with him. Just writing about this most cherished memory of his childhood had made his "slight oppression" vanish as he described the "affectionate need" he had felt for her. He knew that he would have a good night and might even spend the first part of the coming week in the country somewhere. Perhaps he would join her at Zermatt. In the postscript, he requested money (in case he decided to go away), reported on his bowels ("loose"), and announced his decreased consumption of milk, suspected of aggravating his asthma.

New Friends

Marcel took no vacation that summer. Perhaps he had been unable to decide when to leave and where to go. Perhaps he was reluctant to leave Paris because he had begun to form close attachments with two young aristocrats who were to occupy many of his thoughts over the next few years: Prince Antoine Bibesco and Vicomte

Bertrand de Fénelon. Marcel was to fall in love with each of these attractive young men, both of whom were born in 1878.

The Bibesco brothers, Antoine and Emmanuel, lived with their mother, Princesse Alexandre Bibesco, at 69, rue de Courcelles, not far from the Prousts'. The princess, like her sister-in-law Princesse Bassaraba de Brancovan, was an accomplished pianist who had known Liszt, Wagner, and many other musicians, writers, and artists.[55] At twenty-three, Antoine was a diplomat attached to the Romanian legation in Paris.[56] A handsome man, often charming, but fun loving and mischievous sometimes to the point of cruelty, Antoine became Marcel's confidant. A ladies' man who loved gossip and intrigue, he thought Marcel one of the most perplexing and fascinating creatures he had ever met—and no one knew more gossip and secrets about members of high society and the literary world than Marcel.

Like most of the young men in Proust's circle, Antoine dreamed of literary glory: he wanted to be a playwright. In the first months of their friendship, the two decided to translate Henry David Thoreau's *Walden* into French, but they never set seriously to work on the project.[57] Proust had been delighted to discover other common interests: Antoine and especially his brother Emmanuel were passionate amateurs of Gothic architecture.[58] They had even compiled a collection of photographs of churches and cathedrals that Marcel, on more than one occasion, borrowed and studied. In late summer, trying to live on a new schedule that required him to rise shortly after noon, Marcel wrote Antoine, requesting an afternoon appointment to see his photographs: "Now I get up at about two or three o'clock" and "dine at about four." He wondered whether they would recognize each other, never having seen each other except in the evening.[59]

Marcel rapidly became infatuated with Bertrand de Fénelon, as handsome as he was distinguished, who bore a noble title and an impressive literary pedigree. Slightly aloof, blond, dapper, with a dimpled chin, Fénelon was a descendant of François de Salignac de la Mothe-Fénelon (1651–1715), archbishop of Cambrai and author of many literary works, the most famous of which was *Les Aventures de Télémaque,* a treatise on education. An especially enlightened work, *Télémaque* had influenced Voltaire's philosophical stories and other works by eighteenth-century philosophes. In his treatise Fénelon maintained that the law is above the king, a dangerous statement for a subject of the divine-right monarch Louis XIV. The archbishop's rapid rise and equally dramatic fall are depicted in Saint-Simon's *Mémoires,* adding to Bertrand's prestige in Proust's eyes.

When Bertrand de Fénelon walked, Marcel noticed that he displayed all the febrile energy of a thoroughbred of superior bloodlines, embodying speed and dexterity. His "bright blue eyes and flying coat-tails" reappeared among the elements used to create the marquis de Saint-Loup's special appeal in the *Search*.[60] Like Fénelon, Saint-Loup betrays his class by scorning high society and endorsing leftist policies, including lay education and the separation of church and state.[61] For the next two years Proust suffered terrible frustration and jealousy because of Fénelon. When Marcel first became acquainted with him, he had as a mistress Louisa de Mornand, an attractive young woman who aspired to be an actress, but whose talents were best appreciated off-stage by a succession of wealthy men. Proust became closely acquainted with Louisa when Bertrand passed her on to another aristocratic friend, Louis d'Albufera, whose family had earned its noble title under Napoléon. Some years later Marcel discovered that Bertrand was or had become bisexual.[62] Perhaps Bertrand's affair with Louisa had shielded any suspicions that he might be attracted to men as well. Or perhaps he was one of those men, later described by Proust, whose sexual orientation does not remain fixed during the course of a lifetime.

Marcel embarked on a Ruskin pilgrimage on September 7 with Léon Yeatman to Amiens, where they spent the morning and had lunch. In the afternoon they visited Abbeville, where Proust wanted to see the church of Saint-Wulfran as Ruskin had seen it, with the late afternoon sun shining on the towers. At five o'clock the two friends separated when Léon boarded a train for Boulogne. Marcel remained in Abbeville to work for an hour or so. He then took the train to Amiens, where he dined at the restaurant in the train station. Just before leaving for Amiens, Marcel had received a four hundred–franc check from his parents, part of which he decided to use for tickets to a popular stage adaptation of Jules Verne's *Around the World in Eighty Days* and to see *William Tell* at the opera.

The next day he reported his activities to his mother, knowing that she would be pleased to hear about his daytime excursion and consumption of two meals. But he also needed to lower her expectations regarding his weight increase. He blamed the fatigue of the trip to Amiens for having made the "extra flesh around his waist," which he had so wanted to show her, disappear overnight. On Marcel's skinny frame, a few extra ounces showed but could also melt quickly away. Desperate for a remedy to his health problems, Marcel wondered whether he should not try something drastic. Dr. Brissaud recommended mercury enemas, but he was afraid to try that by himself. He asked his mother to consult Robert. If his brother thought that mercury or other untried, powerful enemas might be helpful, he should stipulate what kind by telegram. As for Marcel's other projects, he wanted to go to Illiers sometime soon.[63] He did not say why, but perhaps as a nostalgic side trip from Chartres, where he would take notes on the cathedral in whose shadow his father had attended seminary school so long ago.

Marcel invited Antoine Bibesco to come along on the train trip to Chartres and suggested that they include Fénelon and his friends. Marcel would leave them all at the cathedral while he went to Illiers and then rejoin them at Chartres for the return trip to Paris. He asked Bibesco to lend him a copy of Émile Mâle's book *L'Art religieux du treizième siècle en France (The Gothic Image)*.[64] Marcel had misplaced the copy Billy had lent him and wanted to look at the pages on Chartres again. Mâle's study of Christian iconography and its symbolism, as displayed in the statues, windows, and other architectural motifs on the cathedrals, was to become one of Proust's most valuable companion pieces during his work on Ruskin. In his annotations to *The Bible of Amiens,* Proust quoted frequently from Mâle.

Marcel's friendship with Bibesco and Fénelon progressed sufficiently for him to offer them signed copies of *Pleasures and Days.* In Bibesco's copy Proust inscribed Horatio's adieu to Hamlet, which seemed appropriate now that he knew a handsome nobleman to whom he could apply the words: "Good night sweet prince." To Fénelon, with whom he was on less familiar terms, Marcel wrote "To Bertrand de Fénelon in hopes that he will equal the great literary name he bears, and in the less certain hopes of becoming his friend."[65] Proust's fixation on Fénelon was slow to develop but was to reach an intensity unmatched since his passion for Reynaldo.

Beginning in November, Marcel wrote almost daily to Antoine, making frequent requests that the prince stop by to see him after the theater. Attempting to establish a close bond with him, Marcel often asked for interviews to talk about the future of their friendship. When Bibesco did not come, Proust chided him for neglect. One code name for Bibesco was Téléphas, or "he who talks from far away," because Antoine loved to call his friends on the telephone.[66] This led Marcel to complain that whereas he wrote Antoine real letters, all he received in return were rapid notes that were no different from phone calls. Increasingly he confided in Antoine, telling him more, but not everything, about his relationship with Reynaldo. Marcel offered enticements for Antoine's visits, such as dinner with Henri Bergson, whom Bibesco particularly wanted to meet. When Bergson pleaded fatigue and declined the invitation, Marcel assured Antoine that there were numerous ways he could arrange for him to meet the philosopher. Marcel's frustrating search for companionship and affection led him to conclude one letter to Antoine: "All this pays too much attention to friendship which is not real."[67] Yet he appeared eager to squander his time and energy on this nonentity.

Marcel, apparently at Antoine's urging, joined him and Bertrand in puerile games of anagrams and codes. In their secret society, Fénelon was often referred to as Nonelef, Bibesco as Ocsebib. Marcel had new names based on his first name, such as Lecram, or his last, which yielded Stroup. With Antoine, Marcel played the dangerous game of talking about homosexuality, displaying extensive knowledge about the subject while denying any such proclivities. Although Proust had largely avoided the theme of homosexuality in *Jean Santeuil*—perhaps because he did not wish to offend his mother—he talked about it freely with Reynaldo and Lucien, and now Antoine, who clearly preferred women but was intrigued and tolerant. These conversations allowed Proust to collect gossip, anecdotes, and observations upon which he later drew when he was ready to depict characters who represent the full range of human sexuality.

Marcel offered to teach Antoine how to speak "moschant" language, a code word for homosexual, a lesson that Marcel said would "surprise and charm Reynaldo."[68] Marcel's offer to instruct Antoine in the private language he and Reynaldo used to talk about homosexuals was not intended as a confession of homosexuality but only as an indication of common fascination with homosexuals. To refer to homosexuality in conversations, Proust and his friends often used the noun Salaïsme or the adjective Salaïste, derived from the name of a young nobleman Antoine Sala, who did not hide his homosexuality. Even Sala, Marcel and Antoine later discovered, was distressed by such public allusions to his sex life.

When Antoine suggested that Marcel's interest in homosexuality went beyond the academic, Marcel took pains to defend himself. Regarding "Salaïsme," he said in a letter to the prince, Antoine should be psychologist enough on seeing him so often to know that homosexuality interested him in the same way "Gothic architecture does although a great deal less and that in reality and in the reality of my life, in me, it is as absent as . . . " Marcel ended his sentence there and then observed that he had stopped because he could not think of anything that was as lacking in his experience as was homosexual love. Then, thinking that perhaps he had protested too much, he added: "Furthermore I don't give a damn what you think in that regard since you yourself said that you attach no importance to it."[69] This was the first of many skirmishes on the topic. In the same letter Marcel reported that Reynaldo and Sarah Bernhardt were due back in Paris for separate productions. Marcel, who had asked Reynaldo to give Antoine's play *La Lutte* (The struggle) to Bernhardt, did not know whether the actress had read it.

By December, for reasons unknown, Marcel and Antoine had quarreled and stopped speaking. Upon learning that Bernhardt had refused *La Lutte*, Marcel broke the silence because he did not want Antoine to hear the news from someone else. In his letter reporting the Divine One's rejection, Marcel offered to contact Réjane and other directors on Antoine's behalf. Then, seeking to salve his friend's wounded literary pride, Marcel offered this opinion of Sarah Bernhardt: "I implore you not to be discouraged for a single moment by the judgement of a woman capable of solving the difficult problem of being taken for twenty at the age of sixty by people who once they've seen her close up can't bear to part with her, and who has a kind of genius when she acts—but whose literary judgement (I wouldn't repeat this to Reynaldo) is utterly nil and contemptible, based on nothing at all or on an absence of all feeling, thought or sense of style. It's pleasant to be received by her and still more to be played by her, but to be appreciated by her might give one food for self-doubt."[70]

Proust was clearly exaggerating to make Antoine feel better. If he had such reservations about Sarah's literary tastes, not known to be infallible, he had taken care not to reveal them to Antoine's cousin Anna de Noailles when Sarah had proclaimed the young poet a genius.[71] Marcel promised to persist, with a nod from Antoine, in seeking a producer for *La Lutte*. In closing, Marcel, who claimed not to believe in friendship, reassured Bibesco that "I am entirely at your disposal in this as in everything else and always will be Your most devoted Marcel Proust."[72]

At about this time, Marcel was the recipient of an act of friendship. Fernand Gregh had recently published a collection of prose poems, *La Fenêtre ouverte* (The open window), in which he dedicated the poem "Les Cloches sur la mer" to Proust. Marcel wrote to thank Fernand for this evocation of "our old bells of Honfleur," which belonged to the summer in their youth when they had been in love with green-eyed Marie Finaly. Proust wondered whether "there is another prose poem as beautiful in the French language, and honestly I don't think so (perhaps I ought to except certain of Baudelaire's prose poems, which certainly vie with yours but do not excel it, I think)." He then said how happy he would be to see his old friend, had his illnesses not required a schedule that changed daily.[73]

The publication of Gregh's book reminded Proust that it was seven years since the appearance of his first and only book. Eager to secure a publishing date for his translation of *The Bible of Amiens*, Proust was ready to take seriously Paul Ollendorff's earlier offer to publish the edition; sometime before year's end, Proust sent him the manuscript of the work completed thus far.

11 *His Blue Eyes* ∾

EARLY IN 1902 MARCEL PROFESSED his friendship to Antoine and agreed to a secret pact with the prince, whereby one would inform the other of what friends said about each behind their backs. Bibesco proved to be a bad choice for such a game, for he loved gossip and found it difficult to keep the secrets that Marcel entrusted to him during their late evening tête-à-têtes at 45, rue de Courcelles.

Antoine was especially kind to Marcel just before leaving for Easter vacation in the country. The young diplomat brought Marcel a bag of chocolates and, a few days later, a more princely gift: a rare edition of the *Imitation de Jésus-Christ,* attributed to the medieval writer Thomas a Kempis, whom Marcel had quoted in his epigraphs for *Pleasures and Days.* Such attention and largesse thrilled Marcel. Writing to thank Bibesco, he indicated, perhaps as a reward, that he had had some fairly "profound thoughts about Salaïsm," which he would share during one of their next "metaphysical conversations," by which he meant gossip. Whether or not a person was "Dreyfusard, anti-Dreyfusard, Salaïst, anti-Salaïst," he said, "are just about the only things worth knowing about an imbecile."[1] Marcel later regretted trusting Antoine with so many of his secrets.

As much as Marcel prized Antoine's companionship, it was Bertrand de Fénelon, whom he referred to as Nonelef or His Blue Eyes, who captured his heart.[2]

Because nearly all of Proust's letters to Fénelon have remained in the hands of private collectors, it is difficult to reconstruct the relationship with any certainty. What is certain is that His Blue Eyes was the object of one of Marcel's great crushes, and although Bertrand seems not to have reciprocated the sentiments, he did not totally discourage the attention. Sometime in the spring of 1902 Bertrand made some gesture that Marcel interpreted as "affectionate." Marcel confided this incident to Antoine, using their code for "top secret" *(tombeau secret—*information one would take to the grave, *tombeau,* without divulging). What was not secret and especially irked Marcel had been Fénelon's imitation of him and his refusal to accept the kind of friendship Marcel sought from those he adored: exclusivity, confessions, all sealed by a pact. Marcel's obsession became even more evident when he asked Antoine to spy on Bertrand. He wanted to know how Fénelon had spent a particular evening and, above all, where he dined.[3] Marcel signed the letter Leckram; perhaps the anagrams served the purpose of giving anonymity to a grown man behaving like a lovesick adolescent because of supposed neglect by another man. As Antoine witnessed the state Marcel was in over Bertrand, it became necessary for Marcel to insist even more emphatically that his great affection for His Blue Eyes was platonic.

In another letter, Marcel urged Antoine to tell Fénelon "that I have a great deal of affection for him and that I should be only too happy if, in exchange for mine which is enormous, he would grant me a little piece of his, which he breaks up and disperses among so many people. I, too, disperse myself, but successively. Each one's share is shorter but larger."[4]

Proust wrote to decline Ocsebib's (Bibesco's) invitation to attend his rustic tea party, the sort of entertainment that Parisians considered elegant that year, in addition to wearing half-boots and sprinkling their conversation with English words. To Antoine, Marcel had made it clear that he envied him and Fénelon for being well and able to see each other, while he could only change sides in his bed.

On June 1, Marcel sent congratulations to Antoine's cousin Anna de Noailles, whose volume *Le Cœur innombrable* won the Prix Archon-Despérouse for poetry awarded by the Académie française. The committee split the prize between her and two unknown poets, prompting Proust to write: "Christ suffered the same fate. Posterity has forgotten the names of the two thieves . . . but the name of Christ is immortal. As yours already is."[5] And that was just the beginning of the compliment. Later that month Marcel had occasion to congratulate Anna on a new volume of poetry, *L'Ombre des jours* (The shadow of days). Although he loved *Le Cœur innombrable* with "all his soul," he nevertheless felt the latest volume was something greater, that she had reached a "higher point" within herself. As for his work on *La Bible d'Amiens,* he wrote that he was making progress and expected to finish all his research in the next few days.

During the summer Bibesco's lack of reserve landed him and Marcel in trouble, when Antoine talked openly about young Sala's overt homosexuality and the young man learned of the indiscretion. After reproving Bibesco for his poor judgment, Marcel tried to help him smooth things over by drafting a letter of apology for Antoine to send to "My dear little Sala." Marcel attempted to explain away the remark as having been a misunderstood joke, promising never to repeat the mistake. In the postscript Marcel admonished Antoine: "We must absolutely stop this horrible business of being the public denouncer of Salaïsm."[6] The only way to stop it was for Marcel not to confide in Antoine, but Marcel was to wait a long time before taking such a step.

Sometime in 1902 Proust sketched three new characters and scenes and added them to the *Jean Santeuil* manuscript.[7] One of these scenes was directly inspired by a dashing gesture of kindness that Fénelon made in August at Larue's restaurant.[8] In spite of the summer heat Marcel felt chilly, and Bertrand rushed off to find something to keep him warm. Returning with a borrowed coat, Fénelon leaped up on the cushioned seat along the walls of the crowded restaurant and ran toward his shivering friend; as he ran he jumped over the electrical wires jutting out of the wall to the lamps on the tables. Marcel, amazed and moved by Bertrand's kind, acrobatic gesture, transcribed the scene first for *Jean Santeuil,* where he depicted Bertrand as the epitome of good breeding, grace, and masculine beauty.[9] This moment may well have marked the high point in Proust's crush on Fénelon. Their friendship was to follow a pattern similar to that seen with Reynaldo and Lucien, though Proust and Fénelon were never as close.

By August, Marcel's mother had apparently convinced him to adopt a better schedule. In a letter to Robert Dreyfus, who wanted to come for a visit, he indicated that the next day would bring a change in his regimen—Marcel was careful to include an escape clause, telling Dreyfus parenthetically, "This is not certain."[10] Even though this latest attempt at reform collapsed immediately, Proust's parents were not yet ready to admit defeat.

Having given Dreyfus some hope for a late afternoon visit, Marcel wrote a long letter to Antoine in which he discussed his relationship with Fénelon (referred to throughout as Nonelef), a relationship Marcel wanted to discourage because he thought that no good could come of being more closely attached to Bertrand.[11] The danger for Marcel had begun, he said, when Fénelon had twice behaved in a charming way toward him, once at Mme Lemaire's and then at Larue's, thus sending the viscount's "stock" soaring. Proust feared the "beginnings of an intense affection for Nonelef, ephemeral, like all my predilections, and yet, alas, susceptible of continuing for quite some time." He must thwart this affection before it overwhelmed him by avoiding the object of his love. Having written about his affection at some length, always careful to place it in the context of friendship, but in language and tones that none of his friends would have applied to another man, Marcel added a disclaimer by calling his letter "a gross exaggeration." All that Marcel required to become indifferent was for Nonelef to be no more charming than his other friends, after which Marcel would "no longer have to struggle with that Siren of the sea-blue eyes." Then, indicating his readiness to practice the new policy of avoiding Bertrand, he informed Bibesco: "I am going to the Noailleses' this evening and not asking leave to bring Nonelef. And I'm going to Larue's alone at half-past eleven without letting Nonelef know. What do you think of that?"

One can easily imagine what Antoine thought of that. Marcel was endearing, and maddeningly brilliant, and so transparent. His strategy of indifference toward Fénelon did not last long. Several days later he dashed off a letter to Antoine asking whether he was lunching with Nonelef at Weber's or elsewhere. If so, Antoine should reply immediately so that Marcel, who had just undressed for bed in the middle of the morning, could put his clothes back on and run out to meet them. He thought that this meeting might chase away the "horrible state" he was in, but if he was to come, Antoine must not look at his face because he looked like death. If Antoine could arrange this meeting quickly, without Fénelon's knowing that Marcel had requested it, he would be very pleased. This was certainly an odd way to behave toward someone he had resolved to avoid.

In August, Marcel's parents departed for Évian-les-Bains, leaving three servants behind to look after him: Arthur, who was sick with a chest cold during much of the time, Félicie, and Marie. Marie was Mme Proust's chambermaid, a beautiful young woman with a soft spot for Marcel, to whom she once gave a pink satin quilt she had made.[12] In letters to his mother and to Antoine, Marcel complained about being alone, sick, and miserable. Bibesco, more stagestruck than ever and in love with the actress Lucienne Bréval, spent much of his time with playwrights and producers or lying in his lover's arms. Before departing, Jeanne had urged Bertrand to see Marcel more often during her absence. Her suggestions were ignored, and her son instructed her not to try again.[13]

Not long after his parents left, Marcel experienced an episode—perhaps a panic attack—that sent his pulse racing out of control. He tried unsuccessfully to see Dr. Bize, but did obtain an appointment with Dr. Vaquez, a heart specialist, whose advice Marcel considered useless. Dr. Vaquez warned Marcel against the dangers of two substances: morphine and alcohol. Proust brushed the warnings aside because morphine did not tempt him and he considered the large quantities of beer he was consuming merely therapeutic.

The reports Marcel sent his mother in Évian detailed his continued efforts to improve his schedule. As usual, the results were mixed. His complaints ranged from the relatively minor frustration of not being able to go out for a ride because there were no closed carriages available during the warm months to his profound unhappiness at being so lonely. During the first part of his mother's absence, both Antoine and Bertrand were too busy to see him. In mid-August, Marcel told Antoine that he intended to take a strong dose of Trional in order to sleep, and he complained that his friend had neglected him. Reynaldo stopped by very late, but nothing consoled Marcel for the absence of Antoine and Bertrand.

By the end of the summer Marcel complained to Antoine about the unequal nature of their relationship, saying that whereas he told Antoine everything, Antoine told him nothing, not even those things that concerned him. When would he ever, Marcel lamented, find someone who would treat him as he treated others and with whom he could have an inviolable and bilateral pact? He accused Antoine of neglecting him for the company of actors and theater people, such as the critic Abel Hermant and the playwright Henry Bernstein. Like all Proust's confidants, Antoine found it impossible to meet Proust's enormous need for affection and confessions.

In August, Marcel wrote his mother a soul-searching letter in which he sounded unusually optimistic.[14] At the top of the page he wrote, in an obvious attempt to please her: "Monday evening, after dinner, 9 o'clock in the dining room, 45, rue de Courcelles." He was making a serious attempt to control his schedule and had gone to bed at about three o'clock in the morning to avoid taking any Trional. He stayed in bed for twelve hours, during which time his pulse dropped from 120 to 76. He dined at Durand's with Constantin without having an attack either during dinner or during the night, a rarity since he had begun going out every night. As usual, there were setbacks, but he was smoking less than before. He believed that his asthma had been arrested. Maybe enemas were unnecessary, since he had been skipping them during this period of improvement. He even seemed less chilly and had left off the second pair of drawers he usually wore at night. Even more remarkable, during the day he had not needed to wear his second thick jersey. There was no end to the marvels he told. The many restaurant dinners had given him a "brand-new stomach"; he was eating more, but much more slowly. Then, as though he needed to justify his expenditures in restaurants, he told her that eating out was his Évian, his travel, his summer resort—all the things he had to go without.

Then he raised a subject that he and his mother had often discussed: the kind of life he should be leading if he were well or even if he remained the same: "You tell me there are people who have as many troubles as I do but have to work and support their families. I know that. Though having the same troubles . . . infinitely bigger troubles, doesn't necessarily imply the same amount of suffering." He claimed that he was right to have delayed choosing a career until his condition improved; it would have been dangerous to risk his health and even his life by making such an attempt. "Literary work," he observed, "makes constant demands on those emotions which are connected with suffering." What he really wanted now was "frivolity, entertainment," but he was resigned to the absence of such delights in Paris in the month of August.

On September 6 Marcel left Paris "after an impulsive decision" to visit Lucien and his family at Pray, their country home in Touraine.[15] Fénelon, who had a different destination, boarded the 6:25 P.M. train with Marcel. The two friends traveled together as far as Amboise, where Lucien met Marcel and drove him out to Pray, a lovely estate on the Loire River.

The Daudets, no doubt trembling at the thought of such a taxing houseguest, had placed in Marcel's "delightful room," as he noted, "so many things for warmth, for comfort." But there had been an unfortunate mix-up about his request for à hot-water bottle. In the flurry of contradictory telegrams that Marcel sent before leaving Paris, the telegraph operator read "bouillote à l'esprit de vin" (hot-water bottle with spirit of wine) as "bouillon with spirit of wine," completely mystifying the Daudets and their cook.[16]

The Daudets need not have worried too much about entertaining Marcel, because after midnight, as he conversed with Lucien through a cloud of smoke from his Espic cigarettes, their guest had already decided to leave early the next morning. Lucien, exasperated but not surprised, inscribed a photograph for his eccentric friend as a souvenir: "Mon cher petit, It is two in the morning and it's stupid that you are leaving tomorrow but I'm very fond of you anyway. Lucien Daudet. Pray. 9-6-1902."[17] Léon compared Marcel's sudden arrival and rapid departure to the passage of a "peaky meteor that nonetheless left a trail of light." Proust, Daudet believed, had become "through excessive intellectual activity, phosphorescent."[18]

Marcel left in a rush the next morning with Lucien in an automobile bound for Mme de Brantes's château du Fresne at Authon, a destination that he had long wanted to visit. After a night with little sleep, the two men enjoyed the fine weather as they drove through Touraine. Lucien teased Marcel for being "so effusive" because his breathing had eased and he found the car ride exhilarating.[19] When Marcel returned on the train that night to Paris, he had been gone for little more than twenty-four hours. He wrote to Mme Daudet to apologize for his hasty departure, thanking her "for the delightful hours spent at your admirable Pray, one of the most beautiful places I have ever seen" and one that he would always remember.[20] In his haste to leave the Daudets' house, he had left behind a number of items, ranging in size from a tiepin to a suitcase, which Mme Daudet mailed to him as they were recovered.

In September, Marcel received new proof that Antoine was a poor choice for a confidant. At times the prince enjoyed tormenting Marcel, who now suffered from terrible jealousy over Fénelon's frequent coolness toward him. Antoine asked Marcel in front of a mutual friend, Georges de Lauris, whether he thought His Blue Eyes had been nicer or not so nice to him on a certain evening. In a letter expressing his outrage at Bibesco's betrayal, Proust reminded him that he had "made it absolutely clear that you were the *only* person to whom I had spoken of this business. . . . But it's not only on my account, I also owe it to my family not to let myself be taken for a Salaïst, gratuitously since I'm not one." By the postscript he had forgotten his anger over Bibesco's indiscretions and continued the dangerous game as though he were addicted to confessing: "Very important and *ultra silence tomb*. Since an entire hidden aspect of His Blue Eyes's life may be discoverable this evening," he asked where Antoine would be at all hours of the day and at dinner "in case I want to talk with you, because without you I would not be able to learn anything." His final instructions, obviously ignored by Antoine, were to keep this letter hidden and to return it to him. A few days later he asked Antoine to be ready in case he needed him for "my secret police operation."[21]

Having suffered jealousy and betrayal at the hands of his friends, Proust received a blow from an unexpected quarter. On September 29 he learned that Ollendorff had decided not to publish *La Bible d'Amiens*. Determined to find a publisher for his work, Marcel took the extraordinary measure of rising and going out during business hours to Alfred Vallette's office at the Mercure de France, but the editor was not in. He wrote Vallette that another publishing house had just brought out Ruskin's *Unto This Last* and announced a series of translations of Ruskin's works. Clearly, Ruskin was of great interest to French readers. He urged Vallette to publish his translation of *The Bible of Amiens* and asked him for a decision within the next week or so.[22]

That day Marcel heard the news about Émile Zola's tragic death. The acclaimed author had died of asphyxiation due to faulty ventilation in his apartment. Almost immediately, conspiracy theories began to surface, alleging that the hero of the Dreyfus Affair had been murdered because he had defended the despised Jew. But Marcel's thoughts were occupied with art and love. He had decided to go to Belgium and take as his traveling companion Bertrand de Fénelon.

Belgium and Holland

Taking advantage of what he called an improvement in his health, Proust and Fénelon left Paris on Friday, October 3, on a train for Bruges to visit an exhibition of early Flemish art. Because the exhibition was to close on Sunday, they intended to return home within a day or two. In case he decided to prolong his trip, Marcel took along an itinerary provided by Léon Yeatman, who had recently toured Holland with his wife. During this journey Proust experienced an unprecedented burst of energy and independence, at times offset by bouts of fatigue and moroseness.

After viewing the exhibition, Marcel and Bertrand traveled through Holland to visit its museums and picturesque cities. They had brought along two books on art, Eugène Fromentin's study of Dutch painters, *Les Maîtres d'autrefois* (Old Masters), and Hippolyte Taine's *La Philosophie de l'art dans les Pays-Bas* (The philosophy of art in the Netherlands). As they viewed works of art, Fénelon read to Proust relevant passages from Taine.

Marcel, amazed at his own mobility, sent postcards to various friends. Antoine received at least three cards, but a letter to Reynaldo was the most artistic epistle. It contained a twenty-seven-line poem on Dordrecht and a drawing of the city, where Marcel had climbed to the top of the church tower to enjoy the panoramic views.[23] From Dordrecht, the city that perhaps had pleased him most of the entire trip, he and Bertrand traveled by boat to Rotterdam.

On October 9 Jeanne, on her son's behalf, wrote Antoine to inform him of Marcel's travels.[24] She began by quoting Ponsard: " 'Once the limit is exceeded, there's no stopping,' and having failed to return that same evening, Marcel doesn't seem to be coming back at all." Marcel had asked her to convey his best regards and to tell Antoine that he missed him very much. Jeanne thanked Antoine for having encouraged Marcel: "This little absence is a great step forward—and he owes a good part of his improvement to your warm, comforting friendship." Marcel had remarked, in the letter with the message for Antoine, that his fatigue was making him prolong his trip. Jeanne interpreted this to mean that he feared he would never return to the Netherlands.

After a week of traveling together Marcel and Bertrand parted company for four days in Antwerp, agreeing to meet later in Amsterdam. Sometime during the trip a thief stole Marcel's money, and he appealed to his parents for funds to cover the rest of his stay.[25] On October 14 he arrived by boat in Amsterdam and checked in at the luxurious Hôtel de l'Europe, where Bertrand had booked them rooms. The following day, Marcel, still in a quandary over his feelings for Bertrand, suggested that they separate again. He would go on his own to Volendam and meet Bertrand at The Hague in four days. What Fénelon thought of all this is not known. It seems likely that Marcel was in love and profoundly unhappy. Had Marcel sent Bertrand into brief exiles in order to avoid proclaiming his love, because—though he knew he was wearing his heart on his sleeve—he feared being rebuffed and perhaps humiliated? Or was it simply that Marcel's own emotions were fluctuating between jubilation—over a sudden improvement in his health and ability to travel on his own—and moroseness over his awareness that he could never have the kind of relationship he wanted with a man whom he worshiped? He confessed in his next letter to his mother that he was in "so disastrous an emotional state that I was afraid of poisoning poor Fénelon with my dreariness, and I've given him a breathing spell, far from my sighs."[26]

Marcel set off by tramway to Monnikendam, where he took a boat for Volendam. Exhilarated by the open air and freed from the tension of his self-torturing relationship with Fénelon, Proust enjoyed the ride through the marshes. He remained in good spirits as he viewed the fishing village he found "delicious and unique."[27] Volendam, virtually unchanged since the seventeenth century, was a picturesque port beloved of a small colony of artists but neglected by most others.

On October 17, the day before he was to rejoin Bertrand at The Hague, Marcel journeyed to Haarlem to see the Frans Hals paintings, which he later mentioned in the *Search*. Back in his room at the Hôtel de l'Europe, he described to his mother the places he had visited, underscoring for her his daytime activities.[28] His management of this trip was so conscientious and intelligent that he often went out at half-past nine or ten in the morning and did not return until very late. The news that he could function well at normal hours delighted his parents, but for Marcel, happiness seemed elusive. He mentioned his confused emotional state and having sent Fénelon away for a few days.

He missed his parents, despite the success of his trip, his genuine interest in the towns he had visited, and the remarkable paintings and architecture he had viewed.

He told his mother that he might not have had the courage to bear so long a separation if he had not decided on it all at once; he had never imagined that he could go a fortnight without embracing her.

He was still "awfully unhappy about that theft, which is making my trip a heavy burden to you." But in spite of that "catastrophic adventure," he had been balancing his budget with great ingenuity. He blamed Fenélon for having chosen such an expensive hotel, but apparently the choice had been an excellent one for his lungs. He concluded that if he had not had "so much as a *trace of asthma*" in Amsterdam, "it's because the hotel is heated by hot-water pipes" as opposed to the hot-air heating he feared. If his parents still intended to send him away from Paris for the winter, he hoped to discourage such plans: It would do him "*great harm*" to leave now. "Fénelon was *the only person* I could go away with. If I were not afraid of boring him with my present moroseness and not afraid of running out of funds . . . I would spend another week in Holland or Belgium." But the thought of "going to Illiers or anywhere else, especially at the present time, would be true madness."

Once he had accounted for himself to his mother, Marcel added a cruel little postscript: "I suspect you of not reading my letters, which would be horrid. Since this one has been written during a pseudo-remission, do at least read it." Had his parents' intention of sending him away as part of a strategy to improve his health and make him more independent inspired him to accuse them of indifference? The reference to a "pseudo-remission" brought an ominous prophecy, certain to be fulfilled: he expected his health problems to resume.

The artistic revelation of the trip occurred on October 18 at The Hague, when Proust visited the Mauritshuis Royal Art Gallery. There he saw a picture whose beauty had a profound and lasting effect on him: Vermeer's *View of Delft*, which he called "the most beautiful painting in the world."[29] Vermeer's depiction of his native town as it looked in the seventeenth century captivated Marcel. He later assigned his character Charles Swann the task of writing a study of Vermeer, a mysterious, obscure figure about whom virtually nothing is known.

By October 20, after an absence of nearly three weeks, Proust returned to Paris. His mother's assumption regarding his reasons for prolonging this trip proved correct: the journey to Belgium and Holland was his last outside France. Vermeer's painting of Delft left the most lasting impression, but there are other traces of the Holland trip in the *Search* as well. Perhaps his jealousy of Fénelon—fortified by the later knowledge that his friend did engage in homosexual relations—inspired him to choose Amsterdam as one of the places in which the Narrator imagined Albertine's lesbian "debaucheries."

In late October, Antoine rushed to Bucharest on learning that his mother was gravely ill. She died on October 31, before her son reached her bedside. Marcel expressed his sympathy with such emotion that he feared Antoine might judge it intrusive.[30] After giving his condolences, he offered: "I'll write to you or not, I'll speak to you of your sorrow or not, I'll do whatever you wish. I don't ask you to feel affection for me. All other feelings are certain to be shattered. But I never knew that I felt so much affection for you. I'm very unhappy." Perhaps Marcel's reference to his own sorrows, even after so much sympathy, also struck Antoine as insensitive.

On November 24 Marcel wrote to Constantin de Brancovan, the new editor in chief of the review *La Renaissance latine*. Constantin had been "kind enough" to ask Marcel to contribute an article, and Proust proposed excerpts from his forthcoming Ruskin translation, which he claimed was basically a Latin book "because it was the history of Christianity in Gaul and the Orient, explained by the Amiens cathedral." He told Constantin that the Mercure de France would likely publish his translation next February or March—a proposition that was in fact far from certain. Given that possibility, he urged Constantin to move quickly.[31]

Almost immediately after giving Constantin the impression that the Mercure would publish his translation, Marcel received word from Vallette declining the manuscript. Proust wrote at once to ask the publisher to reconsider, even offering to pay the printing costs, a gesture that proved to be reckless and unnecessary. Proust pressed his case for publication of *La Bible d'Amiens*, telling Vallette that many thought the book Ruskin's finest work. He quoted French critics who maintained that "if any of Ruskin's books should arouse the interest of us French, it is *The Bible of Amiens*, the only one dealing with our history and our monuments."[32] Vallette had made it clear that what he really wanted Marcel to produce for him was an edition of Ruskin's *Selected Writings*. Proust refused to consider an anthology until he found a publisher for *La Bible d'Amiens*. His letter to Vallette contained a hint that he had begun translating another Ruskin work, *Sesame and Lilies*.[33]

The strategy worked: Vallette agreed to publish *La Bible d'Amiens* if Proust would later compile a selection of Ruskin's writings. Proust promised to complete his work on *La Bible d'Amiens* by February 1 and publish by March 1. He intended to ask *La Renaissance latine* to publish its first installment on February 15, two weeks before the publication date for the Mercure. He asked Vallette to return the manuscript immediately so that he could begin work. He then convinced Constantin to publish long excerpts in the February 15 and March 15 issues. Proust got everything he wanted from his editor and publisher but greatly overestimated the speed with which he would complete translating and annotating the book.

Sometime during 1902 Marie Nordlinger returned to Paris and resumed her post as a silversmith in the Art Nouveau workshops. Proust, hard at work on the difficult translation and complicated annotation, was happy to hear that Marie had come back. He began to summon her "frequently, urgently, by phone, by messenger or petit-bleu [pneumatic mail]." Marie described what it was like to work with Marcel. On arriving, Mme Proust welcomed her "graciously in the heavily furnished salon." Although Mme Proust was evidently "much interested in our work" she withdrew discreetly, leaving Félicie to take Marie to Marcel:

> I remember only a few sessions at the large oval dining-room table with its red cover and old-fashioned oil-lamp; he was mostly in bed, swathed in Jaeger woolens and thermogene wadding, but invariably fastidious about his appearance. Whatever the season the room was oppressively warm; Félice [Félicie] would bring me an ice or orangeade and petits fours from Rebattet's and boiling hot coffee for Marcel. The apparent discomfort in which he worked was quite incredible, the bed was littered with books and papers, his pillows all over the place, a bamboo table on his left piled high and, more often than not, no support for whatever he was writing on (no wonder he wrote illegibly); a cheap wooden penholder or two lay where they had fallen on the floor. Only Ruskin mattered. These sessions often continued late into the night, scrutinizing or reviewing a chapter, a sentence or a mere word; any help a dictionary could supply had been exhausted and memorized by him before my arrival. Conversation ranged far and wide, but if anything he was an even more eloquent listener, interrogating, probing with his strangely luminous, omnivorous eyes. Eyes I can recall alight with fun and mimicry or suddenly suffused unaccountably, unashamedly, with tears.[34]

On the day Proust learned that *La Bible d'Amiens* would be published in its entirety by Vallette and excerpted by Constantin's review, he awaited a visit from Fénelon, who was coming to say good-bye before leaving for his first diplomatic post in Constantinople. Although he was eager to see Bertrand and tell him the news about his Ruskin translation, he was tired because an asthma attack had prevented him from getting enough sleep. On awakening and seeking assistance he had experienced several unpleasant encounters with the servants, who were forced to obey his mother's restrictions, intended to encourage him to adopt a more reasonable schedule. She had at last taken drastic measures, ordering the servants not to serve him a meal or make a fire at odd hours. She had even removed an item he considered essential: the bedside table on which he kept his stock of medication and writing materials. Marcel was in a terrible state of nerves when Fénelon arrived with Comte Georges de Lauris, a twenty-four-year-old law student. Marcel, who later became closely attached to Lauris, considered him Fénelon's confidant. During the farewell visit, Fénelon, whether provoked or not is unknown, said something to Proust that was "very disagreeable." Marcel flew at him and began to pummel him with his fists. And then, not realizing what he was doing, Marcel picked up the new hat Fénelon had bought for his trip to Constantinople, "stamped on it, tore it into shreds, and finally ripped out the lining."

No one knows how Fénelon and Lauris reacted to Marcel's fit of anger. His friends must not have taken the matter too seriously, because they all remained on good terms. Perhaps they understood and condoned Jeanne's efforts to force her son to follow a normal, healthy routine, even if this caused him, at times, to fly into a rage. Proust's friends knew that the harmony of the household had been destroyed by his habits, temper, and manipulations. Sick and miserable though he was, Marcel confronted his parents with a powerful will and monstrous ego. That evening after Fénelon and Lauris left, it was too late for Marcel to talk to Jeanne about the various contretemps of the day, so he wrote his "dear little Mama" a long, bitter letter that spoke of his profound misery while condemning her for lacking compassion: "I'm writing to tell you that I fail to understand you. You could guess, if you don't know, that from the time I come in I cry all night, and not without reason; and all day long you say things to me like: 'I couldn't sleep last night because the servants were up and about until eleven o'clock.' I would be only too glad if that were what prevented me from sleeping! Today, because I was suffering, I committed the crime of ringing for Marie (to bring me my asthma powders) who had come and told me she had finished her lunch, and you punished me, as soon as I had taken my Trional, by making people shout and hammer nails all day."

He then blamed her for his state of nerves that led to the attack on Fénelon. In case she thought he was exaggerating about having demolished the hat, he enclosed a piece of the lining. He expressed his relief that the victim was a friend; it was fortunate that his parents were not present to restrain him, because he might not have been able to stop himself from saying something awful to them. He then turned to the matter of the servants and her strategy to protect them and punish him, by forbidding them to come when he rang or to wait on him at the table. Marcel told his mother she had no idea how uncomfortable she was making the servants with her orders.

Then, in his most incredible accusation yet, he said her actions served only to perpetuate his invalid status:

> What afflicts me . . . is not finding the moral comfort I thought I could expect from you in these truly desperate hours. The truth is that as soon as I feel better, the life that makes me feel better exasperates you and you demolish everything until I feel ill again. This isn't the first time. I caught cold last night; if it turns to asthma, which it's sure to do in the present state of affairs, I have no doubt that you'll be good to me again, when I'm in the same state as this time last year. But it's sad, not being able to have affection and health at the same time. If I had both at this moment, it would be no more than I need to help me fight against an unhappiness which, especially since yesterday evening . . . has become so intense that I can no longer contend with it.[35]

His prediction came true. A week later he was still in bed, suffering from asthma.

His mother knew that Fénelon's departure had saddened and discouraged Marcel about finding a friend upon whom he could depend for companionship and affection. Jeanne remained devoted to the cause of reforming her son, but she often despaired for him and for herself and Adrien. She knew that Marcel was immensely talented and incredibly handicapped. The pattern of genuine illness, self-pity, hypochondria, self-medication, bizarre schedules, and rituals had been set for life. Except for occasional, unpredictable periods when he improved enough to rise and go out in the daytime, Proust was never to change his habits. He never quite became the bedridden hermit so often depicted, but for the rest of his life his active hours would be primarily nocturnal.

During Antoine's absence Marcel dreamed of traveling with him to foreign lands or settling near him in Romania. On December 20 he wrote Antoine a long letter in which he talked about his eagerness to travel to see him, the difficulties involved, and his disappointment in himself for having set aside original work for translation. Two important obligations at home would prevent his departing for Romania until the spring: his brother's marriage and his "Ruskin," which he must deliver to the Mercure on February 1. He did not see how he could depart with all thirty volumes of his Ruskin books and his manuscripts, because he needed his research materials. Proust had decided to cross-reference *La Bible d'Amiens* to other Ruskin works and to return to original biblical sources for his notations rather than rely on reference books, which he found incomplete.

While Proust worked on this all-consuming task, he regretted not creating an original work of fiction. He explained his frustration to Antoine:

> What I'm doing at present is not real work, only documentation, translation, etc. It's enough to arouse my thirst for creation, without of course slaking it in the least. Now that for the first time since my long torpor I have looked inward and examined my thoughts, I feel all the insignificance of my life; a thousand characters for novels, a thousand ideas urge me to give them body, like the shades in the *Odyssey* who plead with Ulysses to give them a little blood to drink to bring them back to life and whom the hero brushes aside with his sword. I have awakened the sleeping bee and I feel its cruel sting far more than its helpless wings. I had enslaved my intelligence to my peace of mind. In striking off its fetters I thought I was merely delivering a slave, but I was giving myself a master whom I have not the physical strength to satisfy and who would kill me if I did not resist him. So many things are weighing on me![36]

Proust had again prophesied correctly. He was in the end to give himself a master, the *Search,* that would eventually consume him.

12   *Self-Hypnosis*   ✄

EARLY JANUARY 1903 BROUGHT a letter from Montesquiou referring to Marcel's "long disappearance" and "uncustomary silence."[1] The count wanted to hear from Proust before embarking on an adventure that would take him across the sea. He and Yturri, according to an article Montesquiou had written for *Le Figaro,* were sailing to America as "Missionaries of Literature."[2] The missionaries would preach to the New World heathens until April.

Marcel had undertaken his own impossible mission. Because of his machinations with the Mercure de France and *La Renaissance latine,* he had agreed to a production schedule he could not meet. In early January, when Binet-Valmer, Constantin's editor in chief, had not received the excerpts from *La Bible d'Amiens* due to appear in the February 15 issue, Constantin informed Marcel that publication would be delayed for a month. Marcel cried foul and expressed his vexation with Constantin and Binet-Valmer. Confident that *La Bible d'Amiens* would appear in book form on March 1, Proust feared that *La Renaissance latine* would not publish excerpts from a volume already in bookstores. Discounting his own tardiness, Marcel pressured Constantin to find room for the excerpts in the February issue. He blamed Binet-Valmer for not having told him when the copy was due and Constantin for not being "nice" about the matter. Marcel then boldly asserted that "fifty pages could always be displaced in a review of more than 300 pages." Having done his best to make Constantin feel guilty, Marcel offered to write the Mercure to see whether Vallette would postpone publication of the book until after the excerpts appeared in *La Renaissance latine,* but he worried that this tactic might furnish the Mercure with a pretext to cancel publication of his book.[3]

In early January, Marcel attended a party at the princesse de Caraman-Chimay's. Reporting on his social activities in a letter to Antoine, he proposed a visit to Bibesco in Strehaia from February 15 to April 1.[4] He told Antoine about his article soon to appear in *Le Figaro.* Using the pseudonym Dominique, he had begun to write a series of society pieces, each portraying a leading Paris salon. Nearly eighteen months earlier, he had drafted the first of these, "Le Salon de la comtesse Aimery de La Rochefoucauld," but had abandoned it.[5] The second one, whose publication in *Le Figaro* he believed imminent, depicted the salon of Comtesse Greffulhe. Wishing to portray and flatter Antoine, Marcel had inserted an eighteen-line cameo of him in the text. The countess had reservations, however, and asked *Le Figaro* to withdraw the piece.[6] Marcel, determined to depict Antoine, transferred his portrait to the description of another salon, to be published in April.

The Best Man

On January 19 *Le Figaro* announced the engagement of Dr. Robert Proust and Mlle Marthe Dubois-Amiot. The following week the Prousts gave a dinner party at home in honor of their son's fiancée. The impending marriage terrified Marcel, who, as best man, was expected to attend many daylight functions. The ceremony of signing the marriage contract was set for Thursday, January 29. Then on Saturday at 5 P.M., an hour Marcel could accommodate, although not without difficulty, the civil ceremony would take place at city hall of the eighth arrondissement, including a speech by the mayor. Finally, at noon on Monday, February 2, the grandest of all the events, the religious ceremony, would be performed at the church of Saint-Augustin. Proust complained constantly to all his friends about the wedding extravaganza, difficult for him to bear under any circumstances but especially so while struggling to revise and proof the Ruskin excerpts for Constantin and finish the volume for the Mercure de France. Marcel teetered on the brink of nervous exhaustion. He confided to Antoine that he worried about his ability to maintain self-control during the long wedding weekend: "Will I burst into giggles while passing the collection box at Saint-Augustin—or while listening to the Mayor's speech?"[7] The situation seemed hopeless.

Another crisis related to his Ruskin work erupted in the latter part of January, when Constantin made a thoughtless remark that enraged Marcel. Constantin speculated that Proust's Ruskin translation "must be full of mistakes, because you don't really know English." The offended translator controlled his anger until he returned home, where he wrote Brancovan a thoughtful letter in which he admitted his scant knowledge of English but defended his work. After expressing his fondness for Constantin and thanking him for being "so good to me and my Ruskins," Marcel got to the point: he found it "incredible" that his friend could have said such a thing, knowing how hard he had been working for four years and how important the book was to him. He was sure that his "dear Constantin" had meant no harm, but could someone who "detested" him have said anything worse?[8]

He defended himself further by observing that if his translation had merit it was not because of his talent, which was "negligible," but because of his "conscientiousness, which was infinite." Proust then detailed his research and translation methods, all the English writers he had consulted over the meaning of "every ambiguous expression, every obscure phrase," amassing an impressive correspondence.[9] Proust readily admitted not knowing "a word of spoken English" and not reading English "easily." But he stubbornly maintained that after fours years of tedious work on *The Bible of Amiens,* he knew the text by heart: "I don't claim to know English. I claim to know Ruskin." In fact, although there are a number of mistakes in Proust's translation of *The Bible of Amiens,* his translation of *Sesame and Lilies* was impeccable.[10]

On January 26 Marcel wrote to his "dear little Antoine" to say that he had decided to remain in Paris and not go to Constantinople. Proust had hoped to see Antoine and Bertrand, but he had not wanted the latter to know the visit had been his initiative. It grieved him, he told Antoine, not to see Bertrand and the Hagia Sophia.[11] The recompense for so many disappointments was the thought that he would soon be reunited with Antoine in Paris. He then chided Antoine for having given a completely ambiguous answer to the question of when Fénelon had known that Marcel might come to Constantinople. Proust was eager, without wanting to reveal it, to learn how Fénelon had reacted to news of a possible visit.

Near the end of the month Proust sent the excerpts from the fourth chapter of *La Bible d'Amiens,* entitled "Interprétations," to the typist. After informing Constantin of the status of this chapter, Marcel promised to correct the new proofs just received from *La Renaissance latine.* If all went well, he would by Friday morning, January 30, deliver the Ruskin entirely recopied for the March 15 issue. Knowing that Constantin planned to leave soon for Romania, Marcel asked whether he intended to travel alone and, if so, whether he would mind having a traveling companion as far as Bucharest.[12] Proust still clung to the idea of meeting Antoine.

As the wedding approached, the Proust family experienced a run of bad luck. When Jeanne learned that certain friends had not received invitations, she made inquiries and discovered to her dismay that the postal service had lost at least one hundred invitations sent out by the Proust side. Marcel, horrified at the offense his friends might take on believing themselves snubbed, dashed off notes explaining the fiasco and urging them to attend the various ceremonies. In one such note to Robert Dreyfus, Marcel asked him to inform Daniel: "Unfortunately I cannot notify all the people who may not have received the invitation. And how many of them will be enemies for life!"[13]

On January 29 Marcel sent Constantin the revised Ruskin proofs for the February issue. He thanked his friend for having accepted him as a traveling companion to Bucharest, "because there are times when I suffer from a slight persecution mania and think I annoy everyone."[14] In a postscript he told Constantin that he would have enclosed the March copy in the same packet had his mother, suffering from an acute attack of rheumatism, not forgotten to send those pages to be copied. After promising again to send the remaining pages the following day, Marcel addressed problems with the proofs that concerned him. Were his revisions being carefully followed? He had taken some alarm on seeing that in the latest proofs "the new phrase and the old one were often printed side by side." He also thought the typeface for John Ruskin's name was "much too small." All these matters, he trusted, would be changed on the final proofs.[15]

Once he had mailed the letter, he wrote another postscript to tell Constantin that though his translation in book form would be dedicated to Reynaldo Hahn, the prince would give him pleasure by accepting a dedication of the pages to appear in *La Renaissance latine.* Constantin must have declined the honor, for the excerpts appeared with no dedication. The next day Marcel sent another bulletin to Constantin, telling him that he was "extremely vexed" because the typist now said the copy would not be ready until Saturday at 5 P.M., the time of his brother's civil marriage ceremony. He promised to correct the pages all night and have them delivered to Constantin early Sunday morning. He proposed to meet Constantin on Tuesday to review the copy. Then, remembering the wedding on Monday and certain that he would be ill on Tuesday, he suggested that Constantin come to his bedside and work on the copy. Constantin was learning that being Proust's publisher required special nerves and endless devotion.

Proust's family had anticipated that a wedding in which Marcel played a prominent role would be a difficult undertaking. His state of anxiety and fatigue did not surprise them, but as ill luck would have it, Mme Proust's severe bout of rheumatism persisted and she was unable to attend the civil ceremony on Saturday. On Sunday, Marcel wrote Constantin that the end of La Bible d'Amiens had been copied. He had had to reread it quickly because he was "hard pressed by the misfortunes that have hit me in connection with the marriage," including his mother's illness.[16]

The next day, when Marcel appeared for the noon wedding at the church of Saint-Augustin, the effects of sleepless nights were obvious. Mme Proust, incapacitated by rheumatism, was transported to the church in an ambulance. The bride must have wondered about the strange behavior and delicate health of Robert's mother and brother. Valentine Thomson, a young Proust cousin, had been asked to be a bridesmaid. The pretty girl of eighteen was thrilled to be a member of the wedding and was especially proud of her beautiful dress and the large bouquet Jeanne had sent her. Valentine's anticipation turned to horror when she saw the escort whose arm she must cling to throughout much of the ceremony, including the slow and humiliating trip up and down the aisle, while Marcel passed the collection plate. As Valentine later recalled, Proust arrived at the church grotesquely attired. Deathly afraid of drafts and cold air, he had stuffed his tuxedo with thermogene wadding and put on three topcoats. Marcel looked as though he were headed to the North Pole rather than to an indoor wedding whose guests included many of Paris's most distinguished and fashionable citizens. Valentine was also amazed at the extraordinary pallor of this man who hardly ever went out in sunlight, ate little, and exercised not at all. The bridesmaid thought the best man looked as horrible as Lazarus must have upon emerging from the grave.[17]

Marcel managed to stay on his feet and control his nervous impulses. After the ceremony the bride's family hosted a large reception and luncheon in their home at 6, avenue de Messine.[18] Robert and Marthe were to reside in their new home on the boulevard Saint-Germain, near the School of Medicine. As soon as Marcel could gracefully escape the wedding festivities, he took to bed with the inevitable fever and sore throat.[19] Over the next few days, he wrote various friends to say that Robert's wedding had "killed him."[20] His brother, no doubt as relieved as he was grateful that Marcel was able to fulfill his role as best man, offered him a pelisse. Such a coat seemed ideal for Marcel, who constantly complained of freezing, but for some reason, he declined the offer.

After the wedding Marcel quickly resumed work on the proofs for Constantin, cutting thirty of the sixty-two pages he had translated about the bas-reliefs at Amiens, those describing the virtues, the seasons, and scenes from the life of the Virgin. He also cleaned up the proofs and excised repetitions that Constantin had marked.

In mid-February, Marcel wrote Antoine that he was "fully recovered" and prepared "*to go to Turkey, Romania, Italy or to wait for you in Paris.*" Then Marcel made a startling proposal: he would find it amusing "no end" to read Bertrand's letters to Antoine if Antoine did not consider this an "indiscretion."[21] Although he maintained the pretense of not caring how His Blue Eyes had reacted to his hypothetical visit, Marcel apparently felt no compunction in violating Fénelon's privacy. In the same letter, he expressed his eagerness to travel, to flee the cold Paris winter: "I'm very tired and long to go somewhere, anywhere." Quoting Baudelaire's *Le Voyage*, he said that he longed for " 'light and for flaming skies' after so many electrically lit nights" at his desk.[22]

Marcel had no time to spare for planning a trip, however. He knew that he had fallen far behind on his Ruskin work and would not meet the March 1 deadline for sending the complete translation of *La Bible d'Amiens* to the Mercure de France. Attempting to finish his work as close to March 1 as possible, he relied continually on his friends who knew English well. Robert d'Humières responded to Marcel's call for help, stopping by several times to explain obscure or difficult words and expressions. In mid-February, Marcel asked Pierre Lavallée's permission to borrow a book from the Bibliothèque des Beaux-Arts, "because it is my intention to go and work there once or twice in the next few days, and it would make things much easier for me if I could do it under your protection." Feeling guilty about asking a favor from a friend whom he had lately neglected, Marcel exaggerated his condition: "I have spent more than a year in bed, without getting up for so much as half an hour a day."[23]

Dominique

On March 3 Antoine Bibesco, who loved surprises and practical jokes, rang the bell at 45, rue de Courcelles. As happy as Marcel was to hear the news, he was not prepared to welcome a visitor. Writing a note to the prince who waited downstairs, he began by quoting the fervent words Blaise Pascal had expressed during his religious conversion: "Joy, tears of joy, joy." Marcel then informed the source of such joy that it was "physically impossible" to receive him and proposed that they meet for dinner. Marcel wanted to make certain that if Antoine encountered Lauris, he would not contradict Marcel's version of why he had seriously considered going to Constantinople. He wanted his friends to think that his choice had been determined primarily by Antoine's whereabouts and not because of his eagerness to see Fénelon.[24]

Marcel's great need for love, for exclusivity, had not changed since adolescence, nor was he any closer to obtaining it. His lack of illusions about its attainability only increased his unhappiness. He also knew, as he lay in his bed endlessly ruminating on his friends' characters and motivations, that his expectations exceeded reality. He had lately cast Antoine as the trusted friend and Fénelon as the villain and admitted as much shortly after Antoine's return: "Deep down you're not as good and kind as I manage to suppose when hypnotizing myself in solitude." He knew that, to a large degree, his friends as he saw them were already creatures of his imagination. Such longings and imaginings in which he manipulated his friends eventually gave rise to the cast of characters he created around the Narrator, who shared his many complexes.

On February 25 *Le Figaro* published the first of Proust's series on Parisian salons: "Un salon historique. Le salon de S.A.I. la princesse Mathilde." He had signed the piece Dominique, a nom de plume that was supposed to be *secret tombeau,* but he had, of course, confided in Antoine. "Remember," he admonished Bibesco after the publication, "don't let anyone suspect about the articles, which no one alas dreams of suspecting."[25] Bibesco apparently kept this secret, perhaps because he did not want to anger Marcel before his portrait was published.

Proust depicted Mathilde's salon as he had heard it described in its glory days under the Second Empire. He included a number of anecdotes about famous guests, such as Alfred de Musset, the celebrated poet who showed up late for dinner—already a cardinal sin in the eyes of the princess, who liked to dine sharply at 7:30, early for a Parisian salon. To make matters worse, Musset was drunk and behaved rudely. After a few more amusing anecdotes, "Dominique" took *Le Figaro*'s readers on a tour of the home at 20, rue de Berri, during a typical soirée. Guests glimpsed in the salon included the princess's devoted nephew Comte Joseph Primoli, the Strauses, Mme Lemaire, Charles Ephrussi, Charles Haas, Dr. Samuel Pozzi, Louis Ganderax, Paul Hervieu, Paul Bourget, and the playwright Georges de

Porto-Riche, who pretended to despise the aristocracy but somehow managed to show up in the most conservative salons. Proust shared with the newspaper's readers the princess's famous repertoire of bons mots and anecdotes. These included the stories about her humble origins, the howlers from her reader, the baronne de Galbois, and the account of her falling out with Hippolyte Taine. Proust noted her simplicity and frankness whenever she spoke about matters of birth and rank.

Proust later used elements of his salon depiction of Mathilde for her cameo in the *Search*. "Her Imperial Highness" appears when the Narrator, out for a stroll with M. and Mme Swann, notices "an elderly but still handsome lady enveloped in a dark overcoat and wearing a little bonnet tied beneath her chin with a pair of ribbons." Before making introductions, Swann draws the Narrator aside to explain the lady's importance: "That is the Princesse Mathilde . . . you know who I mean, the friend of Flaubert, Sainte-Beuve, Dumas. Just fancy, she's the niece of Napoleon I. She had offers of marriage from Napoleon III and the Emperor of Russia." Then Proust evokes her character and the bygone era she embodied: "This somewhat rough and almost masculine frankness she softened, as soon as she began to smile, with an Italian languor. And the whole person was clothed in an outfit so typically Second Empire that—for all that the Princess wore it simply and solely, no doubt, from attachment to the fashions she had loved when she was young—she seemed to have deliberately planned to avoid the slightest discrepancy in historic colour, and to be satisfying the expectations of those who looked to her to evoke the memory of another age."[26] Proust saw Mathilde, as he had Mme Bartholoni, as a creature belonging to another era, who had miraculously survived into the present. But as he looked back at their youths and the historical elements that had made them interesting, he stood unknowingly on the divide between then and now. The great prolonged feast of life was ending for his father's generation, whose youth had known the best days of the Second Empire.

Marcel seemed willing to forgo the great need he had felt for Antoine's attention before the departure to Romania. Now he wanted to be motivated by devotion rather than sentimentality, and he concentrated on helping Antoine find a producer for his plays. "My friendship for you," he wrote, "is in a phase that can only please you since I no longer ardently desire to see you, to see you if only for a minute each evening, etc. etc." Then, after the offer to help, he stressed, by underlining the words three times, that "this phase requires *loyalty*."[27] Was this merely the latest version of Marcel's game of possession, loosening but not releasing the leash?

At home his mother persevered in the difficult, frustrating task of trying to limit Marcel's spending and to impose order on his chaotic life. Before Robert's wedding Jeanne had agreed to host a dinner with Marcel for Jules Cardane, editorial secretary at *Le Figaro*.[28] On March 9 she lost patience with her son's lack of progress and warned him in a letter that if he did not change his ways, she would refuse to give any more dinners on his behalf. This provoked Marcel to reply in bitter recriminations: "Even with a mother's inverse prescience, you couldn't have devised a more untimely means than your letter of nipping in the bud the triple reform which was supposed to go into effect the day after my last dinner out . . . which was delayed by my most recent cold. It's a pity, because afterwards it will be too late."[29]

The triple reform apparently involved those she had been encouraging him to implement for several years, amounting to nothing more—and nothing less—than leading a normal life: (1) changing his bedtime to night rather than day; (2) taking his meals at normal hours; and (3) discontinuing the use of sedatives.[30] Like many neurotics Marcel believed that he could make such changes only at some ideal, magical moment. The Narrator, who shares Marcel's invalid, hypochondriacal nature and inability to set to work, responds in similar fashion whenever his mother attempts to influence his behavior in order to ameliorate his lifestyle: "I told my mother that her words would delay for perhaps two months the decision for which they asked, which otherwise I would have reached before the end of that week." In the novel the Narrator is lucid and accepts the responsibility for having failed to heed his mother's and grandmother's "exhortations" to adopt a "healthier way of life."[31] But not Marcel, who accused his mother of cruelty, indifference, and unfair discrimination in gladly hosting dinners for medical luminaries on behalf of his father and Robert while refusing those for his editors that might advance his career. His mother was accustomed to such tactics and, though not optimistic about changing his habits, did not intend to abandon the field without a struggle.

In a letter to his mother defending his behavior and blaming her for his lack of success in mending his ways, Marcel listed all the work that he had accomplished on the translation and the calvary he had endured by attending all the wedding events, observing: "All this isn't enough for you, or rather it's nothing to you, and you'll continue to disapprove of everything I do until I fall ill again as I did two years ago." She had even spoiled his pleasure when the excerpts of his translation appeared in the "wretched *Renaissance latine.*" But that was of little consequence, for he did not "aspire to pleasure," having given up "hope of that long ago." If she forced him "to give a dinner at a restaurant," she would, at a time when she had asked him to balance his own accounts, push him "back into the red." He complained about the freezing room at home that had forced him out in search of warmth, with the result that he had caught a fever. "You can't do me any positive good and you're not on the way to learning how." But she could at least help him avoid catching colds. He expressed his desire to live in his own apartment or pay rent at home, if that was what she wanted. "But considering that I pay for my own powders (which everyone finds incredible but which seems perfectly natural to me), perhaps I should also pay rent." His parents had likely required him to pay for his drugs in hopes the financial burden would decrease his use of sedatives. In closing he professed his own purity of intention and blamed her again for being unfair and cruel: "If I make you unhappy, at least it's over things outside my control." He could not say the same for her; he could not imagine refusing her one hundred dinners. "But I'm not reproaching you, I ask you only to stop writing me letters requiring an answer."[32]

Although he frequently lashed out against the constant pressure from Jeanne to change his self-destructive habits, Marcel worshiped his mother and always expressed his love while acknowledging all she did for him. In one letter written during the same period he speculated about living apart from her and acknowledged the impossibility of not seeing her daily: "Considering my need of being near you, you can be sure that you will not be abandoned and that I shall come twenty times a day—except at mealtimes!"[33]

Jeanne and her difficult son must have reached a compromise or at least a truce. By the end of the month, plans were completed for a dinner party at home on April 1. Those invited included his "dear editor in chief" at *La Renaissance latine,* Constantin, along with Brancovan's sisters and their spouses, the Strauses, Paul Hervieu, Abel Hermant, Antoine Bibesco, and Mme de Pierrebourg, a novelist who wrote under the pen name Claude Ferval.[34]

On Wednesday evening, March 18, Marcel wrote to his mother to say that he would like d'Humières to come the next day and answer additional questions about their translation. In order to be rested for the consultation, he asked her to try and maintain silence in the house. The request seemed to contain a veiled threat that otherwise he might resort to Trional, which he had not taken for some time and wanted to avoid. But what he really preferred was that she send a message to d'Humières and have him to dinner on Friday when the two men could dine alone. A tête-à-tête encounter seemed best, for Marcel was always seized by fits of uncontrollable laughter whenever d'Humières came.

Marcel decided to follow Antoine's suggestion that he pretend to be Antoine and write Fénelon in an attempt to discover the young diplomat's true opinion of him. The fake letter had at least one advantage; it allowed Marcel to engage in an exercise that had always been his forte and that he had been honing recently: writing pastiche, mimicking another's style. Writing as Bibesco, Marcel-Antoine placed some bait to see if Fénelon would take it: "It gave me no pleasure to see him [Marcel] again, I no longer feel any friendship for him. He is even stupider than went I went away." Marcel-Antoine did mention a favorable notice in *Le Figaro* about Proust's Ruskin translation.[35] Fénelon's reaction to the letter is not known. Did Fénelon suspect a trick?

Ruskin Expeditions

The younger Dr. Proust, well-to-do and firmly established in his profession, had recently bought an automobile, an ideal acquisition for the speed-loving doctor. A photograph taken of Robert on a motoring expedition to Illiers shows him standing with the quite elderly Uncle Jules Amiot. Sporting a large motoring cap and beaming at the camera, Robert seemed as healthy, happy, well adjusted, and successful as Marcel was sickly, dependent, and miserable.

In April, Marcel asked his mother to inquire whether Robert might be willing to loan his car now and then, which would permit Marcel "to spend a little time in the country."[36] If so, Marcel would hire a driver from an automobile agency of which Robert approved or ask a new friend, Marquis Louis d'Albufera, to drive him. Proust considered Albufera eminently qualified to handle a motorcar, for he had already driven on tours of Belgium, France, Germany, and Switzerland.

Marcel needed transportation for a Ruskin expedition he was planning with his friends. Emmanuel Bibesco, who had the reputation of being an expert on Gothic architecture, had arrived in Paris in early April to visit his brother. Marcel warned Antoine not to bring Emmanuel unannounced: "*Never come here with your brother.*" Marcel did not want to be seen in an unkempt state by a distinguished stranger. "Mama wouldn't allow it. I wouldn't want to receive him in my soiled jerseys, etc." If Antoine disobeyed, Marcel would not receive him either, and "little by little you would move into the category of friends I receive only when fully dressed, in the dining room, in other words seldom."[37] Proust had first suggested to the Bibesco brothers that they leave one evening and spend the night at Autun, visit Vézelay the following day, and return to Paris in the evening. This plan was dropped, and Marcel chose April 10, Good Friday, for a trip southeast of Paris to visit the medieval cities of Provins, Saint-Loup-de-Naud, and Dammarie-les-Lys.

Accompanying Marcel in addition to the Bibesco brothers were François de Pâris—a member of the Jockey Club and the Yacht Club—Lucien Henraux, who collected Oriental art, Georges de Lauris, and, perhaps, Robert de Billy and his wife. In the days preceding their departure, Marcel gave Antoine and other friends complicated instructions for obtaining information about car rental services and train schedules. Fearing the annual onset of hay fever, Marcel intended to travel in a closed car to protect himself as much as possible from pollen and drafts.

The chief attraction of Provins was a splendid twelfth-century donjon forty-four meters tall, visible from a great distance. At Saint-Loup-de-Naud, the group studied one of the oldest churches in the Parisian region. Its construction as part of a Benedictine priory had begun in the eleventh century. The portal under the western porch, like the royal porch of Chartres Cathedral, features Christ in majesty surrounded by the symbols of the Evangelists. Perhaps the most admirable statue, as befitted the church's namesake, was the one representing Saint-Loup, archbishop of Sens, who died in 623. Proust remembered this name when he created the character Robert de Saint-Loup. Marcel and his companions likely stopped last at Dammarie-les-Lys to inspect the ruins of the Abbey of the Lily.

On April 21 Marcel organized another cathedral expedition, north of Paris to Laon, Coucy, Senlis, Saint-Leu-d'Esserent, and Soissons.[38] His motoring companions were the Bibesco brothers, Georges de Lauris, and Robert de Billy. Marcel, who had stayed up all night to be ready for the early-morning departure, stopped several times en route to drink coffee in order to remain alert. The church of Saint-Leu-d'Esserent, (whose *Leu* is a variation of *Loup*), built on a cliff overlooking the Oise River, contains both Romanesque and Gothic elements. Emmanuel proved an extraordinary tour guide, enthralling his listeners with his extensive knowledge about French medieval architecture, but Antoine, true to character, took matters far less seriously. Always the clown, he approached the organ and banged out Paulus's highly secular song "En revenant de la revue."

At Coucy, Enguerrand III, an intrepid and renowned Crusader, had constructed one of the Middle Ages' most impressive fortified castles. Emmanuel led Marcel up the fifty-four meters of the ancient spiral staircase of the donjon. Once they reached the top, the pristine early spring day allowed the visitors to see for miles beyond the castle's walls, supported by no fewer than twenty-eight towers.

In front of the church at Senlis, Marcel listened attentively as Emmanuel, "with so much modesty . . . explained what characterizes the church towers of the Île de France."[39] These were distinguished by the first representations in Western sculpture of the crowning of the Virgin Mary. Here, as at Saint-Loup-de-Naud, the group observed the similarities between the sculptural groups and those at the cathedrals of Chartres, Paris, Amiens, and Reims. At Soissons, Marcel and his friends inspected the cathedral of Saint-Gervais-et-Saint-Protais, noted for its thirteenth-century purity and simplicity of style.[40]

Laon Cathedral presents a unique feature. Built high on a hill, its twin towers, rising higher still and appearing to touch the sky, serve as the viewing platform for eight majestic oxen. The statues were placed high on the towers because the townspeople had wanted to honor the brave beasts of burden for the years spent dragging the huge stones from the quarries far below to the top of the hill for the construction of the cathedral. Proust found Laon's architecture fascinating, as he later wrote to Mme Catusse, because it was there "better than in the rich subsequent efflorescence, that one can see the first burgeoning of the Gothic and how 'the marvelous flower slowly emerges.'"[41] Laon had been a center of medieval scholasticism, and Proust noted the "delightfully pedantic insistence on the liberal arts in its main portal and in the stained glass of its rose window." He described for Mme Catusse the representations of "Philosophy," with "the ladder (of learning) placed in front of her chest, Astronomy gazing at the heavens, Geometry with her compass, Arithmetic counting on her fingers, Dialectics with the wily snake." Although the architecture was "very splendid," he was somewhat disappointed in the representation of Medicine, which he found "rather banal, not as at Reims, where she is examining an invalid's urine."[42]

Marcel took notes both for translating Ruskin and for original essays he wanted to write about medieval architecture, but his impressions were to be more useful in the creation of fictional churches in his novel: the church of Saint-Hilaire at Combray, much grander than Illiers's modest Saint-Jacques, the church at Balbec, and Saint-André-des-Champs.

In mid-April, Anna de Noailles wrote a charming, affectionate note urging Marcel to come to dinner, anticipating his needs and the complications that might discourage his presence. Of all his friends, she seemed best to understand his anxieties and his temperament. The poet showed not only compassion but other qualities that Marcel prized as well: delicacy, affection, and the ability to put herself in another's place. Such gestures erased any doubts he may have at first entertained about her nature and her goodness. Writing to him as "Dear Friend," Anna said that she would hold his place at table to see whether he felt better at the last minute, in which case, he would find Grüber beer that she had kept warm by leaving it out in the sun.[43] If he could not come, she would be happy to think that he was resting.

After expressing her deep affection, she assured him that he would find her house "still warm because we have not yet turned off the heat."[44]

In late April, Marcel went to the Durand-Ruel Gallery to see an exhibition of paintings by Maxime Dethomas.[45] The motivation to rise from his bed during daylight hours had been Dethomas's studies of Venice, a city that continued to occupy Proust's imagination while he worked on Ruskin and architecture. Marcel left the exhibition, as he explained to the artist, "filled with wonder," but also with sadness because illness made it impossible for him to visit the people and skies Dethomas had captured on the canvases. These paintings had given him "new eyes with which to view life and men and even those little windows on the Grand Canal which I should like to confront with yours."[46] Marcel's vision of his mother framed by one of those little windows, while gazing out at the Grand Canal, remained fixed in his memory.

On Monday morning, May 11, *Le Figaro* published Proust's latest society piece: "La Cour aux lilas et l'atelier des roses: Le Salon de Mme Madeleine Lemaire" (The lilac courtyard and the studio of the roses: The salon of Mme Madeleine Lemaire). "Dominique," as Proust had signed the article, began with a page-long parody of Balzac, describing Lemaire's neighborhood and the small house, which violated a city ordinance by protruding one-half meter onto the sidewalk.[47] After an appropriate tribute to Lemaire, a great artist celebrated for her watercolors, including the well-worn mot about her having created more roses than anyone other than God, "Dominique" evoked the celebrities who frequented the salon. Among these were painters Jean Béraud, Pierre Puvis de Chavannes, Sarah Bernhardt's close friend and portraitist Georges Clairin, the actress Réjane, and the writers Anatole France and Georges de Porto-Riche. Dominique also described the well-born and well-to-do who gladly suffered the indignities of perching on uncomfortable stools in the crowded rooms. Among the eager guests was Boni de Castellane, of whom the chronicler gave a flattering portrait. Marcel-Dominique even provided a blurb about Robert de Flers's and Gaston de Caillavet's "triumphant" new operetta *Le Sire de Vergy.*

Marcel had included the little sketch of Antoine, which described the "secretary of the Romanian delegation" conversing with two political figures. In less than two dozen lines Proust managed to compare Bibesco to Achilles, Theseus, and Apollo. Later came the "veiled reference to Fénelon," for whom, at a party like Lemaire's, Dominique had first felt the bonds of "an affection that was later to bring us nothing but repeated betrayals and final enmity."[48] To express the "melancholy" of days that took away with them "possibilities that never came true," he cited Rossetti's lines: "My name is *might have* been." This cryptic remark must have perplexed everyone who read *Le Figaro* except, presumably, Antoine and Fénelon, and perhaps Reynaldo, in whom Marcel had never ceased to confide. Fénelon's reaction, if he saw himself as the inspiration of such bitterness, remains unknown.

Near the end of the description of the salon, Proust turned the spotlight on "that musical instrument of genius" Reynaldo Hahn. Hahn, throwing his head back as he reached without looking at the keys, the inevitable cigarette dangling from his lips, began to sing one of his most popular numbers, "Le Cimetière de campagne." Lemaire, like the future Mme Verdurin, shushed the playwright Francis de Croisset for chatting too loudly with a lady.

On the day the article on Mme Lemaire's salon appeared in the newspaper, Marcel informed Antoine that he would attend her Tuesday reception because he was eager to hear the habitués' reactions to his piece. That evening, as Proust moved among the guests, he heard talk of little else. Someone compared the column to a Fromentin novel and everyone wanted to know "Who is this Dominique?"[49] Marcel was delighted. He was also highly amused when he encountered Comte Primoli, who, unaware of Dominique's identity, told him that the essay on Princesse Mathilde's salon was "imbecilic."[50] The mysterious Dominique was soon unmasked by an unlikely tattler: Gaston Calmette, a rising star on *Le Figaro*'s editorial staff.

Marcel had become friends with Marquis Louis d'Albufera and his nineteen-year-old mistress Louisa de Mornand, who had once been Fénelon's mistress. Born Louisa Montaud, the pretty blonde actress had altered her name to make it more appealing to producers. Louisa and Louis were passionately in love and he quickly spoiled her, even though she often infuriated him by flirting with other men. Having seen how quickly he became jealous, she tormented him by refusing to allay his suspicions. The stormy relationship between the marquis and the actress gave Marcel the occasion to observe the lovers closely. He remembered them when portraying the marquis de Saint-Loup's infatuation with his mistress, the aspiring but untalented actress Rachel. In spite of Proust's unflagging efforts to secure her roles and publicize her appearances, Louisa was less successful on the stage than the fictional Rachel. Between 1903 and 1910 she appeared in roughly twenty minor plays before her star, which had never shone brightly, dimmed altogether.

Marcel did not hide from Louisa the physical attraction he felt for her, nor was she the only young woman he found desirable during this period. Was it for himself or for a friend that he sought information about l'Hôtel du Paradis, an aptly named *maison de rendez-vous?*[51] Marcel, whose libido had not yet been anesthetized by drugs, began with Louisa an apparently innocent flirtation that grew bolder. Louisa often accompanied Albufera when he made late-night visits to Proust. She would come up to the dining room and "roast so charitably" in the overheated room.[52] Later, when Louisa and Louis were rarely able to see each other because of his marriage, Marcel often filled the role of intermediary, message center, and comforter. Is it possible that Marcel and Louisa, at least on one occasion, gave each other the ultimate consolation for Albufera's absence? In her memoir, Louisa hinted that their relationship went beyond the bounds of friendship.[53] In spite of Proust's flirtation with Louisa, his future testimony indicated that he felt physical attraction only for men.

On May 21, two days before Louisa was to appear with la belle Otero in the sketch *On n'a pas le temps!* (We haven't the time!) at the Mathurins, Marcel had Antoine call the theater critic Abel Hermant to see whether he would insert a few lines to mention that Mlle de Mornand was "charming."[54] The next day he asked Antoine to make the same appeal to the playwright Edmond Sée for *Gil Blas*. Sée obliged and, while commenting ironically about Otero's performance, said that Mlle de Mornand had played with "intelligence and finesse."[55] Marcel, who attended the première, dashed off a similar request to Francis de Croisset for *Le Gaulois* and even provided a short paragraph himself about the "gracious" newcomer appearing in *On n'a pas le temps!* and *Le Coin du feu* (The chimney corner) and predicted that one day this young actress would be "someone."[56] These were the first of many efforts by Marcel to publicize the beginning actress's roles.

Marcel had always loved the theater, an art form whose nocturnal hours matched his own. During the years when he earned Albu's gratitude for promoting Louisa's theatrical career, he attended many performances. Assisting Louisa was another way of indulging his own love of the stage. He attempted to arrange dinners for her and Albu to meet leading playwrights or rising ones like Henry Bernstein. On July 9 Marcel wrote to Louisa, vacationing at Blois, and expressed his admiration of her beauty and his fondness for her, of which she was "well aware." Urging her not to "suppose that this is an indiscreet, pretentious and awkward way of courting" her, which would "be pointless" for she would send him "packing," he maintained that he would "rather die than cast covetous eyes upon the woman adored by a friend whose noble and delicate heart makes him dearer to me with each passing day." He pleaded his case that "at least a little friendship and a great deal of admiration" might persuade his "dear Louisa" to grant him (while he "mentally" requested "Albufera's permission") a favor that would give him "no end of pleasure if it could some day be done otherwise than in a letter," to "embrace you tenderly." In the postscript he added a message to Albu, hoping to advance their friendship: "Tell him, first, to stop calling me Proust and incidentally that I am very fond of him."[57] Marcel, with his extraordinary capacity for tenderness and his keen appreciation of the beauty of both sexes, was enamored of both the marquis and the attractive young actress.

13   *A Happy Man* ∾

IN EARLY JUNE, DR. PROUST WAS INVITED, as a delegate of the Académie de médecine, to give a speech at Chartres on the occasion of the inauguration of the Pasteur monument in the place Saint-Michel. The ceremony took place on Sunday, June 7, at two in the afternoon during the celebration of the agricultural fair. In his address Adrien evoked the magnificent cathedral with its "sculpted encyclopedia of the Middle Ages." After eulogizing Pasteur for his revolutionary scientific discoveries, he observed that "in the twelfth century and even the beginning of the thirteenth century, one did not find medicine among the seven liberal arts, in other words, the sciences. It's only a little later, in the middle of the thirteenth century, that Medicine appears on the portal of Reims cathedral, holding a vial at eye level while attentively examining a patient's urine."[1]

Adrien's and Marcel's interests coincided at last in the images found on the Chartres cathedral, the scientist father and the writer son recounting the evolution of medicine and architecture. In the *Search* the links were to be evident between Adrien's passionate investigations into the biology and pathology of disease and Marcel's no less detailed and passionate study of human psychology and the pathology of obsessions. Each man determined in his different way to illuminate truths about the human condition.

On the morning of June 8 Marcel, bedeviled by the difficulties of translating Ruskin's English, sent Antoine a note asking for help checking the proofs. He needed someone with sufficient command of English to finish a section that d'Humières had not had time to read. Marcel wrote that he could call on Marie Nordlinger to help him, but if Antoine were willing to assist him, the task would most likely take "three long sessions of at least an hour each."[2] Marcel would, of course, acknowledge Antoine's aid in the preface. "But since I address the same thanks to d'Humières," he suddenly worried, "don't you think it might look rather Salaïstic, and wouldn't you rather not?" He then chastised Bibesco for having corrupted him by making him betray so many secrets. In spite of Antoine's kindness to him on the evening past, "you are the buyer of my soul and I wish I could return all your kindnesses and take it back again, and find it as it would have been if I hadn't sold it, with its secrets unbetrayed, its innocence unspoilt, its tombs and altars inviolate." He ended with a diabolical comparison: "no one should be able to buy . . . what in reality only the Devil buys. But alas, 'it may not be mended and patched and pardoned and worked up again as good as new.'"[3]

Perhaps the great medieval sculptural depictions of the Last Judgment influenced Marcel's choice of words evoking resurrections and the diabolical commerce in souls. It must have been difficult for Antoine to separate reality from Marcel's imaginings. The wounds the hypersensitive Marcel had suffered in adolescence, some real, many based on false assumptions, were now colored by images the writer was to use in the elaboration of his own immense cathedral-book.

The June 15 issue of *La Renaissance latine* published Princesse Hélène de Caraman-Chimay's "Impressions of Italy." Marcel wrote to compliment her on her extraordinary gifts as a prose writer, just as he had her sister Anna de Noailles when their brother Constantin's literary review had begun serializing her novel in January.[4] Montesquiou, unimpressed and annoyed by the blatant nepotism, began to refer to *La Renaissance latine* as the Brancovan family chamber pot, because "they all use it."[5] Marcel, however, was enchanted by every word the beautiful sisters wrote.

Shortly after July 3 Fénelon arrived in Paris from Constantinople. In anticipation of his arrival Marcel and Antoine had agreed on a strategy not to see each other privately during his visit, in order to avoid gossip and betraying of confidences. Proust again vowed not to "violate any tombs."[6] The unfortunate Bertrand fell ill almost immediately after his arrival and remained unwell throughout his leave. Marcel, already overwrought because of the seemingly endless work required to complete and publish his Ruskin translation, began playing nurse to Fénelon, calling on him nearly every day.[7] Apparently, he had already forgiven the instigator of "repeated betrayals." The extent of Marcel's devotion to Bertrand can be measured by the extraordinary efforts required for him to alter his schedule and leave the house before late evening. Other than Marcel's visits to comfort and distract Bertrand, nothing is known about their relations that summer.

Meanwhile, Marcel attempted to establish closer ties with another young nobleman. In midsummer Marcel wrote to François de Pâris, whom he had apparently not seen since the Good Friday excursion, and mentioned the possibility of visiting him at his château de Guermantes, about twenty-five kilometers east of Paris. This visit, like most others Marcel dreamed of, never took place. The letter to Pâris is likely the first time Proust ever wrote the name Guermantes—a name that resonated in his memory until he made it one of the most important names in his novel, one of the "two ways" around which he would build his epic story. Regarding names, Marcel pretended to find his own inharmonious and entreated François not to use "Proust" but to call him by his given name.[8]

On Thursday evening, July 16, Mme Proust hosted a small dinner party for Marcel, to which he invited Antoine Bibesco, Léon Yeatman, Bertrand de Fénelon, Georges de Lauris, Francis de Croisset, and René Blum. He had asked Gaston Calmette to be the guest of honor to thank him and *Le Figaro* for publishing his salons. In the invitation, before revealing his intention to make Gaston the center of his party, Marcel chided him and his colleagues at the newspaper. He pointed out that his "incognito of Dominique is much more serious than you think. I was seriously irked when you unmasked me to Mme Lemaire, and I adjure you not to do it again." Marcel had become so annoyed with Jules Cardane for not having published his salon articles biweekly as promised that he threatened to suspend them, for in his view, the lack of regularity had made his articles "utterly meaningless and almost unintelligible."[9]

The dinner party, so long anticipated after the delays caused by illnesses and his skirmishes with his mother, ended badly for Marcel because of Antoine's temper and indiscretions. In a letter written late that evening to thank his mother for "the charming dinner," Marcel reviewed the evening's low point and expressed his rage at his friend. Bibesco, angered by Marcel's telling the dinner guests that he had played the secular song "En revenant de la revue" at the church of Saint-Leu-d'Esserent, retaliated by revealing that Marcel had recently given a sixty-franc tip (more than two hundred dollars in today's money) for some minor service. This "ridiculous" remark and "Papa's unjust repartee" had left Marcel "in tears" after the dinner, "less perhaps because of all the unpleasantness caused" by Antoine's remark "than at seeing that no one can be trusted and that those who seem to be one's best friends have such incredible flaws that all things considered they may be even worse than other people." Marcel had even reminded Antoine before dinner not to make any jokes about tipping. But Marcel's exorbitant tips were no joke, as he well knew; this expensive habit had been observed by all his friends.[10] Marcel told his mother he had refused to forgive Antoine, because he had struck Marcel in his "family affections, which matter more to me than my affection for my friends." Antoine was no more to be trusted than "a man who may have a good heart and no end of estimable qualities but who at times, through the effect of drink or something else, will stick a knife into you."[11]

Marcel did, of course, forgive Antoine, as he had occasion to do again before the year was out. On Christmas Day he reproached Antoine for embarrassing him in front of the servants, who attended him with such unselfish devotion, and even, on occasion, lent him money. Antoine had blurted out that Marcel, who never gave his servants any money, handed out "enormous tips to the waiters at Larue."[12] There was no end to the mischief caused by Antoine's loose tongue.

Proust found an unexpected source of funds for his exorbitant habits. Constantin Ullmann, a young friend of Hahn's, had placed a wager for Marcel at the racetrack and won a considerable sum. Marcel, much to his annoyance, could not arrange a rendezvous with Ullmann to collect his winnings. When the Ruskin proofs finally arrived in mid-July, his mother, despite her best efforts, was too busy to read them at once and left them for him on the desk in the "smoking room," as the family called the room where Marcel burned his antiasthma powders. A week or so later, still frustrated because he had not received his racetrack money, Marcel asked René Peter to find Ullmann and collect the money he desperately needed "because of his mound of debts and . . . increasing penury." As eager as Proust was to have his winnings, however, Ullmann must not ask to see him because, between correcting his proofs and nursing Fénelon, he felt himself "becoming crazed."[13] With his bizarre hours, lack of organization, depleted funds, and frequent illnesses, Marcel felt overwhelmed by the tasks at hand.

Still, he found the time and energy to assist his father with another speech. In July, Dr. Proust returned to his hometown of Illiers as a distinguished native son to speak to the high school students on prize day. First at Chartres and now at Illiers, Adrien had returned to the cradle of his existence to make his valedictories. Adrien shared with the students his memory at age six—lunch basket and book bag in hand—of leaving the house for the daily walk to school. Prepared to be nostalgic, Dr. Proust recited lines from Marcel's favorite poems evoking the vanished, happy moments of youth. He quoted Hugo's "Tristesse d'Olympio," whose title character had also returned to a place where, with every step, he glimpsed ghosts of days that "are no more."[14] Adrien spoke of the walk he had taken the day before, along "your delicious Loir," one of France's "prettiest rivers." Perhaps using words provided by his son, Adrien lauded the Loir's "marvelous natural tapestry," woven from the water lilies floating in the stream and the irises, furze, gladiolas, and buttercups growing along its banks. But Dr. Proust the hygienist, less preoccupied with aesthetics than with stagnation and disease, urged the good people of Illiers to clean out their river, even though the procedure would devastate the flowers.

Marcel had grown concerned about another menace, one that threatened the beauty of France's cathedrals. He deplored the rising tide of anticlericalism, a political and social trend that, if carried to its ultimate conclusion, would convert the magnificent churches into arid museums. The prize ceremony at Illiers, where the priest was no longer welcome, had provided a poignant reminder of how deep anticlerical sentiments ran in France. The little country village of Illiers was hardly a hotbed of radicalism, but the ostracism of the priest, at an event in which practically the entire community participated, pained Marcel, who feared that the anticlerical currents might prove as divisive as the Dreyfus Affair.

One of the consequences of the affair had been to strengthen the anticlerical faction, which demanded strict government control over the religious orders. When Émile Combes became prime minister in 1902, he adopted a strong anticlerical policy and introduced a number of new laws, known as the Combes anticlerical laws. Many religious institutions were closed, including a number of Catholic schools; diplomatic relations were broken off with the Holy See, and Napoléon's concordat with the church was annulled. These measures led in 1905 to the separation of church and state.

One evening while Marcel was conversing with Lauris and Albufera, Lauris defended the new laws.[15] In this Lauris was typical not of his social class but of a French intellectual milieu now dominated by anticlericalism. Albufera did represent his class, which upheld conservative, traditional values. Marcel voiced his opposition to the Combes laws on aesthetic and historical grounds, fearing that the new laws were too radical. Sometime after the debate, he sent Lauris a lengthy letter in which he continued the discussion.[16]

Those like Lauris, who favored the laws, believed that the Catholic schools taught their pupils to hate Freemasons and Jews. Marcel cited Illiers, where "the priest has not been invited to the prize-giving since Ferry's laws," as an example of the ills that might result from overzealous radicalism.[17] The anticlerical camp,

Proust argued, in its ostracism of priests and those who shared their beliefs, was responsible, as much as anyone, for dividing the country. Marcel knew from his childhood visits to Illiers that "the church's pretty steeple" and "the village priest, who taught me Latin and the names of the flowers in his garden," could only be forces of good. He denounced the position taken by Jules Amiot, "my father's brother-in-law, the anti-clerical deputy mayor, who hasn't spoken to the priest since the 'Decrees,' who reads *L'Intransigeant* but who since the Affair has taken also to reading *La Libre Parole.*" Marcel condemned the exclusion of the elderly priest from his father's awards ceremony, for "in the village he stands for something more difficult to define than the social function symbolized by the pharmacist, the retired tobacco-monopoly engineer and the optician," but which deserved just as much respect, "if only because of the intelligence of the pretty, spiritualized steeple, which . . . looks finer, nobler, more disinterested than any of the other buildings."

Proust based his arguments against anticlericalism on aesthetics, common sense, tolerance, and the values of an advanced liberal education. "Rest assured," he wrote Lauris, "the fact that a *licence* in literature is required for military service has done more for the cause of the advanced liberal Republic than any expulsion of monks." Friends like Pâris and Albufera who had not "been to university" reflected "the political ideas of their social group, that is, of their newspapers." At the end of the letter the "exhausted" Marcel shook Lauris's hand and "adjured" him "to burn this idiotic letter immediately." This was not to be Proust's last word on the subject. In September at Évian he began an essay, "La Mort des cathédrales" (The death of cathedrals), in which he defended the church's right to maintain its religious role in French society. Proust proved his independence of thought by espousing causes he considered to be just, no matter who among his friends might be in the other camp. He had condemned anti-Semitic priests during the Dreyfus affair; now he combated radicalism from the other end of the political spectrum.

Near the beginning of August the remainder of the proofs for *La Bible d'Amiens* arrived all at once, in such "disorder and filled with insane inaccuracies" that their deplorable condition "maddened" the author.[18] Marie Nordlinger came to the rescue once again. Not long after he and she had finished making many revisions and corrections, a catastrophe occurred: somehow Marcel lost the proof sheets. Writing to Marie, preparing to return to England, he confessed the terrible loss and his disgust with himself for having lost the sheets on which he had noted her "precious corrections." He did not know whether his "exasperated publisher will be willing to publish a translation by someone so disorganized and tiresome."[19]

During the period when he worked on *La Bible d'Amiens*, Marcel's room, normally in disarray, had become even more chaotic. Gregh, recently vexed with Marcel for having lost within the four walls of his room a book he had lent him, described the room's "beautiful disorder" as having attained "a state of art."[20] There were piles of books by and about Ruskin, studies of medieval history and art, the notes he had taken from written texts and interviews with friends and other translators, his mother's rough drafts, and his usual pile of medications and writing materials. The debris of his disordered life spilled out into other rooms, including the one vacated by Robert. The loss of the proof sheets demoralized an exhausted Marcel, who saw himself again, as he had on aborting *Jean Santeuil,* as someone unable to complete his literary projects. Except for the series of articles on Ruskin and the translation excerpts published in *La Renaissance latine,* he now abandoned another project on which he had labored for nearly four years. At first he did not reveal this decision to his mother, who had encouraged him to undertake the translation and who had shared his hard work.

On August 8 Marcel and Antoine accompanied a weakened but nearly recuperated Bertrand to the train station, where the diplomat departed for Constantinople "in rather good spirits."[21] There are no indications that this separation from His Blue Eyes was especially painful for Marcel, as had been the first departure to Constantinople. Had the daily visits to the sick bed of a Bertrand in less than top form dulled his enthusiasm?[22] Perhaps the primary emotion Marcel felt upon Bertrand's return to his diplomatic post was relief. Not long afterward, Antoine, angry with Marcel for some reason, left Paris, apparently to go to England.[23] Soon Marcel's parents would leave on vacation and he would be alone to contemplate his latest failure and bleak prospects.

Autumn Interlude

In August, Adrien and Jeanne left on a summer holiday. First they traveled to the Swiss health resort at Interlaken, where they had booked rooms at the Grand Hôtel Victoria Interlaken, an immense lodge whose letterhead boasted of 350 rooms and 20 salons. Nestled in the Bernese Alps, Interlaken and its valley region were famous for the magnificent view of the Jungfrau. Adrien and Jeanne intended to enjoy a week of relaxation and sightseeing in the Grindelwald Valley. They took a train excursion, admiring from the comfort of their car, as Jeanne described the scene to Marcel, the valley's splendid views of "beautiful glaciers and snow-covered peaks."[24]

On August 18 Dr. and Mrs. Proust embarked at Ouchy and sailed across Lake

Geneva to Évian-les-Bains, where they would continue their holiday and take the waters. Adrien, now nearly seventy, sought relief from digestive disorders he assumed were caused by his gall bladder; Jeanne hoped that the spa would alleviate the rheumatism that still plagued her. After their arrival at the Splendide Hôtel in Évian, the two were so tired that they went to bed early. Jeanne dreamed about Marcel, as she told him in the next morning's letter. Her poor little unhappy wolf, never absent from her dreams, had appeared before her somewhat melancholy.[25] Turning to more routine matters, his mother informed him that Robert and Marthe had gone to Aix, where they would spend the remaining two weeks of August vacation with her family. Marthe, nearly six months pregnant, was enjoying her last holiday before the responsibility of motherhood.

As Marcel began making his own travel plans, he realized that on the way to Évian, he could make a slight detour and visit the medieval churches at Avallon and Vézelay. On August 15 he wrote to Léon Yeatman, chiding him good-naturedly for not having let him know that he had recently been to Bourges and Vézelay, "I'd have done them with you, and I'll certainly be going there soon by myself." As for today, he was remaining in bed, an exception, he said, because he intended to leave at seven on Sunday morning to spend the day at Trouville visiting Mme Straus. If Léon were free he could come up and see him that evening and tell him the best things to see on the way back from Trouville—Bayeux, Caen, Dives, or Lisieux. After laying out elaborate plans, Marcel added, typically, "But I think I'll be back tomorrow evening." Realizing that Léon might find the invitation to stop by less compelling if he needed no touring advice, Marcel urged his friend to come and say good night to him.[26] The lonely Marcel was eager to attract friends who inhabited the real world to his bedside, the command post from which he later directed the lives of his fictional creatures.

After arriving in Évian, Jeanne entreated Marcel to put his affairs in order, especially his wardrobe, to which end she had left specific instructions for him and Marie. Each article of clothing was to be inspected and, as required, cleaned, mended, hemmed, refitted if any buttons were missing, given new collars if needed, and so on. She was eager for her orders to be heeded so that Marcel would leave on vacation decently attired and his wardrobe in perfect condition. He soon informed her that he had followed her instructions to the letter.

Mother and son began the annual debate about where he should lodge during vacation. Jeanne could not recommend the Splendide because of the crowd and noise, but if he wanted to come, she would try to find him the best room in town, and he could take his meals at the hotel.[27] She finally decided that he would be more comfortable at the Splendide because excessive rainfall had increased the humidity in the area. Sensing that his departure was imminent, Jeanne reminded him of his intention to pay all his bills before he departed. She no doubt recalled past years when she had been obliged to deal with his creditors until he returned.

On August 31 Marcel left for Évian and the Splendide Hôtel, where he stayed until October 10. On the way he visited Avallon, Vézelay, and Dijon, packing enough rapid touring into these side trips to exhaust a healthy young man.[28] On the overnight train ride to Avallon, Marcel, accustomed to staying up all night and even more stimulated than usual because of his planned adventures, did not even consider the possibility of sleeping in the train. He was awed by the view of the sunrise, a spectacle he had not seen for a long time. In a letter to Georges de Lauris, Marcel described the sunrise as "beautiful, an inversion, more charming to my taste, of the sunset." Moving from one side of the train to the other, he gazed at the passing villages, some bathed in the first rays of sunlight, others still lit by the moon. The beautiful and strange lighting effects aroused in him "a wild desire to rape the sleeping little towns (don't mistake towns [villes] for girls [filles]!), those to the west in a dying remnant of moonlight, those to the east full in the rising sun, but I restrained myself and stayed on the train."

It was eleven before he got off the train in Avallon, where he visited the sights on foot. Then he hired a car to take him to Vézelay to visit the church of Sainte-Madeleine. He arrived, after a three-hour drive, in an incredible state. "Vézelay is a fantastic place, in a sort of Switzerland," he wrote Lauris, "all alone on a mountain towering over the countryside, visible from all directions for miles around, in the most strikingly harmonious landscape." He thought the "enormous" church resembled "a Turkish bath as much as it does Notre-Dame, but of alternately black and white stones, a delicious Christian mosque." As he entered the cool sanctuary, he felt "something curious and beautiful," which he promised to describe later in more detail.

When he returned to Avallon late in the evening, he had a fever so high that he was unable to go to bed. So, no doubt imprudently, he "walked about all night." At five in the morning he learned that there was a six o'clock train to Dijon, which he boarded. On the way he caught a glimpse of Semur, an "admirable medieval town." Proust did not tell Lauris whether he managed to nap in the train. If not, by the time he arrived in Dijon at ten o'clock, he had not slept for at least thirty-six hours. In this deplorable condition, he visited the museum, where he saw the enormous tombs of the dukes of Burgundy, in magnificent polychrome and much more impressive than the plaster casts of the tombs that he had seen. His final train did not reach Évian until eleven that night. His appearance had been so altered by "this frantic, sleepless race against illness" that he hardly recognized himself in the mirror; people in the train station asked him if he needed assistance. At the end of the letter to Lauris, Marcel turned to a new source of anxiety: his fear that Fénelon might be in danger because of terrorist acts committed by Bulgarian nationalists in Macedonia and the district of Adrianople.[29] He was worried sick about Bertrand's safety in the politically unstable region, and he wished that his friend would be posted to some safe haven in the Americas. In November, much to Marcel's relief, Bertrand was transferred to Saint Petersburg.

In September, while Marcel was vacationing at Évian, Constantin offered him the theater column in *La Renaissance latine*. He welcomed such an opportunity— and who better than he, rising from his bed a few hours before the lights went down in the theaters, to cover that nocturnal world of fantasy and masquerade? Having failed to win recognition as a serious writer of original works, Proust had long wanted a regular outlet in a respected publication, a forum that carried with it status and influence. The position of theater critic would reduce his expenses as well, for he would receive free tickets to all the openings.

Another of his society pieces, "Le Salon de la princesse Edmond de Polignac: Musique d'aujourd'hui, échos d'autrefois" (Music of today, echoes of days gone by), appeared in *Le Figaro* on September 6.[30] Proust, who signed the piece with his new pseudonym "Horatio," began by paying tribute to the late prince de Polignac and his accomplishments as a composer of religious music and melodies inspired by his forested estate at Fontainebleau. As proof of the prince's modernity, despite his deep interest in ancient music, Marcel described his design for what may have been the first sound and light show. During the playing of his compositions, his guests saw projected on the wall "behind the orchestra immense blowups of photographs taken in the forest." Horatio informed his readers that the prince was one of the earliest promoters of "today's innovations, combining music and projections, accompanied by music and recitations."

Proust mentioned the Polignacs' impressive art collection, which included Claude Monet's *Un Champ de tulipes près de Haarlem*—the painting that "Horatio" named as the most beautiful in the collection—and he provided an amusing anecdote of how the prince met his future wife by losing the bid on this painting to the wealthy American heiress. The prince courted and won the lady and her Monet.

Through her marriage Mlle Singer became the princesse de Polignac and a relative to a number of Paris's most exalted aristocratic hostesses, such as the duchesse de Luynes. The daytime concerts held in the Polignac music hall brought together, Proust observed, "a supremely elegant social bouquet," there to hear "perfect performances of ancient music," as well as the "latest compositions by Gabriel Fauré." The Polignacs' guests often heard Bach sonatas and Beethoven quartets, and it may have been there that Marcel heard for the first time Beethoven's late quartets. Proust-Horatio gave a literary bow in this salon to the three women he considered the most beautiful: Comtesse Greffulhe and the sisters Comtesse Anna de Noailles and Princesse Hélène de Caraman-Chimay, each "richly endowed with the double prestige of literary glory and beauty."

Proust observed that the prince de Polignac's ideas in literature, art, and even politics were so advanced as to be "miraculous," considering he was the son of Charles X's reactionary minister. He then expounded on atavism, using the example of a person who, though individual, bears unmistakable traces of his race or clan. The voice heard in the salon pieces belongs to Marcel the historian and social chronicler—Horatio, the loyal friend and royal attendant. This Horatio had yet to become a Prospero, the principal magician-narrator of a vast and splendid tale.

The Ruskin translations, with the hard discipline of mastering and transcribing another's thoughts and words into a different language, allowed Proust to examine meticulously another writer's preoccupations, aesthetics, and style. If he was writing no fiction, at least the Ruskin work and the "salons" allowed him to experiment with techniques that he was later to use—anecdotes, a bit of dialogue or costume, such as monocles—to construct a character. These society pieces, like everything he had written, were, without his knowing it, rehearsals for the future work.

Little is known about Marcel's stay in Évian. It is believed that, fired by his debates with Lauris over the Combes laws, Marcel began "La Mort des cathédrales" at this time. He also drafted an article on Dante Gabriel Rossetti that *La Chronique des arts et de la curiosité*, the supplement to Ephrussi's *Gazette des Beaux-Arts*, published in November. This essay was inspired by a study of Rossetti and Elizabeth Siddal in the May issue of *Burlington Magazine*.[31] In recounting the love story of these two painters and poets, Proust mentioned Ruskin's enthusiastic defense of the Pre-Raphaelite Brotherhood, of which Rossetti was one of the founders.

Sometime in September, Louisa and Albufera arrived in Évian. Proust joined them for an excursion to Chamonix. This outing may have been inspired by reading Ruskin, who, as Proust wrote, had found in "these marvelous mountain treks . . . the greatest joy" of his life.[32] Marcel and the young lovers mounted mules and ascended Montanvert, where they walked out on the sea of ice. It was one of those brief unpredictable episodes in his adult life when he enjoyed the activities of a healthy person in his prime. The trip to Chamonix sealed Marcel's friendship with Albufera; he began to address the marquis by his nickname Albu.

On October 10, on the way back to Paris, Marcel decided to visit another town with important medieval architecture. He sent Louisa a postcard from Beaune, where he visited the church of Brou and the Hospital of Beaune. After arriving in Paris, he heard from Reynaldo that Marie Nordlinger had returned. He immediately wrote to his "dear friend," telling her not to think that he had forgotten the "young Rose of Manchester." During the period of silence he had been on pilgrimages and had "carried across France, from Romanesque vestibules to Gothic chevets, an ardent curiosity and a more and more ailing body. And of the monuments I've visited, only the Hospital at Beaune was suited to my acute state of illness. I have no doubt that I would have been admitted as an emergency patient."[33]

Motivated by his love of architecture and the need to do original work, if only for newspapers and reviews, Proust wrote to Auguste Marguillier, who edited *La Chronique des arts et de la curiosité,* to inquire whether the article he had written about Charlotte Broicher's book on Ruskin had been published and, if so, how to obtain a copy.[34] In the postscript he came to the real point of the communication and told Marguillier that he had just returned from visiting the "churches at Brou, Avallon, and Vézelay, as well as the Hospital of Beaune!" If Marguillier or Charles Ephrussi needed articles of whatever kind on one of these monuments, he could at least aspire to bring to what he might write on them, minus the talent he modestly claimed not to possess, "memories fresh enough to be precise." His strategy failed; neither editor asked him for an essay on the monuments he had taken so much trouble to visit.

In mid-November, Marcel thanked Maurice Barrès for sending his new book *Les Amitiés françaises.* He had been particularly drawn to the book's evocation of a lost country, with its "mysterious grottoes of the past," a place both "real and ideal" and yet woefully unattainable, like his own lost childhood.[35] Now in his early thirties, Marcel knew that he should think of having his own apartment. Could he manage on his own? Fate was to play a role in his decision. On November 22 Marcel and his father had a silly argument over politics. Upset by what he regarded as Adrien's obstinacy and smugness, Marcel made some cutting, ironic remarks that he soon regretted.

Funeral March

At one o'clock on Tuesday, November 24, 1903, Adrien Proust left the house for the Medical School, where he was to preside at a thesis committee.[36] He told Jeanne that, on the way, he would stop at Robert's to check on Marthe, due to deliver any day. Robert, alarmed by his father's exhausted appearance, took Marthe aside and told her he thought it best if he accompanied his father. Only a few minutes after Adrien's committee began its work, Adrien, suddenly feeling unwell, went to the restroom, where he suffered a massive stroke.[37] When he did not return, Robert and his colleagues rushed to the restroom, where they had to force open the stall door and remove his unconscious father.

On the other side of the Seine, Adrien's elder son lay sleeping. At four o'clock voices in the corridor awakened Marcel. Annoyed at this infraction of the rule that while he slept everyone in the house was to keep silent, he rang the bell. His mother cracked opened the door and told him in the "sweetest" possible manner that he must not be angry because she had just received a phone call that his father had fallen ill at the Medical School and was being brought home on a stretcher. Robert soon arrived with the stretcher bearing his stricken father. The seriousness of Adrien's condition was apparent to all; there was nothing to do but wait and hope.

Word of Dr. Proust's stroke spread quickly among relatives and friends. Lucien called to inquire about Adrien's condition, but Marcel was receiving no one. He sent Lucien a note to say that his father was *très malade* and that his friend should not trouble to come again because Marcel would not leave his father's bedside. He promised to send news as soon as he knew anything definite about his father's condition. "Alas, I greatly fear it will only be sad tidings."[38]

On November 25, as the despairing family kept vigil, Robert received word that Marthe had gone into labor. She gave birth to a girl, the only grandchild Adrien and Jeanne were to have. Robert and Marthe named the baby Suzanne-Adrienne.[39] Robert might well have chosen the feminine version of his father's name for his daughter anyway, but when it became clear that his baby's birth would occur near the time of Adrien's death, it seemed doubly fitting as a tribute. For the moment the new father could think only of his father. Robert could take comfort in knowing that he had fulfilled his father's wishes and made him proud of his accomplishments.

On Thursday morning at 9 A.M. Adrien died. Marcel's friends came to comfort him or sent messages of sympathy and affection. The family made arrangements for the funeral service to take place on Saturday, followed by burial at Père-Lachaise cemetery, where Adrien had recently purchased a family plot. A long, front-page obituary appeared on Friday, November 27, in *Le Figaro*. On the day of the funeral, as the casket was being removed from the house for the ride to the church, an incident occurred that Proust later described in the *Search*:

> Imagine a room in which a man has died, a man who has rendered great services to his country; the undertaker's men are getting ready to take the coffin downstairs and the dead man's son is holding out his hand to the last friends who are filing past it; suddenly the silence is broken by a flourish of trumpets beneath the windows and he feels outraged, thinking that this must be some plot to mock and insult his grief; but presently this man who until this moment has mastered his emotions dissolves into tears, for he realizes that what he hears is the band of a regiment which has come to share in his mourning and to pay honor to his father's corpse.[40]

A large and distinguished crowd representing the government and the scientific community attended Adrien's funeral. Marie Nordlinger took her only day off work for the year to attend the service at Saint-Philippe-du-Roule. Marie observed the huge black palls, with the silver initial *P* in the center, hanging in the church. There were candles everywhere and countless immense wreaths. Later, she watched Marcel, "pale and unsteady," as he and Robert led the procession on foot to Père-Lachaise.[41] Along the way, those who listened heard the band playing a funeral march. Marthe, recuperating from a difficult delivery at her parents' home on the avenue de Messine, had not yet been informed of the family tragedy. On hearing the mournful music, she asked for whom it played. Her maid feigned ignorance, at which point Marthe observed, "Someone famous must have died."[42]

The graveside eulogy was given by Professor Debove, dean of the Medical School, to whom Adrien had once confided the words Debove now repeated to those who came to the graveside: "I have been happy all my life, I have only one wish left, to go away quietly and without suffering." Adrien would be remembered by the medical community as a man "ahead of his time, who had urged the creation of an international health organization."[43]

Adrien had not only achieved fame through distinguished service to his country and profession, but he had been successful in his social and family life. The penniless medical student who had gone on to become a brilliant scientist had been a financial success as well. When Adrien's fifty-eight-page will was probated, he had left a fortune whose net worth, not counting property in Jeanne's name, was

1,430,616 francs, the equivalent of nearly five million dollars in late twentieth-century value. Marcel and Robert each inherited 194,582 francs.[44] This amount, plus the 50,000 francs left to each of his great nephews by Louis Weil, gave Marcel a total of almost 250,000 francs, the modern equivalent of about $850,000.[45] This was a small fortune, but his mother, instead of allowing Marcel to become financially independent, continued to pinch the purse strings, giving him only a small allowance on which to live.[46] The exact sum that she gave him is unknown, but Proust remarked to a friend in the summer of 1905 that once he had paid his carriage bill, he had nothing left.

By early December, Marcel resumed work correcting a new set of proofs of *La Bible d'Amiens*, which he had decided to dedicate to the memory of his father.[47] He explained to Anna de Noailles that it was his mother who, on hearing that he had abandoned Ruskin, "has taken it into her head that this was the one thing that Papa desired, that he'd been looking forward to seeing it published any day now. So I've had to countermand instructions and now I'm starting again on the proofs, etc."[48] His resumption of the task seemed halfhearted, perhaps because he had hoped to begin work on original essays inspired by his recent trips. But there was nothing he wanted to do that really engaged and excited him.

He also abandoned the idea, which he would have been incapable of managing, of moving into his own apartment. After his father's death, Marcel vowed to devote himself to living with and for his mother. He would be alone with her; Robert had his career and a new family. Not long after the funeral, Marcel, lying in bed unable to sleep, explained in a letter to his mother his objectives and the challenges he faced in meeting them. He wanted to be her protector and constant companion. And he might have succeeded had not great obstacles—like the loss of a safety pin—prevented him from partially assuming his father's place as head of the house. Marcel believed that the pin, when fastened to his underpants, held his abdomen in and prevented stomachaches.[49] He wrote his mother about his good intentions, spoiled by the lost pin:

> My dear little Mama, . . . I'm writing you this note to tell you that I'm
> thinking of you. I would so much like, I so much want, to be able soon to
> get up at the same time as you do and drink my breakfast coffee with
> you. To feel our sleep and our waking distributed over the same hours
> would be, will be, such a delight to me. I went to bed at half-past one
> with that in mind, but then I had to get up a second time to go to the
> lavatory, and I couldn't find my safety pin (the one I use to close and

tighten my drawers). Naturally the night was over for me, there was
nothing to hold my stomach. I looked for another pin in your dressing
room, etc. etc., and succeeded only in picking up a bad chill from my
wanderings . . . but no pin. I went back to bed, but by then sleep was out
of the question. Now at least I while the night away with plans for an existence such as you wish, brought closer to you materially by living by
the same timetable, in the same rooms, at the same temperature, on the
same principles, with mutual approval, even though satisfaction, alas, is
now forbidden us. Forgive me for leaving the smoking room in disorder.
I was working hard up to the last moment.

He then instructed her to seal him off again from her life and that of the household:
"Make Marie and Antoine keep quiet and keep the kitchen door closed, so their
voices don't come through." Having dispensed with the thoughts of serious reform
and issued the orders for the resumption of his usual schedule, Marcel informed
his mother in a postscript: "I feel that I'll sleep very well now."[50]

Jeanne, of course, knew better than to rely on Marcel for company or for
practical assistance. She had always known that he depended far too much on her.
Would she have enough time to establish him on his own? Could there ever be
enough time? How would he manage without her? This was her greatest fear and,
now that Adrien was gone, her primary reason for living. Two letters written after
Adrien's death show that Marcel knew she sought the strength to live only for
his sake.[51]

The letters Marcel wrote his friends to thank them for their expressions of
sympathy have a common theme: he was now thankful that his illnesses had kept
him so close to his father. The letter to Montesquiou is typical: "Now I bless those
hours of illness spent at home, which during these last years enabled me to enjoy so
much of Papa's affection and company."[52] In an early December letter to Anna de
Noailles, he spoke about his relationship with his father: "You, who saw Papa only
two or three times, cannot know what a very sweet and simple man he was. I tried,
not to live up to his expectations—for I'm well aware that I was always the dark spot
in his life—but to show him my affection." Marcel recalled their quarrels, the "days
when I rebelled against the excessive certainty of his opinions, and the Sunday
before last, I remember, in a political discussion, I said some things I shouldn't
have. I can't tell you how sad that makes me now." He praised his father's nature, so
much "nobler" than his own complaining one. Although their lives would never be
the same, and he especially worried about his mother in her inconsolable grief, he

felt that "Life has begun again. If I had some aim, some ambition, that might help me to bear it. . . . But that's not the case."[53]

Marcel also wrote to Comte Joseph Primoli, thanking him for the expression of sympathy and voicing his concern about Princesse Mathilde's health. In July the seventy-three-year-old princess had suffered a fall that left her partially paralyzed. After commiserating with the count, who could only watch Mathilde's steady decline, Marcel turned to lighter matters and confessed—after swearing Primoli to absolute secrecy because "no one knew"—that he was Dominique. "I wrote the absurd article in *Le Figaro* on the Princesse. I was greatly amused that evening when you said—and how rightly so—in my presence . . . that the article was imbecilic!"[54] Proust exaggerated the need for secrecy, for Antoine, Madeleine Lemaire, and many others could identify Dominique.

He thanked Laure Hayman with all his heart for the "admirable flowers" and "for always being so kind to Papa. . . . I'm sure you'll remember him always. He spoke of you whenever he wanted to cite an example not only of youthful elegance and beauty, but also of intelligence, taste, kindness, tact, and refinement of feeling."[55] He repeated what he had written so many friends: "For some years, thanks to my poor health, which I bless, I had been living on much closer terms with him. . . . In this day-to-day life, I must have attenuated, sometimes in retrospect I have the illusion that I suppressed them altogether, certain traits of character or thought which may well have displeased him. So I think he was fairly well pleased with me."[56] Adrien had died without seeing proof that Marcel had a toughness, an ability to labor and sacrifice that could match or even surpass his own. In his last years Adrien was drained by overwork and illness but had refused to rest, serving still as an active member of commissions and teaching courses at the medical school. Proust later observed that his father's existence had been one of constant service to others, a life in which nothing is kept for oneself.[57]

Jeanne remained in deep mourning and later commemorated the dates of her husband's attack, death, and funeral. For a time she observed these every week, then every month. Marcel respected his mother's wishes and refused invitations for the twenty-sixth of the month. Although his grief was intense, he began to worry that his mother might never fully recover from her loss. A year after his mother died, Proust discovered among her papers a notebook in which she wrote down hour by hour the final illnesses of her father, her mother, and of her husband. Proust wrote that these accounts were "so distressful that, after having read them, it was difficult to go on living."[58]

A few weeks after his father's death, Marcel received a letter from Edmond

Jaloux, a stranger, who, a decade earlier at the age of fifteen, had read and admired his first stories in *La Revue blanche* and *Pleasures and Days*. Jaloux had discovered in Proust's short stories "observations about high society, succinct psychological analyses" that contained the qualities later called Proustian, and "little prose poems on the sea of memory that reminded him of those in Baudelaire's *Le Spleen de Paris*. Jaloux, who had recently published a short story, had seen in *Pleasures and Days* the promise of greatness where few or none had noticed such qualities.[59] Marcel wrote to thank him, saying that he was always "somewhat surprised" to learn that someone had read his book, especially because the publisher claimed that "no one had ever requested this work." Any author, Proust wrote Jaloux, should be happy to "write for a single, exquisite reader like you," and he added a Proustian analogy comparing Jaloux's contact with his book to pollen intended for "a single tree . . . a pollen useless to all others, but for it, singular."[60]

On Christmas Eve, Anna de Noailles wrote to Marcel from the château de Champlâtreux, where she was spending the holidays, to remind him of her friendship and affection. She encouraged him to work in order to "satisfy those who are here and those who are no longer here." She also praised his "precious and marvelous soul."[61] She sensed that Marcel was capable of greatness, if only he could overcome his physical and nervous disorders.

14 Broken Promises ☙

ON JANUARY 4 *LE FIGARO* PUBLISHED "Le Salon de la comtesse d'Haussonville" by "Horatio," in which Proust evoked the memory of his visit to Coppet. Four days later he attended the funeral of Princesse Mathilde, who had died after a long illness. Through stories heard in Mathilde's salon, Proust had collected vivid anecdotes of writers, artists, and personalities reaching back to the waning days of the Romantic era and the writers who came after them, the most important of whom for Proust were the critic Sainte-Beuve and the novelist Flaubert, as a master of prose style.

During the holidays Antoine told Marcel about his plans to go to Egypt and then travel on to join Bertrand in Constantinople. Jeanne had begun to encourage Marcel to embark on a long voyage without her. She feared that Adrien's death had provided Marcel with an even stronger pretext for spending most of his time with her, further undermining any serious attempt on his part to lead an independent life. Marcel, who was probably no longer capable of undertaking such a trip, remembered his and Antoine's aborted plans to travel together a year earlier and doubted whether Antoine would actually embark. Nonetheless, Antoine departed on January 9. It is unlikely Marcel would have accompanied him in any case; relations between Lecram and Ocsebib had recently reached a low point when they had quarreled, each accusing the other of betraying confidences. Marcel denied categorically that he had ever "violated tombs" and warned that on Antoine's return from Egypt he intended to have it out with him once and for all.[1] When Antoine returned in late March, Proust kept his word. In an accusatory letter he blamed Antoine for certain indiscretions and for having said a number of "truly odious things." Then he announced, "In the true sense of the word I am no longer your friend." He ended by offering Antoine the opportunity to maintain a cordial if more distant relationship, explaining that "since the core of my nature is sympathy, I recreate more readily in myself the tendencies that unite me to people than those which separate me from them forever." If he could ever render any service to Antoine, he stood ready to do so and asked him "to remember that in this exceptional and precise sense I remain Your devoted and grateful Marcel Proust."[2] Such breaks were more dramatic than real and almost always short-lived.

Writing to Anna de Noailles in early January, Marcel shared with her the memory of how his father used to bring him his mail, using a method of which his mother disapproved: "When Papa, who was as active as I am lazy and went out every morning, brought up the mail, he would say to me, knowing my joy: 'A letter from Madame de Noailles,' and Mama would scold him, saying: 'Don't spoil his pleasure by telling him in advance.' And I assure you it was a very touching comedy ... the air of supreme indifference Mama would assume when she brought up a letter from you, as if to say: there's nothing but trivial papers, so that my pleasure would be unalloyed."[3] This little scene of an endearing parental disagreement of how to treat their pampered son was later adapted for the *Search*, in which the Narrator leads an existence not dissimilar to Proust's own.

In his letter to Anna, Proust turned to matters of serious discord and expressed his annoyance with her brother Constantin, who had broken a promise. Constantin had offered Marcel a regular theater column in the *Renaissance latine* but had reneged and given the assignment to Gaston Rageot. Constantin had written Proust "insidiously" that "the decision to deprive me of the critic's appointment" had "been taken in my interest." Although Constantin would be happy for Marcel to contribute as frequently as possible to the review, he believed it would be better for Proust not to take on the responsibility of a regular column, certain to give him a great deal of fatigue and boredom. If Constantin were so concerned about his well being, why, Marcel asked Anna, did her brother not have the same scruples in September when he offered Proust the column?[4]

Anna took Marcel's side against her brother: "I am distraught, appalled, you are prodigiously right, and Constantin's thoughtlessness is so overwhelming that I seem to feel it covering me a little, giving me a sort of mask." She went on to say how "very sad" she was that he would not be writing a regular column for the *Renaissance latine,* because of the joy it would have been for her to read on the fifteenth of every month what he alone could write, that "marvelous mixture of irony and sweetness, like two opposing rivers gliding close to one another."[5] Even though Constantin's decision deprived him of the opportunity to contribute regularly, *La Renaissance latine* did, two years later, publish one of Proust's first pieces in which his mature voice is heard.

During the period when Proust was writing the society pieces for *Le Figaro,* he began to practice in a systematic way the difficult art of parody. On January 18 *Le Figaro* published his account, signed Horatio, of a party at Montesquiou's Pavillon des Muses, "Fête chez Montesquiou à Neuilly." Proust described the "feast" as though the account were written by one of his favorite authors, the duc de Saint-Simon, the prolific memorialist of life at Versailles under Louis XIV. Proust even gave his pastiche the subtitle "Excerpts from the *Mémoires* of the duc de Saint-Simon."[6]

Nothing could have pleased and amused Robert de Montesquiou more than a favorable comparison to the Sun King. As Proust playfully mixed personages of the final years of Louis XIV and Regency with those of his contemporaries, he showed Montesquiou playing the sovereign, merciless in drawing up his exclusive guest lists of the best and the grandest, dispensing rare favors, and casting offenders into disgrace. Many of Marcel's aristocratic friends—the ducs de Luynes, Noailles, and Gramont, the duchesse de La Rochefoucauld—could be depicted as their real ancestors. Proust used Saint-Simon's interest in genealogy to explain the connections between the Clermont-Tonnerre, Gramont, Guiche, and Greffulhe families, while paying compliments to each. He especially singled out Anna de Noailles, about whom he, in the guise of Saint-Simon, promised to say much more later, as though what he said here, in passing, did not suffice: "the finest poetic genius of her century and probably all the others, and who has renewed and . . . increased the miracle of the celebrated Sévigné."

The portrait of Montesquiou, as a grand seigneur, was flattering. Although the count was forty-nine, "Horatio" wrote that at forty, he appeared twenty, and, among other qualities, possessed the most brilliant mind and graces that were uniquely his. Proust included a remark that could have provided the count a clue to Horatio's identity. So superior was Montesquiou that "it was as hard to resist imitating him as it was difficult to succeed in doing so." The parody delighted Montesquiou, who suspected Proust was the author. When the count asked whether he had written it, Proust denied authorship. Was Montesquiou fooled by his denial? In a March letter to Anna, Marcel told her *silence tomb* that he had lied to Montesquiou about being Horatio. "But what do you think Montesquiou has done: he told me that, not having been able to find the author, he had had the article privately printed in a slim volume, making a few corrections to it, merely to the punctuation, he said. I didn't say a word, for fear of giving myself away if I protested, but what do you think of this coup? *Tomb, tomb, tomb.*"[7]

During January, as Proust hurried to finish *La Bible d'Amiens,* he consulted Marie Nordlinger by letter and in person on a number of thorny translation matters. She usually came to his house, for it was difficult for him to dress and be at her apartment before eleven in the evening. Growing weary of the enormous task of translating Ruskin, and unable to find help in any dictionary or from any English speaker about the meaning of certain obscure words and phrases—such as "Ironach, recalling the Thuringian armorial bearings of old"—Proust told Marie, "This old man is beginning to bore me."[8]

La Bible d'Amiens

Writing to Marie later in the month to set meetings to finish correcting *La Bible d'Amiens* proofs, he mentioned another Ruskin project, indicating that perhaps he had not yet had his fill of that old man. He had worked intermittently on the preface to his translation of *Sesame and Lilies,* the first part of which was about what and how to read. He told her that he had totally redone the draft she had provided, but he was being so scrupulous about his work that it would take him ten years to finish—not a pleasing prospect.

To express his gratitude for her aid, Marcel gave Marie his copy of Whistler's book *The Gentle Art of Making Enemies.* The volume, richly bound in gold-stamped leather, was one that Robert de Montesquiou had given Marcel. Rather than grant Marie's request to inscribe the book's fly-leaf—"It really is the book of too great a man to tolerate a name like mine"—he sent her a long poem, "a bit of nonsense," to slip inside the front cover.[9] Proust's admiration of Whistler, whose name he never managed to spell correctly in his letters, was genuine. When he was ready to create his fictional painter in the *Search,* Proust invented the name Elstir, in whose syllables one hears the clear echo of the way the French pronounce Whistler.

Even while struggling to finish *La Bible d'Amiens* for publication later in February, Proust found it hard to resist working on *Sesame and Lilies.* He fretted that he had found only a few of the missing notebooks containing his earlier work on *Sesame*. He sent these to Marie, explaining that the underscored words were those he was uncertain of, the ones left blank those he had not understood. "As for the nuances we will see later."[10]

Soon he wrote Marie again regarding *Sesame*, saying that he had been working exceedingly hard on the translation, redoing the entire beginning and first notebook. "I've written comments on several passages in this first notebook, comments intended to serve either for a preface or as notes. As soon as I'm in a fit state to receive you, I shall write, for I'm all on fire for *Sesame*—and for you."[11] Did Marie believe Marcel was declaring his love or passion for her?[12] If so, she was to be disappointed. In August, when she hinted that she was unhappy, Marcel showed concern and sent his wishes for her better days: "I feel that your letter itself is a charming trellis woven over something dark that I cannot see. Dear friend, I want you to feast on life . . . and not weep sadly beside an urn containing nothing but regrets."[13] The following month, when Marie had the opportunity to travel to America, he encouraged her to go, if the idea amused her and the financial arrangements were favorable. Surely, even if Marie had misread his "fire" for her and *Sesame*, she must have seen that Marcel had no romantic intentions toward her.

La Bible d'Amiens finally appeared on February 27, dedicated with tender affection to the memory of Adrien Proust, "stricken while working" on November 24, 1903. On the dedication page Proust quoted a Ruskin passage that seemed appropriate for his father: "Then comes the time of labour; . . . then the time of death, which, in happy lives, is very short."[14] Marcel and his mother imagined the pleasure Adrien would have taken in seeing this work at last in print as an homage to his memory and as proof of his son's erudition and perseverance. Proust had worked hard to complete the unabridged, annotated translation. In the preface he warned readers about Ruskin's at times difficult style and used it as a caveat and excuse for any errors his translation might contain. Although Proust's purpose in translating Ruskin's book on Amiens had been modest—to give readers "the desire to read Ruskin and revisit a few cathedrals"—the supplementary material was impressive.[15] Ruskin's own preface occupied five pages; Proust's took up ninety-two, most of the material coming from the articles he had published on Ruskin in 1900.

In addition to the preface, Proust contributed 190 original notes.[16] Sometime in 1903 he added a postscript to the preface in which he took issue with some of Ruskin's basic tenets.[17] It was a debate that he was to continue, in a more original form, in the preface to *Sésame et les lys*. Proust labeled Ruskin's fault idolatry. To make his meaning clear to his readers, he chose an example close at hand, whose name did not need to be mentioned: "To have done with idolatry, . . . I would like . . . to call upon one of our most justly famous contemporaries . . . who in his conversations, not in his books, shows this defect carried to such extremes that it is easier to recognize and show it in him without further need to take such pains to magnify it." Proust was speaking about Montesquiou, whose exhibitions of idolatry included his fetishes for objects that "belonged to Baudelaire, to Michelet, to Hugo," objects the count would enshrine "with a religious respect."[18]

Proust could have given as an example of idolatry his own gesture when he took and kept a pair of gloves that Whistler had left behind at a party one evening. But Proust portrayed himself to the readers of his preface as someone untainted by the temptations of idolatry: "No, I shall not find a painting more beautiful because the artist has painted a hawthorn in the foreground, though I know of nothing more beautiful than the hawthorn . . . because I know that the beauty of a painting does not depend on the things represented in it."[19] In order to "find this fragile part" in his "otherwise absolute admiration" for Ruskin, in order "to reproach Ruskin thus," Proust had "had to reach the utmost limits of sincerity" toward himself. Although his admiration for Ruskin remained profound, Proust made certain in his future writings to warn readers against confusing life (objects as fetishes) with art. He did so by showing characters who exhibit idolatry and thereby delude themselves. One of the most striking examples occurs when Swann notices the resemblance between Odette and a woman in a Botticelli painting. He then places a photograph of Odette on his desk and gazes at her as though she were a Botticelli. Making love to her, Swann believes, allows him to comprehend the great painter's art.

Once he received his copies of La Bible d'Amiens, Proust began immediately to inscribe the books for his friends. The inscription he wrote to Reynaldo thanked him on Ruskin's behalf for having composed a memorial elegy: "And it is I who thank you, O my little Reynaldo, O my greatest affection in life; you know that this little book was desdicated to you, as long as my little Papa was still alive. But he so wanted to see it appear that, now, I've decided to take it back from you to offer it to him."[20]

Marcel wrote to Lucien to explain why the dedication he had written in his copy of La Bible d'Amiens might seem more distant than he would have liked. Marcel still remembered how he and Lucien had been accused of being lovers by Lorrain eight years earlier. "I signed your copy of Ruskin at the same time as those of Mme Daudet and of Léon. I didn't put the word admiration in yours, for fear that, since you don't write, it might appear m. g. in the eyes of imbeciles." These initials stand for *mauvais genre* (bad form), but in the usage of Proust and Daudet meant "homosexual."[21] In the postscript he mentioned that his mother had returned from the "country yesterday, still very poorly."[22] While Marcel continued to worry about his mother's health and morale, she did her best to hide her illnesses from him. He later learned that she had been sick with renal colic caused by a kidney stone.

In Louisa de Mornand's copy Proust used biblical language and the etymology of her name to suggest the carnal attraction he felt for the young actress. The first sentence indicated that the inscription was not for all eyes: "*Dedication not to be left lying around.*" Proust declared that for men who have seen Louisa, but have had no success with her—that is to say everyone—other women ceased to be attractive. "Whence this couplet: He who Louisa cannot win / Must be content with Onan's sin."[23] Proust employed the archaic French verb *morner,* which meant to blunt a lance or to render it harmless by fitting a ring to its tip, a clear allusion to copulation. Proust's innuendos suggest that because Louisa refuses to "blunt mens' lances," they must resort to Onan's sin, masturbation.[24]

Sometime in early April, Louisa invited Marcel to her apartment, where he watched her read in bed before she fell asleep. Was he conducting research or engaging in vicarious fantasies or both? Louisa sent Marcel an autographed photograph from "The Original who is so fond of little Marcel. Louisa. April 1904." To express his gratitude for the photograph, which he was "mad about," he sent her a poem of thirty-three lines, in which he evoked the vision of her in bed.[25]

One recipient of an autographed copy of *La Bible d'Amiens* was a Mrs. Higginson, without whom, Proust wrote, he "never could have done the book." It was she, Proust informed Montesquiou, who had given him his first English lessons.[26] Referring to an earlier conversation with the count, Proust regretted a remark that may have led Montesquiou to conclude "that my translation wasn't mine alone. On the contrary I did it entirely on my own. I asked d'Humières for advice here and there, but the whole thing is mine, and rewritten twenty times."[27] Proust had, of course, received a great deal of assistance. The list of collaborators, if he were to include all those he consulted on various matters, would be quite long, with his mother leading the list, followed by, among others, d'Humières, Marie, Reynaldo, and Robert de Billy.[28] And yet, considering the definitive text, the preface, and Proust's own notes, there was some justification to his claim, the immodesty of which was not typical. Did he fear Montesquiou's ridicule or that the count, whose literary output was extraordinary compared to Marcel's, would spread the word in literary circles that Marcel could not even produce a translation on his own? Having heard that Yturri was quite ill, Marcel sought to reassure Montesquiou about his friend's health: "I remember that several years ago my poor Papa found him very ill. And you see how he recovered. I believe he would be wrong to worry, and you too."[29] Yturri's condition, the result of severe diabetes, was far more serious that Proust believed.

In the weeks following publication of *La Bible d'Amiens,* Proust sought to obtain as many press notices and reviews as possible. He instructed Anna de Noailles that if she should see Abel Hermant, who had recently rejoined *Le Figaro*'s staff, she should ask him to slip into the newspaper a word or two about Marcel's book. He further coached her to say that such a mention would give Marcel "great pleasure, for it might sell a few copies in which I have no financial interest but I should like the generous action of my publisher in bringing out the book not to be too disastrous for him. Since I produce a book every ten years, Hermant need not fear this precedent."[30]

On April 3 André Beaunier, writing as Le Masque de Fer (The Iron Mask) on *Le Figaro*'s front page, praised Proust's translation and referred to Marcel as "a young, talented writer," a category that must have pleased the author, who saw himself, at nearly thirty-three, as prematurely old and in danger of an early death.

Maurice Barrès was so impressed with Proust's *Bible* that he apparently urged the author to pursue a career as translator and suggested the works of Walter Pater. Proust wrote Barrès to dismiss the idea, particularly because he still intended to translate *Sesame and Lilies* and a volume of Ruskin's selected writings.[31] "As for Pater, I shall certainly not be the one who translates him. I still have two Ruskins to do, and after that I shall try to translate my own poor soul, if it doesn't die in the meantime."[32] It was nearly two years since he had complained to Antoine about failing to heed the call of "a thousand characters for novels, a thousand ideas" urging him to bring them to life, a dream he seemed no closer to realizing.

Henri Bergson wrote to thank Marcel for his copy of *La Bible d'Amiens* and expressed "the great pleasure he took in reading the preface. . . . It is written . . . in a language full of charm." In late May, Bergson delighted Proust by presenting to the Académie des sciences morales et politiques a short paper about *La Bible d'Amiens,* whose preface the philosopher called "an important contribution to the psychology of Ruskin." Bergson said that Proust's style was "so lively, so original, that one can hardly believe one is reading a translation."[33]

Late in the year Georges Goyau, the historian and critic, and Lucie Faure's husband, published anonymous positive reviews of *La Bible d'Amiens* in the *Revue des Deux Mondes* and *Le Gaulois.* Writing to thank Goyau for the article in *Le Gaulois,* Proust described the responsibility he bore Ruskin: "You know how much I admire Ruskin. And since I believe that each one of us has a responsibility for the souls he particularly loves, a responsibility to make them known and loved, to protect them from the wounds of misunderstanding and the darkness . . . of oblivion, you know with what scrupulous hands—but pious too and as gentle as I was able—I handled that particular soul."[34]

Handling that particular soul had also benefited Proust. While accepting many of Ruskin's aesthetic ideas and contesting others, he had honed his own. While writing the preface and notes, he had begun to develop an intermediate style between the sparse neoclassical writing of *Pleasures and Days* and the untamed lushness of *Jean Santeuil.* In the preface to *La Bible d'Amiens* is for the first time heard clearly, though intermittently, the timbre of the full and unique Proustian voice. His former history professor Albert Sorel had heard this sound and wrote about it in an article on Proust's translation.

One Sunday evening Marcel was leafing through J. M. W. Turner's book *The Rivers of France* when a friend arrived with the issue of *Le Temps* that contained Sorel's review of *La Bible d'Amiens.* Marcel wrote immediately to his former professor and expressed his gratitude and disbelief that "the great historian I so admired" had written a "whole big article about a modest translation by the most obscure of his pupils."[35] Sorel's description of Proust's style still stands: "He writes, when he is cogitating or musing, a prose that is flexible, floating, enveloping, opening on to infinite vistas or colors and tones, but always translucent, and reminiscent at times of those artefacts in glass in which Gallé encloses the intertwining tendrils of his lianas."[36] The voice that Sorel and others heard in Proust's prose was unique and remarkably rich. But Proust himself held serious reservations about this style, which seemed so unwieldy, if not useless, for the purpose for which he would most like to use it: the creation of a work of fiction.

In April, with spring in full bloom, Marcel reminded Marie Nordlinger that he could not dare venture out in the daytime—as though his friends thought this likely—because pollen always aggravated his asthmatic condition. This was why he had missed her the other day when she called. He had been sleeping when he heard the door bell ring, and "in the first stupor of wakening" had not asked who was there. By the time he learned that it was Marie, she had already gone.[37] Because Marcel could not go see the flowers, Marie found a clever and harmless way to bring a bit of springtime to his bedroom. She had gone to a store that sold Japanese imports and discovered tiny packets containing dried paper pellets that, when dropped into water, blossomed into flowers, houses, and doll-like figures.[38] Marie's Japanese garden delighted Marcel, who thanked her for "the miraculous hidden flowers which have enabled me this evening to 'make a spring of my own,' as Mme de Sévigné says, a fluvial and inoffensive spring. Thanks to you my dark electric room has had its Far Eastern spring."

He also thanked her for the "splendid" translation of *Sesame and Lilies,* which he would "go through carefully" and alter with "affectionate respect." He told her that she spoke and wrote French better than a Frenchwoman, but when she translated English "all the original characteristics reappear: the words revert to their own kind, their affinities, their meanings, their native rules." However charming this "English disguise of French words," might be, "all this life will have to be cooled down, gallicized, distanced from the original, and the originality extinguished."[39]

Marie was an artist, not a literary person. She was learning a lesson that had taken some time to register with Proust himself, later recognized as the modern master of the French language: translation is an incredibly difficult proposition. Ruskin's books were often lectures that had been published; these texts were thus written in a spoken style and often contained obscure terms. Rendering Ruskin's words in their French equivalent in a gracious, fluid style made Proust see more clearly the distinct and varied resources of his own language.

On May 13 *Le Figaro* published another society piece by "Horatio": "Le Salon de la comtesse Potocka," reputed to have been one of the most brilliant of the nineteenth century. In this piece Proust quoted a number of his favorite authors—Saint-Simon, Balzac, Stendhal, Baudelaire; he parodied Heredia and evoked a number of his contemporaries, including Barrès, Bourget, Montesquiou, Forain, Fauré, and his friend Reynaldo.[40] Comtesse Potocka, Proust soon learned, was displeased with his portrayal of her. He wrote to the countess, identifying himself at once—so that she would not think him cowardly—as the unintentional offender and promised not to reprint the salon in a collected volume until she revised it to her satisfaction.[41]

Marcel, usually the most sensitive person in the world regarding the feelings of others, seems to have been tone deaf when it came to this hostess, who was, of all those about whom he wrote, the one he knew least well. She had likely taken offense at the lines describing her "disdain for humanity" when she moved to Auteuil to devote herself entirely to taking care of her dogs, including the "poor, crippled strays that she took in." "Horatio" made the absurd claim that her love of the animals she adopted was so strong that "in order to care for them, she had not gone to bed for a year." Although the salon contained a number of Proustian compliments, the countess no doubt resented being portrayed as a misanthropic eccentric.

In late May, Marcel wrote Marie about the family's plan for a memorial to Adrien: "Mama would like, for those who come after us and who may wonder what my father looked like, to have a bust in the cemetery which would answer them as simply and accurately as possible." Jeanne intended to "ask some gifted and amenable young sculptor to be good enough to try, on the basis of photographs, to reproduce in plaster or bronze or marble the shape of my father's features. . . . *Would you care to be this sculptor?*"[42] Marie accepted the commission to produce the bust. She ultimately created a bronze medallion that seems to have satisfied no one completely, including the artist herself. Marcel also informed Marie that "Our *Sesame* will appear in *Les Arts de la vie* as soon as it is ready, but when will it be ready? *I'm re-doing it from top to bottom!* I haven't asked how much we shall be paid but I don't think it will be too bad for this review." This project could advance now because he had found all six of the missing notebooks in which he had kept detailed notes for *Sesame and Lilies.* He was thinking of dispensing with Ruskin's preface, which had been written as a general preface to the volume, whereas Proust intended to translate only the first two books.[43]

In June the prolific Anna de Noailles published a novel, *Le Visage émerveillé* (The enraptured face). Enraptured by her prose, Proust wrote immediately, citing a number of images of "perfect beauty," with which every page was covered. The following day, still bewitched by Anna's prose, he wrote again with more praise. Using Anna's novel as the lens through which to examine a novelist's craft, he had made an important discovery regarding a characteristic of major works of literature: one could hear in the author's words a particular sound or, using a painterly analogy, a certain varnish that distinguished an authentic and great literary narration. Proust called this unity of vision "the varnish of the Old Masters."[44] He had identified a quality with which he was to endow his novel, whose "unity" would be so "transparent" that a number of critics would claim not to see it. In one of the frequently quoted aphorisms from the *Search*, the Narrator says, "Style . . . is a question not of technique but of vision."[45]

He thought he recognized in Anna's writings what he had not yet found within himself, although there were soon signs that he was approaching his goal. A short time later he wrote to her again and identified what he had heard in *Le Visage émerveillé* and even more precisely in her poems: "And if the novel has the inimitable accent of your speech, where else but in your poems do we find the inner music

of your soul?"[46] As he wrote his own preface to *Sésame et les lys,* distancing himself
even further from Ruskin, Marcel began to hear, in the words he chose and
arranged, bits of exceptionally rich music that would later be called Proustian,
although for several years he remained skeptical about the quality and usefulness of
his new style.

On June 7 Proust made one of his rare daytime sorties to the Durand-Ruel
Gallery, where there was an exhibition that he "absolutely must see."[47] The irresistible temptation was a collection of thirty-nine paintings by Claude Monet, among
which was *Londres sous le soleil et le brouillard.* In the coming years as he elaborated
the *Search,* the affinities between Monet's and Proust's visions became apparent.
Proust took advantage of being out of bed and dropped by the Bernheim-Jeune
Gallery, where there was an exhibition of excellent paintings of Venice and Dieppe
by William Sickert, for whose catalog Blanche had written a preface that Proust
admired.

In late June, Louisa learned of Albufera's engagement to Anna Masséna d'Essling de Rivoli, daughter of wealthy Prince Victor d'Essling. *Le Gaulois* heralded the
match as uniting "two of the most distinguished families of the Empire nobility."[48]
Albu's engagement complicated his relationship with Louisa, who responded to the
news with a mixture of wild emotions: despair, jealousy, depression, and outrage.
Marcel stepped in and attempted to befriend Albufera and his unhappy mistress.
Louisa, who found her new role extremely difficult, did not understand that she
must become accustomed to seeing Louis much less often. Albu wanted to marry
well and secretly keep his mistress, while making certain that Louisa did not cause a
scandal that would threaten his marriage. The three friends spent a strained Sunday
evening together, during the course of which Louisa displayed her usual tactics
when Louis's jealousy had been aroused. After Marcel returned home, he sent the
actress some advice about how to behave in a changing relationship: "When, as this
evening, Louis has an unjust suspicion in mind . . . instead of . . . letting him think
what he likes, not deigning to justify yourself, or worse still, amusing yourself by an-
choring him in his misconceptions, show him clearly, gently, kindly, tenderly, that
he is absurdly imagining things, that he is unjust, absolutely on the wrong tack."

Marcel told her that in the past when the lovers had been needling each other,
he had kept silent because "it wasn't my business, and besides, lovers' quarrels are of
no consequence, and your relationship with Louis was in no danger of being
affected by it. Now things are entirely different."[49] The tempestuous scene Marcel
had witnessed at dinner between Louisa and her protector was like many he had

seen before. Observing these lovers—Louisa with the speech and manners of a cocotte, always performing whether on the stage or in the bedroom, and Albufera, an eligible, wealthy aristocrat whose life was spent in drawing rooms or at balls or in his château or in the regiment for the annual reserves training—provided Proust with many details that were to nourish the characters of the marquis de Saint-Loup and his mistress, the prostitute-cum-actress Rachel, in the *Search*. In that relationship, as in so many depicted by Proust, with substantial variations on the theme, obsessive jealousy played a prime role.

Marcel soon wearied of trying to explain and justify Louisa's and Louis's behavior to each other. In midsummer he wrote Louisa and explained that he found his role as mediator intolerable: "Allow me to no longer involve myself with matters that don't concern me, where I understand nothing, and where I am not free to give my opinion freely because each of you would blame me." He asked to withdraw, to return to the shadows from which he never should have emerged.[50] Marcel was to find it difficult to maintain his declared neutrality between the feuding lovers.

During the summer Marcel attended a number of parties to celebrate the engagements of Albufera and Armand de Guiche. One of the parties he had most wanted to attend was a dinner on July 14 at Vallière, the vast nineteenth-century château that was the Guiche country estate at Mortefontaine, north of Paris. But how would he get there? The twenty-five-minute train ride might provoke a severe asthma attack. This could be avoided only if he were willing to accept "unheard-of complications" and travel by automobile, which he feared would be just as lethal in a different way. As usual, Marcel shared his anxieties with his friends while seeking their advice, which he then ignored.

Marcel did attend the party at Vallière, along with approximately thirty other guests, including the comte de Cholet, who had been Proust's superior officer in the military. Marcel later said, as he often did after such exploits, that the trip to Vallière had "killed" him.[51] It had been worth the trouble, though, for not only did he enjoy himself, he collected a number of savory anecdotes, one of which he later used in the novel. He relished sharing these amusing stories with his friends, especially Fénelon, to whom he wrote shortly after the party: "When I arrived the Duc de Gramont asked me to sign the visitors' book which had already been signed by the other guests ... and I was about to append my signature underneath a tiny Gutman followed by an enormous Fitz-James and an immense Cholet, followed by a tiny Chevreau and an equally small Mailly-Nesle-La Rochefoucauld, when the Duc de

Gramont, filled with anxiety by my humble and confused demeanor (in addition to the fact that he knew I wrote), addressed me in a tone at once imploring and peremptory these lapidary words: 'Your name, Monsieur Proust, but *no thoughts.*' "[52]

The next story involved a trait of Marcel's, whose friends knew he enjoyed chatting with servants, concierges, and waiters. "Guiche's sister, Mme de Noailles, told me she was like me and loved chatting with 'inferiors,' her housemaid, her concierge," Proust wrote. "One day when she was speaking about this to her cousin Mme Léonino (Jeanne de Rothschild) she added: 'I feel I have the soul of a concierge. I don't know where I get it from. I must have had a skivvy ancestor.' And Jeanne Léonino, slightly hurt, replied: 'On the Gramont side, perhaps; but on the Rothschild side I can assure you no!' "[53]

At times the thought of all his friends who had married or, like Albu and Guiche, were about to, caused Marcel to reflect on his own life and his lack of a mate. In a letter to Antoine he noted that although he was seeing a lot of Guiche, Albu had been coming around "even more often than before if that's possible and is adorable to me. But I'm well aware that whatever he may say it cannot stay the same afterwards. Still I'm too fond of him to consider his marriage purely from my point of view."[54] Marcel wanted to be happy for his friend's sake, but he knew that he, like Louisa, would have to adjust his expectations and enjoy far less of Albu's time and companionship. He also wrote to Georges de Lauris that summer, remarking about how many of their friends were getting married and wondering whether he and Georges should follow their examples. His own answer was decidedly negative: "I have no taste for it."[55] Proust remained intensely curious about beautiful young society women but sought no romantic attachments with them.

At a dinner party at Anna de Noailles's, Marcel committed a blunder that he thought profoundly humiliating. He later described the incident in a letter to Antoine. Proust had scarcely arrived when he made a sweeping gesture with his hand and knocked over Anna's "finest Tanagra figurine," which fell to the floor and shattered.[56] Proust was mortified and vowed that he would never return to avenue Henri Martin until he had replaced the figurine, thus imposing on himself an exile that lasted nearly a year. The countess, with a poet's divining nature, preserved the broken pieces.[57]

Marcel also brought Antoine up to date on his health news, "since you're interested in medical matters and also like to think I'm a bit mad." He had consulted Dr. Pierre Merklen, a heart and lung specialist, who was considered the best in the field. The doctor told Marcel that his "asthma had become a nervous habit and that the only way to cure it was to go to an anti-asthmatic establishment somewhere in Germany where they would (for I probably won't go) 'get me out of the habit' of my asthma just as they 'demorphinize' morphine addicts."[58] This diagnosis, which certainly cannot have been one that Proust welcomed, seemed to confirm the opinion of his father and Dr. Brissaud.

Having reported his many recent social engagements to his friend, he feared that Antoine might have the impression he had done nothing recently except attend dinner parties. Quoting Ruskin in English from *The Bible of Amiens,* he told Antoine that his social life was but "the apparent life," while "the real life is underneath all this."[59] This concept of a superficial social self, the one visible to one's friends, hiding a private self with rich subterranean fields, was one that more and more occupied his thoughts.

In August he exchanged several letters with Marie, who had rented a summer house in Auteuil, about the medallion of his father. She had already brought the heavy object to the house on one occasion, but he had been unable to rise from the bed. Now that he was about to leave on a yachting trip with Robert de Billy and his wife's family, he suggested that she come on August 8 at 9:30 A.M. with the medallion, if that was not too difficult. His mother would see her back to Auteuil and he would "get up for five minutes to shake hands with you."[60]

Sometime in August, Marie gave him a small watercolor, painted at Senlis in 1898, of a landscape he had admired. He hung her picture by his bed, where it reminded him of one of the "prettiest things I have ever seen . . . once in the country . . . a patch of sky and landscape with a carefully chosen clump of fraternal trees."[61] Proust's fascination with trees and flowers, which he seldom saw except in pictures and drawings, was to provide him with key elements for the Narrator's quest.

This Yachting Life

While his mother vacationed at Étretat on the Normandy coast with Robert, his wife, and baby Adrienne, Marcel accepted Robert de Billy's invitation to go sailing along the northern coast of Brittany on his father-in-law's yacht *Hélène.* Just before leaving for Le Havre, Marcel received the proofs from *Le Figaro* for his article "La Mort des cathédrales." In his usual predeparture stricken state, Marcel returned the proofs without bothering to read them. At Le Havre, Marcel's host, M. Paul Mirabaud, met him at the station and took him by cab to the harbor. Mirabaud, governor of the Bank of France, struck Marcel as being in excellent health. In his first letter to his mother he described the banker as an imposing figure, "magnificent, a huge and powerful Saxon god" with the bluest eyes.[62] Marcel was apparently the only male guest on board. The other passengers were Mme Fortoul, "extremely nice," Mme Jacques Faure, "very pretty," Mlle Oberkampf, who merited no description in the letter to Jeanne, and Mme de Billy "who is charming to me and charming in general."[63]

After a tour of the large, steam-powered yacht, Marcel settled into his cabin at 1 or 2 o'clock in the morning. An asthma attack prevented him from sleeping; he felt so miserable that he did not even undress. Even a dose of Trional at 3 in the morning brought no relief; still awake at 5, he arose and went up on deck, two hours before the yacht set sail. Once they were under way, he improved. Marcel took breakfast, and his asthma eased as the *Hélène* headed out into the calm sea in fine weather. The sea air seemed to increase his appetite, enabling him to enjoy a "big lunch at 12:30," which seemed to make his asthma subside even more. After twelve hours of sailing, at 7 P.M. the boat arrived off Cherbourg. Although the next day "turned out fine again," Marcel missed "the charm of sailing" once they were anchored. He considered leaving the sailing party and taking the train to Paris the following morning, with stops at Caen and Bayeux, to visit the medieval churches described by Ruskin.

Toward the end of the next letter to his mother, Marcel spoke about the special oneness he felt with her as he wrote, although he knew she was far away and would not actually read his letter until the following day: "I speak to you in my imagination a hundred times a minute and hug you no less often." Since his father's death, Marcel had worried even more about her health. Knowing himself to be helpless in that regard, as in so many others, he urged her to talk to Robert about her health whenever she had reason. Although Marcel lived "in close proximity" to her, it was with his "eyes closed." He felt compelled to give her advice about consulting Robert because he knew that unlike him, she did not like to complain and might well "have pains, kidney troubles," without his being aware of it at all. He reminded her that last winter she had been ill without his knowing about it. "So do at least put my mind to rest by always talking to Robert in detail about these things."[64]

As for him, her love remained his surest remedy: "Since writing to you I've warmed up and no longer have any asthma. As in an opera, you were bending over me as I wrote, and the soothing effect of our conversation removed the last traces of oppression." He had only wanted to send her one of "my usual bulletins in which I never tell you anything but the worst so that you know what curve I never went below." He proposed to save the best stories from his trip, "all the beautiful sights to do with nature or people," for their "cozy heart to heart chats, punctuated with kisses."[65]

Marcel decided to stay on board a few more days. A photograph taken by Billy shows him sitting in a deck chair and engaged in conversation. He is wearing his gray overcoat, a boater, and a scarf. Billy remarked that Proust made a poor subject for a photograph because it was difficult to get him to stop talking long enough to take his picture.[66] As luck would have it, M. Mirabaud, who had appeared so fit, became ill. The banker had recently suffered a heart attack and been resuscitated by Dr. Merklen, the specialist Proust had consulted. Mirabaud, wishing to be prudent, ordered the *Hélène* to remain at anchor for two days at Dinard while he rested. On Sunday evening, August 14, Marcel, having remained on board the yacht for the better part of a week, left and returned to Paris. Proust later described succinctly his yachting trip to Antoine: "Pretty boat, pretty sailing, pretty women."[67]

Perhaps some of *Le Figaro*'s readers who thought of Proust as a society-page writer were surprised, when "La Mort des cathédrales" appeared on August 16, to find in him an able polemicist willing to engage in political debate.[68] In May 1904 the French government had broken off relations with the Holy See and recalled its ambassador to the Vatican.[69] In his article Proust stated his fear that "these cathedrals that are the highest and the most original expression of French genius" would become meaningless museums without the religious ceremonies for which they were constructed. Proust advanced a number of religious, aesthetic, and nationalistic arguments, appealing both to common sense and French pride. One can prefer another country's literature, music, or painting, he argued, "but it's in France that Gothic architecture created its first and most nearly perfect masterpieces. Other countries have done nothing but imitate our religious architecture, without being able to equal it." If theaters and museums were subsidized by the state, surely the cathedrals merited as much. The liturgical ceremonies were of "such historical, social, artistic, and musical interest" that "only Wagner had approached its beauty, by imitating it in *Parsifal.*"

Proust, who had grown quite knowledgeable after years of studying Gothic architecture, the Bible, and French medieval history, explained the symbolism of the various Christian sacraments and showed how the architecture, including the stained-glass windows populated by biblical figures and medieval French citizens, related to Christian faith and daily life in the Middle Ages. "Never," he observed, "has a comparable spectacle, has such a gigantic mirror of knowledge, of the soul and of history been offered to the eyes and intelligence of man."[70]

After the article appeared, Proust was horrified at the misprints the piece contained and regretted the mistakes, about three per line, that he had not bothered to correct before leaving for Le Havre. As he unburdened himself to Georges de Lauris, Proust nearly disowned the article, which he had not sent his friend "because I thought it very bad." He characterized it as inaccurate, ingenious, and "overloaded with spurious poetry." Perhaps writing about cathedrals and Catholicism had made him consider religious beliefs and the question of eternal life. Immortality was clearly a subject that he and Lauris had discussed. Proust, unlike Lauris, found the prospect intoxicating: "Would it not be sweet to find again, beneath another sky, in the valleys vainly promised and fruitlessly awaited, all those one has left or will leave behind! And realize oneself at last!"[71]

In late August, Proust answered a questionnaire regarding the role of the state in supporting the fine arts that was sent to "personalities in the field of art, literature and politics" by the journalist Maurice Le Blond under the aegis of the review *Les Arts de la vie*. Marcel did not return the questionnaire to Gabriel Mourey, the review's editor, because he believed that his answers would displease Le Blond, whose motives Proust found suspect. Mourey and Le Blond had a mission: the suspension of state funding of two institutions that taught the fine arts, the École des Beaux-Arts and the French Academy in Rome.[72] Proust instead drafted a letter to Le Blond, which afterward he decided not to send. His remarks are interesting from two perspectives: that of the debate over the state's role in subsidizing instruction in art and, on a more personal note, his opinion about an artist's need for freedom and discipline. "Whether or not the State has 'the *right*' to subjugate artistic personality, . . . in no circumstances will it ever have the *power* to do so." Then, although he did not mention Ruskin, he referred to his own long submission to the influence of the English writer, an apprenticeship he saw as positive: "What *can* subjugate the personality of an artist is . . . the beneficent force of a more powerful personality—and that is a servitude which is not far from being the beginning of liberty."

In his preface to *La Bible d'Amiens*, Proust had attempted to explain why the time and energy he had spent on Ruskin had not been lost: "Mediocre people generally believe that to let oneself be guided by books one admires takes away some of one's independence of judgment. 'What is it to you how Ruskin feels: feel for yourself.' Such an opinion rests on a psychological error" that will be dismissed by those who, having submitted to such influence, "feel that their power to understand and feel is infinitely increased" without ever paralyzing their critical sense. "We are then simply in a state of grace in which all our faculties, our critical sense as much as our other senses, are strengthened. Therefore, this voluntary servitude is the beginning of freedom. There is no better way of becoming aware of one's feelings than to try to recreate in oneself what a master has felt."[73]

Proust believed that an artist needed discipline more than any other attribute: "I believe we are indeed dying, but for lack of discipline not of freedom. I don't believe that freedom is very useful to the artist and I think that, especially for the artist of today, discipline would be as entirely beneficial as it is for the neuropath." Rather than the state, the great tyrant was love because "one imitates slavishly what one loves when one isn't original. The truth is that there is only one real freedom for the artist: originality. The slaves are those who are not original, whether the State interferes with them or not. Do not try to break their chains; they would immediately forge new ones." Writing to Gabriel Mourey in September, Proust referred again to the debate about government's role in art, a question he found pointless to begin with, for he was convinced that "one produces the art of one's temperament."[74]

A Case History

In September, Proust wrote to Dr. Georges Linossier, a friend and colleague of Adrien's, who specialized in gastric disorders. Marcel's original purpose in writing Linossier was to make a simple inquiry, intended as a substitute for a visit unless the doctor would be willing to examine him late in the evening. By the time Marcel finished he had written a twelve-page letter, whose length and details so "overwhelmed" him "with embarrassment at my importunateness" that he dared not mail it.[75] Written in a straightforward manner, this statement is the fullest account we have of Proust's self-diagnosis. It reveals a number of rituals, some of which he eventually gave to the famous comic character Aunt Léonie, a neurasthenic modeled on Proust himself. One such ritual was the consumption of Vichy water, about whose properties Linossier, who practiced at Vichy, should have been well informed.

First Proust wrote about his complicated case: "I am . . . from the medical point of view, many different things, though in fact no one has ever known exactly what. But I am above all, and indisputably, an asthmatic." He then described the origin of his asthma in hay fever, that at first seemed seasonal but then bloomed into "a more or less all-the-year-round ailment." Where Linossier's knowledge might be especially useful was in analyzing the relation between his asthma and his diet, the bizarre nature of which had evolved as a means of controlling his asthma as much as possible: "I eat one meal every 24 hours (. . . two creamed eggs, a wing of roast chicken, three croissants, a dish of fried potatoes, grapes, coffee, a bottle of beer) and in between the only thing I take is a quarter of a glass of Vichy water before going to bed (nine or ten hours after my meal). If I take a whole glass I am woken up by congestion; *a fortiori* if instead of Vichy it's solid food." He then came to the second ritual, the need for his underpants to be tightly bound by a pin to prevent digestive problems: "Asthmatic breathlessness is my only form of trouble. That is the advantage of my strange diet." He observed that when he used to eat several meals and drink between meals, he "constantly suffered dissension, wind, and other discomforts which no longer exist."[76] During the recent period when he had tried to reform, he had managed to take two meals a day. But his digestion operated so slowly that he "found it almost impossible to go to bed because of the number of hours (eight) I'm obliged to spend up (or on a chaise-longue) after a meal." Such efforts also increased his breathlessness, sent more blood rushing to his head, and made him less well than when he followed his own strange regimen.

He also wanted advice about the kind of treatment Dr. Merklen had recommended. Was such a "psychotherapeutic treatment" really necessary "in order to modify" his "pernicious living habits"? He tried to imagine himself undergoing such treatment, which consisted of "isolating the patient, immobilizing him, feeding him up and curing him by persuasion." He wanted to avoid a clinic whose practitioners held to the theory that "all gastric troubles are nervous in origin" and thus were unable to evaluate objectively a patient's condition. Marcel then provided details to give Linossier a clearer idea of his arthritic condition. "My urine shows a marked excess of urea, of uric acid, and a diminution of chlorides. The analysis I had done added imponderable traces of albumin and sugar, but I believe this quite temporary. I have been urinating very little for several years. After twelve days on a milk diet I did not produce half a litre in twenty-four hours."[77]

His bowel movements, Proust went on, were frequent but generally unsatisfactory, and he went "to the privy, always several times running." He offered to have his stool analyzed if the doctor thought that would be useful, but in the meantime he provided a description, saying that his stool "varies according to his different states of health" and frequently contained mucus. Every two weeks he took a powerful laxative in the form of a cascara pill, downed in the middle of dinner, "which makes me go to the privy seven [or] even more times during the following twenty-four hours." As for enemas, he had abandoned them "because they bring me out in the most unbearable sweat."

A third ritual, not mentioned in the letter to Linossier, involved a process he called "cooling down," a slow emergence from his bed that allowed his body to adapt gradually to room temperature. Marcel believed that this process prevented colds and the onset of asthma.

Marcel began rounds of conversations with friends and his mother about where to vacation in the fall, a decision that was more complicated than usual because Albufera and Guiche both had planned their weddings to take place during the fall holiday season. He consulted various friends about Dinard, Trouville, and other spots in Brittany and Normandy. In a letter to his mother he listed the advantages and disadvantages of each destination. Trouville was only a four-hour train ride; at Évian he would be more rested and feel more at home. But at Trouville he would find friends (Mme Straus and Charles Ephrussi) who had automobiles. He might consider going to Dieppe with his mother when she left on September 20. It was an easy train ride from Rouen, where there were frequent trains to Paris, but it would no doubt be overrun with English tourists. Paralyzed by indecision, Marcel remained at home.

Jeanne spent her first vacation alone in Dieppe at the Hôtel Métropole et des Bains. Although being at the seashore without a companion must have been a melancholy experience, she told Marcel only about the good exercise she took every day and how, despite the strong wind and unusually cold temperature, she enjoyed bundling up and making her daily rounds, stopping for little ten-minute breaks whenever there was a little sun. "But Dieppe is exceptionally well arranged for these healthy walks (for it's very good for me to be forced to walk). By the time one has covered the length of that immense esplanade—visited the pier—been to the post—bought a newspaper—everything is so far from everything that my walk is done."[78]

While Jeanne was away, Marcel tried again to reform his hours. Many of these attempts might appear comical had he not been seriously concerned about his condition and how miserable it made him. Recently, attempting to rise earlier than usual—that is, early in the afternoon—he had tried taking tea in bed at 3:30. The cook Marie, feeling ill, had retired to her room. Because he knew that his mother disapproved of Félicie's staying by him, he got up to eat dinner. Having left his bed sooner than intended, he had not had time to cool off, and he ran into the dining room, hoping to keep warm. Alas, no fire had been laid, and he did not know where to go.

For whatever reason, "because of this coldness, fatigue from not having rested, an indescribable malaise set in, sore throat, despair, inability to move, unbelievable pulse, etc. etc." Had he experienced a panic attack, or was this the onset of a real illness? In any event his barber François, whom he had summoned to cut his hair, saw that he was in no shape for a trim and left.[79] Marcel apologized for giving his mother such a dreary report: "I realize how boring it must be to hear all this talk of health. I assure you that when you're here I shall never talk about it again." He changed the subject to a tragedy involving a friend, telling her in absolute confidence, "It was for Gabriel de La Rochefoucauld that Mme des Garets killed herself." The lady, on hearing news of Gabriel's engagement, had shot herself through the heart.[80]

He wrote his mother on September 24, marking the ten-month observance of his father's death. It seemed like yesterday, he wrote, despite their "habit of constantly looking back to that day and to all the happiness that preceded it, the habit of regarding everything that has happened since as a sort of mechanical nightmare.... Such thoughts are less painful when we are near one another but when, as we two are, one is linked by a sort of wireless telegraphy, whether more or less near or more or less far one is always in close communion, always side by side." He had some good health news; he had had his urine checked again and this time there was no trace of sugar or albumin.[81]

His mother replied to his apology for constantly talking about his maladies by assuring him that she could never be bored by anything he had to tell her: "You are wrong, darling, your letters are *all* charming, *all* appreciated by me as I appreciate my little pet from every point of view." Then, vexed that he had dismissed his barber and often paid too little attention to how he looked, she gave him some motherly advice: "Do look after your appearance. If you have to get dressed in the daytime make sure your clothes are immaculate. But above all no more of that looking like a Frankish king—your hair gets in my eyes when I think of you. I hope by the time I finish this you'll have had it done."[82] His mother received news a few days later from her son that he had a toothache, but because his asthma exhausted him, going to the dentist was unthinkable, nor could he consider having the dentist come to him.[83]

In the meantime Marcel had managed to inspect the "splendid column" that his mother had selected at an antique dealer's and had made into an Empire lamp for him to give Albufera as a wedding present. The sight of this gift had "amazed, enchanted, overwhelmed" him.[84]

Marcel postponed treatment he considered indispensable in order to attend Albufera's marriage on October 11, but he missed the ceremony because of illness. Three days earlier he had visited the home of Prince Joachim Murat, whose wife was the bride's aunt, to attend the reception following the signing of the marriage contract. As a present to Marcel on the day of the wedding, Albu sent him a handsome cane inscribed with Proust's initials, those of the bridegroom, and the wedding date. During the difficult period of the honeymoon, Proust resumed the role of the "post office" through which Albu and Louisa communicated. Albu had decided to combine honeymooning with a literary pilgrimage by retracing the journey from Paris to Jerusalem as laid out by Chateaubriand in *L'Itinéraire de Paris à Jérusalem.*

Ten days after the wedding Louisa sent Albufera a wire in which she claimed that it was "beyond her strength to bear this voyage." After accusing him of "having chosen the most terrible of separations for me," she warned him "in all sincerity that life seems to me impossible to endure in these conditions."[85] Albu panicked and, perhaps picturing her already dead like Mme de Garrets, alerted Proust. Marcel consoled, reassured, and advised both the abandoned mistress and the honeymooning Albu. While Albu and his bride journeyed toward Athens, Proust sent telegrams addressed to "M. Thecus," an anagram of Albu's family name Suchet.[86] When it seemed obvious that the crisis had ended, he advised Albu: "At every moment of your voyage think only of making your wife as happy as possible. God will reward you for it."[87] The consolation Marcel offered Louisa was more down to earth: he sent her Trional with recommended dosages and offered to provide names of doctors she might consult.[88] During the late summer and fall Marcel consoled Louisa, meeting her occasionally for dinner. He wrote a cameo portrait of her for *Gil Blas* and was instrumental in landing her a role in a play, *Maman Colibri* by Henry Bataille, to whom Proust had introduced Louisa.

Marcel's poor health had caused him to miss Albu's wedding; now his asthma prevented him from attending the openings of two plays by friends. Writing to Antoine Bibesco on October 5, when *Le Jaloux* was in its final rehearsals, Proust told him that an outing two days earlier had provoked a terrible asthma attack. Part of the portrait he had written of Antoine for the occasion was published in *Le Figaro* on October 8, the day of the dress rehearsal. In the postscript, he stressed again his deplorable condition: "I am at present extremely unhappy from every point of view, morally, physically, intellectually." He asked Antoine to stop by and see him, but only in the evening.[89]

By late October he was busy correcting proofs for his translation of Ruskin's *Of Kings' Treasuries,* the first lecture in *Sesame and Lilies,* due to be published in 1905 in installments in *Les Arts de la vie.*[90] In November he resolved again to reform his hours. He would attend Guiche's wedding and take advantage, he wrote Lucien, of the rare daytime sortie to do a slew of "important and secret things" he had always postponed, chief of which was to see a doctor. "From that day forward my life will be settled one way or the other." His outlook optimistic, he told Lucien that no longer would his friends have to see him "in a disagreeable manner that makes you go out at hours when you would prefer to remain at home." He mentioned his wedding gift to Guiche, a folly because it cost so much: a revolver in a leather case that he had commissioned Coco de Madrazo to paint and inscribe with verses from the bride's childhood poems.[91]

On the day of the wedding Marcel did attend to practical matters, but it is not clear whether he saw a doctor, as promised. He called at the Mercure de France, where he urged Vallette to publish Mme Peigné-Crémieux's translation of Ruskin's *Stones of Venice*. The translator was a relative of Mme Proust's. He may have also obtained information about the cost of having the family grand piano adapted to the Aeolian Company's new device that would allow the instrument to serve also as a player piano. Marcel gave Albu instructions to have the necessary work performed, but for some reason the installation was postponed.

At the wedding Marcel chatted with the bride's beautiful mother, Comtesse Greffulhe, who proudly recited to him some "sublime" lines from her daughter's poems.[92] Marcel informed Mme Greffulhe that Guiche "had envisaged" the marriage to the countess's daughter "as a possible means of obtaining her mother's photograph. She laughed so prettily that I felt tempted to repeat it ten times over." Marcel hoped that his friendship with Guiche "might earn me the same privilege."[93] At the wedding he also saw Anna de Noailles for the first time since July 17, the day of the Tanagra figurine fiasco.

Proust soon received the sort of invitation that he had begun to dread: a summons from Montesquiou to attend his lecture on Japanese engravings. When Proust declined, using the proximity of the date to the anniversary of his father's death as a reason, Montesquiou refused to accept his excuse: "I don't think there can be a better way of celebrating [such anniversaries], and one more in keeping with the inclinations of those who are no more (or who, rather, are elsewhere), than not to turn one's back on a new occasion to thrill with harmony." The count was convinced that if Marcel had consulted his "good and intelligent mother, if you had opened your heart to her on the matter," she would have agreed with Montesquiou's opinion. Ruminating on Marcel's transgressions while thinking of the profit Marcel or anyone might derive from hearing his voice, he reminded Marcel of how he used to imitate him in public: "You claim to possess *all my vocal secrets.* Allow me to disabuse you, or at least persuade you that a certain something will always be missing from these phonetic reproductions. An illusion which may perhaps give me some hope of seeing you again!" In his postscript, perhaps intended to threaten Marcel with extinction among the social elite, Montesquiou referred to noble relatives of high rank who were now "dead" because he had quarreled with them. Using the royal *we* in an example of hauteur worthy of Charlus, he remarked, "The death of Mme de Brantes grieved us *very much* in spite of everything. Whereas that of Mme d'Eyragues leaves us *absolutely* indifferent."[94]

Pricked by Montesquiou's goading, Marcel hastened to defend himself by providing the usual dismal status of his health, while making light of his past imitations, intended only as a homage to the count's genius: "As for . . . my 'Imitations,' they were never more than scales, or rather vocal exercises, making no claim to convey a melody or anything of the genius of the original; better still, they were simple exercises and admiring games . . . naïve canticles in which a youthful admiration exercised and indulged itself."[95] Such admiration had disappeared long ago and was never to be revived.

In the days surrounding the first anniversary of his father's death, Marcel spent evenings sitting up late with his mother. On November 25, the day before the anniversary, he went to Père-Lachaise cemetery and placed flowers on his father's grave. He caught a cold and renewed his determination to see a doctor. He would continue, however, to postpone the visit, even after he became alarmed on reading in Dr. Brissaud's book on asthma that each attack upsets something in the body and hastens death.

Sometime that fall Proust received an unexpected present from Bertrand de Fénelon in the form of "splendid reproductions which are doubly precious to me because of my admiration for Vermeer and my friendship for you." He apologized for taking longer than intended to thank Fénelon, but assured him that he was "often in my thoughts." Just the other day he had written and discarded a letter asking Bertrand's advice, "but I was afraid you might think I was indulging in puerilities which are quite incompatible with my age and which you already found ridiculous when you were the object of them."[96] Who the object of these "puerilities" might have been is unknown. Marcel's assumption that he had outgrown such childish infatuations was overoptimistic.

Proust mentioned a mysterious woman, the "mistress I most loved," in a letter to Gabriel de La Rochefoucauld. He did so in the context of reviewing the manuscript of Gabriel's novel, *L'Amant et le médecin* (The lover and the doctor), in which Proust objected to Gabriel's psychology regarding jealousy:

With my particular temperament, my specific jealousy, what would have made me jealous at once is "Let's just be friends," which I'd have interpreted as an admission of satiety, a mark of indifference, a sign of repulsion. I shall never forget the day when those words were said to me by the mistress I most loved. If I acquiesced, after some resistance, it was from pride. But I considered that from that day onwards her desire for my body had been replaced by desire for another. It was the beginning of our rupture. For years afterwards, years of tenderness and chaste kisses, we never once alluded to that moment, to my caresses, to anything that might have come near to the forbidden spot, the painful scar on my heart. Now, all that has been succeeded by such indifference that I recently hazarded a jesting advance, and she said to me quite harshly: "Don't do that, it's wrong."[97]

This is the most direct testimony we have about how Proust experienced love and jealousy. We do not know who the mysterious woman was, and, given Proust's bizarre schedule and the many letters to friends in which he speaks about his affection, there is no credible candidate for this most beloved mistress. One cannot resist the suspicion that the person described here was not a woman at all but rather Reynaldo Hahn, or perhaps Lucien Daudet, because what we know about Proust's relationships with both men fits the pattern described.[98] His infatuations with Antoine Bibesco and Bertrand de Fénelon did not apparently reach the same degree of intimacy as his earlier attachments.

15 *The Only Honey of My Life* ∿

IN FEBRUARY 1905 MARCEL WROTE TO Marie Nordlinger to thank her for sending him a copy of the English original of *Whistler's Ten O'Clock: A Lecture.* She had been traveling with the American railway tycoon Charles Land Freer, an art collector and a friend of Whistler's.[1] Marcel told Marie that he had begun translating *Of Queens' Gardens,* which he had decided to add to *Sésame et les lys.* During her absence his "old and charming English scholar . . . will act as my 'Mary.' "[2] The scholar was apparently Charles Newton Scott, who had been a friend of Ruskin's.[3] He reminisced about the one time he saw Whistler: "I made him say a few kind words about Ruskin! and appropriated his handsome grey gloves which I've since lost." Marcel asked Marie to tell Mr. Freer about his interest in Whistler: "In my intentionally bare room there is only one reproduction of a work of art: an excellent photograph of Whistler's *Carlyle* in a serpentine overcoat like the dress in his portrait of his mother. The more I think about the theories of Ruskin and Whistler the more I believe they are not irreconcilable. Whistler is right when he says in *Ten O'Clock* that Art is distinct from Morality. And yet Ruskin, too, utters a truth, on a different plane, when he says that all great art is morality."[4]

On March 1 *Les Arts de la vie* published the first part of Proust's translation of the first lecture from *Sesame and Lilies: Des trésors des rois* (Of kings' treasuries).

The review published the remaining installments on April 15 and May 15. The complete translation, containing Proust's preface and the second lecture, retitled *Des jardins des reines* (Of queens' gardens), was not published until May 1906.

In early March, Proust planned a dinner party, chiefly to invite his aristocratic friends. Because of a number of complications, he decided on a tea instead. His mother was still in mourning and felt that an afternoon tea would be more appropriate. That would also simplify the guest list, for more people could be invited. As usual, Mme Straus's name was at the top of the list of those Marcel most wanted to see. Worried that her nervous disorders might prevent her attending, he wrote, urging her to come and offering a remedy for every unpleasant situation she might fear: "You can eat or not, you can drink or not, you can talk or remain silent, and if you get bored you can come with me into another room. And if I bore you I shall leave you on your own."[5] It was no use; she could not come. Marcel and Mme Straus, perhaps the two most thorough neurasthenics in Paris, could rarely meet. At the tea, on March 6—the last such gathering at 45, rue de Courcelles—Reynaldo and the comtesse de Guerne, who often sang together, delighted the guests with their performance, primarily selections from Mozart, always Hahn's favorite. Later in the spring Marcel would thank Mme de Guerne by praising her voice in an anonymous article in *Le Figaro*. But not all the sounds heard on the day of the tea party were as harmonious as Mozart's. The party somehow caused a brawl among the Proust servants and the abrupt departure of their cook Marie.[6]

That evening, after the party, Marcel went to the Vaudeville Theater to see Louisa perform. When he returned home, he found an alarming message from Montesquiou. Propped against Marcel's candlestick, the envelope was addressed in the count's unmistakable, large, ornate hand and postmarked Paris. Proust had not invited the count, as he pointed out in the letter he immediately wrote, because Mme de Clermont-Tonnerre and Lucien had told him that he was away at Artagnan. And Marcel remembered that Montesquiou had said that he would not return until the spring: "All these thoughts go through my head on seeing your envelope post-marked Paris, thoughts of pure rage, the predominant fury of the host cheated of his glory."[7]

On March 10 Proust attended a small supper party given by Reynaldo and Harry Fragson, a celebrated music hall singer who was known to be homosexual. Marcel, as he wrote Louisa at 7 o'clock the next morning, regretted her "strange silence," because he would have liked to bring her to the party. "And I think you would have enjoyed yourself. Because Fragson is charming when seen at close quarters, and sang without stopping." When Marcel was forced to leave the party at 3:30 A.M. because of a terrible asthma attack, Fragson was still singing at the top of his lungs.[8]

When Marcel heard that Mme Straus had left the confines of her home, he expressed his "joy" at the news. Believing that her problems were purely psychological in origin, whereas his own nervous disorders resulted from genuine physiological maladies, he encouraged Mme Straus to believe herself cured. As for himself: "Unfortunately I'm going to be obliged to retire to a sort of sanatorium for three or four months, but I think I'll put it off until after my hay fever." He told Mme Straus that he loved her "to a point which makes me feel your pain like a torture and sing with joy metaphorically (since I can't open my mouth) at your recovery."[9]

Proust kept Mme Straus informed of his progress as he worked on the preface, notes, and translation of *Sesame and Lilies*. In the spring he told her that a "very small piece" of his would appear in the *Renaissance latine* on June 15. Marcel's reappearance in the review's pages marked the full reconciliation between him and Constantin. This "small" piece, "Sur la lecture" (On reading), was in some ways his most important publication so far. Before concluding the letter, he attempted to distract his melancholy friend by relating some amusing remarks overheard after a recent concert. He warned that what followed was not "very proper but then we're both invalids." The lady in question was Mme de Saint-Paul, who, according to Proust, made "unintentionally obscene remarks" every time she opened her mouth. He had overheard her talking to a society hostess: "My dear, say what you like, Madeleine likes good cooking. I prefer to give you good music. Madeleine likes it in her mouth, but I prefer it in my ear. Each to her taste, my dear, it's a free country, after all."[10]

As his work to complete *Sésame et les lys* intensified, Marcel began making serious efforts to avoid at all costs Montesquiou and his emissary Yturri, who sometimes came with a message from the count when Marcel was asleep. The count seemed determined to complicate his life by tormenting him, interfering with his work, and occupying time that Marcel preferred to spend with his mother. Marcel knew that on April 21 the count was to lecture on Hugo's *La Fin de Satan,* an event he intended to miss, even though he feared Montesquiou's wrath at his absence. Shortly before that date Marcel left his mother a note asking her to leave the house only when she absolutely felt it necessary to take some fresh air. He wanted her "to organize an inexpungeable defense" against the count and his factotum.[11]

On the day following the lecture, the absent but unrepentant Marcel received from Montesquiou a letter even angrier and more sarcastic than anticipated: "I know that you are ill. But why do you recover when it's a question of the La Rochefoucauld orangeade. . . . Montesquiou isn't 'small beer' either. 'He' of whom I spoke yesterday would have *laid his hands on you, through my voice.*" Because Marcel had refused divine Hugolian intervention through the mediumistic Montesquiou, the count concluded, not unreasonably, that Marcel should be given some other kind of treatment. Remembering Marcel's frequent talk of going to a sanatorium, the count urged him to go: "Anything would be better than your present state and that sequestered room!"[12] Montesquiou's accusations had stung Proust because they were, for the most part, accurate. Claiming to be "worn out by letters from Montesquiou," Marcel complained to Mme Straus about their mutual friend's treatment of him: "Every time he gives a lecture or throws a party etc. etc. he refuses to acknowledge that I'm ill, and beforehand there are summonses, threats, visits from Yturri who wakes me up, and afterwards, reproaches for not having gone."[13]

In his fury Montesquiou compared his own handwriting to Solomon's and Proust's tiny, nearly illegible scrawl to an ant's.[14] When Marcel wrote to Montesquiou to chide him for taking the *beau rôle,* the count retorted, "Where do you get the idea that I take the *beau rôle.* I don't have to take it, *I already have it.*"[15] Then Montesquiou announced that in order to "console" the "ant" for having missed Solomon's lecture, he intended to give a reading chez Proust "at nine o'clock in the evening on the day of publication of my book, if that would amuse you, in the presence of two or three of our friends, male and female, on the choice of whom we can agree together. And if you consider that it would be another case of me *taking the beau rôle,* at least this time we would be sharing it." Anticipating all Proust's excuses and objections, Montesquiou proposed "an audience of only *three!* At the head of the list: Madame Straus."[16] The count's announcement, so solemn and categorical, terrified Marcel and prevented him from sleeping.

Montesquiou attributed Marcel's "sourness" and inaccuracies merely to *aegri somnia,* "the futile visions of a sick man."[17] Proust yielded and replied, graciously and mendaciously, quoting Racine's *Phèdre,* " 'You cannot read what lies within my heart' if you thought you detected 'sourness' in it. . . . It has nothing but gratitude and admiration for you." The involuntary host even suggested writing an article about the new book but left himself an escape route: "It's sad that I don't do any literary criticism in a newspaper, as I should very much like to write about it."[18]

Proust still led the life he had described in the preface to *Pleasures and Days* nearly a decade before when he compared himself to Noah, confined to his ark while gazing at the world outside. Writing to Albert Sorel in May, he said that his health had accustomed him "to do without nearly everything and to replace people by their images and life by thought."[19] To Robert Dreyfus, during the same period, he confided that he "led a very quiet, restful life of reading and very studious intimacy with Mama."[20]

As he wrote the final drafts of his preface to *Sésame et les lys,* Marcel lacked confidence in his new style. He repeated to Mme Straus and others his lament: "Ah, if only I could write like Mme Straus." He particularly envied her "lucidity, that delightful equilibrium that makes your sentences so enchanting."[21] As though his self-doubts were not enough to contend with, he had to undergo the "favor" Montesquiou was bestowing upon him by coming to his home for a private reading. He was at a loss as to what he should tell the select few whom the count had allowed him to invite. Montesquiou advised him: "Say what is the case: that I am doing you the kindness, since you don't go out, of going to your house to read a (short) chapter of my new book; and that this chapter being the portrait of Mme Aubernon, the guests have been chosen among those who knew her."[22] Montesquiou called the chapter read at Proust's "La Sonnette" (The bell) because Mme Aubernon was famous for using that instrument to moderate the conversations of her dinner guests.

The reading chez Proust on Friday, June 2, was attended by the loyal Yturri, weary from complications resulting from his diabetes. As he listened to Montesquiou read, Marcel compared his own recollections to those of the count. It was in Mme Aubernon's salon that he had met, among others, the outrageous, effeminate Baron Doäzan, who, with Montesquiou, was a primary model for the baron de Charlus.

Shortly after June 2 Marie Nordlinger returned briefly to Paris and paid Marcel a visit. She found him in bed, of course, "his eyes ablaze, with his pale face framed by a thick, black beard." He asked her to embrace him once and told her that she had often been in his thoughts. Then he wanted to know whether she had seen any beautiful things in America.[23] They worked for a while on *Sésame et les lys,* but Marcel had relatively few questions to ask her. "After she left," he wrote in a note to his mother, "I worked alone and perfectly."[24] But as soon as Marie returned to England, Marcel realized that he needed her assistance more than he had thought. He wanted to publish a generous acknowledgment of Marie's aid in the translation, but she insisted that he express his gratitude more discreetly.[25]

A Silkworm or an Earthworm?

"There are perhaps no days of our childhood we lived so fully as those we believe we let slip by without having lived them, those we spent with a favorite book."[26] Thus Proust began the preface to his translation of *Sesame and Lilies,* published in the *Renaissance latine* on June 15 and dedicated to the princesse de Caraman-Chimay. Books were for him more than words on paper; those he had known and loved in childhood held the power to evoke the places in which he had first read them: "If we still happen today to leaf through those books of another time, it is for no other reason than that they are the only calendars we have kept of days that have vanished, and we hope to see reflected on their pages the dwellings and the ponds which no longer exist."[27]

Readers of the *Renaissance latine* cannot have known—nor could Proust himself—that they were being given a foretaste of Combray, one of the major landscapes of the *Search.*[28] The preface does not mention Illiers, but Proust evoked aspects of the little town, many of which he had already sketched in *Jean Santeuil:* the ruins of medieval towers near the river, the general topography, the uncle who loved gardening and cooking.

A distinctive aspect of Proust's mature style is its richness in presenting multiple perspectives or a string of analogies that dazzle by their aptness and their brilliance. The following humorous sketch of family life, from the preface, is an early example of this technique. In the family, someone who took the time to write a letter "was the object of a particular deference" and was told: "You have attended to your 'little correspondence,' with a smile in which there was respect, mystery, prurience, and discretion, as if this 'little correspondence' had been at the same time a state secret, a prerogative, a piece of good fortune, and an ailment."[29] Proust's presentation of multiple views of the same object or action was to be one of several narrative strategies used in the novel to render life in its full richness.

This preface, like the later drafts of *Contre Sainte-Beuve* (Against Sainte-Beuve), his last sketchbook before the full-scale novel, contains a narrative followed by a critical essay. In the last section of the preface and its notes, Proust makes observations about structure in Ruskin's writings. These thoughts would be important to his own slow elaboration of a structure for the *Search.*

In the first note to his translation Proust wrote about the retrospective, organic unity he had found in *Sesame and Lilies* and noticed in other Ruskin works. Ruskin had used as the epigraph a quotation from Lucian, "You shall each have a cake of sesame,—and ten pounds." Proust showed that the word *sesame* "projects like a supplementary ray of light that reaches not only the last sentence of the lecture, . . . but illuminates retrospectively all that preceded." In his extensive note, Proust listed the various meanings of *sesame* that Ruskin drew upon in his lecture, creating not only a structure but a layering effect that was to become a distinctive element of Proust's style: "It is precisely the charm of Ruskin's works that between the ideas of one book and among various books there may be links he does not show, which he hardly lets appear for an instant and which he has perhaps woven as an after-thought, but never artificially, however, since they are always taken from the substance, always identical with itself, of his thought. The multiple but constant preoccupations of this thought, that is what assures these books a unity more real than the unity of composition, generally absent, it must be said." Proust saw that Ruskin's method was to go "from one idea to another without apparent order. But in reality the fancy that leads him follows his profound affinities[,] which in spite of himself impose on him a superior logic. So that in the end he happens to have obeyed a kind of secret plan which, unveiled at the end, imposes retrospectively on the whole a sort of order and makes it appear magnificently arranged up to this final apotheosis."[30] If Proust is correct regarding Ruskin's following his fancy, his own unifying elements were to be more conscious, but the themes and their orchestration (it is no accident that Proust describes Ruskin's style in musical terms) were to be organic, growing out of his own vision, tastes, predilections.[31] His sesame would be the word *time*, occurring first and last in his long, circular narration.

As for a writer's vocabulary and knowledge of literature, Proust maintains that "a great writer knows his dictionary and his great writers before writing. But while writing he no longer thinks of them, but of what he wants to express, and chooses the words which say it best, with the most power, color, and harmony." The words come from the well of a writer's being, from an inner necessity, from the organic requirements of the narration when "his erudition gives way to genius." As he writes, "his language, as learned and as rich as it may be, is only the keyboard on which he improvises."[32] These lines, suggesting that the writer enters a trancelike state, in which he seeks and finds the right "notes," indicate the decreasing impor-tance Proust places on intelligence and erudition. These elements are important, even vital, but for Proust they are no longer primary.

In the preface Proust refuted Ruskin's thesis that "the reading of all good books is like a conversation with the most cultivated men of past centuries who have been their authors."[33] The translator, who found "this kind of fetishistic respect for books unhealthy," argued that "the essential difference between a book and a friend is not their degree of greatness of wisdom, but the manner in which we communicate with them, reading, contrary to conversation, consisting for each of us in receiving the communication of another thought, but while we remain all alone, that is to say, while continuing to enjoy the intellectual power we have in solitude, and which conversation dissipates immediately, while continuing to be inspired, to maintain the mind's full, fruitful work on itself."[34]

We find budding here flowers from the seeds that were sown as far back as *Pleasures and Days*, when the writer warned against the dangers of society, a warning repeated in 1905: "All these compliments, all those greetings . . . we call deference, gratitude, devotion, and in which we mingle so many lies, are sterile and tiresome." In Proust's experience "these agitations of friendship come to an end at the threshold of that pure and calm friendship that reading is." Friendship and social exchanges encourage not profound meditation but vanity—"we speak for others, but we keep silent for ourselves"—and snobbism, which Proust again condemned as "the greatest sterilizer of inspiration, the greatest deadener of originality, the greatest destroyer of talent."[35] Ruskin had presented reading as an end; Proust saw it as a means: "Reading is at the threshold of spiritual life; it can introduce us to it; it does not constitute it." Reading, meditation, and creativity, the highest forms of activity, were possible only when one withdrew from the social whirl and plumbed the depths of one's profound being. There were, of course, many obstacles to finding one's true self. Among those Proust listed were an indolent mind, lack of will, diseases of the nervous system, and cases in which "a kind of laziness or frivolity prevents one from descending spontaneously into the deep regions of self where the true life of the mind begins."[36]

Proust had begun to question the method of the distinguished French critic Charles-Augustin Sainte-Beuve in the preface, and in the notes he observed that "while Anatole France judges his contemporaries admirably well, one may say that Sainte-Beuve did not appreciate any of the great writers of his time." He quoted Sainte-Beuve on the duty of the critic: "Everyone is able to pronounce on Racine and Bossuet. . . . But the sagacity of the judge, the perspicacity of the critic, is proved mostly with new works, not yet tested by the public. To judge at first sight, to divine, to anticipate, that is the gift of the critic. How few have it."[37] Proust later decided to prove that Sainte-Beuve had failed to meet the criteria he had set for himself and others. This detour by Sainte-Beuve's way was to be the last of the circuitous routes that would lead the novelist to the right way, the way that lay beyond reading and translating, beyond polemics and parodies.

As he had in the preface to *La Bible d'Amiens,* Proust used the example of Montesquiou, again unnamed, for a fresh condemnation of idolatry, in this case books or words used as fetishes rather than as sources of enlightenment and inspiration: "Our contemporary idolater, to whom I have often compared Ruskin, . . . at times places as many as five epigraphs at the beginning" of a text.[38] Ruskin, who had originally placed "five epigraphs . . . at the beginning of *Sesame,*" had done so, Proust believed, because he "delighted in worshipping a word in all the beautiful passages of the great writers where it appears." A great writer, as opposed to those of a lesser order, like Montesquiou and Ruskin, would not make a fetish of words in themselves but would see them as a means to reach a larger purpose, the creation of a powerful new vision of the world.[39]

Proust ended the preface with an example of how reading can revive past impressions, a major Proustian preoccupation: "How many times, in *The Divine Comedy,* in Shakespeare, have I known that impression of having before me, inserted into the present actual hour, a little of the past, that dreamlike impression which one experiences in Venice on the Piazzetta, before its two columns of gray and pink granite . . . the columns . . . reserving with all their slender impenetrability the inviolate place of the Past: of the Past familiarly risen in the midst of the present."[40]

Proust's preface "On Reading" concludes with this passage in which the past is restored "familiarly" to the present by those ancient Venetian columns.[41] This resurrection of bygone days by means of a present sensation—here through books and monuments—is, of course, the basis for Proust's famous theory of involuntary memory. In this and other texts Proust wrote over the next several years, he seemed to have gathered all the elements needed to launch his novel, to take the leap from reader to writer. Yet his lack of will and inspiration tormented him. And the thread. Would he ever find the thread? What was the story?

Anna de Noailles and other friends marveled at Proust's essay on reading. She wrote immediately to express her admiration: "My dear friend, I only see people who are dazzled . . . touched . . . by the dear, divine pages you have written." She told him that people were quoting extensively from his article and that she, André Beaunier, and Henri de Régnier had passed his preface back and forth, describing to each other his sentences that were like "adorable threads of silk."[42]

Was he really a silkworm? He refused to believe it. Accustomed as he was to showering the most lavish compliments on his friends' mediocre writings, he could not believe that their words were sincere. He answered by "beseeching" Anna to "stop being so nice . . . for I cannot bear it any longer; the burden of happiness, gratitude, emotion, stupefaction is too overwhelming and I might die of it. There is also the fear that the whole thing may be a joke, for nothing can penetrate the armour of my sadness, my conviction that all those pages are execrable, a sort of indigestible nougat which sticks between one's teeth." He professed to believe that she had always hated "everything I write." He had wanted her "to read a few pages of this (infinitely worse written than what I used to do before being ill)"—a reference to his more subdued style in *Pleasures and Days*—"so that you could see that after all I did think a bit and wasn't quite so sottish as people say." Her words of praise had moved him so that he was "in a state of shame and confusion beyond words, enhanced by the Beaunier piece which I strongly suspect you dictated." Beaunier had hailed "M. Marcel Proust the incomparable translator of Ruskin," whose preface the critic found "charming, moving and often marvelous."[43] Beaunier had taken particular delight in the style: "These long sentences, encumbered with all the details and circumstances, have a strange and delicious charm," which came, Beaunier said, from their "meticulous truth."[44] Writing to Mme Straus, Proust worried that his "indigestible nougat" of an essay might be dangerous for his languid friend to read and urged her to avoid it: "Don't read it, it's a failed effort and horribly wearying to read, with sentences that take up an entire page" of the kind "that Dr. Wiedmer [Widmer] would particularly forbid you to read."[45]

By the end of the month, consumed with self-doubt, Proust had written to Gregh inquiring whether his friend had read the essay in the *Renaissance latine*—if not, he would send him a copy—and asking him to evaluate his prose. He told Gregh that he had "unique confidence" in his friend's taste and would like to know, in all frankness, how Gregh judged his writing, whether he had progressed or regressed since *Pleasures and Days* and the preface to *La Bible d'Amiens*. He even requested a "grade," as though he were still writing compositions in school. "And, if it's not asking too much, corrections in the margins."[46] Proust received no answer because Gregh misplaced the letter before reading it.

There were signs that his mother was not well, though she continued to hide her true condition. Marcel sensed that she might need medical attention, and on several occasions he urged her to consult Robert. Marcel knew that she was often unable to sleep, but she showed no other symptoms of being ill. He may have attributed her insomnia, and the resulting fatigue, to her deep mourning for his father. On Monday evening, June 19, believing that she was sleeping soundly, he left her a note: "My dear little Mama, it's a boon for me, greater than that of having you near me, to sense that you are resting a little. Can I say that you are mending? Can normal sleep suffice to repair so many sleepless nights?"[47]

Writing to Louisa in midsummer, he confessed that he was miserable and felt his life sliding past. He must finally resolve the question of whether he could change the way he lived: "Shall I continue to the end of my days to lead a life that even invalids who are gravely ill don't lead, deprived of everything, of the light of day, of air, of all work, of all pleasure, in a word of all life? Or am I going to find a way of changing? I can no longer postpone the answer, for it's not only my youth but my life that's going by."[48] By the end of the summer Proust showed major resolve in attempting to change his life.

On June 24, instead of going to bed after dawn, he stayed up in order to see the Whistler exhibition. He wrote Marie that he had braved "death" and almost met it when "at the hour of my bedtime, utterly exhausted, I took a cab and went to look at the Whistlers. It's the sort of thing one wouldn't do for a living person." Although Blanche had expressed reservations about Whistler's accomplishments, Marcel had none: "If the man who painted those Venices in turquoise, those Amsterdams in topaz, those Brittanies in opal . . . and above all the sails at night belonging to Messrs Vanderbilt and Freer . . . is not a great painter, one can only think there never was one."[49] He then turned to their collaboration and asked whether he could send to Marie in Manchester "my copy of *Sésame*, in which I've put crosses and underlinings wherever I was in doubt?" He assured her that his queries "never apply to more than one or two words at a time. Does this seem feasible to you?" As usual, Proust sought to make corrections after publication.

Marcel complained about new ailments, some of which were troubling. He confessed to his mother in late June that while at Larue's he had, without paying attention, consumed "many cups of extremely strong coffee and become somewhat rabid!" He had begun the dangerous habit of alternating stimulants and depressants that was to continue the rest of his life. On more than one occasion he admitted that his memory had been "half destroyed" by the numerous drugs he took, whose effects he claimed made proofreading especially difficult for him.[50] Another ailment came from severe eye strain. While hard at work translating *Sesame and Lilies,* writing the preface, and then correcting proofs, he complained that his eyes ached from the many hours spent under an electric bulb with no shade. Anyone else would have quickly obtained a shade to protect his eyes, but not Marcel, who seemed unable to deal with practical matters. In July he wrote Marie that his eyes hurt so much that he could not read his own words as he wrote. This was but one factor contributing to his nearly illegible writing (ant trails, according to Montesquiou), which plagued his friends, editors, and typesetters.

He still expressed doubts about his writing and sought advice from friends in whose literary talent and experience he had some confidence. Now that he had nearly developed his mature style, it frightened him. As adept as he was at recognizing the individual song of other writers, he did not recognize his own voice. Could such a style be applied to a novel or to any literary genre? He had hesitated, he told Dreyfus, to send him a copy of "On Reading" because he was "so disgusted with it" that he "no longer dared. I felt that you who know how to say so much in half a line would be exasperated by sentences that run to a hundred. Ah, how I should like to be able to write like Mme Straus! But I must perforce weave these long silken threads as I spin them, and if I shortened them the result would be little fragments rather than whole sentences. So that I remain like a silkworm and indeed live in the same temperature, or rather like an earthworm ('in love with a star,' that's to say contemplating the unattainable perfection of Mme Straus's concision)."[51] If he had such reservations about his new style, how could he expect anyone else to like it? In any case, he had no ideas for stories, only for characters and scenes that haunted his imagination. He remained at an impasse.

On July 9, having learned that Yturri was gravely ill, he sent his mother to Neuilly to inquire about his condition. When she arrived, she learned that Yturri had died three days earlier. Jeanne returned home but dared not give Marcel the news immediately because she feared the shock would be too great. After she told him, later in the evening, Marcel wrote Montesquiou that he could not console himself for not having seen Yturri again. Then Marcel spoke about Yturri's great affection for Montesquiou and his pride in the count's many achievements. Montesquiou replied that Marcel's words touched him more than those of his other friends, who spoke to him only about his grief rather than about Yturri and their mutual affection.

Marcel resolved to seek treatment for his own health problems. On July 28, when he attended the funeral of Guiche's mother, the duchesse de Gramont, he took advantage of being out in the daytime to see Dr. Brissaud. Marcel described the doctor to Anna de Noailles as "more handsome and more charming than ever," and just as reluctant to discuss medicine.[52] Brissaud finally recommended Dr. Paul Sollier to him. Knowing that Anna had recently undergone similar treatment at Sollier's sanatorium, Marcel wrote that he was eager to discuss the doctor and his clinic. Then he announced, "I am going to write a book about doctors." In an August letter to Montesquiou he mentioned that he had been many times on the point of leaving Paris for a "comforting church" or an asylum, but had each time become too ill to undertake such an ordeal.[53] Did Marcel fail to see the irony in this remark? Montesquiou must have smiled at his impossible friend's notion of how to seek treatment.

In July or August, Marcel sent Antoine a letter that provided a list of all the noble families mentioned in Saint-Simon that were extinct, omitting those that Balzac had used. Proust was apparently providing information that Bibesco had requested, though to what purpose is unclear. Did Antoine have a new play in mind? Proust's extensive list proves how well he knew Saint-Simon and Balzac. Whether inspired by Antoine or not, Proust made good use of this knowledge when he began writing the *Search*.

Louisa, who wanted to spend the summer on the Normandy coast, received these observations from Proust: "Trouville is extremely ugly, Deauville frightful, the countryside between Trouville and Villers uninteresting. But on the heights between Trouville and Honfleur is the most wonderful landscape you could possibly see, beautiful open country with superb sea views." After providing more details, he explained his willingness to discuss the area: "I'm telling you all this because I'm in love with that idyllic region."[54] In August, Louisa mounted a horse and went for a ride in the hills overlooking Trouville. As she rode toward Trouville, the horse threw Louisa, who suffered several nasty contusions and a mild head injury. Marcel sent the shaken actress a get-well message, urging her to heal quickly her "beautiful bruised cheeks and if you have to go to Trouville, take the train!"[55] In spite of his apparent flippancy, Proust knew that such accidents could be extremely dangerous and even deadly. Perhaps he remembered Louisa's fall many years later when writing of Albertine, the girl who, having fascinated and tormented his jealous Narrator, dies after a fall from a horse.

On August 15, in *Les Arts de la vie*, Proust published a signed article on Montesquiou, the title of which indicated one of the count's primary roles for those who knew him well: "Un Professeur de beauté."[56] Proust praised the count's extraordinary gifts as an art critic and a writer, his command of the language, his knowledge of flowers and their depictions in literature and paintings, his keen perception of nuances in color and fabric, and the skill to make these distinctions vividly in his writings. Proust said that Montesquiou and Ruskin possessed the ability "to see and to know" more completely than any others. Although he had warned that such erudition could become a form of idolatry, its virtues, when used properly, more than compensated for the dangers. To illustrate Montesquiou's expertise Proust quoted two of his remarks, one about a variety of pears, another about a particular shade of gray trousers the count called "Balzacian." Proust later attributed both remarks to Charlus, who shared Montesquiou's erudition.[57]

"Steeped in every sorrow"

On September 6 Marcel and his mother left for Évian, where they were to meet Mme Catusse. He had planned the trip in the anticipation that better days lay ahead for both of them. He hoped that the baths and rest by the lake would improve Jeanne's health and that she would begin to recover from the period of intense mourning that had lasted nearly two years since his father's death. He had at last made a major commitment to improve his own health. After accompanying her to Évian, he would cross the lake and enter a clinic, presumably that of Dr. Widmer, to whom Mme Straus had spoken about Marcel.

All Marcel's plans began to fall apart soon after he and his mother checked in at the Splendide Hôtel. Jeanne become violently ill with nephritis, suffering severe nausea and dizziness. Apparently believing that stoicism and a brave face would pull her through this crisis, Jeanne insisted on dressing and going down to the hotel salon the next morning, though it took two people to keep her from falling. Marcel immediately telephoned Mme Catusse to inform her of his mother's illness. Jeanne, feeling wretched and confused, tried to disguise her distress from Marcel. She could not decide whether to have her photograph taken; she wished, he later concluded, to leave her son a last image of herself, but she was afraid that she looked too sorrowful to be photographed.[58]

Although Mme Proust's condition was pitiable, the serious nature of her illness was not confirmed at Évian. Both her sons were eager for her to return home and receive the excellent care available there. Robert rushed to Évian to bring his mother back to Paris. Mme Catusse went to the station with Marcel, Robert, and Jeanne, who was "dragged along" by them to the train.[59] Marcel did not board with them because his mother insisted he stay and proceed with the treatment he had postponed for so long. Marcel agreed to wait at the Splendide for a telegram from Paris. If the news was good, he would go on to the clinic. The alternative was unthinkable. He wrote Marie Nordlinger to inform her of his mother's condition and ended on an optimistic note: "I hope all this will vanish like a bad dream."[60]

But the nightmare did not end. Marcel returned to Paris when his mother showed no signs of improvement. Her attitude bewildered him. He now knew that she had left for Évian very ill with uremia, had refused to have her urine analyzed once she had arrived, and had become even sicker. She was no more cooperative about accepting treatment in Paris. Robert called in Dr. Ladislas Landowski, a former student of Adrien's, in whom he and Marcel had great confidence. But Mme Proust scarcely allowed the doctor to look at her. Marcel explained the predicament to Mme Straus: "Mama who loves us so much does not understand that it's very cruel of her to refuse treatment."[61] Jeanne would not accept food or medication. Had she lost the will to live or had she decided that her condition was hopeless?

In addition to her servants, a nun who specialized in nursing came to look after Jeanne. Around September 23 Dr. Landowski informed Marcel and Robert that he thought he saw a slight improvement in their mother's condition. Marcel was skeptical, convinced instead that his mother knew she was dying, which in turn caused her terrible mental anguish because she worried about how he would survive without her. But she remained so calm that he could not know "what she thought and what she suffered."[62] On Sunday, September 24, she began to suffer from the effects of the disease, experiencing paralysis and aphasia. The end came on Tuesday morning, around eleven o'clock. Mme Gustave Neuburger, "Aunt Laure," was by Jeanne's side when she died; Marcel waited in an adjoining room.

On September 2, Marcel wrote to Anna de Noailles and described his mother in death: "She has died at fifty-six, looking no more than thirty since her illness made her so much thinner and especially since death restored to her the youthfulness of the day before her sorrows; she hadn't a single white hair. She takes away my life with her, as Papa had taken away hers." Marcel explained that because his mother had not given up "her Jewish religion on marrying Papa, because she regarded it as a token of respect for her parents, there will be no church, simply at the house tomorrow Thursday at 12 o'clock . . . and the cemetery. . . . Today I have her still, dead but still receiving my caresses. And then I shall never have her again."[63] Reynaldo Hahn, whose memoirs are strangely reticent about his famous friend, recorded this scene of Marcel grieving by his mother's body: "I still see him by Mme Proust's bed, weeping and smiling through his tears at her body."[64]

Jeanne Proust's surprising rejuvenation in death inspired the description of the Narrator's grandmother on her bier:

A face grown young again, from which had vanished the wrinkles, the contractions, the swellings, the strains, the hollows which pain had carved on it over the years. As in the far-off days when her parents had chosen for her a bridegroom, she had the features, delicately traced by purity and submission, the cheeks glowing with a chaste expectation, with a dream of happiness, with an innocent gaiety even, which the years had gradually destroyed. Life in withdrawing from her had taken with it the disillusionments of life. A smile seemed to be hovering on my grandmother's lips. On that funeral couch, death, like a sculptor of the Middle Ages, had laid her down in the form of a young girl.[65]

The funeral took place on Thursday, September 28. Marcel and Robert and their Uncle Georges Weil led the procession that followed the ambulance, barely visible beneath all the flowers, to Père-Lachaise, where Jeanne took her place beside the husband she had adored. A large crowd of friends from the medical community, government, business, high society, and the arts attended the ceremony, including Mme Félix Faure, Henri Bergson, Comte and Comtesse de Noailles, Comtesse Adhéaume de Chevigné, the marquis and marquise d'Albufera, Baron Robert de Rothschild, and Francis de Croisset. Reynaldo Hahn and Lucien Daudet, Marcel's oldest and most intimate friends, understood better than any who followed the cortège the depth of Marcel's grief.

After the funeral Marcel, who intended to fulfill what he regarded as his duty toward his mother, tried to find the best clinic near Paris for treatment. Through Anna de Noailles, he asked her husband to write to him about the merits of Drs. Sollier and Dubois and the comfort of their clinics. He was particularly eager to know whether Dr. Sollier, whose clinic was located on the outskirts of Paris, would agree to pay house calls. He urged Anna not to ask Sollier directly because he already had so many doctors on his list that he feared entanglements.

Now it was Montesquiou's turn to console Marcel, certain to have been devastated by the worst possible loss he could suffer. Marcel thanked Montesquiou in solemn tones and described his grief: "My life has now forever lost its only purpose, its only sweetness, its only love, its only consolation. I have lost her whose unceasing vigilance brought me in peace and tenderness the only honey of my life." Not only had he lost her, but he must live with the knowledge that he had been the source of his mother's greatest anxiety: "I have been steeped in every sorrow, I have lost her, I have seen her suffer, I can well believe that she knew she was leaving me and yet could not give me instructions which it may have been agonizing for her to hold back; I have the feeling that because of my poor health I was the bane and the torment of her life." And yet leaving him "must have been a very great torture for her too." Proust told Montesquiou that the nun who had nursed Jeanne until the end said that for his mother "I was still four years old."[66]

Two days after Jeanne's funeral Charles Ephrussi died. He had been a central figure in the Parisian art world, particularly as the director of the distinguished *Gazette des Beaux-Arts*. His obituary mentioned his extensive knowledge of art, his essay on Albrecht Dürer, and his "magnificent collection."[67] Proust, who had liked and admired Ephrussi, was saddened by his death. In a few years, when he began creating Charles Swann, Proust used Ephrussi, perhaps unconsciously at first, as a model for certain aspects of this major character. Swann, like Ephrussi, is a Jew and an art connoisseur and collector. Unlike Ephrussi's essay on Dürer, Swann's study of Vermeer is never finished.

Although Marcel's admiration for his mother was boundless, he knew that he was better equipped to deal with life than she had believed. He understood, if he did not yet see it clearly, that he and she had lived in a cycle of mutual dependency— that, if he had been unable to break free, she, too, had been incapable of controlling the great maternal affection that so often spoiled and indulged him. Marcel, who had never known any other life, who had never wanted any other life, was now truly alone. In the questionnaire he had filled out at age thirteen, he had answered that his idea of misery was "to be separated from my mother."[68] That honest, simple answer held true for the rest of his life.

Marcel finally selected Dr. Jules Déjerine's clinic for nervous disorders and reserved a room for three months. On the day in early December when he was to enter the clinic, Marcel hesitated. He contacted Mme Straus for advice and asked her to send Dr. Sollier to see him at home. Marcel still hoped that Sollier might treat him there. The doctor arrived and succeeded in persuading the patient to leave immediately for his clinic for nervous disorders, located just outside Paris at Boulogne-sur-Seine. Given his state of near collapse and unprecedented grief, Marcel dreaded the prospect of the treatment, which called for being kept in isolation in strange quarters.

Once at the clinic Proust was forbidden to write letters, instructions he ignored when he wished or used as an excuse when convenient. Sometimes he compro-mised by dictating. Marcel's friends followed his treatment and hoped that its success would enable him to lead a normal life. Hahn wrote Montesquiou that he had heard good reports about Marcel's progress. It is unlikely that these reports came directly from Marcel, who did not share Reynaldo's optimism. Marcel invited Robert de Billy, soon to leave for an international conference, to visit him at the sanatorium and confided that, rather than improving, his condition was rapidly worsening, but that he "still wanted to extend the trial. Of course, don't tell Dr. Sollier that I am not happy! Because he is charming." In the postscript he also asked Billy not to tell any of their friends that Marcel had written him personally. "For the others I dictate."[69] Marcel's confidence in Dr. Sollier was not enhanced when the physician remarked, rather smugly, about Bergson, "What a confused and limited mind."[70] Marcel became increasingly skeptical about modern treatments of nervous disorders; ultimately he had little or no faith in medicine, but if forced to choose, he preferred traditional medicine to treatments like Sollier's. The stay at Sollier's sanatorium confirmed the opinion he had expressed to Anna de Noailles before entering for treatment: "The ideal doctor according to my tastes," he wrote Anna, "is the one at the cathedral of Reims" who is seen examining a vial of urine.[71]

While Proust languished in Sollier's clinic, the legislature, on December 11, passed the law establishing the separation of church and state. Marcel spent a somber and ascetic holiday season.

A few of Proust's closest friends visited him at the clinic, frustrating Sollier's attempt to isolate the patient. Hahn and Albu stopped by whenever they could, and Robert de Billy found time to visit before leaving to represent France at the Algesiras Conference on Morocco. Lucien came to see him twice, though he seemed to be in a bad mood and said so many "disagreeable things" that Marcel wondered why he had bothered to come.[72]

102, boulevard Haussmann

Marcel's isolation was also broken by an important business matter. On January 11 his brother Robert, accompanied by a lawyer, came to the clinic to sign the papers relating to their mother's will. Each brother received half of the family fortune. After expenses, Marcel's share came to 1,204,155 francs in capital, plus a quarter share in ownership of the boulevard Haussmann building, a share evaluated at 142,029 francs. Proust's total fortune in late-twentieth-century currency would be approximately 23 million francs ($4.6 million), capable of earning, in today's money, a monthly income of $16,000.[73] Proust was a wealthy man, but his attitude about money remained unrealistic. He always thought his fortune was small and feared that he would never earn enough money to support himself. Yet this conservative outlook was to have no restraining influence on the tastes he developed for gambling and wild speculations on the stock market.

On January 24 or 25 Proust, feeling no better than when he had arrived and more skeptical than ever about psychotherapeutic treatment, left Dr. Sollier's clinic and returned home to 45, rue de Courcelles. He had at least fulfilled one of his mother's wishes, even though she would have been discouraged by the outcome. Proust was more convinced than ever that he was incurable. During the coming months Dr. Sollier saw him at home at least once, and Dr. Bize, in whom Proust seemed to have more confidence, saw him whenever the writer requested consultation.

In February, when Maurice Barrès was elected to the Académie française, Marcel sent congratulations. Later in the month, he wrote to thank Barrès for sending a copy of his book *Voyage de Sparte*. Proust paid the new "immortal" some compliments on his prose and then made some critical observations about sections of the book where he believed Barrès had become bored with his subject. Proust stated this belief regarding an artist's work: "If I am convinced of one thing it's that . . . enthusiasm is, for the artist as for the reader, the criterion of beauty, of genius, of truth."[74]

Albufera had been encouraged not long before when Marcel, "although not doing marvelously well," began to see his friends every day between 5 and 10 P.M. Marcel wrote Mme Catusse that he missed her, saying that his affection for her had increased, "if that were possible, since his mother's death." After returning from the clinic, he had been "so fantastically sick" that it had not been "physically possible" to see her. If she were willing to stop by between 5:30 and 7, however, perhaps she would find him up. He warned her that he would be dressed in flannels, for he could rarely tolerate clothes that fit.[75]

Reynaldo was acquiring an international reputation as a conductor, particularly of works by Mozart. In the spring he organized and conducted a Mozart festival in Paris that was a great success. He had accepted an invitation to conduct the Vienna Philharmonic Orchestra for two performances of *Don Giovanni* at the Salzburg Festival in August. Although Reynaldo remained Marcel's most frequent and devoted visitor, his schedule was becoming that of an international star performer. In the fall he sent Marcel a postcard from Venice, where he had sung from a gondola to a large crowd gathered on the piazza.

By summer Marcel had resumed his "bad hours," rising only after dinnertime, usually around ten P.M. His lack of fresh air and adequate nourishment made him weak and anemic. Proust's spirits received something of a boost when *Sésame et les lys* was published on June 2. As with *La Bible d'Amiens*, Proust's own contribution was substantial: in addition to his fifty-nine-page preface, he had added nearly two hundred original notes.[76] Proust immediately began to inscribe and mail copies to friends. He was so unhappy with the way the Mercure had handled the task with *La Bible d'Amiens* that this time he did the work himself. He complained to Lucien that he was "exhausted" from having spent the last few days doing "a grocer's job . . . with balls of string, wrapping paper and volumes of *Tout-Paris*," the definitive address book of the Paris elite.[77] He did not learn until December that the copy he had addressed to Marie Nordlinger in America had been lost in the mail. He sent a copy to his friend and former professor Paul Desjardins, who seemed likely to appreciate Ruskin's Christian-based social reforming zeal, but Desjardins refused to read any of the books Proust sent him because he "abhorred society people," among whom Desjardins numbered Marcel.[78]

Upon receiving Lucien's acknowledgment of the book, Marcel thanked him "with all my heart for everything you say about Mama. She is absent from this preface, and I even replaced the word 'My mother,' which was in any case fictitious and didn't apply to her, by 'my aunt' so that there should be no mention of her in anything I write until I've finished something I've begun which is exclusively about her. It's terrifying how my grief has been transformed in the past few months, it's even more painful now."[79] The remarks about "my mother" and "my aunt" show a conscious transposition into fiction of his recollections of family life at Illiers and Auteuil. It also raises the question: What was the unfinished piece that was exclusively about his mother? Did he finish and discard it? Or was it evolving into the drafts of *Contre Sainte-Beuve,* the final jumping off point for the *Search?*

In a March letter to Lucien, Marcel predicted he would die an early death: "I believe my illness will not last indefinitely, mon cher petit, and I will finally join my dear little Mama."[80] It is possible that his determination to write something lasting about his mother gave him a reason to live—at least until he had finished a memorial to her. According to Maurice Duplay, Marcel told him years later that he had considered suicide after his mother's death. He decided against taking his life because he did not want to be listed as a suicide in the newspapers. Instead, he thought of letting himself waste away by not eating and sleeping—a solution that would require only a slight adjustment to his usual regimen. But then he realized that if he allowed himself to die, the memory he had kept of her "would disappear with him . . . and I would take her away in a second and definitive death and be committing a kind of patricide."[81]

The response Proust received for *Sésame et les lys* should have sufficed to encourage any writer. At first, he responded with delight at the reviews, especially those in the *Figaro.* On June 5 he wrote Gaston to express his "great pleasure" over that day's notice by André Beaunier, who described Marcel as "one of our most delicate, most subtle writers" and praised the quality of the translation.[82] On June 14 Beaunier wrote another article for the *Figaro*'s front page on Proust's translation, calling it "the model of a well-done translation, a masterpiece of intelligent docility, an astonishing success."[83] Beaunier made what was apparently the first comparison of Proust's manner and style to that of Michel de Montaigne: "Proust reads Ruskin in somewhat the same way that Montaigne read Plutarch: he 'essays' his own ideas by bringing them into contact with those of another." Such a method, Beaunier noted, allowed Proust to see clearly his own beliefs. "It's the game of a delicate moralist, irresolute because he has a fine mind (l'esprit de finesse) and sees the diverse aspect of things."[84]

Was he then to become Montaigne's successor? Was this to be his genre, Proust the essayist, capable perhaps of matching the distinguished inventor of the genre? Proust remained unconvinced of the suitability of this "voice." Writing to Robert Dreyfus, who had also been "enchanted" by his book, Marcel expressed the opinion "that I write so much worse than during the era of *Pleasures and Days.*"[85] It was true that translation had increased his already remarkable knowledge of words and their nuances; he had developed a style that, as he and others saw later, was extraordinarily supple and complex while remaining lucid and remarkably light. But his range had been far too narrow and lacked originality; how could he, at age thirty-five, be content with the modest reputation of a Ruskin specialist?

If Proust was not puffed up with pride from all the praise he was receiving, he did want his book to sell and his friends to take note of his accomplishment. He was astounded to learn how many of them, all regular readers of the *Figaro*, claimed not to have seen any of the articles. This confirmed his theory that no one read. In a letter to Lucien, Proust mentioned the long article by Beaunier. Lucien replied: "I saw neither the notice nor the article you mention."[86] Proust listed for Dreyfus those among his closest friends, all daily readers of the *Figaro*, who had not seen the piece: Reynaldo, Lucien, and Albufera. Albu, "whose whole family subscribes to the *Figaro* and who takes it himself, wrote to me to say how strange it was as I knew Calmette that the *Figaro* hadn't mentioned *Sésame*. And when I said that on the contrary they'd talked about it too much, he said to me: "*You must be mistaken,* because my wife reads *Le Figaro* from beginning to end every morning and there was absolutely nothing about you."[87] *Sésame et les lys* did sell well; before the end of the year, it was in its fourth printing.[88]

Such diversions as favorable reviews and the success of his translation did nothing to lighten Proust's mourning. When he was awake his conscious thoughts were directed toward his mother, and when he slumbered she was always present. Marcel wrote Lucien that because he took his sleep in intervals, he dreamed about her several times a day. "But almost invariably she is so sick and so sad that I feel infinite pain."[89]

In June, Robert Proust, who was rapidly becoming a distinguished surgeon, left for America. During his journey he visited the Mayo Clinic in Rochester, Minnesota, then represented the Université de Paris at an international medical meeting in Trois-Rivières, Québec. He remained in America until July 20.

Meanwhile, in the week before Robert's return, Proust and many of his countrymen watched the official dénouement of a national drama that summer. The Dreyfus Affair, which had begun so many years before, came to an official end. Those who had defended Dreyfus were at last fully vindicated. Anna de Noailles attended the session at the Chamber of Deputies on July 14, Bastille Day, a session she found "infinitely moving."[90] On Saturday, July 21, at the École militaire in Paris, France bestowed the cross of Chevalier de la Légion d'honneur on the newly promoted Major Alfred Dreyfus. At the same time, Colonel Picquart, the officer who, at tremendous personal cost and risk, had defended Dreyfus, was reinstated and promoted. Marcel read the newspaper accounts of the ceremony with tears in his eyes.[91] That evening he wrote to Mme Straus and, pensive over the resolution of the affair, drew a parallel to fiction:

> It's odd to think that life—which is so unlike fiction—for once resembles it. Alas, in these last ten years we've all had many a sorrow, many a disappointment, many a torment in our lives. And for none of us will the hour ever strike when our sorrows will be changed into exultations, our disappointments into unhoped-for fulfillments, and our torments into delectable triumphs. I shall get more and more ill, I shall miss those I've lost more and more, everything I aspired to in life will be more and more inaccessible to me. But for Dreyfus and Picquart it is not so. Life for them has been "providential," after the fashion of fairy tales and serial stories. This is because our miseries were founded on truths, physiological truths, human and emotional truths. Their misfortunes were founded on errors. Blessed are those who are victims of error, judicial or otherwise! They are the only human beings for whom there is redress and reparation.[92]

In the same letter to Mme Straus, Marcel began to make inquiries about renting a house for the month of August on the Normandy coast, where a number of his friends would be staying in rented villas near Trouville. Now that his mother was no longer living, he turned to Mme Straus and other friends for advice and assistance. As usual, Marcel's needs and instructions were endlessly complicated: the dwelling must be well constructed, not damp, not dusty, in the modern style and bare, not suffocating behind houses but either on the beach or on a hill, and costing no more than one thousand francs for the month of August. If such a structure could be found, he would take it—"perhaps."[93] Thus began a series of letters to friends he enlisted in the quest for a villa. Meanwhile, Proust, who often remained paralyzed by indecision, traveled vicariously by reading a "frightful" number of train schedules and travel brochures between "two and six in the morning on my chaise longue."[94]

At the end of July, Marcel wrote Mme Straus and expressed concern about his uncle's rapidly declining health. Georges Weil was slowly dying of the disease that had killed his sister: uremia. After that disturbing news, Proust resumed his endless volley of questions about seaside villas, for which he apologized: "Forgive me for bothering you and for asking you to provide the means of bothering you in person."[95] Proust accepted an invitation to share a villa with Albu and his wife. Did Albu intend to use Marcel as an excuse to be near Louisa, already on holiday near Cabourg with the man who had recently become her protector, Robert Gangnat? Proust's plans to vacation with Albu fell through in late July when the marquis's father-in-law, Prince Eugène Murat, was killed in an automobile accident in Germany. Marcel, whose doctors were pressing him to escape the lugubrious atmosphere of the apartment where he had seen both his parents die, resumed his appeals to Mme Straus to help him find the ideal villa. In August she pleaded exhaustion, and Marcel, accepting the blame for her fatigue, abandoned the idea of vacationing on the Normandy coast.

In anticipation of going to Normandy or Brittany, Proust had sent the art historian Émile Mâle a copy of "La Mort des cathédrales." Although it was difficult for him to travel, he wrote that a word from Mâle about recommended sights of architectural or natural beauty would be enough to set him dreaming. Proust admitted that he generally found Romanesque architecture the most moving, but he believed from an article he had read that Mâle preferred the Gothic. Mâle suggested that Normandy would be best for a convalescent, because its medieval towns, like Bayeux and Caen, were not far apart and there were many convenient trains. This too would have to wait.

On August 6 Proust suddenly decided to leave for Versailles, where he settled in a "vast and splendid apartment" at the Hôtel des Réservoirs and immediately became ill. He feared going farther away than Versailles because of his uncle's condition. The Hôtel des Réservoirs, which Proust described as "gloomy, dark and cold," despite its sumptuous furnishings, had been the residence of Mme de Pompadour.[96] Reynaldo, who sometimes retreated to the hotel to compose, may have suggested it to Proust. Because Marcel had not booked in advance, he had to suffer the inconvenience of switching apartments several times during his five-month stay to accommodate arriving guests with long-standing reservations. While at Versailles, Marcel occasionally invited friends to dinner. He particularly enjoyed the company of the playwright René Peter, who lived in Versailles six months out of the year. When Hahn, Lauris, or Billy passed through Paris, normally empty in August, they often made the short trip out to Versailles to visit their reclusive friend.

On August 22 Proust received word that Uncle Georges's condition had become critical. He threw a fur coat over his nightshirt and took the train to Paris. When he arrived at the Weil home, it was too late to say good-bye; his uncle did not recognize him. Proust began to have a severe asthma attack and decided to return to Versailles immediately. On reaching the train station, he was so weak that he could not continue. Finally, after a difficult two hours, during which he consumed strong doses of coffee, he was able to board a train. During his distress, he was befriended by a kind railway worker whose name he forgot to ask. When Marcel arrived in Versailles, he learned that his uncle had died. The trip to Paris left Marcel so weak that it was impossible for him to attend the funeral.

In September, Proust suggested to René Peter that they collaborate on a play. Marcel described the proposed plot in a letter to Reynaldo: The main characters are a married couple who adore each other. On the surface, everything is perfect. The husband, however, has a hidden vice: He is sadistic and hires prostitutes, telling them horrible lies about his wife and instructing them to abuse her similarly. Five minutes later, he is heartbroken over what he has done. One day his wife surprises him during such a session; shocked and incredulous, she faints. She leaves her husband, who attempts to win her back. When she refuses, he kills himself. Proust had long been interested in such characters. He had sketched a sadist in "L'Inconnu," one of the earliest drafts of *Jean Santeuil*.[97] A character caught in a compromising position that is humiliating for a beloved family member was also the theme in "La Confession d'une jeune fille." The project of writing a play with René never came to fruition, apparently because Marcel lacked the energy. Ultimately, this theme of "profanation" led Proust to create Mlle Vinteuil, whose lesbian love affair involves a ritual in which she profanes her father's photograph. Her scandalous behavior causes Vinteuil to die of sorrow and shame.

Proust's lease on the rue de Courcelles apartment was to expire on September 30. He did not wish to renew it because the apartment was too big and too expensive for him, and he considered it a "cemetery," having seen both his parents die there.[98] Proust hired two apartment rental agencies and charged his friends, especially Robert de Billy, René Peter, and Georges de Lauris, to look at some likely apartments. He and his brother now each owned a quarter-share of the building at 102, boulevard Haussmann; the other half-share had been inherited by Amélie, Uncle Georges's widow. Although it had been fifteen years since Marcel had seen the apartment, it held considerable appeal for him—despite its location in a noisy, dusty neighborhood—because it was a dwelling his mother had known. Proust asked his friends to compare each apartment under consideration to boulevard Haussmann. He wanted them to tell him how new each apartment was, its degree of "comfort, dust, silence." Was there an elevator? Common sense told him that a new apartment would be more convenient and contain less dust.

To no one's surprise, Proust chose 102, boulevard Haussmann. He told Mme Catusse that he remembered the apartment "as the ugliest thing I've ever seen, the triumph of the bourgeois bad taste of a period still too close to be inoffensive! It isn't even old-fashioned in the charming sense of the word." Still, he was sure that she would understand the "tender and melancholy attraction" that had drawn him back to it, despite his "even greater horror of the neighbourhood, the dust, the Gare Saint-Lazare, and so many other things."[99] He had written to Mme Straus along similar lines, describing the apartment as "an interim arrangement." "I've sub-rented an apartment . . . where Mama and I often came to dine, and where together we saw our old uncle die in the room I shall occupy. Of course I shall be spared nothing—frightful dust, trees under my window, the noise of the boulevard between the Printemps and Saint-Augustin! If I can't stand it I shall leave."[100] The incessant noise was caused by, among other things, streetcars and other modes of transportation, some still horse-drawn, over the cobblestone streets.

Now that Proust had decided to move to a new apartment, he had to furnish it. He began a complicated series of letters to Mme Catusse, whom he had asked to advise him and help select furniture from the rue de Courcelles. In the coming months he would review with her, in a flood of mail, the furnishing of each room in his parents' apartment, as he consulted her about which pieces to keep and how to decorate his rooms at boulevard Haussmann. Proust later told Mme Catusse that after their mother's death he had wanted to take a small apartment that rented for 1,500 francs, but Robert's refusal to take any of the furniture had forced him to look for larger and more expensive apartments. Marcel had let Robert know how much his refusal annoyed him; Robert replied that Marcel had only to sell what he did not need.

Proust soon complained to Lauris that his "housing problems" were growing "more and more complicated." He had never had to deal with so many practical matters at once and on his own: "I have to write to the architect, the manager, the second-floor tenant, my brother and my aunt as the owners, the concierge, the telephone company, the upholsterer, etc. I must leave you for these graceless tasks."[101] A few days later he wrote to Georges again and listed a number of things that demanded his attention, including a lawsuit he was threatening to bring against the tenant from whom he had sublet the Haussmann apartment.

By the end of October, when the work he was having done in the new apartment was completed and Marcel thought that he was ready to move in, his brother and aunt had the "singular idea" of renting to Dr. Émile Gagey the lower apartment, which would require renovations. Proust decided to remain at Versailles, though he complained to his friends about the extra expense of staying at the hotel—it was cold and damp, and none of the doors and windows shut properly—while paying rent in Paris.[102]

Marcel postponed moving because of the new work on the house and his indecision regarding which pieces of furniture he should keep. Decisions that affected his health were quickly made. There were to be no tapestries in his bedroom, and the carpets and rugs there were not to be nailed down, so that they could be removed frequently and easily beaten. In late October he told Mme Catusse to begin by decorating his bedroom and the small living room. If work on the rest of the rooms was still in progress when he moved in, it would have to cease until he became accustomed to the new apartment. In any case, all work would have to be suspended when he arrived so that his lungs could adapt to the new apartment. His first encounter with new rooms, he informed her, always caused him to be "completely asphyxiated." He wanted her to know that he was still attempting to persuade Robert to take some furniture, but all his brother would say on the subject was "It's all the same to me, anything you do will be fine. The excess can be stored." So Mme Catusse was to take all the furniture he had room for, "selected from the best." Lest she think him "selfish" for taking the best pieces, he assured her that the brothers had an understanding whereby Robert would be compensated. Then, thinking about what to keep, he declared that he wanted no portraits in his room. He considered and rejected his mother's 1880 portrait in oil by Mme Beauvais because he had never found it very lifelike; now that the portrait's "vague resemblance had been made more precise" by his mother's rejuvenation in death, Marcel feared that its presence in his room would only cause him pain.[103]

At some point during the protracted furniture deliberations Marcel's sister-in-law Marthe complained that Robert had given carte blanche to his bizarre brother, who seemed to want all the best pieces. Although she never dared confront Marcel directly, remarks made by Robert and Mme Catusse allowed him to guess her displeasure and her eagerness to be involved in the decisions. Marcel would have none of this; he insisted on dealing exclusively with Robert. Marthe was to have only the piece of furniture—one he knew she coveted—that he intended to give her as a New Year's gift. This piece was one of several with exceptionally fine marquetry that had been gifts to Marcel from his mother. Marcel intended to give another of these to his cousin Valentine Thomson. He warned Mme Catusse about Marthe's possible intervention: "If Robert were to offer my sister-in-law's assistance in arranging the apartment (but he will certainly not!), refuse it!"[104]

During the first week of November, Robert and Marthe were distressed to learn that their three-year-old daughter Adrienne had diphtheria. Although the child never showed signs of being in grave danger, the disease was cause for real concern. Marcel reassured Mme Catusse that she should not worry about catching the disease through contact with the furniture. Meanwhile, decisions about the furnishings were being made. Robert agreed to take "Papa's fine desk" and the superb portrait by Lecomte de Nouÿ of Dr. Proust in his academic robes. Marcel could not bear to part with the old desk in the "smoking" room that his mother had "always seen at her grandparents'. " He would keep it or give it to Félicie, at whose home he could go and see it from time to time. He spoke of the desk as "a very ugly old friend but one who knew so well everything I most loved." He would also keep all the photographs in order to make a selection later, because he wanted to have with him "my grandparents and even their parents, whom I did not know, but whom Mama loved." Proust found it nearly impossible to part with any object that reminded him of his mother.

In early December, Marcel informed Mme Catusse that he planned to keep everything in the drawing room, even the grand piano, for he still intended to have it adapted to function as a player piano.[105] Soon Marcel wrote Mme Catusse again, expressing his nagging frustration over Robert's reluctance to select furniture. He wanted her to know that Robert did not approve of Marthe's displays of bad humor. Marthe, Marcel observed, was "very nice" despite moments of ill temper, which he ascribed to her health. This remark made him pause to assess his own behavior and admit that it was far from perfect: "It's true that my faithful old Félicie maintains that I am, without being aware of it, as disagreeable as anyone could possibly be."[106]

Toward the end of November, Marcel asked Georges whether he owned copies (in French translation) of Emily Brontë's *Wuthering Heights* or Thomas Hardy's

Jude the Obscure that he might be willing to lend. If not, he asked Lauris to have them sent from Mme Paul Émile's bookshop in the faubourg Saint-Honoré. In the postscript, he added a request for Gabriel Mourey's *Gainsborough,* "which I badly need." In his sudden move to Versailles, Proust had lost the copy he was to review for the *Chronique des arts et de la curiosité,* and he was way beyond his deadline.

In spite of his depressed state and wretched health, Marcel knew moments of élan and good humor during his Versailles stay. Such twinklings were usually expressed in letters to Reynaldo, to whom Marcel sent a half-dozen or so poems— including one of twenty-two lines, all rhyming in "-ac," a sonnet, an energetic comic poem about streetcar stock investments, and another of twenty-eight lines just to request an address.[107] Although he rarely left his apartment, he sometimes descended to the ground floor and watched René Peter and other friends challenge proprietor Henri Grossœuvre to a game of billiards.

Proust was delighted to hear finally from Marie Nordlinger and answered immediately: "Dear, dear, dear, dear Mary!" He told her about the copy of *Sésame et les lys* he had attempted to send to her in America. He explained that if she had not yet received any royalties for *Sésame,* it was because the Mercure would not pay royalties until more copies had been sold. He offered to send her an advance, assuring her that "nothing could be easier. . . . Alas, I no longer have to answer to anyone for the use I make of my money." Then he asked whether she was working and indicated that his own lassitude and discouragement had brought him to a halt: "I've closed forever the era of translations, which Mama encouraged. And as for translations of myself, I no longer have the heart."[108]

The brave, patient Mme Catusse must have been relieved when she received Marcel's letter of December 10, saying that he wanted to have as "little furniture as possible, while still having a lot. So keep only the best, what is really of some quality. The rest can wait in a repository." He expressed his pleasure that Robert had selected a desk that had been in storage since the days of the boulevard Malesherbes apartment. As for his own desk, he would take the one that had belonged to Uncle Louis, though he wondered why he would need a desk if he were no longer able to work.

During Proust's stay at Versailles, Albu asked him to try and persuade Louisa to behave in a responsible manner. Louisa, while vacationing at Trouville, had re-warded Albufera's appearance by sending Gangnat away to visit friends nearby. Albufera apparently approved of her being kept by Gangnat and did not want Louisa to spoil the arrangement. Instead, she threw away the money both her protectors gave her and attempted to obtain more. Louisa refused to stop flirting—

and who knows what else—with other men, and when she bought an ermine coat that cost twelve thousand francs, Gangnat had had enough. He felt that she was making a fool of him in front of his friends, who had witnessed her flirtations and knew that he could not afford such a coat. Gangnat threatened to leave Louisa, which upset everyone except the actress. Her mother and Albufera consulted with Marcel, who agreed to intervene.

Responding to Albufera's plea for help, Marcel had René Peter, a tactful and sensitive person and, as a playwright, someone Louisa should want to impress, bring her out to Versailles for a visit. The following day, to thank her for having gone to the trouble and made the "sacrifice" of coming to see him without wearing her perfume, Marcel sent her an immense bouquet of roses.[109] Later in December, Marcel wrote to Hahn and asked him to invite Louisa to dinner with Gangnat and seek to restore harmony.

When Reynaldo visited Proust, he usually brought books with him. Among those he had recently given Marcel was the novel *Le Chevalier d'Harmental* by Alexandre Dumas and Auguste Marquet. The hero, while waiting in Paris for a message from fellow conspirators, sees a girl from the window and falls in love with her. What may have caught Proust's attention was the name of the street where this took place, la rue du Temps-Perdu (the street of lost time). In seclusion at Versailles, Proust, consumed with grief and nostalgia, may have been particularly sensitive to this name.[110]

By mid-December the choices for boulevard Haussmann had been made. The portrait of his mother would go in the drawing room, where he could see it when he wished but not too often. He had found another portrait of his father, by a M. Brouardel, that he would also place there. In the smaller salon he would hang his own portrait by Blanche. Perhaps it recalled for him those happier days when he had written the stories and poems for *Pleasures and Days* and he dreamed of a bright future. In his own room there were to be no paintings. Mme Catusse decided to give him for his bedroom the furnishings of the blue room that had been his mother's. He agreed, saying, "It will be very painful for me." He described for Mme Catusse the cloistered life he had led at the Hôtel des Réservoirs: "Would you believe that except for the first few days when I saw the last rays of the sun from my bed, I have never woken up before nightfall and I know nothing of the charms of the season or the hour. I've spent four months in Versailles as though in a telephone kiosk without being the least aware of my surroundings."[111]

Suddenly, on December 27, Proust, in a "fantastic state," sick with fever and asthma, decided to leave Versailles. He felt so much worse that he feared he might have to take to bed indefinitely, and if so, he would prefer to be in Paris.[112] His unanticipated arrival at 102, boulevard Haussmann surprised concierge Antoine Bertholhomme and Proust's manservant Jean Blanc, who were completely unprepared for a lodger with so many special requirements. In the first days he lacked many necessities. In the letter to Mme Catusse, informing her of his arrival, he mentioned having bought some "little things" at Versailles that he hoped she would accept as a gift. He was, he told her, in "ecstasy" over the "genius" that had inspired her decisions about decorating the apartment; some of the forgotten pieces of furniture from boulevard Malesherbes that she had "exhumed" had "released a symphony" of memories.[113]

He swore Mme Catusse to secrecy about his arrival in Paris. His terrible state required that he not be disturbed by any well-intentioned friends, other than the few he chose to inform himself. As soon as he moved in he began to complain about the noise made by the workers renovating Dr. Gagey's apartment. At least a month's work remained to be done, and the lost sleep was certain to aggravate his asthma. Still profoundly saddened by the death of his parents, sick, discouraged, and at a loss about what to do with himself, Proust intended to remain in seclusion. Marcel was no longer the same person who had set out with his mother on the train journey to Évian in September 1905, a journey that was to have culminated with his undergoing treatment at the clinic in Switzerland. Many years later, he told Céleste Albaret: "I loved my father very much. But the day my mother died, she took her little Marcel with her."[114]

PART V

The Beginning of Freedom (1907–1912)

16 *Filial Sentiments of a Parricide* ∾

ILL HEALTH AND THE NEARLY CONSTANT noise produced by workmen re-modeling surrounding apartments made the first months in his new home miserable for Proust. On days when his asthma attacks were especially severe, he did not allow the servants to enter his room because he needed nothing, being unable even to drink. When he was able to rest, there seemed to be no cessation of the sawing and hammering. Shortly after he moved to his new address he succeeded in bringing the work to a halt for several days. When the workmen resumed, he sought occasional relief through complicated negotiations with his neighbors. Any nervous person might have found such conditions intolerable, but for Proust the banging occurred during his sleeping hours. During the coming months, sick, weary, exhausted, and nearly driven mad by the commotion, he engaged a number of friends who knew the neighbors socially or professionally to intervene on his behalf. Those called upon included the Strauses, Albufera, Georges de Lauris, and Joseph Reinach, who as a high-ranking government official might be able to prevent such disturbances. Marcel tried everything, including paying Dr. Gagey's workers large amounts to do most of their labor at night so that he could sleep mornings.

In February, just as Dr. Gagey's work was nearly finished, Proust heard loud banging in the adjacent apartment. Upon inquiring, he learned that a Mme Katz was having renovations done, including the installation of a new toilet, before moving in. Her bathroom was located right next to his bedroom. In despair, he informed Mme Catusse that the banging chez Katz sounded as if it was right in his room. By mid-March Proust wrote Mme Straus, who knew the Katz family, and proposed that she intervene on his behalf. If the workers were willing to begin at noon or two in the afternoon, he would pay Mme Katz any compensation she wanted.

At first, Proust gave his new address and phone number to a handful of friends, urging them not to reveal that he had returned to Paris. He seemed especially eager to avoid the "fatal count," whom he found the most insistent, most easily offended, and most difficult acquaintance to hold at bay. Early in the year Montesquiou, angry with Marcel for never having visited Yturri's grave at Versailles, attempted a reconciliation through Hahn. Hahn showed the count's letter to Marcel, who provided Hahn with a list (intended for Montesquiou) of excuses for not having gone to the cemetery. He also explained to Reynaldo why he avoided Montesquiou: "When he is back in Paris or Versailles, I shall do my utmost to try to see him one evening, but apart from the fact that it's impossible with everyone, with him the difficulty becomes ever greater, as he is the person with whom I'm most embarrassed, in the bad sense of the word. And even if for once he falls in with my odd hours, the possibility of an untimely attack will prevent me from daring to give him a rendezvous which I'd rather die than break, whereas others would understand."[1]

The move to a new apartment seemed to have aggravated Proust's already lamentable state. Marcel wrote to René Peter in mid-January, "For the first time in my life I've been laid low (four times already) by attacks which last thirty-six, forty, fifty hours! And during this time . . . death!" Nonetheless, he reproached René, whose visits had been one of his favorite distractions at Versailles, for not having come to see him. He held Reynaldo up as the example of a devoted friend, willing to wait and, if necessary, return day after day until Marcel could receive him. Albu, who had been so faithful, was now married and could no longer visit late evenings. "I'd rather die here and now than see people in the daytime these days when I don't dine till ten o'clock (if I dine! for I sometimes go three days without eating)." His doctor had warned that if his condition did not improve, Marcel would have to leave Paris for good. Perhaps, he told René, he would move to Versailles.

On January 24 a tragedy occurred that shocked Proust. An acquaintance of his murdered his mother and killed himself. Proust learned the news the next day when he opened the *Figaro* and saw the front-page headline "An Act of Madness." In graphic detail he read how Henri Van Blarenberghe had fired several shots at his eighty-year-old mother, mortally wounding her. On hearing the gunfire and screams the servants had come running to find their mistress, covered with blood, standing on the staircase and screaming at her son: "Henri, what have you done to me!" Mme Van Blarenberghe then plunged down the steps and died. The police, summoned by the servants, forced open Henri's door. They found him near death; he had punctured his neck with a dagger before shooting himself in the head. His left eyeball, dislocated by the force of the bullet, drooped on the pillow.

Because Proust knew the family, he could easily picture the horrible scene. In his own moments of rage, Marcel had glimpsed the hideous countenance of matricide, the awful, reversed face of filial love: the broken glass paneling and smashed vase, or the occasion when, furious at his mother over her fruitless attempts to force him to lead an ordered life, he had exploded in anger and pummeled Bertrand with his fists before demolishing his new hat.[2]

After reading the Van Blarenberghe story, Marcel recalled his recent exchange of letters with Henri. How could anyone commit such a heinous act, especially someone as sober and distinguished as Henri? Marcel expressed his disbelief in a letter to Mme Catusse: "Can you imagine that I received ten days ago the most sensitive, the saddest, the most touching letter from that unfortunate Van Blarenberghe which would make him more to be pitied than Oedipus. What a shocking story!"

Although the Proust and Van Blarenberghe families were not close, Jeanne had known Henri's mother, and Marcel had dined a few times with Henri when both were young. When Henri's father had died the previous fall, Marcel had written a sympathy letter and received a reply that he felt showed great filial love. Two weeks before the tragedy Marcel had written Henri again, hoping to locate through Henri the kind railway worker who had assisted him at the Gare Saint-Lazare. Because Henri's father had been chairman of Eastern Railways, Marcel had asked for advice about how to proceed. On January 12 Henri replied and expressed his condolences for the death of Marcel's parents. He, too, Henri wrote, found it extremely difficult "physically and mentally [*moralement*] to recover from the shock caused by his father's death. One must always hope." Then Henri wrote a sentence that was to haunt Marcel: "I don't know what 1907 holds for me, but let's hope it will bring us both some improvement and enable us to see each other."

Gaston Calmette, on learning that Proust knew Van Blarenberghe, asked him to write about the tragedy. Proust began at three in the morning and wrote the article "without doing a draft, straight on to the *Figaro*'s copy paper, until eight in the morning," when a cramp in his hand forced him to stop. He decided to sleep, leaving instructions to be woken later in the day to finish the story. But just as he tried to sleep the workers in the apartment below began hammering. Feeling wretched, he sent the story off unfinished, without even rereading it. At eleven that evening the proofs arrived. Instead of correcting them, he added a conclusion he thought was "really rather good." Robert Ulrich, Félicie's nephew, returned the proofs to the *Figaro,* with Proust's instructions that "they could cut whatever they liked but not a word of the ending must be changed."[3]

Cardane, who had little appreciation of Proust's talents, received the proofs. When Ulrich informed Cardane of the author's orders regarding the ending, the editor sneered that Proust was deluding himself "if he thinks anyone will read his article other than himself and the few people who know him!"[4] Ulrich reported the remark to Marcel, who later repeated it to Calmette when protesting the excision of his final paragraph.

In "Sentiments filiaux d'un parricide" (Filial sentiments of a parricide), published February 1 in the *Figaro,* Proust tried to identify the evil, irresistible force that had caused Henri to kill his mother and then himself.[5] He compared Henri to a victim of the Greek gods who, for their own purposes, drove people mad and made them commit horrible crimes. The eyeball stuck to the pillow suggested "the most terrible gesture of human suffering that history has left us, the very eye of the wretched Oedipus!" Toward the end of the article Proust returned to the mother's dying, unanswered utterance, "What have you done to me!" and applied it to all mothers and their sons: "There is perhaps not a genuinely loving mother who could not," with her dying breath, "reproach her son" as had Henri's mother. Proust observed that as we age, we kill those "who love us by the worries we give them, by the anxious love we inspire and constantly alarm."[6]

When Marcel received his newspaper with the Van Blarenberghe story, he was outraged to see that his conclusion had disappeared.[7] He wrote to Calmette to protest: "The only thing I had indicated to M. Cardane as being essential" had been omitted: "Let us remember that for the ancients there was no altar more sacred, surrounded with more profound superstition and veneration, betokening more grandeur and glory for the land that possessed them and had dearly disputed them, than the tomb of Oedipus at Colonus and the tomb of Orestes at Sparta, that same Orestes whom the Furies had pursued to the feet of Apollo himself and Athene, saying: 'We drive from the altar the parricidal son.' "[8]

Proust deplored the cut because, as he explained to Calmette, "the word parricide, having opened the article, closed it," thus giving the article "a sort of unity." Calmette replied that Proust's closing lines had "frightened Cardane" because he "thought they showed insufficient disapprobation for the unfortunate parricide's deed." Proust found the reading of his conclusion as an apology for parricide "a bit much!"[9] Easily overlooked by readers was Proust's subtle suggestion that what the Greeks depicted in their stories as destiny, modern society might attribute to pathological or psychological causes.

Among those most impressed by Marcel's article were Ludovic Halévy and his son Daniel. Ludovic had told Robert Dreyfus: "Your friend, young Proust, has written an astonishing article, full of talent and originality."[10] Daniel found the piece so remarkable that he, ever the archivist, cut it out of the paper, had it bound in leather, and sent it to Proust for him to autograph.[11] Proust, unaccustomed to the idea that someone might be interested in his writings to that degree, thanked Daniel in a letter, telling his old school friend that the servants had turned the apartment upside down looking for Van Blarenberghe's letters.[12] Marcel wanted to give them to Daniel to include in the bound copy of "Sentiments filiaux," but he had already managed to lose the letters in the disorder of his room.

Many friends wrote to express their admiration for "Sentiments filiaux." To close friends Marcel expressed serious doubts about his talent. He did not trust this new voice. He wrote to Lucien: "I really *feel* I have" no talent.[13] Between his translation of *Sésame* and "Sentiments filiaux," he had not written a line: "I can tell you that I am not so modest, and if I consider that I haven't any talent, that for a variety of reasons I haven't been able to make the most of my gifts, that my style has rotted without ripening, on the other hand I'm aware that there are many more real ideas, genuine insights, in what I write than in almost all the articles that are published." He seemed more concerned about Lucien's doubts regarding his talent as a painter. To encourage Lucien, he mentioned an idea that would be important to his own work, although he did not see its full implications: "You are wrong to think of yourself always inside time. The part of ourselves that matters, when it matters, is outside time."[14] Lucien should think of himself "simply as an instrument capable of whatever experiments in beauty or truth you wish to perform, and your gloom will evaporate." If Lucien followed his advice, he would find "joy and a great eagerness for life and work."[15]

Proust's disappointment over Cardane's censorship was mitigated by Calmette's thoughtfulness. Consideration and delicacy on the part of others always had an extraordinary effect on him and were especially welcome from an editor. Writing to Dreyfus in early February, Proust expressed his admiration of Calmette: "For amiability (which to this degree is genuine kindness and charm) I don't know anyone comparable. . . . This newspaper editor has written to me three times in three days, for no other reason than to give me pleasure and in this vein: 'Your article is admirable; it moved me more than I can say; it will be an ornament to the paper; there isn't a reader who won't re-read it and thank you for it with a sense of enchantment etc. etc. etc.' When one hasn't slept for a fortnight and when one's half crazy, I assure you that letters like that—even if he's saying to himself at the same moment 'What a bore that article is'—do one good."[16]

Jacques-Émile Blanche sent congratulations but expressed some doubts about Proust's new style. A sentence that ran for eighteen lines had caught Blanche's attention. Proust, perhaps relishing the opportunity to hint that Blanche had really not paid close attention, replied that the article contained sentences of approximately thirty lines. And that in "On Reading" some occupied eighty lines.[17] If "Sentiments filiaux" contained "so many repetitions," it was because he had written it in one draft without revisions, "But that does not excuse its 'quality,' which I find deplorable."[18]

Soon after leaving the Hôtel des Réservoirs and its attentive staff for his own apartment, he saw the need to hire a new manservant. In mid-February he wrote to Paul Bacart, a valet employed by the princesse de Caraman-Chimay, to see whether any of his acquaintances wanted a job. Proust gave Bacart his telephone number and suggested that he call after five or six in the afternoon, though eight would be the best time to find him able to talk. "When you phone I am usually the one who answers, although sometimes the telephone is in the concierge's lodge."[19] During this period Proust made and received calls, perhaps because his only servant in residence was the elderly Félicie, who, like Françoise in the Search, may have refused to use the strange new device. Before closing the letter to Bacart, Proust apologized to the correspondent for the poor quality of the paper. The stationery he had used was the kind he purchased at the department store Au Printemps and kept next to his bed to light his antiasthma powders. He was always embarrassed whenever he used these sheets for a late night letter. He had begun to write more often in bed and still complained of hand cramps, factors that made his difficult handwriting nearly impossible to read.

Proust had already received one job application from Nicolas Cottin, who had worked for Adrien and Jeanne. There was a risk in hiring Cottin, who had been dismissed by Mme Proust for drinking. Marcel's mother had warned him never to engage Nicolas, but he brought certain advantages—advantages Proust mentioned in his letter to Bacart. Cottin, a stocky man two years younger than Proust, was used to his habits. Because Nicolas knew what to expect, there was a better chance he might stick it out and, perhaps most important, Marcel would be spared the difficult task of interviewing and training a new servant. By the end of the month, Marcel had hired Cottin.[20] In May he hired Nicolas's wife, Céline, to assist the aging Félicie.[21]

Georges de Lauris's mother died on February 15, at the age of fifty-three. This death profoundly affected Proust, who wrote to Lauris, "I feel as if I were losing Mama for the second time." Once again his poor health and impossible routine kept him isolated from a friend he needed to see. Proust's extraordinary sensitivity allowed him to put himself in another's place. His isolation and medicated state may have intensified his reactions. He assured Georges, "I see you, I feel you, I live you, and it's the most hideous experience." He had wanted to write an article about the marquise de Lauris for *Le Figaro,* but he felt too ill and distraught.[22]

Two days later Marcel wrote again to console his grieving friend: "You will know a sweetness that you cannot yet conceive. When you had your mother you thought a great deal about the days when you would no longer have her. Now you will think a great deal about the days when you did have her." Once Lauris had adjusted to the "terrible experience of being forever thrown back on the past, then you will feel her gently returning to life, coming back to take her place again, her whole place beside you." But his friend must never expect to be whole again "because something will always remain broken in you."[23] Proust's theory of loss and grief, remembering and forgetting, continued to evolve.[24]

Marcel, who had not seen Montesquiou for more than two years, wrote in mid-March to congratulate him on his article "L'Académicienne." In January the *Figaro* had announced the publication of the definitive edition of Montesquiou's poems under the general title *Hortensias bleus.* Montesquiou's passion for hydrangeas was well known, and the success of *Hortensias bleus* inspired those who found him ridiculous to refer to him as Hortensiou.[25] Proust, fearing that Montesquiou might expect an article, tried to preempt such a request by saying he regretted having had the "unfortunate idea" of writing another article on short notice. He did not mention that the review was of Anna's forthcoming volume of poems, *Les Éblouissements.* For the moment Montesquiou, who continued to conduct social and literary vendettas against those who displeased him, seemed remarkably tolerant of what he might have taken as Proust's impudence.[26] Perhaps he was amused; more likely he prized Marcel's friendship, limited though it was, and, above all, his extraordinary ability to celebrate and promote Montesquiou on those occasions when he could be persuaded to take the trouble.

Days Spent Reading

After the 1905 essay "On Reading," Proust stopped translating and writing society pieces in order to experiment with more personal essays. He decided to write another article on reading, this one in a lighter vein, inspired by the memoirs of the comtesse de Boigne.[27] "Journées de lecture" (Days spent reading) appeared in the *Figaro* on March 20. Remembering his theory that "no one reads," Proust began the article by observing that people read only as a last resort. Always observant about how the new machines of transportation and communication were altering lifestyles, he wrote a description of the relatively new phenomenon of talking over the telephone. He depicted the mystery of such communication, presided over by "the umbrageous priestesses of the Invisible, the Young Ladies of the Telephone."[28] He later used this passage about telephone operators and long-distance conversations with few alterations in the *Search*.

"Journées de lecture" contained in embryonic form other Proustian concerns, such as the fascination with proper names and the disappointment that often results when we encounter a person or a place whose name has made us dream. Because reality often disappoints, wisdom, Proust suggests, counsels us to "replace all our social relations and many of our voyages by reading the Almanach de Gotha or the train schedules . . . "[29] In the *Search*, Proust was to use the confrontation between dream and reality as an important element of the narrative drive.[30]

The newspaper cut a long section on reading from the article, but not the blurb about Anna de Noailles's new volume of poems, *Les Éblouissements*, for which he was soon to write a separate piece.[31] When Anna read his piece in the *Figaro*, she did so "first with my fingers covering 'my passage' in order not to see it, not to get excited or bursting with vanity." His essay was "the most tender account, and also the clearest, sharpest, most piercing, that could possibly be given of familiar life at the edge of dreams." She took particular delight in the "henceforth divine damsels of the telephone."[32]

When Georges wrote to congratulate him on the article, Marcel pretended that it was his "great" friendship that had made Lauris ascribe to him "as much talent as to poet Francis Jammes." What had moved Proust especially had been Lauris's declaration that he had read the article to his father, a gesture "infinitely sweet to me," because he saw this as a continuation of the "sweet spiritual life you shared with your mother." Proust wondered whether life was worth living now that he had lost his mother and father: "Only our parents can give us that tenderness. Afterwards, when we have them no longer, we never experience it again, from anyone.

Except in the memory of the hours spent with them, which alone helps us to live, and above all will help us to die."[33]

Montesquiou wrote urging Marcel to join him during Holy Week for a visit to Yturri's grave: "I should also like to communicate to you some extracts from the book I am devoting to him." The prolific count was about to publish another volume. Because of Proust's secrecy, Montesquiou thought him still at Versailles, which would have made visiting Yturri's grave relatively easy. Montesquiou complimented Proust belatedly on his "fine Blarenberghe article." About "Journées de lectures," he was more circumspect, having found the piece "digressive but very agreeable."[34]

By late March, Montesquiou had learned that Marcel was no longer at Versailles. "We shall take up again another time the project for a funerary pilgrimage; but, for the moment, I propose as a substitute a reading of the extract of which I speak." Proust replied, feigning "great joy" and his "desire to realize that project immediately." He then described the severe attacks that beset him and, pretending not to have understood that Montesquiou was free to come for a reading, requested that the extract be sent to him—"For me, reading means solitude"—and scolding Montesquiou, he added, "(as you will know if you have glanced through my preface to *Sesame and Lilies*—that preface about which you promised to speak to me, but never let me know that you had even read.)"[35] In the postscript he added more details to discourage the count's visit: "Just imagine, I get up (without dressing) only one day in seven!"

Montesquiou abandoned pursuit, but observed, "I'm inclined to believe that you are, I won't say an imaginary invalid, but a spellbound valetudinarian, in the fairy-tale sense, and that this spell can, will yield to a philtre or a bough, or a word." In the postscript, Montesquiou observed that "meetings are not necessary between people who appreciate one another, but they are agreeable."[36] Even those Proust was willing to receive had to observe new, stricter rules. He detailed these for the playwright Francis de Croisset, who had been told that he might visit late at night "if you have no cigarettes, no flowers in your buttonhole, no cologne."[37] As Proust continued the futile search for the elements that caused his debilitating attacks, the list of forbidden items grew longer.

The noisy neighbors continued to plague him. Geneviève Straus, who found it almost as difficult to leave the house as did Marcel, took the extraordinary step of inviting M. Katz, the judge and the son of his neighbor, to lunch, a gesture that filled Marcel with admiration and gratitude. "It's one of those actions full of wit and kindness that are typical of you. His cow of a mother, alas, hasn't stopped building . . . I don't know what! A dozen workers a day hammering away with such frenzy for so many months must have erected something as majestic as the Pyramid of Cheops which passers-by must be astonished to see between the Printemps and Saint-Augustin."[38]

The constant banging made him resort even more frequently to drugs for sleep, and then, of course, to caffeine for waking and remaining alert. He told Mme Straus that he believed his life had been shortened "by several years as a result of all the attacks and the drugs." When the workers finished remodeling next door, he thought he would have "a new lease on life." Since his mother's death he had rarely stepped outdoors, and then almost always at night. Even under the conditions he had described to Mme Straus, he had managed once during the day to take a "few steps outside in front of the house and on the balcony." Although his bold emergence had brought on new attacks, the brief exposure to light and fresh air had given him "great pleasure. I found the sun a very pretty and a very strange object."[39]

On April 11 Reynaldo took Marcel to a musical soirée at the princesse de Polignac's to hear a performance of two of his works, *Le Bal de Béatrice d'Este* and *La Fontaine de Bandusie.* Writing to express his admiration for the compositions, Proust teased Hahn, who had led the small ensemble from the piano, about his conducting style: "I think you led the first movement and all the last part admirably—brilliantly. . . . Elsewhere you indulge in too many tricks, too many mannerisms, too many grimaces, and that way of bouncing up and down on your bottom which I don't find at all pretty." Marcel had been "impressed that you should have succeeded in forcing so many society people to stop and listen to a fountain weeping in silence and solitude." During the concert Marcel had looked around the room at many of his friends whom he had not seen in several years and observed the effects of time on their faces: "How all the people I used to know have aged!" The ravages of age had made them resemble "portraits of monsters from the time when people didn't know how to draw."[40] He was to use this impression and others to create one of the most famous scenes in his novel, a scene called "the masked ball," at which the Narrator, after an absence of many years in a sanatorium, returns to Paris to attend a ball at the princesse de Guermantes's. On entering the ballroom he at first believes that his former friends, whom he cannot recognize, are wearing masks—as indeed they are, the masks of old age.

Montesquiou informed Marcel that he would soon see "*one* of the *ways* in which I am pleased to associate your name with mine in the march of time." The count had put together a book of his literary portraits, *Altesses sérénissimes* (Serene highnesses), the first chapter of which he had devoted to Gustave Moreau. As a postscript Montesquiou had added Proust's article "Un Professeur de beauté."[41] In late May, Proust attended a reading of Montesquiou's poems at Mme Lemaire's. That evening he sent the count a letter declaring how extremely happy he had been to see and hear the poet again. He informed Montesquiou that while awaiting the asthma attack that would begin when the caffeine wore off, he was reading *Altesses sérénissimes.* Marcel feared that he had wounded the count's pride by comparing him to a moss rose and entreated him not to "believe that it's 'age,' as you said, that gives you the pink and wrinkled face of a moss rose. You know that it has its beauty."[42]

At fifty, Montesquiou's beauty had begun to fade. He had resorted to cosmetics in a vain attempt to hide the deep furrows in his face and other blemishes. Proust, in his next letter, still worried that Montesquiou might resent the comparison to a moss rose, evoked memories of their first meeting at Mme Lemaire's: "As regards the moss rose, I owe my knowledge—as of so many other things—to you alone. In the now distant era when the first fine evenings of spring brought us together at the rue Monceau, as we took off our overcoats beneath the arborescent lilacs, I remember seeing you with a ravishing flower in your button-hole, at a time when it wasn't fashionable to wear one, but became so because of the elegance with which you sported it. You told me then that it was a moss rose." Proust later regretted the attention he had drawn to the moss rose when that flower provided Montesquiou with another clue to connect himself to Proust's character the baron de Charlus. When the Narrator first glimpses Charlus at Balbec, he is fingering "the moss rose in his button-hole."[43]

Had Proust taken notice a month earlier when Baron Doäzan had died?[44] He and Montesquiou were to be the primary models for Charlus. Doäzan had long ago ceased to be prominent in social circles, but Proust remembered from Mme Aubernon's salon her cousin's flamboyant appearance, his makeup and perfume, and his scandalous behavior, and how Montesquiou had lured Yturri away from him. Aspects of Yturri and Delafosse were used in the creation of the violinist Morel, with whom Charlus becomes infatuated.

Proust continued to discourage Montesquiou's visits by describing to him the sacrifices Reynaldo made in order to see him: "How could I demand of you . . . what I demand of him, who though he comes at the most propitious hours, sometimes has to come back three or four times in succession at an hour's interval until an unexpected fumigation is over, and finally, when I see him, often has to speak alone, my answers coming to him on scraps of paper. Even my brother is too busy to put up with these habits and I haven't seen him for months."[45] This account of the saintly patience required to see him became a standard tactic to discourage friends from calling, or at least to warn them not to expect an easy entry, even if they were willing to come late at night.

Proust's article on the comtesse de Noailles's third volume of poems, *Les Éblouissements* (Resplendence), "the masterpiece of literary *impressionnisme*," appeared in the *Figaro*'s literary supplement on June 15.[46] He had wanted to avoid the supplement, because he believed that no one read the section he called the "foretaste of eternal oblivion."[47] Like the other articles he had written since "On Reading," this one contained Proustian themes awaiting their ideal frame. These themes, pressed into service here to praise the poet's work, reappeared in the *Search* as elements of Proust's aesthetics, ethics, and views on sexuality.

Art, Proust maintained, is the real world; the one we muddle aimlessly through in our habitual, conformist ways is the sham existence. In addition to Anna's poems, from which he quoted frequently, Proust used other forms of art or nature as seen in an artist's vision to discuss the countess and her poems. Proust alludes to one of his key themes: androgyny. The first of three canvases by Gustave Moreau to which he compares Anna the "Poète-Femme" is *Le Poète*, a painting that, if examined closely, may represent a female instead of a male poet. Proust wondered whether the painter, in making *The Poet*'s sexuality ambiguous, intended to suggest that the poet who "contains within himself all humanity, must possess a woman's tender nature."[48]

In describing Anna, Proust stated a fundamental belief about human personality. Although each of us contains multiple selves, there is a basic division between what he calls the social self and the profound self. The outward self, the one that we most often show the world (and ourselves), is superficial, vain, and habit bound. To become an artist one must succeed, as Anna has, in removing "everything that constitutes the social self" and must speak from the center of one's being, abode of the "profound self that individualizes works of art and makes them last."[49]

When Anna received her copy of the June 15 *Figaro*, she wrote immediately to tell Marcel that she had read and reread "the divine article" with "infinite emotion and gratitude. I realize that you are one of the all too rare people for whom I write." A few days later she wrote again, saying that she continued to read the article, which outshone the work it praised: "I walk . . . through the gardens you have described, which are so rich, so varied, so tangible that mine seem only a geranium blob, stupidly glaring and flat, in the sunlight." She knew that she owed this "divine incense . . . less to your taste and your judgment than to a friendship for me."[50]

Anna was a gifted, dedicated poet, who recognized a major literary talent in her dear Marcel.

On a rare outing, Marcel went to the *Figaro*'s offices to thank Calmette for publishing his articles. During the conversation with the editor, Marcel mentioned that he would like to invite him to dinner one evening. Marcel had, as he wrote to Mme Straus, "thought that would be the end of it, for how could I have imagined that I should be giving a dinner party for years hence, or even before my death (less distant, perhaps)." But Calmette, courteous, obliging, without suspecting "all the agitation" he was about to cause Proust, "very amiably took out his engagement book and searched for a free date." There was no escape. Marcel especially wanted Mme Straus to attend—the "greatest courtesy I could pay him." At the mention of her name, Calmette had given "a great exclamation of joy."[51]

Proust quickly reserved a private dining room at the Ritz and invited Gabriel Fauré to perform some of his own compositions. Unfortunately, Reynaldo was away in London. Marcel intended to invite about twenty guests for dinner at eight and an equal number for the music at ten. He sought advice from Mme Straus, of the kind he would have asked his mother, about what to serve his guests. To his great disappointment she would be unable to attend. Guiche came to his rescue and selected the menu and wines.

On the eve of the party Fauré became indisposed and had to cancel. Proust immediately called Reynaldo's old friend Édouard Risler, who agreed to step in, asking for and receiving a rather stiff fee of one thousand francs. The dinner was a great success. Among those attending, in addition to Calmette, were Mme d'Haussonville, Anna de Noailles, M. and Mme de Clermont-Tonnerre, Louis d'Albufera, Jean Béraud, Armand de Guiche, Jacques-Émile Blanche, and Emmanuel Bibesco. Those who arrived later for the recital were the Casa Fuertes, the Robert d'Humièreses, the princesse de Polignac, Mme de Chevigné, Édouard Rod, Gabriel de La Rochefoucauld, and Robert Ulrich. Risler, joined by Maurice Hayot, professor of violin at the Paris Conservatoire, and Marguerite Hasselmans, another pianist and pupil of Fauré's, played selections from Fauré, Beethoven, Schumann, Chopin, Chabrier, Couperin, and Wagner. In his letter to Reynaldo, Proust described the evening as "exquisite and beautifully arranged," although he lamented the absences of Hahn, Mme Straus, Mme Gaston de Caillavet, and, especially Gladys Deacon, a Boston girl of renowned beauty.[52] The party's only sour note had come from Félicie and Ulrich, who chose the day of the dinner to announce that they were leaving Marcel's employment.[53] Ulrich, however, was unable to find suitable employment and continued to make himself available to Proust for errands and dictation.

Later in July, Robert de Flers's grandmother, Mme Eugène de Rozière, died. Once again Marcel was devastated: "I can scarcely write to you, as my eyes are blinded with tears, having just read the note in the *Figaro:* I shall never see your dear, your beloved little grandmother again." This time, in addition to weeping and commiserating, he did something more: he wrote an article, "La Mort d'une grand'mère" (The death of a grandmother), and sent it to the *Figaro*. His homage to Mme de Rozière presents a variation of a question that was to reverberate throughout the *Search:* Are those we have lost gone from our lives forever? Dead forever? Proust cannot bring himself to believe that this is true. He had not accepted what he would eventually formulate in the novel as the "general law of oblivion." He refused to accept eternal separation, a belief sustained in the article by a brave exclamation point: "Nothing lasts, not even death!"

If Marcel later caricatured aspects of Montesquiou in Charlus, the count had insights into Marcel's character. Expressing his admiration for Proust's "pretty article" on Flers's grandmother (while making it clear that he did not like the woman Proust had honored), Montesquiou told Marcel that "the most agreeable part of your commentary gives you the opportunity to talk about yourself, by treating of those valetudinarians whose economy of physical expenditure allows them prodigalities of mind and heart." After speaking about maternal love in its "laudable excess," he related a story Marcel may not have known about his father: "It was your father, I remember, who gave me, when I met him one day, that sensation of *the absolute*" in the adoration of one's children. "When I asked him for your news he replied: '*Marcel is working on his cathedrals.*' And the way he articulated the pronoun made me realize that in his eyes the Middle Ages, as was befitting, had striven *for you alone* in chiseling and shaping stone."[54]

Thanking the count for his letter, Proust made a general defense of his friends, some of whom he feared had fallen into Montesquiou's black books, a deplorable situation because "I couldn't love my friends without some pain if they didn't love you." Marcel then touched on the "gentle art" of making enemies, concluding that Montesquiou relished quarrels even more than Whistler: "I don't believe the steadfast cult of enmity procured him that savage and salubrious joy which it seems to inflame in you. One would like to ask you for the sacrifice of an enmity as one asks others for the sacrifice of a friendship. And the difference is that you would refuse it!" Then Proust used an analogy that delighted Montesquiou so much he repeated it in his memoirs: "You rise above incomprehension, like the seagull above the storm, and you would hate to be deprived of this upward pressure."[55]

As late as August 1 Marcel still had not made his vacation plans. He wrote to Reynaldo: "I continue to hesitate between Brittany, Cabourg, Touraine, Germany . . . and Paris." This would be the last year of extended hesitation. He finally chose Cabourg, as he was to do for the next eight years.

Cabourg

On August 5 Proust, accompanied by Cottin and Ulrich, left for Cabourg, the seaside resort he had visited with his mother and grandmother many years before. This time his sudden departure was prescribed by his doctors, who were worried about his condition; aware of his inability to make a decision about vacations, they insisted that he leave with only a few hours' notice. The memory of his mother, as he explained to Mme Catusse, guided him to Cabourg.[56]

A month earlier the seaside town had inaugurated the large, sumptuous Grand-Hôtel. Ads for the event appeared in Paris newspapers, and society columns listed the personalities who had already arrived in the "pretty little town" that proclaimed itself "the Queen of the beaches." The *Figaro* reported that the mayor's guests at the inauguration had been "literally astonished to find themselves facing the sea in front of this incomparable beach," along which ran an "admirable boardwalk."[57] The next sentence certainly caught Proust's eye: the reporter called the Grand-Hôtel "a veritable palace from *The Arabian Nights.*" The article then described the interior design and furnishings of the hotel, each of whose rooms boasted its own bathroom.[58]

During his first summer at the Grand-Hôtel, Marcel reserved judgment on the building, its inhabitants, and its amenities. In the summer of 1907 Proust, accustomed to the most exclusive Parisian society, was amazed at what impressed the inhabitants of the Grand-Hôtel. In a letter to the princesse de Caraman-Chimay, he described the company in the hotel as "odious." The "two most eminent personalities are the manager of a department store and a retired croupier."[59] In fact, the social picture was not quite as bleak as Proust had painted it. Among those the *Figaro* mentioned as having been spotted at teatime at the Grand-Hôtel on August 12 were Tristan Bernard and M. et Mme Francis de Croisset, as well as Proust himself.[60]

In a letter to Reynaldo, Proust amused himself by comparing the hotel to a stage set with a cast of characters worthy of a Feydeau farce. There was Alfred Edwards, proprietor and founder of the popular daily *Le Matin* and a notorious womanizer; Edwards's current mistress, the actress Geneviève Lantelme; his latest wife (number five), née Misia Godebska; the banker Thadée Natanson, cofounder with his brother of *La Revue blanche,* and Mme Edwards's first husband; and Dr. Charcot, the first husband of Mme Edwards number four. "Yesterday evening there was a rumour circulating that Mme Edwards . . . had killed Edwards . . . but there was nothing in it."[61] Proust enjoyed sending Hahn gossip, and the guests at the new hotel provided a rich crop. Also staying in Cabourg were the Belle Époque's celebrated caricaturist Sem and the painter Paul Helleu, both of whom accompanied Proust on some excursions. Helleu, who painted flowers and seascapes as well as other subjects, was later an important model for Elstir in the *Search.*[62]

Proust soon established his own routine. He would take "long drives every day in a (closed) motor-car, visit churches (without any pleasure), watch polo, gamble—and lose—at baccarat every evening, etc.—all this among the commonest set of people in the world."[63] He had also trained the hotel staff to provide extraordinary service and as much gossip as possible. René Gimpel, an art dealer from Trouville who became an acquaintance, remembered how well Proust rewarded waiters: "He gave enormous tips; if a dinner cost him ten francs, he added twenty francs for the waiter." Around midnight Proust would go back up to his room and play checkers with one of the servants, whom he interrogated about everything that was happening in the vast hotel.[64]

That first summer at Cabourg, Proust spent an unprecedented amount of time up and about in the daytime. He was determined to explore all the churches and other architectural sights of interest in the region. And he paid many social calls on his Paris friends who had rented villas in the hills and towns east of Cabourg. These included the Strauses, the Guiches, Louisa de Mornand and Robert Gangnat, and Georges de Lauris and his father. Cabourg and his new routine gave him the opportunity to see people, particularly women, whom he never or seldom saw in Paris because of his bizarre schedule and the nearly impossible conditions for seeing him at home.

Shortly after arriving in Cabourg, Proust wrote Émile Mâle to ask what he should see in the region. He told the art historian that, having "spent an entire year in bed," he would "like to take advantage of what may well be the last journey to be granted me, to visit some monuments or sites which you consider particularly striking." His interest was not limited to "cathedrals or even monuments. Indeed a town that had remained untouched . . . or some old port or whatever that you knew, would provide more food for my imagination than a cathedral that wasn't very special—or really sublime." He intended to take advantage of the new car rental service, "which, if my present sufferings calm down a little, would enable me to explore quite far afield in Normandy."[65] Proust's great burst of activity in exploring the region surrounding Cabourg was similar to that exhibited during the 1902 trip to Holland, when he tried to see everything, fearing that he might never return.

Jacques Bizet, like Robert Proust an early car enthusiast, was apparently one of the founders of the company that built Unic automobiles.[66] In spite of earlier setbacks, Bizet had recently known some success as an entrepreneur. In addition to automobile manufacturing, he also served as the director of one of the first car rental agencies in Paris, Taximètres Unic, which brought the rare luxury of rented cars to vacationers in Cabourg in the summer and in Monaco during the winter.[67] It was through his hiring of Bizet's drivers that Proust met two chauffeurs, Odilon Albaret and Alfred Agostinelli, who were to play crucial roles in his life. For the first of many excursions, Proust hired Agostinelli and his red taxi to drive him to Caen, famous for its medieval churches. Agostinelli, whose father was Italian, was a native of Monaco. At nineteen, although slightly plump, Agostinelli was an attractive young man with thick dark hair and fair skin. His habitual shyness disguised an enthusiasm for the new machines of speed and a daredevil fearlessness.

The stay in Cabourg brought about a dramatic change in Proust, who in recent months had gotten out of bed only once a week, and that without dressing. Now "the pure air joined with a deadly dose of caffeine" allowed him "to go out every day in a closed car."[68] Riding across the Normandy countryside with Agostinelli in his red taxi was, Marcel said, like being shot out of a cannon.[69] As the taxi sped along the road toward Caen, Proust watched the distant spires appear and disappear against the horizon in constantly shifting perspectives, and he marveled at the phenomenon of parallax and relativity so keenly felt in the automobile.

Agostinelli also drove the writer to visit friends. On what Proust described as an "unforgettable outing," he motored with Lauris from Cabourg all the way to Trouville, where they had called on the Strauses at the Clos des Mûriers.[70] At Bénerville, he and Georges visited the Guiches at "Mon Rêve" and Louisa and Gangnat, who were nearby in another villa.[71] When they stopped at Houlgate so that Marcel could meet Georges's father, Georges showed Marcel a photograph of his mother. Proust, who found photographs of his close friends and their families irresistible, persuaded Georges to lend him the photograph. Writing to Georges after he had finished contemplating the picture, Marcel explained that he had insisted on taking it because he needed "to study it alone." The photograph had aroused feelings in him that "surpassed all my expectations." Thanking Georges for the "sweet token of friendship," Marcel gave the results of having scrutinized his father in person and his mother through the picture. Proust, always fascinated by atavism, claimed to have "easily recognized the genealogy, and one after the other all the 'patents' of your intellectual, moral and physical nobility."[72]

Another letter to Georges revealed that seeing his mother's photograph had plunged Marcel back into the pit of remorse and regret. Underneath the tender, loving memories lay an abyss of loneliness and despair: "We really do have with us those whom we love. But to think that they cannot realize that we have them, that they cannot feel and enjoy it, that Mama cannot see me up and about, that you will achieve success without your mother knowing of it, all this is more than enough to confirm a longing for death."[73] Proust also worried about other missed opportunities, of what might have been with Bertrand de Fénelon. Uncharacteristically insensitive to Georges's feelings, he wondered "whether I haven't passed over the only friend I ought to have had, whose friendship could have been fruitful for both of us."[74]

It was Reynaldo who remained closest to him, even though absent. In early September, Marcel sent an intimate letter to his "dear little Birnechnibus," in whose love alone he found solace. "I still have the trembling which prevents me from writing. But how many times a day, how many times a night, does my heart melt at the thought of Buninuls, how many times do I bury myself in him, and indeed always, whatever else I'm thinking of, his dear little muninulserie and face loom up and fill my horizon."

Proust then related to Hahn a recent visit to Édouard Vuillard's studio at Amfreville near Cabourg. Vuillard, who had been "wearing a blue workman's smock," seemed unable to speak without repeating the word *chap*. Marcel gave Reynaldo a sample: " 'A chap like Giotto, d'you know, or then again a chap like Titian, d'you know, knew just as much as Monet.' " But Proust recognized that Vuillard was "no ordinary man, even if he does say 'chap' every twenty seconds." This account is typical of the pattern being established in which Proust related by letter or conversation to a friend or servant something he had witnessed that he was later to develop for the novel. Proust endowed his painter Elstir with a verbal tic similar to Vuillard's.[75]

Emmanuel Bibesco was among those who received letters from an apparently rejuvenated but pessimistic Marcel: "You'd be amazed to see me on the road every day. But it won't last." Perhaps because Emmanuel had teased him about behavior that could have been homosexual, Marcel made a point of telling Bibesco that Guiche had introduced him to two ladies, the baronne d'Erlanger and Mlle de Saint-Saveur, whose beauty had "greatly disturbed" him. He enclosed wishes for

Antoine, hoping he was "well, calm, industrious and happy. Everything that I'm not! I have never been so agitated, so sterile, so miserable."[76] He had bright hopes for Antoine's future and work; as for himself, "I know what's good without having the strength to do it, and besides, for me it's no longer of any importance."[77] In his grief Proust could think only of having disappointed his mother; he had forgotten his duty to himself or to his readers.

At times Proust wondered whether the burst of extraordinary activity that appeared so beneficial to his regimen had not been a mistake. The return to a place where he had been happy with his mother and grandmother only increased his unhappiness. Although Cabourg seemed a positive change, Proust explained to Lauris that appearances were deceptive: "Excursions, 'pleasures,' yet I've never been so miserable. Sorrow is decidedly not meant to be stirred up; a great deal of stillness is needed to enable it to settle and become a little more serene and limpid again. The fact that I no longer eat anything, or practically anything, luckily induces a mental emptiness which prevents me from being aware of very much."[78]

But Proust, who by mid-August had already visited Caen, Bayeux, Dives, and Balleroy, was absorbing impressions and sketches for his future work more effectively than he realized.[79] In the letter thanking Mâle for his recommendations, Proust said that he was "so dazed by living on my feet for a change that I don't enjoy anything. I've spent such a melancholy year."[80] After a few paragraphs he broke off, unable to continue "amid the deafening and melancholy tumult of this appalling and sumptuous hotel."[81] In the postscript, despite his protests of exhaustion, he mentioned having been "charmed by the oriental figures in Bayeux cathedral (in the Romanesque part of the nave), but I can't understand them, I don't know what they are."[82] Then he indirectly requested information about a locale that interested him more and more: "I'm looking for an old, untouched, Balzacian provincial town, but haven't found a complete one."[83]

In mid-September, Proust went to examine some tombstones at the church of Saint-Pierre at nearby Dives and others much farther away at Falaise. While at Falaise he called on the marquise d'Eyragues, a good friend of the Daudets'.[84] Proust's interest in tombstones stemmed from his abiding passion for history and genealogy and the search for a subject that would fire his imagination. He was particularly drawn to those prose writers, like Saint-Simon, who had written history with great narrative skill, or like Balzac, whose numerous novels formed *La Comédie humaine*, a vast panorama of French society during the author's lifetime.[85] He thought he might be inspired by an old provincial village that was still intact, or by ancient tombstones whose lettering may have been nearly effaced by the work of time.

Toward the end of September, Proust hired Agostinelli to drive him back to Paris, with stops in Lisieux and Évreux. The Clermont-Tonnerres had invited Proust to stay with them in their eighteenth-century manor house at Glisolles, but he had declined the invitation, choosing instead to spend four days in nearby Évreux, perhaps still in search of the "provincial Balzacian town."[86] Once in Évreux he suffered a setback: "Just before arriving at Évreux . . . we came down into a valley where the mist was visible from a distance and one sensed the coolness in the air. And from that moment to this . . . I haven't stopped suffocating and having incessant attacks."[87] In order to make certain he was not disturbed by any noisy neighbors, Proust rented two floors of the Hôtel Moderne.[88] No price seemed too high for peace and tranquillity.

Something good did come from the several days Proust spent in Évreux: he observed the stained-glass windows at the cathedral of Notre-Dame. In letters sent just after the stay in Évreux, Proust described visiting the cathedral under "the indifference and opacity of a rain-swept sky," from whose black clouds the windows had managed to "steal jewels of light, a purple that sparkled and sapphires full of fire—it's incredible."[89] He remembered this particular lighting effect later when he created the windows in the church of Combray.

While at Évreux, Agostinelli drove Proust out one evening to visit M. and Mme de Clermont-Tonnerre at Glisolles. To counter his incessant asthma, Proust consumed seventeen cups of coffee, apparently having calculated the required dosage of caffeine.[90] Mme de Clermont-Tonnerre, who was enjoying a quiet evening with her husband, suddenly heard what she thought was the sound of tires on the gravel in the driveway—an impression she conveyed to her husband, who remarked, "You're crazy!" But she was right; it was the sound of Agostinelli's red taxi coming to a stop. Proust stayed and chatted until late in the evening. When it was time to leave, Marcel was shaking so severely from all the coffee he had drunk that he could barely walk. M. de Clermont-Tonnerre took Proust by the arm and guided his "tottering, caffeine-weakened steps down the nocturnal staircase." When Marcel politely declined an invitation to return the next day, Mme de Clermont-Tonnerre protested, "But . . . you won't see my roses!" Proust replied, "Show them to me this evening." Agostinelli moved the car and shone the headlights on the bushes, whose flowers appeared like "beauties who had been awakened from their sleep."[91]

When Proust later described to Mme Straus the short visit to the "very attractive spot" and the caffeine's effects on him, he regretted not having accepted the Clermont-Tonnerres' offer to show him "some very beautiful things in the neighbourhood, but I was so fed up with Évreux that I left the next morning and so did none of those excursions, nor did I visit Claude Monet's garden at Giverny, near the beautiful bend in the river which is lucky enough to see you through its mist in your drawing-room."[92] The allusion was to one of the Monets owned by the Strauses: *An Arm of the Seine Near Giverny, at Dawn.* Proust on a number of occasions admired extraordinary paintings by Monet in private homes and art galleries, but he never met his great contemporary, whose painterly technique and subjects, especially in the famous series of water lilies, have interesting affinities with what Proust achieved in the novel.

Impressions on Riding in an Automobile

Proust wrote an article for the *Figaro,* "Impressions de route en automobile," about the motoring trips with Agostinelli.[93] He described the trip to Caen, where, as the taxi sped toward its destination, he had observed the rapidly shifting positions of the steeples of Saint-Étienne and those of Saint-Pierre. Proust later used this part of the newspaper article, with a few changes, as a text the young Narrator writes—his first and only accomplished writing for many years—when he has a similar experience seeing the steeples of Martinville from a fast-moving carriage near Combray.[94]

For the *Figaro*'s readers, Proust also described his and Agostinelli's arrival at Lisieux after nightfall, when he despaired of being able to see the cathedral façade described by Ruskin. Suddenly, the statues leaped out from the darkness as the "ingenious" Agostinelli trained the headlights on the portals. The author likened Agostinelli to a "nun of speed," because of his motoring attire—boots, a long hooded coat, and goggles—which nearly covered his body. Early chauffeurs were often exposed not only to the elements and the dangers of primitive roads but to untrained drivers speeding toward them from the opposite direction. Proust later interpreted as ominous a passage in the article, referring to the risks of being a driver: "May the steering wheel of the young chauffeur who is driving me remain always the symbol of his talent rather than the augury of his martyrdom!"[95]

Another feature of Proust's article was more remarkable still: he twice mentioned arriving home to see his parents, who were, of course, no longer living. This article and "Sur la lecture" contain the earliest known manifestations of the first-person voice that was to become the Narrator's. If the author had begun to feel at home with the voice and persona of the Narrator, he had still not found the story in which his hero was to live and breathe. The voice we begin to hear in "Impressions de route en automobile" belongs no longer to Proust the man but to the storyteller, the voice behind the Narrator's.

By early October, Proust was back in Paris, where his bad health continued: "Since my return to Paris: attacks, bed and terrible suffering."[96] From now on when he did make one of his rare sorties, Proust hired Agostinelli, Odilon, or Jossien, a third driver from Jacques Bizet's Taximètres Unic, to drive him.[97] On October 7, when Proust left the apartment for the first time since his return, Jossien drove him since "poor Agostinelli had been obliged to leave for Monte Carlo because of his brother's health."[98] Proust had decided to spend the evening at the Théâtre de la Scala, where the popular café singer Félix Mayol, creator of "Viens poupoule!" was singing nightly. Proust found his performances enchanting and went to hear him whenever possible.[99]

Proust wrote to his friends, telling them about his extraordinary adventures at Cabourg, while trying to temper the impression created by his motoring exploits. Even though he had improved, he wanted to make it clear that he was not really well. He had forced himself to get up, bathe, dress, and, fortified by gargantuan quantities of coffee, take off in an automobile. Antoine and Emmanuel, perhaps amazed by their sedentary friend's recent exploits on the roadways, invited Proust to join them for a motor tour of England. Proust declined but admitted that he had indeed become an "automobile enthusiast."[100]

There remained the complicated and perplexing problem of where to live. Marcel and Robert had decided to sell their shares in the building at 102, boulevard Haussmann. Marcel informed Mme Catusse that he had decided not to remain much longer in his apartment. He had seen it as a transition between his parents' last apartment and a place that would be his own. He and his doctors had never thought it was a good choice for his health requirements. Mme Catusse must have dreaded the prospect of any Proustian relocation that might involve her. On November 7, the day before the sale of the building on boulevard Haussmann, he wrote Mme Catusse that he had renewed his lease only until August 1908. His doctors had nearly convinced him that Paris, and in particular his new neighborhood, were bad for his health. When the shares belonging to Marcel and Robert were auctioned, their Aunt Amélie acquired them. Proust missed the sale because he decided to attend a party at Montesquiou's Pavillon des Muses.

On the day after the sale Proust regretted his decision not to attend, as he confided to Billy: "I'm distressed because the boulevard Haussmann house has just been sold, *very badly.* I have a week to make a higher bid, but since the purchaser is my aunt I don't dare. If you had been here I would have asked your advice."[101] Proust did need advice, though the reasons that were later to make the decision to sell one of the worst he ever made were not evident in fall 1907. Marcel painted an ever darker picture of the transaction to Montesquiou: "The sale of the house . . . went very badly and has halved my income. Perhaps I should have gone to my lawyer rather than to you that evening, to the Cabinet of Ruses rather than the Pavilion of the Muses."[102] In fact, the sale had the potential of increasing his income, for he could invest the money from his share of the sale.

In Germany, a sex scandal erupted, involving allegations of homosexuality at the highest levels of Kaiser Wilhelm II's court. Prince Philipp von Eulenburg, the suave, cultivated former ambassador to Vienna, and the kaiser's closest friend, was accused by Maximilian Harden, the muckraking, nationalistic editor of the belli- cose weekly newspaper *Die Zukunft,* of having peopled the kaiser's inner circle with homosexuals.[103] A dismissed minister, who had kept secret files of the private lives of his associates at court, sought revenge by releasing the damaging documents to Harden. Harden and his colleagues believed that Eulenburg and his associates were pacifists and francophiles, whose influence on the kaiser thwarted Harden's own ambitions. Harden's charges resulted in a series of libel trials that ended in Eulen- burg's disgrace and arrest. Not since the trial of Oscar Wilde had there been such public attention to homosexuality.

Proust followed the trials through the press and his contacts with French diplomats who knew the German court. In a letter of November 9 he asked Billy what he thought about "this homosexuality trial? I think they've hit out rather at random, although it's absolutely true about some of them, notably the Prince, but some of the details are very comic."[104] For Proust, whose thoughts often centered on sexual ambiguity and homosexuality, the plight of Eulenburg and others ac- cused of acts considered perverse provided another occasion to ponder same-sex love and society's persecution of such behavior. At some point in late 1907 or early 1908, perhaps inspired by the German trials, Proust began to consider writing an essay about homosexuality.[105]

The French, unaware that the disgrace of Eulenburg and other "catamites" could only work to France's disadvantage as Germany grew more bellicose, enjoyed the embarrassment brought upon the kaiser's court. In Paris one heard references to the "German vice," and Berlin was nicknamed Sodome-sur-Spree. In the places where French homosexuals gathered, "Parlez-vous allemand?"—Do you speak German?—became the password for those seeking partners.[106]

Proust's article on his automobile trips around Cabourg appeared in *Le Figaro*

on November 19. Among the notes friends sent, Proust received one that particularly surprised him. "Can you imagine," he wrote Mme Straus, "which was the
prettiest letter? . . . The one from Agostinelli to whom my manservant had sent a
copy of the article."[107] As far as Proust's writings were concerned, he divided his
friends into two categories, both vexing: those who never read anything and those
who read his articles but did not care for them. He complained about his friends to
Mme Straus, who had encouraged him to write more articles like the ones he had
published that year. Her encouragement brought a welcome "change from those
people who take infinite pains to avoid talking to me about my articles and not to
look as though they are doing it on purpose, because they're afraid of hurting my
feelings by admitting that they find them idiotic and because they attach such
asinine importance to their own words and to *sincerity* that they don't want to pay
me a compliment out of kindness."[108]

When Gustave de Borda died, Proust wrote for the *Figaro* a brief, anonymous
tribute to his old swashbuckling friend who had served him so effectively in his
duel with Lorrain. The author remarked that age alone had forced Borda to retire
from duties as a duelist and recalled ingenuously that "the last person" Borda
"assisted as a second was our contributor M. Marcel Proust, who has always had a
veritable cult for him."[109]

By year's end Proust had published, in addition to the two minor pieces, the
tribute to Borda and the long overdue review of Gabriel Mourey's book *Gainsborough*, four essays ("Sentiments filiaux," "Journées de lecture," the review of *Les
Éblouissements*, and "Impressions de route en automobile") in which are heard
early soundings of future major themes.[110] His days of acting as salon reporter were
over, yet even those apparently frivolous pieces held importance for his novel.
He had outlined characters and told amusing and revealing anecdotes, while re-
creating the atmosphere of rarefied Parisian drawing rooms. The "salons" he wrote
for the *Figaro* were sketches for a vastly larger canvas, on which Proust was to
capture a world on the brink of disappearing.

17   *The Notebook of 1908*   ❧

ON NEW YEAR'S DAY, Mme Straus presented Proust with five pretty little notebooks from Kirby Beard, a smart stationery shop located behind the Opéra. In early February he wrote to thank her: "Madame, I'm enchanted by your little almanacs and the thought that they come from you gives them an added poetry." He also made a remark indicating, for the first time since his Ruskin translations, that he had a new project in mind and was eager "to settle down to a fairly long piece of work."[1] Sometime in January or February, Proust chose the largest of the long, narrow notebooks, whose cover bore a picture of a young man smoking a pipe, and began making notes for a novel. This notebook, known as *Le Carnet de 1908*, is the first in which Proust made annotations for various writing projects that were to slowly converge and lead to the *Search*.[2]

In early January, Proust had written Auguste Marguillier to thank him for mentioning *La Bible d'Amiens* in a column. Then he made an unusual request: "Would it be at all possible for you to send me on approval a few of your English engravings, especially those in which an animal is represented beside the person or persons who are the subject of the portrait."[3] Proust was ready to write an episode, evoking memories of childhood, for what he sometimes referred to as his "Paris novel." He wanted to see the engravings because a particular scene he was writing described the distress and anger of his brother Robert, at age five, when he was forced to part with his pet kid.[4] By summer Proust listed "Robert and the kid, Mama leaves on a trip," as the first scene of the ones already written.[5]

Elements of this episode point to the *Search*. The Narrator's first-person voice is recognizable as the prototype of the voice that attains its full power and range in the novel. The locale is inspired by childhood memories of Illiers and Auteuil used to create Combray. In his early drafts, Proust experimented with geographic locations, as he did with names for characters, trying out several before selecting the right one.[6] Robert was eventually written out of the story altogether and this scene reduced from seven pages to twenty-five lines in which the Narrator, now an only child, bids farewell to his beloved hawthorns at Combray.[7] Other elements recognizable from Proust's earliest writings and *Jean Santeuil* are found here. The Narrator's mother, encouraging him to be brave when she goes away for a few days, quotes inspiring passages about courage and stoicism from Latin and French authors.[8]

Among the first notes that Proust made in the *Carnet of 1908* are two that refer to the psychology of love. Both indicate that the Narrator will not seek to possess the girl he keeps because he is incapable of giving or receiving happiness.[9] This reflects Proust's own bitter experience and his reluctance to consider marriage.[10] The second note about his "incapacity for happiness" adds more details: "In the second part of the novel the girl will be impoverished."[11] From the beginning Proust foresaw the kind of relationship that the Narrator would have with the girl, though in the early drafts there is only Maria, originally inspired by Marie de Benardaky, who will become Gilberte Swann. The girl whom the Narrator keeps and decides not to marry will be a much later creation—Albertine.

Following the first note about the girl, Proust lists a number of Balzac's characters, mainly women, among whom he may have been seeking models for his own female characters.[12] Proust links Balzac's Vautrin, a closet homosexual, with Montesquiou through their choice of words or manner of speaking.[13] A few lines later he refers to the scene in *Illusions perdues* in which Vautrin stops to visit the house of Rastignac, the young man with whom Vautrin had been in love. Proust called this scene the "*Tristesse d'Olympio* de la pédérastie" (the *Tristesse d'Olympio* of pederasty), after a famous Hugo poem in which the hero, Olympio, returns to the idyllic location where he had been in love with his young mistress.[14] Another note mentions Fénelon as the lover of Louisa's sister.[15]

This cluster of notes shows that from the beginning Marcel used friends as primary models for characters. As he developed his characters Proust added new elements that made them fictional. But many of the originals, much to Proust's chagrin, were later to see traces of themselves—usually not of the most flattering kind—and become incensed. Bertrand did not live to find the figments of himself in Saint-Loup and Albertine, nor to see Louisa take her sister's role as the original of Rachel, the actress who is Saint-Loup's mistress. Montesquiou, despite many Proustifying disclaimers, saw aspects of himself in the baron de Charlus.[16]

Proust made entries regarding topics, themes, and characters in the *Carnet of 1908* for several years. Lists of names that might serve for characters; names of people and places he knew well or those he dreamed of knowing, "on whose name one forges dreams like a book unread."[17] He jotted down sensations—odors of rooms, bedsheets, grass, perfume, soap, food—capable of reviving the past; he noted dreams about his parents.[18] The *Carnet of 1908* served as a memo pad and, later, as an inventory of sections already written.

Proust was soon distracted by a scandal involving the De Beers diamond empire. Henri-Didot-Léon Lemoine, who worked for De Beers as an engineer, claimed to have invented a method of manufacturing diamonds. After bogus experiments Lemoine extorted more than a million francs from Sir Julius Wernher, president of De Beers. Lemoine's scheme had been to make the De Beers shares drop drastically, buy shares cheap, and make a fortune when it was learned that his method of fabrication did not work. Lemoine had actually purchased the diamonds that he claimed were the product of his process, so when they were analyzed, they were found to be genuine. Sir Julius became suspicious and decided to sue for fraud. Lemoine fled abroad before he could be apprehended. He landed at the French embassy in Bulgaria, where Robert de Billy was chargé d'affaires. Lemoine attempted to obtain a passport for Constantinople in his brother-in-law's name, but he was arrested and returned to France for trial. Billy related the story to Marcel, who was thrilled by this Balzacian tale. Proust had inherited De Beers stock from his parents, and he worried at first about his investments.[19] Once reassured, he was inspired by the story and saw its rich comic potential.[20]

On February 22 the front page of the *Figaro*'s literary supplement carried Proust's parodies of Balzac, Michelet, the Goncourt brothers, and critic Émile Faguet. On March 14 and 21 the *Figaro* published his parodies of Flaubert, Sainte-Beuve, and Renan.[21] The theme of all these pastiches was the Lemoine Affair; different aspects of the affair were assigned to each writer parodied.[22]

Proust's parodies were generally considered by his peers to be among the best ever written. Because a parody mimics a writer's use of vocabulary, turns of phrases, and other stylistic hallmarks, it is virtually untranslatable. For a parody to be good, Proust said, one must not copy or use words from the original but find words or expressions that the writer might have used. The secret was to catch the particular song or rhythm of the original. During his extensive readings, Proust had learned well the particular "music" of distinguished French authors—and one foreigner, John Ruskin. For example, regarding his parody of Renan, Proust explained to Robert Dreyfus that once he had adjusted his "inner metronome" to Renan's "rhythm," he could have written "ten volumes like that."[23] The pastiches show Proust's extraordinary versatility as a writer and his mischievous sense of humor. His amazing gift for mimicry, seen earlier in his salon imitations of Montesquiou's gestures and speech, served him well in creating the distinctive language of his characters.[24]

Proust's friends, amazed at his tour de force, rushed to congratulate him. He was especially pleased to hear from such fellow writers as Anatole France, Jules Lemaître, and Mme de Noailles, to whom he wrote: "I'm pleased that my pastiches amused you. It's a facile and vulgar exercise. But still I think I put a certain breadth into them all the same, that they're good 'copies' as they say in painting . . . "[25] Writing to Francis Chevassu, editor of the *Figaro*'s literary supplement, Proust coined a phrase, describing what he considered the usefulness of such pastiches, which served as "literary criticism in action."[26] In two mid-March letters to Dreyfus he explained he had written the parodies "because I was too lazy to write literary criticism, or rather because I found it amusing to write literary criticism 'in action.'" He assured Dreyfus, however, that there would be "no more pastiches. What an idiotic exercise."

The "idiotic exercise" had taught him some important lessons. There is surely no more intensive level of reading than the process of translating. From the years Proust spent reading, translating, and annotating Ruskin he had learned much about the nature, resources, and restrictions of the French language. Having written a 1,500-page manuscript for *Jean Santeuil*, translated Ruskin, written salon and miscellaneous articles for the *Figaro*, and, most recently, undertaken the stylistic exercises for the parodies, Proust had completed his long apprenticeship.[27] He had forged his own instrument, a pen that was remarkably supple and fully primed, and yet he still hesitated. His sole ambition was to become a writer, but he remained perplexed regarding the nature of his mission.

The Telegraph Boy

Was Proust's often proclaimed physical attraction to girls genuine? Was he truly attracted to Jacques Bizet's maid or only seeking information for a story when he asked his driver Jossien whether the maid was someone with whom you could sleep? Marcel realized just how indiscreet he had been when Jossien replied: "You're embarrassing me . . . she's my sister-in-law."[28] Proust's rather frequent remarks about being attracted to beautiful girls and young women have been taken as smoke screens to hide his homosexuality, especially when he began to pay a lot of attention to young men he met in Paris, and later at Cabourg.

Proust's conception of the human personality, demonstrated in the *Search*, was that most people are androgynous, containing both male and female elements. This is particularly true, he believed, of artists. He maintained that people are not necessarily fixed in their sexual preferences but may vary over time. Proust was attracted to young men and women and more to males than to females. What he consistently denied were homosexual acts, not homoerotic attraction, which he obviously felt and frankly expressed, both in his letters to male friends and in his writings. He may have been lying, of course, about being attracted to women and about not engaging in homosexual acts, but there is some evidence that he was telling the truth.[29]

Marcel did not help himself by providing an easy target for such accusations. In the spring of 1908 he became particularly interested in two young people of different classes and different sexes: one was a young telegraph operator, whose name he did not know, and the other an aristocratic girl, Mlle de Goyon, said to be exceptionally beautiful and distinguished. Proust began to spin fantasies about both the boy and the girl. In the course of a March letter he asked Albu whether he remembered sending his letters by a certain "young telegraph operator," and if so, could Albu put Marcel in touch with the boy? He needed to become acquainted with a telegraph operator for something he was writing.[30]

Albu provided the boy's name, Louis Maheux, and joked that he had never had intimate relations with him. In the letter thanking Albu for the information, Marcel said the joke

> was unnecessary and the idea would never have entered my head. Alas, I'd
> like to be as sure that you don't have such ideas about me in that respect.
> In any case it would be more explicable since so many people have said it
> of me. However I imagine that whatever your thoughts are about me in

that connection deep down (and I hope with all my heart that they're in accordance with the truth, that is, to say exemplary), they wouldn't occur to you with reference to Louis Maheux. I'm not so stupid, if I were that sort of scum, to go out of my way to let the boy know my name, enable him to get me put in the clink, tell you all about it, etc. Perhaps I'm going on a bit about your joke.[31]

Had Proust heard about the Cleveland Street scandal in London that preceded by six years Wilde's conviction for sodomy? In 1889 when police found a male brothel in Cleveland Street that was frequented by prominent members of the aristocracy, including Lord Arthur Somerset, superintendent of Prince Edward's stables, and the earl of Euston, eldest son of the earl of Grafton.[32] Telegraph boys from the General Post Office were able to increase their legitimate earnings substantially by prostituting themselves to high-ranking aristocrats.[33] Lord Somerset, setting an example that Wilde would have done well to follow, left England for France and Italy when it became clear that he could not escape prosecution.[34] Given Proust's keen interest in what he considered the persecution of homosexuals, illustrated by his close attention to the Wilde and Eulenburg trials, and the extraordinary curiosity about sexual behavior that drove him to collect any gossip or stories about such matters, it seems probable that he had heard of the Cleveland Street telegraph boys. Proust's eagerness to become acquainted with a telegraph boy does not suggest, as Albufera joked, that he was intent on seduction, but he may have wanted to know how such a job might lead to the establishment of a thriving homosexual brothel frequented by wealthy bourgeois and aristocrats. One can only speculate about whether he had heard of Cleveland Street, but the male brothel Proust describes in the *Search* is frequented primarily by members of the aristocracy, whose sexual needs are met by boys from the working class. The two young people Proust was so eager to meet in 1908, the telegraph boy and Mlle de Goyon, must have been related to the research he was conducting for what he called his Paris novel.

In April, Proust informed Albufera that he had decided to leave Paris for good in July. He would be sad, of course, to leave his friends. Then he told Louis what was uppermost in his mind: "I'm about to embark on a very important piece of work."[35] While writing on the topics that interested him most for the important piece, Marcel held on to his old dream of moving to Florence or the south of France.[36] A warmer, drier climate might improve his health and make him happier and more productive.

In spite of his efforts, Proust found it impossible to remain focused on one topic or genre. On May 5 or 6 he wrote Albufera an important letter regarding his writing projects. He informed Albufera that Louis Maheux had called about the interview a week earlier, at a time when he could not see him. Proust had not heard from the telegraph boy since. "In any case I'm not sure I won't abandon my Parisian novel."[37] Marcel, seeking inspiration for a female character and aware that Mlle de Goyon was kin to Albu, asked him:

> Have you by any chance—something that's always so interesting—any family photograph albums? If you could lend me one for a few hours (especially if Mlle de Goyon was in it) I should be delighted. It's true that I should be even more delighted if you came here and could tell me the names. By the same token, do you have your genealogy in a few lines? It's again because of what I'm working on that all this would interest me. For I have in hand:
>
>> a study on the nobility
>> a Parisian novel
>> an essay on Sainte-Beuve and Flaubert
>> an essay on women
>> an essay on pederasty (not easy to publish)
>> a study of stained-glass windows
>> a study on tombstones
>> a study on the novel

These are the topics that interested Proust most in 1907–9, when he clearly began writing the earliest drafts of what was to become the *Search*. Of the eight items listed, seven are called essays or studies, but the "Parisian novel" eventually absorbed all the others.[38] The drafts on these topics contain, not surprisingly, many of the same elements as *Jean Santeuil* and his early stories: the child's nervous dependency on his mother, obsessive jealousy, snobbery in the world of high society, and the arts, especially literature and music.

Immediately after Proust sent the letter to Albu listing his current projects, Louis Maheux came by to be interviewed. After he left, Marcel wrote to Albu again, giving his impressions of young Maheux. Proust had found the boy to be "very nice, very intelligent," and able to provide some information of interest. But the boy was too genteel, and most astounding of all: "He resembles Bertrand de Fénelon, except that he's much better dressed. Speaking of telegraphists he said to me, 'They're rather the Grenelle type than the rue Saint-Dominique.' Rue Saint-Dominique in his mind meant *his* type. He would be a perfect model for a picture of society mores." Grenelle was a working-class district of Paris, the rue Saint-Dominique one of the most fashionable streets in the old aristocratic faubourg Saint-Germain.[39] Proust was more amused than enlightened by Maheux. Snobbery, as he already knew, was not restricted to the upper classes.

Proust began writing drafts for his essay on pederasty, uncertain what form it would finally take. Having been discouraged by Robert Dreyfus's negative reaction to his idea for an essay on homosexuality, Proust considered writing a novella about homosexuals.[40] He decided not to write directly about the trials of Wilde and Eulenburg because it would be a mistake to make "an artistic project depend on notions which are themselves anecdotal and too directly drawn from life not to partake of its contingency and unreality. All of which, moreover, presented thus, seems not so much false as banal and deserving of some stinging slap in the face from outraged existence (like Oscar Wilde saying that the greatest sorrow he had ever known was the death of Lucien de Rubempré in Balzac, and learning shortly afterwards, through his trial, that there are sorrows which are still more real). But you know that such banal aestheticism cannot be my artistic philosophy."[41]

As the 1908 text progressed from essay to fiction, Proust, remembering the examples of Wilde and Eulenburg, called homosexuals "a race upon which a curse is laid."[42] The theme of homosexual love, nearly absent from *Jean Santeuil,* became a major topic in the *Search,* where Proust analyzes erotic love in heterosexual and homosexual couples, showing that the obsessions of love, desire, and jealousy are the same in each, and identically doomed to failure because they are based on illusions. Proust would incorporate all he had to say about sexuality into the *Search.* The final version of his remarks about "an accursed race" became part of the prologue on homosexuality in the opening pages of *Sodom and Gomorrah,* where he describes the difficulties homosexuals face in an intolerant society. Proust's compassion for his characters was evident as early as *Jean Santeuil:* "We cannot approach the most perverse people without recognizing them as human beings."[43] His characters live because he loved them enough to see the redemptive features of each.

A Beautiful Girl

Marcel had begun asking other friends about Albu's distant cousin Oriane de Goyon as well. Having heard how beautiful, distinguished, and well born she was, he wanted to observe her at a party for inspiration. Mlle de Goyon, who was twenty-one years old when Proust became infatuated with her, or with the idea of her, was the daughter of Comte Aimery de Goyon. Her aunt by marriage was Albu's stepmother, the duchesse d'Albufera, née Zénaïde de Cambacérès.[44]

In his genealogical research Proust had consulted not only Saint-Simon but the bible of European nobility, the Almanach de Gotha. Mlle de Goyon's ancestors were mentioned in Chateaubriand's *Mémoires d'outre-tombe* in the same sentence with the place name Combourg, a likely source for Combray. Another of her ancestors had been condemned to death under Napoléon I. She had family ties to the prince of Monaco. But what may have caught Proust's attention in the Almanach de Gotha while reading about the duc de Feltre, of the house of Goyon, was the name that immediately preceded it: Eulenburg-Hertefeld, which followed Essling (the house of Masséna—Albu's wife). After Feltre came Fezensac (the house of Montesquiou).[45] Mlle de Goyon seemed to be at the center of many intersecting lines that tied her to people who might inspire his writings.

Proust began asking for invitations to balls where he might see her or meet her. He seemed strangely unconcerned about the quantities of flowers and perfumes to which he might expose himself at these balls, where he dared to venture in search of a rare young girl in bloom. On June 12 Marcel attended a "truly marvelous and supremely elegant" ball at the princesse de Polignac's, where he lingered trying to obtain an introduction to Mlle de Goyon, the "prettiest girl" he had ever seen, and the best dancer.[46]

Proust finally met the beautiful Mlle de Goyon at Princesse Lucien (Marie) Murat's annual summer ball on June 22. Marcel, who had begun to pay more attention to his appearance, now that he was attending parties occasionally, had sent for his barber, who trimmed his beard; Nicolas laid out his best suit. André Becq de Fouquières, a smart young man-about-town, offered to introduce Marcel to the object of his fascination. After the ball Marcel wrote Albu: "It was a hugely emotional moment for me—I thought I was going to fall—but also quite a big disappointment, for she didn't seem to me so nice up close and a bit irritating when she opens her mouth, and more coquettish than amiable. I shall think about her again more calmly: all my ideas are a bit muddled." Proust turned for a moment to vacation plans. Were he and Albu to spend some time together on the coast, Marcel would prefer not to move around because "I have ideas for work for several months ahead, which moving would interrupt." Writing of the difficulty in finding someone willing to introduce him to Mlle de Goyon, he observed, "it's incredible how unhelpful people are, especially when there is an element of love involved." Then he admitted, "I mustn't exaggerate; it isn't real love; I don't really know what it is."[47] His friends did not know what to make of his infatuation, either. None took it seriously, dismissing it as just another of Marcel's complicated fantasies.

Two remarks made by Proust during this period, one in a letter, the other in the first notebook, may explain the extraordinary trouble he took to meet Mlle de Goyon. In April he observed in a letter to Billy: "It's the privilege of those who always live alone to create in their minds substitutes for real people and to love without ever seeing."[48] And he jotted down in his notebook: "One could imagine a man at work only going out to places where there are beautiful girls, as he would go to concerts to hear beautiful music."[49]

In a letter to Hahn, Marcel gave a full report of meeting the girl, including moments of hilarity. Madeleine Lemaire had "shrilled: 'Suzette, show me the girl Marcel's been talking about.' " After looking her over, Mme Lemaire had "turned away, saying: 'She's very ugly and she looks dirty.' " Suzette was kinder, saying that the young miss was attractive, but then "made matters a hundred times worse by staring at her the whole time, making endless remarks, laughing loudly and continually saying to me: 'Come over here; take a look at her from the doorway, etc. etc.' " Clearly, Madeleine and her daughter found Marcel's crush silly.

But the most embarrassing moments had come when Fouquières escorted him to Mlle de Goyon's side. Although Marcel knew that Fouquières was "completely drunk," until that moment he had behaved properly enough. Fouquières, enjoying himself tremendously, grew boisterous: "He kept saying to me as he effected the introduction, out loud, not merely out loud but bellowing: 'What d'you think of those little cheeks? You wouldn't mind pinching them, eh? And how about a little kiss? Ah! you wouldn't mind, would you, you rascal? What's that? You say you'd like to scrunch those little cherry pippins' (I was saying nothing at all); 'you're quite right . . . ' "[50] Proust had wanted to hide, especially because the girl was accompanied by a young man he believed to be her fiancé.

Albu sent Marcel more information about the young woman, including the news that she was not engaged. Proust replied that her eligibility was "a purely chimerical balm to me since she will never be mine. But still the fact of having spoken to her, to know that I shall be able to speak to her again—above all to have found her a thousand times less wonderful than I thought—all that has done me a great deal of good and given me a great calm."[51] He could, for the moment, put her out of his mind; he had pursued—to what purpose?—a creature of his own imagination.

Had Marcel been seeking material for his Parisian novel?[52] Or was this an elaborate and risky scheme to dispel suspicions of his homosexuality? Perhaps he hoped to make his investigation serve both purposes. It is difficult to imagine Proust going to such lengths to counter suspicions of homosexuality. He could have accomplished that simply by becoming more circumspect in his remarks. In any case, one element from his infatuation was to serve his novel well. He took Mlle de Goyon's given name Oriane for the duchesse de Guermantes, whose genealogy, beauty, wit, taste, and social standing place her salon at the pinnacle of Parisian society.[53]

Less than a week after the Murat ball, the most illustrious host of Paris gave a stellar party. Having striven to avoid contact with Montesquiou, Marcel complained bitterly to the count about not being invited to the gathering at the Pavillon des Muses on Saturday afternoon, June 27. The occasion had been the publication of Montesquiou's book *Le Chancelier de fleurs* (The chancellor of flowers), dedicated to the memory of Yturri. The count had chosen the title as a reminder of Yturri's frequent role as his emissary, bearing flowers to friends.[54] To celebrate the memorial volume Montesquiou invited many friends and distinguished artists, such as Comtesse Greffulhe, Mme Arman de Caillavet, Anatole France, Pierre Loti, Auguste Rodin, Dr. Samuel Pozzi, Maurice Barrès, Madeleine Lemaire, and Paul Helleu.

Proust wrote Montesquiou to say that his feelings had been hurt by the slight: "How unkind of you not to have invited me to the admirable commemorative reading . . . which, as you know well, mine would have been the intelligence and the heart most capable of entirely appreciating."[55] Proust's letter, as he told Reynaldo, unleashed "the exchange of innumerable letters in a pontifical but pressing tone." Then the "fatal count" made amends in a way that took Proust completely by surprise. Montesquiou came to 102, boulevard Haussmann at two in the morning and gave Marcel a private reading. If only Reynaldo could have heard the poet "at two o'clock in the morning, without pity for the Gageys, stamping his heels on the floor and declaiming."[56]

Having leafed through *Le Chancelier de fleurs,* Proust observed to Hahn: "In Montesquiou's book there's a letter from Prince von Radolin assuring him of his sympathy for 'your cruel loss' etc. He'd have done better to keep a little of it for Eulenburg." Proust deplored Radolin's hypocrisy, which matched that of European society in general. A friend of Montesquiou's, Radolin was the German ambassador to France and must have known that Yturri's relationship with the count was no different from that for which Prince Eulenburg and his friends were being persecuted.[57]

On July 12 Proust left his apartment during daylight hours for the first time that year to go to Louveciennes, near Bougival, to visit his brother, whom he wanted to see before leaving for Cabourg. For the second summer in a row, Robert and Marthe had rented the Villa Fiammette, a property belonging to the actress Mlle Léonie Yahne. Robert, unfortunately, had not anticipated such an unlikely apparition and was not at home.[58] Marcel was to enjoy other brief visits to Louveciennes.

Sometime in July, Proust listed the six episodes or sections he had written during the first half of the year.[59] The first of these was "Robert and the kid," followed by "the Villebon Way and the Méséglise Way."[60] The two place names, the first from a château near Illiers and the other from a nearby village, indicate that he had found the "two ways," one of the major unifying elements of the *Search.* Another key episode was the drama of the good-night kiss, in which the child Narrator, unable to sleep, places his mother in the position of making "concessions" and spending the night in his room.[61] This scene was perhaps the primal matter out of which grew all Proustian narration. It had been sketched for a story in *Pleasures and Days,* reprised in the drafts of *Jean Santeuil,* and in the *Search* was to become the pivotal scene, when the Narrator as a child loses his will. The Narrator spends the rest of his life trying to regain independence and strength in order to become a creative person.

The last episode on the 1908 list indicates the story's conclusion: "What I learned from the Villebon Way and the Méséglise Way."[62] Proust had conceived an apprentice novel, in which the Narrator becomes neurotically dependent as a child, grows up to explore the two ways of his world, those of the landed gentry and of Paris salons, fails to find happiness in erotic love, and explores the world of homosexuality.[63] The notation "the maternal face in that of a debauched grandson" suggests two homosexual scenes in the novel. Charlus resembles his mother; such men, whether with male or female partners "consummate upon their faces the profanation of their mothers."[64] Mlle Vinteuil, who resembles her father, brings her lesbian lover home to live with her. Her behavior causes her prudish father to die of grief and shame. Traces of plot survive from "La Confession d'une jeune fille."

In the summer of 1908 Proust made an entry in *Le Carnet de 1908* indicating a source for Mlle Vinteuil's profanation of her father's image. As part of their love ritual, she spits on her father's photograph while her lover (known only as Mlle Vinteuil's friend) watches. Proust notes "the little monster . . . Robin." Proust found his inspiration for the scene in an anecdote then current about Dr. Albert Robin and his mistress, the courtesan Liane de Pougy. Proust stresses that Dr. Robin was, in all other respects, a fine man and devoted to his family, but when making love to Liane, he could achieve climax only by calling his son "the little monster."[65]

Proust's novel was to be circular in time and space. As a child the Narrator believes that the two ways led in different directions and would be forever separated. As an adult, he discovers that the ways are joined in a circular path.[66] The first and last words in the novel contain the word *time*.[67] At the end, the Narrator, having completed his quest and understood at last the true nature of his experience, is fully endowed as a creative person and ready to write the ideal version of the story we have just read.[68] But in the summer and fall of 1908, after listing these episodes, Proust stalled again, unable to see that he had found the "sesame" that would open wide the doors to a new world.

Youth in Bloom

While Proust and Nicolas were preparing to leave for Cabourg, both became ill and received orders to report for their annual reserve training of thirteen days. Proust tried to have them both excused for reasons of health. Just before leaving for Cabourg, Proust attended to his wardrobe. Henry Bernstein had recently told Marcel that he was not dressed well enough to accompany Bernstein to a brothel. Proust had been amused by the remark but had taken notice of the poor figure he was cutting and decided to buy new clothes. He ordered several outfits from the Carnaval de Venise, the fashionable haberdasher on the boulevard de la Madeleine, where Yturri had sold ties so long ago. Montesquiou, who had seen the samples when he came to read from his book on Yturri, had "declared them very ugly," but Proust learned that the following day Montesquiou had gone to the clothier's and placed an order for two suits in the same fabric. Proust had also been measured for an overcoat in plaid with a bright purple lining.[69] He told Lauris that he was going to leave it in the cloakroom, for though he did not fear looking "ridiculous," he did not wish to "inflict ridicule" on his friends. Proust continued, poking fun at himself: "If I unbutton this coat in a car and people see it, they will think a bishop is making his rounds."[70]

Shortly after arriving in Cabourg on July 18, Proust received word that his training orders had been annulled, but Nicolas had to report.[71] Perhaps Nicolas welcomed a brief change in routine. In June, on his valet's behalf, Proust had asked his friends whether they knew anyone who needed a gamekeeper. Nicolas was

"becoming neurotic because of being shut in all day and would like such a job."
Should there be such an opening, Proust was prepared to recommend Nicolas as
"a decent youngster, very intelligent, fundamentally honest, very knowledgeable
about horses, etc."[72] While Nicolas was away, Proust sent for Robert Ulrich to assist
him in Cabourg, lodging him in a modest hotel. Finally, having found nothing for
the young man to do, Proust sent him back to Paris.[73]

Proust was as unimpressed that year as the year before by society at the hotel.
Marcel wrote to Billy that a "few Jewish dry goods merchants make up the hotel's
aristocracy, moreover, haughty."[74] Proust did not lack company, however. Many of
his friends were vacationing near Cabourg. Horace and Mary Finaly, now Mme
Thomas de Barbarin, were at Les Frémonts, where Marcel also saw Billy. Proust
invited these three longtime friends to dinner at the Grand-Hôtel. He visited the
Strauses at Trouville, where he also saw Hervieu and Mme de Pierrebourg. While
visiting Louisa and Gangnat at the Chalet Russe in Bénerville, Marcel met a man
who was to become one of his most important associates: Gaston Gallimard, his
future publisher.

Among new friends he met at the hotel were the vicomte and Mme d'Alton
and their two daughters. Mme d'Alton became another source of information for
Marcel regarding the language and customs of the French nobility. In August,
Marcel invited Henry Bernstein to see him at the hotel. He occasionally took tea
with friends like Mme Edwards, the painter José-Marie Sert, and Mme Forain.[75]
Marcel had tried to persuade Reynaldo to join him at the Grand-Hôtel, describing
it as "admirable," the place to stay on the coast; he reminded his friend that each
room had its own bath.[76]

Proust's work had not progressed well since he had taken stock and listed the
sections already written. His health, as well as doubts about what direction to take,
had frustrated his efforts. On August 6 he complained to Reynaldo of his inability
to work: "I cannot write, as though I'd been struck by paralysis of the hand and
brain."[77] During this period Proust complained of headaches, eyestrain, and lack of
concentration.

That summer's stay was different from the previous one, when Marcel had
shown such energy and determination, moving like a cannonball down the roads
of Normandy. Now he complained of being "ill all the time" and found slight
improvement "only by forgoing my long drives of last year."[78] Occasionally, he took
a stroll on the boardwalk. Once on the beachfront, he saw a vision that made an
indelible impression, which he later described to Louisa, because the woman he
had observed was an actress friend of hers: "I met Lucy Gérard on the front at

Cabourg. It was a ravishing evening and the sunset had forgotten only one colour: pink. But her dress was pink and added the complementary colour of the twilight to the orange sky. I lingered to watch this delicate pink tinge and . . . saw it merge with the horizon, to the utmost end of which she glided like an enchanted sail."[79] He entered this impression in the first notebook. Lucy reminded him of the cocottes and actresses his Uncle Louis used to entertain. Noting how much the man had loved the company of such women, Proust wrote the words "temps perdu etc."[80] Was this lost time or wasted time or both? He had written the words, apparently, without thinking much about them.

In early August, Marcel thanked Lucien for dedicating a story to him, "La Réponse imprévue," published in the *Mercure de France*.[81] He told Lucien that the *Figaro* had declined his "adulatory review" of *Le Chemin mort* (The still path), Lucien's new novel with a discreetly homosexual theme.[82] Proust submitted the review to *L'Intransigeant*, where it appeared on September 8, under a pseudonym, perhaps because he did not want his name to appear in a paper that had adopted such a virulently anti-Dreyfus stance. He had signed "Marc el Dante," with his first name evident, but the typesetters, faced with Proust's illegible script, had misread his pseudonym and printed it as Marc Eodante.

One evening at the hotel casino, the vicomte d'Alton introduced Marcel Plantevignes to Proust.[83] Plantevignes was the good-looking, nineteen-year-old son of Camille Plantevignes, a well-to-do necktie manufacturer who had a villa at Cabourg.[84] Proust welcomed Plantevignes nearly every evening into his room at the Grand-Hôtel, where they chatted for hours. The two Marcels were getting along extremely well until one day when the younger went for a stroll on the boardwalk. While conversing with a woman he met, Plantevignes mentioned the fascinating writer with whom he was spending so much time. The lady, perhaps concerned about the young man's reputation, strongly hinted that Proust was homosexual.[85] Rather than coming to Proust's defense, Plantevignes remained silent. Word of the incident reached Proust, who became furious and sent Plantevignes a letter worthy of Charlus, accusing the youth of having "stabbed him in the back" and saying that he would never see him again: "You have carelessly spoiled what could have been a very beautiful friendship."[86] The insolence of the letter alarmed Plantevignes and his father because they did not understand Proust's rage. When M. Plantevignes went to the hotel to clear things up, Proust challenged him to a duel. Many Proustian complications ensued, involving seconds and a number of friends, before the matter was amicably resolved.

Proust became friends with other young men whose middle-class families owned or rented villas at Cabourg. There were two engineers, for example, both in their mid-twenties: Pierre Parent and Max Daireaux. Proust entered Parent's name several times in his notebook; traits or dialogue from Parent were to inspire aspects of Saint-Loup and Albertine.[87] The older brothers of Max Daireaux had been part of the group at the Neuilly tennis parties where Marcel flirted with Jeanne Pouquet.[88] Marcel now found himself reunited with the Daireaux family, who rented the Villa Suzanne for the summer.[89] There was also twenty-two-year-old Albert Nahmias, a future financial journalist, who was to be an intimate friend.[90] Marcel surrounded himself whenever possible with these men in the flower of youth. Was this group the model for "the little band of girls" that populate the beach and bewitch the Narrator, who falls in love with them as a polymorphous unit before falling in love with them individually? At Cabourg Proust noted this "desire to love that floats between persons who know each other."[91]

On September 25 Proust learned that Lauris had suffered a nasty fracture to his thighbone in an automobile accident. Recovery would be slow. Marcel, who always felt duty bound to make daily visits to friends in such circumstances, decided to move to the Hôtel des Réservoirs in Versailles to be nearer Georges, now confined to his Paris apartment. Proust made his farewells at Cabourg. He would especially miss young Plantevignes, to whom he had grown attached, despite the unpleasantness over the slander the young man had failed to repudiate.

On his last evening Proust attended a movie at the hotel.[92] Just before it began he presented Marcel Plantevignes with a copy of La Bible d'Amiens, with a long dedicatory note, mentioning the "sad September evening at Cabourg, just when the cinematographic Punch-and-Judy show was about to begin." Proust's dedication, which quoted poems about the last flowers of summer by Verlaine, d'Aubigné, and Baudelaire, evoked memories of his parents to encourage Plantevignes to treasure the days while he still had his youth and his parents.[93]

Plantevignes, who had many conversations with Proust during summer stays at Cabourg, remembered being struck by how much, for an older man, the writer seemed to miss his parents. "He never said 'my mother' or 'my father,' but always only 'Papa' and 'Mama' in the tone of an emotional little boy, with tears automatically welling up in his eyes, . . . while the hoarse sound of a strangled sob could be heard in his tightened throat."[94]

Proust hired Alfred Agostinelli to drive him to Versailles and to remain in his service for the duration of his stay. This relocation proved just as impractical as his earlier move to Versailles to stay "near" his dying Uncle Georges. Perhaps his decision had been influenced by Hahn's presence at the hotel, where he was composing *La Fête chez Thérèse,* his ballet for the Paris Opéra.

Marcel's good intentions to comfort and amuse Lauris came to naught because the convalescent was confined to a bed in his father's third-floor apartment, just around the corner from boulevard Haussmann. Twice Agostinelli drove his wealthy, generous employer all the way from the Hôtel des Réservoirs to Lauris's apartment building. Marcel got no farther than the entrance because his asthma made it impossible for him to mount the three flights of stairs to reach his friend's bedside. He attributed this weakness that befell him each time he arrived at Georges's apartment building, no matter how much caffeine he had consumed in preparation, to the difference in altitude between Versailles and Paris.[95] "This impotence of my friendship is a terrible thing for me, a mixture of grief and humiliation." Later, in a letter, when Marcel was unable to rise from his bed, he attempted to imagine Georges's body and give thanks for his having survived: "Each of your limbs so miraculously spared, your beautiful, gentle hands which from time to time, when I express a doubt about your friendship, seek mine in a gesture of persuasive eloquence." By the end of Proust's long paragraph Lauris's body had become the Eucharist: "It seems to me that I have too exclusively loved your mind and your heart hitherto and that now I would experience a pure and exalting joy, like the Christian who eats the bread and drinks the wine and sings *Venite adoremus,* in reciting in your presence the litany of your ankles and the praises of your wrists." Once again Proust had gotten carried away and felt that he must immediately explain himself: "Alas, people have always been so cruel and uncomprehending about me, that these are things which I scarcely dare to say" because of misinterpretations that would "spring up in others' thoughts." But he was certain that Georges, who knew him and could "grasp with your infallible intelligence the palpable reality of what I am, will understand how purely moral and reverently paternal is what I say to you."[96]

Marcel had combined his first trip to Paris to see Lauris with plans to take Marcel Plantevignes and four other young men whom he met at Cabourg to the Théâtre des Variétés to see the revival of Flers and Caillavet's hit play *Le Roi.* Plantevignes considered the evening a huge success. Proust sent Robert de Flers a note to confirm their presence. During each intermission Flers came to the box to chat with Proust and his delighted guests.[97] Plantevignes remembered that Proust's words of praise for the play enchanted the playwright, who left the box with an air "of contentment that was pleasing to behold." After the play Proust took the young men to Prévost's for hot chocolate.[98] Not many days after the evening at the theater,

Proust attempted to organize a dinner party for Plantevignes to meet Albufera, Gabriel de La Rochefoucauld, and Léon Radziwill.[99] Proust clearly wanted to present his young protégé to the cream of Parisian society.

That fall, when Plantevignes was preparing to depart for England to receive training in business, Proust solicited letters to introduce his young friend to London society. He had obtained through Albu one such letter to the marquis de La Begassière. Proust wanted to make certain that the letters presented Plantevignes as the son of friends because he feared that the marquis must have heard some of the "inept calumnies" about his behavior. "As regards me, I don't care. But this boy is such a brave and honest lad, and coming from an ultra-bourgeois milieu where such matters are not discussed as they are quite naturally in the more perverted world of artists, I think he would throw himself in the Thames if he thought anyone had such ideas." By the postscript Proust had decided that if the marquis de La Begassière had heard such slander about him, "after two minutes with the young man he will reject this idea."[100]

At Versailles, Reynaldo came to Marcel's room once or twice to sit by his bed. Hahn kept composing while Marcel, Agostinelli, and Nicolas played dominoes. Proust, who required absolute solitude and silence when writing, was amazed that Hahn could concentrate and work in the middle of such noise.[101]

By the fall Lionel Hauser, three years older than Proust, became his chief financial adviser.[102] Hauser, who had been a childhood friend for a brief period, was a solid fellow, meticulous, scrupulous, and articulate—ideal traits for an accountant and financial adviser. He was also kind, patient, and endowed with a wonderful sense of humor. Hauser's uncle, Léon Neuburger, who also advised Proust, held an important position at the Banque Rothschild, depository of the writer's principal account.[103] Marcel would have fared much better financially if he had simply entrusted his fortune to Hauser and Neuburger, but he believed himself a knowledgeable and gifted speculator.[104] In a November letter to Neuburger, Proust congratulated himself on his financial acumen: "My poor parents were convinced that I would always be incapable of reading a business letter or taking the slightest interest in money matters. I know it was a real source of anxiety to them. And I think with sadness of the pleasure it would have given them to see what a good accountant I am."[105] Their pleasure, had they been naïve enough to take any, would have been of short duration.

On October 23 Marcel wrote to Mme de Pierrebourg to congratulate her on her novel *Ciel rouge* (Red sky). One of her scenes involving maternal love had reminded him of his own depiction so long ago of the good-night kiss in *Jean*

Santeuil, a scene that needed rewriting because it was "alas all too inferior" to what she had written. "*You're* a novelist? If only I could create characters and situations as you can, how happy I should be!"[106]

Mme de Pierrebourg was, indeed, a novelist, as Proust had marveled. But was he? Sometime between September and November, Proust's latest efforts to write a novel were undermined by self-doubt. He felt overwhelmed by all that he wanted to say and his inability to shape and focus the material. Was he not once again "amassing ruins"? He wondered in his notebook whether he should not bless his "bad health, that taught me—through the ballast of fatigue, immobility, silence— the possibility of working."[107] But what good was that if he was getting nowhere? He felt a sense of urgency: "Warnings of death. Soon you will not be able to say all that." Then Proust judged himself severely: "Laziness or doubt or impotency taking refuge in the lack of certainty over the art form." The would-be novelist was stymied by the challenges regarding plot, genre, and structure that had made him abandon *Jean Santeuil.* He asked the same questions that he had been unable to answer a decade earlier: "Must I make of it a novel, a philosophical study, am I a novelist?"

The identity crisis regarding the sort of writer he must become was his most agonizing problem as an artist. At his age, he had little to show for his ambitions and work. While he floundered, so many of his contemporaries were succeeding. Even Lucien, who wanted to be a painter, had published a novel! Continuing to write down his thoughts, Proust found some consolation in the examples of Nerval, Chateaubriand, and Baudelaire, all of whom had treated certain themes in various genres.[108]

There is a beautiful irony in this passage: Proust, while writing about his dilemma as an author, was tracing, without seeing it, the answer to the question that had tortured him for so long. The *Search* is about a man who cannot write and spends his life (lost time, wasted time) pursuing the wrong paths, until at the very end, ill, discouraged, and growing old, just like Proust, he discovers that his vocation is to write the experience of his life—now that he understands it at last and can transpose it into a work of fiction.[109]

Four days after the congratulatory letter to Mme de Pierrebourg, Marcel wrote to Mme Straus and described his frustrating attempts to write: "In my less bad moments I have begun (twice in twenty minutes) to work. It's so annoying to think so many things and to feel that the mind in which they're stirring will soon perish without anyone knowing them. It's true that there's nothing very precious about them and that others will express them better."[110] His discouragement did not last long. A little over a week later, on November 6, he wrote her again, this time a feisty, exuberant letter. Something had happened.

He began by criticizing Ganderax's preface to the *Lettres de Georges Bizet,* in which the editor and critic, merciless when editing others, had resorted to trite phrases. Ganderax had pompously referred to his "little marginal notes" as having been written "in illustration and defense of the French language." Marcel had reached his own conclusion about how a writer should approach the words belonging to the common language: "The only people who defend the French language are those who 'attack' it (like the Army during the Dreyfus Case). This idea that there is a French language which exists independently of the writers who use it, and which must be protected, is preposterous. Every writer is obliged to create his own language, as every violinist is obliged to create his own 'tone.'" There was, he insisted, "between the tone of a run-of-the-mill violinist and that of Thibaud (playing the same note) . . . an infinitesimal difference that represents a whole world!"[111] Marcel allowed that "Correctness, perfection of style do exist, but on the other side of originality, after having gone through all the faults, not this side. Correctness this side of originality" led only to clichés and banalities. Nothing was sacrosanct, certainly not "grammatical dogma" that bound writers like Ganderax "in its chains." Nothing could be taken for granted. "Alas, Mme Straus, there are no certainties, even grammatical ones. And isn't it happier that way? Because in that way a grammatical form can itself be beautiful, since only that which bears the imprint of our choice, our taste, our uncertainty, our desire and our weakness can be beautiful."[112]

Just as Proust had rejected the anecdotal to create a thinly disguised rehash of the Wilde or Eulenburg trials, he now condemned a pedestrian, facile style. Now that he had begun to trust his new voice, it was time to select a topic from the list he had sent Albu back in May. He must narrow the field and begin to work. There were moments when his creative energy elated him, as seen in this entry in *Le Carnet de 1908:* "When the rain beat down I could have created worlds. Voyager!"[113]

Sometime in late 1908 Proust bought a quantity of school notebooks like those he had used when he was a pupil at the Lycée Condorcet. Between that purchase and August 1909 he filled ten of these, writing nearly seven hundred pages for what was published postumously as *Contre Sainte-Beuve,* texts in which he attacked the eminent critic's method and legacy. Some of these drafts constitute parts of the first version of the future novel. By the end of his life Proust had filled more than a hundred such notebooks.[114] This remarkable novel was to take shape on the most modest paper, indicating not only a return to the past but a change in Proust from the *Pleasures and Days* epoch, when he produced a deluxe edition for an exclusive readership. He now wrote for himself and for everyone, as his "particular" monad sought the "universal" monad.[115]

In spite of his new determination and exuberant "attacks" on the French language, there seemed to be no end to bad luck. In early November, he returned from Versailles only to be "plagued by the building work of the dentist who has taken the third floor and nearly asphyxiated me by an ill-functioning water-heater." In the early hours of November 8, he wrote Lauris to complain that he was "coughing endlessly and racked with fever, with three windows open at one o'clock in the morning to combat the water-heater."[116] Marcel then urged his recuperating friend to do what he was attempting, despite all the challenges he faced: "Georges, whenever you can, *work*. Ruskin somewhere said a *sublime* thing which we should keep in mind day after day: that God's two great commandments (the second is almost entirely his but it doesn't matter) were: 'Work while you still have light' and 'Be merciful while you still have mercy.' " Proust then quoted from memory another sentence from the Gospel of St. John: " 'For soon the night cometh when no man can work.' "[117] Then Proust expressed a fear that was to increase in the coming years: "I am already half way into this night. . . . But you still have light and you'll have it for long years to come, so *work*. Then if life brings rebuffs there are consolations, for the true life is elsewhere, not in life itself, nor afterwards, but outside, if a term that takes its origin from space can have a meaning in a world freed therefrom."[118] He had identified the goal he would pursue: how could he as a person and as an artist step outside space and time? He must capture within his pages the "true life" that lay "elsewhere."

By December, Proust howled in protest when Lauris reminded him to follow Ruskin's commandment. "Dear Georges, how do you expect me to work when I can't sleep, can't eat, can't breathe—this letter represents a labour of Hercules."[119] Proust continued to complain of being very ill. Around the same time, he told Albu he had been so sick that it had been four days since he had eaten anything and ten since he had slept. By mid-December, recovered from his most recent ailments, Proust found himself at a writing crossroads. He had apparently abandoned his novel and could not even decide what form best suited the article on Sainte-Beuve. He wrote to Georges and Anna, two friends whose literary judgment he trusted, and asked each to indicate the better of two ideas for attacking the critic.[120] "The idea has taken shape in my mind in two different ways between which I must choose; but I have neither the will-power nor the clear-sightedness to do so. The first would be a classical essay, an essay in the manner of Taine, only a thousand times less good (except for the content which I think is new). The second begins with an account of a morning, my waking up and Mama coming to my bedside; I tell her I have an idea for a study of Sainte-Beuve; I submit it to her and develop it."[121]

Anna's response is unknown, but Georges advised Marcel to choose the conversation with his mother.[122] Thanking Lauris, Proust told him, "It's the right advice. But will I follow it? Perhaps not, for a reason you will no doubt approve. What's annoying is that I have begun to forget that piece on Sainte-Beuve which is written in my head but which I can't put down on paper since I can't get up." In order to write the essay Proust needed to consult a number of volumes by Sainte-Beuve, a difficult task when confined to bed. "And if I have to do it all over again in my head for the fourth time . . . it will be too much."[123]

He soon informed Lauris that he had not started work and had already "forgotten everything I've read of Sainte-Beuve, but if I have the strength as I believe I shall . . . I shall write it out of curiosity to have your opinion." He had stopped reading Chateaubriand and was "deep into Saint-Simon to my vast entertainment."[124] He confessed that he was "mainly preoccupied with nonsense, genealogy etc. I swear it isn't out of snobbishness; it amuses me immensely."[125] Lauris must have wondered whether Marcel would ever follow Ruskin's dictum. Would Marcel ever be anything more than an extraordinarily gifted dilettante?

As the new year approached, Marcel looked at his literary balance sheet and wondered what he might hope to accomplish in 1909. In 1907, having recovered from the worst of the shock over his mother's death, he had published a number of articles on various topics, including "Impressions de route en automobile," several passages and analogies of which he would work into his future novel.[126] In 1908 he had published six parodies, five of distinguished writers, one of a respected critic, and a review of Lucien's novel. This was the last year Proust was to make his pen readily available for minor pieces. This was not initially a conscious decision; his quarrel with Sainte-Beuve soon led him to discover, after so many years of searching, his true vocation as a writer. Proust was thirty-seven years old.

18   *Against Sainte-Beuve*   ❧

IN MID-JANUARY PROUST WROTE LAURIS to say how glad he was that his friend had recovered sufficiently to begin to go out. As for himself, these had been "the worst days" of his life since losing his parents. Marcel was convinced that the thick fog that had blanketed Paris since the beginning of the year had worsened his asthma.[1] He was "for the first time . . . utterly despondent; life isn't possible with such constant attacks." He hoped Georges would understand that if he "selfishly" confided his troubles to him, it was because "you are one of the few to whom I can. Reynaldo feels these things too acutely and makes me even iller by writing me furious letters full of stupid advice."[2] Marcel apologized for his "ignoble cowardice in giving way to this gloom and confessing it to you when I've suffered so much and life no longer counts for anything."[3] Sounding even more disgruntled, he said that he had not yet begun the essay on Sainte-Beuve and repeated that he had forgotten all he had read regarding the critic and his works.

To assist Marcel, Georges lent him seven volumes of *Port-Royal*, Sainte-Beuve's history of the Jansenists. Proust promised to send his piece on the critic to Lauris, if he ever felt well enough to write it; then he could say, like Joubert: " 'Behind the strength of many men there is weakness, but behind my weakness there is strength.' "[4] Proust had yet to prove his strength to himself and to his friends, many of whom remained skeptical.

In mid-February, Proust, suffering from headaches and insomnia and frustrated because he could not find his copy of the Saint-Simon parody *Fête chez Montesquiou à Neuilly,* asked to borrow Montesquiou's copy. "As long as I'm unable to work, I intend to dispose of another few pastiches which I did last year, and perhaps collect them all. While having some Saint-Simon read to me recently, I wondered whether that one would be accurate enough to go with the others." Proust told Montesquiou he was immersed in Saint-Simon and weighing the possibility of revising and expanding the article, but "the pastiche that would most amuse me to do when I can write a bit (without prejudice to more serious studies) is one of you! But in the first place it would probably annoy you, and I don't want anything of mine to annoy you, I'm too fond of you for that, and secondly I feel I should never be able to, never know how to!" Montesquiou, delighted that Marcel had finally admitted his paternity of *Fête chez Montesquiou,* seized the opportunity to pose again, replying that he trusted Proust's "talent," not to mention his "delicacy of feeling."[5] Had the count known that Marcel's additional brushstrokes to his portrait would result in the *Search*'s most notorious character, he might not have rejoiced over the prospect of an expanded pastiche.

In late winter Proust attended a party at the Daudets', where he saw Montesquiou and the critic Jules Lemaître, who showered compliments on him about his pastiches and encouraged him to write more, suggesting Voltaire and Mérimée.[6] On March 6 the *Figaro* published his pastiche *L'Affaire Lemoine de Henri de Régnier,* the last to be published for many years. Although tempted to write new parodies, Proust remained committed to working on *Sainte-Beuve.* In the second week of March he reported his progress to Lauris: "What has the best chance of appearing some day is Sainte-Beuve (not the second pastiche but the study) because that full trunk in the middle of my brain hampers me and I must decide whether to set off or to unpack it." Georges, whose long convalescence was nearly over, had expressed his anticipation of their reunion. Proust replied with a pessimistic forecast: "I feel, contrary to what you say, that when we see each other we shall in no way be able to show our pleasures in doing so, but that's of no importance. Gestures matter less than what one says, what one says less than what one writes—reality is elsewhere."[7] Proust sounded as though he had taken his own and Emerson's view of friendship to heart. As he became more and more absorbed by the story he was creating, he intended to devote less time to his friends.

Although Proust began to tell his friends that he was hard at work on an ambitious project, he found it hard to resist his customary inclinations. He wrote letters to assist servants or working-class acquaintances who sought employment, sent congratulatory letters to friends who received awards, put aside his own work to evaluate their manuscripts, and advised them on submitting their works for publication.[8] Even so the withdrawal to concentrate on his own work had begun. Believing that "reality was elsewhere," Marcel looked inward to capture what he found through memory, contemplation, and imagination for his book. He would demonstrate that art alone, not conversation, allows one to experience the essence of what another person has seen and felt.

In the letters he dashed off to friends, he mentioned, without explaining the reason, his lack of accessibility. In March he told Robert Dreyfus, "I don't ask to see you because my hours now begin at two o'clock in the morning."[9] In early April, while thanking Maurice Duplay for his novel *Léo,* he spoke of his own regimen: "Never have I lived like this, eating once every forty-eight hours, never before three in the morning, etc. etc." Commenting on Duplay's novel, Proust observed that, as in everything his friend wrote, "each word reflects the monad who says it, but this monad is itself a reflection of the universe."[10] In his comments on the works of others, Proust's words reflected his preoccupation with his own writing.

A Different Self

Proust-Noah had begun to see the world outside his ark with remarkable clarity. He was to make the highly particularized individuals and settings he invented part of the universal experience. Like the eminent French moralists he had always admired—Racine, Saint-Simon, La Rochefoucauld, La Fontaine—he sought the general in the particular.[11] A draft note he made during this period for *Against Sainte-Beuve* invokes "the boy" who lives in him, a version of his profound being, and who "dies instantly in the particular, and begins immediately to float and live in the general, the general animates him and nourishes him. . . . But while he lives, his life is only ecstasy and felicity. He alone should write my books."[12] Proust found his sustenance in the harmonies he established between himself, his readers, and the world they inhabit.

With his heavy writing schedule, Proust had less time to devote to his investments, which can only have worked to his advantage. Hauser supplied good financial advice; he even sent him an article on health from a German newspaper that claimed to cure asthma by a series of breathing exercises that strengthened the lungs. Hauser calculated that by curing himself, Proust would save the annual 6,000 francs ($20,000) he spent on medication.[13] Another bit of advice from

Hauser came too late; it would have been useful when Marcel refused to bid against his aunt for the building at 102, boulevard Haussmann: "If I had one piece of advice to give you, it's not to mix charity and business."[14] In May, Hauser wrote again, putting his client on notice that he would not act as his agent to buy stocks that carried too high a risk. Marcel did not so much heed Hauser's advice as ignore it; he had more urgent matters to attend to.

Sainte-Beuve provided a useful negative example by confusing the creative self and the social self. Proust noted in *Le Carnet de 1908* that Sainte-Beuve's error in judging his contemporaries resulted from his failure to "understand the originality of genius and the nullity of conversation."[15] Because Sainte-Beuve wrote that he did not view "literature as a thing apart, or, at least detachable, from the rest of the man and his nature," there were questions he must ask about an author before determining the work's merit: "What were his religious views? How did he react to the sight of nature? How did he conduct himself in regard to women, in regard to money? Was he rich, was he poor? What governed his actions, what was his daily way of life? What was his vice, or his weakness? No answer to these questions is irrelevant in judging the author of a book, nor the book itself." Proust held the opposing view: Sainte-Beuve's "method ignores what a very slight degree of self-acquaintance teaches us: that a book is the product of a different self from the self we manifest in our habits, in our social life, in our vices."[16]

Examining the reasons for Sainte-Beuve's failure as a critic led Proust to formulate his own literary aesthetics. Underlining what literature is not, as illustrated by Sainte-Beuve's errors, allowed its essential features, as defined by Proust, to stand out in relief. Art is the opposite of habit and banality, of what each of us sees readily without the intervention of a writer's unique and profound vision. Literature, like all art, should break "the ice of the habitual and the rational which instantly congeals over reality and keeps us from ever seeing it."[17] This realization caused Proust to assign a secondary role to the intellect and to insist on the primacy of instinct and impressions.[18] "Every day I set less store on intellect. Every day I see more clearly that if the writer is to repossess himself of some part of his impressions, get to something personal, that is, and to the only material of art, he must put it aside. What intellect restores to us under the name of the past, is not the past."[19]

To resurrect the past in its true richness—a richness often unperceived at the time—Proust concentrated on the phenomenon he called involuntary memory, a kind of epiphanic or "invading happiness," not unlike déjà vu.[20] In drafts for the introduction to *Sainte-Beuve*, Proust sketched what would become the primary scene of involuntary memory, the "madeleine scene," in which the Narrator dips a piece of madeleine into tea. Proust wrote: "My old cook offered to make me a cup of tea, a thing I never drink. And as chance would have, she brought me some slices of dry toast." As soon as he dipped the toast in the tea and tasted it, "something came over me—the smell of geraniums and orange-blossoms, a sensation of extraordinary radiance and happiness." He concentrated on the taste of the toast and tea, "which seemed responsible for all these marvels; then suddenly the shaken partitions in my memory gave way, and into my conscious mind there rushed the summer I had spent in the . . . house in the country. . . . And then I remembered."[21]

In his critical remarks about Sainte-Beuve, Proust is writing as himself in a fictional situation, imagining a conversation with his mother before she died. This invented setting for a real person (Proust) commenting on another real person and his work (Sainte-Beuve) served as the incubator for the emergence of the Narrator's full voice. In the *Sainte-Beuve* passages describing involuntary memory, Proust began to transmute his lived experience and his invented ones into the Narrator's life. We can clearly see the transition from essayist to novelist in many of the notations from *Le Carnet de 1908*. A strange but remarkably fecund symbiosis is being created in which Proust is himself and not himself as the Narrator. By the time he had finished, Proust had created what is perhaps the richest narrative voice in literature, a voice that speaks both as child and as man, as actor and as subject, and that weaves effortlessly between the present, past, and future.[22]

In the *Sainte-Beuve* drafts, Proust went on to describe the past resurrected through involuntary memory, using the image of dried Japanese flowers, inspired by the pellets Marie Nordlinger had given him. "A whole garden, up till then vague and dim, mirrored itself, with its forgotten walks and all their urns with all their flowers, in the little cup of tea, like those Japanese flowers which do not re-open as flowers until one drops them into water."[23] This text is only a preliminary sketch of the famous madeleine scene in *Swann's Way*. In *Sainte-Beuve*, the madeleine cake was a humble piece of dry toast. Proust likely chose the madeleine later because its shape resembles the scallop shell, worn by pilgrims who stopped at Illiers's church of Saint-Jacques on their way to Santiago de Compostela.[24] In the *Sainte-Beuve* draft Proust followed this involuntary memory with another evoking Venice.

These rare moments are always triggered by the chance encounter with what Proust calls an object-sensation, an object unconsciously connected to a past impression.[25] Venice is vividly restored to his memory when he happens to step on an uneven paving stone in Paris similar to one he had stumbled over in Venice. Until that moment, "days in Venice, which intellect had not been able to give back, were dead for me."[26] He rocked back and forth on the Paris paving stone, elated by the vision of Venice and Saint Mark's: "The shadow which had lain that day on the canal where a gondola waited for me, and all the happiness, all the wealth of those hours—this recognized sensation brought them hurrying after it, and that very day came alive for me."[27] The draft continues with a series of such experiences. In the *Search,* Proust places the toast and tea episode in the front section of the novel, where it serves as an example of the "true life" and the type of vivid recollection the Narrator would like to capture in his writing, when he feels such joy at being outside of time. Art is removed from the contingencies of time, thus giving the essence of human experience, "true life," a life of its own. All the other involuntary memory experiences from *Sainte-Beuve* would be developed and placed toward the end of the novel, where these felicitous moments create a crescendo effect as the Narrator, after many years of disappointment and inability to work, reclaims his will, forfeited long ago in childhood in the scene of the good-night kiss, and finds his vocation as a writer. He must now transpose the fruit of his experience into a book, as his Narrator concludes in *Time Regained:* "Whether I was concerned with impressions like the one which I had received from the sight of the steeples of Martinville or with reminiscences like that of the unevenness of the two steps or the taste of the madeleine, the task was to interpret the given sensations as signs of so many laws and ideas, by trying to think—that is to say, to draw forth from the shadow—what I had merely felt, by trying to convert it into its spiritual equivalent. And this method, which seemed to me the sole method, what was it but the creation of a work of art?"[28]

At the time of the *Sainte-Beuve* drafts, Proust had not written the passage in which the Narrator discovers his vocation. He later placed the episode near the end of *Time Regained,* after remarks about the secondary role of intelligence that do have their origin in the 1908–9 *Sainte-Beuve* text. It was while denouncing the critic that Proust made the key discovery in his long apprenticeship to become a creative person. The images used in the *Search* to explain why the Narrator had taken so long to discover his vocation include the metaphor of dried seeds, also from *Sainte-Beuve:*

And I understood that all these materials for a work of literature were simply my past life; I understood that they had come to me, in frivolous pleasures, in indolence, in tenderness, in unhappiness, and that I had stored them up without divining the purpose for which they were destined or even their continued existence any more than a seed does when it forms within itself a reserve of all the nutritious substances from which it will feed a plant. Like the seed, I should be able to die once the plant had developed and I began to perceive that I had lived for the sake of the plant without knowing it, without ever realizing that my life needed to come into contact with those books which I had wanted to write and for which, when in the past I had sat down at my table to begin, I had been unable to find a subject. And thus my whole life up to the present day might and yet might not have been summed up under the title: A Vocation.[29]

His subject had been ever present, within himself, in the secret places of the heart. He had been living the story in order to write it: "Marcel becomes a writer."[30] He would find everything he needed for the Narrator within himself. Proust had noted in the *Carnet de 1908,* "I am the only being whom I cannot forget."[31] His character would be a man much like himself, who had lost his will in childhood because of fragile health and excessive dependency on his mother, and who, as an adult, became a neurotic, obsessed with his health and regimen, and who, up until very late in life, had appeared to waste his time.

Sainte-Beuve contains the text that will, with revisions, and the addition of the famous first sentence—"For a long time I would go to bed early"—open the novel. "For a moment I was like those sleepers who wake up in the dark and do not know where they are, who ask their bodies to give them a bearing as to their whereabouts, not knowing what bed, what house, what part of the world, which year of their life they are in." Proust was to develop and enrich this text in a brilliant manner for the opening sentences, which show the Narrator slumbering in chaos, uncertain of who he is, where he is, or even what he is, thus establishing the major theme of the novel: his search for his soul. *In Search of Lost Time* is the quest for his true identity and his reason for living. In *Time Regained,* the Narrator will be whole and confident, at last ready to convert the "egotism" of a life spent in vain pursuits into something "useful to others," by creating a work of art.[32]

Here are the opening lines of the *Search:*

For a long time I would go to bed early. Sometimes, the candle barely out, my eyes closed so quickly that I did not have time to tell myself: "I'm falling asleep." And half an hour later the thought that it was time to look for sleep would awaken me; I would make as if to put away the book which I imagined was still in my hands, and to blow out the light; I had gone on thinking, while I was asleep, about what I had just been

reading, but these thoughts had taken a rather peculiar turn; it seemed
to me that I myself was the immediate subject of my book: a church, a
quartet, the rivalry between François I and Charles V.[33]

Sainte-Beuve contains a hint of the future title: "ma poursuite du passé," "my
pursuit of the past," a less poetical rendition of *À la recherche du temps perdu:* In
search of lost time.[34]

In the preface to *Against Sainte-Beuve,* Proust has an imaginary conversation
with his mother in which he tells her that his article would illustrate how Sainte-
Beuve's vaunted "critical method was absurd, that he was a bad writer, and perhaps
that will lead me to some truths that are more important."[35] This is exactly what
happened. The discovery of those truths was so significant that Proust put the
article on Sainte-Beuve aside for good and began to develop those sections that
contained the seeds of the novel. Proust's mature voice, first heard in "On Reading,"
had become his hero's voice even before the author found all the elements of the
story he wanted to tell.

Proust was to tell a fascinating story as he elaborated his plot and created a cast
of remarkable characters to inhabit his fictional world that embraced the years of
his life, roughly the period from 1871 to 1922.[36] Involuntary memory provides both
the vivid recollections he hoped to capture in his writing and proof that by delving
diligently into the past and bringing all the forces of the creative imagination and
craftsmanship to bear on what could be retrieved from memory, that "true life"—
life in all its rich complexity, and not its "pallid ghost"—could be recaptured.[37]
Proust saw this as the artist's duty: "Basically, my entire philosophy, like all true
philosophy, comes down to justifying, reconstructing what is."[38] By the re-creation
of reality, Proust does not mean annotation or reporting as practiced by the
adherents of "realism," but the depiction of life in its plenitude. What we call reality
or life is often merely the product of habit. In the *Search,* the Narrator will say that
"an hour is not merely an hour, it is a vase full of scents and sounds and projects
and climates." By probing beneath the surface and by articulating what he discovered, Proust sought to render events, emotions, sensations, in their rich complexity, "grandeur, for example, in the distant sound of an aeroplane or the outline
of the steeple of Saint-Hilaire, the past in the taste of a madeleine and so on." In the
concluding pages of the *Search,* the Narrator will show that art, or the creative
process, is the antidote to the dulling effects of habit and incuriosity: "Real life, life
at last laid bare and illuminated—the only life in consequence which can be said to

be really lived—is literature, and life thus defined is in a sense all the time immanent in ordinary men no less than in the artist."[39]

In the drafts of *Sainte-Beuve,* Proust began making notes about important points to remember. "Don't forget: Books are the work of solitude and the *children of silence.*"[40] Proust was to place his ideas about the nature of the creative process at the end of *Time Regained,* when the Narrator discovers his vocation and the lessons learned from the "wasted" years. The notations about books in the Sainte-Beuve drafts resulted in this statement in the finished novel: "Real books should be the offspring not of daylight and casual talk but of darkness and silence. And as art exactly reconstitutes life, around the truths to which we have attained inside ourselves there will always float an atmosphere of poetry, the soft charm of a mystery which is merely a vestige of the shadow which we have had to traverse, the indication, as precise as the markings of an altimeter, of the depth of a work."[41]

Proust's mother had been present in *Jean Santeuil,* whose hero's name is the masculine form of Jeanne. The extraordinary closeness Marcel shared with his mother, an attachment the Narrator feels for his mother and grandmother, who are really two versions of the same woman at different ages, can be explained in part by Marcel's resemblance to his mother. This likeness is mentioned in *Jean Santeuil,* where we read that Jean realized that he had inherited from his mother "his manner of seeing, of judging."[42] In the *Search,* while painting a detailed portrait of the highly sensitive and perceptive Narrator's relationship with the mother, Proust reaches beyond the mother to all his readers by seeking the universal.

Proust had been unable to complete *Jean Santeuil,* a third-person narrative that was perhaps too close to home and lacked a clear point of view. In the *Search,* the "I" of the Narrator easily shifts to its plural "We," intimately involving the reader in his thoughts, perceptions, and emotions. The story he wanted to talk through with his mother in *Against Sainte-Beuve,* though still addressed to her in the *Search,* is now narrated with the same love and compassion for his characters and his readers. This step of freedom beyond his immense love for his mother, while fulfilling her highest aspirations for him, was necessary for Proust to become a great writer. When he abandoned the article attacking Sainte-Beuve, Proust left behind not only his bitterness but his despair and became—if not always a happy man—a man with a purpose. The immense joy he often felt when writing came from the clarity with which he now saw his goal and from his determination to complete his ambitious project. Once he had accomplished his mission, death would be a trifling affair. Life still held much pain in store for Marcel, primarily through disappointments in love and catastrophes that were to befall his friends and his country, but he never again suffered the humiliation of considering himself a failure.

Various dates, some as early as 1907, have been proposed for the time when Proust began writing the *Search*. The 1907 date is based on a letter to Daniel Halévy in which Proust mentioned passages he had written on topography and names that bore some resemblance to pages he had since read in an article by the poet and polemicist Charles Péguy.[43] The presumption is that since passages on villages and their names appear in the "Combray" section of the *Search*, Proust had already conceived the novel before he decided to write the essay on Sainte-Beuve in 1908.[44] This hypothesis does not explain why, if he had indeed conceived the novel, he would have put it aside for the comparatively trivial matter of an essay attacking Sainte-Beuve, especially when Proust had begun to worry about surviving long enough to complete the novel that he now saw as his reason for living.

If earlier texts that Proust used with only minor alterations in the *Search* are the criteria by which we date its beginning, then we can push the date far back to the *Jean Santeuil* era, when Proust wrote the October 1896 letter and text about telephoning his mother from Fontainebleau.[45] There are other 1907 texts that Proust wrote as articles and then used in the *Search*, such as the "maidens of the telephone" passage from "Journées de lecture," where paragraphs are used with no changes or only minor ones. Proust also used parts of the 1907 article "Impressions de route en automobile" for the "steeples of Martinville" episode in *Swann's Way* and for later scenes of Albertine pumping the player piano. In a sense, everything Proust wrote was a rehearsal for the *Search*, but the important point—made clear by his many anguished doubts about whether or not he was a novelist—is that until he found the story line, he did not know whether he would ever write such a book. The moment that marked the conscious, willful beginning of *In Search of Lost Time* is the one when Proust knew that he had begun this particular novel with its circular structure. He was still to have moments of indecision regarding titles and the division of the text into volumes, but the demoralizing days of being at a loss over what to write ended when he realized that the story of his own life could be transfigured into a work of fiction.

It is unlikely that we will ever know the precise date when Proust conceived the broad outline of the novel that became the *Search*. The best we can do is to narrow the time frame to sometime between July 1908, when he listed his "pages written," and the summer of 1909, when he began to speak of a completed novel, by which he apparently meant that he had written drafts of the first and last parts of the *Search* and knew how to fill in the middle. This novel was to acquire a vast range that Proust himself could not have foreseen, for its fate would be determined to some degree by chance and forces beyond his or anyone's control. Sometime in spring 1909 Proust made the last pages of notes and comments regarding Sainte-Beuve. Then he moved entirely to writing the *Search,* still using the obsolete name *Against Sainte-Beuve* as his working title. Although he began to refer to this work as a novel, he still was not always certain about the genre, calling it "a sort of a novel" or, as it assumed larger proportions, "a sort of immense novel." He knew that he was attempting something new. *In Search of Lost Time* was to evolve into an unprecedented work of fiction, perhaps the most remarkable example of a sustained narrative in the history of literature.

After his father's death Marcel had said that he had no ambition to console him; after his mother's, he was so miserable he had wanted to die. Now dying prematurely became his greatest fear, as he noted in *Le Carnet de 1908:* "I know that a trifle can destroy this mind."[46] His one task became the completion of his book.

On May 9 Proust rose and went out in the daytime for the first time in weeks.[47] Although the purpose of this extraordinary event is unknown, it may have been to attend an exhibition of Claude Monet's water lilies that had opened three days earlier at the Durand-Ruel Gallery.[48] Monet was showing forty-eight "sonnets" in a series entitled "Water lilies, series of water landscapes" as a "marvelous explanation for six years of silence" on the part of the master.[49] Proust's fictional painter Elstir was to have many affinities with Monet, especially in the creation of series and in the depictions of water lilies. As a writer, Proust created in the *Search,* as did Monet in the long panels of water lilies *(Grandes Décorations),* a space-time continuum in which the text, with no fixed beginning and ending, except the word *Time,* reflects the shape, harmony, and mystery of the universe.[50]

Later in May, Proust wrote Lauris to ask a question, indicating his return to the novel begun a year earlier: "Do you happen to know whether Guermantes, which must have been the name of some people as well as of a place, was then already in the Pâris family, or . . . whether the name of Comte or Marquis de Guermantes was a title used by relations of the Pâris family, and whether it's entirely extinct and available to an author?"[51] Proust did not explain why he needed this information, and when Georges rightly guessed that he was writing a novel, denied it: "No, Georges, I'm not writing a novel; it would take too long to explain. But if Guermantes is one of the names of the Puységur family, it comes to the same thing as if it belonged to the Pâris family. I only want to annoy unknowns, who aren't related to people I know; I haven't Balzac's nerve."[52] Then he took pains to deny again that he was writing a novel: "This must sound as though I'm doing a novel. First of all I'm not *doing* anything. But I should like to." Proust, having resumed the story whose episodes he had listed in 1908 as "pages written," needed a name that appealed to him, poetically and historically, for the most prominent noble family in his novel.

Proust delayed admitting the truth to Georges, who, along with Reynaldo, was his most trusted confidant. He may not have wanted to take the time to explain, or he may not have realized that he was ready to cut the umbilical cord that bound him to *Sainte-Beuve*. He avoided talk about work in progress, and after so many postponements and false starts, he was reluctant to announce a work he might not finish.

Proust and his doctors were still weighing the advantages of his moving away from Paris. Incredibly, in the midst of all his woes and hard work, Marcel found time to engage in flirtatious fantasies with women. On June 23, he startled Georges with the news, "If I leave Paris, it will be perhaps with a woman. How's that for ridiculous!"[53] This woman's identity remains a mystery. Less than a week later, Proust wrote to Dreyfus and mentioned another woman he had seen once at Cabourg and found attractive: "Do you know (I believe you do), Mme Philippi née Fava. I saw her once at Cabourg and not since. But suddenly I feel just a little bit in love with her. Only just a little bit. I seem to recall that she had dark skin and soft eyes. Oh, well, I like her."[54] More Proustian mystifications? It seems unlikely that these women were meant as shields against accusations of homosexuality, for none were being made, nor was Proust, as far as we know, having an affair with a man that might be revealed and confirm the gossip about him. It is likely that he was acting out parts, experimenting with emotions and situations that he could assign to the protagonist.

In his letters and notes to himself about the novel, Proust usually spoke of the Narrator as "I," making no distinction between himself and his fictional persona. Proust's friends would recognize that voice as the writer's own. Whenever the Narrator speaks about art and literature, he is speaking for Proust. Still, Proust was engaged not in writing his autobiography but in creating a novel in which there are strong autobiographical elements.[55] The symbiosis between Proust and his Narrator can be explained by the hybrid origin of the story. Having begun as an essay in which the "I" was himself, as the text veered more and more toward fiction, the "I" telling the story became both its generator and its subject, like a Siamese twin, intimately linked to Proust's body and soul and yet other. This novel that passionately examines and contrasts the poetry and reality of proper names has none for the Narrator and his family. They are known only as "I," "Mama," and "Papa."[56] The novel's creator was truly "another I," Proust at his best and most profound, reinventing himself for this novel that lacked obvious precursors. Those who had compared his essay on reading to Montaigne's work were close to the mark regarding a literary ancestor. Had Montaigne been a novelist or Proust exclusively an essayist, the books they produced might have been remarkably similar. Each examines in fascinating, lucid detail many facets of the human condition.

But what voice or what guise was he not capable of assuming, Proust-Proteus-Pasticheur? To the drugs and regimen that saved him and damned him, moving him up and down in the vicious circle through which he rotated each day, backward to the moon and sun, Marcel added another stimulant, to him the most powerful and rejuvenating: words. This was the air for which he had gasped so long, words, human breath that must flow from his body to his hands with the mighty weight and ease of tides, waves of words he must ink on paper, preserving the true, rich colors of what he had seen.

On June 18 Montesquiou invited Proust to an afternoon party, the last of the season at the Pavillon des Muses, whose purpose was to bid "Farewell to the poet." The count was to receive the Grand Duke Paul of Russia, Comtesse Greffulhe, and many friends. Proust managed to rise that morning and dress to go to the party at Neuilly, but then he became very ill. Instead of attending the poet's farewell, he went to see his dentist, who found him too ill even to apply gutta percha.[57] Marcel returned to his bed and his notebooks.

Although extremely weak and running a fever, Proust attempted to work on the novel. He wrote Lauris: "Georges, I'm so exhausted from having started *Sainte-Beuve* (*I'm hard at work on it,* though the results are execrable) that I don't know what I'm saying to you. I literally cannot write."[58] Occasionally, as a break from his long hours at work, he attended parties and balls. He did not like to remain cut off too long from his models and the world he was re-creating so vividly in his pages. He attended one soirée, probably at Mme Lemaire's, with Emmanuel Bibesco. Afterward Bibesco convinced Proust to accompany him to the ball at Mme Pierre Lebaudy's. Proust later complained to Emmanuel that he had "dragged" him to the ball, though Proust was too ill, without bothering to tell him that his pants pocket was sticking out and that his appearance was "scandalous."[59]

At the end of June, just when Proust had hoped to work uninterrupted on his novel, the Lemoine trial began and the affair became news again. The *Figaro* asked Marcel for more pastiches. At the same time, Lauris, eager to leave on a trip, asked

Proust to read his novel *Ginette Chatenay*. Lauris had revised his manuscript based on Marcel's earlier recommendations and wanted another reading before sending it to a publisher.[60] Proust suggested postponing this task, but Lauris insisted it was urgent. Then, when Proust tried to write the pastiches, renovations began in a neighboring apartment and he found it impossible to work. By the time Proust could write three pastiches of Maeterlinck, Chateaubriand, and Ruskin, the deadline had passed, and the *Figaro* did not publish them. The newspaper subsequently lost the manuscripts.[61] To fulfill his obligations, Proust reread Lauris's novel and suggested new revisions. The night owl at boulevard Haussmann must have believed all his friends would publish a novel before he finished his own.

In early July, when Proust was finally free to work, he determined to resolve his doubts: Am I a novelist? Will I ever see my novel? On July 7, after one extraordinary work session, he wrote Robert Dreyfus, telling him that the letter might not be "delicious," but if his friend could see his body, he would find the letter "courageous!" For more than sixty hours he had not slept or turned off his light. His valet, who did not "worship" his employer, now thought him endowed with "an old Brahman's mysterious power of resistance. . . . Who would have believed it!" In spite of his exhaustion, Proust felt elated over the work he had accomplished. Because Robert persisted in encouraging him to write more parodies, Marcel added a postscript: "*Merde* on the pastiches!" Then, with great verve, he improvised a pastiche for Robert and gave it the title "Explanation by H. Taine of why you bore me when you speak to me about the pastiches."[62]

Late one evening five days later, Marcel enjoyed a particularly delectable dish of beef in jelly that Céline Cottin had prepared. Afterward, as he was preparing to write, it occurred to him that he would like his readers to be as contented as he after this meal. He wrote a grateful note to Céline, who did not know that she, and especially her *bœuf mode*, were posing as models for the servant Françoise and her gastronomical feats: "Céline, I send you my warmest compliments and thanks for the marvelous *bœuf mode*. Would that I might bring off as well as you what I am going to do tonight, that my style might be as brilliant, as clear, as firm as your *gelée*, that my ideas might be as succulent as your carrots and as nourishing and fresh as your meat. Pending the completion of my work, I congratulate you on yours."[63]

This note, full of Proustian charm and gentillesse, shows Proust ready for a night's work and feeling good about what he was writing. For a Frenchman, what could be more real and at the same time more heavenly than a choice dish cooked to perfection? This classic French concoction of larded beef in jelly appears twice in the *Search*. It is served at a dinner party to M. de Norpois, an ambassador friend and associate of the Narrator's father.[64] Its second appearance, at the end of the novel, as in the note to Céline, is analogical. The Narrator selects Françoise's *bœuf mode* as one of the high standards by which his future novel is to be judged.[65]

I Am a Novelist

A sure indication that Proust had begun writing the *Search* is his July 17, 1909, letter to Hahn. Marcel first told Reynaldo some harmless gossip about Comtesse Greffulhe and asked him not to repeat it. The thought of offending the countess made Proust consider an even larger problem that he would face when his novel appeared, as he explained to Reynaldo in a rhymed couplet:

> Nicens,
> I rather fear my novel on Sainte-Veuve
> May not be very pleasing to the Beuve

His transposition of Sainte-Beuve and Veuve was an obvious reference to the "Widow," Madeleine Lemaire. Proust insisted that Reynaldo return the incriminating letter: "Mum's the word. I unbosom myself to you as I did to Mama. But she gave nothing away."[66]

Why would Mme Lemaire be displeased with his novel? Proust had taken her as the primary model for a major character, Mme Verdurin, one of the *Search*'s great comic figures, the tyrannical society hostess who makes virtual prisoners of the "faithful" members of her salon and frequently behaves in a pretentious, ridiculous manner. His fear of Mme Lemaire's wrath, on the day when she would settle into a comfortable chair and open his book, did not deter him from his caricature. Lemaire's persistent painting of roses would be given—complete with Dumas's quip about her having created more roses than anyone except God—to another character, Mme de Villeparisis.

In early July, Proust had begun to think about possible publishers for the novel he believed he would complete within a few months. He asked Lauris, "Where did Gide's novella appear?" André Gide's third novel, *La Porte étroite*, had been published in three successive issues of the recently founded *Nouvelle Revue française*, soon to become Europe's most influential literary journal.[67] Gide, one of the review's founders and its guiding spirit, had little esteem for Proust. The group at the *NRF*, as the review was known, had also created a publishing house that would become equally distinguished and eventually take the name of its director Gallimard.[68] Proust and Gide, two of France's most celebrated twentieth-century authors, were on a collision course for one of the most memorable misunderstandings in the history of literature.

In August, Marcel told Georges that he would consider Calmann-Lévy as a publisher "if my book were not obscene. But it is and that's impossible."[69] Fearing that his depiction of male and female homosexuals would discourage most publishers, he decided to try Alfred Vallette, publisher of his Ruskin translations, who might be less apprehensive about the book's nature. Vallette's wife, Marguerite, using the pseudonym Rachilde, had published three novels with homosexual overtones: *Madame Adonis, Monsieur Vénus,* and *Les Hors nature* (Unnatural beings). Proust did not know that Vallette had since changed his attitude and now censored daring passages.[70]

The letter Proust sent Vallette in August, offering his book for publication, provides the fullest description we have of its status in the summer of 1909. Proust had outlined his plot and sketched many of his characters. The author emphasized that whether or not Vallette accepted his proposal, the letter's contents must remain confidential:

> You will see why. I am finishing a book which in spite of its provisional title: *Contre Sainte-Beuve, souvenir d'une matinée,* [Against Sainte-Beuve, the memory of a morning] is a genuine novel and an extremely indecent one in places.[71] One of the principal characters is a homosexual. And this I count on you to keep strictly secret. If the fact were known before the book appeared a number of devoted and apprehensive friends would ask me to abandon it. Moreover I fancy it contains some new things (forgive me!) and I shouldn't like to be robbed by others. The name of Sainte-Beuve is not there by chance. The book does indeed end with a long conversation about Sainte-Beuve and about aesthetics (if you like, as *Sylvie* ends with a study of popular song) and once people have finished the book they will see (I hope) that the whole novel is simply the implementation of the artistic principles expressed in this final part, a sort of preface if you like[,] placed at the end.[72]

The "preface" at the end was to contain Proust's observations on life and art that result from the Narrator's illumination, after the long and difficult quest to discover his vocation as a writer. The remarks aimed directly at Sainte-Beuve were later removed for more general aesthetic considerations, all linked to the Narrator's past (as a seeker, struggling to be an artist) and future (as creator).

Before ending the letter to Vallette, Proust summarized his proposal: "Would you consent to give me, from the 1st or the 15th of October, thirty (or more—that would be all the better) pages of the *Mercure* in every number until January, which would amount to roughly 250 or 300 pages in book form. The novel part would thus have appeared. There would remain the long discussion on Sainte-Beuve, the criticism, etc. which would appear only in the book version. The whole would be about the same length as *La Double Maîtresse* (425 pages) and would appear under your imprint if you wished."[73]

Proust, who thought that the book would be ready to appear by January or February, offered to pay the publishing costs, choose his own paper, and organize his own publicity. If Vallette wished to see a sample of the work, Proust said that within a few days he could have the first hundred pages copied for him "very legibly, or even typed. But they are of the greatest purity. If the thought of the others frightens you and you would like to be reassured on the point (there isn't a hint of pornography) I can have a few passages copied for you but the text is not absolutely definitive. But I must ask you not to talk about them to anyone."

Proust had also raised the possibility, if the *Mercure* did not want his pages, of giving them to the *Figaro*. But that would mean suppressing the "obscene sections," which "would upset me considerably, and in the second place it's a book of episodes, of events, and the reflection of events on one another at intervals of several years, and it can only appear in large slices." Proust had identified the obstacles he would face in finding a suitable publisher for his unusual and daring novel. Not only the content but the "large slices" would make serialization difficult.[74]

What remained of the critical essay that had led Proust by an unanticipated route to his novel? He had set out to show that Sainte-Beuve was a bad critic because his method was flawed. In the novel what could be called the "Sainte-Beuve syndrome" is attributed to various characters and dramatized in conversations with them about authors. Mme de Villeparisis exhibits this syndrome when she judges writers not by their works but by whether they are brilliant conversationalists. Mme de Villeparisis finds fashionable men, whose wit makes them sparkle in her salon, superior to men of greater achievement who lack social graces.[75]

No critical commentary or aesthetic theory is necessary to understand the Sainte-Beuve disorder. It is an ordinary human failing, the tendency to judge by appearances rather than substance. Proust's orchestration of the theme is never trivial, however, and serves to remind the reader to trust the inner being rather than the "social self," and not to yield to vanity. Throughout the *Search,* Proust develops intricate, kaleidoscopic variations on this theme, as we watch Swann, Charlus, and for a long time the Narrator fall victim to obsessions that ensnare them and keep them from becoming creative people, the world's true benefactors.[76]

After he sent the letter to Vallette, Proust found himself in the usual quandary about whether to leave for vacation. During the first half of August, he ran a high fever due to an abscessed tooth. The dentist Marcel finally saw refused to treat him because of his exhaustion and multiple health problems. When Dr. Bize saw his patient's condition, he insisted that Proust go on vacation.[77] Just before the middle of the month, Proust informed an acquaintance that he would not go to Cabourg. A day or so later, Proust abruptly changed his mind and left for the coast.[78] Before leaving he ordered some renovations of his own to be done while he was away: the walls of his bedroom were to be lined with cork. Marcel had heard about using cork to muffle sounds from fellow neurasthenic Anna de Noailles, who had received the tip from Henry Bernstein.[79]

Shortly after his arrival at the Grand-Hôtel, Proust dropped Georges a line, saying that he hoped to keep his arrival in Cabourg secret. He added: "Vallette, who had already rejected my *Pastiches, Collected Articles,* etc., has now rejected *Sainte-Beuve,* which will doubtless remain unpublished! But I shall *read* it to you. And besides, Calmette is in the neighbourhood and is so charming that he may perhaps undertake to get it published, but precisely because he is so nice I hesitate to ask him. Yes, it will be very long, four or five hundred pages."[80] Vallette had not even asked to look at his manuscript.

Because he had not intended to go to Cabourg, Proust had not reserved rooms at the hotel. He was so unhappy with the rooms he was given that he almost returned to Paris; he did cancel the order for the cork to be installed in his bedroom, in case he should decide on an early return.[81] Marcel complained to Mme Straus that he had to take "nasty damp rooms where it won't be easy to recuperate. I go from the hotel to the Casino, which is two minutes away, and that seems so exhausting that I wonder how I could get to Trouville. But I shall." Around the time he wrote Mme Straus, Marcel happened to see Calmette, who surprised him with the generous offer of serializing his novel in the *Figaro* and promised to begin publishing it within a week of receiving the manuscript. Though unconvinced that the *Figaro* was the right outlet for his work, Proust replied in such a manner as to keep the door open.

Marcel did not share the details of his novel with Mme Straus, but he did want her to know what he had accomplished: "I think you'll see quite a lot of me in Paris this year. And before that you will read me—more of me than you will want—for I've just begun—and finished—a whole long book. Unfortunately, my departure for Cabourg interrupted my work, and I'm only now about to go back to it. Perhaps a part of it will appear serially in the *Figaro*, but only a part. Because it's too improper and too long to be given in its entirety. But I very much want to get to the end of it. Once everything is written, there'll be a lot of things to recast."[82] Intent on working hard on his book, Marcel urged Mme Straus not to divulge his presence in Cabourg: "I need hardly tell you that I've seen no one on the coast since I haven't seen you. If you run into the Guiches, for I see from the newspapers that you're going about a bit, I don't even want them to know I'm here."[83]

The "whole long book" he mentioned to Mme Straus was the earliest draft of the *Search*, the opening section "Combray"—which establishes the major characters, locations, themes—and the conclusion, in which the Narrator understands the lessons from his apprenticeship. The most important words in the letter to Mme Straus are: "I've just begun—and finished." Since the days when he struggled unsuccessfully to complete *Jean Santeuil*, Proust had never been able to finish any work of fiction because he lacked the story and point of view. He had at last found his structure, one that was to prove ideal for his narrative skills and manner of composition. Proust never composed in a linear manner or according to an outline. He always worked like a mosaicist, taking a particular scene, anecdote, impression, image, and crafting it to completion. In his notebooks, there are many notes to himself about such bits: "To be placed somewhere," or a memo to give a remark or trait to a certain character. Sometimes he listed more than one character or episode as a possible source for a quotation. The story's circular form suited his needs perfectly. As he composed and orchestrated the rich Proustian music, the structure would expand while keeping its basic shape and relation among the parts.

Although Proust soon began to project a lengthy novel, he did not yet foresee the gargantuan proportions his book would assume, proportions due in part to forces beyond his control, which he would use to enhance his story. Proust's self-imposed isolation may have served his writing, but he was often lonely. One evening in late August while lingering in the dining room of the Grand-Hôtel and listening to a gypsy band, Marcel asked the musicians whether they knew anything by Reynaldo Hahn. Proust described what happened next in a letter to Reynaldo: "When they started *Rêverie* I began to cry as I thought of my Bunibuls in the big dining-room surrounded by a score of dismayed waiters who put on long faces! The head waiter, not knowing how to commiserate with me, went to fetch a finger-bowl."[84]

After changing rooms several times, Proust found accommodations that were adequate. The casino, directly connected to the hotel by a corridor, included a theater, a gaming room, a private room for members only, a dance hall, and a grill room.[85] Proust, who seldom went out on the boardwalk, blaming the rarity of his walks along the beachfront on his health, which had "greatly deteriorated in the past year," occasionally enjoyed the casino and its amenities. If he rose from his bed at all, it was usually around ten in the evening. Then, he "went down through the hotel, without going out, into the new Casino[,] where I was immediately grabbed by a group of people who together with me represented every age of life. For on the one side there were some really young creatures and on the other M. and Mme d'Alton and the Pontcharras, Mme de Maupeou and [Charles] Bertrand," the proprietor of the Grand-Hôtel.[86] The Altons had two daughters, Hélène and Colette, who were among Proust's young Cabourg friends. Proust read poems from Anna de Noailles's *Les Éblouissements,* including one entitled "Les Adolescents," to his young friends and wrote the poet that he had left behind him "great, budding affection for you in these young hearts."[87]

Proust enjoyed gambling as much as he did playing the stock market, and he often went to the casino and played baccarat or had someone place his bets for him. The more he worked, the more he seemed to enjoy gambling or speculating on stocks; it was a release from his grinding work and constant preoccupation with his health.[88] Occasionally he saw an opera or a play. On August 25 he went to nearby Villers-sur-Mer to see an act of Massenet's *Werther.*[89] The next evening he attended a performance of the hit play *Arsène Lupin* by Francis de Croisset and Maurice Leblanc, staged in the theater at the hotel.

Eager to find a publisher, Marcel unintentionally complicated the *Figaro*'s consideration of his manuscript. He related the dilemma to Dreyfus, who, as a colleague of Calmette's and Beaunier's, might be able to help straighten things out: "Calmette, whom I've seen here, asked me very nicely and with great insistence if he could publish serially in the *Figaro* a novel I'm in the middle of writing. I may add between ourselves that I don't think I shall give this novel to the *Figaro* or to any newspaper or review and that it will appear only in book form." Proust feared that if Calmette happened to tell Beaunier that "he'd asked me for a serial for the *Figaro,* Beaunier might think it was my critical study and advise against it," reasoning that a serialized critical study might not be right for the *Figaro.* Proust did not tell Dreyfus the main reason he feared Beaunier's opposition to his critical study: the journalist also intended to write about Sainte-Beuve.[90] Earlier Proust had alerted Beaunier to the fact they would be competing. Now he wanted Dreyfus to tell Beaunier that "if

by chance Calmette mentions to him a serial by me . . . it's a question of a novel."
Should Marcel later decide "to publish the novel as a serial, then let Beaunier advise
against it if he finds it bad. All I want is to avoid a muddle."[91]

In late September, Marcel wrote Georges from Cabourg, telling him that one
month of calm was all he needed to resume work on the novel and "finish it
quickly." He listed the reasons he dreaded returning to Paris: "the central heating,
the dentist, maddening attacks of asthma." Under such conditions he feared that
the return to the apartment would be even worse than the "calvary" of last winter.
"How to live like that without being able to work, seeing no one, how to eat, to
breathe? But I really am too tired to try new places if they won't let me stay here, I
don't know what to do."[92]

The Grand-Hôtel closed at the end of September, and Proust had no choice but
to return to Paris. While he recovered a little from his homecoming, he made plans
to see Lauris in early November. He proposed having a legible copy "made from my
untidy scribbles of the first paragraph of the first chapter of *Sainte-Beuve* (it's
almost a book in itself, that first paragraph!) and as soon as it's copied will you give
me an evening and come and read it with me?"[93] He was eager to see what Georges
thought of "Combray."

In mid-November, in a letter apologizing to Hauser for the delay in sending
investment information, Proust mentioned his novel. He had been unwell and was
"in the throes of a work in 3 volumes (!), begun, promised, not ready."[94] He now
saw clearly that his narrative would be longer than he had originally thought. In
spite of earlier reservations, Proust decided to accept Calmette's offer to have his
novel appear in serial form in the *Figaro*. Why did he change his mind? Perhaps he
believed that publishing first his expurgated text in a highly respectable newspaper
like the *Figaro* would facilitate its unabridged publication in book form.

In late November, Lauris must have been startled when he opened a letter from
Proust and read: "You will perhaps soon be hearing news of me, or rather I shall ask
your advice: to make a very young and charming girl share my life, even if she's not
afraid of doing so—would that not be a crime?" Proust had no intention of
committing such a crime. Who she was—if she was—remains a Proustian mystery.[95] He then turned to his true preoccupation. He was eager to "get down to work
again because I've read my beginning to Reynaldo (200 pages) and his reaction has
greatly encouraged me. Any evening you like I'll send it to you. I feel it's now my
duty to subordinate everything else to trying to finish it." He told Georges that he
would return the volumes of Sainte-Beuve's *Port-Royal;* they had not been needed,

after all. For his New Year's present, Marcel asked Georges to give him Émile Mâle's new book, *L'Art religieux de la fin du Moyen Âge en France* (French religious art from the end of the Middle Ages), which he may have wanted to consult for the churches he was to describe in the *Search*.[96]

Marcel had offered to send his manuscript to Georges but wondered whether his friend would be able to read his handwriting—worse even in the heat of composition than in letters, where he at least tried to write legibly. The production of a legible copy of his manuscript was essential for the limited circulation he intended and, above all, for prospective publishers. Marcel hired two brothers who were stenographers, but they soon gave up trying to decipher his handwriting. On November 26 Proust explained the difficulties to Reynaldo, who needed a copy so that he could finish reading "Combray."[97] The stenographers had sent Proust a note "saying they . . . would prefer to carry on by taking it down in shorthand. So in spite of the state I was in I sent for them. They (he) left at half past two [in the afternoon]. Afterward I worked alone, demolishing what was done." The prudent stenographers had also revised their production schedule and asked for an additional week to complete the typescript of the three notebooks containing most of "Combray."

Marcel wrote Louisa that he was "cloistering himself for a long work," but first he had to go out once more because he had made the "insane promise," given his condition, of taking several of the sons of friends from Cabourg to see *Circuit*, a new play by Georges Feydeau and Francis de Croisset, with the actress Geneviève Lantelme, whom he knew from Cabourg.[98] Proust's choice of words reflected his pretense of taking an interest in the young men because they were the sons of friends his age; in fact, he was largely indifferent to their fathers. To treat himself to one more evening basking in a cluster of youthful beauty—before entering the austere cloister of serious work—Proust had reserved three boxes at the Théâtre des Variétés for a few of his Paris friends and the young men of Cabourg.[99] Among his older guests were Emmanuel, Lauris, Louisa, Reynaldo, Bertrand de Fénelon, François de Pâris, and Léon Radziwill and his mistress.[100] Marcel knew that Emmanuel's suspicions would be aroused on hearing that he had invited a number of men who were "somewhat too young" and had protested "Nothing Salaïst!!"[101] This denial must have made Emmanuel smile knowingly.

This evening at the theater may have been the occasion when Marcel surrounded himself, perhaps unintentionally, with a number of friends who were posing for various aspects of his characters—Louisa for Rachel, Bertrand for Saint-Loup and Albertine, and the young men for aspects of the little band of girls at Balbec, the seaside resort based primarily on Cabourg. In his high school stories

Marcel had mingled the sexes, seeking within each the seductions attributed to its opposite. His answers to the second questionnaire confirmed this trait: *My favorite qualities in a man:* "Feminine charm." *My favorite qualities in a woman:* "Manly virtue and openness in friendship." As the mature Proust sketched his characters, it seemed natural to him that young men should contribute to his girls (as did girls also) and that his male characters should bear traces of feminine charm and sensitivity.

By early December, Lauris had read the typescript of the first notebook of "Combray" and sent an enthusiastic letter to Proust, who wrote back: "I know it's to your blind friendship that I owe this divine letter." He told Georges that he did not object if others knew that he had read the typescript. "All I ask is that you shouldn't mention the subject or the title or indeed anything that might be indicative of what I'm up to (not that anyone would be interested). But more than that, I don't want to be hurried, or pestered, or ferreted out, or anticipated, or copied, or discussed, or criticized, or knocked. There will be time enough when my thoughts have run their course to allow free rein to the stupidity of others."[102] He wanted to protect his work from interference. Proust then told Georges that he was sending him the copies of the remaining two notebooks.[103]

In early December, Proust sent the typescript made from the first three notebooks of what would become *Swann's Way* to the *Figaro.* Instead of addressing the typescript to Calmette, to whom he had promised the text by early November, Proust sent it to Beaunier for his opinion, requesting that Beaunier pass it on to Calmette. Proust soon saw the decision to submit his work first to Beaunier as a colossal blunder. He had wanted Beaunier to see that they were no longer competing as essayists, that he had not written a critical study of Sainte-Beuve but a novel whose readers would not suspect that Sainte-Beuve had anything to do with its story. But Proust's strategy of placating Beaunier created a much greater obstacle.[104] He realized too late that Calmette, as director of the *Figaro,* had the authority to accept any manuscript but felt inferior in matters of literary judgment to Beaunier, who held a degree in letters from the prestigious École normale supérieure and was an esteemed novelist and critic. Proust had unwittingly given Calmette, whose background was primarily in law and administration, reason to believe that the author valued Beaunier's opinion over Calmette's own. When Proust realized his gaffe, he was horrified that he might have hurt Calmette's feelings and delayed publication. Although he agonized over the muddle he had created, the delay benefited his book, which was not nearly ready for publication.

By December 5 Beaunier had read Proust's typescript and given it to Calmette.

Proust, who expected serialization of his novel to be announced, waited impatiently, scrutinizing the *Figaro* each day. New serials began appearing, but not his. When Beaunier, unaware of the chain of events and Calmette's pique, periodically reminded Calmette about Proust's serial, the director answered that he had not had time to read it.[105]

On December 13 Marcel sent Georges a rather solemn letter, asking him "whether you think that if I were to die now without any further completion of the book, this part is publishable as a volume, and whether in that case would you look after it."[106] "Combray," with its memories of family life (minus Robert) at Auteuil and Illiers, constituted Marcel's testimony to his great love for his mother. Should he die before he completed the novel, he would like to think that at least that much of her survived. Had Proust chosen Lauris as literary executor because he did not want to disturb his busy brother or simply because Lauris knew his work and had literary instincts he trusted? Reynaldo would have been another obvious choice.

By year's end, Proust regretted having canceled the cork installation in his room, because he did intend to "cloister" himself for his work. Writing at night while listening to his "nocturnal muse" was easy. The difficult part was trying to sleep in the daytime, when the rest of the world was wide awake, banging, yelling, dropping things, playing the piano, and riding around en masse outside his window on all sorts of conveyances making an infernal noise, as hooves and wheels pounded the cobblestones and horns blared. Although he desperately needed peace and quiet, last summer's procrastination meant that the cork installation would have to wait until his next vacation. Even though he remained within walls that seemed to amplify noise, Proust was to spend the coming year, as he had the past one, working intensely on his book.[107]

19   *Gathering Impressions*   ⌘

ON JANUARY 13, 1910, Proust learned that Mme Arman de Caillavet had died at age sixty-six. Along with a huge wreath, Proust sent four sympathy letters to her son Gaston, his wife Jeanne, their sixteen-year-old daughter Simone, and Anatole France. In his letter to Gaston, Proust evoked memories of twenty years earlier, when they had become friends at the salon of Mme Arman, whom "no one loved more, admired more, and knew . . . better than I."[1] In the letter to Jeanne, Marcel asked her not to tell Gaston that he was ignoring his advice and drugging himself in order to attend the noonday funeral. He also told her that he was writing a "long novel" that he would have been eager to show Mme Arman.[2]

Mme Arman's death had made Anatole France, also sixty-six years old, despondent. He wrote Marcel that he no longer wished to live.[3] France's despair, as Proust soon learned, was not caused solely by grief. A year earlier, during a long voyage to South America, France had begun an affair with the actress Jeanne Brindeau. His infidelity had so upset Mme de Caillavet that she considered suicide, going so far as to consult a friend who had attempted to kill herself with a firearm. In late August, when France returned from his voyage and found Mme Arman gravely ill, he immediately broke with the actress. Five months later Mme Arman died.

Proust's grief over Mme Arman's death initiated an exchange of letters with

Jeanne de Caillavet and Simone, who was the same age that her mother had been when Marcel had been infatuated with her. Writing to Simone, Proust requested her photograph, as he had her mother's so long ago without success. He explained to Simone the importance photographs held for him: "I shall think of you even without a photograph but my memory, exhausted by drugs, is so feeble that photographs are invaluable to me. I keep them as reminders and don't look at them too often so as not to exhaust their potency. When I was in love with your Mama I went to fantastic lengths in order to get her photograph from some people in Périgord with whom I made friends only in order to try to get hold of that photograph."[4] This photograph showed Marcel kneeling at Jeanne's feet and strumming a tennis racquet as though serenading the vivacious girl.

Marcel soon received a packet from Jeanne. To his delight, it contained a number of photographs, among them the long-coveted picture taken at the Neuilly tennis court. Jeanne, who had been made miserable by Gaston's many infidelities, may have taken some satisfaction in gratifying the wish of a suitor who had made her husband jealous. As for Marcel, he was grateful and touched: "What emotion! What sweet joy mingled with such a sad sentiment! How many years of my life are brought together in the dear envelope." Opening the package had made him tremble, but then he had realized that so many things had changed since the day the photograph was taken that it could no longer affect him as it would have when he was young and in love with Jeanne Pouquet. At the end of the letter thanking her, he referred obliquely to the rumor he had heard about the profound unhappiness Mme Arman had suffered in her final months, which only increased his grief.[5]

Paris suffered its worst flood in modern times on January 21, as the Seine overflowed its banks and kept rising. The *Figaro* reported that the Gare Saint-Lazare, which was not far from Proust's home, was inundated by water from a broken drain as well as from the flooding river. By January 29 the water, still rising by a centimeter an hour, overflowed the lake that had formed on the west side of the train station and turned boulevard Haussmann into a rushing river. Marcel, writing to Simone, said that he would answer her mother's letter, although he would "probably have drowned in the meantime."[6] Much of central Paris remained closed to traffic until February 2, when the waters receded. Clocks and elevators that depended on forced air stopped working, as did the pneumatic mail service. Many buildings were without gas and electricity. At the Comédie-Française the curtain remained up and actors performed on a stage lit by acetylene.

On Sunday, February 13, Proust must have felt an even closer kinship with Noah when he emerged from his apartment to attend the gala dress rehearsal at the

Opéra of Reynaldo's new ballet *La Fête chez Thérèse.* The performance was being given as a benefit for flood victims. Proust described Hahn's work to Lauris as a "delicious thing," predicting that if the other performances matched the première —during which spectators had frequently shouted "Bravo!"—the ballet would enjoy a grand success.[7]

The flood had serious consequences for Marcel, as he explained to Lauris in mid-February, when his basement was still soaked. Although he dared not complain, given the great misfortunes suffered by all, the methods used to dry out and disinfect the building provoked unremitting asthma attacks. And of course there was a substantial amount of renovating to be done in the basement, where workmen had already begun ripping out the soaked floorboards. Later the boards were replaced, as were those in the nearby shops, the elevator, and so on. Proust wrote Montesquiou that the hammer blows and all the extraordinary noise caused by the endless renovations required him to take daily doses of "Veronal and opium, etc., and since I have some albumin, that brings on a thousand ills."[8]

In April, Proust was asked to intervene again in the Louisa-Albu-Gangnat triangle. A new crisis erupted when Gangnat accused Louisa of having an affair with a "well-known" artist, whose wife, claiming to have proof of the liaison, demanded a divorce. This affair set off a flurry of telegrams. Apparently, Gangnat contacted Albu to inform him of the situation. Marcel and Albufera feared that Gangnat would finally abandon Louisa, as he had threatened to do many times. Proust rose from his bed and went to Louisa's apartment to urge her not to abandon the stable situation she had with Gangnat and Albufera as her protectors, but she was not in. He sent a note, hinting mysteriously that he thought she was in danger and being spied upon. Louisa ignored Proust's warning and his letter. The actress, always a lavish spender, had recently asked Albufera for additional money and had requested that that year's Christmas present be cash.[9] She was sensible enough not to abandon sources of good income and remained with Gangnat.

In letters to Montesquiou and Lauris, Proust complained of a new ailment: angina pectoris. The palpitations he experienced frightened him enough to make him temporarily reduce his caffeine consumption, "the only thing" that brought him any relief from asthma.[10] To make matters worse, his sleep had recently been disturbed by strange noises coming from a wall in his room. He informed the servants, who came to listen and, hearing nothing, suggested that his imagination had tricked him. Finally a chimney-sweep was summoned, and he discovered an enormous pigeon that had come down the chimney and into the wall.

Lauris proposed to the woman with whom he had been in love for some time:

Mlle de Pierrebourg, who had finally divorced Louis de La Salle, rumored to have a mean streak. Marcel, writing to congratulate Lauris, teased him: "I was told on the same day that you are to wed Mlle de Pierrebourg and that you have a ravishing mistress. I thought that one of the two (I don't know which) must not be true at the same time, although such simultaneity is currently very well accepted, by wives at least. Because mistresses like it less." Then Proust reminded him: "You *never* answered me" about the name Guermantes.[11] Lauris, whose manuscript Proust had twice pored over so diligently, ignored this simple request.

Proust sent Hauser a letter proposing certain stocks for investment, but left his financial adviser to act as he saw fit. Although Proust's message sounded fairly conservative, it revealed that he had purchased Para stocks through another agent, despite Hauser's reservations and refusal to buy them for him. Proust was to regret ignoring Hauser's warnings, as he continued to suffer large losses because of his reckless approach to investing.[12]

Writing to Mme Straus on April 24, Proust expressed his one wish: "If only I can keep death at bay until I have fulfilled the principal wishes of my intellect and my heart! For I have no others. Or no longer any others." Once he had finished his long work, he would "choose the folly that appeals to me the most and I shall do it. And it will probably be to try and see you constantly." The long work he was finishing was the first draft of the *Search*, entitled "Combray."[13] "Finishing" for the moment meant expanding and enriching, a process that occupied the coming months, while Proust continued to believe that he would soon complete his novel.

In a late April letter to Lauris, Proust worried that he had alienated Calmette, "the man who has shown me the most exquisite kindness," and spoiled his chances of serializing his novel in the *Figaro*.[14] Five months had gone by since Beaunier passed the manuscript on to Calmette. Proust maintained that he was not impatient for his book to be serialized, for he had "always been hostile to this serialization and only considered it on Calmette's extreme insistence." What he deplored was having disregarded Calmette, who had done so much to publish and advance his work. Gaston had not only promised to serialize the novel but had offered to approach Fasquelle as a possible publisher for the work in book form. Proust feared he had lost his only sure ally.

In 1909 Serge Diaghilev brought from Saint Petersburg to Paris dancers who were on summer leave from the Imperial Ballet. Among the exceptionally talented choreographers, dancers, and composers who came with Diaghilev and the Ballets Russes were Vaslav Nijinsky, Ida Rubinstein, and Igor Stravinsky. Parisians, amazed at the freshness of the program and the lavish costumes and scenery, eagerly awaited their return in the summer of 1910. On June 4 Proust, Hahn, and Jean-Louis Vaudoyer attended a program that included Borodin's *Prince Igor* and Rimsky-Korsakov's *Scheherazade*.[15] These ballets featured dancers soon to become legendary: Nijinsky, Tamara Karsavina, and Rubinstein. The story from *The Arabian Nights* had always been one of Proust's favorites, and the Ballets Russes brought it to life with some of the most sumptuous costumes ever created for the stage.

A week later, Proust accepted Mme Greffulhe's invitation to attend another performance by the Russians: "I feel that the prospect of attending *La Sylphide* in the stage-box of the Sylphide herself, and *Cléopâtre* in the company of the Queen who leaves the Queen of Egypt so far behind her, will give me the elasticity of a Russian dancer to enable me to spring from my bed . . . as far as the Opéra."[16] The ballets enchanted Proust, who in the *Search* was to describe the arrival of the Russian dancers: "[This] charming invasion, against whose seductions only the stupidest of critics protested, infected Paris . . . with a fever of curiosity less agonizing, more purely aesthetic, but quite as intense perhaps as that aroused by the Dreyfus case."[17]

Soon Hahn and Frédéric de Madrazo began to collaborate on a ballet with an exceptional young man who had just been introduced into Proust's circle of friends: Jean Cocteau. It is likely that Proust met Cocteau in March at the Strauses'. It was apparent to everyone who met the twenty-year-old Cocteau that he was a phenomenon. He proved to be one of the twentieth century's most versatile artists: poet, novelist, playwright, designer, painter, and filmmaker. Cocteau, already well known to Diaghilev and his troupe, would, with Madrazo, write the book for Hahn's new ballet for the Russians.

Diaghilev saw ballet as Wagner had seen opera, as a synthesis of the arts: "Perfect ballet can only be created by the fusion of dancing, painting, and music." In addition to the extraordinary talent Diaghilev brought with him from Russia, he collaborated with many of France's finest composers, writers, and artists, such as Debussy, Ravel, Satie, Hahn, Gide, and Picasso, as well as Cocteau. Such collective efforts by writers, artists, composers, dancers, musicians, costumers, and decorators surpassed even Wagner's dreams.[18]

In June, Proust reported to Lauris on his lack of progress with the novel: "I still can't send you my exercise-books as I can't work, but when I can it will go very quickly." In the same letter he mentioned that he had just reread Stendhal's *La Chartreuse de Parme* (The charterhouse of Parma) and asked whether Lauris had a copy of Balzac's preface to the same novel. And he reminded Lauris yet again that he had never answered his query about the name Guermantes.[19]

In early July, Marcel sent Reynaldo a charming humorous drawing of a stained-glass window, detailing his daily activities. The window consists of eighteen panels, each with a numbered legend. In the first panel Proust-Buncht lies in bed listening to Fauré's setting of Verlaine's *Clair de lune*. In the second, Hahn-Bunibuls on the other side of the door plays the overture to *Die Meistersinger*. In another, Céline, in the kitchen, cooks a sole for Buncht. In the last panel Proust-Buncht dies and is buried in a tomb beneath "flowers, trees, hawthorns, and the sun," now that they are no longer harmful.[20]

Marcel had read Lucien Daudet's book of four stories, *Le Prince des cravates*, and recommended it enthusiastically to Max Daireaux. He also congratulated a new author, Albert-Émile Sorel, son of his former history professor, on his first novel, *Le Rival*. Comparing Sorel's book to his own work in progress, Proust observed a fundamental difference: "I would never know how to submit to the kind of novel that describes so objectively a thousand details from daily life. But perhaps it's a weakness and a lack of talent on my part. . . . The path you have taken is the one the greatest writers have followed."[21] Proust sought to capture—perhaps more lucidly that any other writer—impressions and perceptions, and to reveal psychological laws that explained human behavior. He also wanted to raise readers' sights high by revealing the true life, attainable through careful observation, meditation, and creativity, rather than the humdrum affair for which we usually settle. His reinvention of the genre was to confuse some of his early critics.

On July 12, at one in the morning, Proust went on a disheartening mission to the *Figaro*, "this house where I was formerly more pampered," to retrieve the typescript of his novel.[22] Though deeply disappointed, Proust did not realize how much this refusal was to benefit his novel, still several years from its full development. His intention to dedicate the book to Calmette did not waver, despite what he saw as their changed relationship; his decision to do so was based on genuine affection and gratitude and not because he expected something in return.

On July 11 Céline Cottin gave birth to a son, Antoine-André. Thanks to Marcel's encouragement, she had been under Dr. Proust's care. Eager to escape the noisy apartment, Marcel left abruptly for Cabourg on July 17. He again made arrangements for his bedroom to be lined with cork during his absence. He informed Reynaldo that he had brought along to Cabourg, in addition to the new father Nicolas, "innumerable and useless Antoines."[23] These were Antoine the concierge, his wife, known as Mme Antoine, and their son Antoine. Shortly after arriving at the Grand-Hôtel, the servants opened Proust's bags and were astonished to find themselves staring at a lady's hatboxes. Antoine senior had mischecked Proust's bags, which had gone on to Brittany with the owner of the hats. For the next twenty-four hours, while Proust awaited the return of his luggage, he was unable to undress or go to bed. Then Proust discovered that Nicolas was drinking. He also worried that Céline might invite strangers to the apartment and asked Hahn, who would remain in Paris for a while, to drop in unannounced to see whether his cook had anything to hide. The Cottins, as his mother had warned, were proving to be less than ideal servants.

A few days after his arrival at the seashore, Proust received word that Albu had had an emergency appendectomy, and although the patient showed signs of improving, his condition remained serious. Fearing the worst, Proust wrote to Louisa, saying that he would "go mad" with worry. But then Marcel received a wire from his brother and Albu's doctor saying that his friend was out of danger and should fully recover. Marcel informed Louisa that he still intended to return to Paris and visit Albu daily at nearby Bizy. Apparently, he then thought better of this plan and decided to remain in Cabourg.

In mid-August Proust wrote to a new acquaintance, Jean-Louis Vaudoyer, a young art critic and poet, and a great admirer of the Russian ballet. Marcel had already sent him *Pleasures and Days,* for which Vaudoyer had expressed his admiration. Proust, who had begun to consider revising and reprinting his first book, told Vaudoyer that his praise of "La Confession d'une jeune fille" and "L'Éventail" had justified his plan. He then mentioned "the long novel" on which he was working. Vaudoyer's curiosity must have been piqued on reading that "although the book is absolutely serious in intention, and almost too virtuous in certain parts, in others it has a freedom of tone which would be somewhat unsuitable in a review." Proust would be eager to have Vaudoyer's opinion of the new work, "which however imperfect seems to me nonetheless genuinely superior to what I've done up to now."[24]

During September, Proust suffered what he described as a significant decrease in his vitality. He mentioned his weakened condition to Maurice Duplay: "I'm working one day out of ten on the novel . . . which is my supreme effort." As proof of his decline, he observed: "Three years ago I was able to go out all day in a closed car; two years ago the car was no longer possible, but I went out on the beach. Last year I was no longer able to go out, but I went down every evening at about nine o'clock to the public rooms of the hotel (or the Casino which is in the hotel). This year I've only been able to rise from my bed and go downstairs for an hour or two every two or three days. But still that's a great deal more than in Paris."[25]

Proust, in his usual extravagant manner, and for no apparent reason other than a whim, had decided to give expensive watches to both the Alton girls, Hélène and Colette. Those he favored at Cartier's cost four thousand francs ($13,000). Worried about paying this amount and the bill for the cork installation, he wrote to Hahn, now back in Paris, and mentioned the strain on his budget.[26] Reynaldo came to his rescue through the good graces of his sister Maria, who took over the task of finding beautiful watches at a fraction of Cartier's price.

A Room Lined with Cork

Toward the end of September, Odilon Albaret drove Proust from Cabourg to Paris. The writer had spent nearly three months in Cabourg without walking once on the beach or calling on the Strauses at Trouville. He was improved enough in health by early October to attend a concert by Félix Mayol. Marcel wrote Reynaldo that he found Mayol "sublime." On those occasions when Proust went out at night— usually once or twice a month—he often went to hear the effeminate singer, whose performances had two great advantages for Proust: he was talented, and he sang only at eleven in the evening.[27] Then, turning to his health, Marcel told Hahn that he suspected the smell of the new cork was causing his current severe asthma attacks. He wanted to flee somewhere. But where and how?

Proust's days of exploring new geographical locations in the real world had ended long before, with the 1902 trip to Holland. His great journey now turned inward and, except for summer trips to Cabourg, he rarely ventured beyond the bounds of Paris. He grew accustomed to the sound-muffling presence of the cork, which, now fresh and new, soon darkened, like everything else in his room, from the daily "fumigations" of burning asthma powders.

In late October, when Robert Gangnat died, Proust sent his condolences to Louisa. He praised the love that she had awakened first in Albu and then in Gangnat as "perhaps the two purest, most chivalrous, greatest devotions that any woman has ever inspired." He also reproached her indirectly for having neglected him: "I am one of those who are so forgotten that people only write to them when they are unhappy, and I no longer dare open a letter as there seem to be nothing but causes for unhappiness." As his work on the novel increased, so did his isolation. He told Louisa that because of his poor health, he now rarely allowed his servants to enter his room. In a letter to Dreyfus earlier in the month, Marcel had said that only he and Reynaldo were permitted nocturnal visits.[28] Proust, however, did not encourage Dreyfus to call often; Reynaldo remained the only friend who was always welcome and who could come unannounced.

Lauris hurt Proust's feelings by not inviting him to his wedding on October 26, at which Bertrand de Fénelon was a groomsman. On November 1 Marcel wrote Georges to express his disappointment at having been excluded. As though to prove his worthiness, he cited the examples of Albu and Guiche, who had invited him to their weddings. Furthermore, each had paid him a call in the days following the ceremony. Quoting Mme Aubernon, Marcel placed himself in the category of guests the society hostess had described as "presentable" because "they don't need explaining." He warned Lauris, should he drop by or phone regarding this slight, not to say anything the servants might overhear about "my reproaches concerning the wedding. It would be too wounding to my pride."[29]

By November, Proust was hard at work on the section of *Swann's Way* known as "Swann in Love." He asked Robert de Flers to help track down one of his "imbecilic" stories, *L'Indifférent,* written in 1893 for the *Vie contemporaine,* about a woman who falls helplessly in love with a mediocre man.[30] In "Swann in Love" it is the superior man who becomes lovesick over a cocotte, who admires his intellectual prowess and fine taste, neither of which prevents his succumbing to her entirely for a long period of his life and eventually marrying this inappropriate woman.[31]

"Swann in Love" is the only part of the *Search* narrated in the third person, because it tells the story of Swann's infatuation with Odette before the Narrator was born. Proust used the device of having someone tell the story to the Narrator. The inclusion of "Swann in Love" was one of Proust's most brilliant narrative and structural decisions, for in many ways it represents the *Search* in miniature: the Narrator, who comes to know the Swanns after their marriage and falls in love with their daughter Gilberte, will repeat many of Swann's mistakes, with interesting variations, in matters of love, society, and even art.[32] The section also gives the Narrator and reader a sense of history, of the span of time through which his characters lived. Proust later said that one reason he had written such a long novel was that he wanted to show the effects of time on a group of people. "Swann in Love" goes back to the days of the Second Empire; when the *Search* ends some four to six years after World War I, the Narrator is ready to loop back and write the story we have just read. Looking back through history and through the lives of the Swanns and the Narrator and his family, the reader has shared the experience of several generations of characters.

Proust soon had occasion to comfort another grieving friend. In early November, Robert Dreyfus's brother Henri died. While consoling Dreyfus, who had been especially close to his brother, Marcel urged him not to abandon his chronicles in the *Figaro,* which Dreyfus signed simply *D.* Proust had earlier expressed the enormous pleasure he always took, before putting out his light at night, in reading Robert's column about current events. To encourage his grieving friend to persevere, Proust described the creative process in terms that applied as well to himself: "It was you who created D. But D. too, if not created, at least completed you, and has drawn from you many many things. . . . What your life has to give, everything real that it contains, it's yourself, yourself that you will finish perfecting by writing."[33] Proust then used one of his favorite images, found in a number of variations in *Time Regained:* one's inner being, the domain of the creative self, is a rich region that rewards exploration: "In continuing to live thus you will be living in a region of yourself where the barriers of flesh and time no longer exist, where there is no death, because there is no time and no body, and where one lives tranquilly in the immortal company of those one loves." These remarks reflect to some degree the passages he was writing on time and involuntary memory, capable of recapturing the lost past in its true colors. The "all-powerful joy" such moments bring stems in large part from the sensation one has of having stepped outside of time: "I had ceased now to feel mediocre, contingent, mortal."[34]

Marcel wrote to Mme Catusse, expressing his affection and eagerness to see her and evoking his mother's great love for her and their terrible last days together in Évian. Because he wanted to finish his novel, he must postpone such cherished projects as seeing her again until his work was done—a task he saw stretching out before him while his energy diminished. As much as he wanted to see Mme Catusse, he would not write again, he told her, because he must concentrate his strength, "such as it is, on my book."[35]

Proust continued to treat young Plantevignes as his protégé, seeking to present him to the finest society and to young writers in the spotlight, such as Jean Cocteau. In November, Plantevignes asked for assistance of a different kind. There was a young actress he wanted to meet. Proust obliged by having his concierge Antoine give Marcel the princely sum of two hundred francs, apparently for flowers and gifts to send the girl.

Toward the end of the year, Proust obtained from another source the information he had requested so many times from Lauris. François de Pâris told Proust that he could use the name Guermantes, a name that Proust intended "both to exalt and sully."[36] The last comte de Guermantes had died in 1800.[37] With the story of Swann well under way, Proust had acquired the second great family name for his novel.

Pelléas et Mélisande

In January 1911 Proust wrote Lucien to congratulate him on Marcel Ballot's review in the *Figaro* of *Le Prince des cravates.* Although Lucien considered the review lukewarm, Marcel assured him that it would "make a considerable impact." As for himself, he lived "suspended between caffeine, aspirin, asthma, angina pectoris, and in . . . six days out of seven" between "life and death." He reminded Lucien that he had started a book. "God knows if I shall ever finish it."[38]

Proust relayed to Anna de Noailles a request from Cocteau for some of her poems. Anna, who was happy to copy them out, told Marcel that she believed the young poet had "a great deal of talent."[39] In his letter to Jean forwarding Anna's verses, Marcel included advice about how to thank her. Cocteau should be effusive: "A frigid tone whereby out of discretion you said to her only the quarter of what you thought . . . would not impress her. She is at once divinely simple and sublimely proud."[40]

Early in the year Proust subscribed to a new device that brought opera, concerts, and plays into the home. For a fee of sixty francs a month, the subscriber received a theatrophone, a large black ear-trumpet connected through telephone lines to eight Paris theaters and concert halls, including the Opéra, the Opéra-Comique, the Concerts Colonne, and the Comédie-Française.[41] Although the sound quality was often poor, the instrument was a great boon to someone like Proust, who loved opera and the theater but who rarely felt well enough to attend performances. He often listened, even when the sound was so bad that he could barely hear the words. Proust told Lauris that in such cases, if the opera was one of Wagner's that he practically knew by heart, he could supply the missing words as he listened. Then he mentioned "a charming revelation," whose power over him had become tyrannical. The piece he found irresistible was Claude Debussy's opera, *Pelléas et Mélisande,* based on Maeterlinck's play by the same name.[42]

After the broadcast on February 21 Proust wrote to Hahn, whose musical tastes remained more conservative than his. At the end of a long letter Marcel finally dared to admit that he had been listening to two composers for whom Reynaldo had little admiration: "Nicens, I'm going to irritate you horribly by speaking about music and telling you that I heard on the theatrophone last night an act of the *Mastersingers* . . . and this evening . . . the whole of *Pelléas.* Now I know how wrong I am about the artistic arts . . . however, as Buncht won't punish me, I shall confess to an extremely agreeable impression. It didn't seem to me to be so absolutely alien to Fauré and even to Wagner *(Tristan)* as it has the pretension and reputation of being. . . . I'm surprised that Debussy could have written it." Perhaps fearing that he had ventured too far onto Reynaldo's turf, Marcel told an amusing story about himself to prove his musical incompetence. "It's true that . . . musical heresies which may get on your nerves pass unnoticed by me, alas particularly through the theatrophone, where at one moment I thought the rumblings I heard agreeable if a trifle amorphous until I suddenly realized it was the interval!"[43]

Proust, who had paid scant attention when Debussy's *Pelléas et Mélisande* was first performed at the Opéra-Comique on April 30, 1902, had became totally enamored of the work. He confessed as much to Antoine Bibesco in late March, complaining of excessive fatigue because he had had the "misfortune of hearing *Pelléas* on the theatrophone and falling in love with it."[44] Proust kept the theatrophone right beside his bed, and every evening when that opera was on, no matter how sick he was, he placed his ear next to the black trumpet and drank in Debussy's music. On evenings when this opera was not played, he sang Pelléas's part to himself.

Hahn was working on a score, commissioned by Diaghilev, for the Ballets Russes. Stravinsky later said that the impresario needed Hahn because "he was the salon idol of Paris, and salon support was very useful to Diaghilev at that time."[45] When Hahn left in February for Saint Petersburg, he took along the piano score for his new ballet, *Le Dieu bleu,* for which Jean Cocteau and Frédéric de Madrazo had created the story.[46] Diaghilev had invited Hahn to Saint Petersburg to be the guest of honor at a huge banquet attended by the city's most prominent figures in the arts. Among those present were the composer Aleksandr Glazunov, director of the Conservatory, as well as members of Diaghilev's company: Léon Bakst, who designed the sets and costumes, Diaghilev's chief choreographer Michel Fokine, and one of ballet's most sensational dancers, Nijinksy.[47] Hahn and Baron Medem, a professor at the Conservatory, played music from *Le Dieu bleu* on two pianos. The evening ended in wild applause when Hahn sang, accompanied by Glazunov on the piano. Paris had to wait until the spring of 1912 to see Hahn's ballet.

At Antoine Bibesco's urging, Proust had subscribed to the *NRF,* which he called Gide's review. Proust read Gide's novella *Isabelle* in the review and wrote Lauris that he thought the work amounted to "very little." At the end of the letter, he gave Lauris this bleak picture of his life: "I no longer sleep, I no longer eat, I no longer work, there are many other things I no longer do and those I gave up long ago."[48] The last deprivation referred to the complete absence of physical love in his life. Proust had likely reverted to his youthful practice of masturbation. If testimony given later by a male prostitute is accurate, masturbation may already have become his primary, and perhaps exclusive, method of sexual gratification.

To Reynaldo's annoyance Proust continued to talk about music, especially Wagner and Debussy. He wrote Hahn that *Pelléas et Mélisande* had cast a spell over him that he had not felt since his repeated evenings out to hear Mayol. He constantly requested the opera on the theatrophone as obsessively as he had gone to the Concert Mayol. Although Marcel said he liked best the parts where only music was heard, there were some lines—when Pelléas leaves the cave and sings, "Ah! je respire enfin"—which he found "impregnated with the freshness of the sea and the odors of roses wafted by the breeze."[49]

The more important role music had assumed in Proust's life was to be reflected in Swann's and the Narrator's remarkable meditations on music. Not only would Proust associate music with the sacred and profane themes of art and eros, but there would be comic scenes as well, satirizing the phony or reversed values of society snobs who use everything from sex to art to climb to the top of the social ladder, never realizing that the kingdom they conquer is, for all its glitter, a wasteland. The attributes Proust ascribes to such characters and their world are those indicating sterility and aridity. In Mme Verdurin's salon, Vinteuil's first great work becomes "her" sonata because she claims to have "discovered" the work, which, of course, can only be heard to its full effect in her salon. She also puts on a show of being so sensitive to music that listening to works like the sonata is a sort of aesthetic martyrdom, leaving her physically devastated. Dr. Cottard, one of the most faithful of her clan, must promise to be ready to assist her before Vinteuil's piece can be played. Even then M. Verdurin suggests that his wife might be able to tolerate no more than the andante. This suggestion causes her to shriek: "Just the andante! That really is a bit rich! As if it weren't precisely the andante that breaks every bone in my body."[50] Mme Verdurin's guests are so witty—unlike the "bores" who frequent all the other salons—that once the doctor had to "reset her jaw, which had dislocated from laughing too much."[51] Proust's great gift for comedy and satire, not apparent in his earlier works, is evident throughout the novel, but especially in *Swann's Way* and in *The Guermantes Way,* the sections that deal most directly with society people.

In a March letter to Reynaldo, Marcel sent a short pastiche of the opera *Pelléas et Mélisande,* inviting him to sing along while reading.[52] Debussy, who like Proust had been influenced by the symbolist poets and impressionist painters, had attempted to adapt Maeterlinck's play while making as few changes as possible to the text. Debussy was forced to make cuts, but his version is far closer to the original than is usually the case when literary works are adapted to opera. Proust's pastiche of Debussy's version of *Pelléas et Mélisande,* published posthumously, pokes fun at some of the symbolist mannerisms. Marcel sent Reynaldo, along with his pastiches, a bit of gossip about two of their friends who had become extremely close: "The *utmost* intimacy . . . reigns between Lucien and Cocteau, who went to stay with him in the country."[53] Lucien had found himself a brilliant young lover.

Louis de Robert, who had written to Proust so long ago to express his admiration for *Pleasures and Days,* now entered his life again. Robert had just published a well-received psychological novel, *Le Roman du malade* (literally, The novel of the sick man). Proust wrote Louis that a book with such a title must have been intended for him. He knew that Robert had struggled with his own health, but "those who, like me, believe literature is the highest expression of life" would accept without anger inspiration even from illness.[54] In December, Robert's novel won the prestigious Prix Fémina–Vie Heureuse, which included a cash reward of five thousand francs. Lauris's mother-in-law, the novelist Mme de Pierrebourg, presided over the awards committee. Proust began to confide in Robert about his novel; Robert was to provide advice regarding titles and divisions of the text, and assist Marcel in finding a publisher.

On May 21 Proust went to the Théâtre du Châtelet to attend the dress rehearsal of Debussy's *Le Martyre de Saint-Sébastien,* based on a story by Gabriele D'Annunzio. Proust had been eager to hear the latest work by the creator of *Pelléas et Mélisande.* The occasion held great promise because many of the creators of the Ballets Russes had collaborated on the piece. Alas, Proust found the production "very boring." Most of the audience must have shared his opinion because the show had a relatively short run.[55] Someone who did not agree with this assessment was Montesquiou, who had sat next to Proust during the last act. Marcel had been grateful for the company, which relieved the tedium of the performance. He wrote to the count later: "I was so happy to be able to listen to you during the intermissions and to be beside you during that last act when, wired to your enthusiasm by the electrode of your grip, I was convulsed and transported on my seat as if it I had been an electric chair."[56] But the enthusiasm had not been contagious.

Proust had been disappointed by the audience as well as by Debussy's work. His remark in a letter to Mme Straus echoes the satirical portraits of society people he had begun to write about. The people he had glimpsed at the performance "seemed to have greatly deteriorated. Even the nicest of them have taken to intelligence and alas, with society people—I don't know how they manage it—intelligence is simply a multiplier of stupidity, raising it to an unbelievable power and intensity. The only possible ones are those who have had the wit to remain stupid."[57]

In the latter part of May, Proust wrote to Francis de Croisset seeking a position for Agostinelli's wife, Anna, as an usher at the Théâtre des Variétés. Agostinelli must have remembered that Proust knew the playwright and requested his aid. Francis apparently obliged and a position was offered; whether or not Anna accepted the job is not known.[58] Two years were to pass before Agostinelli reentered Proust's life, with tragic consequences.

In the summer, Proust offered to hire, as a secretary, an unknown young man he had met one night at Constantin Ullmann's. Nothing is known about the potential secretary, who apparently worked in a bank.[59] Proust must have found the man attractive, for he wrote him two long letters, detailing all the disadvantages of working for someone with his bizarre schedule and yet encouraging him to accept the position. In his proposal Proust, who desperately needed efficient secretarial assistance, put kindness ahead of practicality. If the young man did not know stenography or how to type, Proust would dictate to him and let him take down the words in longhand. Proust's description of his text left its genre ambiguous: "I am finishing a novel or a book of essays which is an extremely considerable work, at least by its mad length."[60] The novelist made it clear that he was willing to tolerate delays and other complications if the young man wanted the position. Perhaps Proust was lonely for an attractive male companion.

A Garden in a Tea Cup

Proust left for Cabourg, in his usual haste, on July 11, the day following his fortieth birthday, which he seems not to have marked in any special way. From there he wrote to Marie Nordlinger to tell her how happy he had been to hear of her recent marriage to Rudolph Meyer Riefstahl, an art teacher.[61] Shortly after his arrival, Proust learned that the Grand-Hôtel now had on staff a typist available to its clients for a fee. She was Miss Cecilia Hayward, a young Englishwoman, drawn like many of her compatriots to the beauty of the Normandy seacoast. Before hiring Miss Hayward, Proust wrote the second long letter to the unknown young man and repeated his offer. He even suggested sending the man extra money just for the trouble of considering the position and reading his letters. Proust proposed an attractive salary and per diem for meals. The mysterious applicant, who must have been confused and exhausted after trying to determine exactly what Proust did expect, declined the offer.

Miss Hayward, using the copy prepared by Albert Nahmias, began typing the first part of the *Search*—just over seven hundred manuscript pages.[62] She must have understood Proust's instructions in French, though it is unclear how well he communicated in English. Proust joked in a letter to René Gimpel that because his typist knew no "French and I don't know English my novel turns out to be written in an intermediate language in which I hope you will find a certain savour when you receive the book."[63] Proust wondered, given Gimpel's connections with the Japanese art world, whether he might "know the little Japanese . . . game that consists in soaking little scraps of paper in water which then twist themselves round and turn into little men, etc. Could you ask someone Japanese what it's called, and especially whether it's sometimes done with *tea,* whether it's done with either hot or cold water, and in the more complicated ones whether there can be *houses, trees, persons,* or what have you."[64] Proust had returned to the image of tea and dry toast from the *Sainte-Beuve* text and had begun developing that passage on involuntary memory, adding the madeleine cake dipped in tea and expanding the metaphoric role of the Japanese pellets to explain this memory phenomenon and its resurrection of the past. He intended to place the scene in the Combray section of the novel, where it is the first such episode the Narrator relates to the reader.[65] He was curious about the pellets' capacity to form houses and people because when the Narrator bites into the tea-soaked cake, the sensations he felt evoked an entire little cosmos:

> And as in the game wherein the Japanese amuse themselves by filling a porcelain bowl with water and steeping in it little pieces of paper which until then are without character or form, but, the moment they become wet, stretch and twist and take on colour and distinctive shape, become flowers or houses or people, solid and recognizable, so in that moment all the flowers in our garden and in M. Swann's park, and the water-lilies on the Vivonne and the good folk of the village and their little dwellings and the parish church and the whole of Combray and its surroundings, taking shape and solidity, sprang into being, town and gardens alike, from my cup of tea.[66]

This is a good example of a long Proustian sentence that seems to breathe quite naturally as it moves toward its conclusion. The spontaneous musicality of the original is not lost in translation. While at Cabourg, Proust also worked on passages for "Madame Swann at Home," a section that ultimately became the opening chapter of volume two, *Within a Budding Grove.*[67]

In a late July letter Proust expressed his loneliness to Reynaldo: "Imagine, my Bunibuls, that every evening when the sun is setting and I have not yet turned on the light, I think about you somewhat sorrowfully in my little bed, and at that moment large women come and play, far down the beach, waltzes on French horns and cornets until night falls. It's melancholy enough to make you throw yourself into the sea."[68]

Proust was suffering from fatigue and loneliness, resulting from his poor health, peculiar isolation, and hard work on his book. These factors no doubt influenced an angry letter to Antoine Bibesco in which an expression of sympathy gave way to one of bitter estrangement. Proust received a note from Antoine requesting to see him and replied that he was so ill he might leave Cabourg, which made a visit "impossible." Marcel had just read the obituary of Antoine's father and, although he had hardly known the man, his death revived memories of Antoine's mother, whom he "would remember . . . only with tenderness as having united me more completely with you and with Emmanuel"—then in mid-sentence, Proust's words became wrathful and accusatory—"were it not that, as a result of a foul and inept lie which you believed because you repeated it to me, it put an end to our friendship, by preventing me from being able to continue truly to love people who took me for a hypocrite." Proust's rancor stemmed from all the jokes the Bibesco brothers had made at his expense about homosexuality. They must have taken him for a homosexual and a hypocrite, he wrote, because they had refused to take seriously his vigorous denials. Marcel then recalled the early days on the rue de Courcelles when their friendship was new and Antoine had visited so often when Marcel was too ill to go out. That year "was embellished for me by the charm of your first visits, of your friendship in which I then believed, in which I still hoped. How far away it all is. Your old friend."[69]

While Marcel was in Cabourg, Reynaldo was vacationing with Sarah Bernhardt at Fort des Poulains, her estate on Belle-Île-en-Mer. Proust wrote to ask whether his friend had been awarded the Légion d'honneur and whether he had selected the dog that was to be his gift.[70] He reminded Reynaldo not to let anyone in Sarah's entourage know about their private language because ridicule—and perhaps worse—would be heaped on them. Reynaldo had not yet been awarded the Légion d'honneur, but he had bought a black long-haired basset hound from a gypsy at Versailles. Hahn named the dog Zadig, after Voltaire's character who remains puzzled by the radical rises and falls that providence has in store for him.

On September 12 Reynaldo, back in Versailles, wrote Marcel to express his affection for Zadig, who "surpassed all that human imagination could have ever conceived in love, kindness, and Bunchtism. But he loves me too much and is wounded by anything he takes as a sign of indifference. As for me, I have been turned into a nanny, a nurse, a papa, a mama, and my life is nothing but an endless procession of humble and precise tasks such as cleaning Zadig's ears, examining Zadig's stool, washing Zadig, feeding Zadig."[71] Reynaldo had found a companion who needed and loved him, even if it was only a dog.

That September, Gaston's brother, Dr. Émile Calmette, rendered Proust a singular service by having him permanently removed from the active military service rolls.[72] Marcel wrote Gaston to express his gratitude, observing that "if war were to break out, the service you have done me would be greater still, in preventing me from occupying a post for which I've been unable to prepare myself." Should there be a war, he would want to serve as best he could, perhaps even as "a mere clerk . . . so as not to be the only one to remain idle while the others were making themselves useful." But Proust was dreaming; even war, as he would discover, could not make him change his habits. At the end of the letter, Proust mentioned the book he intended to dedicate to Gaston and said that he had dictated a quarter of it to a typist. "And this quarter, or rather fifth, is already the length of a volume. May the whole achieve the stature of a *Book*. I can say like the butcher: I've put in the head and the innards, there's no short measure."[73] No one would ever accuse Marcel Proust of short measure, and he would certainly present Gaston and the world with a *Book*. Miss Hayward and her typewriter had not been idle either; she had nearly completed typing what corresponded to the first three hundred printed pages of *Swann's Way*.[74]

Proust returned to Paris at six on Sunday morning, October 1.[75] That day he wrote a long letter to Maurice Barrès in which he mentioned his book, raising the questions of genre and his intended audience: "One wonders for whom one writes"—he said that he found the *NRF* more intelligent than other reviews, but admitted that its recent article on the novel had puzzled him.[76] A critic by the name of Louis Dumont-Wilden had written that despite recent notable exceptions like Balzac and Flaubert, whose powerful geniuses had created a new genre next to that of the traditional French novel, French taste always returned to narratives that were "generally brief, tightly constructed and that go right to the point, where a few characters, whose traits are rigorously defined, or delicately nuanced, but always precise, develop their characters logically, bringing to light some moral problem." Dumont-Wilden provided current examples for writers to follow, such as Barrès's

Colette Baudoche and Gide's *La Porte étroite,* both books that Proust considered inferior. Furthermore, the critic wrote, novels should have no embellishments, should "seek only sobriety, solidity, rapidity, and precision. Such is the true style of the French novel."[77] If Dumont-Wilden's piece contained the NRF's criteria for manuscripts, Proust cannot have been encouraged by what he read, except for the part about bringing moral problems to light. On the other hand, if he possessed a powerful genius like Balzac and Flaubert, two authors he greatly admired, then French literature would have to make room for his book.

Proust was to reinvent his genre for himself, as must each authentic artist. Perhaps he had felt the kinship with Debussy as a lonely pioneer, risking all as he explores new territory. Debussy's reputation was to grow until he became recognized not only as the greatest French composer of his era but as the "revolutionary who, with the *Prélude à l'après-midi d'un faune* of 1894, set twentieth-century music on its way."[78] Proust was to have an equally revolutionary effect on literature, but, as with Debussy and other original artists, the true scope and influence of his work was not evident for many years.

Proust, who never hesitated to write anyone with whom he felt a sympathetic connection, sent a letter to Reynaldo's dog, Zadig, with whom he had found much in common: "My dear Zadig, I am very fond of you because you have a great deal of chasgrin and love through the same person as I have, and you could not find anyone better in the whole world." Proust then expressed his disdain for intelligence, an attitude he could explain to Zadig because "I have been a man and you haven't: This intelligence of ours only serves to replace those impressions which make you love and suffer by faint facsimiles which cause less grief and induce less tenderness. In the rare moments when I recapture all my affection, all my suffering, it's because my feelings have ceased to be based on these false ideas and reverted to something which is the same in you and in me. And that seems to me so superior to everything else that it's only when I've become a dog again, a poor little Zadig like you, that I begin to write and books that are written like that are the only books I like."[79] Proust's attempts to recapture reality in words must be based on primary sensations he would transpose, not on rational deductions. A book or a painting serves no purpose, he believed, when it reveals what everyone can see. His credo resembled that of the impressionists, who, like his character Elstir, determined to paint what they saw, not what they knew.

Marcel had good cause not to trust his intelligence when it came to investments. At the end of November, Proust told Hauser that he had not a penny to invest. Then a few days later he bought, on Albert Nahmias's recommendation, one thousand shares in the Spassky copper mines. Proust grew closer to Nahmias, whom he began to address as "my little Albert" and whose letters he began to sign "Affectionately yours, Marcel," without his surname.[80] At year's end Marcel told Reynaldo to be thankful that he had not involved him "in my vast speculation, for the only thing vast that remains of it is the enormous loss it showed in the end."[81] While squandering one fortune, he was compiling another, whose shares were to remain solid over time.

Proust's ventures into the normal, daytime world remained complicated and rare. When he went out now it was often with the purpose of acquiring material for his book by pumping friends for information or researching details regarding art or fashion. A chance encounter with an old acquaintance whom he had not seen for a long time confirmed a detail about a hat. Proust went with the art historian Lucien Henraux to the Durand-Ruel Gallery to view an exhibition of Chinese paintings, lacquers, and screens. While there he met Georges Rodier, a rich dilettante who had been a regular at Mme Lemaire's salon. Marcel told Reynaldo that he had consulted with Rodier about the way courtesans used to dress: "As soon as I mentioned a black hat worn by Clomesnil, he exclaimed, 'That's right, a Rembrandt hat.' In short, I was overwhelmed with joy." He had found the perfect hat for Odette de Crécy. Proust, who had used Laure Hayman as one of the models for Odette, feared that he had revealed too much and Rodier might later realize she had been the inspiration for this aspect of the novel's cocotte.[82] Proust had also been struck at the exhibition by how old and nearly unrecognizable Rodier had grown, like so many people he now encountered. The ravages of time on the faces of people he had known when young always impressed him.

Everything had become grist for Proust's mill—not only the past he hoped to recapture but present encounters with people who offered bits to enrich his text. Rodier had provided two: confirmation about Hayman's Rembrandt hat and a remark that revealed his unawareness that he had spent his life pursuing the idle, but highly seductive, pleasures of the Belle Époque.

20　*In Search of a Publisher*　∾

PROUST SPENT THE ENTIRE YEAR EXPANDING his manuscript, having it typed, and looking for a publisher. For the practical but challenging task of completing the typescript of *Swann's Way,* he relied on young Albert Nahmias as a part-time paid secretary. In January, Marcel sent him a note, asking him to "pay attention religiously" to the instructions about how to follow the text that began with loose-leaf pages and continued in different notebooks, from the "red notebook" to the "blue notebook."[1] Sometimes the pagination jumped back and forth between the notebooks. In addition to following this complicated road map through the lush growth of Proustian text, Nahmias had to decipher the author's handwriting on page after page crammed with long, intricate sentences, many of which were crossed out, rewritten, and tangled. Proust paid Nahmias handsomely for his services, but the task, for which the young man had no special training or inclination, was never easy. Proust informed Albert that Miss Hayward had arrived in Paris early in the new year and suggested that they take advantage of her services, if he found her acceptable. If so, Albert should warn her not to plan on too many free weekends and make her understand that typing his manuscript was urgent business.

Proust's mania for speculation led to more heavy losses on the stock market when the large number of gold futures, worth nearly four hundred thousand francs

($1,360,000), he had bought on term in December took a dive.[2] When the bill came due he owed forty thousand francs and found himself short of cash to make the payment, a predicament that forced him to confide his financial situation to Robert de Billy. Proust had been sending five hundred francs a month to Billy's mistress Mme Gartzen. Because Billy was away for long periods serving at a diplomatic post in a foreign country, Marcel let the amount advanced accumulate until Billy remembered to reimburse him. But now he found himself so short of cash he did not even have the monthly amount to send to her. He confessed to Billy that he had spent so much and placed so many bets the previous summer at the casino in Cabourg that his bank accounts were running a deficit and he had a huge bill to pay on the gold futures. If Billy preferred, Marcel could sell some of his solid stocks and send Mme Gartzen the money. And he certainly was not asking Billy to pay what he owed him: "You can pay me whenever you like, or provide me with the sentimental pleasure of never paying me, thus giving me the illusion of keeping a woman with whom you may have had amourous relations."[3] This remark must have reminded him of amorous relations of another sort, for in the next sentence he wondered whether he had told Billy that a "distinguished and competent" Normandy source on homosexuals had said that it was practically certain that British Gen. Horatio Herbert Kitchener was one. Proust was pleased to have such information about a contemporary military hero, confirming what had been demonstrated throughout history: that contrary to stereotypes, being homosexual did not mean being a coward. Proust would remember Kitchener's example when writing the *Search;* next to a conversation between Brichot and Charlus about homosexuality, he made a marginal note: "Stress the fact that homosexuality has never precluded bravery, from Caesar to Kitchener."[4]

Billy immediately sent the money for Mme Gartzen and began to look for ways to ease Marcel's financial crisis. He generously offered to buy some of Marcel's shares, which he could afford to hold, perhaps long enough to make a profit. When thanking Billy, Proust applied to himself Mme de Sévigné's remark about her son through whose fingers money ran like water: "He has found a way to lose without gambling and spend without having anything to show for it."[5] In early February, when he wrote Billy again to ask for his advice about regaining a sound financial footing, Proust admitted to a near addiction to gambling and swore to reform.[6]

Proust took risks with drugs as well. When Mme Peigné-Crémieux died on January 19, Proust decided to knock himself out with Veronal, a powerful barbiturate, in order to sleep through the night and arise in time to attend the funeral. Though deathly afraid of drafts and unspecified germs, Proust proved fearless regarding self-medication and experimenting with new drugs. At midnight he downed the Veronal, but instead of deep sleep, he experienced an incapacitating reaction. By three o'clock the next afternoon he felt somewhat calm, but was unable to rise from his bed. Writing to a cousin to explain his absence from the funeral, he said that he had marked Veronal off his list of acceptable drugs. Proust was no truer to this resolution than to most involving his health and finances; by the following year he admitted to "abusing Veronal."[7]

In late February, Proust paid the three hundred francs he owed Nahmias for dictation and the copy he had made for Miss Hayward to type, telling him in a letter that he had "worked like an angel." Regarding the futures that had nearly ruined him, Marcel told Albert that Billy would acquire a good portion of those, after Proust paid the difference owed for the stocks. Proust, who never allowed anyone to question his status, judgment, or talent in the servants' presence, gently scolded Albert for having alluded to his financial difficulties in front of Nicolas. Ending his letter on a positive note, he thanked Albert for introducing one of his girlfriends, "the exquisite visitor" who had recently accompanied the young man.[8]

A short time later Proust informed Albert that his brother Robert had found out about his most recent fiasco on the market and had made him promise to stop speculating. Robert must have imagined how horrified their parents would have been at the way Marcel was squandering his half of the family fortune. Marcel told Lauris about his disastrous speculation in gold shares: "The very day I liquidated they shot up!"[9] Proust did not want Nahmias, who had urged him to buy the futures, to blame himself. The young man had been so nice about recommending investments and copying his manuscript. If Albert was still willing to help with his book, Proust had much more than usual for him to do: "A real volume!"[10]

By March 1 Proust wrote Albert that he had paid what he owed on the shares but still had a deficit in his accounts at several banks, which perplexed him. "If their statements are accurate I should have been able with the money spent this year, to buy the Mona Lisa and keep ten cocottes." Leonardo's famous painting was presumably for sale on the black market since its theft from the Louvre the previous year.[11] Regardless of the uncertain state of his financial situation, Proust told Nahmias he was eager to resume dictation.

The *Figaro* published on March 21 the first of four excerpts from the unrevised version of *Swann's Way.* Proust had intended these "prose poems" to appear as heralds of his book. He had titled the first excerpt simply "Épines blanches, épines roses" (White thorns, pink thorns), but the newspaper, without consulting him, changed the title to "Au seuil du printemps" (On the threshold of spring) and placed a new phrase in his first sentence, "I was reading, the other day, à propos of this relatively mild winter—*which ends today*—that there have been times over the preceding centuries when the hawthorns have flowered from February onwards." Proust had alerted Montesquiou to watch for the excerpts that contained "the best of my imagination." If these were successful, perhaps he would publish others. Then fearing that he had raised the count's expectations too high about his homage to hawthorns, he said, "But perhaps I think they are better than they really are and you won't like them." He then complained bitterly about the newspaper's tampering with his title and opening sentence but remarked, "It's of no importance since nobody reads that sort of thing."[12]

Montesquiou, whose scathing, sometimes scatological wit can be heard later in Charlus's haughty diatribes, wrote Proust a letter in which he made a wordplay on *épines*, slang for penis (thorns, similar to the English *prick*): "I gathered your pretty pricks, but you did not mention the sexual odor." In another wordplay, he evoked the Narrator kneeling before an altar covered with hawthorns. Alluding to Proust's "bittersweet odor of almonds" emanating from the hawthorns, Montesquiou substituted *amant* (lover), for the nearly homophonic *amandes*.[13]

Proust answered, "I'm grateful to you for mentioning my hawthorns although I have the impression that you don't like them. As for the mixture of litanies and sperm you speak of, the most delectable expression of it that I know is in a piano piece of Fauré's, already some years old but quite intoxicating, which is called, I think, *Romance sans paroles*. It's the sort of thing a pederast might sing while raping an altar-boy."[14] Had Proust already conceived the episode in which Charlus is rumored to have attempted, at his wife's funeral, to seduce a choirboy?

Montesquiou, realizing that Proust had taken his joke about pricks to mean that he did not care for the article, wrote to correct the inference his friend had drawn: "Not at all, dear Marcel, your piece is *charming*. It's a fragment of *Memoirs, recollections of childhood*." If Montesquiou had meant to reassure Proust, he could not have chosen his words more poorly. The novelist protested: "As for your remark about *Recollections of Childhood*, alas it's a condemnation of the idea of writing these articles, since they will create in advance a misunderstanding of my book, which is so carefully constructed and concentric and which people will mistake for mere childhood memoirs."[15] Proust had recognized a principal future criticism of his novel, one that he did not always remember to discourage.

Lauris, with whom Proust exchanged fewer letters since his marriage, had sent his congratulations on the *Figaro* article. Proust replied, expressing his horror of "the nauseatingly banal title" that the newspaper had stuck on his article. He told

Georges that he seldom saw anyone now except Reynaldo, "who in spite of my protests adapted himself to the worst oscillations of my timetable. . . . Then a month ago he stopped coming because his mother fell gravely ill."[16] When Hahn's eighty-one-year-old mother died on March 24, Proust felt too ill to go to his friend and comfort him. Marcel lamented his inability to offer Reynaldo "even the feeblest token of my infinite gratitude for all the kindness he lavishes on me."[17]

A Sort of Immense Novel

Proust asked Lauris's advice about the exasperating dilemma he faced over his novel: "I'm very perplexed about what decision I ought to take about the book. Should it be published as a single volume of 800 or 900 pages? As a work in two volumes of 400 pages each? Or two separate works of 400 pages, each with a different title, under the same general title? This I like less but it's what publishers prefer." Proust had two great fears. *Swann's Way* had become far longer than the average novel, but he did not want to chop the story in two at a place that would leave the reader confused and hanging in midair; nor did he want to publish the first volume unless he had a guarantee that the concluding volume or volumes would appear in a timely fashion. If he gave all five parts of *Swann's Way* in the first volume, "it would amount to 700 pages, leaving only 200 pages for the second."[18]

Proust spent the rest of this year and the better part of the next fretting over such decisions. Calmette, he told Lauris, was "in his infinite kindness" recommending the book to Fasquelle, about whom Proust had some reservations. Was he the right publisher for this book? Eugène Fasquelle had assumed command of a successful publishing house established by Georges Charpentier, who had published Gustave Flaubert and Émile Zola. Proust was consulting Georges and others because he wanted to "know beforehand exactly what to ask for, so as not to let the publisher simply follow his own convenience."[19] He wondered about Lauris's publisher, Bernard Grasset, just over thirty and said to be energetic and very intelligent.

During the refurbishment of his Palais Rose, Montesquiou had been staying at the Hôtel Garnier, near Proust's apartment.[20] The count had offered to come to boulevard Haussmann at any hour of any night that suited Proust's schedule, but he never received an invitation. He knew that Proust had been avoiding him and told him so, underscoring each point: "It was you who did not wish *to see me.* For more than a month and a half I've been only *a few steps away from you.*" He reminded Marcel that if he were too ill to leave his apartment, there was no reason for him not to receive visitors: "Our *prayer-books* still firmly recommend *visits to the sick.* But *the sick don't want them any more!*"[21] The normally temperamental and haughty count showed considerable forbearance and understanding of Marcel. In an April letter Montesquiou called him "the invisible, faithful, and charming friend."[22]

At the end of March, Proust paid Nahmias 1,700 francs for his most recent copying. He thanked him for the work even though he had not seen it, declaring himself "amazed" that Albert had been able to complete everything, calling him "a great worker and a boy worthy of the highest esteem."[23] Proust soon sent Albert more pages to copy, the last section of *Swann's Way,* which was to become "Place-Names: The Name." Additional pages and instructions quickly followed. He urged Nahmias not to go too fast because in the last installment, though Nahmias's copies had been "sublime," he had left out many words.[24] Proust explained again his complicated manner of paginating in different colored pencil or ink and outlined again how to trace his text from one notebook to the next.

In early April, Nahmias sent a second batch of pages to Miss Hayward, urging her to work "every day" so that he could come soon to collect the typescript.[25] Albert also responded to Proust's reproaches with a few pertinent observations. Some of the missing words could be ascribed directly to Proust, who had left blanks here and there and forgotten to fill them in before forwarding the pages to Nahmias. Because Nahmias did not want to attempt this time what he had done before—"sublime" though the results may have been—he asked Proust to check his own notebooks, because only the author could know what he had intended. Nahmias now left large blanks for Proust to fill. When stumped by one of Proust's labyrinthine sentences, the secretary labeled the cryptic words "Impossible to understand."[26] He also brought Proust's attention to inconsistencies, like a feather in a lady's hat that was red on one page and purple on another.

Albert had sent Proust, who lavished gifts on others, an electric chafing dish, which the writer refused. He had also been annoyed at Albert's tossing the word *sublime* back at him: "You're an angel (although I don't much like your sarcasm regarding 'sublime')." Having been "very unwell" for the past few days, Proust had not sent him any more pages to copy. "Besides, the pleasantries about 'sublime' have thrown a discouragingly cold shower . . . " Then, fearing that he had been too harsh, Proust pictured his young assistant's face: "Dear Albert, I wish I were less tired so that I could tell you how fond of you I am: near to my heart and even my eyes, for as I write I seem to see below your hair parted in the middle, the smiling eyes of your good days, and that distension, that swelling of the nostrils which with you is a sign of benevolence and also, when it occurs, a great embellishment."[27]

One day in late April, Proust, thinking that Montesquiou was at the Palais Rose, got up in the late afternoon, called for Odilon's car, slipped his "fur-lined coat over a shirt," and set off for Le Vésinet, fifteen miles west of Paris. Proust and Albaret were going down a muddy country road under a gray sky near Rueil when Proust spotted some apple trees in bloom and asked Odilon to stop.[28] While absorbing his impressions of the beautiful trees, a sight he had not seen for so long, and one that reminded him of his beloved Normandy, Proust noticed the farmers warily staring at him and Albaret. Then he remembered that the French country-side was being terrorized by two bandits named Bonnot and Garnier, who, like Bonnie and Clyde, robbed banks, stole cars, and murdered their occupants.[29] Shortly after looking at the fruit trees, Marcel felt the onset of an asthma attack and decided to turn back. Only later did he learn that Montesquiou had been at Artagnan. Proust enjoyed telling the count and others that he and Albaret had been taken for the killers.

In late spring Proust wrote Jean-Louis Vaudoyer, seeking advice about what to expect from a publisher regarding the number of pages per volume. In the rela-tively brief time since the March letter to Lauris, he had again expanded the novel. He no longer spoke of a total of eight hundred to nine hundred pages but fourteen hundred. His great anxiety remained the division of his book into volumes, espe-cially *Swann's Way*, which, in the current state, was far longer than the remaining sections. Was he even certain of the genre? He explained the dilemma to Vaudoyer: "My novel (?) will consist of two volumes of roughly 700 pages each. . . . But I can't end the first at the precise half-way point. Do you think a work in two volumes would be feasible for Fasquelle or another? Or would there have to be two titles, a general title with 1 above it and the one title for the first volume and a different one for the second . . . or even five volumes of 300 pages, one for each part?"

He also worried about the appearance of the text. If *Swann's Way* were pub-lished in one volume, the text would have to be so dense the reader would suffer eye strain or headaches. Proust asked Vaudoyer "whether the *clarity* of the print de-pends on the number of letters in each line and the number of lines on each page. . . . I need very very full pages so as not to have more than 650 in the first volume, which I believe is the maximum number of pages for any one volume."[30] In the postscript, he acknowledged that he could not have a single volume of 1,300 pages, but he would like two volumes of 650 pages. If there were more than two volumes, should he not insist that each appear no later than three months after the last?[31] Proust continued to agonize over these decisions, which he knew would have a significant influence on the success of his novel.

He kept producing new pages for Albert to copy and Miss Hayward to type. In mid-May, he sent Nahmias this tempting offer: "Do you still want to emulate Oedipus and decipher the sphinx-like riddles of my handwriting? If so I can send you some exercise-books which exceed in obscurity anything you have ever seen. But it's only *if you want to*. Don't do it just to please me."[32] Nahmias, whose skills had increased with the hard work, remained on the production line.

Marcel's poor health prevented him from attending two performances that were important to Reynaldo's career. On April 29 Hahn conducted *Don Giovanni* at the Opéra-Comique, confirming his status as one of the era's foremost interpreters of Mozart. Two weeks later, on May 13, his ballet *Le Dieu bleu* had its Paris première at the Théâtre du Châtelet. Cocteau and Madrazo, influenced by the Orientalism that remained very much in vogue, had set the story in the temple ruins of Angkor. In spite of all the talent of Diaghilev's company, with Fokine's choreography and the dancing of Nijinsky and Karsavina, as well as Bakst's magnificent Oriental costumes, the ballet never caught on with the public and was soon dropped from the repertory.[33]

On May 24 Proust accepted Mme Greffulhe's invitation to attend the dress rehearsal of *Sumurum*, another work inspired by Eastern tales.[34] Mme Greffulhe had invited a friend whom Marcel was eager to meet, Mme Henry Standish, née Hélène de Pérusse des Cars, a legendary beauty of the early days of the Third Republic. Now somewhat elderly at seventy-two, Mme Standish had been an elegant style setter and a friend of the Prince of Wales, later King Edward VII.[35] While watching *Sumurum* from Mme Greffulhe's box, Proust was able to study the dresses of two of the most beautiful and fashionable women of the Belle Époque. He noticed striking differences in the conception each had of fashion, observations that would inspire elements of one of the *Search*'s most famous scenes at the Opéra.[36] After the performance, Proust committed one of his rare social gaffes. Having spotted Montesquiou in the crowded lobby, he left the countess, whom he was to have accompanied home, and ran over to speak to the poet. When Marcel looked for the lady, she had disappeared. The next day he sent Mme Greffulhe roses and apologies.[37]

He wrote Billy about meeting Mme Standish, whom he had found, "(making all necessary allowances for age etc.) splendid in her marinated elegance, her artful simplicity."[38] Over the course of the summer Proust consulted Mme Straus and

Jeanne de Caillavet about details of the two women's style. He asked Jeanne whether she could "by any chance give me some small dressmaking details for the book I'm finishing." Observing the clothes worn by Mme Standish and Mme Greffulhe at the Opéra had left him with the "impression of two very different, if not contrasting ways of understanding clothes and elegance." Above all, the ladies must not know he was interested in their clothes "because the two women whom I shall dress up in their clothes—like two mannequins—have no connection with them, my novel has no key, and if I mention it to them and afterwards my characters turn out to be poisoners or to commit incest, they'll think I mean *them!*"[39] In another letter Proust described to Jeanne how he conducted his research. He mentioned the outing to study the colors of hawthorns and apple trees in bloom. On the rare occasions when he went out to see people, "the dresses of the ladies which are of a less delectable color than those of the apple trees puzzle me just as much. For if I have an impression, I need exact words to express it. And I don't know them. So then I skim through books about beauty, or books about architecture, or fashion journals. And naturally they never provide what I want." The same was often true of his friends, but he enjoyed consulting them.

Proust had included in his letter to Jeanne two amusing anecdotes. Mme Greffulhe had told Mme Standish that she "would know when she was no longer beautiful when the little chimney-sweeps no longer turned round as she passed by. And Mme Standish replied: 'Oh don't be afraid, my dear, as long as you go on dressing like that people will always turn round!' " Proust considered this story so good that he used a version of it in the *Search,* in which the duchesse de Guermantes tells the princesse de Guermantes, "You've only got to go on wearing hats like the one you have on and you can be sure they'll always turn round."

The second anecdote, involving Montesquiou, contained, typically, a degrading remark. The count had written to the immensely wealthy Maurice de Rothschild to ask to borrow some jewelry to wear to a fancy costume ball. Rothschild sent Montesquiou a single tiny brooch, "which he recommended as being a family jewel." To which Montesquiou replied: "I was unaware that you had a Family, but I thought you had some jewels."[40] Proust would give this cutting remark to Charlus.

On June 4, the day the *Figaro* published another excerpt from *Swann's Way,* "Rayon de soleil sur le balcon" (A ray of sunlight on the balcony), Proust called for Albaret to drive him to the Bernheim-Jeune Gallery to see the exhibition "Venice and Claude Monet."[41] Proust had been unable to resist twenty-nine paintings of Venice by the master he admired more than any contemporary painter.[42] Afterward he had wanted to take advantage of being out during normal hours to call on Mme

Straus. He wrote that evening to tell her that, after keeping Albaret waiting for two hours, he abandoned the plan because he had felt too weak.

Proust soon became impatient with Miss Hayward's slow progress on the typescript and told Nahmias it was urgent for him to see the typist and do whatever he could to make her work at a faster pace. Proust said that it was "truly odious to devote one's entire life to the creation of a book and to be stopped cold for more than a month by this!"[43] Still undecided about divisions and titles, Marcel sent Reynaldo a list of sixteen titles, none of which were inspired, but almost all of which contained the word *past* or words that suggested the past: *The Stalactites of the Past, In Front of a Few Stalactites of the Past, Reflections in a Patina, What One Sees in a Patina, The Reflections of the Past,* and so on. Only one title, *The Reflections of Time,* contained the key word *time.* Although the titles conveyed the theme of the past, they lacked the words indicating the elements of a quest: lost and found. Hahn's reaction to this first group of proposed titles is unknown.[44] By June 27 Proust at last had the 712-page typescript of *Swann's Way* in hand and paid Nahmias and Miss Hayward for their work. Proust spent the remainder of the summer correcting this copy. In the meantime he found fresh sources of inspiration and added new scenes to his story.

Proust claimed to have fallen in love with a sixteen-year-old girl, the daughter of a woman he had loved at the same age. He wrote letters to Mme de Caillavet, praising Simone's youthful beauty and marveling at how her blond hair and fair complexion contrasted with her mother's attractive brunette colors. How strange, he said, that "one can love opposite physical types. For here I am in love with your daughter. How cruel of her to be amiable because it's her smile that made me fall in love." Proust then suggested that there were traces, in the novel he was writing, of his infatuation with Simone's mother when she was Jeanne Pouquet, mingled with elements of his earlier crush on Marie de Benardaky: "If ever Calmette finds the time to publish an article of mine . . . which is a recollection of a childhood love—not my love for you, it was *before* that—you will nonetheless find amalgamated with it something of the emotional turmoil I felt when I wondered whether you'd be at the tennis-court. But what's the use of recalling things about which you took the absurd and unkind decision never to have noticed!"[45] At such moments Proust came dangerously close to suggesting that his novel was a thinly disguised autobiography, a charge soon to be leveled by some critics.

Proust was particularly taken with Simone's smile: "How pretty your daughter smiles. How pretty she is. I find her infinitely attractive." Proust supposedly called on the Caillavets late one night after Simone had gone to bed and begged that she be awakened and asked to come down to the drawing room. Marcel wrote Jeanne that Simone's beauty occupied his thoughts: "My memory and my imagination offer me from time to time stereoscopic sessions of your daughter's smile and gramophone records of her voice. I've given these pastimes a rather old-fashioned title, 'The Pleasures of Solitude.' "[46] Many years later, long after Proust had died, Jeanne saw that her daughter had inspired the radiant girl of sixteen who appears in the closing pages of the novel, Mlle de Saint-Loup, whose youth and beauty, the Narrator says, are made up of all the years he had lost.

On August 7 Proust told Armand de Guiche that he was having second thoughts about leaving for Cabourg—which meant, of course, that his departure was imminent. He explained why he always left so precipitously: "I don't yet know whether I shall go to Cabourg. I think not, but I am as impulsive as I am irresolute; when I can no longer bear the weight of my indecision, I leave in order not to suffer any longer."[47] This was to be not his final year at Cabourg, but the last one in which he took any pleasure.

An Impatient Author

Proust wrote to Hahn from Cabourg on August 17 to express his condolences on the death of Jules Massenet, who had been his friend's teacher at the Conservatoire.[48] Proust had recently met Mme Marie Scheikévitch, a friend of Reynaldo's who was staying nearby at Houlgate. Mme Scheikévitch was a Russian, an attractive blonde about thirty years old, divorced from Pierre Carolus-Duran, son of the famous society painter. She was the person whom Mme Arman de Caillavet had consulted about how to kill herself. Mme Scheikévitch had been so miserable in her marriage to Carolus-Duran that she had attempted suicide. She made Marcel's "heart bleed" by telling how "old Mme Arman had come to ask her how she had gone about shooting herself with a revolver." The "only consolation" he found in the story was that it left open to interpretation whether Mme de Caillavet had "intended to miss," having consulted someone who had proved inept in doing away with herself.[49] Since Marie's recovery and divorce she had established herself as a young society hostess with literary interests. After Marcel's second meeting with Mme Scheikévitch at Cabourg, he wrote Reynaldo that he found her company stimulating. Proust began to confide in her about his work. He had made a new friend who was to use her influence to help launch his novel.

Proust was more active that season at Cabourg than he had been in several years. He must have astonished Reynaldo when he wrote that he went dancing every other day in order to "remove the rust from his joints."[50] Marcel had also accepted the invitation from the vicomte d'Alton, president of the Cabourg Golf-Club, to attend the club's annual dinner and ball, considered the highlight of the summer social season in Normandy. On Tuesday afternoon, August 20, the day of the ball, Proust dressed and went out on the beachfront promenade, where he was to meet Nahmias between six and seven. Proust waited in vain for the young man. That evening, before going to dinner, he began a long, scathing letter, telling Albert that for someone in his poor health a small event could assume a great importance, and he had expected his young friend to rush back from Deauville to be on time. Had their roles been reversed, Proust would have hurried to be there "dead or alive."[51]

Proust's choice of words was unfortunate. During the drive from Deauville to keep his rendezvous with Proust, Albert's car hit a little girl, mortally wounding her. Unaware of these tragic events, Proust put his letter aside to attend the gala dinner. Later that evening, still furious with Nahmias, he resumed his indictment of the young man's thoughtlessness. Proust mentioned famous older writers who had gone out of their way to accommodate him, such as Alphonse Daudet, who "at the height of his fame and ill health, when he could scarcely scribble a line without weeping with the pain it caused him all over his body," had written him twice one evening before Marcel was to dine with the Daudets, just to inquire where he would prefer to be placed at table.

In rebuking Albert, Proust used language similar to Swann's when he scolds Odette for being incapable of forgoing the most trivial entertainment to spend some time with him. The "very deep and genuine feelings of friendship" Proust had for Nahmias forced him to observe: "You are not perfectible. You are not even made of stone, which can be sculpted when it is lucky enough to come across a sculptor (and you might well meet greater sculptors than I, though I would have done it with tenderness), you are made of water, commonplace, impalpable, colourless, fluid water, eternally insubstantial, endlessly flowing away." He sounds like Charlus berating the Narrator for having failed an early test to live up to the baron's high opinion of him: "You may say that you chanced upon a first-rate friendship, and that you botched it."[52]

When Proust learned that Albert's car had killed a child, he was horrified and embarrassed. Two days after Nahmias's accident, Henri Bardac, a friend of Hahn's, rented a car at Cabourg that hit a little girl, who died instantly. After these calamities, Proust, whose regular drivers Albaret and Agostinelli were not at Cabourg this summer, became reluctant to hire unknown drivers. He especially regretted being unable to find reliable transportation to call on Mme Straus, whom he wanted to see above all others. He told Mme Straus that he would try to come with Calmette or on the train.

Two days before returning to Paris, Proust finally called on Mme Straus. Taking advantage of the splendid weather, the two friends drove as far as Honfleur. From Paris, Marcel wrote Mme Straus that the day with her had seemed "like a sunny enclave in months of darkness, the day when, in a motor-car which you called a donkey-cart and which was the magic coach in which the fairies enable one to explore the past, we traveled to Honfleur, and a few years back in time." He sent along with the letter a copy of his Sainte-Beuve essay and asked her again for the name and address of her furrier Corby, which he had already misplaced, because he intended to give fur coats to Hélène and Colette d'Alton.[53]

In late October, Proust sought advice about his novel from friends like Antoine Bibesco and Louis de Robert. With Antoine he reviewed his misgivings regarding Calmette and Fasquelle, making clear that he had not yet signed a contract with Fasquelle. He feared that the publisher would not accept a general title for the overall work but would insist on "three different titles . . . and with an interval after each volume." It seemed likely that the NRF would be a "more suitable medium for the maturation and the dissemination of the ideas contained in my book. In short, I should like my book to appear (not as with Fasquelle at the publisher's expense but at mine)" under the imprint of the NRF. "Can you ask them?" Proust had some reservations about the review, pointing out the latest issue contained "plenty of absurdities."[54] But given the choices, it was still "the only review. If they publish me, perhaps they'll read me. On the whole I don't see why they should refuse me. I'd pay for the edition as handsomely as they wish. From the literary point of view (although I suspect that, for reasons which I believe to be false, they may not estimate me at my true worth, which isn't great but higher than they may think) I won't disgrace them."

Proust explained his book to Antoine, in whom he had not recently confided: "The work is a novel; if its freedom of tone seems to give it something of the appearance of an autobiography, in reality a very strict composition (too complex to be immediately perceptible) differentiates it profoundly therefrom: the element of the contingent in it is no more than is necessary to express the part played by the contingent in real life." Because his novel could not be published all at once, Proust feared that its structure would not be apparent. No matter what the decision, he wanted to have it quickly: "I'm ill, I'm in a hurry, and I don't care about the preliminaries."[55]

In postscripts placed at the top of the letter, Marcel referred to the division of the volumes and requested time to think things over, if the NRF should agree. The third postscript countermanded the approach to the NRF he had asked Antoine to make in the letter, then contradicted that by telling Antoine, "You might write to see whether they're interested."[56] Bibesco likely interpreted the last sentence as being authoritative, or he may have been thoroughly confused at that point. In any case, he contacted the NRF, thereby initiating another Proustian imbroglio over negotiations for his book.

At the same time Proust asked Mme Straus to remind Calmette to secure an agreement to publish with Fasquelle, which she did. He told her that he had found two promising titles, *Le Temps perdu* (Lost time) for the first volume and for the third *Le Temps retrouvé* (Time regained). Although Proust still lacked the full version of his general title, he had found its essential contrasting elements, alerting the reader that the concluding volume would rejoin the beginning, elucidating what had come first. In the postscript, he sounded the note of mortality, insisting on the urgency of his enterprise, using the word *time* in its most sinister meaning: "For I haven't much time ahead of me . . ."[57]

Once he learned that Antoine had contacted Jacques Copeau, a cofounder of the NRF, Proust had to write Copeau to explain the status of his negotiations with Fasquelle, whom he did not name. He stressed the "peculiarly awkward situation of seeming no longer to want what I desired so much, and declining the offer which I solicited." This was premature, for the NRF had offered nothing. If he could obtain a release from the other publisher, he would write Gaston Gallimard at once. Proust assumed that because he was willing to pay for publication, there would be no question about whether or not to publish his novel.[58]

At the same time Proust sought advice from Louis de Robert, whose successful novel *Le Roman du malade* had been published by Fasquelle and recently serialized in the *Figaro*. Proust was especially troubled because someone had told him that it would be pointless to "ask Fasquelle to bring out a single work in two or three volumes," that the publisher "would *insist* on different titles for each volume, and a gap between their publication dates." If that were not bad enough, Proust had been told that Fasquelle "examines books severely, demands alterations and won't allow anything that might hold up the action." Because Robert had been published by Fasquelle, Marcel wondered whether he thought that the editor would publish his book "as it stands, with all its lyrical digressions, without tinkering with it?" Or should he give up Fasquelle and go with a "purely literary publication" like the NRF, which "would be more likely to persuade readers to accept a work which it must be said is completely different from the classical novel?" He would gladly pay the costs of publication, if that meant that the publishers would not alter the book.[59] When Louis de Robert learned of his offer to pay the costs, he realized at once that Proust had blundered and explained what seemed evident to everyone but the impatient author: such a proposal implied an inferior work.

Mme Straus wrote Marcel that she had received a letter from Calmette dated October 28, telling her, "Fasquelle should have written to Marcel Proust two days ago asking him to send his manuscript. He will publish it gladly; I have his promise. He will discuss the other two volumes after the publication of the first. I may add that Fasquelle very much appreciates Marcel Proust's talent and is delighted to be able to give him proof of this."[60]

Proust, who had no reason to doubt Calmette's word, wrote immediately to thank Fasquelle.[61] He described his book, making certain Fasquelle understood its *indecent* nature, underscoring the word. Because his novel's strong homosexual theme was not apparent in *Swann's Way,* Proust did not want to mislead Fasquelle about what was to come, nor did he want Fasquelle to publish one volume and then refuse to bring out the remainder of the book. Unless Proust could secure this guarantee, any offer to publish was meaningless to him. He assured Fasquelle that "the overall character of the work will testify to its high moral purpose." Then Proust, requesting confidence, explained his intention in creating Charlus and his method of characterization in general: his characters emerge "as people do in life, that is to say scarcely known at first and often discovered long afterwards to be the opposite of what was thought." He gave as an example the Charlus character, merely glimpsed early in the novel, where he is rumored to be Mme Swann's lover. Later, when Charlus meets the Narrator, he "puts on a show of virility, of contempt for effeminate young men, etc. But in the second part this elderly gentleman of a noble family reveals himself as a pederast who will be portrayed in a comic light but, without any obscene language, will be seen 'picking up' a concierge and 'keeping' a pianist." Proust thought that such a character was new to literature: "the *virile* pederast bearing a grudge against effeminate young men, who trick him on the nature of the goods, by turning out to be indistinguishable from women."[62]

He then discussed the titles. The first volume, assuming Fasquelle would not allow him to put the roman numeral I on the cover, would be *Le Temps perdu* and the concluding one *Le Temps retrouvé*. His general title would be *Les Intermittences du cœur* (The intermittencies of the heart), an expression "which in the psychological sphere alludes to a physical malady."[63] Proust then raised the complicated issue of dividing the book into volumes. The solution he saw as "highly advantageous" would be a "fat" volume including all of *Swann's Way*. "For this first volume, full of preparatory material, a sort of poetic overture, is infinitely less 'public' (except for the section entitled "Un Amour de Swann" [Swann in Love] to which I draw your attention) than the second will be." Proust assessed his work accurately, knowing that the story of Swann and Odette's love affair would have a wider appeal. Preparing to send his manuscript to Fasquelle, he commended it to his care, "as I haven't a draft, at least not an identical one." In a follow-up letter, Proust said that he had forgotten to mention how eager he was to publish by the following March and asked whether he could have the proofs soon.[64]

Louis de Robert initially had doubts about Proust's new style, so different from the one he had admired in *Pleasures and Days*. In late October, after reading "L'Église de village" (The village church) he complimented Proust but observed that "at times your rather long sentences become ravelled and involved."[65] If it were possible for two such invalids to meet, Robert would like to talk to Proust because he "might, with all the modesty arising from my ignorance, suggest to you here and there a word, a point, a trifle that would disentangle a sentence and make it clearer and more limpid. But it's very unimportant, and no one could improve the value, the richness of what you write."

Robert was generally encouraging about Fasquelle's reaction to Proust's book. Having offered to untangle Proust's sentences, he gave the novelist practical advice regardless of the publisher: "A book that is too dense, that takes too long to read, frightens the public a bit. Such considerations ought not to influence you. But if, on re-reading your text, you yourself feel that it can be lightened without serious disadvantage, there's no doubt that you will be presenting yourself in more favourable conditions from every point of view." Robert offered to tell Fasquelle how much he admired Proust's writing and to recommend his work wholeheartedly.

Proust wrote Gaston Gallimard in early November, reminding him that Robert Gangnat had introduced them at Bénerville in 1908.[66] A week later, after several fruitless attempts to reach Gallimard by phone, Marcel received a letter from him. He invited the publisher to stop by one evening to become better acquainted and discuss his novel. Proust reviewed the agreement he believed he had with Fasquelle, without naming the publisher, and stated that he must, out of courtesy, fulfill his obligation to this publisher. But he hinted that he might find a way to extricate himself from the agreement. In the meantime, should he receive the first proofs, it would be too late, and the "NRF will have been only a dream for me." He gave his printing requirements and especially wanted to know when the volumes would go on sale. The book must be easily affordable. "I ask this because I want to be read, and not exclusively by the rich or by bibliophiles. And I don't want my whole book to cost the buyer more than seven francs, even if it resulted in greater expense for me; it's a question of *diffusion*. I once had a de-luxe volume published by Calmann-Lévy which cost 15 francs. It's too dear."[67] Proust had learned his lesson; *Pleasures and Days* had been a young writer's indulgence. He was now a mature artist who sought a much larger audience: everyone.

When Gallimard offered to come by and collect the manuscript, Proust told him that it was too heavy to carry. He would have it delivered, thus depriving himself for the time being of a working copy. He repeated to Gallimard the stipulations he had given Fasquelle, described the homosexual character, and proposed some new titles, including one he was to keep for the second volume, *À l'ombre des jeunes filles en fleurs* (In the shade of girls in bloom).[68]

Proust also wrote to Copeau at the *NRF* and enclosed excerpts from the novel. Although Proust knew that articles for the review were selected long in advance, he hoped that these excerpts might appear no later than February 1, in preparation for the first volume of his novel, which he expected to be out by mid-February. Perhaps Copeau would do him this favor, for he was an author who wrote "very rarely." His last volume, he told the editor, went back to "1893!"[69] Copeau rejected the excerpts.

Believing that Calmette had Fasquelle's promise to publish his novel and having made an offer to Gallimard to pay the publishing costs, Proust assumed he had only to choose between Fasquelle and the NRF. On November 10 he wrote a long letter to Mme Straus, weighing the pros and cons of each publisher. He thought that Gide's group provided a "more literary environment," whereas Fasquelle might be "more glamorous, more flattering." What he had particularly liked about Fasquelle was the opportunity to reach a wider audience, "the sort of people who buy a badly printed volume before catching a train."[70] He confided in Mme Straus that Calmette and Fasquelle had been behaving strangely toward him lately. When he had stopped by recently at the *Figaro,* Calmette pretended not to be in, something he had never done before. Fasquelle did not answer his letters about the manuscript. Proust had nearly decided to send Reynaldo, who was on friendly terms with Fasquelle, to retrieve his manuscript as diplomatically as possible.

He told Mme Straus about a letter from Edmond Rostand, author of *Cyrano de Bergerac* and member of the Académie française, who had written to express his admiration for the excerpts in the *Figaro*.[71] Rostand generously offered to contact Fasquelle on Proust's behalf.[72] Having written a number of pages to Mme Straus about publishing his book, Marcel promised to stop lest she think him "terribly self-interested, and there's no virtue in having written nothing for twenty years only to make up for it in a month by intriguing to get oneself published, behaving like a careerist, getting drunk on printer's ink." But this book, which he already knew would be his life's work, merited such attention: "I feel so strongly that a work of art is something which, though it comes from ourselves, is nevertheless better than ourselves, that I find it quite natural to struggle on its behalf, like a father on behalf of his child." A remark recently made by the novelist and playwright Paul Hervieu struck him as true: "The rules of the game were to work for years only to be judged in a few hours. And at least plays are listened to, whereas books are not read." He wanted those who did read his book to become "happier, in the sense that it's a breviary of the joys that can still be experienced by those to whom many human joys are denied. I didn't in the least intend it to be that. But to some extent it is that."[73]

In early December, Marcel wrote to Reynaldo, who had gone to Bucharest to give a lecture. He felt close to Hahn, even so far away: "You are so mixed up now with my thoughts, my sleep, my reading that writing to you seems as irksome as writing to myself."[74] Marcel was terribly disappointed, after having taken care of himself for a week, that he was not well enough "to go and hear three Beethoven quartets which the Capet Quartet were playing this evening at the Salle Gaveau. And I've had such a moschant attack that it was impossible for me to get up. And I can't tell you how crossch I am."[75] Proust now listened to the compositions of certain composers—Beethoven, Wagner, Franck—with the same hunger that had made him want to hear *Pelléas et Mélisande* night after night. He had been eager to hear the outstanding French string quartet, led by the brilliant violinist Lucien Capet, play late Beethoven quartets. As Proust developed his novel, and particularly the new character Vinteuil, his passion for music grew even stronger.

As Christmas approached with still no word from either Gallimard or Fasquelle, Proust became impatient and anxious. In mid-December he wrote to Gallimard, saying that he hoped "no news is good news." He told Gallimard that he did not want to release the other publisher until Gallimard made up his mind. He reminded the publisher that his decision "must apply to the *whole*. . . . I cannot be left stranded after the first volume." He had assumed that the typescript he sent of seven hundred pages "must suffice to enable you to judge the whole," but he would send the rest of the manuscript in the untyped exercise books at Gallimard's request.[76]

The long search for a publisher was wearing the writer down. The week before Christmas, he expressed his frustration to Louis: "You must feel as I do, that our actual profession seems easy, but trying to get into print, dealing with publishers, seem to be overwhelming tasks. It was so easy to write these volumes, and all the more enjoyable for the demands they made. But how difficult it will be to get them published."[77]

On Christmas Eve, Proust received disastrous news: both Fasquelle and the NRF had rejected his book. Proust wrote to Mme Straus the day after Christmas: "I had said no more to you about my book so as not to exhaust you with all these professional problems. But I must tell you, to get it over with, the latest 'events' are damnable." Proust, who preferred not to tell her that the NRF had rejected his book, said that he had withdrawn the book from Gallimard, giving the reasons he would have used had he done so: "The other day (this is absolutely between ourselves) I abandoned the other publisher I mentioned to you because I felt that the dedication to Calmette, who is of another intellectual breed, offended him and because I'm anxious above all not to be ungrateful. By the very fact of breaking with the other I was resigning myself to the changes which Fasquelle would demand." Then Proust had received a letter from Fasquelle in which "he told me quite simply that he couldn't undertake to publish my book (the whole thing interspersed with compliments but nevertheless strictly negative and completely irrevocable; in any case he sent back my manuscript). Alas I think I was right to suspect that Calmette had had no *promise* from Fasquelle and that was why he avoided me at first." Though financially "ruined," Proust still wanted to give Calmette an expensive present—perhaps a cigarette case, for around "1000–1500 francs"—for his efforts to find a publisher. In the postscript, he reminded Mme Straus that if she wrote or called, she must be very discreet because he did not want the servants to know about this setback.[78]

Fasquelle had sent the manuscript to a reader by the name of Jacques Normand, a jack of all trades—lawyer, archivist, playwright, and poet—who like Proust had frequented the salons of Mmes Aubernon and Lemaire and Princesse Mathilde. Proust had mentioned him in *Pleasures and Days,* in a less than flattering context in his *Bouvard et Pécuchet* parody, placing him in the same category as the vicomte de Borrelli, a society poet.[79] In the reader's report Normand vehemently condemned Proust's manuscript. Fasquelle accepted Normand's appraisal and did not even take the trouble to look at a manuscript recommended by Gaston Calmette, Edmond and Maurice Rostand, Jean Cocteau, and his own highly respected author Louis de Robert.[80] Fasquelle soon realized his mistake.

Proust learned much later that the NRF's decision had been made by one man: André Gide. A liberal intellectual and leader of the literary avant-garde, Gide considered Proust to be the epitome of a bourgeois snob and a dilettante, author of an "exquisite" little book called *Pleasures and Days,* someone who heaped flattery on aristocrats with literary pretensions, like Robert de Montesquiou and Anna de Noailles. Convinced that Proust was the antithesis of the authors the NRF had been created to foster, Gide had read only two passages from his book. Perhaps to save his pride, Proust later told Céleste that the NRF had never opened the package containing his manuscript, because it was returned with Nicolas's careful and particular wrappings and knots untouched.[81]

After a few days, Proust wrote to Louis to assess the situation and to weigh his options. He felt that all publishers would have much the same reaction as Fasquelle: none would "undertake to publish a work of such length, and so different from what the public was accustomed to reading." Proust said that he felt no bitterness toward Fasquelle, for his "point of view, perfectly fair commercially, is not unintelligent from the literary point of view." Proust thought that Fasquelle was wrong, but "there's such a thing as being intelligently wrong. So, in order to avoid exhausting negotiations with other publishers, request for alterations, etc., I'm now determined to have the book published at my expense. Not only would I pay the costs but I would also let the publisher have the profits if there were any, not out of generosity but to give him an interest in seeing the book succeed."[82] Proust remembered Robert's suggestion that he approach Ollendorff. Did he think Ollendorff would accept? Proust, determined to find a publisher at any cost with no further delays, considered paying the publicity costs as well. Would Louis de Robert ask Ollendorff? His conditions were that there be two volumes of roughly 650 pages each, the first to appear in the spring of 1913 and the second in February 1914. "There is only one thing I insist on—that it should be at my expense in order to remain free, and to have a definite *guarantee* of publication." Proust apparently chose to forget his past experience with Ollendorff, who a decade earlier had commissioned his translation of *La Bible d'Amiens* and then gone bankrupt, while still retaining the manuscript.

Fasquelle had said so many complimentary things about his articles in the *Figaro* that Proust decided to approach the editor about publishing his collected articles, parodies, and the preface "On Reading." This volume, Proust wrote Fasquelle, would "obviously" be "a minor thing compared to my magnum opus. But perhaps one small volume will frighten you less than two big ones." Whether frightened or not, Fasquelle again declined the opportunity to publish a book by Proust.[83]

Proust had made up his mind. He would publish his own book at his own expense on his own terms. This decision, reached after so much difficulty and so many disappointments, turned out to be the right decision for his book, which was to go through one of the most unusual, protracted, and expensive productions in the history of publishing. But once *Swann's Way* was in print, Proust would never again have to justify his enterprise or go begging for a publisher.

PART VI

Love and War (1913–1918)

Charles Haas, 1895. The principal model for Charles Swann, Haas was a refined aristocrat associated with the court of Napoléon III. He was the only Jewish member of the exclusive Jockey Club. *Paul Nadar/©Arch. Phot. Paris/CNMHS*

Madeleine Lemaire, 1891. The hostess of a bourgeois salon where artists and aristocrats mingled, she illustrated Proust's first book, *Pleasures and Days. Paul Nadar/ ©Arch. Phot. Paris/CNMHS*

Anatole France, 1893. A distinguished
writer whom Proust admired as a young
man, France wrote the preface to
*Pleasures and Days. Paul Nadar/©Arch.
Phot. Paris/*CNMHS

Sarah Bernhardt, 1893, in her most
famous role, Racine's *Phèdre. Paul
Nadar/©Arch. Phot. Paris/*CNMHS

Edgar Aubert, a young Swiss diplomat introduced to Proust by Robert de Billy.

Willie Heath, 1893, another young friend of Proust's, who, like Edgar Aubert, died young. *Paul Nadar/©Arch. Phot. Paris/* CNMHS

Proust near the turn of the century. *Photo: Bibliothèque nationale de France*

Proust in 1900 on a balcony in Venice, where he worked with Marie Nordlinger on his translation of *The Bible of Amiens. Mante-Proust Collection*

Opposite: Proust in the summer of 1899 with members of the Brancovan family and guests at their Villa Bassaraba, near Évian-les-Bains. Front, left to right, Princesse Hélène de Caraman-Chimay and the writer Abel Hermant; second row, the marquise de Monteynard, Princesse Edmond de Polignac (née Winnaretta Singer), and Comtesse Anna de Noailles; last row, Prince Edmond de Polignac, Mme Anatole Bartholoni, Proust, Prince Constantin de Brancovan, Mlle Jeanne Bartholoni, and the pianist Léon Delafosse. *Mante-Proust Collection*

Marie Nordlinger, the English cousin of Reynaldo Hahn, who assisted Proust with his Ruskin translations. Portrait by Frédéric de Madrazo.

Antoine Bibesco, a Romanian prince and diplomat, Proust's mischievous confidant.
Mante-Proust Collection

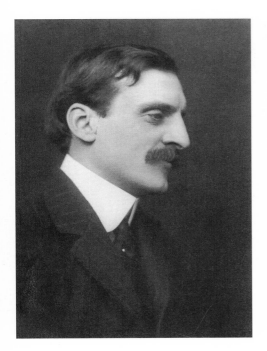

Prince Emmanuel Bibesco, the brother of Antoine, a knowledgeable guide to Proust on his tours of French cathedrals. *Mante-Proust Collection*

Comte Bertrand de Salignac-Fénelon. Proust was infatuated with the handsome young diplomat, referring to him affectionately as "His Blue Eyes."

Louisa de Mornand, an aspiring actress and mistress of Proust's friend the marquis d'Albufera. ©*Collection François-Xavier Bouchart*

Proust chats with Jeanne de Billy aboard her father's yacht *Hélène* in 1904. Her husband, Robert, is at right. *Mante-Proust Collection*

Adrien and Robert Proust on the balcony of
the family apartment at 45, rue de Courcelles,
around 1900. *Photo: Bibliothèque nationale de
France*

Proust on the grounds of the Splendide
Hôtel at Évian-les-Bains around 1905.

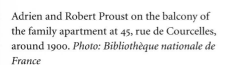

One of the last photographs of Mme Proust, taken around 1904. *Paul Nadar/©Arch. Phot. Paris/* CNMHS

Proust at the home of Reynaldo Hahn around 1905. *Mante-Proust Collection*

Odilon Albaret at the wheel and Alfred Agostinelli, 1907. Both men chauffeured Proust and played important roles in his life. *Photo: Bibliothèque nationale de France*

Céleste Albaret, wife of Odilon, became Proust's housekeeper in 1914.

Paul Morand, a young writer and diplomat who became a friend of Proust's during the war years.

Hélène Soutzo, a wealthy Greco-Romanian princess and future wife of Paul Morand; she often entertained Proust at the Ritz. *Paul Nadar/©Arch. Phot. Paris/*CNMHS

In the spring of 1921 Proust was photographed during a rare daytime sortie to view the Vermeer exhibition at the Jeu de Paume museum. *Mante-Proust Collection*

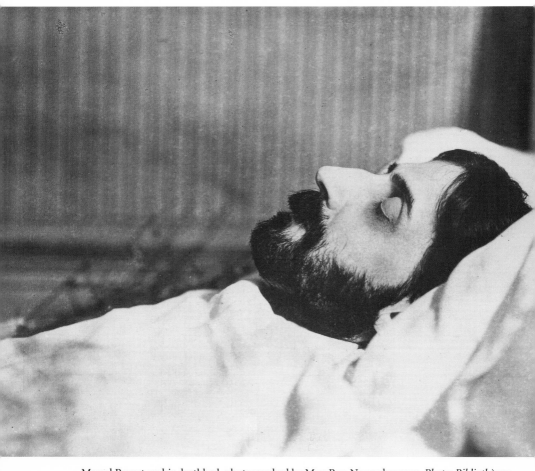

Marcel Proust on his deathbed, photographed by Man Ray, November 1922. *Photo: Bibliothèque nationale de France. © 2000 Man Ray Trust/Artists Rights Society,* NY/ADAGP, *Paris*

21   *Proust's Way* ∾

IN EARLY JANUARY, Marcel wrote Mme Straus that nothing had changed concerning his novel. He wanted to publish it at his own expense, but Louis de Robert had overcome Proust's holiday resolve and convinced him that the idea was "absurd," warning him that such a solution would ruin his reputation as a serious writer. If Proust paid to have his book published, Robert had argued, he and his work would be discredited and he would be considered one of those "idle rich" who publish their "literary elucubrations" out of vanity. Proust was "too great an artist" to abandon hope of finding a publisher who would recognize his worth, treat him as a professional, and pay him royalties.[1] Proust had received Robert's assurance that "he could easily find me a publisher. I'm waiting to see."[2]

Marcel agreed to Louis's plan of submitting the manuscript to Alfred Humblot, general editor at Ollendorff. Humblot had a very high opinion of Robert's writing and had recently approached him about the possibility of publishing his next work. Surely an enthusiastic recommendation by Robert would guarantee an appropriate appraisal of Proust's manuscript. In early January, Marcel wrote Robert that he was sending the "manuscript to M. Humblot with a letter . . . and without offering to pay the costs of publishing since you don't want me to do that either. Since it's you who've done everything, the least I can do is not disobey you."

Yet in the postscript Proust stated his intention to do just that: he would tell Humblot that he "was prepared to subsidize publishing as amply as he considered suitable."[3]

To thank Robert for his efforts and kindness, Proust gave his friend a ring monogrammed with the initials *LR*. Proust was enchanted when Robert accepted the ring and agreed to wear it, but he suggested, because people often misrepresent "friendship between men as soon as it becomes somewhat affectionate," that Louis not say who had given him the ring. "If you want to, you certainly may, naturally it's up to you."[4]

On January 14 Proust went to the *Figaro* with Calmette's New Year's gift, a black moiré cigarette case with a monogram in brilliants that Proust had had made for the editor at Tiffany's. He described the present to Mme Straus: "extremely simple, very pretty, and costs a little less than 400 francs."[5] When Marcel stopped by Calmette's office and placed the wrapped package next to him at his desk, Gaston did not look up or speak, but merely shrugged his shoulders "with an affectionate air."[6] Proust invited Calmette to open the present, but he only gazed at it "in a vague way." The busy editor, preoccupied by the forthcoming presidential elections, only commented: "I really hope Poincaré will be elected."[7] He then walked with Marcel to the door, saying "Perhaps it will be Deschanel." While Calmette was pleasant, he did not say a word about Fasquelle, which convinced Proust that Fasquelle had never promised to publish his novel. Calmette never acknowledged the cigarette case.

While at the *Figaro,* Proust, eager to publicize his novel, met with Francis Chevassu regarding the "prose poems" that he hoped the editor would publish in the literary supplement. Before returning home Proust stopped by Emmanuel Bibesco's apartment and asked him to use his influence with Copeau to publish some excerpts from *Swann's Way* in the *NRF*'s May issue. Chevassu and Copeau both refused Proust's texts.

In their letters, Proust and Louis de Robert compared notes about the life of an invalid. Proust admitted that the long periods of illness, when confined to his bed, had encouraged him "to develop somewhat the mentality of sick, old women," making him distrust those who served him when he entrusted them with letters or errands of a personal nature.[8] Bemoaning his sedentary existence, Marcel told Robert that for a year he had wanted to do only two things: see the exhibitions of the Manzi and Rouart collections, especially the impressionist works, and listen to Beethoven's late quartets. It had been impossible for him to accomplish this. "In fifteen years I believe I was able to go twice to the Louvre. But fortunately, beneficent nature gave me something more valuable than health, illusion. Now, as I write to you, I am convinced that I will be able to go tomorrow to see the Sainte-Anne portal at Notre-Dame Cathedral, my present great desire."[9] Proust was to use details from the statuary at Notre-Dame for his depiction of the church at Balbec.

Proust had written to Mme Straus in mid-January about his daily attempts to leave his apartment early, visit her, and stop at Notre-Dame in front of the Saint-Anne portal, "where for the past eight centuries a human spectacle much more charming than the one we are accustomed to has been visible; but those who pass in front of it never stop or raise their eyes; they 'have eyes but see not.'" His eyes, "perhaps, would look and love; but they don't pass in front of it, they open only in the dark and contemplate only a cork wall."[10] Finally on the last day of January, Proust threw his "fur-lined coat over his nightshirt" and went to stand for two hours in front of the medieval portal.[11] He also went to visit another wonder of medieval Gothic architecture on the Île de la Cité, the Sainte-Chapelle, whose magnificent stained-glass windows partly inspired those in the church of Combray.[12]

By mid-February, Proust, who continued to hope that Fasquelle would publish his collected articles and parodies, wrote to Anna de Noailles, requesting that she lend him her copies of *Les Éblouissements* and "On Reading." He needed these for his proposed volume of collected writings. Proust admitted to Anna that he was some- what discouraged by "everyone's constant refusal to publish anything by me."[13]

When Louis de Robert received Ollendorff's devastating rejection letter, he was so horrified that he asked Humblot to send him a "banal rejection" letter that he could show to the author. Proust expressed his disappointment over Humblot's letter, which he found "very discourteous." He sensed that there was more to the story than Robert allowed, observing, "Here is a man to whom you've spoken of me as only you know how, who has just had 700 pages to consider, 700 pages in which, as you'll see, a great deal of moral experience, thought and pain have been, not diluted but concentrated, and he dismisses it in such terms! It almost makes me wonder whether there isn't another reason. We'll talk about it some day."[14]

Proust kept pressing Robert until he learned more about Ollendorff's report. Ollendorff's reviewer had written, in what became one of the most famous rejec- tion letters ever, "My dear friend, I may be dead from the neck up, but rack my brains as I may, I fail to understand why a man needs thirty pages to describe how he tosses and turns in his bed before falling asleep."[15] Robert was so furious that he threatened to break off relations with Ollendorff and Humblot, but Proust wouldn't permit it: "Allow me to say to you *with the deepest sincerity* that you would cause me real and lasting pain if you altered in any way whatsoever your friendly relations (or your professional relations) with M. Humblot. I shall be entirely frank. I find M. Humblot's letter . . . utterly stupid."[16] But Proust admitted, "Alas, plenty of other readers will be equally severe." Robert scolded Humblot, telling him, "Fortune has knocked at your door and passed you by."[17] Louis promised Proust not to alter his relations with Humblot; "I simply regard him as a fool," he wrote, while predicting that Proust would "triumph in the end and taste the true glory . . . which you deserve as one of the first among us."[18]

As soon as Proust learned of this latest rejection, he decided to follow no one's council but his own regarding the publication of his novel. He wrote immediately to René Blum, who knew Bernard Grasset well, asking him to undertake nego-tiations with Grasset "to publish, at my expense with me paying for the printing and publicity, a major work (let's call it a novel, for it is a sort of novel) which I have finished." Proust outlined, as he had for the other publishers, the work's content and size, saying he was very ill and needed "certainty and peace of mind." The only way he could obtain the immediate and "clear presentation" of his work was by publishing himself. He did not offer Blum or Grasset the opportunity to appraise the manuscript. He wrote that he would like M. Grasset to be involved in the book's success and to that end would be "grateful" if Grasset would take a percentage of the sales. Thus the publisher would have no expenses and might actually "earn a pittance." Even if the book did not sell well initially, Proust thought that it might eventually catch on with the public. But in any event he believed that the work, "far superior to anything I've yet done," would one day "bring honor" to Grasset. Before closing, Proust stressed the need for discretion when telephoning or writing and suggested that Blum and Grasset seal their letters with wax. He insisted that this book was not a collection of articles: "It is on the contrary a carefully composed whole, though so complex in structure that I'm afraid no one will notice and it will seem like a series of digressions."[19]

On Sunday evening, February 23, Proust wrote a letter to Blum to thank him for his trouble. He mentioned the possibility of putting his novel up for the Prix Goncourt, if that would please Grasset. Proust admitted that he was not quite cer-tain what the Prix Goncourt was. He mentioned the Prix Fémina–Vie Heureuse, instituted in 1904 by the *Fémina* and *Vie Heureuse* reviews, but excluded it because of the indecent nature of his work. In the postscript, as an afterthought, the novelist offered this description of the work he wanted to publish: "I don't know whether I told you that this book is a novel. At least it's from the novel form that it departs least. There is a person who narrates and who says 'I'; there are a great many characters; they are 'prepared' in this first volume, in such a way that in the second they will do exactly the opposite of what one would have expected from the first. From the publisher's point of view, unfortunately, the first volume is much less narrative than the second. And from the point of view of composition, it is so complex that it only becomes clear much later when all the 'themes' have begun to coalesce."[20]

Blum, wasting no time, met over the weekend with Grasset and obtained his agreement to publish the book. When Proust woke up late Monday afternoon, Blum's letter with this news was waiting for him. The entire process had taken four days. That evening Proust wrote to Grasset, repeating the offer of a percentage of the sales and asking Grasset to name the figure, "which could increase if the editions multiplied, but leaving me nevertheless the ownership of my work." Proust sought to allay every conceivable hesitation Bernard Grasset might have. The author proposed a publishing schedule of October for volume one and June of the following year for the second. Although Proust was still undecided about divisions and titles, he suggested calling the first volume *Time Lost, Part One,* and the second volume *Time Lost, Part Two,* "since in reality it's a single book. It's as you like. The manuscript you have is Part One. The other part, the one that will appear ten months later, as yet exists only in illegible drafts."[21]

Soon Proust sent another letter to Grasset, saying that his "own financial interest" was less important to him than the "infiltration of my ideas into the greatest possible number of brains susceptible of receiving them." Proust wanted a strategy to earn a wide readership. Grasset went along with Proust's suggestions, although he must have doubted whether such a work would attract many readers. By March 11 Proust and Grasset had settled on a contract, which was signed on March 13.[22] Proust had sent his first payment of 1,750 francs to Grasset when he returned the draft agreement on March 11. All that lay between Proust and publication now was his unusual method of correcting the proofs.

On March 14 Proust related to Blum his recent exchanges with Grasset. During their negotiations Grasset had first asked Proust to price the volumes at ten francs. That way the publisher could give the author four francs per copy, while recovering his expenses. But Proust told Grasset that he did not want his "thoughts to be reserved for people who spend ten francs on a book and are generally stupider than those who buy them for three, so I insist on three fifty." Proust refused to accept more than one franc, fifty centimes as his share of the sales, a gesture that was "noble on my part in that I have all sorts of troubles (please don't tell him this); I hope he will have been touched."[23]

During the winter and spring Proust attended a number of concerts. Always a passionate lover of music, he now concentrated on creating for his fictional composer works that inspired Swann and the Narrator to meditate on the creative imagination. This determination to capture the essence of music gave Proust reason to attend concerts more frequently, providing an enriching supplement to his evenings spent bent over the theatrophone. On February 26 Proust and Lauris attended a concert by the Capet String Quartet at the Salle Pleyel. The program included works that from this time on he would lose no opportunity to hear: two of Beethoven's Late Quartets and the Grosse Fugue.[24]

Proust in Love

Sometime in the spring of 1913, Alfred Agostinelli lost his job as a driver and appealed to Proust for work. Odilon had become Proust's regular driver, but the writer hired Agostinelli as secretary—with some reservations about his capacities in this regard—to finish preparing the typescript of *Swann's Way*. As Proust later explained to Émile Straus, "It was then that I discovered him, and he and his wife became an integral part of my life."[25] Agostinelli, whose refinement and intelligence Proust had noted on earlier occasions, had lost most of his adolescent plumpness and had become something of a daredevil. He had always been fascinated with bicycles and motorcars; now, like many daring young men of his generation, he became passionately interested in the ultimate machine of speed: the airplane.[26] When Agostinelli and Anna, whom the secretary had always claimed was his wife, moved into Proust's apartment, they disrupted to some degree his bizarre but highly organized schedule. But the biggest distraction, far greater than the practical considerations of new lodgers, was to be Proust's emotional involvement with Agostinelli. The writer quickly became infatuated with the young man. Agostinelli, who had been the "artisan of my voyage" in 1907, became, in 1913, the "companion of my captivity."[27]

Anna has been described as ugly and unpleasant. The only known photograph of her shows a rather plain woman with coarse features.[28] Proust, who also found her unattractive and disagreeable, wrote that she was insanely jealous and would have killed Agostinelli had she been aware of his many infidelities. Although he found it difficult to understand how the handsome young Monacan could have fallen in love with such an unappealing woman, this bond confirmed his theory of the subjective nature of love: "Why he fell in love with her cannot be explained, because she is ugly, but he lived only for her."[29] Proust suffered terribly from jealousy over Agostinelli's love for Anna and over his dalliances with other women that were kept hidden from his wife, but he suffered perhaps most of all from the impossible longings he felt for the youthful, athletic man. The full extent of Proust's infatuation was finally exposed by tragedy.

During the time Agostinelli stayed in Proust's employment as his secretary, the writer showered him with money and privileges, despite suffering huge financial losses from his stock market speculations. In letters to friends and publishers, he cautioned them not to mention money matters when writing or phoning. He did not want his servants to know that he was paying to have his novel published—out of pride, perhaps, but also out of prudence.[30] Although Proust was extremely generous to the Agostinellis, he did not want them to know anything about his finances, apparently for fear they might demand even more of him.

For the remainder of the year, in letters to friends, male and female, Marcel made oblique references to the kind of suffering he experienced when in love. The first such letter was sent near the end of March to Mme Straus. He wrote first about how "very, very unwell" he had been and of his ancient dream, to which he still clung, of going to Dr. Widmer's sanatorium. Then, in a likely reference to his feelings for Agostinelli, he told her that he had "a great many other worries too." These troubles "might be a little less painful if I told them to you. And they are sufficiently general, sufficiently human, to interest you perhaps." Marcel did not confide in her, however, turning soon to the safe topic of music and his love of Beethoven. He asked her whether she subscribed to the theatrophone. "They now have the Touche concerts and I can be visited in my bed by the birds and the brook from the *Pastoral Symphony*, which poor Beethoven enjoyed no more directly than I do, since he was completely deaf. He consoled himself by trying to reproduce the song of the birds he could no longer hear. Allowing for the distance between his genius and my lack of talent, I too compose pastoral symphonies in my fashion by portraying what I can no longer see."[31]

On March 27 Proust sent a telegram to Odilon Albaret, who was far away in his native village of Auxillac, in Lozère, a rugged, mountainous region in southern France. Proust wanted to congratulate his driver on an event that proved more important to the novelist than he could ever have imagined. Odilon, thirty-one, received the wire just as he set out to the church to marry a young woman named Céleste Gineste.[32] Odilon soon returned to Paris with his twenty-one-year-old bride, who, never having left her native village, was to have difficulties adapting to a big city so far from home. The couple took a new, small apartment in Levallois-

Péret, on the outskirts of Paris. Near the apartment was a café that stayed open late at night and had a telephone, two necessities for Odilon, who remained on call around the clock, waiting for the summons from Proust.[33]

By early April, Proust had received his first set of proofs from Grasset. He began to correct them, and soon more proofs arrived. On April 12 Proust wrote to Vaudoyer and admitted that the way he was "correcting" the proofs had surprised him: "My corrections up to now (I hope it won't go on) are not corrections. Scarcely one line in twenty of the original text (replaced of course by another) remains. It's crossed out and altered in all the white spaces I can find, and I stick additional bits of paper above and below, to the right and to the left, etc." He knew that this would mean more expense for his publisher and wondered whether he should offer to pay an extra amount. "If so, how much?"[34] In the course of the letter to Vaudoyer, Proust momentarily confused his correspondent's article on Russian Ballet with another on Gautier. He attributed such slips to the "abuse of veronal, aspirin and anti-asthmatic powders."

On Saturday evening Marcel wrote Antoine about the concert he had just attended at the Salle Villiers: "Great emotion this evening. More dead than alive I nonetheless went to a recital hall . . . to hear the Franck Sonata which I love so much." The piece was César Franck's 1886 Sonata in A major for Piano and Violin, performed by the renowned Romanian violinist Georges Enesco and the French pianist Paul Goldschmidt. Proust had never heard Enesco, and he found his playing "wonderful; the mournful twitterings, the plaintive calls of his violin answered the piano as though from a tree, as though from some mysterious arbour. It made a very great impression."[35] Perhaps inspired by the rondeau from Franck's sonata, Proust added a few lines, on galley number 50, to his description of Vinteuil's sonata.[36] Years later, when inscribing an original deluxe edition of *Swann's Way* to a young friend, Jacques de Lacretelle, Proust provided a fairly detailed account of the music that inspired Vinteuil's compositions. He mentioned, as one source of inspiration, Franck's sonata, as played by Enesco, where the "piano and the violin moan like two birds calling each other."[37]

Proust made an effort to strengthen his ties to Mme Marie Scheikévitch. In May he accepted an invitation to dinner, where he amused her guests by making witty comments on a verse line about flowers from Montesquiou's *Hortensias bleus,* in which the poet juxtaposed names of flowers with colors of the same name: "Oh, les lilas lilas! le bleuet bleu! la rose Rose!" The next day Marie sent him a "marvelous bunch of lilacs."[38] Writing to thank her, he promised to detach from the proof pages of his book "(which *no one* but you has seen) a few 'lingering and invisible' lilacs." By the end of the letter, Proust had to admit that he was unable to find his pages about lilacs but said that would send them later. He recalled a vision of Marie at a recent performance by the Ballets Russes where she had been holding red roses close to her white dress. He had been touched by that reminder of how much she had suffered during her marriage and suicide attempt.[39] "I was saying the other day, remembering how your life was once stained with blood, that when I caught sight of you in the distance with that great bouquet of red roses like a wound at your heart, you reminded me of a transpierced Dove." He recalled the day long ago when he had seen such birds on an outing with Reynaldo to the zoo in the Jardin des Plantes. Remembering all the martyrs to love—Reynaldo's explanation for the crimson breasts of the dove—Proust had considered and then abandoned *Transpierced Doves* as a title for his second volume.[40]

Proust encountered Jacques Copeau on May 22 at the Théâtre des Champs-Élysées, where both were attending the première of a new production of *Boris Godunov,* featuring Fyodor Chaliapin. Proust had not shaved for a week and so sat in the stalls wearing his fur coat throughout the performance.[41] He had recently assisted Copeau by making contacts with a number of potential contributors to his new enterprise, the creation of the Théâtre du Vieux-Colombier. After the opera, Proust, who had bought three shares in Copeau's theater, sent him a letter and 750 francs as payment for the first share.

In his fruitless attempts to have the NRF publish his novel or excerpts from it, Proust feared that Copeau had misunderstood the use of memory in his novel. "The memory to which I attach so much importance is not at all what is usually meant by the term. The attitude of a dilettante who is content to delight in the memory of things is the *opposite* of mine." Proust told Copeau that by "reading myself I've discovered after the event some of the constituent elements of my own unconscious." As an example of what he did not mean, he cited a remark that Dostoyevsky made about Raskolnikov, hesitating at the door of the old money-lending woman he is about to kill. Dostoyevsky had written: "the memory of that moment would always remain with him." That memory, Proust explained to Copeau, "is still something extremely contingent and accidental by comparison with 'my' memory, in which all the physical components of the original experience are modified in such a way that from the point of view of the unconscious the memory takes on, *mutatis mutandis,* the same generality, the same force of higher reality, as *the law* of physics, through the variation of circumstances. It is an *act* and not a passive sensation of pleasure."[42] Proust stressed this point because in his novel he intended to reconstruct and interpret past experience, not indulge in tranquil moments of nostalgia.

During the last week in May, Proust and Grasset exchanged letters about progress on the proofs. Earlier in the month Proust had returned the first batch of corrected proofs. Grasset sent an urgent request that the proofs be returned without delay; with so many corrections to make, no time must be lost. Proust had resigned himself "to returning to you these lamentable proofs which fill me with shame." But he had settled on his titles: "The first volume will be called *Du côté de chez Swann*. The second part probably *Le Côté de Guermantes*. The overall title of the two volumes: *À la recherche du temps perdu*."[43] He told Grasset that when all the proofs had been corrected, he would add the dedication to Calmette.[44] He requested that Grasset draw his staff's attention to the "very fragile" nature of his proofs: "I've stuck on bits of paper which could easily tear, and that would cause endless complications. There are galleys which may seem to be half-missing. This is because I've transferred a passage elsewhere." He had abandoned "Intermittences du cœur" in favor of the new general title, but would reserve it as a chapter title for a later volume.[45]

Proust complained to Maurice Duplay about being "broken" by the correction of his proofs, a task that seemed endless because he was "changing everything, the printer can't make any sense out of it, my editor hurries me from day to day, and during this time my health has degraded entirely and I have grown so thin you would not recognize me."[46] As he diminished physically, Proust became alarmed by the length of the first volume and proposed that the dialogue be incorporated into the text without breaks. Grasset reluctantly agreed to this, but Louis de Robert was horrified and thought the best solution was to print "Combray" separately in one volume of roughly normal length.[47] Writing to Grasset, shortly after May 24, Proust said that for the second round of corrections, he would restrict himself to changing a few names. But this wise resolution would not be kept.

Proust admired duelists and so took notice in early June when his publisher fought a duel because he thought that one of his authors had been unfairly attacked. The offender was Henry Postel du Mas, editor of *Gil Blas,* who had written a series of articles unfavorable to Émile Clermont, author of *Laure.* Clermont was in a close contest with Romain Rolland for the Grand Prix awarded by the Académie française. When Rolland won by a narrow vote, Grasset, who felt that the critic's attacks must have influenced the outcome, challenged Mas to a duel. The combat ended when Grasset received a sword cut in the arm.[48] Proust, who thought that such energy and devotion boded well for his novel, wrote Grasset to congratulate him, saying that he did not pity him because he knew from experience "how agreeable such occasions are; a duel is one of my best memories."[49]

Grasset wrote Proust on June 19, telling him that he had glanced at the proofs and noticed that quite a few were still missing from the galleys of the first proofs that the author had corrected. Of the ninety-five galleys that had been sent to Proust, only forty-five had been returned to the publisher.[50] But out of the forty-five returned, thirty-three galleys had been sent back to Proust as second proofs. Grasset felt uncomfortable having two versions of the same text in circulation at the same time and urged Proust to finish correcting the first proofs. Proust asked to be charged for the extra work on the proofs and received a bill from Grasset for the revisions to date that totaled 595 francs.[51]

Proust asked Louis de Robert's advice regarding the myriad solutions to the endless lengthening of his book. After telling Louis that he alone of all his friends would see the entire book before publication, Proust asked him to identify passages in the proofs that seemed too long and could be cut or, perhaps, relegated to notes. He had run the dialogues in, a measure Grasset found very "ugly," but one that Proust claimed was an improvement because his characters' remarks became part of "the flow of the text." Proust, desperate for remedies, later abandoned such extreme solutions to the problem of publishing an unusually long volume. He did not promise to accept Louis's suggestions: "Perhaps I will disobey you because finally I can only obey myself." But he did admit that he had been unable to send the proofs any sooner because he had used them to write a "new book." He then alluded discreetly to his lovesickness over Agostinelli: "I am very ill and what's more I have a lot of sorrow."[52]

By late June, Proust sent Grasset 595 francs and admitted that if *Swann's Way* were published in its present form, it would exceed seven hundred pages, the limit that he and Grasset had set. He saw the necessity of transferring to the "second volume what I thought would be the ending of this one (a good ten galleys). But you yourself are too much of an artist not to realize that an ending is not a simple termination and that I cannot cut the book as easily as a lump of butter. It requires thought. As soon as I've discovered how to end, very shortly . . . I shall return both the first and the second proofs."[53]

Louis de Robert had received from Proust a clean set of second proofs for the first forty-five galleys. Robert read them in amazement as he watched this extraordinary novel expand and take shape. He wrote Proust: "I am still lost in admiration. And I urge you most strongly: make it two volumes of 350 pages each." As for shortening the text, he gave this advice: "Don't cut anything—it would be a crime. Everything must be kept; everything is rare, subtle, profound, true, right, precious, incomparable. But do not pour such a rare liquor into such a big glass." Robert was afraid that most readers would skim a book of seven hundred pages and thus miss "untold beauties, untold original insights, untold observations of astonishing perceptiveness and truth." He had no doubt that "this work will rank you among our foremost writers, and I am deeply delighted." Robert did have one complaint; he hated the title *Swann's Way,* finding it "unbelievably commonplace!"[54]

Soon Louis had another concern. He had apparently learned from Maurice Rostand about the homosexual scenes that occur later in the novel. The anticipation of those, added to Mlle Vinteuil's lesbian love ritual, a scene to which he had always objected, made him fear for the reception of Proust's novel.[55] Proust explained his position of pure objectivity: "I obey a general truth which forbids me to appeal to sympathetic souls any more than to antipathetic ones; the approval of sadists will distress me as a man when my book appears, but it cannot alter the terms in which I probe the truth and which are not determined by my personal whim." He denied a "gift for minute details, for the imperceptible," attributed to him by Louis and others, claiming that he omitted "every detail, every fact, and fasten[ed] on whatever seems to me . . . to reveal some general law." He gave the example of "that taste of tea which I don't recognize at first and in which I rediscover the gardens of Combray. But it's in no sense a minutely observed detail, it's a whole theory of memory and perception." He attempted to explain his title *Swann's Way:* "The point of the title was because of the two ways in the neighbourhood of Combray. You know how people say in the country: 'Are you going round by M. Rostand's?' " It still bothered him that Louis did not like the title, and in the postscript Proust suggested alternative titles.[56]

In subsequent letters Proust continued to defend his title. Louis failed to appreciate how perfectly *Swann's Way* suited the author's needs both thematically —the explorations of bourgeois society *(Swann's Way)* and that of the nobility *(The Guermantes Way)*—while opening windows on French history and contemporary society. The structural function of the two ways (côtés) is vital. As a child the Narrator thinks that the two ways, the walk past Swann's place and the more distant excursions by the Guermantes castle, lie in opposite directions and are distinct geographical unities. In the concluding volume, Gilberte Swann shows him that the two ways are linked geographically and form a circle, just as her marriage to Saint-Loup, a Guermantes, represents the symbolic and biological union of the two ways.

Proust and Robert exchanged further letters regarding homosexuality in the novel. Although Robert's comments revealed him to be somewhat prudish, he was also motivated by a genuine concern that Proust's novel might be shunned because it treated subjects normally considered taboo. Proust tried again to allay Robert's fears about his treatment of sadism and homosexuality: "If, without the slightest mention of pederasty, I portrayed vigorous adolescents, if I portrayed tender fervent friendships without ever suggesting that there might be more to them, I should then have all the pederasts on my side, because I should be offering them what they like to hear! Precisely because I dissect their vice (I use the word vice without any suggestion of blame), I demonstrate their sickness, I say precisely what they most abhor, namely that this dream of masculine beauty is the result of a neurotic defect."[57] Proust's prophecy was accurate; Gide later reproached him for his depiction of homosexuality for precisely these reasons.

On July 26 Proust left suddenly for Cabourg. He described the difficult trip to Reynaldo, to whom he wrote immediately after his 5:00 A.M. arrival: "I'm writing to you after a terribly exhausting journey, the motor-car losing the way, etc., at five in the morning, having just arrived in this hotel to which I've come back for the sixth time and where I'm very comfortable." He told Hahn about having telephoned Mme Jacques Bizet in an effort to find employment for Robert Ulrich, who was "starving to death." He expressed his affection for Reynaldo—"Much love, my dear Guncht"—but said that his letters would be "few and far between as Grasset is clamouring for my proofs, which I haven't begun!"[58] Agostinelli's troubling presence made it difficult for the writer to concentrate on his work.[59]

But Proust had little time to enjoy the Grand-Hôtel's comfort. On August 4, a little over a week after his arrival, while he and Agostinelli were on their way to Houlgate, Proust decided to return immediately to Paris without informing anyone at the hotel. Shortly after his arrival back in the capital, he wrote this account to Charles d'Alton: "It was on the way to Houlgate that suddenly my regret at not being in Paris came back to me so strongly that in order to avoid further hesitations I decided to leave there and then without bag or baggage and without returning to the hotel. I went into a café with Agostinelli and sent a message to Nicolas and Agostinelli sent one to his wife, who joined us after a few hours." Proust prudently asked Alton not to tell anyone that Agostinelli was in his employ as a secretary.[60] A week later, Proust gave a slightly different account to Lauris, saying that when he went to Cabourg, he had left behind "a person whom he rarely saw in Paris and at Cabourg I felt far away and anxious." So he decided to return to Paris, but kept postponing the departure. Then he and "Agostinelli had set off to do some shopping in Houlgate, where he thought I looked so sad that he told me I ought to stop hesitating and catch the Paris train at Trouville without going back to the hotel."[61] Nothing more is known about this bizarre episode, except that it recalled Proust's state of mind when traveling with Bertrand de Fénelon in Holland. Then, miserable and afraid of making Fénelon unhappy by his despondency, he had sent his friend away. Perhaps being constantly in Agostinelli's company in Cabourg reminded him too forcefully of the impossible nature of the love he felt for his secretary. In Paris, Agostinelli would still be in Proust's apartment, but in his presence only when summoned. This situation, which neither man found tolerable, was not to last much longer.

Proust wrote to Nahmias about his sudden return to Paris, where he thought he would stay only a day or two before traveling elsewhere. He now realized that his severe weight loss made another trip too dangerous for his health. In the postscript Proust told Nahmias not to talk about his secretary. "People are so stupid they might see in it (as they did in our friendship) something pederastic. That would make no difference to me, but I would be distressed to place this boy in a bad light." Then, almost as an afterthought, he mentioned that he had dined alone at Larue's, where he had seen a friend of Nahmias's with a blonde whom he found ravishing.[62] Proust's thoughts remained centered to a large degree on his unrequited love for Agostinelli. Though certain that his novel would at last appear, Proust was miserable. Later in August he complained to Charles d'Alton about enduring relentless "mental sorrows, material problems, physical suffering, and literary nuisances."[63] He dared not confide the real reasons for his unhappiness.

Flying Lessons

The year 1913 is known in French aviation history as the Glorious Year. On September 23 Roland Garros became the first aviator to fly across the Mediterranean, and French flyers flew nonstop from Nancy to Cairo. A new speed record of 203 kilometers per hour was set and pilots reached altitudes of six thousand meters. Aerodromes were opened at Buc, near Versailles, and at Issy, drawing crowds of the curious, the idle rich, and brave young men like Agostinelli, who saw a new frontier opening up before them and were eager to fly the new machines.[64] Proust tried to dissuade Agostinelli from taking flying lessons, but his objections were overruled by Anna's determination; she thought that the couple would become fabulously wealthy if her husband could learn to fly an airplane.[65] Proust had warned Agostinelli: "If ever you have the misfortune to have an aeroplane accident, you can tell your wife that she will find me neither a protector nor a friend and will never get a sou from me."[66]

Céleste knew about Agostinelli's passion for sports and his daredevil nature through her husband, Odilon, who had been working with Agostinelli periodically for years.[67] Thanks to Proust's generosity, Agostinelli was able to take flying lessons at Buc, where Roland Garros had an aviation school. Because Agostinelli no longer owned a car, Proust paid Odilon to drive his secretary to and from the airfield.

During the fall, Agostinelli grew restless under Proust's constant surveillance. The sedentary existence of typing a manuscript was hardly the job for a future aviator. He must have spoken at some point of returning home and obtaining his pilot's license at one of the aviation schools that had opened near Monte Carlo. Proust, desperate to keep the young man near him at all costs, did everything possible to make such opportunities available to the young flyer in Paris. He may have hinted at buying Agostinelli a Rolls-Royce if he wanted to resume his profession as a driver, and even an airplane for a career as a pilot.

Toward the end of August, Marcel wrote to Lucien Daudet, saying that he should have contacted Lucien first for his research because he was so knowledgeable: "And doubtless writing to you would have spared me the interminable correspondence I've had with horticulturists, dress-makers, astronomers, genealogists, chemists, etc., which were of no use to me but were perhaps some use to them because I knew a tiny bit more than they did." Proust lamented the "stupid division" of *Swann's Way* and feared that no one would be capable of judging his work until its publication in three volumes, a number he now accepted as necessary. He was not eager for Lucien to read the proofs for *Swann's Way* because he knew that "if one reads a book, one doesn't reread it, and there will be last-minute improvements here and there which I'd like you to be aware of." He then turned to more personal matters, saying that he had been "very ill, very troubled, very unhappy." He would not send another letter: his doctor had ordered him to avoid corresponding because he needed "to regain thirty kilos (!)"[68] Proust could no more stop letter writing than he could reform other aspects of his schedule that undermined his health. The emotional stress that resulted from months of having Agostinelli and Anna in his apartment during this period when he worked so hard on his book had contributed to Proust's phenomenal and alarming weight loss. Nearly every letter he wrote to a close friend that year and next referred to his severe thinness and his unhappiness. Given his lifestyle, regimen, and ailments, it was hardly surprising that he had begun to waste away.

As soon as Lucien read this letter, he begged Proust to send him the proofs as quickly as possible. Two days later they arrived, and Daudet spent that day and part of the night devouring *Swann's Way*. Afterward Lucien had the impression that he had taken a voyage rather than read a book. He wrote immediately to Marcel to tell him that the novel had "dazzled" him.[69] Lucien offered to write an article about *Swann's Way* as soon as it appeared. Marcel, who always melted whenever anyone showed him kindness, was unable to resist the combination of gentillesse and enthusiastic appreciation of his novel.

Marcel began writing long letters of gratitude to Lucien, revealing many details about the remainder of the *Search*, including its plot.[70] In one letter he asked, "My dear Lucien, how shall I ever be able to thank you?" He then inquired whether he could send the new conclusion of *Swann's Way*, for which he had taken some pages from later in the book. He was eager for Lucien to tell him whether these pages made a better ending.[71] The lines Proust had chosen describe a scene where the Narrator, much older and in a nostalgic mood, returns to the Bois de Boulogne, where he used to wait to see Mme Swann pass by. But now everything has changed; not only does she no longer come there, but the horse-drawn carriages have been replaced by noisy automobiles, and the women wear garments he finds much less appealing than the splendid outfits Mme Swann wore. This new state of things leads the Narrator to conclude: "The places we have known do not belong only to the world of space on which we map them for our own convenience. They were only a thin slice, held between the contiguous impressions that composed our life at that time; the memory of a particular image is but regret for a particular moment; and house, roads, avenues are as fugitive, alas, as the years."[72]

In another September letter, Proust showed signs of author's jitters; he worried that Lucien and others could not possibly comprehend the scope of his work from reading *Swann's Way*: "Not only is the work impossible to grasp from this first volume alone, which acquires its full meaning through the others, but the proofs are uncorrected and teeming with misprints, and there are some very important little incidents missing especially in the second part which tighten the knots of jealousy around poor Swann. And even when it's ready to appear, it will be like those themes in an overture which one doesn't recognize as leitmotifs when one has only heard them in isolation at a concert, not to mention all the things that will find their place after the event (thus the lady in pink was Odette, etc.)."[73]

Louis de Robert again urged Proust to delete the lesbian profanation ritual scene because it would delight pederasts and sadists. Using scientific analogy, Proust defended himself by saying that he served a higher cause. It would be unethical to falsify the results of experiments: "I cannot, in the interest of a friendship which is most precious to me, or to displease an audience which I find antipathetic, modify the results of psychological experiments which I am bound to communicate with the probity of a scientist."[74] One can hear Dr. Proust's voice in Marcel's insistence on finding the truth by using rigorous scientific methods.

Sometime during the fall, Proust finally purchased an Aeolian automatic piano player, which was adapted to the grand piano he kept in his room. It seems likely that he did so in part to amuse Agostinelli, who must have pumped the instrument for Proust, as Albertine was later to do for the Narrator. Much to the exasperation of the piano roll suppliers, Proust began to ask for pieces that had never been requested before, such as the piano transcription of Beethoven's late quartets. In early January he complained to Mme Straus about the lack of such rolls: "My consolation is music, when I'm not too sad to listen to it: I've completed the theatrophone with a pianola. Unfortunately they happen not to have the pieces I want to play. Beethoven's sublime XIVth quartet doesn't appear among the rolls."[75]

One September day when Odilon and Céleste were out for a stroll, Odilon decided that they should stop by boulevard Haussmann and inform Nicolas of their return to Paris and Odilon's eagerness to resume work. Nicolas, who admitted them through the servants' entrance into the kitchen, "insisted on announcing that Odilon was there." Céleste recalled the first meeting: "M. Proust . . . was wearing only a jacket and trousers and a white shirt. But I was impressed. I can still see that great gentleman enter the room. He looked very young—slender but not thin, with beautiful skin and extremely white teeth, and that naturally formed curl on his forehead, which he always would have." After Odilon greeted him, Proust noticed Céleste and "held out his hand and said, 'Madame, may I introduce Marcel Proust, in disarray, uncombed, and beardless.'" After the brief encounter, Céleste asked Odilon: "Why did he say 'beardless'?" Odilon replied that Proust had worn, until quite recently, "a magnificent black beard."[76]

On October 10 Louis Brun informed Proust that he had received all proofs from the third set and was sending them on to the printer's with "all your instructions for the new series of proofs that will be sent to you during the week." Brun, eager to speed up the process, pointed out that the "first 257 pages have very few changes" and could be sent to the printer's with the author's "bon à tirer" (permission to print). He asked Proust to indicate how many of those pages could safely be dispatched for final composition.[77] A week later, Grasset asked whether Proust would like to have any deluxe copies printed.[78] Marcel, uncharacteristically conservative, decided to have five copies printed on Japan Imperial paper and twelve on rice paper. Still concerned about the clearest way to announce a work in several volumes, Proust consulted André Beaunier, who suggested that he call it a trilogy. Proust adopted this solution. The announcement carried the general title as well as *Swann's Way,* and announced the titles of the remaining volumes, *The Guermantes Way* and *Time Regained.*

Proust, who had continued to lose money on the Bourse, found himself obliged on October 12 to sell all the Royal Dutch shares held for him by the Warburg Bank in order to pay his rent. Because he remained so unhappy, Proust thought of fleeing Paris and began to inquire about property to rent in Italy. He had not been as unstable and miserable since the period following his mother's death.

Grasset told Proust that he would like to submit *Swann's Way* to the selection committees of the two major literary prizes awarded in December, the Fémina and the Goncourt. Proust complained to Barrès that just at this time, when he was nearly incapable of thinking about the publication of his book, he now must obtain the addresses of jury members and contact them. Was it even proper, he wondered, to submit a book like his, with its unchaste pages, to a committee such as that of the Fémina, presided over by a woman, Mme de Pierrebourg?[79] He was to have the same reservations about sending *Swann's Way* to his younger female friends.

Grasset wrote on October 25, saying that Proust had made so many changes that a new set of proofs was needed, the fourth. He also had some good news. Because his original estimate had assumed a volume of 800 pages—a number now reduced to roughly 530—Grasset was increasing the print run from 1,250 to 1,750. Proust would thus have 250 extra copies to use for the press or give to acquaintances, and 1,500 copies to sell.[80] A few days later, Grasset apologized profusely for presenting Proust with a bill for the four sets of proofs totaling 1,066 francs, of which 595 francs had already been paid. Grasset explained what Proust already knew, that normally such costs are negligible and easily covered by the publisher. Seldom if ever had there been so many galleys and proofs and complicated revisions. By the time Proust had completed his work on volume one, Grasset was to send him a fifth set of proofs.[81] Grasset proposed to publish *Swann's Way* around November 15 if he and Proust could arrange for publicity and reviews, and be certain of obtaining adequate shelf space in bookstores, soon to be crammed with gift books for the holidays.

On October 29 or 30 Grasset finally had a brief interview with the man who was to be his most famous author. Eager to launch the publicity campaign, Grasset and Proust looked over the list of potential reviewers. Ideally, *Swann's Way* should be reviewed by André Beaunier in the *Figaro* and Paul Souday in the *Journal des débats.*[82] Beaunier disappointed them by deciding to wait until the entire novel appeared before giving his opinion.[83] Souday wrote a review that infuriated Grasset and Proust.

In letters to Blum and Robert de Flers written in early November, Proust stressed the great importance he attached to this book, into which he had put "the best of myself, my thought, my very life."[84] He told Blum that everything he had written previously amounted to nothing. This new book was an "extremely real work but propped up, as it were, to illustrate involuntary memory." Proust remarked that although Bergson did not make this distinction, in his view it was the only valid one; he then explained the role involuntary memory played in his novel. He also wanted Blum to understand—a point he would make to other reviewers and readers—that this book was "real, passionate," and "very different from what you know of me, and, I think, infinitely less feeble, no longer deserving the epithet 'delicate' or 'sensitive' but living and true." Such adjectives had hounded him since the publication of *Pleasures and Days,* and, knowing what creatures of habit critics can be, he wanted to insulate his new book from those inappropriate and deadly words. Proust made a similar request to Robert de Flers when he announced the book in the *Figaro.*

On November 8 Grasset asked Proust to send advance copies to the prize committees of Fémina and Goncourt. Among his friends who received autographed copies were Georges de Lauris, Bertrand de Fénelon, posted at the French embassy in Cuba, and Mme de Pierrebourg, with whom he discussed by letter the Fémina, as well as the Goncourt, observing that it was probably already too late to apply. Then he expressed his great fear that no one would read his book because it was so long and dense.[85]

Proust may not have been entirely pleased at Blum's preview in the *Gil Blas* on November 9, just five days before publication. Blum described *Swann's Way* as "the first in a series . . . combining an elegant, ironic study of certain aspects of society and an evocation of tender landscapes and childhood memories."[86] The juxtaposition of "tender landscapes and childhood memories" bothered Proust. Although the relationship between the Narrator and his mother was certainly loving, the Combray landscape contains a number of elements that are far from tender—such as the abandoned and foreboding dungeon of Roussainville, to which, as the Narrator later learns, girls and boys of the village sneak away and engage in youthful sexual experiments. When the child Narrator sees Gilberte for the first time across the hedge, standing in her father's garden, she makes an obscene gesture, which he fails to interpret correctly. The Combray landscape also embraces

Montjouvain, where the young Narrator unintentionally spies on the lesbian lovers who profane images of M. Vinteuil.

Before writing the blurb Blum had visited Proust and listened to him read the most famous passage from the "Combray" section, the madeleine scene. Although incorporated within the pages called "Combray," the scene is not anchored in any definite narrative sequence. It begins, after a break, with a sentence that treats the paucity of voluntary memory: "And so it was that, for a long time afterwards, when I lay awake at night and revived old memories of Combray, I saw no more of it than this sort of luminous panel."[87] When Proust's voice grew tired, he asked Blum to read the conclusion of the madeleine scene: "When from a long-distant past nothing subsists, after the people are dead, after the things are broken and scattered, taste and smell alone, more fragile but more enduring, more immaterial, more persistent, more faithful, remain poised a long time, like souls, remembering, waiting, hoping, amid the ruins of all the rest; and bear unflinchingly, in the tiny and almost impalpable drop of their essence, the vast structure of recollection."[88]

Swann's Way

On November 8 Proust, who did not rise from his bed, received Élie-Joseph Bois, a reporter from the *Temps,* and spoke to him for an hour and a half about "a thousand things."[89] The newspaper's editor Adrien Hébrard, who was Marie Scheikévitch's lover, had arranged for the interview as a favor to her.[90] The primary topic of conversation was, of course, *Swann's Way.* The author explained his views on time, characters, and style. Throughout the interview, Proust quoted passages from *Swann's Way* and remaining volumes, perhaps hoping to thwart criticisms about the lack of a plot by showing some of the lessons the Narrator learns by the novel's end.[91]

In the interview Bois raised readers' expectations about the novel by saying that the copy passed around to "privileged readers" had provoked great enthusiasm.[92] The interviewer wondered whether the book was "a masterpiece, as some had already called it." He also predicted that *Swann's Way* would "disconcert many readers." Though "a book of true originality and profundity to the point of strangeness, claiming the reader's full attention and even seizing it forcibly," Proust's novel lacked a plot in the usual sense "of what we rely on in most novels to carry us along in some state of expectation through a series of adventures to the necessary resolution." Instead, *Swann's Way* was a "novel of analysis," "so deep" that "at times you want to cry out, 'Enough!' as to a surgeon who spares no detail in describing an operation. Yet you never say it. You keep on turning the pages feverishly in order to see further into the souls of these creatures. What you see is a certain Swann in love with Odette de Crécy, and how his love changes into an anxious, suspicious, unhealthy passion tormented by the most atrocious jealousy." Bois told his readers that with Proust "we aren't kept on the outside of things; . . . we are thrust into the mind and heart and body of that man." The interviewer also mentioned similar experiences with a "child's love for his mother, and with a boy's puppy love for one of his playmates. . . . M. Marcel Proust is the author of the disturbing book."

Bois provided a brief summary of Proust's previous work, reprising the hot-house image from France's preface to *Pleasures and Days* to illustrate that the writer had matured: "Marcel Proust, intent upon himself, has drawn out of his own suffering a creative energy demonstrated in his novel." The interviewer described the novelist "lying down in a bedroom whose shutters are almost permanently closed. Electric light accentuates the dull color of his face, but two fine eyes burning with life and fever gleam below the hair that falls over his forehead." Although "still the slave of his illness . . . that person disappears when the writer, invited to comment on his work, comes to life and begins to talk."

Proust wanted potential readers to know that his attempts to bring out all his volumes together had failed because publishers were reluctant to issue "several volumes at a time." Proust explained his notion of the importance of time in his work: "It is the invisible substance of time that I have tried to isolate, and it meant that the experiment had to last over a long period." He gave an overview of his work that showed the union of characters belonging to different social worlds, his presentation of people seen in multiple perspectives, and his concept of multiple selves. "From this point of view," he remarked, "my book might be seen as an attempt at a series of 'novels of the unconscious.' I would not be ashamed to say 'Bergsonian novels' if I believed it . . . but the term would be inaccurate, for my work is based on the distinction between involuntary and voluntary memory, a distinction which not only does not appear in M. Bergson's philosophy, but is even contradicted by it." Proust used the madeleine scene as an example of the extraordinary richness of involuntary memory experiences, indicative of marvelous resources that lie within.

Proust provided examples of the aesthetic lessons the Narrator learns during his long quest to become a creative person. Bois ended with another view of the "ailing author" in his shuttered room, "where the sun never enters." Although the invalid might complain, the "writer has reason to be proud."

A week later Proust granted a second interview, also from his bed, to André Lévy, with whom he talked for an hour.[93] This one appeared in the *Miroir* on December 21. Lévy, who wrote under the pseudonym André Arnyvelde, like Bois noted the pallor of the writer's face. He also mentioned for the first time in print the cork-lined room that was to become legendary. Exaggerating Proust's reclusiveness, Arnyvelde wrote that the writer had retired from the world many years ago to a "bedroom eternally closed to fresh air and light and completely covered with cork." Proust was quoted as saying that his reclusion had benefited his work: "Shadow and silence and solitude . . . have obliged me to re-create within myself all the lights and music and thrills of nature and society."[94]

Arnyvelde, who seemed interested in Proust's working arrangements, described the large bedside table: "Loaded with books, papers, letters, and also little boxes of medicine. A little electric lamp, whose light is filtered by a green shade, sits on the table. At the base of this lamp, there are sheets of paper, pen, inkwell." The array of items may have been ordinary, but not the author's practice of writing at night, and always in bed. The interviewer was struck by Proust's "big invalid's eyes that shine beneath the thick brown hair that falls untidily on the pale forehead."

Proust again outlined his novel and what he had hoped to achieve in writing it. He used Vinteuil as the example of his method of characterization; this apparently dull and banal bourgeois is discovered to be a musical genius. He also made the distinction, first delineated in the essay attacking Sainte-Beuve, between the social self and the creative self. Both interviews stressed the key Proustian point that we must delve deep within ourselves to discover our richest resources.

On November 12, two days before publication, Proust encouraged Calmette to arrange for the novel to be mentioned in the *Figaro*. Back in March the newspaper had published excerpts from *Swann's Way* and *The Guermantes Way* that Proust had edited to create a selection called "Vacances de Pâques" (Easter vacation). But with publication close at hand, Proust told Calmette that it was somewhat "sad to see that the *Figaro* is the *only* newspaper" among those in which literature occupied something of a place that had not announced his novel. Should Calmette insert something, he begged him to avoid the epithets *fine* and *delicate* and any mention of *Pleasures and Days*.[95]

Friday, November 14, was marked by two major events in Proust's life, although the importance of the second was not apparent. The first, of course, was the publication of volume one of his novel. The second event, of which Proust took little notice, was Céleste Albaret's assistance in distributing the copies of *Swann's Way*. Proust's brother Robert had performed gynecological surgery on Céline

Cottin that day. The writer asked Céleste, who had come as a temporary replacement for Céline, to go with her husband in his taxi and deliver the inscribed copies of *Swann's Way* to his friends. Céleste, who had been in Paris for only a few months when she met Proust for the first time, was still afraid of big-city life. She missed her family, especially her mother, and was happy to have something with which to distract herself. From then on Céleste came to 102, boulevard Haussmann to work from nine to five while Proust slept.[96] Nicolas Cottin still waited on Proust personally during hours that matched more closely his employer's nocturnal schedule.

Bernard Grasset had always been professional and courteous in his relations with Proust, but for him the publication of this novel was a business deal. He had tried to read the volume and had found it impenetrable. Grasset had performed his duties well in preparing for publication of *Swann's Way,* but his expectations for sales must have been low. He had told Charles de Richter, a boating friend to whom he gave an advance copy: "It's unreadable; the author paid the publishing costs."[97]

In the week following publication, Proust told Louis de Robert that Grasset had shown himself to be "intelligent, active and charming." But Proust complained about an announcement for bookstores that Grasset had printed without consulting him, "which could not be more objectionable from my point of view." Proust, who had received a copy of the notice from Argus, a clipping service to which he now subscribed, asked Grasset to withdraw this notice, though he feared it was too late: "After a long silence due to his voluntary retirement from life, Marcel Proust, whose debut as a writer elicited unanimous admiration, gives us, under the title, *À la recherche du temps perdu,* a trilogy of which the first volume, *Swann's Way,* is a masterly introduction." Proust considered "voluntary retirement" untrue and objected to the reference to his "debut," which might remind the public of *Pleasures and Days.*[98]

Proust's dedication to the man who had first opened the pages of the *Figaro* to him read: "To M. Gaston Calmette, as a token of profound and affectionate gratitude." Gaston, who had appeared indifferent to the splendid cigarette case, never bothered to acknowledge the dedication of *Swann's Way.*[99] Calmette was engaged in a nasty political press campaign that was to have tragic results. In Mme Straus's copy Proust wrote, "To Mme Straus, the only one of the beautiful things I already loved at the age where this book begins, for whom my admiration has not changed, no more than her beauty, no more than her perpetually rejuvenated charm."[100] He addressed Robert's copy "To my little brother, in memory of Time lost, regained for an instant each time we are together. Marcel."[101] To Lucien he explained why his "dear little one" was "absent from this book: you are too much a part of my heart for me to depict you objectively, you will never be a 'character,' you are the best part of the author."[102] The dedication to Reynaldo is unknown, but certainly it could have expressed the same sentiment, for no one was closer, nor ever would be, to Marcel. Yet in one sense both Reynaldo and Lucien were very much present in the book. Proust had suffered with each of them the tormenting, debilitating jealousy that nearly destroys Swann during his obsession with Odette.

On the day the novel appeared, Léon Daudet, a key figure in any deliberations of the Prix Goncourt committee, wrote his friend Marcel to explain that a majority of the committee objected to voting for an author older than thirty-five. Proust was forty-two. In stating this objection, the members of the Académie Goncourt were following what they believed to be their duty. In his will establishing the prize, Edmond de Goncourt had stated his "supreme wish" that the "prize be awarded to young writers, to original talent, to new and bold endeavors of thought and form."[103] Proust clearly met all the requirements except youth.

Letters written to Robert de Flers, Jean-Louis Vaudoyer, and Anna de Noailles around the time of publication show Proust still profoundly unhappy and making plans to leave Paris and even France. He had recently asked Vaudoyer by mail whether he knew of a "quiet, isolated house in Italy, no matter where, I should like to go away." He then inquired about renting one of the most splendid Renaissance palaces in Italy: "You don't happen to know if that Farnese palace (the Cardinal's), at a place which I think is called Caprarola, is to let? Alas, at the moment when my book is appearing, I'm thinking of something utterly different."[104] Proust had apparently read a recent article in the Revue de Paris saying that the Palazzo Farnese in the hill village of Caprarola, near Viterbo, had been restored and rented to a rich American. Such extravagance seems foolish, given Proust's precarious financial condition, but he was completely demoralized. He wrote Flers that he did not even have the energy and will to recopy the last two volumes of his novel, which were "completely finished." He confided that he had rented a property somewhere outside of Paris, but could not decide to leave.[105] Thanking Anna de Noailles "infinitely for having written him" about his novel, he told her that his book "enjoyed no success." Even if it were to succeed, he would take no joy from it because he was "too sad at present."[106] Proust's distraction resulted from his unhappiness over his relationship with Agostinelli.

Proust had expressed his affection to the young man through constant generosity and favors. But he wanted the impossible—a reciprocated love and devotion. He felt Agostinelli pulling away from him, resentful of his constant and needy presence. Proust knew that the situation was hopeless, but his marvelous lucidity and intelligence remained powerless to unshackle the chains of desire and jealousy that bound him to his secretary. He had depicted Swann's obsessive love for Odette as a malady and then had again caught the disease himself. He believed, according to the image he used for Swann, that the source of the pain within him was "inoperable."

Proust had taken the trouble to send copies of his novel to the group of men who had shunned him, but whom he still wanted to impress more than any other because they were writers. The day after *Swann's Way* was published, he informed Jacques Copeau that he had sent copies for him, Gallimard, and Gide, as well as for M. Paul Claudel, the poet and playwright, whom he "knew only slightly but admired profoundly."[107] While he had Copeau's attention, Proust deplored an indiscretion of Gide's.[108] Word had reached Proust that Gide had gossiped about a matter relating to Copeau's rejection of his excerpts for the *NRF*, a matter Proust and Copeau had agreed to keep confidential. He told Copeau that if Gide knew how many times Proust had tried to refute, for Gide's sake, stories about Turkish baths, Arab boys, and ship's captains on the Calais-Dover run, perhaps Gide would have been more circumspect in tattling about him.[109] Not surprisingly, Proust was well informed about Gide's reputation as a homosexual.

On November 21 Reynaldo wrote to Mme Duglé, Charles Gounod's niece, to express an opinion and make a prediction: "Proust's book is not a masterpiece if by masterpiece one means a *perfect* thing with an *irreproachable design*. But it is without a doubt (and here my friendship plays no part) *the finest book* to appear since *l'Éducation sentimentale*. From *the first line* a great genius reveals itself and since this opinion one day will be universal, we must get used to it at once. It's always difficult to get it into your head that someone whom you meet in society is a genius. And yet Stendhal, Chateaubriand, and Vigny went out in society a great deal."[110] Reynaldo, who had not at first appreciated his friend's remarkable intelligence, now understood Proust's genius and the transformation that had taken place in him through application of his gifts to hard work and to his craft.

The Fugitive

During the fall the relationship between Proust and Agostinelli reached a breaking point. On December 1 Agostinelli and Anna fled Proust's apartment for Monte Carlo, where the secretary's father lived.[111] Distressed and angry, Proust appealed immediately to Albert Nahmias for help. Nahmias received a letter from Proust asking a "strange question." Had Nahmias ever used private detectives to have anyone followed, and if so, could he give Proust their names and addresses? Stressing the urgency of the situation, Proust asked Nahmias to call him—not to talk about the matter openly on the telephone, of course, but perhaps Proust could ask Nahmias "cryptically about an address" or have him visit at once.[112]

Proust, mad with impatience and jealousy, began living scenes from a melodrama. He apparently did employ a private detective to keep informed of the whereabouts of Agostinelli and his father. Soon the desperate writer dispatched Nahmias to Monte Carlo with the purpose of bribing Agostinelli's father into persuading his son to return to Paris. Proust knew that any direct appeal and offers to Agostinelli would meet with categorical refusals. Nor would Agostinelli agree to return if he knew that Proust had paid his father. Nahmias had to keep the negotiations secret.

For a period of five days Proust and his emissary exchanged long, cryptic telegrams under assumed names and using cover stories: one maintained the fiction that Nahmias was there on a mission regarding his own father; another involved a major, top secret stock market speculation. On Wednesday, December 3, at 9:46 P.M., Proust telegraphed Nahmias, under the young man's real name, at the Hôtel Royal in Nice. He gave Nahmias the Monte Carlo address of Agostinelli's father, Eugène, who ran a hotel at 19, rue des Moneghetti. Proust also knew that Eugène was to leave the following morning for Marseilles. Nahmias's instructions were to offer a hefty monthly payment to Eugène if he could persuade Agostinelli to return immediately to Paris, without being told why, and to remain there until April. Above all, Nahmias must not offer money directly to Agostinelli (not named in Proust's wire) because that would guarantee his refusal. And Nahmias must forcefully deny any suggestions on Agostinelli's part that any incentives had been offered to his father.[113] Proust signed the telegram Max Werth.

On December 5 Proust complained in a telegram about the extremely poor telephone connections and urged Nahmias instead to wire quickly and more often. In another telegram of 473 words, Proust expressed his concern about a wire he had sent to Nahmias that had remained unclaimed at the telegraph office. If Nahmias could not collect it, Proust, who always preferred appealing to the highest authorities, would have Prince Louis of Monaco retrieve it. On Saturday afternoon Proust sent a telegram suggesting that Nahmias could sweeten the offer. By Sunday, however, it was clear that the mission had failed and that Agostinelli would remain free. Proust instructed Nahmias to return to Paris and come see him immediately. After closing with love and gratitude, the sender did not sign the wire.

In the *Search* the Narrator becomes infatuated with the girl Albertine. Although such a character had been anticipated from the early stages of the novel, her name appears for the first time in drafts written in 1913. Proust began to adapt elements of his relationship with Agostinelli for Albertine. When Albertine flees the Narrator's apartment, where he had attempted to keep her in loose confinement, the distraught lover sends Saint-Loup to Touraine to convince the girl's guardians that she must return to Paris. Through Saint-Loup, the Narrator offers Albertine's aunt, Mme Bontemps, thirty thousand francs for her husband's political campaign if she can persuade Albertine to return.[114] Saint-Loup's mission also fails. Proust tried again to lure Agostinelli back to Paris in 1914.

In the weeks that followed publication of *Swann's Way,* a number of reviews appeared by friends who were writers. Dreyfus, writing in the *Figaro* as the *Masque de Fer,* characterized the book as a "strong and beautiful work."[115] Cocteau, in *Excelsior* on November 23, called the book a masterpiece, writing that it "resembles nothing I know and reminds me of everything I admire."[116] Cocteau's piece included a picture of Proust in the form of a bust on a pedestal.[117] Lucien, in a long front-page article in the *Figaro* on November 27, praised Proust's novel in terms that still hold. Among his many laudatory remarks, one singles out Proust's profound analytical ability: "Never, I believe, has the analysis of everything that constitutes our existence been carried so far." He called his friend a genius and his book a masterpiece.[118]

On December 8 Proust wrote Beaunier that he had written the remainder of his novel but that everything would have to be looked at again. He had just received a letter from the poet Francis Jammes, who praised *Swann's Way* in terms that would delight any author. But Proust was still depressed. "At any other time," he told Beaunier, "a letter like the one I just received from Jammes in which he says I am the equal of Shakespeare and Balzac (!!) would have made me so happy." His misery did prevent him, he maintained, from being too saddened by articles like that of Chevassu, who accused him of extraordinary carelessness in composition and structure. But in fact such articles bothered Proust a great deal. Before ending the letter to Beaunier, he used the example of his character Vinteuil, prudish and dull but later discovered to be a musical genius: "Isn't that composition?"

As though to counter the words of praise by Robert Dreyfus and Lucien Daudet, the editor of the *Figaro*'s literary supplement, Francis Chevassu, had written an unfavorable account of *Swann's Way* in the December 8 issue. While acknowledging the "highly original" nature of the novel, he criticized it for lacking a plot and a distinct genre; the work resembled an autobiography with no structure.

He ended by warning readers: "You must read M. Marcel Proust's book slowly because it is dense."[119]

After *Swann's Way* had been on sale three weeks, Grasset, pleased overall with the reviews and with the sales, proposed a contract for translations and announced another printing, for which he offered to pay. He suggested a new contract giving Proust the standard 10 percent royalties. Proust made a counterproposal, stalling for time in order to consult Vaudoyer. Above all, Proust wanted to retain the ownership of his work and was uncertain about how to stipulate this in any future contract negotiation.[120]

On December 9 Grasset phoned Nicolas Cottin, "as though war had been declared," to report that Paul Souday, an influential literary critic, had written a "detestable" review in the *Temps*.[121] Souday had sarcastically reproached the author for the banality of his "childhood memoirs." Instead of compelling events, "the matter of the story" comprised vacations and games in the park.[122] Conceding that the contents of a book matter less than the writer's talent, Souday claimed to quote Horace, who had severely criticized cases in which *materiam superabat opus*—the art surpassed the matter. Souday applied this reproach to the first 520 pages of *Swann's Way* and wondered "how many libraries" the author would fill "if he decided to tell his life's story?" Souday complained about the dense, obscure nature of so many pages filled with long sentences, and about the many typos. He had a helpful suggestion for publishers: they should hire some old academic, knowledgeable about grammar and syntax, to proofread copy. The reviewer admitted that the book was a "great original work" that displayed "a lot of talent," but he deplored the lack of order and unity. Souday condemned what he considered the unmeasured, chaotic nature of *Swann,* while acknowledging that the novel did "contain precious elements out of which the author could have made an exquisite little book." The reviewer had mixed feelings about the section called "Swann in Love": "It was not positively boring, but somewhat banal, despite a certain abuse of crudities." Later, when Proust became famous, Souday claimed to have discovered him.[123]

Rather than reply with a letter to the editor, Proust wrote directly to Souday, as he did to nearly every critic he felt had misjudged his work. Addressing the issue of grammatical errors and misprints, Proust admitted that they were too numerous, but fairly obvious. "My book may well reveal no talent; but it presupposes at least, or implies, sufficient culture to make it highly improbable that I should commit such crude mistakes as those you enumerate." Proust pointed out a grammatical error in Souday's article and observed that it did not make him conclude "M. Souday doesn't know that the word *sens* is masculine." Then he made a suggestion for the work schedule of Souday's "old academic": he could be used to check the sources of Souday's Latin quotations. The hypothetical professor might point out that "it was not Horace who spoke of a work in which *materiam superabat opus,* but Ovid, and that the latter poet said it not critically but by way of praise."[124]

As a result of Souday's review, Proust soon received editorial assistance from an unexpected source in the person of Gabriel Astruc, a musical and theatrical entrepreneur who had organized the Ballets Russes' first season in 1909 and recently had founded the Théâtre des Champs-Élysées.[125] After reading Souday's review, Astruc bought a copy of *Swann's Way.* As he read, Astruc found himself unintentionally reverting to old habits, formed in his youth when he had been a proofreader at Ollendorff's. As he underlined the typos and other slips, Astruc, totally captivated by the book, made marginal notes for himself, never dreaming that Proust would read them. When finished he had found nearly a thousand misprints. Reynaldo, who knew Astruc well, told Marcel about Astruc's copy. A new printing of *Swann's Way* was imminent, and Proust wrote and asked to borrow Astruc's copy. Astruc agreed, telling Proust that *Swann's Way* had changed his life and that he now recommended it to all his friends. He felt somewhat sheepish about some of the words he had marked, calling himself overzealous in some of his corrections. He continued with a comparison that can only have delighted Proust: "In a book like *Swann,* the author is always right, just as Debussy is the master of his own harmonies, dissonances, and boldness."[126]

Proust thanked Astruc: "What a delight it is for me to leaf through this copy, and how grateful I feel!" Proust's gratitude was such that he even agreed to help Astruc write his memoirs, if his assistance was kept confidential.[127] The author had found the marginal comments penetrating, like the one next to the descriptions of the water lilies at Combray: "Claude Monet is an inspired guess; I did indeed have him in mind."[128] Proust told Astruc that he had seen Monet's *Water Lilies* years ago in an exhibition. Astruc had also recognized elements of Charles Haas in Swann. Proust denied having portrayed anyone from life, with the exception of a few monocles, because he was "too lazy" to write anything that merely "duplicated reality!" Haas, he allowed, was "in fact the only person, not that I wanted to portray (whom I moreover endowed with a different character), but who was the departure point for my *Swann.*"[129]

Swann's Way had also begun to attract attention abroad, although a translation was many years away. The drama critic of the *Times,* Arthur Bingham Walkley, wrote a long anonymous piece in the December 13 issue of the *Times Literary Supplement.* Walkley found similarities between *Swann's Way* and Henry James's *A*

Small Boy and *What Maisie Knew.* Walkley told his readers that Bergson's influence was obvious. This was a "fascinating book," one whose "weaknesses and strengths accorded admirably with the spirit of our times."[130] Early in 1914 James had lunch with Walkley and Henry Bernstein, who spoke to him about a new writer named Marcel Proust. Edith Wharton later sent James a copy of *Swann's Way*, but it is not certain whether James ever read it.[131]

In Italy on December 10, the writer and critic Renato Manganelli, using the pseudonym Lucio d'Ambra, advised his readers in the *Rassegna contemporanea* to "remember this name and remember this title," predicting that in fifty years their descendants would place Proust and *Swann's Way* in the same category as Stendhal and his novels *Le Rouge et le noir* (The red and the black) and *La Chartreuse de Parme*, generally considered to be among the greatest in the genre. Manganelli also quoted from Daudet's review in the *Figaro*.[132] Proust's novel was rapidly acquiring many foreign admirers.

On December 26, *Comœdia* published Maurice Rostand's highly laudatory review. Agreeing with Cocteau and Daudet that the book was a masterpiece, Rostand said that it was "a soul in the guise of a book." He placed Proust in the company of such great writers as Pascal, Shelley, Goethe, Dostoyevsky, and Shakespeare, saying that like each of them, "Marcel Proust is a universe unto himself."[133]

Between Christmas and New Year's Proust wrote Dreyfus to thank him belatedly for his note in the *Figaro*. He mentioned that one of Dreyfus's colleagues at the newspaper, the essayist and editor Raymond Recouly, had sent him "an amiable and unjust letter."[134] Proust was exasperated that his vivid renderings of impressions, emotions, and perception had been likened to the tedious jottings of a superficial observer. " 'You note everything!' " Recouly had complained. Proust countered: "But in fact I don't note anything. He's the one who notes. Not once does a character of mine close a window, or wash his hands, or put on an overcoat, or say 'How do you do.' Indeed if there were anything new in the book it would be that, but not at all deliberately; I'm simply too lazy to write things that bore me."[135] Proust found such accusations so unjust that he made them part of the wrong-headed reactions to the first writings by the Narrator, who at the end of his quest is ready to write the fictional counterpart of *In Search of Lost Time*.[136]

In mid-December Proust quarreled with Lucien, who had called on two members of the Académie Goncourt to entreat them to read *Swann's Way* and recognize it as an extraordinary work. For some reason, Proust believed a malicious rumor that Lucien had called on the gentlemen to dissuade them from supporting his book. When Proust let his suspicions be known, Lucien became so furious that

Proust was embarrassed that he had been so credulous.[137] Although Lucien quickly forgave him, he had been hurt and disappointed by Marcel's haste to believe such gossip about a friend who was making extraordinary efforts to promote *Swann's Way*. Although Proust's gentillesse was legendary, his friends often needed to call on their own reserves of patience and understanding.

During the year, despite his troubles, Proust had had typed what he believed would be the second volume, *The Guermantes Way*, and had written the story of the Narrator's second stay at the seaside resort he called Balbec. He had named the girl who assumes the dominant female role as the object of the Narrator's desire Albertine, characterized by a love of speed and so elusive that he would call her the fugitive. She came to represent many aspects of desire and unattainability, assuming and enlarging the earlier role of the character he had called Marie. Proust had sketched the Narrator's relationship with her in a single sentence in the *Carnet de 1908:* "In the second part of the novel the girl will be financially ruined and I will support her without attempting to possess her because I am incapable of happiness."[138] This notation, like many utterances of Proust before and after he met Agostinelli, is eerily prophetic. Proust believed that all his efforts to find happiness in reciprocated erotic love were doomed to failure. This is true of the Narrator as well, but the theme assumes universal importance and is linked to the hero's quest to become a creative person, the only role that can bring him real joy.

Swann's Way was widely reviewed and publicized. In 1913, including the two interviews Proust had granted, there were at least nineteen reviews, notices, and reprints in newspapers—sometimes paid—of favorable reviews. A number of papers also published excerpts from the novel. Proust ended the year having successfully launched one of the most ambitious undertakings in the history of literature: the long first installment of a multivolume novel of unprecedented depth and scope. The critical reception had been better than he had dared hope for such a highly unusual work—infinitely better than Grasset had thought possible—but Proust took little satisfaction from this accomplishment. He pined for a young aviator far away by the Mediterranean Sea.

22 *Annus Horribilis* ❧

NINETEEN FOURTEEN WAS TO BE A TERRIBLE year for France and all of Europe. For Marcel, Agostinelli's flight was only the beginning of bad news. Two deaths struck close to home before the horror became universal. As a New Year's gift Henri Ghéon derided Proust's novel in an *NRF* review.[1] Proust was particularly incensed by the critic's opening remark that *Swann's Way* was the result of years of leisure, during which the author obviously had all his time at his disposal. In a private letter to Ghéon, Proust disputed the assertion that his novel had no structure as a consequence of being written willy-nilly in moods of passive recollection. As he had in other letters and the interviews, Proust explained that the work had to be long to show the effects of time on a group of characters. He particularly enjoyed quoting Francis Jammes's letter, which refuted perfectly Ghéon's criticism. Jammes had praised Proust's logic and his sentences "in the manner of Tacitus, showing great skill, subtle, well-balanced," and compared Proust to "Shakespeare, Cervantes, La Bruyère, Molière, Balzac, and Paul de Kocq." It was true that the last name on the list diminished the effect because the popular, often risqué de Kocq was not in the same exalted category as the other authors. At the end of his letter Proust pretended to agree with Ghéon's assessment that "the entire book is very bad."[2]

Ghéon and his colleagues at the NRF were on the verge of recognizing their enormous blunder in rejecting the *Search*. Both critic and writer were soon engaged in a game of diplomatic denial; the critic protested that his review had been laudatory, and Proust called himself "unforgivable" for having misread it.[3] Perhaps Ghéon had in mind this sentence he had written about *Swann's Way:* "With all its faults, it amounts to a veritable treasury of documentation on modern hypersensitivity."[4]

In January, Proust was having the second volume typed but complained that he lacked the strength to correct the typos. Montesquiou sent his congratulations, but the count's praise struck Marcel as being less than unqualified. He characterized *Swann's Way* as a "book that contains *many* books; and as they are all *interesting*, there is *profit* for the reader, as for the author." He, too, compared Proust favorably to Balzac for his creation of the Verdurins and other characters. The count liked the overall title, about which the author still had reservations. Then Montesquiou, in a dramatic gesture, bade farewell to Proust, predicting that they would never meet again due to "divergent predilections" and "adverse friendships."[5] Although Proust told Lucien that the count's letter was "full of reservations," he had been touched by its "extraordinarily friendly and sensitive" nature.[6] Marcel replied immediately to Montesquiou, thanking him for the "splendid things" he said about *Swann's Way*. He attributed his alleged neglect of Montesquiou to wretched health and reminded the count about the times he had set out for Le Vésinet, only to be thwarted. Marcel expressed his great hope of seeing Montesquiou again, although he gave no clue as to when.[7]

The most remarkable letter Proust received came from Gide: "My dear Proust, For several days I have not put down your book; I am supersaturating myself in it, rapturously, wallowing in it. Alas! why must it be so painful for me to like it so much?" Then Gide made a statement and a confession: "The rejection of this book will remain the gravest mistake ever made by the NRF—and (for I bear the shame of being largely responsible for it) one of the most bitterly remorseful regrets of my life." Gide admitted having formed a false image of Proust, based on a few encounters in society that went back twenty years. For Gide, Proust had remained the "man who frequented the houses of Mmes X, Y or Z, the man who wrote for the *Figaro*. I thought of you—shall I confess it?—as belonging to the Verdurin clan: a snob, a dilettante socialite—the worst possible thing for our review." Proust's offer to pay for the publication of his novel had only confirmed Gide's impressions. As for Proust's manuscript, Gide admitted to having glanced at no more than a couple of sentences, the one about some tea and, a few pages later, the "only one in the book that I don't understand very well—up to now . . . in which a forehead with vertebrae showing through is mentioned." He would never forgive himself, Gide said, but he had written to "alleviate my pain a little" while "begging you to be more indulgent towards me than I am myself."[8] Gide had made a rare gesture, one certain to win Proust's forgiveness and affection: he had frankly and graciously admitted his mistake and apologized for it.

Proust replied immediately: "My dear Gide, I have often found that certain great pleasures are conditional on our having first been deprived of a lesser one, which we deserved, but without the denial of which we could never have known the other, greater pleasure." The "joy" of receiving Gide's letter "infinitely surpasses any I might have felt from being published by the NRF."[9] He told Gide that he should feel no remorse, "for you have given me a thousand times more pleasure than pain." Proust now had what he had wanted: to be read and respected by the group of men he considered his peers.

During the first half of 1914 Proust paid for a number of ads and reprints of favorable reviews to run in newspapers. Sometimes these ran free of charge. On May 1, for example, the *Mercure de France,* fulfilling Proust's request to Alfred Vallette, reprinted most of Jacques-Émile Blanche's laudatory article. Along with the generally good reception of his novel, Proust was enjoying better health. Whatever the reasons for his alarming weight loss of the previous year, his appetite had returned. On January 21 he reported to Reynaldo that, despite the onset of a cold, he had consumed "macaroni, a liter and a half of milk, roasted veal, three croissants and an enormous raspberry tart."[10]

Proust always enjoyed exchanging stories with Montesquiou about the unintended insults writers received from well-meaning friends, and now had new ones to tell about *Swann's Way.* Without mentioning Jeanne de Caillavet's name, he quoted her recent letter: "I constantly re-read the passage . . . about First Communion, as I experienced the same panic, the same disillusionment." As the count knew, of course, there was no First Communion in the book. Proust also reported that "Albufera . . . can't remember whether or not he has read *Swann.* 'If I received it,' he told me, 'you can be sure I read it, but I'm not sure I received it.' "[11]

Proust soon heard from another member of Gide's group. Jacques Rivière, one of the founders of the NRF, had assumed, at age 27, the duties of editor when Copeau left. The most brilliant critic of his generation, Rivière immediately recognized Proust as a great writer: "I shall never forget the wonderment, the depth of emotion into which I was at once plunged." Rivière was to devote himself to defending and promoting the *Search.* When Proust received a letter in which Rivière expressed his admiration and his sense of the work's overall design, he wrote back: "At last I find a reader who has *grasped* that my book is a dogmatic work with a structure. And what a stroke of luck for me that this reader should be you." He then explained in more detail his strategy in the novel: "I thought it more honorable and tactful as an artist not to let it be seen, not to proclaim that I was setting out precisely in search of the Truth, nor to say what it consisted in for me. I so hate those ideological works in which the narrative is a constant betrayal of the author's intentions that I preferred to say nothing. It's only at the end of the book, when the lessons of life have been grasped, that my design will become clear." Proust explained that the end of *Swann's Way* was the "*opposite*" of his conclusion, a "stage, apparently subjective and dilettante, on the way towards the most objective and affirmative conclusion." If he "had no intellectual beliefs, if I were simply trying to remember the past and to duplicate actual experience with these recollections, ill as I am I wouldn't take the trouble to write. But I didn't want to analyse this philosophical evolution abstractly, I wanted to recreate it, to make it live. I'm therefore obliged to depict errors."[12]

The depiction of errors was, of course, a staple of literature, especially, perhaps, of quests like the one on which Proust's Narrator had embarked. These errors included various manias, such as snobbery, obsessive jealousy, and confusing eros and art—for example, Swann's reducing Vinteuil's music to his and Odette's "song" and believing that she was a Botticelli woman. All these mistakes, if not overcome, prevent one from becoming a creative person. A creative person is, by definition for Proust, an altruist, someone who learns how to make his egotism useful to others.[13] This conversion of lost time into time regained had become Proust's sole occupation.

In an early March letter, Proust told Gide that he was incapable, "perhaps from fatigue, or laziness, or boredom, of recording anything which hasn't produced in me an impression of poetic enchantment, or in which I haven't somehow perceived a general truth."[14] Most of these general laws, especially those regarding the creative process and his purpose in writing the *Search*, were not revealed until *Time Regained*, when the Narrator discovers them.

During the months Proust defended *Swann's Way*, the man to whom he had dedicated the work launched a political offensive. Calmette's conservative newspaper waged a heated campaign against Joseph Caillaux, a former prime minister and head of the leftist Radical Party.[15] These sustained attacks, often libelous and personal, reached a low point on March 13, when Calmette violated an unwritten code among Paris newspapers by publishing an item from the politician's private correspondence, a letter to his former mistress signed "Ton Jo" (Your Joey). This latest blow was perhaps the most intolerable for a Frenchman, who abhors, above all else, ridicule. On March 16, at six in the evening, Caillaux's wife, Henriette, came to Calmette's office and asked to see him. Paul Bourget, who had just concluded a meeting with Gaston, advised him not to receive her. But Calmette, displaying those manners Proust found so admirable, remarked that he "could not refuse to receive a woman." When Mme Caillaux entered, the editor noticed that she was elegantly dressed in a gown, as though for a soirée, and wearing a fur coat, to which was attached a large fur muff. Before Calmette could speak, she asked if he knew why she had come. When he replied, "Not at all, Madame," she drew a Browning automatic from the muff and rapidly fired six shots. Calmette fell to the floor, mortally wounded.

During the night, Proust wrote to Mme Straus, who he knew would be as devastated as he was by the brutal murder of her dear friend. "I'm desperately sorry about Calmette's death." He told her how, on hearing the news, he had rushed "to the *Figaro* with a feeling of dread and the need to see once more that corridor along which he escorted me so often and that frightful woman followed him." He shared his grief with Robert Dreyfus and Jacques Bizet and his wife, who had come on Mme Straus's behalf. Proust later contributed three hundred francs for a bust in Calmette's memory.[16] The editor's murder was the harbinger of this *annus horribilis*.

Meanwhile, Proust's prospects for establishing his reputation as an important writer could not have been brighter. Two of the publishers who had rejected *Swann's Way* now sought the right to publish the remaining volumes. A few days after Calmette was killed, Proust received a letter from Gide, who had heard that Proust was not bound to Grasset by "any definite contract" and therefore not obligated to let Grasset publish *The Guermantes Way* and *Time Regained*. Gide could hardly believe such an opportunity existed: "Would it be possible, really?" Gide then made Proust the offer that had been voted the previous day, he said, unanimously and enthusiastically, at the editorial meeting. The NRF was prepared to "defray all the costs of publication, and to do its utmost to ensure that the first volume is reunited with its successors as soon as the present edition runs out." Gide told Proust that he had come back from Florence for the sole purpose of attending this important meeting of the editorial board regarding the *Search*.[17]

Proust replied the next day, saying that he would answer Gide's offer as soon as he was well enough to rise from his bed and look for his contract, whose terms he claimed to have completely forgotten. He mentioned that Fasquelle had recently approached him indirectly with a similar offer that he had not even considered, because he did not want to leave Grasset. Being published by the NRF was a different matter; it was the honor he had most coveted, and he asked Gide to thank his friends. Should he accept their offer, there would be one absolute condition: he must bear entirely all the costs of publication.[18]

Proust consulted Émile Straus in his capacity as lawyer to find out whether his Grasset contract prevented his giving the second volume to another publisher. Although his contract with Grasset had not anticipated a third volume, Proust did not want to take advantage of such a loophole. He asked Straus to keep the matter confidential, for he had not said anything to Grasset. Did Grasset suspect what Proust was considering? He may have learned of the approaches being made by Fasquelle and the NRF, because on March 26 Grasset wrote Proust, suggesting the second volume be published at the end of May or the beginning of June, a date the publisher must have known was impossible.[19] Grasset may have wanted to signal his eagerness to proceed with the remainder of the *Search.*

Proust answered Grasset, saying that he had heard "very upsetting things" about "our book." What Proust meant by "upsetting" is unclear, but he told Grasset that Fasquelle had made a very attractive offer to publish the remaining volumes, as had the NRF. He then repeated to Grasset what he had told Gide: Fasquelle's offer did not interest him, but the NRF's did because its directors were writers by whom he wanted to be read and respected. Lest Grasset think the decision was motivated by financial gain, Proust told him about his condition of paying the publishing costs. Regarding a publication schedule for volume two, Proust told his publisher that it would be difficult for him to have the book ready before October.

When Proust's letter arrived, Grasset was in bed with a terrible cold. What he read cannot have made him feel better. If any doubts remained in Grasset's mind about the literary value of Proust's work, the offers from Fasquelle and the NRF erased them. He instructed Louis Brun to write Proust at once, explain that he was ill, and tell him that Grasset wanted very much to publish the second and third volumes of the *Search.* Grasset would have done well to stop there, but in a subsequent letter he made a serious tactical mistake by mentioning contractual obligations. Proust shot back immediately: "You evoke our contract (and speak of *constraint*—this word, which you underline, 'is harsh to my ears'). . . . Your letter was unnecessary since I consulted you only about your *wishes* and you had already made them known to me some days ago."[20]

Grasset immediately understood his mistake and tried to make amends: "I must have expressed myself very badly," he wrote, for Proust had interpreted his letter "exactly contrary to my intentions." Observing that their contract called for Grasset to publish the entire work, he nonetheless admitted that Proust certainly retained ownership of *In Search of Lost Time.* Then Grasset wrote the magic words:

he proposed putting the contract completely aside; he wanted to remain Proust's publisher for the sequel, only if "you give me your total trust." And summing up, the publisher said that Proust should not consider himself bound in any way, that Grasset released him from everything in their first agreement that might constitute "the slightest obligation." Proust, he insisted, was entirely free to choose.[21]

Proust cannot have been happy to read Grasset's words, for they were the very ones that would bind him more tightly to the publisher than any contract. Proust wrote to Gide a few days later, saying that he was "defenseless against such magnanimity." He would give the NRF as many excerpts as they liked, but he would stay with Grasset for the remaining volumes, at least in their first edition.[22] Then Proust informed Grasset of his decision: Grasset would publish the first editions of volumes two and three, but future editions would be reserved for his "friends at the NRF."[23] On April 30 Grasset offered a new contract whereby the publisher would pay the publication costs, print three thousand copies, and give Proust sixty-five centimes per copy sold. The author's only expenses would be for revisions.[24] Grasset, who now understood this author and his methods of creating prose that readers and critics had begun to recognize as extraordinary, knew that Proust's revisions would be extensive and the costs in time and labor high.

Robert Proust was pleased with the reception of Swann's Way. At last, Marcel, who had been so unhappy and apparently so foolish in many regards, had shown himself capable of producing a remarkable work. Dr. Proust, meanwhile, had established his own reputation as an eminent surgeon. In the spring he and Marthe sailed for New York, where he was to read a paper on April 9 at a meeting of the American Surgery Association. In his paper, quoted in the New York Times, Robert described how he had successfully performed open-heart surgery on a young man who had been shot. By the summer Dr. Proust's surgical skills were to be put to tests he never imagined.

Proust wrote Jacques Rivière, who planned to publish long passages from the forthcoming volumes of the Search, telling him that he had been touched by Rivière's letter and wanted no other newspaper or magazine to publish his excerpts. Rivière proposed, rather naïvely, that the NRF print Proust's entire volume. The writer was wise enough not to accept the generous offer: "I fear that the publication of the whole volume (which will be at least as long as the first, if not longer), even with cuts, would clutter up your review dreadfully."[25] Rivière would publish long excerpts of nearly fifty pages in both the June and July issues. Grasset endorsed Proust's decision to give excerpts to the NRF, saying that he considered this review the most "interesting artistic manifestation of our day, and I admire it while being somewhat jealous of it."[26] Grasset could afford to be magnanimous; he had kept the prize.

In early May, Proust contacted Hauser with the urgent request to sell enough of his Royal Dutch shares to raise roughly ten thousand francs. Hauser phoned and left a message with Nicolas, reminding Proust that he had already sold all his Royal Dutch shares held by the Warburg Bank. Proust, mortified, apologized for his confusion.[27] It is unclear why Proust needed so much cash in a hurry. Did he need to cover his speculation debts or to replenish his cash account, or was he accumulating liquid assets for the final attempt to lure Agostinelli back to Paris? By month's end, Proust dangled before his former secretary one of the most generous offers ever made to a runaway.

Because of his reckless way with money, Proust soon proclaimed himself ruined. He wrote Robert de Flers, Calmette's successor at the *Figaro,* that he was broke and looking for work. He would take any column, he told Flers: the weather, gossip, music, theater, or the stock market—one can imagine the results of making Marcel Proust financial adviser to readers of a major newspaper—or even the society page. Proust assured his friend that such an opportunity would delight him, and Flers would "see that I'm capable of abstaining myself from literature and being brief and practical."[28] Flers soon made such an offer, but by then Marcel had changed his mind and proposed instead that the *Figaro* publish a long novella, *Odette Married,* pieced together from forthcoming sections of the *Search.* Proust had apparently already forgotten the wish expressed to Rivière that the *NRF* be the exclusive outlet for excerpts. Flers, who must have recognized his extraordinary good luck, accepted the proposal, but circumstances interfered to prevent publication.

"The sea will be my tomb"

On May 28 Proust arranged the sale of some stocks in order to raise enough money to buy gifts for Agostinelli.[29] Two days later he wrote a long letter to his former secretary, telling him that he had spent twenty-seven thousand francs to buy an airplane for him. Proust began by thanking Agostinelli for his recent letter, from which he quoted a line later attributed to Albertine: "Thank you very much for your letter—one sentence was *ravishing* (crepuscular etc.)."[30] Agostinelli had sent Proust a wire and a letter, whose contents are unknown, probably in reply to letters from Proust. Proust's letter on May 30 to Agostinelli is the only one that survives.

Proust had evidently written asking Agostinelli to cancel the order for the airplane and another, unnamed gift—most likely a Rolls-Royce—that Proust intended for him as well, both of which Agostinelli had declined.[31] Without explaining why, Proust had thought it "indelicate" to ask Agostinelli to cancel the order for the unnamed gift. Exactly what Proust intended and what game he was playing here is not clear from the ambiguous remarks in the only extant letter. Perhaps he thought that Agostinelli would not have the will to resist such magnificent gifts if he had to cancel the orders himself. The cost of a Rolls (26,200 francs) in 1914 was almost the same as the price of an airplane (27,000 francs).[32] If Proust decided to keep the airplane, he would have lines from Mallarmé's poem that the young aviator admired inscribed on the fuselage: "You know: it's the poem you loved even though you found it obscure, which begins: *Le vierge, le vivace et le bel Aujourd'hui.* Alas, 'today' is neither 'virgin' nor 'vivacious' nor 'beautiful.'" Knowing how interested Agostinelli was in sports, Proust enclosed with the letter an article on *Swann* from a sports newspaper. As usual, he asked Agostinelli to return the letter, making certain that it was well sealed; Proust observed that his young friend had so far failed to follow these instructions.[33]

In early spring Agostinelli, aged twenty-five, had enrolled in the aviation school run by the Garbero brothers at La Grimaudière, near Antibes. He registered as Marcel Swann, in bizarre homage to his benefactor. After two months of training, during which he made rapid progress, Agostinelli was ready for his second solo flight. On Saturday, May 30, the day Proust sent his offer of regal gifts, Agostinelli was at the airfield taking flying lessons. Around five o'clock, the apprentice pilot took off in a monoplane.

Anna and Émile, Alfred's brother, also an apprentice pilot, watched Agostinelli go through his maneuvers. Agostinelli's half-brother, Jean Vittoré, was also in Antibes, though it is not known whether he was at the airfield. Elated by his success, Agostinelli ignored the warnings of chief pilot Joseph Garbero, left the designated flying area, and flew out over the Bay of Angels. Attempting a turn, the inexperienced pilot forgot to increase his altitude, and the right wing skimmed the water, pulling the plane into the sea. Anna, Émile, and the others watched in horror. Once Agostinelli recovered from the shock of finding himself plunged into the water, he noticed that the plane, though three-fourths submerged, seemed to be floating. He stood atop the pilot's seat and screamed for help. Those on shore quickly launched a boat and began rowing frantically toward the downed aviator. But suddenly the monoplane sank beneath the waves, taking Agostinelli with it. He was known to be a good swimmer, and his friends were later puzzled that he disappeared without a struggle.[34] Some said that sharks had been seen in the area, while others claimed that the spot where the plane went down was known for its swift currents. Search boats plied the waters in the bay until darkness forced them back to port.

Proust learned of the tragedy that evening when he received a telegram from Anna.[35] On Sunday morning a boat found the sunken plane, but the body had been swept away. The family provided newspapers with a description of Agostinelli's clothes: a khaki one-piece flying suit, a brown rubber helmet, gray shirt, black pants, black shoes, and a signet ring with the initials *AA*.[36] In addition to the heavy clothing, Agostinelli had on his person all his money, a considerable sum of about five or six thousand francs, apparently the remainder of what Proust had given him. Agostinelli's father and brother quickly realized that if the body were found, all the money would go to Anna, whom everyone thought was the pilot's legal wife. The Agostinellis allegedly turned against her and sent a wire to the prince of Monaco, telling him that she was only Alfred's mistress.[37]

Jean Vittoré rushed to Paris, where a profoundly aggrieved Proust wept in his arms. Vittoré had come to entreat the author to hire divers to search for the body.[38] The divers, who would have to come from faraway Toulon, wanted five thousand francs for their trouble. Proust was willing to help but realized that his debt payments alone would probably deplete all the cash Hauser had raised for him.[39] Agostinelli's body was found by fishermen eight days after the accident.

On June 1 the *NRF* published extracts from *The Guermantes Way*. Proust continued to receive proofs for the next volume, but he was too upset to work, and his inaction risked delaying publication.[40] Soon Proust had Anna and Émile to worry about. Immediately after Agostinelli's funeral, they had come running back to Paris, confident that Marcel would help them despite his earlier warnings that they would never receive a penny from him if Agostinelli died in a plane crash. As was his nature in such circumstances, Proust relented and did everything he could to help, trying to find them employment, enlisting the aid of friends such as Émile Straus on their behalf, and even writing to the prince of Monaco to support Anna's claim, as Agostinelli's widow, to any recovered property. A week after the accident, Proust, having just learned that Anna and Agostinelli apparently had not been legally married, sent a letter to Straus asking him to write the prince and apologize on Proust's behalf for having unintentionally misled him about Anna's marital status. He explained to Émile why Anna deserved to be designated Alfred's rightful heir. Proust believed that while Agostinelli's initial love for her was inexplicable, he knew that Agostinelli had "lived for her alone and would have left her everything he had." Proust did not have a high opinion of the rest of the family, describing them as "not worth much." But the business about fighting over money retrieved from the dead body did not strike him as behavior particular to their class: "This sort of thing, horrible though it is, happens every day among the La Rochefoucaulds or the Montmorencys whenever a question of pecuniary interest arises." The Agostinellis, he observed, were no different.[41]

In appealing to his friends to help the Agostinellis, Proust stressed his former secretary's intellectual gifts.[42] In a letter to Gide, Proust spoke of his great sorrow over "the death of a young man whom I loved probably more than all my male friends[,] since it has made me so unhappy." He maintained that although the unnamed young man was of humble origins, he was extremely intelligent and wrote letters like "those of a great writer." It was only after falling in love with him that Proust discovered in him "those qualities that were so marvellously incompatible with everything else he was—discovered them with amazement, though they added nothing to my affection for him: I simply took pleasure in making him aware of them. But he died before he realized what he was, before he even became it entirely."[43]

In the weeks following Agostinelli's death, Anna tried several times to commit suicide, and Proust was afraid that if her situation grew desperate enough, she might succeed.[44] Proust himself was not immune to death wishes. Later that fall, he confided to Lucien that in the days following Agostinelli's accident he had longed to die: "After having put up so well with being ill without feeling sorry for myself, I found myself hoping, with all my heart, every time I got into a taxi that an oncoming bus would run me down."[45] Proust had not only lost someone he loved passionately, but he felt responsible for Agostinelli's death. Had he not lavished money on Agostinelli, "Marcel Swann" probably could not have afforded to relocate in Antibes and enroll in the aviation school. Proust had tried at first to discourage Agostinelli from becoming a pilot, but later he had taken advantage of the young man's passion for flying by promising him an airplane if he returned.[46]

In early June, Proust exchanged letters with Gide, who had read the excerpts in the *NRF.* Gide told him, "I am enchanted. Through the strange and powerful subtlety of your style I seem to be reading . . . my own memories and my most personal sensations."[47] Proust explained to Gide his conception of Charlus, infatuated with virility because, without knowing it, he was a woman. Proust readily conceded that Charlus was not the only homosexual type, but was one that had not been portrayed in literature. He paraphrased for Gide a remark the Narrator makes after having understood Charlus's true nature. The Narrator believes that if Charlus is "so much more subtle and sensitive" than his rather boorish brother the duc de Guermantes, it is due to his homosexuality.[48]

Gide replied, expressing his admiration for Charlus but noting that Proust had "contributed to the habitual confusion between the homosexual and the invert." For Gide, the homosexual, a man in love with another man, carried on a noble tradition dating from the ancient Greeks, whereas Charlus, who wanted to become a woman for another man, represented a modern, decadent variety. Turning to Proust's concerns about his titles, Gide told him that he must on no account change them, calling them "excellent." Gide believed that Proust was "ill-placed to know how familiar they have become to so many readers." Gide ended by saying that he longed to see the sequel to Charlus.[49] But Marcel questioned whether Gide or anyone else would see the sequel; since the death of his "poor friend," he had not the strength to open a single one of the packages of proofs that arrived daily from the printers.[50]

The End of an Era

June 28, 1914, was the day the Belle Époque came to an abrupt end. The event that triggered its demise happened not in Paris but in faraway Sarajevo, where the heir to the Hapsburgs, Archduke Francis Ferdinand, and his wife had come for a state visit. Earlier in the day Bosnian Serb nationalists had attacked the archduke's car with a bomb, injuring two of his officers. Unintimidated, the archduke continued to city hall, where other Bosnian Serb conspirators waited in the crowd. After the welcome by the mayor, the archduke decided to visit a hospital. His driver took an immediate wrong turn down a narrow street and, unable to turn around, had to back up. Gavrilo Princip, armed with a handgun, stood watching from only ten yards away as the archduke's car backed toward him. Princip stepped forward and fired two shots, mortally wounding the archduke and his wife.[51]

In Paris, in a phone conversation shortly before the assassination, Hauser uttered words that rang prophetically in Proust's ears: "In the possible event of a European conflagration . . . " Proust began immediately to reduce his financial commitments by selling a number of stocks; but unfortunately, with a generally depressed market, he was unable to liquidate as much as he would have liked. Then came the "thunderbolt of the Austro-Serb incident." Proust knew that he faced even greater losses, but that was of little consequence, he admitted, "amid the immense disasters it may well let loose upon Europe."[52]

Proust's efforts to put his finances in order on the eve of war required him to outline all his holdings and thereby confess to Hauser his foolish speculations. In the closing days of June, Proust received a check for twenty thousand francs from the Warburg Bank in Germany, which held an important portion of his remaining resources. He quickly had the bank sell another twenty-five thousand to thirty-five thousand francs' worth of shares. Proust managed to cash the first check on the Warburg Bank but not the one for thirty thousand francs that he received on July 31, because all banking operations between France and Germany were suspended due to the threat of imminent hostilities.[53]

On the eve of war, Proust and many of his friends were outraged when the jury found Mme Caillaux not guilty for the murder of Gaston Calmette. Her *crime passionnel* defense had persuaded the jury not to convict her. A petition protesting the verdict ran in the *Figaro* on August 1, and Proust was among the many who signed.[54] Events surrounding a much larger crisis moved swiftly, as military leaders urged their governments not to lose a second in the race to mobilize. On August 2 the French government ordered the mobilization of the army, and on August 3 Germany declared war on France. On hearing of the declaration of war, General Gérald Pau, a veteran of the humiliating defeat by the Germans in 1870, declared: "I have been waiting forty years for this day. It is the most glorious day of my life." In *Time Regained,* after the war has ended, Charlus quotes General Pau's statement as an example of excessive nationalism.[55]

Proust's brother Robert was in the first group to be called up. Although Marcel and Marthe admired Robert's courage, they were dismayed at his insistence on being sent to the front. At midnight on Sunday, August 2, Marcel accompanied his brother to the Gare de l'Est. Dr. Proust had been assigned to a place whose name would be associated with one of the longest and bloodiest episodes of the war: Verdun. Before boarding the train, Robert entrusted Marcel with two important missions. The first was to look after Marthe and his daughter Adrienne, now eleven years old; the second was confidential and involved the other woman in Robert's life. Dr. Proust's life, like that of millions of others, had changed in a matter of minutes; in preparing to leave for the front, he had not had time to inform Mme Fournier, his mistress of nine years, of his departure and destination. He asked Marcel to do so.[56] Marcel promised Robert to do his bidding, but he was soon relieved of the duty to Robert's family when Marthe decided to join many of her compatriots who sought refuge in Pau, in France's southwest corner.

Marcel watched as the train pulled out of the station, carrying his brother and hundreds of men away into the night. He had no illusions about the hell that awaited them. The machines of war had, like all the others, greatly multiplied their power, speed, and efficiency. The arms used in the Franco-Prussian War, just before Marcel and Robert were born, now seemed primitive. And this war would have a new force: airplanes that would drop bombs onto battlefields and cities. Proust wrote Lucien that from the moment he accompanied his brother to the train station, he could think of nothing but the war. He began following the development of French strategy on military maps and reading seven newspapers a day to keep abreast of developments.[57]

After saying farewell to Robert, Marcel wrote Hauser, describing his brother's departure. His own financial predicament, as complicated and onerous as it was, seemed "very unimportant when I think of the millions of men who are going to be massacred in a *War of the Worlds* comparable to that of Wells, because the Emperor of Austria thinks it expedient to have an outlet onto the Black Sea."[58] In his reply, Hauser asked that Robert be informed that Hauser's brother-in-law Victor Schwenk had also been sent to Verdun. Hauser described Victor as "a very charming young man," married for only a year and a half and the father of a little girl.[59] Proust agreed to relay the message to his brother.

As late as August 16 Mme Straus remained in Trouville, but she was soon to join the other refugees in Pau. Marcel worried about her son's safety, until he learned that Jacques had been attached to an ambulance crew. His servant Nicolas, Proust reported to Mme Straus, had made a wildly optimistic assessment of his and his country's position on the day war was declared. Because he belonged to the territorial reserves, a group that had not been called up in the first mobilization order, Nicolas told Proust and Céleste the war would be over too quickly for him to worry: "They won't call me for another fortnight, and by that time we'll have killed them all and be in Berlin; I shan't have to go, you'll see."[60] Perhaps Nicolas had been drinking again. Two weeks passed; the Germans were in France, and Nicolas was in the army.

Nicolas's departure left Proust alone at night, but soon he had another attendant. Because Odilon had been called in the first mobilization, Céleste soon moved into Proust's apartment to avoid the daily trek from Levallois and back. Her assumption of some of Nicolas's duties was meant to be temporary while Proust looked for another manservant. He considered it improper for a bachelor to keep a female servant under his roof, especially a young and pretty one like Céleste.

With his sister-in-law and niece safe in Pau, Proust began to consider leaving for Cabourg, despite the increasingly chaotic state of rail transportation. In a letter to Albufera written a day or so before his departure, Proust described a nocturnal stroll in Paris under a moonlit sky two or three days before the victory in the Marne, when the siege of Paris seemed imminent. He arose one evening and went out into moonlight that was "luminous, brilliant, reproachful, serene, ironic, and maternal, and on seeing this immense Paris that I had not realized I loved so much, waiting, in all its powerless beauty, for what seemed the inevitable onslaught, I could not hold back a sob."[61] Paris and so many other cities would find their beauty powerless to prevent the murderous transformations that the nations at war had decided were worth the gamble. The great city would endure four nerve-racking years under the threat of bombs, siege, and invasion by a hated enemy.

Proust later learned that two of his friends had been declared unfit for duty and assigned to the Red Cross. Lucien had been sent to Tours, where he was staying in the Hôtel Brunswick.[62] Cocteau set out for the front as a volunteer male nurse, but not before adding a bit of chic to the terrible duty that awaited him: the astonishing Jean had gone off to war in a uniform made for him by the distinguished designer Paul Poiret.[63] Reynaldo had been mobilized as soon as fighting began and sent to Melun, southeast of Paris.[64] Marcel wrote him on August 30, saying that because he could not possibly come to Melun, he had decided to leave for Cabourg, if the trains were running. The war already seemed like a terrible nightmare from which he longed to wake: "How wonderful it will be to see each other again when these terrible days are over and if we haven't too many friends to mourn. But in fact I weep just as much for the unknown. I no longer live." He knew that Reynaldo was worried about the safety of his close friend Henri Bardac in the Marne: "I think you are wrong to be worried for if the absurd 'No news is good news' is true anywhere it's in war; because families are immediately informed of deaths or serious wounds." In the great confusion of World War I battlefields, this axiom was to prove false, as Proust soon learned.[65] Within a week Henri Bardac, an infantry sergeant, was wounded in the battle of the Marne.

Proust told Hahn about his futile search for a manservant. How could he find anyone suitable when all able-bodied men—and then some—had been called up? Frédéric de Madrazo had recommended one young servant, but when he arrived Proust found himself confronted with "Galloping Consumption in person." This unpromising youth was soon drafted, to the author's relief. Proust told Reynaldo that, given the circumstances, it seemed perfectly reasonable to take Mme Albaret to Cabourg. Céleste had even offered to dress in men's clothes.[66] Although Proust declined her offer, he was highly amused by her pluck and spirit of adventure. This young woman from nowhere—even Proust seemed confused about where Auxillac was, believing it to be in the Auvergne rather than Lozère—sounded like an excellent companion for a fiction writer. At the end of his letter Proust expressed his strong disapproval of Hahn's determination to go to the front. He urged Reynaldo to remain at Melun or to seek a post in Bordeaux or Toulon, somewhere thought safe.

Proust considered vacationing in Nice, an area he had long wanted to visit, but a new friend, Louis Gautier-Vignal, had warned him that with the vast movements of soldiers and civilians fleeing south the trip would take at least thirty hours.[67] Just before leaving for Cabourg, Proust interviewed a young Swedish manservant by the name of Ernest Forssgren. A tall, remarkably handsome Nordic blond, Forssgren looked the picture of health and sounded ideal. It seemed unlikely that a Swede would be drafted anytime soon. Proust hired Forssgren immediately. On September 3 Proust, Céleste, and Forssgren, as his new manservant, left for Cabourg.[68] Céleste, able to look at Forssgren more objectively than Proust, said that the attractive youth was "so pleased with himself, as if he were the King of Sweden, if not God Almighty."[69]

Proust had traveled to Cabourg for long summer stays every year since 1907. This visit, his last, proved difficult from the moment he and his servants tried to board the train, so jammed with soldiers and civilians that it was nearly impossible to sit down. Some passengers chose to ride on top of the cars. Instead of the customary four hours, the trip took twenty-two. Proust arrived to find the first two floors and the dining room of the Grand-Hôtel transformed into an auxiliary hospital and the casino closed due to lack of personnel and clients.

In spite of the ordeal of getting to Cabourg and the somewhat chaotic nature of life at the Grand-Hôtel, Proust remained there for nearly a month and a half. During his stay, two old acquaintances from the beau monde called to see him, counts Greffulhe and Montesquiou, but he was too ill to receive them.[70] He corresponded with his friends, especially those who had loved ones at the front. Proust had been worried about the safety of Mme Catusse's son Charles and was relieved to hear that he had received only a superficial wound. He wrote to her on September 15, saying that he hoped the wound would be slow to heal so that Charles would not have to return to the front. He told her that there were hundreds of wounded at Cabourg, whom he visited every day, bringing them whatever small items he could afford with his sharply reduced resources. The soldiers recuperating at the hotel were not seriously wounded, he told her. Each day as he watched the men eating, sleeping, walking, he hoped that her Charles was "doing as well!"[71]

On October 13 or 14 Proust left Cabourg to return home. Between Cabourg and Évreux, he suffered an unusually violent asthma attack. Céleste, not knowing that she must bring his medicine with them into the compartment, had packed it in the luggage now secured in the baggage car. Faced with a surly conductor who was unsympathetic to her employer's extreme discomfort, Céleste was unable to talk her way into the baggage car. At the first stop she leaped to the platform and convinced a kinder railway employee to allow her to retrieve Proust's antiasthma powders from the suitcase. Proust immediately began his "fumigation," filling the compartment with smoke.[72] The asthma attack was so severe that Proust could not write for several days.[73] Forssgren left Proust's employment shortly after the return to Paris. Apparently under threat of being drafted in the Swedish army, he emigrated to New York. He was to reappear near the end of Proust's life.

Proust returned to Paris just in time to receive news from Marthe of his brother's courageous actions under fire. Dr. Proust's heroism, along with his promotion to captain in the Medical Corps, was mentioned in the dispatches.[74] According to the military citation, Robert had shown remarkable courage at Étain by keeping his field hospital in full operation August 22–26, performing surgery on wounded soldiers while being fired on by the enemy. Shell splinters fell on the operating table while the doctor, forgetting his own safety, continued to save lives.[75]

Reynaldo had earlier expressed his concern that the trip to Cabourg might be painful for Marcel because of memories of Agostinelli associated with the difficult trip the year before and the first time they met at the seaside resort in 1907. Proust reassured Reynaldo, telling him that his thought had been "sweet," that, to his "shame," the return to Cabourg without Agostinelli had not been "as painful as I might have expected . . . and the journey marked a first stage in detachment from my grief. . . . At Cabourg, without ceasing to be just as sad and to miss him just as much, I found there were moments, perhaps hours, when he disappeared from my thoughts." He told Hahn that he had really "loved" Alfred; more than that he had "adored him." Why, Proust wondered, was he already using the past tense when he still loved Agostinelli? It was because in "feelings of grief there is an element of the involuntary and an element of duty which sustains the involuntary part and ensures its durability. This sense of duty doesn't exist in the case of Alfred, who behaved very badly towards me; I give him the regrets that I cannot help but give him. I don't feel bound to him by a duty of the sort that binds me to you, that would bind me to you even if I owed you a thousand times less, even if I loved you a thousand times less." If during the few weeks at Cabourg, he had been relatively unfaithful to Alfred's memory, then he should not be blamed for being "fickle." The person to blame was Agostinelli, for having been "incapable of deserving fidelity."[76]

Once Marcel was back in Paris, to his "great joy" the pain of losing Alfred returned. Proust then formulated for Hahn his theory about grieving, which was explained by his theory of multiple selves: "It isn't because others have died that grief diminishes, but because one dies oneself." This was a lesson Proust had already learned and, he confided to Reynaldo, described in the unpublished part of his novel: "For a long time now life has only presented me with events I've already described. When you read my third volume . . . you will recognize the anticipation and the unerring prophecy of what I've experienced since." Marcel entreated Reynaldo to remain in Albi, where he had recently been transferred, far from the front. In his postscript Marcel, as he often did, compensated for what might have seemed too cold in the body of the letter. In spite of the distance he now felt between himself and Agostinelli, he would not hesitate to cut off an arm or a leg if such measures would bring his former secretary back to life.[77]

Proust's regular physician, Dr. Bize, now a major in the Army Medical Corps, had also been posted at Albi. Reynaldo, worried that by some fluke Marcel might be declared fit for service by a military medical examiner, some of whom had the reputation of taking anyone with a beating pulse, asked Bize to produce a certificate testifying to Marcel's unfitness.[78] Proust was moved by Hahn's solicitude but knew that such a document lacked official status.[79] He was relieved that Hahn had been taken under the wing of Lt.-Col. Louis Cuny, commanding officer at Albi, whose sister was a singer at the Opéra-Comique.[80] Although Marcel knew that Reynaldo could not be counted upon to take advantage of this connection, he hoped that Cuny shared his sister's love of music and would frustrate Hahn's efforts to be sent to the front. The musician seemed determined to fight. When his sister Maria and Marcel learned that he had put in another request to be sent to the front, they did everything possible to make him change his mind. Proust asked for Hahn's permission to write his commanding officer and inform him about Hahn's fragile bronchial tubes, frequent colds, and bouts of laryngitis. How, Marcel demanded, could his friend possibly tolerate the freezing trenches when he often caught a cold on leaving the opera and stepping out in the chilly air?[81] Hahn, bent on discouraging such initiatives on Proust's part, replied testily that he had lungs of iron and did not even know what a sore throat was.[82]

By November, Marcel feared that none of his letters were reaching his brother, because he had not heard from him since he left for the front.[83] He knew that Robert had little time to write, but it was unlike his brother not to try to contact him. On the home front, Proust was disgusted by the excessive chauvinism of many reporters, and—even more disappointing—artists he respected. In letters to Daniel and Lucien, Proust deplored what he called the "disarmament of intellects." The press was filled with jingoistic articles referring to Germans as "Boches"—the disparaging French equivalent of "Krauts"—or, even worse, attacks on German artists and even the German language. Frédéric Masson, a historian and member of the Académie française, wrote an article in *L'Écho de Paris* that reviled Wagner and characterized anyone who liked his music as a victim of Wagneritis.[84] Camille Saint-Saëns attacked the German composer in the *Figaro*. In his letter to Lucien, Proust asked what would have happened if France had been at war with Russia instead? Presumably, statements similar to Masson's would have been made about Tolstoy and Dostoyevsky. In another letter to a friend, Proust decried the "low standards in the press, what stupidity! Fortunately it can't tarnish the heroism, but it will lessen the significance of victory."[85] Before ending his letter to Lucien, Proust may have encouraged the disarmament of intellects by praising Léon Daudet's *L'Avant-guerre*, which the novelist thought was "confirmed and immortalized" by this war. Although Proust's remark was made in a private letter, in which he states that he had not actually read Léon's articles about the crimes allegedly committed by German-Jewish spies in France since the Dreyfus Affair, his friendship may have blinded him to the excesses of the elder Daudet brother, who remained as rabidly anti-Semitic as ever.[86]

In early September the poet and essayist Charles Péguy was killed leading his company at the battle of the Marne. Péguy had begun his career as a fiery anticlerical socialist but had evolved into a patriot and fervent Catholic.[87] At forty-one, he had volunteered for military service. In late November, as the list of dead and wounded swelled daily, Proust expressed his admiration for Péguy's heroism but not for his writings. He had the same criticism of Péguy's style that he had at times voiced against Ruskin, who had a similar tendency to yield to the temptation of the "law of association." Proust explained to Lucien: "As a rule an art . . . in which something is repeated ten times, leaving a choice between ten formulations none of which is the true one, is for me the opposite of art." Proust still grumbled about his subscription years ago to *Les Cahiers de la Quinzaine*, founded by Péguy and Halévy, in which Proust had found "an unbearable hotchpotch" of writing that had put him in a terrible mood.[88]

In a letter on November 21 Proust asked Reynaldo whether he had read about the death of the cellist Marcel Casadesus, killed by a shell on October 10 in the Pas-de-Calais. Proust had heard him play on several occasions as a member of the Capet String Quartet.[89] France, like the other nations, continued to lose its artists and writers to the war.

Proust had to worry about his own military status, primarily because he had committed a blunder. Because he had been released from all military obligation when struck from the lists in 1913, he was required to do nothing. Instead, knowing that he was unfit to serve, he had signed up for a medical examination to verify that condition. This led to a string of Proustian complications involving men whose time would have been better spent on other matters. On November 22 Proust wrote Joseph Reinach to thank him for having been so charming and kind when Frédéric de Madrazo approached him on the novelist's behalf regarding the status of his military obligations.[90] Reinach confirmed that being struck from the lists released Proust from "all military obligation without any doubt."[91] Proust had also been pleased at Reinach's remark that the novelist was in "no way a shirker." Proust informed Reinach that, in addition to his daily war column, signed "Polybe," in the *Figaro,* Proust was rereading the statesman's volume *La Révision,* from his great history of the Dreyfus Affair. Proust was eager for Reinach to know that he re- mained unswayed by nationalistic propaganda and had told Léon Daudet how he felt: "As I wrote to Léon the other day, I remain as Beethovenian and Wagnerian as ever, and I find the articles of Masson and Saint-Saëns idiotic."[92] Reinach's family had suffered terrible losses in the opening days of conflict. Proust expressed sympa- thy for the death of Reinach's son-in-law Pierre Goujon and his fervent hope for the safety of his son Adolphe, missing in action. This hope was in vain; Adolphe had also been killed.

Because men and lead were needed for meaner tasks than typesetting books, Grasset and other publishers ceased operations. Proust found himself without a publisher, a press, and a deadline. Nonetheless, he kept writing, expanding his novel, intent on creating the cycle of Albertine. He wrote far more than originally planned about homosexuality, enlarging its female branch. Proust ultimately chose *Sodom and Gomorrah* as the title of the *Search's* fourth part, inspired by a line from Alfred de Vigny's poem "La Colère de Samson" (The wrath of Samson): *The women shall have Gomorrah and the men shall have Sodom.*[93] For Proust, Sodom indicates the world of male homosexuality, Gomorrah that of female homosexuality. He linked these themes, as he had the character of Mlle Vinteuil from its original conception, to the Narrator's search for a vocation. During the long period of waiting for publication to resume, Proust added the war years to the novel, includ- ing his observations of the changes in society. In the *Search,* reversing roles, Proust compares a general diverted from his battle plan to a novelist: "A general is like a writer who sets out to write a certain play, a certain book, and then the book itself, with the unexpected potentialities which it reveals here, the impassable obstacles which it presents there, makes him deviate to an enormous degree from his preconceived plan."[94] Agostinelli and the Great War had certainly presented such potentialities and obstacles for Proust, who was to write a much longer novel of greater scope than originally intended, although without changing the basic circular structure of his story, which is that of a quest.

By late December, Proust decided to simplify his existence by canceling the telephone, which meant that he would no longer have the theatrophone. Perhaps he felt that the player piano and its rolls were all he required for the moment. No telephone meant that Céleste had to cross the street to a little café, where she made calls for Proust whenever he had an urgent message for the outside world.

Proust was unaware that Bertrand de Fénelon, who could have fulfilled his obligation to his country by staying in his diplomatic post, had volunteered for active service. As of December, His Blue Eyes was missing in action. Nineteen fourteen had been, as Marcel wrote in a letter to Reynaldo, a hellish year.[95]

23   *Shattered Hearts*   ∾

IN THE FIRST FIVE MONTHS OF THE WAR French casualty figures totaled a staggering three hundred thousand dead and six hundred thousand wounded, captured, or missing.[1] And 1915 brought no letup in the blood being spilled in the trenches east of Paris. A mid-January offensive alone cost the lives of some forty thousand French and English soldiers.[2] Because of the threat posed by the new German airships called Zeppelins, which dropped bombs on cities, the military governor of Paris issued strict orders regarding blackouts.

Since the beginning of the war Proust had eaten little on a daily basis, relying hourly on medication. He explained in a letter that Céleste was the "charming and perfect chambermaid" who served as "valet de chambre and nurse—I don't say cook, except for herself, because I eat nothing."[3] Proust worried constantly about the safety of his friends and relatives, especially his brother, Robert, and Reynaldo.

The war did not make Proust fear for his personal safety, but it did complicate what had for some time been his greatest worry: having to wake and go out during daylight hours for appointments. Now it was the army medical board that insisted on examining him to see whether he was fit to serve. Proust would turn forty-four in July, but men up to the age of forty-five were being sent into combat. Proust wished that his health would allow him to serve at least in an administrative post, but he was convinced that if he went into the service, what remained of his fragile health would fail, dooming his work to incompletion and oblivion.[4]

Proust had seldom gone out in the evening since his fall return from Cabourg. As the death toll mounted, he paid visits of condolence or, more rarely, attended a party. He continued to study his models and glean information about fashion and paintings, and he still registered particular scenes, such as musicians performing pieces that inspired him, usually the works of Franck, Fauré, and Beethoven.[5] At the end of January, Proust went to a party around midnight at the home of Mme Edwards, née Misia Godebska, who inspired a minor character in the *Search*, Princesse Yourbeletief, a sponsor of the Ballets Russes.[6] During the winter, now that so few of his friends were in Paris and he had a housekeeper with no culinary skills, Proust occasionally rose from his bed in early evening and dined at the Ritz. In January he suggested that Albufera, eager for a visit while on leave, come to his bedside no earlier than nine or meet him later at the Ritz.[7]

Proust continued to borrow traits of friends, to which he added the products of his imagination, creating characters for his novel. He described this technique in the *Search*: "More even than the painter, the writer, in order to achieve volume and substance, in order to attain to generality and, so far as literature can, to reality, needs to have seen many churches in order to paint one church and for the portrayal of a single sentiment requires many individuals."[8] He gave Mme Straus's knowledge of Hugo's poetry, as he had her witticisms, to the duchesse de Guermantes. During the year Proust paid two visits to Comte Joachim Clary, whom he described in a letter as "old and inert, half-paralyzed, and nearly blind." He used his observations of the decrepit count to depict Charlus in his dotage.[9] As he incorporated the war years into his tale, Marcel, who had what he described as a "passion for military art," discussed strategy with Antoine and other friends much in the same way as do the Narrator and Saint-Loup.[10] In the fall Proust called twice on Mme de Chevigné. The first time he found Cocteau present, but on the second occasion, the mischievous, talkative Jean was absent, and Proust asked the countess for information about women's fashion and recipes for his book.

Among friends and relatives whose lives the war had already claimed were Jean Bénac, the son of his old friends at Beg-Meil, and Jean-Louis Cruppi, a distant relative on his mother's side. Marcel tried to console friends whose relatives had been killed: Marie Scheikévitch lost her brother; Louis Gautier-Vignal lost a brother and a brother-in-law. As much as Proust wished for victory that would end the carnage and the fears, he did not believe that it was close at hand.[11] In addition to the war dead, some in Proust's extended circle succumbed to natural causes. On January 8

Hugo Finaly died at the age of seventy-one. Writing to Mme Finaly, Proust told her "how profoundly" her husband "was linked to my most cherished memories of the irreparable, sweet, and heart-rending past," a past that included his youthful vacations with the Finalys in Ostende and at Les Frémonts.[12]

Less than a week after Finaly's death, Gaston de Caillavet died from uremia after a long illness. Proust wrote immediately to Jeanne de Caillavet: "If only I could shed with you the tears that are choking me! I adored Gaston, my affection for him was infinite, my heart is torn with pain, I cannot stop weeping. I had no idea of his condition: for me the news came as a bombshell." Marcel recalled Gaston's unwarranted jealous rage over his fruitless attempts to obtain Jeanne's photograph. "How absurd it is that I, the useless one, the invalid, the good-for-nothing, should remain while he, full of strength, already famous, on the eve of election to the Academy . . . should disappear." Meanwhile, the war provided constant reasons to mourn: "As a final blow to my shattered heart, which has already taken the most terrible punishment during the past year, I have just learned that there is no news of Fénelon, that it's feared he may be a prisoner or even worse."[13]

Over the next several months Proust grasped at any shred of hope concerning Bertrand's fate. Marcel would gladly have accepted the news that his friend was a prisoner of war or convalescing in a military hospital. He wrote to Antoine that the missing soldier had appeared to him in a dream: "I told him we believed he was dead."[14] Jacques Berge, Antoinette Faure's young son, had been missing in action since one of the earliest battles. When Marcel heard that the youth had been seen in a prisoner of war camp, he rejoiced for Antoinette and took Jacques's survival as a sign that Bertrand must have shared a similar fate. Joy soon turned to sorrow when it was learned that Jacques had been killed in battle.

On February 17 Bertrand's sister, the marquise de Montebello, sent Proust more discouraging news: an officer, interviewed in a prisoner of war camp, had reported seeing Bertrand fall on the battlefield, mortally wounded. Proust wrote to Mme de Montebello, saying that although her letter made him despair, he found it difficult to believe that an officer, under such circumstances, could judge the seriousness of a wound. Marcel admitted that he was clinging to the "the slightest hope for a joy after which I would be willing to die." A few days later, Proust seemed to have abandoned hope, writing to an acquaintance that he was crushed by the death of friends he deeply loved, and, above all, by the disappearance of Fénelon: "You can't imagine how much intelligence, how much heart, how much heroism there was in that exquisite creature."[15]

By early March, Robert and Reynaldo were both in the Argonne.[16] Reynaldo sent Proust a postcard of himself in uniform, a photograph the composer described as "crappy" looking but that he had sent anyway to amuse Marcel and his sisters. The extreme cold, Reynaldo wrote on the card, made everything more difficult for the men in the trenches.[17]

Gaston Gallimard had no intention of sharing such hardships while exposing himself to enemy fire. He paid two thousand francs to have a government official produce a document that declared him dead. He then made himself sick by not eating. Drinking just enough to stay alive, Gaston let his beard grow, feigned incoherence, and shook with chills whenever anyone approached him. This performance convinced his closest friends that he was incurably ill. Gaston's doctor diagnosed his symptoms as stemming from appendicitis and hepatitis. After losing nearly sixty pounds Gallimard was transported in an ambulance to a hospital, where he was examined by an eminent surgeon, Dr. Gosset, and a military doctor, who declared him unfit for military service. Having achieved his goal, Gaston kept a promise he had made himself: he got a shave and a haircut and went alone to Maxim's, where he enjoyed a sumptuous dinner, after which he vomited in the street outside the restaurant. Gallimard was passionately devoted to literature, not to defending his country.[18] Jacques Rivière, on the other hand, managed to combine patriotic and literary gestures. Rivière, who had joined the army as a sergeant, was captured in the early fighting and spent the war years in a prisoner of war camp at Königsbrück.[19] During his imprisonment, he wrote a novel and studied Russian to distract himself from his miserable existence as a prisoner, which severely undermined his nerves and health. Rivière's wife, who could never be certain of Jacques's fate, had lost her brother Henri, known as Alain-Fournier, in 1914 in the first battle of the Marne. He had been one of France's most promising young writers, and his novel Le Grand Meaulnes (1913) quickly became a classic.

In late winter Mme de Chevigné began telling friends that when anyone asked Marcel about the war he replied: "The war? I haven't yet had time to think about it. At the moment I'm studying the Caillaux affair." Marcel, perplexed and offended, protested in a letter to Lucien that despite his grief and outrage over Calmette's assassination, he had never paid any attention to the Caillaux affair. But he had not stopped thinking about the war since the first day, when he accompanied his brother to board the train for the front. He even followed troop movements and strategy "in a rather touching and ridiculous way on a General Staff map. It's true that 'Boche' doesn't figure in my vocabulary."[20] Proust soon learned, as he related to Lucien, that Cocteau had invented this story about the Caillaux affair and told it to his neighbor Mme de Chevigné, who had not questioned its authenticity. When

Proust confronted Cocteau, the young poet admitted to "synthesizing" Proust's "hothouse life and was quite astonished" that the novelist was not "delighted." This experience made Marcel reflect on the differences between Jean Cocteau on the one hand and himself and Lucien on the other: "For the two of us, while there is communication on the 'outward' journey, from life to literature (life feeding literature), there is no equivalent communication, no 'return' journey from literature to life. We don't allow literature to tinge, to distort our social relations, and to corrupt the habitual moral basis of these relations."[21]

Proust suspected Cocteau of using material from their conversations in his magazine articles. The novelist found this only mildly annoying and even somewhat amusing, for Cocteau was not an author who needed to poach in another's domain. In a March letter to Lauris, Proust apparently referred to Cocteau when he wrote about "a certain friend of ours whom you know and whom Gide knows too, above whose signature I come across everything I said to him a week ago, although he is quite rich enough to do without these slender acquisitions."[22] Proust likely had Cocteau in mind when he wrote this passage about Bloch stealing from the Narrator, a crime that incenses Françoise, who does not know the word for plagiarism but understands the offense: " 'You're too trustful,' she would say, 'all those people are nothing but copiators.' And it was true that, whenever I had outlined to Bloch something that I had written and that he admired, he would provide a retrospective alibi for himself by saying: 'Why, isn't that curious, I have written something very similar myself, I must read it to you one day,' from which I inferred that he intended to sit down and write it that very evening."[23]

With each rumor that seemed to confirm Fénelon's status as missing in action, Proust wept, fearing the worse. In early March, Antoine came to tell Marcel of his conviction that Bertrand had been killed. Proust seemed to accept this, writing to Louis de Robert that one of the people he had "loved most dearly, Bertrand de Fénelon, whom I first believed dead, then a prisoner, seems alas, . . . to have been killed. He was needed in his diplomatic post, and the ministry tried to keep him, but he was determined to join up, and it was while leading his platoon into battle that he 'disappeared.' " But soon Proust wrote Lauris that half the time he thought Fénelon was still alive: "From one hour to the next I see our misfortune differently and my mind, like a kaleidoscope successively breaking up images and forming others with the same elements, presents me alternately with Bertrand as a prisoner and Bertrand no longer alive."[24] Rumors fed such hopes; recently there had been a mysterious report that someone riding in an automobile had spotted Bertrand by the roadside. By March 13 denial was no longer possible when confirmation of

Bertrand's death appeared in the papers. The testimony of the interviewed prisoner had been accurate: Fénelon had received a bullet in the head during a heroic but futile action in the heavy fighting on December 17. His body had been identified by family photographs found in his uniform.[25]

Proust wanted to talk to Lauris at "greater length" about Bertrand's death but was "utterly prostrate." He compared Fénelon's death to his other great losses of Gaston de Caillavet and Agostinelli, saying that this death was "the least cruel . . . since I hadn't seen Bertrand for more than twelve years and it's an additional sadness that such a prolonged absence, together with my life perpetually under drugs which have destroyed my brain and killed my memory, weakens the resources of grief and prepares the way for it." Yet despite his diminished capacity for mourning, his grief was so immense that if one were to "join end to end all the pain caused to the vast majority of people by the deaths of their closest friends and even their family, you will not match the pain I feel." Turning from death to debts, Proust mentioned an appointment he must keep regarding his disastrous futures speculations and his total neglect of his financial affairs. He had recently made a mistake of ninety-eight thousand francs in a calculation and confessed that he never bothered to open the regular statements from his banks and brokers.[26] Proust not only neglected to read his statements, he completely baffled his brokers by the letters he sent. The broker David Léon recalled that he often received letters four or five pages long, brimming with Proustian orders, counterorders, and various hypotheses, attenuated with exquisite, unbusinesslike considerations that left him and his colleagues unable to determine whether the novelist wanted to carry forward or liquidate his holdings.[27]

Regarding the deaths of his three friends, Proust had left unstated a major distinction. Though deeply grieved over Gaston's death, he had never been infatuated with him, as he had with Fénelon and Agostinelli. In his tribute to Fénelon in the *Search*, the Narrator calls him "my dearest friend, the best, bravest, most intelligent of men, whom no one who knew him could forget: Bertrand de Fénelon."[28] The two men with whom Proust had fallen in love shared an important trait: both were fugacious, embodying speed and freedom of movement. Long ago in *Jean Santeuil*, Proust had depicted the scene of Bertrand running along the restaurant banquettes to bring him a coat. In the *Search* this gesture is given to Saint-Loup, who does the same favor for the Narrator.

Proust soon met Paul Morand, a diplomat who had known Fénelon and whose memoir confirmed the bisexuality of His Blue Eyes. According to Morand, Proust "invented nothing" in his sexual characterization of Saint-Loup—who first appears as the ardent lover of the actress Rachel. Proust had obtained his information about Fénelon from what Morand called the best sources: "The ravishing blond young man with blue eyes, the darling of the ladies of 1900, who served as a model for Saint-Loup, was indeed to end in heresy, or more precisely to use the jargon of the time, 'bimetallism.' "[29] *Bimétallisme* was a slang term for bisexuality. Fénelon's having kept Louisa de Mornand as a mistress may have inspired Saint-Loup's infatuation with Rachel, the aspiring actress.

There are, of course, many differences between Fénelon and Saint-Loup. After Saint-Loup marries Gilberte, he uses her and other women as a shield to hide his homosexuality, the revelation of which startles the unsuspecting Narrator, who had every reason to believe Saint-Loup to be a ladies' man. Although very much a military man and a patriot, Saint-Loup refuses, as did Fénelon, to be tainted by jingoistic or nationalistic prejudices, and like Proust's friend, he dies a hero's death: "Robert de Saint-Loup, killed . . . while covering the retreat of his men. Never had any man felt less hatred for a nation than he (and as for the Emperor, for particular reasons, very possibly incorrect, he thought that Wilhelm II had tried rather to prevent the war than to bring it about). Nor had he hated Germanism; the last words which I had heard on his lips, six days before he died, were the opening words of a Schumann song."[30] Proust had written a friend that Fénelon's "courage was all the more sublime for being totally unadulterated by hatred. He had a profound knowledge of German literature, of which I am completely ignorant."[31]

Within two months of the confirmation of Fénelon's death, Proust learned that Lt. Robert d'Humières had met a similar fate. Leading the Fourth Zouave regiment in the first wave of an attack, d'Humières had been shot in the heart. Proust remembered his friend's insatiable curiosity, "so eager to learn everything, to experience everything, that it's hard to believe such an incandescent flame has been extinguished." It was d'Humières, the translator of Kipling and Conrad, who had helped Proust with his Ruskin translations and increased his knowledge of Victorian literature.[32] When the war broke out, d'Humières had completed a third of his translation of Edith Wharton's *The Custom of the Country*.[33] Under threat of a homosexual scandal, d'Humières had asked to be posted to a Zouave regiment at the front.[34] A married man like Saint-Loup, d'Humières was another homosexual who had died bravely. The heroic deaths of Fénelon and d'Humières confirmed to Proust's satisfaction his earlier observation that homosexuals were as capable of bravery as heterosexuals.

Agostinelli is not mentioned by name in the *Search*, but many of Proust's emotions and actual experiences with Agostinelli are transfigured into the Narrator's experience with Albertine. Although Proust's experience with Agostinelli influenced the course of the plot, his early notes and sketches for the novel anticipated a character like Albertine, the Narrator's great erotic obsession. She bears traces of Fénelon (dating from the last pages Proust added to *Jean Santeuil*) and of Agostinelli in her love of speed and in certain physical characteristics that can be interpreted—once the Narrator suspects her of homosexual behavior—as masculinizing elements, an aspect she shares with Mlle Vinteuil.[35] Nearly all the major characters—the notable exceptions being Swann and the Narrator—display the androgynous characteristics that had fascinated Proust since adolescence. Fragments of the description of Albertine's legs pumping the player piano come from the descriptions of Bertrand de Fénelon (as Bertrand de Réveillon in *Jean Santeuil*) bringing Marcel the coat and of Agostinelli driving the car in "Impressions de route en automobile." The surviving remnants of real people in fictional characters—traces that are appropriately obscure—inspire the Narrator to observe: "A book is a huge cemetery in which on the majority of the tombs the names are effaced and can no longer be read."[36]

With the exception of Céleste's being as his sole servant, Proust's household routine changed little during this period. An early March letter to Lucien indicated that the writer spent six waking hours each day bent over his asthma powders, struggling to breathe, and three hours blackening his hands with ink as he feverishly dipped his pen in the inkwell, covering the pages with his rapid, small, and barely legible script.[37]

The war gave Proust more time to write and additional material to consider; Agostinelli's death lent new life and direction to the novel, leading to the development of Albertine, in whom he would concentrate all that remained for him to say about erotic love, jealousy, death, memory, oblivion, and the relationship of suffering to the creative act. In *Time Regained* the Narrator observes that "it is our passions which draw the outline of our books, the ensuing intervals of repose which write them."[38] During the war years Proust worked hard as he expanded his manuscript of roughly half a million words to approximately 1.25 million, or some three thousand printed pages.[39] Proust wrote about the war in a section called "M. de Charlus during the war."[40] But most of his efforts by far went into creating the cycle of Albertine, whose story stretches from the Narrator's first sighting of her, in *Within a Budding Grove,* pushing a bicycle on the beach with the little band of girls whom he watches with astonished admiration as they move across the sand "with a sort of shimmering harmony, the continuous transmutation of a fluid, collective and mobile beauty," through her confinement in *The Captive* and her flight, death, and his mourning for her in *The Fugitive.*[41] In *Time Regained,* the Narrator's passionate but pathologically jealous obsession with Albertine, like all his past life that he believed wasted or lost, becomes the inspiration and substance of his future work. This joyful transformation of his life's experience into a book is explained in a series of remarkably fine passages and includes his realization that the suffering he experienced because of Albertine has "impregnated" him and made him plumb the depths of his being and discover himself as a creative person: "She had fertilised me through unhappiness and even, at the beginning, through the simple effort which I had had to make to imagine something different from myself. Had she been capable of understanding my pages, she would, for that very reason, not have inspired them."[42]

Céleste remembered that the war years encouraged their late night conversations, which became ever more familiar. She described life with Proust as a "sort of upside-down and almost completely closed world where we seemed to have our own special calendar . . . and our own clock whose hours were dicated by M. Proust and had nothing to do with other people's hours."[43] Proust, curious as always, asked many questions about Céleste and her family, and especially about her childhood, remarking that it is in our earliest years that "everything is formed, paradise as well as hell." He even told her that he wanted to write a book about her, an idea at which she scoffed: "You're making fun of me!" But she found him equally fascinating as he listened intently to her reminiscences, "his cheek resting gracefully on his hand and his eyes now gentle, now laughing."[44] Céleste had four brothers and one sister; her father had died in September 1913. Not surprisingly, Proust wanted to know all about her mother. She spoke at length about her mother's goodness, leading Proust to observe that even in the best of men goodness never attained the purity, the naturalness it found in a woman. When Céleste showed him family photographs, he discovered a strong resemblance between her and her mother and observed that they were also alike in character: "There is an innocence about you that you certainly must have inherited from her." To which she replied, paying him an unexpected compliment that greatly pleased him: "That is because I find my mother again in you, monsieur. By that I meant the same care, the same warmth, the same kindness towards me."[45]

Among the extraordinary services Céleste rendered Proust, none is perhaps more noteworthy than one regarding his revisions and proofs. When he rang for her one day, she came to his room and found him beside himself with worry. When she inquired what was wrong, he said that he had filled all the margins of the exercise book, "and I still have corrections to make and lots of things to add." If he inserted extra pages, "the printer will get them all mixed up and it won't make sense. What on earth am I to do?" Céleste, "almost without thinking," replied: "If that's all, monsieur, there's no problem." Proust was incredulous: "No problem, Céleste, I would like to see you solve it!" She told him how simple it was: "Just write your extra pages, making sure you leave a bit of blank space at the top and at the bottom. And when you've finished I'll stick them in as carefully as I can at the right place. In that way you can add as much as you like—all we have to do is fold the paper. Then the printer will have to unfold the strips . . . in the right order." Proust's face "lit up. He was beside himself with relief." He was "so pleased he told everyone about it. . . . And that's how the exercise books containing the manuscript expanded."[46] From that time until the end, Céleste assisted Proust by pasting on many additions to the pages of his exercise books. One of Céleste's paste-ons, consisting of a number of separate additions, reached true Proustian proportions. When unfolded it measured one and a half meters.

The army sent Proust a notice ordering him to come to the Hôtel de Ville at 3:30 A.M. on Thursday, April 8, for a medical examination. Those who failed to report, the order warned, would be considered fit for combat.[47] The time of the appointment was obviously an error, but one that uniquely suited Proust. Unfortunately, he knew that no one else would take the hour seriously. Proust, who feared any obligation that upset his strange routine, anxiously awaited the corrected summons. Meanwhile, he asked Dr. Bize to certify that he was too ill to appear before the review board. Dr. Bize submitted the letter on April 10; the next day Proust received a new order to report for a medical exam on April 13, at 8:30 A.M. He sent a messenger to take his medical certificates to the president of the commission and asked to be excused from the formality of the standard medical examination. On returning from a doctor's appointment at the end of April, a consultation made necessary by a "strange pain in his head," Proust received a new summons to appear before the medical board. Uncertainty about his medical classification remained his greatest torment, but regardless of his fears, he was never to serve. He was eventually declared unfit and given the necessary papers, which he soon lost in the disorder of his apartment. For the duration of the war he lived in fear of being asked to produce his papers and being arrested as a draft dodger or deserter.

On April 20 Céleste entered Proust's room "screaming with sorrow." She had just received news of her mother's death. Proust wept with her and urged her to return home immediately for the funeral, telling her that even though her mother was dead, she must see her again before the burial. Having received Proust's encouragement and an embrace, Céleste left immediately for Auxillac, where she arrived too late to attend the burial.[48] The next day, Proust sent Céleste two wires. The first, at 6:30 P.M., was to let her know that he was thinking about her in her sorrow. Twenty minutes later he sent the second wire, informing her that Jean Albaret, Odilon's youngest and favorite brother, had been wounded at Vauquois. In fact, Proust, who had promised Céleste to forward any news from the front, knew through Reynaldo that Jean had been killed, but he dared not give her the awful news because she already had too much grief.[49] The same evening Proust wrote to Céleste's niece, Marcelle Larivière, asking her to take care of Céleste, to think for her, to see that she stayed warm and avoided drafts. Proust, who took a maternal interest in his young housekeeper, explained to Marcelle that by observing Céleste every day, he had come to understand her constitution. Marcelle must do everything in her power to help Céleste's "poor body bear with the least possible ill the most horrible blow that could befall her."[50]

During Céleste's absence, she was replaced by her sister-in-law Léontine Albaret, in whom Proust had little confidence, as he explained to Jeanne de Caillavet, because he did not know Léontine and "what is worse she doesn't know the apartment, can scarcely find my room if I ring, could not make my bed if I were to get up." This detail was important because Proust insisted that his sheets be changed daily during the time when he decided to leave his bed.[51] Céleste, who had found her own sanctuary at 102, boulevard Haussmann, quickly returned to Paris. When she entered his room, he told her: "My thoughts were with you all the time."[52]

Reynaldo was another who was always in his thoughts. Marcel worried constantly about his exposure to danger, in the form of both deadly munitions and inclement weather. At first, Proust could not understand why Hahn refused to take leave. Later in the summer he concluded that Reynaldo's odd behavior resulted from his profound sadness over the slaughter he witnessed daily. How could one expect Reynaldo's "adorable goodness" to withstand "the spectacle of such suffering."[53] Marcel had recently forwarded to Maria de Madrazo another photograph of Reynaldo that showed the composer rehearsing his march *Aux morts de Vauquois* (To the dead of Vauquois), commissioned by General Gouraud to honor those who died taking Vauquois, in the Argonne. Hahn, who had formerly composed lyrical love songs and light operas, now wrote funeral marches.

In late April, Proust heard from Jeanne de Caillavet, who wanted to see him. Shortly before Gaston died, he had asked his wife to tell Marcel a secret about their unhappy marriage. Although Proust was "a little embarrassed at letting a woman— especially a woman with whom I was once in love—come to visit me on my sickbed," he sent a cab for her.[54] According to Céleste, Proust was "shattered" by what

Gaston's widow told him. Gaston had fallen "madly in love with another woman—
a dancer." He ultimately broke off the affair because of Jeanne's protests, but the
playwright "never got over it." He had made her swear to tell Proust about the affair
and its aftermath. Proust, who still thought of Jeanne Pouquet as the beautiful,
vivacious girl with braided hair, listened with affliction to the white-haired woman
seated before him. After she left, Proust remarked to Céleste, "Poor Gaston, she
ought never to have made him break it off."[55]

With the approach of May, Proust began to think about the first anniversary of
Agostinelli's death. In a letter to Clément de Maugny, Proust said, without naming
his former secretary, that it had been a year since he lost a friend who "with my
mother, my father, is the person I loved most." He contacted Mme Catusse in Nice,
requesting that she send forty francs' worth of flowers to be placed on Agostinelli's
tomb. He urged her not to spend much time selecting something tasteful because
the intention would be lost on the Agostinellis. A year earlier, Agostinelli's family
had complained because the magnificent four hundred–franc bouquet Proust sent
contained real flowers instead of artificial ones. In addition to sending flowers, he
wrote Mme Jean Vittoré, Agostinelli's sister-in-law, that the war alone prevented
him from visiting his secretary's grave.[56]

On May 7 a German submarine, without warning, fired a single torpedo at the
British liner *Lusitania* off the southern coast of Ireland. The steamer, advertised as
the "fastest and largest" on the Atlantic crossing, sank in eighteen minutes. Despite
the loss of 1,198 civilian lives, including 128 Americans, President Wilson remained
firm in his determination to keep the United States out of the war. On May 23 Italy
abandoned its position of neutrality and declared war on Austria-Hungary, opening a new front.[57] In the *Search,* Proust used the sinking of the *Lusitania* in a scene
of biting satire to illustrate Mme Verdurin's shallowness. For the wealthy, social-
climbing society hostess, the war's greatest hardship has been the difficulty of
obtaining her favorite buttered croissants. Mme Verdurin uses her faithful friend
Dr. Cottard to obtain what she wants despite war shortages and rationing:

> Mme Verdurin, who suffered even more from her headaches now that
> she could no longer get croissants to dip in her breakfast coffee, had
> eventually obtained a prescription from Cottard permitting her to have
> them specially made in a certain restaurant. . . . The first of these special
> croissants arrived on the morning on which the newspapers reported the
> sinking of the *Lusitania.* As she dipped a croissant in her coffee and read
> the news account, she said, "How Horrible! This is something more hor-

rible than the most terrible stage tragedy." But the death of all these drowned people must have been reduced a thousand millions times before it impinged upon her, for even as, with her mouth full, she made these distressful observations, the expression which spread over her face, brought there . . . by the savour of that so precious remedy against headaches, the croissant, was in fact one of satisfaction and pleasure.[58]

During the summer Proust learned from Céline Cottin that Nicolas had become seriously ill from constant exposure to the elements. Proust wrote to reassure her about Nicolas and other matters of grave concern. Céline was worried about being unable to pay her rent, but Proust told her that she should not have to pay until after the war because her husband was mobilized and she had taken in refugees. He acknowledged his own inability to pay his rent due to the chaos reigning in the financial markets.[59] Proust wrote to Nicolas, sending news from the home front and attempting to raise the soldier's morale. Nicolas's recovery proceeded slowly; by late October he remained hospitalized in Ain.[60] Céline came one last time to boulevard Haussmann while Nicolas was still in the hospital. Weeping, she told Proust that her husband was cold and had asked for a blanket. No one could appreciate better than Proust the horrors of lying ill and shivering from the lack of adequate bedclothes. He instructed Céleste to give Céline the "red satin quilt he had never used," made for him so long ago by the pretty chambermaid Marie. Proust told Céleste afterward that the young servant girl had been "one of his sweethearts when he was still a young man."[61]

Bernard Grasset had been called up in the first mobilization on August 2, 1914. Shortly afterward, he became ill with typhoid fever and was given a temporary discharge. His publishing firm had nearly ceased to function because all his male employees had been mobilized. Grasset, whose recovery was slow, obtained authorization to complete his convalescence at the Chanet-Neuchâtel Clinic in Switzerland. In the summer of 1915, before leaving for Switzerland, an ailing and discouraged Grasset called on Proust.[62] The convalescent was touched by the author's friendly reception. Proust, on seeing how depressed the man appeared, was careful not to "breathe a word about business matters, or literature, or editions, or anything."[63] This was the last mercy Proust showed his publisher.

Although Proust still read seven newspapers a day, he found the press "greatly inferior to the great events about which it spoke."[64] In letters to Cocteau and Mme Catusse, he bemoaned the "stupidity" of the newspapers. The only columns he liked were Henri Bidou's "The Military Situation" in the *Journal des débats* and Colonel

Feyler's in the *Journal de Genève*. As for war literature in general, Proust felt that too many authors were rushing into print: "I've just received a book by Léon Daudet called *Hors du joug allemand* and one by Montesquiou, *Les Offrandes blessées* (188 elegies on the war). He must have started on the first day of mobilization. What fecundity!"[65] Thanking Montesquiou for his inscribed copy of *Offrandes blessées*, Proust intended to compliment the prickly count, writing among other things: "At last, thanks to you, Art and War have coincided!" But Marcel added a gentle reproach, "I don't understand why you say we liked Wagner too much."[66] Montesquiou interpreted this remark and Proust's faint praise as "insults." The count, who continued to read Proust's feelings accurately, wrote that he did not believe the recluse would keep his word and come for a visit: "There is between us, henceforth, a wall of ice. It contains, retains, maintains fresh, bright flowers; one sees them without being able to reach them."[67] Proust, having apparently learned everything he needed from Montesquiou, now seemed to despise him.

During the spring Jacques-Émile Blanche contributed to the mounting flow of war literature by serializing in the *Revue de Paris* his letters, *Lettres d'un artiste (1914–1915)*—observations of life in France during the first year of the war. The NRF now intended to publish a selection of these in a book under the title *Cahiers d'un artiste, juin–novembre 1914*. Proust, who had read the letters, wrote Blanche to share his thoughts, whereupon the painter asked Proust to read his proofs and make suggestions regarding grammar and style. Proust agreed, provided that Blanche would send the proofs rather than oblige him to read them in Blanche's presence: "I live on the surface of myself and it is only when I am alone that I redescend into the hole in which I see somewhat clearly."[68]

One evening around eleven Blanche's concierge woke him. Proust had decided to pay him a surprise visit. The drowsy artist found Marcel waiting outside in a taxi. At first Proust insisted that Blanche come and dine with him, but Blanche persuaded the nocturnal novelist to come in. Although it was June, the weather remained cool and Proust had bundled himself up in a fur coat and scarf; he reminded Blanche of someone on an expedition to the North Pole. Once inside, fearing an attack of hay fever, Marcel asked Jacques to close the windows overlooking the garden. Proust enumerated his fallen friends while lamenting the bad health that made him unable to do his duty and fight with the others.[69] He stayed until dawn, helping the painter with the proofs of his war journal and laying out, as Blanche remembered, his "*plan, the architectural structure* of his work, by which he set great store; he explained to me what *Sodom and Gomorrah* would be like . . . I closed the door, because his courageous projects horrified me, and he talked very loudly."[70] If Proust's intention to write about homosexuals alarmed a worldly artist like Blanche, the novelist must have felt that his trepidations about the subject were justified, but his determination to explore in detail the forbidden topic remained firm. Finally, an asthma attack forced Proust to leave the weary Blanche and hurry home.

On the visit to Blanche in Auteuil, Proust caught a chill, after which he ran a high fever.[71] If Montesquiou had felt a wall of ice between himself and Marcel, the novelist had experienced a similar frigid environment during his visit to Blanche. After complaining in a letter to Blanche about the doleful amnesia that plagued him, a condition he admitted aggravating by taking so many stimulants and depressants, Marcel thanked the artist for his many kindnesses during the visit: "You lent me your overcoat like a good Samaritan, you closed the window, you offered me your help with the army. But of the affectionate smile which once seemed so happy to see me again . . . not a sign. An impeccable and icy welcome. Why?"[72] Proust, who sometimes turned up unexpectedly to rouse his friends from their sleep, does not seem to have considered that such a disruption and being kept up all night, even by someone eager to see him, might have a dampening effect on the person's enthusiasm, especially an older man like Blanche, not known for his bonhomie under the best of circumstances.

While Proust bemoaned Blanche's icy reception, Montesquiou, newly offended, expressed his amazement that Proust had recently visited Mme de la Béraudière, a society hostess, friend of Reynaldo's, and the acknowledged mistress of Henri Greffulhe.[73] Writing to defend himself, Proust managed to hide his extreme annoyance at having to justify his actions to the count. After complimenting Montesquiou again on *Offrandes blessées,* he accused the count of being blind to the difficulties of his life, the daily asthma attacks that lasted until evening and left him "enveloped in a cloud of smoke which would reduce you to coughing and spluttering if you ventured to penetrate it." Marcel said that he suspected on Montesquiou's part "some sort of cruel sadism, intent on exacerbating my sorrowful Regret into Remorse." In this the count would fail, Proust maintained, because his conscience was clear. Adding another charge to his indictment, Proust said that Montesquiou, who understood "everything," had "decided . . . to indulge in the demoniacal pleasure of pretending not to understand." Proust's systematic denials of ever being well enough to visit or receive those he wanted to avoid had landed him in trouble again, and in defense he cast himself as a victim of persecution. He complained to Louis Gautier-Vignal that "people don't allow someone who seldom goes out to go out once."[74]

Montesquiou delighted in Proust's acrimonious letter, replying that although he had been in a "state of *sadness*" on reading Proust's attack, when he "reached the passage about the 'sadism' and 'demonicalness' of my persecution of you, my chagrin couldn't hold out, and gaiety broke through." The count told him about having felt obliged to "concur with one of our celebrated contemporaries who said to me last year . . . that you would always remain 'our young man.' " In his postscript the relentless Montesquiou vowed to see Proust "between a medical board and a fumigation."[75] Resigning himself to the inevitability of the visit, Proust warned the count he would find him "in bed in the midst of great disorder and with a week's growth of beard."[76] Montesquiou, seeking to ease Proust's apprehension, promised to stay no more than five minutes. Had Proust really known what to expect, he certainly would have barred the door on July 13, when the count came to his bedside and talked—as though he might never have such an opportunity again— for seven hours.[77] Marcel found Montesquiou's talk "brilliant but extenuating."[78] The unwanted nightlong visit had given Proust a dose of his own medicine, although less bitter for him than when he awakened friends from sleep and kept them up all night. Proust later made a point of describing to Montesquiou the consequences of the prolonged visit. After the count left, Marcel felt so ill that he took an enormous amount of caffeine. For several days, the palpitations and severe asthma he suffered made him think the end was near. Montesquiou, who had long ago abandoned any pretense of believing Marcel was genuinely ill, shrugged off these insinuations of attempted homicide.[79]

Proust heard several times from Agostinelli's younger brother Émile, whom he had assisted after Agostinelli's death. On Proust's recommendation, the Rostands had hired Émile as a driver. The writer had also given the threadbare youth what was left of Dr. Proust's clothes to wear. Recently Émile, who had a wife and children to support, contacted his benefactor because he feared losing his job if the Rostands left Paris for a safer region. Although Marcel rarely saw Émile, he intended to maintain contact with him in order to learn more about Agostinelli's life between the time he fled Proust's apartment and his death. Proust reminded Maurice Rostand that he had never answered his questions about whether he had learned anything of interest from Émile regarding Agostinelli or the pilots he had known at Antibes. In case Maurice suspected his motives, Marcel explained that such matters intrigued him as a "Balzacian reconstitution."[80] Sometime after Agostinelli's death, Proust had visited Buc airfield to question such aviators as Louis Gautier-Vignal, who had learned to fly in Nice.[81] Proust's persistent questioning of those who knew

Agostinelli matched the Narrator's endless investigations into Albertine's activities after her death: "My jealous curiosity as to what Albertine might have done was unbounded."[82]

Although his curiosity about Agostinelli remained keen, Proust also worried about the living. Lucien had become depressed in Tours, where he had never liked working at the Red Cross canteen, despite its proximity to the family country home at Pray. Unable to shake off his moroseness, Daudet often took long walks at night.[83] Bored and lonely away from his family and friends, he requested a transfer to one of the Red Cross ambulance convoys that ran between the first and second lines.[84] In August, Marcel wrote to Lucien, seeking to distract him with news from Paris. He knew that his friend, a devout Catholic, would be interested in Céleste's connection to Tours: "Do you remember my housekeeper (the one you thought was Swedish)? Her brother has been married for some years to Mlle Nègre, beloved niece of the Archbishop of Tours. They live with my housekeeper's family, and Monseigneur Nègre came to perform the marriage ceremony in person." Marcel also gave Lucien the startling news that the army doctor, whose competence he questioned, had found him fit for combat. But the doctor had heard so many "rales" in his lungs that he gave Proust a six-month deferment, after which another examination would be necessary.[85] These "new military doctors" had not even known that Marcel's father and brother were doctors and inquired on each visit: "You are an architect, aren't you?" If Proust felt confident about the outcome of these visits because he knew he was genuinely ill, he may have had some misgivings when he related to Lucien the account of a military medical exam Reynaldo had witnessed:

> The doctor asked the man, "Do you have any health problems?"
> "I have a heart condition."
> "No. You're fit to serve in the army."
> At that the candidate dropped dead on the spot.

Marcel told Lucien the same might happen to him. If it did, he would not regret dying, for the invalid existence he had led for the last twelve years was too cheerless to regret.[86]

Proust began to express his concern to friends about his brother's refusal to think about his own health, despite being seriously ill. Robert had been suffering from dysentery for eight months but had kept his condition hidden from his superiors, as Proust explained to Hauser, because he did not want to suspend his "horrible" work. What disturbed Robert most was a choice he had to make repeatedly; he abhorred sawing off the arms and legs of wounded soldiers and "suffered visibly" when he had to perform an amputation.[87] The bloody, grinding work of field surgeon often required him to wake up and leave his tent many times during the night to tend to the wounded and dying. Robert, who remained so close to the lines that Marcel later described him as a "very combatant" surgeon, seemed determined to push himself beyond the limit.[88] Though proud of Robert's courage, energy, and dedication, Marcel wrote a friend that his brother was a "fanatical" soldier.[89] The army eventually recognized Dr. Proust's exemplary and courageous service and rewarded him with citations and a promotion.[90]

Financial Strategies

Beginning in the summer of 1915 and through 1916, Proust and Hauser developed and implemented a strategy to bring the writer back from the brink of financial disaster, a task complicated by the war's many calamities and uncertainties. On August 24 Hauser sent Proust a plan to improve his financial position by liquidating nearly all his stocks, especially those that paid no dividends. He explained the advantage of selling off the foreign shares because, although stocks had declined, the exchange rate, in most instances, had improved, partly offsetting losses. Hauser enjoyed teasing Marcel about his new military status: "I was delighted to learn that the major who examined you found you fit for the armed services, and if in six months his opinion has not changed, I hope one day to see your chest decorated with the *croix de guerre*."[91]

Proust thanked Hauser for the financial advice, concluding his paean of gratitude: "You have therefore been nice, good, delicious, in all your advice." Then he told Hauser "very affectionately" that the remarks about his military classification had been unkind, for active duty would mean his death within forty-eight hours. Death would be a relief for him were it not that his work would die with him, a work in which he wanted to deposit "truths" that others might find "nourishing."[92]

Hauser replied in a conciliatory but jocular tone, saying that he hoped Proust was wrong about his health, but if that was not the case he could only suggest that Proust follow the example set generations earlier by his colleague Voltaire, who, despite lifelong complaints about frail health, had buried all his contemporaries.[93] Although Proust relished Hauser's wit, he found nothing amusing about references to his health, especially suggestions that he might not be as sick as he claimed. Hauser's attitude reminded him in a painful way of his father's diagnosis of his condition. But in the *Search*, Proust makes fun of his reclusive, hypochondriacal life in the person of Aunt Léonie, whose attitude about references to her health are similar to her creator's:

> My aunt had by degrees dropped every other visitor's name from her list because they were all guilty of the fatal error, in her eyes, of falling into one or other of the two categories of people she most detested. One group, the worst of the two . . . consisted of those who advised her not to "coddle" herself, and preached . . . the subversive doctrine that a sharp walk in the sun and good red beefsteak would do her more good (when she had had only two wretched mouthfuls of Vichy water on her stomach for fourteen hours!) than her bed and her medicines. The other category was composed of people who appeared to believe that she was more seriously ill than she thought, in fact that she was as seriously ill as she said. . . . In short, my aunt demanded that whoever came to see her must at one and the same time approve of her way of life, commiserate with her in her sufferings, and assure her of ultimate recovery.[94]

The extensive, detailed exchanges between fantastical Proust and common-sensical Hauser about stock market liquidations, bank loans, and interest rates often yielded to remarks about philosophy, religion, or literature. Each man enjoyed the other's wit and cleverness. In one letter Proust wrote Hauser that he had sought to console their friend Léon Neuburger, who in 1912 had lost his son Georges, only twenty-eight years old. Proust explained to Hauser that he had attempted to hold out some hope that Neuburger might see his son again in another life: "Although . . . I have no faith, on the other hand religious preoccupations are never absent from my life for a single day. But the more religious one is, the less one dares to venture in affirmation beyond what one believes. I deny nothing, I believe in the possibility of everything, objections based on the existence of Evil, etc. seem to me absurd, since suffering alone seems to me to have made, and to continue to make, man something more than a brute. But it's a long way from there to certainty, or even Hope. I haven't got there yet. Will I ever get there?"[95] The answer was apparently No.

Because operations on the Bourse had been suspended at the end of July, Proust thought that the liquidation would be postponed until the end of the war and he would not have to pay the piper until that distant date, by which time he hoped that the value of his holdings would have substantially increased. Instead, the liquidation took place at the end of September. Proust wrote Gautier-Vignal that "the liquidation of the Paris Stock Exchange has caused me endless worries and obliged me to write almost as many letters."[96]

While preparing his income tax form, Marcel realized that because of the exorbitant interest rate he was being charged on the overdue loan payments that had been mounting in the year since the war began, he was paying a rate that came to approximately 80 percent, a drain that could quickly diminish even the greatest fortunes.[97] In addition, he was paying the fairly high interest rate of 7 percent a month on the large advance from the Crédit Industriel that had financed his stock purchases.[98]

The real threat of financial ruin forced Proust to examine his position. After he sent Hauser a detailed list of his holdings at the Rothschild and Crédit Industriel banks, Hauser replied that he and his colleagues were "plunged in the study" of his accounts and would have a report in several days. He observed rather caustically that success in the market depended on the skill of the manager; Marcel belonged to the category that gets "burned."[99] On October 29 Hauser sent his report. After opening with a sentence that characterized Proust's most recent letters as "sparkling with wit" while exhibiting "an admirable insouciance of reality," Hauser handed down the verdict: Proust's debt after the Bourse liquidation reached the staggering total of 274,183.04 francs ($932,000 in late twentieth-century dollars).

Hauser followed that blow with a plan that would begin to set Proust back on a relatively stable financial footing. By selling those stocks that could be liquidated immediately, the novelist would be able to pay approximately half the debt and lose only 5,388 francs in annual dividend income while saving 22,000 francs per year on interest. Hauser's strategy called for Proust to pay off the balance of the debt as quickly as possible by selling additional stocks. Hauser concluded that once Proust paid his debts, primarily owed on futures and interest on the bank loan, he could count on a yearly income of 27,390 francs ($67,000).[100] Although Proust's speculations had reduced his fortune by approximately a third, 27,000 francs was nearly four times the sum needed to support a family of four. Toward the end of the year Hauser presented Proust with another element of his strategy for regaining financial health. Although a number of Proust's shares could not be sold through the Bourse because of the war, Hauser thought that, with enormous patience, they could sell most of them off bit by bit. Hauser began to think about transferring the balance of Proust's debt to a bank with a lower interest rate.

Grieving and Forgetting

In early November, Proust revealed the future course of the *Search* to Marie Scheikévitch, whose copy of *Swann's Way* he had not returned because he intended to do far more than just autograph it: Proust wanted to introduce Mme Scheikévitch to the character "who plays the biggest role and brings about the peripeteia, Albertine."[101] The letter summarizes the Narrator's experience with Albertine: the initial attraction, first suspicions of lesbian contacts, appeasement, boredom—a condition that befalls Proustian lovers whenever they feel secure in their possession of the desired person—and his intention of breaking with her. After Albertine reveals to the Narrator that her childhood friend, with whom she still maintains the most affectionate relations, is Mlle Vinteuil, whose homosexuality scandalized Combray, the Narrator spends "a terrible night . . . at the end of which I come in tears to my mother to ask her permission to get engaged to Albertine. Then you will see our life together during this long engagement, the slavery to which my jealousy reduces her and which, by successfully assuaging my jealousy, dispels, or so I believe, the desire to marry her." In letters to friends, Proust nearly always speaks of the Narrator as "I," referring to himself. Proust did not portray the Narrator as as the real Marcel Proust, but when speaking about his book he often assumed his protagonist's voice. As Proust lived more and more in the world he invented, he came to embody the Narrator rather than the other way around.

The marriage, of course, never takes place, because Albertine, like Agostinelli, flees the apartment where the Narrator tried to make her his captive and, shortly thereafter, is killed in a horseback riding accident. After Albertine's death the Narrator realizes that she is alive in him: "In order to enter into us, a person is obliged to assume the form, to comply with the framework of Time; appearing to us only in a succession of moments, he has never been able to reveal to us more than one aspect of himself at a time, to present us with more than a single photograph of himself. A great weakness no doubt for a person, to consist only in a collection of moments, a great strength too; for he is a product of memory." After observing that "memories of love are no exception to the general laws of memory, itself ruled by Habit, which weakens everything," the Narrator notices that he had begun "gradually to succumb to the force of forgetfulness, that powerful instrument of adaptation to reality, destructive in us of the surviving past which is in perpetual contradiction with it." As he expounded his theory of remembering and forgetting to Mme Scheikévitch, Proust spoke about "the cruelty of memory" and concluded with this example: "After a certain time, a patient suffering from cancer will be dead. It is very uncommon, after the same length of time, for an inconsolable widower not to have been cured."[102] Swann dies from a real tumor and not the metaphorical one to which Proust often compares his pathological love of Odette before their marriage.

Albertine's role as a new central character would greatly alter the original content, though not the substance, of his novel.[103] Texts that predate *Swann's Way* and his infatuation with Agostinelli contain the essential components of Proust's analysis of love. The conclusion of one sentence from the *Carnet de 1908* sums up succinctly the experience of all Proustian lovers: "In the second part of the novel the girl will be financially ruined and I will keep her without seeking to possess her owing to an incapacity for happiness."[104] All Proust's lovers suffer from this "incapacity for happiness," with variations on the theme of obsessive jealousy over heterosexual or homosexual infidelities: Swann and Odette, Saint-Loup and Rachel, the Narrator and Albertine, and Charlus and Morel.[105]

Proust's isolation and his disappointments in love and friendship—upon which he had made, as do Swann, the Narrator, and Charlus, impossible demands—led him to some somber conclusions regarding sentimental attachments: "The bonds between ourselves and another person exist only in our minds. Memory as it grows fainter loosens them, and notwithstanding the illusion by which we want to be duped and with which, out of love, friendship, politeness, deference, duty, we dupe other people, we exist alone. Man is the creature who cannot escape from himself, who knows other people only in himself, and when he asserts the contrary, he is lying."[106]

The sorrows of the lover and of the mourner will play an important role in the creation of art, as the Narrator learns upon discovering the secrets of his vocation, but particular sorrows and regrets are in themselves transitory, for we are not capable of sustaining such emotions over protracted periods of time: "In this world of ours where everything withers, everything perishes, there is a thing that decays, that crumbles into dust even more completely, leaving behind still fewer traces of itself, than beauty: namely grief."[107]

Sometime before mid-November, Reynaldo finally came home to a Paris shrouded in fog and blanketed in snow. Mme Duglé, a society hostess, arranged a soirée at which the pianist Édouard Hermann joined Reynaldo in performing his new waltzes for four hands: *Ruban dénoué, suite of waltzes for two pianos.* Hahn had composed the waltzes at Vauquois and dedicated them "To the armies of 1915." Marcel arrived at Mme Duglé's a few minutes late, dripping with rain and shivering from the cold; he kept on his pelisse during the concert. In a letter to Maria, he praised Reynaldo's "sublime waltzes, to my mind the highest point his art has ever reached, which together with certain Beethoven quartets made on me the most extraordinary impression I have experienced in music." Hahn had managed to conjure up "in his desolate solitude the purest and most heart-rending strains I know."[108] Afterward Proust felt too unwell to stay for the party in Hahn's honor.[109] Having waited for months for Reynaldo to come home, Marcel became so ill with incessant asthma attacks that he had to receive his friend in the midst of his fumigations, where the two could barely see each other through the dense swirls of smoke. Yet he saw clearly enough to note that Reynaldo looked "superbly well."[110]

If the war had taken away many of Proust's friends, either permanently or for its duration, it had brought him new acquaintances as well. A few of these, like Henri Bardac, whom he had known slightly before, became good friends, bringing with them other unknown and fascinating young men. Bardac, son of a wealthy financier, was a friend of Reynaldo's. When Marcel first met him in 1906, he thought Bardac resembled a "pink coral guinea-pig."[111] After receiving a serious head wound in the battle of the Marne, Bardac was sent to London as an attaché at the French embassy.[112] While there, Bardac spoke about a remarkable new book called *Swann's Way* to a young diplomat and writer named Paul Morand. Henri made frequent, extended trips to Paris, where he soon became part of Proust's intimate circle. In June, when Proust believed that Bardac was about to return to the front, he paid the attaché a visit. By July 1915 Proust was increasingly interested in Bardac and aware of his many fine qualities. By fall the exchange of visits between Bardac and Proust had grown more frequent. Occasionally, Proust asked Henri, as he had Albert Nahmias, to meet with his broker David Léon and discuss matters pertaining to the Bourse.[113] It had taken him a long time to appreciate Bardac's dry wit and to recognize how "remarkably intelligent and excessively nice" the wounded soldier really was; he found Henri "truly perfect."[114]

With Henri, Marcel could observe the ravages of war at close hand. In a letter to Hauser, the novelist enumerated Bardac's various incapacities, most of which resulted from the serious head injury that had left a deep scar curving from his forehead down over his right temple. Bardac had "lost an ear, his facial nerve," and "part of the use of a leg, and many other things, it's rather sad. He still has infinite resources of wit and soul."[115] Henri's facial scar may have inspired a similar cicatrix on Saint-Loup's forehead. Bardac was linked to the homosexual world of Paris high society. His great passion appears to have been a valet by the name of Charlie Humphries, whom Bardac designated as his heir.[116]

As much as Proust admired Bardac's pluck and enjoyed his quiet company, he was even more impressed by Bardac's friend Paul Morand, a twenty-seven-year-old diplomat and writer, whose circle the novelist would soon join. Morand's true vocation was writing, but he had been an attaché at the French embassy in London since the spring of 1913. In early September, Bardac wired Proust, telling him of Morand's great admiration for *Swann's Way* and informing him that the young diplomat was coming to Paris to spend four days in Bardac's apartment.[117]

One evening at 11:30 Paul Morand was wakened by the doorbell, which signaled the beginning of the most extraordinary night.[118] Without bothering to put on a bathrobe over his pajamas, Morand, who was expecting no visitors, opened the door. He saw standing before him a "very pale" man, wearing a thick but worn fur coat and a scarf, despite the warm evening. Morand, although half-asleep, had a writer's eye and quickly took in the features of the strange personage in the doorway. Proust's black hair was so thick that it pushed back the gray bowler, he carried a cane and wore slate-colored kid gloves, his teeth were large and perfect, with heavy lips set off by a mustache and large dark eyes whose gaze was both soft and magnetic. The nocturnal visitor announced in a "ceremonious" and "tremulous" voice: "I am Marcel Proust."

The astonished Morand invited him in. Proust, who asked permission to keep on his pelisse, began to speak in an insinuating but authoritative voice which Morand immediately recognized as the one he had found so spellbinding in *Swann's Way*. After telling Morand to get back into bed, Proust explained that he could go out only late at night and had taken the liberty of ringing the doorbell because Bardac had told him how much Morand liked *Swann's Way*. Morand later remembered that he "had even cried out, after having read *Swann:* 'It's so much better than Flaubert!' This cry of enthusiasm had reached Proust," who was now sitting down in front of the white marble chimney at the foot of Morand's bed. So began a long visit.

Morand had first heard of Proust through Bertrand de Fénelon in the fall of 1914, when Bertrand passed through London on his way to joining the army, having resigned his diplomatic post. Fénelon said that Proust was the author of two books he had paid to have published. (Bertrand was mistaken; *Pleasures and Days* had been published without any subvention from the author.) Marcel was a "Saturnian," by which, Fénelon apparently meant, sullen and "very difficult in matters of friendship."[119] What he had said of *Swann's Way* had greatly interested Morand. When it came to Proust the man, Bertrand spoke only in veiled terms; the novelist's admirers gave the impression of belonging to a secret society. When Morand read *Swann's Way* he knew that he was in the presence of something new and great.

When the usually articulate Morand tried to express what *Swann* meant to him, he heard himself muttering sentences that sounded awkward and insufficient. He noticed a nervous fluttering of Proust's long eyelashes, which he took as a signal that the novelist found his clumsiness appealing. Paul's impression was accurate; Proust was immediately drawn to the handsome, blond, baby-faced attaché.

The diplomat, who harbored ambitions to be a writer, found himself matched with the man whose conversation was said to be the most brilliant in a city of legendary oral wits. The Proustian spoken sentence, as registered by Morand that evening, was "singsong, caviling, reasoned, answering objections the listener would never have thought of making, raising unforeseen difficulties, subtle in its shifts and pettifoggery, stunning in its parentheses—that, like helium balloons, held the sentence aloft—vertiginous in its length . . . well constructed despite its apparent disjointedness; as you listened spellbound, you risked becoming enmeshed in a network of incidents that was so tangled that you would have been lulled by its music had you not suddenly been alerted by an observation of unbelievable pro-fundity or brilliant comedy."[120] Morand remained dumbstruck in admiration. What he felt most strongly in the room that evening was the presence of genius.

"I'm going," Proust would say, without making any move to leave. Morand, though fascinated and grateful for the extraordinary visit, felt heavy with sleep and watched for any sign that Proust might be ready to leave. When Proust crossed his legs, his black socks fell down around the gray uppers of his patent leather ankle boots. When he grew tired of that position, Proust uncrossed his legs, straightened his cane on his knees and—head thrown back—recommenced his monologue.

Proust said that he had made an exception to come out and meet Morand that night, an exception he would pay for afterward. He then described the "art of living" with this famous traitor known as illness, how he changed—to the amaze-ment of specialists—the prescribed doses of stimulants and depressants, how he consumed huge quantities of caffeine in pill form, or brewed, which he often laced with bromide, as a corrective to coffee's stimulating properties. Morand, aghast at what he heard, remarked that Proust was applying the accelerator and the brakes at the same time. Proust replied that he knew better than anyone what was good for him, adding, "We are never cured; at best we learn to live with our maladies." By now it was two in the morning, and despite his admiration of *Swann's Way* and his intense curiosity about the contents of the future volumes, Morand dared not question Proust. The novelist continued to talk for a long time, in the affectionate tone, mildly teasing, that older, experienced men use to talk to young women.

When he finally prepared to leave, Proust extended an invitation to Morand to stop by 102, boulevard Haussmann or perhaps meet him at Larue's for dinner one evening. If Morand liked music, and Poulet had not been drafted, Proust could rent a room somewhere and engage the Poulet Quartet to play. Standing, but not moving toward the door, Proust continued to chatter like a sleepwalker, Morand thought, for whom time is suspended, and who, as the hour advances, becomes more and more brilliant and seductive to prevent you from going to bed. "I could invite whomever you'd like, except Mme Straus who doesn't go out and your friend Mme Scheikévitch whose perfumes would give me an asthma attack. Don't worry it would not be like the tête-à-tête I imposed on you tonight." Proust left around 3:30 in a taxi that had been waiting at the door for four hours. Morand understood from the beginning why Proust found him appealing: because of his connections as an embassy attaché and his possession of what Proust admired above all, for sexual and aesthetic reasons: youth.

The Private Life of a Genius

For what fault have you most toleration?
For the private life of geniuses.

Even at age thirteen, Marcel understood the importance of tolerance.[121] He extended this compassion to friends and to his characters. In order to create those characters, Proust drew from many sources: from his own experiences and observations, from his extensive readings, and from a network of informants. Many of those who supplied him information did so casually in conversations at parties, where he would learn all he could from the hostess and her guests, as well as the servants, with whom he would speak on arriving or leaving.

Proust depended on two primary sources of information, and he was willing to pay. Both men were specialists, each highly knowledgeable in his domain: Olivier Dabescat's restaurant at the Ritz served the wealthy elite from all over Europe, and Albert Le Cuziat operated a male brothel and Turkish baths for men who wished to remain anonymous. Proust was a client of both Olivier and Albert. Although being seen at the Ritz could be pleasant, Proust feared staying long at Le Cuziat's brothel, which was often the target of police raids.

He was frank with Céleste regarding the nature of Le Cuziat's establishment, which it was rumored Proust had helped finance initially. He often interviewed Albert at home or went to the brothel, located in the Hôtel Marigny at 11, rue de l'Arcade, not far from his apartment. Céleste remembered the first time she saw Le Cuziat, when he answered one of Proust's summons to come to boulevard Haussmann. She described Albert, whom she detested, as "a bean-pole of a Breton, slovenly, fair, with cold blue eyes like a fish—eyes that matched his soul. The precariousness of his profession was in his face and his look, a hunted look, which was not surprising, seeing that . . . he often did short spells in jail." Le Cuziat had started his career as a footman in the service of the Russian Count Orloff before coming to Paris to serve Prince Constantin Radziwill, who hid his homosexual proclivities from no one, including his wife. Céleste believed that it was at Prince Radziwill's home that Proust met Le Cuziat. Having become expert in the practices and needs of the closeted homosexuals of Paris, Le Cuziat opened a succession of brothels and Turkish baths. Céleste was well informed about the history of his businesses: He had "started near the Bourse" in 1913 and "then kept a bathhouse on rue Godot-de-Mauroy, a street near la Madeleine." Two years later "he opened a . . . male brothel . . . on rue de l'Arcade." Céleste denied the rumors that Proust gave Albert money or furniture from storage to get his business going, but she did admit that when "Le Cuziat told M. Proust he didn't have enough money to buy furniture for his own bedroom," the writer "let him have the key to the shed and told him to take what he wanted. He only took a green half-length chaise-longue—a sort of reclining arm chair—and one or two other chairs and a pair of curtains."[122]

If, as Céleste recorded, Proust paid Olivier Dabescat to "keep him informed of such details as who dined with whom, what dress Mme so-and-so wore, and what sort of etiquette was observed at the various tables," Le Cuziat provided information of a more intimate and potentially scandalous nature, such as "the names of people who used to frequent the house in rue de l'Arcade—they included politicians and even ministers. Albert supplied details about their vices." When Proust wanted information from the brothel, he sent Céleste with a note to the rue de l'Arcade to summon Albert, always warning her, "And don't forget, Céleste, ask for him and give him the letter personally. And whatever you do, see that he *gives it back to you*." Proust did not want anyone to know about his relationship with Le Cuziat. He also feared being caught on the premises, as he admitted to Céleste: "I don't like to stay there too long when I go." Proust added, "You never know when there will be a police raid. I shouldn't like to see myself all over tomorrow's papers!"

Proust was using the details about what he saw at Le Cuziat's for the creation of Jupien's male brothel in the *Search*.[123] Céleste found it strange that Proust would call her to his room as soon as he returned from Le Cuziat's and relate to her, in rather graphic language, what he had seen through the peephole, "just as if he'd come back from an evening at comte de Beaumont's or Comtesse Greffulhe's." When she told Proust that it was incomprehensible that he would receive someone like Le Cuziat and, even worse, go to his establishment, he replied, "I know, Céleste. You can't imagine how much I dislike it. But I can only write things as they are, and to do that I have to see them."

One afternoon Proust received a message from the Hôtel Marigny, telling him to come that evening if he wanted to see a spectacle Albert had told him about that had made him intensely curious. Afterward, when he returned home, Céleste noticed that he "came in with his hat cocked, which meant he hadn't been wasting his time." He told her that what he had seen that evening was "unimaginable." He had watched "through a little window in the wall" as a man was being whipped. The client was supposedly a "big industrialist who comes down from the north of France specially for that. Imagine—there he is in a room, fastened to a wall with chains and padlocks, while some wretch, picked up heaven knows where, who gets paid for it, whips him till the blood spurts out all over everything. And it is only then that the unfortunate creature experiences the heights of pleasure." His incredulous housekeeper asked, "And did you have to pay a lot of money to see it?" Proust answered, "Yes, Céleste. But I had to."

Céleste expressed her disgust with Le Cuziat, saying that he deserved to die in prison. Proust, who found redeeming qualities in everyone, pointed out that the pander adored his mother and did everything possible for her when she was alive.[124] But Proust did not, despite Céleste's assertions in her book to the contrary, tell her everything. A young prostitute who worked for Le Cuziat left his testimony, which the novelist Marcel Jouhandeau recorded in a notebook.[125] Some nights Proust went to the brothel and "looked through a glass pane into a room where a game of cards was in progress. He selected his partner and went upstairs," said the young man, who was often chosen by Proust. "A quarter of an hour later, I knocked on the door, went in, and found Marcel already in bed with the sheet drawn up to his chin. He smiled at me. My instructions were to take all my clothes off and remain standing by the closed door while I satisfied myself under the anxious gaze of Marcel, who was doing the same. If he reached the desired conclusion, I left after having smiled at him and without having seen anything other than his face and without having touched him. If he didn't reach the desired conclusion, he would make a gesture for me to leave and Albert would bring two cages." Each cage contained a famished rat. Albert would set the cages together and open the doors. The two starving beasts would attack each other, making piercing squeaks as they clawed and bit each other. This spectacle allowed Proust to achieve orgasm.[126] The prostitute's testimony about Proust's wanting no physical contact sounds authentic, given his poor condition and especially his germ phobia, which Céleste saw become intense during the final years.

After Proust's death, Céleste scoffed at the rumors about the caged rats, as she did at any gossip that might discredit him. But Proust admitted to Gide, whose credibility seems unquestionable, that he engaged in such practices. Gide recalled the conversation in his posthumously published memoir *Ainsi soit-il:* "During a memorable nighttime conversation (of which there were so few that I remember each of them well) Proust explained his preoccupation with combining the most diverse sensations and emotions in order to achieve orgasm. That was the justification for his interest in rats, among other things; in any case Proust wanted me to see it as such. Above all, I saw it as the admission of some type of psychological inadequacy."[127] To which Gide might have added a physiological inadequacy as well, given Proust's peculiar regimen and excessive use of drugs and caffeine. Marcel apparently never had a sexually fulfilling relationship with a companion whom he loved. If he did, there are no traces of it in his letters and writings. The Narrator observes in his account of Swann's love affair with Odette: in "physical possession . . . the possessor possesses nothing."[128]

Another aspect of the rumors regarding Proust's sexual practices is more questionable. Proust allegedly showed photographs of his distinguished lady friends to male prostitutes, who had been instructed to spit on them. According to Maurice Sachs, as the prostitutes defiled the photograph of "the princesse de C***," they asked, "Who's that whore?"[129] Other accounts claim Marcel subjected photographs of his mother to such defilement.[130] Sachs is not an especially credible witness. Céleste's objection to this story is practical, however, rather than moral. Because Proust would ring for her to come to his room and hand him any item he needed that was not on the bedside table, she simply could not imagine Proust, with no assistance, finding the box of photographs, wrapping them up, taking them to a brothel, and then returning home with them. "The only thing he ever took out with him was sugar, which he had me do up in a parcel to give as a present to my sister-in-law, Adèle Larivière, when it was rationed during the war."[131]

The theme of parents who are saddened or destroyed by their children appears in Proust's earliest work. Matricide had been at the center of Proust's early story "La Confession d'une jeune fille." Traces of this theme remain in the *Search,* in the good-night kiss scene and in the guilt the Narrator feels over the grandmother's death, and in the case of Vinteuil, who dies of a broken heart because of his daughter's lesbian affairs.[132] The sacred and profane theme of love is skillfully woven throughout the *Search*. Ultimately, the nameless lesbian friend of Vinteuil's daughter redeems herself and Mlle Vinteuil by transcribing and publishing his compositions, which were long thought illegible and irretrievable. Some have seen the *Search* as an act of redemption for all the pain Proust caused his parents. Whether this was conscious or not is difficult to say, but surely any great work that enriches the lives of others is redemptive.

The details of the amorous relationship between Proust and the men to whom he was attracted are likely to remain unknown. Louis Gautier-Vignal, who often saw Proust during the period after Agostinelli's death and observed his poor health and dependence on others—especially Céleste—believed that all of Proust's crushes on young men were platonic and that moreover Proust was probably impotent.[133] The only putative eyewitness account of Proust's having sex is that of the anonymous prostitute. That partner—the term seems overstated, for there was no contact—watched Proust presumably masturbating under the covers. This testimony sounds plausible, especially for Proust of the later years, when he was nearly incapacitated by illnesses and self-medication. No other documents are available to serve as a peephole that would allow us to look at Proust naked and exposed.

24 *A Fortuny Gown* ∾

IN HIS NEW YEAR'S MESSAGE TO ANTOINE, Marcel sent "all the best of wishes in these sad days, which remind us that the years return laden with the same natural beauties but without bringing back people with them. Alas, 1916 will have its violets and apple blossoms, but there will never be a Bertrand again."[1] Proust sent Odilon a New Year's greeting that was affectionate but brief, because his eyes were bothering him.[2] He had never worn glasses and began to complain constantly to friends about eyestrain. In the summer, Hauser urged him to consult an optometrist. Finally realizing that Proust would never take such a practical step, Hauser offered to see whether his optometrist would be willing to come to boulevard Haussmann in the evening and examine Proust's eyes.[3] The writer continued to complain but did nothing to alleviate the problem.

Early in the year Emmanuel Berl, a sixteen-year-old soldier with literary ambitions, wrote Proust from the trenches.[4] Proust was amazed to find little pieces of shrapnel still attached to the letter when it was handed to him. Berl had received a copy of *Sésame et les lys* from the English poet and critic Mary Duclaux and had been impressed with the essay "On Reading." In replying to Berl, Proust engaged the young man in a debate about friendship and made this observation about himself: "I am myself only when alone, and I profit from others only to the extent that they enable me to make discoveries within myself, either by making me suffer (hence rather through love than through friendship) or by their absurdities (which I don't like to see in a friend), which I don't mock but which help me to understand human character." Proust sent Berl a copy of *Swann's Way* and a number of letters, which the soldier lost in the mud of Lorraine. Berl visited Proust several times in 1917.[5] On one occasion the two men continued the debate about love and friendship. When Berl, who was madly in love with his fiancée, insisted that happy couples do exist, Proust grew annoyed at what he considered the young man's naïveté and remarked that Berl would be better off if the girl were dead. Berl recoiled and Proust, furious, told Berl he was stupid and threw his slippers at the astonished young man, who became angry in turn and left.[6]

As he completed *Within a Budding Grove* and other episodes of the Albertine cycle, Proust called on younger friends to provide details about the lives of adolescent girls. He consulted Céleste's niece Marcelle Larivière about two high school French compositions he was to attribute to Gisèle. He had selected as topics for the compositions works by his mother's and grandmother's favorite seventeenth-century writers: Racine, Mme de Sévigné, and Mme de La Fayette.[7] Marcelle, as bright as she was diligent, provided excellent summaries, for which Proust thanked her, finding them to be "quite perfect."[8] He wrote to Gautier-Vignal to ask him about the aviators he had known at nearby Buc as well as in Antibes.[9] Later in the year he contacted Albert Nahmias, requesting information about what sort of clothes young ladies wore to dine out while on seaside vacation. He also questioned Albert about all the nicknames of the little train that served the coastal resorts.[10]

In addition to working on texts for the Albertine cycle, Proust wrote the first drafts of his pages on Paris during the war. A conversation he had with Mme de Chevigné, "very charming and very worried about her son's safety," and M. Greffulhe, both of whom told stories about the old days, reinforced his impression that the war had created a "formidable" earthquake throughout French society, making the years before 1914 appear as far from the present as the days of the ancien régime. In the *Search,* Proust commented on this watershed. Although it had been a relatively short time since the decadelong Dreyfus Affair had sharply divided French society, people's memories were so short that few remembered who had been Dreyfusards and who had not: "All *that* had been a very long time ago, a 'time' which these people affected to think longer than it was, for one of the ideas most in vogue was that the pre-war days were separated from the war by something as profound, something of apparently as long a duration, as a geological period, and Brichot himself, that great nationalist, when he alluded to the Dreyfus case now talked of 'those prehistoric days.' "[11]

On February 21 the Germans launched a fierce offensive against a small fortified town on the River Meuse. The French, under General Pétain, adopted the slogan "Thou shalt not pass." Before the battle of Verdun ended in December, more that two million men were engaged, half of whom were killed. It was the longest and bloodiest battle of the war.

In February, Proust worked on a leitmotiv he was creating for scenes in the two sections that close the Albertine cycle, *The Captive* and *The Fugitive*. He wrote to Hahn's sister, Maria de Madrazo, to obtain information about Fortuny dresses. Mariano Fortuny y Madrazo, the famous Venetian couturier who made his own fabrics by a secret process, was the nephew of Maria's husband and cousin to Marcel's friend "Coco" de Madrazo. But first, Marcel wanted Maria's investment advice. He had recently sold "some minor shares" at a loss in order to reduce a bank loan and remembered she had told him once about some "astonishing tips about American shares." Did she have any leads on "American stocks or gold-mines, which might compensate a little for the loss I've incurred with the bank."[12] Such a request sounded like the old, reckless Marcel, not the "burned," reformed speculator who had made so many pledges to Hauser never to take such risks again. Fortunately for Proust, Reynaldo advised Maria not to "bother to reply to Marcel in detail; he gets rather fussy about his shares and has got into the habit of writing to all and sundry."[13] Broaching a safer topic, Proust asked Maria for "advice about female costumes, not for any mistress but for fictional heroines." He particularly wanted to know whether or not Fortuny had ever used as motifs "for his dressing-gowns . . . those coupled birds, drinking for example from a vase, which are so recurrent on the Byzantine capitals in St Mark's." And if so, did she know "whether there are pictures in Venice (I should like a few titles) showing cloaks or dresses from which Fortuny drew (or might have drawn) inspiration. I would find a reproduction of the painting and see if it might inspire me."

A few days later Proust sent Maria a second letter in which he summarized the role of Fortuny dressing gowns in the Albertine episode, explaining why he wanted to know which Carpaccio paintings might have inspired the couturier: "At the beginning of my second volume a great artist with a fictitious name, who symbolizes the Great Painter in my book as Vinteuil symbolizes the Great Composer (such as Franck), says in front of Albertine (who I don't yet know will one day be my adored fiancée) that according to what he has heard an artist has discovered the secret of the old Venetian materials etc. This is Fortuny." During the period of her engagement to the Narrator, he gives her some Fortuny dresses, a brief description of which "illustrates our love scenes," and "since, as long as she is alive, I don't realize how much I love her, these gowns chiefly evoke Venice for me, and the desire to go there, a plan to which her presence is an obstacle etc."[14] Later, after Albertine's death, the Narrator goes to Venice "where in the paintings of X (let's say Carpaccio) I find one of the dresses I gave her. In the past this dress evoked Venice for me and made me want to leave Albertine; now the Carpaccio in which I see it evokes Albertine and makes Venice painful to me." Proust concluded by telling Maria that while the "Fortuny leitmotiv" was "not very extensive," it was "crucial," and was "partly sensual, poetic and sorrowful." In early March, Proust described *The Fugitive* as being "almost entirely about death and survival in the memory."[15]

Maria replied by lending Marcel a book about Carpaccio with two of the paintings that had apparently inspired Fortuny, *The Holy Cross* and *The Legend of St. Ursula*. In thanking her, Proust made an additional request: "When you see Fortuny I'd be most grateful if you could ask him for the most direct possible description of the cloak."[16] Whether or not Fortuny provided the description is not known, but Proust's consultation of a modest schoolgirl and a renowned artist illustrates his constant search for precise details to enrich his palette. Lucien, who now visited more frequently, was asked for advice concerning Albertine's gold vanity case, one similar to the ones Proust had given the Alton girls in 1911.[17] Marcel asked Lucien whether a girl could take one along in an automobile. Proust was to use Albertine's vanity case, ordered from Cartier's, to demonstrate the Narrator's obsessive jealousy. When they take the train out to La Raspelière for dinner with the Verdurins, he realizes that if she had a vanity case, she could do her sprucing up in the train and would not have to leave his side when they arrived at the villa.

In the Narrator's recollection of how Albertine looked in the Fortuny cloak she had worn on their last excursion to an airfield near Paris, Proust used a detail from his correspondence with Agostinelli. He attributed to Albertine a line from Alfred's last letter: "that melancholy occasion which she was to describe in her last letter as 'a double twilight since night was falling and we were about to part.' "[18] Agostinelli, like Albertine, like all those lost and mourned, had been consigned in Proust's emotions to the general law of oblivion.[19]

That spring, as the battle raged, Proust wrote at least the first draft of Paris during the war.[20] In its pages he observed the changing face of the city: "There was a march past of allied troops in the most variegated uniforms; and among them, the Africans in their red divided skirts, the Indians in their white turbans were enough to transform for me this Paris through which I was walking into a whole imaginary exotic city."[21]

Opium or Dynamite?

In mid-May Hauser found a bank willing to refinance Proust's loan at a rate of 5.5 percent with no commission. The London County and Westminster Bank, a reputable English firm, would charge him only eleven thousand francs in annual interest instead of the sixteen thousand he had been paying. If the loan went through, Proust's net income would increase by 25 percent.[22] Hauser also sent encouraging news regarding the shares in the Russian Doubowaia Balka iron mines; it should be possible to sell them on the Bourse in lots of twenty-five or fifty shares. If so, Proust could further reduce his debt by approximately one hundred thousand francs, which would nearly put him in the black.[23]

Hauser next urged Proust to withdraw all his funds from the Crédit Industriel. The accountant had found the bank guilty of so many irregularities, including sloppy bookkeeping, that he advised Proust to clear all his accounts there, even if he might wish to reopen them afterward.[24] Proust declined to do so, saying that because of family attachments he preferred to keep "something" at that bank. This lack of cooperation drew a sharp rebuke from Hauser, who had earlier warned Proust about mixing business and sentimentality. In order to serve the writer's best interests, Hauser needed to be "entirely free to act."[25] He compared Proust's attitude in sticking with the inefficient bank to a "woman beaten by her husband."[26] The comparison offended Proust, who scolded Hauser gently and advised him that "a friendly word of comfort such as I have often had from you would have done me more good than your sarcasm." After expressing his deep gratitude for all Hauser's efforts, Proust admitted, "There are times when I find it difficult to accept your severities."

Instead of being moved or persuaded, Hauser admonished Proust again, adopting the tone of a family member responsible for a wayward child. Saying that he had no intention of changing the way he treated Marcel, Hauser observed: "You have grown since your childhood, but you haven't aged, you have remained a child who will not accept being scolded even when he is disobedient. This is why you have eliminated from your circle all those who, refusing to succumb to your wheedling, have had the courage to scold you when you were naughty. The consequence is the situation in which you now find yourself." Hauser agreed with Proust that "man is not entirely the master of his destiny, but this fact ought not to encourage you to abandon the helm while your mind, lulled by delightful dreams, floats above your languishing body. Meanwhile, I shall do all I can to waken you, which explains why instead of opium I employ dynamite." Having subjected his

sentimental client to a strong cautionary blast, Hauser directed Proust's attention
to the loan forms to sign from the London County and Westminster Bank and the
"list of the shares agreed upon by the above establishment as security for the
advance designed to repay your debt to the Crédit Industriel."[27]

In his reply, Proust declined to debate the "question of mental maturity, moral
aging, the parallelism between spiritual and physical growth, a dissertation which
would bore you without convincing you," and he "would leave it to neurologists to
decide whether opium or dynamite is more effective in treating neurotic persons."[28] In another letter, Proust acknowledged that his huge financial losses were
the result of his own stupidity: "I regret them deeply, but I don't speak about them
in the elegiac mode." What he did lament were "the deaths and sufferings of the
others." He agreed to sell everything that Hauser proposed in order to pay off his
huge cash advance at the bank. Should there be any income left over, he would
request funds to pay a portion of what he owed on his rent and what he called
Céleste's grocery bills, for he did not eat.[29]

On June 21 Hauser wrote to give Proust the good news about his relatively
healthy financial status. Hauser calculated that Proust's income had risen to about
eighteen thousand francs, plus fifteen hundred francs in interest earned by the loan
of stocks to the Treasury, an increase of 80–95 percent, according to Hauser's calculations. Proust still needed to liquidate the remaining Doubowaia Balka stocks,
which were earning no income. (Hauser's liquidation of the Russian stocks proved
timely, coming just nine months before the outbreak of the Russian Revolution.)
One month later Hauser wrote that he had sold 102 shares of Doubowaia Balka,
leaving Proust with 400 shares.[30] Marcel was delighted with results of the sale and
congratulated Lionel: "If Napoléon lived in our time, instead of making Ney Prince
of the Moskova, he would have made Hauser Prince of the Doubowaia." Then,
referring to other shares he held, Proust added: "Let us hope that the titles of Duke
of Mexico and La Plata and Prince Suzerain of Egypt will soon be added to it."[31]

The Incommensurable Keyboard

In early March, Proust went out once to hear Beethoven's Twelfth Quartet.[32] In a
letter written at the time, he told a friend: "For several years Beethoven's late
quartets and Franck's music have been my primary spiritual nourishment."[33] Later
in the month he wrote to Mme Catusse that he was feeling rather well: he had been
able to get up more often, and he was working. It pained him that his mother could

not have foreseen this improvement in his health; how many worries that would have spared her. Still, his life remained complicated by his inability to predict when he would feel better and by the consequences suffered whenever he increased his activity. If he went out to hear one of Beethoven's late quartets, he paid for the pleasure by spending the following week in bed.[34]

As Proust attended concerts where he listened to pieces by Beethoven, Franck, and Fauré, he developed the Narrator's meditations on music that occur at key moments on his journey to self-discovery. Works by these composers and others, such as Mozart, Schumann, and primarily Wagner, provided the inspiration for the compositions of Proust's fictional composer Vinteuil, whose works move Swann and the Narrator to meditate on music and the creative imagination. One work Proust was eager to hear again in the late winter of 1916 was César Franck's Quartet in D as performed by the Poulet Quartet. One evening at a concert by this ensemble, Proust approached the viola player Amable Massis during the intermission and asked him whether the group would be willing to come and play for him in a private concert. Massis agreed in principle and thought no more about it.

One night around eleven Gaston Poulet, the leader of the quartet, heard his doorbell ring.[35] Poulet, already in his pajamas, opened the door to find himself face to face with a thin, pale man with a moustache, who said, "I am Marcel Proust." The caller made an unusual request: he wanted to hear Franck's Quartet that very night. There was a cab waiting that could round up the other members of the quartet. Poulet agreed. Once in the cab Poulet directed the driver to the homes of Louis Ruyssen, cellist, Victor Gentil, second violin, and Amable Massis, viola. When Massis entered the taxi, he saw Proust wrapped in a huge eiderdown; there was a bowl of mashed potatoes sitting on the folding seat. Massis, suddenly disconcerted by the oddity of the situation, received a reassuring smile and gesture from the driver, signaling that his employer was somewhat bizarre, but harmless.[36] By the time Proust had collected all the musicians and their instruments and arrived back at boulevard Haussmann, it was nearly one in the morning.

Céleste opened the door and greeted the group. Massis, like everyone who saw her the first time, noted that she was tall for a woman, svelte, and very pretty. The men removed their overcoats, opened their cases, and took out their instruments. Massis remembered playing in a bedroom lighted solely by candles. Just beyond a circle of light a divan covered in green velvet had been placed in the semidarkness; near the bed stood a mountain of manuscripts. The opening of the chimney had been covered, as Poulet had recommended, to prevent any of the sound from escaping. While Céleste assisted the musicians in setting up makeshift music stands, Proust stretched out on the divan.

During the playing Proust lay with his eyes closed, without making the slightest movement. So solemnly eerie was this concert deep in the night that the musicians dared not speak to each other between movements. When the last notes of the Franck piece were no longer audible, Proust opened his eyes and asked the musicians to begin again. The stricken instrumentalists looked at each other. The Franck quartet took forty-five minutes to perform. It was now around two in the morning, and the musicians felt dead with fatigue. Sensing their distress, Proust asked Massis to bring him a small Chinese box from a nearby shelf. The novelist opened it and removed a stack of fifty-franc bank bills redeemable for gold. He handed each musician three of the bills. According to Massis's recollection, 150 of these gold francs were worth 45,000 ordinary francs. Their energy restored at the sight of so much money, the musicians immediately began again to play the entire quartet. The room filled once more with the strains of the Pater Angelus.

Afterward, Proust thanked the musicians warmly and told them that he would like to have them back again under similar conditions. Céleste came in with champagne and fried potatoes. Shortly before dawn the musicians stepped out onto the boulevard Haussmann to find four taxis waiting to take them home.[37]

Proust saw Massis now and then when the quartet performed in concert halls. On one occasion he told Massis that his dream was to spend a moonlit night in a Venetian palace, where he would await the sunrise while listening to beloved musical works. When Massis observed that wartime conditions made it impossible for men like himself, convalescing from a terrible war wound, to leave the country, Proust assured him that he could pull strings and arrange for the musicians to accompany him to Venice.

In April the Poulet Quartet returned to Proust's apartment and performed Beethoven's Thirteenth Quartet and Franck's Quartet.[38] Poulet said that Proust called on the quartet several times to play Mozart, Ravel, and Schumann, but, above all, Fauré and Franck. Proust's knowledge about everything that was happening in the music world, despite his apparent reclusiveness, impressed Poulet. The members of the quartet found him a "marvelous listener: simple, direct, who never sought to pontificate," a man who "drank in music effortlessly." Poulet believed that Fauré was the composer whose music was the closest to the novelist's own sensitivity. In an interview given years after Proust's death, Massis observed that the pieces by Franck and Fauré that Proust knew and loved were not well known in the circles Proust frequented. Massis attributed such knowledge and taste to Hahn's influence.

Although Saint-Saëns had provided the inspiration for one of Vinteuil's key phrases, known as the "little phrase" that plays a major role in the love affair between Swann and Odette and in the Narrator's meditations on music, Poulet said that Proust did not like Saint-Saëns's music and never requested it.[39] According to Poulet, the writer cared deeply for chamber music and loved Mozart for his purity, Fauré for his atmosphere, Franck both for his human qualities and his seraphic radiance. Proust told Poulet that he found Beethoven "hermetic and heartless." The novelist was less interested in the technicalities of music than in its inspirational powers, for its encouragement to turn inward and seek one's profound being.

When the Narrator hears Vinteuil's sonata and its little phrase for the first time, he comments: "Since I was able to enjoy everything that this sonata had to give me only in a succession of hearings, I never possessed it in its entirety: it was like life itself. But, less disappointing than life, great works of art do not begin by giving us the best of themselves." Using Beethoven's late quartets to epitomize musical greatness, the Narrator realizes that such works must create their own posterity: "The reason why a work of genius is not easily admired from the first is that the man who has created it is extraordinary, that few other men resemble him. It is his work itself that, by fertilising the rare minds capable of understanding it, will make them increase and multiply."[40] In another scene Charlus comments to Morel regarding his playing of the piano transcription of Beethoven's Fifteenth Quartet: "It is meant for people whose ears are offended by the overtaut strings of the glorious Deaf One. Whereas it is precisely that almost sour mysticism that is divine."[41]

Proust had written *Swann in Love,* of course, before the series of private concerts at boulevard Haussmann. In that early section of the novel, when Swann hears the Vinteuil sonata again, he meditates on music and creativity:

> The field open to the musician is not a miserable stave of seven notes,
> but an immeasurable keyboard (still almost entirely unknown) on
> which, here and there only, separated by the thick darkness of its unex-
> plored tracts, some few among the millions of keys of tenderness, of pas-
> sion, of courage, of serenity, which compose it, each one differing from
> all the rest as one universe differs from another, have been discovered by
> a few great artists who do us the service, when they awaken in us the

emotion corresponding to the theme they have discovered, of showing us what richness, what variety lies hidden, unknown to us, in that vast, unfathomed and forbidding night of our soul which we take to be an impenetrable void.[42]

This passage bolsters Proust's argument, frequently made in the coming years, for the highly structured nature of his novel. Swann, who in many ways functions as a father figure to the Narrator, lacks the ability to fathom his own soul. In a note to himself in one of his notebooks for the *Search*, Proust indicated that Swann's failure to distinguish between eros (Odette) and art (Vinteuil's music, which is trivialized as Swann and Odette's song, "their national anthem") and to follow the path of art is perhaps the most important point in the entire novel. When the Narrator discovers his vocation as an artist, he undertakes to find the riches that lie undiscovered within himself and transform them into a work of art. At one point during a failed meditation on music the Narrator compares Swann to Moses, who never made it to the promised land.[43] The Narrator will, after years of wandering in the desert of high society, make his way there, guided largely by the inspiration he finds in music.

On April 14 Proust attended the Festival Gabriel Fauré at the Odéon, featuring the composer himself at the piano, as well as Lucien Capet, André Hekking, and a young violist, Raymond Pétain.[44] After the performance, Proust asked Fauré to introduce him to the musicians. Proust intended to hire the Poulet Quartet for another private performance but was faced with the problem of finding a tuner for his pianos, both of which were seriously out of tune. And he would have to find a pianist, for the work he most wanted to hear again was one he had heard at the Odéon: Fauré's Quartet for Piano, Violin, Viola, and Cello No. 1 in C minor, Op. 15. Proust was collecting impressions and thoughts for the key scene toward the end of the novel, when the Narrator hears Vinteuil's septet.

Shortly after the Odéon concert, Proust wrote Pétain, telling him about a recent private concert and his intention to bring the Poulet Quartet back again. He hoped that Pétain would join the group for the next concert and made him a generous offer. Proust seemed particularly taken with Raymond and told him to name his fee, without divulging the amount to the other musicians. Proust wanted Pétain to play the viola part in the Fauré piece while Massis listened. During the Franck Quartet, Pétain would listen with Proust.[45] Marcel also wondered whether Pétain might be willing to come over now and then and read certain scores with him, an arrangement that would avoid the complications of dealing with a quartet.

He preferred very young men for such tasks, he said, because their age made them "indulgent."

The novelist quickly developed an interest in Raymond that went beyond music. He wanted to watch the young man play because Pétain, without knowing it, was posing for a character Proust would introduce in *Sodom and Gomorrah*. When Pétain came to boulevard Haussmann, Proust told him that during his performance of Fauré's Quartet at the Odéon a ray of sunlight had struck the performer's forehead at the very moment a lock of his hair had fallen loose.[46] While relating this account to the musician, Proust cried out, "and then, suddenly . . . the Lock!" A few weeks later Pétain joined the 22d Artillery Regiment in Versailles. When he came back to see Proust, he was in uniform and his beautiful locks had been shaved. Proust, assuming, as he sometimes did, the role of Charlus, told Pétain: "Ah, I miss the lock . . . how I miss the lock!"

Pétain may have lost his marvelous lock to army barbers, but it is preserved on the head of the violinist Charles Morel, a character inspired in large measure by the pianist Léon Delafosse, whom Montesquiou had adopted as his protégé. Morel, like Delafosse, is a young man of humble origins, who through his remarkable talent becomes a virtuoso performer. By making Morel the object of Charlus's infatuation, Proust examines the aspects of an obsessively jealous homosexual passion, as he had in his heterosexual couples. After a concert Charlus organized to present Morel to the beau monde, the baron is in a fit of ecstasy over his protégé's triumph: " 'Do admit, Brichot, that they played like gods, Morel especially. Did you notice the moment when that lock of hair came loose? Ah, my dear fellow, then you saw nothing at all. There was an F sharp which was enough to make Enesco, Capet and Thibaud die of jealousy. Calm though I am, I don't mind telling you that at the sound of it I had such a lump in the throat that I could scarcely control my tears. The whole room sat breathless. Brichot, my dear fellow,' cried the Baron, gripping the other's arm and shaking it violently, 'it was sublime.' "[47]

Proust consulted Pétain about the instruments used by street merchants, such as the porcelain mender, the chair-bottomer, and the goatherd.[48] Pétain told him that the chair-bottomer used a trumpet and the goatherd a flute. Proust wanted the information about the street cries for his own Paris symphony composed of bits taken from the cries of ambulatory peddlers who hawked their wares, sounds that rapidly became extinct in postwar Paris. In *The Captive*, Proust presents a variety of vendors hawking fruits, vegetables, periwinkles, and all sorts of mending services. To capture their voices and styles, he evoked a number of musical works and their composers, including Mussorgsky's *Boris Godunov* and Debussy's *Pelléas and*

Mélisande, in which Proust heard "the vague sadness of Maeterlinck" transposed into music.[49]

One spring day Henri Bardac drove Proust to Versailles to hear Hahn's new opera *Nausicaa.* At the Trianon Palace, Proust met Mme Straus and Princesse Polignac. Marcel was delighted to encounter Mme Straus, who, next to him, was Paris's least visible inhabitant. No details are known about this meeting, but it was likely the last time the two old friends saw each other. They continued to exchange letters, though these became less frequent. Before returning to Paris, Marcel accompanied Princesse Polignac to visit Mme de Madrazo, which afforded him the opportunity to thank her again for lending him the book on Carpaccio.[50]

As Proust developed the passages on Vinteuil's septet, he compared the composer at work to Michelangelo "strapped to his scaffold" and "hurling tumultuous brush-strokes on to the ceiling of the Sistine Chapel." Although Vinteuil had been dead for some years, the Narrator hears in "the sound of these instruments which he loved" Vinteuil's life or "a part at least of his life" that lives "for an unlimited time." This leads him to ask himself whether "art was indeed but a prolongation of life, was it worth while to sacrifice anything to it? Was it not as unreal as life itself? The more I listened to this septet, the less I could believe this to be so."[51] In his paean to music, the Narrator "wondered whether music might not be the unique example of what might have been—if the invention of language, the formation of words, the analysis of ideas had not intervened—the means of communicating between souls."[52] Art, in this case in the form of music, gives us what we can never find, despite Swann's and the Narrator's obsessions, in the possession of another: "Music, very different . . . from Albertine's society, helped me to descend into myself, to discover new things. . . . As the spectrum makes visible to us the composition of light, so the harmony of a Wagner, the colour of an Elstir, enable us to know that essential quality of another person's sensations into which love for another person does not allow us to penetrate."[53]

The Break with Grasset

Proust's concerted move to break with Grasset had begun back in the winter, with visits by Gide and Gallimard to boulevard Haussmann. In late February, on an evening of heavy snowfall, Gide made his first visit to Proust's apartment to discuss the NRF's desire to become his publisher. Gide wrote in his diary the next morning that he had not seen Proust since 1892, twenty-four years earlier.[54] A few days later,

Gallimard wrote Proust, expressing his eagerness to publish the remaining volumes of the *Search*. Gaston, who said he would always "reproach" himself for his "past negligence," offered to publish the novel "tomorrow and have it on sale within a month."[55] Furthermore, he would accept all Proust's conditions and be personally responsible for seeing his novel through publication. The NRF wanted to make amends for having rejected *Swann's Way*.[56]

In a letter to Gallimard, Proust questioned the sincerity of Grasset's earlier magnanimity—when the NRF had made its first prewar overtures—in saying the novelist was free to choose the publisher he wanted. Grasset's gesture, Proust now professed to believe, had merely been "a clever ploy, but at the time I was very touched." He also suspected that Grasset had been less than candid about the number of printings and the royalties owed on them.[57]

In mid-May, Gallimard answered Proust, who had listed a number of problems the publisher might encounter in publishing his book. He said that the novel's length mattered little, nor was he deterred by the boldness of certain passages, referring to their homosexual content. If readers or critics were shocked to the point of assailing his publishing house, he would have no regrets. Gallimard's commitment to Proust's novel was total: "I will take your books as you give them to me, happy to publish them in their entirety."[58]

Gallimard needed to know the length of the *Search* in order to obtain enough paper, a commodity made precious by the war. Proust replied that it was difficult to estimate the total number of pages because the manuscript consisted of proofs, typed pages, and notebooks in script. He estimated that the remainder of the novel would equal three volumes, each as long as *Swann's Way*, a guess that proved to be only half the ultimate length. Given the choice, Proust would prefer the volumes to appear at the same time so that the reader could appreciate their "true composition."[59]

At the end of May, René Blum, who had negotiated the original contract with Grasset, came to see Proust and offered to act as the agent for the break.[60] Before leaving Grasset, Proust had to convince himself that his publisher had treated him badly and to make certain Gallimard's commitment was absolute. He wrote Gallimard, again outlining the disadvantages and dangers of publishing the *Search*: chiefly, its excessive length and homosexual content.[61] Proust could not afford to take the chance of abandoning Grasset if the NRF had any misgivings: "If at the last minute you refused to publish me or asked me for unacceptable changes," it would be impossible for him to return to Grasset. Proust's poor health was also an important consideration, causing him to fear "anything that might delay or even completely jeopardize the putting into safe keeping . . . in a book which may perhaps outlive me, of all that I have thought and felt most deeply."

After Gallimard assured him again that the NRF was totally committed to the *Search,* Proust gave him the reasons, for the most part fabricated or exaggerated, that he would use to break with Grasset: "I can perfectly well tell him that it's difficult for me to wait until the end of the war and the re-opening of his firm, when the NRF can print me immediately." He repeated to Gallimard his preference for publishing, after the war, "all the volumes at one go, so that the whole thing explains and justifies itself."[62]

Proust set this plan in motion by writing to Blum on May 30, and listing the reasons—candidly admitting that they were pretexts—to use in his letter to Grasset: "Marcel Proust has lost" most of his fortune and needed money; Grasset's publishing company had been forced to close because the war had reduced the office staff to his accountant's wife, who was a seamstress.[63] The NRF was still operating and could publish the remaining volumes immediately.[64] Blum was instructed to ask for Proust's release to allow the NRF to publish the remaining volumes and to reclaim *Swann's Way.* Proust then made a concession that he would regret; out of largesse or perhaps guilt, he said that the NRF would pay Grasset an indemnity for his loss. Proust later remarked to Blum that such an offer seemed unnecessary, for he had paid a lot for printing *Swann's Way* and given Grasset most of the profits. Proust ended his letter to Blum: "Dear friend, if you think you can bring about this divorce without paining Grasset, that would make me very happy."

Proust was being naive. In addition to losing his most promising writer, Grasset was wounded by Proust's eagerness to leave him for the NRF. In a subsequent letter to Blum, Proust listed additional reasons for his unhappiness with Grasset, including his having paid for a volume of seven hundred pages whereas *Swann's Way* was only five hundred printed pages, and Grasset's having failed to pay any royalties since the spring of 1914. Blum should inform Grasset that Proust had kept the NRF waiting for months because he did not want to do anything without Grasset's assent, but he had been unable to locate him.[65] It was true that Grasset had failed to pay Proust the royalties earned on copies sold since 1914, but Proust had forgotten that, as compensation for the lower number of pages in *Swann's Way,* Grasset had provided him with many additional copies for gifts and publicity purposes.

Grasset replied to Blum from the clinic in Switzerland. Not surprisingly, Grasset wrote that the request to relinquish the rights to publish Proust's books "gives me great pain." He spoke about "all the trouble I had establishing and developing" the publishing house, which was "the thing I care about most in the world." Grasset was also "painfully surprised that, in the middle of a war, when all my staff are mobilized, when I myself, after serving for a year, am ill and remote from business concerns, when everyone, engrossed by other preoccupations than those of business, respects this truce and postpones outstanding questions until the resumption, one of the authors I care most about should suddenly ask to sever our relationship." Nonetheless, if Proust insisted "on a rupture," Grasset had "too much pride to retain an author who no longer has confidence in me and I will facilitate the complete restoration of his freedom. But I am anxious that you should first of all communicate my letter to him and that he should weigh up all sides of the question."[66]

Proust received Grasset's letter from Blum just as he was becoming quite ill with fever, pain, and palpitations, apparently resulting from dental problems, from which he suffered for the next two weeks. This condition may have contributed to his fury on reading Grasset's letter, which the publisher obviously considered inoffensive since he had asked Blum to forward it to Proust. Interpreting Grasset's remarks in the worst possible light, Proust found insults where none were intended. When Proust forwarded Grasset's letter to Gallimard, he characterized it as "hypocritical and mendacious" and said that he was highly offended. In his anger the novelist discouraged the idea of paying Grasset an indemnity, saying that such an arrangement would be "an unjustified gift" for "bad conduct. I fought a duel once with Lorrain for less than that."[67]

In his next letter to Blum, Proust outlined his reply to Grasset and suggested that Blum join him in anticipating "the inevitable day when he (Grasset) will launch a press campaign against my book and say he refused to publish such filth."[68] Proust's anger and vilification of Grasset was unwarranted, as was the tone of the letter he sent his publisher. Marcel began by recalling better days when he had considered leaving Grasset: "You said to me then that it would be regrettable from your point of view and I at once withdrew and formally apprised the NRF of my decision. But you said it to me affectionately without a hint of anger, entirely understanding my motives and indeed . . . very magnanimously, giving me complete liberty which, because of that very magnanimity, I there and then absolutely forswore." Now he was offended because Grasset had accused him before Blum of being an "egotist, alone among all Frenchmen in thinking only of himself" and "taking advantage of the war to air a grievance against a sick man for not having published his book because all his workers had been called up." Marcel, who should have pleaded guilty to most of the charges, claimed to be "more reasonable and fair-minded than that. But I believe the war has made a lot of lives difficult, including mine, and that by the force of circumstance it has severed many a contract more solemn than ours (which in any case doesn't exist)."

Proust then enumerated the reasons he had given Blum: his heavy financial losses due to his "absurd speculations," a terrible situation made worse by the outbreak of war, all of which nearly bankrupted him. Later, with his "landlady demanding rent," Proust thought "it would have been wise this time to succumb to the solicitations of the NRF." He mentioned Gide's visits and entreaties, which he had not even considered accepting. The long war, with no end in sight, "has dictated all kinds of adjustments which could not have been foreseen." Then, coaching Grasset, Proust said that he had "expected the affectionate response of 1914 with this difference, that you would add: 'But naturally, there's the war, and it's only too understandable.'"

The novelist assured Grasset that allowing him to go to the NRF would be no loss. Far from being "a star" among Grasset's authors, Proust claimed to be "no more than an imperceptible grain of sand." But for him, his novel was everything and he did not know whether he would "live to see it *appear* at last, and it is fairly natural that, with the instinct of an insect whose days are numbered, I should be in a hurry to find a resting-place for what has come from inside me and will represent me." In the postscript Proust returned to money matters, saying the "small indemnity" would in "no way preclude" his receiving the royalties owed on *Swann's Way*. He closed by saying he hoped that "this time, by explaining myself, I shall be better understood, and that in losing a publisher I shall regain a friend."[69]

Grasset replied that he was "very surprised" that his letter had offended Proust and that no matter what it cost him, he would forgo publishing the *Search*.[70] Proust agreed to wait until all the figures were available on the copies sold by Grasset before reaching a financial settlement. Having obtained what he wanted, Proust addressed Grasset as a "dear friend," whom he hoped to see soon in a "victorious and peaceful France."[71] In a subsequent letter, Grasset specified that the indemnity was not compensation for relinquishing the copyright, but what he would have earned on publishing the first edition. He closed by wishing Proust success with his book and expressing his "affectionate devotion."[72]

In early July, Proust received news that Nicolas Cottin had died of pleuresy in a military hospital.[73] Proust, worried about Céline, who was left with a small son to raise on her own, sent his former cook some money, though he bemoaned his inability to provide as much as he would have liked. As for taking Céline back as a servant, that was impossible, as he explained to Hauser, because of her intense hatred of Céleste, with whom he was entirely satisfied.[74]

Sometime in September, Gaston called on Proust and spent nearly the entire night talking with his newly acquired author, sealing their agreement for publication of *In Search of Lost Time*. On September 20 Gallimard wrote to Gustave Tronche, marketing director at the NRF since 1912, to inform him that the novelist had joined their group. Gaston provided his colleague with this portrait of Proust: "I found him as he appears in his work; his conversation is like his style, lively, full of twists and turns, of incidents, charming, full of affection."[75]

There is no question that Grasset regretted losing Proust. He may have smiled, though, as he pictured Gallimard trying to deal with this nearly impossible author whom Grasset once described as "the most complicated man in Paris."[76]

"Now I can die"

The one prospect Proust feared was dying before completing his work, a dread that Céleste described as "the leitmotiv of his life."[77] He told her that "death was hounding him and that he wanted to finish his work and that he would be distressed, after having worked so hard, to leave it all unfinished."[78] That was why he worked so hard; his life had only one purpose. Céleste recalled: "I think that even when he was drowsing the work must have gone on. It was like a fever in him." She tried to reassure him but had little success: "There couldn't have been one day when at some moment or other there wasn't some sign of his fear that he might not be able to finish what he had started." She tried to resist his talk about death, insisting that he would outlive her. To which he replied: "My life is not normal, no air, no food. Ever since I was a child my health has been ruined by asthma. I don't know how many times I have told you my bronchial tubes are like old elastic, my heart scarcely breathes any more—it is worn out by years of gasping for air. I am a very old man, Céleste—as old as my old tubes and my old heart. I shan't live long."[79]

One afternoon, Céleste heard the bell ring around four o'clock. "He'd only rung once, so I went in empty-handed (he would ring twice for the tray). He was resting in bed, his head and shoulders slightly raised on the pillow as usual, with the light of the little lamp leaving his face in the shadow except for the eyes, the look that was always so strong that you felt it watching or following you." She noticed that he had not had his fumigation. "He looked very tired, but he smiled at me as I came in. Suddenly I was struck by the radiance of his expression. As I came up to the bed he turned his head slightly toward me, opened his lips, and spoke. It was the first time he'd ever spoken to me immediately . . . before having had his first cup of coffee." He reminded her of "a child who had found the most beautiful toy and the greatest happiness.

> He said, "Dear Céleste, I have great news to tell you."
> I said, "Well, what? What happened last night in this room that was so important?'
> "Something tremendous. Something so wonderful!"
> "Well, what happened?"
> He sat up in bed, smiled at me and said: "I have written the words 'The End.' Now I can die."
> So I said to him, "But what about all the bits of paper I still have to paste together? And all the corrections you still have to make?"
> "That, my dear, that's something else."[80]

Proust had written the word *Fin* and underlined it. Although Céleste, in her memoirs, said that she was certain this extraordinary moment took place in 1922, it could have occurred much earlier, perhaps as early as 1916.[81] On November 6 of that year Proust informed Gallimard that he was ready to send him a package containing the beginning of the rest of his novel. The novelist, who seldom liked his titles, said that he did not care for the one he had given the next volume, *À l'ombre des jeunes filles en fleurs,* and considered it provisional. Proust asked that the proofs be prepared immediately. He included information about the following two volumes, *Sodom and Gomorrah* and *Time Regained,* and he confirmed to his publisher that he had completed the manuscript for the entire book.[82] Were he to die, he felt his work could appear as a coherent, finished whole. It seems unlikely that Proust would have given such an authorization to Gallimard if he had not written the conclusion. For as long as he lived, Proust expanded and revised his manuscripts, but sometime in 1916 or not long afterward, he gave his book its ultimate shape if not its final dimensions.

The parcel sent to Gallimard also contained the first twenty pages of Grasset's proofs for *The Guermantes Way.*[83] Gallimard should tell the printer not to consider the corrections and additions on Grasset's proofs as changes "because what were proofs for Grasset will be for your printer the original manuscript. The corrections will begin on the first proofs I receive from him." Proust outlined his production plan: The day after he received proofs for the first packet, he would send the next two notebooks and so on two by two until he had all the proofs. He wanted to avoid having more than one set of proofs in circulation at a time because in a work of such length repetitions might slip in. To avoid this error he intended to read the first proofs of the entire novel.[84] Proust later abandoned this method in order to speed up the process, a step made necessary by problems with Gallimard's printer, who had difficulty retaining competent, efficient workers because of the war.

On December 20 Proust was unable to attend an afternoon lecture given by Montesquiou, who had engaged Ida Rubinstein to read poems from *Les Offrandes blessées*. Afterward Montesquiou sent Marcel a letter bidding him "Adieu! I will soon send you a volume which, I hope, will earn me fewer insults from you than the last one. Your friend, Robert de Montesquiou." In a postscript the count said that, in the meantime, he would send Marcel "some *white violets* and *gold-wrapped chocolates,* if it does you no harm."[85] Céleste remembered what Proust told her to do with any gifts that arrived from Montesquiou: "If he does send any chocolates, throw them straight into the dustbin without opening them. It wouldn't surprise me in the least if they were poisoned."[86] Proust, who daily feared he might die of natural causes, had no intention of letting himself be poisoned by Montesquiou. That Proust could entertain such an idea, even in jest, indicates how thoroughly demonized the count had become in the novelist's mind.

25 *Proust of the Ritz* ⌒

NO ONE WAS IN A MOOD TO CELEBRATE the dawn of 1917 with the war raging and no end in sight. In January, Proust wrote Mme Straus that as long as the Germans remained in France, "We are like people in deepest mourning."[1] Each month brought new reasons to grieve and new hardships to endure. On January 11 the government began rationing sugar.[2] The supply of food, which until now had been adequate, was to become increasingly scarce during the year. Although Parisians never endured the hardships seen by those during the previous German invasion and siege, for those of Proust's generation the shortages and inconveniences, not to mention the lethal threat of new German weapons, constituted a new and harrowing experience.

Proust's ailments remained the same, though he soon found them less inhibiting: asthma, eyestrain, palpitations, and insomnia. In an early January letter to Lucien, Marcel compared himself to a character out of an H. G. Wells novel because he had been up for fifty hours straight.[3] In spite of his concentrated labor on his novel, he received a number of visitors. Antoine, when he left his post in London, made a quick trip over to Paris. Old friends like Lucien and Clément de Maugny stopped by boulevard Haussmann when on leave. And Proust had three new friends named Jacques: Jacques de Lacretelle, a tall, handsome young man with literary ambitions; Jacques Truelle, who had lost a leg to the war and now served as an embassy attaché; and Jacques Porel, son of the famous actress Réjane. Porel had been released from the army after suffering injuries from mustard gas.

Proust did not see Gallimard during this period because the publisher had been in Switzerland taking a cure since December. While there, Gaston contacted printers, thinking that a press in a neutral country might provide steady, reliable work.[4] Gallimard had left in charge his secretary Berthe Lemarié, an unusually able woman who endeared herself to Proust with her unflagging devotion to his book. In January, Mme Lemarié wrote Proust to clarify a misunderstanding about how the author wished to proceed. She told him that Gallimard had thought Proust wanted all the volumes set at once. Now that Gallimard understood each was to be set and corrected before proceeding to the next, production would go faster.[5] As one measure to move the process along, Gallimard had arranged to have typed the revised manuscript of *Within a Budding Grove*. Because of the threat posed by the war and his health, Proust had taken the precaution of showing Céleste where he kept the notebooks containing his manuscripts so that if he died, Gallimard would know where to find "the essential part of me, that is, my book," and publish it, alerting readers that this version was "only a draft."[6]

Since the evening when Proust had turned up unexpectedly at Morand's door, the two men had become friends. Not long after that impromptu encounter, Morand met and fell in love with a beautiful princess, Hélène Soutzo, whose only shortcoming was that she was already married to a prince. Proust was soon to become a regular fixture of the Morand-Soutzo circle, which usually gathered at the Ritz Hotel.

Princesse Soutzo, at thirty-eight, was nearly a decade older than Morand. Considered one of the most ravishing Parisian beauties, the princess was also intelligent, witty, and extremely rich. Born Hélène Chrissoveloni, the daughter of a Greek banker, she was unhappily married to the Romanian prince Dimitri Soutzo-Doudesco, whom she later divorced to marry Morand. The princess gave brilliant dinner parties in her luxurious apartment at the Ritz, to which she invited such writers as Morand, Proust, and Cocteau, along with members of the Paris beau monde.[7]

By the winter of 1917 Proust had heard so much about the princess from Morand that he was eager to meet the mysterious lady. While dining at Larue's on February 22, Proust heard that Morand and Mme Soutzo were at Viel's, a restaurant just around the corner. He sent the doorman to Viel's with a note for Morand, suggesting that they meet later in the evening.[8] But the couple had other plans, and Proust had to wait. In a March 1 letter Proust evoked the lady whom Morand called "the most beautiful and intelligent of them all." Could it be true? Did such a creature exist? Proust expressed his skepticism: "People disappoint me so much that I am more curious about flowers, and many other things that one can't see from one's bedroom. But when people don't disappoint, nothing is more marvellous."[9]

Three days later, Morand introduced Proust to Princesse Soutzo at a dinner at Larue's. The novelist was immediately taken with the Greek beauty. Wanting to mark the occasion with a Proustian gesture combining largesse and art, Proust suggested hiring the Poulet Quartet to come to the princess's apartment and play Franck's Quartet. The proposal delighted everyone, and Proust rushed off to round up the musicians. He returned an hour later to the Ritz, his plans thwarted because cellist Ruyssen had just undergone an appendectomy.[10]

Proust began to dine out several times a week at the Ritz, often as the princess's guest. In his memoir Morand described a typical evening in Mme Soutzo's apartment, where Proust and other guests talked until the early morning hours. Proust usually sat near the corner of the Louis XVI fireplace. Finally, "Proust would rise and announce that he was going to leave. While saying good-bye to everyone, he took off his overcoat, that he had kept on all evening." If anyone showed surprise at his removing it just before leaving, "he would explain that he was thus reestablishing a momentary equilibrium between the indoor temperature and the one outdoors." This removal of his fur coat in front of guests was the social version of his cooling-down ritual. "Proust would then put back on his coat, catch someone's offhand remark on the fly, begin developing it, introducing first one incident and then another, a thought or a portrait, and finally sit back down with no thought of leaving."[11] When Proust entertained friends at the Ritz, he usually ended the evening by going up to Mme Soutzo's apartment to chat with her and other guests who lingered.

As Proust became a regular at the Ritz, either as Mme Soutzo's guest or when he entertained others, or dined alone, late in the evening, he came to consider the exceptionally well-trained staff at the hotel as an extension of his household servants. He would rely on the Ritz staff for food, for information about matters political and social in France and even throughout Europe and in America, and for its supply of attractive young waiters, one of whom was to become his first male "secretary" since Agostinelli.

The person at the Ritz upon whom Proust came especially to rely was its remarkable first maître d'hôtel, Olivier Dabescat. Dabescat had been trained by none other than César Ritz at Le Paillard before the hotelier opened, in June 1898, the establishment bearing his name that would set the standard for luxury hotels throughout Europe. Now Olivier often served Proust in a private room at whatever hour of the evening or early morning the writer chose to arrive. Another advantage of the exceptionally late hour and private room was that Proust could engage Dabescat or other members of the staff in conversation for lengthy periods and learn a great deal about guests and personnel. The duchesse de Clermont-Tonnerre remembered often seeing Dabescat talking to Proust for hours at a stretch. The Proustian charm and generosity, both of which seemed to be in endless supply, worked their magic on Dabescat and his underlings, who soon devoted themselves to Proust with a thoroughness and enthusiasm that surpassed even the exceptionally high standards of service given to ordinary guests. Not since his eight straight years of summer vacation at the Grand-Hôtel in Cabourg had Proust enjoyed such attention and such well-informed sources of information about the high and low jinks of Europe's wealthiest and most pampered citizens. Dabescat's position allowed him to yield great power over the mighty or those who took themselves as such or wanted others to do so; a person's social standing could often be determined by the table to which the headwaiter assigned him.

The combination of Mme Soutzo and Dabescat allowed Proust to rejoin the mainstream of Parisian society during the war years as he developed his novel and traced the evolution of society from its post-Dreyfus configurations to the postwar upheavals, many of which the novelist anticipated. Proust recognized the importance of Mme Soutzo's hospitality and understanding of his peculiar hours in a letter to a friend: "Thanks to the kindheartedness of a lady who understands the hours of sick people," he could now "leave his bed once or twice a week and dine out."[12] Through this "impromptu arrangement," he could see friends, some old and some new, in an elegant setting and in the company of a pair of attractive lovers, allowing him a luxury unknown since the days of Albufera and Louisa. He dined so often with the princess at the Ritz that he insisted on sharing the bill and asked her to keep this arrangement secret.[13] Proust was so taken with Morand that he offered to read the youthful diplomat's stories even though his eyes hurt too much for him to correct his own proofs.[14]

Proust's expenses, which he and Hauser had worked so hard to rein in, were henceforth greatly increased by the lobster dinners and champagne consumed several times per week with Mme Soutzo at the Ritz or the equally expensive Hôtel Crillon, all of which, of course, called for enormous Proustian tips for those who served him.[15] Proust was so pleased by everything at the Ritz that he told Morand he was considering the possibility of living at the hotel.[16]

In March, Léon Daudet published a book entitled *Salons et journaux,* in which he depicted Proust as he used to appear at the Café Weber around the turn of the century. Daudet wrote that Marcel, who arrived around 7:30, was a "pale, doe-eyed young man, sucking on or fingering the ends of his dark, drooping moustache, and swaddled in layers of wool like a Chinese curio." After the physical portrait, Daudet mentioned Proust's exceptional gifts as a conversationalist: "Soon there fell from his lips, in hesitant bursts, remarks of an extraordinary originality, observations of fiendish acuity." Daudet ended by saying: "This was the author of that original, and often stupefying, book *Du côté de chez Swann:* this was Marcel Proust."[17]

Proust wrote to thank Daudet: "Dear friend, I know what it means to find *Swann* stupefying, to think that it isn't condensed and ultra-condensed, that I don't know how to keep within bounds, that I let myself be carried away by fortuitous associations of ideas. I don't agree with this judgement though I understand the reasons behind it." Proust flattered Daudet, saying that only his friendship mattered, before returning to what most concerned the novelist: Daudet's failure to appreciate *Swann's Way:* "Truth, even literary truth, is not the fruit of chance. . . . I think truth (literary truth) reveals itself, whenever it does, like a physical *law.* One discovers it or one doesn't. All that chattering around the required word, and the *unique* connection between two psychological facts, is as though they didn't exist. If I had chattered (alone, because one can chatter to oneself) through *Swann,* I would never have published it."[18]

On March 13 Marcel had several callers, including Antoine and Reynaldo; Hahn remained until three in the morning. To Proust's dismay, Reynaldo soon reverted to his practice of refusing to take his military leave, a pratice that he maintained throughout the year.[19] Proust despaired, observing to Lucien that this was Reynaldo's stoic side, "his death of the wolf" side, referring to a poem by Alfred de Vigny in which a brave wolf, mortally wounded, suffers and dies in silence.[20]

At a mid-March dinner Proust hosted at Ciro's, to which he invited Mme Soutzo, Morand, and Antoine, he was distraught over the poor impression he must have made on the "glamorous" princess. In the course of the evening Marcel was "mortified to discover" that Céleste had let him go out "with a shirt that had been drenched by the barber's soapy water and an old waistcoat."[21] Proust had hardly progressed beyond those days in young manhood when his mother anguished over his sloppy appearance and neglect of his wardrobe.

On April 2 the United States entered the war against Germany, bolstering French hopes for a victorious conclusion to the conflict. That evening, Proust hosted a small dinner party at the Ritz, to which he invited Princesses Soutzo and Lucien Murat, as well as Morand.[22] Such expenditures at the Ritz constantly drained his resources, and he appealed to Hauser, saying that he needed cash to pay his bills. He failed to mention all the lobster and champagne he and his guests had been consuming at the Ritz. Instead, Proust talked about the rising costs of Legras powders. Perhaps seeking sympathy from his financial adviser, whose careful plan to restore his financial security was being wrecked by Proust's sudden shift in his lifestyle, he told Hauser that he weighed only ninety-nine pounds.[23]

Hauser replied that he was worried about all the shares in Mexico Tramways the writer still owned, which constituted a "gaping wound in your treasury." Hauser suggested selling them at the best offer, thus ridding Proust forever of the bitter "aftertaste of your financial orgies." Proust agreed to this proposal. By early May, Hauser had sold the seventy-five shares at an unexpectedly good price and informed Proust that he need no longer fear any "bloodlettings" and could hence-forth establish his budget on a solid footing.[24] Hauser reminded Proust that he still owned one hundred shares of Mexican Tramways, purchased as futures; the war regulations for the Bourse prohibited the liquidation of such stocks.[25]

Jacques-Émile Blanche had asked Proust to accept the dedication of his volume of collected essays on painters and to write a preface for the book *Propos de peintre: De David à Degas.* On April 15 Proust wrote saying he was "touched and honored," and he accepted despite "my exhaustion, my eyes, my feverish haste to finish my book before I die." These were "so many obstacles I am prepared to surmount with joy."[26] Proust set a single condition: absolute secrecy. He did so because he had recently declined similar requests from others, including Gide.[27] Once Blanche's book was published, everyone would know, but Proust wanted to delay the excuses and explanations for as long as possible. Marcel requested copies of Blanche's articles about painters and a copy of the dedication to use as the beginning point for his preface. Blanche's dedication evoked their youth: "To Marcel Proust, as a token of great admiration, these pages that will remind him of the Auteuil of his childhood, of my youth and my old friendship."[28]

Sometime in early April, Proust saw Emmanuel Bibesco, who had come from London for a visit. It was a disturbing interview because the remarkably handsome Emmanuel had fallen victim to a degenerative disease that had begun to disfigure him. Antoine had come that evening with Emmanuel to boulevard Haussmann to collect Proust and Morand. After being admitted by Céleste, Antoine informed his friends: "You know, Emmanuel is below, but he stayed in the cab because he doesn't want people to see him." When the three men arrived at the cab, Emmanuel tried, out of politeness, to move to one of the jump seats. Proust later remembered the "gentle and imperious authority" with which Antoine sat his "brother down again in the back as if to show him that this was perfectly natural, and also to provide him with a screen," saying: " 'The two Bibesco brothers will ride in the back.' " Emmanuel, whose mind was as sharp as ever, saw the opportunity for a joke and asked: "Why doesn't the cabman drive backwards so that Marcel Proust and Paul Morand will be facing forwards?" Emmanuel remained silent for the rest of the evening. Proust later told the Princesse Hélène de Caraman-Chimay that he had "wept all through the night, my only witness being my housekeeper."[29]

An American Friend

Among Proust's new friends was a prominent member of what he called the "American colony" in Paris. In the summer of 1916 Proust had received in the mail a present that delighted him from a stranger named Walter Berry. Berry, who lived in Paris, had read and admired *Swann's Way*. One day while browsing through the bins of secondhand books along the Seine, Berry came across an eighteenth-century volume stamped with the arms and coronet of Prondre de Guermantes. Remembering that this was the name of the noble family in Proust's novel, Berry purchased the book and sent it to Proust.[30] The delighted author wrote to thank Berry: "You probably think as I do that the wisest, the most poetic, the best, are not those who put all their poetry, all their kindness and all their knowledge into their work but those who have the adroitness and prodigality to keep some of it for their lives."[31] Thus began a friendship that was to be one of the most rewarding of Proust's final years.

Descended from an old New York family, Walter Van Rensselaer Berry was born in Paris, where he spent his early years. He had returned to the United States with his parents, attended Harvard, and decided to pursue a career in international law and diplomacy. Berry was a close friend of Henry James and Edith Wharton, who called Berry "the love of my life."[32] Before returning to France, Berry had served as a judge at the International Tribunal of Egypt, 1908–11. When Proust met him, Berry was fifty-seven, handsome and tall (six feet, three inches), with blue eyes that sparkled mischievously. An avid tennis player, Berry often rose for early morning matches in the Bois de Boulogne. Remarkably fit for his age, Berry enjoyed fine foods and wine and played tennis, Proust told Blanche, "as if he were twenty years old."[33]

During the war years Berry and Wharton, another American expatriate, toured battlefields as part of their campaign to assist the French. Wharton made important contributions to relief work by setting up a number of charities, while Berry lobbied hard to bring the United States into the war. Berry, who spoke fluent, eloquent French, was, after the U.S. ambassador, the most influential American in Paris and the most revered.[34] His ready wit and endless supply of charm and kindness enchanted Marcel. When Proust began dining at the Ritz several times a week, he and Berry saw each other more often. When he visited Berry's apartment in spring 1917 and saw the Indian and Chinese objets d'art Berry had acquired during his voyages to the Far East, Proust began to dream again of travel.[35]

Berry's importance to his country's business interests was demonstrated when he was elected president of the American Chamber of Commerce in Paris. He was also knowledgeable about prehistoric art and in April was invited to Barcelona to give a lecture on prehistoric cave paintings. Berry delivered his lecture, which he entitled "Mediterranean Art," in French and later lent the manuscript to Proust, who expressed his opinion to Scheikévitch: "It's astonishing that an American jurist should write so admirably in French. Who would not be proud to have written that!"[36]

In mid-April, Marcel grew concerned about Reynaldo, of whom he had received no news for some time. He knew that Hahn's headquarters had recently been subjected to the longest and most terrible bombardment of the war, in the course of which Hahn's general had been wounded.[37] Proust soon learned that Reynaldo had escaped harm.

On April 22 Proust dined at the Ritz as Mme Soutzo's guest, along with Comtesse Chevigné, her neighbor Jean Cocteau, the marquise de Ludre, Paul Morand, and Abbé Mugnier. Abbé Arthur Mugnier had been educated at the seminary of Nogent-le-Rotrou, twenty miles west of Illiers. In 1896 he was named vicar of the fashionable church of Sainte-Clothilde, in the heart of the faubourg Saint-Germain, where he became a regular guest at dinner parties.[38] Mugnier, who ministered to the poor and heard their confessions wherever he encountered them, even on the street or in train stations, was soon the darling of the most aristocratic salons. He once described himself in his journal as the "Plural Abbé."[39] Of the side of himself that was drawn to the faubourg, Mugnier noted: "What I like in society is the setting, the names, the beautiful homes, the reunion of fine minds, the contact with celebrities . . . "⁴⁰ The feeling was mutual: those who entertained the abbé found in him an appealing combination of holiness, worldliness, and wit. Once an aging actress told Mugnier, "When I pass in front of my mirror, I cry out 'How beautiful I am! Is that a sin?' 'No,' murmured the abbé, 'It's only an error.' "⁴¹

Although Mugnier's wit and sense of humor was a match for the best of the faubourg, his clothes hardly suited those of a salon habitué—and not simply because they were priestly robes, but because of their unkempt condition. Mugnier looked like a country priest in his big, square shoes, threadbare cassock, and quaint three-cornered hat. So shabby was his appearance that often society hostesses resorted to having their maids secretly take his coat and gloves while he was at the dinner table and mend them or sew on buttons.⁴²

If Mugnier's vocation was holy, all his secular passion was devoted to literature: "All my loves have been literary. My vows having prohibited women, my heart has gone entirely to books."⁴³ Of all writers, Mugnier adored the works of Chateaubriand, especially his posthumous autobiography *Les Mémoires d'outre-tombe,* a work Proust particularly admired and considered an important precursor of the *Search.* The priest adopted as his special charges men of letters. Mugnier's most remarkable conversion had been that of the distinguished novelist Joris-Karl Huysmans, whom he had sent to a Trappist monastery in 1892.⁴⁴

After meeting Proust at Mme Soutzo's dinner party, the priest wrote in his diary that "Marcel Proust is rather distinguished." Proust, according to Céleste, had been "fascinated by the abbé's manner and wit" but had found him rather "ugly . . . with warts all over his face." But Proust had been touched by his threadbare appearance, "for he is as poor as a saint." As the priest talked, he kept "toying with a lock of gray hair and gazing" at Marcel "with . . . childlike blue eyes." Proust thought "you would have to be the devil not to love him. And what brilliant conversation!"⁴⁵

On the evening of their first encounter at the Ritz, Proust recounted for the abbé some of his favorite quotes and anecdotes, including the story of the duc de Gramont's saying, as Proust leaned over his guestbook, "Sign, but no thoughts." Then the novelist told the priest about his work and another great passion, cathedrals, especially those of Chartres and Reims. The famous statues of angels at Reims had, according to Proust, da Vinci smiles. Proust said the Germans had pockmarked the cathedral by shelling it to avenge themselves for being unable to capture it. The writer and the priest discussed other cities with notable Christian architecture: Vézelay, Amiens, and Venice. Wanting to tease the abbé, Proust asked him whether he had read Baudelaire's *Fleurs du mal.* The priest "patted his cassock and said, 'My dear fellow, I carry it about with me. Without the smell of sulfur, how should we appreciate the scent of virtue?' " At the dinner party there was talk of a Viennese psychologist who had developed astounding new theories to explain human behavior. Mme Soutzo promised to tell Mugnier more about a Jewish doctor in Vienna by the name of Freud, who had an "unusual theory about dreams, release from conflicts. etc."[46] Proust, like his contemporary Freud, was fascinated by sleep and dreams, which become important themes in the *Search*. Blanche once described the *Search* as a book about insomnia.[47] In a number of passages the Narrator examines the sensations of falling asleep, dreaming, having nightmares, and awakening to interpret his dreams in a way not unlike Freud's. Swann's obsessive jealousy over Odette provokes erotic dreams which he interprets on awakening. Toward the end of the novel, the Narrator speaks about the "great interest" he has always taken in dreams and the role they may play in writing his novel by reawakening in him "something of the desire, the regret for certain nonexistent things which is the necessary condition for working, for freeing oneself from the domination of habit, for detaching oneself from the concrete. And therefore I would not disdain this second muse, this nocturnal muse."[48]

There was an awkward moment during Mme Soutzo's dinner party. Proust, who had rarely seen Mme de Chevigné in recent years, told her that he never went out in the evening. Mme Soutzo, "unaware of this white lie," told the countess that Proust called on her so often that the elevator boy brought him directly to her living room without announcing him. Proust, for once at a loss for words, stammered desperately, "which proves that I have customs at the princesse's that I no longer have at the comtesse's."[49] Mme de Chevigné was furious with Proust for lying to her in front of everyone, and perhaps somewhat jealous of Mme Soutzo, who now occupied a position the countess had held and disdained so long ago: being an idol of Marcel's.

Proust and Mme de Chevigné slowly reconciled. Later in the year he invited her to the Ritz, where they dined tête-à-tête. He wrote to her in the fall, assuring her that though they lived only a "few houses apart, and even closer, whether you wish it not, you live in me in 'the light of an Eternal Morning.' " Proust informed the countess that a friend with whom he had dined recently, on hearing him speak about his admiration for her, stared at him silently afterward. When Proust asked him what was wrong, the man replied that he had never heard anyone speak about a woman with such passion.[50]

On May 15 Proust had dinner with Armand de Guiche and his wife to bid the duke farewell. Armand was leaving the next day for Washington, D.C., on a scientific mission to help the U.S. military with airplane construction for the war effort. Guiche was to remain in Washington until early September. During Guiche's Atlantic crossings, Proust worried that a German submarine might sink his ship.[51] The day of Guiche's departure coincided with the publication of Morand's novella *Clarisse, ou l'amitié* in the *Mercure de France*. Proust had read Morand's proofs in April and encouraged the young author to collect and publish his stories in a volume.[52]

Proust attended a performance at the Théâtre du Châtelet of Cocteau's remarkable ballet *Parade,* written for the Ballets Russes, with modern choreography by Léonide Massine and music by Erik Satie, who, for his first orchestral score, made use of typewriters, sirens, and other modern sources of sound. Picasso made his debut as a set and costume designer, marking the first time Cubist art was seen in a theater. The poet and art critic Guillaume Apollinaire, a longtime champion of Picasso, coined the word *surrealist* in writing the program notes for the ballet. Writing to congratulate Cocteau on the ballet, Proust said that the other ballets on the program, including Stravinksy's *Petrouchka,* were "nothing special," but Cocteau's ballet was "poignant and continues to generate in me untold regrets." One regret he felt was never "to have known the sawdust of circuses." In the postscript Proust proved that his eyes had not been restricted to what he saw on stage: "How *handsome* Picasso is."[53] *Parade,* for all its innovations and daring avant-gardism, did not succeed with the public, nor did it win over Simone de Caillavet, whose adolescent beauty had dazzled Proust. Now twenty-two, Simone panned the show in a scathing review that she wrote for *Le Gaulois.*[54] *Parade*'s creators withdrew the ballet.

In the summer Proust gave two dinners at the Ritz. On June 7 his guests included Mme Soutzo, Paul Morand, and Princesse Lucien Murat. A few evenings earlier Proust had dined there with Mme Soutzo, Paul Morand, Abbé Mugnier, and Jean Cocteau. Still bitter over the failure of his ballet, Cocteau denigrated the public's taste. Mugnier remembered that Proust, "a very likable invalid," told him about Illiers, its customs and environs. The two men discovered their shared admiration of Chateaubriand. Mugnier was delighted when Proust quoted passages from *Les Mémoires d'outre-tombe.*[55] Proust wanted Céleste to meet Mugnier and kept telling her that he intended to invite him home one evening. Finally, he said that she would certainly meet the abbé because she must promise to ask Mugnier to come and pray at his bedside after his death.

On July 14 Proust gave a more intimate dinner, to which he invited Comte and Comtesse Étienne de Beaumont, Mme Soutzo, and Paul Morand.[56] Proust's new friends Comte Beaumont and his wife, née Édith de Tasine, were part of Cocteau's circle. The wealthy Beaumonts enjoyed throwing lavish parties and costume balls that brought together aristocrats and members of the avant-garde.[57]

In early June, Proust wrote Louisa de Mornand to express his sympathy for the loss of her brother Ernest, killed on the Chemin des Dames during General Nivelle's notorious April offensive. Proust told Louisa that he recalled having seen a photograph of Ernest that had made him eager to meet the young man, "for I have always been curious about the effects of the transposition of a friend's or loved one's face from the masculine sex into the feminine and vice versa." He then described an accident that occurred that morning while he was preparing for his fumigations. A "pinch" of his antiasthma powders "caught fire and flared into my eyes, burning a corner of one of them. I haven't seen a doctor and I imagine it will be nothing but it continues to hurt a good deal."[58] The pain lasted several days.

As food shortages worsened, Olivier Dabescat proved especially resourceful in procuring for Proust a quantity of dry tea biscuits known as "petits-beurres." Proust wrote Mme Soutzo that the headwaiter had provided enough for "thirty years' captivity."[59] Dabescat may have been the source of sugar that Proust obtained for Adèle Larivière, who needed a supply for her restaurant and who thanked the novelist for the favor.[60]

Toward the end of June, Hauser managed to sell some of Proust's holdings, including nineteen Doubowaia mine shares at the "fantastic" rate of 185 francs each.[61] Thanks to Hauser's diligence, Proust's financial situation continued to improve, despite his lavish spending. He was soon to have a new partner to assist him in depleting his liquid assets.

Bombs over Paris

On July 27 Proust attended a dinner party given by Mme Soutzo in her apartment at the Ritz. The guests included the Beaumonts, Joseph Reinach, Jacques Porel, Jean Cocteau, and Paul Morand. After dinner there was a session with a hypnotist.[62] The novelist was amused when the hypnotist asked Princesse Eugène Murat whether she had a special request while she underwent hypnosis, and the lady "could think of nothing else to ask but to be cured of grinding her teeth." Proust remarked of this rather "modest request" that it was "extraordinary the extent to which contact with mystery makes people trivial."[63]

At 11:30, the sirens on the Eiffel Tower began to wail, and Cocteau remarked:

"There goes the Eiffel Tower again, complaining because someone's trodden on her toe."[64] In late May the Germans had launched the first air raids with new bombers named Gothas, each capable of carrying thirteen bombs and much more deadly than the Zeppelins.[65] Risking a cold, Proust followed the other guests to the balcony, where he remained for an hour "watching this wonderful Apocalypse in which the airplanes climbing and swooping seemed to complement and eclipse the constellations." A painterly analogy came to mind: "The unbelievable thing was that, as in the Greco painting in which there's the celestial scene above and the terrestrial scene below, while we watched this sublime mid-air spectacle from the balcony, below us the Hôtel Ritz . . . appeared to have turned into Feydeau's *Hôtel du libre échange*. Ladies in night-dresses or bathrobes roamed the 'vaulted' hall clutching their pearl necklaces to their bosoms." As was often the case in Proust's letters, this description of an air raid sent to Mme Straus served as a draft for the scene he included in the war years in the *Search*.[66]

When August came, Proust grew nostalgic about Normandy and the many summers he had spent there. With the Allies and the Germans dug in, Mme Straus had decided it was safe to return to her villa near Trouville. Writing to her at Le Clos des Mûriers, Proust said that he knew of no place "as full of feminine charm, as the Normandy countryside."[67] He longed to see those fields again, even those surrounding Paris and in the fall he proposed that Montesquiou join him on an excursion to Versailles. He told the count that after so many years of not having left Paris, he needed to see the colors of the countryside one more time in order to finish his novel.[68] Proust did not object to seeing Montesquiou on his own terms outside his apartment, but the proposed excursion never took place.

On August 22 a tragic event occurred in London that deeply saddened Proust, though he had anticipated it. Emmanuel Bibesco, waiting until Antoine left him alone, hanged himself in his hotel room.[69] Proust grieved for his handsome, gifted friend who had proved such an excellent guide on his Ruskin pilgrimages to Gothic cathedrals. The number of Proust's closest friends who met with violent death is remarkable, even taking the war into account. The death toll had begun with Agostinelli and Calmette, and now an ailing, depressed friend had taken his own life. Emmanuel was not the last to select such a death.

Proust sent letters of sympathy to Antoine and his cousins. Writing to the princesse de Caraman-Chimay, with whom he had not corresponded for years, he evoked the last time he had seen Emmanuel, in April, huddling in the darkness of the cab. Proust found the way Emmanuel killed himself too horrible to contemplate: "I don't want to talk to you about an end which I, alas, too soon and too accurately foresaw." Turning to more pleasant matters, he told the princess that he had been "glad to meet Constantin, after so many years, at the Princesse Soutzo's." He wondered whether she and her sister "had ever received a book of mine called *Swann* (for the only persons who have never acknowledged it are you, Princesse, Mme de Noailles and Constantin. But I attach no importance to my book which I no longer remember myself, though I shall send you nonetheless its interminable sequels, and if you are kind enough not to forget my humble self that will be more than enough for me)."[70] It had been four years since the publication of *Swann's Way*, and Proust wondered if the war would ever end, allowing him to publish his remaining volumes.

In October, Proust wrote Gide to thank him for sending him a copy of a new edition of *Les Nourritures terrestres*, first published in 1897.[71] After complimenting Gide on these "*Fruits of the Earth* which have already nourished a generation and on which many others will live in the future," Proust made a statement about his own attitude toward literature, preparing to share with Gide a parody by Céleste that he found delightful: "Dear friend, I believe, contrary to the fashion among some of our contemporaries, that one can have a very lofty idea of literature, and at the same time have a good-natured laugh at it." Having said that, Proust was certain that Gide would not be offended by the informal pastiche of Céleste, who was so "unbelievably ignorant" that he "had to explain to her recently that Bonaparte and Napoléon were one and the same person; I've never managed to teach her to spell, and she has never had the patience to read even half a page of my book." Yet Céleste was "full of extraordinary gifts," as had been proven recently, when Proust, suffering from eyestrain, asked her to read *Les Nourritures terrestres* aloud to him. Céleste, for all her ignorance, had quickly caught on to Gide's style in the book, whose pages contain verse and prose fragments addressed to a youth Nathanaël, who is urged to live fully and freely. Proust gave Gide several examples of his housekeeper's parody, such as her reply when asked to phone Mme Soutzo: "Nathanaël, I will speak to thee of the lady-friends of Monsieur. There is she who has made him go out again after many years, taxi to the Ritz, bell-hops, tips, exhaustion."

Gide's reaction to Céleste's poking fun at his style is unknown, but it seems unlikely he was as amused as Proust. Gide was not an author endowed with a strong sense of the comic, nor was he capable, as was Proust, of self-parody. At the end of his letter, Proust said that he sometimes sensed between himself and Gide "certain affinities, and perhaps the possibility of friendly relations between us[,] which would give me great pleasure."[72] He assured Gide that he was eager to see him and dine with him. But Proust and Gide never became close friends; they were too different in too many ways to trust each other. What Proust wrote about homosexuality further estranged the two authors when *Sodom and Gomorrah* was published. Proust and Céleste continued to amuse themselves at Gide's expense, finding him to be, in his self-righteousness and his proselytizing on behalf of his own brand of hedonism and self-gratification, a "fake monk."[73]

During the summer and fall Proust made several attempts to see Montesquiou, none of which succeeded. Now that he was once again leading an active social life, with a new group of friends, Marcel seemed less reluctant to see the count. He soon learned that Montesquiou abhorred his new friends and refused to accept any invitations that included them. Proust wrote Mme Scheikévitch that Montesquiou was "stubborn in his prejudices and perhaps the only person with whom my peacemaking efforts fail. Peace can be made to reign on earth between men of good-will. But his will is not altogether good."[74] Proust had not hidden his admiration and affection for Mme Soutzo from Montesquiou, having told him that among his new friends "(those who far from being ridiculous are charming) I love Princesse Soutzo."[75]

In the fall, Proust invited Montesquiou to dinner at the Ritz with Princesse Soutzo and the Beaumonts, but Montesquiou replied testily that it was apparent that Proust could no more envisage a meal without Mme Soutzo than he could one without bread—"panis salsus, mollis esca"—"since I am never invited without her."[76] Montesquiou wanted to see Proust alone. When the novelist proposed, as he had in August, an excursion to the countryside, the count again declined; he wanted to engage the novelist in tête-à-tête conversation for as long as he liked.

In mid-October, Proust wrote Mme Catusse that he had sent a cyclist from the Ritz to her house to inquire whether she could see him. He had wanted to consult her again about the disposal of a number of remaining household items. He told her that he had begun correcting the proofs for the next volume of his novel, complaining that he had just received "five thousand-page proofs" for *Within a Budding Grove,* and because he had to correct them "three times," that would "make 15,000" pages. He wondered how he would ever accomplish that "insane task," especially with no glasses and exhausted eyes.[77] Proust exaggerated the total number of pages received, but not the intensive labor required by his way of revising and augmenting his pages. He soon saw that he must abandon this practice if he were to stand even a chance of finishing his novel and publishing it.

On October 17 Gallimard went to Grasset's office and negotiated the purchase of the remaining 206 copies of *Swann's Way* for 2.35 francs each. Within a few days, Gallimard ordered new covers, bearing the NRF imprint, for these copies, which he believed would sell while the remainder of the novel, including a new edition of *Swann's Way,* was being readied for publication. Thus Proust could reprint *Swann's Way* with the corrections he had always wanted to make and place all his volumes on sale at once.[78] Gallimard was being overoptimistic.

Trying to calculate for his publisher the number of pages for the remaining volumes, Proust concluded that each would be as long as *Swann's Way.* He mentioned, perhaps as a justification for a new volume featuring Albertine and her girlfriends at the beach, that "since Albertine through the whole story of my keeping her and of her death, the story of which is the subject of the fourth volume, has become the true dramatic center of the work there is an advantage . . . in having her introduced well ahead of time during the first stay at Balbec, in the second volume." Proust, fearing that Gaston might be horrified at the unprecedented length to which his novel was stretching, proposed that if publishing him became a bad business venture, Gallimard could reduce his royalties.[79] This generosity toward his new publisher was not to last long.

On October 30, in his haste to leave on a goodwill mission to the United States, Gallimard said that he would write Proust from on board the ship. On his return to France he hoped to "find the five volumes typeset because I am eager to read the continuation."[80] Gallimard and the rest of Proust's readership had to wait much longer than anyone anticipated.

Proust received some encouragement from the journalist Olivier Flament, who printed a notice in *Excelsior* on October 17, informing his readers that the remainder of the *Search* would be published in five large volumes, of which the newspaper gave the titles. Flament wondered how those who had been "stupefied" by the "thick *Swann's Way*" would react on learning the "author had prepared for us no fewer than four other books as heavy, as detailed" as the first. Flament said that Proust's novel would be in "five panels," constituting "an immense fresco of a thinker's entire life." The grateful author invited Flament to meet him at the Ritz and thanked him for reminding the public that his vast work would indeed appear.[81]

With the war casualties reaching unprecedented levels and French troops demoralized to the point that desertions became more and more frequent, Proust grieved for all those being slaughtered. In a letter to Mme Soutzo, he wondered what had "happened to all these young men." Observing that "*Le Gaulois* would especially grieve the death of a duke, I weep for everyone's death, even for the men I never saw. The war had given us a new sense, through the appalling exercise of daily anguish, that makes us suffer for unknowns."[82]

Because he always worked at night, Proust began to take proof sheets with him when he went to the Ritz. He would have preferred to remain there until the early-morning hours, "where the staff is so considerate that I feel right at home," but the Ritz had to observe the blackout beginning at 9:30 because it was located next to the Ministry of Justice.[83] This forced Proust to go to the Hôtel Crillon, adjacent to the American embassy on the place de la Concorde, where the lights stayed on until 2 A.M.[84] Proust never grew accustomed to the Crillon, as he had the Ritz, saying that the environment was "very hostile, and except for a charming old concierge" who was on duty at night, "everyone else was odious."[85]

After a small dinner party at the Crillon, Mme Scheikévitch revealed to Proust the extent of her financial difficulties. Like many well-to-do Russians who lived abroad, she found herself without funds as a consequence of the onset of the revolution.[86] Two days later Proust wrote Mme Catusse, saying that he wanted to assist a lady who had been shaken by a "great misfortune." He intended to organize a sale of furnishings and to split the proceeds with Mme Scheikévitch. In addition to Mme Catusse, Proust involved the Strauses and Walter Berry in the sale. Berry, he told Mme Catusse, was "a man of refined taste who spends his life in antique shops and, what's more, knows all the rich Americans."

Writing to Mme Straus, he listed a number of items in storage—carpets, an armoire, bronzes, and so forth. He had decided to sell all his mother's flatware, which was still in boxes in his dining room, where he had "never taken a meal." Mme Straus would be relieved to learn that he had emptied a storage space in the basement to give household items to refugees.[87]

Mme Scheikévitch wrote to thank Proust for his kind offer of help and to say that she had been both right and wrong to speak so freely about her problems. Right because no one was "so understanding" and "wrong because there is no remedy." She must decline his generous offer because she had to envision the future as well as the present.[88] Mme Scheikévitch's eventual remedy was to marry a second time, but the match was no more enduring than the first.

Proust also sought to assist Morand and Mme Soutzo. He had known since the summer that she needed an appendectomy; now he began to worry about the impending operation.[89] In mid-October, he offered to consult his brother about various surgeons. He wrote Morand about Dr. Charles Walther, of whom he had a high opinion, stressing that he was not making a recommendation, but simply starting a list of the best qualified doctors. Marcel explained that it might be difficult to contact his brother because Robert's ambulance division was constantly moving as the front lines shifted.

Robert would soon be operating on a new front in another country. In late October, after the Italian defeat at Isonzo, where the Germans had been concentrating an offensive, the Allies decided to send British and French troops to reinforce the Italians.[90] General Mangin asked Robert Proust, whose bravery and surgical skills he greatly admired, to accompany his division to Italy.[91] Robert arrived on November 24, in charge of Surgical Ambulance Unit number 25.[92] Marthe began to make plans to join her husband at the Italian front, where she would serve as a volunteer nurse. She asked Marcel to seek the assistance of Morand, who was soon to join the French diplomatic corps in Rome, in obtaining the necessary papers for her to go to Italy.[93]

By December, Proust could no longer find taxis or gasoline in the evening.[94] With the war entering its fourth winter, Parisians were experiencing more shortages in food and fuel; there were longer blackouts in central Paris, where strategic buildings were located.[95] Occasionally, the night concierge sent a car from the Ritz to collect Proust, or Mme Soutzo dispatched her chauffeur to bring him.[96]

Proust's friends responded to his appeal for help with the furniture sale. Mme Catusse sent two women who were antiques dealers to his apartment at two in the afternoon, the first time anyone had ever called at such an "early" hour. One evening Proust went over to the Strauses' and woke Émile up at eleven. M. Straus, "the nicest possible person" even after being roused from his sleep, offered to accept anything that Proust sent over, even the rugs. Straus would invite a number of antiques dealers to bid on the items. If Straus succeeded in selling the chairs and rugs, the silver would remain, "so monstrously useless in crates." Proust began to think about sending everything to the auction house.[97]

Proust attempted to assist Bardac in finding new employment for a valet. He wrote Paul Goldschmidt about Charlie Humphries, who belonged to one of the homosexual circles the writer frequented. Humphries, a young Englishman, had served as valet de chambre to Henri Bardac, who became so enamored of Charlie that he made him his heir. In the letter to Goldschmidt, an extremely wealthy clubman whose secretary Humphries had been, Proust described his efforts to find Charlie a position with a Mme de Salverte, but said that he had been instructed by Henri and Charlie to tell the lady that Charlie was Goldschmidt's secretary instead of Bardac's. Goldschmidt ignored Proust's instructions to destroy the letter and returned it to the author, who left it among his papers.[98] Nothing more is known about this mysterious matter: why did Charlie need a position if Bardac was his protector? Why must the lady not know Charlie was Bardac's protégé? Perhaps Bardac feared a scandal.

Proust shared, at least partly, his extensive knowledge of the world of Parisian homosexuality with Céleste, for he "made no bones of the fact" that Goldschmidt "belonged to the 'Sodom party,'" as Céleste called it. She also remembered that Proust was fascinated by Goldschmidt's unrelenting formal elegance and the way Charlie "dressed, particularly by his waistcoats." Céleste said that this curiosity about fashion was "the only reason" Proust "allowed him to come to the apartment twice—to study his dress, for the book," which she remembered his doing, "down to the last detail" of the former valet's attire.[99] Humphries may have contributed his first name to Morel the violinist, just as Pétain had provided the seductive lock. Charlus falls madly in love with Morel, who, like Humphries, comes from the servant class.[100] It is obvious that the name Charles appealed strongly to Proust. He gave the name to Charles Swann and a variation of it to Charlus. Pronounced in French, the names Charles and Marcel echo each other.

Proust had begun to suffer the pangs of anticipated separation from Morand. He wrote Mme Soutzo about these and about his fears that she was not resting enough before surgery. He told her, as he did Morand the following day, that the "infinite sorrow" he felt over the young man's departure was "egotism," caused by the dread of seeing the self that loved his friend destroyed by becoming accustomed to his absence. "The present Proust is not at all like that. I have never loved Morand as much as I do this evening." The thought of Morand's departure made him "want to turn his face to the wall and take such a strong dose of Veronal that he would not wake up" until Morand was in Rome. He had told Morand none of this, but his "heart was overflowing" with such feelings. "But I don't know how to say nice things. And besides he doesn't give me much encouragement."[101] Grasping at straws, Proust had found some encouragement recently when Paul accompanied him home. Morand's kindness on waiting to see whether he would be all right when he could not open his door had moved and surprised him, making Proust draw some "very happy conclusions" regarding his friend's "literary destiny."[102] A few days later, Proust, identifying himself with the Narrator, wondered whether Morand had "read in the NRF the pages in which I show how I finally reconcile myself to the departure of my friends," that "what saddens me most," is the knowledge "that a day will come when, a new 'self' having formed, I shall no longer miss you." Proust felt, however, that Morand might prove the exception to the rule.[103]

Once Morand's departure date was fixed, Proust urged Mme Soutzo to proceed with the operation, assuming that her doctors would advise the same, and he gave her a reason he must have felt would be important to her. If vanity, as he feared, was giving her any cause to delay, she should go ahead. The anesthesia and the operation "will transform you momentarily into a marble statue which those who have seen it will never forget." She would become, for a while "the most transparent and sublime alabaster."[104]

Proust devoted the evening of December 9 to Morand, who was leaving the next day for his new diplomatic post in Rome. In order to spend the final hours with Paul, Proust had declined an invitation to a dinner followed by an organ concert at the princesse de Polignac's. He reported to Morand that Céleste was weeping over his departure, but being "Celestial," she had read in her stars that Morand would not be like "my other friends and that I will never forget you."[105]

On the same day Proust said good-bye to Morand, Émile Straus wrote him a note to say that four antiques dealers had come to look at Proust's furnishings. The highest offer was fifteen thousand francs for all the furniture and tapestries. Proust agreed to accept the offer, and because the Strauses lived nearby, he proposed stopping by for a visit and to pick up the money from the sale.[106]

On December 16 Proust had another opportunity to attend a dinner and organ concert at the princesse de Polignac's. Afterward, when he proposed to accompany Princesse Soutzo home, she answered him coldly, "No, the Beaumonts will see me home." Proust was deeply wounded. He reported the incident to Morand, saying that Mme Soutzo's kindness toward him had been diminished by Paul's departure. "You have in some way taken away with you the present you had given me." He assured Morand that his own devotion and attention to the princess had in no way decreased; he continued to be "assiduously importunate" and would keep Morand fully informed by telegrams during her convalescence. Morand should follow his example and say nothing to Mme Soutzo about the "threat of being disgraced" that her words to him after the Polignac party seemed to convey.[107] Mme Soutzo's rejection of Proust as an escort home was a reenactment of a key scene in "Swann in Love," in which Odette, who has been Swann's mistress for some time and has always let him take her home, allows the Verdurins and Forcheville to accompany her instead. Perhaps Mme Soutzo resented his intrusiveness in his role as inter-mediary, or perhaps she simply lacked the stamina and patience to tolerate large doses of Proustian solicitude as she gathered her strength to undergo surgery.

Early in December, Gallimard's printer, La Semeuse at Étampes, frustrated at being unable to find competent workers, began firing his typesetters, so that by Christmas, production had come to a halt. Proust, who received no more proofs for *Within a Budding Grove,* wrote Gide a few days before Christmas that "even my most modest work is interrupted."[108] The novelist was to wait nearly a year for the remaining proofs.

Two days before Christmas, Proust wrote Morand that Céleste's prediction had come true: he had not forgotten his young friend. Proust assured him that previous cases had made him think forgetting Morand would be "very quick. But exceptions to the rule make life enchanting." He professed his inability to understand how Morand's "face can be so continuously present, how I can remember the slightest expansions of your smile, the simplicity in which your goodness cloaked itself, so many things that when you are near pass unnoticed."[109] Although Paul was no doubt cheered by this news, he may also have been puzzled: he had been gone less than two weeks.

In spite of the war, there was no shortage in Paris of attractive young men in whose company Proust could console himself. Earlier in the year he had begun corresponding with Jacques de Lacretelle, an aspiring writer who later became a respected critic and novelist and the third in his family to be elected to the Académie française.[110] In a short time Lacretelle became a regular visitor. On Christmas Eve, after first meeting Mme de Chevigné at the Ritz, Proust and Lacretelle attended a party given by Princesse Marie Murat.[111]

Dr. Antonin Gosset removed Mme Soutzo's appendix in her apartment at the Ritz on December 29.[112] Gosset was a respected urologist who had called on the Prousts just before Mme Proust's death. The operation on the princess was a complete success, and her recovery was rapid. Proust wired Morand immediately to announce the good news.[113]

That evening he wrote to Mme Straus, thanking her for arranging the furniture sale. As a token of his gratitude, he sent her an enormous box of chocolates. Thinking of New Year's Eve, he said that if he were "not feeling too unwell on Monday evening, I shall come and wish you what in other days used to be called a 'happy New Year.' Life changes the sense of words, deprives usages of all meaning, and War as well as life." The year about to begin was to be the last of the Great War.[114]

26   *A Walk in the Snow*   ❧

JANUARY 1918 BEGAN WITH UNUSUALLY COLD temperatures and a freezing mixture of snow and rain that lasted for several days, aggravating the hardships and despair that often seemed unbearable. The snow was so heavy in many areas that it interfered with trains and telegraphic communications.[1] In the misery of what promised to be another hard winter, everyone had the same New Year's wish: that the war would end quickly and well.

On the second day of the new year, Proust went out late at night to take a stroll in the snow. As he walked and slipped on the ice, two American soldiers approached him and asked for directions to the Hôtel Bedford. Because the soldiers spoke little French and Proust had forgotten his English, the three set out in silent search of the hotel, and they soon found it. Relating the incident to Walter Berry, Proust said that he had been unaware that the hotel was in the rue de l'Arcade, "right around the corner from me." Proust knew the short, narrow street quite well, for he often went down it late at night to visit Le Cuziat's brothel. He had been moved, he told Berry, at the thought of how far from home the two soldiers had come. He lamented the ever-mounting war dead, observing that those spared by the war were ruined financially. But an end to the fighting appeared more likely now that the Americans had arrived, for which he credited Berry.[2]

Antoinette Allavena, Mme Soutzo's chambermaid, brought news daily to Céleste about her mistress's recovery, news that Proust forwarded to Morand in
Rome. One day the maid told Céleste that it was impossible to imagine how
beautifully pale the princess was, fulfilling Proust's prophecy about the alabaster
effects of surgery. Proust wrote Princesse Soutzo and said his walk in the snow and
fog had given him a touch of bronchitis, which made his asthma attacks last until
eleven in the evening. When she was well enough, he would "attempt something
energetic, even if dangerous": he would come to chat with her from nine to ten, at
which time he would leave so as not to risk making her tired. If her servant
Antoinette had not outlawed food odors, he would dine in her company. Proust
had become so accustomed to the pleasures of his Ritz routine and visits with the
beautiful, witty princess that he eagerly awaited their resumption. He told the
convalescent that he could see in his mind that "room where I spent all my hours
'out' for a year." No doubt it would have been better for him to have seen some
friends during her convalescence, but he was "too sad, too tied to your suffering.
What a way for the year to begin."[3]

On January 9 Proust returned to Mme Lemarié two batches of proofs for 277
pages of *Within a Budding Grove*, explaining that he had waited until after the
holidays to send them, when there was less danger of packages going astray. He
asked that she be careful not to mix them up, for the pages through 172 were second
proofs and the others first proofs. He attached "particular importance to this
package because of three pages that bear extensive handwritten additions of which
I don't have a copy." If she could not guarantee safe delivery to the printer, she
should return the pages to him for copying. After the third set of proofs, he would
likely ask for supplementary proofs of the three pages with all the additions, but he
could not write their definitive version until he corrected the pages surrounding
them. Mme Lemarié, who appreciated Proust's unique qualities as a writer, assured
him that she had sent his packet to the printer by registered mail. "So far we have
never lost anything."[4]

In mid-January, Blanche threatened to drop the preface that Proust was writing for his book, which was "already too long." Marcel seized the opportunity to tell
Blanche that because he suffered constantly from eyestrain, he did not want to
write a preface that would later be discarded. The two argued about whether or not
Blanche's book should include his earlier essay on Forain. Proust strongly advised
against using the piece because he considered Forain a despicable person and a
rabid anti-Semite. When Blanche changed his mind about dropping the preface,
Proust sent him the text, along with all the books and articles the painter had

loaned him. Proust told him to "throw my pages in the fire if you wish," but should Blanche publish the preface, he would be "very proud and happy."[5] Blanche followed Proust's advice and omitted the essay on Forain.[6] But the harmony between the painter and his prefacer was short-lived. When friends told Proust that they had heard about the preface, which he had hoped to keep secret as long as possible, he wrote Blanche, saying he was "infinitely vexed" that the painter had failed to keep his word.

If Proust was "infinitely vexed," Blanche, on reading his letter, became incensed. He wrote Proust that his letter had struck him like a meteorite. Blanche denied the mysterious informers' allegations and expressed his fury at Proust's refusal to name them. Blanche's first inclination had been to refuse the preface and demand that Proust return his oil portrait. After a night's sleep, the painter decided against such drastic measures. But he would not forget: "Never have I felt more mortally offended."[7]

Insisting that his letter had been "entirely affectionate," Proust expressed his dismay at Blanche's reaction.[8] Marcel had seen a Blanche he did not know, but would choose to forget, having been fond of him since the portrait he had painted so long ago. Their friendship remained intact, and Blanche proved to be one of the keenest admirers and most effective defenders of the *Search*.

Having forgiven Blanche's alleged indiscretions, Proust found himself defending his own ability to keep a secret. Gide had recently alluded somewhat mysteriously to his "good fortune," by which he meant a young man by the name of Michel, with whom he had been in love since the previous summer. Gide had decided to say no more because he believed Proust indiscreet. Proust protested that just the opposite was true, explaining to Gide, as he often had to others, that although he could never help himself in matters of love, he could always assist others. "Thus I chose the wrong vocation, which should have been that of a matchmaker or professional second for duelists."[9]

Gide had nearly finished *Corydon*, his proselytizing book on homosexuality, but he waited until Proust published *Sodom and Gomorrah* to bring out his very different book. He had recently considered writing his memoirs but quickly changed his mind after reading a few passages aloud to a friend. Gide had immediately felt disappointed with his texts, saying that comparing them to "the pages of Proust's marvelous book, which I was rereading anyway," completely discouraged him.[10]

Mme Scheikévitch was another friend with whom Proust's relationship became strained, due primarily to her inability to keep a secret, even as he sought to alleviate the financial straits in which she found herself. Proust wrote to say he was "*very* hurt" by remarks she had made about him since they last met. At first, he had decided to keep quiet, but events in Russia had made him worry about her, so he wanted to forgive her indiscretions and turn a new page. He could not forget her past kindnesses regarding publicity for *Swann's Way.* "Your Russian origin is another reason for us to love you more, since it has become for you a source of chagrin." He assured her that he would "always remain true to the Russia of Tolstoy, Dostoyevsky, Borodin, and Mme Scheikévitch."[11]

Because she had declined an earlier offer of money from his furniture sale—while ignoring his entreaty to keep the matter secret—he now presented a fantastical scheme to help her. He would ghostwrite a daily literary column for the *Temps,* where, Proust said, she had excellent connections, an oblique reference to the newspaper's publisher Adrien Hébrard, who had been her lover. How happy he would be to spare her the thankless boredom of writing; he wanted her to receive her guests, to gaze at her flowers and dream while he wrote the column for her. Each evening Céleste would deliver to her the copy for the newspaper. "Would you like that, dear collaborator?"[12] Proust remembered to compliment her on her drawings, saying that she was "admirably gifted" and that her portraits of Abbé Mugnier were "masterpieces."

The incorrigible Mme Scheikévitch promptly told Mme Soutzo about Marcel's dotty offer to ghost a column in order to help her financially. Proust expressed anew his annoyance at her complete lack of discretion, which he again offered to forgive and forget, if only she would learn to be discreet. She wisely declined his proposal to collaborate. Regarding her finances, there was a reprieve. The French government had announced that it would continue to pay, in the short term, coupons on Russian loans.[13]

Marcel wrote Lucien, who, in late January, had been given a desk job at a military office in Paris. Proust would try to visit him, but he complained about suffering from palpitations, which made it difficult for him to mount even three steps. He received an invitation from Lucien's mother to attend a reception in honor of Francis Jammes. Thanking Mme Daudet, he wrote "I am always astonished when someone knows I'm still alive."[14] On February 4 Proust attended the party, where he saw the Daudet brothers, Jacques Truelle, Louis Gautier-Vignal, and Anna de Noailles, whom he had not seen in years. And he met a young writer, François Mauriac, whom he found "charming" and who was to become a great admirer of the *Search,* though with serious reservations about the many passages on homosexuality. The program included hymns declaimed and sung by Jammes and a soprano.[15] Mugnier noticed that Anna found it impossible to disguise her feelings of being a superior poet; she acknowledged Jammes's greatness as a poet but told the priest that the pieces heard that evening were "catechism for sheep." After the party, Proust and Jacques Truelle accompanied Abbé Mugnier to his home on the rue Méchain. Marcel delighted in the abbé's rather licentious choice of words. A little over a week later Proust saw Mugnier, along with Cocteau and Gautier-Vignal, at another party given by Mme Soutzo.[16] Proust and Mugnier talked about hawthorns and medieval architecture, especially Vézelay.

Blanche wrote again to say that he had reduced his volume on painters to about three hundred pages. In the postscript he voiced his trepidations about the artistic world that awaited them after the war, which was merely "the prodrome of the Great Terror." As examples of the horrors that lay in wait, Blanche cited the Picasso exhibition—a show of works by Matisse and Picasso had opened in January—and the current floor show at the Casino de Paris, featuring a "Yankee" orchestra with cymbals, banjos, and drums, all of which made a terrific noise. Henri Ghéon, in Paris on leave, had told Blanche that this spectacle heralded "the end of the world."[17]

Like many of his compatriots, Proust knew that the war was profoundly changing society. Part of what he was writing in "M. de Charlus during the war" reflected these developments, many of which, such as realignments in the salons and changes in women's fashion, were further proof of human folly. Mme Verdurin and Mme Bontemps, two bourgeois ladies, are now "the queens of this wartime Paris." As for fashion, "young women went about all day with tall cylindrical turbans on their heads . . . and from a sense of duty wore Egyptian tunics, straight and dark and very 'war,' over very short skirts. . . . They did not forget that it was their duty to rejoice the eyes of these 'boys at the front.' "[18] The boys at the front had no time to ponder rising skirtlines. The Germans were preparing to begin their last major offensive.

Gothas and Berthas

In midwinter the German army, under Gen. Paul von Hindenburg, launched an all-out offensive, unleashing terrible new weapons of destruction. Late in the evening of January 30, thirty-one new twin-engined Gothas made their first air raid on Paris. Within a short period of time the planes had dropped 267 bombs on the city, killing or injuring 259 Parisians.[19] The sound of the planes and the bombs exploding startled Mme Daudet, who noted in her diary that the raid began at 11:30. She listened in terror as the repercussions from the explosions shook her windows.[20]

Proust had gone to a party at Gabriel de La Rouchefoucauld's to hear Borodin's Quartet no. 2.[21] The concert ended and Proust was entering a taxi to go home when the sirens began to wail. He should have reached the nearby boulevard Haussmann and been inside before the first bombs exploded, but the taxi, driven by an elderly chauffeur, traveled a short distance and stalled in the rue Murille. A good thirty minutes later, the chauffeur got the car moving only to have it break down for another half-hour on the avenue de Messine. Proust, by now extremely impatient, stepped out of the taxi to watch and listen. He heard the sirens blaring and saw the airplanes diving from the sky and releasing their bombs, which exploded in nearby streets. The chauffeur finally deposited the novelist at boulevard Haussmann. Proust, concerned for the old man's safety, offered to put him up in the little salon. He realized that the driver was deaf when he answered, "Oh, no! I'm headed for Grenelle. That was only a false alarm." At that moment a bomb landed in the rue d'Athènes, only five minutes away.

From then on the Germans bombed or shelled Paris almost daily, killing dozens of civilians. Proust described the air raids in his novel: "It was the period when there were constant Gotha raids; the air was perpetually buzzing with the vibration, vigilant and sonorous, of French aeroplanes. But at intervals the siren rang out like the heart-rending scream of a Valkyrie—the only German music to have been heard since the war—until the moment when the fire-engines announced that the alert was over, while beside them, like an invisible street-urchin, the all-clear at regular intervals commented on the good news and hurled its cry of joy into the air."[22]

Lucien's desk job in Paris had done little to lift his spirits. Proust sought to encourage his friend. On one occasion he compared his own poor health and bleak prospects for a long, happy life to Lucien's, whose situation seemed enviable. Marcel agreed to read the typescript of Lucien's new novel *La Dimension nouvelle*, saying that he would find such work much less fatiguing than his own proofs, whose print was so tiny that he remained blinded for hours, unable "to distinguish any object." In exchange, he would send Lucien the proofs of *Within a Budding Grove*. Thinking about the party the Daudets had given for Jammes, Proust expressed his affection for Mugnier and said he had never seen "Mme de Noailles looking prettier, and your mother exactly as she was when I met you."[23]

Writing to Mugnier in mid-February, Proust said that he was in a quandary as to which of his books he should send the priest: "*Swann,* so discouraging by its length, so shocking by its licentious nature, above all so sorrowful? *Pleasures and Days* is valuable because of France's preface," but his own pieces were written when he was in high school, as was only too evident. (As usual, Proust made himself younger than he really had been when he wrote those early stories.) His prefaces and "annotations to Ruskin are of interest only to an admirer of Ruskin." Proust finally decided to send his excerpts on hawthorns, "tearing the bouquet . . . from the forbidden book."[24]

In March, Proust confided to a few friends his anxiety about a new illness. He thought himself threatened by facial paralysis and aphasia, which he took as indications that death was even closer at hand than he had feared. Among new friends listening to Proust's complaints was the twenty-five-year-old Jacques Porel, who occasionally dined with Proust and Mme Soutzo at the Ritz. When Porel introduced his wife to Proust at a dinner, the writer, as he later told Porel, was so struck by her beauty that "for an hour the Ritz became a museum." Toward the end of the month, Proust complained to Porel that he was losing his memory. Even though he did not fear death, he wanted to hide from his friends the facial paralysis, whose source he did not know and which he assumed would worsen. "Death would obviously be the desired outcome. Unfortunately, I have five volumes to correct, and because of that I would like . . . to live." Proust was thinking of his mother's inability to speak in the days preceding her death, and he feared a similar fate.[25]

On March 8 German planes dropped more than ninety bombs on Paris. Although Parisians appeared calm, within a short time some two hundred thousand of them decided to leave for the safety of the countryside, far from the front lines.[26] On the morning of March 23, the Germans at Crépy-en-Laonnoise, seventy-four miles from Paris, aimed their monstrous long-range cannons at the city and began shelling. The first shell landed in Paris four minutes later at 7:16.[27] These cannons, known as Berthas, had been especially designed and manufactured by the Krupp family, leaders of the German munitions industry. The Germans fired more than twenty rounds, killing 256 civilians. On March 29 a shell hit the church of Saint-Gervais at 4:33 in the afternoon, just as the Good Friday services began, killing seventy-five worshipers and wounding ninety. After a week of murderous shelling, many more Parisians made plans to leave, fearing an invasion.[28] The German bombardment was to last until April 27.

The danger was real, but Proust was not affected. Writing to Mme Catusse, he claimed not to fear the Gothas and Berthas that terrified his neighbors and friends. It was not bravura, he told her, for he often feared smaller things, such as mice and germs. The only problem caused by his refusal to go down to the basement during raids was the bad impression he created. Because he was the sole person in the building who did not take shelter, his neighbors mistakenly thought that he scorned those who did. His insouciance was not shared by Céleste. Proust wrote Hauser that Céleste frequently "descended from her empyrean to the depths" of the cellar, where she caught colds.[29] He dared not try to keep her out of the cellar, because he would feel great remorse if she were harmed.

Mme Catusse, concerned for Proust's safety, offered him a refuge in her property in Nice. It was primarily for Céleste's sake that Proust considered leaving for Nice or Biarritz, where Mme Soutzo had gone to seek safety, or even for Cabourg. He would have rented Mme Catusse's tower at Mont Boron were he not afraid of the lush growing season, with all its pollen. What troubled him most, however, and kept him from leaving, was the uncertainty regarding his military classification; he still could not find his certificate confirming that he was unfit to serve. Céleste was indignant, he wrote Princesse Soutzo, because Mme Catusse had offered him "her empty villa overlooking Nice and I prefer to remain in Paris." No one should think badly of his "dear Céleste" for fearing the bombs, because in many other ways she was "so valiant." But Proust, who had always hesitated until the last minute before leaving Paris, had become incapable of freeing himself from the bonds of habit. While he postponed making a decision, between March and July, the direction of the war began to change, as the Allies launched a counteroffensive, catching the Germans off guard.[30]

Marcel wrote Lucien that "death was nothing"; what really worried him was his facial paralysis and his doctors' refusal to tell him the truth. "I have, unfortunately, the art of wringing it from them, which isn't the same at all as if they said it, because they say nothing, their hesitation alone betrays them, and one remains both threatened and poorly informed." Believing that his days of lucidity and vitality were numbered, he complained bitterly to Lucien about the printer who left him for months on end with no proofs.[31]

Mme Catusse was not the only friend who worried about Marcel's safety. Félicie Fitau, the Prousts' former cook, now quite elderly, wrote from Lupiac, offering him "a place to sleep." Though moved by her kindness, he scoffed at "her insane notion that Paris has been ravaged." In the sanctuary of the cork-lined room he no more "heard the cannon than the clock." Montesquiou, safe in the family château of Artagnan, may have worried also; he sent Proust some magnificent violets. Although Proust had warned Céleste about the dangerous nature of gifts from the count, he did not throw out the flowers.[32]

In early April, Robert Proust asked to return from Italy to his native soil for the big German offensive. One evening Robert turned up at boulevard Haussmann for a brief visit. Marcel, who thought his brother was still on the Italian front near Padua, described to Lucien "the great joy of seeing him and of seeing him alone."[33]

Proust wrote to Maugny that the war made one anxious and miserable on everyone's behalf. Nothing caused more anguish than seeing parents sincerely grieving the death of a child. He observed that it was scarcely to the credit of high society's honor that this sensitivity appeared stronger among common people than among socialites, who seemed to console themselves with a "terrible facility." There were exceptions, such as the duc de Luynes, greatly distraught over the loss of his son. In another letter to Maugny, Proust referred to "a young man of the people," one of a "number of soldiers to whom I send each week tobacco, gifts, and chocolate."[34] Proust sometimes noted on a manuscript page the name and address of a soldier, presumably with the intention of sending the youth some treats.[35] Since childhood Proust had corresponded with servants, and he still kept in touch with a footman he had met at the casino in Cabourg, as well as a former hotel manager. He enjoyed hearing about their marriages and sudden rises up the socioeconomic ladder. A former valet at the casino, for example, had recently married a woman whose brother "owned almost all the villas at Houlgate."[36] The *Search* contains a number of examples of members of the servant class who reach new financial and social heights.

Jacques de Lacretelle, with all the determination of a passionate bibliophile, had managed to procure one of the five copies of *Swann's Way* printed on Japan Imperial paper. Lacretelle sent the rare copy to Proust, asking him to autograph it. Proust, claiming to be poorly informed about what pleased bibliophiles, asked Lacretelle for advice. Would his young friend like him to write out certain pages from *Swann's Way* or excerpts from an unpublished volume? Or put in the margin of this copy rare notes indicating the few keys to characters in the *Search*? Or would he like some proof sheets to have bound in the book? Proust told Lacretelle that his request had not interrupted his work because for months, unable to obtain his proofs, he had done nothing. A few galleys had just arrived, and though his head and eyes were too tired for him to correct them, he would nevertheless try. In the postscript Proust asked for the "great pleasure of reimbursing" Lacretelle for the book. Thus he would have the illusion of having given him the rare copy.[37]

On April 20 Proust dedicated Lacretelle's copy of *Swann's Way,* revealing some of the keys that inspired his characters and his fictional musical compositions.[38] At the beginning of the dedication, the novelist wrote the date and place, describing Paris as a "beach at the end of the season, very deserted since the cannon and the

Gothas." Addressing Lacretelle as "Dear friend," he opened by saying there were "no keys to the characters of this book; or rather there are eight or ten for each one; the same is true of the church of Combray; many churches posed for me in memory. I no longer even remember whether the paving comes from Saint-Pierre-sur-Dives or from Lisieux. Certain windows are certainly those of Évreux, others from the Sainte-Chapelle, and some from Pont-Audemer."[39] Regarding Vinteuil's sonata, Proust's recollections were more precise. "To whatever extent I made use of reality, actually, a very slight extent, . . . the little phrase of the sonata is, and I have never told this to anyone, the charming but infinitely mediocre phrase of a sonata for piano and violin by Saint-Saëns, a musician I don't like. (I will show you the exact passage, which recurs several times and which was the triumph of Jacques Thibaud.)"[40] Proust listed other works that he "shouldn't be surprised" had contributed to the music, such as Wagner's "Good Friday Spell," from *Parsifal,* and later at the Sainte-Euverte soirée, "when the piano and violin sigh like two birds answering each other's call, I thought of the Franck sonata (particularly as played by Enesco), whose quartet will appear in subsequent volumes. The tremolos that overlay the little phrase at the Verdurins were suggested to me by a prelude to *Lohengrin,* but the prelude itself, at that moment, was suggested by something of Schubert. In that same soirée at Verdurin's there is a ravishing piano piece of Fauré."

One of the most delightful comic descriptions in the novel is set at the Sainte-Euverte soirée, where Proust describes the monocles, very much in fashion, of society gentlemen. In his inscription he revealed to Lacretelle some of the men whose monocles and mannerisms he remembered for that scene.[41] Proust also evoked Mlle Benardaky, "today Princesse Radziwill (though I haven't seen her for . . . many years)," as the model for Gilberte on the Champs-Élysées. Clomesnil, a "wonderfully beautiful cocotte of the period," had posed "for a minute, when Mme Swann walks near the pigeon-shooting gallery" in the Bois de Boulogne. At the end of the dedication, Proust reminded Lacretelle again that "the characters are entirely invented and there is no key, so that no one is less like Madame Verdurin than Madame de Briey. Nevertheless, she does laugh the same way." Proust apologized for "very ineptly showing my gratitude for the touching pains you have taken to get a copy of this volume by messing it up with these handwritten notes." He regretted that there was no room for him to copy the passage Jacques had requested.

Proust soon received a literary avowal from a surprising source: Lionel Hauser told him, "My dear friend, I have come to make a confession to you because I have on my conscience a horrible sin. Just imagine . . . I have written a book." Hauser's opus was called *Les Trois Leviers du monde nouveau: Compétence, probité, altruisme*

(The three levers of the New World: Competence, probity, altruism), in which he explained why he was a theosophist and how the tenets of this philosophy could benefit contemporary society. Hauser had one request: that Marcel "read my work without any preconceived ideas and describe for me, with brutal frankness, your impression."[42] Hauser's statement of his beliefs inspired Proust to summarize his own ideas, many of which he had already developed in unpublished portions of the *Search*.[43] Regarding style, he told Hauser it was wrong to think of style as "an embellishment that one adds as a kind of Sunday best. It is inseparable from thought or impression. And that's why your style is excellent."

As for the education of young men, Proust told Hauser that he had observed many youths, raised according to the rules of strict morality, become "dried academic fruit useless to anyone," whereas drunken poets such as Musset or Verlaine, or those with what he referred to as the "perversions" of Baudelaire and Rimbaud, found "a new voice that reveals an unknown fragment of mind, a supplementary nuance of tenderness." He expressed his belief in the creative power of suffering, "physical maladies of the body being (in our degenerate days) almost a condition of intellectual force that is somewhat brilliant." Proust was referring to his theory that it is often neurotics who become creative people and thus humanity's great benefactors. He believed that "all the good that has been done on earth by artists, by writers, by scientists has been accomplished in a manner that is not strictly speaking egotistical (since their object was not the satisfaction of their personal desires, but bringing to light an inner truth that had only been glimpsed) but, in any case, without directly concerning themselves with others. Altruism for Pascal, Lavoisier, Wagner, did not consist in interrupting or falsifying their solitary work to busy themselves with charitable works. They made their honey as do the bees, and in truth this honey benefited all others, but could be made only on condition of not thinking about others while they made it." Proust ended by telling Hauser that he remained "totally astonished on seeing him suddenly become, with so much competence, charm, and authority, a legislator and a writer."

Proust stated in the *Search* his theory about creativity: "Everything we think of as great has come to us from neurotics. It is they and they alone who found religions and create great works of art. The world will never realise how much it owes to them, and what they have suffered in order to bestow their gifts on it. We enjoy fine music, beautiful pictures, a thousand exquisite things, but we do not know what they cost those who wrought them in insomnia, tears, spasmodic laughter, urticaria, asthma, epilepsy, a terror of death which is worse than any of these."[44]

In late April, Proust informed Mme Lemarié of an important decision

intended to speed up publication of his novel. Instead of waiting for each completed section to come back to him in galleys or proofs and then sending them back
for second and third versions, he would take the galleys and proofs of *Within a
Budding Grove* and make one version to which no further changes would be made.
He would proceed in the same manner with *The Guermantes Way*, parts 1 and 2,
and the other two projected volumes.[45] Then when the projected four volumes
were ready, he would make a few minor changes that would be required to assure
the "equilibrium of the parts." There was cause for alarm: the notebook that
contained the end of *Within a Budding Grove* had not been returned or made into
galleys.[46] Known as the "purple notebook," lost and then found, it had been at the
printers for a long time and Proust had no copy.

A few days later Proust wrote to the NRF, saying that he intended to send the
copy for *The Guermantes Way*, whose beginning portions were contained in the old
Grasset proofs, "heavily supplemented, alas, by little pieces of paper added by me
and even by big pieces of paper." Thinking of the constant threat of annihilation by
German bombs and shells, he prudently suggested that he and the NRF each keep a
copy of *Within a Budding Grove*. Proust's greatest fears, however, were not of
external forces. In late May, still alarmed at his difficulty in speaking and what he
believed to be impending facial paralysis, he told Mme Scheikévitch that he intended to consult Dr. Joseph Babinski, a distinguished neurologist who had studied
with Charcot.[47]

With the enemy offensive showing no sign of relenting, Proust informed
Hauser that Céleste, extremely worried that the Germans would capture Paris, had
been urging him to make plans to flee if the shelling intensified. Proust agreed to
form a plan, though he apparently remained indifferent to the German threat. He
asked Hauser how to obtain enough money to take with him were he to flee. He
calculated that he would need thirty thousand francs and assumed that he could
easily draw this sum against his credit at the London County Bank. Hauser consulted Proust's bankers, who found the sum excessive. They recommended twenty
thousand francs, more than enough to lodge the writer and his servants comfort-
ably for a period of six months. Hauser arranged for Proust to cash a check in that
amount.[48]

On May 29 the Germans retook Soissons and pillaged the cathedral town.[49] In
late May and early June the casualty figures rose as French villages were overrun by
enemy soldiers, who often shelled churches and cathedrals as they advanced.
Proust expressed his anguish over the loss of lives and, to a lesser degree, the
destruction of medieval churches. He wrote Mme Straus: "I had never felt how

much I loved France. You, who love so much the paths near Trouville, will understand how I feel about Amiens, Reims, Laon, where I went so often." No matter how precious the things that were lost, "one must love people even more . . . and I weep for and admire the soldiers of France more than the churches, which were only the fixation of a heroic gesture, gestures that today are renewed at every moment."[50]

Proust walked home one night during intense shelling, believing that he had nothing to fear from "this artificial storm," and he was surprised to find in the courtyard "pieces of exploded shells."[51] When he came inside and Céleste helped him remove his things, she noticed that the brim of his hat "was full of bits of shrapnel." She showed him "all this metal," but he said that he had not been afraid.[52] Proust often found himself near German engines of destruction. One night in late June, while he was talking to Mme Soutzo in her apartment at the Ritz, a bomb landed right outside in the place Vendôme.[53]

During the war, Proust made a strategic decision regarding the geography of the *Search:* he moved Combray from its Beauce location near Chartres, where Illiers lies on the map, to the north of Paris, near Laon, in order to place the little village in the path of the German advance. Gilberte Swann, who by the time of the war is married to Saint-Loup, flees Paris because of the "constant Taube raids on the city," making her fear for her little daughter's safety. She arrives at Tansonville, Swann's country estate, only two days before the Germans arrive. For more than eight months the French and the Germans, in the battle of Méséglise, fight over Combray and its environs. Gilberte describes in a letter to the Narrator how his beloved hawthorn path that rises up a slope has become an important military objective. "The huge field of corn upon which it emerges is the famous Hill 307. . . . The French blew up the little bridge over the Vivonne . . . and the Germans have thrown other bridges across the river. For a year and a half they held one half of Combray and the French the other."[54] The Narrator's childhood paradise is annihilated by the opposing armies.

When Charlus visits the ruins of his ancestral home at Combray, he laments the loss of the church: "And now this church has been destroyed by the French and the English because it served as an observation-post to the Germans. All that mixture of art and still-living history that was France is being destroyed, and we have not seen the end of the process yet." Proust evoked, through Charlus, the destruction of the cathedrals of Reims and Amiens, leading the Narrator to observe to Charlus that these churches, as glorious and beautiful as they were, constituted symbols: "Do not sacrifice men to stones whose beauty comes precisely from their having for a moment given fixed form to human truths."[55]

Proust did not believe in the eternity of human works or in the sanctity of works as material objects. He avoided idolatry. Those who believe he worshiped art as a substitution for humanity have misunderstood him. Proust saw art not as an escape from what it is to be human but as the only way to see what our lives would be if we did not yield to the weaknesses of habit and sloth. As the Narrator says near the end of his quest, we must follow our heart or instinct. "For instinct dictates our duty and the intellect supplies us with pretexts for evading it. But excuses have no place in art and intentions count for nothing: at every moment the artist has to listen to his instinct, and it is this that makes art the most real of all things, the most austere school of life, the true last judgment."[56]

On June 2 Proust had an appointment with Dr. Babinski. He went to the doctor's office convinced that his problems were caused by a brain disorder and determined to undergo a trephination, a procedure in which holes are drilled in the skull. The neurologist categorically refused such radical treatment, saying that Proust's self-diagnosis was clearly mistaken.[57] Babinski's diagnosis, Proust told Hauser, was "very reassuring." Marcel later joked that the consultation proved what an obscure writer he was, for the doctor asked him, "Do you have a profession? Which one?"[58] What was Babinski's diagnosis? Proust apparently never divulged it to his friends, so one can only assume that the doctor must have asked many questions, some a great deal more personal than "What is your profession?" Did he probe far enough to discover that Proust had begun to poison himself with intoxicants? Although Proust's race against time to complete his life's work was to grow more desperate, he must have known that he was engaging in a kind of Russian roulette: would the lifestyle he felt necessary to write the book kill him before he could finish it?

On June 13 a tragedy occurred that saddened Proust and his friends. One of the most famous doctors of Paris and a long-time Proust family friend and colleague, Dr. Samuel Pozzi, was murdered by a patient. Robert Proust, who had been Pozzi's assistant from 1904 until the war began, was devastated by the loss. The patient, on whom Pozzi had performed surgery, had come for a consultation, after which he drew a gun and shot Pozzi three times before killing himself.[59] Pozzi, remarkably handsome and vain, a gifted surgeon, member of the Académie de médecine, and former senator, had been immortalized in one of Sargent's great portraits, which depicted him as a Renaissance prince.[60] Knowing how saddened Mme Straus would be by the death of her old friend, Proust wrote to her at Saint-Germain-en-Laye, where she and Émile were convalescing from colds—too far from him but too near the Germans, he said. He told Mme Straus how deeply Robert grieved for

Pozzi. Marcel had known Pozzi, he told her, for as long as he could remember; at fifteen his first invitation to dinner in society had been to Pozzi's home in the place Vendôme.[61]

Pozzi's murder reminded Proust of that awful day when Mme Caillaux had assassinated Gaston Calmette. The "singular awfulness" of Pozzi's death made him think about the ruined towns like Soissons, among whose church pillars the battle had been fought. He wondered whether the mysterious sacrifice of an innocent man like Calmette, in whose death one felt the war coming, was somehow matched now, so that peace would finally come in the wake of Pozzi's death. Had those dear friends been the two bloody pillars setting the boundaries of the war?[62]

In mid-June Proust sent Gallimard, back in France since May, the corrected proofs for *Within a Budding Grove* and the manuscript of *The Guermantes Way*. Although Gallimard remained in France for less than three months, he took care of a number of business matters before returning to the States with Jacques Copeau and his troupe of actors. Gallimard told La Semeuse to print *Within a Budding Grove*. Then he suggested to Proust that he collect and publish his pastiches and articles. On June 23 Proust signed a contract with Gallimard to publish *Pastiches et mélanges* and the remaining volumes of the *Search*, estimated to be "five or six" in number.[63] Proust decided that he would like all three volumes to be published simultaneously: the new edition of *Swann's Way*, *Within a Budding Grove*, and *Pastiches et mélanges*. He began collecting the parodies and articles from newspaper archives and friends. Halévy loaned Proust his leather-bound copy of "Sentiments filiaux."

In July, Proust corresponded with Grasset about their final settlement. Grasset calculated that Gallimard should pay him an indemnity of 750 francs for income lost on relinquishing *Within a Budding Grove*. Grasset owed Proust 550 francs in royalties, so that figure would leave Proust in debt to his old publisher. Because Grasset did not want that to be the case, he lowered the indemnity to 300 francs, which left him owing Proust 250 francs. Grasset asked Proust whether he would accept this proposal, which the publisher saw as generous. Proust's position was that because the NRF had purchased the remaining copies of *Swann*, a volume for which he had paid the printing costs and shared the profits with Grasset, he should owe the publisher nothing.[64]

Just after this exchange of letters, Gallimard returned to New York, further delaying a settlement. Grasset refused to pay Proust the royalties until all parties had agreed on the terms. On the day of Gallimard's departure, Proust wrote Grasset, saying that he would await payment of royalties until Gallimard and Grasset conferred. He told Grasset that he would soon send him copies of two new volumes, one containing his collected pastiches and articles and the other, *À l'ombre des jeunes filles en fleurs,* which he referred to as "the title of a chapter in my work. But that has taken on the proportions of a thick volume."[65] Proust, who assumed that Grasset had read *Swann's Way,* told him that the new volumes would contain "many things you don't know," especially the two volumes of *Sodom and Gomorrah,* which had been written during the war and included passages about its effects on France. "Thus I will have a collection of six volumes to give you. But don't worry, not all at once." Then, almost as an afterthought, he returned to the indemnity that bothered him, saying he did not understand exactly what it was that Grasset was "giving up" that entitled him to an indemnity.[66]

Grasset replied that it was so painful for him to have a discussion, even the most courteous, about money with Proust, and he was turning the matter over to his assistant Louis Brun, giving him a single instruction: "to do whatever pleased" the author. Regarding the new volumes, Grasset would have preferred to offer them to Proust: "I am too much a publisher, in fact, for the pleasure I would take on reading you not to be mingled with a very great bitterness and a lot of jealousy." These were sentiments Proust could understand perfectly well, though it pained him to be blamed for having inspired them.[67]

With the Grasset business set aside for the moment, Proust turned to the urgent problem of obtaining galleys for *The Guermantes Way,* which he wished to correct as soon as possible. Lemarié parried his query by telling him that she had found a printer, Louis Bellenand, for *Pastiches et mélanges* and would deliver the manuscript as soon as she received it from Proust. Lemarié kept the pressure on La Semeuse to produce *The Guermantes Way* proofs and on Proust to send the copy for *Pastiches et mélanges.*[68]

On June 25 Proust received a second letter—he had ignored the first—from Calmann-Lévy, saying that he had in stock, out of 1,500 copies printed of *Pleasures and Days,* 1,100 unbound and 71 bound.[69] The binder had kept these books on hand for more than two decades. The sale of the book having "completely stopped long since," Calmann-Lévy would, "to his great regret," be forced to sell the remaining copies at a "very low price." He had written Proust first to let him know that he could purchase the remaining copies for three francs each.[70] Proust took offense at what he saw as a heartless, wholesale effort to dump his book. Neither the author nor Calmann-Lévy seemed to appreciate the rarity of Proust's first book, printed in a limited deluxe edition.[71] Was it pride that kept him from informing Gallimard, who might well have bought the unbound copies and issued them in his own covers?

On June 28 the Allied counteroffensive began. Two days later Proust, unable to sleep for three consecutive days, left his bed and went to the Ritz for lunch. Having decided to write a new parody of Saint-Simon to include in *Pastiches and mélanges,* he requested copies of the first Saint-Simon pastiches from the *Figaro,* whose archives were much better organized than his own.[72] In the new pastiche, he intended to include Guiche, the Strauses, and the maître d'hôtel Olivier Dabescat.[73] Still, he did not let the pastiche distract him from his main purpose; before July was over he again expressed his impatience at not having received any galleys for *The Guermantes Way,* which he wished to begin correcting immediately.[74]

In a July letter Proust thanked Mme Soutzo for her willingness to find him a house near Biarritz in case the Germans drew too close to Paris, but he said that it was impossible for him to travel to Biarritz or anywhere because Céleste "was rather seriously ill."[75] Céleste, exhausted by the constant bombardment and uncertainty about their safety, had caught the Spanish flu. This particularly virulent strain of influenza had broken out on the front in 1917 and spread through France and Germany. It was estimated that the flu killed sixty-two thousand American soldiers alone, far more than German bullets.[76] Although Céleste had a remarkably strong constitution, she decided to leave Proust for two weeks and recuperate in Lozère.[77] Adèle Larivière replaced Céleste as best she could. André Foucart, on leave, visited Marcel, making him dream again of going to Cabourg for a brief stay; but Proust's chronic indecisiveness, complicated by the war and his anxiety about proofs, made such a salutary change impossible.

Mme Soutzo was no longer in Biarritz, as Proust thought, but at the seaside Grand-Hôtel Eskualdune at Hendaye, near the Spanish border. During this period she was cooler toward Proust, who remained as taken with her as ever. He wrote to tell her how much he would like to be "near you to kiss your hand and have you assure me that there is no sugar on my mustache." In the postscript he urged her to tell Morand again of his tender friendship, which had not "weakened like a dead memory, but had grown deeper like a living, fecund reality." Mme Soutzo remained indifferent; when she returned to the Ritz on August 28, she did not inform Proust. When he learned from Morand in mid-September that she had kept her return a secret from him, Proust was deeply hurt.[78]

By August, Proust had decided there were two indispensable changes to make on the proofs of *Within a Budding Grove.* In typical Proustian fashion he offered not only to pay the press for the trouble but to overcompensate for the modifications by paying triple the amount the press would charge. The change he regarded as the more important had to do with the way Odette and Gilberte sprinkle their conversations with English words and expressions, thought to be very chic during the fin-de-siècle years. Proust said that the changes were so vital that he did not even care if they delayed publication.[79] Mme Lemarié first replied that it was impossible, but she finally agreed and went to the printer's at Étampes to oversee all the changes the author wanted.[80] Mme Lemarié was, like everyone at the NRF— despite Proust's frequent suspicions and castigations—devoted to his novel.

Although Proust had told Gallimard that he did not intend to dedicate the separate volumes of the *Search* to friends, in September he changed his mind. Encouraged by Morand, he decided to dedicate *Within a Budding Grove* to the prince de Polignac. He wrote the princess to ask her permission, assuring her that the volume contained no characters resembling her or her late husband. But he made obscure allusions to a friend of hers who was an enemy of his and to one of his friends, with whom she had fallen out and who would soon become an enemy of his. Proust was anticipating the day when Montesquiou discovered the traits he shared with Charlus. Mme de Polignac could make so little sense of Proust's letter that she was not certain whether he truly wanted to dedicate the volume to the prince. Proust had asked her to reply by simply sending a yes or no answer without explaining her reasons—the only part of his letter that she found heartening. The princess declined a distinction that sounded dubious if not dangerous. To draw the public's attention to the resumed publication of his novel, Proust offered *Figaro* editor Alfred Capus an excerpt from *Within a Budding Grove*. In mid-September Capus refused, pleading lack of space in the paper.[81] The war continued to dominate the news, leaving little room for other stories.

On August 10 Reynaldo, sensing that the Allies would soon be victorious, came home on leave and dined at the Ritz with Marcel and Armand de Guiche. A few days later Proust dined by himself at the Ritz to allow Odilon, who had come home on leave, to be alone with Céleste. Henri Ellès, manager of the Ritz, in a gesture intended to show special consideration, posted himself next to the writer's table, an honor Proust found "tiresome," because he had come to the hotel to "ruminate and rest." Ellès informed Proust that the British minister of munitions, Winston Churchill, and his entourage were dining at the adjoining table. With Churchill were his cousin Charles Spencer Churchill, duke of Marlborough, and Lord Bertie, the British ambassador. The duke eventually married Gladys Deacon, a beautiful young woman Proust had tried to glimpse years ago at Versailles. Another table was occupied by the American Edward Riley Stettinius and his party.[82] Churchill and Stettinius, the chief purchasing agent in the United States for the Allied governments, had met that day as part of the new Inter-Allied Munitions Council.[83]

Proust wrote Lucien that a certain group was not at their accustomed table that evening—an allusion to Comte Antoine Sala and his homosexual friends—and service was unusually good because the "waiters did not have to flee in desperation to the kitchen except to serve the dishes."[84]

On August 29 the *Action française* informed its readers that the "NRF would continue the publication of Marcel Proust's memoirs, these so slightly structured books, yet so rich in sensitivity, nuances, humour, finesse, and tender love that *Sivan's* [*sic*] *Way* appeared to us one of the best books of 1914!" The note announced the forthcoming titles, misspelling Guermantes (Guernantes). Although grateful for any publicity, Proust was annoyed by the two misspellings and especially by the remark that his books lacked structure. Proust wrote Lucien that the terms of the notice "were certainly meant to be amiable," which made him believe that Léon was behind it.[85]

"An incorrigible Penelope"

By the middle of the summer Proust had a new reason to dine at the Ritz. He had become attracted to a young Swiss waiter named Henri Rochat.[86] Camille Wixler, a waiter at the Ritz during the same time as Rochat, gave an interview nearly six decades later about Proust's attraction to young waiters.[87] Swiss like Rochat, Wixler was only nineteen when he met Proust. One day Olivier told Wixler that Proust had noticed him and wondered whether he would be willing to wait his table. The innocent Camille gladly accepted, having heard about the lavish tips. The first time he served Proust a meal, the novelist arrived around 11:30, after everyone else had left the kitchen. During the meal, and afterward in the small salon, where Proust consumed a dozen or so demitasses of coffee, Proust chatted and asked Camille questions about the personnel. The writer was especially curious about Henri Rochat, whom Camille described as a "handsome waiter." Could Wixler ask Rochat to serve his table? "I agreed to this, naturally, and instructed Rochat on what he liked." Rochat soon became Proust's regular waiter. Not long afterward, when Wixler asked whether Rochat was proving satisfactory, Proust answered in the affirmative but said that he had found Rochat an occupation that suited him much better, an apparent reference to the position of secretary. Wixler had noticed when he and Rochat changed from street clothes into their uniforms that his colleague had suddenly acquired handsome suits and underclothes of the finest quality. Camille, still the innocent, knew that Henri's salary from the Ritz did not allow such luxuries and asked how he could afford them. Rochat "answered frankly and even with pride that he did so with the aid of M. Proust."

Wixler finally realized that Proust was using him to procure young waiters for sexual trysts at boulevard Haussmann. The moment of illumination occurred when Proust asked him to send another young waiter by the name of Vanelli to boulevard Haussmann at night. Wixler, who thought Vanelli was not the type to accept such a proposition no matter how large the tips, was astounded when Vanelli asked Wixler to send him to Proust, even before Wixler had broached the subject. According to Wixler, Vanelli became Proust's favorite when Rochat left for America. It seems unlikely that everything in Wixler's account is true. If Vanelli did become Proust's "favorite," he did so without leaving any traces, which is not, of course, impossible. What the young men did to repay Proust's gifts is likely to remain unknown, but it seems fair to assume that Proust expected sexual favors of them.

Sometime in late 1918 or early 1919 Proust made Rochat his secretary, though the waiter seemed to have few qualifications for such a position. His handwriting was beautiful, but his spelling was atrocious. Not highly educated, Rochat was rather dull and taciturn, though he believed himself gifted as a painter. The young man proved to be expensive to keep. Proust soon spent his twenty thousand francs set aside as emergency funds reserved to flee Paris and borrowed another ten, just to keep Rochat happy.[88]

Proust's letters began to refer vaguely to a "sentimental" attachment or express lovesick complaints unheard since the days of Agostinelli. In mid-September, Proust wrote Hauser that for two months he had suffered great heartaches. To Blanche he spoke of a "great mental chagrin of which I shall certainly die and which is poisoning my life." To Mme Straus he announced that his health was "rather less poor, but I have embarked on sentimental things without resolution, without joy," which were "perpetual sources of fatigue, suffering, and absurd expenditures." Hauser replied that Proust's letters showed "how greatly he needed to become a theosophist in order to glide above the nothingness that constitutes our wretched lives."[89] The novelist answered that "when one is not a theosophist and one loves someone . . . from the people . . . the heartaches are generally accompanied by considerable financial difficulties." Proust then quoted La Bruyère: "It is sad to love without a large fortune."[90] He commented that "God knows I don't regret having given up society, which is boring. But it at least had the advantage of being extremely economical." This observation may have been intended to prepare Hauser for a revelation Proust could not hope to hide much longer.

On September 26 Proust congratulated Walter Berry on being awarded the Légion d'honneur.[91] The following day the Allied counteroffensive began to produce results when French and American troops advanced by several kilometers along the front. On October 2 Proust learned that his brother had been seriously injured in an automobile accident. He immediately informed Mme Catusse, underscoring the irony: Robert, "who for four years sought the most dangerous, exposed points in France and Italy without being wounded, has just been hurt and nearly killed in a stupid car accident at the front." Robert had been inspecting sanitation facilities when his car collided head-on with another vehicle. The impact of the crash threw him against the windshield, breaking it and making a deep gash in his head. Robert, who refused to leave his post, nearly bled to death.[92] Fortunately, there was a château only two kilometers away, where he was carried on a stretcher. Before Marcel could obtain a pass to visit his brother, Robert had removed his bandages and come to spend several days in Paris. Proust visited him and caught a cold, which prevented him from correcting the proofs he had just received of his preface for Blanche.[93] Robert soon returned to the front—an "insane" course of action for someone with an open head wound, according to his brother.

On October 6 the German line that stretched forty-five kilometers drew back. The cathedral city of Reims was freed. The Germans asked for an immediate armistice and peace negotiations, which the Allies rejected. Seeing the inevitability of their defeat, the Germans hoped to end the fighting without accepting prior conditions that would be to their disadvantage.[94] On October 13 French soldiers under Generals Debeney and Mangin drove the Germans out of Laon, a city that had been occupied for more than four years.[95]

Proust sought to renew his friendship with Mme de Chevigné, whose lineage and birdlike features had inspired elements of his leading fictional aristocratic hostess, the duchesse de Guermantes. He invited Mme de Chevigné to dine alone with him at the Ritz. He gazed at her eyes, which he had given to Oriane de Guermantes and which always reminded him of forget-me-nots.[96] In November he wrote Mme de Chevigné, expressing the hope that she would allow him, one day before he died, to show her all the passages in his novel where "a glance, a pose, something magical . . . are yours."[97] Still, their relationship remained somewhat strained; she had never really trusted Marcel since those days when he used to linger in the avenue Gabriel just to watch her pass by. He wanted to convince her that the details he had borrowed from her to portray Oriane constituted the highest form of compliment; she remained skeptical, fearing, on the contrary, that the identification between her and the duchesse de Guermantes might be something less than flattering.

Proust was also eager for Mme Straus to read those pages in *The Guermantes Way* where he attributed her witticisms to the duchesse de Guermantes. In the new Saint-Simon pastiche written for inclusion in *Pastiches et mélanges,* he said of Mme Straus: "You could make an entire book if you recorded everything she had said that was worth remembering."[98] His new parody and the creation of Oriane's wit were intended as lasting monuments to the admired and beloved friend whose illness was even more confining than his own.

Proust heard from Mme Lemarié, who assured him that she was sending reminders daily to pressure the printer to produce proofs for *The Guermantes Way* but had as yet received none. Bellenand was ready to begin setting *Pastiches et mélanges,* which she estimated would make a volume of approximately 250 pages. She lamented the lack of progress: "But everything is horribly LONG at this time." Yet it seemed evident that the war could not last much longer: "Finally, the end is near!"[99]

In mid-October, Proust wrote Hauser, finally confessing his misdeeds regarding money. Without naming Rochat, Marcel informed his financial adviser that because of "a love—non-Theosophist—for a commoner, and its attendant philanthropic assistance, he had made a lunch of the 20,000 francs" in his war chest. But even that princely sum had not sufficed. Proust had taken another ten thousand from his accounts at the Rothschild Bank and London County Bank. It was true that he had not spent it all, and a portion had gone to pay for his own "food (meager) and his pharmacy bill (huge)." Proust professed to be concerned again about his long-range financial situation, for Babinski believed that he might live somewhat longer than he had thought.[100] Rochat, who loved to spend Proust's money, apparently had a fondness for jewelry—it is not known whether for himself, for his fiancée, the daughter of a concierge, or as an investment. Proust, excessively generous with his friends, was incapable, when in love, of denying any whims.

Proust's caprices would have severely tested even the most virtuous and indulgent theosophist. Hauser, totally exasperated, wrote back and scolded Proust, saying that he felt like a doctor who, having struggled for months like a madman to save a patient, saw that patient, just on the verge of recovery, behave in such a reckless manner that he risked losing all that had been gained.[101] The situation would have been more bearable if Proust showed some remorse. "But no, you are still smiling, obvious proof of your complete disregard." If it were in his power, he would give Proust a legal guardian. But failing that, he advised Proust to use what remained of his fortune to buy an annuity. Hauser believed that Proust would live for a long time, like Voltaire, he said, and was glad Babinski concurred with his optimistic prognosis.

Having vented his frustration, Hauser turned to practical matters. He had prepared a letter for Proust to sign in order to cancel the standing order to sell the Mexican Tramways stocks. These shares had risen somewhat in value, and it would be wise to hold them for a while longer. Hauser assumed, wrongly, as it turned out, that if the London County Bank had sold the shares, Proust would have been informed. He wondered whether Proust still had any Royal Dutch stocks, because these petroleum shares had risen sharply in the past two years. In this regard, Proust's lack of diligence in managing his affairs served him well. He later discovered a few remaining Royal Dutch shares that he had not sold because he had forgotten he had them in another portfolio. In the years following the war these multiplied and became worth a small fortune.

Proust replied to Hauser that he was crushed and touched by his adviser's feeling that he "had failed him, that I lacked kindness by undoing with my hand like an incorrigible Penelope what you had so expertly woven for my good with your hand." After more humorous words and compliments to Hauser for all his good financial counsel, Marcel took exception to Hauser's assessment of his health. He did not have the reserves of a Voltaire and would not live long. Thus he hoped to obtain an annuity at the high rate of 20 percent.[102]

Hauser answered from his theosophist high horse, claiming that he would have done for anyone what he had done for Proust, that gratitude as Proust conceived it did not exist. Based on that principle, Marcel was free to dispose of his heart and his money as he saw fit. But if Proust did so in a reckless manner, he should be prepared to bear the consequences. Toward the end of the letter Hauser mellowed, saying that if he had expressed his opinion about how Proust spent his money without being asked, it was because he had been alarmed by the deep cuts Proust was making in his capital. He realized that if Marcel behaved otherwise, he would not be a poet, for one's flaws are the obverse of one's virtues. Although Hauser had little hope of influencing Marcel, he felt compelled to suggest an annuity out of the affection he still felt for Proust's "admirable mother," who despite her great love for her son would certainly disapprove of the way he managed his fortune. Hauser made another suggestion: Proust should find a more modest apartment, one that would suit him perfectly while allowing him to economize.[103]

Proust said that he had no illusions about love, even if he were unable to resist it. "Nothing is further from the 'heart' than this egotistical sentiment called love." He noted that in Racine's plays love, when not reciprocated, led to assassinations and suicide. But awareness of this perverse principle did not mean that Marcel found such love uninteresting. "It is important for the philosopher, full of instruction for the one who analyzes it, atrocious, as I know only too well, for the one who feels it. But I never meant to assimilate it to good-heartedness." As for his apartment, living there had nothing to do with vanity, for he never received guests and had a dining room filled with crates and other items in storage. If he stayed at 102, boulevard Haussmann, where his annual rent was 6,500 francs, that was because his asthma bothered him less there than it would elsewhere. He shuddered at the thought of the asthma attacks he would have to endure and the efforts to adapt to a new place.[104] Proust did not mention his sentimental attachment to the house, knowing that Hauser found such reasons ridiculous.

Proust, still estranged from Princesse Soutzo, wrote to broach a reconciliation. "Is it really over, our seeing each other?" He had tried to overcome the black mood into which he fell on picturing her room at the Ritz during the weeks when she kept her return secret from him. Now when he entered the Ritz, before going to the dining room, he forced himself to turn and look at the elevator door in order to prevent a phobia from developing around the idea of no longer being allowed to go up to her apartment. Even if they were reconciled, he feared she would soon invent, as was her custom, some new grievance against him.[105]

On October 24 Proust wrote to Mme Hugo Finaly to express his deep sorrow over the death of her "adorable daughter," Mary de Barbarin.[106] The green-eyed girl, with whom Marcel had been in love so many summers ago when he recited Baudelaire's poems to her, had died from the Spanish flu, contracted while nursing wounded soldiers. Marcel assured her mother that "Nothing from the past is lost to me."[107]

By the end of October, war or no war, Proust had run out of patience with Gallimard. He sent letters detailing his grievances.[108] Describing his missives as business letters and cries of "desolation," he reminded his publisher that in June, on submitting the complete manuscript of *The Guermantes Way*, the printer promised to send him the "proofs almost immediately." Four months had passed and the writer had received nothing. The difficulty in obtaining proofs had made Proust suggest earlier that Gallimard use separate printers. He predicted that it would take eight years at the current slow rate to publish the remaining volumes, the last three of which were "the longest, the most striking." Proust described *Within a Budding*

Grove as the "somewhat languishing prologue for those volumes," and if all the volumes appeared together around 1925, at the earliest—assuming that he was still alive to correct the proofs—readers would have long since forgotten *Swann,* and his life's work would have been in vain.[109]

Proust discussed his need for money, saying that he earned no regular income as a columnist and had no royalties coming in. He broached his idea for a special edition of *Within a Budding Grove,* in which would be bound signed proof sheets and perhaps a photograph, signed by Blanche, of his oil portrait of Proust. Proust thought that such a limited edition could sell for three hundred francs a copy.[110] He also expressed his annoyance at his inability to collect the royalties due since 1914 because Gallimard had not taken the time to reach an agreement with Grasset regarding the indemnity. Proust praised Mme Lemarié, who had been "charming" and had behaved toward him with "a goodness, an energy, and an obligingness" that Proust described as "delicious." Proust's complaints regarding Gallimard were accurate, and yet everything depended, to a large degree, on something beyond the publisher's control: the war.

On November 9, Céleste's sister Marie Gineste arrived in Paris.[111] Three years older than Céleste, Marie became a permanent part of Proust's household and relieved her sister of many duties, primarily errands and shopping done in the daytime, when Céleste needed to sleep. When Marie arrived and Proust did not offer her the maid's room upstairs, Céleste, too proud to ask for it, arranged for Marie to stay with her sister-in-law. In the beginning Marie came only at lunch and stayed until the evening. Céleste sensed that Proust was jealous of Marie. She knew his reaction came from "the possessive side of him; the fonder I was of my sister, the less affection there was for him." Proust eventually grew fond of Marie. After Marie moved in, she assisted Céleste with the housework, always done late at night when Proust went out, as a precaution against aggravating his asthma. On one occasion, when Céleste was away, Proust talked to Marie about his father. When Céleste returned, she noticed that Proust was "radiant." He was extremely pleased with something Marie had said about Dr. Proust: " 'Lives like that of your father, monsieur, are lives offered up.' That is beautiful, and I shall put it in my book."[112]

"A miraculous and vertiginous peace"

On Monday, November 11, the war officially ended. All across France church bells rang out in celebration. Proust wrote to Mme Straus, saying that they had "both thought about the war too much not to say a tender, joyful word on the day of victory, a word made joyous" because of the victory, "sorrowful because all those they loved had not lived" to see the day. "What a marvelous allegro presto is this finale after the infinite slow movements of the beginning and all that followed."[113]

The war had been cruel down to the final minute. Émile Agostinelli, only twenty, was killed on armistice day. He left a young wife and children. In his sympathy letter to Émile's half-sister Mme Vittoré, Proust mentioned "a slight grievance that I had against him and it pains me even more to see him disappear before I was able to clear it up with him. Above all he was Alfred's brother, Alfred for whom I had such great affection. I had always hoped to be able to speak to him about this dear late friend whose life he must have known so well."[114] Had Émile been reluctant to discuss Alfred with Proust, whose posthumous curiosity and jealousy matched the Narrator's in its pathological persistence? Alfred and Émile had come to France to seek their fortune and had lost their lives instead—one fleeing an obsessed writer in the guise of a generous benefactor, the other defending his adopted country in the closing minutes of a global war. The Great War had been framed not only by the murders of Proust's prominent friends Calmette and Pozzi, but by the deaths of two obscure Agostinelli brothers, neither of whom, thanks to Proust's fictional, fugitive girl named Albertine, would be forgotten.

Proust's letters to Mme Straus celebrating victory and bemoaning the deaths of friends gave him the occasion to renew the practical matter of selling his carpets, furniture, and other items in storage. He asked her to send a truck and moving men to haul everything off to the auction house. He no longer needed the silverware now that he took most of his meals at the Ritz; if he stayed home, he usually just drank café au lait in his bed. Within a short time, Proust informed her that everything had been sent to the auction house, except the carpets that she was going to sell for him. He retained the large, ancient Persian rug the shah had given his father in 1859 because he intended to dispose of it separately. He would send, for her approval, the proofs of the Saint-Simon pastiche as soon as he received them.[115]

Right after the armistice, Proust wrote to Mme Soutzo, hoping that peace would extend to their relationship. He admitted being under the "demonic empire of an idée fixe" concerning her. He had worried for some time about their relationship and the misunderstandings between them: "It would be too sad if we, who became friends at the beginning of the war, should become disunited just when the miraculous and vertiginous, enchanting Peace ended it like the vivace of the slowest symphonies!"[116] Once Morand returned to Paris, he and Mme Soutzo resumed friendly relations with Proust.

Proust learned that in April the London County Bank had sold one hundred shares of Mexico Tramways below the price authorized by Proust.[117] He calculated that the transaction had cost him at least five thousand francs. Thus began a dispute with the bank over who was responsible for the error, whether Proust's instructions had been clear, and what remedy, if any, was appropriate. The matter of the Mexico Tramways shares and the impossibility of cashing the thirty thousand–franc War-burg check that he had held during the war dragged on without a satisfactory resolution, despite Proust's involving a number of his knowledgeable and influential friends, including Lionel Hauser, Walter Berry, Mme Soutzo, Paul Morand, Robert de Billy, and Émile Straus.

On November 30 the printer finished *Within a Budding Grove,* the proofs of *The Guermantes Way,* parts 1 and 2, and *Pastiches et mélanges.* As he had feared, Proust at last had his pages and his proofs all at once. He wrote Gallimard, who lingered in the United States, requesting a type size as large as that used by Grasset for *Swann's Way* because "correcting proofs, so wearying in my current state, when everything arrives at once, will be easier with characters that are less fine." Proust, who still wore no glasses, continued to suffer from eyestrain.

On Christmas Day, Proust wrote two letters, one to Mme Soutzo, the other to Mme Straus. He told the princess that he had seen Reynaldo at Princesse Murat's party, where he had been seated in the place of honor "to her right!!" Reynaldo had returned practically overnight to the orchestra pit as conductor at the Opéra-Comique.[118] The battlefield dirges now yielded to Offenbach and make-believe tragedies.

Proust thanked Mme Straus for having arranged the sale of his carpets, which had brought him three thousand francs. He would respect Mme Straus's wishes and not portray her in the Saint-Simon pastiche as a lofty Vasthi. He would tone down the portrait of her, but, because of the publishing schedule, she would have to accept his new version or he would drop it from the pastiche. There was no time for additional changes. He told her that it was because of problems with printers that he was bringing out only one volume of his novel, along with *Pastiches et mélanges,* instead of the third, fourth, fifth, and sixth volumes of the *Search.* Gallimard had finally hired two printers in an effort to speed the process.[119]

The war had ended and despite constant exposure to danger, Marcel's brother Robert, like Reynaldo, came home unharmed. Although Proust's fortune was greatly reduced, enough remained for him to live as he wished. A staggering amount of work remained to be done on his book, but Babinski's diagnosis gave him reason to believe that no grave illness threatened to shorten his days. Yet Proust could not dismiss the fear that he would die, a fear so often expressed to friends that they generally ignored it. In his memoir about Proust, Morand wrote that he had never known anyone who seemed to have "stopped living" so early in life and "had abandoned all earthly pleasures without regret or disgust."[120] Proust had long since given up hope of finding happiness. He had one reason to stay alive: the completion of his book.

In the final days of the year Proust was invited to a number of dinners and parties. On December 28 he attended a dinner at the Ritz given by Mme Soutzo, with whom he had finally made peace. Two days later a cold prevented his accepting Mme Hennessy's dinner invitation, but not from going to the party afterward. On New Year's Eve he attended a grand dinner given by the Beaumonts in honor of the British ambassador Lord Derby. The ambassador was accompanied by his secretary, whom a contemporary described as "the noble and tall and handsome Reginald Francis Orlando Bridgeman." Proust, too, had noticed the attractive first secretary and told Cocteau, in a letter written after the party, that Bridgeman "pleases me more and more."[121] Rochat's presence did not make Marcel indifferent to other handsome men.

The year that had begun in the freezing, bleak snow and despair over the endless war ended with France victorious. The country had been severely bled of the lives of at least 1,384,000 men who would never come home again and who had carried to their graves infinite promises that would never be fulfilled.[122] Proust now lived in the new world he had anticipated with some foreboding because "so many beloved faces had disappeared."[123]

PART VII

The Fountain of Youth (1919–1922)

27 *Homeless* ∾

AT THE BEGINNING OF 1919 LARYNGITIS and a high fever slowed the pace of Proust's work. By mid-January he had not corrected a single proof. Mme Lemarié sent letters urging him to work at a faster pace.[1] Just as he began to feel more like working, disaster struck. On returning home from a dinner with Berry at the Ritz, Proust found a letter from his Aunt Amélie Weil, informing him that she had sold 102, boulevard Haussmann to a banker, who intended to convert the building into a bank and offices. Proust was incredulous that she had said nothing to him about the possibility of selling the property. He had no lease, only a verbal understanding with his aunt, and he feared that the new owner might evict him, while demanding immediate payment of approximately twenty-five thousand francs he owed for past-due rent.[2] Rather than finding out what his rights were, he stepped up his efforts to sell furniture and tapestries. Hauser, rather naïvely, saw Proust's "eviction" as a providential opportunity to find a more suitable and less expensive apartment.[3] The financial adviser failed to foresee the housing shortage that followed the war; Proust would have to pay higher rent for a smaller, less desirable apartment.[4]

On January 21 Proust wrote Berry to detail the disaster that had befallen him and to solicit his aid in selling furnishings. Would Berry be willing to receive and show at the American Chamber of Commerce "two large greensward tapestries, an antique oriental rug, a magnificent antique easy-chair, sconces, and an antique settee?" Marcel believed that these items would sell for "much more than 25,000 francs," because he had already declined an offer of five thousand francs just for the chair. He also asked Berry how he should approach the French government regarding the Warburg check and his remaining assets at that bank. He had waited years for the war to end so that he could at last obtain the funds represented by the uncashed check; now that he sought to raise money to pay his back rent, the matter became more urgent. Proust wanted to settle with the new owner quickly because he might not live long: "for an asthmatic, moving to new quarters is usually fatal." In late February he wrote Gide that changing apartments was certain to aggravate his serious asthma condition. While the attacks themselves were survivable, his heart condition could no longer tolerate such suffering. He now understood that "death is our only hope."[5] Even while despairing, Proust determined to use his remaining physical resources to serve his only reason for living: the completion of his book. The Narrator's commitment to his projected book at the end of the *Search* sounds as heroic: "Since strength of one kind can change into a strength of another kind . . . since the dull pain in our heart can hoist above itself like a banner the visible permanence of an image for every new grief, let us accept the physical injury which is done to us for the sake of the spiritual knowledge which grief brings; let us submit to the disintegration of our body, since each new fragment which breaks away from it returns in a luminous and significant form to add itself to our work."[6]

Eager to honor Berry for his service to France during the war, Proust asked him to accept the dedication of *Pastiches et mélanges* or *The Guermantes Way*. The *Pastiches* dedication would have the advantage of appearing sooner. Looking far ahead, he told Berry that he did not intend to dedicate the three volumes of *Sodom and Gomorrah* to anyone because of their subject matter. Berry answered that he would be "enchanted" to receive Proust's furnishings and would show them to his friends and others without revealing the owner's name. He was "profoundly touched" by Marcel's intention to dedicate a book to him and said it must surely be *The Guermantes Way*, because the name Guermantes had brought them together.[7] Within a few weeks Proust received disappointing news from Berry regarding the items for sale: the offers were extremely low.[8] Proust's furniture remained at the American Chamber of Commerce until summer, when a dealer came to collect it.[9]

As news of Proust's loss of his apartment spread, friends, many of whom he had never suspected were "so nice," offered him "their town houses, castles, which, naturally, I refused."[10] He spoke often of finding an apartment high above the ground, on the eighth or ninth floor, presumably to be far from street noise and perhaps because he thought that the air would be purer. Hauser urged him not to act too quickly but to see what his rights were regarding his current apartment. He suggested that the new owner might have to pay Proust an indemnity to move out. Sometime in late winter or early spring Hauser, in some distress, called on Proust for assistance. Because of his contacts with the Warburg Bank, Hauser had been accused of pro-German sympathies. Proust contacted Berry and both men vouched for Hauser's innocence.[11] Strangely, after little more than a year, Hauser did not recall that Proust had assisted him.

By January 10 Proust had received the proofs for *Pastiches et mélanges,* as well as the new edition of *Swann's Way.*[12] A little more than a week later, he received an advance copy of *Within a Budding Grove* from Mme Lemarié. Although Proust found the cover extremely attractive, he became distressed when he opened the book and saw the "microscopic" characters and tight lines. *Within a Budding Grove* was 443 pages long—eighty fewer than *Swann's Way.* Gallimard had cautioned Proust that the second volume could not be printed in larger type than the first, but had promised that it would be set in an equivalent type size. Had this been done, each volume should have had approximately the same number of pages. Proust expressed his dismay to Mme Lemarié: "To have worked so hard for this." Convinced that no one would read such tiny print, he considered having the volume reprinted at his own expense. But Gallimard remained in New York, and it was impossible to do anything in his absence. Proust aired additional grievances to Mme Lemarié. He had heard that when people asked for a copy of *Swann's Way* at Grasset's office, his employees did not tell them the book was available at the NRF. But what really stupefied Proust was that recently Étienne de Beaumont had asked the NRF for *Swann's Way* only to be told they did not have a copy.[13] Grasset's remaining copies of the book should have been available in new covers at the NRF.

By January 22 Proust had received the proofs of his Blanche preface, which he corrected almost immediately and sent on to the editor. Having heard rumors that Blanche was "frightened" by the preface, Proust urged him not to publish it "just to please me." Marcel had reason to be unhappy with Blanche. The painter had revised his book since the early version Proust had read, adding discussions of paintings by Paul Cézanne, Edgar Degas, and Auguste Renoir. Blanche asked Proust to cut what he had written on Vuillard and Denis, depriving him of the opportunity to discuss two artists whose works he knew and admired. He suggested that Proust revise the preface, but the novelist refused because of the demands made upon him by his own work. As a result, Proust had great misgivings about his preface, in which he criticized Blanche for, among other things, talking too much about Manet the man, who coveted medals and decorations, rather than about the revolutionary artist. Blanche had committed the Sainte-Beuve sin. Proust praised Blanche for having selected major painters and explaining to readers how they modified their palettes and reworked their canvases. Before publication, Proust persuaded Blanche to insert a few lines in the preface praising the "admirable" Picasso portrait of Cocteau, which "concentrated all Cocteau's traits in an image whose rigor was so noble" that it rivaled the "most charming Carpaccios in Venice."[14]

In early February that inveterate prankster Antoine Bibesco played a trick on Céleste and Proust. Antoine decided to break one of the most rigid rules that protected the writer in his inner sanctum by sneaking a beautiful, distinguished young woman into the cork-lined bedroom. The young lady was Antoine's fiancée, Miss Elizabeth Asquith, daughter of Herbert Henry Asquith, the first earl of Oxford, who had served as British prime minister from 1908 to 1916. As Céleste related the story, Antoine came one evening with Miss Asquith, whom he left on the landing. The prince asked Céleste if he might go into Proust's room and was told she would have to go in and see. When she turned and walked toward the bedroom, Antoine quietly picked up his fiancée "like a doll" and followed Céleste into the room. Proust was "horribly embarrassed" as he lay there "with his face in the shadow and his hands folded over his sweater and the sheet." Turning to Céleste, Proust said, " 'You see, Céleste? I told you he was crazy!' "[15] Proust described to a friend the "martrydom" he suffered when Miss Asquith saw him in bed, "wearing my sweaters with holes burned in them, etc." Nonetheless, he and the young lady took an immediate liking to each other and later exchanged letters.[16]

In February, Proust sent Berry a copy of the dedication for his approval. He had decided not to wait for publication of The Guermantes Way, at least a year away, and instead wrote the dedication of Pastiches et mélanges, due out in the spring. It read "To Mr. Walter Berry, lawyer and man of letters who, from the first day of the war, confronting an indecisive America, argued France's cause with an incomparable energy and talent, and won. His friend, Marcel Proust."[17] Proust later told Berry that he considered him the "victor in the greatest war of all the wars." The delighted Berry replied that Proust was "mad on grandeur—for me! I expect I'll end up in the Panthéon!"[18]

In spite of his illnesses and mounting piles of proofs, Proust kept a fairly busy social calendar that spring. He attended an engagement dinner for Antoine and Elizabeth, who married in London on April 30, in a ceremony attended by Queen Alexandra and Princess Victoria.[19] In early March he went to a dinner party at the Ritz given by Princesse Soutzo in honor of diplomats who were in Paris for the peace conference. Marcel was particularly impressed by British diplomat Harold Nicolson. Afterward, Proust told Antoine that he found Nicolson "exquisite, exceptionally intelligent!" Nicolson, who was surprised that Proust spoke to him with no hint of affectation, did note the Frenchman's unkemptness: "White, unshaven, grubby, slip-faced." When Nicolson saw Proust again at the end of April at another dinner party, attended by Princesse Lucien Murat and Gladys Deacon, the diplomat was struck by the contrast between Miss Deacon, who looked "Very Attic," and Proust, who looked "Very Hebrew."[20] Proust's resemblance to his mother, always strong, had grown more marked as he aged. If Proust knew the story of Nicolson's marriage, he would certainly have found it intriguing. Nicolson, a homosexual, was married to the novelist Vita Sackville-West.[21] Vita enjoyed sleeping with women as well as men—not unlike a number of Proust's female characters. Vita's most noteworthy affair was with Virginia Woolf, who drew inspiration from it to create *Orlando*, an androgynous hero who changes sexes in the course of a number of reincarnations.[22]

In late winter or early spring Proust experienced new, troubling symptoms. He had difficulty speaking, finding certain words nearly impossible to pronounce. He confided his difficulty to Berry, fearing that he might have a serious neurological problem. Yet he knew that the symptoms were not the beginning of general paralysis because all his reflexes were excellent and he had never had a venereal disease. His only hope was that this difficulty was "due to an abuse of Veronal. But I fear there is little likelihood that this is the true cause." All he wished for was to remain mentally alert as long as necessary to finish all his volumes. In the meantime, he would drink a lot of water and go out for a bit of air to detoxify himself, in case his careless self-medication was really the cause.[23] A short time later, when Proust consulted Bize, the doctor correctly diagnosed his problems as resulting from drug intoxication and recommended that in addition to exposing himself to fresh air, Marcel take fewer drugs. Proust chose not to believe Bize's diagnosis and for the most part ignored his recommendations.

When Blanche's book *Propos de peintre* went on sale March 10, Proust sent copies of the "ravishing volume" to friends, including Mme Souzto, telling her that he was ashamed of the "stupid preface" he had written so "distractedly one evening in a bad mood." To the extent that his embarrassment was genuine, the reactions of readers would change his mind. Proust wrote Blanche that he had, at first, thought the preface "detestable" but had begun to receive "flattering letters from 'prominent' men" who praised it. One evening in early spring Princesse Lucien Murat came to Proust's door at eleven in the evening to congratulate him on the preface. He had Céleste tell the princess that he had gone out, because he did not want her to see him in bed.[24]

In late March, Mme Hennessy invited Proust to a dinner in his honor. Replying to the invitation, which he yearned to accept though he feared that he would be able to attend only the party afterward, he provided her with a list of practical suggestions on how to prepare for his arrival, including the following:

> If your house is warm, if the windows are closed everywhere in the dining room, but above all in the room where we will be afterward, I will do everything possible to come. . . . I will phone around eight if I feel well enough to come to dinner and you will tell me if that is convenient for you or not. You must tell me very frankly. . . . I have no special diet, I eat everything, I drink everything, I think I don't like red wine but I like every white wine in the world, beer, cider. My only dietary request would be to bring a bottle of Contrexéville or Évian, of which I will drink a little from a separate glass. Forgive me for speaking to you so candidly. But I find it ridiculous to talk pompously about practical matters. And you are too intelligent not to understand that all this is quite simple and that I cannot risk my life over a question of drafts.[25]

Proust did attend Mme Hennessy's party in his honor, arriving, as he had predicted, after dinner.

Gaston Gallimard finally returned to France on March 25. Proust anticipated long sessions of correcting the proofs for his various volumes, while friends looked for an apartment for him. Proust wrote Gallimard, as did Hahn, to explain their concerns about the font size and many errors they had found in *Within a Budding Grove*.[26] The publisher proposed no solution.

That spring, Proust replied to his first letter from Sydney Schiff, a wealthy English publicist and novelist.[27] Schiff, who was fifty-one, wrote under the pseudonym Stephen Hudson. He and his wife, Violet, who both knew French, had been among the first in Britain to discover and love *Swann's Way*. Schiff had another reason for writing: he hoped that Proust would publish in his review *Art and Letters,* whose contributors included Edith Sitwell, Katherine Mansfield, and T. S.

Eliot. Proust replied that he might be willing to answer some sort of literary survey.[28]

On receiving Proust's letter, Schiff wrote again to express his and Violet's admiration for Swann, who had become "a close friend whom we love and whom we comprehend as one comprehends those one has loved for a long time." Schiff said they had often laughed at Dr. Cottard's jokes and silly puns. He even invited Proust to stay with them London, offering him a room with a study where he could rest and where they would leave him "completely free." To reassure Proust that they would understand his needs, Schiff then revealed something about himself: "I am a nervous, moody creature, but I understand the nerves of others." Proust answered that the invitation touched and delighted him; then he explained that his asthma attacks and other health problems required isolation from others and from any noise.[29]

Jacques Rivière, whose health and nerves had been nearly ruined by four years in a German prisoner of war camp, was now editor in chief of the *NRF*. As soon as he read *Within a Budding Grove,* he wrote Proust to express his profound admiration. Rivière was eager to publish an excerpt from the volume in the June 1 *NRF,* the first since 1914, of which he planned a large printing. Rivière suggested the passages on the Narrator's falling out of love with Gilberte.[30] Because this issue would be read by a much wider audience, he wanted Proust, as the "preeminent novelist" of the day, to have the lead article. He then touched on a question of capital importance to Proust: the editor did not think that the excerpt's appearance in the *NRF* would delay publication of the novel by more than ten days.

Proust, who had been waiting six long years to resume publication of his novel, at first expressed his unqualified opposition to this idea. He was fed up with the endless delays. Even though convinced that his books would "appear under deplorable conditions," he still wanted his volumes out well before June, which he thought was a very bad time to publish. Having said this, Proust wrote: "I hasten to add that all reasons yield and all objections vanish immediately" if publishing the excerpt "pleases you, which will with the same stroke please me also." Jacques replied that he could think of no better way to call readers' attention to Proust's books.[31] In fact, because the new NRF edition of *Swann's Way* was not ready until June 23, Gallimard ultimately decided to hold *Within a Budding Grove* and *Pastiches et mélanges* in order to put all three volumes on sale at once.[32] Each delay infuriated Proust, who thought such tactics cost him readers.

Shortly before April 26 Proust wrote Mme Catusse and told her about his speech problems and why he had dismissed Bize's diagnosis of too many drugs: "I think it's the beginning of a state like the one in which my poor Mama ended her days." He did have some good news: the settlement Guiche had negotiated with the banker René Varin-Bernier, the new owner of 102, boulevard Haussmann.[33] The banker agreed to forgive the rent owed and pay Proust an indemnity of three years' rent plus twelve thousand francs.[34] In exchange, Proust had to vacate his apartment by June 1.

As Proust considered where to live, he remained fascinated by the idea of inhabiting Mme Catusse's tower overlooking the sea at Nice. Such a location would be an ideal starting place to fulfill another old dream of visiting those Italian cities he had longed to know: Pisa, Siena, Perugia, and, above all, Florence. It was even possible that he would remain in Italy. He had discussed these plans with Dr. Bize, who would give him an injection on his departure; another doctor, chosen by Bize, would accompany him, along with a nurse, who would give Proust injections along the way. But such trips were dreams with which he consoled himself for no longer being able to travel. He abandoned the idea of renting the tower when Bize told him that if he made it to Nice, the doctor could not guarantee that he would be strong enough for the return trip.[35]

Guiche had masterfully solved Proust's most pressing financial problem. There remained the question of the Warburg check, as Proust explained to Berry. Given the impending and complicated move, the proofs to correct, and his poor health, he had no time for such matters. He also alluded mysteriously to "an unhappy love that is ending." Proust apparently meant his attraction to Rochat, which had indeed been short-lived. Having made the young man a part of his household, Proust could not bring himself to evict him. In the spring, when Proust invited a friend to dine at his bedside, he told him that no one else would be present "except a boy I took in several months ago, but who will not bother us since he says nothing."[36] Rochat seemed content to stay in "his room daubing at his painting," or to hang around and play checkers.[37] He occasionally took dictation when Proust's eyes were too tired for him to write letters that were not personal. Being in Proust's employ was certainly easier and more remunerative for Rochat than any jobs for which he could apply. Rochat contributed several details to characters in the *Search*: Albertine's ambition to become a painter and Morel's beautiful handwriting and bad spelling.[38]

Proust heard from Louis de Robert, who still regretted that Marcel had not followed his advice and published a shorter *Swann's Way*. Louis remained firm in his belief that so many pages discouraged readers. Marcel, "greatly perplexed" by his friend's reservations, had to confess to Louis that the three-volume work they had discussed before the war had expanded into four additional volumes, each as long as *Swann*. And Proust had not yet finished revising. Louis expressed surprise at such length and added, "So much the better for me, for those who first read you." Had Proust decided to "write only for the restricted circle of elite readers who already admire you" and abandon the attempt to "touch, to win over the many delicate and profound souls who will pass by your books without knowing what treasures are hidden within?"[39] Proust's intention, of course, was just the opposite. He wanted to write a book for people who took the train and bought a third-class ticket or for electricians, who, he thought, would be more appreciative of his books than dukes and duchesses.[40] But Louis's reservations troubled him. Proust knew that he was taking the greatest gamble of any novelist in history: he had decided to put everything into one book of unprecedented scale. Could Louis de Robert be right? Could *In Search of Lost Time,* at least ten times the length of an average novel, appeal to large numbers of readers, or would it be a colossal failure?

On May 22 Proust sent his "Dear friend and publisher" a letter in which he released his pent-up anger at what he viewed as Gallimard's shortcomings. He scolded Gaston for having stayed in New York so long as a theater administrator. Gallimard's negligence had resulted in a completely "botched" edition of *Within a Budding Grove.* Even if all the errors were the author's, Gallimard's proofreaders should have caught them. He was furious at having waited so long and worked so hard to obtain such poor results. And his books were still not on sale! Now, after pleading for proofs for years, he had received them all at once: "I no longer have the same strength and perhaps it's my turn to be somewhat slow. It would be good for the entire work to appear while I'm still alive and should things turn out differently, I have left all my notebooks numbered so that you could take them, and, therefore, I am counting on you to complete the publication."[41] Proust had given his final instructions in case death took him before he finished.

On the same day Proust heard from his former publisher Grasset, who proposed "the most amiable solution" to the indemnity matter. Grasset would forgo the indemnity in exchange for Proust's forfeiture of the much smaller royalties owed him. He asked only that Proust give him in the future whatever excerpts or articles he could for a new magazine, *Nos Loisirs,* a review of modern literature that Grasset intended to launch in July. Grasset had ambitious plans for this review, telling Proust that the first printing would be an unprecedented three hundred thousand copies.[42] Proust, who assumed that Grasset would pay him handsomely for a publication with a huge circulation, decided, without telling Rivière, to reserve excerpts from *The Guermantes Way* for *Nos Loisirs.* He ignored Grasset's "amiable solution" to the indemnity settlement, which was less advantageous than the previous proposal.

Meanwhile, Proust's friends, neighbors, and servants continued to look for an apartment with no success. By May 26 Proust had no choice but to accept an offer from Jacques Porel, who suggested as a temporary solution that Proust sublet a furnished apartment in a building that belonged to his mother, Réjane. The actress lived on rue Laurent-Pichat, "a little street between avenue Foch and rue Pergolèse."[43] Réjane occupied the second floor; Jacques, his wife, and their child lived on the third. The fourth-floor apartment that Proust rented for the month of June belonged to Réjane's daughter, who was away in America. This solution to his housing crisis brought new difficulties. Proust would have to move twice, once to the temporary apartment and then to a more permanent dwelling, which he still must find. Marcel, who waited until the last minute to organize his move, was horrified to discover that the unused rooms at boulevard Haussmann contained enough items "to furnish many houses."[44] Réjane's apartment was smaller and furnished, so he would have to store nearly everything he owned.

All the complications and the rapidity with which decisions had to be made and action taken overwhelmed Proust. Céleste, exhausted from all the extra errands and work, suffered from lack of sleep and became "unbearable" with him. When Proust realized how much there was to sort and move, he took the uncharacteristic action of burning a quantity of items. In a letter to Abel Desjardins, Marcel said he burned "precious autographs, manuscripts of which there are no copies, and photographs that had become rare."[45]

Céleste insisted in her memoirs that no such burning took place when they left boulevard Haussmann.[46] She did recall that sometime "between 1916 and 1917, after he'd finished *Within a Budding Grove* and had all the rest in his head," Proust asked her to burn, "one or sometimes two or three at a time, as he came to have no further need of them," what she referred to as "the old exercise books, which were the nucleus of the *Search* and of all his work. They contained the first drafts of his book, long fragments and even whole chapters written in the course of earlier years, even of his youth." On Proust's last trip to Cabourg in 1914, these notebooks "were the only part of his work he didn't take with him." Proust referred to them as the " 'black books' because they had black imitation-leather covers. There were thirty-two of them, numbered with big white figures that looked as if they'd been written with a finger dipped in paint or white ink. They were big school exercise books." When Proust needed to consult one, he would ask Céleste for the number required. She remembered seeing "them open in front of him. The white pages were covered with perfectly even writing without any smudges or crossings-out. I don't think they had been written in bed for they dated from the time when he still wrote sitting down, a period I never knew." Céleste was convinced that "they already contained the essence of his work. Starting from them he reworked, developed, expanded, embellished." Whatever they contained, "no trace remains . . . because at a certain point he made me destroy them, and all thirty-two of them were burned to ashes in the big kitchen stove."[47] No one knows what Proust and Céleste destroyed, but it is generally believed that he burned notebooks containing early drafts that he had already used, recopied, or revised. Proust's normal method of working was not to throw away any text that might later be useful. It is possible that Proust, exhausted and harried, burned notebooks containing sketches for characters he no longer intended to use and of which he kept no copies.[48]

Proust had hired an electrician to go to the new apartment and install an electrical outlet over the place where his bed would be. There would be "three switches, one for the bell, one for the bedside lamp, and one for the kettle."[49] Proust dispatched Odilon to supervise the electrician. When the installation seemed to be progressing very slowly, despite a workday that lasted from nine in the morning until seven in the evening, Proust concluded that Odilon must be telling his war stories to the electrician. Réjane's concierge was asked to oversee Odilon's supervision of the electrician.

Before leaving the only place he had considered home since the death of his parents, Proust took one last look at the dress his mother had worn to Robert's wedding. Long ago, Marthe had asked Marcel for the dress, but he had refused to give it to her. Realizing that "the style of those days had come back," he asked Céleste, "maddened by twenty nights with no sleep," to take the dress to Mme Catusse. He had heard that her son Charles was planning to wed. No doubt Proust hoped his mother's dearest friend would be able to wear the dress. Marcel, who had kept a number of his mother's garments for purely sentimental reasons, sent three dresses to close relatives.[50]

Proust took to the new apartment all the essential items from his bedroom: the brass bed, "tarnished by the fumigations. . . . The little Chinese cabinet he was so fond of . . . and the three little tables with all he needed for his work: the exercise books of the manuscripts and notes, the pile of handkerchiefs, the box of paper for lighting Legras powder, the glasses, the watch," and the light with the green lampshade.[51] The bed being used by Rochat was moved to the room the "secretary" would occupy. Proust brought with him the oil portraits of his parents and his own by Blanche. The other items, including the cork and the grand piano, went to storage. In late May, Proust wrote Porel, telling him how pleased and proud Céleste was to be moving to such a "marvelous apartment, in the shadow of Mme Réjane's glory." He wanted no one except Reynaldo, who already knew it, to have his new address.[52] Proust was to find the apartment anything but marvelous.

Chez Réjane

On May 31 an exhausted Proust left boulevard Haussmann and moved to 8 bis, rue Laurent-Pichat. He had hoped to do nothing but rest for a month while friends and a rental agency looked for more suitable lodgings, but he developed such a high fever and was so miserable that he wanted to leave immediately.[53] Proust remained at Réjane's for four months, during which time he suffered terrible attacks of asthma and complained about the noise that came through walls made of "paper." He felt so wretched that he did not even inform his brother of the new address. Céleste recalled: "Death began for him with our leaving boulevard Haussmann."[54]

The day after Proust moved, the June issue of the *NRF* appeared with an excerpt from *Within a Budding Grove*, about the young Narrator's gradual falling out of love with Swann's adolescent daughter Gilberte. This was Proust's and the *NRF*'s first publication in five years; on July 1, 1914, just a month before the outbreak of war, the review had published excerpts from *The Guermantes Way*. Proust's pages had a powerful effect on Berry, who wrote the author that they "awakened all my painful memories—because I have lived all that, down to the last line—but the wound has not healed. In order to elude the obsession, I walked along the quais under the mournful Moon. God, everything today is lamentable—and what . . . an incomparable artist you are—and how I admire you . . . and how everything is sad sad sad—Walter Berry."[55]

In early June, Proust became annoyed at what he considered Gallimard's inaccessibility and wrote that he had been unable to reach his publisher by phone and wondered why he kept such odd hours. He remarked sarcastically, "It was slightly more convenient when you were in America, because there was at least the boat 'that was going to set sail.'" Proust informed Gaston that on the day he moved, while going through drawers and boxes, he found the original proofs of *The Guermantes Way*, made long ago when Grasset was preparing what was then the second volume. Once he recovered from his asthma and fever he would correct them. "I hope to begin within forty-eight hours and then will go like the wind." Gallimard explained that Proust's last letter sent to his home address had gone unanswered because he, too, had a new address.[56] Gaston, who did not reveal that address, said that Proust should send all his mail to the NRF office.

Proust negotiated with Gallimard concerning the deluxe edition of *Within a Budding Grove*. The publisher estimated that the cost would be approximately three thousand francs. Hoping to sell fifty copies at five hundred francs, Proust asked whether the profits from the sales would be entirely the author's. "My question may be stupid, but I haven't the foggiest notion about this." Gallimard answered that all the revenue would go to Proust, "after deduction of the expenses, which had actually just increased because of the institution of the eight-hour workday."[57]

Around June 7 Proust wrote Tronche because he was furious that his three volumes, whose publication had been announced for the first week in June, had not appeared. Furthermore, friends who went to the NRF offices in the rue Madame to obtain his books came away empty-handed. Would they even bother to try again? Proust beseeched the NRF at least not to announce a date again until it was certain the books would be available. Tronche explained that the delay was due primarily to strikes by typesetters.[58] The next week Proust wrote Gallimard to express his fear that everyone would leave Paris for summer vacation before his books were available. Tronche responded on Sunday, June 15, the day the strikes ended, assuring him that his three volumes would be in all the bookstores by the end of the week. He apologized for their having failed to "better satisfy you despite all our goodwill and this imperious desire that we have to serve your work."[59]

Certain at last that his books were to appear, Proust wrote Robert de Flers to request an article in the *Figaro* announcing their publication.[60] No one, he said, would do that as well as his old friend Robert Dreyfus. If Flers thought it impossible to place a literary piece on the front page at the moment, the novelist would resign himself to a brief notice. That was the solution adopted by Flers. The Versailles Peace Conference, nearing an agreement, had dominated the news for weeks, crowding other items off the front page.

On June 21 Proust began autographing and sending friends copies of *Within a Budding Grove, Pastiches et mélanges,* and *Swann's Way.* He soon discovered that these copies were not first editions. Dismayed, he sent Odilon and Marie to bookstores to look for first editions. Proust learned that an "Association of Bibliophiles" had reserved all copies of the first edition. This circumstance forced him to write his closest friends, telling them why they had not received signed copies of his books. Proust urged Antoine, if he happened to see "Anna de Noailles, Princesse de Chimay, Princesse de Polignac, Comtesse Greffulhe, Maurice Barrès, etc.," to explain his predicament. Marcel continued to inscribe copies, hoping to replace them later with first editions, if any were to be found. When he apologized to Cocteau for sending an edition that was not the first, he received a charming note: "My dear Marcel, I am not a bibliophile—any edition becomes precious when inscribed by you."[61]

Although Proust was still smarting from Léon's qualification of *Swann's Way* as "stupefying," he paid his friend a large compliment in his copy: "To Léon Daudet, who does not like my book which does not prevent me from worshipping his (See *Pastiches et mélanges*, p. 37) and himself . . . " Proust referred to the page from his 1907 parody of the Goncourts' *Journal,* in which Lucien describes Proust as a person who is "completely enamored of Léon's novels."[62] Proust was mistaken about Léon's opinion of his work; Daudet was about to become one of the most important champions of the *Search*.

When Proust inscribed a copy of *Within a Budding Grove* for Réjane, he congratulated the actress on her great roles, especially as Germinie, a performance that left him with a "recurrent fever," and for the "most beautiful" of all her roles as Jacques's mother. "Respectful homage from an unbearable tenant."[63] Proust could observe another famous actor, who lived in a neighboring apartment. Céleste recalled: "On the other side of the courtyard we could see the actor Le Bargy, of the Comédie-Française, coming and going in his bathroom, occasionally letting out great howls, either declaiming his lines or quarreling with his wife—it was sometimes hard to tell. M. Proust was very amused by this."[64] Proust worried about Réjane's health. Although she remained active at sixty-three, she suffered from a weak heart. Remembering her long and remarkable career, Proust noted his intention to use impressions of Réjane in old age for an episode recounting the last days of his fictional actress Berma.[65]

On June 23 Berry returned from Tours and found his copy of *Pastiches et mélanges.* Writing Proust to say how "delighted" he had been to find "your book— or rather *my* book," Berry noted the historical moment: "The war ends today." Germany had just accepted the conditions of the Versailles Treaty.[66] In less than a month, France prepared a grand victory celebration for the first peacetime Bastille Day since 1914. It soon became evident, however, that the diplomatic, political, and economic difficulties resulting from the Great War were far from over. Proust later told Berry that he had his own idea regarding a peace accord. If France intended to ask Germany and Austria for artistic reparations, why not take the Vermeer paintings in Dresden and Vienna. "The world's greatest painter is unknown in France (*La Dentellière* at the Louvre is exquisite but hardly sufficient)."[67]

At the end of June, Tronche wrote Proust requesting a list of critics to receive press copies. He enclosed a royalty check, the first Proust had received in years, in the amount of 2,430 francs as an advance on the sale of the first one thousand copies of *Swann's Way* and the first three thousand copies of *Within a Budding Grove* and *Pastiches et mélanges*.[68] Proust questioned the terms and payment. His contract called for him to receive a generous 18 percent on the price of the volumes sold, but he wanted his percentage to be calculated on the full price (7.50 francs), and he wanted to be paid immediately for all three thousand copies of each volume. This was the first of many skirmishes regarding contracts and royalty payments. After explaining to Proust that the royalties for all authors were calculated on the amount remaining after 2.50 francs in state taxes were deducted—which made 5 francs in his case—the NRF yielded. Tronche warned the writer, however, that such payment might mean the price of his volumes would have to be increased.[69] Proust soon received another, recalculated royalty check for 5,490 francs.[70]

Although Proust's fascination with Henri Rochat had not lasted long, he was too kindhearted to dismiss the young man. The novelist found it nearly impossible to get rid of his "secretary," even though he tried several times. On one occasion Rochat expressed an impulse to return to Switzerland. Eager to encourage such a move, Proust obtained a pass, still necessary in the immediate postwar period. Rochat had the clever idea of waiting for his papers on the Riviera, where he quickly squandered all the money Proust had given him for the trip to Switzerland. He apparently spent some of the funds on prostitutes. The wayward secretary contracted a venereal disease, and he returned to Proust's apartment so ill that he required nursing. In the summer, Proust tried again to send Rochat home to seek regular employment. This time he obtained a pass through Jacques Truelle. On July 9, to make certain that Rochat left for Switzerland, Proust saw him off at the Gare de Lyon.[71] Afterward, a relieved Proust joined his guests Walter Berry, Mme Soutzo, and Paul Morand for a small dinner party at the Ritz.

Rivière informed Proust of his decision to write a study of the author's work to date. Jacques, who feared that his condition might make it impossible for him to write an article worthy of his subject, predicted that he would have to struggle against an "unbearable mental fatigue." Proust, who knew how severely the critic's health had been undermined by all he had suffered during the war, expressed his gratitude but urged Rivière to abandon the idea and rest.[72]

Violet Schiff received a letter in which Proust expressed his "despair" that she had ordered his books rather than waiting for him to send copies. He enumerated all his problems in his new apartment, including the noise made by hammers from work being done nearby and his terrible asthma attacks. He had not slept "for a minute" and was in "such a weakened condition" that he had taken as "much caffeine as possible" to be able to write to her. He asked whether she knew any friends who might like copies of the deluxe edition. Proust was drawing up a list of potential subscribers. He had been "very moved" by an objection that Violet, who shared her husband's great affection for Swann, had made regarding the turn this character was taking: "I feel I am going to have many regrets." He assumed the Schiffs meant that they considered "Swann to be a living person" and had been "disappointed to see him become less likable and even ridiculous." Proust assured them that transforming Swann had been painful: "But I am not free to go against truth and violate the laws of character. *Amicus Swann sed magis amica veritas.* The nicest people sometimes have odious periods. I promise you that in the following volume, when he becomes a Dreyfusard, Swann will again become likable. Unfortunately, and this causes me great distress, he dies in the fourth volume." Swann was not the book's main character: "I would have liked it to be he. But art is a perpetual sacrifice of sentiment to truth."[73] Violet acquiesced; what else could she do after such a charming and convincing letter?

Blanche visited Proust in his temporary lodgings and found him looking well, though rather plump. Marcel seemed very animated and spoke of leaving soon for Cabourg. Céleste served Blanche a sumptuous snack. Proust entreated her to do some of her imitations, for which, he said, she had a kind of genius, but Céleste refused to perform. Blanche remembered his last dinner with Proust as only laughter and enchantment, as the two old friends evoked their youth.[74]

Princesse Soutzo, who during her morning walks looked for an apartment for Marcel, had found one at thirty thousand francs a year, which she thought was "quite expensive, even for Céleste." Proust passed this amusing comment on to Porel. He then reported that another tenant in the building had complained about a noisy neighbor. Proclaiming his innocence, the writer asked Jacques to tell his mother that Proust did not have in his apartment "either a piano or a mistress." He did, however, have an idea about the source of the noise: "The neighbors in the adjoining room make love . . . every day with a frenzy which makes me jealous. When I think that for me this sensation is weaker than that of drinking a cold beer, I envy people who can scream so that the first time I thought someone was being murdered, but very soon the cry of the woman repeated an octave lower by the man, reassured me about what was happening."[75] Proust concluded, he told Porel, from the sounds heard that as soon as their lovemaking ended the couple leaped from their bed to take a sitz-bath before performing the necessary household chores, which included taking care of children. Then Proust made an unusually frank and intimate confession—though vague, and with no indication of the identity or sex of the partner. He said that "The total absence of any transition makes me tired for them [the lovers overheard], for if there is anything I detest *afterward,* at least *immediately afterward,* it's moving, no matter how much egotism there is in keeping in the same place the warmth of a mouth that no longer has anything to receive."[76] Proust's description of his preferences when engaged in sex suggests fellatio. Why did he make such an extraordinary admission to Porel? It is true that there is nothing in the letter that suggests a homosexual rather than a heterosexual partner, but such a comment proves at least that Proust discussed his sexual habits frankly with a number of people whose discretion he apparently trusted.

In the opening pages of *Sodom and Gomorrah,* which he did not publish until 1921, Proust uses a description similar to the one in the letter to Porel when the Narrator overhears two men, Jupien and Charlus, who engage in sex, apparently anal intercourse: "From what I heard at first in Jupien's quarters, which was only a series of inarticulate sounds, I imagine that few words had been exchanged. It is true that these sounds were so violent that, if they had not always been taken up an octave higher by a parallel plaint, I might have thought that one person was slitting another's throat within a few feet of me, and that subsequently the murderer and his resuscitated victim were taking a bath to wash away the traces of the crime. I concluded from this . . . that there is another thing as noisy as pain, namely pleasure, especially when there is added to it . . . an immediate concern about cleanliness."[77]

This scene between Jupien and Charlus, and others that occur later in the book, demonstrate the daring nature of Proust's narrative. Balzac had only hinted at Vautrin's desire for Lucien de Rubempré; Proust actually described, at least through sounds and a minimum of dialogue, a homosexual encounter. After Proust, there was no way to deny the existence of what he called a large colony of homosexuals.

By the end of July, Rochat was back. Unable to obtain the job he wanted with an aviation company in Switzerland, he returned to Paris without informing Proust. At first he did not dare come to Proust's apartment. The novelist speculated that Rochat might have wanted to spend the first days back in Paris with his fiancée. Proust told Truelle that once Rochat realized that the hotel was costing him fifty francs a day compared with "nothing in my apartment, he came and asked me for hospitality, which I did not dare refuse him, but which poisons my existence." When Proust learned that the fiancée, who was "delicious, although the daughter of a concierge," intended to visit her grandmother in Deux Sèvres in western France, he urged Rochat to accompany her. But Rochat worried that his presence "might compromise her. Meanwhile it is my repose which is compromised."[78] Proust described Rochat to Porel as a burden who filled his "moments with a dead weight."[79] Because Rochat was "very nice" and "knew how to play checkers," Proust put aside his proofs to "maneuver men on the board." A year later, when a friend asked Proust how he viewed company and people in general, the novelist replied: "I do my intellectual work within myself, and once I am with others, it almost doesn't matter to me if they are intelligent, provided they are nice, sincere, etc."[80] Rochat, like many other male servants Marcel knew through the years, seems to have met those modest requirements.

Proust complained to friends that the constant noise and his asthma attacks made him suffer so much that he could "neither work, or do anything, or speak, or write."[81] Mme de Ludre, a friend with whom he sometimes dined, sent him some Quiès cotton wool balls to use as ear plugs. Proust used his perceptions of noises muffled by the Quiès balls for a passage on sounds and silences when the Narrator visits Saint-Loup's barracks in Doncières.[82] He might have felt wretched, but the strange apartment did stimulate him to create new scenes, especially ones involving sound effects.

Around this time, Proust and Daniel Halévy engaged in an epistolary debate over France's role as an intellectual leader. When Halévy signed a manifesto in the *Figaro,* "Pour un parti de l'intelligence," intended as an answer to the Communist Manifesto, Proust wrote to express his disapproval.[83] The only criterion, the only law one should seek was truth. "If France is to watch over the literature of the entire world, that is a mandate one would weep with joy to learn has been entrusted to us, but it's somewhat shocking to see us assume for ourselves. This hegemony, born with 'Victory' makes one think immediately of 'Deutschland über alles' and for that reason is slightly disagreeable." After Halévy attempted to justify his position by stating the rectitude of those with whom he sided, Proust warned: "It is very dangerous to adhere to false ideas because of the virtues of those who proclaim them." This very practice explained why military men who leaned toward support-ing Dreyfus had been against revision because they knew what a good man General Gonse was and had "more trust in the Chiefs of Staff than in the anarchists." Turning to personal matters, he told Daniel not to "imagine that 'my lot' is good. It's atrocious. I am weaving nothing but my shroud, and so slowly and so painfully."[84]

Yet his lot was in fact very good, at least as far as reaction to his novel was concerned. Proust's friends with literary ambitions, such as Halévy and Gregh, found his position enviable. Praise for *Within a Budding Grove* continued to arrive from friends and admirers. Blanche wrote that if Montaigne had been tempted to "write a novel, he would not have surpassed or even attained, in his analysis, what each page of your astonishing book possesses." Proust should not be surprised, Blanche said, if critics write many articles on his work; even those who, like Vandérem, admire him "hatefully" admire him "passionately." The painter ended by saying, "I live with your books and am returning to them immediately."[85]

Proust was delighted when Comte Jean de Gaigneron compared his books to a cathedral. Thanking the count, the author said that it was impossible "not to be moved by an intuition which permits you to guess what I have never told anyone and that I am writing here for the first time: I have wanted to give to each part of my book the title: Portal I Stained Glass Windows of the Apse etc., to answer in advance the stupid criticism . . . over the lack of construction in a book where I will show that the only merit is in the solidity of the most minor parts." Proust abandoned the idea of "architectural titles" because he found them "too pretentious." The cathedral analogy occurs again in a letter to François Mauriac, a fervent Catholic. Proust, perhaps apprehensive about Mauriac's reaction to *Sodom and Gomorrah,* recalled that Jammes had asked him to cut the scene between Mlle Vinteuil and her friend. Proust would have liked to grant Jammes's request, "but I had constructed this work so carefully that this episode in the first volume explains the jealousy of my young man in the fourth and fifth volumes, so that by ripping out the column with the obscene capital, I would have brought down the arch. That's what critics like to call works without composition and written according to random memories."[86]

For the rest of his life, with the publication of each successive volume, Proust was to defend his work against those critics who, even while praising the *Search* as an extraordinary accomplishment, said that it lacked structure and composition. The accusation that he was writing thinly disguised memoirs or free associations of ideas amounted to the same, for either charge meant that he had not had to be selective and create a plot.

On August 15 Proust was Berry's guest at a small dinner party at the Ritz that included Princesse Lucien Murat. Marcel arrived late and was unhappy to see they were to dine in the garden. Noticing his downcast look, the "charming" Princesse Murat stopped the dinner and insisted that the table be moved inside. This infuriated the waiters, who tried to convince the diners that it was warmer outside. After leaving the Ritz, Proust decided to enjoy the lingering effects of Berry's excellent champagne by taking a long ride until five in the morning in the Bois de Boulogne, "sublime in silence, solitude and moonlight." Such a sight was one of his favorites, and one he rarely saw. Walter later told Marcel that if he had stayed a little longer in the Bois, they would have met at 7:30, when Berry came to play tennis.[87]

Toward the end of August, Proust wrote Montesquiou, apologizing for not having sent first editions of his new volumes. Regarding *Pastiches et mélanges,* he wrote: "You must have known . . . that I had done, using Saint-Simon as my cover, a long portrait of you . . . which is not a mere reproduction of the one that appeared years ago in the *Figaro,* but contains new parts and new praises. And for that I hoped to receive a note from you." Such a note, Proust wrote, "would have been for me a beneficial balm during these days when I have suffered so much." Montesquiou replied, thanking Marcel for the books and the parody, in which he did indeed recognize himself. Here the count quoted a line from Virgil's *Aeneid* describing Hector "covered with wounds"—apparently an indication that he found Proust's portrait less than flattering. But the count had been moved by the remembrance of Yturri, the "shade which will always be dear to me and about whom you speak so well."[88] Montesquiou wrote again in the fall, complimenting the parody, saying that it "was a marvelous success, better, a miracle in the genre." What Proust had referred to as "my 'vice' "—that is, the count's frequent feuds with friends—"I call the art of pruning the tree of friendship." The count concluded his long letter of praise, "So with this you've become a thaumaturge, therapeutist, and a friend," this last being "the most beautiful title of the three." Montesquiou said that Proust would read his "memoirs since you will outlive me"; he hoped his recollections would please the novelist and inspire him to visit his last resting place.[89] It is odd that the count thought that Proust would be pleased by his memoirs, which depict the author as suffering from "megalomania."[90] Montesquiou was right about Proust's outliving him, but wrong about his surviving long enough to read the dreaded memoirs.

In early September, when Reynaldo returned from a stay at the Daudets' country estate at la Roche, he informed Marcel that Rosny the Elder, a writer and member of the Académie Goncourt, intended to vote for *Within a Budding Grove* for the Prix Goncourt, as did Léon Daudet, who wielded tremendous influence. Reynaldo had strongly urged that Proust be given the prize. On learning of Rosny's and Daudet's intention to vote for him, Proust "quickly sent" his "book to the other members."[91] Because there was no way to campaign openly for the prize, Proust's gesture of sending copies of his book to the ten members of the academy was interpreted as a declaration of his candidacy.[92]

Proust abandoned hope of finding first editions of *Within a Budding Grove* and inscribed a copy of a later printing to Mme Catusse. He paid tribute to his mother's great friendship for her, saying that in "those hours in which I adhere to the most recent philosophy—and so old—that maintains that souls survive," he turned toward his mother "so she will know that I tell you everything, everything she owes you." He ended by saying that he had "placed all my heart in these pages. Receive them in memory of my Mother."[93] His own desire to be reunited with his mother and his ability to communicate with her silently are described in two passages from *Within a Budding Grove* in which the Narrator enjoys the same relationship with his grandmother. The Narrator, who fears eternal separation from his grandmother, seeks to exorcize that horrible thought by saying to her "in the most casual tone but . . . taking care that my grandmother should pay attention . . . what a curious thing it was that, according to the latest scientific discoveries, the materialist position appeared to be crumbling, and what was again most likely was the immortality of souls and their future reunion."[94] The young Narrator, at Balbec with his grandmother, is constantly reassured by his extraordinary closeness to her: "I knew, when I was with my grandmother, that however great the misery that there was in me, it would be received by her with a pity still more vast, that everything that was mine, my cares, my wishes, would be buttressed, in my grandmother, by a desire to preserve and enhance my life that was altogether stronger than was my own; and my thoughts were continued and extended in her without undergoing the slightest deflection, since they passed from my mind into hers without any change of atmosphere or of personality."[95]

In keeping with his understanding with Grasset, Proust offered him the choice of excerpts from *The Guermantes Way.* He told his former publisher that he had thought himself unknown but had been deluged by requests for excerpts from newspapers and reviews. He had said yes to only a few, including *Le Matin,* to which he had sent a fragment of Mme de Villeparisis's stay in Venice.[96] He had chosen that paper because he admired Colette, who was working as an editor there. Unfortunately, Grasset was plagued by internal problems with his new magazine and did not publish any excerpts from the *Search.*

In September the rental agency found Proust a fourth-floor apartment, in a building with an elevator, in the eighth arrondissement.[97] Proust liked the location, and he sent Céleste to the rue Hamelin to inspect the apartment and find out who lived in the building. After Céleste reported back, the novelist made up his mind, but with a typical Proustian variation. He wanted the landlady to empty the fifth-floor apartment and rent it to him at the furnished rate.[98]

44, rue Hamelin

On October 1, Proust moved the relatively short distance from 8 bis, rue Laurent-Pichat to the rue Hamelin. His new fifth-floor apartment lay on a line between the Arc de Triomphe and the Eiffel Tower. Before moving in, he hired workers to make the necessary installations: carpets everywhere to insulate against the noise, the electrical outlet above his bed for his bell, lamp, and kettle, but nothing else, no other installations, not even the cork, for he did not regard his new quarters as permanent.[99] Proust's entourage followed him to rue Hamelin: Céleste and Odilon, Marie, and the barnacle-like Rochat, "without employment" and with no plans. Proust's rent was sixteen thousand francs a year, nearly three times as much as his old apartment.

Céleste described their new neighborhood as "quiet, middle-class . . . with nice people." There was a baker's shop on the ground floor owned by a M. Montagnon, with whom Céleste "arranged to do her telephoning. I used to go straight into his dining room without asking." Proust's apartment possessed, Céleste recalled, essentially the same floor plan as at boulevard Haussmann, though on a smaller scale: "salon, small salon (or rather boudoir) and bedroom. That was the route for visitors. I usually went by the corridor and the boudoir, and entered the bedroom through a double door . . . across the hall. After the bathroom came a bedroom full of books and silver not in use."

The essential items for writing and burning the antiasthma powders, including the candle that stayed lighted all night on a table in the hallway, were placed in their positions. Daylight was blocked out as it had been at boulevard Haussmann by "long, very handsome window curtains of blue satin." The "boudoir now contained the black bookcase that used to be in the small salon, with his favorite authors: Mme de Sévigné, Ruskin, Saint-Simon in a beautiful binding stamped with the initials M. P. Instead of the armchairs, there were now low fireside chairs."

The only differences Céleste recalled, once Proust settled in and the "machinery of his habits resumed," were that he said more frequently: " 'I haven't much time, Céleste . . . ' " She also thought he "smoked" less. In her memory, she later saw "those last two years of his life . . . in an atmosphere which already resembled the grave." The new apartment had little charm and no warm memories. Nor did the "very small" fireplace produce the desired heat. "He couldn't stand central heating because of the dust, I tried to light a fire. . . . But the draft wasn't good and the smoke seeped back into the room. 'The smoke makes me ill, Céleste,' he said, 'I can taste it in my mouth and chest. I can't breathe. We will have to give it up.' So I didn't light a fire any more. I can see him as he lay there in bed, with the little green light falling on the pages he was writing or correcting, and the sweaters slipping down one after the other behind him as he asked me for another to put around his shoulders. And never a complaint." When she worried about his catching cold in the freezing room, he answered that they were " 'only passing through. When I have finished we will be more comfortable.' " He told her that they would go south for a holiday after the *Search* was completed.

Soon after Proust moved to rue Hamelin, Tronche somehow obtained for him copies of the first editions of *Swann's Way* and *Within a Budding Grove*. Tronche informed the author that the deluxe edition, with its corrected proof sheets and the photogravure of the Blanche portrait, was advancing well.[100]

In October, Paul Morand angered Proust by publishing an "Ode to Marcel Proust," in which he depicted Proust as someone who always claimed to be on the verge of dying. But what shocked Proust were the indiscreet insinuations and the public disclosure of details regarding his private life.[101] What late night revels, Morand asked in verse, did Proust attend to return home with "eyes so weary and so lucid?" In spite of the "Ode," Proust did not break with Morand; he was indulgent, but he scolded Paul, saying that the "Ode" could be interpreted as an indication of his having been caught in a raid or left for dead by hooligans. Proust had good reason to fear being caught in a raid; had his friends or others found out about his late night visits to Le Cuziat's brothel? He did mete out a form of punishment to Paul. It had been his intention to write another volume of pastiches entirely devoted to Morand and Mme Soutzo, "your accomplice for the Ode." Because the book was "infinitely laudatory," Proust said, he could not "publish it . . . without looking like a coward." Reminding Morand that the "artist's duty is to Truth," Proust complained that the "Ode" had embarrassed him publicly with no justification. As for Morand's "charming dedication," in Proust's copy, it was handwritten and private, and could not counteract the poem, "where you threw me into this Hell that Dante reserved for his enemies."[102]

In a mid-October letter to Porel, Proust said, "Not only am I sicker but I fired Céleste. And then, naturally, I took her back." The cause of this dismissal, which Céleste does not mention in her memoirs, is unknown. It seems likely that Céleste became "unbearable" again under the stress of the second move, as when she had nearly collapsed from exhaustion during the frantic days that preceded Proust's first relocation.[103] Even the normally valiant, all-suffering Céleste could be at times pushed to her limit by the demands of the most complicated and least practical man in Paris.

Rivière, struggling with his essay on the *Search,* wrote Proust that it had been madness to announce that "I was writing an article on your novel!" Jacques worked also to expand the *NRF,* creating new columns for it. Having engaged writers for the columns about poetry and painting, he "suddenly became exceedingly ambitious for the column about the novel," which he wanted to give to "the current master of the genre."[104] This was the column formerly entrusted to Henri Ghéon, who had written the negative review of *Swann's Way.* In earlier years Proust would have welcomed such an assignment; he declined the offer in order to devote himself entirely to finishing the *Search.*

Proust contacted his old friend Mme Lemaire, saying that he would send her a copy of *Pastiches et mélanges,* the publication of which had resulted in a break with the Murats and Albufera. These ruptures "pained" him a "great deal," but as "for society I don't give a damn," as his parodies proved.[105] The Murats were furious with him because he had depicted them as pretentious courtiers, intriguing to be granted the same rank as foreign princes. Albufera, who was related to the Murats by marriage, also took offense. To make matters worse, Proust's intended compliment to the nobleman had been turned into an insult by a printer's error. Proust had written of his "infinite esteem" for Albufera, but the typesetter had read *infime* for *infinie,* which changed the phrase to "minute esteem."[106] Albufera did not acknowledge receiving any of his books. Proust did not care, he told Hauser, that the Murats were incensed, but to lose an old friend like Albu, "*tried and true,* pains me infinitely."[107]

Rosny wrote Proust at the end of October to express the "intense joy" he had felt on reading *Within a Budding Grove:* "I am indebted to you for having rejuvenated this literature with which I am saturated!" Rosny, who admitted having had reservations about *Swann's Way,* offered to support Proust for the Prix Goncourt.[108] Seemingly more moved by Rosny's testimony than by the prize held out to him, Proust answered: "I don't know if I will win the prize, I don't even know when it's given, but I am happy in any case that it exists, because it has permitted me . . . to know your gentle goodness, the kind interest you show those whose books you like." On November 3 Rosny sent a confidential letter, telling Proust that he already had six of the ten votes. The president, as things stood, also intended to vote for Proust. If that decision held, Proust would certainly win. Rosny wrote again a month later to assure Proust that he need fear no surprises.[109]

That fall, when Robert de Billy visited Proust for the first time since the armistice, he found the writer in a "very somber" mood. Marcel admitted that he was in a difficult position financially. When Proust explained the dilemma regarding the Warburg check and his need for cash, Billy proposed a solution that relieved, at least temporarily, one of Marcel's long-standing financial frustrations. Robert arranged for Proust to receive an advance of thirty thousand francs on the check by giving his personal guaranty. A grateful Proust insisted on sending a receipt so that if he died, his heirs would pay Billy immediately.[110] Billy noted in his memoirs the "extremely complicated nature" of Marcel's mind and wondered: "Did he need the money or not? I don't know, but I do know that he needed to believe in me and . . . my friendship."[111]

With his financial status looking brighter, Marcel was tempted to revert to his old habits as a speculator. Not long after receiving the advance on the Warburg check, he wrote Hauser. After complaining about his new apartment—which he described as a sixteen thousand–franc slum—he asked whether Hauser knew anything about various stocks, such as Transatlantic Cables, in which he might invest. Proust was thinking about selling his surplus at London County Bank and buying new shares.[112]

Hauser replied at once that Marcel's letter absolutely appalled him. Obviously, Proust had not suffered enough from his close brush with bankruptcy. How, Lionel asked, could Marcel ever hope to maintain a sound financial footing if he continued to gamble? The stock market tips Marcel had received were exactly the kind that had led to his ruin. If he had more money to throw away, fine, "only don't try to make me your accomplice." Hauser marveled that Proust did not believe in God but put faith in tips from financiers. "Admit, my dear Marcel, that you are not very logical." He then enumerated what he viewed as Proust's excessive habits, including a household of four servants. "If I remember correctly, you had left something like 25,000 francs for income. Now, if you are currently paying 16,000 francs in rent and still keep a valet and a housekeeper . . . you will soon discover that after having paid the wages of your servants and their board, which must certainly be substantial, you will have just enough left to buy a package of eucalyptus cigarettes."[113]

Proust waited several weeks before answering. He had not been "wounded" by the letter but complained that Hauser's remarks about Proust's financial ruin, his "follies, etc.," had been dictated to Hauser's secretary. Then Proust, who had failed to do so earlier, brought Hauser up to date regarding the large indemnity that he had received on leaving boulevard Haussmann. He also asked his financial adviser to confirm that his portfolio still contained seven shares of Royal Dutch, each of which should be worth more than thirty thousand francs.[114]

Hauser seized the opportunity to cut himself free from Proust and his endless financial complications: "Not only are you not financially ruined, you are almost in an enviable situation given the hard times in which we are living." Lionel announced that he considered his "mission accomplished," and while remaining at Proust's "entire disposition," he hoped the writer would never again need to have recourse to his financial rescue services. At the beginning of the letter he had brushed Proust's complaints aside, saying that he had not been indiscreet because his employees were familiar with all aspects of Proust's financial portfolio. The novelist had in their eyes "the prestige of someone like Balzac." Hauser had recently spotted a copy of *Swann's Way* on his accountant's desk.[115] Proust was always delighted to hear that a particular individual was reading his book, especially someone who did not belong to the leisured class.

Proust was caught off guard by Hauser's resignation, but he had no choice but to accept it. He later wrote that although Hauser's letter had been "very nice," it had caused him "a lot of pain. You told me: 'I quit.' " Proust considered this "materially a great misfortune for me. But even if it were a good fortune, the pain would still be the same. I cannot get used to things that end. I would be as sad to leave a slum for a palace, as a palace for a slum (now I'm in a slum)."[116]

That November, Proust suffered from unrelenting asthma. He wrote to Rosny on November 10 that his attacks often lasted "forty-eight hours," during which he gasped for air "like a half-drowned person pulled out of the water, unable to say a word or make the slightest movement."[117]

Proust finally yielded to Montesquiou's request and gave him the rue Hamelin address. Having read *Within a Budding Grove,* the count sent Proust his impressions, complete with a list of quotations. He compared Proust, in a Montesquiouan way, to "two masters of the Divisionist School" of painting, Giovanni Segantini and Henri Fantin-Latour, a "comparison which seems to me laudatory." What had struck Montesquiou was Proust's "multiplicity of brushstrokes that make the composition vibrant and bring the subject to life." He had noticed Marcel's remarkable gift for creating maximlike reflections that often terminate passages describing a character's actions or the Narrator's reflections: "Your quotations, your observations, fly like multicolored confetti." Montesquiou, at no loss for airborne analogies, compared the pithy observations to flower petals tossed in the air or snowflakes or butterflies. The count's favorite quotation, the "most beautiful," spoke of glory and mortality: "Men who believe that their works will last—as was the case with Elstir—form the habit of placing them in a period when they themselves will have crumbled into dust. And thus, by obliging them to reflect on their own extinction, the idea of fame saddens them because it is inseparable from the idea of death."[118]

Albert Thibaudet, a professor and critic who wrote for the *NRF,* contributed an article on Gustave Flaubert for the November issue: "Reflections on Literature: On Flaubert's Style." Proust, who had long been interested in Flaubert, took issue with some of Thibaudet's statements. In mid-November, Proust wrote Rivière and offered the *NRF* a letter on Flaubert's style, which would serve as a reply to Thibaudet. Proust contended that the way critics viewed the most distinguished French authors was so "defective" that it was time to "redress the many false judgments." Proust insisted that he would write a very short article or note; he knew that it would be wiser to work on the Guermantes volume because the moments when he could read a newspaper or correct a proof page were "so rare."[119] Proust may have offered Rivière the Flaubert piece because he had told his young friend, without saying why, that it would be impossible to give him excerpts from *The Guermantes Way.*

Rivière was delighted for his review to be the stage of a debate between Proust and Thibaudet. He told Proust that he wanted the Flaubert essay by November 30 at the latest, for inclusion in the January issue. Proust became confused about the date and nearly missed the deadline, but when he realized his mistake, he rushed to finish. Because the books he needed were in storage, he quoted Flaubert from memory, often accurately, sometimes in error. Proust apparently located his essay on Flaubert, begun before the war; his original intention to write a note quickly swelled to a manuscript of sixty-two pages.[120]

One week before the Prix Goncourt was to be announced, Proust wrote Gallimard to express his concern that *Within a Budding Grove* would soon be out of print. By December 3, of the 3,242 copies originally printed, there were only 225 in stock at the printer's.[121] Marcel had not expected the volume to enjoy such success. He had even told Gallimard, as he reminded him now, that he had been "somewhat ashamed to bring out all by itself this languishing interlude." To his amazement, "this book is enjoying a hundred times the success of *Swann.*" He observed proudly, having been informed no doubt by his friends in the diplomatic corps, that "there were copies on all the tables in China and Japan." He enumerated the various places copies had been seen in France: on his accountant's desk, "in houses in the Pyrénées or in the North, in Normandy, or in Auvergne." This "direct contact with the reader," which he had not had with *Swann,* delighted Proust, but he claimed to take no pride in this, noting that "often the worst books are the most popular." If he drew no vainglory from his success, he did expect to earn some money. He also wanted to know whether Gallimard had chosen a translator for England. Here, too, Proust suspected his publisher of procrastinating. Anticipating the popularity his novel would enjoy in English-speaking countries, he stressed once more the importance of signing a contract for the translation as soon as possible: "The English like my books better than the French." Had Gallimard received the proofs for *The Guermantes Way* or the typescript for *Sodom and Gomorrah*? If so, sending them without delay would help him to make up for "lost time."[122]

Reynaldo wrote that he had been so busy with such "intolerable obligations" as "lectures, conducting, etc.," that he had not been able to come any evening to rue Hamelin. Because Proust had no phone, Hahn never knew when his friend might be out until all hours. He gently reproached Marcel for never telling him anything, "although you have four people in your service." Mme Gregh wanted to nominate Proust for the Prix Fémina and had asked Hahn whether the novelist was a candidate for the Goncourt. Proust's friends and admirers were eager to see his accomplishment officially recognized. In early December, Proust learned that Henri de Régnier and his wife wanted him to receive the Grand Prize for Literature given by the Académie française.[123]

"Now you are famous"

On Wednesday, December 10, the members of the Académie Goncourt met at their annual luncheon at the Restaurant Drouant and voted, six to four, to give their prestigious prize to *Within a Budding Grove*. The minority votes had gone to a war novel, *Les Croix de bois* (The wooden crosses), written by a thirty-three-year-old veteran named Roland Dorgelès.[124] The award carried a cash purse of five thousand francs. The academicians sent the headwaiter to announce the winner to the press, while they drafted a short letter to Proust.[125]

Léon Daudet and several academicians set out for the rue Hamelin to inform Proust.[126] On hearing the news, Gallimard, Rivière, and Tronche rushed out to congratulate their first Prix Goncourt winner.[127] Both delegations arrived at the same time; the laureate was asleep.[128] Céleste, who was authorized on exceptional occasions to enter Proust's bedroom without being sent for, gave him the news. After brief, separate interviews with Daudet and Gallimard, Proust issued strict orders to Céleste that no reporters or photographers were to be admitted.[129]

Proust later attributed some of his negative reviews to his refusal to see journalists who came seeking him for front-page stories. He also blamed Gallimard and his colleagues at the NRF office for failing to give the offended reporters a better reception.[130] Gallimard countered by saying that he did not understand why "you are advising me to be nice to reporters; I am seeing a lot of them these days and I am trying hard to satisfy them, and by talking to them about the Prix Goncourt, to clear things up." He urged Proust to accept Gide's suggestion that the NRF give a large banquet in his honor.[131] Gaston pressed the idea repeatedly, but Proust never responded.

The day following the announcement the remaining copies of *Within a Budding Grove* sold out. Proust was furious with Gallimard on learning that there were no more copies available, though the publisher had admitted a week earlier that the stock was quite low.[132]

Letters of congratulation arrived by the hundreds; within three days Proust received 886. Louis de Robert wrote, "Bravo, cher Marcel. The surprise increases my joy. Now you are famous." Bernard Grasset sent his "most affectionate congratulations. I don't need to tell you to what degree I share the joy of your friends and admirers." He regretted only that he had not been the one to publish Proust's "beautiful book."[133] With Colette's congratulations came the promise to publish immediately in *Le Matin*—if Proust could cut thirty lines—a page describing the Narrator's stay in Venice.[134] Colette had been holding the excerpt since September; now Proust's sudden fame inspired her to publish it. Jacques Porel came on his mother's behalf to ask what Proust would like as a present to express her happiness over the award.[135] Marcel requested the photograph of Réjane dressed as the prince de Sagan, an androgynous vision that thrilled him. The actress signed the picture, "Homage from a Prince, Admiration from an artist, Friendship from a friend."[136]

On December 12 Léon Daudet published a front-page article in the *Action française:* "A New and Powerful Novelist, Marcel Proust." Daudet wrote that since the creation of the Académie Goncourt in 1903, "we have not, in my opinion, crowned a work as vigorous, as new, as full of riches." He had already "read these 440 pages twice. One regrets on closing the book that there are not 880 pages." Daudet placed Proust among the best *moralistes* and chroniclers of the human heart, such as Saint-Évremond, La Bruyère, La Rochefoucauld, and novelists such as Meredith and Sterne. In her congratulatory note, Anna de Noailles placed Proust in the first rank of France's greatest novelists: "Dear friend . . . we are reading, rereading, interpreting your works, comparing you to Balzac, Stendhal." Daudet's article had "expressed well and in magnificent terms the miracle that you are."[137]

Daudet's opinion of the excellent work done by the Académie Goncourt was not widely shared. Between 1914 and 1918 all the Prix Goncourt had been awarded to war novels.[138] In 1919 many critics and four members of the Académie Goncourt believed that *Les Croix de bois* was the best of the genre and clearly more deserving than a lengthy book about young girls in bloom, apparently the work of a wealthy aging dilettante who had never served a day during the war, not even at a desk job. Critics agreed that Dorgelès had written an outstanding war novel.[139] As soon as Proust's prize was announced, journalists began attacking the decision. On December 11 Gérard Bauer, in *L'Écho de Paris*, noted that Marcel Proust was neither young nor poor, though it was true that he had come late to literature, "at his leisure and with a sort of attentive dilettantism." Bauer complimented certain aspects of Proust's novel but lamented his being chosen over Dorgelès. *Les Croix de bois* was "a human story, moving and true, of perfect and profound beauty." Proust's defenders also made themselves heard. Rivière published, on the same day as Bauer's essay, an article in *Excelsior* in which he said Proust's novel was the most important "monument" of psychological analysis since Saint-Simon's *Mémoires*.[140]

Immediately following the announcement that Proust had won the Prix Goncourt, some thirty articles on the novel appeared. By the end of January commentators would have written more than one hundred articles on *Within a Budding Grove*.[141] Proust understood the value of negative criticism, even as he abhorred it, and he explained to Souday that though the attacks were somewhat humiliating, if it brought him readers, he preferred such attention to "all honors."[142]

Jean Binet-Valmer, a conservative critic and militarist, praised elements of Proust's work but thought it was "prewar." He would have favored giving the Prix Goncourt to *Swann's Way* in 1913 but blamed the Académie Goncourt for passing over Dorgelès's patriotic novel for one whose morality appeared suspect. Proust wrote Binet-Valmer that he was eager to read Dorgelès's novel once his sight improved: "Since I have not been well enough to go see an optometrist, I'm going to buy all kinds of glasses, and if I succeed in finding the right lenses, I will read . . . *Les Croix de bois*."[143]

Proust dispatched Céleste to buy glasses, instructing her "to bring back a selection of spectacles with the lenses already in, for him to try." When she hinted that an eye examination might be in order, he said that it would take too long. "Just bring me the most ordinary kind there is—steel rims will do." Céleste returned with a dozen or so glasses in steel frames. He tried them, chose a few that improved his vision and told Céleste to keep them all. The ones that suited him best remained on his bedside table.[144]

On December 12 Dorgelès won the Prix Fémina. In the controversy over the Prix Goncourt selection, Dorgelès's publisher Albin Michel saw an opportunity to increase sales. He had bands printed and placed around each copy of *Les Croix de bois* that read "Prix Goncourt: Roland Dorgelès. *Les Croix de bois*," and in finer print, "four votes out of ten. Winner of the Prix Vie Heureuse." Albin Michel also ran this text as advertisements in various newspapers.[145] Proust noticed Dorgelès's publisher was taking better advantage of the Prix Goncourt than was Gallimard.

Less than a week after winning the prize, Proust asked Céleste to telephone the NRF and express his amazement that there were no more books in stock. A few days later, he sent Marie to bookstores, looking for copies of *Within a Budding Grove*. There were none; nor did the merchants know when they would receive any. He sent Gallimard an "urgent" letter, informing him of the situation, which Proust said made him weep. As to the misleading advertisements suggesting that Dorgelès had won the Prix Goncourt, Proust found them "rather inelegant."[146]

Gaston replied by return mail, blaming Proust partly for the delay by having waited a week to answer his question about the division of *Swann's Way* and *Within a Budding Grove* into two volumes each.[147] He informed Proust that the day after the prize announcement he had gone to the printer's at Abbeville. The new editions of the first two volumes had been completed in the record time of three working days. To make certain that the delay did not work against them, Gallimard had sent a notice to all Paris bookstores and placed an announcement in the *Bibliographie de France* that the new edition would be in bookstores by the end of the week. Regarding Albin Michel's bands and advertisements, Gallimard said that they were not only inelegant but illegal, and he announced his intention to sue.[148] In May the court ordered Albin Michel to remove all the misleading bands, pay a one hundred–franc fine and two thousand francs in damages, and publish the verdict in two newspapers of the plaintiff's choice. Gallimard used the fines to publicize *Within a Budding Grove*.[149]

In spite of the record time in which Gallimard produced the new editions, Proust remained discontented. The day after Christmas the author again pressed his publisher to secure an English translator. That his Prix Goncourt had been "sabotaged" by Gallimard's negligence did not matter to him, but it could have consequences that would make him unhappy. Proust was thinking of the loss in sales that resulted from his book's going out of print on the day he won the prize. Proust apparently had reservations about Gallimard's new two-volume editions. Although the new format satisfied his wish for a larger font and more inviting pages, he feared that the slightly higher price and the complication of purchasing two volumes might discourage some readers. "Everyone" had told Proust that the Prix Goncourt should produce in rapid succession "thirty printings" of the winning book. Marcel told Gaston that although this figure was no doubt greatly exaggerated, "our" missteps would force a considerable scaling back of their expectations.[150] Proust's confidence in his publisher was rapidly eroding. He did accept Gallimard's objection to Grasset's offer to publish selections from *The Guermantes Way* in a new series of deluxe books. Gaston pointed out that if excerpts were published, the Gallimard volume could not be presented as an "original" first edition. Proust would not be so pliant in the future, especially when larger sums of money were offered.[151]

Paul Souday, who had not reviewed *Within a Budding Grove* because of his wife's recent death, told Proust in mid-December that he would soon devote a column to the book.[152] Anticipating another negative review, Proust wrote the critic. He lamented the confusion caused by his general title, *In Search of Lost Time*, which "perpetuates the misunderstanding between me and my readers, even the most eminent, who believe" that the book was "an unfurling of memories."[153] Proust told Souday that his novel was "so meticulously 'composed' . . . that the last chapter of the last volume was written right after the first chapter of the first volume. Everything in between was written afterward, but long ago. The war made it impossible to have proofs, now illness prevents me from correcting them. Otherwise, critics would have long since finished with me."[154]

Jacques Boulenger, who wrote for the *Opinion*, praised *Within a Budding Grove* as a remarkably rich and concise "psychological novel," saying that what Proust had written would fill fifteen ordinary volumes. Among the work's admirable qualities the critic specified were "the acuity of emotions and impressions, the delicacy and depth of its analyses." Boulenger, however, joined the chorus of those who deplored the absence of "composition, artistry," in the sense of shaping the text into a plot. In France especially, Boulenger observed, "art means choice."[155]

Rosny, who was preparing an article on Proust for *Comœdia*, requested a biographical sketch. Proust sent a long letter, summarizing his career and providing a few details about his lifestyle.[156] Because of his asthma, he explained, for fifteen years "I have lived in bed. I mean entirely in bed." As for his religious life, "I have never been to mass since my first communion, which must have been more than thirty years ago." He referred to his role in the Dreyfus case, of which he remained proud. After reviewing his early works and translations, Proust came to the *Search* and said that he could not remember exactly when he had begun writing it. Only his "unfortunate valet" Nicolas, who died during the war, could have determined the exact date because he "took care of my notebooks." Proust thought that he must have begun his novel "around 1906 and finished it around 1911. When *Swann's Way* appeared in 1913, not only were *Within a Budding Grove, The Guermantes Way* and *Time Regained* written, but also most of *Sodom and Gomorrah*.

But during the war (without altering the novel's conclusion, *Time Regained*) I added something on the war that was well suited to M. de Charlus's character." In the postscript Proust said that after receiving the Prix Goncourt he had received nearly nine hundred congratulatory letters, including "ten from members of the Académie française to whom I did not even send my book. How am I going to manage!"[157] Proust was exaggerating somewhat; the entire Albertine cycle had not been written in 1913. But Proust's essential point was true: the plot, with its quest narrative whereby the end rejoins the beginning after the hero discovers his vocation, had been in place for years.

Rosny's article, which defended the decision of the Académie Goncourt, hailed *Within a Budding Grove* as "a *great* book, such as rarely appears. It teems with treasures, with ingenious images, with fine and original observations; it has flashes of genius." It "will endure after the immense majority of others are completely forgotten. That anyone could reproach us for having been *unfair* in selecting it astonishes me. Marcel Proust is one of our finest choices, one of those of which I am most proud."[158]

At year's end, Boulenger wrote to express his regrets at not having better expressed his high opinion of Proust's "fine book." The critic sought to clarify what he had meant by the lack of composition: "No doubt, your book is marvelously composed according to the laws of your own sensitivity. But it seems to me that it is not according to those that preside over the composition of most" French works. "If you don't find this distinction very clear, don't hold it against me, please, because I boxed a lot before dinner and I am dead tired." Boulenger told Proust that one of his detractors, Jean de Pierrefeu, intended to discuss in the *Journal des débats* "The Case of Marcel Proust. I will answer him in the *Opinion*. . . . So I've become your champion." Boulenger was happy to defend the *Search*, "certainly the most 'original' book published . . . since X time. And I love it with all my heart. Furthermore, it's one of those books that one could not love without taking a keen liking to their authors." Boulenger had charmed the charmer. And Proust was delighted to have a champion who boxed for sport.[159]

Proust had waited six long years for the publication of his novel to resume. With roughly one-third of the work in print, he had won France's major literary award and become famous. With such recognition, he could anticipate, even though many hours of revising remained, a triumphant conclusion to his vast undertaking. This was the moment to enjoy success and to select the best strategy for reaching his goal. But he did nothing to alter his regimen and his dangerous practice of taking drugs in heavy dosages. That December he wrote Robert de Billy that he had not "slept for fifteen minutes" in the previous ten days despite taking a number of depressants and stimulants, of which he listed five, including Veronal and digitalis. On Christmas Eve he wrote Mme Straus, who knew something about drugs, that he took "1.5 grams of Veronal daily without sleeping."[160] His mother's old nightmare had come true: Marcel was addicted to a variety of substances.

28   *The Idea of Death*   ❧

ON JANUARY 1, 1920, PROUST'S ARTICLE "On Flaubert's Style" appeared in the *NRF*.[1] Proust disagreed with Thibaudet's assessment that Flaubert was not a particularly talented writer. The author of the *Search* maintained that Flaubert's use of certain pronouns and verb tenses "had renewed our vision of things almost as much as had Kant." He conceded that Flaubert's use of metaphors and analogies did not measure up to Proust's own standards for writers. Proust believed that "metaphor alone can give a kind of eternity to style and there is perhaps not in all Flaubert a single beautiful metaphor." But any reader who had ever, even for a single day, stepped on board Flaubert's "great rolling sidewalk cannot fail to realize that it is without precedent in literature. Perhaps nothing "touched" Proust more, given his own "modest research," than the mastery with which Flaubert gives "the impression of time." After defending his own work, once again, against the accusations of being formless, of stemming from free associations provoked by "madeleine crumbs dipped in tea," Proust hinted that his "entire theory of art" was based on the phenomenon of involuntary memory, and he named two writers whom he considered his major precursors: Chateaubriand and Gérard de Nerval. Proust referred to the scene in *Les Mémoires d'outre-tombe* in which Chateaubriand, at Montboisier, hears the thrush singing, and suddenly this songbird that he had heard so often in his youth transports him, and the reader along with him, in memory back to Combourg. The bird's song had suddenly moved him back through time and space. Citing a similar example in Nerval, Proust remarked that this great genius could have used one of Proust's titles for nearly all his works: "The Intermittencies of the Heart."[2]

With Proust's burgeoning fame, foreign presses and publishers were curious to know more about the author of what appeared to be a novel of unprecedented scale. In early January, Proust sent Gallimard two photographs that the publisher had requested on behalf of a Mr. Sanborn, who represented American magazines.[3] As Proust attempted to win over the critics who wrote for the major dailies of Paris, he not only exchanged letters with them but often invited them to dinner, either at his bedside or in a private room at the Ritz. These literary pundits included Boulenger, Souday, and Pierrefeu, whose initial articles were decidedly hostile.[4]

Early in the new year, Proust invited Boulenger, along with Pierre de Polignac, Jean de Gaigneron, and Georges Casella, the publisher of *Comœdia,* to dine at his bedside. Boulenger declined, but the others accepted. Henri Rochat was also present, and the small bedroom was filled. The novelist understood that his critics— given the vastness of his novel and the slowness of its publication—might easily believe his narration had no particular goal in view. Without revealing details, he assured them that long ago he had written the conclusion of his novel, which would circle back and connect with the beginning, while resolving the themes sounded in the opening pages. He explained his method of characterization, whose aim was to endow his players with "the movement of life, which means that one only meets characters in my books as one does in life, that is to say one is at first mistaken about them." By underscoring the originality of his method, Proust sought to convince critics not to draw conclusions until they had read the entire *Search,* "this work to which I am sacrificing my pleasures, my health, my life."[5]

Proust thanked Mme Alfred Vallette, alias Rachilde, who had accused him in an article of being a socialite who sought readers in the upper class. Proust observed that choosing society people for many of his characters did not imply that he sought them for readers. "If my work is refined, society people, as regards literature, are the least refined people." He would do better to seek electricians as readers. Far from seeking the Prix Goncourt as she had alleged, he had been approached by members of the Académie Goncourt. Proust must have enjoyed reminding Rachilde that he had been obliged to pay for the publication of *Swann's Way,* which had been declined by the major publishers, including her husband.[6]

Proust's insomnia worsened, and in turn he again increased his dosage of depressants. In mid-January, he wrote Boulenger that he had been unable to sleep, despite having taken three grams of Veronal each evening. Rather than writing letters, he "would do better to correct my proofs. I won't do that either. Playing checkers is my maximum effort."[7]

No longer trusting Gallimard to see that his books remained in stock, Proust sent Odilon to bookstores to look for copies. He found several stores that had no copies; nor could the clerks tell him when delivery was expected. Gallimard assured Proust that there were seven thousand copies in stock and that if bookstores ran out, it was due to their failure to reorder, or to a temporary shipping delay.[8] Proust remained skeptical. A few days later he wrote Gallimard that while Odilon was waiting at the NRF, someone came in to ask for *Within a Budding Grove* and received the astonishing reply that there were no copies. Although Proust was unable to tell his publisher when the proofs of *The Guermantes Way* would be ready, he had reached a conclusion that he knew would please Gallimard: he had abandoned the idea of publishing the remaining volumes at the same time.[9] Gallimard was relieved, primarily because Proust's texts were such a challenge for the printer, not only because huge amounts of lead stayed immobilized while Proust corrected proofs but because of the nearly illegible manuscripts, and proof pages that came back covered with corrections and additions. Proust failed to appreciate how difficult his texts were for the printer, who left blanks for the author to fill in, as Nahmias had done when preparing the typescript of *Swann's Way.*

Gallimard urged Proust not to worry about printer's errors in the second set of proofs for *The Guermantes Way.* Before the final print run, the publisher would go himself, with Rivière, to the printer's and verify that all the corrections had been made. He wondered when Proust could give him the revised text for *Sodom and Gomorrah,* for which Gallimard had earlier sent him the typescript. Concerning the supply of Proust's books in stores, the publisher asked for his trust. Gallimard insisted that the books were never unavailable, no matter what Proust's spies reported.[10] Proust at first declined Gallimard's offer to go to the press and check the proofs, saying that it was too much trouble. In any case, he could not accept the offer because Gallimard refused to accept the compensation Proust offered. Meanwhile, Proust thought the process of correcting proof would advance more rapidly if he could find someone to read his texts aloud to him.[11] Rochat, useless in so many ways, was unable to help with this task because he read poorly in French, making it difficult for Proust to distinguish words and verb tenses.

In February, Gallimard reassured Proust about the constant availability of *Within a Budding Grove.* The publisher had ordered another printing, after which the book would have sold fifteen thousand copies—"a beautiful number," said Gaston, who hoped to sell even more.[12] Gallimard soon reported that the printer was "tormenting" him because the longer Proust kept the proofs the longer the printer's lead remained immobilized. A Proust volume used far more lead than the average book; and paper was still scarce and becoming increasingly expensive. Gallimard feared that if they delayed too long, he might have to raise the price on *The Guermantes Way.*[13]

Rivière's article "Marcel Proust and the Classical Tradition" appeared in the February *NRF.* Jacques had given Proust the proofs to read in January, after writing to say that this article was not the one he dreamed of writing but the best "his brain has allowed him to produce so far." In the essay Rivière compared Proust to Racine, saying that the novelist had renewed the great French classical tradition by examining himself in order to understand others. The *Search* was indeed a "psychological novel, but one imbued with lyricism." In a long letter thanking Rivière, the novelist assured him that "no one could have for you more admiration, gratitude and affection than your Marcel Proust." Proust soon informed Rivière of his intention to dedicate *The Guermantes Way* to Léon Daudet for helping him obtain the Prix Goncourt.[14]

In late winter, Proust offered Rivière financial assistance if he had trouble making ends meet. Rivière, deeply touched, said that he would not hesitate to accept Proust's generous offer, if need be. Jacques's wife was expecting in March, and he worried about the delivery because their first child, a girl now eight, had been delivered by cesarean section. In early March, Proust paid a late afternoon visit to the NRF offices. Rivière, whose health remained fragile, asked whether Robert Proust could recommend a neurologist; he planned to see a specialist immediately after his wife's delivery. On March 11 Rivière announced to Proust the birth of his son Alain, who arrived "in the best possible conditions." Relieved at how well his wife and baby were, he made plans to see Dr. Gustave Roussy in early April. Rivière hoped that the neurologist recommended by Dr. Proust would "bring me out of this awful languor in which I am stuck."[15]

As Proust wrote to friends or attempted to answer the hundreds of congratulatory letters he had received, his fears regarding his own health became a constant theme. Though made miserable by his usual ailments and deplorable use of stimulants and depressants, the writer worked hard correcting proofs. Proust gave his own race against time and preoccupation with death to the Narrator, who discovers his vocation as a writer at the same time he realizes that he has grown old. "The idea of death took up permanent residence within me in the way that love sometimes does. Not that I loved death, I abhorred it. But after a preliminary stage at which, no doubt, I thought about it from time to time as one does about a woman with whom one is not yet in love, its image adhered now to the most profound layer of my mind, so completely that I could not give my attention to anything without that thing first traversing the idea of death . . . the idea of death kept me company as faithfully as the idea of my self."[16]

In mid-March, Proust received a letter from Mme Straus. She had intended to write three months earlier but had fallen seriously ill and spent seven weeks in bed. She told him that when he won the Prix Goncourt, Montesquiou had wanted to send his congratulations, but because the count's letter praising *Within a Budding Grove* had gone unanswered, he could not, "given his age, his correctness, etc., write a second letter before receiving a reply." Instead, he asked Mme Straus to congratulate Marcel on his behalf. Having been "foolish enough to recover," she wanted to keep her promise to Montesquiou.[17]

Proust answered her immediately, saying how distressed he was to know that she had been so ill. "What a blessing that you have recovered!" He wanted to come and sing hosannas to her for escaping death. He also gave Mme Straus—survivor of so many Proustian furniture sales—the good news that he had discovered twelve forgotten Royal Dutch shares, which had allowed Céleste to sport some very ugly feathers from a bird of paradise on her hat. Proust dutifully sent Montesquiou a brief, dry note, claiming that his brush with "Death" had prevented his writing sooner.[18]

Hauser kept Marcel's New Year's letter—the one in which the novelist had said that he could "not get used to things that end"—for three months before answering it in a rather distant tone. Lionel preferred to drop their debate about Proust's powers of psychological analysis, which was pointless in any case, because the financial adviser was talking about psychology as applied to practical matters, whereas Proust applied his remarkable analytical skills to personality, motivation, and understanding one's profound self. In an April letter, Hauser repeated his accusation of Proust's behaving like a spoiled child. The accountant shared Montesquiou's view that Proust's fame had gone to his head; unlike Montesquiou, Hauser told him so: "I fear, my dear Marcel, that glory has somewhat intoxicated you." After they exchanged a few more letters, Hauser relented a little by offering to examine Proust's account at the London County Bank and bring his financial statement up to date. Although their friendship might have seemed to have survived all the misunderstandings, too many acrimonious words had been exchanged for either man to enjoy corresponding as in the past.[19]

Rivière had his first appointment with Dr. Roussy in early April and was "delighted" with the man, in whom he had "complete confidence." Roussy, because of his friendship with Proust, would not accept a fee for his services. Rivière, obviously buoyed by the consultation, failed to appreciate Proust's state of fatigue and urged him to write an article on Sainte-Beuve for the July issue of the NRF.[20] Proust declined, while holding out the tantalizing offer of novellas, presumably excerpts from the *Search* that he could shape into anthology-like pieces. Proust soon told Rivière that he must devote what little energy he had to completing the novel.[21]

Late on a rainy spring evening, Proust attempted to call on Tronche. Gustave heard the bell ring, but incredulous that anyone would call at such an hour, especially in bad weather, he ignored the sound. Proust, who waited for a while in the rain, may have wanted to thank Tronche for the ten thousand–franc check he had received as a partial payment on royalties due.[22]

On April 16 Gallimard sent the second corrected proofs of *The Guermantes Way*, part 1, with a typescript of the author's additions, from which the printer insisted on working. The workers who composed on monotype had begun to refuse copy that was too difficult to read because they were paid per thousand letters. The time they spent trying to decipher Proust's handwriting lowered their wages considerably.[23] Gallimard asked Proust to fill in a few blanks in these proofs, passages where no one had been able to determine what he had written.

Proust told Morand that he was being urged to present himself as a candidate for one of the three vacant seats at the Académie française. Were he to do so, "it must be now, because after *Sodom*, it will no longer be possible." Proust sounded out acquaintances who were members of the august body and sent them copies of his books. Henri de Régnier was caught off guard when Marcel broached his possible candidacy. In a letter to Régnier, Proust admitted that his candidacy presented "numerous drawbacks." His contacts with members he knew, such as Gabriel Hanotaux and Pierre Loti, were old and tenuous. Of course, if he became a candidate, he would visit them as well as the others. He told Régnier, rather naïvely, that he thought he could count on the support of the war hero General Mangin, "a *close* friend of my brother . . . and a friend of my books."[24]

Régnier replied tactfully but advised Proust not to seek election at that time. Proust said that he could not promise to follow the poet's advice, but he identified two unsurmountable obstacles to his candidacy: his close friendship with Léon Daudet, who had many enemies in official circles, and the nature of his forthcoming volumes on homosexuality.[25] He would be averse to changing the nature of his books for a seat in the Académie française. His original intention had been to write about homosexuality in an objective way. "But to my great chagrin" the fate of the characters led him "to write a sort of pamphlet, a sermon, very different from the impartial depiction I had intended. I see in this a literary drawback about which I can do nothing." If Régnier informed members of the Académie française that Proust depicted the dangers and difficulties of homosexuality, it would reassure them. "I add that if condemnation breaks through everywhere, on the other hand, the depiction is not insipid, far from it. And this, doubtless, is not very academic although fairly religious." If Régnier thought his election possible, Proust would engage Guiche, who had excellent contacts, to lobby on his behalf. Although Proust had not seen "Masters" like Anatole France for twenty years, he was certain that they viewed him kindly: "I don't know if all these puzzle pieces of friendship add up to a vote." Régnier again cautioned Proust not to put himself forward, observing that he had waited too late to launch a successful campaign; members were already committed to other candidates. Régnier advised him to wait for the next vacant seat and to announce his candidacy immediately. As a gesture of his friendship, Régnier offered his vote and support should Proust become a candidate.[26]

In early May, Proust called on Maurice Barrès late one evening to solicit his support. Barrès did not care for Proust's works; he had only "leafed through *Swann's Way*, whose style, content and characters he deprecated."[27] When Proust called at approximately ten P.M., Barrès was outraged at Proust's presumption and his appearance. Fulminating later to his secretary, Barrès expressed his annoyance that Proust, whom he had not seen "in twenty years," would knock on his door at such an "impossible hour." And "what a man! Muffled up in an enormous scarf, unshaven, looking exactly like someone who had just climbed out of bed" at an hour when normal people were retiring to theirs. The academician wondered aloud why Proust had "risked dying en route" to come and "ask me if I didn't think it was time for him to respond to the wishes of those who were calling him to the Académie française. What a singular idea! No one, there, is expecting anyone!" Barrès was surprised at Proust's "exaggerated opinion (and yet quite legitimate) of his own importance."[28]

Proust had little choice but to follow Régnier's advice and wait. Still, he hesitated, weighing an immediate move against a future one. He asked Rivière whether a seat in the Académie française would be good for his books and for the NRF. Jacques, who understood that Proust's stature rendered such distinctions meaningless, assured the novelist that his work was "too vigorous, too real, too true" for members of the Academy. "Most of them cannot understand you; their slumber is too deep."[29] Marcel was not to fulfill his father's prophecy and become a member of the Académie française.

Natalie Clifford Barney, a wealthy American expatriate who lived openly as a lesbian, sent Proust a copy of her recent book *Pensées d'une amazone* (Thoughts of an Amazon), bearing the inscription (in French): "To Marcel Proust, whose understanding merits this unexpurgated copy—between pages 72 and 73— . . . where he will find himself mentioned." In this passage, she writes about the amorous relationship between Socrates and Alcibiades, as described in Plato's *The Symposium*. Proust wrote immediately to thank her for the book, which was "ravishing and profound and puts mine to shame."[30] Thus began an exchange of letters that continued for some time in a fruitless attempt to arrange a rendezvous. Had Proust met Miss Barney, he would presumably have asked many questions of this outspoken proponent of Gomorrah.

Proust sent a brief description of himself and his career to the Italian bibliophile and historian Alberto Lumbroso, who like many of Proust's foreign admirers was eager to know about the man who wrote such extraordinary prose. In evoking his youth Proust spoke of the "great indulgence" from which he had "benefited and which should have," without his bad health and extreme laziness, "encouraged me to work." He reviewed his early stories and the volume into which they were collected, saying that he did not repudiate them but remembered vaguely that they contain the "embryo of today's books"; reading them again, though, as enjoyable as that might be, would also "pain me because then I had a certain gift for style." He started writing again "twenty-five years later," when he was too sick to do anything else. Although his looks had not changed and he did not have a single gray hair, he had lost all the "suppleness of the craft." Nor did he "share at all Francis Jammes's opinion who saw in *Swann* the model of the most perfect language he knows since Tacitus!"[31]

It is surprising that Proust misrepresented his career, for he had never really stopped writing. By glossing over the "twenty-five years" that separated *Pleasures and Days* and his first drafts of the *Search*, Proust left out the abandoned *Jean Santeuil*—more important in the development of his themes and style than *Pleasures and Days*—his Ruskin translations, his articles, and his pastiches. The biographical sketch describes the Narrator's career more accurately than Proust's. His hero, when young, wrote only one article for the *Figaro* and then floundered for years before discovering his vocation late in life. Proust, in his final years, often adopted his protagonist's persona. At the end of the letter to Lumbroso, Proust anticipated his own legend. After referring to his pages on Italy, Proust explained that his travels were now limited to his imagination because he had cloistered himself "in this extraterrestrial place which is my cork-lined room, whose blinds are always closed, and where the only light is electric." Not only had Proust not spent twenty-five years without writing anything, he was no longer surrounded by cork.

The Enchanter

Although only two volumes of the *Search* had appeared, readers and critics began to speak of the creation of a new world. Abel Bonnard wrote Proust, saying that his pages captured the very essence of the "most fleeting emotions," that the completed novel would contain "your own universe where you will reign like an Enchanter."[32] Blanche, in the *Revue de Paris*, likened the *Search* to a "rising whirlwind" that surprises and changes the world as we know it," creating "a public granary that will nourish other writers."[33] The painter wrote, "There is nothing like it in the plastic arts."[34] Proust, who recognized an excellent blurb, sent this quotation to Rivière, urging him to use it in the forthcoming issue of the *NRF*. Rivière declined, saying that he had received the quotation too late and did not have room to insert it. Proust replied that his excuses were preposterous, but, as usual with Jacques, he showed remarkable patience and forbearance.[35]

Proust finished the proofs for *The Guermantes Way*, part 1, in two days and on May 18 gave them to Tronche to deliver to Gallimard. Gaston, noting the rapidity with which the proofs had returned, told Proust that this was a "good sign" for his health and for the NRF.[36] Gallimard sent the proofs on to the printer, instructing him to use the greatest care in making corrections. In spite of Proust's refusal to accept help, Gallimard intended to go to the printer's for a final reading to make certain that all the author's changes had been made. By May 20 the deluxe edition of *Within a Budding Grove* was finished, though it would not be available to subscribers until the end of July.

The Schiffs, on their way south to Roquebrune, stopped briefly in Paris and met Proust. Marcel enjoyed telling the story of how Schiff, after meeting him, would stop his friends on the streets of London to tell them that the most remarkable thing he and Violet had seen in Paris was Marcel Proust: "I was very happy to hear this, but then Schiff added 'because he's the only man we've ever seen who dines in a fur overcoat.'"[37] Nothing else is known about the first encounter. The Schiffs returned to Paris in the spring of 1922 to become better acquainted with the writer whose books enthralled them.[38]

Rivière had taken the *Guermantes* proofs with him on the train to Cenon, a quiet little town near Bordeaux, where, following doctor's orders, he would rest for the month of May. In a letter to Proust, Jacques told him that as the train rolled south, he had read the proofs, "with irresistible emotion, enthusiasm, transport. You are a great writer." Rivière found the opening pages of the new volume "even more poetical than psychological." He asked whether he had already told Proust, "this will no doubt amuse you, that André Breton, the head Dadaist, came to help us correct your proofs, and declared to me an intense admiration for you, based precisely on the poetic treasures he discovered in your work."[39]

A group of Proust's friends, led by Hahn, began work to obtain the Légion d'honneur for Proust by July 14, the French national holiday. Although they did not meet that deadline, they succeeded before year's end. In a May letter regarding contacts to be made for the decoration, Reynaldo told Marcel that Lucien wanted him to know that "he loves you despite your total abandonment." Proust, tremendously preoccupied with correcting proof and courting critics, appeared to neglect his old friends.[40] His health and the race to finish kept him from seeing Reynaldo, the person "I love most in the world." To a friend, he described Hahn as "another me."[41]

In May, Proust received a letter from Colette, along with the proofs of *Chéri*, her latest novel, due out soon and destined to become one of her most famous works. And what about his books? Colette hoped to be fortunate enough to have a new "Marcel Proust for summer vacation. That and the sea together, what bathing!"[42] Proust believed that there were many who, like Colette, wanted new books for vacation reading. By midsummer he expressed his annoyance to Gallimard regarding the publication date, telling him that if *The Guermantes Way*, part 1, could not be placed on sale by August 1, he would prefer to wait until after October 1, when Parisians returned to the city.[43] Gallimard agreed to a fall publication.

On June 14 Princesse Soutzo invited Proust to her box at the Opéra for the dress rehearsal of Shakespeare's *Antony and Cleopatra*, translated by André Gide and set to music by Florent Schmitt. Ida Rubinstein, whose exotic beauty had captivated audiences at the Ballets Russes, had the starring role. Gide also had offered Proust tickets and suggested that he escort Miss Barney or anyone he liked.[44] During the intermission, Proust learned that Réjane had just died. He rushed to rue Laurent-Pichat, where Jacques Porel let him in.[45] Two days later Marcel wrote Jacques that he grieved for Réjane as though he had lost a member of his own family. Porel, touched by Proust's kind gesture and words, gave Proust the cameo that Anatole France had presented to Réjane so long ago at the première of *Le Lys rouge*. Proust insisted on returning the cameo, saying that the souvenir he would keep would be one he could not "misplace or lose," the memory "of those sublimely atrocious evenings" when Porel's mother had incarnated Germinie Lacerteux.[46] In July, Porel asked Proust, through Gallimard, to write an article about his mother for the *NRF*. Again Proust's "terrible state of health" and his intensive work on the *Search* forced him to decline.[47]

On June 26 Proust informed Gallimard that *The Guermantes Way*, part 1, would be followed by *The Guermantes Way*, part 2, and *Sodom and Gomorrah*, part 1, published together in the same volume. *Sodom and Gomorrah*, part 1, would be a relatively short text. He predicted that two or three months after the publication of *Guermantes* 1 they should be ready to publish the next volume, concluding *The Guermantes Way* and introducing the reader to the cities of the plain. That day Proust sent Gallimard another letter, which began well—if not quite sincerely—by expressing his close attachment to the NRF and Gide. Then came the reproaches directed at Gallimard, whom Proust accused of avoiding him: he did not know where his publisher lived; he seldom found Gallimard at his office, and so on. Proust made the practical suggestion that the back cover of the forthcoming volume be used to announce the December publication of *The Guermantes Way*, part 2, and *Sodom and Gomorrah*, part 1.[48] In fact, Gallimard announced more "cautiously" that *The Guermantes Way*, part 2, *Sodom and Gomorrah*, parts 1 and 2, and *Time Regained* were in press.[49]

Proust wrote to Rivière, accusing the NRF of having failed to publicize *Pastiches et mélanges*, which had "fallen flat on its face." He also announced his intention of giving excerpts from *The Guermantes Way* to Belgian and American reviews, "since the *NRF* had not asked him for them." And he was still unhappy with what he believed was Gallimard's procrastination in signing a contract for an English translation of his novel, observing pointedly that his "daily" arguments in favor of "an English translation had resulted in . . . a Spanish translation." Proust referred to Gallimard's recent signing of a contract with a Spanish publisher for *Swann's Way* and *Within a Budding Grove*.[50] When Rivière read Proust's letter he was beside himself. He answered from Cenon that he had written five or six times requesting excerpts from *The Guermantes Way*, but Proust had said that they were promised to Grasset. Rivière did not mince words, telling Proust, "You are appallingly unfair!" All Rivière's work, articles, and blurbs to launch *The Guermantes Way* "should mean one thing: Proust is a great writer. Proust is our only great writer."[51]

In June, Proust asked Tronche to send half of the page proofs to Ezra Pound at *The Dial* and the other half to the *Revue latine*, published in Bruges, Paris, and Rome. Pound wrote Gallimard, in nearly impeccable French, to acknowledge receipt of Proust's pages: "Quel enchantement que il [*sic*] y a dans cette prose" (What enchantment there is in this prose).[52] An excerpt from *The Guermantes Way,* "Saint-Loup: A Portrait," appeared in *The Dial* in October 1921.[53]

With the deluxe edition of *Within a Budding Grove* ready to go on sale at the end of July, Proust drew up a list of his wealthy friends, including the Schiffs, who might be interested in acquiring the rare, expensive book. Designed to appeal to collectors, the volume sold for three hundred francs and included a photogravure of the Blanche portrait, fragments of the manuscript, and corrected proof sheets.[54] Berry, who invited Proust to accompany him to Venice in September—"Doesn't that tempt you?"—subscribed to three copies of the deluxe edition. Proust expressed his astonishment at Walter's generosity: "I don't know how to thank you for this 'folly.' " Marcel found the photogravure in the deluxe edition "hideous," saying that it made him look as if he had "a black, hairy nose." He asked Berry not to repeat his complaints about the NRF, because despite numerous "faults," the NRF group showed him "many great kindnesses and I know that I am not an easy author."[55] Rivière's chastisement had at least made Proust more discreet.

During the year Proust answered several surveys from newspapers. In the middle of the summer, he replied to two queries from *L'Intransigeant.* If he were obliged to work as a manual laborer, what sort of work would he choose? Proust answered that he would take "the very same one that he currently practiced: that of writer. And if paper became absolutely unavailable, I would, I think, become a baker. It is honorable to give men their daily bread."[56] A short time later, the newspaper asked what he thought about lending libraries that would charge for rental. Proust answered in a humorous tone, saying that those who were very poor and those who were very rich were unable to buy books, the first because of poverty, the latter because of avarice. Such libraries would only regularize an existing situation and create the "unheard of innovation of being required to return the books on loan." He concluded by observing that when one's taste for something was whetted, the result was more often "abuse than restraint; just as taking riding lessons made one want to have his own horse, by dint of renting books, perhaps one would finally buy some if not read them."[57] Back in February, Proust had given his answer to a survey from the *Opinion* about which paintings, limiting the choice to eight, should be selected for a French Tribune at the Louvre. Proust named the paintings he would choose in a letter to Vaudoyer, not intending that his list be published. Vaudoyer, an editor at the paper, printed Proust's choices on February 28. The novelist's selection included several works by Chardin, indicating his great admiration for that painter: *Portrait de Chardin, Portrait de Mme*

Chardin, and *Nature morte.* To these he added "Millet's *Le Printemps,* Manet's *Olympia,* an unspecified Renoir or *La Barque de Dante,* or Corot's *La Cathédral de Chartres;* Watteau's *L'Indifférent* or *L'Embarquement.*"[58] When Proust saw Blanche's list, he noted that it was remarkably similar to his. Each had selected works by Watteau, Millet, Chardin, Corot, and Manet.[59]

Rivière persisted in asking Proust for more articles. In late July, while planning the September issue, he reminded Proust that he had given the *NRF* nothing since the essay on Flaubert. The editor feared that if "your silence continues, people will think you have withdrawn your collaboration from me." Rivière was reserving the lead story for him.[60] Marcel answered a few days later, saying that the *Revue de Paris* wanted to publish excerpts from *The Guermantes Way.*[61] He told Rivière again that after he finished the novel he intended to write critical articles for the *NRF.*[62]

One consequence of the Prix Goncourt was Proust's appointment to a number of honorary committees and panels. At the end of July he was asked to serve on the selection committee of a new American institution, the Blumenthal Foundation, created by Florence Blumenthal. The purpose of the committee was to encourage French thought and art by awarding ten stipends of twelve thousand francs each. Among Proust's distinguished fellow panelists were Anna de Noailles, Maurice Barrès, Henri Bergson, Edmond Jaloux, André Gide, Paul Valéry, and Robert de Flers.[63]

Proust missed the first board meeting. Knowing that Rivière neglected his own writings while struggling to edit the *NRF* and support his family, Proust asked whether he would like to be considered for one of the Blumenthal stipends. If so, Proust would speak to the other committee members on his behalf. Rivière, touched by such kindness, replied that the prize "would be extremely advantageous" for him. Proust promptly wrote to other committee members, stressing Rivière's severely damaged health and true promise as a writer, citing his book *L'Allemand* and his essays on Rimbaud and Russian music.[64]

On the last Thursday in September, Proust stayed up all day in order to attend the five o'clock meeting of the Blumenthal committee. He was so shaky on arriving that he nearly "fell first on Henri Bergson and then on René Boylesve!" With Proust's sponsorship, Jacques Rivière was awarded a stipend. Immediately after the meeting, Proust went to announce the news to Rivière, who was profoundly grateful. During the visit Proust asked Rivière to insert five lines in an article for the *NRF* about Lucien Daudet's new book, *Évidences.* Rivière refused. Proust did not hold this against his protégé, because, as he explained to a friend, Rivière was not ungrateful; he simply held a different opinion and "he is a Conscience."[65]

After Proust made a sales pitch about the deluxe edition to the Schiffs, those "charming friends of my thought," they ordered a copy. Even so, Schiff sent Proust a letter explaining his misgivings about such editions, which he found "artistically unjustifiable." Proust, clearly annoyed, wrote back and asked whether Schiff thought that "authors should have to starve to death?"[66] Schiff made matters worse in a subsequent letter, showing himself to be something of a snob by saying, "It bothers me to know that any idiot can, by paying 300 francs, lead himself to believe he loves your pages as much as I do." Schiff also held the taste of his fellow Englishmen in rather low esteem. "The English public that wants good literature is very small, especially for good French literature, and that public, the most learned, reads those books in French." Schiff did not believe that translations of the *Search* would earn much money. "There is also the important question of the translator. I know no one except myself who would do a suitable translation." He suggested translating *Un Amour de Swann* first as a "trial balloon."[67] Schiff was wrong, of course, in his pessimistic forecast about the success of the *Search* in English, but right in seeing that *Un Amour de Swann,* which could be read as a complete story, with its remarkably fine analysis of jealous love, would become the most popular portion of Proust's novel.

Proust complained frequently to Paul Morand, another Gallimard author, about what he perceived as negligence on Gaston's part. Morand, not always objective in his own assessments of the publisher, often fed Proust's discontentment with erroneous information about Gallimard's business practices. Toward the end of August, Proust grumbled to Paul that he had not received any copies of *The Guermantes Way,* part 1, ready since August 17, nor had Gallimard reprinted *Within a Budding Grove.*[68] In a subsequent letter Proust said he was considering canceling his contract with the NRF. "But at present it's only a desire." Then he went on to say that "death is a terrible thing. For the past week I have been offered all the situations that I would have loved only a year ago. But now death." On an equally somber note, at the end of a letter to Berry, who was enjoying his Venetian holiday, Proust wrote that "death," with which he lived, "prevents everything."[69]

On August 31 Proust began reading *The Guermantes Way,* part 1, and discovered numerous errors that, as he complained to Gallimard, "rendered the sentences unintelligible," and "faced with my dishonor I understood why Vatel threw himself on his sword."[70] The reference to François Vatel was one that any Frenchman would understand. Vatel was steward to the Grand Condé, who during the reign of Louis XIV distinguished himself as the victor in the battle of Rocroi against the Spaniards. When the king visited Condé's château de Chantilly, Vatel ran out of roast meat. Then panic seized the steward when he realized that fresh fish would not be delivered on time for Friday's dinner. Believing himself irrevocably dishonored, Vatel committed suicide.[71] Proust was not quite ready to throw himself on his sword, but he insisted on preparing an errata because the pages were not yet bound. He blamed himself for not having insisted on additional proofs, to which he had a "right," and for having said, "Let's go with what we've got!" Still, he was astounded that with all the reading by Rivière and the "charming Dadaist" Breton, blatant errors had so often gone unnoticed by such trained eyes. The proofreaders had failed to see that each time the name of Proust's fictional novelist Bergotte occurred, the printer had put Bergson.[72]

Within a few days Proust regained his aplomb and told Gallimard not to be upset about the many errors. He had gotten over the disappointment in a few hours and was resigned to inserting the errata. Marcel turned to other problems: he was eager to have the proofs for *The Guermantes Way,* part 2, and he reproached Gallimard again for not having sold the rights for an English translation.[73] Someone had told Proust that the translation was being held up because Gallimard had demanded fifty thousand francs for the rights. Defending himself, Gallimard told Proust that such a sum was impossibly high. Like a lawyer preparing a brief, the publisher outlined his contacts with English and American publishers, enclosed copies of correspondence, giving figures that were in line with other contracts for foreign translations. Ezra Pound was one editor with whom Gallimard was discussing rights and whose letter confirmed that the NRF's terms for Proust's novel were reasonable.[74] Then Gallimard invited Proust to set his figure. "I have but one goal, to satisfy you."[75] In his letters and conversations, Gaston constantly expressed his friendship and devotion to Marcel and his eagerness to see him whenever possible. The novelist may have been "the most complicated man in Paris," but Gallimard never doubted the importance of Proust's book.

On September 5, when Proust attended a dinner at Princesse Elizabeth Bibesco's, he had an earache, which marked the beginning of a painful infection. One of the Quiès balls he used to stifle noises had become lodged within his ear, and he had been able to remove only a portion of it. Dr. Gagey, his former neighbor at boulevard Haussmann, examined Proust's ear and called in a specialist. The otolaryngologist, as Proust explained to a friend, "miraculously turned out to be the famous Alexis Wicart, who had treated Reynaldo Hahn and Georges Clemenceau." Wicart, who found the infected ear entirely blocked, cleared it out as best he could and then left on vacation. Marcel wrote his brother: "Unfortunately," Wicart "informed me that he would return to finish his work, which seems to be not only unblocking my ear, but to cure me of asthma, etc. He is charming, but too intelligent for me. Ah! how restful are doctors like good old Bize, who hasn't auscultated me in ten years."[76]

Lucien, who had read his advance copy of *The Guermantes Way* twice, wrote to express his wonderment at his friend's accomplishment. Proust's "projection" of what seemed to be every human thought and emotion "caused a special happiness: one no longer had the impression of reading." He congratulated the author on his "incredible sense of dialogue," citing examples, as Montesquiou had done. "One could make of this third volume an entire book of maxims," the "most beautiful" ever written, and a "psychological manual more complex than all the others, a totally new artistic 'doctrine' and the most amusing of all the novels" ever written. Lucien was awed. "How is it that you possess all this too, in addition to all the rest?" He continued in this vein, saying that Proust had encapsulated life, accomplishing even more than Balzac and Stendhal. "You have re-created the novel, and you are the greatest novelist who has ever lived in any epoch in any country. Because you have everything that all the others had and, in addition, everything that is yours. It's magnificent." Lucien saw, as Gide had, the challenge Proust posed for other writers: "But you are a monster, you exhaust every subject. How can you expect anyone else to write a novel?"[77]

On September 21 Proust wrote to inform Gallimard that he had completed the errata for the first three-fourths of *The Guermantes Way*, part 1. He had spent his time looking for printer's mistakes rather than working on the preface for Morand's *Tendres Stocks*. Then, having found more than two hundred errors, he stopped because his eyes had grown too weak. Nonetheless, he reminded Gaston of his eagerness to begin work on the proofs for *The Guermantes Way*, part 2.[78]

A Vocation

When it was announced that Marcel Proust, "a man of letters," would be awarded the Légion d'honneur, he received a new stack of congratulatory letters. Henri Bergson told his "dear cousin" that *Within a Budding Grove* was "the worthy continuation" of *Swann's Way*: "Rarely has introspection been carried so far. It's a direct and continuous vision of inner reality." Artist Paul Helleu, ready to embark for New York, sent congratulations and said that he had always wanted to do an etching of Proust's head, "but you never come to see me anymore." From his vacation spot at Le Piquey near Bordeaux, Cocteau wrote, "On you—the red ribbon has meaning. I embrace you." As usual, Walter Berry managed to be charming and witty. Having noticed that Édouard Branly was being honored in the same group as Proust, Berry wrote that the "government has brought honor on itself by decorating two great Frenchmen—the only truly modern novelist and the inventor of the wireless, Branly. Basically, you both practice the same trade, but I prefer your waves!"[79] When Proust learned that Berry had ordered two more deluxe copies of his book, for a total of five, he teased the American about being so wildly extravagant and threatened to give him a legal guardian.[80]

On learning that he was to receive the Légion d'honneur, Marcel confided to his brother his fears that the committee might think the *Sodom and Gomorrah* volumes were "pro-sodomy and pro-gomorrah books," whereas they were the opposite. It "would be truly ridiculous, if having been decorated, I were subjected to disciplinary actions for writing indecent books." While he certainly did not "disdain honorary distinctions," they were "secondary"; the only thing that mattered was the work.[81] He told Robert that *The Guermantes Way,* part 1, would be published at the end of October, and, although the next installment was only half as long as the others, "I am certain you will not read it."[82]

Robert answered from his vacation spot in Stresa, on the western shore of Lake Maggiore, saying that he had brought along with him, as he put it, Marcel's "Girls in Bloom" (*À l'ombre des jeunes filles en fleurs*). Contrary to Marcel's assumption, Robert had read much of the volume and was finishing it in a "hotel very like 'Balbec.'" He expressed his joy that Marcel was to receive the Légion d'honneur and promised that he would come to congratulate and embrace his brother.[83]

In mid-October, Cartier's notified Proust of a delivery they wished to make. René Gimpel had commissioned a magnificent Légion d'honneur cross studded with diamonds. Proust thanked Gimpel for his munificence, which moved him more than he could say: "Dear friend, you cannot imagine the hell my life has become because of my health" and "bad hygienic habits." As for the "ravishing cross," Proust wondered where he could hide it; he would have no occasion to wear it, because he never attended "official receptions." Marcel requested that Robert, a longtime member of the Légion d'honneur, be authorized to bestow the cross on him. Moved by his brother's thoughtful gesture, Robert obtained permission to present the award. On Sunday, November 7, at the Proustian hour of ten in the evening, Robert placed the red ribbon bearing the cross around Marcel's neck.[84] Robert stayed and dined at Marcel's bedside, where the two brothers evoked memories of their parents and childhood.[85]

As publication of the next installment drew near, Proust tried to prepare critics for the course his novel would take in the opening section of *Sodom and Gomorrah*. Léon Daudet's article announcing a new book by Proust appeared on the front page of *Action française* on October 8. Proust alerted Paul Souday that in the next volume things were going to "take a bad turn through no fault of mine. My characters don't turn out well; I must follow them where their serious defects or vices lead me."[86] Proust was capable, depending on the person and concern he addressed, of presenting his treatment of homosexuality as condemnatory, sympathetic, objective, or exculpatory.

On October 10 Proust wrote André Chaumeix, editor of the *Revue de Paris*, and offered him the preface he had written for Morand's volume containing three novellas. Proust told the editor that the preface was in part a response to Anatole France's article on Stendhal, in which his former mentor had made some remarks about style and French literature with which Proust disagreed.[87] Marcel mentioned how sick he was. A few days earlier he had caught cold, after which his asthma attacks returned with an "unprecedented violence." Because he was running such a high fever, Dr. Bize gave him "morphine shots, the first in my life," which had "so far only resulted in making me entirely stupefied." He feared that his spasms made his handwriting illegible for Chaumeix. After meeting with Proust at rue Hamelin, Chaumeix agreed to publish the preface in the November 15 issue.

Proust was delighted to learn of a sign of his growing international reputation: readers in various countries, including Holland, Belgium, and England, had founded Marcel Proust Societies. The English Proust club was modeled on the Browning Society. Proust informed a correspondent that his novel "was commented upon in nearly every country (even in China)."[88]

On October 18 Proust sent out the first signed copies of *The Guermantes Way*, part 1, to his friends. Under the printed dedication in Léon's copy, he wrote a few lines to express his "affection" that he had not "dared" include in the printed text lest his friend think him "too familiar." The published dedication was "To Léon Daudet," the author of "so many masterpieces, to the incomparable friend, as a token of gratitude and admiration, M. P."[89] It was a grand Proustification to call Daudet's works masterpieces and a potential ongoing embarrassment to have done so indelibly. But Proust had always prized "tendresse" and the expression of gratitude much more than he feared derision.

On the same day, Proust sent Mme Straus her copy of *The Guermantes Way*. "*Everything* in it that's witty comes from you." She had refused to let him put her name next to her witticisms because this was a novel. He asked her, should she see Montesquiou, to tell him that he had run a high fever for ten days, which had prohibited answering the count's letter. He wanted Montesquiou to appreciate that "I might appear negligent while being fidelity personified."[90]

In his publisher's copy, he wrote: "To my dear Gaston, I hardly suspected when I saw you for the first time . . . that I would one day owe you so much gratitude, and the absurd fidelity that this real and sometimes imaginary cuckold has to the NRF, Affectionately, Marcel Proust."[91] Even his dedication (of this and future volumes) to Gaston contained explicit or barely veiled reproaches.

Proust answered Clément de Maugny's request to preface a slender volume of his wife's drawings. He was eager to accommodate the Maugnys but wondered whether he could write about something "so new for me." Perhaps he could write instead a brief notice for the *Revue hebdomadaire.* It would be pointless to ask the *NRF,* where all he had to do was to recommend someone for them to refuse. Describing how he lived, Marcel told Clément that so much time in bed had fattened him. From time to time he went to the Ritz so that his room could be cleaned. Because he had difficulty speaking, it was painful to dine with friends, and so he often dined alone in a private room, where he corrected proofs. If he took "enough caffeine" beforehand, his speech difficulty would disappear for an hour or two.[92] Proust finally agreed to write a brief preface for Rita de Maugny, whom he greatly admired for her service to France as a nurse in the war against her native Germany. He wrote to tell Rita that, after announcing his "death in Morand's preface," he would use hers to make a kind of "pilgrimage to Lausenette and Maugny." It was regrettable that her illustrations had not been reproduced in color, for this voyage in his mind was inseparable from "the pure tones and perspectives of your landscapes."[93]

On October 22 Gallimard sent Proust a letter to announce that *The Guermantes Way,* part 1, was in bookstores. Anticipating Proust's canvassing, Gallimard had phoned stores throughout Paris to make certain the copies were on the shelves.[94] Critical reception was generally favorable. Still, with the appearance of this volume, which describes the Narrator's entry into the exclusive aristocratic salons of Paris, Proust found himself depicted again as a snob. He immediately launched a counteroffensive. In a letter to Jacques Boulenger, Proust observed that because he had lived from the age of fifteen in the midst of ladies like Mme de Guermantes, he had the "strength to brave in the eyes of those who ignore it the opinion that I am a snob, by depicting snobbery, not from the outside and ironically as would a novelist who was a snob, but from the inside by giving myself the soul of someone who would like to know a duchesse de Guermantes." He admitted to Boulenger that when "excessively fatigued," he occasionally dispensed with inventing and gave his own traits to the Narrator. "But would an author who is a snob . . . say that he desired to know a Mme de Guermantes?" He described "so many different things in his work that truly one cannot think that everything is me. Without being enraptured like the 'Dadaists' over my pages about deafness . . . nonetheless they are true. Now I am not in the least deaf."[95]

A recent remark published by Paul Souday alarmed Proust even more. He wrote the critic that "one thing pained him" in the review, although he knew that "it was not intentional!" What disturbed Proust, especially in anticipation of the publication of *Sodom and Gomorrah*—after which "no one" would dare defend him—was Souday's characterization of him as "feminine. From feminine to effeminate, there is only a step. Those who served as my seconds in duels will tell you if I am soft like men who are effeminate."[96] Souday had used the word in comparing Proust's style to Saint-Simon's. Although Proust's style did share many characteristics with Saint-Simon's, Souday wrote, "Marcel Proust is above all a highly sensitive aesthete, somewhat morbid, almost feminine."[97]

Proust's prophesy came true rather quickly. Jacques Patin, writing in the *Figaro*'s literary supplement of November 14, quoted at length from Souday, including the description of his "feminine" quality.[98] Souday wrote Proust and asked: "What kind critic would refrain from criticizing?" To which Proust replied, after treating Souday to dinner at the Ritz, "Allow the author the right . . . to find that such and such a criticism is more or less fair."[99]

In addition to sparring with critics, Proust received and answered letters of congratulations from his friends. Mme Straus wrote that she had been reading "with passion," this "beautiful book that evokes many memories of boulevard Haussmann." Because it was unlikely that the two of them would see each other again, she suggested that Proust send the "beautiful Céleste" to report on his health and work, and thus spare himself the trouble of writing. As for her, she had to put down her pen and "die again for today."[100] Around this time, Proust somehow broke his glasses, which caused quite "a drama." But his fever and cough had disappeared.[101]

Schiff wrote to say that Violet had been ill and had undergone surgery but was expected to make a full recovery, to which *The Guermantes Way* had already contributed. Sydney had not yet finished the volume because he was savoring Proust's sentences as one did the "bouquet of an old Chambertin." He preferred Proust to Henry James because the American "never succeeds" in making the reader feel his characters are "living beings." Most of all, Schiff wrote, "you give us yourself, whom we love and whom we keep in our heart like a part of ourselves." In the spring the Schiffs planned to spend several weeks in Paris on their way to Rochebrune and hoped to see him.[102]

On November 15 Proust's preface for Morand's *Tendres Stocks* appeared in the *Revue de Paris*, under the title "For a Friend: Remarks on Style."[103] Although Proust said that Morand's "delicious little novellas" needed no introduction, he would have undertaken a "real preface" had not "a sudden event prevented me from it. A strange woman took up residence in my brain. She came, she went," so often that soon he "knew all her ways. Moreover, like a boarder who is too attentive, she insisted on establishing direct relations with me. I was surprised to see that she was not beautiful. I had always thought that Death would be." Some of Proust's friends were disturbed to hear him thus announce his death; others, who had heard it so often, thought he lacked originality; still others thought that such a proclamation seemed out of place in a preface for a young writer's first publication. When Reynaldo read the preface, he became furious at Marcel for calling Léon Daudet and Charles Maurras "my masters."[104] Hahn knew that Proust was like the Himalayas compared with those two minor elevations.

For those who pitied Morand for his choice of presenter, matters only got worse in the following paragraphs. The only direct remark about Morand as a writer was critical: Proust said that his metaphors always fell short.[105] Did the preface come too soon after Morand's "Ode"? Was Proust trying to avoid paying Morand any compliments? He was certainly much less gracious than Anatole France had been in prefacing *Pleasures and Days*. Now Proust used his forum to launch a gentle attack against France, who had recently made some rather absurd remarks about style. France had expressed the opinion in the *Revue de Paris* that "any singularity in style must be rejected" and that since the eighteenth century French writers had written poorly. Proust did employ Morand's style as ammunition against France's argument. Morand's "style was certainly singular." Were Proust to see France, he "would ask him how he can believe in the unity of style since sensitivities are singular." Proust used examples from France's own books to prove his point, as well as from Baudelaire's poetry. Then he revived his attack on Sainte-Beuve, using material from earlier notebooks on Baudelaire and Sainte-Beuve.[106]

In the articles and prefaces Proust wrote during his final years, he took advantage of the opportunity to put forward his own ideas on art and literature. In the Morand preface, Proust paraphrased this passage from *The Guermantes Way,* part 2, which was to be published the following year. Original artists are always singular, he observed, and that is why it takes a while for them to be recognized and appreciated:

> People of taste tell us nowadays that Renoir is a great . . . painter. But in so saying they forget the element of Time, and that it took a great deal of time . . . for Renoir to be hailed as a great artist. To succeed thus in gaining recognition, the original painter or the original writer proceeds on the lines of the oculist. The course of treatment they give us by their painting or their prose is not always pleasant. When it is at an end the practitioner says to us: "Now look!" And, lo and behold, the world around us (which was not created once and for all, but is created afresh as often as an original artist is born) appears to us entirely different from the old world, but perfectly clear.[107]

Just when it looked as though Proust and Miss Barney might meet at last, he had an accident with drugs that forced him to postpone their rendezvous. Enraged at being unable to sleep, Proust said, he took an entire box of Veronal, along with Dial, another barbiturate, and opium. The dangerous mixture resulted not in sleep but in "terrible suffering."[108] Proust was apparently exaggerating about the amounts he swallowed, because that many barbituates would likely have killed him. Céleste described in her memoirs a 1917 incident during which he did not ring for two days. As Céleste waited anxiously, she feared he had died of drug intoxication.[109] In his final years, Proust repeatedly risked accidental poisoning.

At the end of November, Proust wrote Montesquiou: "If by chance you learn that I have published a new book (an event of little importance and of which you will probably be unaware), I entreat you to believe if I have not yet sent it to you, it's not through neglect." Proust blamed the diabolical maneuverings of his publisher, the confusion over various editions, and other factors beyond his control. Montesquiou, in top form, sent a withering answer from Le Vésinet: "How would I not know that you have published your book? Do you think I am deaf? Not to the point of being unable to hear the trumpets blaring. How could all this not interest me? Why must you put on airs?" He advised Marcel to learn simplicity, as he had, and he blamed Proust for not sending the book that "everyone has had for a very long time." It was quite simple: if Proust did not want the count to read his books, so be it.[110] Of course, Proust and Montesquiou were only playing games; the count would read every book—how could he afford not to see what became of Charlus?—and the novelist would always insist that he wanted the poet to have the best editions of his volumes.

At the beginning of December, Proust sent Émile Henriot, editor at the *Temps*, brief answers to a survey on classic and romantic writers. Proust's answers were to appear in January 1921 in *La Renaissance politique, littéraire et artistique*.[111] "I believe all true art is classical, but the laws of the mind rarely permit it to be, when it first appears, recognized as such." Proust used the example of Manet's *Olympia*, which scandalized the public at first and seemed such a departure from the classical tradition, and Baudelaire's *Les Fleurs du mal*. These great innovators are the only true classics, Proust wrote, and form an almost continuous line. Proust became his own advocate when he commented: "innovators worthy of becoming classics one day obey a strict inner discipline, and are builders above all. But precisely because their architecture is new, it takes a long time for people to discern it."[112]

Proust wrote Louis Martin-Chauffier regarding a review planned for the February issue of the *NRF*. The novelist counted on him to "make it very clear that *The Guermantes Way* is the exact opposite of a snobbish book. . . . The truth is that by natural logic after having confronted the poetry of the name Balbec with the triviality of the place Balbec, I had to proceed in the same manner for the proper name Guermantes. That's what critics call books that are barely composed or not composed at all." Proust then revealed to Martin-Chauffier how the Narrator's lifelong quest concludes: "The only thing I don't say about the Narrator is that at the end he is a writer, because the entire book could be called a vocation . . . but which is not discovered until the last volume."[113]

29   *I Am Finishing a Great Task*   ∾

ONE OF THE LAST LETTERS PROUST wrote in 1920 was to the duchesse de Clermont-Tonnerre. He praised a letter he had received from her, comparing it to a painting by Watteau and a poem by Verlaine, both of whom had treated the subject of a fête galante—an old-fashioned aristocratic garden party.[1] It is evident that Mme de Clermont-Tonnerre was one of several society women with whom Marcel enjoyed sharing gossip and anecdotes about homosexuals in Paris society. The mention of Verlaine in such a context reminded Proust of handsome blond footmen wearing liveries of blue panne. This set off a series of comments about such footmen recruited by Prince Constantin Radziwill, who, though married, was a notorious homosexual, of whom Montesquiou had poetically remarked, "To speak of women would be uncivil / In the house of Constantin Radziwill." Of Polish origin and immensely wealthy, the prince kept a staff of twelve handsome valets, to each of whom he gave a pearl necklace.[2] As Proust reminisced about such characters with the duchess, he recalled the occasion when a new, uninitiated valet, angered by the prince's advances, attempted to throw his employer out the window. The prince's wife intervened, scolding the "recalcitrant valet, 'If you didn't want to do that, you had only to refuse. But you shouldn't try to kill people over such matters.' A maxim that would prevent many wars." Proust recalled another occasion when Lady Pirbright was caught performing fellatio on the energetic Prince Constantin. Marcel also evoked Ernest Forssgren, a handsome blond valet who had been in his own employ. Proust quickly added that the young Swiss was not kept for the same purposes as those who worked for Prince Constantin.

The duchesse de Clermont-Tonnerre, flattered in her literary ambition by Proust's high praise of her letter, requested its return. Upon sending back the "masterpiece so rightly reclaimed," he asked her to destroy his letter containing comments about handsome blond footmen.[3] This request must have given him pause as he remembered all the other letters whose recipients he had asked to burn or return them. Few had heeded his instructions. Céleste remembered Proust's fears regarding his correspondence: "I shall hardly be cold and everyone will start publishing my letters." He sought advice from such friends as Henry Bernstein, Horace Finaly, and Émile Straus, but uncertain of what measures to take, he did nothing to prohibit publication of his letters.[4]

On January 11 Proust sent Gallimard a thoughtful letter about his circumstances and the work remaining. Since the beginning of the year he had been suffering from bronchitis and a high fever, and he could barely speak. He managed to get up from time to time so that Céleste and Marie could clean his room. As for his novel, there remained four "colossally long" volumes, which Proust referred to as *Sodom and Gomorrah*, parts 2, 3, and 4, and *Time Regained*. He hoped that these volumes, which would succeed each other at fairly long intervals—"If God gives me life"—would give Gallimard "an idea of my talent that will make you not regret having chosen me as one of your authors." As a first step, he needed the proofs for *Sodom and Gomorrah*, part 1, which had to be published with the remainder of *The Guermantes Way*. He urged Gallimard to do everything possible to hasten the printer's work. Next, Proust broached the matter of royalties. The ten thousand–franc check of last summer had been only a partial payment; the balance had been promised by mid-September at the latest. Nearly half a year had passed and he had not "received a sou." Nor had Gallimard paid any royalties from the deluxe edition, although there were a fair number of subscribers. Gaston was woefully behind on payments to his most famous author.[5] By the summer he would owe Proust fifty thousand francs, a large sum by any measure.

Gaston immediately sent Proust another partial payment of 7,500 francs.[6] Proust offered to lend 3,000 francs back to Gallimard if he needed it.[7] The publisher explained that his real difficulty was in collecting more than half a million francs due him from bookstores. He promised to send Proust 2,500 francs a month, beginning on February 15, as installments on royalties past due. Regarding titles for the forthcoming volumes, Gallimard feared that readers would be confused if the title *Sodom and Gomorrah* appeared on different volumes.[8] Proust eventually recognized this danger and created different titles for parts 3 *(The Captive)* and 4 *(The Fugitive)*.[9]

Proust spent all night Friday, January 14, correcting the proofs of "Un baiser" (A kiss), an excerpt Rivière needed for his February issue. The following morning he wrote Rivière that he felt well enough to correct many proofs, if only he had them.[10] Producing the *Search* one volume at a time had become a full-time job not only for the novelist himself but for Gallimard, his staff, and the printer. Writing, typing, setting, proofreading, revising, reprinting, and correcting the three thousand pages of complex Proustian prose became one of the most demanding productions in the history of publishing.

In mid-February, Henri Bergson asked Proust to grant an interview to Algot Ruhe, a Swedish gentleman who had written an essay on *Swann*. After the interview with Ruhe, Proust was inspired to create a minor character, a Norwegian philosopher, who makes a brief, essentially comic appearance as a guest of the Verdurins at La Raspelière.[11] The Norwegian philosopher pops up again briefly to quote Bergson—the Narrator says that he cannot vouch for the accuracy of the attribution—about memory, including all those forgotten moments of our past, and its implications for the immortality of the soul. The Narrator's own conclusion is that the immortality of a soul makes no more sense than possessing memories one cannot recall: "The being that I shall be after death has no more reason to remember the man I have been since my birth than the latter to remember what I was before it."[12] As he revised the final portions of his book, Proust found that minor characters like the Norwegian philosopher could easily be appended to his vast panoramic—and often satirical—view of Parisian society.

Rivière informed Proust in February that the "chorus of praises rising around 'An Agony' is becoming prodigious." This excerpt, an account of the grandmother's death, published in the January issue of the *NRF*, had put new life into the review; subscriptions were pouring in.[13] Jacques also made a request: he wanted Proust to read his novel *Aimée*, written in 1915 in a single burst during his internment as a prisoner of war.[14] Proust obliged without delay and soon advised Jacques to publish his "masterpiece," after changing a few details. On the same day, Rivière wrote Proust that he should soon receive the proofs for *The Guermantes Way*, part 2. As for *Sodom and Gomorrah*, part 1, the printer was working without respite; the delay had been caused by the preparation of a typescript.[15]

Proust had given a third excerpt from *The Guermantes Way,* part 2, to the *Revue hebdomadaire.* On February 26 the review published "Une soirée de brouillard" (A foggy evening) with a brief introductory essay, "The Art of Marcel Proust," by the novelist François Mauriac. Mauriac praised Proust's novel for having renewed the genre and said that the *Search,* of all contemporary works of literature, was the most likely to survive. What some critics mistakenly called Proust's snobbishness was "only curiosity about these imperceptible differences of status." Noting the writer's ability to render finely nuanced differences among all the social classes, including the subdivisions within each, Mauriac considered the *Search* to be a remarkable "summa of contemporary sensitivity."[16] Proust, obviously pleased with Mauriac's appraisal, invited him to a bedside dinner in the presence of Henri Rochat. Afterward he presented Mauriac with an autographed copy of *Pleasures and Days.*[17]

By the evening of March 6, Proust had finished a "colossal" task, and he sent an "important, urgent" message to Gallimard, along with the packet containing all of *The Guermantes Way,* part 2. Working "against wind and tide," Proust was ready to "take the plunge" and publish the second part of the Guermantes volume and the opening pages of *Sodom and Gomorrah,* which Tronche already had.[18] Given Proust's nearly constant state of intoxication, the arduous work that he performed over the next year and a half, requiring tremendous concentration and presence of mind, seems extraordinary. But it became increasingly clear that the work and the drugs were taking a toll.

That spring, not only did he continue to write and revise, he attempted to orchestrate publicity and reviews. Proust wanted to prepare readers and critics for the opening pages of *Sodom and Gomorrah,* and he asked Boulenger to quote Mauriac, a fervent Catholic whose morals were beyond reproach. On March 12 Boulenger alerted readers of the *Opinion* that the forthcoming volume would "depict audacious, bold, daring scenes, but in the case of M. Marcel Proust the question of morality or immorality does not arise." Then he cited Mauriac: "The examination of one's conscience is the basis of all moral life, and Proust projects a terrible light on our inner depths."[19] Curious readers had to wait another two months before they could see how Proust illuminated their inner beings.

In a short time Proust wrote Gallimard to convey some important information: "*Sodom and Gomorrah,* Part II . . . is the only volume which requires a true reshaping." As for the remaining volumes, "if I were to die they could appear as they are or nearly so. It is thus highly desirable that while I am able (?) still to work that I receive without delay the proofs for *Sodom and Gomorrah,* Part II."[20]

Gallimard assured Proust that he was doing everything possible to speed up the printer; he had ordered his personnel, as their first duty every morning, to phone the printer and keep him moving.[21]

Meanwhile, Proust and Hauser exchanged letters about the author's regimen. Hauser observed that Proust's behavior was self-destructive. The two elements most necessary for good health, he wrote, were sun and pure air, both of which Proust shunned. It was wrong to use drugs, like morphine, which soothed pain and nerves but did not cure, and which had to be taken in increasingly larger and more dangerous doses: "The only thing for which I bitterly reproach you is your fierce determination to commit suicide."[22] Proust not only disregarded Hauser's advice, he seemed not to have read it. In April he wrote Hauser and listed the most recent medicines his "excellent doctor was using on his body" to relieve a painful flare-up of rheumatism. Among the drugs prescribed were morphine and adrenaline. "The result," Proust reported, was "negligible, except for a great soddenness."[23]

Montesquiou and Proust exchanged testy letters, each taking offense where none was intended. When the count's copy of *The Guermantes Way,* part 1, finally arrived, he wrote that he had received the "somewhat mutilated, not at all timely, edition, in no sense rare, of your book that you gave everyone else six months ago. If this is an example of what you call deference, I no longer know what the word means and I prefer not to know in this topsy-turvy world. You were always so kind to me that I cannot at all understand this sudden change and this new manner. The only explanation that I can see is the entry in the lower house of your zodiac, of a sign that could well be named Cancer." Proust, less conversant with astrology than the count, was offended that Montesquiou thought him terminally ill with cancer. The count explained then that the novelist's sign was entering a period that alienated friends. Montesquiou revealed that he was under observation in a medical facility, the Clinique Vieux jardin, in Lilas.[24] He promised to send Proust his latest books when he returned home: *Les Délices de Capharnaüm* (The delights of Capharnaum) and *Diptyque de Flandre, triptyque de France* (Diptych of Flanders, triptych of France). In the postscript, he told Marcel that "instead of a nurse I have your book, which is acquitting itself well."[25]

Proust occasionally consulted Mme Straus about drugs and now wrote her that he felt intoxicated from taking too much Veronal. Mme Straus, who had become as reclusive as he, revealed that by "swallowing a quantity of various poisons" she had been able to wean herself from Veronal. Then she had tried taking nothing, "which was leading me to consider suicide. Then I replaced Veronal with Dial Ciba . . . and I am staying with that. Only I take too much of it." She suggested that he try two barbiturates, Dial and Didial, "but not daily." She admitted that she was once again in a crisis of melancholy and anxiety. "Adieu, mon petit cher Marcel. How sad it is not to be able to laugh together—at everything that is sad!"[26] One of the saddest cases, which she did not mention to Marcel, was her son Jacques's state of acute depression. Addicted to morphine and alcohol, his second marriage falling apart, Jacques, like his mother, fought suicidal impulses.

It seems unlikely that Proust made a serious effort to reduce his drug intake or seek a less intoxicating combination. In the last two years of his life Proust suffered a number of mishaps due to his increasingly shaky condition. In April he had an accident while boiling milk to take with his Veronal. He made a clumsy movement and knocked over the kettle, spilling scalding milk on himself and his bedclothes. His skin was burned and his sweaters and bed soaked, which made the bed too cold afterward and brought back his sore throat.[27]

Gallimard informed Proust that he, Rivière, and another editor, Jean Paulhan, were rereading the proofs of *The Guermantes Way,* part 2, sheet by sheet as the pages became available, every day until the last hour. To gain more time Gallimard took the corrected sheets back to the printers in the evening for final corrections.[28] Proust, touched by this "revision," of which he had known nothing, thanked Gallimard for being "too nice."[29] This gratitude did not last long.

Montesquiou, eager to identify the models for various Proustian characters, kept pressing Marcel for answers. Proust adopted the strategy of giving the count just enough information to satisfy his curiosity, while steering him away from identifying himself with the baron de Charlus. Proust was especially eager to obscure this connection in light of the volume that was about to appear. When the count wrote that he had identified the "likable and impatient Robert [de Saint-Loup]," Proust acknowledged that there were at most "two or three keys" for the entire novel, and even they "opened for only an instant." Yes, he had thought of Bertrand de Fénelon for the scene in the restaurant where Saint-Loup runs to bring the shivering Narrator a borrowed coat. But for the remainder of the novel, Saint-Loup bore none of Bertrand's traits. Many of Proust's friends, he told the count, equated Saint-Loup with Albufera, but he claimed never to have thought of his former friend while creating that character. "I suppose he believes it himself; that is the only explanation I can think of for his break with me."[30]

Proust knew that a more direct reason was Albufera's furor over the depiction of his family in the Saint-Simon pastiche, but he thought that Albu's erroneous self-identification in the novel might be exemplary for Montesquiou. To throw Montesquiou off the scent, Proust admitted that in the scene where the baron de

Charlus "stares at me . . . near the Casino, I thought for an instant of the late Baron Doäzan, an habitué of the Aubernon salon and very much the type. But I dropped him afterward and constructed a Charlus that is much more vast, entirely invented."[31] As for Montesquiou's notion that Proust was enjoying newfound celebrity and prosperity, the novelist asked: "What pleasure is there for someone who can no longer pronounce words?" He related a recent incident in a restaurant, where he asked for mineral water and had to repeat the word *Contrexéville* more than ten times before making himself understood.

Although Proust was uncertain about the nature and seriousness of the count's illness, he felt compassion. The tone of his letters became more affectionate and deferential, as of old. That spring Boulenger received a letter from Proust, urging him to ask Montesquiou to contribute articles to the *Opinion*. He said that the count, "the best art critic of our epoch," was unjustly neglected because no one asked him for articles. In the summer Proust informed Montesquiou that he had spoken to Boulenger several times about how welcomed and "useful" articles by the count would be. Proust had praised Montesquiou to Boulenger as "a marvelous essayist" whose style was unequaled when writing about "a painter or sculptor he loves."[32] But when Boulenger approached Montesquiou about writing for the newspaper, the count replied with a "terrible letter" attacking the critic. Montesquiou's legendary irascibility spoiled the opportunity.[33]

By April, Proust had decided to write an article on his favorite poet, Charles Baudelaire, for the June 1 *NRF*, in part because he found it scandalous that the "*NRF* alone had remained silent" on the centennial of the poet's birth.[34] He worked "double time" to redress the lack of a commemorative article. Although he had obtained the authoritative Crépet edition of Baudelaire's poems, he told Rivière that he was quoting from memory, as he had when writing the essay on Flaubert.[35] He placed Baudelaire in the same category as Dostoyevsky—that is, writers whose neuroses inspire them to far surpass others and to renew literature. He found in the poet a distinguished successor to Racine: "nothing is so Baudelairian as *Phèdre*, nothing so worthy of Racine . . . as *Les Fleurs du mal*."[36] He praised the poet for conveying with such intimacy, sincerity, and conviction the sentiments of "suffering, death, and humble fraternity" among men.

On April 21 Proust, no longer feeling fraternal, sent Gallimard a letter that read like an indictment. Saying that he was in a black mood because he wondered whether he had not been the "cuckold" of the NRF for some years, Proust raised the issue of hiring an arbiter or breaking altogether with Gallimard. He was furious about several matters that he found detrimental to the publication of his book.

Having told Gallimard that *Sodom and Gomorrah,* part 2, was the only part of the novel that needed reshaping, he had not yet received a single page proof. He had concluded that it would be impossible, at the current pace, to bring out the remainder of *Sodom and Gomorrah* before May 1922.[37] In fact, Proust had returned the corrected typescript to Gallimard on April 8, less than two weeks earlier. True, Proust had been insisting since January on the need to work as rapidly as possible to allow him time for the needed modifications, but it is difficult to see how, given the complexity and scope of the manuscript, the work could have gone at a faster pace. Another sore spot with Proust was that *The Guermantes Way,* part 2, and *Sodom and Gomorrah,* part 1, scheduled for publication in early May, had not been announced in the April issue of the *NRF.* Scolding Gallimard for this neglect, Proust complained that *Pastiches et mélanges* and the deluxe edition of *Within a Budding Grove* had been "sabotaged in the same way." Gallimard had not acted quickly enough to publicize the current volume. The publication of *The Guermantes Way,* part 2, and *Sodom and Gomorrah,* part 1, was to be announced on page 4 of the *NRF*'s May 1 issue.[38]

Proust's letters, containing such accusations and the threat to withdraw his books, shook Gallimard and Rivière. Rivière informed Proust of the consternation Gaston had experienced on receiving his complaints. Rivière underscored their many fruitless attempts to move the printer. So devoted was everyone at the NRF to Proust's work that the previous week all other work had been put aside to check his proofs. Rivière had not even worked on the review or his personal correspondence during those five days. This was not a lament, because he had never before performed "such an absorbing task."[39] Gallimard wrote Proust that the charges dismayed him and that rather than seeing himself as the NRF's "cuckold [*cocu*]" Proust should think of himself as its "heart [*cœur*]."[40]

If Proust needed additional proof of where he stood with the founders of NRF, Gide provided it. Gide was generous and sincere in his public praise of Proust. In an *NRF* column he wrote that Proust's style was "so disconcerting in its suppleness that any other style appears stilted, dull, imprecise, sketchy, lifeless. Should I admit that when I plunge again into this lake of delights, for many days afterward I remain afraid to pick up the pen, no longer believing myself capable—as happens during the time a masterpiece holds us in its sway—of writing well, seeing in what you call the 'purity' of my style only 'poverty.' "[41]

Since early February, Antoine Bibesco and his wife had been in Washington, D.C., where he was a member of the Romanian delegation. When Antoine read Gide's comments about Proust's novel, he wrote from Washington: "AT LAST. The simple truth. And to think the NRF refused the manuscript [of *Swann*] that Emmanuel delivered to them."[42]

Proust wrote to the critic Fernand Vandérem in late April, just a week before the publication of *Sodom and Gomorrah,* part 1, to explain his intentions. Vandérem should not think that the author had "wanted to strike sodomites with all his might." If that was the impression he had created, he was "terribly sorry." He had aimed for objectivity, intending not to write a "speech for the defense" or a "condemnation," but rather to give a "frank, unadorned depiction," an "impartial one without the intervention of the moral element, which has no business here."[43]

Proust's attitude about sex had not changed since "Avant la nuit." In expressing physical love one must be true to one's own sexual nature, which might evolve during a lifetime. What some critics failed to appreciate was that in the case of Charlus's obsession with Morel, Proust was condemning not homosexuality but a jealous obsession that is as destructive, in that it diverts one from higher purposes, and as pointless as Swann's infatuation with Odette.

Sodom

On May 2 *The Guermantes Way,* part 2, and *Sodom and Gomorrah,* part 1, appeared in bookstores.[44] Their publication coincided with a worsening of Proust's condition. Intoxicated by his excessive use of drugs, he found it impossible to go from his bed to the door without falling.[45] A week later, feeling well enough to go out for the first time in more than a month, he sent word to Gaston to meet him at the Ritz for dinner. After waiting in vain for Gaston to appear, Proust concluded that his publisher chose to neglect him. As soon as Gallimard learned what had happened, he expressed his "infinite" regrets: he had never received Marcel's message.[46] Proust's vexation broke through when he inscribed a book for Gallimard: "To you, my dear Gaston, whom I love with all my heart (although you sometimes think the opposite is true!) and with whom it would be so nice to spend long and cheerful evenings." Then came the reproaches that showed why Gallimard might well doubt such declarations: "But you never take the initiative." He accused his publisher of remaining as aloof as "during the time when you refused *Swann.* Your very grateful and very faithful and very affectionate friend."[47]

Proust made yet another plea to Gallimard for the proofs of *Sodom and Gomorrah,* part 2, stressing the urgency of his request because this volume would also be long and difficult to reshape. Because he wanted to leave Gallimard his "work in its entirety," he broached the question of the rights to *Pleasures and Days*.[48] A short time later Proust contacted Calmann-Lévy, who reminded him that no contract existed for *Pleasures and Days*. Calmann-Lévy would be happy to cooperate and make it possible for Gallimard to republish Proust's first book.[49] Proust hesitated about whether or not to proceed.

The recent recipient of honors himself, Proust decided to give an award. When he inscribed Céleste's volume, he bestowed upon her a number of distinguished crosses for extraordinary service and friendship: "To my faithful friend of eight years, but in reality so united with my thoughts that I would be closer to the truth in calling her my friend of always, not being able to imagine a time when I did not know her . . . to Céleste the War Cross because she tolerated Gothas and Berthas, to Céleste who has borne the cross of my temperament, to Céleste the Cross of Honor, Her friend Marcel."[50]

Proust did not have to wait long for the reactions of friends and critics to *Sodom and Gomorrah*.[51] Gide was one of the first to express his displeasure. Proust's depiction of homosexuals appalled him, but for reasons that differed from those of other disapproving readers. Gide blamed Proust for having made his homosexuals so unappealing. Jupien and Charlus, two aging and effeminate inverts, were the opposite of the virile type Gide celebrated in his unpublished *Corydon*. Proust first learned of Gide's disapproval in a letter of May 3. Although he had no intention of criticizing Proust publicly, Gide told him what he would have said in a review. Although Proust had adopted an "impartial point of view, that of a true naturalist," he had given of this particular " 'vice' a portrait that was far more stigmatizing than all invectives"; he has "branded this subject with a red-hot iron that served conventional morality far more effectively than the most emphatic moral treatises." In the postscript Gide added that "a pederast (in the full Greek sense of the word), would never consent to recognize himself in the portrait you give of homosexuals."[52] In spite of Gide's misgivings, he saw that Proust's book was the talk of Paris. A few weeks after its publication he wrote Proust: "Wherever I go everyone talks of nothing but you. Princesse Murat reads certain passages about Charlus" to friends "over the telephone!"[53]

In mid-May, Gide visited Proust several times to discuss homosexuality. On the first visit, he brought a copy of *Corydon* and left it for Proust to read, asking him not to talk to anyone about the book. Four days later Proust, feeling somewhat better, sent Odilon to return Gide's copy of *Corydon* and to bring Gide back to rue Hamelin for a visit.[54] Gide came and spent the entire evening talking with Proust.

Gide recorded in his diary his impressions and a summary of these conversations with Proust. Gide was shown into a room that was suffocatingly hot but where Marcel was shaking with cold. Proust complained that his life had become a slow agony. Gide noticed that Proust looked "fat or rather bloated," resembling Jean Lorrain, Proust's ancient nemesis and dueling opponent. Almost immediately, Proust began talking about homosexuality, occasionally interrupting himself to ask his visitor about Christ's teachings. Proust gave Gide the impression that he hoped to find in Christ's words some relief from his "atrocious" ills. His frankness in talking about homosexuality amazed Gide, who noted that "far from hiding his homosexuality, he exposes it and I could almost say prides himself on it."

Proust confided that he had "never liked women except platonically and had only known love with men." This admission surprised Gide, who had never thought that Proust was exclusively homosexual.[55] In order to depict the attractive features of the girls of the little band, of which Albertine is the most important representative, Proust told Gide, he drew upon memories of homosexual experience. Having given all the attributes that were tender, graceful, and charming to the girls, he had nothing left for his homosexual portraits but "mean and grotesque qualities." Proust apparently did not reveal Saint-Loup's evolution as a homosexual who dies a hero on the battlefield, a portrait that seems to meet all of Gide's positive criteria.

When Gide said that the stigmatization of homosexuals in the *Search* seemed intentional, Proust became upset and protested. Gide finally understood "that what we find ignoble, derisive or disgusting, does not seem to him so repulsive." When Gide asked Proust whether "we will ever see this Eros in types that are young and handsome," Proust replied that "what attracts him is almost never beauty, and he thinks beauty has little to do with desire."[56]

After the interviews with Gide, Proust wrote Boulenger that *Sodom and Gomorrah* had "angered many homosexuals." He deeply regretted this reaction, but "it's not my fault if M. de Charlus is an old gentleman. I could not suddenly give him the appearance of a Sicilian Shepherd such as one finds in Taormine's engravings." Proust later told Boulenger that Gide was "a very difficult man" to whom he should not even mention *Sodom and Gomorrah,* for it had caused their friendship "to cool."[57]

Among those whose ire was raised by *Sodom and Gomorrah* was the nationalist and militarist Binet-Valmer, who scolded Proust for using his "admirable, prodigious analytical qualities to create abnormal, antisocial" types rather than depicting those "true sons of France . . . that gave our army its most humble but most virile chiefs." Léon Daudet explained to Proust that, given his newspaper's readership, he could not even mention the title *Sodom and Gomorrah*. Daudet promised to compensate for this omission "in a more serious form." His strategy would be to praise Proust's novel in general terms, thus avoiding references to the title. Even sympathetic critics like Jacques Boulenger feared public reaction. Late in the year Boulenger told Proust that it would be impossible to write an article on *Sodom and Gomorrah* for the *Opinion* without causing massive cancellations. He suggested an interview instead.[58]

Many friends and writers congratulated Proust on his courage and his achievement. Blanche praised him for having treated the subject with such thoroughness and dignity. Proust had endowed the subject of homosexuality with "a tragic nobility" that derived from its author's being such a "learned" and "profound *moraliste*." In early July, Proust heard from Colette, to whom he had sent a copy of *Sodom and Gomorrah*. "No one in the world has written pages such as these on homosexuals, no one!" She particularly admired the Charlus-Jupien encounter, but found it all "magnificent."[59]

Antoine Bibesco had been so eager to read the remainder of *The Guermantes Way* and begin *Sodom and Gomorrah* that, rather than wait for his inscribed copy to arrive, he purchased one at the French bookstore in Washington. He wrote Marcel that the "sound effects" of Charlus and Jupien's lovemaking were somewhat shocking, but the section on the grandmother's death was "the most sublime of all." Antoine asked Marcel to send him the proofs for the last volumes; it was unbearable to have to wait for "these slices . . . when one is so hungry" for more.[60]

Mauriac also praised the description of the agony and death of the Narrator's grandmother. There was "not a line that did not captivate me." Regarding the opening pages of *Sodom and Gomorrah,* however, Mauriac had experienced the "most contradictory feelings: admiration, repulsion, terror, disgust," but he believed in the "fate of a work of art: It was impossible for you not to bear this terrible fruit. It had to fall to you and not to another to assume the role of the angel who makes the accursed cities rise from their ashes." The younger writer trembled "at the thought of all those who closed their eyes" in order not to recognize themselves and "whose secret and shameful wound you probe with a brutal finger."[61]

When Proust inscribed his copy to Geneviève and Émile Straus, he entreated them to read the episode about the duchesse de Guermantes's red shoes, "which I came one evening to find" so long before. Proust had sought inspiration for the scene from a stunning red dress and matching shoes that he had remembered Mme Straus wearing years earlier. This episode, which concludes *The Guermantes Way,* reveals Oriane de Guermantes's vain, shallow nature.[62] Late for a grand dinner party, which she and her husband pretend that they must attend out of social duty, but which they would rather die than miss, the couple hurries to their carriage, accompanied by Swann, who had stopped by unannounced for a brief visit. When Oriane invites him, her oldest and dearest friend, to accompany them to Italy the next spring, he declines. Swann resists answering her questions as to why he cannot come, but finally, after she insists, he admits that it is because he will be dead by then. He has an inoperable tumor. Swann urges Oriane to hurry on to the party, "because he knew that for other people their own social obligations took precedence over the death of a friend, and he put himself in their place thanks to his instinctive politeness. But that of the Duchess enabled her also to perceive in a vague way that the dinner-party to which she was going must count for less to Swann than his own death." Oriane is about to abandon, with much regret, the dinner party until the duke insists that she come along. They must not arrive late. Just as she is getting into the carriage, the duke notices that she is wearing black shoes instead of red and orders her to go back and put on shoes that match. Not only is a dinner party more important than staying with a close friend who has just announced his impending death, but so are appearances. This scene, one of the most bitterly satirical in the novel, shows that Proust, far from being in thrall to high society, sees it for the vain and sterile world he knew it to be.[63]

Mme Straus thanked Marcel for his "audacious and magnificent book." As for the portrayal of homosexuality, she was "not at all scandalized" and remembered that "we used to talk about it when you called in the evening."[64]

"The little patch of yellow wall"

On April 21 an exhibition of old and modern Dutch masters opened in the Jeu de Paume.[65] Morand, who knew how delighted Proust would be, had used his influence as a diplomat to insist that the Dutch organizers of the exhibition include Vermeer's View of Delft. A short while after the exhibition opened, Morand asked whether Proust had gone to see the painting. "If not, you will have to get up and go. Are you better at this moment?"[66]

Proust decided that he might see two exhibitions on the same outing: the Vermeer exhibition and another of works by Jean-Auguste-Dominique Ingres at the Hôtel des Antiquaires et des Beaux-Arts.[67] On May 9 Proust sent Étienne de Beaumont a word of thanks for trying to arrange for a special pass to visit the Ingres exhibition one evening after hours. On those rare occasions when Proust planned a daytime excursion, he simply did not go to bed the night before. This was the solution he adopted in order to see the two exhibitions. One morning in the latter part of May, he sent a note to the art critic Jean-Louis Vaudoyer, inviting him to come along. Just after the exhibition opened, Proust had read and admired Vaudoyer's article on the "mysterious" Vermeer and knew that he would be an ideal companion.[68]

On the morning that Proust felt well enough to attend the exhibitions, he waited until the last minute to send a note to Vaudoyer, asking whether he would be willing to lead to the exhibitions "the dead man I am and who will lean on your arm. I will be alone, except perhaps for Morand. If you say yes I will send for you around 9:15 (later in the day I will be too tired)."[69]

That day someone photographed Proust standing on the terrace next to the Jeu de Paume. These were to be the last photographs of Proust's life.[70] His demeanor is both proud and slightly confused, as he squints against the bright sunlight. He looks pale and puffy, and not altogether healthy, but he is impeccably dressed and, posing for the camera, superbly erect and dignified.

The scene of Bergotte's death in *The Captive* was long thought to have been inspired by Proust's visit to the Vermeer exhibition. This myth apparently originated with Robert Proust, who had read the passage and, knowing that his brother had not been well around the time of the museum visit, believed that Marcel had attributed his own malaise that day to the fatal attack Bergotte suffers at the same exhibition.[71]

It had been almost twenty years since Proust had last seen "the most beautiful painting in the world." In the scene preceding Bergotte's death, the painting plays a vital part in the narration. Staring in awed admiration at the painting, Bergotte suffers the awful realization that, despite a highly successful career and his reputation as a distinguished writer, he is a failure as an artist. Admiring Vermeer's brushstrokes and use of color, Bergotte sees that his own books were far too intellectual. "His dizziness increased; he fixed his gaze . . . on the precious little patch of wall. 'That's how I ought to have written,' he said. 'My last books are too dry, I ought to have gone over them with a few layers of colour, made my language precious in itself, like this little patch of yellow wall.' " As Bergotte begins to faint, he has a vision: "In a celestial pair of scales there appeared to him, weighing down one of the pans, his own life, while the other contained the little patch of wall so beautifully painted in yellow. He felt that he had rashly sacrificed the former for the latter. 'All the same,' he said to himself, 'I shouldn't like to be the headline news of this exhibition for the evening papers.' " As Bergotte sinks down onto the settee in the museum room, he keeps repeating to himself, "Little patch of yellow wall, with a sloping roof, little patch of yellow wall." He rolls to the floor and dies.

In this scene, Proust reprises the theme of death and survival through art. He comes as close as he ever did in the novel or in life to declaring his belief in some sort of afterlife when the Narrator asks of Bergotte:

> Dead for ever? Who can say? Certainly, experiments in spiritualism offer us no more proof than the dogmas of religion that the soul survives death. All that we can say is that everything is arranged in this life as though we entered it carrying a burden of obligations contracted in a former life; there is no reason inherent in the conditions of life on this earth that can make us consider ourselves obliged to do good, to be kind and thoughtful . . . nor for an atheist artist to consider himself obliged to begin over and over again a score of times a piece of work the admiration aroused by which will matter little to his worm-eaten body, like the patch of yellow wall painted with so much skill and refinement by an artist destined to be for ever unknown and barely identified under the name Vermeer. All these obligations, which have no sanction in our present life, seem to belong to a different world, a world based on kindness . . . self-sacrifice, a world entirely different from this one and which we leave in order to be born on this earth, before perhaps returning there to live once again beneath the sway of those unknown laws which we obeyed because we bore their precepts in our hearts, not knowing whose hand had traced them there—those laws to which every profound work of the intellect brings us nearer and which are invisible only . . . to fools. So that the idea that Bergotte was not dead for ever is by no means improbable.

After Bergotte's burial, "all through that night of mourning, in the lighted shop-windows, his books, arranged three by three, kept vigil like angels with outspread wings and seemed for him who was no more, the symbol of his resurrection."[72] The symbol but not the certainty. Proust was unable to account for the nobility of human striving in the face of an unjust, absurd world, but he always left the ultimate question unanswered. Dead forever? Perhaps. Perhaps not.

By June, Rochat had at last made preparations to leave for a far country. Proust had asked his banking friend Horace Finaly to find a position for the young man. On June 4 Rochat embarked for Argentina, where he was to work at the Buenos

Aires branch of the Banque de Paris et des Pays-Bas.[73] Before he left, Rochat, who had become mean and mendacious in his conduct toward his fiancée, finally broke off his engagement, a despicable act that Proust used for his character Morel. In a letter to Schiff, Proust said he feared that after the estrangement, Rochat would become bored at rue Hamelin. It was that concern, the writer said, that inspired him to secure a "good situation" for Rochat in South America.[74]

The day after Rochat's departure, Proust dictated a letter to Céleste for his publisher. He complained that he still had no proofs for *Sodom and Gomorrah,* part 2, despite having given Gallimard the manuscript four months earlier. "I have spent many fertile weeks without working because I have no material, and since Rochat left yesterday for several years my work . . . will necessarily be slower."[75] This last remark was probably an exaggeration, but it justified his having kept Rochat on for so long and might make Gallimard more concerned about additional delays. Gallimard answered that he had been hounding the printer to send the proofs, but the delay was due to a shortage of lead. The printer had promised to produce a considerable number of pages during the first third of June. Still searching for ways to speed up the process, Gallimard said that he would adopt Proust's suggestion of having a blank page glued onto each proof sheet for his revisions and additions.[76]

This delay was not Proust's only frustration. He was annoyed by what he considered Mme de Chevigné's ungrateful reaction on noticing aspects of her appearance and lineage in the attractive, elegant, and socially prominent duchesse de Guermantes. Writing to Guiche, Proust had nothing but insults for Mme de Chevigné, whom he continued to envisage as a fowl: the duchesse de Guermantes "resembles somewhat the tough old hen I once took for a bird of Paradise and who could only answer me like a parrot, 'Fitz James is waiting for me,' when I tried to capture her under the trees along the avenue Gabriel. By making her a powerful Vulture, I have at least prevented her being taken for an old magpie."[77] Marcel made similar complaints to Mme de Chevigné's neighbor Jean Cocteau. He even suggested that Cocteau read passages from his novel to the lady to make her see that instead of being offended, she should be flattered. Cocteau made an amusing and appropriate observation: "Marcel, that would be like Mr. Audubon asking the birds to take an interest in what he had written about them."[78]

Montesquiou sent a letter expressing his admiration for the latest volume. Proust, knowing how many traits, rejoinders, gestures, and attitudes he had borrowed from Montesquiou to create Charlus, stressed again his creation of composites. Even when describing "inanimate objects (or so called), I extract a generality from a thousand unconscious reminiscences. I can't tell you how many churches 'posed' for my church of Combray in *Swann's Way*. The characters are even more invented, the monuments each having brought . . . one its steeple, another its dome."[79] He signed the letter, "Au revoir, cher Monsieur, I hope you are completely cured and that your entire resurrection will come at the same time as my death, that is to say soon. Your affectionate and grateful admirer. Marcel Proust."

Montesquiou wrote again in early June, avoiding even a hint that he saw himself as the principal model for Charlus. He did recognize himself as the object of a remark made by that character who refers to "the test that the one eminent man of our world has ingeniously named the test of untoward kindness, and which he rightly declares to be the most terrible of all, the only one that can separate the wheat from the chaff." The count often applied this test to a friend or someone who wanted to be friends by treating the candidate with excessive kindness. Then when the person on probation invariably failed to meet Montesquiou's impossible standards, the count dismissed the "chaff," often in public. Montesquiou, pretending to be flattered, called Charlus's allusion to him—"the one eminent man"—and his test "fine praise, which compromises or satisfies no one since it is anonymous."[80]

A week later Montesquiou returned to his favorite topic: the keys for characters. He did not know Albufera, but he thought Guiche had posed for Saint-Loup, and he liked Charles Haas much better than Charles Ephrussi as the model for Swann. As for the duc and duchesse de Guermantes, it seemed so obvious; surely they were inspired by the Greffulhes. Then, again without betraying any sign that he saw himself in Charlus, the count acknowledged Proust's role as a pioneer in bringing onto center stage a cast of characters who were homosexual or bisexual: "You wanted to widen the field of literature and open it to the immense space of inversion, which has been forbidden until now, and which can provide . . . beautiful and perilous works." Would Proust succeed? Montesquiou thought it "possible, but not certain. The adversary is strong." To Proust's annoyance, the count also recognized the androgynous nature of Proust's seaside girls from *Within a Budding Grove*.[81]

Montesquiou may have been uncertain how he should confront Proust on this issue. To other friends he expressed his anger and his vexation. If he succeeded in convincing himself and Proust that he did not see himself caricatured in Charlus, he apparently fooled no one else. Anna de Noailles, whose imitation of Montesquiou's voice rivaled Proust's earlier mimicry, began reciting Charlus's tirades at after-dinner parties. Those who arrived late and heard her voice as they climbed the stairs "thought for a moment that Montesquiou had emerged from his hermitage."

In spite of dissimilarities between him and Charlus, in particular the baron's corpulence, Montesquiou knew that he would forever be identified with Proust's character. "He confided to a friend: 'I am in bed, ill from the publication of three volumes which have bowled me over.'" The count was indeed ill, although he himself did not yet appreciate to what degree. He asked Mme de Clermont-Tonnerre, in desperation: "Will I be reduced to calling myself Montesproust?"[82]

Montesquiou hid his anger and distress from Proust, to whom the count began to send extremely kind letters. Proust denied to Boulenger—calling the idea "absurd"—that it had been his intention to portray Montesquiou as a homosexual. Had such a portrayal been voluntary, that would be "even worse, because, if I have known in society an enormous number of homosexuals whom no one suspected of being that way, in all the years I've known Montesquiou, I have never seen him, at home or in a crowd or anywhere, give the slightest indication of that. Despite that, I think (?) he believes that I intended to portray him. Since he is infinitely intelligent, far from seeming to believe it, he was the first to write me the warmest letters on *Guermantes* and *Sodom*. But I still think he believes it. And so the kindness of his letters torments me." Proust described Montesquiou as a "mean man who through madness made many of his relatives suffer." Now that Montesquiou was sixty-six, and Marcel saw him in "his sad old age in which he is deprived of the glory that he believed was rightly his . . . it breaks my heart." Proust's professed pity soon turned to fear as he contemplated how Montesquiou's memoirs would depict him.[83]

A Case of Jealousy

In September, Marcel fell in his room. Dr. Babinski gave him another examination, about which little is known; presumably, the consultation differed little from the first. Proust told Hauser that the doctor asked him to pronounce certain sentences, so apparently he still had difficulty speaking. Marcel had one wish: "If only I could finish my books. Ars longa, vita brevis."[84] Proust had corrected only the first chapter of *Sodom and Gomorrah,* part 2, and offered to send it to Gaston if that would speed the process. Gallimard replied that he was eager to have those 160 pages and the entire next volume, if it was completely ready. If he could have the copy for both volumes, he would hire another printer and produce them simultaneously. He and Rivière would correct the proofs. Once all the *Search* was in print, Gallimard intended to proceed immediately with Proust's *Selected Writings.*[85] Gallimard's ambitions for Proust's work appealed to the novelist, who was working hard to finish revising *Sodom and Gomorrah,* part 2; only then could he begin to reshape the volume that was to become *The Captive.*

Jacques Boulenger had told Proust in July about the recently founded *Les Œuvres libres.* Arthème Fayard had created the review to specialize in publishing new novels in an affordable format. Each issue contained several works. When Proust considered selling a long segment from the cycle about Albertine, he told Boulenger that he thought Gallimard would "take to his bed" if he published "anywhere else other than the *NRF.*"[86] By early September, Proust received Fayard's offer to pay two francs per line for an unpublished novel of five thousand lines, for a total of 10,000 francs.[87] Proust, always short of cash, and annoyed that Gallimard had failed to pay his monthly installments of 2,500 francs on royalties past due, found the proposition very tempting.

Meanwhile, Proust heard from Rivière, who had taken with him to Cenon the manuscript of *Sodom and Gomorrah,* part 2. Jacques had been unable to put it down because it was "so admirable, of such powerful and profound beauty! especially the return to Balbec and the grief over the grandmother's death." The Narrator had never really felt the deep and true loss of his grandmother until he returned to the seaside hotel where they had stayed in adjoining rooms. Because of his inability to undo his own boots each evening, his grandmother would bend over to unlace and remove them. On the second visit to Balbec, when the Narrator returns to his hotel room and makes the same gesture to take off his boots, he suddenly feels the full weight of his loss. This passage, "The Intermittencies of the Heart," on grieving and forgetting, is one of the novel's most poignant. Rivière begged Proust to give it to him for the October issue, saying it was the natural complement to the account of the grandmother's death that had appeared in the *NRF*'s January issue.[88]

Proust wrote to Rivière, not revealing that his reluctance to give Rivière excerpts was due to his fear of undermining the negotiations with *Les Œuvres libres.* Rivière continued to press his case: *NRF* was planning a brochure to be sent out in thousands of copies that would attract new readers; if Proust's pages appeared anywhere else, it would be a "catastrophe." The public would not understand; Proust must appear when he was expected, where he would be read. Jacques asked Proust, when making his selection for the review, to "avoid anecdotes of which M. de Charlus is the hero. I have been reproached a lot for the growing licentiousness · of the review." Apparently, these reproaches came from Paul Claudel, a rather stern and conservative author also published by Gallimard. Rivière soon regretted having made this restriction and rescinded it.[89]

On September 8 Gallimard spent the entire evening, from six o'clock until one in the morning, talking with Proust. The novelist extracted from Gaston permission to publish a long section from the next volume in *Les Œuvres libres*. Gallimard tried to hide his dismay over Proust's betrayal, because he did not want to spoil the fine evening. Earlier that day Proust, having decided to accept Fayard's offer, sent Jean Paulhan the pages Rivière wanted for his October issue. Two days later Proust sent Rivière a telegram, telling him not to worry: Proust would give him "The Intermittencies of the Heart."[90]

The morning after his long visit with Proust, Gallimard, who had spent a sleepless night, wrote and asked the novelist never to reach such an agreement with another publisher.[91] Gallimard called the publication in *Les Œuvres libres* a book in disguise: same format, same appearance, same price, and same distribution. Fayard might print as many as forty thousand copies, but if Proust calculated his fee, he would see that Fayard was paying him a mere twenty-five centimes per copy. Gallimard's royalties on the same number of copies would be twenty-five thousand francs, compared with Fayard's ten thousand. Gallimard, who wanted to make certain he never found himself in the same situation again, offered to pay the same amount as Fayard or anyone else. He would even pay any difference that forgoing such an opportunity would cost Proust. In the present case, he asked Proust to give Fayard the fewest pages possible, with a special title, and to include the mention that these pages were an excerpt from a volume to be published by the Editions of the NRF.[92]

Proust gave his word and reminded Gallimard that the authorization was for only this one time. True, he was unhappy over renouncing any future proposals, but he did not want to vex Gallimard. He did point out that Gallimard owed him a large sum of money, approximately sixty thousand francs.[93] As he kept giving the NRF new books, the amount Gallimard owed him would increase. Proust said that he did not intend this observation as criticism or a request for money, but he did regret that Gallimard would not let others compensate somewhat for the NRF's inability to pay him in a timely fashion.[94]

That evening Proust wrote Henri Duvernois, Fayard's editor, relating his discussions with Gallimard. Proust was as accommodating with Duvernois as he had been cool with Gaston. Duvernois could send him the initial payment in a month or two; "I don't need money." Proust scoffed at Gallimard's request that *Les Œuvres libres* notify its readers that his contribution was excerpted from a forthcoming NRF volume. He told Duvernois: "Don't commit such a folly . . . to which I moreover am opposed." Two days later, Fayard sent Proust a check for ten thousand francs.[95] In November, *Les Œuvres libres* published 150 pages entitled *Jalousie* (Jealousy) as "a new and complete novel."[96]

On September 13 Paulhan wrote Proust that he would receive the proofs of *Sodom and Gomorrah,* part 2, within a week.[97] In the meantime, Rivière, unaware that Proust had sent additional pages for "The Intermittencies of the Heart" directly to Paulhan, wrote to inquire why Proust had not provided enough copy. Upset and annoyed over the confusion, Proust wrote Rivière, "Your letter made me absolutely crazy. I gave you everything you wanted, more than you wanted."[98] Paulhan, seeking to gain time, had forwarded the pages directly to the printer rather than to Rivière. Once Jacques realized his error, he apologized for the trouble he had caused.

The grievances continued. On September 19 Proust sent Gallimard a long list of complaints, many of which might have been meant to disguise his own despicable behavior and guilt over having betrayed his publisher.[99] He began by relating a recent accident: he had fallen in his room, and in trying to catch hold of the door had bruised himself as he crashed to the floor. Proust claimed that to torment him, the NRF had two directors: Rivière, who kept hounding him for copy, and Gallimard, who was always absent or unreachable. He even accused Gallimard of having his secretary deny that he was in when Proust called. This suspicion revived the memory of the rejection of *Swann,* after which Proust had naïvely phoned three times a day, expecting to talk to someone. He regretted having sold the excerpt to *Les Œuvres libres,* but that, too, was Gallimard's fault. The publisher had not been available when he tried to consult him: "You didn't even answer my letter." Fearing retaliation, he attributed to Gaston the base intention of promoting the next volume halfheartedly to prove the detrimental effects of publishing in *Les Œuvres libres.* Proust wanted Gallimard to work even harder to launch this volume—"(or two volumes, it's very long)"—to efface the wrong that publication in *Les Œuvres libres* might do and to "compensate me for my sacrifice since I henceforth refuse their collaboration," a gesture Proust thought was "extremely nice . . . dear prior, because our contract contains no vow of celibacy, chastity, poverty."

Gallimard had heard enough about his having refused *Swann's Way,* a decision in which he had no part, and he asked Proust to drop that charge. The publisher assured Proust that everything owed him would be paid; if the writer wanted the money immediately, Gallimard would arrange for him to receive it. Inasmuch as Proust had referred to their contract, Gaston reminded him of clause 6, which stipulated that authorization to reproduce any text must be agreed to by both parties. Furthermore, any money Proust earned from such publications was to be divided equally between the author and the NRF. Gaston repeated that he mentioned the contract only because Marcel had; he preferred to base their understandings on mutual affection—an indication that he understood Proust's psychology perfectly. If Proust was tempted by other offers, Gaston would pay him all money owed by January. It was as a "friend" that he had asked to pay monthly installments. If bookstores had paid him the approximately six hundred thousand francs they owed, he would not have delayed payment. He brushed aside the innuendo that he "could have the petty intention" of not properly launching the next volume. Gallimard had for Proust's novel a "jealous affection: therefore demand of me, brutally, what you want and I will use all my strength never to disappoint you." In the postscript he reminded Proust of his eagerness to publish *Selected Writings* and reprint *Pleasures and Days*.[100] Gallimard's forgiveness, generosity—even self-abasement—made Proust's behavior look even more contemptible.

Proust answered that Gallimard should not worry about immediate payment. He did not need any money, for his life was reduced to "consultations" with Gallimard and Babinski.[101] Proust offered to drop his own peculiar interpretation of clause 6 in their contract, saying that his desire was "to do only what you wish." The clause in question was a standard one that protected copyright and clearly prohibited such publications as the one in *Les Œuvres libres* without the NRF's permission. Proust had contended, rather ridiculously, that because the pages he sold to *Les Œuvres libres* had never been published anywhere, their publication did not constitute a "reproduction." Although it had been just two weeks since he had received Fayard's check, Proust already regretted the decision, telling Gallimard that "despite the extraordinary kindness of Duvernois and the vertiginous and honest rapidity of Fayard"—clearly an invitation to Gallimard to compare his own way of doing business and paying his authors—he wished that he had not "embarked on this slave-ship." Proust had failed to calculate that he would receive a mountain of proofs from Fayard, which would require "secretaries, and the profit would be zero." In the postscript he thanked Gaston for the 2,500-franc check and urged that regular payments be made.[102]

Gallimard feared, based on what Proust said about length, that *Sodom and Gomorrah,* part 2, would not be ready for several months. "I, therefore, insist that you allow me to publish a new edition of *Pleasures and Days*. It could be ready in several weeks and would require no proofs to correct."[103] Proust replied that although the next volume was long, he was working on it constantly and exclusively and would have it ready for May publication. He intended to give Gallimard the entire revised manuscript in a month or a month and a half. Regarding *Pleasures and Days,* Proust opposed immediate publication because he feared that readers would be confused by the appearance of a separate and unrelated volume "in the midst of the long convoy that is already so difficult to follow." Once the *Search* was finished, he hoped that *Pleasures and Days* would find new readers and "live to an old age."[104]

When Rivière requested an essay for Dostoyevsky's centennial, Proust refused to be distracted from revising his manuscript. Although he admired "the great Russian passionately," he knew his works "imperfectly." The necessary reading and rereading would interrupt his own work for months. "I can only answer as did the prophet Nehemiah (I believe), who from his perch on a ladder" said to someone who called him: "I cannot come down, I am finishing a great task."[105]

Proust, who had great respect for Rivière's judgment and knew him to be candid, asked for his opinion about *Sodom and Gomorrah,* part 2. Jacques, who had already told him how "admirable" it was, observed that "no human work is perfect." Listing what he saw as the defects of Saint-Simon, Balzac, and Stendhal, Rivière asked, "Yet what do we have that is greater (with Racine)? . . . I put you with those four." Proust, like the others, did "not avoid imperfection." It was difficult for Rivière to define Proust's shortcoming, but "I suspect it must be there." Perhaps "such and such a sentence might be clearer, or a particular articulation in the story might be more accentuated, or a digression" such as "Brichot's etymologies" could have been somewhat shorter. "But what does that matter next to the continuous sublimeness of the book?" He congratulated Proust on being "the creator of a society as complete and complex as the *Comédie humaine.* You have the additional merit over Balzac of not having just presented and described it, but explored it and explained it." Rivière said that "personally," he thought Proust's most "amazing" faculty was his "extraordinary analytical ability." This succinct assessment, given before Rivière or anyone had read the complete novel, seems fair and accurate. Proust must have found it so, for he did not contest any of Rivière's reservations concerning style and content.

On October 13, the day of Rivière's letter, Proust suffered a terrible accidental poisoning. His own drug abuse was the underlying cause, but the direct blame fell on the pharmacist, who had mislabeled the medication. Proust described the incident in a letter to Gallimard. Thinking that he was taking seven Veronal cachets of "one-tenth gram" each, Proust had swallowed "seven one-gram doses." When he tried to stand, he "suffered terrible vertigo, etc. I could have died from it."[106]

Proust seems to have recovered fairly quickly. A few days later he answered a survey for André Lang that was published in *Les Annales politiques et littéraires* the following February.[107] Among Lang's questions was the following: "When someone makes a distinction between an analytical novel and an adventure novel, does that mean anything, according to you, and if so what?" Proust, who knew that it would be several years before the publication of his concluding volume, *Time Regained*, which contains his literary credo, seized this opportunity to explain to readers his (and the Narrator's) ideas about literature. What he sought was not the analysis of minutiae, but the truth, the laws that govern human behavior and the universe. This was why he did not like the expression "analytical novel," which had come to mean "study under the microscope." His preferred instrument was the telescope. "But I had the misfortune of beginning a book by the word 'I' and immediately everyone thought that instead of seeking to discover general laws, I 'was analyzing myself' in the private and detestable meaning of the word. I would replace 'analytical novel' by the 'novel of introspection.' "[108] In his novel, Proust urges readers to engage in introspection. He viewed reading, as he had in the 1905 essay on the subject, as the beginning of self-knowledge. Toward the end of the *Search,* when the Narrator anticipates his future novel, he recognizes the reader's independence and duty to himself: "For it is only out of habit, a habit contracted from the insincere language of prefaces and dedications, that the writer speaks of 'my reader.' In reality every reader is, while he is reading, the reader of his own self. The writer's work is merely a kind of optical instrument which he offers to the reader to enable him to discern what, without this book, he would perhaps never have perceived in himself."[109]

On October 20 Proust gave Rivière an excerpt from *Sodom and Gomorrah*, part 2, for the December *NRF*.[110] The episode describes the train rides of the Narrator and Albertine from Balbec to visit the Verdurins, who had rented the villa La Raspelière. While they are there, Charlus makes an entry in which his homosexual nature is apparent to the Narrator. Proust described Charlus as seeming "ladylike" and embodying the soul of a female relative.[111] After sending these pages to Jacques, Proust wrote Gaston, saying that he wanted to finish the volume as quickly as possible and then rest for three or four days, which he "had not done since 1915." Then he would begin to perfect *Sodom and Gomorrah,* part 3 *(The Captive).*

In November, Proust received a letter from Bernard Faÿ, a historian and biographer who spent his winters at Columbia University, where he lectured on contemporary French authors.[112] Faÿ was about to return to New York, and Proust was to be the topic of one of his first lectures. The scholar expressed his desire to meet Proust and discuss the lecture. "Your work is greatly admired in certain American intellectual circles and is beginning to be more widely known" to the general public. "Last year at Columbia University several of my students (male and female) showed an interest in studying and writing . . . dissertations on you." Faÿ wanted to consult Proust about how to encourage these students and which of his works the author would like to see translated. In his reply, Proust explained his bizarre hours to the professor, whom he invited to dine at his bedside. Faÿ agreed and spent his last night in Paris listening to the strange genius, upon whose works the professor would soon be expounding to students at Columbia.[113] Those students, like everyone else, had to wait six more years before all the *Search* was published.

At the end of the month Proust heard from Binet-Valmer that with Christmas approaching, there were, in the aftermath of the war, "100,000 children living in the ruins of France who are counting on me and I am working like a ditch digger." Proust sent two thousand francs for the children, for whom he would have liked to write something, but his high fever made that impossible. He told Binet-Valmer that he had taken three adrenaline shots just to summon the energy to write this short letter.[114]

Proust sent Gallimard his recommendations for the division and titles of the next installments: "Sodom and Gomorrah, Part II will fill two volumes published together." Part 3, on which he was ready to begin working hard, would be called *The Captive,* "a brief volume of dramatic action." This was the first hint that the writer was seriously considering making a large cut in the original manuscript.[115] He expressed to Gallimard his outrage that a satirical newspaper had announced a new pen called "Swan's Way Proust Stylograph, manufactured by Marcel Proust." Should he not write the newspaper a stern letter of protest, something he had never done before?[116] Proust raised one more issue of concern: Morand had told Proust that a German firm's efforts to secure translation rights to the *Search* had fallen through because the NRF's demands were too high.[117]

Gallimard, who disliked Morand for his loose tongue, replied that the fees he sought for Proust's works were "never any higher than those obtained for other writers whose reputations are far from the equal of yours." It was "certain that sooner or later *In Search of Lost Time* will be translated into all languages." As for answering those satirical journals, he advised against it, saying that they were of "no importance. They would publish your answers while ridiculing them."[118]

A week later Gaston informed Proust that he had sent the corrected manuscript to the printer and was certain *Sodom and Gomorrah,* part 2, could appear May 1. He agreed to use a larger font but reminded Proust that the price of the book would rise. To increase the type size the volume had to be completely reset and that cost reabsorbed. Gaston refused to let the author pay.[119] Marcel replied with an economical proposal. He suggested making only a typescript for *Sodom and Gomorrah,* part 3. That would be the definitive text, and there would be no proofs or typesetting to pay for. He would hire a typist and have all the work done at rue Hamelin. "Am I not an accommodating author? (which will compensate somewhat since you say, it appears, that I am an expensive author.)"[120] Gallimard accepted Proust's suggestion, telling him, "You are, it is true, a very accommodating author, and I have never said that you were an expensive author." He informed Marcel that only nine copies remained of the deluxe edition of *Within a Budding Grove.*[121] Proust hired another member of Céleste's family, Odilon's young niece Yvonne Albaret, as a secretary. During her first stay, Yvonne was to prepare the typescripts of *The Captive* and *The Fugitive.*[122]

On December 8 Proust wrote Berry that after "seven months in bed," he had gone at midnight to the Ritz, where he had asked the "good Olivier" if he might dine. In a sentimental mood after downing a bottle of Porto 345, Proust had thought how "sweet" was the time when he used to "come to the Ritz with M. Berry! And I asked myself: 'Have I passed the age of loving?' (La Fontaine without any Charlus)." The port had made him "only slightly drunk," but Berry should not "attribute his tender effusions solely to the '345.' . . . Is there no way before dying (I am talking about me) to see each other again, to tell each other those things whose seeds will perhaps sprout in Eternity?" Remembering Faÿ's visit, Proust said that Berry's countrymen were kind to request so many lectures on the *Search.* This reminded Proust of an amusing letter he had recently received from an American woman living in Rome whose name he had already forgotten. After assuring him that she remained very beautiful at twenty-seven, she confessed that for three years she had done nothing night and day except read his books. That sounded fine until he reached the end of her letter, which was "humiliating," because the woman expressed her utter perplexity: "I don't understand a word, absolutely nothing. Dear Marcel Proust, stop playing the poseur, come down for once from your empyrean. Tell me in two lines what you meant." Proust thought it "pointless to reply," since "she had not understood in 2,000 lines."[123]

Berry was also eager to see his old friend: "When you go out, even at eleven, why not have Céleste phone me, and we will go and empty together a flacon of 345?" Regarding the American lady, Berry knew a hundred like her. He said that whenever one of them asked him if he "liked your books, I would answer: 'Yes, but they have a grave defect: they are so short.' And the poor lady would walk away dumbfounded. I should have added they have an even more serious defect: after having read them, one cannot read books by others."[124]

On December 16 Parisians received confirmation of Montesquiou's death at Menton, five days earlier. At sixty-six, "The Sovereign of Transitory Things" had succumbed to uremia. The next day Marcel, who had not gotten out of bed for days, "dragged himself to the dining room" to await the duc de Guiche, whom he had invited to relate "the details of Montesquiou's death."[125] Guiche had other obligations that kept him away, but Berry, who was free, came and dined with Proust.

Writing to Guiche's wife the following day, Proust said that he could fill volumes for her on Montesquiou, "the subject is so inexhaustible." He remembered all the times that Montesquiou, "with a smile," had allowed Proust "to reproach him for the way he had treated so many people." As for his own relationship with the count, Proust said, there had never been a "cloud," which he certainly would have known, because Montesquiou "was not a man to ignore clouds, but [one] whose manner was rather to hurl thunderbolts." Montesquiou's memoirs, which Proust secretly dreaded, "would settle the matter." Proust saw a great injustice in the "small success of my books and the appalling obscurity where his have been forgotten." Proust, however, refused to believe that the count was "literally" dead.[126] Montesquiou, who had always seemed larger than life, would surely surprise them all by turning up alive and well.

Montesquiou's intense dislike of his family survived him. He left everything to his secretary, Henri Pinard, except for certain legacies, some of which went to the library at Versailles, in memory of Yturri. Only a handful of friends attended the service in the small chapel dedicated to Sainte-Élisabeth at Versailles, where Montesquiou was laid to rest beside Yturri under the watchful Angel of Silence.[127]

A week before Christmas, Gallimard informed Proust that he had received the unbound pages, for the author's inspection, of the English translation of *Swann's Way*. He reminded Proust that Chatto and Windus could not publish it without the author's approval: "Would you like to see it?" Proust regretted not having asked earlier for two or three sample pages, but if the job was done, he might as well accept it sight unseen.[128] When the English translation appeared nine months later, Proust did not remember giving his consent.[129]

Between Christmas and New Year's, Proust received urgent requests from Daniel Halévy, now editing a Grasset series called the *Cahiers verts*. Daniel wanted to publish a long section from one of Proust's forthcoming volumes. Proust declined, having just been through the contretemps with Gallimard over *Les Œuvres libres*. He told Halévy that his contract prohibited such a publication. He distinguished between *Les Œuvres libres*, which appeared as a review, with each issue containing "four or five things," and *Cahiers verts,* each number of which was a volume by a single author. It was unfortunate that Daniel had not asked him earlier, before he became aware of Gallimard's "intransigence," because he would have given "A Case of Jealousy" to the *Cahiers verts* instead of Fayard, "because of you and Grasset to whom I owe so much."[130]

On December 28 Proust wrote Gallimard about two preoccupations. The first was the lamentable state of his health, which was so bad that he "regretted not having any cyanide" to swallow. The second was whether or not he could, without delaying *Sodom and Gomorrah,* part 2, "make a few minor additions." Proust even considered going to the printer at Abbeville. Given the rapid decline in his health, such a dangerous excursion tempted him as a way out of "my hell."[131] Gallimard replied that Proust should put his health first. Gaston, who thought it unlikely Proust would actually rest, given his determination to finish, offered to come to his bedside every evening for a month and assist him, if he wished. As for Marcel's going to Abbeville, that was out of the question; Gallimard offered to retrieve the proofs and bring them to him.[132]

Although he alluded to suicide, Proust felt well enough to attend the Beaumonts' lavish New Year's Eve costume party. He wrote well before Christmas to inquire how late he could come without inconveniencing the hosts, and whether the house would be warm. Proust liked to arrive late, after the other guests had "warmed" the room, "which is delicious (according to my taste)." On New Year's Eve, he dictated to Céleste a note for Comte Beaumont, warning that he, "the most boring of guests," would attend. In preparation, he had taken "such large quantities of drugs" that his hosts would be receiving "a man half-aphasic and especially unsteady on his legs due to vertigo." He had two requests: first, on arriving, "a cup of tea . . . so boiling hot that it burns your throat"; second, "not to meet too many intellectual and tiresome ladies."[133] The Beaumonts must have met his requirements, because Paris's most famous nocturnal creature stayed at the party all night.

30 *The End of Time* ॐ

NINETEEN-TWENTY-TWO BROUGHT no relief to Proust's many ailments. He complained of difficulty speaking, and he continued to take dangerous adrenaline injections. Now he felt that he needed such stimulation not just for extraordinary . efforts but simply to go out for some air while Céleste and Marie cleaned his room.[1] In a note to Tronche thanking him for the New Year's gifts, Proust described the "terrible days I have spent, an infinite mental distress combining with physical suffering. It's useless for the doctors to be clever at dodging the difficulties because my awful clairvoyance sees right through their contradictions and deprives me of any hope. How unfortunate that doctors must be 'conscientious' and that instead of 'treat me' you cannot say to them 'kill me' since they are unable to cure you." This was at least the second time, since the previous year's wish for a cyanide pill, that Proust expressed an eagerness to die. He no longer knew moments of repose; he vacillated between the highs and lows resulting from the strange mixtures of drugs he took and the unknown quantities of his will and appetite for life that occasionally surfaced. On January 8 he went to the Ritz for dinner and, finding himself in the midst of a noisy crowd arriving for a ball, "fled" upstairs to a private dining room where he "devoured a leg of lamb."[2] How Proust treated his body and the sad results had become predictable, yet his mind remained lucid when he revised his pages.

If he seemed no longer able to rescue himself from the downward slide, Proust still went to no end of trouble to help his friends. On learning that Clément de Maugny and his wife were destitute to the point of not knowing when they went to bed whether they would have enough to eat the next day, he attempted to find them a situation in Paris. Though fond of Clément, Marcel considered Rita an "angel a thousand times superior" to her husband.[3] Maugny was another friend whose financial security had been undermined by the Russian Revolution and the war. His deceased mother's inheritance was tied up in Russia. Commiserating with Clément, Marcel told him that Reynaldo was forced to spend each winter wasting "his energy and his talent . . . as musical director of the Casino Théâtre de Cannes." In his determination to assist the Maugnys, Proust wrote letters throughout the spring to friends in diplomatic and official circles, such as Paul Morand, Robert de Billy, and Mathieu de Noailles, who had connections with the recently founded Société des nations. At one point, Proust even thought of engaging Maugny as his secretary, but he wrote Clément that he had not dared suggest this, even if his friend were able to adapt to the "slum where I now live."[4]

Although Proust continued to have periodic suspicions of Gallimard's actions and motives—largely because Morand kept telling him stories about Gaston's lack of competence or goodwill—on occasion he felt sympathy toward his publisher over the enormous burden of bringing out the *Search*. He was also touched by Gallimard's repeated offers to assist with the proofreading, offers that Proust continued to decline. In mid-January, fearing that Gaston might somehow regret having undertaken the publication of a novel whose "proportions were somewhat vast," Proust offered to free the publisher from his contractual obligations. If Gallimard wanted out, he should not fear "hurting my feelings"; while "no longer being one of your authors, I would remain your friend."[5]

Gaston replied that he had "never thought for one minute that publishing the *Search* was a burden." Not only was he "satisfied to publish" Proust's books, but he "wished it would never stop and that there would be many of them and that I will always have the opportunity to prove to you my devotion and my admiration." He assured Marcel that he was "of all the authors published by the NRF the most beloved and the most admired." If Marcel were able to attend the receptions Gallimard gave for his authors, he would see that the other writers considered him their "maître."[6]

Proust's solicitous attitude toward his publisher lasted less than a week. Fearful that Gallimard's proposal to bring out *Sodom and Gomorrah*, part 2, in three volumes—and thus at an increased price—would reduce the number of readers,

Proust sent him another list of accusations. Proust's letter is missing, but the charges are clear from Gallimard's letter defending himself and asking that he be allowed to confront his accusers. Proust seemed to have revived every old grievance, from Gaston's negligence during the years when he was in New York with the theatrical troupe, to his ineffective launching of *Within a Budding Grove,* to his inadequate response to the opportunity presented by the Prix Goncourt.

Trying once again to placate Proust, Gaston said that if the author thought that agreeing to three volumes would be a "new capitulation," then two it would be. He also guaranteed that if Proust sent him part 3 (eventually called *The Captive*), Gallimard would have it set immediately and publish it in October. In the postscript, Gallimard, who suspected that Morand was behind all the complaints, asked Proust's permission to speak directly to Morand.[7] Proust asked Paul to talk to Gallimard, but the diplomat entreated Proust not to identify him as the source of any remarks critical of Gallimard. Morand claimed that he could not remember making such comments, but if he had "it must have been terrible because I am so blunt."[8]

On the evening of January 28 Proust made an effort to go out, despite feeling "much sicker," to celebrate his niece's eighteenth birthday. Although Suzy (as Adrienne now preferred to be known) had turned eighteen on November 25, Robert and Marthe had postponed the big party until after the holidays. As Proust explained to Gallimard, Suzy knew that he had attended the Beaumonts' gala New Year's Eve party, and she might hold it against him if he did not put in an appearance. He feared that all he would accomplish would be to "catch cold between three and four in the morning."[9] Proust performed his avuncular duty and, as he noted in a letter to Morand in the early hours after returning home, the party had been the first such "medical" gathering he had attended at which there had been no "smell of iodoform." He trusted that his "presence as a resurrected Lazarus had not cast too great a chill" on the party. He was ready, however, "to return to the tomb."[10]

By February, Proust had grown discouraged about all the work remaining for the forthcoming volume and what he viewed as the printer's refusal to produce the proofs in a timely manner. He expressed to Gallimard his doubts that the book would be ready May 1. If not, he would rather wait another year, for he believed that October would not be a good time to publish.[11] A few days later Proust wrote again, complaining that the late arrival of proofs meant that he had less time to complete his work. He resented being treated like a "machine that one can regularly oil so that it will work to maximum capacity," but he would continue to work hard as though May 1 were the "real date," convinced though he was that the book would not be published until May 1923. That would be a "disaster" because by then "the characters of May 1922 will be even more forgotten." This disaster loomed because Gaston had "*no authority* over your printer. He's making fools of us." But in the same letter Proust suggested that he wanted more time and was even considering further expansion of the *Search:* "I have so many books to give you that if I die will not be published (*À la recherche du temps perdu* has hardly begun)." Proust conceded that because he was making additions to *Sodom and Gomorrah,* part 2, perhaps three volumes would be appropriate after all. He would leave the decision to Gallimard.[12] His hesitation about the desirable publication date and his reference to "so many books to give you" indicate his inability to make firm decisions regarding the definitive shape of his novel.

Gallimard promised Proust that the book would appear in May 1922; if not, Gaston would pay him a heavy forfeit. Frédéric Paillart agreed to let two typesetters work full time on the book. Furthermore, if Gallimard received the definitive text of *Sodom and Gomorrah,* part 3, in May, he would guarantee its publication for October 15, which was "as good a date as May 1." He gently rebuked Proust for having recently hurt his feelings again by another allusion to Gallimard's rejection of *Swann's Way.* Gallimard had repeatedly explained that he had nothing to do with that decision. "Once I was in charge, my first step was to contact you." Proust was pleased with Gallimard's initiatives and guarantees. He took an additional step: he instructed Gallimard to offer the printer on Proust's behalf a one thousand–franc bonus for finishing the job by May. Gallimard assured Proust that such a reward was unnecessary, but he did "not dare contradict" the author.[13] Proust kept his word; in early April, when the volume was printed, he sent Paillart one thousand francs.[14]

In spite of his chronic health problems and hard work, Proust went out relatively often in the first months of the year. Twice in early February he attended parties given by Mme Soutzo in her apartment. At the first, Proust asked Mlle d'Hinnisdaël to show him some of the latest dance steps. Céleste recalled that Mlle d'Hinnisdaël intrigued Proust because her family, "although still very formal, stiff, and traditional as they were despite the changes in postwar society, couldn't help accepting people and things they wouldn't have tolerated in the old days." Proust was amazed at how naturally and "with exquisite gracefulness" Mlle d'Hinnisdaël performed the latest and most popular "1922 dances," while maintaining her aristocratic bearing.[15] The party must have been a fairly wild affair. Writing to Mme Soutzo afterward, Proust recalled the moment when "you dragged me over to Mme [Wanda] Landowska who was biting Mlle [Hélène] Vacaresco's buttocks." (No doubt this is not to be taken literally, but Proust says nothing more about meeting the famous Polish pianist, composer, and teacher.) Marcel feared he had made a terrible gaffe in addressing Mme Scheikévitch by that name rather than as Mme Vial. He was relieved to learn that he had made no blunder; she had divorced Vial and was indeed once again Mme Scheikévitch.[16]

In late February, Proust wrote Robert de Flers to congratulate his old friend on becoming director of the *Figaro*. Proust had canceled his subscription months before, when the newspaper had become "something unmentionable," but now he renewed it. Proust mentioned his own "odious existence" and said that he awaited someone whose specialty was simplifying all matters: "Her name is death."[17] Flers, like most of Proust's old friends, had no particular reason to take alarm at such pronouncements of doom. Marcel had been complaining about his health and claiming to be at death's door for as long as any of them could remember. The note to Flers was dictated to Proust's new secretary, Odilon's niece Yvonne, whom the author described as "a pretty Lozèroise from Monjézieu."[18]

Proust still felt indebted to Léon Daudet and announced his intention to write an article about him. Léon urged Marcel to abandon the idea and spend his time and energy on the *Search*. Daudet did not need a tribute to appreciate Marcel's profound friendship, which was reciprocated. Writing to Marcel and thinking about his health had made Daudet, who had long ago abandoned medicine for journalism, "feel more like a doctor than ever. But you would never heed my advice, which would be, in your eyes, extremely upsetting."[19]

Proust did take someone's advice regarding a shield against contagious diseases. This step had been prompted by the concierge's young daughter, who often brought Proust's mail to his apartment and who seemed to be constantly sick with infectious childhood diseases. Proust's germ phobia, which had become even more marked, made him fear that, in his weakened condition, touching the envelopes that the child brought up in her unclean hands might give him the measles or whooping cough. He instructed Céleste to buy a "long metal box and put formol in it to disinfect the letters before he opened them." Proust would not take an envelope in his hands until it had been exposed to the formaldehyde solution for two hours.[20]

English Visitors

On April 7, in anticipation of the Schiffs' visit to Paris, Proust drafted a letter for Rivière to send Sydney upon his arrival in Paris. The letter, to be written as though from Rivière to Schiff, explained that Proust, due to illness and other distractions, had failed to forward in a timely manner Schiff's novel for Jacques's consideration to publish in the *NRF.* Proust had forgotten Schiff's pseudonym (Stephen Hudson) and the book's title *(Elinor Colhouse)* and asked Jacques to supply them if he knew them. In the postscript "Jacques" invited Schiff to stop by for a visit at the NRF offices. Rivière, after going to a fair amount of trouble, even having Schiff's novel translated into French, rejected the manuscript. *Elinor Colhouse* was later published by Schiff's friend T. S. Eliot in his new review *The Criterion.*[21]

Rivière was not having a good year. He had spent January in Luxembourg, where he finished revising his novel *Aimée.* Jacques, whose health was declining but whose ambitions for himself and the *NRF* remained strong, found it increasingly difficult to work and concentrate. When Schiff met Rivière at the NRF's offices in early May, he thought the editor looked "very sick, to the point of dying." Schiff reported his impressions to Proust, including Jacques's desperate practice of taking arsenic and strychnine injections just to get through the day.[22]

The Schiffs proved to be difficult guests, especially for two men whose lives were as complicated by literature and illness as were Proust's and Rivière's. The visit began badly when the Schiffs changed hotels even before arriving but neglected to inform Proust. They decided at the last minute to go to the Hôtel Foyot, known for its excellent restaurant and accommodations. Certain that his English friends would be staying at the Ritz, Proust took his various fortifying shots and waited in vain for them to arrive at the hotel. When Proust learned what had happened, he sent a letter to the Schiffs, saying that he did not know whether he would be able to rise again soon.[23]

During part of the Schiffs' two-month stay in Paris, Violet felt ill. Sydney was often reduced to lunching and dining alone at the Ritz, where he hoped that Proust, who found all other hotels unacceptable, would join him. Sleeping poorly and coughing through the night, Schiff soon became fatigued. A nervous man under normal conditions, Sydney resorted to his usual medecine in stressful situations: he began to drink too much champagne. He later admitted to Proust that the excessive wine only made him "stupid as well as deafer."[24]

Proust had little time for the Schiffs because he was occupied with preparations for the publication of *Sodom and Gomorrah,* part 2. He was eager for Rivière to publish an article, as part of the publicity campaign, in which Camille Vettard compared Proust to the physicist Albert Einstein. Proust believed that Jacques was reluctant to print the piece because readers might be put off by the comparison to the scientific genius, but Marcel saw the comparison as "the most immense honor and the keenest pleasure one could grant me." In fact, Rivière hesitated because of the highly personal tone of some passages in Vettard's piece.[25] Once those were cut, the essay appeared in *NRF*.

Before the publication of *Sodom and Gomorrah,* part 2, Proust gave excerpts to two reviews, apparently in the belief that exposure to different audiences increased his readership. In April, *Intentions* published an excerpt about the "strange and sorrowful reason" for which the Narrator intends to marry Albertine ("Étrange et douloureuse raison d'un projet de mariage"). At the end of the month, "Une soirée chez les Verdurin" (An evening at the Verdurins') appeared in the April–May issue of *Les Feuilles libres.*

On April 26, Gallimard reported to Proust that copies of the volume should be delivered to bookstores by Saturday morning, April 29, "exactly as you wished." He enclosed the press list and invited Proust to mark the names of those he wanted to receive a copy directly; Gallimard would bring him the others to sign. At the end of his letter, Gallimard expressed concern about Proust's condition: "It seems to me that this year has been difficult enough for you so that you must try everything to get better."[26]

Proust did make sporadic attempts to improve his health, or at least to eat more. Sometime in late April he wrote a note to Céleste, asking her to "warm up a little bit of Vichy water" because the water in his glass was flat. He had decided not to request any potatoes, because the "horrible tart" had made him nauseated. "I'm freezing. Is it warmer in the kitchen than here? Do you have any croissants, I'm afraid the potatoes will take too long. How much time for the noodles? Forgive me for ringing so much." If Proust listed so many things that he might eat, it was because he had no appetite and nothing appealed to him.[27]

On the last day of April, Mme Straus sent her "dear little Marcel" a melancholy note, in which she said, "Life is passing by—especially mine—and we are still kept apart by sleep!" She doubted they would see each other again "in this world, and I am hardly counting on 'the other' to facilitate our friendship." She was eager to read his new book before she was "completely dead." Mme Straus urged him to rise early—around eight in the evening—and come dine on a "sachet of caffeine." Failing that, she asked him to send the "beautiful Céleste" to report when she might "read, even in proofs, the desired volume." If Marcel waited too long and she went "up there," she certainly would not be able to receive *Sodom and Gomorrah.* "I was the first to know and to love you. Furthermore I still love you tenderly."[28] Mme Straus's apprehensions proved true; she and Marcel never saw each other again, but he was the first to leave. Proust, who spent time with his new friends, apparently had no particular desire to see his oldest friends. He seemed happy to see those, like Reynaldo and Lucien, who called on him, but he made no special effort.

On May 1 Proust was amazed to find himself surrounded by the "pile of volumes" that Gallimard had sent. "Apparently, this is my book," he wrote Binet-Valmer. Indeed, it was one hundred copies of the three-volume edition of *Sodom and Gomorrah,* part 2. Strapped for cash, as always, Proust complained to Gallimard about the publisher's "restrictions," by which he meant the clauses of his contract. It was clear from what he wrote Gallimard that he was tempted to sell another long episode from the *Search* in order to earn extra money: "Being able to give from time to time an unpublished episode" to *Les Œuvres libres* "would have made my life easier from a monetary point of view and would have caused me no fatigue." Forgetting all the extra work required to provide a separate novella for Fayard, Proust thought only of the extra money he could earn from such a publication.[29]

The day proved fateful for Proust. His carelessness with drugs resulted in another accident, one with permanent consequences. Although he did not feel like going out, he agreed to accompany the Schiffs to the Ritz for dinner. His note to Schiff said that he had not slept for a week and that he was having his worst day in a while. He described himself as "a misshapen and staggering thing." No matter: he agreed to be ready at eight o'clock, when Violet was to call for him in a car. But the visit must be short because he was exhausted. He included instructions for the staff at the Ritz: Olivier must close all the windows in the restaurant and the gallery. Schiff received Proust's message at four and soon reported that he had spoken to Olivier and arranged everything as requested.

While signing his books, Proust decided to take some dry adrenaline in a very strong dose. He neglected to dilute it sufficiently, and when he swallowed the powder, it severely burned his digestive tract. He dropped his books and howled in pain. For three hours he suffered a "veritable martyrdom." Once the worst pain subsided, he decided to meet the Schiffs anyway. When Violet came to pick him up, his eagerness to go out was apparent; as Proust later described to Sydney, he had "jumped" in the car. A few hours after Proust returned home, however, he came down with a high fever. Although he described himself as "very well cared for" by his servants and doctors, he endured weeks of fevers during which he could take no solid food. He sent Odilon to the Ritz every night to bring back ice cream, "the only thing I can swallow."[30] From that time on Proust ate and drank little other than ice cream and iced beer from the Ritz.[31]

In the days following the accident, the doctors considered washing out his stomach but abandoned the idea. Instead, they put plasters on his stomach in an attempt to heal the ulcerations. Proust's discomfort was so great that he found it difficult to turn over in his bed. He assured Sydney that if the Schiffs remained in Paris, as soon as he was able to leave his bed, "my first visit will be for you." There are indications that by mid-May, Proust was giving serious thought to entering a sanatorium. He advised Maurice Duplay to use the NRF address when writing him because he might leave for a clinic.[32] By the last week in May, though, Proust was able to go to the Ritz for the first time since the accident.

During his latest health crisis, Proust heard from friends who had read *Sodom and Gomorrah,* part 2. Morand wrote to say that the publication had gotten off to a good start: the volume "was in all the bookstores, very much in view, and everyone is talking about it," even the foreign press. Morand referred to the critic J. Middleton Murry's article in the *Times* of London. Writing about French literary taste, Murry cited Proust's success with the *Search* as an example of an author who appeals to the "general public despite his rare qualities." According to Murry, French readers had purchased forty thousand copies of each of the five volumes to date of this "remarkable and demanding story."[33] In August, Léon Daudet sounded the same theme, calling Proust a "popular" author whose books "sell thousands and thousands of copies, [one] who is read, reread, interpreted, admired in every milieu."[34] Although Murry's figures are inflated, he and Daudet had observed correctly: the *Search* did sell well, especially given the demands it made on the reader's attention and pocketbook.

There was surprisingly little reaction to Proust's having populated his novel with a high percentage of characters who engage in homosexual acts. François Mauriac did tell Proust that he had gone too far in depicting so many homosexuals. "Your cursed cities lack the ten righteous men that, it's true, God did not find therein. Without the ten righteous men," Mauriac, like other readers, felt the proportion was out of balance and that "Sodom and Gomorrah were becoming one with the Universe. A single saintly figure would have sufficed to set everything right."[35] Walter Berry, however, approved of Proust's frank talk about sexuality; Berry wrote a friend that the volume was "terrific . . . nothing like it outside of Krafft-Ebing."[36] The book predated by nearly three decades the first scientific surveys, such as the Kinsey reports, which validated a number of Proust's observations about human sexual behavior, many of which involve bisexuals or individuals whose sexual orientation changes with time. Proust was the first novelist to present what Dr. Albert Kinsey later described as the continuum of human sexuality.[37]

Mme Straus sent her congratulations on the new volume, which absorbed her so completely, she wrote, that she did not even hear the servant call her to dinner.

She expressed her regret that she might never see Proust again and thanked him for the "immense joy" his book had given her. The daughter of Fromenthal Halévy had been very touched by Proust's quoting an aria from the composer's most famous opera, *La Juive*.[38]

Proust performed a remarkable nonliterary feat in honor of the Schiffs: he entertained in his apartment during daylight hours so that the Schiffs could meet his sister-in-law and niece. Marcel received his guests in the small living room, where he stretched out on a chaise longue. During the visit, Suzy saw how much Mr. Schiff idolized her uncle. After their return to London, Violet, without consulting Proust, wrote directly to Suzy and invited her to visit them in England. Suzy felt that her Uncle Marcel was "violently opposed" to her accepting the invitation. Violet may have had this impression also, for she later wrote to Proust and apologized, only to have him tell her that there was no cause. Suzy later learned that the Schiffs hoped to marry her to their nephew.[39]

On May 15 Schiff sent Proust a note to congratulate him on his book. Sydney mentioned that he and Violet planned on Thursday to attend the première of Stravinsky's new ballet *Renard*. After the performance, they were hosting a supper party for the composer, Diaghilev, and some members of his troupe at the Hôtel Majestic. Schiff had rented a private salon at the Majestic because the Ritz allowed no music after 12:30. If, "by some miracle," Proust could attend, he would find the party "on the ground floor around 12:30."[40] Schiff listed the other guests, including Picasso and his wife.[41] A guest not mentioned by Schiff was the Irish writer James Joyce, whose sensational novel *Ulysses* had been published only two months earlier in Paris. Marcel, whose fever had subsided, went out for the first time since his accident to the Schiff's party at the Majestic.

Joyce, who arrived before Proust, apologized to the Schiffs for being late and for not having dressed; at that time he had no formal clothes.[42] The Irish author began drinking heavily to hide his embarrassment. Suddenly, the door opened and Proust appeared, wearing a fur coat. Eager to meet Proust, Joyce followed the Schiffs to the door and attached himself to Proust for the rest of the evening. Perhaps geniuses attract, or perhaps Joyce, underdressed and slightly drunk, felt more comfortable in the company of a fellow practitioner of his craft. Neither writer knew the other's work. In October 1920 Joyce had mentioned Proust in a letter to Frank Budgen: "I have read some pages of his. I cannot see any special talent but I am a bad critic."[43] The creators of Leopold Bloom and Charles Swann had little to say to each other. Nonetheless, there are many versions of the meager exchange. The variations in the tale apparently resulted from Joyce's relish in retelling the encounter, remembering it differently each time. Proust, presumably unimpressed with Joyce, never related the encounter to anyone who recorded it. According to William Carlos Williams, Joyce complained about headaches and his eyes, while Proust bemoaned his poor digestion. But Joyce told Jacques Mercanton that "Proust would only talk about duchesses, while I was more concerned with their chambermaids." Violet Schiff remembered that the party broke up when Proust suggested that the Schiffs accompany him to his apartment in a taxi. Joyce, very tipsy, climbed into the taxi with them and promptly opened the window. Schiff, knowing Proust's deadly fear of drafts, immediately closed the window. When they arrived, Proust, in a polite gesture that also served to get rid of Joyce, urged the Irishman to let the taxi take him home. Joyce lingered, eager for more drink and badinage. Proust fled to his apartment, leaving the Schiffs to persuade Joyce to return home on his own.

Joyce wrote Sylvia Beach in October, saying, with typical Joycean wordplay, that he had "read the first two volumes recommendés by Mr. Schiff of À la Recherche des Ombrelles Perdues par Plusieurs Jeunes Filles en Fleurs du Côté de chez Swann et Gomorrhée et Co. par Marcelle Proyce and James Joust."[44] Nothing more is known about his opinion of Proust; apparently, Joyce continued to see "no special talent."

Proustian Monsters

Around the time of the Schiff party Proust received a letter from a woman who was outraged because she recognized herself as Odette. Without naming Laure Hayman, Proust lamented his situation to Gallimard: "A woman I loved thirty years ago wrote me a furious letter to tell me that she is Odette and I am a monster. Such letters (and the replies!), that's what kills all work. I am not speaking of pleasure. I renounced that long ago."[45]

Proust answered Laure, expressing his astonishment that she had found any resemblance between herself and Odette: "Odette de Crécy is not only not you, but your exact opposite. This seems to me overwhelmingly obvious in every word she speaks." Proust chose to overlook the fact that he had given Laure's address in the rue La Pérouse, behind the Arc de Triomphe, to Odette de Crécy. He cited the example of a woman, whom he did not name but who belonged to high society and whose flowers he had described for Odette's apartment. The lady had thanked him "without believing for a second that she might, therefore, be Odette." The

flowers in question were Mme Straus's "guelder-rose snow-balls."[46] Using the tactic
he had employed to throw Montesquiou off the scent, Proust named other courtesans, such as Clomesnil, who had inspired a particular dress worn by Odette. He
paraphrased for Laure a passage in *Sodom and Gomorrah,* part 2, that had been
published in *Les Œuvres libres,* in which he remarked how silly society people were
for believing that "a book is a sort of cube one side of which has been removed, so
that the author can at once 'put in' the people he meets."[47] In such cases, society
people "generally choose a person who is exactly the opposite of the character. . . .
Alas, did I overrate you? You read me and find yourself resembling Odette! It's
enough to make one give up writing books." He knew that society women had no
idea of what literary creation is, except those who were "remarkable. But remarkable is just what you were in my memory. Your letter has disillusioned me. I lack the
strength to go on, and in saying good-bye to the cruel correspondent who writes
only to cause me pain, I place my respects and my tender memory at the feet of her
who used to think better of me."[48] In his charming, ingratiating, and perhaps
convincing way, Proust had maneuvered from offender to innocent victim.

Fortunately, not all reactions to his book put him on the defensive. Henri
Bidou, whose articles on the war Proust had found superior, praised the novel.
Being with Proust's characters, the critic wrote, was like "being in a lively crowd."
The *Search* was much more than a reading, it was a "presence."[49] Cocteau sent a
note saying that next to Marcel's books all others seemed "boring." Among the
pages Jean particularly admired were those on Céleste, "which are of a celestial
poetry." Proust paid tribute to Céleste and her sister, Marie Gineste, in a humorous
passage in which the two meet the Narrator at Balbec, where the sisters are staying
in the servants' quarters, performing the service of messengers. "I had very soon
formed a mutual bond of friendship, as strong as it was pure, with these two young
persons, Mlle Marie Gineste and Mme Céleste Albaret." Proust evoked the sisters'
home in central France, describing them as products of that particular landscape.
Françoise, the fictional servant, is favorably impressed on learning about the
marriage of Céleste and Marie's brother to the niece of the archbishop of Tours.
Céleste and Marie taunt the sedentary Narrator about being spoiled and playing
the prince. Proust ended the passage with a moving portrait of Céleste, in which the
Narrator teases her about reproaching her husband for failing to understand her,
"and I myself was astonished that he could put up with her. For at certain moments,
quivering, raging, destroying everything, she was detestable." He compared her
humors to the elements and to the "rhythm of her native streams. When she was
exhausted, it was after their fashion; she had literally run dry. Nothing could then

have revitalised her. Then all of a sudden the circulation was restored in her tall, slender, magnificent body. The water flowed in the opaline transparence of her bluish skin. She smiled in the sun and become bluer still. At such moments she was truly celestial."[50]

In late May, Edmond Jaloux, now Grasset's literary editor for novels, invited Proust to dinner with Middleton Murry and his wife, the writer Katherine Mansfield, at the Bœuf à la Mode. Jaloux was certain that Proust knew "how much they admire you."[51] The previous December, Mansfield had written Schiff from Switzerland to express the couple's intense admiration of the *Search:* "We lived Proust, breathed him, talked and thought of little else for two weeks." Proust was unable to accept the invitation.[52]

By late May, Proust, ready to try solid food, communicated with Céleste by note. "You could always buy some asparagus and prepare them right away. I will have them or not have them. Wait until I ring to bring them." Proust ate the asparagus but found it indigestible. Three nights later he ordered a "monstrous dinner" from the Ritz and had it delivered to his apartment. Whether he ate any of it is unknown. He complained to friends about the huge tab he was running at the Ritz because of his constant need for ice cream and iced beer.[53]

Shortly before the Schiffs were to return to London, Proust took Sydney to Le Cuziat's brothel. Apparently, Schiff did not enjoy the experience, for Proust later wrote to apologize for having "inflicted" the visit on his English friend. Marcel caught a cold during the outing, which apparently prevented his seeing the Schiffs again before their June 1 departure.[54]

On June 4 Lucien wrote and asked to visit Marcel "one evening when you can receive me without tiring yourself too much."[55] Lucien found Proust "even paler than usual, with deep black circles around his eyes." As they talked about the old days, something reminded Lucien of the little ivory box Marcel had given him. "God!" Proust exclaimed, "How could you have kept that box? Surely it's very ugly? Is there not something prettier that you'd like to have?" Lucien replied that nothing could rival the box. When it came time for him to leave, the past overwhelmed Lucien, the "memory of the little box moved me to tears, and I tried to embrace him; he drew back in his bed and said to me: 'No, don't embrace me, I haven't shaved,' then I quickly seized his left hand and kissed it."[56] When Lucien went through the door, he turned and looked at Marcel, who was staring at him. It was the last meeting of the two friends.

That week Antoine Bibesco, his wife, and Princesse Marthe Bibesco came to Proust's apartment.[57] Antoine was in Paris for summer vacation and had wanted to see Marcel before going on to Romania, where the three would stay through the fall. Proust, weary and unkempt, allowed Antoine to come to his bedside for a visit, while Céleste entertained the ladies.

He also received Rivière in an emotional meeting. Proust demonstrated his great friendship for Jacques, whom he wanted to encourage and aid. He asked Rivière to take leave from the *NRF* and devote himself to revising the remaining volumes of the *Search,* but Rivière felt that he could not leave the review. Though moved by Proust's kindness and affection, Rivière was upset by one remark. He wrote Proust afterward: "Why do you despair of finishing your work? I am certain you will finish it." So "great was the need" everyone felt for the book that Proust could not "leave it unsatisfied."[58]

On June 10 Proust wrote Berry about his intention of going to Mme Hennessy's party the following week. Because she had no doubt "invited hundreds of guests whose heat will revive me . . . I could risk this exception. But yesterday after eating ice cream and drinking iced beer in my bed, where I was too hot, I developed a sore throat and I don't know if, between now and Monday . . . I will be recovered." He told Berry he had already spent "850 francs this month for ice cream, which I find excessive."[59] Proust did attend the Hennessy party, where he met Marie de Benardaky, now the "white-haired Princesse Radziwill." According to Céleste, when Proust offered to take Jeanne home and she declined, saying, "Another evening, perhaps," he said that he would never see her again.[60]

A few days later, Proust told Lacretelle that he had "eaten nothing in the last ten days and had hardly slept three hours in all" during that time. "Every day I try a new remedy," and while he no longer expected to be well, he would at least like to "go out and above all to work again."[61] Proust's biggest problem apart from his health was his need for money. Gallimard contacted Proust with what sounded like a possible opportunity to obtain needed funds. Jacques Doucet, renowned couturier and collector, who was amassing important documents for the creation of an important library that he intended to leave to the state, had offered to buy Proust's manuscripts. Proust first set the figure at seven thousand francs, which Gallimard thought was too high, observing that Gide's manuscripts had sold for a third as much.[62] The negotiations continued into the fall, with Proust alternately raising and reducing the price. Finally he rejected an offer of ten thousand francs from Serge André for the manuscript of *Sodom and Gomorrah.*[63] Pleased that the offer showed how prized his manuscripts were, Proust nonetheless hesitated to sell them. As he explained to Schiff, he dreaded the notion that when Doucet's library became state property "anyone (if anyone still cares about my books) will be allowed to go through my manuscripts, compare them to the definitive text, and reach conclusions, which will always be erroneous, about my way of working, on the evolution of my thought, etc."[64]

Meanwhile, in London, Violet Schiff posed for a drawing by Wyndham Lewis. Sydney wrote Proust that after Lewis finished Violet's portrait he would draw one of him. If they turned out well, Schiff would send the drawings to Proust. "Lewis is our Picasso but a difficult person, hard and without charm." Schiff said that Proust was the "only man I like and I don't intend to like any other." His intense admiration for Proust led him to inquire, "Would you allow Picasso to draw you if I ask him to portray you for me? Just a drawing—it would only take an hour." Schiff had also been thinking about the English version of the *Search* and had concluded that his "sympathetic intuition, literary taste and mental faculties" made him the "only one who could do this translation." He added: "I often think about this. Would I not do better to put my own work aside and undertake the translation of the entire *Search*?"[65]

In the summer the Schiffs sent the charmless Wyndham Lewis to call on Proust and make a drawing. Lewis, who had the wrong address, did not reach Proust until near the end of a brief stay. By the time Proust received Lewis's note asking for an appointment, he felt too unwell to see the painter. He wrote Lewis that he regretted the missed opportunity, for being portrayed by him "would have been my only chance to be remembered by posterity!" Later in the summer, Schiff sent Lewis to call on Proust again, but nothing came of the proposed drawing.[66]

Proust invited Edmond Jaloux to dinner in his apartment on June 23 but had to postpone the meeting after experiencing "malaises" that made Dr. Bize believe he might be suffering from uremia. Bize intended to come the next day and draw blood to send to the laboratory for analysis. Until the results were known, Proust could make no plans. It seems likely that his only serious problems stemmed from excessive self-medication. The evening after Proust canceled dinner with Jaloux, he felt well enough to receive Gide. During the visit, Gide, though by that time somewhat estranged from the NRF, declared that Proust's "unfairness and ingratitude toward the NRF were revolting." Proust denied the charge.[67] Gallimard had written that day, asking when Proust would send "the remainder of 'Sodom' for typesetting." Gaston hoped to take advantage of the vacation lull to print the next volume, even if Proust chose a later date for publication.[68]

Perhaps inspired by Schiff's interest in translating the *Search*, Proust asked Gallimard whether his book had been or was being translated into English. Proust apparently remembered none of the earlier details Gaston had supplied or the translation copy sent for approval. He informed Gaston that although he had both the manuscript and the typescript of the next two volumes, *The Captive* and *The Fugitive,* the "revising of the typescript, where I am making additions everywhere and am changing everything, has hardly begun."[69]

Gallimard reminded Proust that he had negotiated with Chatto and Windus of London for rights in England and America and had written him when the contracts were signed. Gaston probably learned from Rivière that Proust had decided to give excerpts from the next volume to the *Revue de France,* and he wanted to make certain the *NRF* was not slighted: "You know my detestable jealousy concerning you. So if you must give excerpts to the *Revue de France,* I would be greatly saddened if the *NRF* did not receive its share."[70] Proust also heard from Rivière, who expressed his displeasure with the decision. Rivière said he did not deserve such treatment and, "moreover, the *Revue de France* was in steep decline and . . . had no right to present itself to you as a better embarkation than the *NRF.* You can ask any bookseller; I am confident about the answer you will receive." Proust consoled and reassured Jacques, telling him that there was no one he "liked, esteemed and admired more than you. And I always manage, by my clumsiness, to vex you, even, you tell me, to 'discourage' you, you the person to whom I would most love to give additional encouragement." He insisted that Jacques was not to worry; Proust had no formal agreement with the *Revue de France.*[71]

As Marcel's friends began to leave for vacation, he envied their freedom. He bemoaned his sedentary, isolated, nocturnal existence in a letter to Jaloux, saying that he had not been able to "leave Paris even for an hour in eight years. I see no reason why this year should be different." But he did not even see Paris, "only the awful walls of his room, never illuminated by daylight."[72]

When Proust did not receive his royalty check at the end of June, he waited a few days before sending a polite reminder to Gallimard. The author attributed the delay to Gallimard's needing a little more time to calculate the royalties for the previous volume. This was an indirect way of saying that he had not yet received the advance royalties on the first three thousand copies of *Sodom and Gomorrah,* part 2, as stipulated in the contract. But because he had agreed to monthly payments, he was not entitled to receive any more than the usual amount.[73] Proust probably saw matters otherwise, given the large sum that Gallimard owed him and his own pressing need for cash. He told Gallimard that he could announce the next two volumes for 1923, but he was not certain that they would be ready. He did not want to give Gallimard "botched work, but the best possible given my limited abilities." Proust also believed his public was somewhat "sated" from the three most recent volumes and it might be a good idea to let his readers "catch their breath a little and let their appetite return." There was a new factor regarding the titles. Another publisher had just brought out a book by Rabindranath Tagore whose title had been translated as *The Fugitive.* Therefore, Proust said, no *Fugitive* and no *Captive,* for the titles were clearly in opposition.[74]

Gallimard replied that Proust had not received the regular monthly check because Raymond Gallimard, who had taken Tronche's place as business manager, had been away. The publisher ignored the hint about the advance on royalties. So far as the forthcoming volumes were concerned, it was better to announce books even if they did not appear, rather than the other way around. Gallimard had received a request from the American magazine *Vanity Fair* to publish a photograph of Proust in its monthly "Hall of Fame" column. Gaston had on file the Nadar photograph of Proust at sixteen, which he intended to send to the magazine.[75] In January 1923 *Vanity Fair* published the column with an 1896 photograph of Proust, apparently the first to appear in the American press.

Proust received a letter from Schiff that he apparently threw away because it revolted him. One can judge its contents only by Proust's response. Schiff had clearly committed two cardinal sins: he had spoken like a snob (or as though Proust wrote for snobs) and he had expressed a viewpoint that matched Sainte-Beuve's. Marcel gave him a severe dressing down. He began by saying that if Schiff really read his book he would see that he cared nothing for society and had given it up years ago. "But you don't read my book because like all socialites who don't care for it, in Paris you are too nervous, in London you are too busy, in the country you have too many guests." Proust blamed himself, or rather his book, "because if it were really a fine book it would unite spirits and calm troubled hearts. Yet from the day it was published, the book's true friends read it . . . in the métro . . . oblivious to those sitting next to them and ride past their stops." When Schiff reiterated his Sainte-Beuvian belief that "when one knows a person one does not need to read a book by that person," Proust denounced the idea as "absurd" and explained his theory of the profound self: "Between what a person says and what he extracts through mediation from the depths where the integral Spirit lies covered with veils, there is a world. It is true there are people who are superior to their books, but that's because their books are not *Books.*"[76]

In early July letters to Schiff and Gallimard, Proust said that he was enjoying a sudden improvement in his health. His vertigo and speaking difficulties had all but disappeared, and he felt many years younger. Proust wrote Princesse Soutzo that he was once again dining nightly or nearly so at the Ritz. One wonders on what he dined, given his recent diet of ice cream and iced beer. He asked her to keep his reemergence secret, because he sometimes dined at the hotel when friends were expecting him for dinner. Proust's return was a windfall for the Ritz staff. Having sent out for ices, beer, and beef vinaigrette during recent months, he now arrived to see "unknown waiters come out of the cellars and kitchens to assure me that they are the ones who made the raspberry ice cream or cut the meat." He felt obliged, of course, to tip them all in the grand Proustian manner.[77] Had Proust eaten the beef vinaigrette or ordered it for his bedside guests?

Le Bœuf sur le Toit had officially opened on January 10 in the rue Boissy d'Anglas. Its proprietor, Louis Moysès, had asked permission of Cocteau and Milhaud to use the title of their spectacle-concert for his new bar and restaurant. Cocteau and his entourage attended the gala opening of the Bœuf, which became an overnight sensation and favorite spot of the smart set. Cocteau later described the Bœuf as "not a bar at all, but a kind of club, the meeting place of all the best people in Paris, from all spheres of life—the prettiest women, poets, musicians, businessmen, publishers—everybody met everybody at the Bœuf."[78] Those present on July 15 could have met or at least seen Marcel Proust, who put in his first and only appearance as the guest of Edmond Jaloux and Paul Brach, a young poet and novelist who sometimes visited rue Hamelin. Brach and Jaloux had difficulty persuading Proust to forgo the Ritz for an evening. When Jaloux called for Proust, Céleste was knotting his dress tie for him. Jaloux observed in amazement how helpless Marcel seemed. When Proust complained that his cup of tea was lukewarm and not, as he had requested, boiling hot, Céleste seemed hurt. Sensing this, Proust praised the cup of tea, saying that, given his condition, Céleste had been right to serve it to him at that temperature. Jaloux noticed that "All this was said with infinite kindness."[79]

On arriving at Le Bœuf sur le Toit, Jaloux sensed that Proust felt rather edgy. Soon, however, it was obvious that he felt completely at ease. When Jaloux left early to keep another engagement, Proust and Brach were joined at the bar by some of Brach's inebriated friends. In fact, everyone at the bar seemed drunk except Proust, who later said he had nothing to drink. At the other end of the bar, where there was a noisy group of revelers, a brawl broke out between the party of Comte Charles de Maleissye-Melun and a group of men whom Proust took to be "unbelievable pimps and queers."[80] Proust had the impression that the bar's proprietor Moysès sided with the "pimps and queers." In the meleé, Proust almost received a hot roast chicken and ice bucket on his head, leading him to conclude, punning on his host's name, that this "Moses keeps tables that are not those of the Law."[81] The loud, violent scene stirred Marcel, making his natural adrenaline flow. He said afterward that he "had believed that the charming time of duels was going to be born again for me."

The next day Proust opened the *Figaro* and saw Jean Schlumberger's article, "*À la recherche du temps perdu:* Une Nouvelle *Comédie humaine*," in which the critic compared Proust's work to Balzac's remarkable re-creation of French society from Napoléon through the Restoration.[82] Proust wrote immediately to offer Robert de Flers his "tender admiration" and profound gratitude for publishing Schlumberger's article. Proust expressed his amazement that *Sodom and Gomorrah* had caused "so little scandal!" Was it because France had been through the long trauma of the war, in whose aftermath society's mores had grown more lax? Or was it because the prestige of the Prix Goncourt had sanctioned his enterprise? "*Le Gaulois,* where I know no one, has already done five articles on my last book, *L'Écho de Paris* is asking that I be given the Nobel Prize, the *Revue de Paris,* the *Revue de France* praise me as though I were as innocent as Madame de Ségur. Léon Daudet, who finds Hervieu putrid and Bataille fetid, celebrates in me a genius, alas, that doesn't exist." Proust apologized to Flers for his dreadful handwriting, "due to drug intoxication," which made him fall with every step he tried to take and left his hand so twisted and stiff that he could hardly write, "and the most horrible thing about it is that it's my fault." Proust saw what he was doing to himself but lacked the willpower to stop.[83]

Proust compiled a mental list of Gallimard's recent transgressions. Soon his letters contained hints that should have alerted Gallimard that a new crisis was building. It did not really matter if Proust were sick during the vacation season, because he had so little money that it would be difficult for him to "go on vacation, the first in eight years, and the first I could have really enjoyed." For someone like him, even a ride around town in a closed car was a "voyage." Gallimard soon received a reprimand for not having done a better job publicizing *Sodom and Gomorrah,* part 2. All publicity, Proust maintained, had been arranged by himself and his friends. He wanted the Schlumberger piece to be placed as a paid advertisement in the Académie française's *Revue des journaux.* Gallimard defended himself and assured Proust that he was neglecting nothing and had gone to no end of trouble to obtain Schlumberger's article. Proust replied that Gallimard's letter "touches me without convincing me." He complained that there had been nothing in the *NRF* about the important article by the distinguished German scholar Ernst Robert Curtius. In February, Curtius had published in *Der neue Merkur* "Marcel Proust," the first of his several articles on the novelist. Here Proust was mistaken;

Rivière had published a detailed notice of the Curtius review in the July *NRF*. Proust leveled another charge against Gallimard: other writers were paid more than he. If the better-paid writer were someone of Gide's stature, he approved. But there were others that Gallimard himself judged third-rate who were "paid a great deal more than I." Addressing his publisher as "Dear Gaston," he told him that "this eternal question of all the money" owed him was what so often divided them. He hated to talk about "such vulgar matters." Then, realizing that he had been a little harsh, Proust wrote in the postscript that "Someone who lives as I do and suffers endlessly is almost a monster."[84]

Gallimard reassured him: "You are by far the highest paid author here." Saying that he would "welcome the opportunity to prove" this, Gaston provided details about what others received and what Proust earned. He asked Marcel to name at once the mendacious "hidden enemy" who kept feeding the novelist's discontent with falsehoods. Gallimard asked for sympathy: "You can well see that my life is not beautiful because . . . I must defend myself against calumnies and constantly justify myself to you, while you are assuredly the author I admire most, the friend whom I prefer."[85] Proust had little time for sympathy, and he did not believe Gaston's protestations.

Rivière, whose spirits had been even lower than usual, waited until he reached his resting spot in Haute Savoie before rereading *Sodom and Gomorrah*. Afterward, he wrote to Proust and expressed his admiration: "My dear Marcel, how beautiful it is! It's life itself." Rivière had noticed for the first time Proust's "relationship to the Cubist movement" and his "profound immersion in contemporary aesthetics." Jacques explained what he meant: "Never have things said to be the same been shown in so many different lights—to the point . . . where they seem to be coming apart, where they would come apart if the movement, the implacable continuation of your narrative did not guarantee their reconstruction." He then talked about Charlus, who was "prodigious!" Charlus was "greater than Balzac's Vautrin because he was better analyzed." Jacques regarded one aspect of this characterization as nearly "miraculous." After having first shown Charlus "in circumstances that were quasi-repugnant," Proust made him "progressively likable." As the reader learned more and more about Charlus, "one discovered . . . his bond with normal humanity. It's magnificent!" Regarding the Narrator's infatuation with Albertine, Rivière found "the way in which you study the generation of love by jealousy . . . admirably new and profound."[86]

In spite of such praise, Proust feared that if the next two volumes were shorter than the earlier ones, his admirers and detractors might conclude that he was falling off. He wrote Gallimard on July 22 that he would soon send the manuscript of *Sodom and Gomorrah*, part 3 *(The Captive)*, in order to have proofs made that he would then greatly rework. He was eager to see whether *The Captive* would be short enough to publish at the same time as *The Fugitive*, because if it was "certain that short books sell better, in my case, since I have managed until now not to fall into a slump, I would like to avoid, even if I publish a work that is not as long, having people say: 'He is really declining.'" He hoped to rest for two weeks and resume work with renewed vigor.[87]

At Proust's urgings, Gallimard placed ads in newspapers. One in a woman's magazine, *Eve*, warned that *Sodom and Gomorrah* was "Not for young ladies"; an ad in *Le Gaulois* recommended Proust's books "For Vacation Reading." Because Proust had complained so bitterly about the lack of publicity, Gaston pleaded once again for a résumé, which he described as indispensable, and for photographs for American magazines. As for giving the impression that Proust was in a "decline," Gallimard did not see how anyone could believe that; just one of the volumes of *Sodom and Gomorrah*, part 2, seemed more substantial than many complete works by others.[88]

By the end of the month the improvement in Proust's health began to wane. One evening, after dispatching Odilon to the Ritz for iced beer, Proust wrote Brach and described how miserable he felt. If he remained in bed too long, he began to sweat so profusely that every fifteen minutes he had to get out of bed and change pajamas while Céleste put fresh sheets on the bed; each time he arose from the bed and stripped, he suffered chills. His neck ached from a new crick. Proust now viewed his life, he told Brach, as a kind of "horror." He managed to distract himself somewhat in the evening by giving history lessons to Odilon and his "charming family to whom I teach night school."[89] Céleste remembered one occasion near the end, when Proust, up at an unusually early hour for him, came home around six or seven in the evening. Odilon and Marie were also present and Proust's "look embraced us, and he added, smiling with heartrending tenderness: 'I love you all so much.' Then, more gently still: 'You are my children.'"[90]

Proust heard from Schiff, who, though "tired and depressed," wrote to say how much he admired Proust's work "as much for its philosophical erudition as for precise knowledge, and as a literary and artistic encyclopedia." Schiff praised him as "the equal of the greatest authors of the past; your works will have a permanent, definitive place in the literary history of Europe above everyone else since Balzac. Therefore, your manuscripts, your proofs will have historical value." Schiff, convinced that the manuscripts would end up in some museum, offered to buy them.

He announced that as soon as he finished his "little book," he and Violet would come to Paris for three days and stay at the Ritz, solely to see Proust.[91]

T. S. Eliot contacted Gallimard and Proust, requesting an excerpt from the next volume for *The Criterion,* the first issue of which would appear in October. Gallimard consulted Proust, who replied rather vaguely that the most practical solution would be to send Eliot an excerpt from a volume that had been published but not translated.[92] Gallimard pressed Proust to make certain that he wanted to give Eliot an excerpt. If so, the publisher would find out how much the American would pay. This time Proust remained silent, and nothing came of the proposal.[93]

The *NRF* finally published Camille Vettard's article "Proust et Einstein" on August 1. Although Proust told Gallimard that Vettard "flatters me too much," the novelist was delighted by the comparison.[94] Vettard had found, among other similarities, that Proust and Einstein "have the sense, the intuition, the comprehension of the great natural laws." Eager to proceed with the hard work that remained for *The Captive,* Proust engaged Yvonne Albaret again as a typist. During the next ten weeks she typed three successive versions.[95]

On August 9 Proust went out in the daytime and returned home early in the afternoon. This unusual occurrence most likely was the result of relentless insomnia. He sat down immediately, without shedding any of the heavy clothes he wore even in summer, and wrote Paul Brach. Proust apologized for not being able to meet Brach in the grill room at the Ritz because he had already been out and expended all his energy. He had been looking forward to their meeting and to seeing the grill room, which was, he told Brach, the only part of the Ritz he did not know. Proust related that he often accompanied waiters late at night to the icebox, where their sudden arrival made the roaches run for cover. He boasted that he even knew how to work the showers at the Ritz.[96] Proust thanked Brach for having sent a magazine clipping that showed James Tissot's painting *Le Balcon du Cercle de la rue Royale en 1867.* Proust knew three of the men in the painting: Charles Haas, Edmond de Polignac, and Saint-Maurice, all eminent society figures of the Second Empire, the epoch depicted in *Swann in Love.* "But what a pleasure to see them again."[97] Having evoked the ghosts of Napoléon III's court and models for his characters, Proust returned to reality, which, for him, had grown somewhat grim. It was now two in the afternoon and, as he wrote Brach, he still had on his hat and overcoat. When would he be able to go out again? He knew that Brach was preparing to leave on vacation and seemed resigned to being left alone in Paris: "That's all very well, one thinks of people and one gets by without them so easily. I had something to ask you but I can no longer remember what. I am beginning to say a little less often: 'I will drown you in an ocean of shit.' "[98] What Proust meant by this last sentence is unclear. Had he resigned himself to his status as a permanent invalid, someone who could not take a vacation or enjoy the company of friends? Had Proust lately been giving free expression to scatological outbursts—a tendency he shared with Montesquiou and which he gave to Charlus? Or was the frequent use of such language the "return to a very infantile anal stage, which also characterized his sexuality"?[99] Gide, to whom Proust had spoken so frankly about his homosexuality, did not record the use of such language.

Rivière was preparing to leave for Pontigny in Burgundy in order to attend an annual meeting at which writers and philosophers from France and other countries gathered to debate philosophical and moral issues. The conference, held in an old abbey, had been founded by Marcel's former teacher and friend Paul Desjardins. This meeting was the first since the war began. Jacques was to participate in the sessions on literature, along with André Gide, Jean Schlumberger, Edmond Jaloux, and Ernst Robert Curtius. On the eve of his departure, Rivière asked Proust for the passage "Albertine sleeping" for the *NRF*'s October issue. If Proust agreed, he should send the text before the end of August. Rivière later reported to Proust that everyone at Pontigny had been talking about his novel. When a foreigner would ask Rivière who was the greatest French novelist of the day, "I invariably answered: Proust."[100]

During late spring and summer, Proust answered several surveys for newspapers and reviews. *Le Gaulois* asked three writers considered to be in the avantgarde for their thoughts on the work and influence of the Goncourt brothers. The paper described Proust as a Goncourt laureate who represented the "new psychology." Proust, who did not consider the Goncourts accomplished writers, answered candidly that the brothers "took notes, kept a diary," which did not make one "a great artist, a creator." Nonetheless, he found the diary's pages "delicious and entertaining." Remembering his 1907 pastiche of the Goncourt *Journal*, he cited the parody as a "laudatory criticism." Always eager to promote his novel, Proust alerted the newspapers' readers to a pastiche that was to appear in *Time Regained*, in which the Goncourt diary plays an important role in the Narrator's discovery of his own vocation as a writer. In the *Search*, the Goncourts' superficial jottings about life among the leisured classes first cause the Narrator to despair; if their work represents good literature, he realizes, he cannot compete because it is impossible for him to write in that manner. Then he sees that his own observations not only describe the surface but probe more deeply to reveal the profound psychological causes of human folly and vanity.[101]

The survey from *La Renaissance politique, littéraire et artistique* allowed Proust to give a more straightforward answer. "Are we," the review wanted to know, "in the presence of a renewal of style?" Proust replied briefly that "the continuity of style is not compromised but rather assured by a perpetual renewal. Writers should not be concerned " 'with originality of form' "—Proust was quoting from the questionnaire—but "only by the impression or idea to be translated." One must "look inward and force oneself to render with the greatest possible fidelity the interior model." Vain attempts to "shine" usually spoiled everything.[102] Proust was stating his conviction that each writer must find his own voice. A writer's style results from the rendering in his voice what he alone has discovered and beheld. In the *Search* Proust defines genius as the ability to mirror, to make visible, new truths about the human condition. That is why the Narrator says that "style for the writer, no less than colour for the painter, is a question not of technique but of vision."[103]

Proust's succinct answer to the third and most poignant survey appeared in *L'Intransigeant* on August 14. Other than excerpts from his novel, this was the final publication of his life. The newspaper asked "A Simple Question: If the world were about to end, what would you do?" Proust gave the rather standard answer for which this question begged, but with Proustian touches. The awareness of an approaching catastrophe, he wrote, would suddenly make us want to surmount our habitual laziness. "If only we can be spared we will visit the new exhibition rooms at the Louvre, we will throw ourselves at the feet of Mlle X, we will visit India. The cataclysm does not occur," and we quickly resume our normal routine, "where negligence dulls desire." We should need no disaster to make us "love life today. We need only to remember that we are humans and death may come this evening."[104]

A second accident that apparently contributed to Proust's physical deterioration occurred on August 20, when the chimney caught fire, filling his room with smoke. He wrote Princesse Soutzo that he had to leave his apartment at three in the morning because he could not stand the fumes. Although Proust repeatedly mentioned the chimney accident and decried the menace of asphyxiation, Céleste denied that such an incident ever took place.[105] Is this because Proust blamed her for the accident, for which she and Odilon may have been partly responsible if they failed to report a defective chimney? Proust was convinced that the noxious fumes aggravated his precarious condition.

On the day of the chimney fire, Proust informed Gallimard that he was thinking again about breaking not just his contract but his word. His need for money and his exasperation with Gallimard's slow payments had brought him to this point. As a pretext Proust used the recent example of Paul Morand. In September *Les Œvres libres* was to publish Morand's novella *La Nuit de Putney Common*. Proust hoped this publication signaled an end to Gallimard's misgivings about his authors' works appearing in Fayard's review. Marcel wrote that he was thinking of giving a large portion of *The Captive* to *Les Œuvres libres* before the volume was published by Gallimard. He stressed the advantages of being read by the "vast public" that subscribed to *Les Œuvres libres* rather than being read twice by essentially the same audience in the *NRF* and then in book form. If Proust did give *The Captive* to *Les Œuvres libres*, he assured Gallimard that he would offer Jacques other texts as compensation. Proust, who held his excerpts hostage while he negotiated, asked Gallimard to answer quickly because Rivière wanted texts for the October and November issues.[106] The new dispute was essentially a replay of the previous year's battle, with the same results.

Furious on reading Proust's letter, Gallimard waited a week before answering. After reminding Proust of his pledge never to break ranks again, Gaston, as the "Administrative Delegate of the NRF," reviewed the provisions of their contract. He concluded his letter, as he should have begun, by saying that "personally I have only one wish: that of pleasing you." By ending on a note of personal affection and trust, Gallimard hoped to persuade Proust not to give his excerpts to *Les Œuvres libres*. Proust blamed him, however, for having spoken first as an administrator rather than as a friend and observed that "the interest alone" of what Gallimard had owed him since the publication of *Within a Budding Grove* was greater than the fee offered by *Les Œuvres libres*.[107] Proust acknowledged that his contract required him to give the NRF half the ten thousand francs he would earn from Fayard.[108] For good measure, Proust sent along a postscript reminding Gallimard of his promise to match any such offer. Then Proust emphasized the enormous amount of work that he had to provide because "I don't want to give you books that are too bad. And I am starting over again for the third time my *Captive*, with which I am not happy, and I am having an infinitely difficult time trying to decipher the corrections and additions that I wrote on the pages of my typescript that otherwise would be very clear." Proust was also having difficulty reading his proofs because he had broken his glasses a few weeks earlier and needed to buy new ones or find another pair in the stockpile Céleste had brought home. He described the ruined glasses as "a real drama for me."[109]

In early September a contrite Gaston answered Proust's letter, which "had pained him infinitely." Gallimard offered to calculate the interest he owed Proust and pay him.[110] With the publisher groveling at his feet, Marcel, having obtained everything he wanted, became charming again. He wrote Gallimard immediately, saying that the excerpts on "Albertine sleeping" that he had promised Rivière were the "best things I have ever done." And he "would not accept a penny for these excerpts in order to acknowledge your kindness." Nor did he want Gallimard to hasten the settling of accounts; Proust had agreed to monthly payments and it would be better to leave things as they were. It was only his need for money that had made him raise the question of interest payments. If Proust had accepted the offer from *Les Œuvres libres,* it was because he had believed the NRF was unable to make him such an advance.[111] Gallimard replied that it was "out of the question" that Proust not be paid for the excerpts. As for *Les Œuvres libres,* he asked Marcel to choose another title for the piece and to make cuts in it so that the "volume we publish will have its raison d'être." He also wanted to know the approximate date for typesetting *The Captive* so that he could reserve time at the printer's.[112]

On September 4 Proust wrote Rivière and promised him the passage "Albertine sleeping" and many other excerpts, "on condition you don't say which volume they are from." He confided to Jacques that his most alarming symptoms had returned: "I am suffering too much today (I fell down five times today from vertigo. Please don't talk about this—to *anyone*)." A day or so later Marcel sent Guiche a letter and mentioned his deteriorating health, though in less specific terms than to Jacques. He observed that when he went out to dine at four in the morning, his symptoms seemed to vanish, which made him blame his troubles on the fumes emanating from the cracks in the chimney. But it was also possible that death was approaching. "That's bothersome before my book is finished."[113]

In Proust's final months, Montesquiou threatened to return from the grave and haunt the novelist. Proust became somewhat obsessed with the fear that the count had attacked him in his memoirs, which were being prepared for publication. In the summer Proust raised the issue with Paul Brach. If Montesquiou attacked him, could Proust sue Dr. Paul-Louis Couchoud, whom the count had chosen as literary executor? Marcel asked Tronche to go to Grasset's, where Montesquiou's memoirs, *Les Pas effacés* (Vanished footsteps), were being edited, and discover what the count had written about him. Tronche apparently learned nothing. In mid-October, Jaloux, who had heard about Proust's concerns, told him not to worry. Jaloux had not read the memoirs yet, but Grasset had charged him with editing them. Jaloux intended to cut any denigrating passages on Proust or other prominent figures—a condition he had set before agreeing to be the editor. But

Proust wanted stronger assurance; he asked Jaloux to remove his name altogether, for if he succumbed to the strange illness from which he suffered, he would be unable to answer any attacks Montesquiou might have made.[114]

Remembrance of Things Past

Of greater importance to the reputation of Proust's novel was the publication in English of Charles Kenneth Scott-Moncrieff's translation of *Swann's Way*. A native of Scotland, the translator had served as a captain in the Scottish Borderers during World War I. Before reading *À la recherche du temps perdu*, he had already made a name for himself as the translator of major French works, such as *La Chanson de Roland* (The song of Roland) and Stendhal's two masterful novels *Le Rouge et le noir* and *La Chartreuse de Parme*. After the war he had served as secretary to Lord Northcliffe, in addition to being an editor at the *Times* of London. In January 1920 the thirty-year-old Scott-Moncrieff had resigned his post at the *Times* in order to devote himself entirely to translating *La Recherche*. In September 1921 Sir Edmund Gosse, the English poet and critic, wrote Scott-Moncrieff and attempted in vain to persuade him to abandon the idea of translating the *Search* because Gosse thought Proust's work stood little chance of being remembered.[115] Considered by many to be one of the most accomplished translators of modern times, Scott-Moncrieff combined a knowledge of French and a command of Victorian English that allowed him to render Proust's complex style in a version that remained the standard over many decades for Anglophone readers.[116]

Proust was unaware of his good fortune in having such a translator; his misgivings were founded on a letter from Sydney Schiff. In London on September 9, Schiff read this announcement in the *Athenaeum:* "Messrs Chatto & Windus, as publishers, and Mr Scott-Moncrieff, as author, have almost ready the first installment of M. Marcel Proust's '*Remembrance of Things Past*' in the English translation. The title of this initial volume is '*Swann's Way*.' " Schiff, who had long thought he was the only Englishman capable of translating the *Search*, abhorred Scott-Moncrieff's titles. Schiff did not realize that the overall title came from the opening lines of Shakespeare's sonnet 30: "When to the sessions of sweet silent thought / I summon up remembrance of things past . . . " In his letter to Proust, Schiff lamented the loss of the French title's double meaning—time wasted and lost, with its "melancholy nuance, etc."[117] An even more surprising blind spot was Schiff's total misreading of *Swann's Way*, rendering it for Proust as the title "À la manière de Swann" (In the manner of Swann), as though that were its only possible meaning. Naturally, Proust, who knew something about the art of translation, was alarmed by Schiff's misleading letter.

Proust answered Schiff, indicating that he certainly did not intend to "let *Du côté de chez Swann* appear under the title you gave me. I knew nothing about this translation." Of course, Proust did know—or should have known—about Scott-Moncrieff's translation; the previous December he had declined Gallimard's offer to inspect it. Proust, whose condition was worsening again, waited nearly a week before writing Gallimard about the translation. Now, he said, in addition to "falling with every step," his speech troubles had returned. He then conveyed Schiff's concerns about the translation to Gallimard. The author could not accept a title that meant "In the manner of Swann." That was "intolerable." He reminded Gaston that *Du côté de chez Swann* and *Le Côté de Guermantes* indicated the two separate walks at Combray. The English title was "nonsense"; surely it must be an error. Proust concluded: "I value my work too much to allow an Englishman to demolish it."[118]

Gallimard replied that such a distortion of Proust's titles was indeed out of the question, and he would do everything in his power to prevent it. Gaston soon received the advance copies of *Swann's Way* in English. He had also found in the files for Proust's inspection the contract with the English publisher and his own letter to Proust offering to let him approve Scott-Moncrieff's translation. And Gallimard had some encouraging news: he had spoken to Victor M. Llona, his agent for America and England, "who knew English admirably well" and who assured him that *Swann's Way* was not at all bad for the title; it was in fact "quite good."[119]

In October, Proust, who did not live long enough to appreciate the excellence of Scott-Moncrieff's work, exchanged letters with his translator: "I was very flattered and touched by the trouble you took to translate my *Swann*." Because of his terrible health, Proust said that it was a miracle that he could thank Scott-Moncrieff. Although he had not read the entire volume, the author did have "one or two criticisms." The first was to explain that the general title did not mean at all *Remembrance of Things Past*. Proust regretted the omission of "lost time," which "is found again at the end of the work: *Time Regained*. As for *Swann's Way* that can mean *Du côté de chez Swann*, but also Swann's manner. By adding *to* you would have made it all right." Proust's second suggested correction seems to confirm his admission in the next sentence that he had forgotten all his English.[120]

Scott-Moncrieff's reply, written on Saville Club letterhead, was modest and brief: "My dear Sir, I beg that you will allow me to thank you for your very gratifying letter in English as my knowledge of French—as you have shown me, with regard to your titles—is too imperfect, too stunted a growth for me to weave from it the chapelet that I would fain offer you." After expressing his regret that Proust was so unwell, the translator continued, "I am making my reply to your critiques on another sheet, and by the aid of a machine which I hope you do not abominate: it is the machine on which *Swann* and one-third of the *Jeunes Filles* have been translated. Thus you can throw away this sheet unread, or keep it, or inflict it upon M. Gallimard. Charles Scott-Moncrieff."[121] The second sheet was discarded or lost, so we do not know how the translator justified his choice of the general title that Schiff and Proust were the first, but far from the last, to criticize.

In mid-September, Proust heard from Ernest Forssgren, his former Swedish valet, whose tenure had been so short. Forssgren was in Paris for a brief stay and hoped to see Proust before embarking for New York. Ernest had gone to boulevard Haussmann, only to find a bank where the apartment had been. He called at Dr. Proust's house and left a note for Marcel, saying that he was staying at the Riviera Hôtel. Then one night, not having heard from Proust, Ernest "got swept away in the whirlwind of Paris" and stayed out until three in the morning. When Forssgren returned to the hotel, the owner told him that a distinguished-looking gentleman had come to the hotel at eleven and waited for nearly three hours, shivering in the hallway, despite being clad in a heavy fur coat.[122] Finally, the gentleman asked for a piece of stationery and left a note to "Dear Ernest," saying he was "terribly sorry to have missed" him. Forssgren should not come to his apartment, but should keep him informed of his departure date. "Write to me at the Hôtel Ritz, place Vendôme, please forward." The note was signed "Marcel."[123] The rest of Forssgren's memoir claims that he called at rue Hamelin and found Céleste and Robert Proust extremely distressed because of Marcel's poor condition. Forssgren was told Proust had fallen critically ill after having stayed out until three in the morning in the course of a "mysterious visit." No one at rue Hamelin could imagine anyone being so important for Proust to have taken such risks.[124] According to Ernest, he felt so guilty and horrified at the thought that the illness had been his fault, even indirectly, that he dared say nothing. He left because Proust was too ill to receive anyone. This last part of Ernest's story sounds like pure invention. It is fairly certain that Forssgren left Paris for New York on September 20—a month before Proust became seriously ill.

In the third week in September, Proust complained to Gallimard of terrible asthma attacks, saying that he found it impossible under such conditions to work on *The Captive*, which he was rewriting for the fourth time. Proust sent Rivière a note, along with the excerpt for November's *NRF;* the titles for the piece would be "La regarder dormir" (Watching her sleeping) and "Mes réveils" (My wakings). Proust was so weak that the only way he had found the strength to work for an hour was to take an injection combining antiasthma medication and stimulants. When "Dr. Bize saw me killing myself on your excerpts he thought I was crazy to work in my condition."[125]

Rivière read the passages and wrote back at once: "It's admirable! I don't know if you have ever written anything as moving." Jacques expressed his heartfelt gratitude for the effort it had taken on Proust's part. Tronche had seen Proust and told Rivière how sick the writer looked. "I am completely ashamed." Jacques, however, knew no shame when it came to copy for the *NRF;* he still needed double the number of pages Marcel had sent to make the required twenty-five to thirty pages. For once Proust said no, he would not be able to send more copy. Were he to improve, the recovery would take a long time. Rivière had always asked him to reduce by half the copy he sent because readers preferred shorter texts. This time Proust said: "*Alea jacta est* and I'm not changing it." In case Rivière was having second thoughts about using the excerpt, Proust insisted on a November 1 publication or he would withdraw the offer. "You know I have always been superstitious about certain months."[126] Rivière published the excerpt as agreed.

With the latest controversy over *Les Œuvres libres* settled, Gallimard resumed regular payments to the author in early October. Proust, who now had to file his income tax report for 1921, thanked Gallimard for the check and asked him to provide the figure for the total amount of royalties paid to date. Proust had earned thirty thousand francs—an impressive figure. Soon Proust had another complaint for his publisher. Friends had told him that they were unable to find copies of *The Guermantes Way,* part 1, or *Sodom and Gomorrah,* part 2. "Is it possible," Proust asked, "that these recent volumes are out of print?" He asked Gallimard to be extremely diligent because if this were true, such a shortage would be the source of severe distress. "Others . . . enjoy the entire universe. I can no longer move, speak, think, or simply enjoy the well-being of not suffering. Thus, expulsed from myself, so to speak, I seek refuge in my books, which I touch, being unable to read them, and I have for them the wariness of the burrowing wasp." Like the wasp, and "deprived of everything, my only care is to give my [books], through their absorption by other minds, the expansion that is refused me."[127]

Again Gallimard proclaimed his innocence: "I don't know who told you *Sodom and Gomorrah,* part 2, was out of print." But he did admit that *The Guermantes Way* was "temporarily" out. The publisher had been meeting requests by having new covers placed on three hundred returned and damaged copies. He assured Proust that he had ordered a reprinting of 4,400 copies, which would be completed by December. In a letter to Tronche, Gallimard was more candid: "*The Guermantes Way* has in fact been out of print since July and I have been meeting demands with the returned copies." A few days later Gallimard informed Proust that Davis Erdtracht, director of the publishing house La Renaissance in Vienna, had written and requested rights for German and Polish translations of the *Search*. Gallimard, who had proposed to Erdtracht a 10 percent royalty on the retail price of each volume sold, sought Proust's approval.[128]

On October 12, as Proust's condition worsened, Rivière wrote to thank him for having returned the proofs of the passage "Albertine sleeping." After saying how dismayed he had been to learn of Marcel's illness, Jacques gave him good advice: "Let your brother do everything possible to treat you." Rivière was convinced that Robert could set Marcel on the path to recovery. Thanking Proust again for the "magnificent passage," Jacques could not resist adding, "whose only fault is being too short." But the editor was pleased because Proust had promised him a longer excerpt for December on "The Death of Albertine."[129]

As Proust's bronchitis developed into pneumonia, he began having terrible coughing fits. Finding it nearly impossible to speak, he scribbled notes to Céleste on the backs of envelopes or any scrap of paper lying about; often those closest at hand were the papers he used to light his antiasthma powders. He continued writing these little notes to her until the day he died: "I have just coughed more than three thousand times and no longer have a back or a stomach or anything. It's madness. I need very warm linens and woolens. Just remember one thing. All your linens have a pungent odor that provokes my coughing fits, which are so pointless. I hope you are going to follow *my orders* to the letter. If not, I will be *more than angry.*" After writing such a note, Proust would look up at Céleste and smile so that she could see both the importance of his orders and the humor of his threats. He considered his coughing fits useless because he never expectorated. Other notes asked: "Should aspirin be taken on an empty stomach? Why were the hot water bottles or ear plugs not warm enough?" In one note he wrote that his fever was so high he thought it would prevent "new coughing fits. What was that beer I drank two hours ago? I would like a hot water bottle wrapped in wool. (I already asked you for it.) I wrote some tender and pretty verses on you."[130] Teasing Céleste about being abrupt with him, Proust wrote a short poem to her in which all the rhymes end in -*aigre* (which suggests tartness); the last lines of which refer to her uncle by marriage Archbishop Nègre:

Grande, fine, belle et maigre,	Tall, slender, beautiful, rather thin,
Tantôt lasse, tantôt allègre,	Now tired, now gay.
Charmant les princes comme la pègre	Charming both princes and riff-raff,
Lançant à Marcel un mot aigre,	Throwing Marcel a harsh word,
Lui rendant pour le miel le vinaigre	Returning him vinegar for honey,
Spirituelle, agile, intègre,	Witty, nimble, upright,
Telle est la nièce de Nègre.	Such is the niece of Nègre.[131]

Proust occasionally tried to eat solid food. One day he wrote Céleste a note to apologize for ringing so much. Although he had gone back to bed, he thought she had remained up for a bit: "I think despite my stomachache, the stewed peaches instead of pears would do me some good. And my box of bicarbonate of soda so that I can take some with it."[132]

Léon Daudet came to see Marcel, who was too sick to receive him. Around October 21 Robert Proust wrote that he would like to see Marcel but had a bad cold and doubted whether he could come in the evening. Robert would do so, if Marcel requested it, but he would prefer the daytime. Robert reported that Bize had received the results from the analysis of Proust's sputum: "It's indeed pneumococcus. You should have Bize come back, we would all be very pleased. I embrace you profoundly. Your little brother." Rather than consult Bize or even his brother, Proust took a circuitous and peculiar route. He had Jacques write his brother, Dr. Maurice Rivière, who practiced in Bordeaux, and ask him to explain what the presence of pneumococcus portended. Proust asked Jacques not to tell Robert that he had consulted another doctor. Dr. Rivière confirmed that pneumococcus is present in nearly all sputum from healthy individuals. His letter was scientific to a fault; he asked no questions and made no recommendations. Dr. Rivière's letter may have encouraged Proust to believe that his body could cure itself.[133]

The End of Time

There are several theories of how Proust caught his final cold, which led to bronchitis, pneumonia, and death. Forssgren was convinced the writer caught it that night while waiting three hours for him to return. Céleste said that Proust caught his cold one October night when he went to a big party at the Beaumonts'.[134] And Proust? He blamed Odilon and especially Céleste. Writing to Morand in the first half of November, Proust explained that he had not been well for a month: "Odilon had

caught a cold that lasted only a day, but Céleste, refusing to put on any rhinogomenol, gave me the cold with a rapidity such that one would have thought she
was in a hurry for me to catch it. For a little more than a month I have been reduced
to coughing fits, fever, etc., asthma revived from my youth. Alas, youth itself has
not revived." Marcel gave Paul gossip about new divorces, including some humorous comments about Mme Scheikévitch's brief marriage. Then he mentioned a
recent obsession. He was worried that he had written Jean Giraudoux a "delirious"
letter and feared that Giraudoux might read in it "a touch of Charlus." Surely, it was
mad to think that. He also worried about his tax form. Morand, seeking to relieve
Proust's mind, asked Giraudoux about the letter and was told that the playwright
had received no such mail.[135]

Sometime around October 21 Proust's asthma and coughing grew even worse.
Dr. Bize told Proust that he had only "a slight attack of influenza" and that
"camphorated shots" should "relieve the congestion of the lungs and bronchial
tubes." If Proust followed his advice and agreed to look after himself, as Bize
suggested, he would be well in a week. Proust rejected the idea of any shots on
principle, believing that they were ineffective and only prolonged suffering. He
answered the doctor in a "gentle, rasping voice: 'My dear doctor, I must and shall go
on correcting the proofs. Gallimard is waiting for them.'" After the doctor left,
Proust, as usual, instructed Céleste to buy the medication Bize had recommended,
and, as usual, he took none.[136]

Dr. Bize, alarmed that pneumonia was about to set in, called Proust's brother
and asked that he try to persuade Marcel to accept treatment. His illness was
reaching a critical point and if action was not taken soon, it would be too late.
When Dr. Proust came that evening, Céleste witnessed a "painful" scene between
the two brothers.[137] Robert tried to convince Marcel that he should accept treatment at once, for his own sake and that of his work. When reasoning failed, Robert
said in an exasperated tone: "Well, we will have to look after you in spite of
yourself." This remark greatly "offended" Proust, who exclaimed: "What! You
mean to force me?" Robert denied any such intention and stressed the advantages
of entering a clinic: "Just around the corner in rue Puccini there is a marvelous
clinic, very well run, very well heated, with excellent doctors. You'd have a nurse to
do all that was necessary." If Marcel would enter the clinic, Robert assured him, he
would improve rapidly. Robert even promised that Céleste could have a room next
to his at the clinic. Proust answered in an explosion of anger, sending Robert away.
"I forbid you to come back here if it's to impose anything on me." And he ordered
Céleste not to let his brother or Dr. Bize in again. She must promise to obey him on

that point and one other: "Never let them give me an injection." She protested that she had no authority over his doctors. "But still I promised." Seeking to make things better, Robert had only made them worse, if that was possible.

After leaving Marcel's apartment building, Robert encountered Reynaldo, to whom he appealed as his last, best chance for assistance in persuading his brother to accept medical treatment. Hahn must have told Robert that for years Marcel had refused to listen to his advice regarding health. Nonetheless, the next day the composer typed a long letter to Marcel. In the first half he summarized his conversation with Robert, regarding Marcel's condition and prognosis: "Here is exactly what he told me. 'Marcel does not have anything serious, it's a pneumococcus, that is, something which can be treated and easily cured. But you must treat it and Marcel refuses to accept treatment.' " Robert had admitted to Hahn that he had spoken to Marcel "too much like a doctor and I now realize I was quite wrong and I upset him." Robert promised not to mention clinics, or nurses, or anything that might upset his brother, and he would stay away from rue Hamelin until Marcel invited him to return. But Robert had told Reynaldo, "It is very painful for me to see him refuse treatment when nothing would be easier." If, while making his hospital rounds, Robert "met a patient in Marcel's condition, [he] would say, 'He's a sick person who hasn't been treated.' " Robert would like to be his brother's "nurse and would do it in such a way that would not annoy Marcel or we'd find some arrangement that would work, but it's not natural for me to leave him sick, with no care, when he is in great need of it." Reynaldo explained Robert's fear that Marcel would contract pneumonia if he did not receive treatment soon. Then Reynaldo spoke directly to Marcel: "I don't need to tell you how much I regret not having the least influence on you; it pains me a great deal to think that you even refused to try and eat a little purée, as you had promised me, and persist in fasting, which cannot be good at this time. I know that no one can influence your decisions and I can do nothing I consider reasonable or beneficial for my dearest friend, for one of the people I have loved most in my life." At the conclusion Hahn said: "I will do as you wish and I resign myself, since I must, to obtain nothing. With great affection from your Reynaldo."[138]

Shortly after the scene between Marcel and Robert, all was forgiven. Soon Marcel had Céleste sending phone messages to Robert, who was again welcome at rue Hamelin, not as his doctor but as his brother. Dr. Bize also came to see him, but there was nothing he could do, given Marcel's stubbornness. Marcel, son and brother of distinguished doctors, refused all medical treatment, trusting instead to his own and Céleste's remedies.

Céleste, who wanted him to receive treatment as much as did Robert and Reynaldo, had no choice but to respect his wishes and prepare whatever food and drink he thought he might be able to digest. Most of her preparations went untouched. "He was always ringing the bell, either for a hot-water bottle, or a woolen, a book, an exercise book, a bit of paper to be stuck in." When he wanted some stewed fruit, he expected it "right away." If he asked Céleste for "some lime tea, he would just have one tiny sip and then put the bowl aside or hand it back to me. The same with the stewed fruit. He hardly tasted it. Probably because of the fever, all he fancied was cold beer."[139]

As pneumonia set in, Proust wrote notes, because as soon as he tried to speak a coughing fit began. In one late October note he gave Céleste instructions regarding his typescript for *The Captive*. "You see my coughing fits recommenced because I spoke to you. Cut everything (except what we left in *Albertine disparue*)—up to my arrival in Venice with my mother."[140] A similar notation was made on one of the two copies of the typescript. The proposed cut would have reduced the typescript by 250 pages. Proust indicated a major change in the locale of Albertine's death from a horseback riding accident: in the proposed short version she would die not in the neutral area of Touraine but at Montjouvain, scene of the lesbian trysts between Mlle Vinteuil and her friend, whose presumed influence on Albertine had driven the Narrator nearly mad with jealous despair. Proust may have changed his mind about excising so many pages, but death intervened before he could make the many changes required by this cut or give more detailed instructions.

When Proust received the proofs for the excerpts on "Albertine sleeping," he hated the way the passage ended. By the time he notified Jacques of his displeasure, the printing had already begun in Bruges. On October 24 Proust wrote Rivière to "wire Bruges" and stop the presses. Proust said that he would pay all the costs, but the excerpt "cannot end like that." Jacques answered that he had followed Proust's instructions and begged him to send the ending he wanted as rapidly as possible.[141]

The next day Proust sent Rivière the preferred ending. Then he asked Jacques to leave him alone; he was only "a wretched person who could stand it no longer and who, feeling better yesterday, had corrected an entire book for Gaston and written on your behalf for the Prix Balzac." He blamed Jacques for having made him believe that corrections had been made in *Sodom and Gomorrah,* part 2. Proust was confused on this point, because he had instructed Georges Gabory, the young man the NRF hired to read the proofs, to look for duplicate passages, not typos and other errors. Now Proust told Rivière: "I no longer trust you." The letter upset

Jacques, who did not understand what he had done wrong. If, while only seeking to be agreeable, he had been maladroit, he asked to be forgiven.[142]

Toward the end of October, Proust received postcards from Antoine and Marthe Bibesco, who were enjoying their vacation on the family estate in Corcova. Antoine had encouraging news regarding Scott-Moncrieff's translation: "Dear Marcel, You will no doubt be happy to learn that the translation is Remarkable. See you soon I hope, Antoine." Marthe's postcard showed the irises of Mogosëa. If Proust had seen the irises, she wrote, surely he would have placed them with "the hawthorns and apple trees in blossom" that he had "immortalized at Méséglise and Balbec." Under Marthe's signature, Antoine again scribbled "See you soon."[143] Antoine's assessment of Scott-Moncrieff's translation was confirmed by many readers, including a number of distinguished writers. F. Scott Fitzgerald wrote, in a letter to his daughter, "Scott-Moncrieff's Proust is a masterpiece in itself."[144]

On November 1 Proust requested from Rivière a copy of the *NRF* to read that evening, "while I am lucid." He said that earlier he had been a little delirious. It was regrettable, Proust wrote, that Jacques had not received the Prix Balzac.[145] Gaston sent a note, inquiring when he might have the next volume. Gallimard would have stopped by to see him, but he feared exposing Proust to a bad cold that he had been unable to shake.[146]

Proust answered Gallimard, thanking him for a recent check for four thousand francs. Then he spoke of his own distress: "I think now the most urgent action is to deliver all my books to you. The sort of tenacious work that I have done for *The Captive* . . . especially in my terrible current state . . . forced me to set aside the following volumes. *The Captive* is ready but needs to be read again. (The best thing would be for you to make the first proofs that I will correct.) But three days of rest will be enough, I am stopping here, farewell dear Gaston." In the postscript he wrote: "Letter will follow when able."[147] This was his last word to Gallimard. A few days later Proust had one typescript of *The Captive* delivered to Gallimard; that copy did not contain the notation prescribing the large cut.

On November 7 Gallimard acknowledged receipt of the manuscript for *The Captive*, which he was sending to be typeset. "I will send the proofs as soon as I have them." Did the delivery of the complete typescript version indicate that Proust had changed his mind about cutting so many pages—a cut that may have been motivated by his eagerness to publish the episodes of Albertine's death and the Narrator's phases of grieving and forgetting? A year earlier, Proust had described these episodes to Gallimard as the "best" he had written.[148] It was unlike Proust to discard material, especially pages he judged "aesthetically perfect."[149] The pages marked for omission include the Narrator's investigations at Balbec regarding Albertine's possible trysts with laundry girls, an investigation carried out with the assistance of Aimé; the first two stages on the road to indifference over Albertine's death (the Venice episode begins with the third and final stage); and Mme de Guermantes's changed attitude toward Swann's wife and daughter after his death. The pages to be omitted contain many fine Proustian observations about love, jealousy, memory, death, and forgetting. Knowing Proust's method of composition, it appears likely that had he made such cuts, he would have reworked some of this material back into the concluding volume. One can only speculate about the results. The standard edition, known and loved by three generations of readers, will probably endure.

On November 4 Jacques Bizet took his own life by shooting himself in the head. Bizet had been long been tormented by his private demons as well as a demanding mistress. If Proust learned the news of Jacques's death, he was apparently too ill to send Mme Straus a letter of condolence. She had lost her only child and was soon to lose Marcel. When Robert Dreyfus did not hear from Marcel regarding Bizet's death, he inquired about the novelist's health and was told that it was very bad.[150]

In early November, Proust wrote a note to Céleste, saying that he would take a spoonful of vinegar and a bean salad, immediately. She had not given him enough vinegar before, he complained. He kept spitting everything up. In another note to Céleste, written about the same time, he said: "I don't think I will have anything. But what if I were to ask (on condition that I might not drink it) for some café au lait that Marie could keep ready and be warned that what I want indeed is milk that has no odor."[151]

When Proust's copy of *Aimée* arrived, he was unconscious. Céleste read Rivière's dedication: "To Marcel Proust, great portrayer of love, this unworthy sketch is dedicated by his friend J. R." She wrote to thank Jacques: "M. Marcel Proust is aware of nothing, that's why he does not know that you have sent him your book. But if he recovers, you may be certain that nothing will captivate him as much as reading your book *Aimée*, which he so much enjoyed reading on an earlier occasion." Proust had taught her well.[152]

Schiff, unaware of Proust's critical condition, wrote in mid-November, complaining that his last two letters had gone unanswered. He congratulated Marcel on "Albertine sleeping," which was "a delicious fragment." Sydney had kept all the clippings from the reviews of *Swann* in translation, and he assumed that Gallimard had done likewise. The press, he thought, had been good. Its effect on Schiff, however, was to make him "want to vomit when I read again the effusive praise heaped on your translator but I swallow them with the most grace I can muster, and while thinking of the advantages for you, I enjoy them in your place." Schiff then revealed his tearful, emotional state, for which he seemed to blame Proust: "A letter from you would have been the prayer that my lips no longer lend themselves to sigh, the tears that my eyes are no longer willing to shed." Was Proust still there? Perhaps he, like everything and everyone else except Violet, had "flown away and left the earth barren." Schiff ended by sending Marcel "all my affection. Your S."[153] By the time Schiff's letter arrived, Proust was barely conscious. In retrospect, Céleste realized that Proust "knew he was going to die, and I still thought he'd live to a fine old age."[154]

On the last day of Proust's life, Céleste broke the two promises she had made, but only out of desperation. The evening before—Friday, November 17—Robert had come around eight or nine, just as Céleste was preparing a meal for Proust.[155] The patient had said that he did "not feel too bad this evening." But Céleste had been urging him to eat, and he told her that he thought he could eat some sole. Robert asked to see Marcel before she served the sole. Céleste remembered that the two brothers were together for a long time before "M. Proust called me in and said: 'I don't think I shall have the sole after all, Céleste.'" When Robert came out he told her that he had examined his brother and thought his heart sounded weak. He expressed his relief that Céleste would sit all night with Marcel. Céleste later realized that she "was probably the only one still under the illusion that he would recover. It wasn't that I rejected the idea of his dying—it simply didn't enter my head." Later she remembered signs that should have alerted her. He had asked her to send flowers to Dr. Bize, not "out of remorse," as some later claimed, but "out of gratitude for the doctor's care and kindness over many years." Léon Daudet also received flowers to thank him for his recent article on Proust.

After Robert left, Proust said to Céleste that she should settle down in the chair by the bed so that they could begin to work. "If I get through the night, I shall have proved to the doctors that I know better than they do." Although it seems unlikely that Proust was in any condition to work, Céleste recorded that he dictated to her until about half past three, when he decided it would be less tiring to write than to dictate, "because of the breathing." Then, after a few minutes, he declared himself too tired to continue but asked her to stay with him. (Dr. Proust later explained to Céleste that it was "probably then the abscess burst and septicemia set in.") Proust wanted to write a letter to her, but she must promise not to read it until after he died. She protested, saying that he would live. Attempting to lighten the moment, she teased him by saying, "Women are inquisitive, monsieur. How could I resist?" Proust may have believed her or may simply have been too exhausted to move; for whatever reason he did not write the letter. Céleste realized later that he had wanted to leave her something.[156]

Toward morning Céleste noticed that Proust looked much worse: "His eyelids would sometimes flutter rapidly, and his breathing was very difficult." Around seven he asked for some coffee, to please her and Robert. He would "have it hot, if it is ready and you bring it right away." Proust drank a little and gave the cup back to Céleste. Then he asked to lie quietly for a moment and signaled for her to leave. She went out but was so concerned by the changes in him that she remained in the corridor outside his room as she had done once so many years before at boulevard Haussmann, when he went two days without ringing for her. This time he rang:

"What were you doing behind my door, Céleste?" he asked. She tried to deny she had been there.

"Céleste, Céleste, don't lie." She admitted wanting to remain near, in case he needed anything. He said nothing for a moment, and then: "You won't switch off my light, will you?

"Monsieur," she replied "It's you who give the orders."

"Don't switch it off, Céleste. There's a big fat woman in the room . . . a horrible big fat woman in black. I want to be able to see . . . "

Thinking he was having a nightmare or was delirious, she reassured him: "Just wait—I'll chase her away. Is she frightening you?"

"Yes, a bit. But you must not touch her . . . "[157]

While Proust spoke to her, Céleste noticed him "pulling up the sheet and picking up the papers strewn over the bed," something he never did. She had never been with someone who was dying, but she remembered that in her village she had "heard people say that dying men gather things." She became truly alarmed and thought for the first time that Proust might die. She broke her first promise by sending for Dr. Bize, then ran down to the baker's to telephone Dr. Proust. Mme Proust said that her husband was teaching at Tenon Hospital, but she would send a "message to him at once."

Dr. Bize arrived around ten. Earlier Proust had requested cold beer, and Odilon had left for the Ritz. Before the doctor entered Proust's room, Céleste broke her second promise and begged Bize to save Proust by giving him an injection. The doctor responded: "But you know he doesn't want it." Céleste, nearly mad from exhaustion and fear, led the doctor into the bedroom. Although she thought it impossible to trick Proust, desperate measures were needed. Dr. Bize had been passing by, she said, and just stopped in to see how M. Proust was feeling. She had invited the doctor to come up, thinking that Proust would like to see him. Proust said nothing. Céleste recalled: "All he did was just look at me—so that I should see, once again, that one couldn't lie to him." He refused to acknowledge Bize's presence, but when Odilon arrived with the beer, Proust greeted him affectionately: "Good morning, my dear Odilon. I am so glad to see you." But Marcel did not touch the beer. Dr. Bize, very ill at ease, prepared the injection, then whispered to Céleste: "How am I going to manage?" She asked where he would give the injection. When he answered that it would be in the thigh, she volunteered to lift up the sheet. She did so "carefully, doing everything not to offend M. Proust's modesty." He was "lying on the edge of the bed with one arm hanging down over the side." Céleste noticed the arm was "slightly swollen," probably an indication of poor circulation. When the doctor leaned over to administer the shot, Proust "reached out his other arm and pinched" her on the wrist, crying out, "Oh, Céleste . . . oh, Céleste!" Her remorse was "all the greater" when she realized that "by then the injection was useless." Bize left. When Dr. Proust arrived, she explained what she had done and how terrible she felt about it. Robert tried to comfort her by saying, "You've nothing to regret, Céleste. You did quite right."

Robert saw that the situation was hopeless and left, promising to return soon. When he came back at around one, he asked Odilon to find some cupping glasses and Céleste to bring an eiderdown and more pillows. Robert raised Marcel as gently as possible while Céleste arranged the pillows.

Robert said: "I'm tiring you, my little Marcel."

"Yes . . . yes, Robert dear."

Odilon returned with the cupping glasses, which were to be placed on the skin and heated, in an effort to improve circulation by creating a partial vacuum. But they did not hold on Marcel's skin and hence were useless. Then Robert sent Odilon for some oxygen cylinders. As Robert gave his brother a little oxygen, he leaned over and asked whether that felt "a bit better, my little Marcel?"

"Yes, Robert."[158]

A short time later Robert sent for Drs. Bize and Babinski. At approximately four o'clock, the three doctors conferred in the bedroom while Céleste listened, fearful that Proust heard everything. Robert suggested an intravenous injection of camphor, but Babinski said: "No, my dear Robert. Don't make him suffer. There is no point." Then Bize left. When Céleste showed Dr. Babinski to the door, she made a desperate plea: "Professor, you *are* going to save him, aren't you?" Babinski took her hands in his and looked into her eyes: "Madame, I know all you have done for him. You must be brave. It is all over."

At approximately half past four, Céleste returned to the sickroom and stood beside Dr. Proust. No one else was present. She felt certain that Proust had never taken his eyes off them. "It was terrible. We stayed like that for about five minutes, and then the professor suddenly moved forward, and bent gently over his brother, and closed his eyes. They were still turned toward us. "I said: 'Is he dead?' 'Yes, Céleste. It is over.'"

Robert asked Céleste to help lay out his brother. Céleste was so upset that she forgot Proust's request to "entwine his fingers with the rosary Lucie Faure had brought back for him from Jerusalem." Robert said, "He died working. We will leave his hands as they were." She did remember that Proust had wanted Abbé Mugnier to come and pray at his deathbed. Robert asked Céleste to cut off two locks of Marcel's hair, one for him and the other for her. Then he contacted Mugnier, but the priest was ill and unable to come.

Soon Hahn arrived and took charge of notifying Marcel's closest friends. After phoning Lucien Daudet, Reynaldo sent a note by pneumatic mail to Rivière: "Sir, it is my duty to inform you that our dear Marcel Proust died this evening at 5:30. His brother and I wanted you to be one of the first to know. Marcel had a special friendship and esteem for you, and we know his death will aggrieve you deeply."[159] Léon Daudet arrived and wept for a long time by the body. Proust's friends and acquaintances had heard him speak of dying so often that many could not believe the news.

Robert thought Marcel "looked so 'well'" that he postponed the funeral until Wednesday, which would allow friends to pay their last respects on Sunday and Monday before the body was placed in a coffin on Tuesday. Reynaldo stayed through the night. Sometimes he sat with Céleste next to the body; sometimes he went into another room and wrote music.[160]

Among those who came to pay their respects were Anna de Noailles, Robert Dreyfus, Jacques Porel, Paul Morand, Fernand Gregh, and Jean Cocteau. Someone placed a large bunch of Parma violets on Proust's chest. Céleste, weeping, asked Dreyfus whether he wished to see Proust one last time, but he did not feel up to it. He preferred to remember the Marcel of long ago when they had first become friends playing in the gardens along the Champs-Élysées.[161] Porel did enter the bedroom because he had brought something for Marcel to carry with him on his final journey. Porel placed on Proust's finger the cameo ring that Anatole France had given Réjane at the première of *Le Lys rouge*.[162] When Paul Morand viewed the body, he told Céleste: "Sometimes when I came to see him he would say: 'Forgive me, Paul, if I shut my eyes for a little. I am tired. But go on talking, please, and I shall answer. I am only resting.' And he would shut his eyes, but he would leave one eye just slightly open to watch. Well, I don't know if you noticed it, Céleste, but he is doing that still even now; one lid is just slightly raised."[163]

Lucien later wrote that when he viewed Marcel's body, he noticed all "traces of care and the black circles around the eyes had disappeared. On his solemn face, the candlelight showed an inkling of a smile that was neither bitter nor haughty, the smile that follows a hard-won victory: his rejuvenated features proved that Marcel Proust, after so much suffering and resignation, had finally discovered Eternity— and regained true Time."[164]

In a passage toward the end of the novel, when the Narrator is obsessed by death, Proust makes this comparison: "In my awareness of the approach of death I resembled a dying soldier."[165] When Cocteau paid his respects, he was especially moved by the stack of Proust's notebooks on the mantel: "That pile of paper on his left was still alive, like watches ticking on the wrists of dead soldiers."[166] Proust had left his novel unfinished, yet, as he had predicted, somehow complete.

Sunday afternoon, around two, the painter Paul Helleu came at Robert's request to do an etching. Those who called to view the body marveled at how beautiful Proust's features and skin looked in death. Perhaps no one did so more effusively than Helleu, who had long wanted to depict Proust: "Oh! it was horrible, but how handsome he was! I have done him dead as dead. He hadn't eaten for five months, except for café au lait. You can't imagine how beautiful . . . can be the corpse of a man who hasn't eaten for such a long time; everything superfluous is dissolved away. Ah, he was handsome, with a beautiful, thick black beard."[167] Helleu worked hard, afraid of botching the job, because his eyes had grown weaker with age and he was etching under an electric light, which reflected on his copper-plate and prevented him from seeing clearly. The artist, who talked to Céleste as he worked, asked why Proust had spoken as he had about Montesquiou. Helleu was referring to the portrayal of Charlus. "It killed Montesquiou," Helleu told her. Céleste amazed him by showing a kind of "fierce delight" at the thought.[168] Two proofs were made of the etching. Robert Proust was pleased with the result; he kept a copy and gave the other to Céleste.[169] That afternoon André Dunoyer de Segonzac drew a charcoal sketch of Proust.

With Robert's permission Cocteau phoned Man Ray, an American artist and photographer, who had come to Paris a year earlier. Ray, severely depressed to the point of being suicidal, managed to pull himself together long enough to go to rue Hamelin and photograph Proust on his deathbed.[170] It was impressed upon Ray that the photograph was for private use. The family would keep a print; Cocteau was to receive one, and Ray, if he wished, could keep a print for himself.[171]

On Tuesday, before the body was put into the coffin, Robert stayed a long time alone in the room; then he let Céleste go in to say good-bye.[172] The next day, funeral services were held at noon in the church of Saint-Pierre de Chaillot. Military honors, to which Proust was entitled as a knight of the Légion d'honneur, were provided by a squadron of officers from central Paris. After the service, Maurice Barrès stepped outside the church, put on his bowler, and found himself standing next to François Mauriac. "Ah well," Barrès said, "so that's the end of our young man."[173] Unnoticed, apparently, by any of Proust's friends, was James Joyce, who had come to pay his respects to the one author whose achievement in the novel rivaled his own.[174]

As the funeral procession set out on its journey across Paris to the Proust family plot in Père-Lachaise, Fernand Gregh's little dog Flipot, who had been hiding under the hearse, ran out and disappeared into the crowd, never to be seen again by his master.[175] Cocteau and a few friends slipped away from the long procession and stopped off at the Bœuf sur le Toit before taking a taxi to the cemetery.[176] At last the procession reached the Proust family plot, where the likeness of Dr. Proust, as captured in Marie Nordlinger's medallion, gazed out over Paris's most famous necropolis. Marcel was laid to rest beside his parents.

Those dark, hypnotic, penetrating eyes were closed. But Proust had left behind, in the pages of his book, a new way of seeing. The Proustian lenses, which he urges the reader to throw away if they fail to improve his vision, invite us to take a marvelous, exhilarating trip: "The only true voyage, the only bath in the Fountain of Youth, would be not to visit strange lands but to possess other eyes, to see the universe through the eyes of another, of a hundred others, to see the hundred universes that each of them sees, that each of them is; and this we can do with an Elstir, with a Vinteuil; with men like these we do really fly from star to star."[177]

Notes ∾

Abbreviations for Works by Proust

Corr.
Correspondance de Marcel Proust, edited by Philip Kolb, Paris: Plon, 21 vols., 1970–93.

CSB 5
Contre Sainte-Beuve, edited by Pierre Clarac with the collaboration of Yves Sandre, Paris: Gallimard (Pléiade), 1971.

JS 4
Jean Santeuil, preceded by *Les Plaisirs et les jours,* edited by Pierre Clarac with the collaboration of Yves Sandre, Paris: Gallimard (Pléiade), 1971.

PJ
Les Plaisirs et les jours, edited by Thierry Latget, Paris: Gallimard (Folio), 1993.

PR
Pleasures and Regrets, with a preface by Anatole France, a translation of *Les Plaisirs et les jours* by Louise Varese, New York: Crown, 1948.

Recherche OP
À *la recherche du temps perdu,* edited by Pierre Clarac and André Ferré, Paris: Gallimard (original Pléiade edition), 3 vols., 1954.

Recherche NP
À *la recherche du temps perdu,* general editor Jean-Yves Tadié, Paris: Gallimard, 4 vols., 1987–89.

Search
In Search of Lost Time (formerly *Remembrance of Things Past*), translated by C. K. Scott-Moncrieff and Terence Kilmartin, revised by D. J. Enright, New York: Modern Library, 6 vols., 1992–93. This English

translation is referred to as the *Search* by volume number: 1, *Swann's Way;* 2, *Within a Budding Grove;* 3, *The Guermantes Way;* 4, *Sodom and Gomorrah;* 5, *The Captive* and *The Fugitive;* 6, *Time Regained.*

SL 1   *Selected Letters in English, 1880–1903,* edited by Philip Kolb, translated by Ralph Manheim, introductions by J. M. Cocking, New York: Doubleday, 1983.

SL 2   *Selected Letters, 1904–1909,* vol. 2, edited by Philip Kolb, translated with an introduction by Terence Kilmartin, London: Collins, 1989.

SL 3   *Selected Letters, 1910–1917,* vol. 3, edited by Philip Kolb, translated with an introduction by Terence Kilmartin, New York: HarperCollins, 1992.

STW   *On Art and Literature, 1896–1919,* translated by Sylvia Townsend Warner, with an introduction by Terence Kilmartin, New York: Carroll and Graf, 1984.

Unless otherwise indicated, all attributed dates for the events in Proust's life are those established by Philip Kolb in his edition of the letters. Unless otherwise stated, all translations are my own. Any emphasis in quoted material is in the original.

1 Secret Places of the Heart

1. According to the census of 1859, in all of France, there were only 6,600 people whose income exceeded ten thousand francs. Claude Francis and Fernande Gontier, *Marcel Proust et les siens, suivi des souvenirs de Suzy Mante-Proust,* Paris: Plon, 1981, 45.
2. Philippe Michel-Thiriet, *The Book of Proust,* translated by Jan Dalley, London: Chatto and Windus, 1989, 130.
3. Jean-Yves Tadié, *Marcel Proust,* Paris: Gallimard, 1996, 41.
4. Tadié, *Marcel Proust,* 32.
5. Michel-Thiriet, *Book,* 122.
6. Tadié, *Marcel Proust,* 29.
7. When I refer to Proust's novel, I always mean *In Search of Lost Time,* referred to hereafter as the *Search.*
8. *Jean Santeuil,* 738–39. It was not known until several decades after Proust's death that he had begun a novel at age twenty-four, worked on it for several years, and then abandoned it. These drafts were left unrevised by Proust, who did not even indicate a title for the work. When the manuscript was published by Gallimard in 1952, the editors named it *Jean Santeuil* after the hero. Proust's drafts are of considerable interest because of their autobiographical nature and because they contain many of the major themes that will be fully developed in the *Search.* I will use such passages from *Jean Santeuil,* when their autobiographical content is clear, to illustrate his childhood and adolescence. I always refer to this work as *Jean Santeuil.* When possible I used the English translation by Gerard Hopkins, New York: Simon and Schuster, 1956. Unless otherwise stated all translations from *Jean Santeuil* are from this edition. However, there are passages and fragments of interest in the French editions that were not included in the translation. I have translated these and refer to them as *JS* 4.

9. Tadié, *Marcel Proust*, 36.

10. Robert Le Masle, *Le Professeur Adrien Proust (1834–1903)*, Paris: Librairie Lipschutz, 1935, 32.

11. Philibert-Louis Larcher, *Le Temps retrouvé d'Illiers*, Illiers: Mairie d'Illiers, 1971, 71.

12. Le Masle, *Adrien Proust*, 32–33, 38.

13. Larcher, *Illiers*, 63.

14. For my description of Dr. Proust's war on cholera, I am particularly indebted to Francis and Gontier, *Proust*, 45–53.

15. Honoré de Balzac, "Lettres sur Kiev," *Œuvres Complètes*, Paris: Gallimard, 23: 533. Quoted in Francis and Gontier, *Proust*, 47 and n. 1.

16. Michel-Thiriet, *Book*, 125.

17. André Ferré, *Les Années de collège de Marcel Proust*, Paris: Gallimard, 1959, 38.

18. For my description of the siege of Paris and the Commune, I am particularly indebted to Rupert Christiansen's *Paris Babylon: The Story of the Paris Commune*, New York: Viking, 1995.

19. Michel-Thiriet, *Book*, 121.

20. See Denise Mayer, "Le Jardin de Marcel Proust," *Cahiers Marcel Proust*, n.s. 12, *Études proustiennes*, V, 9.

21. Tadié, *Marcel Proust*, 18.

22. "Mon petit loup" is a standard term of endearment in French.

23. *Marcel Proust: Letters to His Mother*, translated and edited with an introduction by George D. Painter and with an essay by Pamela Hansford Johnson, London: Rider, 1956, 32.

24. Fernand Gregh, *L'Âge d'or: Souvenirs d'enfance et de jeunesse*, Paris: Grasset, 1947, 154.

25. Robert Proust, "Marcel Proust Intime," *Hommage à Marcel Proust, La Nouvelle Revue Française*, n.s., 112, 20 (January 1923): 24. This volume is subsequently cited as *NRF Hommage*.

26. Francis and Gontier, *Proust*, 138.

27. Tadié, *Marcel Proust*, 48.

28. Tadié, *Marcel Proust*, 16. Uncle Louis was the model for Uncle Adolphe in the *Search*, a man who adored cocottes and actresses and at whose home the Narrator as a youth first sees Odette de Crécy.

29. Quoted by George D. Painter, *Marcel Proust*, vol. 1, *The Early Years*, Boston: Little, Brown, 1959, 12. This volume is hereafter cited as Painter, *Proust* 1.

30. Mayer, "Jardin," 14.

31. Mayer, "Jardin," 11.

32. Tadié, *Marcel Proust*, 19.

33. Michel-Thiriet, *Book*, 127. The "train de ceinture," or Zone railway, appears in the *Search* 1: 489.

34. Mayer, "Jardin," 12–13.

35. *Corr.* 21: 542, 547.

36. See Proust's preface to Jacques-Émile Blanche's *Propos de peintre: De David à Degas, CSB* 5: 570–76.

37. Preface to Blanche, *Propos de peintre, CSB* 5: 572–73.

38. *Corr.* 21: 540–41, and n. 3.

39. *Corr.* 17: 349.

40. *Corr.* 12: 142.

41. Sand's novel is also used to illustrate how we remember books we read.
42. Ferré, *Collège*, 81. Ferré points out that Marcel also found *Wilhelm Meister, Consuelo,* and *Le Roman comique* boring.
43. *JS* 4: 214.
44. In the abandoned manuscript, Proust, still hesitating at the border between reality and fiction, at times calls the town Illiers; at others, he uses a name that rhymes with the hero's family name Santeuil: Éteuilles. Both of these rhyme with Auteuil, the place that, along with Illiers, will be the primary inspiration for Combray in the *Search*. The sound of the second syllable, dear to Proust because it contained the resonances of the happy days spent at Auteuil, will be maintained in the final syllable of the *Search*'s great composer, Vinteuil.
45. *Jean Santeuil*, 83.
46. *Search* 1: 65.
47. Archives Musée Marcel Proust, Illiers.
48. Ernestine, referred to by her real name in *Jean Santeuil*, is the primary model for Françoise in the *Search*. See, for example, *Jean Santeuil*, 86.
49. *Jean Santeuil*, 86.
50. "Journées de lecture," *CSB* 5: 162.
51. *Search* 1: 10–11.
52. In the early 1950s a citizen of Illiers, Philibert-Louis Larcher, created the Society of the Friends of Marcel Proust, which ultimately acquired Jules's house from the heirs. An inspired local booster, Larcher re-created "Marcel's room" and "Aunt Léonie's room" based on descriptions in the *Search*.
53. Proust consulted Marquis's history of Illiers, *Archives historiques du diocèse de Chartres, 1904,* when writing the pages of the *Search* inspired by memories of the childhood visit to the town. The canon is mentioned in a letter of July 29, 1903, as "the village priest, who taught me Latin and the names of the flowers in his garden." *SL* 1: 343.
54. *SL* 1: 343.
55. Mayer, "Jardin," 15.
56. *Jean Santeuil*, 122.
57. In 1971, on the centennial of Proust's birth, Illiers officially changed its name to Illiers-Combray, in a brilliant public relations initiative and perhaps unique example of reality yielding to fiction.
58. *Search* 1: 180–89.
59. Proust sometimes refers to Swann's way as the Méséglise way, for the walk past Swann's also goes by Méséglise.
60. Proust remembered the connection between the pilgrims and the madeleines, when he described the cakes in the *Search*: "the little scallop-shell of pastry, so richly sensual under its severe, religious folds." *Search* 1: 63. The stairs leading up to the tower and the sixteenth-century steeple of Saint-Jacques contain, like the Church of Saint-Hilaire in *Swann's Way,* ninety-seven steps; Lucien Goron, *Le Combray de Marcel Proust et son horizon,* Toulouse: Imprimerie Julia: 1956, 25.
61. Philibert-Louis Larcher, "Marcel Proust et la magie de Combray," *Histoire locale, Beauce et Perche,* Illiers: Mairie d'Illiers, 4.
62. Larcher, *Illiers,* 99–100.
63. *Search* 1: 121.

64. *Search* 1: 120.
65. André Maurois, *The World of Marcel Proust,* translated by Moura Budberg with the assistance of Barbara Creed, New York: Harper and Row, 1974, 13.
66. See *Corr.* 1: 46.
67. *Search* 1: 158.
68. See *Recherche* (NP) 1: 860.
69. Gregh, *L'Âge d'or,* 156.
70. Robert Proust, "Marcel Proust Intime," 24.
71. *L'Indifférent,* introduced and edited by Philip Kolb, Paris: Gallimard, 1978, 42–43. An appropriate English title would be *A Man with No Feelings.* By coincidence, the last sentence quoted contains two words that are the keys to the *Search: loss* and *recapture.* In the original text, the two words used are forms of the verbs *perdre* and *retrouver,* the two key words of Proust's titles modifying the word *time: le temps perdu, le temps retrouvé*—time lost, time regained.
72. *Corr.* 6: 28.
73. *JS* 4: 202.
74. *Corr.* 20: 403.
75. Dr. François-Bernard Michel, a distinguished French specialist on asthma, has concluded that Marcel's asthma was not psychosomatic in origin, was debilitating, and was probably life-threatening. Michel validates the anxiety felt by Dr. Proust, who knew that asthma can kill quickly. François-Bernard Michel, *Proust et les écrivains devant la mort,* Paris: Bernard Grasset, 1995, 22, 67.
76. *Corr.* 2: 122.
77. *Search* 1: 12. And from another passage: "My grandmother . . . held that when one went to the seaside one ought to be on the beach from morning to night sniffing the salt breezes." *Search* 1: 182.
78. *Corr.* 21: 541. Kolb indicates that the year 1881 is approximate.
79. See *Corr.* 1: 59, 108. *SL* 1: 15.
80. *Recherche* (NP) 4: 1128, n. 1.
81. *Jean Santeuil,* 125.
82. *Search* 5: 885–86.
83. *Jean Santeuil,* 104.
84. *Search* 1: 260.

2 A Sentimental Education

1. Class 5 is roughly equivalent to seventh grade in the current U.S. education system. The French secondary system consists of thirteen grades, counting in reverse order in relation to the U.S. system: the first grade is 12, second 11, and so on, until the first grade is reached, comparable to our twelfth grade. Then French students matriculate for one more year, called the terminal year. In Proust's day the school system was not coeducational, and all of his professors were men. The lycées were college preparatory schools, and the qualifications for teachers were higher than in the typical American high school. For documentation about Proust's secondary education, I am particularly indebted to André Ferré's book *Les Années de collège de Marcel Proust.*
2. Robert Dreyfus, *Marcel Proust à dix-sept ans,* Paris: Simon Kra, 1926, 12–13.

3. Dreyfus, *Dix-sept ans,* 11.

4. Gregh, *L'Âge d'or,* 137.

5. Tadié, *Marcel Proust,* 67.

6. See Dreyfus, *Dix-sept ans,* 9–10, 53.

7. André Berge, "Deux lettres," *Bulletin de la Société des Amis de Marcel Proust et de Combray* 7 (1957): 272. The *Bulletin* is hereafter abbreviated *BMP.*

8. Comtesse Sibylle de Riqueti de Mirabeau wrote under the pseudonym Gyp. See Gyp, *La Joyeuse Enfance de la Troisième République,* 207. Quoted by Ghislain de Diesbach, *Proust,* Paris: Perrin, 1991, 53.

9. The titles of these popular books were *La Famille Fenouillard* (1895), *Le Sapeur Camember* (1896), and *L'Idée fixe du savant Cosinus* (1899). Colomb published them under the pseudonym Christophe, thus assuming, in French, the name of Christopher Columbus, Christophe Colomb.

10. Francis and Gontier, *Proust,* 146.

11. Ferré, *Collège,* 99.

12. Tadié, *Marcel Proust,* 82.

13. Quoted in *Voyager avec Marcel Proust: Mille et un voyages,* texts selected and introduced by Anne Borrel, Paris: La Quinzaine Littéraire, Louis Vuitton, 1994, 86–87.

14. Dreyfus, *Dix-sept ans,* 15, n. 1.

15. *Search* 5: 919.

16. "Le Gladiator mourant," *CSB* 5: 321, n. 1.

17. Tadié, *Marcel Proust,* 83.

18. *The Odyssey of Homer,* translated by Richmond Lattimore, New York: Harper and Row, 1965, book 5, ll. 306–7.

19. "Composition française," *CSB* 5: 324.

20. *JS* 4: 263.

21. Borrel, *Voyager,* 39–40.

22. *Corr.* 21: 543–46.

23. *SL* 1: 5–7.

24. See *Corr.* 21: 548, n. 4.

25. Borrel, *Voyager,* 47–49.

26. See "L'Éclipse," *CSB* 5: 325–27.

27. Ferré, *Collège,* 137.

28. "Les Nuages," *CSB* 5: 328.

29. Tadié points out the romantic themes that still survive in 1885 among the young generation of symbolists: anguish, reverie, pantheism. See his *Marcel Proust,* 85.

30. See *Corr.* 1: 110, n. 6.

31. See Hayden White's article "Romantic Historiography," in *A New History of French Literature,* edited by Denis Hollier, Cambridge: Harvard University Press, 1989, 632–38.

32. *Marcel Proust: Textes retrouvés,* collected and edited by Philip Kolb and Larkin B. Price, Urbana: University of Illinois Press, 1968, 179.

33. *Textes retrouvés,* 178–79. The early drafts for the *Search* are even more autobiographical than the published novel.

34. *Search* 1: 218–19. The Narrator, at the end of his quest, is finally ready to write his version of the story we have just read.

35. Ferré, *Collège,* 68.

36. The questionnaire was in English, but Proust's answers were in French. No one knows Marcel's exact age when he filled out the questionnaire. According to Kolb's chronology he did so in 1886, when he was fourteen or fifteen. See *Corr.* 1: 51. When he was about twenty, Proust filled out a similar questionnaire. For my translation of the questionnaire, I consulted those of Roger Shattuck in *Marcel Proust*, Princeton: Princeton University Press, 1982, 12, and Jan Dalley in Michel-Thiriet, *Book*, 57–58. I have omitted five questions—soliciting the respondent's "chief characteristic," favorite color and flower, favorite food and drink, favorite names, and "present state of mind"—that Proust left unanswered, though it might be said that some of his omissions are as telling as his replies. For the original text, see [Questionnaire], *CSB* 5: 335–36.

37. Maurice Duplay, *Mon Ami Marcel Proust: Souvenirs intimes, Cahiers Marcel Proust*, n.s., 5, Paris: Gallimard, 1972, 7.

38. My account is based primarily on Robert Dreyfus, "Marcel Proust aux Champs-Élysées," *NRF Hommage*, 27–30.

39. See Duplay, *Mon Ami*, 7.

40. Dreyfus, "Champs-Élysées," 28.

41. Ferré, *Collège*, 155.

42. *Corr.* 15: 75.

43. Dreyfus, "Champs-Élysées," 28.

44. See *Corr.* 17: 175, 194.

45. *Jean Santeuil*, 46. In *Jean Santeuil*, Marie and her sister Nelly appear with their real names and family circumstances, including the house in the sixteenth arrondissement in the rue de Chaillot.

46. Ferré, *Collège*, 136.

47. Ferré, *Collège*, 153, n. 1.

48. Charles Rearick, *Pleasures of the Belle Époque: Entertainment and Festivity in Turn-of-the-Century France*, New Haven: Yale University Press, 1985, 12.

49. *SL* 1: 7–8. In July 1886 the singer Paulus created at the Alcazar the immensely popular song "En revenant de la revue," which celebrated General Boulanger and marked the peak of his appeal. See Duplay, *Mon Ami*, 8.

50. *Search* 2: 90.

51. *Marcel Proust: Écrits de Jeunesse, 1887–1895*, selected and edited by Anne Borrel, Illiers-Combray: Institut Marcel Proust International, 1991, 141. See also Dreyfus, *Dix-sept ans*, 44–45.

52. *Marcel Proust: Correspondance avec Daniel Halévy*, edited by Anne Borrel and Jean-Pierre Halévy, Paris: Éditions de Fallois, 1992, 169–72.

53. *SL* 1: 9–10.

54. *SL* 1: 12.

55. Dreyfus, *Dix-sept ans*, 16.

56. Quoted by Tadié, *Marcel Proust*, 91.

57. See "Dissertation française," *CSB* 5: 329–32.

58. Quoted by Tadié, *Marcel Proust*, 90–91.

59. *SL* 1: 14, n. 7. The last sentence quoted is not in *SL*. See *Corr.* 1: 107, n. 7.

60. See *Corr.* 1: 106–7, n. 4.

61. *SL* 1: 13.

62. "Le Salon de la Princesse Edmond de Polignac," *CSB* 5: 466.

63. See *JS* 4: 258, *Corr.* 1: 107, n. 9.

64. Gregh, *L'Âge d'or,* 136.

65. *Proust-Halévy Corr.,* 7.

66. Description of Halévy from Gregh, *L'Âge d'or,* 137.

67. Dreyfus, *Dix-sept ans,* 27.

68. Tadié, *Marcel Proust,* 94.

69. Proust, *Jeunesse,* 140–41. The date of May 13, 1888, is taken from Halévy diary entry.

70. Proust, *Jeunesse,* 136.

71. Dreyfus, *Dix-sept ans,* 28–29.

72. Dreyfus, *Dix-sept ans,* 25.

73. Proust, *Jeunesse,* 41.

74. Echoes of his rebellion against his parents' severity are found in the Narrator's desire to defy them, "the people I loved best in the world." See *Search* 5: 833. See also *JS* 4: 709. Quoted in Tadié, *Marcel Proust,* 54.

75. *SL* 1: 10–11.

76. Pascal's *Pensées* were part of the curriculum that year at Condorcet. See Jean-Yves Tadié, *Proust,* Paris: Pierre Belfond, 1983, 240.

77. Quoted in Proust, *Jeunesse,* 38.

78. See *SL* 1: 11, n. 4. The translation mistakenly gives Halévy's name as "Cléry."

79. Jacques-Émile Blanche, *Mes Modèles: Souvenirs littéraires,* Paris: Stock, 1928, 1984, 100.

80. This common sexual activity was condemned by parents, priests, teachers, and doctors, including Adrien Proust. See Adrien Proust and Gilbert Ballet, *L'Hygiène du neurasthénique,* Paris: Bibliothèque d'hygiène thérapeutique, 1897, 154. Masturbation is the only overtly sexual expression the Narrator experiences, and that as an adolescent.

81. For the letter and Halévy's comments, see *Proust-Halévy Corr.,* 42–44.

82. The ellipsis is Proust's. He often uses it to create suspense before a surprise.

83. *Letters of Marcel Proust,* translated and edited with notes by Mina Curtiss, with an introduction by Harry Levin, New York: Random House, 1949, 3–4. The French word *pédéraste,* less specific than the English cognate, can mean any homosexual, not only a pedophile.

84. *Corr.* 21: 550–51.

85. *JS* 4: 243, 245. Quoted by Tadié, *Marcel Proust,* 36.

86. Tadié, *Marcel Proust,* 32.

87. See Proust, *Jeunesse,* 56–58; *Proust-Halévy Corr.,* 39–41; *Corr.* 21: 553–54.

88. Marcel said that he held in horror critics who adopted an ironical attitude toward the decadent writers. A contemporary critic, Paul Bourde, had named Verlaine and Mallarmé as the "two columns" of the decadent school. See Proust, *Jeunesse,* 59, n. 2.

89. See Proust, *Jeunesse,* 62, n. 10.

90. The word Proust uses for unclean is *malpropre,* and for normal, *habituel.*

91. "Avant la nuit" is not included in *Pleasures and Days,* no doubt because of its scandalous nature.

92. Tadié, *Marcel Proust,* 110.

93. The French is *une grande saleté.* Tadié acknowledges that we cannot know whether this confession is true because Raoul destroyed most of Marcel's letters. See *Marcel Proust,* 110, n. 3.

94. Tadié, *Marcel Proust,* 110.

95. Proust, *Jeunesse*, 149–51.
96. Ferré, *Collège*, 87–88.
97. *SL* 1: 15–16.
98. *SL* 1: 17–18.
99. *Search* 4: 32.
100. Acacia Gardens, now named Allée de Longchamp, remained a stylish venue from the time of the horse-drawn carriages of Proust's youth, through the era of the first automobiles, until sometime after World War I.
101. *SL* 1: 19–20.
102. See Tadié, *Marcel Proust*, 35, where he compares Laure's relationship with Adrien to Odette's with Dr. Cottard in the *Search*. Adrien kept all such friendships and liaisons secret from his wife.
103. Cf. *Search* 1: 102, where the Narrator speaks about his uncle's actress friends: "Now my uncle knew many of them personally, and also ladies of another class, not clearly distinguished from actresses in my mind." See Tadié, *Marcel Proust*, 51, *Corr.* 1: 47; and Robert Soupault, *Marcel Proust: Du côté de la médecine*, Paris: Plon, 122–23.
104. Maurois, *World*, 78.
105. *SL* 1: 21–22 and n. 1. Dreyfus identified the courtesan as Clomesnil because he was mistaken about the date when Proust first met Hayman. See Dreyfus, *Dix-sept ans*, 47, n. 1, and *Corr.* 1: 118, n. 2.
106. See Paul Desjardins's article "Un Aspect de l'œuvre de Proust: Dissolution de l'individu," *NRF Hommage*, 150.
107. See Desjardins, "Un Aspect," 146.
108. *Jean Santeuil*, 72–73.
109. Another work of considerable interest to Proust was France's 1874 booklet on Racine. In the *Search*, Proust to a large degree based his fictional author Bergotte on France. Bergotte also writes a booklet on Racine, source of the Narrator's initial admiration.
110. *SL* 2: 40. Proust read *The Arabian Nights* in Antoine Galland's translation. At Illiers, he had been able to contemplate scenes from the story on the Creil plates in his Aunt Amiot's dining room. Proust saw the Narrator as a modern Scheherazade, the creator of the Arabian tales of his era. See *Search* 6: 524–25.
111. *Jean Santeuil*, 72–73.
112. For the pupils' opinion of Darlu, see the passage on Professor Beulier in *Jean Santeuil*, 159.
113. This description is based on that of Professor Beulier's late arrival on the first day of class in *JS* 4: 260. All of Proust's classmates who lived long enough to read the manuscript of *Jean Santeuil* when it was published in 1952 immediately recognized Beulier as Darlu.
114. *Jean Santeuil*, 160.
115. *SL* 1: 22–23.
116. This is the standard scale in the French grading system.
117. See Philip Kolb's essay "The Making of a Novel" in *Marcel Proust, 1871–1922: A Centennial Volume*, edited by Peter Quennell, New York: Simon and Schuster, 1971, 25, n. 1.
118. Henri Bonnet, *Alphonse Darlu: Maître de philosophie de Marcel Proust*, Paris: Nizet, 7–8.
119. Robert Proust, "Marcel Proust Intime," 25.
120. Gregh, *L'Âge d'or*, 142–43.

121. Tadié, *Marcel Proust*, 107.

122. Bonnet, *Darlu*, 27–28.

123. *SL* 1: 24–25.

124. *Corr.* 2: 464.

125. Dreyfus, *Dix-sept ans*, 50.

126. See Painter, *Letters to His Mother*, 38; *SL* 1: 40, n. 2.

127. Dreyfus, *Dix-sept ans*, 42.

128. Maurois, *World*, 59, 66.

129. *Proust-Halévy Corr.*, 63.

130. Tadié, *Proust*, 240.

131. See Robert Dreyfus, *Souvenirs sur Marcel Proust, accompagnés de lettres inédites*, Paris: Grasset, 1926, 68; Ferré, *Collège*, 143–44, and *Jeunesse*, 91–109. *Jeunesse* provides evidence indicating that *Le Lundi* and the little review previously known as *La Revue de Seconde* were one and the same.

132. *Les Causeries du lundi*, Sainte-Beuve's famous weekly essays that appeared on Mondays for more than two decades, may have inspired the title of the boys' first review.

133. Most notably in the 1908 series of parodies he wrote for *Le Figaro*.

134. *Jeunesse*, 106.

135. *Corr.* 20: 292.

136. Daniel Halévy, *Pays parisiens*, Paris: Grasset, 1932, 118.

137. *Jeunesse*, 78.

138. The probable date of composition is October 1888. For the two versions of this poem and Proust's critique, and documentation, see *Jeunesse*, 156–67, and *Proust-Halévy Corr.*, 54–61.

139. *Proust-Halévy Corr.*, 207.

140. *Jeunesse*, 159–67.

141. *Juvenilia, CSB* 5: 868, n. 3.

142. *La Revue verte, CSB* 5: 332–33.

143. See *Jeunesse*, 118.

144. Dreyfus, *Dix-sept ans*, 54.

145. These texts are reprinted in ["Le ciel est d'un violet sombre . . . "], *CSB* 5: 333–34. One of the texts may date from 1886, but that hypothesis does not seem likely. See *CSB* 5: 333, n. 1.

146. Rereading these pages many years after his friend's death, Dreyfus says that in these lines he recognizes the true voice of Proust. See Dreyfus, *Dix-sept ans*, 62–64. Proust resumed this practice only very late, when he "found his voice" in the early drafts of the *Search*.

147. Dreyfus, who preserved the original manuscript, omitted the sentence about sitting in Bizet's lap when he first published the text. The complete version can be in found in *Jeunesse*, 123–24.

148. Dreyfus, *Dix-sept ans*, 62–64.

149. *Jeunesse*, 121–22.

150. According to Philip Kolb's chronology for 1888, the productions Marcel attended in the. fall were *Cendrillon, Athalie, Pied de mouton, Mimi, Amante du Christ*, and Ambroise Thomas's opera *Mignon*, based on Goethe's *Wilhelm Meister*. See *Corr.* 1: 53–54.

151. Dreyfus, *Dix-sept ans*, 60. For the complete text of Proust's theater notes, see *Impressions de théâtre*, in *Jeunesse*, 126–27.

152. See *Proust-Halévy Corr.*, 176–80.

153. Edmond and Jules de Goncourt, *Journal: Mémoires de la vie littéraire,* Paris; Robert Laffont, 1989, 2: 1028. Entry dated Wednesday, November 21, 1883.
154. Goncourt *Journal* entry dated Saturday, August 14, 1886, 2: 1262.
155. Gregh, *L'Âge d'or,* 168.
156. Goncourt *Journal* entry dated Monday, March 28, 1887, 3: 25–26.
157. It is possible that young Proust met the American novelist Henry James when he attended Mme Straus's salon on December 18, 1888. See Leon Edel, *Henry James: A Life,* New York: Harper and Row, 1985, 351.
158. In the *Search,* the duc de Guermantes, constantly unfaithful and rather indifferent to his wife's affection, takes great pride in her salon and repeats her witticisms, directly inspired by those of Mme Straus, to everyone he wishes to impress with the superiority of her intelligence and the enviability of belonging to their salon.
159. Quoted in *Corr.* 1: 328, n. 7.
160. Ferré, *Collège,* 161.
161. Dreyfus, *Dix-sept ans,* 53.
162. *Corr.* 21: 556 and n. 2.
163. See Proust's preface to Paul Morand's *Tendres Stocks, CSB* 5: 608. Tadié sees a more profound influence from Renan on Proust's style: the search for laws determining behavior, and the depiction of France's historical past. See *Marcel Proust,* 184.
164. André Maurois, *Proust: Portrait of a Genius,* translated by Gerard Hopkins, New York: Carroll and Graf, 1984, 27.
165. Henri Chantavoine wrote the negative review in the *Journal des débats,* May 15, 1889. *SL* 1: 26, n. 2.
166. In *Swann's Way,* the Narrator has the same admiration for Bergotte, whom he imagines to be "a frail and disappointed old man." See *Search* 1: 134. Later the Narrator is surprised to meet "a youngish, uncouth, thickset and myopic little man, with a red nose curled like a snail-shell and a goatee beard" (*Search* 2: 165). Some have seen this as a description of Anatole France. *SL* 1: 26, n. 5. Others believe that Proust was describing Renan.
167. *SL* 1: 25–26.
168. Bonnet, *Darlu,* 68.
169. Tadié, *Marcel Proust,* 92.
170. Dreyfus, *Dix-sept ans,* 14.
171. Ferré, *Collège,* 255.
172. Marcel's diploma for the Bachelor of Letters was awarded several months later.

3 Private Proust

1. Mayer, "Jardin," 31.
2. *Corr.* 1: 126–27.
3. *Corr.* 1: 132.
4. *Corr.* 1: 128–29.
5. *Corr.* 1: 131. See also *Corr.* 19: 558–59.
6. Maurois, *World,* 77.
7. This observation is made by Anthony Powell in his article, "Proust as a Soldier," in Quennell, *Marcel Proust,* 149. See also Pierre-Edmond Robert, "Marcel Proust ou le paradis militaire," *BMP* 33 (1983): 87.

8. Clovis Duveau, "Proust à Orléans," *BMP* 33 (1983): 12.
9. *PR*, 150–51.
10. *Jean Santeuil*, 437.
11. *Jean Santeuil*, 471.
12. *SL* 1: 144.
13. Powell, "Soldier," 151.
14. Powell, "Soldier," 150.
15. Pierre Gallante, "Le Jockey: The World's Most Exclusive Club," *Town and Country*, April 1987, 204 ff.
16. Georges de Lauris, *Souvenirs d'une belle époque*, quoted by Duveau, "Proust," 67.
17. For distinctions that Proust noted between ancien régime nobles and those of the empire, see *Jean Santeuil*, 435–39.
18. "I saw Captain de Borodino go majestically by, putting his horse into a trot, and seemingly under the illusion that he was taking part in the Battle of Austerlitz." *Search* 3: 182.
19. Émile Hovelaque, quoted by Élisabeth de Gramont in "Proust's France," *American Vogue*, January 1948, 126.
20. Powell, "Soldier," 153. Jeanne-Maurice Pouquet, *Le Salon de Madame Arman de Caillavet*, preface by Gabriel Hanotaux, Paris: Hachette, 1926, 106–7.
21. *Corr.* 19: 137. See Pouquet, *Salon Caillavet*, 84.
22. Pouquet, *Salon Caillavet*, 109.
23. Maurois, *Genius*, 41.
24. *Corr.* 19: 138.
25. Quoted by Duveau, "Proust," 33–34.
26. Pouquet, *Salon Caillavet*, 107.
27. Quoted by Maurois, *Genius*, 41.
28. Pierre Corneille, *Le Cid*. See *SL* 1: 28, n. 5.
29. *Search* 4: 230.
30. Maurois, *Genius*, 70.
31. Duveau, "Proust," 44.
32. From the *Journal du Loiret*, February 7, 1890, quoted by Duveau, "Proust," 16.
33. A prefect is the chief administrator of a department, which is the basic administrative and political division of France, roughly equivalent to an American state.
34. Robert de Billy, *Marcel Proust: Lettres et conversations*, Paris: Édition des Portiques, 1930, 22.
35. Robert de Billy, "Une Amitié de trente-deux ans," *NRF Hommage*, 31. In *Jean Santeuil*, Proust endowed his hero with the same intensive curiosity that had amazed Billy: "Extremely curious about every detail of army routine . . . and eager to learn in what precise way the military mind differs from others, Jean never tired of questioning his new friends, asking them . . . who they considered to be the most remarkable of the senior officers." *Jean Santeuil*, 436. See also Billy, *Lettres et conversations*, 21.
36. See Billy, *Lettres et conversations*, 21.
37. *SL* 1: 28–29.
38. From the May 9 issue of the *Journal du Loiret*, quoted by Duveau, "Proust," 37.
39. There is a similar episode in the *Search* in which the Narrator, who has not expressed his grief over the death of his beloved grandmother, leans over to unbutton his boot and feels his "entire being disrupted." See *Search* 4: 210. Proust's grandmother may have helped him remove his boots because of the difficulty an asthmatic has in bending over.

40. *Corr.* 1: 142.
41. *Corr.* 1: 147.
42. *Corr.* 15: 149.
43. *Corr.* 1: 155.
44. Powell, "Soldier," 152.
45. *Corr.* 1: 157.
46. Painter, *Letters to His Mother,* 206.
47. *Corr.* 1: 159–60.
48. Philip Kolb, "Historique du premier roman de Proust," *Saggi e ricerche di letteratura francese* 4 (1963): 253–54.
49. *SL* 1: 189. For the Narrator's rapturous description of life in the barracks, see *Search* 3: 96–97.
50. See *Corr.* 19: 688, and *Corr.* 21: 160. In *Jean Santeuil,* Proust recalled his military service with nostalgia: "When you who have tasted the pure pleasures of the earthly Paradise come to search your memories, I have an idea that you will dwell with particular affection on the thought of the barrack-room bed where you took your noon siesta during your time in the army, of the roads along which you marched." *Jean Santeuil,* 428.
51. Anthony Powell maintains that there is no English equivalent for the rank of sous-officier. See Powell, "Soldier," 151.

4 A Modest Literary Debut

1. *SL* 1: 31.
2. For Proust at the École libre des sciences politiques, see Billy, *Lettres et conversations,* 23–25.
3. Michel-Thiriet, *Book,* 70.
4. Billy, "Amitié," 31.
5. "Les Phares" means lighthouses. Richard Howard's translation of the title as "Guiding Lights" nicely conveys Baudelaire's intent. Charles Baudelaire, *Les Fleurs du mal,* translated by Richard Howard, Boston: David R. Godine, 1982, 16.
6. See *JS* 4: 81. This poem was ultimately published in *Pleasures and Days* in a section called "Portraits of Painters and Musicians," not included in Louise Varese's English translation of the work.
7. See *Jeunesse,* 169–203.
8. Other articles, published under pseudonyms or even anonymously, a common practice in Proust's time, may be attributed to him.
9. *Jeunesse,* 172–73.
10. *Jeunesse,* 174.
11. *Jeunesse,* 194, n. 2, and *Corr.* 1: 200.
12. ["Sur Réjane"], *CSB* 5: 600–601.
13. *Corr.* 1: 162.
14. The exact date of this letter is unknown, but it is thought to date from 1891. *SL* 1: 32.
15. The date of Proust's and Gide's first encounter was established by Gide's biographer Jean Delay. See his *La Jeunesse d'André Gide,* Paris: Gallimard, 1957, 2: 128. See also Proust, *Jeunesse,* 201, n. 7.
16. Delay, *Gide,* 129.

17. This description of Marcel at the "court of love" is based on Pouquet, *Salon Caillavet*, 108–9.

18. Years later, this villa inspired Proust to create the fictional Raspelière with similar sweeping vistas of sea and farmland.

19. *Jeunesse*, 195.

20. *Corr.* 21: 560 and n. 2.

21. *Corr.* 1: 164–65.

22. Philippe Jullian, *Oscar Wilde*, translated by Violet Wyndham, New York: Viking, 1969, 66.

23. Richard Ellmann, *Oscar Wilde*, New York: Knopf, 1988, 341.

24. Ellmann, *Wilde*, 344.

25. Ellmann, *Wilde*, 346.

26. Quoted in Ellmann, *Wilde*, 355. See also André Gide, *Journal: 1889–1939*, Paris: Gallimard (Pléiade), 1965, 28.

27. Ellmann, *Wilde*, 357.

28. The grandsons first told their story to Wilde's French biographer Philippe Jullian. Their account has been repeated since by other biographers, including Richard Ellmann. See Jullian, *Oscar Wilde*, 241–42; Ellmann, *Wilde*, 347. Painter corrects the address to 9, boulevard Malesherbes. Maurois omits the encounter altogether. Proust's encounter with Wilde was essentially as meaningless as that, late in his life, with another legendary Irish writer, James Joyce.

29. See *Proust-Halévy Corr.*, 74; Dreyfus, *Souvenirs*, 67, 80–81. Bonnet believed the title was chosen to oppose the reigning philosophical doctrine of the time: positivism represented by the writings of Auguste Comte and Herbert Spencer. Positivism was to be the doctrine espoused by M. Santeuil, no doubt modeled on Dr. Proust, in *Jean Santeuil*. See Bonnet, *Darlu*, 40.

30. Fernand Gregh, *Mon Amitié avec Marcel Proust: Souvenirs et lettres inédites*, Paris: Grasset, 1958, 153.

31. Gregh, *Amitié*, 41, 46.

32. Gregh, "L'Époque du *Banquet*," *NRF Hommage*, 41–42; *Amitié*, 32–33.

33. Gregh, *Amitié*, 48–49, 153.

34. *Corr.* 1: 166.

35. Princesse Mathilde's personality traits and the details about her life and salon are based primarily on two Proust texts, particularly the 1903 article he wrote for *Le Figaro* describing her salon, "Un Salon historique: Le Salon de S. A. I. la Princesse Mathilde," signed Dominique, in *CSB* 5: 445–55.

36. Gregh, *Amitié*, 154. Popelin had conspicuously betrayed the princess by having an affair with the youngest of her maids-in-waiting, Maria Abbatucci. See Léon Daudet, *Fantômes et vivants, Souvenirs et polémiques*, Paris: Robert Laffont, 1992, 124 and n. 1.

37. Léon Daudet (1867–1942) was the elder son of the famous writer Alphonse Daudet, with whose family Proust was soon to become acquainted.

38. Daudet, *Fantômes et vivants, Souvenirs et polémiques*, 126.

39. "Un Salon historique," *CSB* 5: 447; and *Search* 3: 750.

40. See *Corr.* 7: 240. Years later Proust could not recall which of the two salons (Mme Mailly-Nesle later became Mme Reszké) he had attended that evening, but he did remember the red dress.

41. See *Corr.* 1: 382. Marcel was capable, when exceptionally motivated, of rising in the early morning.
42. *PJ*, 65–66. In the original *Le Banquet* text, the comparisons of the lady to a bird were more abundant. Proust retouched the text slightly for *PJ*, where the resemblances between the lady and her sons and nephews were added.
43. *Search* 3: 69.
44. Painter, *Proust* 1: 149.
45. Billy, *Lettres et conversations*, 37–38.
46. *SL* 1: 38.
47. For "Snobs, 1:" see *PR*, 66–67.
48. *SL* 1: 41.
49. " 'Tel qu'en songe' par Henri de Régier," *CSB* 5: 354.
50. *SL* 1: 33.
51. *SL* 1: 35, n. 1.
52. [Preface], *CSB* 5: 570.
53. Tadié, *Marcel Proust*, 176.
54. Blanche, *Modèles*, 188–89.
55. [Préface], *CSB* 5: 571.
56. Daudet, "L'Entre deux-guerres," *Souvenirs et polémiques*, 276.
57. Jacques-Émile Blanche, "Quelques instantanés de Marcel Proust," *NRF Hommage*, 53.
58. Blanche, *Modèles*, 111; quoted in Maurois, *Genius*, 33.
59. [Préface], *CSB* 5: 572.
60. Blanche, *Modèles*, 112.
61. Blanche, *Modèles*, 110.
62. Blanche, *Modèles*, 100–101.
63. *PR*, 123–25.
64. *PR*, 122–23.
65. *PR*, 143.
66. *Corr.* 1: 174.
67. *Corr.* 1: 199.
68. *Corr.* 1: 176, n. 2.
69. "Un Salon historique," *CSB* 5: 447.
70. *Corr.* 1: 176–77.
71. Gregh, *L'Âge d'or*, 163.
72. Gregh, *L'Âge d'or*, 154.
73. Painter, *Proust* 1: 144.
74. Gregh, *L'Âge d'or*, 164, 166; *SL* 1: 36, n. 3.
75. Charles Baudelaire had become Marcel's favorite poet—a poet whose major themes included time and memory and some of whose poems, such as *Le Flacon* and *Le Balcon*, contained elements of the Proustian phenomenon of involuntary memory. Proust was familiar with Fauré's musical rendering of "Chant d'automne." Fernand Gregh recollected having often seen Marcel, his eyes half-closed, humming Fauré's "enchanting music" to "Chant d'automne." See *L'Âge d'or*, 167. I have used Richard Howard's translation of *Les Fleurs du mal*, 62.
76. *Corr.* 1: 183–84.

77. *Corr.* 1: 184.

78. "Violante, or Worldly Vanities," *PR*, 87–99. *Corr.* 1: 185, n. 1. When Proust published the story in the February 1893 issue of *Le Banquet*, he dedicated it to Anatole France, who in September 1892, in the collection of stories *L'Étui de nacre*, had dedicated "Madame de Luzy" to Proust.

79. "La Mer" appeared in the November 1892 issue of *Le Banquet*. See *PR*, 167–69. The sea always reminded Proust of his mother and grandmother. Tadié observes that the "nocturnal anguish" stems from "the absence of his mother." Tadié, *Marcel Proust*, 120. In French, it is nearly impossible not to associate sea and mother, for the words *mer* and *mère* are homophonic. Marcel's behavior, as observed from his activities and letter writing, do not indicate that he missed his mother exceptionally during this holiday.

80. *SL* 1: 38.

81. *Corr.* 1: 64.

82. Gregh, *L'Âge d'or*, 164.

83. *Corr.* 1: 188, n. 5.

84. *SL* 1: 39.

85. *Corr.* 1: 190.

86. Gregh, *Amitié*, 51–52.

87. Gregh, *L'Âge d'or*, 156, n. 1.

88. *SL* 1: 41–42.

89. *Corr.* 7: 329.

90. Gregh, *L'Âge d'or*, 173.

91. Gregh, *L'Âge d'or*, 326–27, n. 2.

92. *SL* 1: 42–43.

93. *SL* 1: 43.

94. "La Conférence parlementaire de la rue Serpente," *CSB* 5: 356.

95. Dreyfus, *Souvenirs*, 83.

5 A Man About Town

1. Lemaire, née Jeanne-Magdeleine Coll (1845–1928), served as a primary model for Proust's domineering, aggressive society hostess Mme Verdurin. Lemaire's painting skills, especially her endless depictions of roses, were used for another character, the bluestocking aristocrat Mme de Villeparisis.

2. Quoted by Proust in his dedication to *Les Plaisirs et les jours* in *JS* 4: 5. "La Cour aux lilas et l'atelier des roses: Le Salon de Mme Madeleine Lemaire," *CSB* 5: 458. Robert de Montesquiou had nicknamed her the "Empress of Roses." See Philippe Jullian, *Prince of Aesthetes: Count Robert de Montesquiou, 1855–1921*, translated by John Haylock and Francis King, New York: Viking, 1968, 145.

3. Élisabeth de Clermont-Tonnerre, *Robert de Montesquiou et Marcel Proust*, Paris: Flammarion, 1925, 23; Daudet, *Fantômes et Vivants*, 119.

4. These details and others about Yturri's background and arrival in Paris and quotations from Montesquiou's memorial volume to Yturri, *Le Chancelier de fleurs*, are all from Edgar Munhall, *Whistler and Montesquiou: The Butterfly and the Bat*, New York: Frick Collection, and Paris: Flammarion, 1995, 39–41.

5. Élisabeth de Clermont-Tonnerre, quoted by Munhall, *Whistler and Montesquiou*, 40–41.

6. Jullian, *Montesquiou,* 113.

7. Jullian, *Montesquiou,* 112. Others say that he sold gloves.

8. Proust remembered elements of both men later when creating the baron de Charlus. The physical traits of Charlus in his later years are primarily based on corpulent Doäzan rather than svelte Montesquiou.

9. Jullian, *Montesquiou,* 112.

10. *SL* 1: 46.

11. *Corr.* 1: 204. The volume appeared with a preface by Leconte de Lisle.

12. *Corr.* 1: 206.

13. Blanche, "Quelques instantanés," 57.

14. Maurois, *Genius,* 34.

15. *Jean Santeuil,* 715. Kolb speculates that Proust attributed the painting to Blanche's rival because he and Blanche had fallen out over the Dreyfus Affair; see *Corr.* 1: 174, n. 2; see also *Album Proust,* edited by Pierre Clarac and André Ferré, Paris: Gallimard (Pléiade), 1965, 138–39.

16. *Jean Santeuil,* 715. M. Sandré is Jean's maternal grandfather.

17. Painter, *Proust* 1: 123. Painter incorrectly identifies the place of honor as that on Mme Proust's left.

18. Tadié discovered that Heath's and Aubert's mothers were sisters. See *Marcel Proust,* 191, n. 1.

19. This description contained in a sentence from the dedication of *Pleasures and Days* provides virtually all the information that is known about Marcel's relationship with Heath. See Maurois, *Genius,* 54.

20. This remark from Painter has been repeated by Diesbach and other biographers. Painter, *Proust* 1: 123.

21. *Corr.* 1: 221.

22. *Corr.* 1: 213, nn. 1, 2.

23. *SL* 1: 50.

24. *Corr.* 1: 216.

25. See Daudet, *Souvenirs et polémiques,* 337, n. 7.

26. See *PR,* 100–108.

27. In the *Search,* Proust's narrator concludes that in society any serious conversation is taboo.

28. *Jean Santeuil,* 738.

29. These anecdotes are related by Proust in the preface he wrote for Jacques-Émile Blanche in 1918. See [Préface], *CSB* 5: 574–75.

30. *SL* 1: 50–51.

31. Jullian, *Montesquiou,* 66.

32. *Corr.* 1: 219, n.3.

33. *SL* 1: 51.

34. *Corr.* 1: 220.

35. *L'Indifférent* was published on March 1, 1896, in a short-lived review, *La Vie contemporaine et Revue parisienne réunies.* The story was quickly forgotten by everyone but Proust until Philip Kolb unearthed it and reprinted it in 1978. This is the story in which Proust compared being abandoned by the beloved to suffocation from asthma.

36. For this story, like several Proust wrote in 1893 and 1894, he put himself in the guise of a female narrator. See "Mélancolique Villégiature de Mme de Breyves," "Avant la nuit," "La

Confession d'une jeune fille," and the epistolary novel, undertaken with friends and quickly abandoned, in which he assigned himself the role of Pauline. For the three letters Proust wrote as "Pauline," see *Jeunesse*, 250–58, 264–71.

37. Lepré's "vice" could mask another that Proust was eager to depict and that also makes love between a man and a woman impossible: homosexuality. In stories written this year and the next Proust begins to study aspects of behavior that he, following society's lead, characterizes as vice.

38. For the text of "The Melancholy Summer of Madame de Breyves," see *PR*, 172–91.

39. For the original version of this text, see *JS* 4: 167–71. Proust did not retain this story for *Pleasures and Days*. Thierry Latget, in his edition of *Les Plaisirs et les jours*, suggests that Proust omitted it because he had used material from this story in several others that were reprinted in that volume. See Marcel Proust, *Les Plaisirs et les jours, suivi de L'Indifférent et autres textes*, edited by Thierry Latget, Paris: Gallimard (Folio), 1993, 346–47.

40. Proust borrowed the image of the jellyfish from Michelet's *La Mer* (1861) and reprised it many years later as one of several illustrations of homosexual attraction in the extensive discourse on the topic that opens the fourth part of the *Search, Sodom and Gomorrah*. *Search* 4: 36.

41. *Corr.* 4: 419, n. 6, and 420. This translation *(L'Intrus)* marked the beginning of the Italian writer's popularity in France.

42. "Bodily Presence," *PR*, 158.

43. *Tout-Paris* and *La Société et le High-Life* were social registers published in Paris. *L'Almanach de Gotha* was a genealogical directory of nobility published in Gotha, Germany, from 1763 to 1945; see *PJ*, 313.

44. *PR*, 69.

45. *Jeunesse*, 229, n. 2.

46. *SL* 1: 57. In "Présence réelle" (Bodily presence) and "Rêve" (Dream), both stories Proust wrote at Évian, the narrator is attracted to phantom lovers. These stories, to be published in *La Revue blanche*, were reprinted as part of *Pleasures and Days*.

47. *SL* 1: 62. The license that concerned Marcel was in stories involving illicit sex. In *PR* he would retain one such story published earlier, "La Confession d'une jeune fille," but not "Avant la nuit," with its lesbian theme.

48. *SL* 1: 56.

49. *SL* 1: 58, n. 1.

50. *SL* 1: 57, 58.

51. *SL* 1: 61, n. 1.

52. *SL* 1: 62

53. *SL* 1: 61–62.

54. Billy mentions "certain scruples" on the family's part in "Amitié," 34.

55. *Corr.* 1: 239.

56. *Corr.* 1: 260.

57. Published in July–August 1893, *La Revue blanche*. See *PR*, 77.

58. *Corr.* 1: 281 and n. 2.

59. *Corr.* 1: 276 and n. 2.

60. *Corr.* 1: 291, n. 1. This aspect of the relationship between Montesquiou and Delafosse was to be the model in the *Search* for Charlus's presentation of the violinist Morel, like Delafosse of humble origins, to high society.

61. The literal translation of the title of the second part of the *Search, À l'ombre des jeunes filles en fleurs,* is "In the shade of girls in bloom." The translator chose as the title *Within a Budding Grove.*

62. *Corr.* 1: 278 and 285, n. 3.

63. *Corr.* 1: 282–83.

64. *Corr.* 1: 286.

65. Quoted in Elaine Brody, *Paris: The Musical Kaleidoscope, 1870–1925,* New York: George Braziller, 1987, 241.

66. *Corr.* 1: 288.

67. *SL* 1: 69.

6 A Musical Prodigy

1. For additional information about the early part of Reynaldo Hahn's life, especially up until the time he met Proust, I have relied upon Bernard Gavoty's biography *Reynaldo Hahn: Le Musicien de la Belle Époque,* Paris: Éditions Buchet/Chastel, 1976. Gavoty, who knew Hahn in the years following Proust's death, had access to his diary and many of his letters. The published portion of Hahn's memoirs, *Journal d'un musicien* (Paris: Plon, 1933), is rich in details about his taste in music, his travels, and anecdotes about society people and artists, but is silent on personal matters, and especially about his relationship with Proust.

2. *Marcel Proust: Lettres à Reynaldo Hahn,* edited by Philip Kolb with a preface by Emmanuel Berl, Paris: Gallimard, 1956, 13.

3. Gavoty, *Hahn,* 90.

4. Both letters were written in 1893. Quoted in Gavoty, *Hahn,* 91. Hahn's emphasis on the word *homosexuals*—in French, *pédérastes.*

5. This quotation is from Proust's account of the Lemaire salon, "Le Salon de Mme Madeleine Lemaire," *CSB* 5: 463.

6. *Corr.* 1: 293, n. 4. Only Bernhardt merited having her full name printed.

7. *Corr.* 1: 300.

8. *Corr.* 1: 305.

9. See *Corr.* 1: 310, 311, n. 2.

10. *Corr.* 1: 311.

11. *SL* 1: 71. I have modified the translation, which omitted the negative from "Let's have no more jokes about articles" ("Plus de plaisanteries d'articles," *Corr.* 1: 313), thus reversing the intention of Yturri's request.

12. *Corr.* 1: 315–16.

13. *SL* 1: 77.

14. *SL* 1: 75. On May 7, 1894, the Opéra gave its one hundredth performance of *Lohengrin,* hailed as "a brilliant triumph." See *Corr.* 1: 327, n. 7.

15. *SL* 1: 75–76.

16. Hahn's description is from a letter to Marie Nordlinger, quoted in Gavoty, *Hahn,* 89.

17. See *Corr.* 1: 75.

18. This account of Proust at Réveillon is from Hahn's posthumous tribute, "Promenade," *NRF Hommage,* 39.

19. Hahn, "Promenade," 39–40.

20. *Recherche* (NP), Esquisse 62, 1: 860. This passage was not retained for the novel. Before writing the *Search*, Proust developed earlier versions of this incident in *Jean Santeuil*, 264, and *Contre Sainte-Beuve*. See Prologue, STW, 23–24.

21. *SL* 1: 73–74.

22. *SL* 1: 74, n. 4.

23. *SL* 1: 75.

24. *Corr.* 4: 412, n. 5.

25. *SL* 1: 76–78. Loute was Mme Lemaire's dog, whom she considered to be exceptionally intelligent.

26. *Corr.* 1: 330, n. 4. The castle sketch was not retained.

27. *SL* 1: 78–79

28. *Corr.* 1: 341.

29. *SL* 1: 79–80.

30. "Je vous aime, bien cher ami," *Corr.* 1: 333.

31. The god in disguise appeared again at the end of another story, "Promenade," *PR*, 119. In "La Mort de Baldassare Silvande," written in late summer and fall of 1894, Proust used an epigraph for each of the five sections gleaned from his extensive readings and his favorite authors. In addition to the American essayist and poet Emerson, the other quotations come from Mallarmé, Mme de Sévigné, and two from Shakespeare—Macbeth's famous speech about "sound and fury" and, from *Hamlet,* one of Proust's favorite quotations, Horatio's farewell to the dying hero. Proust grew fond of the name Horatio and later used it when he needed a pseudonym for the society pieces for *Le Figaro*.

32. Latget believes that Proust was inspired by reading an anthology of Tolstoy's death scenes. Published in France in 1886, *La Mort* contained, in addition to "The Death of Ivan Ilich," death scenes from *Anna Karenina* and *War and Peace*. See *PJ*, 68, n. 2. Latget's contention that the story is a parody of Robert de Montesquiou and contains satirical elements is less convincing; see his introductory note to "Baldassare," *PJ*, 304.

33. In *PJ*, Proust favored names with an exotic or outdated air. Those he chose seem to evoke especially Central Europe, the Balkans, Italy, or such enchanted realms as those used by Gérard de Nerval or Shakespeare. See *PJ*, 45, n. 2.

34. *PR*, 17.

35. *SL* 1: 81 Proust tends to use the ellipsis for suspension after expressing an emotion or alluding to one.

36. See *PR*, 31–47. I have modified the translator's title of "La Confession d'une jeune fille" from "A Young Girl's Confession," because *jeune fille* in French means "girl." At the moment of her attempted suicide and subsequent death, the "girl" has become a young woman of twenty; she is hardly innocent and is engaged to be married. "Confession" was the story Marcel had intended to dedicate to Montesquiou, perhaps because he considered it the finest in the book. His own favorite seems to have been "La Fin de la Jalousie." His dedication of "Baldassare" to Hahn can only indicate that Proust was pleased with that story also. This story is Proust's only first-person narrative other than the *Search;* its storyteller, like the future Narrator, has no name; *PJ*, 333.

37. [Marcel Proust par lui-même], *CSB* 5: 337.

38. This is the first instance in which Proust takes the good-night kiss drama from life and uses it in a story. He continued to develop the scene in the drafts of *Jean Santeuil*.

39. See Céleste Albaret, *Monsieur Proust,* edited by Georges Belmont and translated by Barbara Bray, New York: McGraw-Hill, 1976, 196–98. In the *Search,* Proust created a similar scene, with comic overtones, for Charlus, who despairs of finding a genuine sadist to whip him.

40. See *PR,* 192–221. The behavior of the lovers and the invention of a special language was no doubt inspired in part by Proust's and Hahn's similar actions: "Giving themselves up without thinking to the inventive and fertile genius of their love, it had, little by little, provided them with a language, as nations are provided with arms, games and laws"; *PR,* 193. This last image is the cell from which much of the imagery used to represent love in the *Search* was to grow: the beloved as a country with its own flag and national anthem.

41. The story includes a scene in which jealousy triggers severe asthma.

42. Although Honoré dies as the result of an accident, he speaks of his jealous passion for Françoise as "this disease that was killing him."

43. See "The End of Jealousy," *PR,* 193–94.

44. "The End of Jealousy," *PR,* 196.

45. *SL* 1: 83–84.

46. Proust relates his consultation with Mme de Thèbes (1865–1916), the celebrated palmist, in *Jean Santeuil,* 45–46.

47. Kolb observes that this is the conclusion regarding love and friendship found at the end of the *Search; Corr.* 1: 350, n. 5.

48. *Corr.* 1: 80, and 4: 370.

49. Quoted by Kolb in *Corr.* 1: 80.

50. Jean-Denis Bredin, *The Affair: The Case of Alfred Dreyfus,* translated by Jeffrey Mehlman, New York: George Braziller, 1986, 3. Dreyfus had been arrested on October 15, 1894. On November 1, *La Libre Parole* had identified the guilty party and said that he was a Jew. This was the beginning of the virulent anti-Semitic campaign in Paris newspapers. See Émile Zola, *L'Affaire Dreyfus: La Vérité en marche,* chronology and preface by Colette Becker, Paris: GF-Flammarion, 1969, 11.

51. Bredin, *Dreyfus,* 4–5.

52. Bredin, *Dreyfus,* 8.

53. *SL* 1: 87 and n. 1.

54. *Corr.* 1: 363 and n. 2.

55. *SL* 1: 88–89.

56. *Corr.* 1: 370.

57. The discreet young woman was Anna de Noailles, later a poet and Proust's great friend. Then unmarried, she was known as the princesse de Brancovan; *Corr.* 1: 322, n. 2.

58. Montesquiou's volume was published on June 7, 1895; "Sérée" bore the dedication "To M. Marcel Proust." *Corr.* 1: 372 and n. 2.

59. *Corr.* 1: 375; *Corr.* 2: 162.

60. À *la recherche du temps perdu, Sodome et Gomorrhe I et II,* text established, edited, and annotated by Françoise Leriche, Paris: Librairie Générale Française (Livre de Poche), 1993, 367, n. 2.

61. Goncourt *Journal,* 3: 1104–5.

62. *Corr.* 1: 379.

63. *SL* 1: 90.

64. Goncourt *Journal*, 3: 821.

65. H. Montgomery Hyde, *The Trials of Oscar Wilde*, with an introduction by Sir Travers Humphreys, London, 1948, 99.

66. *SL* 1: 91–92.

67. *SL* 1: 93.

68. *Search* 5: 344.

69. *SL* 1: 92–93.

70. The artists to whom Proust paid homage were Aelbert Cuyp, Paul Potter, Anthony Van Dyck, and Antoine Watteau; the composers were Chopin, Gluck, Schumann, and Mozart.

71. See *SL* 1: 95–96.

72. *Corr.* 1: 393, n. 2

73. Philip Kolb, "Marcel Proust et les dames Lemaire, avec des lettres de Proust à Suzette Lemaire et quelques autres," *BMP* 14 (1964): 131–32 and n. 1.

74. *Corr.* 1: 85.

75. See *Corr.* 1: 87.

76. Soupault, *Médecine*, 194, 195.

77. *Corr.* 1: 413.

78. Gavoty, *Hahn*, 103.

79. *Corr.* 1: 420–21.

80. *Corr.* 7: 333, n. 3.

81. *Marcel Proust, 1871–1922: An Exhibition of Manuscripts, Books, Pictures, and Photographs*, Manchester, England: Whitworth Art Gallery, 1956, exhibition, No. 86, 25.

82. In a July 1896 letter to Reynaldo, Proust wrote, "I am not, like the Lemaires, hostile to all places where we cannot be together." See *SL* 1: 127, *Search* 1: 265–68.

83. Hahn's Trio for Violin, Cello and Piano in F Major eventually became a symphonic suite entitled *Illustration pour le Jardin de Bérénice, June 1895–January 1896*. See *Corr.* 7: 331–32 and n. 4.

84. *Corr.* 2: 493.

85. *SL* 1: 101–2.

86. *SL* 1: 101 and n. 2. The line of poetry is from Alfred de Vigny's *La Maison du berger*.

87. See *Jean Santeuil*, 363–64; and *Corr.* 1: 429–30, n. 2.

88. Kolb, "Historique," 224. Harrison lived from 1853 to 1930. In my description of Proust's stay at Beg-Meil and the origins of *Jean Santeuil*, I am particularly indebted to Philip Kolb's article "Historique du premier roman de Proust."

89. Kolb, "Historique," 226.

90. *Lettres à Reynaldo Hahn*, 15.

91. Although Elstir bears vestiges of Harrison, he evolved to embody aspects of other painters such as Whistler, Monet, Manet, and Renoir.

92. *Corr.* 1: 430, n. 3.

93. *SL* 1: 349–50, and 351, n. 1. See *Search* 2: 592, where Elstir says of Carquethuit in Brittany: "I know nothing in France like it, it reminds me rather of certain aspects of Florida." Harrison knew Florida, having spent some years there making topographic drawings. Harrison's description of Penmarch may have inspired Proust's description of Elstir's masterpiece *Le Port de Carquethuit*.

94. See *Jean Santeuil*, 406–10. The title, "Impressions Regained," is not Proust's; he rarely provided titles for the drafts of *Jean Santeuil*.

95. *Jean Santeuil,* 409; I have modified the translation from "imprecision of feeling."
96. *Corr.* 1: 419, n. 2.
97. *Jean Santeuil,* 69; *JS* 4: 234–35.
98. See *Corr.* 21: 562, n. 2.
99. *SL* 1: 350.
100. *Corr.* 1: 435.

7 Pleasures and Days

1. *Corr.* 2: 51–52.
2. *Corr.* 1: 441 and 443, n. 3.
3. *Corr.* 1: 442. The ellipsis is Proust's.
4. For the complete text of this long, thoughtful letter, see *SL* 1: 105–7. In the letter Proust numbers his grievances against the host and dinner guests.
5. Goncourt *Journal,* 3: 1193.
6. "Contre l'obscurité" appeared in the July 15, 1896, issue of the *Revue blanche.* The little study on Chardin was not published during Proust's lifetime. See *Corr.* 1: 446.
7. *Search* 6: 333.
8. *Corr.* 1: 448 and n. 3.
9. Bredin, *Dreyfus,* 66–67.
10. *Corr.* 1: 449 and n. 1.
11. Lucien Daudet, *Autour de soixante lettres de Marcel Proust, Les Cahiers Marcel Proust* 5, Paris: Gallimard, 30.
12. *SL* 1: 108.
13. *Corr.* 2: 494 and n. 3.
14. *Textes retrouvés,* 82–83 and n. 2.
15. See *Jean Santeuil,* 660. On inscribing Jacques de Lacretelle's copy of *Swann's Way,* Proust identified Saint-Saëns's composition as the source of Swann and Odette's song. See [Dédicace], *CSB* 5: 565.
16. *Corr.* 2: 128; *SL* 1: 109.
17. *Corr.* 2: 50–51.
18. *Corr.* 2: 45 and n. 3.
19. *SL* 1: 118–19.
20. See Daudet, "L'Entre Deux-Guerres," in *Souvenirs et polémiques,* 386.
21. *Corr.* 2: 59–60.
22. *SL* 1: 119–20.
23. *SL* 1: 120.
24. *SL* 1: 121.
25. Mayer, "Jardin," 40.
26. *Jean Santeuil,* 723. In the *Search,* there is an echo of this text, and therefore of Auteuil, when the Narrator remembers his childhood and the scene of the good-night kiss: "Many years have passed since that night. The wall of the staircase up which I had watched the light of his [the father's] candle gradually climb was long ago demolished." *Search* 1: 49.
27. *SL* 1: 121.
28. *Corr.* 2: 68.

29. *Corr.* 2: 71 and n. 3.

30. In the first edition, France's preface bore no title. See *JS* 4: 3, n. 1. For a translation of the preface, see *PR*, vii–ix.

31. Gregh, *Amitié*, 9–10.

32. Pouquet, *Salon Caillavet*, 109–11.

33. *PJ*, 350.

34. Jean-Jacques Brousson, *Itinéraire de Paris à Buenos Aires*, 1927; quoted in *JS* 4: 4, n. 2.

35. Tadié dismisses Brousson's allegation as "anachronistic." *Marcel Proust*, 303, n. 3.

36. *SL* 1: 123 and n. 1.

37. See *PJ*, 289–92.

38. *PR*, "Regrets, Reveries, Changing Skies," 6: 123.

39. See *PJ*, 292.

40. *SL* 1: 124 and n. 2.

41. See *PJ*, 292–93.

42. For a reprint of Lorrain's article, see *PJ*, 294–95.

43. Jullian, *Montesquiou*, 162.

44. Quoted in the "Notice" to *Les Plaisirs et les jours;* see *JS* 4: 907.

45. Gregh, *L'Âge d'or*, 158.

46. Gregh, *Amitié*, 65.

47. Hahn, *Journal*, 139.

48. "Éros et Vénus," *CSB* 5: 388.

49. *SL* 1: 129, n. 2.

50. *SL* 1: 129.

51. *SL* 1: 127.

52. Mayer, "Jardin," 40–41.

53. *SL* 1: 130 and n. 3.

54. *SL* 1: 131.

55. *Corr.* 2: 94.

56. Certain of Brissaud's traits were given to Dr. du Boulbon, who treats the Narrator's grandmother in the *Search; SL* 1: 145, n. 5.

57. Michel, *Proust*, 29. Michel says that these manuals combined popular notions, unsubstantiated observations, Dr. Proust's and Dr. Ballet's own prejudices, and what little science was known. He also observes that, in spite of the impressive progress made in medicine since Adrien's day, hygiene remains the number one weapon in the arsenal against worldwide epidemics: condoms against AIDS, mosquito nets against malaria, and bleach to combat a number of infectious diseases.

58. Michel, *Proust*, 28, 36–37.

59. Proust and Ballet, *L'Hygiène du neurasthénique*, 30–31.

60. *SL* 1: 205.

61. Proust and Ballet, *L'Hygiène du neurasthénique*, 32.

62. Proust and Ballet, *L'Hygiène du neurasthénique*, 78.

63. Proust and Ballet, *L'Hygiène du neurasthénique*, 94.

64. Proust and Ballet, *L'Hygiène du neurasthénique*, 75.

65. *Search* 6: 212.

66. Proust and Ballet, *L'Hygiène du neurasthénique*, 168–69.

67. *SL* 1: 132.

68. *Corr.* 2: 100–101.
69. *SL* 1: 136, n. 2.
70. See *PJ*, 293–94.
71. See *Lettres à Reynaldo Hahn*, 17. The Narrator later defines, in a similar way, his and Albertine's love, seeing it clearly, like Marcel's love for Reynaldo, only after he had destroyed it: "I was perhaps the person whom she distinguished least from herself." *Search* 5: 81. There are fewer details about the relationship between Hahn and Proust in the years after Marcel's annulment of the pact because nearly all the letters they exchanged between 1897 to 1903 are missing. Many of the letters he exchanged with Lucien Daudet and Bertrand de Fénelon are in the hands of private collectors. The unpublished portion of Reynaldo Hahn's diary is deposited at the Bibliothèque nationale but is not available for consultation. See Tadié, *Marcel Proust*, 236, n. 2.
72. *Marcel Proust, Mon cher petit: Lettres à Lucien Daudet*, edited by Michel Bonduelle, Paris: Gallimard, 1991, 19–20.
73. *Corr.* 2: 122, n. 3.
74. Painter, *Letters to His Mother*, 60, 62.
75. *Corr.* 2: 125; Painter, *Letters to His Mother*, 64–65.
76. Painter, *Letters to His Mother*, 63.
77. *Corr.* 2: 131–32.
78. *SL* 1: 142–43.
79. *SL* 1: 277.
80. This passage is one of the rare ones to which Proust assigned a title in *Jean Santeuil*, perhaps indicating its importance. In the first draft, he set the scene at the Hôtel des Roches Noires in Trouville; later, he changed the scene and the title to "Jean at Beg-Meil: The telephone call to his mother." See *JS* 4: 356, n. 1, and *Jean Santeuil*, 365–70.
81. *SL* 1: 143–44.
82. Quoted in *Corr.* 2: 134, n. 1.
83. See Léon Daudet, *Rive droite, Souvenirs et polémiques*, 988.
84. *SL* 1: 147–48.
85. *Corr.* 2: 145–46.
86. Painter, *Letters to His Mother*, 71–72.
87. *Corr.* 2: 150–51.
88. *Corr.* 2: 149, n. 1. See *JS* 4: 833–36.
89. Bredin, *Dreyfus*, 175.
90. *SL* 1: 153–54.
91. *Corr.* 2: 157, n. 4.

8 The Duelists

1. *SL* 1: 163.
2. *SL* 1: 153 and n. 1.
3. See Albaret, *Monsieur Proust*, 180–81.
4. Gloves eventually became one of Proust's fetishes; he owned many pairs and insisted that they be in perfect condition. If not, new pairs were immediately purchased.
5. This information about the unpublished letter is from Tadié, *Marcel Proust*, 350.
6. *Corr.* 2: 164.

7. See *SL* 1: 154–55 and nn. 3, 5, and 156–57.

8. *PJ*, 295–96.

9. *Corr.* 20: 430, n. 2.

10. The Narrator refers to a number of duels he fought over the Dreyfus Affair. See *Search* 4: 11; 5: 387.

11. Bonduelle, *Mon cher petit*, 130.

12. Proust's recollections on this point varied over the years. See *SL* 1: 158, n. 2, and *Corr.* 2: 174, n. 2; *Corr.* 20: 288.

13. Hahn, *Journal*, 54.

14. Dreyfus, *Souvenirs*, 152–53.

15. From a film interview in Roger Stéphane and Roland Darbois, *Portrait-Souvenir: Marcel Proust*, directed by Gérard Herzog, 1962.

16. *Corr.* 2: 174, n. 2.

17. *SL* 1: 158.

18. Except for the satirical portrait of the duc de Réveillon, we do not know for certain what he wrote in 1897. By mid-1897 Proust had written no more than one half of *Jean Santeuil*. See Kolb, "Historique," 243–45.

19. This description of Bizet's apartment and the satirical review is based on Dreyfus's memoirs: *Souvenirs*, 116–25.

20. Larkin B. Price, *Materials for a Critical Edition of Marcel Proust's* Les Plaisirs et les jours, Ann Arbor: University Microfilms, 1965, 81.

21. *Proust-Halévy Corr.*, 70.

22. *Corr.* 2: 192.

23. *Corr.* 2: 184–85 and n. 5.

24. Munhall, *Whistler and Montesquiou*, 148–50.

25. Patrick Chaley, *Robert de Montesquiou: Mécène et dandy*, Paris: Somogy, 1992, 78.

26. See Munhall, *Whistler and Montesquiou*, 46.

27. Philippe Jullian, *Jean Lorrain ou le Satiricon 1900*, Paris: Fayard, 1974, 259.

28. Rearick, *Pleasures of the Belle Époque*, 191–92.

29. Robert Dreyfus, quoted in Chantal Bischoff, *Geneviève Straus: Trilogie d'une égérie*, Paris: Éditions Balland, 1992, 147.

30. Jullian, *Montesquiou*, 169.

31. *Corr.* 2: 189, and n. 2. See Gregh, *Amitié*, 74–75.

32. For details about the dinner, see *Corr.* 2: 188 and nn. 2, 3.

33. Montesquiou, quoted by Munhall, *Whistler and Montesquiou*, 46.

34. Jullian, *Montesquiou*, 170.

35. *Corr.* 20: 615, n. 2, and 616, n. 2.

36. *Corr.* 2: 194.

37. Jullian, *Montesquiou*, 173

38. Jullian, *Montesquiou*, 173–74.

39. *Corr.* 2: 194.

40. *Search* 3: 765.

41. Munhall, *Whistler and Montesquiou*, 47.

42. *SL* 1: 163 and n. 1.

43. *SL* 1: 164.

44. *Corr.* 2: 216–17.

45. *SL* 165.
46. See "La personne d'Alphonse Daudet, 'Œuvre d'art,' " *CSB* 5: 399–402.
47. *SL* 1: 167.
48. See *SL* 1: 169–70.
49. Dreyfus, *Souvenirs*, 125.
50. *SL* 1: 171.
51. *Corr.* 16: 393 and n. 2.
52. *Corr.* 2: 19.
53. See Zola, *Affaire*, 71.
54. *Proust-Halévy Corr.*, 82.
55. Bredin, *Dreyfus*, 228.
56. *Proust-Halévy Corr.*, 83.
57. *Proust-Halévy Corr.*, 83, 86–87.
58. See Tadié, *Marcel Proust*, 349.
59. *Proust-Halévy Corr.*, 83–84.
60. *Proust-Halévy Corr.*, 214.
61. "Adieux," *CSB* 5: 402–3.
62. Quotations about Zola and "J'accuse" are from Bredin, *Dreyfus*, 247–49.
63. Bredin, *Dreyfus*, 276. "The Dreyfus Affair . . . marked the first time that intellectuals acted as a self-conscious group in attempting to influence public events." Susan Rubin Suleiman, "The Literary Significance of the Dreyfus Affair," in *The Dreyfus Affair: Art, Truth, and Justice*, edited by Norman L. Kleeblat, Berkeley: University of California Press, 1987, 121.
64. *Corr.* 2: 20. Yeatman's name was misspelled as Jeatman.
65. Tadié, *Marcel Proust*, 368; Soupault, *Médecine*, 107.
66. Bredin, *Dreyfus*, 255.
67. *Jean Santeuil*, 320. In the *Search*, it is Bloch, the Narrator's Jewish friend who seeks to hide his ethnic identity and become assimilated, who attends the Zola trial. *Search* 3: 315.
68. *Jean Santeuil*, 333; for the remark about Picquart as philosopher, see *Jean Santeuil*, 343.
69. In *Jean Santeuil*, there is an occasional mention of anti-Semitism but no real discussion or development of the effect of the scandal on society. For example, a young duchess tells Jean that she never receives any Jews. This remark is conveyed in one sentence in the text without any comment. See *JS* 4: 706.
70. *Search* 3: 252.
71. Odette must hide from her husband, Charles Swann, the only Jewish member of the Jockey Club, her shameless maneuverings to ally herself with women in league against Dreyfus. Swann had been so thoroughly assimilated that everyone, including himself, had forgotten he was a Jew. Because of the virulent, unmerited attacks on his people, Swann rediscovered his race and heritage, which he proudly acknowledged, taking care not to denigrate the army in which he had served with distinction and whose mission and ideals he still respected.
72. *Search* 4: 384.
73. Billy also remarks that Marcel's health prevented him from taking an even more active role; *Lettres et conversations*, 126–27.
74. Tadié, *Marcel Proust*, 368–69.
75. Letter to Robert Dreyfus, May 29, 1905; *SL* 2: 188 and n. 4.

76. *SL* 1: 183.
77. Blanche, *Modèles*, 117.
78. My description and quotations for the breakup between the Halévys and Degas are taken from Linda Nochlin, "Degas and the Dreyfus Affair: A Portrait of the Artist as an Anti-Semite," in Kleeblat, *The Dreyfus Affair*, 96–116.
79. Léon Daudet, *Au temps de Judas, Souvenirs et polémiques*, 572.
80. *Corr.* 2: 248.
81. *Corr.* 2: 253, n. 10.
82. "Un esprit et un génie innombrables: Léon Daudet," *CSB* 5: 603, n. 4. In *Jean Santeuil*, Jean is stupefied to hear someone say that "if Dreyfus were innocent it would be the government's painful but necessary duty to hide this fact and declare him guilty for the greater good." *JS* 4: 485.
83. *SL* 2: 222.
84. "Le Destin," signed and dated "Reynaldo Hahn, Octobre 1898, Dieppe, Chez Mme Lemaire." See *Corr.* 3: 474, n. 2.
85. An allusion to Vigny's poem *La Maison du berger*, *Corr.* 3: 474, n. 4.
86. See *Corr.* 2: 472–73.

9 Am I a Novelist?

1. *Corr.* 2: 260, n. 2. The dates of the Rembrandt exhibition in Amsterdam were September 7–October 31 1898; see *SL* 1: 184, n. 1. See also Kolb, "Historique," 262.
2. Borel, *Voyager*, 151.
3. Kolb, "Historique," 261.
4. "Rembrandt," STW, 338.
5. "Rembrandt," STW, 339.
6. "Gustave Moreau," STW, 355.
7. ["Notes sur le monde mystérieux de Gustave Moreau"], *CSB* 5: 969.
8. "Gustave Moreau," STW 352.
9. In December, Picquart won a high court ruling that resulted in his case being transferred to a civilian court; Nochlin, "Degas," x.
10. *SL* 1: 187, n. 2.
11. Proust presumably wrote to *L'Aurore*'s director Ernest Vaughan on November 26 or 27; *SL* 1: 187.
12. *Corr.* 2: 269, n. 3.
13. The unlucky Yeatman's name had been misspelled again, as "Yestman."
14. See *SL* 1: 188.
15. A similar, more tentative, exploration of this theme is found in the scene called "Beg-Meil in Holland," presumably inspired by the 1898 trip. This passage contains an important element: such experiences give Jean the strength to "stop, to exert the energies of my mind on it (the involuntary memory experience) and this time setting me, indeed, to work." See *Jean Santeuil*, 401–4. One recognizes in this single line the key episode at the conclusion of the *Search*, in which, after a series of involuntary memory experiences, the Narrator, his will restored and his enthusiasm boosted, is ready to create his great work.
16. It is possible, of course, that he wrote the scene first for *Jean Santeuil*.
17. *Jean Santeuil*, 464.

18. All artists hope to "seduce" their public. Proust always wanted to please everyone he met and certainly he wanted to enchant his readers. His intensely seductive voice is similar to Walt Whitman's, whose sounds and words constantly seem to urge the reader to lie with him and exchange caresses. Both the *Search* and Whitman's *Leaves of Grass* have famous, powerful opening lines in which each author offers an "I" the reader can immediately assume. Proust begins "For a long time I used to go to bed early," Whitman "I celebrate myself / And what I assume you shall assume, / For every atom belonging to me as good belongs to you." Both writers are ones with whom, as Shelby Foote said of Proust, the reader can easily "hook atoms." *Conversations with Shelby Foote,* edited by William C. Carter, Jackson: University Press of Mississippi, 1989, 205.

19. The collection of poems was published by Fasquelle in the fall of 1898.

20. "To Marcel Proust, his friend, Anatole France," *Corr.* 2: 276, n. 2.

21. *SL* 1: 190.

22. *Corr.* 2: 333–34.

23. William L. Shirer, *The Collapse of the Third Republic: An Inquiry into the Fall of France in 1940,* New York: Simon and Schuster, 1969, 64.

24. David Levering Lewis, *Prisoners of Honor: The Dreyfus Affair,* New York: Holt, 1994, 263.

25. Bredin, *Dreyfus,* 372; Shirer, *Collapse,* 64.

26. *SL* 1: 193, n. 3. See *Corr.* 2: 280, n. 3, and Pouquet, *Salon Caillavet,* 193.

27. *SL* 1: 192.

28. *Corr.* 2: 283–84.

29. *Corr.* 2: 282, n. 4.

30. *SL* 1: 193–94.

31. *Corr.* 2: 287, n. 3.

32. *Corr.* 19: 538.

33. Proust remembered this image and used it as an analogy for Vinteuil's music in *Swann's Way* and *The Captive.*

34. *SL* 1: 194–95.

35. *SL* 1: 196.

36. See *Corr.* 2: 298–300.

37. Nadine Beauthéac, *Les Promenades de Marcel Proust,* with photographs by François-Xavier Bouchart, Paris: Éditions du Chêne, 1997, 53–54.

38. Beauthéac, *Promenades,* 58.

39. *Corr.* 2: 344. According to Painter, she played Chopin "beautifully, but reluctantly." Painter, *Proust* 1: 136.

40. *SL* 1: 199.

41. Marie de Chevilly, "Marcel Proust en Savoie," *BMP* 24 (1974): 1822.

42. The Brancovans' garden and yacht are the models for those of Mme de Cambremer at her Brittany château in the *Search* 4: 226. See *SL* 1: 202, 203, and n. 2.

43. Marie de Chevilly, "Marcel Proust en Savoie," *BMP* 23 (1973): 1591.

44. *SL* 1: 197.

45. *SL* 1: 201.

46. Not even the elevator boy was exempt. When the boy, who Marcel suspected was Jewish, came to tell him good-bye, the youth informed him that he "had to leave his post earlier than planned because his support of Dreyfus had made him too many enemies." *Corr.* 2: 354.

47. *SL* 1: 199.

48. *SL* 1: 197.

49. *Corr.* 2: 307.

50. *SL* 1: 202, 204, n. 4. Eppler is the model for the tailor Jupien, whose shop is located in the courtyard of the Guermantes's large town house, where the Narrator's family takes an apartment. See *Search* 1: 25; 3: 14–18.

51. Chevilly, "Proust en Savoie," 23: 1588, 1591.

52. *SL* 1: 199.

53. *Corr.* 2: 330.

54. Almost nothing is known about Poupetière, who was born in 1867; see *Corr.* 2: 325, n. 14.

55. Painter, *Letters to His Mother*, 95–96; *Corr.* 2: 332–33.

56. *SL* 1: 200. See *Corr.* 2: 336.

57. *SL* 1: 207.

58. *Corr.* 2: 326.

59. Chevilly, "Proust en Savoie," 24: 1826.

60. *SL* 1: 202–3.

61. *Corr.* 2: 330.

62. ["Le déclin de l'inspiration"], *CSB* 5: 422–34.

63. Painter, *Letters to His Mother*, 96. Did the little wrist massage inspire a scene in *Jean Santeuil*? Jean, at midnight at the bedside of a female friend, tells her that his wrist hurts. This woman whom he had never desired, but whose affection he would have welcomed, takes his hand and massages it. This intimate act of kindness arouses him and he asks permission to kiss her. She stops his advances. *JS* 4: 837–42. This is an earlier version of the Narrator's first attempt to kiss Albertine.

64. *SL* 1: 206.

65. Marcel had made one quick trip alone to Geneva, where, not feeling well, he did nothing but obtain the addresses of several cocottes for Abel Hermant; *Corr.* 2: 317.

66. For a study of modernity in the *Search* see William C. Carter, *The Proustian Quest*, New York: New York University Press, 1992.

67. *SL* 1: 205–6.

68. *Corr.* 2: 292–93.

69. *SL* 1: 207.

70. *Search* 4: 695.

71. Painter, *Letters to His Mother*, 116. *Corr.* 2: 359.

72. *Corr.* 2: 357.

73. Painter, *Letters to His Mother*, 116. *Corr.* 2: 358.

74. La Sizeranne's book was published in Paris by Hachette, 1897; see *Corr.* 2: 348, and 350, n. 16.

75. Coco was already in Rome; Marcel considered joining him there. *Corr.* 2: 359.

76. *Corr.* 2: 352. Proust frequently borrowed money from his friends. In August 1898 he wrote to Yeatman about repaying him the "ridiculous sums" he owed. See *Corr.* 2: 241.

77. *Corr.* 2: 357. In 1901 Suzanne Thibault (1881–1918) married Captain Henri Mollin; *Corr.* 2: 358, n. 8.

78. *Corr.* 2: 357.

79. *Corr.* 2: 359–62; Painter, *Letters to His Mother*, 117–22.

80. Hubert Juin, Introduction to John Ruskin, *La Bible d'Amiens*, translated by Marcel Proust, edited by Juin, Paris: Union Générale d'Editions (10/18), 1986, x.

81. See *Textes retrouvés*, 24, n. 4, and *JS* 4: 556, n. 2.

82. Tadié, *Marcel Proust*, 429.

83. *Corr.* 2: 348.

84. Tadié, *Marcel Proust*, 429, n. 6.

85. *Corr.* 2: 366.

86. *JS* 4: 181.

87. "Notice" to *JS* 4: 983.

88. *JS* 4: 181. *Jean Santeuil*, 1. I have modified the translation, which omitted most of this passage. The continuation of the quotation contains a jibe at society: views of nature, he says, "free him for an instant" from the brilliant but frozen "ice of high society." In another passage, Jean makes a similar remark about society: "society seemed to him something brilliant and cold like one of the princesse de Durheim's witticisms." *JS* 4: 497.

89. *SL* 1: 57, 58.

90. Quoted in Diesbach, *Proust*, 184.

91. In one passage in which Jean is talking to Charlotte, whom he hopes to make his mistress though she is married, he attempts to persuade her to call him by his given name. She remarks, "It would be better if I called you Marcel and you called me Charlotte." *JS* 4: 831. (In the English translation "Marcel" is changed to "Jean" for the sake of uniformity; *Jean Santeuil*, 682.) Such a slip indicates Proust's identification with his hero, which became even more marked during the writing of the *Search*. A similar conversation occurs there between Albertine and the Narrator, who hints that his name might be Marcel. Still, in spite of Proust's close identification with his protagonist, the *Search* is not an autobiography.

92. See *Jean Santeuil*, 701–2. Jean recognized snobbery, the "frivolity, eloquence, pride" that had made him want to shine in the salons, as "the true evil." See *Jean Santeuil*, 702–3. If Jean had not yet discovered his vocation, he did feel that he had been sent on a mission by a deity that dwelled in him and that he must not allow to perish. This mission, the expression of his entire being through poetry, now forms, he said, "the center of his moral being." Good was anything that favored his inspiration; evil, anything that paralyzed it.

93. *Search* 1: 243–44. See also *Search* 1: 244: "This lack of genius, this black cavity which gaped in my mind when I ransacked it for the theme of my future writings"; *Search* 1: 251: "How often . . . in the course of my walks along the Guermantes way, and with what an intensified melancholy, did I reflect on my lack of qualification for a literary career, and abandon all hope of ever becoming a famous author."

94. The Narrator, in a moment similar to Proust's abandonment of *Jean Santeuil*, concludes that he had "no aptitude for writing. And so, utterly despondent, I renounced literature for ever." *Search* 1: 245.

95. Kolb believes that Jeanne proposed the project; "Historique," 269.

96. *SL* 3: 4.

97. "What I need is to concentrate, to probe deeply within myself, to seek the truth, to express my entire soul, which is true, and not all these things that are, in short, frivolous." *JS* 4: 440. Proust does not yet see how the frivolous things will form a marvelous counterpoint to the deeper currents of the *Search* by illustrating the errors of a number of his characters while amusing the reader with their follies.

98. *SL* 1: 210–11.

10 Ruskin and Certain Cathedrals

1. See A. D. Trottenberg's introduction to *Eugène Atget, a Vision of Paris,* New York: Macmillan, 1963, 11–28.
2. See *JS* 4: 499, 739.
3. See *JS* 4: 63–64, "La Bénédiction du sanglier," *CSB* 5: 202, and the *Search* 4: 290.
4. *SL* 1: 211.
5. *Corr.* 2: 381–82.
6. *SL* 1: 212.
7. The unidentified friend was probably Douglas Ainslie or Charles Newton Scott; *Corr.* 2: 385, n. 3.
8. *SL* 1: 212, n. 2.
9. *SL* 1: 212–13.
10. *SL* 1: 216 and n. 5.
11. Proust called his years spent studying and translating Ruskin a "voluntary servitude." See his preface to *The Bible of Amiens, On Reading Ruskin: Prefaces to* La Bible d'Amiens *and* Sésame et les lys, translated and edited by Jean Autret, William Burford, and Phillip J. Wolfe, with an introduction by Richard Macksey, New Haven: Yale University Press, 1987, 60.
12. *SL* 1: 213–14.
13. *SL* 1: 214, n. 1.
14. See *SL* 1: 215–16 and n. 2; the Hugo quotation is from *Les Contemplations,* book 1, chapter 8: "Car le mot qu'on le sache est un être vivant." See *Search* 1: 118.
15. *On Reading Ruskin,* 9. Proust dedicated the piece to Léon Daudet, an odd choice, for Daudet despised Ruskin's work. Daudet confided to his memoirs, published after Proust's death, that Ruskin was "unbearable," that "nothing seemed more removed from Venice than Ruskin and his *Stones of Venice,*" and that Proust's work on Ruskin was "stupid." See Léon Daudet, *L'Entre Deux-Guerres,* 387, and *Rive Droite,* 984, in *Souvenirs et polémiques.*
16. *On Reading Ruskin,* 19.
17. *On Reading Ruskin,* 29.
18. This essay became the first section of part 3 of his preface to *La Bible d'Amiens;* see *On Reading Ruskin,* 29–38.
19. The situation is similar in the *Search* when the Narrator's family seeks a more secluded neighborhood with purer air because of concerns about the grandmother's health. *Corr.* 2: 395, n. 3; *Search* 3: 3.
20. In the translation of *The Bible of Amiens,* she became "the eminent artist." *Corr.* 2: 396, n. 2.
21. *Corr.* 2: 395–96.
22. From "Huit lettres inédites à Maria de Madrazo," presented by Marie Riefstahl-Nordlinger, in *BMP* 3 (1953): 36, n. 4.
23. Marcel Proust, *Lettres à une amie, recueil de quarante et une lettres inédites adressées à Marie Nordlinger, 1899–1908,* Manchester, England: Editions du Calame, 1942, ix.
24. Ruskin's 1877 guidebook to Venice. *Corr.* 2: xiii; *SL* 2: 89 and n. 5.
25. *On Reading Ruskin,* 59.
26. Nordlinger, *Lettres à une amie,* ix.
27. *Search* 5: 853.
28. *On Reading Ruskin,* 77–78. Ruskin had gone to Venice to study Carpaccio from September 1876 to May 1877.

29. Preface to *La Bible d'Amiens* in *On Reading Ruskin*, 91, 92.

30. Nordlinger, *Lettres à une amie,* ix.

31. *Corr.* 2: 30.

32. *Search* 5: 874–75.

33. *Search* 5: 845–47.

34. *Search* 5: 876.

35. *Corr.* 7: 174, n. 5. The year before, Proust had read Ruskin's *Flors Clavigera,* which made him eager to see the magnificent Giottos in the Scrovegni Chapel in Padua.

36. *Search* 1: 460.

37. *SL* 2: 289 and n. 2.

38. *Search* 5: 848, 868.

39. Wilde's remains were moved to Père-Lachaise Cemetery in 1909, when the famous funerary monument by Epstein was placed there. See Ellmann, *Wilde,* 588–89.

40. Proust's review appeared in the January 5 issue of *La Chronique des arts et de la curiosité.* See "Pays des aromates," *CSB* 5: 444–45. The details about the exhibition are from Jullian, *Montesquiou,* 205.

41. "Notre Amour," *La Revue de Paris,* February 1, 1899; *SL* 1: 221, n. 5.

42. Tadié, *Marcel Proust,* 453.

43. *SL* 1: 221.

44. *SL* 1: 223–24. In a late-summer letter to her cousin Antoine Bibesco, Marcel again declared his love for the princesse de Caraman-Chimay; *Corr.* 2: 440.

45. *SL* 1: 223–24.

46. As noted in both *Le Gaulois* and *Le Figaro;* see *Corr.* 2: 430, nn. 5 and 6.

47. *Corr.* 2: 431.

48. This description of the dinner party and the quotations are from Daudet's memoirs; see *Salons et Journaux, Souvenirs et polémiques,* 505. Proust gave a series of dinner parties in fairly rapid succession. He hosted another on June 21; on July 1 Proust gave a more intimate dinner for Montesquiou and Yturri. See *Corr.* 2: 32 and 435, n. 3.

49. *SL* 1: 217.

50. *SL* 1: 218.

51. "Le salon de la comtesse d'Haussonville," *CSB* 5: 486 and n. 2.

52. *SL* 1: 223.

53. *SL* 1: 228, nn. 2, 3.

54. See *SL* 1: 228, n. 4. Details of the prince's grand funeral later inspired in part Saint-Loup's funeral in the *Search.*

55. Antoine's mother was born Hélène Costaki Epureano. *SL* 1: 271, n. 2.

56. *SL* 1: 225, n. 1.

57. In 1903 Proust's friend the princesse de Polignac, writing under her maiden name W. Singer, published her translation of *Walden. Corr.* 209, 210, n. 8.

58. Billy had been particularly impressed by Emmanuel's knowledge and wrote that the prince "had studied Gothic architecture in depth." Billy, *Lettres et conversations,* 121.

59. *SL* 1: 226.

60. George de Lauris, quoted in Maurois, *Genius,* 91.

61. Tadié, *Marcel Proust,* 461.

62. *Corr.* 4: xiv. Proust wrote in the first notebook for the *Search:* "Bertrand lover of Louisa's sister." Louisa de Morand's sister, Suzanne Montaud, was a minor actress who performed

under the name Jane Moriane. See Marcel Proust, *Le Carnet de 1908,* edited by Philip
Kolb, *Cahiers Marcel Proust,* n.s., 8, Paris: Gallimard, 1971, 49 and n. 15. (This little notebook, hereafter cited as *Carnet 1908,* contains the first notes Proust made that eventually
led to the *Search.*) Whether Fénelon was the lover of either or both sisters is not well established. Apparently, Proust believed that he was. The sources of the information about
Fénelon's bisexuality are rather vague. Among those closely associated with Marcel, it was
Paul Morand who recorded, without giving details or the date, Proust's discovery of this
aspect of Fénelon's private life. We do not know how Proust reacted to this revelation. See
Morand's memoirs about Proust, *Le Visiteur du soir, suivi de quarante-cinq lettres inédites
de Marcel Proust,* Geneva: La Palatine, 1949, 26.
63. *Corr.* 2 449–52.
64. The full title of Mâle's important 1898 study is *L'Art religieux du treizième siècle en France:
Étude sur l'iconographie du moyen âge et sur ses sources d'inspiration.*
65. *Corr.* 4: 423.
66. *SL* 230, n. 5; *Corr.* 2: 465, n. 6.
67. *Corr.* 2: 464.
68. *Corr.* 2: 470. There are times when Proust uses *moschant* in its usual meaning of *méchant,*
bad, wicked, or mean.
69. *Corr.* 2: 470.
70. *SL* 1: 234–35.
71. Proust's admiration for the great actress, especially as Phèdre, is found in the *Search's*
actress La Berma, Bernhardt's fictional counterpart. Although La Berma has more than
one real-life model, as Phèdre she is clearly the Divine Sarah.
72. *SL* 1: 234–35.
73. *SL* 1: 232–33.

11 His Blue Eyes

1. *SL* 1: 242.
2. *Corr.* 3: 129, 132, 135. This nickname for Fénelon may have been an allusion to
Thomas Hardy's novel *A Pair of Blue Eyes* (1873); *Corr.* 3: 129, n. 5. Tadié provides a
more likely choice, Henry Bernstein's play *Ses Yeux bleus;* Tadié, *Marcel Proust,* 461 and
n. 9.
3. *Corr.* 3: 64–65. Proust's future characters who are consumed by jealousy—Swann, the
Narrator, and Charlus—ask friends to spy on the men and women who become objects
of their obsessions.
4. *SL* 1: 244–46.
5. *SL* 1: 243–44.
6. See *SL* 1: 248–49.
7. These are believed to be the last additions to the *Jean Santeuil* manuscript. In the scene
from *Jean Santeuil* depicting the race across the restaurant to bring Jean a coat, the beau
geste is made by Jean's friend Bertrand de Réveillon, whose name echoes that of his real-
life counterpart.
8. Kolb dates this incident in May or June 1902. See *Corr.* 3: 8, and Kolb, "Historique," 264.
9. In the *Search,* Fénelon was a model not only for Saint-Loup but for Albertine in the scene
in which the Narrator admires her beautiful legs pumping the pianola. This vision of the

athletic girl inspired thoughts identical to those when Proust admired Fénelon running toward him with the coat. See *Search* 5: 515.

10. *Corr.* 3: 84.
11. *SL* 1: 251–54.
12. See Albaret, *Monsieur Proust*, 44, 176.
13. *Corr.* 3: 92.
14. *SL* 1: 258–60.
15. *Corr.* 3: 128.
16. *SL* 1: 265.
17. *Corr.* 3: 131.
18. Léon Daudet, *Salons et Journaux, Souvenirs et polémiques*, 505.
19. *Corr.* 3: 248.
20. *SL* 1: 263–64.
21. *Corr.* 3: 137.
22. See *SL* 1: 266 and nn. 1, 2. The periodical had the same name as the publishing house; the title of the journal will be italicized as the *Mercure de France* or simply *Mercure*, while the name of the publishing house will appear in roman type.
23. See *Corr.* 3: 160–62, and 21: 615. During his Ruskin years, Proust often sketched churches and religious scenes depicted on portals or in stained-glass windows. Reynaldo was usually the recipient of these drawings, some of which were humorous and contained captions in their private language. Many of the sketches were quite detailed, like the one he did of the cathedral of Amiens. Many of these drawings can be seen in *Lettres à Reynaldo Hahn*.
24. See *SL* 1: 267.
25. This incident, about which nothing more is known, is mentioned in the letter to his mother of October 17; see *SL* 1: 268.
26. See *SL* 1: 268.
27. *Corr.* 21: 614.
28. *SL* 1: 268–69.
29. It is possible Proust first glimpsed Vermeer's painting on his 1898 trip to Holland. *Corr.* 20: 226. In the *Search*, Proust uses the painting as a touchstone of artistic achievement.
30. *SL* 1: 271–72.
31. *SL* 1: 274–75.
32. *SL* 1: 276 and n. 3.
33. *SL* 1: 277, n. 5.
34. See Marie Nordlinger, "Proust and Ruskin," Whitworth exhibition catalogue, 9–10. Marie says that her visits were to boulevard Malesherbes, apparently having forgotten that the Prousts moved to the rue de Courcelles in 1900. She also forgot the servant's name.
35. *SL* 1: 280–82. This letter reveals how Mme Proust struggled to force Marcel to adopt healthier habits. Proust's Narrator demolishes Charlus's top hat as revenge for an insult. *Search* 3: 766.
36. *SL* 1: 282–84.

12 *Self-Hypnosis*

1. *Corr.* 3: 205.
2. *SL* 1: 320, n. 3; the article appeared in the December 5, 1902, issue. Marcel, who saw the

notice of Montesquiou's return from New York in *Le Figaro* on April 10, 1903, wrote a welcome-home note in which he told the count of his joy on learning that "the waves have at last brought back to us the vessel bearing Virgil." *SL* 1: 319.

3. *Corr.* 3: 206–8. Constantin's review published thirty-one pages of *La Bible d'Amiens* in its February 15 issue and twenty-three pages in the March 15 issue; *Corr.* 3: 208, n. 5.

4. *Corr.* 3: 209.

5. See "Le Salon de la comtesse Aimery de La Rochefoucauld," *Textes retrouvés*, 38–40, and *CSB* 5: 436–39.

6. Not only did this salon description not appear, it disappeared and has remained lost. See *Corr.* 3: 290, n. 2.

7. *SL* 1: 288–89.

8. *SL* 1: 289–91.

9. *SL* 1: 291, n. 3.

10. *SL* 1: 291.

11. *SL* 1: 291–93.

12. *Corr.* 3: 225.

13. *SL* 1: 295.

14. *SL* 1: 294. I have modified the translation from "Everyone is bored with me."

15. *SL* 1: 294.

16. *SL* 1: 296.

17. Valentine Thomson, "My Cousin Marcel Proust," in *Harper's Magazine* 164 (May 1932): 717.

18. *Corr.* 3: 231, n. 6.

19. *Corr.* 3: 235.

20. *Corr.* 3: 249.

21. *SL* 1: 306.

22. *SL* 1: 297–99.

23. *SL* 1: 305.

24. *SL* 1: 308. Proust used the Pascal quote again in July when he wrote to Robert de Billy to congratulate him on his being awarded the Légion d'honneur; *Corr.* 3: 341–42 and n. 1.

25. *SL* 1: 309.

26. *Search* 2: 157–58.

27. *Corr.* 3: 261.

28. Jules Caradon, known as Cardane.

29. *SL* 1: 309–12.

30. *SL* 1: 312, n. 1.

31. *Search* 4: 567–68.

32. *SL* 1: 311.

33. *SL* 1: 323.

34. See *Corr.* 3: 20 and 279, n. 2.

35. On February 19, André Beaunier had praised Proust's "fine translation." See *SL* 1: 313, n. 4.

36. *Corr.* 3: 292.

37. *SL* 1: 317, 318, n. 4.

38. There are various accounts of the Good Friday trip. Billy's and Lauris's accounts have Bertrand de Fénelon present, but other evidence places Fénelon in Constantinople at the time. For this reason some, like George Painter, believe that the trip took place in 1902.

Lauris, like Billy, writing many years after the event, recalled that the group was at Coucy on Good Friday. According to Lauris, Fénelon, worried that Marcel's lungs would not allow him to make the dizzying ascent, held him by the arm while intoning "The Good Friday Spell" from Wagner's *Parsifal*. See Georges de Lauris, "Quelques années avant Swann," *NRF Hommage*, p. 47. According to Kolb's chronology, the first trip occurred on Good Friday (April 10), but Kolb believed that the trip to Coucy took place on April 21. See *Corr.* 3: 20, 21. Tadié suggests that there may have been more than two trips in 1903. See Tadié, *Marcel Proust*, 481, n. 5. There seems to be no way to resolve the disparities. I have adopted Kolb's chronology.

39. Lauris, "Quelques années avant Swann," 45.
40. Beauthéac, *Promenades*, 86.
41. The internal quotation has not been identified.
42. *SL* 2: 167–68.
43. Marcel consumed beer with meals because he thought it was good for his condition. See *Corr.* 3: 377.
44. *Corr.* 3: 299.
45. Maxime Dethomas (1867–1929) was an artist to whose studies of Venice Proust gives the highest praise in his *Séjour à Venise* (*Search* 5: 848). An exhibition of Dethomas's drawings was held at the Durand-Ruel Gallery, April 15–29, 1903. *SL* 1: 323, n. 1.
46. No. 29 in the catalogue of the exhibition: *View of the Grand Canal in Venice. SL* 1: 323, n. 2.
47. See "Le Salon de Mme Madeleine Lemaire," *CSB* 5: 457–64.
48. See *SL* 1: 325, n. 1.
49. *Corr.* 3: 313–14 and n. 2.
50. *Corr.* 3: 22.
51. Kolb thinks that Marcel made this inquiry in 1903; see *Corr.* 7: 334.
52. *Corr.* 4: 183.
53. In 1928, when Louisa de Mornand published Proust's letters to her, she said, in an interview: "We had a loving relationship which was neither an idle flirtation nor an exclusive liaison, but, on Proust's side, a keen passion balanced between affection and desire, and on mine a deeply felt attachment which was more than friendship." "Mon amitié avec Marcel Proust," *Candide*, November 1, 1928, quoted in Michel-Thiriet, *Book*, 207. Painter states that Proust and Louisa did have intercourse: "Proust made love to her, first platonically, then physically." See Painter, *Letters to His Mother*, 42.
54. *Corr.* 3: 321 and 322, n. 3.
55. See *Corr.* 3: 323, and 324, n. 3.
56. See *Corr.* 3: 325 and n. 2, 327.
57. See *SL* 1: 337–38.

13 A Happy Man

1. *Textes retrouvés*, 123.
2. See *SL* 1: 332–33. There is no indication that Antoine ever helped with the proofs.
3. "Quoted in English, and drawn, except for the first four words, from *The Bible of Amiens*, ch. iv." *SL* 1: 333, n. 3.
4. *Corr.* 3: 347.
5. *SL* 2: 9, n. 7. Montesquiou's scatological diatribes inspired those of the baron de Charlus.

6. *Corr.* 3: 355.

7. *Corr.* 3: 378–79.

8. See *Corr.* 10: 397, and *Corr.* 3: 398, n. 2.

9. *SL* 1: 339.

10. Lauris, "Quelques années avant Swann," 45.

11. *SL* 1: 340.

12. *Corr.* 3: 464.

13. *Corr.* 3: 379.

14. Adrien also quoted from Baudelaire's *Le Cygne,* Sully Prudhomme's *Les Vieilles Maisons,* and Leconte de Lisle's *Midi.*

15. *SL* 1: 347, n. 1. See Lauris, *À un ami,* 23.

16. See *SL* 1: 342–46.

17. *SL* 1: 347, n. 4. Ferry's "laws" or "decrees," sponsored by Jules Ferry (1832–93), then minister of education, and promulgated on March 29, 1880, called for the dissolution of the teaching order of Jesuits.

18. *Corr.* 7: 333.

19. *SL* 1: 348.

20. Gregh, *Amitié,* 89.

21. *SL* 1: 348, n. 1.

22. In the *Search,* Swann and the Narrator respond in similar fashion whenever Odette and Albertine became readily available and thereby lose, even temporarily, their evanescent natures. At such moments Proust would compare the formerly desirable "winged creatures" to "burdensome slaves." *Search* 5: 500–501.

23. *SL* 1: 350. Marcel does not say why Antoine was angry with him.

24. *Corr.* 3: 393.

25. *Corr.* 3: 393. Jeanne conveyed the information about his sadness by quoting from La Fontaine's fable "Les Deux Amis," "Vous m'êtes en dormant un peu triste apparu" (While I was asleep you appeared before me somewhat sorrowful). *Corr.* 3: 394, n. 2.

26. *SL* 1: 349.

27. Apparently, Adrien and Jeanne left around the time of Marcel's arrival. Adrien selected Aix-les-Bains, where he arrived on September 3. We do not know where Jeanne continued her vacation. See *Corr.* 3: 413 and 414, n. 4.

28. The details about the trip are from Proust's letter to Georges de Lauris. See *SL* 1: 351–52.

29. *SL* 1: 353, n. 2.

30. See "Le Salon de la princesse Edmond de Polignac: Musique d'aujourd'hui, échos d'autrefois," *CSB* 5: 464–69.

31. This text is in "Dante Gabriel Rossetti et Elizabeth Siddal," *CSB* 5: 470–74. Proust signed the article M. P.

32. Kolb notes that Proust cites the epilogue of *Modern Painters,* in which Ruskin, like Proust after him, writes "Chamouni" for Chamonix. See *Corr.* 3: 426, n. 2.

33. *SL* 1: 353.

34. Proust's review of *John Ruskin und sein Werk* by the German scholar Charlotte Broicher appeared on January 2, signed M. P. See *CSB* 5: 478–81. *SL* 2: 241, n.2

35. *Corr.* 4: 430, n. 2.

36. *Corr.* 16: 395.

37. In the *Search* the Narrator's grandmother suffers a mild stroke in the public toilets

adjacent to the Champs-Élysées. This attack marks the beginning of her decline and leads, within a relatively short period of time, to her death.

38. *Corr.* 3: 439–40.
39. Robert Proust's only child later chose to be called Suzy.
40. In the novel, the scene is used as an analogy for a misunderstanding. *Search* 6: 281–82. The Narrator's parents do not die in the novel. Once their essential narrative functions have been fulfilled (primarily in the good-night kiss drama and other scenes from childhood), they fade into the background.
41. Marie-Nordlinger, "Fragments d'un journal," *BMP* 8 (1958): 526–27.
42. Albaret, *Monsieur Proust,* 141.
43. From Maurice Bariéty's eulogy, reprinted in Christian Péchenard, *Proust et son père,* Paris: Quai Voltaire, 1993, 255, 260.
44. Roger Duchêne, *L'Impossible Marcel Proust,* Paris: Laffont, 1994, 464.
45. Tadié, *Marcel Proust,* 56.
46. Duchêne, *L'Impossible Proust,* 464–65.
47. *SL* 1: 358, n. 1.
48. *SL* 1: 360.
49. *SL* 2: 84.
50. *SL* 1: 358.
51. *Corr.* 3: 459–60, 16: 395–96.
52. *SL* 1: 361. In the *Search,* the portrait of the father was softened in comparison with the rather harsh and at times caricatural portrait that Proust created in *Jean Santeuil.*
53. *SL* 1: 359–60.
54. *Corr.* 3: 453–54.
55. Tadié sees Marcel's letter as proof that Adrien had been Laure's lover and refers to the same relationship between Dr. Cottard and the cocotte Odette, to whose portrait Laure contributed a number of elements. Tadié, *Marcel Proust,* 35.
56. *SL* 1: 361–62.
57. Ferré, *Collège,* 41.
58. *Corr.* 11: 138.
59. Jaloux's story was "Le Triomphe de la frivolité," which he sent along with his letter. See *Corr.* 3: 458, n. 2; Edmond Jaloux, *Avec Marcel Proust, suivi de dix-sept lettres inédites,* Paris: La Palatine, 1953, 14–16.
60. *Corr.* 3: 457. In the *Search,* Proust developed a similar image, that of a rare insect alone able to fertilize a particular plant, applying the analogy to Charlus's chance encounter with Jupien, his exceptional and ideal homosexual partner.
61. *Corr.* 3: 462–63.

14 Broken Promises

1. See *Corr.* 4: 6–7.
2. *SL* 2: 34–35.
3. *SL* 2: 8.
4. *SL* 2: 10–11.
5. *SL* 2: 12.
6. See *Textes retrouvés,* 140–43.

7. *SL* 2: 29.

8. This letter was written at the end of January. The meaning of Ironach had plagued Proust for some time. He would ultimately mistranslate Ruskin's "Thuringian armouries" as *armoiries,* French for "armorial bearings. See *Corr.* 4: 48–49, and *SL* 2: 14, n. 3. As Proust began to discover and elaborate his own beliefs by questioning Ruskin's, he often expressed his growing frustration with the Englishman's writings: "The old fellow's a nuisance," or "he's beginning to bore me," or even, "I haven't a notion what he means and I couldn't care less." See Nordlinger, *Lettres à une amie,* 10.

9. *SL* 2: 18–19.

10. *Corr.* 4: 55–56.

11. *SL* 2: 20.

12. Kolb believed that Marie expected a proposal from Marcel. *Corr.* 4: xvi.

13. *SL* 2: 79.

14. *On Reading Ruskin,* 3.

15. "Journées de pèlerinage: Ruskin à Notre-Dame d'Amiens, à Rouen, etc.," *CSB* 5: 76.

16. These notes are the equivalent of another thirty full pages. The calculations of the length of Proust's additions to Ruskin's text are from Jean Milly's article, "Proust traducteur de Ruskin," in *Acclimater l'autre: La Traduction littéraire et son contexte culturel,* Budapest: Editions Balassi, 1997, 82.

17. *Corr.* 3: viii.

18. *On Reading Ruskin,* 55–56.

19. *On Reading Ruskin,* 57. For Proust the beauty of a work of art depends on the artist's vision, as he demonstrates in the *Search* through his fictional painter Elstir, whose beliefs embody impressionistic doctrine.

20. Hahn had composed in 1902 and dedicated to Proust *Les Muses pleurant la mort de Ruskin.* See *SL* 2: 20–21. "Desdicated" and other such words in the letter are part of the private language Proust and Hahn often used when writing to each other. See *SL* 2: 21, nn. 3, 5. In 1906 Proust dedicated the translation, *Des Trésors des rois,* the first part of *Sésame et les lys,* to Hahn. See *Corr.* 4: 67, n. 3.

21. *SL* 2: 23, n. 6.

22. *SL* 2: 22–23.

23. *SL* 2: 23–24.

24. See *SL* 2: 24, n. 3.

25. *SL* 2: 37–38 and n. 4.

26. See *Corr.* 20: 621 and n. 4. Almost nothing is known about Mrs. Higginson; she and her sister Miss Mary Dutton were friends of Mme de Brantes'. See *Corr.* 2: 206 and nn. 2, 6.

27. *SL* 2: 32.

28. The Bibliothèque nationale has notebooks containing, in Mme Proust's handwriting, translations from Ruskin's *The Bible of Amiens, Sesame and Lilies, Mornings in Florence,* and *Deucalion.* Tadié, *Marcel Proust,* 254, n. 1.

29. *SL* 2: 31–32.

30. Hermant did not oblige. *SL* 2: 29 and n. 4.

31. In 1906 Proust learned that Robert de La Sizeranne was preparing a similar volume and asked Vallette to release him from the obligation. After some hesitation, Vallette acquiesced. See *Corr.* 21: 608, 609, n. 2, and 612.

32. *SL* 2: 33–34.

33. *SL* 2: 44, n. 2; *Corr.* 20: 622; see *Corr.* 4: 138, n. 2.

34. *SL* 1: 124.

35. In his letter to Sorel, Proust referred to an article in which his former professor spoke a great deal about Mme de Combray, a real person who was a model for Balzac's baronne de la Chanterie in *L'Envers de l'Histoire contemporaine.* This name was used by Proust not for a person but for an essential geographical spot in his novel. See *Corr.* 4: 178, n. 3.

36. See *SL* 2: 58, n. 6, and *Corr.* 4: 179, n. 6.

37. *SL* 2: 39.

38. Kuychiro Inoué, "Un Morceau de madeleine et des comprimés japonais," *BMP* 22 (1972): 1347.

39. *SL* 2: 39.

40. See "Le Salon de la comtesse Potocka," *CSB* 5: 489–94.

41. *Corr.* 4: 121.

42. *SL* 2: 46–47.

43. *SL* 2: 46–47 and n. 7.

44. See *SL* 2: 50; *Corr.* 4: 155–57.

45. *Search* 6: 299.

46. *SL* 2: 52.

47. To Lucien Daudet, from unpublished chronological information provided to the author by Philip Kolb.

48. *SL* 2: 56, n. 2; *Corr.* 4: 174, n. 3.

49. *SL* 2: 54.

50. *Corr.* 4: 192–93.

51. *Corr.* 4: 192.

52. Agénor, duc de Gramont, Guiche's father, was a model for the duc de Guermantes. *SL* 2: 61–62 and n. 1.

53. Guiche's sister was Comtesse Hélie de Noailles, née Corisande de Gramont. *SL* 2: 62, n. 3. The countess's word for "skivvy" in the original is *pipelette,* from a character who is a concierge in E. Sue's *Mystères de Paris.*

54. *SL* 2: 60.

55. *Corr.* 4: 206.

56. A similar incident occurs in the *Search:* Bloch, who is endowed with a number of Proust's less endearing characteristics, knocks over and breaks Mme de Villeparisis's vase. *Search* 3: 289. *SL* 2: 61, n. 16.

57. When Anna de Noailles's memorabilia were exhibited at the Bibliothèque nationale in 1953, the broken figurine was item no. 84: "Tanagra broken by Marcel Proust." *SL* 2: 61, n. 16.

58. *SL* 2: 60.

59. *SL* 2: 61, n. 12.

60. *SL* 2: 65.

61. *SL* 2: 65–66 and nn. 1, 2. In his will, Proust left her watercolor to Reynaldo Hahn.

62. *SL* 2: 68.

63. *SL* 2: 67.

64. *SL* 2: 68–69.

65. *SL* 2: 69, 71.

66. Billy, *Lettres et conversations,* 143.

67. *Corr.* 4: 224.

68. "La Mort des cathédrales," *CSB* 5: 141, n. 2. See *CSB* 5: 141–46. In a note added some years later, he explained that he had written this "quite mediocre study" to fight one article in the law governing separation of church and state. If the law passed, Proust observed, after five years the government could convert the cathedrals into museums, lecture halls, or even casinos.

69. "La Mort des cathédrales," *CSB* 5: 144, n. 1.

70. "La Mort des cathédrales," *CSB* 5: 146.

71. *SL* 2: 87–88.

72. For the complete text of Proust's reply to Le Blond, see *SL* 2: 76–78.

73. *On Reading Ruskin*, 60.

74. *Corr.* 4: 257.

75. The letter was found among his papers after his death. *SL* 2: 85, n. 5. For the complete text, see *SL* 2: 83–85.

76. *SL* 2: 83–84.

77. In the *Search*, Cottard recommends a milk diet for the Narrator.

78. *SL* 2: 91.

79. François Maigre (1864–1930), formerly barber to Napoléon III. *SL* 2: 93, n. 4.

80. *SL* 2: 92–93 and n. 7; *Corr.* 4: 282, n. 11.

81. *SL* 2: 98.

82. *SL* 2: 102.

83. Proust's dentist was Dr. Paul Ferrier. See *Corr.* 4: 303 and 304, n. 2.

84. *SL* 2: 103.

85. *Corr.* 4: 319 and n. 2.

86. *Corr.* 4: 327, n. 1. When the couple reached Cairo in mid-November, Marcel sent one wire, asking for a safe address, and signed it Marcelle Paris. *Corr.* 4: 345.

87. *Corr.* 4: 320.

88. *Corr.* 4: 328.

89. *Corr.* 4: 310.

90. *Corr.* 4: 324, 325 and n. 3.

91. *Corr.* 4: 330–31.

92. See *SL* 2: 111–12 and n. 10.

93. The Narrator makes a similar appeal to Saint-Loup in an attempt to obtain a photograph of his aunt, the duchesse de Guermantes, for whom Mme Greffulhe was one of the chief models.

94. *SL* 2: 109–10 and n. 2. The marquise d'Eyragues, née Henriette de Montesquiou-Fezensac, was Montesquiou's cousin.

95. *SL* 2: 113.

96. *SL* 2: 117 and n. 1.

97. *SL* 2: 105–6. Gabriel de la Rochefoucauld took Proust's advice and revised his novel. Proust makes an appearance as the character Larti, a hypochondriac who is not attracted to women, who travels to Holland with his best friend Hermois and believes that happiness cannot be found in love. See Tadié, *Marcel Proust*, 501, n. 2.

98. Tadié has also concluded that the person in question seems to be Hahn. See Tadié, *Marcel Proust*, 502.

15 *The Only Honey of My Life*

1. *SL* 2: 138, n. 1. Freer later gave his Whistler collection to the Smithsonian Institution.
2. *SL* 2: 137. See also *SL* 2: 138, n. 5.
3. Scott is the only person other than Marie thanked in the acknowledgments of *Sésame et les lys*.
4. *SL* 2: 137. I have substituted *bare* for the translator's *naked*.
5. *SL* 2: 143.
6. *SL* 2: 141, n. 3, and 147.
7. *SL* 2: 145.
8. Fragson's real name was Victor Pot (1869–1913). See *SL* 2: 149, n. 1.
9. See *SL* 2: 153–55.
10. *SL* 2: 164–65.
11. *Corr.* 5: 103 and n. 7.
12. *SL* 2: 158–59. I have modified the translation from "enclosed nun's room."
13. *SL* 2: 164–65.
14. Montesquiou mockingly alluded to the fable of "Solomon and the Ants," on which he had based a poem, "La Makédienne" (in *Le Parcours du rêve au souvenir:* 1895). *SL* 2: 162, n. 1.
15. *SL* 2: 175.
16. *SL* 2: 172.
17. See *SL* 2: 170. The quotation is from Horace's *Ars Poetica* 2: 7. *SL* 2: 170, n. 4.
18. *SL* 2: 171.
19. *Corr.* 5: 140.
20. *SL* 2: 179.
21. *SL* 2: 176.
22. *SL* 2: 182.
23. The description of Proust and his conversation is from Nordlinger, *Lettres à une amie*, x. Her account differs from Proust's on one point; she recollected that they worked on the translation until dawn. See *SL* 2: 197.
24. *Corr.* 5: 192.
25. In the book he thanked his "friend Marie Nordlinger" for "having carefully reviewed this translation, often making it less imperfect." See *Sésame et les lys*, preceded by "Sur la lecture," with an introduction by Antoine Compagnon, Paris: Éditions Complexe, 1987, 37.
26. *On Reading Ruskin*, 99. I have modified the translation from "we left without having lived them."
27. *On Reading Ruskin*, 99–100. The beginning of the preface, with its shifts in time and place, is an early sketch for the first paragraph of the *Search*, in which the Narrator, in bed and falling asleep while reading, is uncertain of where he is, who he is, and even what he is, for in his slumbering state he confuses his own identity with that of the book he is trying to read. The preface ends with another resurrection of the past.
28. Quotations are from *On Reading Ruskin*, 101 and 107. In the preface Proust wrote Méséglise, a name he used in the *Search* for an area near Combray, instead of Méréglise, a real place near Illiers. Was this merely a slip or had he already begun fictionalizing Illiers and its environs for a story? See *On Reading Ruskin*, 101. Later in the essay Proust informs his reader that he has fictionalized scenes from his travels to illustrate points: "The channel I placed in Utrecht is in Delft," for example. See *On Reading Ruskin*, 137. Proust's friends

and first readers of the *Search* were quick to observe the importance of the preface as a precursor of the novel. See Dreyfus, *Souvenirs*, 178 and n. 1: "These pages contain a very developed sketch of [the Narrator's] memories of Combray." Dreyfus, who quotes Benjamin Crémieux, considered this essay on reading to be "the basis for Proust's work."

29. *On Reading Ruskin*, 101. Proustian richness or layering, as demonstrated in his novel, involves his theory of personality, according to which we each contain multiple selves. This notion is expressed later in this preface: "Diverse personalities are to be found in the breast of each of us, and often the life of more than one superior man is nothing but the coexistence of a philosopher and a snob." See *On Reading Ruskin*, 152.

30. See *On Reading Ruskin*, 143–46.

31. Robert de Billy links Proust's analysis of Ruskin's style and structure and his fascination with the English critic's subjects to Proust's Wagnerian side. As evidence of this Billy mentioned the seven themes, organic structure, and retrospective unity that Proust found in *Sesame and Lilies*, which lead to the final apotheosis. Billy, *Lettres et conversations*, 133.

32. *On Reading Ruskin*, 156.

33. From Proust's essay "Sur la lecture." See *On Reading Ruskin*, 111. Proust observes that the thesis is the same as Descartes's.

34. *On Reading Ruskin*, 120, 112.

35. *On Reading Ruskin*, 162.

36. *On Reading Ruskin*, 116–17.

37. *On Reading Ruskin*, 138. Kolb suggests that this note, which he dates from the first months of 1905, is the point of departure for Proust's essay *Contre Sainte-Beuve* (Against Sainte-Beuve). Proust took this up again several years later. He never completed it because it was the springboard for something far greater: *In Search of Lost Time*. See *Corr.* 5: 10.

38. *On Reading Ruskin*, 145; see also 157.

39. Ruskin and Montesquiou also shared a fascination with etymology, a trait given to the pedantic Brichot in the *Search*. Proust had acknowledged, in a passage already quoted here, that a writer must know these things, but his choice of words will be determined not by erudition (idolatry) but by something more profound summoned by the organic nature of his vision.

40. *On Reading Ruskin*, 128–29.

41. This example of Venice may be the inspiration for the episode of the uneven paving stones that sets off the final crescendo of involuntary memories, bringing the Narrator at last to discover his vocation and accept the challenge of fulfilling it.

42. *Corr.* 5: 229.

43. *SL* 2: 191–92 and n. 2.

44. *Corr.* 5: 234, n. 3. Proust's first critics sought the right adjectives to describe his unprecedented style. Their word choices are understandable, even if Proust, while appreciative and often flattered, later protested against "delicate," "fine," "meticulous," and so on.

45. *Corr.* 5: 243.

46. *Corr.* 5: 275

47. *Corr.* 5: 237.

48. *SL* 2: 196–97.

49. *SL* 2: 197–98 and 199, n. 8. For the painter Elstir in the *Search*, Balbec bay was the "the gulf of opal painted by Whistler in his *Harmonies in Blue and Silver*," *Search* 3: 27. This

passage is a good example of Proust's technique of juxtaposing the real-life model and the character he or she inspired. *SL* 2: 199, n. 8.

50. *Corr.* 5: 267, 283.

51. *SL* 2: 200.

52. Proust jokingly called Brissaud "our dear 'Doctor in spite of himself,'" after Molière's farce by that title. Is this a mere pleasantry, as Kolb believed, or part of a list of topics that Proust wanted to write about, comparable to items in the list that he was to develop in 1908, just before beginning the *Search?* See *Corr.* 5: xxv, 318, and 319, n. 5.

53. *Corr.* 5: 337.

54. *SL* 2: 184–85.

55. *Corr.* 5: 335.

56. See "Un Professeur de beauté," *CSB* 5: 506–20. Montesquiou liked the article and had it reprinted in *Altesses sérénissimes* (1907).

57. "Un Professeur de beauté," *CSB* 5: 514. For the pears "bon chrétien," see *Search* 4: 556. Both these remarks fall under the category of idolatry, one of Charlus's errors inherited from Montesquiou. Among a number of Montesquiou's traits, Charlus possesses the same erudition regarding fabric, fruit, and literature, particularly Montesquiou's great admiration of Balzac. Because Charlus is essentially a satirical figure, a caricature, Proust portrayed only the talented dilettante side of Montesquiou. Although the count was clearly a talent of the second order, many of his articles on art reveal an astute critic. And Montesquiou was a determined and prolific writer, even if the quality of his work was often unexceptional.

58. *Corr.* 10: 215. Such a photograph, similarly motivated, is used in the episode at Balbec when the grandmother experiences her first attack. The photograph will reveal to the Narrator aspects of his grandmother's character and his own reactions to grieving and forgetting. *Search* 2: 500–501, 4: 237–43.

59. *Corr.* 10: 215.

60. *Corr.* 5: 338.

61. *Corr.* 5: 342–43.

62. *Corr.* 5: 342.

63. *SL* 2: 207.

64. Hahn, *Journal,* 99.

65. See *Search* 3: 470–71. Anna de Noailles received a letter from Marcel in which he described in detail his mother's death. This letter was later stolen from her, but she maintained that the grandmother's death in *Search* was described in the same terms. In any event, Marcel had not witnessed his grandmother's death, because he was at Orléans at the time, serving in the military. See *Corr.* 5: xxvi and n. 81.

66. *SL* 2: 208.

67. See *Corr.* 12: 402 and n. 3.

68. *CSB* 5: 335.

69. *Corr.* 5: 379–80 and n. 2.

70. Lauris, *À un ami,* 206, quoted in *Corr.* 5: xxviii.

71. *Corr.* 5: 346.

72. *Corr.* 6: 49

73. See Duchêne, *L'Impossible Proust,* 530. I have used Duchêne's conversion figures for 1994 francs, which I have converted to dollars according to contemporary exchange rates.

74. Proust quoted Renan's observations that "one only writes well about what one loves." *Corr.* 6: 38.
75. *Corr.* 6: 50.
76. See Milly, "Proust traducteur de Ruskin," 83.
77. *SL* 2: 211.
78. *Corr.* 6: 103, n. 2.
79. *SL* 2: 211.
80. *Corr.* 6: 48–49.
81. Duplay, *Mon Ami Marcel Proust,* 112.
82. *Corr.* 6: 104.
83. *Corr.* 6: 117–18 and n. 2.
84. In July, Marcel Cruppi, a distant relation of Proust's, also compared him to Montaigne. *Corr.* 6: 147, n. 4. In a review that did not appear until the following year, Jean Bonnerit also saw the similarities between Proust and Montaigne. See "Journées de lecture," *CSB* 5: 160, n. 1.
85. *Corr.* 6: 115.
86. *Corr.* 6: 120, n. 6.
87. *SL* 2: 214. This statement is given to the duc de Guermantes in the *Search.*
88. *CSB* 5: 789, n. 2.
89. *Corr.* 6: 124.
90. *Corr.* 6: 154.
91. *SL* 2: 222.
92. *SL* 2: 222.
93. *Corr.* 6: 161. This part of the letter is omitted in the English translation.
94. *Corr.* 6: 167. This passion for train schedules as a substitute for travel will be given to Swann and the Narrator. See *Search* 1: 415.
95. *Corr.* 6: 168–69.
96. *Corr.* 6: 265, n. 1.
97. See *Jean Santeuil,* 4: 23–31.
98. *SL* 2: 235. See also *Corr.* 6: 312.
99. *SL* 2: 235.
100. *SL* 2: 227.
101. *SL* 2: 228.
102. *Corr.* 6: 256.
103. *Corr.* 4: 259–62.
104. *Corr.* 6: 274.
105. This apparatus was manufactured by the Aeolian Company, located nearby at 32, avenue de l'Opéra. *Corr.* 6: 294, n.3. This decision was postponed until 1914.
106. *Corr.* 6: 302–3.
107. See *Corr.* 6: 64–66, 214–15, 282–83, 294–95, 298–99, 300, 316.
108. *SL* 2: 230. In June, Proust had told Beaunier there would be no more translations: "I am ending the series . . . with *Sésame et les lys,* be assured!" *Corr.* 6: 106.
109. *Corr.* 6: 18.
110. See *Corr.* 6: xxv and 332, n. 4. This is Kolb's hypothesis.
111. *SL* 2: 235.
112. *Corr.* 6: 344, 345 and n. 1.

113. *Corr.* 6: 346.
114. Albaret, *Monsieur Proust,* 135.

16 Filial Sentiments of a Parricide

1. See *SL* 2: 238–39.
2. In *The Guermantes Way* the Narrator has a nightmare in which he tortures his parents. In *Sodom and Gomorrah* the author refers to a future chapter to be called "The Profanation of the Mother." Apparently, Proust never wrote this chapter. It would probably have resembled the scene in which Vinteuil's photograph is profaned as part of a lesbian love ritual engaged in by his daughter and her friend. See *Search* 1: 226–30.
3. *SL* 2: 253–54. Ulrich (born 1881?) sometimes ran errands for Proust. *SL* 2: 296, n. 9.
4. *Corr.* 7: 52.
5. See "Sentiments filiaux d'un parricide," *CSB* 5: 150–59. Proust included his final exchange of letters with Van Blarenberghe in the article.
6. Proust had not yet read Wilde's similar observation. See *Corr.* 10: 184–85. After his parents' deaths, the two shortcomings for which Marcel reproached himself were the worry he caused his mother and his lack of success. In the good-night kiss scene in the *Search,* there is a subtle allusion to matricide: "I felt that I had with an impious and secret finger traced a first wrinkle upon her soul and brought out a first white hair on her head." *Search* 1: 52.
7. Proust's article almost completely filled four columns on the *Figaro*'s front page of February 1. See *Corr.* 7: 108, n. 3.
8. *SL* 2: 249. There are some interesting parallels between Proust's ideas and those of Freud. Freud had begun developing his theory of the Oedipus complex around 1897, a theory he was to develop substantially over the years; Peter Gay, *Freud: A Life for Our Time,* New York: Norton, 1988, 100. It was more than a decade before Freud began to be known in France, where the first article about him appeared in 1911; Theodore Zeldin, *France, 1848–1945,* vol. 2, *Intellect, Taste and Anxiety,* Oxford: Oxford University Press, 1977, 867.
9. *SL* 2: 250–51. For the details of Proust's defense and his explanation of Greek morality regarding such parricides, see this letter.
10. Dreyfus, *Souvenirs,* 202.
11. See *Corr.* 7: 320–21.
12. *Corr.* 21: 627.
13. *SL* 2: 251–52.
14. *SL* 2: 252. He also urged Lucien to "stop thinking of wasted time [*temps perdu*]." It is the double meaning in French of *temps perdu,* "wasted time" and "lost time," in the sense of time retrievable and thus potentially useful, that eventually led Proust to choose his resonant title. He was to write in an article on Anna de Noailles's latest poems a sentence that applies particularly well to the themes he was to develop for the *Search:* "She knows that a profound idea which has time and space enclosed within it is no longer subject to their tyranny, and becomes infinite." *SL* 2: 293, n. 1.
15. *SL* 2: 252–53.
16. *SL* 2: 255.
17. Hahn had reproached Proust for a sentence of more than fifty-five lines in "On Reading." See *Corr.* 5: 245, n. 2.

18. *Corr.* 7: 90–91; see 91, n. 5.

19. *Corr.* 7: 79.

20. *Corr.* 18: 582. In April, Proust again made inquiries about a manservant, indicating perhaps that he was displeased with Nicolas, who may have started drinking. *Corr.* 7: 135, n. 6.

21. *Corr.* 7: 11. Céline, too, contributed elements to the servant Françoise in the *Search*.

22. *Corr.* 7: 84.

23. *SL* 2: 257.

24. He gave his final statement on the phenomenon of love and eternal separation in the section of the *Search* known as "The Intermittencies of the Heart." At one point, Proust considered using "The Intermittencies of the Heart" as the general title for the novel.

25. Maurois, *World*, 225.

26. In *Hortensias bleus,* Montesquiou had dropped a number of the original dedications to friends who had fallen from grace.

27. The publisher Émile-Paul had begun to bring out the first volumes of *Les Récits d'une tante: Mémoires de la comtesse de Boigne, née d'Osmond, 1781–1866.*

28. *Search* 3: 174.

29. "Journées de lecture," *CSB* 5: 531. Ellipsis is Proust's. Proust later demonstrated that if reality disappoints us, it is often because we have failed to understand the true meaning of the experience.

30. Proust also uses an analogy comparing a name to a magic lantern that summons up visions of medieval times. This seems to be a precursor of the scene in Combray in which the child Narrator watches the projection of the story of Golo and Geneviève de Brabant. See "Journées de lecture," *CSB* 5: 531.

31. The passage cut by the newspaper contains an early sketch of the *Search*'s Mme de Villeparisis.

32. *SL* 2: 262.

33. *SL* 2: 265–66.

34. *SL* 2: 266.

35. *SL* 2: 267–68.

36. *SL* 2: 270.

37. *Corr.* 7: 160.

38. *SL* 2: 273.

39. *SL* 2: 274.

40. *SL* 2: 276–77. Cf. *Search* 6: 374.

41. *SL* 2: 278 and n. 1.

42. *SL* 2: 286 and nn. 1, 2.

43. *SL* 2: 288, n. 2. *Search* 2: 453.

44. *Corr.* 7: 11.

45. *SL* 2: 288. Proust believed that when he spoke too soon after a fumigation it gave him a sore throat. Albaret, *Monsieur Proust,* 63.

46. See "*Les Éblouissements,* par la comtesse de Noailles," *CSB* 5: 533–45. In this article Proust says that he would like to write a book called *The Six Gardens of Paradise,* each inhabited by a different artist he admired: Anna de Noailles, John Ruskin, Maurice Maeterlinck, Henri de Régnier, Francis Jammes, and Claude Monet. He gives a sample of what each garden would be like.

47. *Corr.* 7: 106–7.

48. "*Les Éblouissements,*" *CSB* 5: 534. The other two paintings are *La Péri* and the *Indian Poet.*

49. "*Les Éblouissements,*" *CSB* 5: 536, 537.

50. *SL* 2: 293.

51. *SL* 2: 300.

52. See *SL* 2: 302–3 and nn. 4, 5.

53. *SL* 2: 303. In a January letter Proust had written: "Félicie made a frightful scene this evening." *SL* 2: 245.

54. *SL* 2: 310–11.

55. *SL* 2: 315–16 and n. 3.

56. *Corr.* 7: 285–86.

57. The inauguration took place on July 7; The *Figaro* and *L'Écho de Paris* were among the papers that carried stories about the event; see *Corr.* 7: xv. The boardwalk is today named the Promenade Marcel Proust.

58. *Corr.* 8: 188.

59. *Corr.* 7: 259.

60. *Corr.* 7: 266, n. 8.

61. *SL* 2: 325.

62. *SL* 2: 326, and 327, n. 3. Sem's real name was Georges Goursat (1863–1934).

63. *SL* 2: 333.

64. René Gimpel, *Diary of an Art Dealer,* translated by John Rosenberg, with an introduction by Sir Herbert Read, New York: Universe, 1987, 174.

65. *SL* 2: 318–19.

66. Unic was the trademark name of the cars built at Puteaux by Georges Richard. Bizet had been one of the founders of the Unic model and one known as Le Zèbre. *Corr.* 7: 290, n. 10.

67. *Corr.* 7: 290, n. 10. See Henri Bonnet, *Marcel Proust de 1907 à 1914,* Paris: Nizet, 1971, 47, n. 29. According to Céleste Albaret, the automobile rental company was created by the Rothschilds, who were related to Émile Straus, and was managed by Straus's stepson, Bizet. See Albaret, *Monsieur Proust,* 101–2.

68. *Corr.* 7: 285–86.

69. *SL* 2: 325.

70. *Corr.* 7: 252, nn. 1, 2.

71. *Corr.* 7: 254, n. 4.

72. *SL* 2: 320, and 321, n. 1.

73. See *SL* 2: 326–27.

74. *SL* 2: 327.

75. *SL* 2: 329, nn. 3, 5. See *Search* 2: 574.

76. *Corr.* 7: 259.

77. *SL* 2: 321.

78. *SL* 2: 326.

79. He wrote to ask Emmanuel Bibesco whether the Bayeux tapestry, which he had been unable to see, was "something truly beautiful and interesting" that he should return and see. See *Corr.* 7: 255, and *SL* 2: 322. Before returning to Paris, Proust also visited Jumièges, Lisieux, and Saint-Wandrille.

80. *SL* 2: 322.

81. Madeleine Lemaire, impatient with Proust's endless complaints, answered one letter and told him that surely he could find something more interesting to tell her about than "the noise in the hotel." *SL* 2: 324.

82. *SL* 2: 322. "I much preferred Bayeux cathedral to the churches of Caen." See *SL* 2: 326. He said that he was "too tired" to explain why. Could it have been because of the elements he called Oriental? The Narrator is just as puzzled when Swann speaks of Persian art in the Balbec church. During the Narrator's first trip to Balbec, Elstir explains the church's Oriental elements to the Narrator.

83. *SL* 2: 322. It is possible Proust envisioned some sort of novel at this time, but we do not know why he wanted to see such a town. Perhaps he was looking for inspiration and thought an old "Balzacian" town would yield secrets about novel writing.

84. *Corr.* 21: 616. See also *Corr.* 18: 583, and 584, n. 4. Eight months later Proust wrote Albufera that he was "writing a study on tombstones." See *Corr.* 8: 113. All this is reduced to a single sentence in *Swann's Way*. See *Search* 1: 80.

85. The period of French history embraced by *La Comédie humaine* is roughly from the Consulate through the July monarchy.

86. *SL* 2: 332 and n. 1. It is not known whether Proust ever found what he was looking for. When he invented Combray, the provincial town in the *Search*, he was inspired primarily by memories of Illiers and Auteuil, though Combray is a product of the creative imagination. The arrival at Glisolles with Agostinelli is mentioned in *Carnet 1908*, 52: "Hector, Agostinelli à Glisolles," 52.

87. *SL* 2: 333.

88. Clermont-Tonnerre, *Montesquiou et Proust*, 101.

89. *SL* 2: 332, 334 and n. 3. These windows of Saint-Hilaire were "never so sparkling as on days when the sun scarcely shone, so that if it was dull outside you could be sure it would be fine inside the church." *Search* 1: 80.

90. *Corr.* 7: 295, 19: 712.

91. These details from Proust's visit are from Mme de Clermont-Tonnerre's memoirs, *Montesquiou et Proust*, 101–2.

92. *SL* 2: 334–35, 336, n. 7.

93. See "Journées en automobile," *CSB* 5: 63–69.

94. For the Narrator's text, see *Search* 1: 255–56.

95. "Journées en automobile," *CSB* 5: 67.

96. *Corr.* 7: 286.

97. Jossien is thought to have inspired the name of Jupien in the *Search*. *SL* 2: 335 and n. 5.

98. *SL* 2: 334.

99. *Search* 4: 632, 735. *Corr.* 7: 14.

100. *Corr.* 7: 296.

101. *SL* 2: 336.

102. *SL* 2: 337.

103. Barbara W. Tuchman, *The Proud Tower: A Portrait of the World Before the War, 1890–1914*, London: Folio, 1995, 309.

104. *SL* 2: 336. For Charlus's remark about the dignity and courage of those accused in the scandal, see *Search* 4: 471.

105. In 1906 and 1907 Proust had asked Auguste Marguillier whether there were any essays by the American art critic Bernard Berenson available in French translation. Kolb writes

that Proust may have known through Robert de Rothschild, or a member of his circle, that Rothschild's cousin Baronne Léon Lambert had entreated Berenson to explain homosexuality to her. Berenson had responded by writing an essay in which he was completely frank about his homosexuality. See *Corr.* 7: vii and n. 14; see also *Corr.* 7: 26, and 27, n. 6.

106. See *Recherche, Sodome et Gomorrhe,* Poche, xxv.

107. *SL* 2: 338 and n. 2. See *Search* 5: 799, where the Narrator receives, in similar circumstances, a letter of congratulation "in an illiterate hand and a charming style."

108. *SL* 2: 341.

109. "Gustave de Borda," *CSB* 5: 549.

110. "*Gainsborough* par Gabriel Mourey," was published in *La Chronique des arts et de la curiosité,* March 9, 1907; see *CSB* 5: 524–26.

17 *The Notebook of 1908*

1. *SL* 2: 348.

2. In three of the remaining notebooks Proust made notes about readings, aristocratic names, gossip, and other material that interested him. In other notebooks and, more rarely, on loose-leaf paper, he wrote drafts on topics or episodes listed in *Carnet 1908.* Although the notebook is known as *Le Carnet de 1908,* it contains entries that date to as late as 1912. See the chronology in *Carnet 1908,* 38–42. In reminders made to himself in other notebooks, Proust referred to this one as "The big notebook Kerby [*sic*] Beard young man." See *Carnet 1908,* 164, n. 221.

3. *SL* 2: 345.

4. Robert is seen with his pet goat and toy cart "seated on the ground beside his kid, fondling its head and kissing it on its innocent reddish nose. . . . He and his pet bore but a scant resemblance to that popular theme of English painters, a child fondling an animal." Robert, dressed in his finest clothes to be photographed, "looked as sumptuous as any English child beside his animal friend." This scene, and some of the others published by Bernard de Fallois as part of the drafts for *Contre Sainte-Beuve,* are available in STW. For "Robert and the kid goat," see STW, 257.

5. *Carnet 1908* contains a list, dating from the summer of 1908, of six scenes already written, "Pages écrites." See *Carnet 1908,* 56. The texts grouped by the editor in *Contre Sainte-Beuve* are drafts, not intended for publication, of episodes, characters, and themes that foreshadow the *Search.* Fallois changed Proust's titles, which were more like working names. For the episode of Robert and the kid ("Robert et le chevreau, Maman part en voyage"), Fallois used the title "The Return." See STW, 248–64.

6. In the sketch about Robert and the kid, part of this action takes place near Chartres, but elsewhere Proust mentions Évreux.

7. *Search* 1: 204.

8. STW, 255, 261. The narrator describes his eagerness to join his mother in terms of an asthmatic: "I was bent on getting to you as a stifling man is bent on drawing breath." STW, 262. Trying to reassure his mother, concerned about how he would manage if something happened to her, he admits: "For the first week, I am demented. After that, I can go on by myself for months, for years, for ever." That evening, however, a different topic makes him tell her that "contrary to what I had previously believed, the latest sci-

entific discoveries and the most advanced philosophic inquiries demolished materialism and made out death to be something merely phenomenal; that souls were immortal and eventually met again. . . . " STW, 262–64. Ellipsis is Proust's. This sketch contains the name of Mme de Villeparisis, one of the novel's important characters, the bluestocking of the Guermantes family.

9. See *Carnet 1908*, 48 and n. 5.

10. Cf. *Search* 4: 713, 5: 615.

11. See *Carnet 1908*, n. 23, 135–36.

12. Kolb suggests that Proust was seeking models for Odette; *Carnet 1908*, 133, n. 6.

13. Vautrin was one of the rare—and very discreet—homosexual characters in French literature before Proust's era. *Carnet 1908*, 48.

14. This remark will be given to Charlus, who quotes Swann as the originator of the witty comment; *Search* 4: 611. See *Carnet 1908*, 48 and n. 13.

15. Fénelon will be the principal model for Saint-Loup, who is in love with the actress Rachel, for whom the primary model was Louisa de Mornand. Proust knew Louisa much better than her sister, Suzanne Montaud, who played at the Bouffes under the stage name Jane Moriane. *Carnet 1908*, 134, n. 15.

16. Proust sometimes joined the game, tipping his hand to reveal the original models, as he did in the 1918 dedication to Jacques de Lacretelle. See [Dédicace], *CSB* 5: 564–66.

17. This is one of the major themes and structural devices of the *Search*: the difference between dream and reality. Examples are the Narrator's anticipation of meeting the duchesse de Guermantes and going to Balbec. Each experience disappoints him. Later he promises himself to discover the laws that control the phenomena of anticipation, disappointment, illumination. *Search* 5: 223–24, 6: 263–74.

18. As he noted, "the past lingers obsessively in odors," *Carnet 1908*, 91; for dreams, see 50–51.

19. See *Corr.* 8: xxii.

20. See Billy, *Lettres et conversations,* 170. See also *CSB* 5: 7, n. 1. See Proust's own note in the 1919 edition of *Pastiches et mélanges.* On July 6, 1909, Lemoine was sentenced to six years in prison. Parodies had long been an aspect of Proust's writing, from the early (1893) pastiche of Flaubert's *Bouvard et Pécuchet* in *Pleasures and Days,* to the 1903 description of Mme Lemaire's salon in the manner of Balzac, to the 1904 "Fête chez Montesquiou à Neuilly," in the manner of Saint-Simon. In the *Search,* Proust used this talent when he created dialogues for characters, newspaper articles (an obituary, or articles on fashions, receptions, the war), and the remarkable parody of the Goncourt brothers' *Journal.* This parody is given an important structural and thematic role at the conclusion of the *Search.* It illustrates why Proust never kept a diary and believed that such copying from real life was not art.

21. *Corr.* 8: 43, n. 4.

22. The pastiches can be found in "L'Affaire Lemoine," *CSB* 5: 7–59. The Saint-Simon parody includes the earlier one of "Fête chez Montesquiou à Neuilly." Proust left unpublished Lemoine parodies in the styles of Sainte-Beuve, Chateaubriand, Maeterlinck *(Pelléas et Mélisande),* and Ruskin describing Giotto's frescoes as representing the Lemoine scandal for the edification of young students. See [Appendice], *CSB* 5: 195–207.

23. *SL* 2: 356–57. During the time of the parodies, he mentioned this ability in a note for the Sainte-Beuve essay: "As soon as I read an author, I quickly distinguished beneath the

words the air of the song that is different in each . . . and, as I read, without realizing I was doing so, I hummed it." ["Notes sur la littérature et la critique"], *CSB* 5: 303. Cf. *Search* 5: 146–51. Gregh, who considered the parodies "masterpieces of critical thinking," urged Proust to publish them. See Gregh, *Amitié*, 136–38.

24. Gregh realized this when he observed that "everything Norpois says results from this 'in the manner of' and mimics deliciously the sort of speech one heard among elderly diplomats." Gregh, *L'Âge d' Or*, 159, n. 1.

25. *SL* 2: 350. Ellipsis is Proust's.

26. See *SL* 2: 353, 355, and 356–57. Barrès congratulated Proust on having created "a delicious form of literary criticism."

27. In a 1919 letter to Ramon Fernandez, Proust saw in retrospect that the parodies had served to purge him of the "natural vice of idolatry and imitation," allowing him to become only "Marcel Proust when I write my novels." *Corr.* 18: 380.

28. *Corr.* 8: 104.

29. His temperament in this regard resembles Walt Whitman's. The leaves of the *Search* would be as all-embracing as Whitman's *Leaves of Grass*. Proust's earliest texts, written during adolescence, contain traces of androgyny and homoeroticism.

30. *SL* 2: 360.

31. *SL* 2: 365. I have modified the translation from "get me put inside."

32. Wolf Von Eckardt, Sander L. Gilman, and J. Edward Chamberlin, *Oscar Wilde's London: A Scrapbook of Vices and Virtues, 1880–1900*, New York: Anchor, 1987, 259.

33. H. Montgomery Hyde, *Oscar Wilde: A Biography*, New York: Farrar, Straus and Giroux, 1975, 118.

34. Ellmann, *Oscar Wilde*, 282.

35. *SL* 2: 365–66.

36. In June he told Albufera: "Once my work is done I think I shall leave for Italy and if I can't settle near you in Paris I shall buy a little house above Florence." *SL* 2: 381.

37. *SL* 2: 371.

38. Duchêne remarks that Proust, as in his university days, remained a literary man and a philosopher. *L'Impossible Proust*, 583.

39. *SL* 2: 372 and n. 1. Proust often noticed unexpected refinement and distinction among members of the working class. Agostinelli provided one example, as did Céleste Albaret, whom Proust came to regard, despite her remarkable ignorance on a number of subjects, as a kind of genius.

40. See *SL* 2: 373–74.

41. *SL* 2: 374.

42. See *Search* 4: 20–44. The Eulenburg case is followed closely by Charlus because of his "own tendencies." See *Search* 4: 471. From the early sketches, Charlus, like almost all Proust's "homosexual" characters, is capable of heterosexual experience. Guercy, an earlier version of Charlus, remained married for fifteen years, until his wife died. Charlus was also married and left a widower. See STW, 229.

43. *JS* 4: 872. Jean's attitude influences his mother to be more tolerant without compromising her own moral standards. M. Sandré, on the other hand, would have chased such creatures from his house by beating them with a stick.

44. *SL* 2: 354, n. 2.

45. These observations are all from Kolb's foreword to *Corr.* 8: x–xi.

46. *SL* 2: 376. The purpose of the letter had been to explain his way out of another awkward situation. At the ball, he had told Vicomte François de Pâris that Mme Proust had thought his "the most handsome face of any man she knew, and she knew that I also admired your looks. If you pretended to find something funny in the way I told you this, it's because I didn't want to embarrass you with a compliment *coming from me* in front of Madame de Chimay." Marcel continued with more justifications of his remarks: "I would never link Mama's memory with anything that wasn't the *very truth itself*." He ended the paragraph: "You are not worth my having tired myself writing you all this. But the truth is worth it." *SL* 2: 376. Duchêne, who does not believe Marcel's frequent protests, suggests that this is a form of profanation, taking his mother's name in vain. Duchêne, *L'Impossible Proust*, 584. See *Corr.* 8: 139, n. 3 for the *Figaro*'s account.

47. *SL* 2: 380–81. I have modified the translation from "so nice close to."

48. *Corr.* 8: 84.

49. *Carnet 1908*, 69.

50. *SL* 2: 382–83.

51. *SL* 2: 387.

52. According to Kolb, Mlle de Goyon is a likely model for girls the Narrator pursues and dreams of possessing. See *Corr.* 8: xiii. The closest match in this category for Mlle de Goyon is a character with a lovely name, the elusive Mlle de Stermaria.

53. The duchesse de Guermantes's cousin, like Mlle de Goyon's aunt, is called Zénaïde. *SL* 2: 354, n. 2. For her appearance and noble birth, Oriane de Guermantes is modeled upon the comtesse Greffulhe, whose cousin Montesquiou is the chief model for Oriane's cousin the baron de Charlus. One can name obvious traits in his friends that inspired Proust's characters, but they are not merely composites but unique fictional beings. To create the duchesse de Guermantes's wit Proust borrowed a number of bons mots from Geneviève Straus. See *Search* 4:216.

54. Munhall, *Whistler and Montesquiou*, 40.

55. *SL* 2: 383

56. *SL* 2: 386.

57. *SL* 2: 386–87, n. 7.

58. *Corr.* 8: 179. Proust made a note to remember the odor of the grass at Louveciennes. *Carnet 1908*, 51.

59. *Carnet 1908*, 56.

60. Sometime around May 1909 Proust changed Villebon to the more euphonious Guermantes. *Carnet 1908*, 141, n. 61. Proust slightly changed the name of Méréglise, a village located four kilometers from Illiers; *Carnet 1908*, 14. Villebon is a castle located twelve kilometers from Illiers.

61. In the brief descriptions of these "pages already written," words for mother or grandmother occur four times, as does the word *visage*, face. The face in question is either the mother's as seen directly or profaned in the resembling face of a debauched offspring.

62. Kolb believed that this followed the plan sketched in a note to *Sésame et les lys*, where the ending explains what has preceded; *Carnet 1908*, 13.

63. The failure to find contentment in sexual possession is the basic outline of Swann's experience with Odette and the Narrator's with Albertine. Proust will use the two couples to portray variations on the major theme of obsessive, jealous love, one of several manias that pre-

vent Swann, Charlus (who is similarly infatuated with Charles Morel), and, for a while, the Narrator from exerting their will. In depicting homosexual love in the same manner and as thoroughly as heterosexual love, Proust was a courageous pioneer. Before the *Search*, the full spectrum of human sexuality had been largely left unexplored by serious writers.

64. *Carnet 1908*, 142, n. 64. *Search* 3: 338, 4: 416.

65. See Louis de Robert, *Comment débuta Marcel Proust*, Paris: Gallimard, 1969, 105–6; Clermont-Tonnerre, *Montesquiou et Proust*, 146. For Proust's notation "le petit monstre Gabardine de Robin," see *Carnet 1908*, 54. This anecdote may also have been the inspiration for the play Proust wanted to write with René Peter.

66. As usual in Proust, there are layers to this aspect. The two ways have also been joined in the flesh by the marriage of Gilberte (Swann's way) to Saint-Loup (the Guermantes way). The Narrator finds the crossroads of his entire experience bound up in their child, Mlle de Saint-Loup. See *Search* 6: 501–7.

67. The first word is *longtemps*, translated as "For a long time," and the last words are *dans le Temps*, "in Time."

68. Proust later realized that he had found the ideal structure for the kind of novelist he proved himself to be. One of Proust's many fascinating tricks as narrative enchanter is to have his reader follow the Narrator through three thousand pages of dazzling prose—Iris Murdoch said Proust wrote like an angel—all the while proclaiming his lack of talent and inability to write. That is why at the end, in a superb mirror trick that awed another literary magician, Nabokov, the Narrator is ready to write the master version of what we have just read. Vladimir Nabokov, "The Walk by Swann's Place," in *Lectures on Literature*, edited by Fredson Bowers and with an introduction by John Updike, New York: Harcourt Brace Jovanovich, 1980, 210–11.

69. *Corr.* 8: 183, 185.

70. Lauris claimed that Proust had not selected the color but had accepted the lining that came with the coat, having specified only that the garment was to be padded with wool. See Lauris, *À un ami*, 29.

71. *Corr.* 8: 187.

72. *SL* 2: 381.

73. *Corr.* 8: 14.

74. *Corr.* 8: 193.

75. *Corr.* 8: 14.

76. *Corr.* 8: 188.

77. *SL* 2: 392.

78. *SL* 2: 390.

79. *SL* 2: 391, n. 8, 392. See *Corr.* 8: 201, n. 6; *Carnet 1908*, 55, 56, 39. This vision may have inspired Proust to use Lucy's dress as the model for the scene in which the child Narrator meets, without learning her name, Odette de Crécy. Odette, a cocotte like Louisa and Lucy, wears a pink dress at his Uncle Adolphe's. Until he learns her true identity as Mme Swann, he thinks of her as "the lady in pink." Of all the Proustian characters, many of whom can be quite protean, Odette has the most different identities and names. Odette, like her model Laure Hayman, was raised by her mother to be a courtesan. She would play her roles as actress and prostitute to please men and work her way up in society.

80. *Carnet 1908*, 55–56.

81. *SL* 2: 389–90, 391, n. 1.

82. *SL* 2: 391, n. 2.

83. See Marcel Plantevignes, *Avec Marcel Proust*, Paris: Nizet, 1966, 15–17.

84. *SL* 2: 399, n. 3.

85. Tadié, *Marcel Proust*, 615.

86. *Corr.* 8: 208.

87. *Carnet 1908*, 99, 101, and 59, where he is mentioned in a passage with Fénelon, another model for Saint-Loup.

88. *SL* 2: 434, n. 1. Jeanne Pouquet inspired aspects of Gilberte.

89. Tadié, *Marcel Proust*, 615, n. 7.

90. *SL* 2: 457, n. 1.

91. *Carnet 1908*, 58.

92. This was apparently Proust's first movie; it may also have been his last. The cinema was one of the modern inventions that interested him little.

93. *Corr.* 8: 222.

94. Plantevignes, *Avec Marcel Proust*, 40.

95. See *SL* 2: 398–99.

96. *SL* 2: 399.

97. *Corr.* 8: 15.

98. Plantevignes described his recollection of the evening in his memoirs *Avec Marcel Proust*, 251–54. Odette also goes Chez Prévost for chocolate.

99. *Corr.* 8: 227.

100. *Corr.* 8: 255–56, 257.

101. *SL* 2: 405–6.

102. *SL* 2: 408, n. 1; *Corr.* 8: 219, n. 17.

103. *SL* 2: 408, n. 3.

104. *Corr.* 8: 243–44.

105. *SL* 2: 415.

106. *SL* 2: 402.

107. *Carnet 1908*, 60–61.

108. Their example he called a "noble lineage." *Carnet 1908*, 61 and nn. 94, 95. In *Time Regained*, Proust uses the same example and same phrase. *Search* 6: 334–35.

109. A few pages later Proust asked the same question, this time using an expectant mother as the image for the creator and wondering whether she will ever find the strength, before dying, to give birth to the child she carries: "Will I ever see you?" *Carnet 1908*, 69. Similar images are used in the *Search* 6: 507–8, 522.

110. *SL* 2: 405.

111. See *SL* 2: 410, n. 4. Jacques Thibaud (1880–1953), a famous violinist, is mentioned twice. *Search* 5: 63, 383. Proust had heard him play Fauré and Franck. Tadié, *Marcel Proust*, 620, n. 1.

112. *SL* 2: 409–10.

113. *Carnet 1908*, 80, dated November 1908.

114. Today there are seventy-five notebooks containing manuscripts for the *Search* at the Bibliothèque nationale. Céleste affirmed having burned thirty-two similar notebooks on Proust's instructions. Tadié, *Marcel Proust*, 622 and n. 4.

115. "Moréas," *CSB* 5: 311.

116. *SL* 2: 412.

117. *SL* 2: 411–12. In the letter Proust remarked that Léon Blum "has never said anything as good." Then he admitted that he often found Ruskin's words "stupid, cranky, exasperating, wrong, preposterous, but they are always estimable and always great." See also *Corr.* 8: 288, n. 5, where Kolb observes that Proust quotes Ruskin's version of the same commandment when he sketches the beginning of *Against Sainte-Beuve,* shortly after this letter to Lauris. John 12:35 reads, "Yet a little while is the light with you. Walk while ye have the light."

118. *SL* 2: 410–11. See Tadié, *Proust,* 263, n. 1.

119. *SL* 2: 419.

120. The only difference in the letters is that Proust did not forget Anna's unquenchable thirst for compliments: "It's because you are our greatest writer that it's monstrous to bother you with these trifles, but it's also for that reason that your advice is irreplaceable." *SL* 2: 416. For the letter to Lauris, see *Corr.* 8: 320. Just before December, Proust made many notes for *Against Sainte-Beuve; Corr.* 8: xxiv.

121. *SL* 2: 416.

122. The fragments we have include a scene in which he calls his mother to his room to read such an essay to her. Just as he is about to discuss Sainte-Beuve, the fragment ends. Proust apparently stopped there because he continued to hesitate between a number of topics and because he was headed for a work of fiction and not a critical essay.

123. *SL* 2: 417.

124. During this time, Proust wrote the unpublished parody of Chateaubriand. *Corr.* 8: 16.

125. *SL* 2: 420.

126. In July, Proust had noted in his *Carnet:* "Agostinelli at Glisolles," *Carnet 1908,* 52. See *Search* 5: 514–17.

18 Against Sainte-Beuve

1. *Corr.* 9: v.

2. We do not have any of these letters. Reynaldo may have told Marcel some things he did not want to hear about self-medication and dependency on drugs.

3. *SL* 2: 421–22.

4. *SL* 2: 421–22. Joseph Joubert (1754–1824) was a French moralist whom Proust admired and about whom he drafted a brief article of unknown date. See *Search* 6: 650–51 and STW, 371–72.

5. *SL* 2: 425, n. 7; see *Corr.* 9: 42.

6. *SL* 2: 430. It is unclear exactly when Proust attended this party.

7. *SL* 2: 428–29.

8. He read Lauris's novel twice and attempted to help the young writer Max Daireaux place a text. Judging by the number of letters we have, Proust apparently did write fewer letters in the 1909–11 period.

9. *SL* 2: 432.

10. *Corr.* 9: 71. A note on Moréas around this time shows Proust concerned with the idea of various "selves" and the relation of the particular to the universal. "Moréas," *CSB* 5: 311.

11. Two volumes of maxims from the *Search* have been published. Proust, despite his reputation for being long-winded, could be as pithy as any of his great predecessors in the maxim genre.

12. ["Notes sur la littérature"], *CSB* 5: 303–4; STW, 265–66: "This young man who . . . plays among my ruins lives on air; the pleasure he draws from the sight of the idea he has discovered is all the food he needs; he creates the idea and is created by it; he dies, but an idea survives him—like those seeds which suspend the process of germination in too dry an atmosphere and are lifeless; but a little moisture and warmth is enough to bring them back to life."

13. *Corr.* 9: 49–50.

14. *Corr.* 9: 78.

15. See *Carnet 1908*, 19, 71. In a sense, Proust's argument with Sainte-Beuve continues his contention with Ruskin in "On Reading," that the experience of literature is superior to conversations with friends, no matter how learned: "Reading is at the threshold of spiritual life; it can introduce us to it; it does not constitute it." In another draft for *Sainte-Beuve*, Proust wrote that other authors cannot serve as our guides "since we possess within us, as the compass dial or the carrier pigeon, the sense of our orientation." Text omitted in English edition. "Moréas," *CSB* 5: 311.

16. STW, 98–100. "La Méthode de Sainte-Beuve," *CSB* 5: 221–22. Proust had understood this in *Jean Santeuil*, where he expressed it differently: "Each time an artist, instead of depending on his work for happiness, depends on his life, he feels a disappointment that is almost remorseful and which gives him clear warning that he has made a mistake." *JS* 4: 490.

17. STW, 267.

18. STW, 25–26.

19. STW, 19.

20. STW, 21.

21. STW, 19.

22. There are other aspects of this voice. For example, the Narrator as a man reflects on his childhood and his present. Sometimes when he considers the past from the viewpoint of the present, he draws certain conclusions that are corrections of what he thought earlier, but then may add, "however, as I was to learn later. . . . " After the Narrator discovers his vocation as an artist, he reflects on the work he is about to create in relation to the story which we have just read.

23. STW, 20.

24. *Search* 1: 60.

25. "All the efforts of our intellect" to recapture the past "must prove futile. The past is hidden somewhere outside the realm, beyond the reach of the intellect, in some material object (in the sensation which that material object will give us) of which we have no inkling. And it depends on chance whether or not we come upon this object before we ourselves must die." *Search* 1: 59–60.

26. STW, 20.

27. STW, 21.

28. *Search* 6: 273.

29. *Search* 6: 304.

30. This is the plot synopsis proposed by Gérard Genette. See *Narrative Discourse: An Essay in Method*, translated by Jane E. Lewin, Ithaca: Cornell University Press, 1980, p. 30.

31. *Carnet 1908*, 54.

32. I have modified the translation because "an egotism which could be put to work for the benefit of other people" seems too wordy and lacks the clarity of Proust's simple "utilisable pour autrui." See *Search* 6: 513.

33. *Search* 1: 1.

34. STW, 23. *CSB* 5: 214.

35. [Projets de préface], *CSB* 5: 218.

36. This chronology is approximate. Proust never concerned himself greatly with linear narration and precise dates, so it is not possible to establish an exact time frame for the *Search*. The most comprehensive attempt to do so can be found in Gareth H. Steel's "Chronology and Time" in *À la recherche du temps perdu*, Geneva: Librairie Droz, 1979.

37. STW, 22.

38. From the 1909 draft "Romain Rolland," *CSB* 5: 309. Text omitted in English version. This draft contains a variation of this remark about intelligence: "More and more I believe it [intelligence] powerless in this recreation of reality that constitutes all art." *CSB* 5: 216.

39. See *Search* 6: 289, 298.

40. From the 1909 draft "Romain Rolland," *CSB* 5: 309. Text omitted in English version.

41. *Search* 6: 302. Traces of Proust's remarks about "materialist art" from his draft in *Sainte-Beuve* about Romain Rolland in 1909 remain in *Time Regained* just before the quotation about "real books." Proust wanted to avoid the superficial, conversational style of Sainte-Beuve. See *Corr.* 9: vii–viii.

42. *JS* 4: 856.

43. See *Proust-Halévy Corr.*, 92, 97 and nn. 47, 48, 221–22. The editors date this letter between mid-October and mid-December 1907. Kolb dates it as January 1908; see *Corr.* 21: 628. Péguy's essay "De la situation faite au parti intellectuel dans le monde moderne devant les accidents de la gloire temporelle," in which Proust found passages that he said bore some resemblance to what he had written on topography and names, appeared in *Les Cahiers de la Quinzaine* on February 3, 1907. See *Proust-Halévy Corr.*, 216, n. 39.

44. Duchêne followed the *Proust-Halévy Corr.* editors on this point; *L'Impossible Proust*, 575 and n. 5. Tadié does not; see *Marcel Proust*, 601, n. 4.

45. This text, with slight alterations, became the telephone call the Narrator makes to his grandmother in *The Guermantes Way*.

46. *Carnet 1908*, 61; last quarter of 1908.

47. *Corr.* 9: 92.

48. Kolb believes that Proust saw the exhibition, but we do not know for certain that he did. *Corr.* 9: x.

49. Monet had insisted on this title. This was the largest number of paintings Monet had ever exhibited of any single series. See Paul Hayes Tucker, *Claude Monet: Life and Art*, New Haven: Yale University Press, 1995, 191–96.

50. Monet's *Grandes décorations* found their home in rooms especially designed for them in Paris's Musée de l'Orangerie.

51. *SL* 2: 435. See *SL* 2: 436, n. 3. "François de Pâris's aunt, the baronne de Lareinty, née Puységur, had inherited the château de Guermantes, near Lagny, Seine-et-Marne."

52. *SL* 2: 436.

53. *Corr.* 9: 117.

54. *Corr.* 9: 119. She lived on avenue Henri-Martin and had vacationed at Cabourg in August, 1907. *Corr.* 9: 121, n. 21.

55. He had first used an autobiographical "I" in the 1905 text "On Reading," though even there he had begun to fictionalize it, having indicated in the first drafts that "mother" was not really his mother, and in any case, he later changed "mother" to a fictional "great aunt." In 1907, in "Impressions de route," he had mingled autobiographical and fictional elements. From 1908 on, the "I" who spoke for Proust the storyteller shared many traits with the real person known as Marcel Proust. But there are many differences between Proust and the Narrator, the most obvious of which are found by comparing the family situations: the Narrator's parents are both Catholic; he is an only child; his father is not a scientist; he has no homosexual tendencies, although he is suspiciously well informed about and fascinated by the subject. As Proust developed the plot, the list of similarities and dissimilarities lengthened.

56. There is a draft in which Proust rather coyly says that if the Narrator had the same given name as the author, his name would be Marcel. This rather oblique hint at what the Narrator's name might have been should not be read as a confession. What Proust unquestionably sought to capture in his book was the essence of his life, not the banal details.

57. *Corr.* 9: x–xi.

58. *SL* 2: 438.

59. *Corr.* 9: 122.

60. See *Corr.* 9: 131–32. A young publisher by the name of Bernard Grasset, who ultimately published *Swann's Way,* brought out Lauris's novel in 1910, after it had been refused by Calmann-Lévy and Fasquelle. Lauris most likely paid for publication. See Franck Lhomeau and Alain Coelho, *Marcel Proust à la recherche d'un éditeur,* Paris: Olivier Orban, 1988, 117.

61. The parodies were found and published posthumously.

62. See *Corr.* 9: 134–35.

63. *SL* 2: 439.

64. *Search* 1: 493–94.

65. *Search* 3: 1091. Proust occasionally slips into a letter a passage or fragment he is writing for the novel. Tadié, *Marcel Proust,* 628, n. 6.

66. *SL* 2: 440–41. Kolb dated this letter July 17 or 18.

67. *SL* 2: 439, n. 3.

68. The acronym of the periodical will be italicized as the *NRF,* while the name of the publishing house will appear in roman type.

69. *Corr.* 9: 152.

70. *SL* 2: 444, n. 3.

71. Proust considered his book "obscene" by the standards of his time. It would be so judged, he feared, because he depicted homosexuals (not their acts) in pursuit of partners, a topic that had been taboo.

72. *SL* 2: 442. *Sylvie,* by Gérard de Nerval, was one of Proust's favorite books.

73. *SL* 2: 443. *La Double Maîtresse* was a novel by Henri de Régnier that Mercure de France had published in 1900. *SL* 2: 444, n. 6.

74. *SL* 2: 443.

75. *Search* 2: 394–95.

76. An early example occurs in the novel when Swann, deeply moved by a new sonata, attempts to learn who composed it. The music has extraordinary power, and listening to it Swann discovers "many of the riches of his own soul," releasing him briefly from his obsession with Odette. All he can find out is that the composer's name is Vinteuil. At Combray, Swann has a country neighbor named Vinteuil, who is the local piano teacher. Could he be the composer? Swann pictures the man, prudish, apparently dull, not in any way fashionable, and immediately rejects the thought that such a man could have written the remarkable sonata capable of moving a man like himself. In the *Search*, when Proust speaks of the "artist" in general (as opposed to a specific writer, painter, composer), he means the creative person. In Swann's meditation on Vinteuil's sonata, he calls such artists "explorers of the unseen" and gives as examples two scientists, Lavoisier and Ampère. *Search* 1: 496, 498–99.

77. *Corr.* 9: 154.

78. *Corr.* 9: 12.

79. Tadié, *Proust*, 269.

80. *SL* 2: 444.

81. Proust had "kept writing to my architect" from Cabourg, " 'I may come back tomorrow,' they were unable to get down to work." *SL* 2: 466, 467, n. 1.

82. *SL* 2: 445–46. The excessive dampness in his room soaked his writing sheet after fifteen minutes, and the walls were covered with damp stains of moisture.

83. *SL* 2: 446.

84. *SL* 2: 447.

85. Tadié, *Marcel Proust*, 629 and n. 3.

86. *SL* 2: 466, 467, n. 5.

87. *Corr.* 9: 197 and n. 7.

88. Tadié, *Marcel Proust*, 619.

89. *Corr.* 9: 171 and *SL* 2: 447.

90. *Corr.* 9: xix.

91. *SL* 2: 448–49.

92. *Corr.* 9: 191.

93. *SL* 2: 451.

94. *Corr.* 9: 210, n. 2.

95. Kolb wonders if the girl in question might have been one of Albert Nahmias's sisters, Estie or Anita, about whom virtually nothing is known. *Corr.* 9: xxii.

96. See *SL* 2: 458, 459, and nn. 9, 10.

97. *SL* 2: 459.

98. Tadié, *Marcel Proust*, 630.

99. *Corr.* 9: 222.

100. *Corr.* 9: xxii.

101. *Corr.* 9: 215.

102. *SL* 2: 460.

103. Proust had crossed out "a few enormities," misreadings by the copyists.

104. My account of the Proust-Beaunier-Calmette misunderstanding is based on Kolb's foreword in *Corr.* 9: xxiv–xxv.

105. Proust found this out several months later. *SL* 3: 9.

106. *SL* 2: 461.
107. During 1908 Proust had begun and abandoned notebooks containing a hybrid genre consisting of an essay and a narrative *(Against Sainte-Beuve)* and had filled twenty bound notebooks of drafts for the *Search* (still without a title). He had written first versions of "Combray," "Swann in Love," a description of a seaside sojourn at Querqueville (to become Balbec), and passages about Gilberte and her mother. Proust's method of composition had become fixed. Some notebooks, like *Le Carnet de 1908*, contained notes, preliminary sketches; or reminders. In other notebooks he organized these sketches and revised them. See *Recherche* 1 (NP): cxxx.

19 Gathering Impressions

1. *Corr.* 10: 24.
2. *Corr.* 10: 31.
3. *Corr.* 10: 28.
4. *SL* 3: 1. Proust gave his fascination with photographs and the Périgord anecdote to the Narrator, who attempts in vain to obtain Gilberte's photograph. See *Search* 1: 103–4. Simone de Caillavet became the primary model for the daughter of Saint-Loup and Gilberte Swann; her brief appearance at the end of the *Search* has an important structural and symbolic role. *Search* 6: 502–7.
5. *Corr.* 10: 45–46.
6. *SL* 3: 2.
7. See *Corr.* 10: 49–50 and n. 5.
8. *Corr.* 10: 49, 51.
9. *Corr.* 10: 68, n. 2.
10. See letters to Montesquiou and Lauris; *Corr.* 10: 71, 72–73.
11. *Corr.* 10: 73.
12. Proust sought and took advice from friends, some well placed and knowledgeable, others mere novices and dreamers. He also followed the recommendations of columnist Yvel in the *Figaro,* a practice he admitted did him "no good. The rubber and oil and all the rest of the shares invariably wait for the day after my purchases to come tumbling down!" *SL* 3: 7.
13. *SL* 3: 6–8. See also *SL* 2: 446, n. 1, where Kolb says this text, begun in 1909, may be the "earliest draft" of the *Search,* "consisting of its long overture, *Combray,* and its conclusion as then envisaged."
14. See *SL* 3: 8–9.
15. See *Corr.* 10: 114, 115, n. 3; 120, n. 3. See *Corr.* 11: 346, n. 2.
16. *SL* 3: 11, n. 2.
17. *Search* 5: 314.
18. Brody, *Kaleidoscope,* 130.
19. *SL* 3: 12.
20. *Corr.* 10: 122–24.
21. *Corr.* 19: 715.
22. *Corr.* 10: 136, 137.
23. *Corr.* 10: 144, and 146, n. 2.
24. *SL* 3: 14.

25. *SL* 3: 16–17 and n. 7.
26. *Corr.* 10: 169.
27. *Corr.* 10: 215.
28. *SL* 3: 20–21.
29. *SL* 3: 22–23.
30. *Corr.* 10: 197–98.
31. "Swann in Love" ends with this diatribe by its main character: "To think that I've wasted years of my life, that I've longed to die, that I've experienced my greatest love, for a woman who didn't appeal to me, who wasn't even my type!" *Search* 1: 543. Before the long flashback of "Swann in Love," Proust had shown the reader glimpses of Mme Swann in the garden at Combray. At the conclusion of "Swann in Love," the reader guesses that, despite Swann's final words, he married the cocotte known as Odette de Crécy. The next volume begins with a section entitled "Mme Swann at Home."
32. Swann's jealous obsession with Odette will be repeated, with variations, in the Narrator's youthful crush on Gilberte, in his mature involvement with Albertine, and in Charlus's fixation on the violinist Morel. Proust masterfully orchestrates the theme, which runs in profane counterpoint to the sacred theme of creativity.
33. Proust knew that if he succeeded in writing the *Search,* he would have created himself as the man capable of writing such a book. Some years after Proust's death, Robert de Billy reflected on how his friend would have been remembered had he died in 1910. Proust "would have very rarely been mentioned as a writer of note." He was considered "bizarre," someone amiable who loved society and art. Billy, *Lettres et conversations,* 14.
34. *Search* 1: 60.
35. *Corr.* 10: 214–15.
36. *Corr.* 10: 217.
37. Tadié, *Marcel Proust,* 624, n. 4. Proust had first used the name Guermantes in May 1908 in *Carnet 1908.* Once he was certain that the title was clear, he substituted it for the name Villebon. See *Carnet 1908,* 94 and n. 392. Entries dating from February 1909 show that he had also found the names Swann, Combray for the little provincial town, and Saint-Hilaire for its church. See *Carnet 1908,* 97 and n. 407.
38. *SL* 3: 27.
39. *SL* 3: 27.
40. *SL* 3: 28.
41. See *SL* 3: 33, n. 24; *Corr.* 10: 253, n. 22.
42. *Corr.* 10: 254.
43. *SL* 3: 30–31.
44. *Corr.* 10: 273.
45. Quoted in Francis Steegmuller, *Cocteau: A Biography,* Boston: David R. Godine, 1986, 75–76.
46. *Corr.* 10: 260, n. 115. *Le Dieu bleu,* a ballet by Cocteau and Frédéric de Madrazo with music by Reynaldo Hahn, was first performed in Paris at the Théâtre du Châtelet on May 13, 1912.
47. *Corr.* 10: 258, n. 2.
48. *Corr.* 10: 254.
49. *Corr.* 10: 256–57.
50. *Search* 1: 291.

51. *Search,* 1: 267.
52. *SL* 3: 33–34. See "Pastiche de *Pelléas et Mélisande,*" *CSB* 5: 206–7.
53. *SL* 3: 34.
54. *Corr.* 10: 271. Proust wrote "collaboratrice inspirée," whose feminine form with the adjective *inspired* seems to indicate that he had in mind a "muse" who inspires through illness.
55. In spite of the reputation of the creators and performers—Ida Rubinstein played the saint, Bakst had provided the set and costumes, Fokine the choreography—the show closed after eleven performances. See *Corr.* 10: 289 and n. 7.
56. *SL* 3: 41. In the *Search,* Proust frequently used scientific analogies to explain perception, the way impressions are recorded by the body.
57. *SL* 3: 40 and n. 3.
58. *Corr.* 10: 294 and n. 5.
59. *Corr.* 10: 317, n. 5.
60. *Corr.* 10: 308.
61. *SL* 3: 42 and n. 1.
62. *Corr.* 10: 317, n. 4.
63. *SL* 3: 43–44 and n. 1.
64. *SL* 3: 43.
65. This scene occurs in the opening section of the book, sometimes referred to as the overture—indeed Proust himself once called it that in a letter—and is not, therefore, anchored chronologically in the Narrator's experience. The succession of involuntary memory experiences at the conclusion of the book does occur chronologically at the end of the Narrator's quest.
66. *Search* 1: 64.
67. Phrases he mentioned in a letter to Reynaldo are attributed to Odette in this section. See *Corr.* 10: 332 and 335, n. 13; *Search* 2: 109. This English title needs to be replaced by one closer to the original. The literal meaning of Proust's title *À l'ombre des jeunes filles en fleurs* is "In the shadow of girls in bloom." The traditional English title unfortunately loses the key element of girls in the flower of youth.
68. *Corr.* 10: 323, 324.
69. *SL* 3: 45.
70. *SL* 3: 52, n. 1.
71. *Corr.* 18: 588–89.
72. See *Corr.* 10: 344–45.
73. *SL* 3: 48–49 and n. 8.
74. An unknown typist produced part of the typescript (beginning at *Search* 1: 430); see *Corr.* 10: 350, nn. 5, 6.
75. *Corr.* 10: 359, n. 3.
76. See *Corr.* 10: 353 and nn. 23, 24 for details; *Corr.* 10: 356, n. 24.
77. Quotations from Dumont-Wilden are in *Corr.* 10: 356, n. 24.
78. Harold C. Schonberg, *The Lives of the Great Composers,* revised edition, New York: Norton, 1981, 466.
79. *SL* 3: 52.
80. *Corr.* 10: 382 and 19: 716.
81. *SL* 3: 54. See *SL* 3: 56, n. 17: in recent speculations at the Bourse, Proust had lost, in less than a month, nearly 10 percent on two large transactions. Cf. *SL* 3: 8, n. 13.

82. *SL* 3: 53, 55, n. 9. Léonie de Clomesnil, a celebrated courtesan, was one of the models for Odette. See *Search* 1: 340–41, where Swann sees Odette in a fashionable new outfit, "a cape trimmed with skunk, a Rembrandt hat, and a bunch of violets in her bosom."

20 In Search of a Publisher

1. *Corr.* 11: 25–26.
2. Tadié, *Marcel Proust,* 667.
3. *Corr.* 11: 28.
4. *Corr.* 11: 28 and n. 4. See the *Search* 5: 406, n. 20.
5. *Corr.* 11: 32. Proust frequently quoted this line to friends when speaking about his bad luck at the Bourse.
6. *Corr.* 11: 41.
7. *Corr.* 11: 34 and n. 4.
8. *Corr.* 11: 43–44.
9. *SL* 3: 63.
10. *Corr.* 11: 46.
11. *Corr.* 11: 51 and n. 3. The painting, stolen on August 21, 1911, was found in Florence on December 12, 1913.
12. *SL* 3: 58 and n. 13. Italics indicate the *Figaro*'s interpolation.
13. *Corr.* 11: 66 and n. 6.
14. *SL* 3: 65 and n. 4. Fauré's composition, which apparently induced erotic fantasies in Proust, is *Trois Romances sans paroles pour piano,* op. 17 (1863).
15. *SL* 3: 65–66.
16. *SL* 3: 62.
17. *SL* 3: 65.
18. *SL* 3: 63–64 and n. 7. It is difficult to refer to the various parts of Proust's novel as volumes, because the number of volumes varies considerably among editions. The best way to refer to the Search is by the seven main divisions of the story: *Swann's Way, Within a Budding Grove, The Guermantes Way, Sodom and Gomorrah* (formerly entitled *Cities of the Plain*), *The Captive, The Fugitive* (formerly entitled *The Sweet Cheat Gone*), and *Time Regained.*
19. *SL* 3: 62–63.
20. The palace was located at Le Vésinet, about fifteen miles west of Paris. *SL* 3: 66, n. 8.
21. *SL* 3: 65–66.
22. *Corr.* 11: 93.
23. *Corr.* 11: 84–85.
24. *Corr.* 11: 86 and n. 3; *SL* 3: 68, n. 2.
25. *Corr.* 11: 88.
26. *Corr.* 9: viii.
27. *SL* 3: 67–68. Ellipsis is Proust's. I have modified the translation from "cold douche."
28. *SL* 3: 74, 78.
29. *SL* 3: 70, n. 7.
30. *SL* 3: 71.
31. *Corr.* 11: 118–19.

32. *SL* 3: 72. In December, Proust quoted Montesquiou, who "says paleographers spend years deciphering my letters." *SL* 3: 139.

33. Steegmuller, *Cocteau*, 76–77.

34. *Sumurum*, performed at the Théâtre du Vaudeville, was Max Reinhardt's mime adapted from tales by Friedrich Freska. Victor Hollaender wrote the music. *SL* 3: 74, n. 6.

35. *SL* 3: 74, n. 5, where Edward VII is incorrectly referred to as Edward VIII.

36. See *Search* 3: 62–67, in which the duchesse de Guermantes and the princesse de Guermantes sit together in the duchess's box at the Opéra and are observed by the Narrator.

37. *Corr.* 11: 125.

38. *SL* 3: 74.

39. *SL* 3: 76–77.

40. *SL* 3: 78–79 and n. 5; *Search* 4: 731; addendum to *Search* 4: 157.

41. *Corr.* 11: 142.

42. *SL* 3: 76 and n. 1.

43. *Corr.* 11: 143–44.

44. *Corr.* 11: 151. The exact date of this letter is not known. It was obviously sent well before October 12, when Proust had chosen most of his titles, *Le Temps perdu,* and *Le Temps retrouvé,* Time lost, Time regained. See *Corr.* 11: 257.

45. *SL* 3: 74–75.

46. *SL* 3: 79.

47. *SL* 3: 81.

48. Hahn wrote Massenet's obituary in *Le Journal,* August 18, 1912. *Corr.* 11: 186, n. 2.

49. *SL* 3: 88; *Corr.* 11: 194, n. 5.

50. *Corr.* 11: 185.

51. See *SL* 3: 85–87.

52. *SL* 3: 86–87 and n. 6; see *Search* 1: 412. Proust made a remark in the letter to Nahmias that hints at the famous scene in which the duchesse de Guermantes, Swann's oldest friend, is running late for a dinner party and does not have time to listen to him, even though he has, at her insistence, begun telling her that he has a terminal illness and will soon die. Proust to Nahmias: "One day I shall describe those characters who, even from a vulgar point of view, will never understand the elegance, when one is dressed and ready for a ball, of forgoing it in order to keep a friend company." See *Search* 3: 816–19. For the scene in which Charlus berates the Narrator, see *Search* 3: 760–65.

53. *SL* 3: 93–94 and n. 6. The text of the Sainte-Beuve essay was lost.

54. *SL* 3: 99 and n.6. The issue contained an article by Ghéon "mocking the naïve piety of Francis Jammes" that would have certainly irritated Proust.

55. *SL* 3: 97–98.

56. See *SL* 3: 97–99.

57. *SL* 3: 100–101; ellipsis is Proust's.

58. *SL* 3: 104–5.

59. *SL* 3: 106–7.

60. *SL* 3: 108.

61. *SL* 3: 108–10.

62. *SL* 3: 120.

63. This title was eventually given to one of the novel's most remarkable episodes, in which

the Narrator returns to the Grand-Hôtel and experiences a much-delayed reaction to his grandmother's death and meditates on grieving and forgetting, formulating what Proust called "the general law of oblivion."

64. *Corr.* 11: 264.
65. *SL* 3: 111–12. On September 3 the *Figaro* had published "L'Église de village," the third of four excerpts from the novel to appear in the newspaper.
66. *Corr.* 11: 276, n. 3; *SL* 3: 121, n. 2.
67. See *SL* 3: 117–19.
68. *SL* 3: 120–21.
69. *SL* 3: 122.
70. *SL* 3: 123–24.
71. *SL* 3: 126, n. 7; *Corr.* 11: 295, n. 9.
72. Marcel later learned that Cocteau had contacted Rostand and urged him to write Fasquelle. *SL* 3: 134.
73. *SL* 3: 124–25.
74. *Corr.* 11: 310, n. 2.
75. *SL* 3: 128–29, n. 1.
76. *SL* 3: 129–30.
77. *SL* 3: 135.
78. *SL* 3: 135–36. Fasquelle, who had relied on a reader's report, returned Proust's manuscript on Christmas Eve. *Corr.* 11: 333, n. 3. In a mid-January letter to Antoine Bibesco, Proust said that he had withdrawn the manuscript over a disagreement about length: "Since Fasquelle wouldn't allow me the volume length I believe necessary for the presentation of my book, I've taken back my manuscript, which will probably be published by Ollendorff while Fasquelle in exchange will publish a collection of my articles." *SL* 3: 146.
79. See *JS* 4: 64; *Corr.* 11: xxviii.
80. See *Corr.* 11: xxviii, 295, 335. Maurice had sent a long telegram to Fasquelle.
81. *Corr.* 11: xxvii.
82. *SL* 3: 137–38.
83. *SL* 3: 140–41.

21 Proust's Way

1. Louis de Robert, *Comment débuta Marcel Proust*, Paris: Gallimard, 1969, 8.
2. *Corr.* 12: 22.
3. *SL* 3: 141.
4. *Corr.* 12: 39.
5. *SL* 3: 144.
6. Proust described this visit to Mme Straus and Reynaldo in separate letters. See *SL* 3: 144 and *Corr.* 12: 48–49.
7. Raymond Poincaré was elected January 17. *Corr.* 12: 69, n. 7.
8. *Corr.* 12: 37. The mentality of a sick old woman, comically portrayed in Aunt Léonie, becomes that of the Narrator.
9. *Corr.* 12: 42–43.
10. *SL* 3: 143.
11. Proust had read Mâle's descriptions of the sculptures illustrating such biblical scenes as

the life of the Virgin and the kings of Judah, which he used as models for the porch of the church at Balbec. *SL* 3: 145, n. 4. See *Search* 2: 573–76.

12. *Corr.* 12: 45 and 46, n. 19.

13. *Corr.* 12: 70.

14. *SL* 3: 148.

15. See Robert, *Comment débuta Marcel Proust,* 9. The reader, long thought to have been Humblot, was Georges Boyer, the sixty-two-year-old playwright, lyricist, and theater critic for the *Petit Journal.* See *Corr.* 12: 87, n. 6.

16. *SL* 3: 153–54.

17. Robert, *Comment débuta Marcel Proust,* 10. *SL* 3: 149, n. 1.

18. *SL* 3: 156–57.

19. *SL* 3: 149–52.

20. *SL* 3: 158–59.

21. *SL* 3: 159–61.

22. *SL* 3: 163, n. 3.

23. *SL* 3: 164.

24. *Recherche* 1 (NP): cxxxii, and *Corr.* 12: 10.

25. *SL* 3: 261.

26. This fascination with sports and machines of speed is a trait given to Albertine in the novel. Albertine and the Narrator make their last excursion together to an airfield. *Search* 5: 132.

27. See "Impressions de route," *CSB* 5: 66.

28. See Albaret, *Monsieur Proust,* 189: See the photograph published opposite 385 of the original French edition of *Monsieur Proust,* Paris: Laffont, 1973.

29. *Corr.* 13: 239. The Narrator has difficulty comprehending Saint-Loup's infatuation with Rachel. The actress-cum-prostitute is not attractive when seen up close and has a face that is pockmarked. *Search* 3: 231–32.

30. Robert Vigneron, "Genèse de *Swann,*" in *Études sur Stendhal et sur Proust,* Paris: Nizet, 1978, 106.

31. *SL* 3: 165.

32. *Corr.* 12: 118, n. 2. Albaret, *Monsieur Proust,* 3.

33. *Corr.* 21: 660, n. 2. See Albaret, *Monsieur Proust,* 4.

34. *SL* 3: 168–69. Proust waited nearly a month before he wrote Grasset, offering to pay more for the heavily revised proofs, saying that it would be "dishonest of me to regard such an enormous number of corrections as being covered by our agreement." *SL* 3: 173.

35. *SL* 3: 169 and n. 1. Proust gave his own fictional violinist Morel an "F sharp [that] was enough to make Enesco, Capet and Thibaud die of jealousy." Enesco, Lucien Capet, leader of the Capet Quartet, and Jacques Thibaud were the three most famous violinists of Proust's era. See *Search* 5: 383. Shortly after hearing this performance, Proust added the passage on Vinteuil's sonata. See *Search* 1: 493–94. As late as April, Proust fused two characters to create Vinteuil: the naturalist Vington, who had a lesbian daughter, and a composer named Berget. See *SL* 3: 204, n. 13. See also Alison Winton, *Proust's Additions: The Making of* À la recherche du temps perdu, 2 volumes, Cambridge: Cambridge University Press, 1977, 1: 334. Proust took the first syllable of Vington, to which he added the beloved suffix *-teuil.* The name of this composer, whose works resound thematically in some of the *Search*'s most beautiful passages throughout, contains the magical sound found in

Auteuil and Santeuil, which evoked many memories for Proust, chiefly of his mother and her family.

36. *Corr.* 12: 149, n. 4. The galley bears the date May 13, 1913. See *Search* 1: 498–500.
37. See *Corr.* 17: 193–94.
38. See *SL* 3: 174; for example, "rose Rose" in French means pink rose.
39. *SL* 3: 173–74 and n. 2, 175, n. 12. Proust attended the ballet on May 15. According to Maurice Rostand, Proust attended the Ballets Russes again on May 17 and saw Nijinsky dance Debussy's *L'Après-midi d'un faune*. Afterward, Proust went with Maurice and Nijinsky to dine at Larue's. See *Corr.* 12: 12.
40. *SL* 3: 207.
41. See also *Corr.* 12: 181, n. 3.
42. *SL* 3: 175–76, nn. 1, 2. See *Corr.* 12: xv.
43. *Corr.* 13: 381–82.
44. Gaston had written Marcel to accept the dedication of *Swann's Way* with "great joy." *Corr.* 12: 105.
45. *SL* 3: 177.
46. Proust corrected the second proofs between May 30 and September 1. Proust mentioned to a number of friends that he had been so ill and lost so much weight they would not recognize him. *SL* 3: 179–80 and n. 1.
47. Robert, *Comment débuta Marcel Proust*, 12–13.
48. Jean Bothorel, *Bernard Grasset: Vie et passion d'un éditeur*, Paris: Grasset, 1989, 76–77.
49. *Corr.* 13: 389–90. See also *SL* 3: 203–4 and n. 22.
50. Galley 95 of the first proofs bears the date June 11. *Corr.* 12: 213, n. 5.
51. *Corr.* 13: 391.
52. *Corr.* 12: 211–12.
53. *SL* 3: 185–86 and n. 1; Proust transferred the greater part of the chapter entitled "Mme Swann at Home" to the second volume, where it became the first part of *Within a Budding Grove*, but he kept the ending—the description of a visit to the Bois de Boulogne—as a coda to *Swann*. Because Grasset did not want two books sold together, Proust decided to publish a single volume of 527 pages instead of one of 680. "I shall make it 520." *SL* 3: 195. *Swann's Way* was to have 525 pages.
54. Louis de Robert had opposed the idea of using notes because it would make Proust's novel look too scholarly. *SL* 3: 188–89.
55. Francis Jammes, who would express his profound admiration of *Swann's Way*, had also asked for suppression of the Montjouvain scene. *Corr.* 13: vi–vii.
56. *SL* 3: 190–92. This letter is one of many in which Proust speaks as the author and as the Narrator.
57. *SL* 3: 194. See *Search* 4: 479–80.
58. *SL* 3: 192–93. Ulrich became the model for Françoise's erudite young footman, Joseph Périgot. *SL* 3: 193, n. 2.
59. *Corr.* 12: xxi.
60. *SL* 3: 195–96.
61. *SL* 3: 197.
62. *Corr.* 12: 248–49.
63. *Corr.* 12: 252.
64. *Corr.* 12: 209–10.

65. *Corr.* 13: 228–29.
66. See *SL* 3: 261.
67. Albaret, *Monsieur Proust,* 190.
68. *SL* 3: 198–99.
69. Daudet, *Soixante lettres,* 67.
70. *SL* 3: 200–203.
71. *SL* 3: 200–201.
72. *Search* 1: 606.
73. *SL* 3: 205.
74. *SL* 3: 206.
75. *SL* 3: 221 and n. 1. See *Search* 5: 514–16, where Albertine is described as an "angel musician" playing Rameau and Borodin on the pianola.
76. Albaret, *Monsieur Proust,* 5–6. See *Corr.* 12: 267, n. 15.
77. *Corr.* 13: 401 and n. 2.
78. *Corr.* 13: 402.
79. *Corr.* 12: 285.
80. *Corr.* 13: 405.
81. *Recherche* 1 (NP): cxxxii.
82. *Corr.* 13: 408–9.
83. The danger here, one clearly recognized by Proust, was mortality. Beaunier did not live to see the *Search* completed.
84. See *SL* 3: 207 and *Corr.* 12: 298–99.
85. *Corr.* 12: 304–5.
86. *SL* 3: 208, n. 3.
87. *Search* 1: 58. The conclusion of the scene ends "Combray I." "Combray II" goes back to the Narrator's childhood and the family vacations to Combray.
88. *Corr.* 12: 300, 319. *Search* 1: 63–64.
89. *Corr.* 12: 300.
90. Michel-Thiriet, *Book,* 223.
91. Proust likely quoted these passages from memory for future volumes that he was to develop. For a translation of the complete interview, see Shattuck's *Marcel Proust,* 167–72. All the quotations are from Shattuck's translation.
92. The interview appeared in the edition of the *Temps* published on November 12, dated November 13.
93. See *Textes retrouvés,* 221–24 and n. 3.
94. See "À propos d'un livre récent: L'Œuvre écrite dans la chambre close. Chez M. Marcel Proust" (About a recent book: The work written in a shuttered room. At M. Marcel Proust's), *Textes retrouvés,* 221–22.
95. *Corr.* 12: 308–9.
96. *Corr.* 12: 15.
97. Bothorel, *Bernard Grasset,* 92.
98. *SL* 3: 212 and n. 11.
99. *SL* 3: 178, n. 2.
100. *Corr.* 21: 657.
101. *Corr.* 12: 320.

102. *Corr.* 21: 658.

103. See Lhomeau and Coelho, *Recherche d'un éditeur,* 360.

104. *SL* 3: 209.

105. *Corr.* 12: 326.

106. *Corr.* 12: 336.

107. *Corr.* 12: 321.

108. This involved a literary indiscretion that would have been minor for anyone but Proust: Gide had gossiped about Proust's having temporarily misplaced a letter from Emmanuel Bibesco regarding the NRF's rejection of *Swann's Way.*

109. *Corr.* 12: 322.

110. *Corr.* 12: 333 and n. 7. Flaubert published *L'Éducation sentimentale,* a novel some critics prefer to *Madame Bovary* (1857), in 1869.

111. Céleste believed that Anna was largely responsible for the sudden departure of the Agostinellis. According to her, Anna did not like living in Paris and was eager to return to the Riviera. See Albaret, *Monsieur Proust,* 190. The date of their departure was determined by Kolb in *Corr.* 12: 15.

112. See *SL* 3: 214.

113. For the correspondence between Proust and Nahmias regarding Agostinelli, see *Corr.* 12: 355–66.

114. The volume telling of Albertine's disappearance is called *The Fugitive,* formerly *The Sweet Cheat Gone.* A letter from the Narrator to Albertine ends with a postscript in which he denies sending Saint-Loup to bribe Mme Bontemps. Proust was as mendacious in his dealings with Agostinelli as are the Narrator and Swann with the women they pursue. Proust had instructed Nahmias to make a similar denial; see *Corr.* 12: 357. There are echoes of this episode throughout *The Captive* and *The Fugitive.* Saint-Loup is sent to spy on Albertine as he tries to win her return through negotiations with Mme Bontemps; in *The Captive,* there is probably a direct transposition of Proust's suspicions concerning Agostinelli's infidelities to his wife. Albertine, who had been taken to Auteuil by a chauffeur, does not dare go out for fear of being seen. The insanely jealous Charlus has Morel tailed by a private detective agency. See *Search* 5: 283.

115. Lhomeau and Coelho, *Recherche d'un éditeur,* 270.

116. Lhomeau and Coelho, *Recherche d'un éditeur,* 271. Cocteau also used the term *overture* to describe the opening volume, a choice of words that would have pleased Proust, extremely sensitive to the connections between what he was trying to achieve in the novel and what Wagner and other composers he admired had achieved in music.

117. *SL* 3: 210 and nn. 1, 3.

118. Lhomeau and Coelho, *Recherche d'un éditeur,* 271–76.

119. Lhomeau and Coelho, *Recherche d'un éditeur,* 276–81.

120. *Corr.* 12: 371.

121. *Corr.* 12: 372–73.

122. Souday's review is reprinted in Lhomeau and Coelho, *Recherche d'un éditeur,* 281–87.

123. *Corr.* 12: xxvii.

124. *SL* 3: 215. The Ovid quotation is from *Metamorphoses,* book 2, 1. 5. *SL* 3: 216, n. 4.

125. *Corr.* 12: 384, n. 2.

126. *Corr.* 12: 385–86.

127. *Corr.* 12: 388–89.
128. Proust later had Céleste call and ask to borrow the copy a second time. See *Corr.* 12: 391, n. 2.
129. *Corr.* 12: 387.
130. Lhomeau and Coelho, *Recherche d'un éditeur*, 287–91.
131. Edel, *Henry James*, 688.
132. *Corr.* 13: 76, n. 7; see also *SL* 3: 230, n. 4.
133. Lhomeau and Coelho, *Recherche d'un éditeur*, 296–98.
134. *SL* 3: 219, n. 3.
135. *SL* 3: 218.
136. *Search* 6: 522.
137. This is Lucien's version from *Soixante Lettres*, 214, n. 1. See also *Corr.* 12: 392.
138. *Carnet 1908*, 49.

22 *Annus Horribilis*

1. Ghéon's real name was Dr. Henri Vangeon. *SL* 3: 220, n. 2.
2. *Corr.* 13: 22–27.
3. *Corr.* 13: 37.
4. Lhomeau and Coelho, *Recherche d'un éditeur*, 310.
5. *SL* 3: 221–22.
6. *SL* 3: 229.
7. *SL* 3: 223–24.
8. *SL* 3: 225–26. Gide had read too quickly the sentence in which Proust describes Aunt Léonie's "false hair . . . through which the bones shine." See *Search* 1:71.
9. *SL* 3: 226.
10. *Corr.* 13: 68.
11. *SL* 3: 231–32.
12. *SL* 3: 232–33.
13. *Search* 6: 513.
14. *SL* 3: 235.
15. This account of Calmette's murder is based on Edward Berenson's from his book *The Trial of Madame Caillaux*, Berkeley: University of California Press, 1992, 1–2.
16. *Corr.* 13: 11.
17. *SL* 3: 237.
18. Fasquelle had made his offer through Maurice Rostand; see *SL* 3: 237–38.
19. *SL* 3: 242.
20. *SL* 3: 245.
21. *SL* 3: 247.
22. *SL* 3: 249.
23. *Corr.* 13: 157.
24. *Corr.* 13: 167–68.
25. *SL* 3: 252.
26. *Corr.* 13: 179–80.
27. *Corr.* 13: 186–87.
28. *SL* 3: 255.

29. See the letter to Lionel Hauser in *Corr.* 13: 213 and 214, n. 2.

30. *Corr.* 13: 217–21. Other details from Agostinelli's and Proust's letters and from events about to unfold were to be attributed to Albertine in the *Search*. The Narrator, in his vain attempts to lure her back after she flees his apartment, offers her a Rolls-Royce and a yacht, the latter gift being more suitable for a young woman than an airplane. The details about the Mallarmé poem, about engraving on the fuselage the word *Swann* or *Cygne*, French for swan, quotations from Albertine's letter, and so on, have their direct origin in Agostinelli. See *Search* 5: 614, 632–33. Albertine falsely predicts that the sea will be her tomb.

31. See Bonnet, *Proust, 1907–14*, 195.

32. *Corr.* 13: 221, n. 8.

33. *SL* 3: 258–59. Agostinelli ignored Proust's request to return all his letters, later destroyed by the young man's family, who said they were love letters. The one surviving letter, returned because Agostinelli died before he could receive it, does not read like a love letter. See Tadié, *Proust*, 280, n. 3. Had Proust wanted the letters back in order to use them in his novel? This is Kolb's thesis. If he is right—the fact that Proust preserved this letter may be an important indication of his intention to use it in the novel—then the novelist had already decided to use Agostinelli as one of the models for Albertine before the pilot's death. See *Corr.* 13: 220–21 and 223, n. 25.

34. The idea that Agostinelli drowned because "he had never learned to swim" apparently originated with Painter, who does not cite a source for this information. See George D. Painter, *Marcel Proust*, vol. 2, *The Later Years*, Boston: Little, Brown, 1965, 213. This volume is hereafter cited as Painter, *Proust 2*. Vigneron says that the young aviator was known to be a good swimmer. In fact, none of the earlier accounts say that Agostinelli could not swim. For press accounts of Agostinelli's death, see Vigneron, "Genèse de *Swann*," 339; *Corr.* 13: 242, n. 3.

35. The Narrator learns of Albertine's death in a telegram sent by Mme Bontemps (*Search* 5: 642).

36. Albertine has mysterious rings that bear eagles with spread wings and her initial, *A*, which, when inverted, resembles the *V* symbol for velocity. See *Search* 5: 75, 623–24.

37. *Corr.* 13: 238.

38. *Corr.* 13: 225 and n. 2.

39. *SL* 3: 260.

40. *Corr.* 13: 241, 243; *SL* 3: 267.

41. *SL* 3: 265.

42. *Corr.* 13: 228 and n. 3.

43. *SL* 3: 267–68. In a letter to Émile Straus, written three days after Agostinelli's death, Proust called Agostinelli an "extraordinary person who possessed perhaps the greatest intellectual gifts I have ever known." *SL* 3: 261. Cf. *Search* 5: 668.

44. *Corr.* 13: 239.

45. *SL* 3: 293.

46. *Corr.* 13: 228. *SL* 3: 261. Proust made the same remark to Gautier-Vignal. See Louis Gautier-Vignal, *Proust connu et inconnu*, Paris: Laffont, 1976, 243. The Narrator's guilty feelings over Albertine's death are harder to justify than Proust's regarding Agostinelli's. There is a direct reference in the novel to the guilt the writer felt over the aviator's death in the aftermath of Albertine's death: "From my prison she had escaped to go and kill herself on a horse which but for me she would not have owned." *Search* 5: 674.

47. *SL* 3: 264.
48. *SL* 3: 268. See *Search* 4: 479–80.
49. *SL* 3: 270.
50. *Corr.* 13: 254.
51. My account is based primarily on Martin Gilbert's in *The First World War: A Complete History*, New York: Holt, 1994, 16.
52. *SL* 3: 271.
53. *SL* 3: 272–73.
54. *Corr.* 13: 278.
55. *Search* 6: 157.
56. *Corr.* 13: 290 and 291, n. 3.
57. Daudet, *Soixante Lettres*, 135.
58. *SL* 3: 274.
59. *Corr.* 13: 286.
60. *Corr.* 13: 292, n. 4; Albaret, *Monsieur Proust*, 25.
61. *Lettres retrouvées*, 109–10.
62. Daudet, *Soixante Lettres*, 107.
63. Steegmuller, *Cocteau*, 124.
64. *Corr.* 13: 298, n. 2.
65. In the fall, Proust inquired about Jacques Berge, the young son of Antoinette Félix-Faure and René Berge. Although he was killed at the battle of Charleroi in August, his fate was not known until months later. *Corr.* 13: 324, n. 4.
66. *SL* 3: 276.
67. *SL* 3: 277.
68. *Corr.* 13: 302, n. 2.
69. Albaret, *Monsieur Proust*, 29.
70. *Corr.* 13: 309.
71. *Corr.* 13: 303.
72. Forssgren and Céleste both claimed to have retrieved the medicine. See Albaret, *Monsieur Proust*, 36–37, and Ernest Forssgren, "Les Mémoires d'un valet de chambre," *Cahiers Marcel Proust*, n.s. 12, *Études proustiennes*, II, 119–37.
73. *SL* 3: 278.
74. *Corr.* 13: 305 and n. 3.
75. *Corr.* 13: 327, n. 4. See also *SL* 3: 280, n. 9
76. See *SL* 3: 280–82. This is the fullest statement we have by Proust of his affection for Agostinelli and the relatively brief period of his intense mourning. In November, Proust wrote a similar statement to Lucien; see *SL* 3: 293.
77. See *Search* 2: 254–55; 5: 751.
78. *SL* 3: 282, n. 1
79. For Bize's certificate, see *Corr.* 13: 310, n. 2.
80. *Corr.* 13: 314.
81. *Corr.* 13: 219.
82. *Corr.* 13: xviii, 592.
83. *Corr.* 13: 328.
84. *SL* 3: 284, 285, and 288, n. 2.
85. *SL* 3: 295.

86. *SL* 3: 285–86.
87. Barbara W. Tuchman, *The Guns of August,* New York: Macmillan, 1962, 45.
88. *SL* 3: 293.
89. *Corr.* 13: 349, n. 25.
90. See *SL* 3: 291–92.
91. *Corr.* 13: 351, n. 2.
92. See *Search* 3: 402.
93. *Search* 4: 1.
94. *Search* 6: 102.
95. *Corr.* 13: 345, 360.

23 Shattered Hearts

1. This figure was "more than the total number of British war dead in the whole of the Second World War." See Gilbert, *Complete History,* 123.
2. *Corr.* 15: 15.
3. *Corr.* 14: 121.
4. *Corr.* 14: 63.
5. *Corr.* 14: xvi.
6. Misia soon divorced Edwards and married José-Maria Sert. *Corr.* 14: iv. See *Search* 5: 314–15: "Under the auspices of Princesse Yourbeletief . . . an exquisite supper brought together every night the dancers themselves . . . their director, their designers, the great composers Igor Stravinsky and Richard Strauss, a permanent little nucleus around which . . . the greatest ladies in Paris and foreign royalty were not too proud to gather." See also *Search* 4: 193, where Princesse Yourbeletief is described as "the youthful sponsor of all these new great men," including Bakst, Nijinksy, "and the genius of Stravinsky."
7. *Corr.* 16: 412–13.
8. *Search* 6: 316–17.
9. *Corr.* 14: iv, x. See *Search* 6: 244–52.
10. See *Corr.* 20: 154, 14: x–xi. Tadié finds in Proust's letters of June 1915 to Antoine Bibesco (*Corr.* 14: 144, 221) proof that Proust was a "fine military critic." Tadié, *Marcel Proust,* 744.
11. *Corr.* 14: 23–24, nn. 3, 4.
12. *Corr.* 14: 27.
13. *SL* 3: 295–96.
14. *Corr.* 14: 56.
15. *Corr.* 14: 52–54.
16. *Corr.* 16: 26.
17. *Corr.* 14: 58.
18. Pierre Assouline, *Gaston Gallimard: Un Demi-siècle d'édition française,* Paris: Balland, 1984, 78–79.
19. *Corr.* 15: 148, n. 9.
20. *SL* 3: 298. Proust did use the word *Boche* at least once in a February 27, 1917, letter to Mme Scheikévitch, but not in a context in which he denounced Germans or their culture. See *SL* 3: 365.
21. *SL* 3: 300–301. In May, Proust wrote to Charles d'Alton that he thought about the war night and day, sorrowfully, because he was unable to participate. See *Corr.* 14: 130.

22. *SL* 3: 305 and n. 9.

23. *Search* 6: 510. *Copiator* is Françoise's word for plagiarist.

24. *SL* 3: 298–99, 303–4.

25. See *Corr.* 14: 90, n. 2

26. *SL* 3: 306–7.

27. From a piece by Constantin Ullmann in *Le Monde*, July 6, 1986, quoted by Tadié, *Marcel Proust*, 745, n. 1. Proust's usual practice, as Tadié observes, was to borrow on shares he owned and use the money to speculate by buying futures on other stocks based on tips he had gathered from various sources.

28. *Search* 4: 231–32. This tribute appears in a passage on how the Narrator's mother pronounced certain words. She stressed the second syllable of Fénelon, just as had Proust's mother. Those Marcel loved dearly do not die in the novel; Bertrand's death is not mentioned. This passage is typical of those in which it is virtually impossible to distinguish Proust from the Narrator. In his descent into the "rich mine" of his creative imagination, Proust occasionally brought particles from the other side, from his lived experience, and set them in his book, either neglecting or not caring to submit them to artistic transformation.

29. Morand, *Le Visiteur du soir*, 26.

30. *Search* 6: 226. For Saint-Loup's knowledge of German literature and music (Nietzsche and Wagner), see *Search* 2: 246 and 6: 93. Bonnet sees Proust's denunciation of jingoism as part of his heritage from Darlu. Bonnet, *Darlu*, 25.

31. *SL* 3: 299.

32. Billy, *Lettres et conversations*, 130.

33. Gide apparently approached Proust about the possibility of completing the translation. See Shari Benstock, *No Gifts from Chance: A Biography of Edith Wharton*, New York: Scribner's, 1994, 316, 420.

34. See Michel-Thiriet, *Book*, 196, and Tadié, *Marcel Proust*, 739 and n. 3.

35. Albertine may owe her big cheeks to Agostinelli, who in that regard resembled Proust's mother and Proust himself in the periods when he put on weight. It is impossible to sort out the autobiographical elements in the development of Albertine and Saint-Loup in relation to Agostinelli and Fénelon, and that is as it should be. Although one can enumerate those elements Proust's two friends share with Albertine, it is important to remember that her major function as a character and her relationship to the Narrator were outlined in a note found in the *Carnet 1908* long before Proust fell in love with Agostinelli. The note could describe Proust's experience with Fénelon, but it is also the same as that of anyone who experiences unrequited love or, like Proust and his Narrator, has impossible expectations regarding love. Such expectations can be fulfilled, Proust concluded, only through the creative experience.

36. *Search* 6: 310.

37. *Corr.* 14: 86.

38. *Search* 6: 317.

39. *SL* 3: xvii.

40. *Search* 6: 46–237. This is a rare passage in which Proust provides dates in the novel, mentioning August 1914 and the Narrator's return to Paris in 1916, after a stay in a sanatorium.

41. *Search* 2: 505.

42. *Search* 6: 328. The entire last movement of Proust's "symphonic novel," in which all the

themes are reprised and resolved and in which he gives his artistic credo, begins at *Search* 6: 238. For his explanation of the salutary nature of suffering, see 6: 301–19.

43. Albaret, *Monsieur Proust*, 333.

44. Albaret, *Monsieur Proust*, 106.

45. Albaret, *Monsieur Proust*, 110. See also 90: "What was so marvelous was that with him there were moments when I felt I was his mother, and others when I felt I was his child."

46. Albaret, *Monsieur Proust*, 276–77.

47. *Corr.* 14: 96.

48. Albaret, *Monsieur Proust*, 111–12.

49. *Corr.* 14: 107–8 and n. 4.

50. *Corr.* 14: 109–10.

51. *Corr.* 14: 105. Proust also deplored Léontine's indiscretion in gossiping with the servants in the building. See Albaret, *Monsieur Proust*, 112.

52. Albaret, *Monsieur Proust*, 112.

53. *Corr.* 14: 164.

54. *SL* 3: 340.

55. Albaret, *Monsieur Proust*, 184.

56. *Corr.* 14: 135, 137, 140. In 1916 Proust asked Adèle Larivière, traveling in the south, to sign his name in the book in the church of Saint-Pierre in Monte Carlo at the mass for the anniversary of Agostinelli's death. See *Corr.* 15: 175.

57. Gilbert, *Complete History,* 157, 166–67.

58. *Search* 6: 120–21.

59. *Corr.* 14: 173–74.

60. *Corr.* 14: 247 and 248, n. 2.

61. Albaret, *Monsieur Proust*, 44.

62. See *Corr.* 15: 213, 247.

63. See *Marcel Proust–Gaston Gallimard: Correspondance,* edited by Pascal Fouché, Paris: Gallimard, 1989, 28, n. 3, and *SL* 3: 359.

64. *Corr.* 16: 23–24, nn. 3, 4. See *SL* 3: 300.

65. *SL* 3: 311. Proust had become disillusioned with Joseph Reinach when the chronicler wrote him a letter stating that he could not be certain whether Proust was sick. From that time forward, Proust had only disparaging comments about Reinach's war columns. His admiration of Reinach's history of the Dreyfus Affair remained constant. See *Corr.* 14: 33, 36.

66. *Corr.* 14: 166, 167 and n. 2.

67. See *Corr.* 14: 169, 171.

68. *Corr.* 14: 156. When Blanche's war letters were published, Proust declared them "a masterpiece," a quality, he told Blanche, that he had not seen while reading the proofs. *Corr.* 14: 199 and n. 4. This appraisal sounds like a Proustification.

69. Blanche described this visit in "Quelques instantanés," 58–59. Billy also heard Proust express his sorrow over being isolated by his illness from active life. Billy, "Amitié," 38. Blanche reflected that for Proust the "front" was a darkened bedroom with "fumigations, drugs, gossips, and notebooks to blacken with his handwriting in order to finish his work."

70. Blanche, "Quelques instantanés," 58. Emphasis and ellipses are Blanche's.

71. *Corr.* 14: 162, 177–78.

72. *SL* 3: 314.

73. *SL* 3: 316, n. 5. Greffulhe's infidelities to his beautiful wife are reflected in the duc de Guermantes's many open affairs with society ladies.

74. *SL* 3: 315–16, 317.

75. *SL* 3: 317–18 and n. 2. See *Corr.* 14: 188, n. 4. The Montesquiou quotation is from *Les Pas effacés*, Paris: Émile Paul, 1923, 2: 284.

76. *Corr.* 14: 188.

77. *Corr.* 20: 372.

78. These were the terms Proust used in 1921 to describe Montesquiou's verbal fireworks. *Corr.* 20: 192.

79. *Corr.* 14: 189, 194.

80. *Corr.* 14: 201.

81. Tadié, *Marcel Proust,* 732. *Corr.* 15: 32, n. 8. See *Corr.* 15: 31.

82. *Search* 5: 689.

83. *SL* 3: 301.

84. *Corr.* 15: 249, n. 2.

85. *SL* 3: 318–19 and n. 5. *Corr.* 14: 207.

86. *Corr.* 14: 228.

87. Robert Soupault, "Robert Proust, frère de Marcel," *BMP* 17 (1967): 558.

88. *Corr.* 14: 207, 19: 688.

89. *Corr.* 15: 53.

90. Robert Proust was promoted to the rank of commandant on January 16, 1916; see *Corr.* 15: 205.

91. *Corr.* 14: 209.

92. *Corr.* 14: 211–13.

93. *Corr.* 14: 215.

94. *Search* 1: 94–95.

95. *SL* 3: 320.

96. *SL* 3: 323, 324, and n. 3.

97. *Corr.* 14: 230.

98. *Corr.* 14: xi–xii. In a February 1916 letter Proust gave the interest rate as 8 percent. *SL* 3: 334.

99. *Corr.* 14: 244–45.

100. See *Corr.* 14: 257–60 and Tadié, *Marcel Proust,* 744–46. See also *Corr.* 14: 257, 259.

101. See *SL* 3: 325–29.

102. In the letter to Mme Scheikévitch, Proust copied passages from his notebooks (*Cahiers* 55, 56), which contained drafts for future volumes of the *Search;* see *Corr.* 14: 286, n. 16.

103. See Jean Milly, *La Prisonnière,* Paris: GF-Flammarion, 1984, 12–13. There are other traces of "Albertine" episodes in *Carnet 1908.* See nn. 21, 77.

104. See *Carnet 1908,* 48 and n. 5, 135–36, n. 23.

105. Henri Bonnet, *Les Amours et la sexualité de Proust,* Paris: Nizet, 1985, 47–48. Tadié makes the same point; see *Proust,* 269–70. Kolb notes that the episode of the refused kiss belonged to a character named Charlotte in *Jean Santeuil* but was given to Albertine in the *Search,* leading him to conclude: "Charlotte was . . . a model for Albertine long before Agostinelli, whom Proust did not meet until 1907." Kolb, "Historique du premier roman," 247.

106. *Search* 5: 607.

107. *Search* 6: 7. See *Search* 5: 874, where Proust states what he calls "the general law of oblivion," when the Narrator realizes that he has ceased to love and mourn Albertine.

108. *SL* 3: 335.

109. *Corr.* 14: 290–91, nn. 6, 12.

110. *SL* 3: 335.

111. Jullian, *Montesquiou,* 205.

112. *Corr.* 13: 298, n. 8.

113. Tadié, *Marcel Proust,* 744.

114. *Corr.* 14: 176.

115. *Corr.* 14: 296.

116. Albaret does not mention Bardac in her chapter about the young men with whom Proust was rumored to have been in love. But Céleste was well aware that Humphries belonged to the Sodom side. See Albaret, *Monsieur Proust,* 185–98, 240.

117. In early September, Proust wrote Lauris that "a charming attaché from the French embassy in London who knows many of your friends (and knew poor Bertrand) is in Paris for four days and would like to meet you as well as Gide." See *Corr.* 14: 219.

118. This account of the first encounter between Proust and Morand is taken from the latter's memoir, *Le Visiteur du soir,* 9–30.

119. Paul Morand, "Notes," *NRF Hommage,* 93.

120. Morand, *Le Visiteur du soir,* 11–12, 22.

121. Epigraph from the first questionnaire, *CSB* 5: 333.

122. For Albaret on Le Cuziat, see *Monsieur Proust,* 192–93. In the *Search,* the Narrator gives some of the furniture inherited from Aunt Léonie to a female brothel. *Search* 2: 208.

123. See *Search* 6: 182–85, 195–201.

124. Proust shows the same compassion for his characters. Even the detestable Verdurins are the donors of anonymous gifts. *Search* 5: 436, 440. The Narrator attributes his inability to condemn others to the influence of his mother and grandmother. *Search* 2: 455.

125. Bonnet, *Amours de Proust,* 79–85.

126. Bonnet admitted that the key word in the notebook, which he transcribed as *pleasure,* meaning orgasm, is illegible and therefore dubious. Bonnet, *Amours de Proust,* 80, n. 1. In one passage of the novel, the Narrator has a nightmare in which he performs a sadistic act against his parents; such visions are, he says, inherent in the family picture album. *Search* 3: 109.

127. André Gide, *Ainsi soit-il,* in *Journal, 1939–49, Souvenirs,* Paris: Pléiade, 1966, 1223.

128. *Search* 1: 331.

129. See Maurice Sachs, *Le Sabbat,* Paris: Gallimard, 1960, 285, 287. Sachs's book, which reads like memoirs, bears the disclaiming subtitle "roman" (novel). Sachs was for a time a protégé of Cocteau and Gide who influenced Gallimard to hire Sachs in 1933. Sachs thought nothing of stealing original drawings and manuscripts from his friends, selling them, and keeping the money for himself. Among the books sold by Sachs were autographed editions of Proust and Apollinaire. When he was caught at such thievery, he forged a letter from Cocteau authorizing him to sell rare papers and editions. It was not long before the furious Gaston Gallimard fired Sachs. See Assouline, *Gaston Gallimard,* 175–77. For more on Sachs's escapades and misadventures, see Henri Raczymow's biography, *Maurice Sachs ou Les Travaux forcés de la frivolité,* Paris: Gallimard, 1988.

130. George Painter says that Proust had the act of spitting performed on a photograph of his

mother and cites as proof an article by Sachs written on the occasion of Albert Le Cuziat's death. Contrary to Painter's assertions, however, there is nothing in the sources cited by him that states that such a ritual of profanation was performed on a photograph of Proust's mother. See Painter, *Proust* 2: 268–69. Painter gives the wrong month for Sachs's reminiscence, "Historiette," which appeared under the rubric "L'Air du mois." It was in the May 1938 issue (pp. 863–64)—not July—of *NRF*. Sachs does not mention Proust's mother as a victim of profanation in either account, but in *Le Sabbat* he does speak of the *Search* as a shrine to Marcel's mother. See *Le Sabbat*, 285, 287.

131. Albaret, *Monsieur Proust*, 196.
132. Traces of this theme are found in the title "Le Visage maternel dans un petit-fils débauché," used by Proust in *Le Carnet de 1908*, the first notebook of the *Search*. In Kolb's introduction to *Carnet 1908*, he traces this theme for us, as Proust developed it in the *Search*. See *Carnet 1908*, 15. In a passage in *Sodom and Gomorrah*, Charlus is described as having a woman's soul within a man's body. Proust writes that profanation of the mother merits a special chapter: "Besides, can one entirely separate M. de Charlus's appearance from the fact that sons, who do not always take after their fathers, even without being inverts and even though seekers after women, may consummate upon their faces the profanation of their mothers? But let us not consider here a subject that deserves a chapter to itself: the Profanation of the Mother." *Search* 4: 416. We do not know what Proust intended to write in this chapter, but the Vinteuil/Mlle Vinteuil episode probably provides a clue.
133. See Gautier-Vignal, *Proust connu et inconnu*, 246–47.

24 A Fortuny Gown

1. *SL* 3: 330.
2. *Corr.* 21: 667.
3. *Corr.* 15: 200–201, 298.
4. Berl wrote to Proust from "Hartmanswillerkopf, a peak in the southern Vosges, the scene of bitter fighting in early 1915, culminating in a French victory on March 26." See *SL* 3: 332 and nn. 1, 2, 6.
5. *Corr.* 16: 18.
6. From Berl's interview in the documentary film *Portrait-Souvenir*. See Tadié, *Marcel Proust*, 764, n. 4; Diesbach *Proust*, 624.
7. *Corr.* 15: 43, n. 2.
8. *SL* 3: 332. *Search* 2: 668–75.
9. See *Recherche* 2 (NP): 264–65 and n. 1, 268, n. 2
10. *Corr.* 15: 257. The little train appears in the Narrator's two stays in Balbec: the first in *Within a Budding Grove*, the second in *Sodom and Gomorrah*: "Albertine would wait for me . . . upon the beach and we would return together after dark. I went to take the train on the little local railway, of which I had picked up from Albertine and her friends all the nicknames current in the district, where it was known as the *Twister* because of its numberless windings, the *Crawler* because the train never seemed to move, the *Transatlantic* because of a horrible siren which it sounded to clear people off the line, the *Decauville* and the *Funi*, albeit there was nothing funicular about it but because it climbed the cliff, and, though not strictly speaking a Decauville, had a 60 centimetre gauge, the

B.A.G. because it ran between Balbec and Grattevast via Angerville, the *Tram* and the
T.S.N. because it was a branch of the Tramways of Southern Normandy" (*Search* 4: 249).
See also *Search* 2: 609, 623. The little train that ran along the coastline of Lake Geneva resembles the train in the novel. Proustian geography usually consisted of real elements to
which he added many of his own invention or relocated on his own fictional map. What
interested him most was the etymology of place names rather than their geographical location. For details and references, see *Recherche* 3 (NP): 180, n. 4. In his preface for Rita de
Maugny, Proust describes the train that stopped at Thonon in terms similar to those he
used for the little train at Balbec. See "Au royaume de bistouri," *CSB* 5: 567.

11. *Search* 6: 53.
12. See *SL* 3: 334–35.
13. *SL* 3: 336, n. 6.
14. In May 1915 Proust had expressed a similar interest in Fortuny, and Mme Straus offered
    to lend him one of her Fortuny coats. Proust declined the offer, apparently because he
    needed to see dressing-gowns, as he later explained to Mme de Madrazo. *SL* 3: 335.
15. *SL* 3: 341.
16. For passages in which Proust used the information regarding Fortuny's garments, see
    Search 5: 497–501, 531, 538, 554.
17. See *Corr.* 15: 111, 10: 358–59 and n. 2. Daudet, *Soixante Lettres*, 164–67. *Recherche* 3 (NP):
    424, n. 1.
18. *Search* 5: 877.
19. On recovering from the loss of Albertine, the Narrator observes: "I had finally ceased to
    love Albertine. So that this love . . . had ended too, after having proved an exception to it,
    by succumbing, like my love for Gilberte, to the general law of oblivion." *Search* 5: 873–74.
20. *Recherche* 4 (NP): 315–34, 1167.
21. *Search* 6: 106.
22. *Corr.* 15: 122–23.
23. *Corr.* 15: 91–92.
24. *Corr.* 15: 119–20.
25. *Corr.* 15: 143–44.
26. *Corr.* 15: 126; *SL* 3: 344.
27. *Corr.* 15: 136–37.
28. *SL* 3: 350.
29. *Corr.* 15: 159–60.
30. See *Corr.* 15: 186–87, 189, n. 3, and 232.
31. *SL* 3: 356. The Crédit Industriel had claimed it could not sell a single share of Doubowaia
    Balka. By late August, Hauser had managed to sell sixty thousand francs' worth and to in-
    crease Proust's annual income by approximately thirty-two hundred francs. See *Corr.*
    15: 274.
32. *SL* 3: 340.
33. *Corr.* 15: 61.
34. *Corr.* 15: 74.
35. This account of the private concerts given in Proust's apartment by the Poulet Quartet is
    based on interviews with Gaston Poulet and his viola player Amable Massis, published in
    "Proust et la musique," *BMP* 11 (1916): 424–34, and on Albaret, *Monsieur Proust*, 327–32.
    Massis tells a similar story of Proust ringing his doorbell around midnight. Céleste's rec-

ollections are at odds on several points with the musicians' and with Proust's letter to Raymond Pétain in April 1916. Céleste insisted that only one such private concert took place, in 1920, when Proust was living in the rue Hamelin apartment. This letter indicates that she was mistaken. Proust's letter and the musicians' memoirs all indicate 1916 as the date and that more than one private concert took place. For details about the members of the Poulet Quartet, see *Corr.* 15: 79, n. 7 and 85, nn. 2, 3, 7–9.

36. In his recollection, Massis identified the driver as Odilon Albaret, but that seems unlikely, for in 1916 Albaret was in the army, not driving for Proust. Céleste scoffed at the notion that Proust would have taken the eiderdown (one he never used because the stuffing bothered his allergy) and a bowl of mashed potatoes in a car with him. Albaret, *Monsieur Proust,* 330.

37. On what was apparently another occasion, Proust accompanied the musicians and treated them to supper, Céleste thought, at the Brasserie Lipp, where he continued to ask them questions about the music. Albaret, *Monsieur Proust,* 331.

38. *Corr.* 15: 77–78.

39. Bardac asked Reynaldo Hahn about the genesis of the little phrase: "Most of it," said Reynaldo, "is a passage from Saint-Saëns's Sonata in D Minor, but Marcel has embroidered it with things he has remembered from Franck, Fauré, and even Wagner." Maurois, *Genius,* 270.

40. *Search* 2: 141–42. In this passage, Proust named Beethoven's Twelfth, Thirteenth, Fourteenth and Fifteenth Quartets.

41. *Search* 4: 555. In 1918 Proust wrote Montesquiou that "the most beautiful music he knew was the intoxicating finale of Beethoven's quartet XV," which he characterized as "delirium of a convalescent who would, moreover, die a short time later." *Corr.* 17: 109.

42. *Search* 1: 497. In the continuation of the passage, the author observes that this richness will be condemned to nothingness if one does not undertake a diligent and arduous exploration of one's inner being. Swann and Charlus, who both act as foils to the Narrator, are unable to carry out such a difficult task. Only after many postponements and wrong turns does the Narrator regain his will and understand clearly his mission as a creative person.

43. This varient is found in one of Proust's notebooks (*Cahier* 57), quoted in Milly, *La Prisonnière,* 41.

44. Kolb described Pétain as a "young violinist," *Corr.* 15: vi, but Proust refers to him only as a viola player. See *Corr.* 15: 77, 17: 393.

45. Céleste recalled that Massis visited Proust several times in the middle of the night at boulevard Haussmann to discuss music. On those occasions Proust asked her to make fried potatoes, which Massis washed down with champagne or cider. Albaret, *Monsieur Proust,* 328. There is no mention of Raymond Pétain in her memoirs.

46. This incident is related by Kolb in his foreword to *Corr.* 15: vi.

47. *Search* 5: 382–83. Enesco, Capet, and Thibaud were three of the era's most accomplished violinists.

48. *Corr.* 15: v–vi.

49. For the Paris street cries, see *Search* 5: 148–50, 161, 175–76. No more is known about Proust's relationship with Pétain, except that during the war years the musician continued to visit 102 boulevard Haussmann. See *Corr.* 17: 393.

50. *Corr.* 15: 17.

51. *Search* 5: 339.
52. *Search* 5: 345.
53. *Search* 5: 206, 343.
54. Gide also wrote in his diary that he had promised himself to "relate the visit at length" in his journal. Unfortunately, the next morning he "no longer had the heart to do it." Gide, *Journal*, 543.
55. Gallimard, who chafed at Proust's references to the NRF's rejection of *Swann's Way*, later denied having had anything to do with that decision.
56. See *Proust-Gallimard*, 26.
57. *SL* 3: 339–40.
58. *Proust-Gallimard*, 40.
59. *Corr.* 15: xix, 732–33.
60. See *Proust-Gallimard*, 41, n. 3, and *Corr.* 15: 17.
61. *SL* 3: 345–48.
62. *SL* 3: 348.
63. *Corr.* 15: 213, n. 4.
64. See *Corr.* 15: 144–46.
65. *SL* 3: 354–55.
66. *SL* 3: 357–58.
67. *Corr.* 19: 739–40.
68. *Corr.* 15: 259.
69. *SL* 3: 358–60.
70. *Corr.* 16: 279.
71. *Corr.* 15: xv, 295–97.
72. *Corr.* 19: 752–53.
73. *Corr.* 15: 205.
74. *Corr.* 15: 257. Céleste and Céline were extremely jealous of each other. See Albaret, *Monsieur Proust*, 41–44.
75. *Proust-Gallimard*, 60 and n. 1.
76. *Corr.* 16: 87.
77. Albaret, *Monsieur Proust*, 334.
78. Interview in *Portrait-Souvenir*.
79. Albaret, *Monsieur Proust*, 333–35.
80. There are two records of Céleste's account of this exciting moment. The first is in the 1962 documentary *Portrait-Souvenir: Marcel Proust;* the second is in her memoirs. In both versions the contents of the conversation with Proust are the same, but the film interview is more lively. I have combined the versions here. Excerpts of Céleste relating this incident and speaking about Proust's health and eating habits can be seen in the 1993 documentary made for American television: *Marcel Proust: A Writer's Life*, produced by William C. Carter, George Wolfe, Sarah B. Patton, and Sarah Mondale, directed by Sarah Mondale, 1992.
81. It was while attempting to date this event that Céleste wrote she particularly regretted not having kept a diary during the years she was with Proust. Albaret, *Monsieur Proust*, 335. It is impossible to date this moment, but it most likely occurred well before 1922, which is the date Tadié, following Céleste, accepts. Tadié, *Marcel Proust*, 887, 892. Duchêne favors, as do I, an earlier date. He believes that Proust wrote "the end" in 1919. Duchêne, *L'Impossible Proust*, 751. No one knows for certain; I believe that Proust wrote "the end" be-

tween 1916 and 1919, based on *Corr.* 16: 417 (letter to Gallimard of November 1916) and 18: 226 (letter to Gallimard of May 1919).

82. *Corr.* 16: 417.
83. Proust revised and expanded *The Guermantes Way* for the next several years. In June 1919 he received the first proofs of this volume, which was printed by August 17, 1920.
84. *Corr.* 19: 758-59.
85. *Corr.* 15: 342.
86. Albaret, *Monsieur Proust,* 265.

25 Proust of the Ritz

1. *Corr.* 16: 32.
2. *Corr.* 16: 15.
3. *Corr.* 16: 29
4. *Corr.* 19: 762, n. 2. See *Proust-Gallimard,* 76, n. 3.
5. *Proust-Gallimard,* 77-78.
6. *Corr.* 19: 761.
7. See Diesbach, *Proust,* 615-16. Tadié, *Marcel Proust,* 768.
8. *Corr.* 16: 56.
9. *SL* 3: 366.
10. *Corr.* 16: 15.
11. Morand, *Le Visiteur du soir,* 54-55.
12. *Corr.* 17: 173.
13. See *SL* 3: 380 and *Corr.* 16: 223.
14. *Corr.* 16: 145.
15. *Corr.* 16: xvii.
16. *Corr.* 16: 50.
17. *SL* 3: 370, n. 7.
18. *SL* 3: 368-69.
19. *Corr.* 16: 381.
20. *Corr.* 16: 380-81.
21. *SL* 3: 371.
22. See *Corr.* 16: 16-17, and 75, n. 2.
23. *Corr.* 16: 83.
24. *Corr.* 16: 114-16.
25. *Corr.* 16: 172.
26. *SL* 3: 373.
27. See *Corr.* 16: xiii, 250.
28. *Corr.* 16: 123.
29. *SL* 3: 396-97.
30. *SL* 3: 354, n. 1.
31. *SL* 3: 353. In July 1916 Berry had called on Proust, who had invited him after receiving Berry's gift. The two men did not begin corresponding and meeting on a fairly regular basis until 1917. See *Corr.* 15: 18.
32. Benstock, *No Gifts from Chance,* 49.
33. *Corr.* 16: 123.

34. Benstock, *No Gifts from Chance*, 49, 400.
35. *Corr.* 16: 103.
36. *SL* 3: 389, n. 6, and 395. *Corr.* 16: 190, n. 9.
37. *Corr.* 16: 103.
38. See Painter, *Proust* 2: 276–77.
39. Arthur Mugnier, *Journal de l'Abbé Mugnier, 1879–1939*, edited by Marcel Billot, with a preface by Ghislain de Diesbach, notes by Jean d'Hendecourt, Paris: Mercure de France, 1985, 171.
40. Mugnier, *Journal*, 104. Ellipses are Mugnier's.
41. Mugnier, *Journal*, 16.
42. This description is based on Diesbach's preface to Mugnier, *Journal*, 9–10.
43. Mugnier, *Journal*, 81.
44. See Mugnier, *Journal*, 59–77.
45. For Céleste's recollections of Proust's encounters with Mugnier, see Albaret, *Monsieur Proust*, 126–27.
46. Mugnier, *Journal*, 309–10.
47. From Blanche's review of *Swann's Way* in *L'Écho de Paris*, April 15, 1914, quoted in Lhomeau and Coelho, *Recherche d'un éditeur*, 330.
48. *Search* 6: 327.
49. From Morand's diary, quoted in *Corr.* 16: 105, n. 4.
50. *Corr.* 16: 284–95. Proust uses the term "eternal morning" to characterize the impression made by Vinteuil's septet. *Search* 5: 333.
51. *Corr.* 16: 224.
52. *Corr.* 16: 166, n. 7.
53. *SL* 3: 378 and nn. 1, 3.
54. *Corr.* 16: 147, n. 8.
55. Mugnier, *Journal*, 312–13.
56. *Corr.* 16: 19.
57. *SL* 3: 388–89.
58. *SL* 3: 383 and 384, n. 1.
59. *SL* 3: 384–85.
60. *Corr.* 16: 384.
61. *Corr.* 16: 174.
62. This account is based on Proust's description of the evening in a letter shortly afterward to Mme Straus. See *SL* 3: 391–93.
63. Proust makes a similar observation in the *Search*: "In the survivors of battle . . . or in living men hypnotised or dead men summoned by a medium, the only effect of contact with mystery is to increase, if that be possible, the insignificance of things people say." *Search* 6: 97.
64. The Germans had launched an air raid on Le Bourget, the first in the Paris region since January 1916. *SL* 3: 393, n. 9.
65. The Gothas were first used on May 25 in an air raid on London. See Gilbert, *Complete History*, 334.
66. See *Search* 6: 97–100.
67. *SL* 3: 395.
68. *Corr.* 16: 244–45.

69. *Corr.* 16: 213, n. 3.
70. See *SL* 3: 396–98. Anna de Noailles apparently had thanked Proust for her copy of *Swann's Way.* Her letter is missing. See *Corr.* 12: 336.
71. *Corr.* 16: 227.
72. *SL* 3: 404–5.
73. See Albaret, *Monsieur Proust*, 293–300.
74. *SL* 3: 395.
75. *Corr.* 16: 245.
76. *Corr.* 16: 247.
77. *Corr.* 16: 257.
78. *Proust-Gallimard*, 88.
79. *Corr.* 19: 764–65.
80. *Proust-Gallimard*, 91.
81. *Corr.* 16: 280–81 and 282, n. 6.
82. *Corr.* 16: 272.
83. *Corr.* 16: 302.
84. *Corr.* 16: 287.
85. See *Corr.* 16: 339–40.
86. *Corr.* 16: 305 and 315, n. 3.
87. See *Corr.* 16: 311–12, 314.
88. See *Corr.* 16: 318–19.
89. See *Corr.* 16: 208, 254–55.
90. Gilbert, *Complete History*, 370.
91. Soupault, "Robert Proust," 555. Proust later wrote Hauser that although Robert had been exhausted after nearly four years at the front, he had wanted to go to Italy for the Isonzo offensive. See *Corr.* 17: 123.
92. *Corr.* 16: 382, n. 11.
93. *SL* 3: 410. See letter of December 6 to Morand: "My sister-in-law has received the authorization from her husband, which apparently might be necessary. She has also obtained a doctor's certificate explaining the health reasons which oblige her to spend the winter in Rome." *SL* 3: 408–9.
94. *Corr.* 16: 353.
95. *Corr.* 16: i.
96. *Corr.* 16: 289.
97. *Corr.* 16: 323–24.
98. *Corr.* 16: 329, n. 6.
99. See Albaret, *Marcel Proust*, 187, 240. Proust dined occasionally with Bardac and Humphries at Ciro's. See *Corr.* 16: 329, n. 2.
100. In the manuscript for *Le Temps retrouvé*, the character is called Bobby. See *Recherche* 3 (OP): 702, n. 1.
101. *Corr.* 16: 330–31.
102. *Corr.* 16: 333.
103. *SL* 3: 408–9. Proust was referring to a passage published in the *NRF,* July 1, 1914. *Corr.* 16: 346, n. 8.
104. *SL* 3: 407.
105. *Corr.* 16: 350.

106. *Corr.* 16: 351, 363.
107. *Corr.* 16: 367.
108. *Corr.* 16: 365–66.
109. *Corr.* 16: 369–70.
110. *Corr.* 16: 142, n. 2.
111. *Corr.* 16: 23.
112. Tadié, *Marcel Proust,* 767, n. 2.
113. *Corr.* 16: 374. In May 1918 Morand was transferred to Madrid, where he would serve as interim attaché to the ambassador. See *Corr.* 17: 272, n. 12.
114. *SL* 3: 414 and n. 1.

26 A Walk in the Snow

1. *Corr.* 17: 33, n. 10.
2. *Corr.* 17: 42–43.
3. *Corr.* 17: 39–40.
4. *Proust-Gallimard,* 100.
5. *Corr.* 17: 69.
6. Blanche included the essay in the second part of his series on painters, published in 1920. *Corr.* 17: 61, n. 6.
7. *Corr.* 17: 81–83.
8. *Corr.* 17: 84.
9. *Corr.* 17: 64 and 67, n.2.
10. See Gide, *Journal,* 643–44. Gide had a long and distinguished career, winning the Nobel Prize for literature in 1947. He died in 1951 at the age of eighty-two.
11. *Corr.* 17: 75–76. According to Mme Scheikévitch's memoirs, Proust told her one evening at Cabourg in 1912 that Borodin's Third Symphony had given him the idea for the famous "little phrase" in Vinteuil's sonata. Marcel Proust, *Lettres à Madame Scheikévitch,* Paris: Librairie des Champs-Élysées, 1928, 26. Kolb observed, however, that Proust never gave this source to anyone else. See *Corr.* 17: 78, n. 10. Perhaps Proust was trying to flatter her by selecting a Russian composer as the primary inspiration.
12. *Corr.* 17: 78–79.
13. *Corr.* 17: 88–89 and n. 5.
14. *Corr.* 17: 89–90, 92, and 171, n. 3.
15. *Corr.* 17: 101, n. 7. See *Corr.* 17: 100, nn. 12, 13.
16. *Corr.* 17: 18, 98–99. See Mugnier, *Journal,* 327–28.
17. *Corr.* 17: 96–97 and nn. 7, 8.
18. *Search* 6: 47.
19. Gilbert, *Complete History,* 396. *Corr.* 17: 98, n. 10, and 282, n. 5.
20. *Corr.* 17: 171, n. 3.
21. This is Proust's account as related to Mme Straus in a letter written shortly after the air raid. See *Corr.* 17: 104.
22. *Search* 6: 127.
23. *Corr.* 17: 18, 107–8.
24. *Corr.* 17: 113.
25. *Corr.* 17: v, 152.

26. Gilbert, *Complete History,* 403.

27. Details about this shelling are from Gilbert, *Complete History,* 407.

28. *Corr.* 17: vi and 161, n.8.

29. *Corr.* 17: 159, 161, n. 7.

30. *Corr.* 17: vii, 167, 176, 179.

31. *Corr.* 17: 169–70.

32. *Corr.* 17: 173, 174, n. 4.

33. *Corr.* 17: 178, 190–91.

34. *Corr.* 17: 178, 203.

35. Tadié, *Marcel Proust,* 802, n. 1.

36. See *Corr.* 17: 327–28. Proust does not give their names.

37. *Corr.* 17: 189–90.

38. See *Corr.* 17: 193–95.

39. All quotations from this letter can be found in Curtiss, *Letters,* 362–64.

40. Proust may have forgotten that he had made similar revelations to Antoine Bibesco in the fall of 1915: "The Vinteuil sonata is not Franck's." If Bibesco was interested, Proust would tell him "all the works which 'posed' for my sonata. Thus the 'little phrase' is a phrase from a sonata for piano and violin by Saint-Saëns which I'll hum to you (tremble!); the restless tremolos above it come from a Wagner prelude; the opening with its plangent rise and fall, is from the Franck sonata; the more spacious passages from Fauré's *Ballade,* etc., etc., etc. And people think that these things are written at random, 'off the cuff.'" See *SL* 3: 322. In any case, Proust's closest friends had long known the origin of the little phrase.

41. *Search* 1: 465.

42. *Corr.* 17: 207–8, 218, n. 2, and 250.

43. See *Corr* 17: 212–17. Many of the ideas expressed in the letter to Hauser come to the Narrator, near the end of his quest, as revelations when he finally understands the nature of his life's experience and its relation to his vocation as a writer.

44. *Search* 3: 414.

45. Proust himself did not know at this point exactly how the remaining sections of the *Search* would be divided into volumes. His count of volumes thus remained hypothetical.

46. See *Corr.* 17: 220–21, 222, n. 3.

47. *Corr.* 17: 234, 261. In June, when Gallimard transported the "principal paintings" from his father's valuable collection to safekeeping in Bénerville, he offered to take Proust's manuscripts with him and put them safely away with the paintings. See *Proust-Gallimard,* 114.

48. *Corr.* 17: 274–75, 276–77.

49. *Corr.* 17: 286, n. 7.

50. *Corr.* 17: 270.

51. *Corr.* 17: 281. On May 21 Proust walked home from Mme Hennessy's during another air raid. *Corr.* 17: 20.

52. Albaret, *Monsieur Proust,* 93–94.

53. *Corr.* 17: 292.

54. *Search* 6: 88–89, 95–96.

55. *Search* 6: 154.

56. *Search* 6: 275.

57. *Corr.* 17: 282.

58. See *Corr.* 17: 279–80 and n. 8.

59. *Corr.* 17: 286, n. 2.

60. *SL* 1: 181, n. 4.

61. *Corr.* 17: 331–32.

62. *Corr.* 17: 284–85.

63. *Corr.* 17: 507, n. 5; *Proust-Gallimard*, 113 and n. 1.

64. *Corr.* 17: 303, 305.

65. This title was listed in the Grasset edition of *Swann* announcing the remaining two volumes as part of *Time Regained*. See *Proust-Gallimard*, 84, n. 1. See also *Corr.* 12: 368, n. 2.

66. *Corr.* 17: 310–11.

67. *Corr.* 17: 315.

68. *Corr.* 19: 776 and n. 2, 19: 778.

69. See *Corr.* 17: 262.

70. *Corr.* 17: 290.

71. According to Céleste, Proust did understand how valuable the copies would be one day and told her, "What a pity I haven't anywhere to store them. They will sell one day, I can tell you." Albaret, *Monsieur Proust*, 312.

72. *Corr.* 17: 21.

73. Proust sent the Saint-Simon parody to the *NRF* on October 1. *Corr.* 17: 23.

74. *Corr.* 17: 281.

75. *Corr.* 17: 322.

76. Gilbert, *Complete History*, 540.

77. *Corr.* 17: 22 and 324, n. 3.

78. *Corr.* 17: 335 and 380, n. 3.

79. *Corr.* 17: 336–37, 339.

80. See *Corr.* 17: 340, 19: 782.

81. *Corr.* 17: 351–53, 361.

82. *Corr.* 17: 22, 343 and nn. 5–9.

83. Gilbert, *Complete History*, 452.

84. *Corr.* 17: 344, n. 10. Proust made a similar reference in an October letter to Ramon Fernandez. In the absence of "the Table of Sala," diners were able to enjoy good service from the waiters, who had not been obliged to flee outside to the place Vendôme because of homosexual advances made by Sala and his companions. *Corr.* 17: 387.

85. *Corr.* 17: 355 and n. 6.

86. Tadié, *Marcel Proust*, 798.

87. This account is taken from Wixler's interview "Proust au Ritz: Souvenirs d'un maître d'hôtel," *Adam International Review* 40, nos. 394–96 (1976): 14–21.

88. *Corr.* 17: xi.

89. *Corr.* 17: 360–61, 363, 384, 483.

90. *Corr.* 17: 367.

91. *Corr.* 17: 371. After the war ended, Proust told Hauser that he did not share Berry's evident hatred of Germans and that Berry's "Germanophobia" did not suit "my temperament or my taste." *Corr.* 17: 491.

92. Soupault, "Robert Proust," 557.

93. *Corr.* 17: 23, 374–75, 384, 392.

94. *Corr.* 17: 383, n. 6.

95. Gilbert, *Complete History*, 478.

96. See *Search* 5: 369, where Charlus says, "Her very eyes say to use 'Forget me not!', for they remind one of those flowers."

97. *Corr.* 17: 456.

98. "L'Affaire Lemoine dans les *Memoires* de Saint-Simon," *CSB* 5: 53.

99. *Corr.* 19: 783–84.

100. *Corr.* 17: 405.

101. *Corr.* 17: 409–11.

102. *Corr.* 17: 423–24.

103. *Corr.* 17: 430–31. Proust later asked Hauser to believe the sincerity of his "feelings of gratitude and affection that theosophy forgoes but which are necessary to the heart of your *evolved* one." *Corr.* 17: 492.

104. *Corr.* 17: 433–34.

105. *Corr.* 17: 415–16.

106. Mary Finaly had married Roger Thomas de Barbarin in 1897. See *SL* 1: 36, n. 3.

107. *Corr.* 17: 427–28, n. 3. The Spanish flu also claimed one of France's most accomplished poets and art critics and a close associate of Picasso's, Guillaume Apollinaire. *Proust-Gallimard*, 135, n. 3.

108. See *Corr.* 17: 435–36, 441–44.

109. Proust's guess was off by two years. *Time Regained* was published in 1927.

110. In Gallimard's absence Lemarié suggested that Proust consult Gide about the deluxe edition, which he did in a letter of November 21, 1918. See *Proust-Gallimard*, 145, n. 2.

111. Marie Gineste (1888–1978); *Corr.* 17: 505.

112. Albaret, *Monsieur Proust*, 114. For the passage inspired by Marie's remark about lives sacrificed for others, see *Search* 4: 334.

113. *Corr.* 17: 448.

114. *Corr.* 17: 457.

115. *Corr.* 17: 452–53, 478–79.

116. *Corr.* 17: 458.

117. *Corr.* 17: 19.

118. *Corr.* 17: 523.

119. *Corr.* 17: 524. Gallimard took *The Guermantes Way* from La Semeuse and entrusted it to Louis Bellenand. See *Corr.* 17: 525, n. 5.

120. Morand, "Notes," 93.

121. *Corr.* 17: 531 and 532, n. 6.

122. See Gilbert, *Complete History*, 541.

123. *Corr.* 17: 123.

27 Homeless

1. *Corr.* 18: 44–45, 75.

2. In a late January letter to Robert de Billy, Proust said he might be put out in the street from one day to the next and quoted Luke 9:58, in which Jesus says, "Foxes have holes, and birds of the air have nests; but the Son of man hath not where to lay his head." Proust quoted from memory the Bible text he had translated from a passage in Ruskin. See *Corr.* 18: 47, nn. 4, 5.

3. *Corr.* 18: 91.

4. *Corr.* 18: 51–54.

5. *Corr.* 18: 109.

6. *Search* 6: 315.

7. *Corr.* 18: 55–56.

8. Berry later told him that in the postwar period modern furnishings were selling better than antiques. *Corr.* 18: 233.

9. The dealer's name was André Imbert; see *Corr.* 18: 281 and 291, n. 3. Over the next several years, Proust called on Mme Catusse and the Strauses to assist him in selling various lots of furnishings.

10. *Corr.* 18: 89.

11. *Corr.* 18: 18.

12. The most important change in the new edition was the removal of Combray from near Chartres to its final location near Reims, so that it would lie in the path of the invading Germans during World War I. The name Doncières appears for the first time as that of the garrison town near Balbec, where the Narrator visits Saint-Loup, who is on military service there. *Recherche* 1 (NP): 1052.

13. *Corr.* 18: 48–49. In March, Proust was still so concerned by the appearance of *Within a Budding Grove* that he had Hahn, who shared his misgivings, write Mme Lemarié regarding the tiny font and the countless missing punctuation marks, saying that it would be a great pity to publish in this condition "a book of such importance." *Corr.* 18: 145.

14. See *Corr.* 18: 77–79 and *CSB* 5: 580. See Diesbach, *Proust,* 649–50.

15. Albaret, *Monsieur Proust,* 227.

16. *Corr.* 18: ii–iii, 90.

17. Benstock, *No Gifts from Chance,* 400.

18. See *Corr.* 18: 113, 116.

19. *Corr.* 18: 20, 122, n. 6.

20. Quoted by Kolb in *Corr.* 18: 123, n. 4.

21. *Corr.* 18: 122, n. 2.

22. Woolf's biographer Hermione Lee sees *Orlando,* in part, as a parody of the Nicolson marriage. See *Virginia Woolf,* New York: Knopf, 1997, 484. Nigel Nicolson recounted the story of his parent's unusual union in *Portrait of a Marriage,* New York: Atheneum, 1973.

23. *Corr.* 18: 135.

24. *Corr.* 18: 137, 138, 157.

25. *Corr.* 18: 142–43.

26. *Corr.* 18: 154.

27. *Corr.* 18: 166 and n. 2. After Proust's death, Schiff wrote a novella, *Céleste,* based on Proust's housekeeper.

28. *Corr.* 18: 165–66 and 167, n. 8. Morand believed that the Schiffs were the only English readers who knew *Swann's Way* from its first French edition. See *Visiteur du soir,* 13. It seems likely that Charles Kenneth Scott-Moncrieff was an early reader of the original edition.

29. *Corr.* 18: 167–68, 196–97.

30. *Corr.* 18: 169.

31. *Corr.* 18: 173, 175–76.

32. *Corr.* 18: 50, n. 6.

33. The Varin-Bernier bank still occupies 102, boulevard Haussmann. In recent years Proust's bedroom, which had become the president's office, has been emptied and opened to visi-

tors, who can judge its dimensions, admire the marble fireplace whose fires warmed Proust, and do something the writer never did: look out the windows. Some of Proust's original bedroom furnishings, including the bed, screen, tables, and lamp, are on display in the reconstituted cork-lined room at the Musée Carnavalet. Proust's neighbor at the Musée Carnavalet, in her own cork-lined bedroom, is Anna de Noailles.

34. *Corr.* 18: 187, n. 6.
35. *Corr.* 18: 177–78, 190, 232.
36. *Corr.* 18: 199–200, 205.
37. Albaret, *Monsieur Proust,* 188.
38. Tadié, *Marcel Proust,* 799, n. 6. See *Search* 4: 534–35, 589.
39. *Corr.* 18: 215, 216–17.
40. See *Corr.* 19: 55.
41. *Corr.* 18: 225–26.
42. *Corr.* 18: 223–24.
43. See Albaret, *Monsieur Proust,* 319–20.
44. *Corr.* 18: 294.
45. *Corr.* 18: 231, 337–38.
46. Albaret, *Monsieur Proust,* 324.
47. For Céleste's description of the notebooks she burned, see Albaret, *Monsieur Proust,* 273–74. Scholars have speculated that the notebooks contained the original volume of *Time Regained* offered to Fasquelle, or the completed version of the essay attacking Sainte-Beuve that Proust proposed to Vallette in 1909, or the manuscripts of *Swann's Way* and *Within a Budding Grove.* See Tadié, *Proust,* 297 and n. 2.
48. He wrote to Mme Garrett, on April 25, that "what I wrote on you are pages that will not be printed, that I may well have burned." See *Corr.* 18: 182.
49. Albaret, *Monsieur Proust,* 322.
50. *Corr.* 18: 248–49.
51. Albaret, *Monsieur Proust,* 324–25.
52. *Corr.* 18: 240–41, 249.
53. *Corr.* 18: 249.
54. Albaret, *Monsieur Proust,* 315.
55. *Corr.* 18: 255.
56. *Corr.* 18: 251–52, 251, n. 2.
57. See *Corr.* 18: 234, 258, and *Proust-Gallimard,* 177–78.
58. *Corr.* 21: 673 and 674, n. 6, and 18: 259, n. 2. There had been a series of strikes, sometimes violent, by workers in many trades in favor of the eight-hour workday.
59. *Corr.* 18: 258, 262.
60. *Corr.* 18: 265–66.
61. *Corr.* 18: viii, 368.
62. *CSB* 5: 24.
63. *Corr.* 18: 271.
64. Albaret, *Monsieur Proust,* 322.
65. *Cahier* 60 contains a note in Proust's hand: "Réjane's old age, Le Bargy's for notebook XX." See *Recherche* 4 (NP): 576 and var. a, n. 1 (p. 1299). The episode describing Berma's death does not resemble Réjane's; *Search* 6: 479–80.

66. *Corr.* 18: 275–76 and n. 5.
67. *Corr.* 18: 321.
68. *Corr.* 18: 277.
69. See *Corr.* 18: 307, n. 2.
70. See *Corr.* 18: 384.
71. *Corr.* 18: vi–vii, 243, 284–85, 313.
72. See *Corr.* 18: 316, 318.
73. *Corr.* 18: 296 and nn. 5, 6. This Latin proverb had its origin in Aristotle's *Nicomachean Ethics,* book 1, chapter 4.
74. Blanche, "Quelques Instantanés," 60–61.
75. *Corr.* 18: 330–31.
76. The complete version of the letter, not given in full by Kolb in *Corr.* 18: 331, is quoted by Tadié, *Marcel Proust,* 817, n. 1.
77. *Search* 4: 12.
78. *Corr.* 18: 355–56.
79. Proust used similar language to describe the Narrator's disenchantment with Albertine once he had made her a "prisoner" in his apartment. "I had clipped her wings, and she had ceased to be a winged Victory and become a burdensome slave of whom I would have liked to rid myself." *Search* 5: 500–501.
80. *Corr.* 18: 373, 19: 435.
81. *Corr.* 18: 356.
82. *Search* 2: 91–96.
83. "Pour un parti de l'intelligence" appeared on the front page of the *Figaro*'s literary supplement, July 19, 1919, and was signed by, among others, Daniel Halévy, Paul Bourget, Binet-Valmer, Henri Ghéon, Edmond Jaloux, Charles Maurras, and Jean-Louis Vaudoyer. See *Corr.* 18: 336, n. 5. The Communist Manifesto had appeared on the *Internationale*'s front page on June 7. See *Corr.* 18: 336, n. 6.
84. *Corr.* 18: 369.
85. *Corr.* 18: 347–48. Vandérem's article appeared in the *Revue de Paris* on July 15, 1919. See *Corr.* 18: 332, n. 7.
86. *Corr.* 18: 359, 404–5.
87. *Corr.* 18: 373–76.
88. *Corr.* 18: 385–86. The reference to the *Aeneid* is from book 2, line 274; see *Corr.* 18: 392–93 and n. 8.
89. *Corr.* 18: 414–17.
90. Robert de Montesquiou, *Les Pas effacés: Mémoires,* Paris: Émile Paul, 1923, 3: 292; see *Corr.* 18: 450, n. 3.
91. *Corr.* 18: 390, 535.
92. Lhomeau and Coelho, *Recherche d'un éditeur,* 372, n. 61.
93. *Corr.* 18: 397.
94. *Search* 2: 419.
95. *Search* 2: 335.
96. See *Corr.* 18: 404, nn. 4, 5. This fragment was from *The Fugitive,* a future volume that was to be published posthumously.
97. *Corr.* 18: 381.

98. See Albaret, *Monsieur Proust,* 322.

99. For Céleste's description of the apartment in rue Hamelin and their first days there, see Albaret, *Monsieur Proust,* 322–26.

100. *Corr.* 18: 409.

101. *Corr.* 18: 27. The "Ode" was published in a collection of poems by Morand entitled *Lampes à arc.*

102. *Corr.* 18: 421–25 and nn. 3, 8.

103. *Corr.* 18: 231, 427.

104. See *Corr.* 18: 437–38.

105. *Corr.* 18: 440, nn. 2, 3.

106. Albufera would be even more offended when he saw that he and Louisa de Mornand were likely models for certain scenes with Saint-Loup and Rachel.

107. *Corr.* 19: 37.

108. *Corr.* 18: 441. In an article in which he defended the Goncourt decision, Rivière described Proust as not the "youngest" but "the most rejuvenating of all the novelists" whom the Académie Goncourt could have chosen. See *Corr.* 18: 553, n. 3.

109. *Corr.* 18: 454–56, 494.

110. *Corr.* 18: 446–47.

111. Billy, *Lettres et conversations,* 233–34.

112. *Corr.* 18: 453.

113. *Corr.* 18: 457–58.

114. *Corr.* 18: 480–82.

115. *Corr.* 18: 484–85.

116. *Corr.* 19: 41.

117. *Corr.* 18: 466.

118. *Corr.* 18: 468–69; *Search* 2: 576.

119. *Corr.* 18: 495–96 and 471–72, n. 3.

120. *Corr.* 18: 477 and 502, n. 4. Proust's text was nineteen pages in print.

121. *Proust-Gallimard,* 207–8.

122. *Corr.* 18: 490–92. A Mrs. Gertrude Joakes had written Proust offering to translate his novel into English; her letter has been lost. *Corr.* 18: 493, n. 7.

123. *Corr.* 18: 492, 497, 511, and 493, n. 10.

124. *Corr.* 18: 513, n. 4. Léon Hennique, a member of the Académie Goncourt, wrote Proust to explain that he had not voted for him because of his age. Proust was forty-seven, too old, Hennique thought, to satisfy the provisions of Goncourt's will. See *Corr.* 18: 531.

125. Jacques Robichon, *Le Défi des Goncourt,* with an afterword by Hervé Bazin, Paris: Denoël, 1975, 59; *Corr.* 18: 505.

126. *Corr.* 18: 508, n. 2.

127. Over the next half-century his publishing firm won twenty-six additional Prix Goncourt—an extraordinary record. Robichon, *Le Défi des Goncourt,* 60.

128. *Corr.* 18: 535.

129. Albaret, *Monsieur Proust,* 304.

130. *Corr.* 18: 535.

131. *Proust-Gallimard,* 218.

132. *Proust-Gallimard,* 208.

133. *Corr.* 18: 29, 511–14. Louis de Robert said he was pleased that the Académie Goncourt had broken its tradition of giving the prize as a "bonus" for starving writers. Only talent and achievement should matter.

134. This page came from a future volume, *The Fugitive*.

135. Albaret, *Monsieur Proust*, 305.

136. *Corr.* 18: 509.

137. *Corr.* 18: 516–17 and n. 3. The French term *moraliste* designates primarily those French writers like Pascal and La Rochefoucauld whose self-examination led them to formulate maxims, capturing brilliant or biting observations about human behavior. Proust excelled at this. At least two volumes of Proust's "maxims" have been published. See Justin O'Brien, *The Maxims of Marcel Proust*, New York: Columbia University Press, 1948, and Bernard de Fallois, *Maximes et pensées dans* À la recherche du temps perdu, Paris: France Loisirs, 1989.

138. Céleste erroneously states that the Prix Goncourt was not given during the war. Albaret, *Monsieur Proust*, 301. The prize for 1914 was not awarded until 1916. For a list of Prix Goncourt winners, see Robichon, *Le Défi des Goncourt*, 355–69.

139. *Les Croix de bois* is generally considered one of the three best novels of World War I. The others are Henri Barbusse's *Le Feu* (the 1916 Prix Goncourt winner) and Erich Maria Remarque's *All Quiet on the Western Front*. Robichon, *Le Défi des Goncourt*, 60. Duchêne writes that *Les Croix de bois* was "the masterpiece" of the genre. *L'Impossible Proust*, 739. Jacques Boulenger, a critic who greatly admired Proust's work, thought Dorgelès's novel the best to come out of the war. See Boulenger, quoted in Lhomeau and Coelho, *Recherche d'un éditeur*, 243.

140. Quoted in Lhomeau and Coelho, *Recherche d'un éditeur*, 373, n. 63.

141. Lhomeau and Coelho, *Recherche d'un éditeur*, 241.

142. *Corr.* 18: 535.

143. *Corr.* 18: 528.

144. Albaret, *Monsieur Proust*, 271–72. The exact date on which Proust began wearing glasses is not known. Judging from Proust's letter to Binet-Valmer, it was shortly after mid-December 1919.

145. *Corr.* 18: 542 and 543, n. 4.

146. *Corr.* 18: 549–50.

147. See *Proust-Gallimard*, 212–13.

148. *Corr.* 18: 542 and 543, n. 4.

149. *Proust-Gallimard*, 249.

150. *Corr.* 18: 567–68. The old 7.50 price of each book was raised to 10 francs for the two volumes of *Swann's Way* and to 11 francs for the two volumes of *Within a Budding Grove*. *Corr.* 18: 30.

151. See *Proust-Gallimard*, 220, 222.

152. *Corr.* 18: 538, n. 12.

153. *Corr.* 21: 676.

154. *Corr.* 18: 536–37.

155. *Corr.* 18: 543, n. 3.

156. See *Corr.* 18: 544–45.

157. *Corr.* 18: 546–47.

158. *Corr.* 18: 548, n. 2.
159. *Corr.* 18: 567–68.
160. See *Corr.* 18: 534, nn. 9–13, and 18: 554.

28 The Idea of Death

1. In March, Proust was invited to join the committee planning to erect a statue of Flaubert in the Jardin de Luxembourg on the centennial of his birth. *Corr.* 19: 154 and n. 8.
2. "À propos du 'style' de Flaubert," *CSB* 5: 586–87, 595, 598–99.
3. *Corr.* 19: 43. *Proust-Gallimard*, 229.
4. *Corr.* 19: ii. See *Corr.* 19: iii. Jacques Boulenger's brother Marcel was a literary critic who wrote for *Comœdia*. On January 12 he wrote an article about Proust called "La Noblesse magique" (The magical nobility). Defending himself against another accusation of being infatuated with the upper crust, Proust told the critic that in future volumes the nobility was the class he slandered for being "always wrong . . . vulgar and detestable." Boulenger's article was far from negative. "Nothing," he wrote, was as "original, interesting, fascinating even, as admirably intelligent" as Proust's book. See *Corr.* 19: 93–94 and nn. 2, 5.
5. *Corr.* 19: 17, 77–78. The dinner took place on January 3.
6. Proust also refuted Rachilde's accusation that his style and content were "prewar" and therefore outdated. See *Corr.* 19: 55–56. Rachilde's article on recent novels had appeared in the *Mercure de France* on January 1. Proust also wrote Boulenger, entreating the critic not to think him a snob because "I always give my family and myself the most modest situation." *Corr.* 19: 35–36.
7. *Corr.* 19: 64.
8. See *Proust-Gallimard*, 231 and n. 4. Gallimard had ordered 6,600 copies printed in December 1919; the same number were printed in February 1920.
9. *Corr.* 19: 90–91.
10. *Proust-Gallimard*, 235. In this letter, Gallimard said that the printer shipped five hundred copies daily.
11. *Corr.* 19: 125.
12. *Corr.* 19: 121, n. 11. During the same period, Dorgelès's novel sold 85,000 copies. See Duchêne, *L'Impossible Proust*, 741. Over the next half-century Dorgelès's novel sold 827,000 copies and *Within a Budding Grove* 509,000. See Robichon, *Le Défi des Goncourt*, 61. This figure, which represents the French sales until 1975 of only one volume of the *Search*, is an example of how well Proust's massive novel sold and continues to sell.
13. *Proust-Gallimard*, 238.
14. *Corr.* 19: 65, 100, 103, n. 16, and 172.
15. *Corr.* 19: 115, 172, n. 2, and 179. Proust sent his congratulations with "profound joy." See *Corr.* 19: 153.
16. *Search* 6: 523.
17. *Corr.* 19: 158.
18. *Corr.* 19: 159–61 and n. 11, 161–62.
19. *Corr.* 19: 40, 181–82, 232.
20. *Corr.* 19: 192. The preface on Flaubert, published in January, contained a short version of Proust's condemnation of Sainte-Beuve as a critic, as did the preface for Morand's *Tendres Stocks*, which appeared later in the year.

21. See *Corr.* 19: 269, 277, 283.
22. *Corr.* 19: 209–10.
23. *Proust-Gallimard*, 246–47.
24. *Corr.* 19: 213–15.
25. On Daudet, see *Corr.* 19: 220.
26. *Corr.* 19: 228–29, 232–33.
27. *Corr.* 19: 22.
28. This account of Barrès's reaction to Proust's visit are from Jérôme and Jean Tharaud, *Mes Années chez Barrès*, Paris: Plon, 1928, 180–82, quoted by Kolb in *Corr.* 19: xi–xii.
29. *Corr.* 19: 284.
30. *Corr.* 19: 256, nn. 2, 5.
31. *Corr.* 19: 265–66.
32. *Corr.* 19: 252.
33. See *Corr.* 19: 272 and n. 4.
34. Proust quoted this passage from Blanche's article in a letter to Rivière on July 26–27. See *Corr.* 19: 374–75.
35. *Corr.* 19: 407.
36. *Proust-Gallimard*, 247–48.
37. Morand, *Le Visiteur du soir*, 22.
38. *Corr.* 19: 420, n. 2
39. *Corr.* 19: 337. André Breton worked for Gallimard from April through July, mainly correcting proofs of *The Guermantes Way*, part 1. *Proust-Gallimard*, 267, n. 2.
40. *Corr.* 19: 279–80.
41. See *Corr.* 20: 236, his 1921 dedication of *The Guermantes Way*, part 2, to Hahn, "My little Reynaldo, whom I no longer see." See also his letter to the duchesse de Clermont-Tonnerre, mid-June, 1921, *Corr.* 20: 334.
42. *Corr.* 19: 282.
43. *Corr.* 19: 373. The volume was ready by August 17.
44. *Corr.* 19: 304.
45. *Corr.* 19: 301, n. 3.
46. *Corr.* 19: 312, 313, n. 3.
47. See *Corr.* 19: 344–45. In January, when Réjane was awarded the Légion d'honneur, Proust spoke about the actress to journalist Louis Handler, to whom he also lent the photograph of her as the prince de Sagan. He told the reporter that Réjane's transvestite costume was the only one he knew that was not "ridiculous" and that he had "a cult for Réjane, this great actress, who by turns wore the two masks, who placed all her intelligence and all her heart in innumerable and magnificent 'creations,' among which must be counted her son and her daughter." See ["Sur Réjane"], *CSB* 5: 600–601 and n. 1.
48. *Corr.* 19: 323, 324–25.
49. *Proust-Gallimard*, 253, n. 1.
50. *Corr.* 19: 346–47. Proust's Spanish publisher was Compania Anonima Calpe of Madrid and Barcelona; see *Corr.* 19: 348, n. 12.
51. *Corr.* 19: 359–60.
52. *Proust-Gallimard*, 256, n. 3, and 257.
53. See *Corr.* 19: 348, n. 8, and *Proust-Gallimard*, 256, n. 3. See Elyane Dezon-Jones, "La Ré-

ception d'*À la recherche du temps perdu* aux États-Unis," in *The UAB Marcel Proust Symposium,* edited by William C. Carter, Birmingham: Summa, 1989, 35.

54. See *Corr.* 19: 355–56; *Proust-Gallimard,* 255, n. 3.

55. *Corr.* 19: 368, 388–89.

56. *L'Intransigeant* printed Proust's answer on August 3, 1920. See also *Corr.* 19: 290.

57. *CSB* 5: 605–6. Proust's reply was printed in the paper on August 28, 1920. See also *Corr.* 19: 362–63.

58. See ["Une Tribune française au Louvre?"], *CSB* 5: 601.

59. See *Corr.* 19: 271 and 273, n. 12.

60. *Corr.* 19: 378.

61. Proust did not give this review any excerpts from the novel but did offer it the preface to *Tendres Stocks,* under the title: "For a Friend: Remarks on Style." See *Corr.* 19: 387, n. 4.

62. *Corr.* 19: 385–86. ·

63. *Corr.* 19: 396–97, n. 2.

64. *Corr.* 19: 396–97, n. 2, and 404, 487.

65. *Corr.* 19: 496, 510.

66. *Corr.* 19: 419, 423, 435.

67. *Corr.* 19: 450–51. Proust confessed that he would have to forgo the pleasure of reading Schiff's novel *Richard Kurt,* for he no longer knew a word of English. He was amazed at how many English newspapers were "so nice to me and refer familiarly to such tiny details of *Swann* that this proves they know it really well." And this was before an English translation was available. *Corr.* 19: 436.

68. *Proust-Gallimard,* 263, n. 2. On August 31 Gallimard sent Proust the unbound pages for *The Guermantes Way,* part 1. *Proust-Gallimard,* 265.

69. *Corr.* 19: 430, 432.

70. *Corr.* 19: 437. Proust certainly knew Mme de Sévigné's version of the story, given to her daughter in letters of April 24 and 26, 1671.

71. See *Proust-Gallimard,* 266, n. 3.

72. *Corr.* 19: 437–38. In the fall Proust unsuccessfully nominated André Breton for the Prix Blumenthal. See *Corr.* 19: 439, 556.

73. *Corr.* 19: 442–43.

74. Gallimard quoted Pound from a letter, of which the publisher sent a copy to Proust. Subsequently, both original and copy were lost. *Proust-Gallimard,* 295 and n. 2.

75. See *Proust-Gallimard,* 287–89.

76. *Corr.* 19: 446, 453, 468.

77. *Corr.* 19: 455–58.

78. *Corr.* 19: 471–72, 474. See *Proust-Gallimard,* 280, n. 2.

79. *Corr.* 19: 492, 498, and 505 and n. 2. The official announcement came on October 4. Many of Proust's friends with government connections learned the news earlier.

80. See *Corr.* 19: 495, 510–11.

81. On October 22, Proust wrote Natalie Clifford Barney that by publishing *Sodom and Gomorrah,* he "renounced—gladly—all future honors. . . . The nature of my characters makes my book something less 'objective' than I would have wished." *Corr.* 19: 543.

82. *Corr.* 19: 467–68.

83. *Corr.* 19: 501.

84. *Corr.* 19: 544–45, 570–71.

85. Albaret, *Monsieur Proust*, 307.

86. *Corr.* 19: 513–14.

87. *Corr.* 19: 517 and n. 4. France's article "Stendhal" had appeared in the *Revue de Paris* on September 1.

88. *Corr.* 19: x, 518, 661.

89. Proust listed five of Daudet's books. *Corr.* 19: 532. In March, to satisfy his eagerness to demonstrate his gratitude and friendship, Proust wrote an article on Daudet, calling him a genius while comparing him to Saint-Simon and Balzac. The article, far too dithyrambic to appear in a respectable review, was published posthumously. See "Un Esprit et un génie innombrables: Léon Daudet," *CSB* 5: 601–4, and STW, 395–96.

90. *Corr.* 19: 530–31.

91. *Proust-Gallimard*, 290.

92. Proust had given a similar description a few days earlier to Dr. Landowski, saying that his regimen had made him look healthier, but "unfortunately, this was only an appearance." See *Corr.* 19: 534.

93. *Corr.* 19: 507–9, 535, 537–38. See "Au royaume de Bistouri," *CSB* 5: 566–68.

94. *Proust-Gallimard*, 291.

95. *Corr.* 19: 580–81. In another letter written a short while later, Proust assured Boulenger that in a future volume "my hero will love women who are not duchesses at all, and love them much more." *Corr.* 19: 588.

96. *Corr.* 19: 574–75. Proust also addressed the issue of snobbery in this letter. Saying that "society people were so stupid" that when it was time to illustrate the duchesse de Guermantes's wit, the only model he could find was that of a commoner, Mme Straus. The scene in which the Narrator thinks he has received an invitation by mistake to a grand social event came from the memoirs of M. d'Haussonville père. "These are perhaps the only two times in my entire work when I did not completely make things up." See *Corr.* 19: 574–75. Souday called Proust a "nervous aesthete."

97. Quoted in *Corr.* 19: 576, n. 12.

98. Quoted in *Corr.* 19: 595, n. 7.

99. *Corr.* 19: 623, 626.

100. *Corr.* 19: 596–97.

101. *Corr.* 19: 561–62.

102. *Corr.* 19: 591–93.

103. See [Préface], *CSB* 5: 606–16. Proust thought that Morand's title was "awful." See *Corr.* 19: 519.

104. *Corr.* 20: 65. Hahn wrote from Cannes on January 21. Aside from the offending comparison, he told Proust that his article on style "delighted me. It seemed to me that I was seated on your bed chatting with you."

105. See [Préface], *CSB* 5: 616. Proust used an image similar to one in the *Search*. In the preface, he said that a good metaphor must seem inevitable: water boils at 100 degrees centigrade; near misses do not count.

106. See [Préface], *CSB* 5: 609, n. 5. See also "Sainte-Beuve et Baudelaire," *CSB* 5: 242–62.

107. *Search* 3: 445. For the version in the preface to *Tendres Stocks*, see [Préface], *CSB* 5: 615.

108. *Corr.* 19: 618.

109. This brief chapter was omitted from the English translation. See the chapter "Deux jours d'angoisse" (Two days of anguish), in the original French edition; Albaret, *Monsieur Proust* (1973), 333–38.
110. *Corr.* 19: 626–27, 635–36.
111. See *Corr.* 19: 642–43.
112. ["Classicisme et romantisme"], *CSB* 5: 617–18.
113. See *Corr.* 19: 646–47. Proust gave Mme de Chevigné a similar explanation: "It was necessary to show that Places and People lose" some of their mysterious charm "when one approaches them. Balbec for the places, Guermantes for People." *Corr.* 19: 680. For the passage in which the Narrator discovers his vocation, see *Search* 6: 304.

29 I Am Finishing a Great Task

1. See *Corr.* 19: 695–96.
2. Michel-Thiriet, *Book*, 216.
3. *Corr.* 20: 35.
4. Albaret, *Monsieur Proust*, 201.
5. *Corr.* 20: 53–55. Proust mentioned two rumors. The first was that Gallimard had taken the money due his authors and used it to create a new bookstore. The second, which Proust did not believe, was that Gallimard had avoided serving in the war by wearing fake beards and hiding out in Normandy. One reason for his disbelief regarding Gallimard's military service was the "avalanche of false information" about Proust that resulted from the extensive press coverage of the Prix Goncourt. *Corr.* 20: 555–56.
6. Proust received seven thousand, two hundred francs for the first three thousand copies of *The Guermantes Way*, part 1, and three hundred francs for the excerpt "An Agony," which describes the grandmother's death and was published in the January *NRF*.
7. *Corr.* 20: 73.
8. *Proust-Gallimard*, 311, 323.
9. For *The Captive* and *The Fugitive* (or *The Sweet Cheat Gone*) Proust retained as subtitles "Sodom and Gomorrah, Part III," and "Sodom and Gomorrah, Part IV," for they belonged to the cycle of Albertine and the depiction of same-sex love.
10. *Corr.* 20: 59, n. 2, and 62.
11. See *Search* 4: 446–48, 453–54, 520–22.
12. See *Search* 4: 521–23.
13. *Corr.* 20: 94–95.
14. According to Tadié, *Aimée (Beloved)* is the story of Rivière's platonic love for Gaston Gallimard's wife. Tadié, *Marcel Proust*, 833.
15. *Corr.* 20: 99, 100.
16. *Corr.* 20: 109, n. 3, and 20: 117, n. 4. For Mauriac's foreword, see François Mauriac, *Œuvres autobiographiques*, Paris: Gallimard (Pléiade), 1990, 315–17.
17. See *Corr.* 20: 109, n. 3; 113, n. 4; 366. Mauriac's son Claude later married Proust's great-niece.
18. *Corr.* 20: 119.
19. *Corr.* 20: 118, n. 7, and 141, n. 5.
20. *Corr.* 20: 147–48. Proust's question mark suggested that he was not certain how long his strength would last.

21. *Proust-Gallimard,* 336.
22. See *Corr.* 20: 135–38.
23. *Corr.* 20: 163.
24. *Corr.* 20: 146, 149–50, 157, 185.
25. *Corr.* 20: 169–70, nn. 5, 6.
26. *Corr.* 20: 175–76.
27. *Corr.* 20: 174.
28. *Proust-Gallimard,* 346.
29. *Corr.* 20: 183–84.
30. *Corr.* 20: 194–95.
31. *Corr.* 20: 194. In another letter Proust repeated the remark about two keys that open only briefly and again identified Doäzan as the model for the first scene where Charlus stares at the young Narrator. *Corr.* 20: 281.
32. *Corr.* 20: 192, 371, 378.
33. See *Corr.* 21: 64.
34. For Proust's article on Baudelaire, see "À propos de Baudelaire," *CSB* 5: 618–39. Proust wrote that he considered Baudelaire, along with Alfred de Vigny, the greatest poet of the nineteenth century, but his choice for most beautiful poem was Hugo's "Booz endormi." *CSB* 5: 618.
35. *Corr.* 20: 181, 197, 206.
36. "À propos de Baudelaire," *CSB* 5: 627.
37. *Corr.* 20: 200.
38. See *Corr.* 20: 205–6, n. 6.
39. *Corr.* 20: 202–3.
40. *Proust-Gallimard,* 354.
41. "Billet à Angèle," quoted in *Corr.* 20: 210, n. 5.
42. *Corr.* 20: 236.
43. *Corr.* 20: 217.
44. The opening section of *Sodom and Gomorrah* contains a passage that is sometimes referred to as a sermon on sexuality; it contains what is thought to be the longest sentence in literature, running, in Scott-Moncrieff's translation, to 958 words. The sentence begins (*Search* 4: 21), "Their honour precarious" and ends (p. 24) "similar to themselves."
45. *Corr.* 20: 241.
46. *Proust-Gallimard,* 362.
47. *Corr.* 20: 253.
48. *Corr.* 20: 254 and 255, n. 4.
49. On May 9, 1923, Robert Proust signed the contract with Gallimard for a new edition of *Pleasures and Days.* See *Proust-Gallimard,* 420, nn. 2 and 3.
50. *Corr.* 20: 228.
51. Louis de Robert, who had always objected to the profane love ritual between Mlle Vinteuil and her girlfriend, was shocked by Proust's depiction of male homosexuality. In June, Robert confided to Paul Faure, "I find the pages of *Sodom and Gomorrah* profoundly disgusting." *Corr.* 20: 294, n. 2.
52. *Corr.* 20: 240–41.
53. *Corr.* 20: 262–63, n. 7. Gide, *Journal,* 691–92.
54. Gide, *Journal,* 693.

55. Gide, *Journal*, 691–92. Proust's word, which I have translated as *platonically* was *spirituellement*.

56. Gide, *Journal*, 694.

57. *Corr.* 20: 272, 275, 565.

58. *Corr.* 20: 310, 352, and 565, n. 3. Proust's response is unknown, but the interview did not take place.

59. *Corr.* 20: 247–49, 381–82.

60. *Corr.* 20: 236.

61. *Corr.* 20: 268–69.

62. *Corr.* 20: 285.

63. *Search* 3: 815–19.

64. *Corr.* 20: 285–86.

65. It was scheduled to run through May 31; *Corr.* 20: 223, n. 2.

66. *Corr.* 20: 222–23.

67. *Corr.* 20: 251.

68. Vaudoyer's article "The Mysterious Vermeer, I," appeared in the *Opinion* on April 30. *Corr.* 20: 226 and 227, n. 4.

69. *Corr.* 20: 289. The exact date that Proust visited the exhibitions is unknown. Kolb dated it sometime between May 18 and May 24.

70. Proust was also photographed on his deathbed.

71. This is Kolb's hypothesis. He also interviewed Céleste Albaret, who said that Proust did not experience any unusual malaise that day. See *Corr.* 20: x–xii. On April 8, five weeks before the exhibition opened, Proust wrote Gallimard and mentioned the scene of Bergotte's death, referring to it as "entirely new." See *Corr.* 20: 166. Before the exhibition opened, Proust wrote Beaumont, saying that he did not want to spoil the exhibition "of so many masterpieces" by suffering an attack or sudden death and having his name appear in the papers as a news item. Kolb interpreted this remark as another indication that the scene with Bergotte at the exhibition had already been written, for this is exactly what does happen to the fictional writer. See *Corr.* 20: 251–52 and n. 6.

72. The scene of Bergotte's death appears in the posthumously published *The Captive*. See *Search* 5: 238–46.

73. *Proust-Gallimard*, 365, n. 2.

74. *Corr.* 20: 402, 405.

75. *Corr.* 20: 300–301.

76. *Proust-Gallimard*, 366 and n. 2.

77. *Corr.* 20: 349.

78. Cocteau in film interview, *Portrait-Souvenir*. In the same interview he said that Mme de Chevigné did not care for Proust's books because she kept "tripping over his sentences."

79. *Corr.* 20: 281.

80. *Corr.* 20: 321 and 328, nn. 4, 5. See *Search* 3: 762. Proust had written to Montesquiou about this test on July 16, 1895. Another letter attributes the same test, perhaps a notion popular among the social set, to the prince de Polignac. See Clermont-Tonnerre, *Montesquiou et Proust*, 236.

81. *Corr.* 20: 337–39.

82. Jullian, *Montesquiou*, 264, 266, 268.

83. *Corr.* 20: 372.
84. *Corr.* 20: 431.
85. *Proust-Gallimard*, 381–82.
86. *Corr.* 20: 396 and n. 7.
87. *Corr.* 20: 432.
88. *Corr.* 20: 425. For "The Intermittencies of the Heart," see *Search* 4: 204–45.
89. *Corr.* 20: 434–36, n. 2, and 488.
90. *Corr.* 20: 439.
91. *Corr.* 20: 443.
92. *Proust-Gallimard*, 385–86.
93. Proust's calculation is not far off for mid-September. As of July 15, Gallimard owed him 50,185 francs. See *Proust-Gallimard*, 388, n. 2.
94. *Corr.* 20: 440–41.
95. *Corr.* 20: 444–445, 449.
96. *Corr.* 20: 446, n. 5. These pages came from *Sodom and Gomorrah*, part 2, the volume published in May 1922.
97. *Proust-Gallimard*, 389. *Sodom and Gomorrah*, part 2, appeared in three volumes.
98. *Corr.* 20: 456.
99. See *Corr.* 20: 462–65.
100. For Gallimard's reply, see *Proust-Gallimard*, 397–400.
101. See *Corr.* 20: 469–71.
102. *Corr.* 20: 470–71, 478.
103. *Proust-Gallimard*, 405–6.
104. *Corr.* 20: 477–78. In fact, by 1927 *Pleasures and Days* had sold eighteen thousand copies—success at last for Proust's first book. See *PJ*, 20–21.
105. *Corr.* 20: 479. "If 'magnum' is taken as praise, I can't apply it to *In Search of Lost Time*. But if it means length, Jacques has no idea of the work I am doing in making this book." The reference is to Nehemiah 6:3. In a note contained in material to be used for *Le Temps retrouvé*, Proust likens himself to Nehemiah and says that his refusal to descend from his perch— "Non possum descendere magnum opus facio"—should be the motto of every writer. See Marcel Proust, *Matinée chez la princesse de Guermantes, Cahiers du Temps retrouvé*, edited by Henri Bonnet in collaboration with Bernard Brun, Paris: Gallimard, 1982, 309.
106. *Corr.* 20: 491.
107. Published on February 26, under the title: "Voyage en zigzags dans la République des lettres: M. Marcel Proust."
108. *Corr.* 20: 496–97 and 498, n. 2.
109. *Search* 6: 321–22.
110. This excerpt, "En tram jusqu'à la Raspelière" (In the little train to La Raspelière), was composed of passages found in the *Search* 4: 358–458. *Corr.* 20: 501, n. 7.
111. This presentation of a homosexual as a woman in disguise angered Gide, who wrote in his diary that Proust was "not sincere" and wrote such scenes in order "to protect himself." Gide believed that "*Sodom* more than any other work will sink public opinion deeper in error." Gide, *Journal*, 705. Gide, who wanted homosexuals to be depicted as healthy, youthful, virile men, in what he considered the Greek pederast tradition, did not yet know about the evolution of Saint-Loup, who was to meet these criteria.

112. *Corr.* 20: 523 and n. 3.

113. *Corr.* 20: 524–25 and n. 3. Faÿ had only a few hours of sleep before rushing, on the morning of November 18, to catch the boat train to Le Havre, where he set sail on the S.S. *Touraine*. Faÿ paid a final visit to Proust in August 1922. *Corr.* 21: 17.

114. *Corr.* 20: 530, 555.

115. Proust's ultimate instructions for *The Captive*, issued just before his death, remained unknown for decades, and when revealed, in the late 1980s, provoked a major literary controversy in France.

116. Proust also expressed his vexation to his brother; perhaps he feared that he had brought embarrassment on his family by having the name appear in a satirical newspaper. See *Corr.* 20: 538–39 and n. 13; 549–50. The gag ad ran in the *Le Merle blanc* on November 19.

117. *Corr.* 20: 549.

118. *Proust-Gallimard*, 427–28.

119. The three volumes of *Sodom and Gomorrah*, part 2, sold for 6.75 francs each. *Proust-Gallimard*, 436 and n. 1.

120. *Corr.* 20: 568.

121. *Proust-Gallimard*, 439.

122. *Corr.* 20: 551, n. 16. Apparently Yvonne did not remain long beyond April 19, 1922. See *Corr.* 21: 135, n. 3.

123. *Corr.* 20: 570–71.

124. *Corr.* 20: 583.

125. *Corr.* 20: 584 and n. 2; 593.

126. *Corr.* 20: 586–87.

127. Jullian, *Montesquiou*, 270; Clermont-Tonnerre, *Montesquiou et Proust*, 243.

128. *Corr.* 20: 592.

129. *Proust-Gallimard*, 441, n. 2, and 443.

130. *Corr.* 21: 680–81.

131. *Corr.* 20: 598–99.

132. *Proust-Gallimard*, 446–47.

133. *Corr.* 20: 591, 601–2.

30 The End of Time

1. *Corr.* 21: 31, 42.

2. *Corr.* 21: 27, 30.

3. *Corr.* 21: 288.

4. *Corr.* 21: 32–33, 37, n 2.

5. *Corr.* 21: 39–40.

6. *Proust-Gallimard*, 458–59.

7. See *Proust-Gallimard*, 463–64, 467.

8. *Corr.* 21: 51.

9. See *Corr.* 21: 48–49 and n. 6.

10. *Corr.* 21: 50. In a May 1 letter to Mauriac, Proust compared himself to "Lazarus still in his winding sheet who had risen from the depth." *Corr.* 21: 159.

11. *Corr.* 21: 53.

12. *Corr.* 21: 55–56. *Sodom and Gomorrah,* part 2, would be published on April 29, in three volumes of 232, 240, and 240 pages. The remaining three sections would appear posthumously.

13. *Proust-Gallimard,* 478–79, 480.

14. *Corr.* 21: 110. The printing was completed on April 3; Tadié, *Proust,* 314.

15. Albaret, *Monsieur Proust,* 248.

16. *Corr.* 21: 58

17. *Corr.* 21: 67–68.

18. See *Corr.* 21: 67 and n. 2.

19. *Corr.* 21: 97.

20. Albaret, *Monsieur Proust,* 341; *Corr.* 21: 117.

21. *Corr.* 21: 117–18, 239, n. 7, and 392, n. 13.

22. *Corr.* 21: 175–76.

23. *Corr.* 21: 117–18.

24. *Corr.* 21: 295.

25. *Corr.* 21: 140, 293.

26. *Proust-Gallimard,* 509–10.

27. *Corr.* 21: 146.

28. *Corr.* 21: 157.

29. *Corr.* 21: 160.

30. *Corr.* 21: ii, 162, 221.

31. *Proust-Gallimard,* 522, n. 2.

32. *Corr.* 21: 168–69, n. 2., 185, 193, 236.

33. *Corr.* 21: 171–72 and n. 3.

34. Léon Daudet's article "Sur la misère du théâtre contemporain" was published in the *Action française* on August 18. See *Corr.* 21: 429, n. 6. In a summer letter to Sir Philip Sassoon, Proust poked fun at himself and at Daudet. He told Sassoon that he had not read a single line by Pierre Benoit. "Léon Daudet from time to time writes that I am the première French writer, which gives me a certain satisfaction, and that after me comes Benoit, which destroys any pleasure." *Corr.* 21: 326–27.

35. *Corr.* 21: 166.

36. Benstock, *No Gifts from Chance,* 389–90. Berry's reference is to Richard von Krafft-Ebing, a German neuropsychiatrist and pioneer in the study of human sexuality. His *Psychopathia sexualis* was published in 1886. Proust may have known this work, which presented many case studies of what were considered sexual perversions.

37. "Males do not represent two discrete populations, heterosexual and homosexual. The living world is a continuum in each and every one of its aspects. The sooner we learn this concerning human sexual behavior the sooner we shall reach a sound understanding of the realities of sex." Alfred C. Kinsey, Wardell B. Pomeroy, and Clyde E. Martin, *Sexual Behavior in the Human Male,* Philadelphia: Saunders, 1948, 639.

38. *Corr.* 21: 184. See the *Search* 4: 331. The quotation from *La Juive* is followed immediately by the scene in which the real Céleste Albaret and her sister Marie Gineste visit the Narrator at the Grand-Hôtel. Proust also used the name of *La Juive*'s most famous aria, "Rachel, quand du seigneur," in *Within a Budding Grove,* as a nickname for Saint-Loup's mistress, whose name is Rachel. The Narrator refers to her as "Rachel when from the Lord." See, among other passages, *Search* 2: 206–7.

39. See *Corr.* 21: 374, n. 9; *Marcel Proust et les siens,* 164–65.

40. Richard Ellmann's information that the Schiffs did not invite Proust because they knew that he rarely left his apartment is mistaken. *James Joyce,* New York: Oxford University Press, 1982, 508.

41. *Corr.* 21: 195–96 and n. 3.

42. My account of the Joyce-Proust encounter is based primarily on that in Ellmann's distinguished biography *James Joyce,* 508–9.

43. *The Letters of James Joyce,* edited by Stuart Gilbert, New York: Viking, 1957, 148.

44. Ellmann, *Joyce,* 508.

45. *Corr.* 21: 206.

46. *Corr.* 21: 210, n. 6. See *Search* 2: 289.

47. *Search* 4: 90.

48. Curtiss, *Letters of Marcel Proust,* 391–92.

49. *Corr.* 21: 282, n. 5.

50. *Search* 4: 331–37.

51. Jaloux had become an editor for Grasset in 1920; Bothorel, *Bernard Grasset,* 141.

52. *Corr.* 21: 225–26.

53. *Corr.* 21: 228, 229, 238–39.

54. *Corr.* 21: 235, 238.

55. *Corr.* 21: 15.

56. Daudet, *Soixante Lettres,* 241.

57. *Corr.* 21: 15.

58. *Corr.* 21: 16, 250–51.

59. *Corr.* 21: 254–55.

60. Albaret, *Monsieur Proust,* 338. Céleste incorrectly identified Princesse Radziwill as the former Jeanne Pouquet. It was Marie de Benardaky who married Prince Michel Radziwill.

61. *Corr.* 21: 284.

62. *Proust-Gallimard,* 537.

63. In July, Proust offered the manuscript to Schiff for five thousand francs, saying that he thought seven thousand, offered by Doucet, was too much. *Corr.* 21: 372. Kolb observes that Proust apparently misrepresented the situation to Schiff, because Gallimard had said that he would try to obtain seven thousand francs from Doucet. There is no indication that Doucet was willing to pay that much. *Corr.* 21: 374, n. 6. For Serge André, owner of the *Opinion,* see *Corr.* 21: 409, 423; *Proust-Gallimard,* 548, n. 4. In October, when Proust had become too ill to respond, Gallimard told him that Doucet was interested in acquiring the manuscript of his preface to Morand's *Tendres Stocks,* which the collector intended to have bound with Morand's manuscript. See *Proust-Gallimard,* 633.

64. *Corr.* 21: 372–73.

65. *Corr.* 21: 295, 303–4. Proust's response to the possibility of being sketched by Picasso is unknown.

66. *Corr.* 21: 347, 441, n. 6.

67. *Corr.* 21: 301, 307. Proust reported Gide's remark in a letter to Vettard.

68. *Proust-Gallimard,* 543.

69. *Corr.* 21: 310–11.

70. See *Corr.* 21: 300; *Proust-Gallimard,* 547–49.

71. *Corr.* 21: 314, 317.

72. *Corr.* 21: 320.

73. *Proust-Gallimard*, 552. n. 1.
74. *Corr.* 21: 331–32. Proust's title *La Prisonnière (The Captive)* was maintained; *Albertine disparue* (rendered in the English translation as *The Sweet Cheat Gone*) was used as the other title until the 1954 Pléiade edition. Some recent editions have reverted to *Albertine disparue.*
75. *Proust-Gallimard*, 553, 555, 557.
76. *Corr.* 21: 341–42, 363.
77. *Corr.* 21: 329, 341–43.
78. Steegmuller, *Cocteau*, 281.
79. Jaloux, *Avec Marcel Proust*, 12–13.
80. See *Corr.* 21: 351 and 352, n. 3
81. See *Corr.* 21: 351, 358.
82. *Corr.* 21: 355, n. 8. In his letter thanking Schlumberger, Proust scolded him very mildly for saying the novelist often "transposed the sexes." The critic's remark was fairly general and did not seem to refer specifically to homosexual characters. See *Corr.* 21: 355–56.
83. *Corr.* 21: 351–52. Proust was exaggerating his reputation; *Le Gaulois* had published two articles on *Sodom and Gomorrah*, part 2. *Corr.* 21: 354, n. 4. On June 8 *L'Écho de Paris* reported that Proust's name had been mentioned as a contender for the Nobel Prize for literature. Writing to Gallimard, two weeks later, Proust mentioned this and said that he thought the paper was "exaggerating a bit." *Corr.* 21: 298–99, n. 16. Mme de Ségur was famous for her stories for children.
84. *Corr.* 21: 70, 71, n. 4, 345–46, 361, 367–69. Curtius eventually wrote a monograph, *Marcel Proust.*
85. *Proust-Gallimard*, 568.
86. *Corr.* 21: 376–77.
87. *Corr.* 21: 379–80.
88. *Proust-Gallimard*, 573–74.
89. *Corr.* 21: 386.
90. Albaret, *Monsieur Proust*, 340.
91. *Corr.* 21: 389–91.
92. *Corr.* 21: 345, 401. Proust's correspondence with Eliot was not preserved. See *Corr.* 21: 346, n. 6.
93. *Proust-Gallimard*, 576.
94. *Corr.* 21: 396, n. 2, and 400.
95. *Proust-Gallimard*, 579, n. 4. The three versions, made from notebooks, were required because of Proust's many corrections. Tadié, *Proust*, 313.
96. Blanche remembered the last time he saw Proust at the Ritz, dining alone in a private room and surrounded by waiters, whom the novelist "seemed to be teaching, in my honor, how to work all the light switches, whose every location he knew precisely. Suddenly, light flooded the deserted salon." Blanche noticed that Proust was somewhat bloated, but still handsome, though more mature, full of authority and happy with his success. "Quelques instantanés," 61.
97. *L'Illustration* had reproduced James Tissot's painting *Le Balcon du Cercle de la rue Royale en 1867* on June 10, 1922. See *Corr.* 21: 410, n. 9, where Kolb observes that Proust knew another man depicted by Tissot: Général de Galliffet.
98. *Corr.* 21: 409.

99. This is Tadié's thesis; *Marcel Proust,* 900. Painter, who often took liberties in his biography, has Proust scream this very sentence at Céleste and her family when he gives them history lessons in the evening. Not only is there no evidence of this, but it would be highly uncharacteristic of Proust to use such language in front of people, especially women, he loved and respected. Painter, *Proust* 2: 344: "At his bedside he gave lessons in French history to Céleste, Marie Gineste, Yvonne Albaret, and Odilon, scolding them when he was displeased with the awful menace: 'I'll drown you in an ocean of *merde!*'"
100. *Corr.* 21: 413–14 and n. 2, 429–30.
101. See *Search* 6: 27–38. Proust's answer to the survey was published in *Le Gaulois* on May 27.
102. Proust's answer appeared in the July 22 issue of *La Renaissance politique, littéraire et artistique.* See *CSB* 5: 645.
103. *Search* 6: 299.
104. See ["Une petite question: Et si le monde allait finir . . . "], *CSB* 5: 645–46.
105. *Corr.* 21: 427. See *Corr.* 21: vii. See Albaret, *Monsieur Proust,* 341. In the same passage, Céleste asserts that "there was no heating of any kind at rue Hamelin after we noticed that the chimneys were too narrow and the smoke came back into the room." The absence of fires and "the icebox of a room" is contradicted by Proust's letters and by Gide, among others, who wrote about the suffocating heat of Proust's room. Gide recorded that Proust received him in a different room, stifling hot, because Proust's room was so incredibly hot that it was nearly unbearable even for Proust, who sweated profusely.
106. *Corr.* 21: 424.
107. *Corr.* 21: 452–53. On Proust's death, Gallimard owed the novelist approximately twenty thousand francs. See *Proust-Gallimard,* 594, n. 2.
108. Proust did not live long enough to enjoy any of the money. He promised half of it to Binet-Valmer's charity for children who were victims of the war. *Corr.* 21: 474.
109. *Corr.* 21: 425–26, 455–56.
110. *Proust-Gallimard,* 597–98.
111. *Corr.* 21: 457–58. See *Proust-Gallimard,* 600, n. 3, and *Corr.* 21: 37. In the latter half of the month, Proust was still trying to raise cash. He wrote Hauser and asked what shares he should sell. Lionel offered to study Marcel's portfolio and advise him. Time was running out, and Proust took no action.
112. *Proust-Gallimard,* 602–3.
113. *Corr.* 21: 459–60, 461.
114. *Corr.* 21: 358–59, 468, 509, and 510, n. 3. Proust had nothing to fear. There was one scandalous aspect of Montesquiou's memoirs: they were boring. Painter quotes the count's cousin Mme Greffulhe, who could hardly hide her disappointment: "One expects more of a dead man." Montesquiou rather tamely derided Proust's ugly furnishings. Painter, *Proust* 2: 346. I have modified the translation from "It's not quite what one expects" to better express Mme Greffulhe's disappointment.
115. *Corr.* 20: 27, and 21: 500, n. 2. Scott-Moncrieff died in 1930, at age forty, leaving untranslated *Le Temps retrouvé.* His task was completed by Sydney Schiff; the last volume had another English translator, Andreas Mayor.
116. The rights Gallimard sold to the English publisher Chatto and Windus allowed them to distribute the translations of Proust in the United States. *Swann's Way* appeared in New York in 1922, distributed by Holt. See *Proust-Gallimard,* 486, n. 5. Scott-Moncrieff's translation was revised and updated by Terence Kilmartin, an Englishman, in 1981.

Kilmartin's work was needed primarily because Scott-Moncrieff had worked from the often defective French first edition. Kilmartin, however, did not always have Scott-Moncrieff's ear for rendering Proust's music into English.

117. *Corr.* 21: 470, n. 2. Schiff later made amends and become a good friend of Scott-Moncrieff's. *Proust-Gallimard*, 610, n. 1.

118. *Corr.* 21: 473–76.

119. *Proust-Gallimard*, 612–13, 618. Scott-Moncrieff's titles endured for the next seven decades as the titles in English. The Modern Library edition was the first complete translation to adopt a title that mirrors Proust's original: *In Search of Lost Time*—but even here the double meaning of *perdu* as "lost" and "wasted" is more potential than virtual.

120. *Corr.* 21: 499.

121. *Corr.* 21: 501.

122. See Ernest Forssgren, "Une Visite: Paris, 1922," *Cahiers Marcel Proust*, n.s. 12, *Études proustiennes*, II, 138–39. The only account of this visit and the only record of Proust's note to Forssgren is the valet's account. Céleste makes no mention of Forssgren's last visit to Proust when he was near death or the "mysterious visit" to the Riviera Hôtel, to which, according to Forssgren, the doctors in attendance on Proust attributed his death. See "Une Visite," 123, n. 2.

123. *Corr.* 21: 480.

124. Forssgren, "Une Visite," 140.

125. *Corr.* 21: 483, 484–85, and see 485, n. 2. The corresponding passages in *The Captive* are 84–91. *Search* 5: 84–91.

126. *Corr.* 21: 486, 489.

127. *Corr.* 21: 493–94. Proust had referred to Jean-Henri Fabre's studies of the burrowing wasp as an analogy, in a different context, in *Swann's Way*. See *Search* 1: 173. In fact, this particular wasp is mentioned not in Fabre but rather in the work of Élie Metchinikof, who vulgarized aspects of Fabre's studies; see *Recherche* 1 (NP): 122, n. 1.

128. *Proust-Gallimard*, 625, 627, 630.

129. *Corr.* 21: 502.

130. *Corr.* 21: 503–4, 505.

131. Albaret, *Monsieur Proust*, 107.

132. *Corr.* 21: 509–10.

133. *Corr.* 21: 511–12, 528.

134. Albaret, *Monsieur Proust*, 341–42. There is no other record that he attended such a party.

135. *Corr.* 21: 531–32 and n. 9. Rhinogomenol was a salve that was used to treat head colds and that Proust apparently believed made them less contagious.

136. The conversation with Dr. Bize is from Albaret, *Monsieur Proust*, 345–47.

137. My version of the scene between the two brothers is based on Albaret's account in *Monsieur Proust*, 346–48.

138. *Corr.* 21: 513–15.

139. See Albaret, *Monsieur Proust*, 343–44, 348–49.

140. *Corr.* 21: 515 and n. 4. Kolb dates this letter simply as October, based on coughing fits that had started again. The date Proust came down with the cold was determined by Kolb to be shortly after October 12; see *Corr.* 21: 504, letter 351 to Céleste. It is obviously impossible to date the instructions to Céleste with much certainty. Kolb places it between a letter he dated shortly after October 21 and another of October 23 or 24. If Kolb is right about

the date, there are several lucid letters written between that date and mid-November. Proof of Proust's instructions were not be found until nearly seven decades later, when Claude Mauriac discovered a typescript in whose margins one finds the same instructions in Proust's hand as in the note to Céleste. Because Proust died before he could make the changes required by cutting so many pages, Gaston Gallimard and Robert Proust ignored the author's instructions. Once the typescript was discovered, it set off a controversy in France. Those who wish to follow the debate in France should read *Albertine disparue*, edited by Nathalie Mauriac and Étienne Wolff, Paris: Grasset, 1987; *Albertine disparue*, edited by Jean Milly, Paris: Champion, 1992; *La Fugitive*, edited by Nathalie Mauriac Dyer, Paris: Livre de Poche, 1993. Many other articles in France have debated which version is the authentic one. See Nathalie Mauriac Dyer, "Les Mirages du double: *Albertine disparue* selon la Pléiade," *BMP* 40 (1990): 117–53. See also the new Pléiade edition, *À la recherche du temps perdu*, vol. 4, Paris: Gallimard, 1989, which essentially maintains the original Gallimard edition, the one translated by Scott-Moncrieff. Because no new English translations have been made since the discovery of the Mauriac typescript, the controversy over which edition of Proust is the authentic one has not yet affected English readers of the *Search*. A new Penguin translation under the general editorship of Christopher Prendergast of Cambridge University is scheduled for 2001.

141. *Corr.* 21: 517–18.
142. *Corr.* 21: 48, 518–19, 520.
143. *Corr.* 21: 523.
144. Quoted by Elyane Dezon-Jones in *Proust et l'Amérique: La Fiction américaine à la recherche du Temps Perdu*, Paris: Nizet, 1982, 47, n. 67.
145. *Corr.* 21: 527, 528, n. 6.
146. *Proust-Gallimard*, 634.
147. *Corr.* 21: 529. *The Captive* was published in November 1923 with this preliminary note: "The typescript of this work . . . was sent to us by M. Marcel Proust shortly before his death. Illness did not leave him strength to correct the text completely. A very careful revision of the manuscript was undertaken after his death by Dr. Robert Proust and Jacques Rivière." *Proust-Gallimard*, 637, n. 2.
148. *Corr.* 20: 500. See *Recherche* 4 (NP): 58–223, *Search* 5: 642–874.
149. Tadié, *Marcel Proust*, 906.
150. Dreyfus, *Souvenirs*, 340.
151. *Corr.* 21: 530, 534.
152. *Corr.* 21: xi, 455, n. 2, and 530.
153. *Corr.* 21: 534–35.
154. Albaret, *Monsieur Proust*, 343.
155. Céleste was the only witness who was constantly present for the last twenty-four hours of Proust's life and the only person who left a memoir about his death. My account relies heavily on hers. See Albaret, *Monsieur Proust*, 343–62.
156. Later, she learned that Proust had consulted Horace Finaly on her behalf. Proust left no will. When Robert Proust asked if his brother had left any instructions regarding what should be done for Céleste and Odilon, she said that he had not and that she wanted nothing. Albaret, *Monsieur Proust*, 364.
157. Proust, who was no longer eating and drinking, had also stopped taking barbiturates. Because Proust had long been accustomed to heavy doses, Dr. Dominique Mabin be-

lieves this sudden change was the cause of his hallucination. Mabin, *Le Sommeil de Marcel Proust,* with a preface by Philip Kolb, Paris: Presses universitaires de France, 1992, 144.

158. According to Céleste, Proust's last words had been the last two exchanges with his brother. "Despite what people have said— . . . for literature's sake, I suppose—he didn't say 'Mother.' " Albaret, *Monsieur Proust,* 359. She is refuting Painter's version of the story, for which he cites no evidence. Painter, *Proust* 2: 362.

159. *Corr.* 21: 535–36. That evening Hahn sent a shorter note to Léon Yeatman, giving the time of death as six o'clock.

160. Albaret, *Monsieur Proust,* 359–60, 361.

161. Dreyfus, *Souvenirs,* 341.

162. *Corr.* 19: 313, n. 3.

163. Albaret, *Monsieur Proust,* 361.

164. Daudet, *Soixante Lettres,* 242.

165. *Search* 6: 524.

166. Steegmuller, *Cocteau,* 296.

167. Quoted by Gimpel, *Diary of an Art Dealer,* 195. Proust had anticipated his own loss of substance in the character of his novelist Bergotte, who grows quite thin before his death: "The bulk of his thought had long since passed from his brain into his books. He had grown thin, as though they had been extracted from him by a surgical operation." *Search* 3: 447.

168. Gregh, *Amitié,* 34–35.

169. Albaret, *Monsieur Proust,* 361.

171. Steegmuller, *Cocteau,* 296.

172. Albaret, *Monsieur Proust,* 362.

173. Maurois, *World,* 286.

174. Ellmann, *Joyce,* 509.

175. Michel-Thiriet, *Book,* 187.

176. Steegmuller, *Cocteau,* 296.

177. *Search* 5: 343.

Index ∾

Adam, Paul, 236

Agostinelli, Alfred: hired as chauffeur, 433, 437–38, 456–57, 458; letter to Proust, 440; asks Proust to find employment for "wife" Anna, 501; Proust hires as secretary, 536; Proust's love for, 536–37, 554–55; accompanies Proust to Cabourg, 543–44; Proust pays for flying lessons, 544–45; offers of gifts from Proust, 545; flees to Monte Carlo, Proust sends Nahmias to offer money for his return, 555–56; model for Albertine, 557, 589–90, 603–4, 616; plane crash, 569–72; Proust on grief, 578–79; anniversary of his death, 594; Proust investigates, 598–99, 678

Agostinelli, Anna (common-law wife of Alfred Agostinelli), 501, 537, 543, 544, 545, 555, 570, 571–72

Agostinelli, Émile, 570, 571, 598, 678

Agostinelli, Eugène, 556

Alain-Fournier, Henri-Alban, 586

Albaret, Céleste, née Céleste Gineste: Proust confides in her about Le Cuziat, 179, 608–12; marriage to Odilon, 537; meets Proust, 547; delivers copies of Swann's Way, 553; becomes Proust's housekeeper, 575; last trip to Ca-

bourg, 576–78; makes phone calls from café, 582; on war years, 591, 656, 660, 664, 665; paste-ons, 591–92; death of her mother, 592–93; on Poulet Quartet, 619–20; on completion of Search, 629–30; Proust shows her where he keeps his notebooks, 633; her parodies of Gide, others 645–46, 698; Spanish flu, 669; on Antoine Bibesco, 686; denied Proust burned photos, 692; rue Hamelin, 703, 704; Proust fired, rehired, 705; buys eyeglasses, 713, 792; her hat, 721; on Proust's use of drugs, 738; Proust's tribute, 749, 798–99; on Proust's germ phobia, 772; on his diet, 774, 801–2; in Search, 779–80; her attentiveness, 785; Proust considers her family his own, 788; denies chimney fire, 791; notes to her, 798–99; revision of The Captive, 801–2; on Proust's last days, 801–10; note to Rivière, 804

Albaret, Jean, 593

Albaret, Léontine, 593

Albaret, Odilon: Proust hires as chauffeur, 433, 438, 494; becomes Proust's regular driver, 536; marries Céleste Gineste, 537–38; drives Agostinelli to airfield, 545; war years, 593,

Daudet, Léon (*continued*)
  the *Search,* 671, 734, 750–51, 786; in Proust
    parody, 696; Proust dedicates *The Guer-
    mantes Way* to him, 737; urges Proust to
    forgo article on him, 772; calls Proust a pop-
    ular author, 776; Proust sends flowers, 805
Daudet, Mme Léon, 169, 656
Daudet, Lucien, 219, 245, 297, 307, 353, 492, 497,
    500, 616, 632, 729; Proust meets Lucien and
    family, 183; Proust attracted to him, 186;
    mad laughter and "louchonneries," 206;
    Proust becomes intimate friend, 208, 210,
    212; Proust offers photograph, 223; relations
    cool, 223, 227–30, 237; photographed with
    Proust and Robert de Flers, 233; Lorrain
    insinuates that he and Proust are lovers, 235;
    Proust visits at Pray, 314–15; Proust inscribes
    La Bible d'Amiens, 364–65; Proust promises
    to see doctor and reform, 381–82; visits
    Proust at clinic, 402; Proust confides doubts
    about his talent, 421; dedicates story to
    Proust, 455; Proust consults regarding novel,
    545; reads *Swann's Way,* 546; Proust inscribes
    Swann's Way, 553–54, reviews *Swann's Way*
    for *Le Figaro,* 557; supports *Swann's Way*
    for Prix Goncourt, is wrongly accused by
    Proust, 560–61; war years, 575, 599, 656, 658;
    on *The Guermantes Way,* 732; last visit, 780
Deacon, Gladys, 670, 687
Debeney, Gen. Marie-Eugène, 673
Debove, Dr. (dean of the medical school), 354
Debussy, Claude, 151, 155, 491, 497–98, 499, 500,
    505, 524, 623–24
Degas, Edgar, 93, 166, 247, 253–54, 685
Déjerine, Dr. Jules, 401
Delafosse, Léon, 155, 171, 206, 269, 274; model
    for Morel, 155, 427, 623; and Montesquiou,
    162–64, 168, 170, 240, 243–44, 270; dedicates
    song to Proust, 165
Delaunay, Jules-Élie, 95
Delibes, Léo, 76
Denis, Maurice, 685
Derby, Lord Edward, 680
Desbordes-Valmore, Marceline, 169, 219
Deschanel, Paul, 39
Des Garets, Marie-Louyse, 380, 381
Desjardins, Abel, 72, 692
Desjardins, Paul, 78, 117, 404
Detaille, Édouard, 144
Dethomas, Maxime, 337

Diaghilev, Serge, 490, 491, 498, 514, 777
Dickens, Charles, 245
Diderot, Denis, 63
Dion, Comte Albert de, 169, 242
Doäzan, Baron Jacques, 147, 282, 389, 427, 746
Dorgelès, Roland, 710, 711–12, 713
Dostoyevsky, Fyodor, 70, 245, 539, 560, 580,
    656, 746, 762
Doucet, Jacques, 781
Douglas, Lord Alfred, 125, 189
Dreyfus, Captain Alfred, 44, 183–84, 185, 204,
    205, 230, 270–71, 406, 700
Dreyfus, Henri, 496
Dreyfus, Mathieu, 247
Dreyfus, Robert, 142, 311, 482, 448, 496, 494–95,
    695, 804, 808; on Marcel and Condorcet, 38,
    40, 55, 65–67, 75–76, 84, 89, 90, 95; *Le Ban-
    quet,* 126; anonymous review of *Swann's
    Way,* 557, 560
Dreyfus Affair, 189, 204, 211–12, 230–31, 242,
    247–54, 263–64, 266, 270–71, 316, 345, 406,
    460, 580, 581, 614, 714
Du Bellay, Joachim, 49
Dubois, Dr. Paul, 400
Dubois-Amiot, Marthe. *See* Proust, Mme
    Robert
Duclaux, Mary, 613
Duglé, Mme Joseph, 604
Dumas, Alexandre, 128, 146, 223, 331, 413
Dumas, Alexandre fils, 103, 145, 162, 471
Dumont-Wilden, Louis, 504–5
Du Paty de Clam, Lt. Col. Mercier, 250, 256
Duplay, Maurice, 465, 776
Duplay, Dr. Simon, 33, 298
Duplay, Mme Simon, 33, 298
Durand-Ruel gallery, 337, 370, 473, 506
Dürer, Albrecht, 129, 401
Duvernois, Henri, 759, 761

Édouard, Julien, 291
Edward VII, 511
Edwards, Alfred, 431–32
Edwards, Mme Alfred, née Misia Godebska,
    431–32, 454
Egger, Victor, 178, 182
Eiffel, Gustave, 96–97
Einstein, Albert, 773, 789
El Greco, 644
Eliot, George, 55, 79, 126, 131, 229, 237–38, 285
Eliot, T. S., 688, 789

Nietzsche, Friedrich, 291
Nijinsky, Vaslav, 490–91, 498, 514
Nivelle, General, 643
Noah, 389, 465, 488, 742
Noailles, Anna de, 271, 274, 308, 342, 396, 533,
    645, 808; in *Jean Santeuil*, 261; Proust visits
    at Amphion-les-Bains, 268–70; Dreyfusard,
    270–71, 406; Proust admires her poems,
    hosts party in her honor, 300–301; wins
    Archon-Despérouse Prize, 310; affection for
    Proust, 336–37, 358; takes Proust's side in
    disagreement with her brother, 360; her
    "inner music" in writings, 369–70; Proust
    breaks her figurine, 372, 382; compliments
    Proust on preface "On Reading," 393–94;
    Proust's article on *Les Éblouissements*, 428–
    29; Proust consults about Sainte-Beuve
    essay, 461–62; Proust reads her poems to
    young friends, 482; on Cocteau, 497; her
    pride, 497, 656–67; congratulates Proust on
    Prix Goncourt, compares him to Balzac and
    Stendhal, 711; imitations of Montesquiou as
    Charlus, 756–57. *See also* Proust, Marcel,
    Writings, Miscellaneous writings
Noailles, Mme Hélie de, 372
Noailles, Comte Mathieu de, 260, 268, 271, 300,
    400
Nordlinger, Marie: meets Proust, 231; accom-
    panies him to Louvre and Harrison's studio,
    240; card from Proust describing an invol-
    untary memory experience, 260; Proust
    announces intention to write about Ruskin,
    285; sends Proust articles on Ruskin, 292–93;
    collaborates on Ruskin translations, 295–96,
    320, 346, 362–63, 365, 389, 395, 412; describes
    Proust, 320, 354, 389; gives him Japanese
    paper pellets, 367–68, 467; creates medallion
    of Adrien, 369, 373; marries Rudolph Meyer
    Riefstahl, 501
Normand, Jacques, 525
Northcliffe, Lord Alfred, 794
Nouÿ, Jules Lecomte de, 48, 411

Oberkampf, Mlle, 374
Offenbach, Jacques, 18, 88, 96, 166
Ollendorff, Paul, 292, 308, 315, 526, 531, 533
Oncieu, François d', 281, 282
Orloff, Comte, 609
Otero, Caroline Puentovalga, 164, 339
Otto (photographer) 222, 223

Oulman, Amélie. *See* Weil, Mme Georges
Ovid, 559

Paderewski, Ignacy Jan, 243
Paillart, Frédéric, 771
Parent, Pierre, 456
Pâris, François de, 335, 343, 346, 473, 496
Pascal, Blaise, 69, 85, 330, 663
Pasha, Grand Vizier Ali, 11
Pasteur, Louis, 341
Pater, Walter, 366
Patin, Jacques, 736
Pau, Gen. Gérald, 574
Paul of Russia, Grand Duke, 475
Paulhan, Jean, 745, 760
Paulus (Jean-Paul Habans), 335
Péguy, Charles, 472, 580
Peigné-Crémieux, Mme Mathilde, 382,
    508
Pellieux, Gen. Georges de, 250, 256
Pericles, 52
Perret, Paul, 214
Pétain, Gen. Philippe, 615
Pétain, Raymond, 622–23
Peter, René, 344, 408, 409, 412, 413, 418
Petronius, 62, 213
Philip II, King of Spain, 58
Philippe, Charles-Louis, 204
Philippi, Mme, née Fava, 474
Picasso, Pablo, 491, 642, 657, 686, 777, 782
Picquart, Col. Georges, 230, 251–53, 256, 257,
    259, 406
Pierrebourg, Mme Marguerite de, 333, 458–59,
    500, 548, 549
Pierrefeu, Jean de, 715, 718
Pinard, Henri, 766
Pinel, Philippe, 8
Pirbright, Lady Sarah, 741
Piso, Gaius Calpurnius, 42, 44
Plantevignes, Camille, 455
Plantevignes, Marcel, 455, 456, 457–58, 496
Plato, 83, 126, 724
Pliny the Younger, 52, 53
Plutarch, 405
Poincaré, Raymond, 103, 187, 199, 212
Poiret, Paul, 576
Polignac, Prince Edmond de, 185, 268–69, 303,
    350, 351
Polignac, Princesse Edmond de, née Win-
    naretta Singer, 185, 268–69, 272, 303, 426,